ISC Exams 2026

All in One®

Chemistry

Class 11

Simplified Theory

Topic & Chapter Exercises

Exam Pattern Questions

Author
Shahana Ansari
Neha Miglani

arihant
SUCCESS AND NOTHING LESS

arihant
SUCCESS AND NOTHING LESS

ARIHANT PRAKASHAN
(School Division Series)

卐 *ADMINISTRATIVE & PRODUCTION OFFICES*

Regd. Office
'Ramchhaya' 4577/15, Agarwal Road, Darya Ganj, New Delhi -110002
Tele: 011- 47630600, 43518550; Fax: 011- 23280316

卐 *Head Office*
Kalindi, TP Nagar, Meerut (UP) - 250002, Tel: 0121-7156203, 7156204

卐 *SALES & SUPPORT OFFICES*
Agra, Ahmedabad, Bengaluru, Bareilly, Chennai, Delhi, Guwahati, Hyderabad, Jaipur, Jhansi, Kolkata, Lucknow, Nagpur & Pune.

PO No : TXT-XX-XXXXXXX-X-XX

Published By Arihant Publications (India) Ltd.

For further information about the books published by Arihant, log on to www.arihantbooks.com or e-mail at info@arihantbooks.com

Follow us on

卐 *PRICE* ₹590.00

PRODUCTION TEAM

Publishing Managers
Mahendra Singh Rawat & Keshav Mohan

Cover Designer
Salman Shaikh

Inner Designer
Ankit Tyagi

Project Head
Akansha Tomar

Page Layouting
Sanjay Yadav

Proof Reader
Sarthak

Index *cum* Study Planner

One Book- Endless Features

to Help you Succeed

In this Chapter

At the start of each chapter, all the chapter topics of have been listed, so that students may know what they are going to study.

CHAPTER

02

Struture of Atom

TOPIC 01 Sub-atomic Particles and Some Atomic Models

In the previous chapter, you have read about the atom and Dalton's atomic theor that consider atoms as fundamental building of matter. Also, proposed that, matter was composed of extremely small particles called atoms which are structureless, possessed, fixed mass and were indivisible.

- Sub-atomic Particles and Atomic Models
- Dual Nature, Heisenberg's Principle and Quantum Mechanical Model
- Quantum Numbers and Electronic Configuration

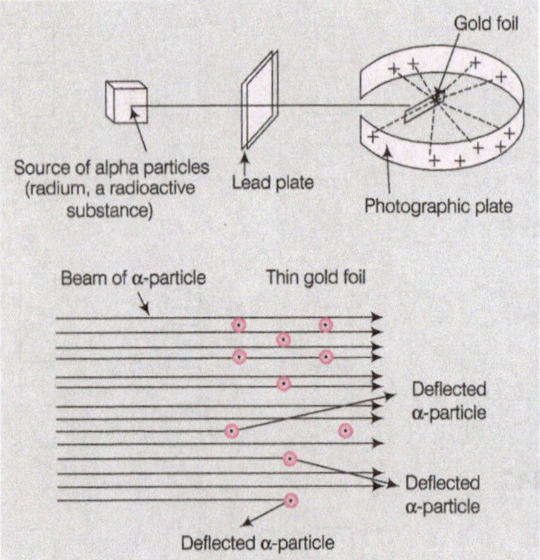

Schematic molecular view of the gold foil

Complete Theory in Each Chapter

To make the students understand the chapter completely, each chapter has been divided into Individual Topics and each such topic has been treated as a separate chapter. Each topic has detailed theory, supported by examples, well labelled diagrams, tables etc.

Illustrative Figures

To make the concepts completely visible, illustrative diagrams have been given at various place.

TOPIC 01 **Sub-atomic Particles and Some Atomic Models**

In the previous chapter, you have read about the atom and Dalton's atomic theory that consider atoms as fundamental building of matter. Also, proposed that, matter was composed of extremely small particles called atoms which are structureless, possessed, fixed mass and were indivisible.

The discoveries of several scientists like Faraday, Thomson, Rutherford, etc. clearly revealed that the atom is divisible and composed of several smallest particles like electrons, protons, neutrons, etc. although atom is the smallest particles that take part in a chemical reaction.

Subatomic Particles

At the end of 19th century, the discovery of radioactivity, Faraday's law of electrolysis and other observations proved that atom is divisible into three fundamental particles like electron, proton and neutron. These particles are collectively known as **subatomic particles.**

Topic Practice 2

Very Short Answer Type Questions

(1 Mark)

1 Fill in the Blanks

(i) The maximum number of electrons that an orbit can have is given by ...... where, n is the number of the orbit.

(ii) The energy of electrons in atom is ....

(iii) The probability of finding an electron at a poin with an atom is .... to the .... of the orbital wave function, i.e. $|\psi|^2$ at that point.

(iv) An orbital is a region in space around the nucleus where the .... of finding the electron i ......

Topical Exercises

To make students understand the chapter in a smooth part-by-part manner, Topical Exercises have been given in each chapter. These Exercises help students to assess the understanding of related concepts at regular interval.

One Book- Endless Features

to Help you Succeed

Chapter Summary

Summary of chapter given at the end helps to revise the chapter quickly at the time of examination or routine school tests.

SUMMARY

- The smallest particle taking part in a chemical reaction is called atom.
- Electron is one of the fundamental constituent of an atom. (Charge $= -1.6 \times 10^{-19}$C and mass $= 9.1 \times 10^{-31}$ kg).
- Protons and neutrons are other fundamental particles of an atom. Proton (charge $= +1.6 \times 10^{-19}$C and mass $= 1.6 \times 10^{-31}$ kg). Neutron (charge = 0, mass $= 1.67 \times 10^{27}$ kg). These are present in the **nucleus** of an atom.
- An atom can be represented as ${}^A_Z X$, where, A = mass number, Z = atomic number
- An atom can be represented as ${}^A_Z X$, where, A = mass number, Z = atomic number. Atomic species can be classified as :
  - (i) **Isotopes** Species having same atomic number but different mass number. These are chemically same.
  - (ii) **Isoelectronic** Species having same number of electrons.
  - (iii) **Isobars** Species with same mass number but different atomic number are called Isobars.
  - (iv) **Isotones** Species having same number of neutrons.
- Two preliminary models are :
  - (i) Thomson's model assumed atom as a pudding of positive charge with electrons embedding in it.
  - (ii) Rutherford's model assumed that protons and neutrons are present in the nucleus and electrons revolve around it.
- Wavelength (λ), frequency (ν), velocity (c) and wave number ($\bar{\nu}$) are related as $c = \nu . \lambda$ and $\bar{\nu} = \frac{1}{\lambda}$.
- EMR spectra is used to detect wavelengths. It shows increasing order of wavelengths.
- Bohr's model assumes electrons revolve only in stationary orbits of fixed energy.

Bohr radius, $r_n = a_0 \cdot \frac{n^2}{Z}$ ($a_0 = 52.9$ pm), Calculation of energy, $E = -2.18 \times 10^{-18}\left(\frac{Z^2}{n^2}\right) \cdot J$

Calculation of velocity, $v = 2.19 \times 10^6 \times \left(\frac{Z}{n}\right)$ms^{-1}, Calculation of spectral lines, $x = \frac{(n_2 - n_1) \cdot (n_2 - n_1 + 1)}{2}$

Chapter Practice

Very Short Answer Type Questions

1 Mark

1. **Fill in the Blanks**
   - (i) l describes the ...... of the orbital occupied by the electron.
   - (ii) The wave function ψ describes properties of the orbital and the ...... that occupies the orbital.
   - (iii) $|\psi|^2$ and ψ at any point is ...... to the probability of finding that ...... at that point
   - (iv) ...... determined the charge on the electron.
2. **Objective Type Questions**
   - (i) Which of the following will violates Aufbau principle as well as Pauli's exclusion principle?

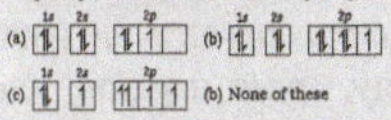

(b) None of these

   - (ii) The atomic number of an element is 35 and its mass is 81. The number of electrons in its outermost shell is
     (a) 3 (b) 5 (c) 7 (d) 9
   - (iii) Total number of orbitals associated with third shell will be [NCERT Exemplar]
     (a) 2 (b) 4 (c) 9 (d) 3
   - (iv) Number of angular nodes for 4d orbital is [NCERT Exemplar]
     (a) 4 (b) 3 (c) 2 (d) 1

Codes

	A	B	C	D
(a)	(i)	(iii, iv)	(ii)	(iii)
(b)	(iv)	(v)	(ii, iii)	(i, iii)
(c)	(i)	(ii)	(iii)	(iv)
(d)	(iv)	(iii, i)	(ii)	(i)

4. Calculate the amount of energy required to remove the only electron present in the hydrogen atom.
5. The minimum energy required to eject an electron from a metal is 4.34×10^{-19} J. What is the minimum frequency of light required for photoelectric effect in the metal?
6. Give the name and atomic number of the inert gas atom in which the total number of d-electrons is equal to the difference between the numbers of total s-electrons.
7. What is the difference between ground state and excited state?
8. Write the electronic configuration of a divalent ion of a coinage metal.

Short Answer Type I Questions

2 Marks

9. Show that ground state energy of electrons in hydrogen atom is equal to the first excited state energy of electron in He^+ ion, assuming that their Rydberg's constants are equal.

Chapter Practice

The Exercise contains questions in that format in which these are asked in the examinations. Questions have been categorised as 1 mark questions, 2 marks questions, 3 marks questions, 4 marks questions. All the questions given here are fully solved.

Sample Question Papers

To make students practice of examination in real sense, there are 5 Sample Question Papers at the end. All these Sample Questions Papers are exactly prepared on the latest syllabus & pattern of examination.

SAMPLE QUESTION PAPER 1

A Highly Simulated Sample Question Paper for ISC Class XI

CHEMISTRY (Fully Solved)

Time : 3 hours Max. Marks : 70

GENERAL INSTRUCTIONS

- This paper is divided into four Section A, B , C and D. Answer all questions.
  Section A consists of one question having sub-parts of one mark each.
  Section B consists of ten questions of two marks each.
  Section C consists of seven questions of three marks each, and
  Section D consists of three questions of five marks each.
- Internal choices have been provided in one question each in Section B, Section C, Section D.
- All working, including rough work, should be done on the same sheet as, and adjacent to the rest of the answer.

Section-A [14 Marks]

1. (A) Fill in the blanks by choosing the appropriate word(s) from those given in the brackets. [4 × 1]
   [subshell, main shell, sigma, pi, isobaric, orbitals, isothermal, adiabatic, Lavoisier, Proust, heat, energy, Dalton, SO_2, CO_2, O_3]
   - (i) ...... and ...... are mainly produced by burning of fossil and fuel.
   - (ii) Principal quantum number and azimuthal quantum number represents .... and .... respectively.
   - (iv) The system, which does not exchange the .... with its surrondings is known as......... system.

   (B) Select and write the correct alternative from the choices given below. [7 × 1]
   - (i) The ratio of K_p / K_c for the reaction, $CO(g) + \frac{1}{2}O_2(g) \longrightarrow CO_2(g)$, is
     (a) 1 (b) RT (c) $(RT)^{1/2}$ (d) $(RT)^{-1/2}$

Latest Course Structure

PAPER I THEORY 70 Marks

S. No.	UNIT	TOTAL WEIGHTAGE
1.	Some Basic Concepts of Chemistry	Physical Chemistry 41 Marks
2.	Structure of Atom	
3.	Classification of Elements and Periodicity in Properties	
4.	Chemical Bonding and Molecular Structure	
5.	Chemical Thermodynamics	
6.	Equilibrium	
7.	Redox Reactions	Inorganic Chemistry 6 Marks
8.	Organic Chemistry: Some Basic Principles and Techniques	Organic Chemistry 23 Marks
9.	Hydrocarbons	
	TOTAL	**70 Marks**

1. SOME BASIC CONCEPTS OF CHEMISTRY

General introduction: Importance and scope of chemistry.

Study of matter. Understanding laws of chemical combination. Dalton's atomic theory: concept of elements, atoms and molecules. Isotopic (atomic) and molecular masses, mole concept and molar mass, percentage composition, empirical and molecular formula. Stoichiometry and calculations based on chemical reactions.

(i) *Precision and accuracy: Quantities and their measurements in Chemistry, significant figures, SI units.*

(ii) *Dimensional analysis: Conversion of units, numericals and applications of units.*

(iii) *The concept of atoms having fixed properties in explaining the laws of chemical combination.*

Study about atoms. Dalton's atomic theory: Main postulates of the theory; its limitations.

Laws of chemical combinations, Law of conservation of mass, Law of definite proportions, Law of multiple proportions, Law of reciprocal proportions, Gay Lussac's law of gaseous volumes.

Statement, explanation and simple problems based on these laws.

(iv) *Atomic (isotopic masses) and molecular mass. Relative molecular mass and mole:*

The atomic mass unit is one of the experimentally determined unit. It is equal to 1/12 of the mass of the carbon 12 isotope.

Numerical problems based on mole concept, Avogadro's number and gram molecular volume.

(v) *Empirical and molecular formula: Numericals based on the above.*

(vi) *Chemical equivalents, volumetric calculations in terms of normality. C = 12.00 should be taken as a standard for expressing atomic masses.*

Equivalent weight expressing the combining capacity of the elements with the standard elements such as H, Cl, O, Ag, etc.

Variable equivalent weight. Gram equivalent weights, relationship between gram equivalent weight, gram molecular mass and valency.

Determination of equivalent weight of acids, alkalis, salts, oxidising and reducing agents. (experimental details not required).

Terms used in volumetric calculations such as percentage (w/w and w/v), normality, molarity, molality, mole fraction, etc. should be discussed. Students are required to know the formulae and normality and molarity equations.

Simple calculations on the above topics.

(vii) *Chemical reactions – stoichiometric calculations based on mass-mass, mass-volume, volume-volume relationships and limiting reagent.*

2. STRUCTURE OF ATOM

Discovery of fundamental particles electron, proton and neutron), atomic number, isotopes and isobars. Thomson's model and its limitations. Rutherford's experimental model and its limitations. Dual nature of matter and light. Bohr's atomic model and its limitations (de Broglie's equation, Heisenberg's uncertainty principle), concept of shells, subshells, orbitals. Quantum numbers, shapes of *s*, *p* and *d* orbitals. Rules for filling electrons in orbitals - aufbau principle, Pauli's exclusion principle and Hund's rule of maximum multiplicity. Electronic configuration of atoms, stability of half-filled and completely filled orbitals.

(i) *Subatomic particles (electrons, protons and neutrons) their charges and masses: Concept of indivisibility of atom as proposed by Dalton does not exist. The atom consists of subatomic fundamental particles. Production of cathode rays and their properties. Production of anode rays and their properties.*

Chadwick's experiment for the discovery of neutron and properties of neutron.

(ii) *Rutherford's nuclear model based on the scattering experiment: Rutherford's scattering experiment. Discovery of nucleus. Rutherford's nuclear model of atom. Defects of Rutherford's model. Electromagnetic wave theory and its limitations (Black body radiation and photoelectric effect)*

Planck's quantum theory.

Numericals based on the above.

(iii) *Types of spectra: emission and absorption spectra. Band and line spectra to be discussed.*

(iv) *Bohr's atomic model.*

Postulates of Bohr's theory – based on Planck's quantum theory. Merits of Bohr's atomic model and explanation of hydrogen spectra. Calculations based on Rydberg's formula.

Numericals on Bohr's atomic radii, velocity and energy of orbits (derivation not required).

Defects in Bohr's Model.

(v) *Quantum mechanical model of an atom - a simple mathematical treatment. Quantum numbers; shape, size and orientation of s, p and d orbitals only (no derivation). aufbau principle, Pauli's exclusion principle, Hund's rule of maximum multiplicity. Electronic configuration of elements in terms of s, p, d, f subshells.*

- *de Broglie's equation. Numericals.*
- *Heisenberg's Uncertainty Principle. Numericals.*
- *Schrodinger Wave Equation – physical significance of ⊠ and* $|\Psi|^2$.
- *Quantum numbers – types of quantum numbers, shape, size and orientation of the s, p and d subshells. Information obtained in terms of distance of electron from the nucleus, node, nodal planes and radial probability curve, energy of electron, number of electrons present in an orbit and an orbital.*
- *Aufbau principle, (n+l) rule.*
- *Pauli's exclusion principle.*
- *Hund's rule of maximum multiplicity.*
- *Electronic configuration of elements and ions in terms of s, p, d, f subshells and stability of half-filled and completely filled orbitals.*

3. CLASSIFICATION OF ELEMENTS AND PERIODICITY IN PROPERTIES

Significance of classification; study of Mendeleev's periodic law and its limitations; Modern Periodic Law and the present form of periodic table leading to periodic trends in properties of elements - atomic radii, ionic radii, valency, ionisation enthalpy, electron gain enthalpy, electronegativity. Nomenclature of elements with atomic number greater than 100

(i) *Modern Periodic Law*

Mendeleev's periodic law, defects in the Mendeleev's periodic table. Advantages and disadvantages. Modern periodic law (atomic number taken as the basis of classification of the elements).

(ii) *Long form of Periodic Table.*

General characteristics of groups and periods. Division of periodic table as s, p, d and f blocks. IUPAC nomenclature for elements with Z> 100.

(iii) *Periodic trends in properties of elements.*

Atomic radius, ionic radius, ionisation enthalpy, electron gain enthalpy, electronegativity, metallic and non-metallic characteristics.

- *Periodic properties such as valence electrons, atomic and ionic radii and their variation in groups and periods.*
- *The idea of ionisation enthalpy, electron gain enthalpy and electronegativity must be given and their variation in groups and periods may be discussed.*
- *The factors (atomic number, screening effect and shielding effect, the number of electrons in the outermost orbit) which affect these periodic properties and their variation in groups and periods.*

(iv) *Periodic trends in chemical properties – periodicity of valence or oxidation states. Anomalous properties of second period elements.*

Diagonal relationship; acidic and basic nature of oxides.

NOTE: Recommendations of the latest IUPAC for numbering of groups to be followed. Numbering 1 – 18 replacing old notation of I – VIII. Details given at the end of the syllabus.

4. CHEMICAL BONDING AND MOLECULAR STRUCTURE

Valence electrons, ionic bond character, covalent bond of ionic bond, covalent bond, bond parameters, Lewis structure, polar character of covalent bond, VSEPR theory, geometry of covalent molecules, valence bond theory, concept of hybridisation involving *s, p* and *d* orbitals and shapes of some simple molecules. Coordinate bond. Molecular orbital theory of homonuclear diatomic molecules (qualitative idea only). Resonance and hydrogen bond.

(i) *Kossel-Lewis approach to chemical bonding. Octet rule, its application to electrovalent and covalent bonds.*

(ii) *Electrovalent or ionic bond: Lewis structures of NaCl,* Li_2O*, MgO, CaO,* MgF_2 *and* Na_2S*.*

Definition of ionic bond.

The conditions necessary for the formation of ionic bonds such as: low ionisation enthalpy of metals, high electron gain enthalpy of non-metals, high lattice energy.

— electronegativity difference between the reacting atoms.

All these points must be discussed in detail.

The formation of cations and anions of elements and their positions in the periodic table.

Variable electrovalency; reasons for variable electrovalency i.e, due to inert electron pair effect and unstable core, by using suitable examples.

Calculation of lattice enthalpy (Born-Haber cycle).

Characteristics of electrovalent bond.

(iii) *Covalent Bond – Bond parameters, Lewis structure, polar character of covalent bond, shapes.*

Sigma and pi bonds e.g. formation of ammonia, nitrogen, ethene, ethyne, and carbon dioxide.

Definition of covalent bond, conditions for formation of covalent bonds, types of covalent bonds, i.e single, double and triple bonds. Sigma and pi bonds: H_2, O_2, N_2.

Classification of covalent bonds based on electronegativity of atoms - polar and non-polar covalent bond, dipole moment.

Formation of CH_4, NH_3, H_2O, ethane, ethene, ethyne and CO_2, etc. and their electron dot structure or Lewis structure.

Characteristics of covalent compounds. Comparison in electrovalency and covalency.

Reason for variable covalency e.g. Phosphorus 3 & 5 and sulphur 2, 4, 6 & chlorine 1, 3, 5 and 7.

Formal charge of ions.

(iv) *Deviation from octet rule and Fajan's rules.*

Definition of octet rule.

Failure of octet rule, due to either incomplete octet or exceeding of octet with suitable examples.

Fajan's rules: statements, conditions for electrovalency and covalency. Polar and non polar bonds should be correlated with Fajan's rules.

(v) *Valence Shell Electron Pair Repulsion (VSEPR) Theory; Hybridisation and shapes of molecules: hybridisation involving s, p and d orbitals only.*

Concept of electron-pair repulsion and shapes of molecules using suitable examples.

Hybridisation and molecular shapes – definition, hybridisation of orbitals involving s, p and d orbitals (using suitable examples).

(vi) *Molecular orbital theory: Qualitative treatment of homonuclear diatomic molecules of first two periods (hydrogen to neon), Energy level diagrams, bonding and antibonding molecular orbitals, bond order, paramagnetism of O_2 molecule. Relative stabilities of O_2, O_2^-, O_2^{2-}, O_2^+ and N_2, N_2^+, N_2^-, N_2^{2-}.*

(vii) *Co-ordinate or dative covalent bond, e.g. formation of oxy-acids of chlorine: Co-ordinate or dative covalent bonding: definition, formation of chlorous acid, chloric acid, perchloric acid, ammonium ion, hydronium ion, nitric acid, ozone.*

(viii) *Resonance in simple inorganic molecules: Resonance in simple inorganic molecules like ozone, carbon dioxide, carbonate ion and nitrate ion.*

(ix) *Hydrogen bonding: the examples of hydrogen fluoride, water (ice), alcohol, etc. may be considered.*

H-bonding – definition, types, condition for hydrogen bond formation, examples of inter-molecular hydrogen bonding in detail taking hydrogen fluoride, water and ice and ethanol into account. Intramolecular hydrogen bonding.

5. CHEMICAL THERMODYNAMICS

(i) Introduction, concepts, types of system, surroundings, extensive, intensive properties and state functions.

(Types of system – ideal system, real system, isolated system, closed system, open system. Meaning of surroundings.

Properties of the system: macroscopic, intensive and extensive properties.

State of the system.

Main processes the system undergoes: reversible, irreversible, adiabatic, isothermal, isobaric, isochoric, cyclic.

Meaning of thermodynamic equilibrium. Meaning of thermodynamic process.

(ii) First Law of Thermodynamics and its significance, work, heat, internal energy, enthalpy (ΔU or ΔE and ΔH), heat capacity and specific heat. Hess's law of constant heat summation, enthalpy of bond dissociation, combustion, formation, atomisation, sublimation, phase transition, ionisation, solution and dilution.

Meaning of: internal energy of the system, work done by the system, by the surroundings at constant temperature, heat absorbed by the system and by the surroundings at constant temperature.

The sign convention for change in internal energy, heat given out or gained, work done by the system or by the surroundings.

State function and path function - meaning with examples. Internal energy change, work done and heat absorbed in a cyclic process.

Internal energy change in an isolated system and in a non-isolated system. Total internal energy change of a system and surroundings. Mathematical statement of the first law.

Significance of first law of thermodynamics. Need for enthalpy – constant pressure or open vessel processes. Enthalpy - a thermodynamic property, state function. Mathematical form of enthalpy.

Heat - the energy in transit. Conditions for the transfer of heat. Limitations in conversion of heat into work. Condition at which heat transfer ceases, unit of heat.

Meaning of work, capacity to do work, types of work. Mathematical form of reversible work and irreversible work. Difference between the reversible and irreversible work done – graphically.

Relationship between C_v and internal energy change. Relationship between C_p and C_v.

Definitions of the following:

Heat of reaction: Heat of formation – standard heat of formation, Heat of solution, Heat of dilution, Heat of neutralization, Heat of combustion.

Constancy in the heat of neutralisation: Experimental verification in case of strong acids and strong bases. Reason for that observation – ionic neutralisation and the heat evolved.

Definition of Calorific value of a fuel.

Statement of Hess' Law and its application.

Problems based on Hess' Law.

(iii) Second Law of Thermodynamics and its significance, spontaneity of a chemical change; Entropy, Free Energy. Inadequacy of First Law and need for Second Law; Ideas about reversible (recapitulation), spontaneous and non-spontaneous processes

Meaning of entropy – derived from Second Law – statement of Second Law in terms of entropy; Physical significance of entropy; State function and not path function. Entropy change of the universe, reversible isothermal process and irreversible process. Meaning of thermal death, Gibb's free energy of the system and Helmholtz free energy. Relationship between Gibb's free energy and Helmholtz's free energy.

Relationship between change in Gibb's free energy and equilibrium constant of a chemical reaction. Defining the criteria for spontaneity of a chemical change in terms of Gibb's free energy.

Note: Numericals based on the First Law, Second Law of Thermodynamics and Hess' Law.

(iv) Third Law of Thermodynamics – statement only.

Self-explanatory.

6. EQUILIBRIUM

(i) Chemical Equilibrium

Introduction of physical and chemical equilibrium and its characteristics

Dynamic nature of equilibrium, law of mass action, equilibrium constant and factors affecting equilibrium. Le Chatelier's principle and its applications

(Irreversible and reversible reactions).

Physical equilibrium: solid-liquid, liquid-vapour, solid-vapour; Characteristics of Physical equilibrium.

Chemical equilibrium: Characteristics of chemical equilibrium; dynamic nature. Law of mass action; Equilibrium constant in terms of concentration K_c. Gaseous reactions; Equilibrium constant in terms of partial pressures K_p. Relationship between K_p and K_c (derivation required); Characteristics of equilibrium constant; Units for equilibrium constant; Simple calculations of equilibrium constant and concentration.

The following examples should be considered to show maximum yield of products:

Synthesis of ammonia by Haber's process, The dissociation of dinitrogen tetra oxide, Hydrolysis of simple esters, The contact process for the manufacture of sulphuric acid, Le Chatelier's Principle. Statement and explanation.

Factors affecting chemical and physical equilibria should be discussed in the light of Le Chatelier's principle.

Change of concentration, Change of temperature, Change of pressure, Effect of catalyst, Addition of inert gas.

(ii) Ionic Equilibrium

Introduction, electrolyte (strong and weak), non-electrolyte, ionisation, degree of ionisation of polybasic acids, acid strength, concept of pH, pH indicators, buffer solution, common ion effect (with illustrative examples). Henderson equation, hydrolysis of salts, solubility and solubility product.

Ostwald's dilution law and its derivation. Strength of acids and bases based on their dissociation constant. Problems based on the Ostwald's dilution law.

Arrhenius, Brönsted-Lowry and Lewis concept of acids and bases, multistage ionisation of acids and bases with examples.

Ionic product of water – definition, pH, pOH, pK_w of solutions.

pH indicators and their choice in titrimetry.

Numericals on the above concepts.

Common ion effect – definition, examples (acetic acid and sodium acetate; ammonium hydroxide and ammonium chloride), applications in salt analysis.

Salt hydrolysis – salts of strong acids and weak bases, weak acids and strong bases, weak acids and weak bases and the pH formula of the solutions of these salts in water with suitable examples.

Buffer solutions: definition, examples, action; its interpretations based on Le Chatelier's principle. Henderson equation.

Solubility product: definition and application in qualitative salt analysis (Group II, III and IV cations).

Numericals on pH, buffer solutions, solubility and solubility product.

7. REDOX REACTIONS

Concept of oxidation and reduction, redox reactions, oxidation number, change in oxidation number, balancing redox reactions (in terms of loss and gain of electrons). Applications of redox in various types of chemical reactions.

- Concept of oxidation and reduction in terms of oxygen, hydrogen, electrons.
- Redox reactions – examples.
- Oxidation number: rules for calculation, simple calculations of oxidation state in molecules and ions like $K_2Cr_2O_7$, $S_2O_3^{2-}$ etc.
- Oxidation and reduction in terms of change in oxidation number.
- Balancing of redox reactions in acidic and basic medium by oxidation number and ion-electron method

8. ORGANIC CHEMISTRY - SOME BASIC PRINCIPLES AND TECHNIQUES

General introduction, classification and IUPAC nomenclature of organic compounds and isomerism.

Methods of purification, qualitative and quantitative analysis. Electron displacement in a covalent bond: inductive effect, electromeric effect, resonance and hyperconjugation.

Homolytic and heterolytic bond fission of a covalent bond: free radicals, carbocations, carbanions, electrophiles and nucleophiles, types of organic reactions.

(i) Introduction to organic chemistry:

Vital force theory, reason for separate study of organic chemistry and its importance, characteristics of carbon atoms (tetra valency), Reasons for large number of organic compounds: catenation, isomerism and multiple bonding, etc.

(ii) Classification of organic compounds: (definition and examples): open chain, closed chain, homocyclic, hetrocyclic, aromatic, alicyclic compounds, homologous series and its characteristics, functional groups.

(iii) IUPAC rules for naming organic compounds. Aliphatic, alicyclic and aromatic compounds.

(iv) Definition and classification of isomerism:

Structural isomerism: definition, classification, examples.

Chain isomerism, Positional isomerism, Functional isomerism, Metamerism, Tautomerism - examples for each of the above.

Stereoisomerism: definition and classification, examples.

Geometrical isomerism: Definition. Conditions for compounds to exhibit geometrical isomerism; types and examples, cis and trans, syn and anti. Examples.

Optical isomerism: Definition, Nicol prism, plane polarised light.

polarimeter. Method of measuring angle of rotation. Specific rotation. Conditions for optical activity. d, l form; External compensation, Internal compensation, racemic mixture & meso form. Examples – lactic acid and tartaric acid.

(v) *Analysis of organic compounds:*

Detection of elements (qualitative analysis) such as carbon, hydrogen, nitrogen, halogens and sulphur should be considered by using Lassaigne's test and reactions involved in it.

(vi) *Estimation of carbon, hydrogen, nitrogen, halogens, sulphur and phosphorous:*

Estimation of carbon and hydrogen – Leibig's method.

Estimation of nitrogen - Kjeldahl's method.

Estimation of halogens sulphur and phosphorous - Carius method. Numericals included. Experimental details required.

(vii) *Types of chemical reactions and their mechanisms.*

Substitution, addition, elimination reactions: definition and examples.

Homolytic and heterolytic fission – definition and examples. Free radicals, carbocation, carbanion (their reactivities and stabilities).

Electrophiles and nucleophiles – definition and examples (including neutral electrophiles and nucleophiles).

Inductive, electromeric, mesomeric effect and hyperconjugation – definition, examples.

(viii) *Free radicals and polar mechanisms*

In terms of fission of the bonds and formation of the new bonds including S_N1, S_N2, E1 and E2 mechanisms. Explain with relevant examples and conditions.

9. HYDROCARBONS

Classification of Hydrocarbons

I. Aliphatic Hydrocarbons

(i) Alkanes - Nomenclature, isomerism, conformation (methane and ethane), physical properties, chemical properties including free radical mechanism of halogenation, combustion and pyrolysis

Occurrence, conformation (Sawhorse and Newman projections of ethane).

General methods of preparation: from sodium salts of carboxylic acids (decarboxylation and Kolbe's electrolytic method); from alcohols and alkyl halides (Wurtz reaction, Coreyhouse Synthesis). From aldehydes and Grignard's Reagent.

Physical and chemical properties of alkanes.

Physical properties: state, freezing point, melting point, boiling point, density.

Chemical properties: combustibility, reaction with chlorine (free radical mechanism), reaction with oxygen in presence of catalyst (formation of alcohol, aldehyde, and carboxylic acid). Cyclisation, aromatisation, isomerisation and pyrolysis.

Uses of alkanes.

(ii) Alkenes - Nomenclature, structure of double bond (ethene), isomerism; methods of preparation; physical properties, chemical properties; addition of hydrogen, halogen, water, hydrogen halides (Markownikoff's addition and peroxide effect), ozonolysis, oxidation, mechanism of electrophilic addition.

General methods of preparation – dehydration of alcohols, dehydrohalogenation of alkyl halides (from vicinal dihalides), Kolbe's electrolytic method and from alkynes.

Physical Properties: State, freezing point, melting point, boiling point, dipole moment, density.

Chemical properties - addition reactions (hydrogen, halogens, hydrogen halides, sulphuric acid, water).

Markownikoff's rule and anti-Markownikoff's rule with mechanism and examples.

Oxidation: complete combustion, hot and cold alkaline $KMnO_4$ (Baeyer's reagent), ozonolysis.

Polymerisation. Saytzeff's rule and its application.

Uses of alkenes.

(iii) Alkynes - Nomenclature, structure of triple bond (ethyne), methods of preparation; physical properties, chemical properties: acidic character of alkynes, addition reactions - hydrogen, halogens, hydrogen halides and water.

General methods of preparations of alkynes. Manufacture of ethyne by calcium carbide and from natural gas. Dehydrohalogenation and Kolbe's electrolytic method.

Physical properties of alkynes: State of existence, freezing point, melting point, boiling point, density.

Chemical properties of alkynes – addition reactions (hydrogen, halogens, hydrogen halides and water), acidic nature of alkynes, formation of acetylides.

Oxidation: complete combustion, hot and cold alkaline $KMnO_4$ (Baeyer's reagent), ozonolysis.

Polymerisation.

Uses of alkynes.

Distinguishing test between Alkane, Alkene and Alkyne

II. Aromatic Hydrocarbons

Introduction, IUPAC nomenclature, benzene: resonance, aromaticity, chemical properties: mechanism of electrophilic substitution. Nitration, sulphonation, halogenation, Friedel Crafts alkylation and acylation, directive influence of functional group in monosubstituted benzene. Carcinogenicity and toxicity.

Structure: Resonance structures (Kekule's) of benzene.

Benzene: Preparation from sodium benzoate and from phenol.

Physical properties: State of existence, freezing point, melting point, boiling point, density.

Chemical properties:

- Electrophilic substitution reactions with mechanism (halogenation, nitration, sulphonation).

- Alkylation, acetylation – Friedel Crafts reaction.

- Directive influence (o-, p-, and m-) of substituents in electrophilic and nucleophilic substitutions (with mechanism).

- Oxidation: catalytic oxidation, reaction with ozone.

- Addition reactions with hydrogen, chlorine, bromine.

- Pyrolysis (formation of bi-phenyl).

Carcinogenicity and toxicity of benzene may be discussed. Uses.

CHAPTER

01

Some Basic Concepts of Chemistry

Chemistry deals with the composition, structure and properties of matter. The basic constituents of matter are atoms and molecules, so chemistry is called the science of **atoms** and **molecules**. In this chapter, we will discuss about matter and its properties alongwith discussion of constituent particles of matter.

- General Introduction, Nature of Matter and Laws of Chemical Combination
- Atomic and Molecular Masses, Mole concept and Formulae of Compounds
- Chemical Reactions and Stoichiometric Calculations

TOPIC 01 General Introduction, Nature of Matter and Laws of Chemical Combination

Chemistry is the branch of science that deals with structure, properties, interaction, transformation of a matter and the energy changes accompanying these transformations. It also plays an important role in daily life.

Importance of Chemistry

Chemistry has helped us to meet with all our requirements that are necessary for the advancement of life such as food additives, health care products, plastics, dyes, polymers etc. Chemistry is involved in each and every aspect around us. From man-made furniture to acid rains and from artificial medicines to natural grains all have their own chemical aspects or roles.

A few important such roles are listed below :

(i) **In the Existence of Life** As metabolic reactions, i.e. chemical reactions necessary for life.

(ii) **In Meterological Process and Geographical Occurrences Around us**
- As composition of soil and rocks.
- As composition of atmosphere around us.
- As the occurrence of acid rains etc.

(iii) **In Economy of a Country**
- As the foundation stone of industries like soap, paints, cement, processed foods, etc.
- As a principle procedure in agriculture based industries like fertilizer, pesticide.

(iv) **In Making Our Life Easier**

- As its involvement in construction of various man made articles like buildings, vehicles etc.
- As polymers with predefined role in making synthetic articles like pen, paints, plastic items, road.
- As a support system of our daily usage products like food preservatives, cosmetics, perfumes, soaps and detergent items etc.

Nature of Matter

Matter is anything that has mass and occupies space, e.g. book, pen, pencil etc.

Another term widely used in chemistry is **material** but it has a limited meaning as it corresponds to matter having specific uses, e.g. glass, cement, paper etc.

Classification of Matter

There are two ways to classify matter, viz

(i) **Physical classification** based upon the physical properties.

(ii) **Chemical classification** based upon the chemical composition.

Physical Classification of Matter

Depending upon their physical characteristics, matter is generally classified as solids, liquids and gases.

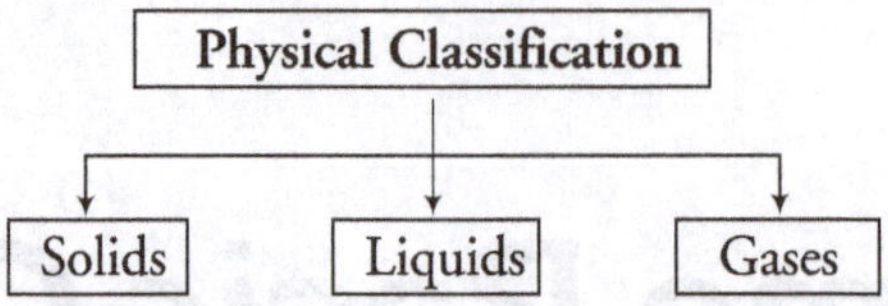

(i) **Solids** The particles in solids are held very close to each other in an orderly fashion and there is no much freedom of movement.

(ii) **Liquids** The particles in liquids are close to each other in an orderly fashion but they can move around.

(iii) **Gases** The particles are far apart as compared to that present in solids and liquids states and their movement is easy and fast.

The three states of matter are interconvertible under different conditions of temperature and pressure as given below.

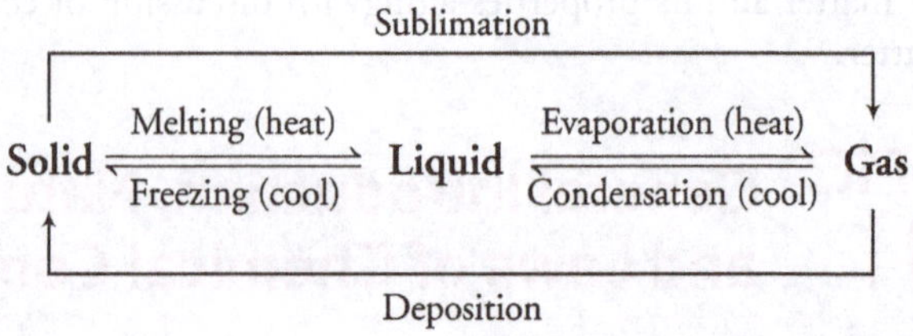

Chemical Classification of Matter

Depending upon the chemical composition, at the macroscopic or bulk level, matter is classified as:

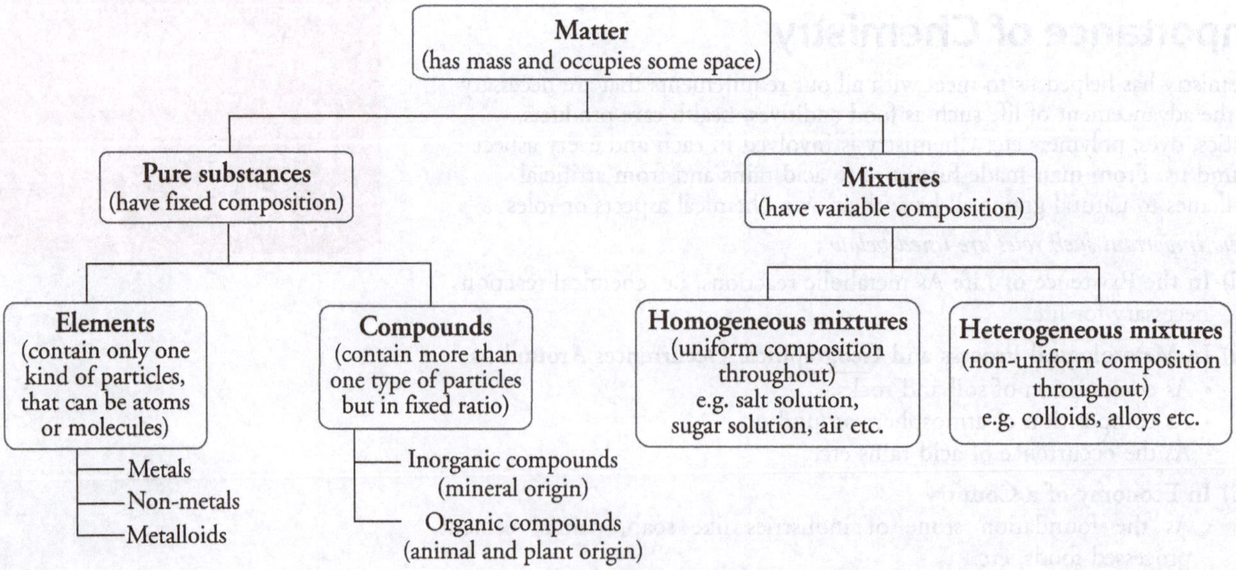

A brief description based on chemical classification of matter is given below:

1. Mixture

Two or more substances mix together in any ratio to give **mixture**, e.g. air, milk, tea etc. A mixture can be classified as homogeneous or heterogeneous.

(i) **Homogeneous Mixture** A mixture having uniform composition throughout is called homogeneous mixture, e.g. salt solution, air etc.

(ii) **Heterogeneous Mixture** A mixture in which the composition is not uniform throughout and different components can be observed is called heterogeneous mixture, e.g. mixture of salt and sugar, cereals and pulse etc.

2. Pure Substance

They have fixed composition and their constituents cannot be separated by physical methods. e.g. gold, silver, water etc.

(i) Elements

An element is defined as a pure substance that contains only one kind of particle which may be an atom or a molecule.

Depending upon the physical and chemical properties, the elements are further divided into the following three categories:

I. **Metals** Metals are those elements which reflect light and hence possess lustre. They are good conductor of heat and electricity, malleable and ductile (can be drawn in wire). At room temperature, metal exist as solid, e.g. silver, aluminium.

II. **Non-metals** Non-metals are those elements which do not reflect light and hence do not possess lustre. They are brittle, poor conductor of heat and electricity (except graphite).

III. **Metalloids** Metalloids are those elements which possess the characteristics of both metals as well as non-metals. e.g. bismuth, antimony etc.

(ii) Compounds

A molecule of a compound is formed by the combination of two or more atoms of different elements in a fixed ratio by mass.

Depending upon the compound may be categorised into two types:

I. **Organic Compound** Those compound which contains carbon and a few other element like hydrogen, nitrogen, sulphur etc. These are originally obtained by plants and animals.

II. **Inorganic Compound** The compounds which are obtained from non-living sources, e.g. sea water, rocks etc; are called in organic compounds. These are of non-organic nature and are the compounds of all elements (except those compounds of carbon which are of organic nature).

Some Physical Quantities

Several properties of matter like length, area, volume, etc; are quantitative in nature and are called physical quantities.

1. Mass and Weight

Mass (m) is the amount of matter present in a substance. It remains constant for a substance at all the places. Its unit (SI unit) is kilogram (kg) but in laboratories usually gram (1 kg = 1000 g) is used. Analytical balance or electrical balance is used to measure the mass of a substance.

Weight (w) is the force exerted by gravity on an object. It varies from place to place due to change in gravity. Its unit is Newton (N).

$$\boxed{w = m \times g}$$

where, m = mass, g = gravity.

2. Volume

The space occupied by matter (usually by liquid or a gas) is called its **volume**.

$$\text{Volume} = (\text{length})^3 = \text{m}^3$$

Thus, SI unit of volume is m^3. However, in laboratory, smaller volumes like cm^3 (or mL, i.e. millilitre) or dm^3 (or L, i.e. litre) are used. These terms are correlated as :

$$1 \text{ L} = 1000 \text{ mL} = 1000 \text{ cm}^3 = 1 \text{ dm}^3$$

$$1 \text{ m}^3 = (100 \text{ cm})^3 = 10^6 \text{ cm}^3 = 10^3 \text{ dm}^3 = 10^3 \text{ L}$$

In the laboratory, volume of liquids or solutions can be measured by graduated cylinder, burette, pipette etc.

Example 1 Convert the following into basic units.

(i) 28.7 pm (ii) 15.15 μs (iii) 25365 mg

Sol. The basic units for length is meter (m), for time is second(s) and for mass is kilogram (kg).

(i) $28.7 \text{ pm} \times \dfrac{10^{-12} \text{ m}}{1 \text{pm}} = 2.87 \times 10^{-11} \text{m}$

(ii) $15.15 \mu\text{s} \times \dfrac{10^{-12} \text{s}}{1 \mu\text{s}} = 1.515 \times 10^{-5} \text{ s}$

(iii) $25365 \text{ mg} \times \dfrac{1\text{g}}{1000 \text{ mg}} \times \dfrac{1\text{kg}}{1000 \text{ g}} = 2.5365 \times 10^{-2} \text{ kg}$

3. Density

It is defined as the amount or mass per unit volume and has units kg m^{-3} or g cm^{-3}. (Here kg or g represents mass and m^3 or cm^3 represents volume).

$$\boxed{\text{Density} = \text{Mass/Volume}}$$

Example 2 A liquid has a volume of 49.0 cm^3 and a mass of 57.642 g. Find out the density of this liquid in SI unit.

Sol. $$\text{Density} = \frac{\text{Mass (kg)}}{\text{Volume } (m^3)}$$

$$\text{Mass} = 57.642 \text{ g} = 57.642 \times 10^{-3} \text{ kg}$$

$$\text{Volume} = 49.0 \text{ cm}^3 = 49.0 \times (10^{-2})^3 = 49.0 \times 10^{-6} \text{ m}^3$$

$$\therefore \text{Density} = \frac{57.642 \times 10^{-3}}{49.0 \times 10^{-6}} = 1.176 \times 10^3 \text{ kg/m}^3$$

4. Pressure (p)

Pressure of the gas is the force exerted by the gas molecules per unit area on the walls of the container in all directions. Instrument used for the measurement of the pressure of a gas is called **manometer.**

$$\text{Pressure} = \frac{\text{Force}}{\text{Area}}$$

Atmospheric pressure is defined as the pressure exerted by the gases of the atmosphere at the sea level. Instrument used for the measurement of atmospheric pressure is called a **barometer.**

$$\boxed{\text{Atmospheric pressure} = \rho g h}$$

where, h = height of mercury column (in barometer)
g = acceleration due to gravity
ρ = density of the mercury at room temperature

The SI unit of pressure, is pascal (Pa). It is defined as 1 newton per metre square (1 Pa = 1 N m^{-2}).

5. Temperature

It is defined as the degree of hotness or coldness. Several scales are used to measure temperature. Common three scales are °C (degree celsius), K (Kelvin) and °F (degree Fahrenheit). These scales are shown in the below figure:

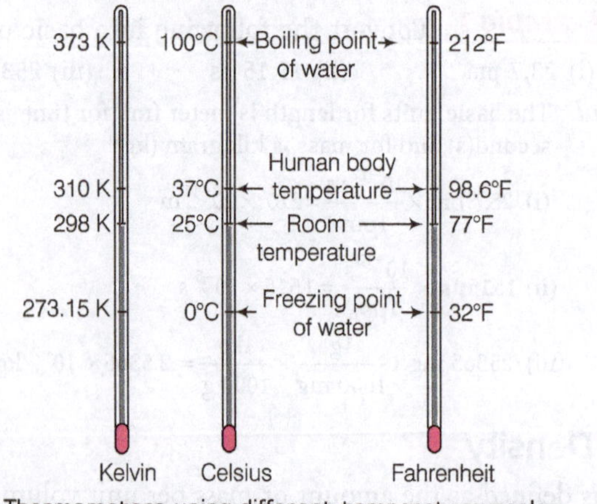

Thermometers using different temperature scales

From the above figure, it is clear that on the kelvin scale freezing point of water is taken as 273.15 K and boiling point of water as 373.15 K, at normal atmospheric pressure.

Similarly, on the celsius scale, freezing point of water is taken as 0°C and boiling point of water is taken as 100°C. Thus, both the scales are divided into 100 equal parts. The relationship between kelvin and celsius scale is

$$°C = K - 273.15 \quad \text{or} \quad K = °C + 273.15$$

Practically speaking, the lowest temperature permitted in nature is – 273.15 °C (0 K). This temperature is known as **absolute zero.** Similarly, the celsius and Fahrenheit scales are related as

$$\boxed{°C = \frac{5}{9}(°F - 32) \quad \text{or} \quad °F = \frac{9}{5}(°C) + 32}$$

Example 3 Convert the following temperatures into degree Fahrenheit.

(i) 25°C, physiological (human body) temperature.
(ii) 35°C, the room temperature.

Sol. (i) Given, C = 25°C

$$°F = \frac{9}{5}C° + 32 = \frac{9}{5} \times 25 + 32 = 45 + 32 = 77°F$$

(ii) Given, C = 35°C

$$°F = \frac{9}{5}C° + 32 = \frac{9}{5} \times 35 + 32 = 63 + 32 = 95°F$$

Example 4 A measured temperature on Fahrenheit scale is 200°F. What will this reading be on celsius scale?

NCERT Exemplar

Sol. There are three common scales to measure temperature °C (degree celsius), °F (degree Fahrenheit) and K (kelvin). The K is the SI unit. The temperatures on two scales are related to each other by the following relationship

$$°F = \frac{9}{5}t°C + 32$$

Putting the values in above equation,

$$200 - 32 = \frac{9}{5}t°C \Rightarrow \frac{9}{5}t°C = 168$$

$$\Rightarrow \quad t°C = \frac{168 \times 5}{9} = 93.3°C$$

6. Length

Though the SI unit of length is metre, yet it is very common to express length in Angstrom (Å) or nanometre (nm) or picometre (pm). These are related to SI unit as follows.

$$1 \text{ Å} = 10^{-10} \text{ m}, \ 1 \text{nm} = 10^{-9} \text{ m}, \ 1 \text{ pm} = 10^{-12} \text{ m}$$

Unit of Measurement

In order to measure physical quantities some standard reference is choosen, which is called the **unit of measurement**. Thus, "A unit is defined as the standard of reference choosen to measure a physical quantity".

The International System of Units (SI Units)

This system was established by 11th General Conference on weights and measurements and in French is called 'Le systeme International d' unites.

1. Fundamental Units

In this system there are seven base units, called the **fundamental units,** which are independent and cannot be derived from any other units. These units along with their symbols are tabulated below.

Base Physical Quantities and their Units

Base physical quantity	Symbol for quantity	Name of SI unit	Symbol for SI unit
Length	l	metre	m
Mass	m	kilogram	kg
Time	t	second	s
Electric current	I	ampere	A
Thermodynamic temperature	T	kelvin	K
Amount of substance	n	mole	mol
Luminous intensity	I_v	candela	cd

The definitions of the SI base units are given in the following table:

Definitions of SI Base Units

Units of length	Metre	The metre is the length of the path travelled by light in vacuum during a time interval of 1/299 792 458 of a second.
Unit of mass	Kilogram	The kilogram is the unit of mass, it is equal to the mass of the international prototype of the kilogram.
Unit of time	Second	The second is the duration of 9192 631 770 periods of the radiation corresponding to the transition between the two hyperfine levels of the ground state of the caesium 133 atom.
Unit of electric current	Ampere	The ampere is that constant current which, if maintained in two straight parallel conductors of infinite length, of negligible circular cross-section and placed 1 metre apart in vacuum, would produce between these conductors a force equal to 2×10^{-7} newton per metre of length.
Unit of thermodynamic temperature	Kelvin	The Kelvin, unit of thermodynamic temperature, is the fraction 1/273.16 of the thermodynamic temperature of the triple point of water.
Unit of amount of substance	Mole	(i) The mole is the amount of substance of a system which contains as many elementary entities as there are atoms in 0.012 kilogram of carbon-12; its symbol is "mol". (ii) When the mole is used, the elementary entities must be specified and may be atoms, molecules, ions, electrons, other particles, or specified groups of such particles.
Units of luminous intensity	Candela	The candela is the luminous intensity, in a given direction, of a source that emits monochromatic radiation of frequency 540×10^{12} hertz and that has a radiant intensity in that direction of 1/683 watt per steradian.

2. Derived Units

The other physical quantities such as speed, volume, density etc., can be derived from the above given base quantities and are called **derived quantities** and their units are derived from fundamental units.

e.g. density, $d = \dfrac{\text{mass}, m}{\text{volume}, V}$

Volume = length × breadth × height = $(\text{length})^3$ [for a cube]

$\therefore \quad \text{Density} = \dfrac{\text{mass}, m}{(\text{length})^3}$

On putting the units, we get density, $d = \dfrac{\text{kg}}{\text{m}^3} = \text{kg m}^{-3}$

Therefore, the unit of density is kg m^{-3}.

Some commonly used derived quantities and their units are tabulated below.

Physical Quantity	Formula	Unit	Symbol
Area	Length square	Square metre	m^2
Volume	Length cube	Cubic metre	m^3
Density	Mass/volume	Kilogram per cubic metre	kg m^{-3}
Velocity	Distance/time	Metre per second	ms^{-1}
Acceleration	Speed change/ time	Metre per second square	ms^{-2}
Force	Mass × acceleration	Newton	$N = kgms^{-2}$
Pressure	Force/area	Pascal (Newton per square metre)	$Pa = Nm^{-2} = kgm^{-1}s^{-2}$
Work, energy	Force × distance	Joule	$J = Nm = kgm^2s^{-2}$
Frequency	Cycles/sec	Hertz	$Hz = s^{-1}$
Electric charge	Current × time	Coulomb	C = A s
Potential difference	——	Volt	$V = kgm^2 s^{-3}A^{-1} = JA^{-1}s^{-1} = JC^{-1}$
Electric resistance	Potential difference/ current	ohm	$\Omega = VA^{-1}$

3. Supplementary Units

These include radian (rad) for angle and steradian (Sr) for solid angle. This class of unit was created in 1960 to cover those units which are neither base units nor derived from base units.

Prefixes

Some physical quantities are either too small or too large. To change the order of magnitude, these are expressed by using prefixes before the name of the base units.

The various prefixes are listed in the following table:

Prefixes Used in SI System

Multiple	Prefix	Symbol	Multiple	Prefix	Symbol
10^{-1}	deci	d	10^{1}	deca	da
10^{-2}	centi	c	10^{2}	hecto	h
10^{-3}	milli	m	10^{3}	kilo	k
10^{-6}	micro	μ	10^{6}	mega	M
10^{-9}	nano	n	10^{9}	giga	G
10^{-12}	pico	p	10^{12}	tera	T
10^{-15}	femto	f	10^{15}	peta	P
10^{-18}	atto	a	10^{18}	exa	E
10^{-21}	zepto	z	10^{21}	zeta	Z
10^{-24}	yocto	y	10^{24}	yotta	Y

Measurement in Chemistry

Many times during the study of chemistry, one has to deal with experimental data as well as theoretical calculations. While dealing with the calculations, the meaningful way is to handle the numbers conveniently and present the data realistically with certainty to the extent possible. These ways are scientific notation, significant figures and dimensional analysis.

Scientific Notation

It is the greatest way to represent very small or very large numbers conveniently. In scientific notation, any number can be represented in the form $N \times 10^n$ where n is an exponent having positive or negative values and N is a number (called digit term) which varies between 1.000... and 9.999....

(i) **Calculations involving Multiplication and Division**
These two operations follow the same rule which are there for exponential numbers i.e. the number N before the factor 10^n in scientific notation are multiplied and the exponents of 10 are added up.
While, in division, the N are divided and the exponents (n) are subtracted.

(ii) **Calculations involving Addition and Subtraction**
For these two operations, first the numbers are written in such a way that they have some exponent. After that, 10^n is taken out as common and the coefficients are added or substracted as the case may be.

Thus, in general number (N) is written in scientific notation as number with a single non-zero digit to the left of decimal and the number of places the decimal point has moved, is the exponent (n) of 10 with (+) sign if moved left and (–) sign if moved right. e.g. 943.876 is written as 9.43876×10^2 in scientific notation, i.e. decimal is moved two places towards left so that only one non-zero digit is left and the number of places moved (2) is the exponent of 10 in scientific notation.

Example 5 Express the following in the scientific notation.

(i) 0.000968 (ii) 157428
(iii) 90,000 (iv) $(5.7 \times 10^6) \times (4.2 \times 10^{-2})$
(v) $(6.8 \times 10^{-9}) \div (1.4 \times 10^{-6})$
(vi) $(4.56 \times 10^3 + 2.62 \times 10^2)$
(vii) $(9.87 \times 10^{-3} - 2.26 \times 10^{-4})$

Sol. (i) $0.000968 = 9.68 \times 10^{-4}$ (ii) $157428 = 1.57428 \times 10^5$

(iii) $90{,}000 = 9 \times 10^4$

(iv) $(5.7 \times 10^6) \times (4.2 \times 10^{-2}) = (5.7 \times 4.2)(10^{6-2})$
$= 23.94 \times 10^4 = 2.394 \times 10^5$

(v) $(6.8 \times 10^{-9}) \div (1.4 \times 10^{-6}) = \left(\frac{6.8}{1.4}\right) \times (10^{-9-(-6)})$
$= 4.857 \times 10^{-3}$

(vi) $(4.56 \times 10^3 + 2.62 \times 10^2)$
$= 45.6 \times 10^2 + 2.62 \times 10^2 = (45.6 + 2.62) \times 10^2$
$= 48.22 \times 10^2 = 4.822 \times 10^3$

(vii) $(9.87 \times 10^{-3} - 2.26 \times 10^{-4})$
$= 9.87 \times 10^{-3} - 0.226 \times 10^{-3}$
$= (9.87 - 0.226) \times 10^{-3} = 9.644 \times 10^{-3}$

Accuracy and Precision

Accuracy is the agreement of a particular value to the true value of the result or it is a measure of the difference between the experimental value or the mean value of a set of measurements and the true value.

$$\text{Accuracy} = \text{Mean value} - \text{True value}$$

Smaller the difference between the mean value and the true value, the larger is the accuracy. Accuracy also expresses the correctness of measurement.

When the true value of a quantity is not known then it becomes very difficult to calculate the accuracy. In such cases, precision of the measurements is calculated.

Precision refers to the closeness of various measurements for the same quantity or it is expressed as the difference between a measured value and the arithmetic mean value for a series of measurements.

Precision = Individual value – Arithmetic mean value

Smaller the difference between the individual values of repeated measurements, the greater is the precision.

Note Accurate results are generally precise but precise results need not be accurate.

e.g. if true value of the mass of a given salt is 10.5 g and four students reported the result of their three measurements as follows:

Measurement (g)	1	2	3	Average (g)
Student *A*	10.3	10.4	10.5	10.4
Student *B*	10.0	10.1	10.2	10.1
Student *C*	10.4	10.6	10.5	10.5
Student *D*	10.8	10.7	10.9	10.8

(i) Measurement by student *A* has not so good accuracy and good precision.

(ii) Measurement by student *B* has poor accuracy but good precision.

(iii) Measurement by student *C* is both accurate and precise.

(iv) Measurement by student *D* has poor accuracy and poor precision.

Example 6 Two students performed the same experiment separately and each one of them recorded two readings of mass which are given below. Correct reading of mass is 3.0 g. On the basis of given data, what would you infer about the accuracy and precision in the readings of students *A* × *B* ? **NCERT Exemplar**

Students	Readings	
	(i)	(ii)
A	3.01	2.99
B	3.05	2.95

Sol. Average readings of student, $A = \frac{3.01 + 2.99}{2} = 3.00$

Average readings of student, $B = \frac{3.05 + 2.95}{2} = 3.00$

Correct reading = 3.00. For both the students, average value is same as the correct value. Hence, readings of both are accurate. Readings of student *A* are close to each other (differ only by 0.02) and also close to the correct reading, hence, readings of *A* are precise. But readings of *B* are not close to each other (differ by 0.1) and hence are not precise.

Significant Figures

Significant figures are meaningful digits which are known with certainty and the uncertainty is indicated by writing the certain digits and the last uncertain digit. e.g. if we write a measurement as 49.6 g, we say that 49 is certain and 6 is uncertain and the uncertainty would be ±1 in the last digit.

Thus, "the total number of digits in a number including the last digit whose value is uncertain is called the number of **significant figures**," e.g. there are 4 significant figures in 3.200 but only two significant figures in 3200.

Note The number of certain digits depends upon the precision of the instrument used for the purpose.

Rules for Counting the Number of Significant Figures

The following rules are followed to count the number of significant figures in a particular number:

(i) All non-zero digits are significant, e.g. in 285 cm, there are three significant figures and in 0.35 mL, there are two significant figures.

(ii) Zeros between two non-zero digits are significant. e.g. there are four significant figures in 1007.

(iii) Trailing zeros are significant only if the digit contains a decimal point. e.g. 1.560 have 4 significant numbers whereas 450 has 2 significant figures. Such numbers are better represented in scientific notation.

(iv) Leading zeros are not significant because their purpose is simply to place the decimal point.

e.g. In 0.05, there is only one significant figure whereas 0.0060500 have five significant figures.

(v) Defined values or counting numbers have infinite number of significant figures, as these are exact numbers and can be represented by writing infinite number of zeros after placing a decimal.

i.e. $2 = 2.000000$

or $20 = 20.000000$

(vi) If numbers written in scientific notation, then all digits are significant, e.g. 4.01×10^2 has three significant figures, and 8.256×10^{-3} has four significant figures.

Significant Figures in Operational Calculations

1. In Case of Addition and Subtraction

When the two or more digits are added or substracted the result cannot have more digits to the right of the decimal point than either of the original numbers. e.g.

(i)	6.611 5.234 +2.021	Each number has three decimal places, so the answer has to be reported upto three decimal places. The significant figures in each of the terms is 4 but the result has 5 significant figures.
Actual sum	13.866	
Reported sum	13.866	
(ii)	19.26 −11.02534	The first number has 2 decimal places and the second has 5 decimal places, so the answer is reported upto 2 decimal place only.
Actual difference	8.23466	
Reported difference	8.23	

2. In Case of Multiplication and Division

In these operations, the result must be reported with no more significant figures as there in the measurement with the least significant figures. e.g.

	41.012 × 1.21	The first term has 5 significant figures, while the second term has 3 significant figures, so the result can have only 3 significant figures.
Actual product	49.62452	
Reported product	49.6	

The presence of exact numbers in an expression does not affect the number of significant figures in the answer because exact numbers have infinite number of significant figures.

e.g. $\frac{4.28 \times 0.146 \times 3}{0.0418} = 44.84784$

Correct answer is 44.8.

Example 7 How many significant figures should be present in the answer of the following calculations?

(i) $\frac{0.02856 \times 298.15 \times 0.112}{0.5785}$ (ii) 5×5.364

(iii) $0.0125 + 0.7864 + 0.0215$ **NCERT Textbook**

Sol. (i) Least precise number of the calculation is 0.112.
Number of significant figures in the answer = Number of significant figures in the least precise number = 3.

(ii) Least precise number of calculation = 5.364.
Number of significant figures in the answer = Number of significant figures in 5.364 = 4.

(iii) Since, the least number of decimal places in each term is four, the number of significant figures in the answer is also 4.

Rounding off the Numbers

The numbers are rounded off to limit the result of a mathematical operation to required number of significant figures. While rounding off the numbers, keep following points in the mind.

(i) If the rightmost digit to be removed is more than 5, the preceeding number is increased by one, e.g. 1.386. If we have to remove 6, we have to round off it to 1.39.

(ii) If the rightmost digit to be removed is less than 5, the preceeding number is not changed. e.g. 4.334 if 4 is to be removed, the result is rounded off to 4.33.

(iii) If the rightmost digit to be removed is 5, then the preceeding number is not changed if it is an even number, but it is increased by one if it is an odd number. e.g. if 6.35 is to be rounded off by removing 5, we have to increase 3 to 4 giving 6.4 as the result. However, if 6.25 is to be rounded off, it is rounded off to 6.2.

Note In multiple step calculations, do not round off until the end, however keep significant figure in mind.

Example 8 Round off the following upto three significant figures.

(i) 34.216 (ii) 10.4107 (iii) 0.04597 (iv) 2808

Sol. (i) 34.216
The digit to be removed is less than 5, therefore the preceeding digit is not changed.
∴ 34.216 rounded upto three significant figures = 34.2

(ii) 10.4107
The digit to be removed is less than 5, therefore the preceding digit is not changed.
∴ 10.4107 rounded up to three significant figure = 10.4

(iii) 0.04597
The digit to be removed is more than 5, therefore the preceeding digit is increased by one.
∴ 0.04597 is rounded upto three significant figures = 0.0460

(iv) 2808
The digit to be removed is more than 5, therefore the preceeding digit is increased by one.
∴ 2808 rounded up to three significant figures = 2810

Example 9 Express the result of the given calculation to the appropriate number of significant figures.

$$\frac{3.24 \times 0.08666}{5.006}$$

Sol. $\dfrac{3.24\times 0.08666}{5.006} = 0.0560883$ (Actual result)

As 3.24 has least number of significant figures, *viz* 3, the result should contain 3 significant figures only. Hence, the result will be reported as 0.561 (after rounding off).

Conversion Factor (Dimensional Analysis)

The numerical value which must be multiplied or divided to the original unit to convert it into other unit is called **conversion factor** (CF). A conversion factor must always have the numerator and denominator representing equivalent quantities.

Information sought = Information given × CF

or $\quad \text{Unit}_2 = \text{Unit}_1 \times \text{CF}$

To take a simple example, suppose you want to know how many seconds there are in 1 minute (min). First write the unit you want to convert and then multiply it by an appropriate conversion factor.

$$1\text{ min}\times\frac{60\text{ s}}{\text{min}} = 60\text{ s}$$

The conversion factor has two effects:

(i) it introduced a new unit and

(ii) it allowed the cancellation of the old unit (units as well as number can be cancelled)

Let us look at the reverse of the problem; how many minutes are there in 60s? We write the unit we want to convert and multiply it by an appropriate conversion factor

$$60\text{ s}\times\frac{1\text{ min}}{60\text{ s}} = 1\text{ min}$$

The reason, we can use either form of conversion factor can be seen by writing it as a solution to an algebraic expression

$$1\text{ min} = 60\text{ s}$$

so, $\quad \dfrac{1\text{ min}}{60\text{ s}} = 1 \quad \text{and} \quad \dfrac{60\text{ s}}{1\text{ min}} = 1$

Thus, $\quad \dfrac{1\text{ min}}{60\text{ s}} = \dfrac{60\text{ s}}{1\text{ min}}$

A conversion factor does not change the size of a number or measurement, only its name.

e.g. there are three common scales to measure temperature — °C (degree celsius), °F (degree fahrenheit) and K (Kelvin). Kelvin (K) scale represents the SI unit (° degree) of temperature.

The relationship between various temperature units are as follows:

Temperature in K = Temperature in °C +273.15

Temperature in °C = Temperature in K −273.15

Thus, $\quad ^\circ\text{F} = \left(\dfrac{9}{5}\times{}^\circ\text{C}\right)+32^\circ$

$$^\circ\text{C} = \frac{5}{9}(^\circ\text{F}-32)$$

Some important conversion factors (CF) listed in the below given table:

Conversion Factors

1 m	= 39.37 inch
1 mile	= 5280 ft = 1.609 km
1 inch	= 2.54 cm
1 L	= 1000 mL = 1000 cm^3 = $10^{-3} m^3$ = 1 dm^3
1 gallon (US)	= 3.785412 L
1 lb	= 453.59237 g
1 cal	= 4.184 J = 2.613×10^{19} eV
1 eV	= 1.602189×10^{-19} J = 3.827×10^{-20} cal
1 eV/atom	= 96.485 kJ mol^{-1}
1 amu	= 1.6605653×10^{-27} kg = 931.5016 MeV
1 kilo watt hour (kWh)	= 3600 kJ
1 horse power (hp)	= 746 watt
1 J	= 10^7 erg
1 esu	= 3.3356×10^{-10}C
1 dyne	= 10^{-5}N, 1 atom = 760 Torr, 1 Torr = 133.32 Pa
1 atm	= 101325 N m^{-2} = 101325 Pa = 1.01325 bar
1 bar	= 1×10^5 Nm^{-2} = 1×10^5 pascal
1 L atm	= 101.3 J = 24.21 cal
1 year	= 365 days = 3.1536×10^7 s
1 debye (D)	= 1×10^{-18} esu cm
1 mole of a gas	= 22.4 L at STP
1 mole of a substance	= N_0 molecules
1 g atom	= N_0 atoms
1 g cm^{-3}	= 1000 kg m^{-3}

Example 10 How many seconds are there in 2 days?

Sol. *Step* I Here, we know 1 day = 24 hours (h)

or $\quad \dfrac{1\text{ day}}{24\text{ h}} = 1 = \dfrac{24\text{ h}}{1\text{ day}}$ then 1 h = 60 min

or $\quad \dfrac{1\text{ h}}{60\text{ min}} = 1 = \dfrac{60\text{ min}}{1\text{ h}}$

so, for converting 2 days to seconds.

i.e. 2 days ...... = ... seconds

Step II The unit factors can be multiplied in series in one step only as follows :

$$2\text{ day}\times\frac{24\text{ h}}{1\text{ day}}\times\frac{60\text{ min}}{1\text{ h}}\times\frac{60\text{ s}}{1\text{ min}}$$

$$= 2\times 24\times 60\times 60\text{ s} = 172800\text{ s}$$

Example 11 What is the mass (in grams) of a copper block whose dimensions are 5.0 inch × 6.0 inch × 4.0 inch and whose density is 8.96 g/cm^3? Given that 1 inch = 2.54 cm.

Sol. Here, unit conversion factors are $1 = \frac{2.54 \text{ cm}}{1 \text{ inch}} = \frac{1 \text{ inch}}{2.54 \text{ cm}}$

Hence, required mass (in g) = 5.0 inch × 6.0 inch × 4.0 inch

$$\frac{2.54 \text{cm}}{1 \text{ inch}} \times \frac{2.54 \text{ cm}}{1 \text{ inch}} \times \frac{2.54 \text{ cm}}{1 \text{ inch}} \times \frac{8.96 \text{ g}}{1 \text{ cm}^3} = 1.76 \times 10^4 \text{ g}$$

Laws of Chemical Combinations

Elements combined to form molecules in accordance to the following five basic laws, called the laws of chemical combinations.

Law of Conservation of Mass

This law was put forth by Antoine Lavoisier in 1789. According to this law, **"matter can neither be created nor destroyed but one form of matter can be converted into other."**

This law is also known as **law of indestructibility of matter**. The other statement for this law is **"In all physical and chemical changes, the total mass of the reactants is equal to that of the products."**

i.e. Sum of masses of reactants = Sum of masses of products.

Example 12 If 6.3 g of $NaHCO_3$ are added to 15.0 g of CH_3COOH solution, the residue is found to weigh 18.0 g. What is the mass of CO_2 released in the reaction ?

Sol. $$NaHCO_3 + CH_3COOH \longrightarrow \underbrace{H_2O + CH_3CO\overset{-}{O}\overset{+}{Na}}_{\text{Residue}} + CO_2$$

Sum of the masses of reactants = 6.3 + 15 = 21.3 g

Sum of the masses of products = $x + 18$

$21.3 = x + 18$; $x = 21.3 - 18 = 3.3$ g

Thus, the mass of the CO_2 released is 3.3 g.

Law of Definite Proportions

This law was given by, a French chemist, **Joseph Proust in 1799**. According to this law, **"a given compound always contains exactly the same proportion of elements by weight."** It is sometimes also referred to as **law of definite composition**, e.g. pure water obtained from any source (well, river, lake or sea) or any country (India, Russia, America etc.) will always be made up of only hydrogen and oxygen combined together in the same fixed ratio of 1 : 8 by mass.

Example 13 Copper oxide was prepared by the following methods.

(i) In one case, 1.75 g of the metal was dissolved in nitric acid and igniting the residual copper nitrate yielded 2.19 g of copper oxide.

(ii) In the second case, 1.14 g of metal dissolved in nitric acid were precipitated as copper hydroxide by adding caustic alkali solution. The precipitated copper hydroxide after washing, drying and heating yielded 1.43 g of copper oxide.

(iii) In the third case, 1.46 g of copper when strongly heated in a current of air yielded 1.83 g of copper oxide. Show that the given data illustrate the law of definite composition.

Sol. *Step* I and II : In the first case,

2.19 g of copper oxide contained 1.75 g of Cu.

∴ 100 g of copper oxide contained

$$Cu = \frac{1.75}{2.19} \times 100 = 79.91 \text{ g, i.e.\% of Cu} = 79.91$$

In the second case,

1.43 g of copper oxide contained 1.14 g of copper.

∴ 100 g of copper oxide contained

$$Cu = \frac{1.14}{1.43} \times 100 = 79.72 \text{ g},$$

i.e. % of Cu = 79.72

In the third case,

1.83 g of copper oxide contained 1.46 g of copper

∴ 100 g of copper oxide contained

$$Cu = \frac{1.46}{1.83} \times 100 = 79.78 \text{ g},$$

i.e. % of Cu = 79.78

Step III The percentage of copper in copper oxide derived from all the three cases is nearly the same. Hence, the above data illustrate the law of definite composition.

Law of Multiple Proportions

This law was proposed by **Dalton in 1803.** It states that **"if two elements can combine to form more than one compound, the masses of one element that combine with a fixed mass of the other element, are in the ratio of small whole numbers,"** e.g. two compounds, water and hydrogen peroxide are formed when hydrogen combines with oxygen.

Hydrogen	+ Oxygen →	Water
2 g	16 g	18 g

Hydrogen	+ Oxygen →	Hydrogen peroxide
2 g	32 g	34 g

Here, the masses of oxygen (i.e. 16 g and 32 g) that combine with a fixed mass of hydrogen (i.e. 2 g) bear a simple ratio, i.e. 16 : 32 or 1 : 2.

Example 14 Three oxides of nitrogen contained 63.6%, 46.7% and 30.4% nitrogen, respectively. Show that these figures illustrate the law of multiple proportions.

Sol. **In first case,**

Step I The oxide of nitrogen contains 63.6% N

i.e. 63.6 g of N reacts with (100 − 63.6) g of O = 36.4 g of O.

Step II $\therefore$ 1 g of N will react with $\frac{36.4}{63.6}$ g of O = 0.57g of O.

In second case,

Step I The oxide of nitrogen contains 46.7% N,

i.e. 46.7g of N reacts with (100 −46.7) g of O = 53.3 g of O.

Step II $\therefore$ 1g of N will react with $\frac{53.3}{46.7}$ g of O = 1.14 g of O.

In third case,

Step I The oxide of nitrogen contains 30.4% N,

i.e. 30.4 g of N reacts with (100 − 30.4) g of O = 69.6 g of O.

Step II $\therefore$1g of N will react with $\frac{69.6}{30.4}$ g of O = 2.26 g of O

This means the ratio of the masses of oxygen which combine with 1 g of nitrogen is 0.57 : 1.14 : 2.26, i.e. 1 : 2 : 4. is obviously in accordance with the law of multiple proportions.

4. Law of Reciprocal Proportions

This law was given by Richter in 1792. It states that, "the ratio of the masses of two elements *A* and *B* which combine separately with a fixed mass of the third element *C* is either the same or some simple multiple of the ratio of the masses in which *A* and *B* combine directly with each other." This can be illustrated by the following examples.

Example 15 The element H and O combine separately with the third element S to form H_2S and SO_2 respectively, then show that they combine directly with each other to form H_2O.

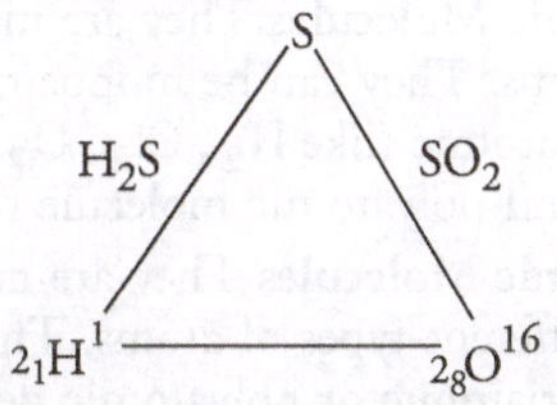

Sol. As shown in figure, the masses of H and O which combine with the fixed mass of S, i.e. 32 are 2 and 32, i.e. they are in the ratio 2 : 32 or 1:16. When H and O combine directly to form H_2O, the ratio of their combining masses are 2:16 or 1 : 8.

These ratio are related to each other as $\frac{1}{16} : \frac{1}{8} = 1:2$,

i.e. they are simple multiple of each other.

Example 16 The percentage composition of elements in NH_3, H_2O and N_2O_3 is given below:

$NH_3 \longrightarrow$ 82.35% N and 17.65% H

$H_2O \longrightarrow$ 88.90% O and 11.10% H

$N_2O_3 \longrightarrow$ 63.15% O and 36.85% N

Show that these data are in accordance with the law of reciprocal proportion.

Sol. (i) NH_3 : 1 part of H reacts with $= \frac{82.35}{17.65} = 4.67$ part of N

(ii) H_2O : 1 part of H reacts with $= \frac{88.90}{11.10} = 8.01$ part of O

Thus, the ratio N : O :: 4.67 : 8.01 = 1 : 1.72

(iii) N_2O_3 :

Here, N and O reacts with each other in the ratio N : O :: 36.85 : 63.15 = 1 : 1.71. Thus, the two ratios are the same. Hence, it illustrates the law of reciprocal proportions.

5. Gay Lussac's Law of Gaseous Volumes

As the name implies this law was given by Gay Lussac in 1808. He stated that "when gases combine or are produced in a chemical reaction they do so in a simple ratio by volume provided all the gases are at same temperature and pressure". e.g. one volume of hydrogen and one volume of chlorine always combine to form two volumes of hydrogen chloride gas.

$$\underset{1\text{ vol}}{H_2} + \underset{1\text{ vol}}{Cl_2} \longrightarrow \underset{2\text{ vol}}{2\,HCl}$$

The ratio between the volumes of the reactants and the product in this reaction is simple, i.e. 1 : 1 : 2

Hence, it illustrates the law of combining volumes.

Example 17 N_2 reacts with H_2 to form NH_3. If 10 L N_2 reacts with 30 L H_2 to form 20 L NH_3 under same conditions of pressure and temperature. Show that the given data is in accordance with law of gaseous volumes.

Sol. The reaction taking place is $N_2 + 3H_2 \longrightarrow 2NH_3$

The ratio of $N_2 : H_2 : NH_3$ :: 10 : 30 : 20, i.e. 1 : 3 : 2.

Since, the ratio is simple and whole number, thus law of gaseous volume is proved.

6. Avogadro's Law

It is the modified form of Gay-Lussac's law which states that, "**equal volumes of all gases under the same conditions of temperature and pressure contain equal** number of molecules". e.g. consider the following reaction,

$$\underset{\substack{1\text{ V} \\ n\text{ molecules}}}{H_2} + \underset{\substack{1\text{ V} \\ n\text{ molecules}}}{Cl_2} \longrightarrow \underset{\substack{2\text{ V} \\ 2n\text{ molecules}}}{2\,HCl}$$

As per the Avogadro's law, if 1 volume each of H_2 and Cl_2 are reacted to form 2 volumes of HCl, then it means equal number of molecules of both H_2 and Cl_2 reacted to form the double number of molecules of HCl.

Dalton's Atomic Theory

The concept that matter is composed of very tiny particles was given by Indian and Greek philosophers. The *Greek* philosopher Democritus (460-370 BC) suggested that the ultimate particle of a matter is atom. The word 'atom' has been derived from the *Greek* word *'atomos'* meaning **indivisible**. The old ideas were put on a scientific scale by John Dalton in the form of a theory, known as Dalton's atomic theory.

Main postulates of this theory are as follows:

(i) Matter consists of minute, indivisible, indestructible particles, called **atoms.**

(ii) Atoms of the same element are identical to each other. They have the same mass and size.

(iii) Atoms of different elements differ in properties and have different masses and sizes.

(iv) **Compounds** are formed when atoms of different elements combine with each other in simple numerical ratios and the relative numbers and kind of atoms are always the same in a given compound.

(v) Chemical reactions involve reorganisation of atoms. These are neither created nor destroyed in a chemical reaction.

Explanation of the Laws of Chemical Combination by Dalton's Atomic Theory

Dalton's theory could explain the laws of chemical combination.

(i) **Law of Conservation of Mass** Matter is made up of atoms [postulate (i)] which can neither be created nor destroyed [postulate (v)]. Hence, matter can neither be created nor destroyed.

(ii) **Law of Constant Composition** Law of multiple proportions and law of reciprocal proportions follows directly from postulate (iv).

Limitations of Dalton's Atomic Theory

Dalton's atomic theory gave a powerful initiative to scientists in the beginning of the 19th century.

But the discoveries in the beginning of 20th century by Sir J J Thomson, Rutherford, Neils Bohr and others, resulted in a reviewed and modified theory.

The main drawbacks of Dalton's atomic theory are:

(i) It could explain the laws of chemical combination by mass but failed to explain the law of gaseous volumes.

(ii) It could not explain why atoms of different elements have different masses, sizes, valencies etc.

(iii) It failed to explain the nature of forces that bind together atoms in a molecule.

(iv) It could not explain how and why atoms of different elements combine with each other to form **compound, atoms** or **molecules.**

(v) It does not make any distinction between ultimate particle of an element or a compound.

Concept of Atoms and Molecules

When the shortcoming of atomic theory was highlighted, Avogadro came with the concepts of atoms and molecules which are widely accepted.

A glimpse of this concept are discussed below:

Atom

The smallest unit of an element that takes part in a chemical reaction is called **atom.** It is the smallest particle that consists all the chemical properties of its element. Atom of an element (except the inert gases) does not have independent existence.

Hydrogen has the smallest atom with its radius being 0.931 Å (9.31×10^{-11} m).

Molecule

The smallest particle of a substance which is capable of independent existence and which has all the properties shown by the substance is called **molecule,** e.g. H_2, N_2, Ne, H_2O etc.

Types of Molecules

Molecules are divided into two types based on nature of atoms they consist.

(i) **Homoatomic Molecules** They are made up of same type of atoms. They can be monoatomic (like He, Ne, Ar), diatomic (like H_2, Cl_2, O_2), triatomic (like O_3) and polyatomic molecule (like P_4, S_8).

(ii) **Heteroatomic Molecules** They are made up of two or more different types of atoms. They can also be diatomic, triatomic or polyatomic depending upon number of atoms they contain, e.g. HCl, H_2O, CO_2, NH_3 etc.

Modified Atomic Theory

The following are the modified views of Dalton's atomic theory:

(i) The atom is no longer supposed to be indivisible. It is not a simple particle but a complex one.

(ii) Atoms of the same element may not necessarily have the same mass but have the same atomic number and show similar chemical properties (**discovery of isotopes**).

(iii) Atoms of the different elements may have the same mass but they always have different atomic numbers and differ in chemical properties (**discovery of isobars**).

(iv) Atoms of one element can be transmutated into atoms of other element (**discovery of artificial transmutation**).

(v) In certain organic compounds, like proteins, starch, cellulose, etc., the ratio in which atoms of different elements combine cannot be regarded as simple. There are a number of compounds which do not follow the law of constant proportions. Such compounds are called **non-stoichiometric compounds.**

(vi) The mass of atom can be changed into energy according to Einstein's equation, $E = mc^2$

where, E = energy, m = mass

and c = velocity of light.

Topic Practice 1

Very Short Answer Type Questions

1 Mark

1 Fill in the Blanks

(i) The elements which posses the characteristics of both, metals as well as non-metals, are termed as ....

(ii) The basic fundamental units are .... in number.

(iii) The relationship between Kelvin and Celsius scale is related as: K = °C+ ....

(iv) 'The matter can neither be created nor destroyed but one form of matter can be converted into other' the said law is known as...... .

2 Objective Type Questions

(i) Which of the following statements about a compound is incorrect?

(a) A molecule of a compound has atoms of different elements

(b) A compound cannot be separated into its constituent elements by physical methods of separation

(c) A compound retains the physical properties of its constituent elements

(d) The ratio of atoms of different elements in a compound is fixed

(ii) A measured temperature on Fahrenheit scale is 200°F. What will this reading be on Celsius scale?

(a) 40 °C (b) 94 °C (c) 93.3 °C (d) 30 °C

(iii) If the density of a solution is 3.12 g mL^{-1}, the mass of 1.5 mL solution in significant figures is ....

(a) 4.7 g (b) 4680×10^{-3} g

(c) 4.680 g (d) 46.80 g

(iv) Which of the following reactions is not correct according to the law of conservation of mass?

(a) $2Mg(s) + O_2(g) \longrightarrow 2MgO(s)$

(b) $C_3H_8(g) + O_2(g) \longrightarrow CO_2(g) + H_2O(g)$

(c) $P_4(s) + 5O_2(g) \longrightarrow P_4O_{10}(s)$

(d) $CH_4(g) + 2O_2(g) \longrightarrow CO_2(g) + 2H_2O(g)$

(v) Which of the following statements indicates that law of multiple proportion is being followed?

(a) Sample of carbon dioxide taken from any source will always have carbon and oxygen in the ratio 1 : 2

(b) Carbon forms two oxides namely CO_2 and CO, where masses of oxygen which combine with fixed mass of carbon are in the simple ratio 2 :1

(c) When magnesium burns in oxygen, the amount of magnesium taken for the reaction is equal to the amount of magnesium in magnesium oxide formed

(d) At constant temperature and pressure 200 mL of hydrogen will combine with 100 mL of oxygen to produce 200 mL of water vapour

3 Match the terms of Column I with the items of Column II and choose the correct option using the codes given below:

Column I (Basic physical quantity)		Column II (Symbol for quantity)
A. Moles of a substance	(i)	I
B. Temperature	(ii)	T
C. Mass	(iii)	n
D. Luminous intensity	(iv)	I_v
E. Electric current	(v)	m

Codes

	A	B	C	D	E
(a)	(iii)	(ii)	(i)	(v)	(vi)
(b)	(i)	(ii)	(iii)	(iv)	(v)
(c)	(iii)	(ii)	(v)	(iv)	(i)
(d)	(i)	(ii)	(v)	(iv)	(iii)

4 What is the SI unit of mass? How is it defined? **NCERT Textbook**

5 What do you mean by significant figures? **NCERT Textbook**

6 How many significant figures should be present in the answer of the following calculation? **NCERT Exemplar**

$$\frac{2.5 \times 1.25 \times 3.5}{2.01}$$

7 If the speed of light is 3.0×10^8 m s^{-1}, calculate the distance covered by light in 2.00 ns. **NCERT Textbook**

8 What mass of silver nitrate will react with 5.85 g of sodium chloride to produce 14.35 g of silver chloride and 8.5 g of sodium nitrate, if the law of conservation of mass is true?

9 Two substances X and Y combine to give a substance Z. The process is exothermic and Z has properties different from those of X and Y. Is the substance Z, an element, a mixture or a compound? Give explanation to support your answer.

10 How can you prove that red oxide of copper is not an element?

11 Suppose the length of a cardboard has been reported to be 31.24 cm. What is the minimum uncertainty implied in this measurement?

12 What is the difference between 5.0 g and 5.00 g?

13 Why is the law of Gay Lussac's not obeyed if any reactant or product is not a gas?

Short Answer Type I Questions

2 Marks

14 Match the following with their multiples. **NCERT Textbook**

	Prefixes	Multiples
(i)	micro	10^6
(ii)	deca	10^9
(iii)	mega	10^{-6}
(iv)	giga	10^{-15}
(v)	femto	10

15 The water level in a metric measuring cup is 0.75 L before the addition of a pebble weighing 150 g. The water level after submerging the pebble is 0.82 L. Determine the density of the pebble.

16 Express each of the following in SI units.
(i) 14 pound per square inch (atmospheric pressure)
(ii) 100 mile per hour (iii) 5 feet 2 inch
(iv) 150 pound

17 For precious stone, carat is used for specifying its mass. If 1 carat = 3.08647 grains (a unit of mass) and 1 gram = 15.4324 grains. Find the total mass in kilogram of a ring that contains 0.700 carat diamond and 5.00 gram gold.

18 If the density of a solution is 3.12 g mL^{-1}, what will be the mass of 1.5 mL solution in significant figures? **NCERT Exemplar**

19 5.975 g of the higher oxide of metal gave 5.575 g of lower oxide on heating. The quantity of the lower oxide gave 5.175 g of metal on reduction. Prove that these results are in accordance with the law of multiple proportions.

20 If ten volume of dihydrogen gas react with five volume of dioxygen gas, how many volume of water vapour would be produced? **NCERT Textbook**

21 Air contains 20% oxygen by volume. Calculate the theoretical volume of air which will be required for burning completely 500 m^3 of acetylene gas. All volumes are measured under the same conditions of temperature and pressure.

22 Pressure is determined as force per unit area of the surface. The SI unit of pressure, pascal is as shown below 1 Pa = 1 N m^{-2}. If the mass of air at sea level is 1034 g, calculate the pressure in pascal. **NCERT Textbook**

23 One of the statements of Dalton's atomic theory is "compounds are formed when atoms of different elements combine in a fixed ratio". Which laws of chemical combination is not related to this statement? **NCERT Exemplar**

Short Answer Type II Questions

3 Marks

24 Perform the following calculations and express the results to proper number of significant figures.
(i) 144.3 m^2 + (2.54 m × 8.4 m)
(ii) (4.05×10^2 mL) – (0.0225×10^2 mL)
(iii) (3.50×10^2 cm) (4.00×10^6 cm)

25 If two elements can combine to form more than one compound, the masses of one element that combine with a fixed mass of the other element, are in whole number ratio. **NCERT Exemplar**

(i) Is this statement true?
(ii) If yes, according to which law?
(iii) Give one example related to this law.

26 A box contains some identical red coloured balls, labelled as *A*, each weighing 2 g. Another box contains identical blue coloured balls, labelled as B_1 each weighing 5 g. Consider the combinations *AB*, AB_2, A_2B and A_2B_3 and shows that law of multiple proportion is applicable. **NCERT Exemplar**

27 45.4 L of dinitrogen reacted with 22.7 L of dioxygen and 45.4 L nitrous oxide was formed. The reaction is given below

$$2\,N_2(g) + O_2(g) \longrightarrow 2\,N_2O(g)$$

Which law is being obeyed in this experiment? Write the statement of the law. **NCERT Exemplar**

28 Two oxides of a metal contain 27.6% and 30.0% of oxygen respectively. If the formula of the first oxide is M_3O_4, find that of the second.

29 10 mL of H_2 combine with 5 mL of O_2 to form water. When 200 mL of H_2 at STP is passed over heated CuO, the CuO loses 0.144 g of its weight. Does the above data correspond to the law of constant composition?

Long Answer Type Questions

5 Marks

30 The following data are obtained when dinitrogen and dioxygen react together to form different compounds.

	Mass of dinitrogen	Mass of dioxygen
(i)	14 g	16 g
(ii)	14 g	32 g
(iii)	28 g	32 g
(iv)	28 g	80 g

(i) Which law of chemical combination is obeyed by the above experimental data? Give statement.
(ii) Fill in the blanks in the following conversion
(a) 1 km = ... mm = ... pm
(b) 1 mg = ... kg = ... ng
(c) 1 mL = ... L = ... dm^3 **NCERT Textbook**

31 Define the law of multiple proportions. Explain it with two examples. How does this law point to the existence of atoms? **NCERT Exemplar**

32 A mixture of oxalic acid and formic acid is heated with concentrated H_2SO_4 and the gas evolved is collected. On treating the solution with KOH, the volume of the solution decreases by 1/6th. Calculate the molar ratios of two acids in the original mixture.

Hints & Solutions

1. (i) metalloids
(ii) seven
(iii) K = °C + 273.15
(iv) law of conservation of mass.

2. (i) (c) The properties of a compound are quite different from the properties of constituent elements. e.g., water is a compound containing hydrogen and oxygen combined together in a fixed proportion. But the properties of water are completely different from its constituents, hydrogen and oxygen.

(ii) (c) The temperatures on two scales (°F and °C) are related to each other by the following relationship:

$$°F = \frac{9}{5} t°C + 32$$

Putting the values in above equation,

$$200 - 32 = \frac{9}{5} t°C$$

$$\Rightarrow \quad \frac{9}{5} t°C = 168$$

$$\Rightarrow \quad t°C = \frac{168 \times 5}{9} = 93.3°\,C$$

(iii) (a) Given that, density of solution = 3.12 g mL^{-1}
Volume of solution = 1.5 mL
For a solution, Mass = volume × density

$$= 1.5\ mL \times 3.12\ g\ mL^{-1} = 4.68\ g$$

The digit 1.5 has only two significant figures, so the answer must also be limited to two significant figures. So, it is rounded off to reduce the number of significant figures. Hence, the answer is reported as 4.7 g.

(iv) (b) In this equation,

$$\underset{44g}{C_3H_8(g)} + \underset{32g}{O_2(g)} \longrightarrow \underset{44\,g}{CO_2(g)} + \underset{18\,g}{H_2O(g)}$$

i.e. mass of reactants ≠ mass of products.
Hence, law of conservation of mass is not followed.

(v) (b) The element, carbon combines with oxygen to form two compounds, namely, carbon dioxide and carbon monoxide. In CO_2, 12 parts by mass of carbon combine with 32 parts by mass of oxygen while in CO, 12 parts by mass of carbon combine

with 16 parts by mass of oxygen. Therefore, the masses of oxygen combine with a fixed mass of carbon (12 parts) in CO_2 and CO are 32 and 16 respectively. These masses of oxygen bear a simple ratio of 32 : 16 or 2 : 1 to each other.
This is an example of law of multiple proportion.

3. (c) (A) → (iii), (B) → (ii), (C) → (v), (D) → (iv), (E) → (i),

4. SI unit of mass is kilogram (kg). It is equal to the mass of international prototype of the kilogram.

5. Refer to text on page 7. (Significant figures).

6. Least precise term i.e. 2.5 or 3.5 has two significant figures. Hence, the answer must have two significant figures.

$$\frac{2.5\times 1.25\times 3.5}{2.01} = 5.4415 \approx 5.4$$

7. Time 2.00 ns = 2.00×10^{-9}s ($\because$ 1 ns = 10^{-9} s)
Distance covered = speed × time
$= 3.0\times 10^8 \text{ m s}^{-1} \times 2.00\times 10^{-9} \text{ s} = 0.6 \text{ m}$

8. According to law of conservation of mass,
mass of reactants = mass of products.

$$\underset{x\text{ g}}{AgNO_3} + \underset{5.85\text{ g}}{NaCl} \longrightarrow \underset{14.35\text{ g}}{AgCl} + \underset{8.5\text{ g}}{NaNO_3}$$

$\therefore$ $x + 5.85 = 14.35 + 8.5$ or $x = 17.0$ g

9. The substance Z is a compound. This is because
I. heat is evolved during the formation of Z.
II. the properties of Z are different from those of X and Y.

10. On heating red oxide of copper in the presence of hydrogen, its mass decreases and it forms shining metallic copper which is chemically different from the original compound.

$$Cu_2O + H_2 \longrightarrow 2Cu + H_2O$$

11. The minimum uncertainty implies in this measurement is ± 0.01 cm.

12. Though the two values seem to be equivalent but scientifically they are different. 5.0 g has two significant figures and hence, its precision is 0.1 part in 5, 5.00 has three significant figures and hence, its precision is 0.01 parts in 5. Hence, 5.00 g is more precise measurement than 5.0 g.

13. If any reactant or product is a liquid or solid, the volume occupied by them is extremely small as compared to the gas and hence, the law is not obeyed.

14. Micro $=10^{-6}$, deca $=10$, mega $=10^6$, giga $=10^9$ and femto $=10^{-15}$. [2]

15. The volume displaced by the pebble
$= 0.82 - 0.75 = 0.07$ L $= 70$ mL [1]
Mass of the pebble = 150 g
Therefore, density of the pebble is

$$\text{Density} = \frac{\text{Mass}}{\text{Volume}} = \frac{150}{70} = 2.14 \text{ g mL}^{-1}$$ [1]

16. (i) 1 pound per square inch = 6894.76 Nm^{-2}
$\therefore$ 14 pound per square inch
$= 14\times 6894.76 = 96526.64$ Nm^{-2}

(ii) $1 \text{ mile/h} = \dfrac{1.6\times 10^3 \text{ m}}{3600 \text{ s}} = 0.444 \text{ ms}^{-1}$

$\therefore$ 100 mile/h = 44.4 m/s

(iii) 5 feet 2 inch = 1.5748 m
[$\therefore$ 1 feet = 12 inch, 1m = 39.37 inch]

(iv) 1 pound = 0.454 kg
$\therefore$ 150 pound = 68.1 kg [½ × 4]

17. Finding mass of diamond in kg.
1 carat = 3.08647 grains
$\therefore$ 0.700 carat = 0.700 × 3.08647 grains = 2.16 grains
Also, 1 gram = 15.4324 grains

$\therefore$ $1 \text{ grain} = \dfrac{1}{15.4324} = 0.064799$ grams [1]

and 2.16 grains = 2.16 × 0.064799 = 0.1399 grams
1 gram $= 10^{-3}$ kg $\Rightarrow$ 0.1399 g $= 1.399\times 10^{-2}$ kg
Total mass of the ring in kg
$= 1.399\times 10^{-2}$ kg $+ 5\times 10^{-3}$ kg $= 1.899\times 10^{-2}$ kg [1]

18. Given that, density of solution = 3.12 g mL^{-1}
Volume of solution = 1.5 mL
For a solution, Mass = volume × density
$= 1.5 \text{ mL}\times 3.12 \text{ g mL}^{-1} = 4.68$ g [1]

The digit 1.5 has only two significant figures, so the answer must also be limited to two significant figures. So, it is rounded off to reduce the number of significant figures. Hence, the answer is reported as 4.7 g. [1]

19. As 5.575 g of lower oxide on reduction gives 5.175 g of the metal, the mass of the oxygen is 5.575 − 5.175 = 0.4 g

For 1 g of metal, mass of oxygen is $\dfrac{0.4}{5.175} = 0.077$ g

In case of higher oxides, mass of metal is 5.175 g
Mass of oxygen is 5.975 − 5.175 = 0.8 g [1]

For 1 g of metal, mass of oxygen is $\dfrac{0.8}{5.175} = 0.155$ g

For a given mass of metal, the ratio of oxygen is 0.077 : 0.155 or 1 : 2. Hence, the law of multiple proportion is proved. [1]

20.
$$\underset{2\text{ V}}{2H_2(g)} + \underset{1\text{ V}}{O_2(g)} \longrightarrow \underset{2\text{ V}}{2H_2O(g)}$$

According to Gay Lussac's law of gaseous volumes, 2 volume of dihydrogen react with 1 volume of dioxygen to produce 2 volume of water vapour. Therefore, 10 volumes of dihydrogen on reaction with 5 volumes of dioxygen will produce 10 volume of water vapour. [2]

21.

$2C_2H_2$	$+5O_2$	$\longrightarrow 4CO_2$	$+2H_2O(g)$
2 vol	5 vol	4 vol	2 vol (Gay-Lussac's Law)
or 1 vol	5/2 vol	4/2 vol	2/2 vol
500 m^3	$5/2 \times 500 m^3$	$4/2 \times 500 m^3$	$2/2 \times 500 m^3$
500 m^3	1250 m^3	1000 m^3	500 m^3

[1]

Thus, 1250 m^3 oxygen is required for burning 500 m^3 of acetylene. But the percentage of oxygen in air is 20%

$\therefore$ Volume of air required $= 1250 \times 100/20 = 6250\ m^3$ [1]

22. (i) The SI unit of mass is kilogram and of length is metre so convert gram to kilogram and cm^2 to m^2 as pressure is to be calculated in SI units.

(ii) Write $1\ kg\ m\ s^{-2} = 1\ N$ and $1\ N\ m^{-2} = 1\ Pa$ to obtain pressure in pascal.

Pressure is the force or weight per unit area.

$$\text{Pressure} = \frac{1034\ g \times 9.8\ ms^{-2}}{1\ cm^2} \quad [\because F = ma]$$ [1]

$$= \frac{1034\ kg \times 100 \times 100 \times 9.8\ m\ s^{-2}}{1000\ m^2}$$

$$= 101332.0\ N\ m^{-2} \quad (\because 1N = 1\ kg\ m\ s^{-2})$$

$$= 1.01332 \times 10^5\ Pa \quad (\because 1\ Pa = 1\ Nm^{-2})$$ [1]

23. Law of conservation of mass and Avogadro's law because law of conservation of mass is simply the law of indestructibility of matter during physical or chemical changes.

Avogadro law states that equal volumes of different gases contain the same number of molecules under similar conditions of temperature and pressure. [2]

24. (i) $(144.3\ m^2) + (2.54\ m \times 8.4\ m)$

$2.54\ m \times 8.4\ m = 21.336$ or $21\ m^3$

(upto 2 significant figures)

$$\begin{array}{rl} 144.3 & m^2 \\ +\ 21 & m^2 \\ \hline 165.3 & m^2 \end{array}$$

(As 144.3 contains (1) one digit (SF) after the decimal point.) [1]

(ii) $(4.05 \times 10^2\ mL) - (0.0225 \times 10^2\ mL)$

$= 4.0275 \times 10^2\ mL$ or $4.03 \times 10^2\ mL$ [1]

(upto two decimal place as in 4.05)

(iii) $(3.50 \times 10^2\ cm) \times (4.00 \times 10^6\ cm)$

$= 14.0 \times 10^8\ cm^2$ (upto 3 significant figures) [1]

25. (i) Yes [1/2]

(ii) According to the law of multiple proportions. [1]

(iii) $\underset{2\,g}{H_2} + \underset{16\,g}{O} \longrightarrow \underset{18\,g}{H_2O}$ [1/2]

$\underset{2\,g}{H_2} + \underset{32\,g}{O_2} \longrightarrow \underset{34\,g}{H_2O_2}$ [1/2]

Here, masses of oxygen, (i.e. 16 g in H_2O and 32 g in H_2O_2) which combine with fixed mass of hydrogen (2 g) are in the simple ratio i.e. 16 : 32 or 1 : 2. [1/2]

26.

Combination	Mass of *A* (g)	Mass of *B* (g)
AB	2	5
AB_2	2	10
A_2B	4	5
A_2B_3	4	15

[1]

Mass of *B* which is combined with fixed mass of *A* (say 1 g) will be 2.5 g, 5 g, 1.25 g and 3.75 g in *AB*, AB_2, A_2B and A_2B_3 respectively. They are in the ratio 2 : 4 : 1 : 3 which is simple whole number ratio. Hence, the law of multiple proportion is applicable. [2]

27

$$\begin{array}{ccccc} 2N_{2(g)} & + & O_{2(g)} & \longrightarrow & 2N_2O_{(g)} \\ 2V & & 1V & & 2V \\ 45.4L & + & 22.7L & & 45.4L \\ \frac{45.4}{22.7} = 2 & & \frac{22.7}{22.7} = 1 & & \frac{45.4}{22.7} = 2 \end{array}$$

Hence, the ratio between the volume of the reactants and the product in the given question is simple i.e. 2 : 1 : 2. It proves the Gay Lussac's law of gaseous volumes. [2]

For Gay Lussac's law of gaseous volumes :

Refer to text on page 11. [1]

28. In the first oxide, oxygen = 27.6

Metal = 100 − 27.6 = 72.4 parts by mass.

As the formula of the oxide is M_3O_4, it means 72.4 parts by mass of metal = 3 atoms of metal and 4 atoms of oxygen = 27.6 parts by mass.

In the second oxide, oxygen = 30.0 parts by mass and metal = 100 − 30 = 70 parts by mass.

But 72.4 parts by mass of metal = 3 atoms of metal.

$\therefore$ 70 parts by mass of metal $= \frac{3}{72.4} \times 70$ atoms of metal

= 2.90 atoms of metal [1]

Also, 27.6 part by mass of oxygen = 4 atoms of oxygen.

$\therefore$ 30 part by mass of oxygen $= \frac{4}{27.6} \times 30$ atoms of oxygen

= 4.35 atoms of oxygen. [1]

Hence, ratio of *M* : O in the second oxide

= 2.90 : 4.35 = 1 : 1.5 or 2 : 3 [1/2]

$\therefore$ Formula of the other metal oxide is M_2O_3. [1/2]

29. In the second experiment 0.144 g weight is lost from CuO. This is due to the reduction of CuO into Cu. In other words, 0.144 g oxygen combined with 200 mL H_2. [1]

32 g oxygen occupies 22400 mL volume at STP.

$\therefore$ 0.144 g oxygen will occupy $= 22400 \times \frac{0.144}{32}$ [1]

$= 100.8\ mL\ O_2$

It means the ratio of H_2 and O_2 in water is 200 : 100.8 = 2 : 1. The same ratio is in first case (10 : 5 or 2 : 1). Thus, the law of constant composition is proved. [1]

30. (i) On fixing the mass of dinitrogen as 28 g, the masses of dioxygen combined are 32, 64, 32 and 80 in the given four oxides. These are in the simple whole number ratio i.e. 2 : 4 : 2 : 5. Hence, the given data obey the law of multiple proportions. [2]

Law of multiple proportions Refer to text on page 10.

(ii) (a) $1\text{km} = 1\text{ km} \times \frac{1000\text{ m}}{1\text{ km}} \times \frac{100\text{ cm}}{1\text{ m}} \times \frac{10\text{ mm}}{1\text{cm}} = 10^6\text{ mm}$

$$1\text{ km} = 1\text{ km} \times \frac{1000\text{ m}}{1\text{ km}} \times \frac{1\text{pm}}{10^{-12}\text{ m}} = 10^{15}\text{ pm}$$

$\therefore 1\text{ km} = 10^6\text{ mm} = 10^{15}\text{ pm}$ [1]

(b) $1\text{ mg} = 1\text{ mg} \times \frac{1\text{g}}{1000\text{ mg}} \times \frac{1\text{ kg}}{1000\text{ g}} = 10^{-6}\text{kg}$

$$1\text{ mg} = 1\text{ mg} \times \frac{1\text{ g}}{1000\text{ mg}} \times \frac{1\text{ ng}}{10^{-9}\text{ g}} = 10^6\text{ng}$$

$\therefore 1\text{ mg} = 10^{-6}\text{ kg} = 10^6\text{ng}$ [1]

(c) $1\text{ mL} = 1\text{ mL} \times \frac{1\text{ L}}{1000\text{ mL}} = 10^{-3}\text{L}$

$$1\text{ mL} = 1\text{ cm}^3 = 1\text{ cm}^3 \times \frac{1\text{ dm} \times 1\text{ dm} \times 1\text{ dm}}{10\text{ cm} \times 10\text{ cm} \times 10\text{ cm}}$$

$$= 10^{-3}\text{ dm}^3$$

$\therefore \quad 1\text{ mL} = 10^{-3}\text{L} = 10^{-3}\text{dm}^3$ [1]

31. Refer to the text on pages 10 and 11. Law of multiple proportions.

32. Let x mole of oxalic acid and y mole of formic acid be heated with conc. H_2SO_4 according to the following equations.

$$\underset{x\text{ mol}}{\begin{matrix}COOH\\ |\\ COOH\end{matrix}} \xrightarrow{H_2SO_4/\text{heat}} \underset{x\text{ mol}}{CO(g)} + \underset{x\text{ mol}}{CO_2(g)} + H_2O(l)$$

$$\underset{y\text{ mol}}{HCOOH} \xrightarrow{H_2SO_4/\text{heat}} \underset{y\text{ mol}}{CO(g)} + H_2O(l)$$ [2]

Total moles of gaseous mixture = Moles of CO + Moles of $CO_2 = (x + y)$ mol $+ x$ mol $= (2x + y)$ mol

Now, KOH absorbs only CO_2 i.e. x moles and the volume of the solution decreases by 1/6th of its volume. Since equal volume of gases have equal number of moles according to Avogadro's law,

$$\therefore \quad \frac{\text{moles of }CO_2}{\text{moles of both the gases}} = \frac{x}{(2x + y)} = \frac{1}{6}$$ [2]

or $6x = 2x + y$

or $4x = y$

or $\frac{y}{x} = 4$

$\therefore$ Molar ratio of formic acid : oxalic acid = 4 : 1 [1]

TOPIC 02 Atomic and Molecular Masses, Mole Concept and Formulae of Compounds

Atomic Mass

It is defined as a number that expresses how many times an atom of the element is heavier than 1/12th of the mass of carbon atom (^{12}C). Therefore,

$$\text{Atomic mass} = \frac{\text{mass of an atom}}{(1/12) \times \text{mass of a carbon atom } (^{12}C)}$$

The scale of relative masses of atoms is termed as **atomic mass unit (amu) scale.** However, the new symbol used is u (known as unified mass) in place of amu. In this system, ^{12}C is assigned as mass of exactly 12 atomic mass units and masses of all other atoms are given relative to this standard. Hence, **one atomic mass unit is defined as the mass exactly equal to 1/12th of the mass of an atom of carbon** (^{12}C).

$$1\text{ amu} = 1.66056 \times 10^{-24}\text{ g}$$

Since, the atomic mass is the ratio of the masses, so it has no units. However, we express it as amu, which only signifies that it is taken on atomic mass unit scale in which 1/12th of carbon atom is fixed as 1u.

C-12 is chosen as standard because in such case the masses of most of the elements are whole number or nearest to the whole number, which corresponds closely to the mass of a proton or neutron. More recently, these units have been called **Daltons** (Da).

$$1\text{ Da} = 1\text{ u}.$$

Mass of an atom of hydrogen $= 1.6736 \times 10^{-24}$ g

Thus, in terms of amu, the mass of hydrogen atom

$$= \frac{1.6736 \times 10^{-24}\text{ g}}{1.66056 \times 10^{-24}\text{ g}}$$

$$= 1.0078\text{ u} = 1.0080\text{ u}$$

Similarly, the mass of oxygen 16 (^{16}O) atom would be 15.995 u.

Average Atomic Mass (Isotopic Masses)

Many naturally occurring elements exist as mixture of several isotopes [Isotopes are the different atoms of the same element having same atomic number and different atomic masses] in which the atomic mass of an element is equal to the average of atomic masses of all the isotopes. Thus, it is termed as average atomic mass and is generally fractional. **Average atomic mass is, thus, defined as the average relative mass of atoms of an element as compared with an atom of carbon-12 taken as 12.** It is determined with the help of mass spectrometer. If we have the percentage abundances of all the isotopes, the average atomic mass is calculated by the expression,

Average atomic mass $= \frac{\Sigma p_i A_i}{100} = \frac{p_1 A_1 + p_2 A_2 + \ldots}{100}$ where,

p_i is the percentage abundance of isotope having atomic mass A_i. Fractional abundances, f_i can also be used to obtain the atomic mass of an element.

Fractional abundance is the total number of atoms that is comprised of that particular isotope. Thus,

Average atomic mass $= \Sigma f_i A_i = f_1 A_1 + f_2 A_2 + \ldots$

e.g. nitrogen has the following two isotopes with relative abundance and atomic masses as shown against each of them.

Isotope	Relative abundance %	Atomic mass (amu)
^{14}N	99.33%	14
^{15}N	0.67%	15

From the above data, the average atomic mass of nitrogen can be calculated as:

$$(0.9933 \times 14) = (0.0067 \times 15) = 14.0067 \text{ u}$$

Example 1 Boron occurs in nature in the form of two isotopes having atomic mass 10 and 11. What are the percentage abundances of two isotopes in a sample of boron having average atomic mass 10.8?

Sol. Let the % abundance of ^{10}B isotope $= x$

Then % abundance of ^{11}B isotope $= 100 - x$

The average atomic mass $= \frac{x \times 10 + (100 - x) \times 11}{100}$

But, average atomic mass = 10.8

$$\therefore \quad \frac{x \times 10 + (100 - x) \times 11}{100} = 10.8$$

or $\quad 10x + 1100 - 11x = 10.8 \times 100$

or $\quad -x = -1100 + 1080$ or $x = 20$

Thus, percentage abundance, $^{10}B = 20\%, {}^{11}B = 80\%$

Note In the periodic table of elements, the atomic masses mentioned for different elements actually represented their average atomic masses.

Gram Atomic Mass

Atomic mass of an element expressed in gram is called its **gram atomic mass** or **gram atom.** It may also be defined as that quantity of the element whose mass in gram is numerically equal to its atomic mass.

e.g. the atomic mass of hydrogen is 1.008 amu and thus, a gram atom of hydrogen is 1.008 g.

Gram atomic mass = Atomic mass expressed in gram
= gram atom

Never get confused between the terms gram atom and mass of an atom of the element.

e.g. The mass of one atom of oxygen is only 2.66×10^{-23} g whereas, its gram atomic mass is 16 g. The mass of one atom of an element is known as the actual mass of the atom.

Molecular Mass

Molecular mass is the sum of atomic masses of the elements present in a molecule.

Thus, it is obtained by multiplying the atomic mass of each element by the number of its atoms and then adding them together e.g.

Molecular mass of methane CH_4 can be calculated as:

$$= 1 \times \text{atomic mass of C} + 4 \times \text{atomic mass of H}$$
$$= (12.011\text{u}) + 4\ (1.008\text{ u}). = 16.043\text{ u}$$

Example 2 Calculate molecular mass of glucose ($C_6H_{12}O_6$) molecule. **NCERT**

Sol. Molecular mass of glucose ($C_6H_{12}O_6$)

$$= 6\ (12.011\text{u}) + 12\ (1.008\text{u}) + 6\ (16.00\text{u})$$
$$= (72.66\text{u}) + (12.096\text{u}) + (96.00\text{u}) = 180.162\text{u}$$

Gram Molecular Mass or Gram Molecule

Molecular mass of a substance expressed in gram is called its **gram molecular mass** or **gram molecule.**

Gram molecular mass or gram molecule
= Molecular mass expressed in gram

e.g. the molecular mass of oxygen is 32 and, therefore, its gram molecular mass is 32 g. Gram molecular mass should not be confused with the mass of one molecule of the substance in gram.

e.g. the mass of one molecule of oxygen is only 5.32×10^{-23} g, whereas the gram molecular mass is 32 g. The mass of one molecule of a substance is known as its **actual molecular mass.**

Example 3

(i) Calculate the gram molecular mass of sugar having molecular formula $C_{12}H_{22}O_{11}$.

(ii) Calculate

(a) The mass of 0.5 g molecule of sugar and

(b) Gram molecule of sugar in 547.2 g.

Sol. (i) Molecular mass of sugar $(C_{12}H_{22}O_{11})$

$= 12 \times$ atomic mass of C $+ 22 \times$ atomic mass of H $+ 11 \times$ atomic mass of O

$= 12 \times 12 + 22 \times 1 + 11 \times 16 = 342$

$\therefore$ Gram molecular mass of sugar = 342 g

(ii) (a) 1 gram molecule of sugar = 342 g

$\therefore$ 0.5 gram molecule of sugar $= 342 \times 0.5 = 171$ g

(b) 342 g of sugar = 1 gram molecule

547.2 g of sugar $= \frac{1}{342} \times 547.2 = 1.6$ gram molecule

Formula Mass

Ionic compounds do not contain discrete molecules as their constituent units. In these compounds, positive and negative ions are arranged in a three-dimensional structure. Thus, the formula of such compounds is used to calculate the formula mass instead of the molecular mass.

Formula mass of an ionic compound = number of cations × its atomic mass + number of anions × its atomic mass

e.g. formula mass of sodium chloride

= atomic mass of sodium + atomic mass of chlorine

= 23.0 u + 35.5 u = 58.5 u

Formula mass expressed in grams is called **gram formula mass.**

1. Chemical Equivalents

In most of the chemical reactions, a fixed mass of a particular substance combines with a fixed mass of some other substance, e.g. 1g of hydrogen will always combine with 8g of oxygen or with 35.5 g of chlorine. This equivalence can be expressed in terms of specific mass, called equivalent mass or equivalent weight.

2. Equivalent Weight (Equivalent Mass)

Equivalent weight or equivalent mass of a substance is the number of parts by mass of the given substance which combines with or displaces directly or indirectly 1.008 parts by mass of hydrogen or 8 parts by mass of oxygen, or 35.5 parts by mass of chlorine.

Mathematically,

$$\frac{\text{Eq. wt. of substance } A}{\text{Eq. wt. of substance } B} = \frac{\text{Wt. of substance } A}{\text{Wt. of substance } B}$$

For example in the following process

$$\underset{65}{Zn} + \underset{98}{H_2SO_4} \longrightarrow ZnSO_4 + \underset{2}{H_2}$$

In said reaction, 65 parts by mass of zinc combine with 98 parts by mass of H_2SO_4 and displace 2 parts by mass of hydrogen.

Thus,

2 parts by mass of hydrogen ≡ 65 parts by mass of zinc

$\therefore$ 1 part by mass of hydrogen $\equiv \frac{65}{2}$ parts by mass of zinc

Hence, the equivalent weight of zinc $= \frac{65}{2} = 32.5$

In the same way,

2 parts by mass of hydrogen ≡ 98 parts by mass of H_2SO_4

$\therefore$ 1 part by mass of hydrogen $\equiv \frac{98}{2}$ parts by mass of H_2SO_4.

Hence, the equivalent weight of $H_2SO_4 = \frac{98}{2} = 49$

Note Equivalent weight is simply a number and does not have any units.

Determination of Equivalent Weight

There are many methods to determine the equivalent weight of acids, bases (or metal oxides) etc. Some important are as follows:

1. Hydrogen Displacement Method

This method is useful to find the equivalent masses of metals which displace hydrogen from acids like zinc, calcium, magnesium, tin, iron, etc.

Procedure

In this method, a known quantity of the metal will react with dilute sulphuric acid or dilute hydrochloric acid and the volume of hydrogen thus collected is measured. This volume is converted to the volume at STP with the help of the gas equation.

As, 22400 mL of hydrogen at STP weighs 2 grams, the mass of the hydrogen displaced by the metal can be calculated.

Knowing the mass of the metal and that of hydrogen displaced by the metal, the equivalent mass of the metal can be calculated as shown below:

Calculation

Let the mass of the metal used be equal to w_1 g and the volume of hydrogen collected at T_1 °C and p_1 mm pressure (the temperature and pressure of the experiment) be V_1 mL. Let the volume of this hydrogen at STP be equal to V_2.

According to the gas equation,

$$\frac{p_1V_1}{T_1+273}=\frac{p_2V_2}{T_2}$$

or
$$\frac{p_1V_1}{T_1+273}=\frac{760\times V_2}{273}$$

[$\because T$ and p at NTP are 273 K and 760 mm]

or
$$V_2=\frac{273\times p_1V_1}{760\times(T_1+273)}$$

[$\because 2g\ [H_2(g)] \equiv 22400$ mL at STP]

Mass of V_2 mL of $H_2=\frac{2}{22400}\times V_2=w_2 g$ (say)

Now, w_2 g of H_2 are obtained from the metal weighing $=w_1$ g

$\therefore$ 1 g of H_2 will be obtained from the metal weighing

$$=\frac{w_1}{w_2}$$

Hence, equivalent weight of the metal

$$=\frac{w_1}{w_2}=\frac{\text{Mass of metal taken}}{\text{Mass of } H_2 \text{ evolved at STP}}$$

2. Oxide-Formation Method

This method is useful to find the equivalent masses of those metals which easily combine with oxygen to form oxides like zinc, copper, magnesium, calcium, mercury, etc.

Procedure

In this method, a known mass of the metal is converted into its oxide by a direct or indirect method.

Metal + Oxygen $\longrightarrow$ Metal oxide (Direct method)

Metal + HNO_3 $\longrightarrow$ Metal nitrate $\xrightarrow{\Delta}$ Metal oxide (Indirect method)

The mass of the oxide thus formed is noted.

The calculations are carried out as follows :

Calculation

Let the mass of the metal taken be w_1 g and that of the oxide formed be w_2 g.

$\therefore$ Mass of oxygen that combines with w_1 g of metal $=(w_2-w_1)$ g

By definition, the equivalent weight of a substance is the mass of the substance which combines with 8 g of oxygen.

Hence, mass of the metal which combines with 8 g of oxygen $=\frac{w_1}{w_2-w_1}\times 8$

Thus, the equivalent weight of the metal

$$=\frac{w_1}{w_2-w_1}\times 8=\frac{\text{Mass of the metal}}{\text{Mass of oxygen}}\times 8$$

3. Oxide-Reduction Method

This method is useful to find the equivalent weights of the metals, whose oxides can easily be reduced, e.g. iron, tin, etc.

Procedure

In this method, a known mass of a metal oxide is heated strongly in an atmosphere of hydrogen for reduction of metals oxide into the corresponding metal. The mass of the metal thus obtained is noted:

$$\text{Metal oxide}+H_2\longrightarrow \text{Metal}+H_2O$$

The calculations are carried out as follows:

Calculation

Let the mass of the metal oxide be w_1 g and that of the metal obtained on its reduction be w_2 g.

$\therefore$ The mass of oxygen that combines with w_2 g of metal $=w_2-w_1$ g

Hence, the mass of the metal that combines with 8 g of oxygen $=\frac{w_2}{w_1-w_2}\times 8$

Hence , equivalent weight of the metal

$$=\frac{w_2}{w_1-w_2}\times 8=\frac{\text{Mass of the metal}}{\text{Mass of oxygen}}\times 8$$

4. Chloride Formation Method

This method is used to find the equivalent masses of metals which easily combine with chlorine to form chlorides, e.g. sodium, potassium, silver, gold, etc.

Procedure

A known mass of the metal is heated in an atmosphere of chlorine. The mass of the chloride thus obtained is noted.

$$\text{Metal + Chlorine}\longrightarrow\text{Metal chloride}$$

Calculation are carried out as follows :

Calculation

Suppose the mass of the metal taken is w_1 g and that of the chloride formed is w_2 g.

$\therefore$ Mass of chlorine that combines with w_1 g of the metal $=(w_2-w_1)$ g

By definition, the equivalent mass of a substance is that mass of the substance which combines with 35.5 g of chlorine.

$\therefore$ Mass of the metal that combines with 35.5 g of chlorine

$$= \frac{w_1}{w_2 - w_1} \times 35.5 \text{ g}$$

Therefore, the equivalent weight of the metal

$$= \frac{w_1}{w_2 - w_1} \times 35.5 = \frac{\text{Mass of the metal}}{\text{Mass of chlorine}} \times 35.5$$

5. Metal Displacement Method

This method depends upon the fact that certain metals can displace some other metals from their salt solutions. For example, when a piece of iron is immersed in a solution of copper sulphate, copper gets displaced and a precipitate of copper is obtained.

$$Fe(s) + CuSO_4(aq) \longrightarrow FeSO_4(aq) + Cu(s)$$

This is due to phenomenon of electropositive nature. A more electropositive metal can displace a lesser electropositive metal from its salt solution.
The determination of equivalent weight is based on the fact that the masses of the two metals bear the same ratio as their equivalent weights.

Procedure

A known mass of the more electropositive metal is added to an aqueous solution of a salt of lesser electropositive metal. The more electropositive metal displaces the lesser electropositive metal from its salt solution which gets precipitated.
The precipitate thus obtained is filtered, washed, dried and weighed.

$$\text{Metal}_1 + Aq. \text{ solution of salt of metal}_2 \longrightarrow Aq. \text{ solution of salt of metal}_1 + \text{metal}_2$$

The masses of metal_1 and metal_2 are always in the ratio of their equivalent weights. Therefore, knowing the masses of metal_1 and metal_2 and the equivalent weight of one metal, the equivalent weight of the other metal can be calculated as given below:

Calculations

Suppose, Mass of the metal_1 taken $= w_1$ g
Mass of the metal_2 precipitated $= w_2$ g
Equivalent weight of $\text{metal}_1 = E_1$
Equivalent weight of $\text{metal}_2 = E_2$

Thus,
$$\frac{\text{Mass of metal}_1 \text{ taken}}{\text{Mass of metal}_2 \text{ precipitated}} = \frac{\text{Equivalent weight of metal}_1}{\text{Equivalent weight of metal}_2}$$

or
$$\frac{w_1}{w_2} = \frac{E_1}{E_2} \text{ or } E_1 = \frac{w_1}{w_2} \times E_2$$

6. Electrolysis Method

Electrolysis is a process in which electric energy is used to bring some chemical changes. It is carried out in an electrolytic cell which involves conversion of electric energy to chemical energy.
The electrolysis of an electrolytic solution is governed by two important laws, known as **Faraday's laws of electrolysis.** These laws may be used to find the equivalent mass of a substance.

The two laws are discussed as follows:

(i) **First Law** It states that deposited mass of the substance is directly proportional to passed charge in a voltameter.

$$w \propto Q, \; w = ZQ, \; w = Zit$$

where, w = mass, Q = charge (in Coulomb)
i = current (in Amperes), t = time (in second)
Z = electrochemical equivalent.

$$= \frac{\text{equivalent weight}}{96500 \text{ C}}$$

$$\left[\text{Equivalent wt.} = \frac{\text{Atomic weight}}{\text{Valency}}\right]$$

(ii) **Second Law** It states that the number of equivalents of any substance produced by a given quantity of electricity during electrolysis are same.

$$\frac{w_A}{w_B} = \frac{E_A}{E_B}$$

where, w_A = deposited mass of substance A
E_A = equivalent weight of A
w_B = deposited mass of substance B
E_B = equivalent weight of B

The method for the determination of equivalent weight of a substance can be determined with the help of Faraday's law as follows:

(i) **Using Faraday's First Law of Electrolysis According to the Faraday's First Law of Electrolysis,**

$$w = ZIt$$

or
$$w = \frac{\text{Equivalent weight}}{96500} \times I \times t$$

Thus, by knowing the amount of substance discharged by passing a current of I amperes for t second, the equivalent mass of the substance can be calculated with the help of above equations.

(ii) **Using Faraday's Second Law of Electrolysis** When the same amount of current liberates w_1 g of a substance A in voltameter (A) and w_2 g of some other substance B in voltameter (B) connected in series, then according to Faraday's second law of electrolysis,

$$\frac{\text{Mass of substance } A \text{ deposited}}{\text{Mass of substance } B \text{ deposited}} = \frac{\text{Eq. weight of } A}{\text{Eq. weight of } B}$$

i.e. $$\frac{W_1}{W_2} = \frac{E_1}{E_2}$$

where, E_1 and E_2 are respectively the equivalent weights of A and B.

Thus, by knowing w_1 and w_2 and the equivalent mass of one of the substance, the equivalent mass of the other substance can be calculated with the help of above equation.

Calculation of Equivalent Weight

Equivalent weight of various types of substances can be calculated as given below :

(i) Equivalent weight of metal

$$= \frac{\text{mass of metal}}{\text{mass of hydrogen displaced}} \times 1.008$$

or $$= \frac{\text{mass of metal}}{\text{mass of oxygen combined}} \times 8.0$$

or $$= \frac{\text{mass of metal}}{\text{mass of chlorine combined}} \times 35.5$$

(ii) Equivalent weight of acid

$$= \frac{\text{molecular weight of acid}}{\text{basicity (number of replaceable } H^+)}$$

e.g. Equivalent weight of HCl $= \frac{36.5}{1} = 36.5$

(iii) Equivalent weight of base

$$= \frac{\text{molecular weight of base}}{\text{acidity (number of replaceable } OH^-)}$$

e.g. Equivalent weight of NaOH $= \frac{40}{1} = 40$

(iv) Equivalent weight of salt

$$= \frac{\text{molecular weight of salt}}{\text{total positive valency of metal atoms}}$$

e.g. Equivalent weight of NaCl $= \frac{58.5}{1} = 58.5$

(v) Equivalent weight of $Na_2CO_3 = \frac{106}{2} = 53$

(vi) Equivalent weight of an oxidant (oxidising agent) or a reductant (reducing agent)

$$= \frac{\text{Formula mass of oxidant or reductant}}{\text{Number of electrons gained or lost by one molecule}}$$

Variable Equivalent Weight

As we know,

Equivalent weight of an element

$$= \frac{\text{Atomic mass of the element}}{\text{Valency}}$$

The atomic mass of an element is always constant but its valency may change. Thus, '**the equivalent weight of an element inversely proportional to its valency**'. The equivalent weight of an element is constant only when its valency is constant.

Thus, the equivalent weight of an element depends upon the valency, oxidation state and mode of reaction.

(i) **Dependence of Equivalent Weight upon Valency** When an element has variable valencies, its equivalent weight is also variable. For example,

Equivalent weight of copper in cuprous salts.

$$= \frac{\text{Atomic mass}}{\text{Valency}} = \frac{63.6}{1} = 63.6$$

Equivalent weight of copper in cupric salts

$$= \frac{\text{Atomic mass}}{\text{Valency}} = \frac{63.6}{2} = 31.8$$

(ii) **Dependence of Equivalent Weight upon Oxidation State** When an element exists in more than one oxidation state, it has different equivalent weights.

For example,

Equivalent weight of Fe in FeO (+2)

$$= \frac{\text{Atomic mass}}{\text{Oxidation state}} = \frac{55.85}{2} = 27.925$$

Equivalent weight of Fe in Fe_2O_3 (+3)

$$= \frac{\text{Atomic mass}}{\text{Oxidation state}} = \frac{55.85}{3} = 18.616$$

(iii) **Dependence of Equivalent Weight upon Mode of Reaction** The equivalent weight of an element also depends on the way the reactants take part in a reaction.

For example, let us consider the following reactions:

$$Fe + 2HCl \longrightarrow FeCl_2 + H_2 \quad \text{.... (i)}$$

$$2Fe + 3Cl_2 \longrightarrow 2FeCl_3 \quad \text{..... (ii)}$$

In reaction (i), 55.85 parts by weight of iron give 2.016 parts by weight of hydrogen from hydrochloric acid.

∴ Equivalent weight of Fe in reaction (i)

$$= \frac{55.85}{2.016} \times 1.008 = 27.925$$

In reaction (ii), 2×55.85 parts by weight of iron combine with 3×71 parts by weight of chlorine.

$\therefore$ Equivalent weight of Fe in reaction (ii)

$$= \frac{2 \times 55.85}{3 \times 71} \times 35.5 = 18.616$$

Gram Equivalent Weight

The mass in grams of a substance numerically equal to its equivalent weight is called the gram equivalent weight or **one gram equivalent** of that substance.

For example,

1 gram equivalent of HCl = Eq. weight of HCl = 36.5 g

1 gram equivalent of H_2SO_4

= Eq. weight of H_2SO_4 = 49g

1 gram equivalent of NaOH = Eq. weight of NaOH = 40 g

Number of gram equivalents

$$= \frac{\text{Mass of the substance in grams}}{\text{Gram equivalent weight}}$$

Relationship between Gram Equivalent Weight, Gram Atomic Mass and Valency

Let the equivalent weight, atomic mass and valency of an element be E, A and V respectively.

The valency of an element is defined as the number of atoms of hydrogen which combine with 1 atom of the given element.

$\therefore V$ atoms of hydrogen combine with 1 atom of the element. It implies that $V \times 1.008$ parts by weight of hydrogen combine with A parts by weight of the element.

$\therefore$ 1.008 parts by weight of hydrogen would combine with $\frac{A}{V \times 1.008} \times 1.008 = \frac{A}{V}$ parts by weight of the element.

As we know, the equivalent weight of an element is defined as the number of parts by weight of the element which combine with 1.008 parts by weight of hydrogen hence, by definition.

$$E = \frac{A}{V} \text{ or } A = E \times V$$

Thus,

i.e. Atomic mass = Equivalent weight × Valency

Gram atomic mass = Gram equivalent weight × Valency

Mole Concept and Molar Masses

The word **mole** (means heap or pile) was introduced by **Wilhelm Ostwald** and is defined as **"the amount of a substance that contains as many particles or entities as there are atoms in exactly 12 g (or 0.012 kg) of the ^{12}C isotope"**. The mole of a substance always contain the same number of entities independent of the nature of the substance taken.

The number of atoms in 12 g of ^{12}C is calculated as

Mass of a carbon atom = 1.992648×10^{-23} g

(Determined by mass spectrometer)

1 mol of carbon = 12 g

$\therefore$ The number of atoms in 12 g C

$$= \frac{12 \text{ g/mol } ^{12}C}{1.992648 \times 10^{-23} \text{ g}/^{12}C \text{ atom}}$$

$$= 6.0221367 \times 10^{23} \text{ atoms/mol}$$

This number or entities in 1 mol is so important that it is given a separate name and symbol.

It is known as **Avogadro constant,** denoted by N_A in honour of **Amedeo Avogadro.**

In other words, we can say a mole is a collection of 6.022×10^{23} particles.

Thus, 1 mole of atoms = 6.022×10^{23} atoms

≡ gram atomic mass of the elements

1 mole of molecules = 6.022×10^{23} molecules

≡ gram molecular mass

The mass of one mole of a substance in grams is called its **molar mass.** The molar mass in grams is numerically equal to atomic/molecular/formula mass in '*u*'.

e.g. Molar mass of water = 18.02 g mol^{-1} and it contains 6.022×10^{23} H_2O molecules.

Moles in Case of Ionic Compounds

The mass of one mole formula units in gram is equal to formula mass expressed in grams or gram formula mass of the compound. Thus, mass of 6.022×10^{23} formula units (or one mole formula units) of any ionic substance in grams is equal to its **gram formula mass.**

Moles in Case of Gases

In case of gases, a mole is defined as that amount of the gas which occupies a volume of 22.4 L at STP, which is called its **molar volume.**

The mass of one mole of a substance in gram is called its **molar mass.** Its units are g mol^{-1} or kg mol^{-1}. The molar mass in gram is numerically equal to atomic/molecular /formula mass

The above relations can be summarised as:

(i) Number of moles of atoms $= \frac{\text{mass of element}}{\text{atomic mass}}$

(ii) Number of moles of molecule

$$= \frac{\text{mass of molecule}}{\text{molecular mass}}$$

(iii) Number of moles of gas

$$= \frac{\text{volume of the gas (STP)}}{22.4\ \text{L}}$$

(iv) 1 mol $= 6.022 \times 10^{23}$ particles

= Gram atomic/ molecular mass.

(v) Number of molecules = Number of moles $\times N_A$, where, N_A = Avogadro number $= 6.022 \times 10^{23}$

(vi) Number of atoms = Number of molecules × atomicity (or number of atoms in the molecular formula or in 1 mole).

Note The problems based on mole concept can be solved by unitary method or by directly applying formulae.

Example 4 Calculate the number of molecules present 0.0896 L of O_2 gas at STP.

Sol. Applying mole concept,

$$\frac{\text{Volume of gas at STP (L)}}{22.4\ \text{L}} = \frac{\text{Number of molecules of gas}}{\text{Avogadro's number}}$$

$$\frac{0.0896}{22.4} = \frac{\text{Number of molecules of } O_2 \text{ gas}}{6.022 \times 10^{23}}$$

∴Number of molecules of O_2 gas

$$= \frac{0.0896 \times 6.022 \times 10^{23}}{22.4}$$

$$= 2.40 \times 10^{21}$$

Example 5 Calculate the number of moles in the following.

(i) 7.85 g of iron (ii) 4.68 mg of silicon

(iii) 65.6 μg of carbon **NCERT**

Sol. (i) Moles of iron $= \frac{\text{given mass of iron}}{\text{atomic mass of iron}}$

$$= \frac{7.85}{55.8} = 0.141\ \text{mol}$$

(ii) Moles of silicon $= \frac{\text{given mass of silicon}}{\text{atomic mass of silicon}}$

$$= \frac{4.68 \times 10^{-3}}{28.1}$$

$$= 1.67 \times 10^{-4}\ \text{mol}$$

(iii) Moles of carbon $= \frac{\text{given mass of carbon}}{\text{atomic mass of carbon}}$

$$= \frac{65.6 \times 10^{-6}}{12}$$

$$= 5.47 \times 10^{-6}\ \text{mol}$$

Example 6 Calculate the number of atoms in each of the following.

(i) 52 mole of Ar (ii) 52 u of He

(iii) 52 g of He **NCERT Textbook**

Sol. (i) 1 mole of Ar contains 6.022×10^{23} atoms

∴ 52 moles of Ar will contain $6.022 \times 10^{23} \times 52$

$= 3.13 \times 10^{25}$ atoms

(ii) 4 u of He = 1 atom

∴ 52 u of He $= \frac{1}{4} \times 52 = 13$ atoms

(iii) 4 g of He contains 6.022×10^{23} atoms

52 g of He will contain $\frac{6.022 \times 10^{23} \times 52}{4}$

$= 7.83 \times 10^{24}$ atoms

Empirical Formula

An **empirical formula** of a compound represents the simplest whole number ratio of various atoms present in one molecule of the compound.

Determination of Empirical Formula

The steps to calculate the empirical formula is summarised below:

(i) Calculate the amount of elements and their percentage composition using the formula given below:

Mass % of an element

$$= \frac{\left[\begin{array}{l}\text{Mass of the element in one}\\ \text{mole of the compound}\end{array}\right]}{\text{Molar mass of the compound}} \times 100$$

(ii) Divide the percentage of each element by its atomic mass. It gives atomic ratio of the elements present in the compound.

(iii) Divide the atomic ratio of each element by the minimum value of atomic ratio as to get simplest ratio of the atoms of elements present in the compound.

(iv) If the simplest ratio is fractional, then multiply the values of simplest ratio of each element by a smallest integer to get a simplest whole number for each of the element.

(v) To get the empirical formula, write symbols of various elements present side by side with their respective whole number ratio as a subscript to the lower right hand corner of the symbol.

Molecular Formula

The molecular formula shows the exact number of different types of atoms present in a molecule of a compound.

Determination of Molecular Formula

Step I Determine the empirical formula as described above.

Step II Calculate the empirical formula mass by adding the atomic masses of the atoms in the empirical formula.

Step III Determine the molecular mass by suitable method.

Step IV Determine the value of n as $n = \dfrac{\text{molecular mass}}{\text{empirical formula mass}}$.

Change n to the nearest whole number.

Step V Multiply empirical formula by n to get the molecular formula.
Molecular formula = $n \times$ empirical formula

Example 7 An organic substance containing carbon, hydrogen and oxygen gave the percentage composition as C = 40.687%, H = 5.085%.
The vapour density of the compound is 59. Calculate the molecular formula of the compound.

Sol. *Step* I To calculate empirical formula of the compound.

Here, % of $O = 100 - (40.687 + 5.085) = 54.228\%$

$\therefore$ Empirical formula is $C_2H_3O_2$.
(See table below)

Step II To calculate the empirical formula mass. The empirical formula of the compound is $C_2H_3O_2$.

$\therefore$ Empirical formula mass $= (2 \times 12) + (3 \times 1) + (2 \times 16) = 59$

Step III To calculate the molecular mass of the salt. The vapour density of the compound = 59 (Given)

Using the relation between vapour density and molecular mass.

Molecular mass $= 2 \times$ vapour density $= 2 \times 59 = 118$

Step IV To calculate the value of $n = \dfrac{\text{molecular mass}}{\text{empirical formula mass}} = \dfrac{118}{59} = 2$

Step V To calculate the molecular formula of the salt, Molecular formula = $n \times$ empirical formula

$= 2 \times C_2H_3O_2 = C_4H_6O_4$

Thus, the molecular formula is $C_4H_6O_4$.

Element	Symbol	Percentage of element	Atomic mass of element	Moles of the element = $\frac{\text{Percentage}}{\text{Atomic mass}}$ (Relative number of moles)	Simplest molar ratio	Simplest whole number molar ratio
Carbon	C	40.687	12	$\frac{40.687}{12} = 3.390$	$\frac{3.390}{3.389} = 1$	2
Hydrogen	H	5.085	1	$\frac{5.0885}{1} = 5.085$	$\frac{5.085}{3.389} = 1.5$	3
Oxygen	O	54.228	16	$\frac{54.228}{16} = 3.389$	$\frac{3.389}{3.389} = 1$	2

Topic Practice 2

Very Short Answer Type Questions

(1 Mark)

1 Fill in the Blanks

(i) One atomic mass unit is defined as the mass exactly equal to ...... of the mass of an atom of ....

(ii) Atomic mass of an element expressed in .... is called its gram atomic mass or gram atoms.

(iii) Equivalent weight of an element is .... proportional to its valency.

(iv) Mole is a collection of .... particles.

(v) An ...... of a compound represents the simple whole number ratio of various atoms present in one molecule.

2. Objective Type Questions

(i) The number of atoms present in one mole of an element is equal to Avogadro number. Which of the following element contains the greatest number of atoms?

(a) 4 g He (b) 46 g Na
(c) 0.40 g Ca (d) 12 g He

(ii) 'X' is the amount of a substance that contains as many particles as there are atoms in exactly 12 g of the Y isotope. X and Y respectively are

(a) $A \rightarrow$ one mole, $B \rightarrow {}^{14}C$
(b) $A \rightarrow$ percentage composition, $B \rightarrow {}^{12}C$
(c) $A \rightarrow$ one mole, $B \rightarrow {}^{12}C$
(d) $A \rightarrow$ percentage composition, $B \rightarrow {}^{14}C$

(iii) The mass of one mole of a substance in gram is called its

(a) Avogadro mass
(b) molar mass
(c) atomic mass
(d) formula mass

(iv) The equivalent weight of an element is 4. Its chloride has a vapour density 59.25. Then the valency of the element is

(a) 4 (b) 3
(c) 2 (d) 1

3 Match the following Columns and choose the correct option using the codes given below:

	Column I		Column II
A.	88 g of CO_2	(i)	0.2 mol
B.	6.022×10^{20} molecules of H_2O	(II)	2 mol
C.	5.6 L of O_2 at STP	(iii)	1 mol
D.	96 g of O_2	(iv)	6.022×10^{23} molecules
D.	1 mole of any gas	(v)	3 mol

Codes

	A	B	C	D	E
(a)	(ii)	(iii)	(i)	(v)	(iv)
(b)	(i)	(iii)	(ii)	(iv)	(v)
(c)	(i)	(ii)	(iii)	(iv)	(v)
(d)	(iii)	(i)	(iii)	(v)	(iv)

4 One mole of oxygen gas at STP is equal to? **NCERT Exemplar**

5 What will be the mass of one atom of C-12 in gram? **NCERT Exemplar**

6 Why are the atomic mass of most of the elements is fractional?

7 A black dot used as a full stop at the end of a sentence has a mass of about one attogram. Assuming that the dot is made up of carbon, calculate the approximate number of carbon atoms present in the dot ?

Short Answer Type I Questions

(2 Marks)

8 Calculate the atomic mass (average) of chlorine using the following data. **NCERT Textbook**

Isotope	% natural abundance	Molar mass
${}^{35}Cl$	75.77	34.9689
${}^{37}Cl$	24.23	36.9659

9 Calculate the average atomic mass of hydrogen using the following data. **NCERT Exemplar**

Isotope	% Natural abundance	Molar mass
${}^{1}H$	99.985	1
${}^{2}H$	0.015	2

10 Use the data given in the following table to calculate the molar mass of naturally occurring argon. **NCERT**

Isotope	Isotopic molar mass	Abundance
^{36}Ar	35.96755 g mol^{-1}	0.337%
^{38}Ar	37.96272 g mol^{-1}	0.063%
^{40}Ar	39.9624 g mol^{-1}	99.600%

11 Which one of the following will have the largest number of atoms? **NCERT Textbook**

(i) 1g Au (*s*) (ii) 1g Na (*s*)
(iii) 1g Li (*s*) (iv) 1g of $Cl_2(g)$

12 Chlorophyll, the green colouring matter of plants contains 2.68% magnesium by weight. Calculate the number of magnesium atoms in 2.00 g of chlorophyll (Atomic mass of Mg = 24).

13 The empirical formula and molecular mass of a compound are CH_2O and 180 g, respectively. What will be the molecular formula of the compound? **NCERT Exemplar**

14 A compound on analysis was found to contain C = 34.6%, H = 3.85%, and O = 61.55%. Calculate its empirical formula.

15 What is the molecular mass of a substance each molecule of which contains 9 atoms of carbon, 13 atoms of hydrogen and 2.33×10^{-23} g other component?

Short Answer Type II Questions

3 Marks

16 Calculate the molar mass of the following.
(i) H_2O (ii) CO_2 (iii) CH_4 **NCERT Textbook**

17 In three moles of ethane (C_2H_6), calculate the following.
(i) Number of moles of carbon atoms.
(ii) Number of moles of hydrogen atoms.
(iii) Number of molecules of ethane.

18 Determine the molecular formula of an oxide of iron in which the mass per cent of iron and oxygen are 69.9 and 30.1 respectively. Given that molar mass of the oxide is 159. 898 mol^{-1}

19 The average molar mass of a mixture of methane (CH_4) and ethane (C_2H_4) present in the ratio of $a : b$ is found to be 20.0 g mol^{-1}. If the ratio were reversed, what would be the molar mass of the mixture?

20 Calculate the total number of electrons present in 1.6 g of methane.

21 A 0.005 cm thick coating of copper is deposited on a plate of 0.5 m^2 total area. Calculate the number of copper atoms deposited on the plate (density of copper = 7.2 g cm^{-3}, atomic mass = 63.5).

Long Answer Type Questions

5 Marks

22 A welding fuel gas contains carbon and hydrogen only. Burning a small sample of it in oxygen gives 3.38 g carbon dioxide, 0.690 g of water and no other products. A volume 10.0 L (measured at STP) of this welding gas is found to weigh 11.6 g. Calculate (i) empirical formula (ii) molar mass of the gas and (iii) molecular formula. **NCERT Textbook**

23 A compound made up of two elements *A* and *B* has *A* = 70%, *B* = 30%. Their relative number of moles in the compound are 1.25 and 1.88. Calculate
(i) atomic masses of the elements *A* and *B*
(ii) molecular formula of the compound, if its molecular mass is found to be 160.

Hints & Solutions

1. (i) $\frac{1}{12}$ th, carbon - 12 (ii) grams
(iii) inversely (iv) 6.022×10^{23}
(v) empirical formula

2. (i) (*d*) The number of atoms is related to Avogadro's number (N_A) by

$$\text{Number of atoms} = \text{moles} \times N_A$$

The number of atoms of elements can be compared easily on the basis of their moles only because N_A is a constant value. Thus, element with large number of moles will possess greatest number of atoms.

For comparing number of atoms, first calculate the moles as all are monoatomic and hence,

$$\text{moles} \times N_A = \text{number of atoms.}$$

$$\text{Moles of 4 g He} = \frac{4}{4} = 1 \text{ mol}$$

$$46 \text{ g Na} = \frac{46}{23} = 2 \text{ mol}$$

$$0.40 \text{ g Ca} = \frac{0.40}{40} = 0.1 \text{ mol}$$

$$12 \text{ g He} = \frac{12}{4} = 3 \text{ mol}$$

Hence, 12 g He contains greatest number of atoms as it possesses maximum number of moles.

(ii) (c) One mole is the amount of a substance that contains as many particles or entities as there are atoms in exactly 12 g (0.012 kg) of the ^{12}C isotope.

(iii) (b) The mass of one mole of a substance in grams is calles its molar mass.

(iv) (b) Vapour density of chloride = 59.25

Molar mass of chloride = $59.25 \times 2 = 118.5$

If formula is MCl_n

$$M + (n \times 35.5) = 118.5$$
$$x_n + 35.5n = 118.5 \text{ [as eq. wt } (x_n) = M]$$
$$4n + 35.5n = 118.5$$
$$39.5n = 118.5$$
$$n = 3$$

Formula is MCl_3 or valency of M is 3.

3. (a) A → (ii), B → (iii), C → (i), D → (v), E → (iv)

A. Number of moles of CO_2 molecule

$$= \frac{\text{Weight in gram of } CO_2}{\text{Molecular weight of } CO_2} = \frac{88}{44} = 2 \text{ mol}$$

B. 1 mole of a substance = N_A molecules

$= 6.022 \times 10^{23}$ molecules = Avogadro number

$= 6.022 \times 10^{23}$ molecules of H_2O = 1 mol

C. 22.4 L of O_2 at STP = 1 mol

5.6 L of O_2 at STP $= \frac{5.6}{22.4}$ mol = 0 . 25 mol

D. Number of moles of 96 g of $O_2 = \frac{96}{32}$ mol = 3 mol

E. 1 mole of any gas = Avogadro number = 6.022×10^{23} molecules

4. 1 mole of O_2 gas at STP = 6.022×10^{23} molecules (Avogadro number) of O_2 = 32 g of O_2

Hence, 1 mole of oxygen gas is equal to molecular weight of oxygen as well as Avogadro number.

5. Mass of 1 atom of $^{12}C = \frac{\text{Atomic mass of C}}{\text{Avogadro's number}}$

$$= \frac{12 \text{ g}}{6.022 \times 10^{23}} = 1.9927 \times 10^{-23} \text{ g}$$

6. It is because most of the elements occur in nature as a mixture of isotopes and their atomic masses are the average relative atomic masses of the isotopes depending on their abundance.

7. Mass of carbon in the dot = 1 attogram = 10^{-18} g

Gram atomic mass of carbon = 12 g,

i.e. 12 g of carbon contains 6.022×10^{23} atoms of carbon.

∴ 10^{-18} g of carbon will contain carbon atoms

$$= \frac{6.022 \times 10^{23}}{12} \times 10^{-18}$$
$$= 5.02 \times 10^4 \text{ atoms}$$

8. Average atomic mass is the sum of the products of fractional abundances (f_i) of the isotopes and their corresponding mass number (A_i). Average atomic mass,

$$\overline{A} = \Sigma f_i \cdot A_i = f_1 \times A_1 + f_2 \times A_2 + \ldots\ldots \quad [1]$$

Average atomic mass,

$$A = 0.7577 \times 34.9689 + 0.2423 \times 36.9659$$
$$= 26.4959 + 8.9568 = 35.4527 \quad [1]$$

9 Many naturally occurring elements exist as more than one isotope. When we take into account the existence of these isotopes and their relative abundance (per cent occurrence), the average atomic mass of the element can be calculated as.

Average atomic mass

$$= \frac{\{(\text{Natural abundance of } ^1H \times \text{ molar mass of } ^1H) + (\text{Natural abundance of } ^2H \times \text{ molar mass of } ^2H)\}}{100}$$

$$= \frac{99.985 \times 1 + 0.015 \times 2}{100}$$

$$= \frac{99.985 + 0.030}{100} = \frac{100.015}{100} = 1.00015 \text{ u} \quad [2]$$

10. Average molar mass of Ar = $\Sigma f_i \times A_i$

$= (0.00337 \times 35.96755) + (0.00063 \times 37.96272) + (0.99600 \times 39.9624)$

$= 0.121 + 0.024 + 39.803 = 39.948 \text{ g mol}^{-1}$ [2]

11.

> **Key Idea** We know that number of atoms = moles × N_A × atomicity, so first calculate the number of moles by using the formula,
>
> Moles of a substance = $\frac{\text{mass of a substance } (g)}{\text{molar mass}}$

Then, find number of atoms from moles of the substance and compare them.

(Atomic masses : Au = 197, Na = 23, Li = 7, Cl = 35.5 u)

(i) 1 g Au $= \frac{1}{197}$ moles of Au $= \frac{1}{197} \times 6.022 \times 10^{23}$

atoms of Au = 3.057×10^{21} atoms

(ii) 1 g Na $= \frac{1}{23}$ moles of Na $= \frac{1}{23} \times 6.022 \times 10^{23}$ atoms of Na = 2.6×10^{22} atoms

(iii) 1 g Li $= \frac{1}{7}$ moles of Li $= \frac{1}{7} \times 6.022 \times 10^{23}$ molecules of Li $= 8.60 \times 22^{22}$ atoms

(iv) 1 g $Cl_2 = \frac{1}{71}$ moles of Cl_2

$= \frac{1}{71} \times 6.022 \times 10^{23}$ atoms $Cl_2 = 8.48 \times 10^{-21}$ atoms

Hence, 1 g Li have the largest number of atoms. [4 × ½]

12. Mass of chlorophyll = 2.0 g

Percentage of Mg = 2.68 g

Mass of Mg in 2.0 g of chlorophyll $= \frac{2.68 \times 2.0}{100} = 0.054$ g

6.022×10^{23} atoms of magnesium = 24 g

$\therefore$ 24 g of Mg contains 6.022×10^{23} atoms

$\therefore$ 0.054 g of Mg contains $\frac{6.022\times 10^{23}}{24}\times 0.054 = 1.3\times 10^{21}$ atoms [2]

13. Empirical formula mass = $CH_2O = 12 + 2\times 1 + 16 = 30$

Molecular mass = 180

$$n = \frac{\text{Molecular mass}}{\text{Empirical formula mass}} = \frac{180}{30} = 6$$ [1]

Molecular formula = $n\times$ empirical formula

$= 6\times CH_2O = C_6H_{12}O_6$ [1]

14. Calculation of the empirical formula.

Element	Percentage	Atomic mass	Gram atoms (Moles)	Molar ratio	Simplest whole number ratio
C	34.6	12	$\frac{34.6}{12} = 2.88$	$\frac{2.88}{2.88} = 1$	3
H	3.85	1	$\frac{3.85}{1} = 3.85$	$\frac{3.85}{2.88} = 1.335$ or $\frac{4}{3}$	4
O	61.55	16	$\frac{61.55}{16} = 3.85$	$\frac{3.85}{2.88} = 1.335$ or $\frac{4}{3}$	4

$\therefore$ The simplest whole number ratios of the different elements are, C : H : O :: 3 : 4 : 4 and the empirical formula of the compound = $C_3H_4O_4$. [2]

15. Mass of 9 atoms of carbon = 9×12 amu = 108 u

Mass of 13 atoms of hydrogen = 13×1 amu = 13 u

Mass of 2.33×10^{-23} g of other component $= (1\text{ u})\times \frac{(2.33\times 10^{-23}\text{ g})}{(1.66\times 10^{-24}\text{ g})} = 14.04$ u [1]

Molecular mass of the substance = (108 + 13 + 14.04) u = 135.04 u [1]

16. (i) Molar mass of $H_2O = 2\times$ atomic mass of hydrogen $+ 1\times$ atomic mass of oxygen

$= 2\times 1.0079\text{ u} + 1\times 16.00\text{ u} = 18.0158$ u [1]

(ii) Molar mass of $CO_2 = 1\times$ atomic mass of carbon $+ 2\times$ atomic mass of oxygen

$= 1\times 12.01\text{ u} + 2\times 16.00\text{ u} = 44.01$ u [1]

(iii) Molar mass of $CH_4 = 1\times$ atomic mass of carbon $+ 4\times$ atomic mass of hydrogen $= 1\times 12.01\text{ u} + 4\times 1.0079\text{ u} = 16.0416$ [1]

17. (i) 1 mole of C_2H_6 contains 2 moles of carbon atoms.

$\therefore$ Number of moles of carbon atoms in 3 moles of $C_2H_6 = 2\times 3 = 6$. [1]

(ii) 1 mole of C_2H_6 contains 6 moles of hydrogen atoms.

$\therefore$ Number of moles of hydrogen atoms in 3 moles of $C_2H_6 = 3\times 6 = 18$. [1]

(iii) 1 mole of C_2H_6 contains 6.022×10^{23} molecules of ethane.

$\therefore$ Number of ethane molecules in 3 moles of $C_2H_6 = 3\times 6.023\times 10^{23} = 1.8069\times 10^{24}$ [1]

18

Element	Symbol	% by mass	Atomic mass	Relative number of moles of element	Simple molar ratio	Simple whole number molar ratio
Iron	Fe	69.9	55.85	$\frac{69.9}{55.85} = 1.25$	$\frac{1.25}{1.25} = 1$	$1\times 2 = 2$
Oxygen	O	30.1	16.00	$\frac{30.1}{16.00} = 1.88$	$\frac{1.88}{1.25} = 1.5$	$1.5\times 2 = 3$

$\therefore$ Empirical formula = Fe_2O_3, Empirical formula mass of $Fe_2O_3 = (2\times 55.85) + (3\times 16.00) = 159.7\text{ g mol}^{-1}$

$$n = \frac{\text{moler mass}}{\text{empirical formula mass}} = \frac{159.8}{159.7} = 1$$

Hence, molecular formula of the compounds is Fe_2O_3. [3]

19. Molar mass of $CH_4 = 16\ g\ mol^{-1}$

Molar mass of $C_2H_4 = 28\ g\ mol^{-1}$

When they are present in the $a : b$, their average molar mass

$$= \frac{a \times 16 + b \times 28}{a + b} = 20\ g\ mol^{-1} \text{ (Given)}$$ [1]

i.e. $16a + 28b = 20(a + b)$

or $4a + 7b = 5(a + b)$ or $a = 2b$

or $\frac{a}{b} = \frac{2}{1} = 2:1$ [1]

If the ratio is reversed, now the ratio $a : b = 1 : 2$

$\therefore$ Average molar mass $= \frac{1 \times 16 + 2 \times 28}{1 + 2} = 24\ g\ mol^{-1}$ [1]

20. (i) Molar mass of methane $(CH_4) = 12 + 4 \times 1 = 16$ g

16 g of methane contains $= 6.022 \times 10^{23}$ molecules

1.6 g of methane will contain

$$= \frac{6.022 \times 10^{23}}{(16\ g)} \times (1.6\ g)$$

$= 6.022 \times 10^{22}$ molecules [1]

(ii) 1 molecule of methane contains $= 6 + 4 = 10$ electrons.

Thus, 6.022×10^{22} molecules of methane contain electrons $= 6.022 \times 10^{22} \times 10 = 6.022 \times 10^{23}$ [1]

21. Area of plate $= 0.5\ m^2 = 0.5 \times 10^4\ cm^2$

Thickness of coating = 0.005 cm

Volume of copper deposited $= 0.5 \times 10^4 \times 0.005$

$= 25\ cm^3$

Mass of copper deposited $= 25 \times 7.2 = 180$ g

Now, 63.5 g of copper contains atoms $= 6.022 \times 10^{23}$

$\therefore$ 180 g of copper will contain atoms $= \frac{6.022 \times 10^{23}}{63.5} \times 180$

$= 1.71 \times 10^{24}$ atoms

22. (i) 44 g CO_2 = 12 g carbon

3.38 g $CO_2 = \frac{12}{44} \times 3.38\ g = 0.9218$ g carbon

18 g H_2O = 2 g hydrogen

0.690 g $H_2O = \frac{2}{18} \times 0.690\ g = 0.0767$ g hydrogen

Total mass of compound = 0.9218 + 0.0767 = 0.9985 g (because compound contains only carbon and hydrogen)

% of C in the compound $= \frac{0.9218}{0.9985} \times 100 = 92.32$

% of H in the compound $= \frac{0.0767}{0.9985} \times 100 = 7.68$

Calculation for Empirical Formula

Element	Per cent by mass	Atomic mass	Relative number of moles of elements	Simplest molar ratio
C	92.32	12	$\frac{92.32}{12} = 7.69$	$\frac{7.69}{7.68} = 1$
H	7.68	1	$\frac{7.68}{1} = 7.68$	$\frac{7.69}{7.68} = 1$

Hence, empirical formula = CH [3]

(ii) **Calculation for molar mass of the gas**

10.0 L of the given gas at STP weigh = 11.6 g

$\therefore$ 22.4 L of the given gas at STP will weigh

$$= \frac{11.6 \times 22.4}{10} = 25.984\ g$$

Molar mass $= 25.984 \approx 26\ g\ mol^{-1}$. [1]

(iii) Empirical formula mass (CH) = 12 + 1 = 13

$\therefore$ $n = \frac{\text{molecular mass}}{\text{empirical formula mass}} = \frac{26}{13} = 2$

Hence, molecular formula

$= n \times CH = 2 \times CH = C_2H_2$ [1]

23. Relative number of moles of an element

$$= \frac{\text{\% of the element}}{\text{atomic mass}}$$

or atomic mass $= \frac{\text{\% of element}}{\text{relative number of moles}}$

$\therefore$ Atomic mass of $A = \frac{70}{1.25} = 56$

and Atomic mass of $B = \frac{30}{1.88} = 16$ [1]

Calculation of Empirical Formula

Element	Relative number of moles	Simplest molar ratio	Simplest whole number molar ratio
A	1.25	$\frac{1.25}{1.25} = 1$	2
B	1.88	$\frac{1.88}{1.25} = 1.5$	3

$\therefore$ Empirical formula $= A_2B_3$ [2]

Calculation of molecular formula

Empirical formula mass $= 2 \times 56 + 3 \times 16 = 160$

$n = \frac{\text{molecular mass}}{\text{empirical formula mass}} = \frac{160}{160} = 1$ [2]

$\therefore$ Molecular formula $= A_2B_3$

TOPIC 03 Chemical Equations and Stoichiometric Calculations

Chemical Equations

A chemical equation is a brief representation of a chemical change in terms of symbols and formulae of substances involved in it, e.g. the reaction of silver nitrate with sodium chloride to give silver chloride and sodium nitrate can be represented as:

$$\underbrace{AgNO_3 + NaCl}_{\text{Reactants}} \longrightarrow \underbrace{AgCl + NaNO_3}_{\text{Products}}$$

The substances which react among themselves to bring about the chemical changes are known as **reactants** whereas, the substances which are produced as a result of the chemical change, are known as **products**.

Reactants and products of a chemical equation are separated by arrow pointing towards the products.

Characteristics of a Chemical Equations

A chemical equation must fulfill the following conditions:

(i) It must be consistent with the experimental facts.

(ii) It should have molecular species.

(iii) It should be balanced, i.e. it follows the law of conservation of mass and have equal number of atoms of each elements on both the sides.

Stoichiometry and Stoichiometric Calculations

The word '**stoichiometry**' is derived from the combination of two Greek words, i.e. *stoicheion* (means element) and *metron* (means measure). Stoichiometry, thus, deals with the calculation of masses (sometimes volumes also) of the reactants and the products involved in a chemical reaction. In other words, the relationship between the amounts of reactants and products is called the **stoichiometry.**

The number before the formula unit or molecules used to balance the equation are called **stoichiometric coefficients.** These shows the number of moles/molecules of that particular substance.

Calculations based on chemical equations are termed as **stoichiometric calculations.**

Algorithm for Stoichiometric Calculations

The general steps involved in all types of stoichiometric calculations are as follows:

***Step* I** Write the balanced chemical equation.

***Step* II** Write the stoichiometric coefficient that shows the moles of the respective substance.

***Step* III** Convert moles into required quantity (if needed).

***Step* IV** Write the given data.

***Step* V** Calculate the required information by unitary method.

The calculations are of the following types :

1. Calculations Involving Mole-Mole Relationship

In such problems, the moles of one of the reactant/product can be calculated, if the moles of others are given.

Example 1 How many moles of CO_2 will be obtained when 0.274 mole of C_2H_5OH is burnt?

Sol. *Follow the following steps to solve such problems:*

Step I Write down the balanced equation for the given reaction and then write the stoichiometric coefficient followed by given moles.

	C_2H_5OH	+ $3O_2 \longrightarrow$	$2CO_2$	+ $3H_2O$
Stoichiometric coefficients	1 mol		2 mol	
Given moles	0.274 mol		?	

Step II Calculate the amount of the CO_2 by unitary method.

1 mole of C_2H_5OH produces 2 moles of CO_2

$\therefore$ 0.274 mole of C_2H_5OH will produce CO_2

$$= \frac{2}{1} \times 0.274 = 2 \times 0.274 = 0.548 \text{ mol}$$

Thus, 0.548 moles of CO_2 is obtained from 0.274 moles of C_2H_5OH.

2. Calculations Involving Mass-Mass Relationship

In such problems, the mass of one of the reactant/product can be calculated if we have the mass of others.

Example 2 Calculate the amount of water (*g*) produced by the combustion of 16 g of methane. **NCERT Textbook**

Sol. Such problems involve following steps:

Step I Write the balanced chemical equation.

$$CH_4(g) + 2O_2(g) \longrightarrow CO_2(g) + 2\,H_2O(g)$$

Step **II** Write the stoichiometric coefficients of each substance. These represent mole of that particular substance.

$$\underset{1\text{ mol}}{CH_4(g)} + \underset{2\text{ mol}}{2O_2(g)} \longrightarrow \underset{1\text{ mol}}{CO_2(g)} + \underset{2\text{ mol}}{2H_2O(s)}$$

Step **III** Convert moles into mass by multiplying them with molar mass.

$$\underset{\substack{1\text{ mol}\\=16\text{ g}}}{CH_4(g)} + \underset{\substack{2\times 32\\=64\text{ g}}}{2O_2(g)} \longrightarrow \underset{\substack{1\times 44\\=44\text{ g}}}{CO_2(g)} + \underset{\substack{2\times 18\\=36\text{ g}}}{2H_2O(g)}$$

Step **IV** Write the given mass under the respective substance.

$$\underset{16\text{ g}}{CH_4(g)} + \underset{64\text{ g}}{2O_2(g)} \longrightarrow \underset{44\text{ g}}{CO_2(g)} + \underset{36\text{ g}}{2H_2O(g)}$$

Step **V** Calculate the mass of unknown substance by unitary method. From the equation, it is already clear that 16 g of methane produces 36 g of water.

3. Calculations Involving Mass-Mole or Mole-Mass Relationship

In such problems, the mass or mole of one of the reactant/product can be calculated if we have the mole or mass of others.

Example 3 Oxygen is prepared by the catalytic decomposition of potassium chlorate ($KClO_3$). Decomposition of potassium chlorate gives potassium chloride (KCl) and oxygen (O_2). If 2.4 moles of oxygen is needed for an experiment, how many grams of potassium chlorate must be decomposed?

Sol. The balanced equation is

$$\underset{\substack{2\text{ mol}\\2\times(39+35.5+3\times 16)=245\text{ g}}}{2KClO_3(s)} \longrightarrow \underset{2\text{ mol}}{2KCl(s)} + \underset{3\text{ mol}}{3O_2(g)}$$

$\because$ 3 moles of O_2 is produced by decomposition of $KClO_3 = 245$ g

$\because$ 2.4 moles of O_2 will be produced by the decomposition of

$$KClO_3 = \frac{245\times 2.4}{3} = 196.0\text{ g}$$

4. Calculations Involving Mass-Volume Relationship

In these problems, mass or volume of one of the reactants or products can be calculated from the mass or volume of other substances.

Example 4 Calculate the amount of $KClO_3$ needed to supply sufficient oxygen for burning 112 L of CO gas at NTP.

Sol. Calculation of O_2 gas required to burn 112 L of CO.

$$\underset{\substack{1\text{ mol}\\=22.4\text{ L}}}{CO} + \underset{0.5\text{ mol}}{\frac{1}{2}O_2} \longrightarrow \underset{1\text{ mol}}{CO_2}$$

22.4 L of CO at NTP require $O_2 = 0.5$ mol

112 L of CO at NTP will require O_2

$$= \frac{0.5}{22.4}\times 112 = 2.5\text{ mol}$$

This O_2 is obtained by heating $KClO_3$.

$$\underset{\substack{2\text{ mol}\\2(39+35.5+3\times 16)=245\text{ g}}}{2KClO_3} \xrightarrow{\Delta} 2KCl + \underset{3\text{ mol}}{3O_2}$$

3 moles of O_2 are produced from $KClO_3 = 245$ g

2.5 moles of O_2 will be produced from $KClO_3$

$$= \frac{245\times 2.5}{3} = 204.167\text{ g}$$

5. Calculations Involving Volume-Volume Relationship

In these problems, the volume of one of the reactant/product is given and that of the other can be calculated.

Example 5 What volume of oxygen at STP is required to effect complete combustion of 200 cm^3 of acetylene and what would be the volume of carbon dioxide formed?

Sol. The balanced chemical equation is

$$\underset{\substack{2\text{ mol}\\2\times 22400\text{ cm}^3}}{2C_2H_2} + \underset{\substack{5\text{ mol}\\5\times 22400\text{ cm}^3}}{5O_2} \longrightarrow \underset{\substack{4\text{ mol}\\4\times 22400\text{ cm}^3}}{4CO_2} + 2H_2O$$

$\because$ 2×22400 cm^3 of acetylene require O_2 for complete combustion $= 5\times 22400$ cm^3

200 cm^3 of acetylene will require O_2 for complete

combustion $= \frac{5\times 22400}{2\times 22400}\times 200 = 500$ cm^3 at STP

Further 2×22400 cm^3 of acetylene produce CO_2

$= 4\times 22400$ cm^3

$\therefore$ 200 cm^3 of acetylene will produce CO_2

$= \frac{4\times 22400}{2\times 22400}\times 200 = 400$ cm^3 at STP

Limiting and Excess Reagents

The reactant which is present in the lesser amount and gets consumed after sometime, i.e. which limits the amount of product formed is called the **limiting reagent.**

The reactant other than the limiting reagent, which is in somewhat excess is called the **excess reagent.**

The remaining amount of excess reagent is calculated by subtracting the available amount of limiting reagent from the amount of the excess reagent.

Note Remember that in stoichiometric calculations, it is very important to choose the limiting reagent as it decides the amount of the product obtained.

Example 6 50.0 kg of $N_2(g)$ and 10.0 kg of $H_2(g)$ are mixed to produce $NH_3(g)$. Calculate the $NH_3(g)$ formed. Identify the limiting reagent in the production of NH_3 in this situation. **NCERT Textbook**

Sol. *Step* I A balanced equation for the above reaction is written as follows.

$$N_2(g) + 3H_2(g) \rightleftharpoons 2NH_3(g)$$

Step II Calculation of moles.

$$\text{Moles of } N_2 = 50.0 \text{kg } N_2 \times \frac{1000 \text{ g } N_2}{1 \text{ kg } N_2} \times \frac{1 \text{ mol } N_2}{28.0 \text{g } N_2}$$

$$= 17.86 \times 10^2 \text{ mol}$$

$$\text{Moles of } H_2 = 10.0 \text{ kg } H_2 \times \frac{1000 \text{ g } H_2}{1 \text{ kg } H_2} \times \frac{1 \text{mol } H_2}{2.016 \text{ g } H_2}$$

$$= 4.96 \times 10^3 \text{ mol}$$

Step III Then, find out the limiting reagent.

$$17.86 \times 10^2 \text{ mol } N_2 \times \frac{3 \text{ mol } H_2 (g)}{1 \text{ mol } N_2 (g)}$$

$$= 5.36 \times 10^3 \text{ mol } H_2$$

But we have only 4.96×10^3 mol H_2. Hence, dihydrogen is the limiting reagent in this case. So, $NH_3(g)$ would be formed only from that amount of available dihydrogen, i.e. 4.96×10^3 mol.

Step IV After that, find out the amount of ammonia.

Since, 3 mol $H_2(g)$ gives 2 mol $NH_3(g)$

$$4.96 \times 10^3 \text{ mol } H_2(g) \times \frac{2 \text{mol } NH_3 (g)}{3 \text{ mol } H_2 (g)}$$

$$= 3.30 \times 10^3 \text{ mol } NH_3 (g)$$

3.30×10^3 mol $NH_3(g)$ is obtained from 4.96×10^3 mol $H_2(g)$.

If they are to be converted in grams, it is done as follows:

$1 \text{ mol } NH_3(g) = 17.0 \text{ g } NH_3(g)$

$$3.30 \times 10^3 \text{ mol } NH_3 (g) = \frac{17.0 \text{ g } NH_3 (g)}{1 \text{ mol } NH_3 (g)}$$

$$3.30 \times 10^3 \times 17 \text{g } NH_3(g) = 56.1 \times 10^3 \text{g } NH_3 = 56.1 \text{ kg } NH_3$$

Volumetric Calculations

The quantitative analysis of the strength of an unknown solution with the help of a solution of known strength is called volumetric analysis. The procedure used is called titration. A titration is an experiment where the volume of reactant solution (titrant) needed to react exactly with some amount of another reactant is measured. The point at which the reaction gets completed is referred to as the end point of the titration.

If concentration of a substance can be known simply by dissolving its known amount in a given volume of solution, then the substance is called **primary standard and the solution formed as primary standard solutions,** e.g. oxalic acid, potassium dichromate. In most cases, concentration can be determined by standardisation against primary standard solution. Such solutions are called **secondary standard solutions.** e.g. Ferrous sulphate, mineral acids (e.g. H_2SO_4, HNO_3). Their solutions are prepared by dissolving a known amount or volume but they have to be standardised using primary standard. Thus, all these are secondary standards.

Concentration of Solution

(Terms used in Volumetric Calculations)

Most of the reactions occurring in the laboratories are carried out in solutions. In solutions, generally two components are present.

The one which is in lesser amount is called the **solute** and the other one which is in higher amount is called the **solvent.** The amount of solute present in a given quantity of solvent or solution is expressed in terms of **concentration.**

The concentration of the solution is usually expressed in the following ways:

1. Mass Per cent

It is the mass of a component per 100 g of the solution. In a solution of the two components

$$\text{Mass per cent} = \frac{\text{mass of solute}}{\text{mass of solution}} \times 100$$

e.g. 10 % (w/W) solution of sodium chloride means that 10 g of sodium chloride is present in 90 g of water so that the total mass of the solution is 100 g.

Example 7 A solution is prepared by adding 2 g of substance A to 18 g of water. Calculate the mass per cent of the solute. **NCERT Textbook**

Sol. Mass per cent of $A = \frac{\text{Mass of } A}{\text{Mass of solution}} \times 100$

$$= \frac{2 \text{ g}}{2 \text{ g of } A + 18 \text{ g of water}} \times 100$$

$$= \frac{2\text{g}}{20\text{g}} \times 100 = 10\%$$

2. Volume Per cent

It is defined as the volume of the component per 100 parts by volume of the solution, e.g. if V_A and V_B are the volumes of two components A and B respectively in a solution, then
Volume per cent of A

$$= \frac{\text{Volume of } A}{\text{Volume of } A + \text{volume of } B} \times 100$$

This may be expressed as v/V.
Sometimes, we express the concentration as weight/volume, e.g. a 10% solution of sodium chloride (w/V) means that 10 g of sodium chloride is dissolved in 100 mL of solution.

3. Parts Per Million

When a solute is present in very minute amounts (trace quantities), the concentration is expressed in parts per million, abbreviated as ppm. It is defined as the parts of a component per million parts of the solution. It is expressed as

$$\text{ppm of } A = \frac{\text{mass of component } A}{\text{total mass of solution}} \times 10^6$$

For example, suppose a litre of public supply water contains about 3×10^{-3} g of chlorine.

$$\therefore \text{ ppm of chlorine} = \frac{3 \times 10^{-3} \times 10^6}{1000} = 3$$

Atmospheric pollution in cities due to harmful gases is generally expressed in ppm. Though in this case the values refer to volumes rather than masses, e.g. the concentration of SO_2 in Delhi has been found to be as high as 10 ppm. This means that 10 cm^3 of SO_2 are present in 10^6 cm^3 (or 10^3 L) of air.

4. Mole Fraction (χ)

It is the ratio of number of moles of a particular component to the total number of moles of the solution.
In case of a solution of two components A and B,
Mole fraction of A,

$$\chi_A = \frac{\text{number of moles of } A}{\text{number of moles of solution}} = \frac{n_A}{n_A + n_B}$$

(where n_A and n_B are the moles of A and B respectively).
Mole fraction of B,

$$\chi_B = \frac{\text{number of moles of } B}{\text{number of moles of solution}} = \frac{n_B}{n_A + n_B}$$

Also, remember that $\chi_A + \chi_B = 1$
Mole fraction is independent of temperature.

Example 8 A solution contains 25% water, 25% ethanol and 50% acetic acid by mass. Calculate the mole fraction of each component.

Sol. Let the total mass of solution = 100 g
Mass of water = 25 g, Mass of ethanol = 25 g
Mass of acetic acid = 50 g

$$\text{Moles of water} = \frac{25}{18} = 1.388 \quad (\because \text{Molar mass of } H_2O = 18)$$

Moles of ethanol = 25/46 = 0.543
($\because$ Molar mass of $C_2H_5OH = 46$)
Moles of acetic acid = 50/60 = 0.833
($\because$ Molar mass of $CH_3COOH = 60$)
Total number of moles = 1.388 + 0.543 + 0.833 = 2.764

$$\text{Mole fraction of water} = \frac{1.388}{2.764} = 0.502$$

$$\text{Mole fraction of ethanol} = \frac{0.543}{2.764} = 0.196$$

$$\text{Mole fraction of acetic acid} = \frac{0.833}{2.764} = 0.302$$

5. Molarity (*M*)

It is defined as the number of moles of the solute in 1 L of the solution. It is denoted by M. Thus,

$$\text{Molarity } (M) = \frac{\text{number of moles of solute}}{\text{volume of solution in litres}}$$

As we know, number of moles of solute

$$= \frac{\text{given mass of solute}}{\text{molar mass of solute}}$$

$$\therefore \quad \text{Molarity } (M) = \frac{\text{mass of solute } (W)}{\text{molar mass of solute } (M) \times \text{volume} (V) \text{ of solution } (L)}$$

or

$$M = \frac{\text{mass of solute} \times 1000}{\text{molar mass of solute} \times V \text{ (in mL)}}$$

The units of molarity are mol L^{-1} or mol dm^{-3}.
If we have % by mass and specific gravity or density, the molarity is calculated by the expression,

$$M = \frac{\% \text{ by weight} \times \text{specific gravity} \times 10}{\text{molar mass}}$$

In case of dilution, $M_1V_1 = M_2V_2$, where, M_1V_1 are respectively the molarity and volume before dilution and M_2V_2 are molarity and volume after dilution.
Molarity of a solution depends upon temperature because volume of a solution is temperature dependent.

Example 9 Calculate the molarity of NaOH in the solution prepared by dissolving its 4 g in enough water to form 250 mL of the solution.

Sol. Since, molarity $(M) = \frac{\text{number of moles of solute}}{\text{volume of solution in litres}}$

$$= \frac{\text{Mass of NaOH / Molar mass of NaOH}}{0.250 \text{ L}}$$

$$= \frac{4 \text{ g}/40 \text{ g}}{0.250 \text{ L}} = \frac{0.1 \text{ mol}}{0.250 \text{ L}}$$

$$= 0.4 \text{ mol L}^{-1} = 0.4 \text{ M}$$

Example 10 What volume of 10 M HCl and 3 M HCl should be mixed to get 1L of 6 M HCl solution?

Sol. Suppose volume of 10 M HCl required to prepare 1L of 6 M HCl = x L

Volume of 3 M HCl required = $(1 - x)$ L

Applying molarity equation, $\underbrace{M_1V_1}_{10\text{ M HCl}} + \underbrace{M_2V_2}_{3\text{ M HCl}} = \underbrace{M_3V_3}_{6\text{ M HCl}}$

$$10 \times x + 3(1 - x) = 6 \times 1$$

$$\Rightarrow \quad 10x + 3 - 3x = 6 \Rightarrow 7x = 3 \quad \text{or} \quad x = \frac{3}{7} = 0.428 \text{ L}$$

$\therefore$ Volume of 10 M HCl required = 0.428 L = 428 mL

Volume of 3 M HCl required = 1 − 0.428

= 0.572 L = 572 mL

6. Molality (*m*)

It is defined as the number of moles of solute present in 1 kg of solvent. It is denoted by *m*.

Thus, molality $(m) = \frac{\text{number of moles of solute}}{\text{mass of solvent in kg}}$

or $$m = \frac{\text{mass of solute} \times 1000}{\text{molar mass of solute} \times \text{mass of solvent (in g)}}$$

Molality is considered better for expressing the concentration as compared to molarity because molarity changes with temperature because it is volume dependent entity which varies with temperature. But, molality does not change with temperature as the mass of the solvent does not change with change in temperature. However, molarity is widely used because it is easier to measure the volume of a solution.

Example 11 Calculate the molality of a solution containing 20.7 g potassium carbonate dissolved in 500 mL of solution (assume density of solution = 1 g mL^{-1}).

Sol. Mass of K_2CO_3 = 20.7 g

Molar mass of $K_2CO_3 = 2 \times 39 + 12 + 3 \times 16$

$= 138 \text{ mol}^{-1}$

Moles of $K_2CO_3 = \frac{20.7}{138} = 0.15$

Mass of solution = (500 mL) × (1 g mL^{-1}) = 500 g

Amount of water = 500 − 20.7 = 479.3 g

$$\text{Molality} = \frac{\text{moles of solute}}{\text{mass of solvent in gram}} \times 1000$$

$$= \frac{0.15}{479.3} \times 1000 = 0.313 \text{ m}$$

Example 12 The density of 3 M solution of NaCl is 1.25 g mL^{-1}. Calculate molality of the solution.

NCERT Textbook

Sol. $M = 3 \text{ mol L}^{-1}$

Mass of NaCl in 1 L solution = 3 × 58.5 = 175.5 g

Mass of 1 L solution = 1000 × 1.25 = 1250 g

(since density = 1.25 g mL^{-1})

Mass of water solution = 1250 − 175.5

= 1074.5 g = 1.0745 kg.

$$\text{Molality} = \frac{\text{number of moles of solute}}{\text{mass of solvent in kg}}$$

$$= \frac{3 \text{ mol}}{1.0745 \text{ kg}}$$

$$= 2.79 \text{ m}$$

7. Normality (*N*)

It is defined as the number of gram equivalents of solute present per litre of solution. It is denoted by '*N*'.

$$\text{Normality } (N) = \frac{\text{number of gram equivalents of solute}}{\text{volume of solution in litres}}$$

$$\text{Number of gram equivalent of solute} = \frac{\text{mass of solute}}{\text{equivalent mass}}$$

The unit of normality is g equiv L^{-1}. In case of dilution, $N_1V_1 = N_2V_2$, where N_1V_1 are respectively the normality and volume before dilution and N_2V_2 are normality and volume after dilution.

Like molarity, normality of a solution also changes with temperature.

Note Often in a chemical laboratory, a solution of a desired concentration is prepared by diluting a known solution of higher concentration. The solution of higher concentration is also known as Stock solution.

Example 13 Calculate the normality of solution containing 62.3 g of hydrated copper sulphate ($CuSO_4 \cdot 5H_2O$) in 500 mL of solution.

Sol. Mass of solute = 62.3 g

$$\text{Equivalent mass of oxalic acid} = \frac{249.5}{2} = 124.75 \text{ g}$$

$$\text{Gram equivalents of oxalic acid} = \frac{62.3}{124.75} = 0.5$$

Volume of solution = 500mL

$$\text{Normality} = \frac{0.5}{500} \times 1000 = 1 \text{ N}$$

Topic Practice 3

Very Short Answer Type Questions

1 Mark

1 Fill in the Blank.

(i) Calculations based on chemical equations are termed as .... calculations.

(ii) The reactant which is present in lesser amount, i.e. which limits the amount of product formed is called ....

(iii) In a binary solution, the component present in large excess is called ....

(iv) Molarity is defined as number of .... of the .... dissolved in 1L of the solution.

(v) Mole fraction is independent of ....

2 Objective Type Questions

(i) What is the mass per cent of carbon in carbon dioxide?

(a) 0.034% (b) 27.27%
(c) 3.4% (d) 28.7%

(ii) What will be the molarity of a solution, which contains 5.85 g of NaCl(*s*) per 500 mL?

(a) 4 mol L^{-1} (b) 20 mol L^{-1}
(c) 0.2 mol L^{-1} (d) 2 mol L^{-1}

(iii) If 500 mL of a 5M solution is diluted to 1500 mL, what will be the molarity of the solution obtained?

(a) 1.5 M (b) 1.66 M
(c) 0.017 M (d) 1.59 M

(iv) What will be the molality of the solution containing 18.25 g of HCl gas in 500 g of water?

(a) 0.1 m (b) 1 M
(c) 0.5 m (d) 1 m

(v) If the concentration of glucose ($C_6H_{12}O_6$) in blood is 0.9 g L^{-1}, what will be the molarity of glucose in blood?

(a) 5 M (b) 50 M
(c) 0.005 M (d) 0.5 M

(vi) Sulphuric acid reacts with sodium hydroxide as follows:

$$H_2SO_4 + 2NaOH \longrightarrow Na_2SO_4 + 2H_2O$$

When 1L of 0.1M sulphuric acid solution is allowed to react with 1L of 0.1M sodium hydroxide solution, the amount of sodium sulphate formed and its molarity in the solution obtained is

(a) 7.10 g, 0.1 mol L^{-1} (b) 7.10 g, 0.025 mol L^{-1}
(c) 3.55 g, 0.025 mol L^{-1} (d) 3.55 g, 0.1 mol L^{-1}

3 Match the items of Column I and Column II and choose the correct option using the codes given below :

Column I	Column II
A. Mole fraction	(i) $M_2 \times V_2$
B. Molarity	(ii) The solution of higher concentration
C. Molality	(iii) It is defined as the number of moles of solute present in 1 kg of solvent.
D. $M_1 \times V_1$ is equal to	(iv) It is the ratio of number of moles of a particular component to the total number of moles of the solution.
E Stock solution	(v) It is defined as the number of moles of the solute present in 1 L of the solution.

Codes

	A	B	C	D	E
(a)	(i)	(ii)	(iii)	(iv)	(v)
(b)	(iv)	(v)	(iii)	(i)	(ii)
(c)	(i)	(ii)	(v)	(iv)	(iii)
(d)	(iii)	(ii)	(i)	(iv)	(v)

4 Volume of a solution changes with change in temperature, then, will the molality of the solution be affected by temperature? Give reason for your answer. **NCERT Exemplar**

5 Calculate the mass of sodium acetate, CH_3COONa required to make 500 mL of 0.375 molar aqueous solution. Molar mass of sodium acetate is 82.0245 g mol^{-1}. **NCERT**

6 How many moles of iron can be made from Fe_2O_3 by the use of 16 moles of carbon monoxide in the following reaction?

$$Fe_2O_3 + 3CO \longrightarrow 2Fe + 3CO_2$$

7 If 2 L of N_2 is mixed with 2 L of H_2 at a constant temperature and pressure, then what will be the volume of NH_3 formed ?

Short Answer Type I Questions

2 Marks

8 The reactant which is entirely consumed in reaction is known as limiting reagent. In the reaction $2A + 4B \rightarrow 3C + 4D$, when 5 moles of A react with 6 moles of B, then

(i) which is the limiting reagent?

(ii) calculate the amount of C formed? **NCERT Exemplar**

9 How are 0.50 mole Na_2CO_3 and 0.50 M Na_2CO_3 different? **NCERT Textbook**

Short Answer Type II Questions

3 Marks

10 Calculate the amount of carbon dioxide that could be produced when
(i) 1 mole of carbon is burnt in air.
(ii) 1 mole of carbon is burnt in 16 g of dioxygen.
(iii) 2 moles of carbon are burnt in 16 g of dioxygen. **NCERT Textbook**

11 If 4 g of NaOH dissolves in 36 g of H_2O, calculate the mole fraction of each component in the solution. Also, determine the molarity of solution (specific gravity of solution is 1 g mL^{-1}). **NCERT Exemplar**

12 Dinitrogen and dihydrogen react with each other to produce ammonia according to the following chemical equation,

$$N_2(g) + 3H_2(g) \longrightarrow 2NH_3(g).$$

(i) Calculate the mass of ammonia produced if 2.00×10^3 g dinitrogen reacts with 1.00×10^3 g of dihydrogen.
(ii) Will any of the two reactants remain unreacted?
(iii) If yes, which one and what would be its mass? **NCERT Textbook**

13 If the density of methanol is 0.793 kg L^{-1}, what is its volume needed for making 2.5 L of its 0.25 M solution? **NCERT Textbook**

14 Chlorine is prepared in the laboratory by treating manganese dioxide (MnO_2) with aqueous hydrochloric acid according to the reaction,

$$4\,HCl(aq) + MnO_2(s) \longrightarrow 2H_2O(l) + MnCl_2(aq) + Cl_2(g)$$

How many gram of HCl reacts with 5.0 g of manganese dioxide? **NCERT Textbook**

Long Answer Type Questions

5 Marks

15 (i) A sample of drinking water was found to be severely contaminated with chloroform $CHCl_3$ which is carcinogenic in nature. The level of contamination was 15 ppm (by mass).
(a) Express this in per cent by mass.
(b) Determine the molarity of chloroform in the water sample.
(ii) Calculate the molarity of a solution of ethanol in water in which the mole fraction of ethanol is 0.040. **NCERT Textbook**

16 Calcium carbonate reacts with aqueous HCl to give $CaCl_2$ and CO_2 according to the reaction,

$$CaCO_3(s) + 2\,HCl(aq) \longrightarrow CaCl_2\,(aq) + CO_2\,(g) + H_2O\,(l)$$

What mass of $CaCO_3$ is required to react completely with 25 mL of 0.75 M HCl? **NCERT Textbook**

17 Calcium carbonate reacts with aqueous HCl to give $CaCl_2$ and CO_2 according to the reaction given below:

$$CaCO_3(s) + 2HCl\,(aq) \longrightarrow CaCl_2(aq) + CO_2(g) + H_2O\,(l)$$

What mass of $CaCl_2$ will be formed when 250 mL of 0.76 M HCl reacts with 1000 g of $CaCO_3$? Name the limiting reagent. Calculate the number of moles of $CaCl_2$ formed in the reaction. **NCERT Exemplar**

Hints & Solutions

1. (i) stoichiometric (ii) limiting reagent.
(iii) solvent (iv) moles, solute
(v) temperature

2. (i) (b) Molecular mass of $CO_2 = 1\times 12 + 2\times 16 = 44\,g\,mol^{-1}$

1 g molecule of CO_2 contains 1g atoms of carbon

$\because$ 44 g of CO_2 contain C = 12 g atoms of carbon

$\therefore$ % of C in $CO_2 = \frac{12}{44} \times 100 = 27.27\%$

Hence, the mass per cent of carbon in CO_2 is 27.27%.

(ii) (c) Since, molarity (M) is calculated by following equation,

$$\text{Molarity} = \frac{\text{weight} \times 1000}{\text{molecular weight} \times \text{volume (mL)}}$$

$$= \frac{5.85 \times 1000}{58.5 \times 500} = 0.2\ mol\ L^{-1}$$

(iii) (b) For dilution, a general formula is

$$\underset{\text{(Before dilution)}}{M_1V_1} = \underset{\text{(After dilution)}}{M_2V_2}$$

$$500 \times 5M = 1500 \times M$$

$$M = \frac{5}{3} = 1.66M$$

(iv) (d) Molality is defined as the number of moles of solute present in 1 kg of solvent. It is denoted by m.

Thus, $\text{Molality}\,(m) = \frac{\text{Moles of solute}}{\text{Mass of solvent (in kg)}}$ ...(i)

Given that, Mass of solvent (H_2O) = 500 g = 0.5 kg

Weight of HCl = 18.25 g

Molecular weight of HCl $= 1 \times 1 + 1 \times 35.5 = 36.5$g

$$\text{Moles of HCl} = \frac{18.25}{36.5} = 0.5$$

$$m = \frac{0.5}{0.5} = 1\text{ m} \qquad \text{[from Eq. (i)]}$$

(v) (*c*) In the given question, 0.9 g L^{-1} means that 1000 mL (or 1L) solution contains 0.9 g of glucose.

$\therefore$ Number of moles in 0.9 g glucose

$$= \frac{0.9}{180}\text{ mol glucose}$$

$$= 5 \times 10^{-3}\text{ mol glucose}$$

(where, molecular mass of glucose $(C_6H_{12}O_6) = 12 \times 6 + 12 \times 1 + 6 \times 16 = 180$ u)

i.e. 1L solution contains 0.005 mole glucose or the molarity of glucose is 0.005 M.

(vi) (*b*) For the reaction,

$$H_2SO_4 + 2NaOH \longrightarrow Na_2SO_4 + 2H_2O$$

1L of 0.1 M H_2SO_4 contains = 0.1 mole of H_2SO_4

1L of 0.1 M NaOH contains = 0.1 mole of NaOH

According to the reaction, 1 mole of H_2SO_4 reacts with 2 moles of NaOH. Hence, 0.1 mole of NaOH will react with 0.05 mole of H_2SO_4 (and 0.05 mole of H_2SO_4 will be left unreacted), i.e., NaOH is the limiting reactant. Since, 2 moles of NaOH produce 1 mole of Na_2SO_4.

Hence, 0.1 mole of NaOH will produce 0.05 mole of Na_2SO_4.

Mass of Na_2SO_4 = moles × molar mass

$$= 0.05 \times (46 + 32 + 64)\text{ g}$$

$$= 7.10\text{ g}$$

Volume of solution after mixing = 2 L

Since, only 0.05 mole of H_2SO_4 is left behind as NaOH completely used in the reaction. Therefore, molarity of the given solution is calculated from moles of H_2SO_4.

H_2SO_4 left unreacted in the solution = 0.05 mol

$$\therefore \text{ Molarity of the solution} = \frac{0.05}{2} = 0.025\text{ mol L}^{-1}$$

3. (*b*) (A) → (iv), (B)→(v), (C) → (iii), (D)→(i), (E)→(ii).

4. No, molality of solution does not change with temperature since mass remains unaffected with temperature.

5. $$\text{Molarity} = \frac{w \times 1000}{m \times \text{volume of solution (mL)}}$$

where, w = mass of solute and m = molar mass of solute.

Given, molarity of the solution = 0.375 M

Molar mass of solute, $m = 82.0245$ g mol^{-1}

Volume of solution = 500 mL

Mass of solute = ?

$$\therefore \text{ Mass of solute, } w = \frac{0.375 \times 82.0245 \times 500}{1000} = 15.379\text{ g}$$

$$\approx 15.38\text{ g}$$

6. $$\underset{}{Fe_2O_3} + \underset{16\text{ mol}}{3CO} \longrightarrow \underset{?}{2Fe} + 3CO_2$$

3 moles of CO are used to produce 2 moles of Fe.

Hence, 16 moles of CO are used to produce

$$= \frac{2}{3} \times 16 = 10.67\text{ mol}$$

7. $N_2(g) + 3H_2(g) \longrightarrow 2NH_3(g)$

1 L of N_2 reacts with 3 L of H_2.

Therefore, 2 L of N_2 will react with 6 L of H_2 but we have only 2 L of H_2, therefore, H_2 is the limiting reactant.

Since, 3 L of H_2 gives 2 L of NH_3.

$$\therefore 2\text{ L of } H_2 \text{ gives} = \frac{2}{3} \times 2 = \frac{4}{3} = 1.33\text{ L of } NH_3$$

8. $2A + 4B \longrightarrow 3C + 4D$

According to the given reaction, 2 moles of A react with 4 moles of B.

Hence, 5 moles of A will react with 10 moles of

$$B\left(\frac{5 \times 4}{2} = 10\text{ moles}\right)$$

(i) It indicates that reactant B is limiting reagent as it will consume first in the reaction because we have only 6 moles of B. [1]

(ii) Limiting reagent decide the amount of product produced. According to the reaction, 4 moles of B produces 3 moles of C.

$$\therefore 6 \text{ moles of } B \text{ will produce} = \frac{3 \times 6}{4} = 4.5 \text{ moles of } C.$$ [1]

9. Molar mass of $Na_2CO_3 = (2 \times 22.99) + 12.01 + (3 \times 16)$

$$= 105.99 \approx 106\text{ g mol}^{-1}$$ [1]

0.50 mole $Na_2CO_3 = 0.50 \times 106$

$$= 53\text{ g } Na_2CO_3$$

0.50 M Na_2CO_3 means 53 g Na_2CO_3 is present in 1 L of the solution. [1]

10. In order to find the moles of different elements/ compounds taking part in the reaction, write a balanced chemical equation for combustion of carbon in dioxygen (air). Calculate the amount of CO_2 produced with the help of information available from the balanced chemical equation.

$$\underset{1\text{ mol}}{C(s)} + \underset{\substack{1\text{ mol}\\32\text{ g}}}{O_2(g)} \longrightarrow \underset{\substack{1\text{ mol}\\44\text{ g}}}{CO_2(g)}$$

(i) According to the equation, when 1 mole of carbon is burnt completely, CO_2 produced is 44 g. [1]

(ii) 1 mole of carbon requires 32 g dioxygen from the reaction. But we have only 16 g dioxygen. Hence, dioxygen is the limiting reagent. So, the amount of CO_2 produced by 16 g dioxygen is 22 g. [1]

(iii) In this case again, dioxygen is the limiting reagent. 16 g dioxygen can react only with 0.5 mole of carbon and produce 22 g CO_2. [1]

11. **Key Idea** To proceed the calculation, first calculate the number of moles of NaOH and H_2O.
Then, find mole fraction of NaOH and H_2O by using the formula,

$$\chi_{NaOH} = \frac{n_{NaOH}}{n_{NaOH} + n_{H_2O}} \left(\text{or } \chi_{H_2O} = \frac{n_{H_2O}}{n_{NaOH} + n_{H_2O}} \right)$$

Then, calculate molarity $= \frac{W \times 1000}{m \times V}$, so in order to calculate molarity we require volume of solution which is, $V = \frac{m}{\text{specific gravity}}$.

Number of moles of NaOH,

$$n_{NaOH} = \frac{4}{40} = 0.1 \text{ mol} \quad \left\{ \because n = \frac{\text{Mass (g)}}{\text{Molar mass (g mol}^{-1})} \right\}$$

Similarly, $n_{H_2O} = \frac{36}{18} = 2$ mol

Mole fraction of NaOH,

$$\chi_{NaOH} = \frac{\text{moles of NaOH}}{\text{moles of NaOH} + \text{moles of } H_2O}$$

$$\chi_{NaOH} = \frac{0.1}{0.1 + 2} = 0.0476$$ [1]

Similarly, $\chi_{H_2O} = \frac{n_{H_2O}}{n_{NaOH} + n_{H_2O}} = \frac{2}{0.1 + 2} = 0.9524$

Total mass of solution = mass of solute + mass of solvent
$= 4 + 36 = 40$ g [1]

Volume of solution

$$= \frac{\text{mass of solution}}{\text{specific gravity}} = \frac{40 \text{ g}}{1 \text{ g mL}^{-1}} = 40 \text{ mL}$$

$$\text{Molarity} = \frac{\text{moles of solute} \times 1000}{\text{volume of solution (mL)}} = \frac{0.1 \times 1000}{40} = 2.5\text{M}$$ [1]

12. (i) $N_2(g) + 3H_2(g) \longrightarrow 2NH_3(g)$

$\quad$ 1 mol $\quad$ 3 mol $\quad$ 2 mol
$\quad$ 28 g $\quad$ 6 g $\quad$ 34 g

28 g N_2 reacts with 6 g H_2.

$\therefore$ 1 g N_2 will react with $\frac{6}{28}$ g H_2.

$\therefore$ 2000 g N_2 will react with $\frac{2000 \times 6}{28}$

$= 428.57$ g H_2

Hence, N_2 is the limiting reagent and H_2 is in excess. N_2 limits the amount of ammonia produced.

28 g N_2 produces 34 g NH_3 and 1 g N_2 produces $\frac{34}{28}$ g NH_3

$\therefore$ 2000 g N_2 will produce $\frac{34}{28} \times 2000 = 2428.57$ g NH_3 [1]

(ii) Yes [1]

(iii) H_2 is in excess so, it will remain unreacted. Amount of H_2 remains unreacted $= 1000 - 428.57 = 571.43$ g. [1]

13. Given, $d = 0.793 \text{ kg L}^{-1} = 0.793 \times 10^3 \text{ g L}^{-1}$

Mass of methanol $(m) = 0.793 \times 10^3$ g [if volume = 1 L]

Final volume, $V_2 = 2.5$ L
Final molarity, $M_2 = 0.25$ M
Molarity of initial solution $M_1 = ?$
Initial volume $V_1 = ?$.
Molar mass of methanol,

$CH_3OH = (1 \times 12.01) + (4 \times 1.0079) + 16.00$
$= 32.0416 \approx 32 \text{ g mol}^{-1}$ [1/2]

$$\text{Molarity} = \frac{0.793 \times 10^3 \text{ g L}^{-1}}{32 \text{ g mol}^{-1}} = 24.781 \text{ mol L}^{-1}$$

$\Rightarrow \quad M_1V_1 = M_2V_2$ [1]

$24.781 \times V_1 = 0.25 \times 2.5$ [1/2]

$$V_1 = \frac{0.25 \times 2.5}{24.781} = 0.02522 \text{ L} = 25.22 \text{ mL}$$ [1]

14. $4\text{HCl}(aq) + MnO_2(s) \longrightarrow 2H_2O(l) + MnCl_2(aq) + Cl_2(g)$

$\quad 4 \times 36.5 \quad$ 87 g

According to the balanced chemical equation,
87 g of MnO_2 reacts with 4×36.5 g HCl
$\therefore$ 5 g of MnO_2 will react with

$$\frac{4 \times 36.5 \times 5}{87} = 8.39 \text{ g HCl}$$ [3]

15. (i) (a) 15 ppm means 15 parts in one million $(10)^6$ parts.

Therefore, % by mass $= \frac{15 \times 100}{10^6} = 1.5 \times 10^{-3}\%$ [1]

(b) Molar mass of $CHCl_3 = 119 \text{ g mol}^{-1}$ [1/2]

$1.5 \times 10^{-3}\%$ means 1.5×10^{-3} g chloroform is present in 100 g sample.

$$\text{Molarity, } M = \frac{w \times 1000}{m \times \text{volume of sample}}$$ [1/2]

(For water, density = 1 g cm^{-3}, so mass = volume)

$$M = \frac{1.5 \times 10^{-3} \times 1000}{119 \times 100} = 1.26 \times 10^{-4} \text{ M}$$ [1]

(ii) Molarity is defined as the moles of solute (ethanol) in 1L of the solution.

1L of ethanol solution (as it is diluted) = 1L of water

Number of moles of $H_2O = \frac{1000 \text{ g}}{18} = 55.55$ mol [1/2]

$\chi_{H_2O} = 1 - n_{C_2H_5OH}$

$\chi_{H_2O} = 1 - 0.040 = 0.96$ [1/2]

$$\chi_{H_2O} = \frac{n_{H_2O}}{n_{H_2O} + n_{C_2H_5OH}}$$

$$\Rightarrow 0.96 = \frac{55.55}{55.55 + n_{C_2H_5OH}}$$ [1/2]

or $$n_{C_2H_5OH} = \frac{2.222}{0.96} = 2.3145 \text{ mol}$$ [1/2]

16. **Key Idea** To calculate the mass of $CaCO_3$ required to react completely with 25 mL of 0.75 M HCl first we will calculate the mass of HCl in 25 mL of 0.75 M HCl.
Now, calculate the mass of $CaCO_3(g)$ by using the information available from a balanced chemical equation.

(i) Calculation for mass of HCl in 25 mL of 0.75 M HCl

$$\text{Molarity} = \frac{w \times 1000}{m \times \text{vol (mL)}}$$

$$\Rightarrow \quad 0.75 = \frac{w \times 1000}{36.5 \times 25}$$

(Molar mass of HCl = 1 + 35.5 = 36.5 g/mol)

$$w = 0.75 \times 36.5 \times \frac{25}{1000} = 0.6844 \text{ g}$$ [2½]

(ii) Calculation for required mass of $CaCO_3$ to react completely with 0.6844 g HCl.

$$\underset{100\text{ g}}{CaCO_3(s)} + \underset{2 \times 36.5 = 73\text{ g}}{2HCl(aq)} \longrightarrow CaCl_2(aq) + CO_2(g) + H_2O(l)$$

According to balanced chemical equation,
73 g HCl completely reacts with 100 g $CaCO_3$

1 g HCl completely reacts with $\frac{100}{73}$ g $CaCO_3$

$\therefore$ 0.6844 g HCl will completely reacts with

$$\frac{100 \times 0.6844}{73} = 0.9375 \text{ g}$$ [2½]

17. Number of moles of HCl

$$= 250 \text{ mL} \times \frac{0.76 \text{ M}}{1000} = 0.19 \text{ mol}$$

$$\text{Number of moles of } CaCO_3 = \frac{1000 \text{ g}}{100 \text{ g mol}^{-1}} = 10 \text{ mol}$$ [2]

For the 10 moles of $CaCO_3(s)$, number of moles of HCl required would be $10 \times \frac{2}{1} = 20$ mol HCl (aq) [1]

But we have only 0.19 mole HCl (aq), hence, HCl (aq) is the limiting reagent. Since, 2 moles HCl (aq) forms 1 mole of $CaCl_2$, therefore, 0.19 moles of HCl (aq) would give

$$0.19 \times \frac{1}{2} = 0.095 \text{ mol}$$

Mass of $CaCl_2 = 0.095 \times 111 = 10.54$ g [2]

SUMMARY

- Anything which is having mass and occupying some space is called matter.
- Matter can be a pure substance or a mixture. Pure substance with only one kind of atoms are known as elements.
- Pure substance having fixed composition are called compounds.
- When composition of various components is not fixed it is called mixture.
- Composition of components of a mixture is uniform through out is called **homogeneous mixture**. If it is not uniform through out, it is known as heterogeneous mixture.
- A matter possess properties like mass, volume, density, temperature, etc.
- Representation of number as $N \times 10^n$ (where, N = number, n = power over 10) is called scientific notation (n is (–) ve if decimal moves to right and is (+) ve if it moves towards left).
- All certain digits with last digit uncertain are called significant figures. Dimensional analysis can be done by using the concept, Required unit = given value × conversion factor.

Law of Chemical Combinations

(i) Law of conservation of mass.
(ii) Law of definite proportion.
(iii) Law of multiple proportion.
(iv) Gay Lussac's law of gaseous volume.
(v) Avogadro's law ($V \propto n$).

- Dalton's atomic theory states that matter is made up of tiny indivisible particles called atoms.
- Atoms of same elements are identical to each other. Compounds have different atoms but in fixed proportion.
- Masses can be expressed in various ways:
  (i) Mass of an atom relative to the mass of C_{12} is called atomic mass.
  (ii) Amu (atomic mass unit) is the mass exactly equal to $\frac{1}{12}$th mass of C-12 atom
  (1 amu or $1 - u = 1.66056 \times 10^{-24}$ g).
  (iii) Average atomic mass is average of all isotopic atomic mass. It is given as:
  Average atomic mass $= \frac{\Sigma\, x A}{\Sigma\, x}$ (where, x = % abundance, A = atomic mass).
  (iv) Molecular mass is the sum of atomic mass of all the elements present in a compound.
  (v) Molecular mass in case of ions is called formula mass.
- Formula showing exact number of atoms, present in a molecules is called molecular formula.
  Molecular formula = n × empirical formula.
- Mass of constituents in 100 parts of a compound is known as percentage composition.
- The number of parts of a substance that combines with or displaces, directly or indirectly, 1.008 parts by mass of hydrogen or 35.5 parts by mass of chlorine or 8 parts by mass of oxygen is called the equivalent mass of the substance.
- Values (number of moles) used for calculation based on balanced chemical equations are called stoichiometric calculations.
- Mole concept is the relation in terms of moles and other properties like number of particles, volume of gas, mass etc.
  (i) 1 mole of particles = 6.023×10^{23} particles.
  (ii) 1 mole = 22.4 L (for gases at NTP).
  (iii) Number of moles $= \frac{\text{mass of substance } (w)}{\text{atomic or molar mass } (m)}$
  (iv) Number of atoms = Number of molecules × atomicity.
- The reagent which limits the amount of product formed is known as limiting reagent.
- The simplest whole number ratio of different atoms present in a compound is known as empirical formula.
- Reaction occurs in aqueous medium are called reactions in solutions.
- Relation between solute and solvent can be expressed as:
  (i) Mass per cent is the mass of substance (solute/solvent) per 100 g of solution.
  (ii) Mole fraction is ratio of moles of substance (solute/solvent) to the total number of moles present in the solution.
  (iii) Molarity (M) is the number of moles of solute present per litre of solution (V).
  $M = \frac{w \times 1000}{m \times V}$ (m = molecular mass of solute)
  (iv) Molality (m) is the number of moles of solute present per kg of solvent.
  $$m = \frac{w \times 1000}{M \times W}$$
  (w = mass of solvent)

Chapter Practice

Very Short Answer Type Questions

1 Mark

1 Fill in the Blanks

(i) SI unit of electric current is ....

(ii) According to law of definite proportion, a given compound always contain exactly the .... of elements by ....

(iii) Molecular mass of a substance expresesed in gram is called its ....

(iv) For gases, a mole is defined as amount of gas, which occupies a volume of .... at STP.

(v) .... = $\frac{\text{number of moles of solute}}{\text{volume of solution in L}}$.

2. Obejctive Type Questions

(i) The sulphate of a metal *M* contains 9.87% of *M*. The sulphate is isomorphous with $ZnSO_4 \cdot 7H_2O$. The atomic weight of *M* is

(a) 40.3 (b) 36.3
(c) 24.3 (d) 11.3

(ii) The equivalent weight of H_3PO_2, when it disproportionates into PH_3 and H_3PO_4 is

(a) 82 (b) 61.5
(c) 33 (d) 20.5

(iii) How much mass of NaOH is required to neutralise 1500 cm^3 of 0.1 N HCl? (Na = 23)

(a) 40 g (b) 4 g
(c) 6 g (d) 60 g

(iv) 5 mL of N HCl, 20 mL of $N/2H_2SO_4$ and 30 mL of $N/3HNO_3$ are mixed together and volume made upto 1 L. The normality of resulting solution is

(a) 0.45 (b) 0.025
(c) 0.9 (d) 0.05

(v) If 0.5 moles of $BaCl_2$ are mixed with 0.2 moles of Na_3PO_4, the maximum number of moles of $Ba_3(PO_4)_2$ that can be formed, is

(a) 0.7 (b) 0.5 (c) 0.30 (d) 0.10

(vi) The empirical formula and molecular mass of a compound are CH_2O and 180 g respectively. What will be the molecular formula of the compound?

(a) $C_9H_{18}O_9$ (b) CH_2O
(c) $C_6H_{12}O_6$ (d) $C_2H_4O_2$

3. Match the Column I with Column II and choose the correct option using the codes given below:

Column I	Column II
A. Mass of H_2 produced when 0.5 mole of zinc reacts with excess of HCl.	(i) 3.01×10^{23} molecules
B. Mass of all atoms of a compound with formula $C_{70}H_{22}$.	(ii) 6.023×10^{23} molecules
C. Number of molecules in 35.5 g of Cl_2.	(iii) 1.43×10^{-21} g
D. Number of molecules in 64 g of SO_2.	(iv) 1 g

Codes

	A	B	C	D
(a)	(ii)	(i)	(iv)	(iii)
(b)	(i)	(ii)	(iii)	(iv)
(c)	(iv)	(iii)	(i)	(ii)
(d)	(iv)	(iii)	(ii)	(i)

4. What is the mass in gram of one molecule of caffeine ($C_8H_{10}N_4O_2$)?

5. Calculate the number of moles of sulphur atom.

6. Explain, why diamond is considered as an element, not as a compound?

7. Round up the following upto three significant figures.

(i) 38.216 (ii) 10.4107

8. 32 g of sulphur reacts with 32 g of oxygen even if more than 32 g of sulphur are available. Which law of chemical combination does this illustrate?

9. Give the empirical formulae of the following substances.

(i) C_6H_6
(ii) Graphite
(iii) Magnesium chloride

10. Write balanced chemical equation for the following.

Elemental phosphorus (P) reacts with concentrated nitric acid to give nitrogen dioxide and phosphoric acid.

11. 3 L of water is added to 2 L of 5 M HCl. What is the molarity of HCl in the resultant solution?

Or

Calculate the mass of a molecule of carbon dioxide ($^{14}CO_2$)?

Assertion-Reason

Directions (Q. Nos. 12-16) In the following questions, a statement of Assertion is followed by a corresponding statements of Reason of the following statements, choose the correct one.

(a) Both (A) and (R) are correct and (R) is the correct explanation of (A).
(b) Both (A) and (R) are correct but (R) is not the correct explanation of (A).
(c) (A) is correct and (R) is incorrect.
(d) (A) is incorrect and (R) is correct.

12. **Assertion** (A) Significant figures for 0.200 is 3 whereas for 200 it is 1.

Reason (R) Zeros at the end or right of a number are significant provided they are not on the right side of the decimal point.

13. **Assertion** (A) The empirical mass of C_2H_4 is CH_2.

Reason (R) The empirical formula represent the simplest whole number ratio of various atoms present in a compound.

14. **Assertion** (A) Equal moles of different substances contain same number of constituent particles.

Reason (R) Equal weights of different substance contains the same number of constituent particles.

15. **Assertion** (A) A reactant that is entirely consumed when a reaction goes to completion is known as limiting reaction.

Reason (R) The amount of limiting reactant limits the amount of product formed.

16. **Assertion** (A) Molarity of a solution does not represents its concentration.

Reason (R) Molarity is the number of moles of solute per litre of solution.

Case-Study

17. The identity of a substance is defined not only by the types of atoms or ions it contains, but by the quantity of each type of atom or ion. The experimental approach required the introduction of a new unit for amount of substances, the mole, which remains indispensable in modern chemical science.

The mole is an amount unit similar to familiar units like pair, dozen, gross, etc. It provides a specific measure of the number of atoms or molecules in a bulk sample of matter.

A **mole** is defined as the amount of substance containing the same number of discrete entities (atoms, molecules, ions, etc.) as the number of atoms in a sample of pure ^{12}C weighing exactly 12g. One Latin connotation for the word "mole" is "large mass" or "bulk," which is consistent with its use as the name for this unit.

The mole provides a link between an easily measured macroscopic property, bulk mass, and an extremely important fundamental property, number of atoms, molecules and so on.

The number of entities composing a mole has been experimentally determined to be $6.02214179 \times 10^{23}$, a fundamental constant named Avogadro's number (N_A) or the Avogadro constant in honor of Italian scientist Amedeo Avogadro. This constant is properly reported with an explicit unit of "per mole," a conveniently rounded version being 6.022×10^{23}/mol.

Consistent with its definition as an amount unit, 1 mole of any element contains the same number of atoms as 1 mole of any other element.

The masses of 1 mole of different elements, however, are different, since the masses of the individual atoms are drastically different. The molar mass of an element (or compound) is the mass in grams of 1 mole of that substance, a property expressed in units of grams per mole (g/mol).

(i) A sample of copper sulphate pentahydrate contain 8.64 g of oxygen. Calculate grams of Cu present in the sample.

(ii) A gas mixture contains 50% helium and 50% methane by volume. What is the per cent by weight of methane in the mixture?

(iii) Calculate the mass of oxygen gas which occupies 5.6 litres at STP.

18. A chemical reaction is a change in which one or more substance(s) react(s) to form new substance(s) with entirely different properties.

A chemical equation is a brief representation of a chemical reaction in terms of symbols and formulae of substances involved in it, e.g. the reaction of silver nitrate with sodium chloride to give silver chloride and sodium nitrate can be represented as

$$\underbrace{AgNO_3 + NaCl}_{\text{Reactants}} \longrightarrow \underbrace{AgCl + NaNO_3}_{\text{Products}}$$

The substances which react among themselves to bring about the chemical changes are known as reactants whereas, the substances which are produced as a result of the chemical change, are known as products.

Reactants and products of a chemical equation are separated by arrow pointing towards the products.

Quantitative information conveyed by a chemical equation is as follows

- The relative number of reactant and product species (atoms or molecules) taking part in the reaction.
- The relative number of moles of the reactants and products.
- The relative masses of the reactants and products.
- The relative volumes of gaseous reactants and products.

The reactant which is present in the lesser amount and gets consumed after sometime, i.e. which limits the amount of product formed is called the limiting reagent.

The reactant other than the limiting reagent, which is in somewhat excess is called the excess reagent. The remaining amount of excess reagent is calculated by subtracting the available amount of limiting reagent from the amount of the excess reagent.

Remember that in stoichiometric calculations, it is very important to choose the limiting reagent.

(i) What will be the volume of the mixture after the reaction?

$$\underset{1\,L}{NH_3(g)} + \underset{1.5\,L}{HCl(g)} \longrightarrow NH_4Cl(s)$$

(ii) For the formation of 3.65 g hydrogen chloride gas, what volume of hydrogen gas and chlorine gas are required at NTP conditions?

(iii) A gas mixture contains 50% He and 50% CH_4 by volume. What is the percentage by weight of methane in the mixture?

Short Answer Type I Questions

2 Marks

19. The molality and molarity of a solution of sulphuric acid are 4.13 mol/kg and 11.12 mol/L respectively. Calculate density of the solution.

20. The "star of India" sapphire weighs 563 carats. If one carat is equal to 200 mg, what is the mass of the gemstone in gram?

21. Give one experiment involving a chemical reaction to prove that the law of conservation of mass is true.

22. Naphthalene (compound of C and H) contain 93.71% carbon. If its molar mass is 128 g mol^{-1}, calculate its molecular formula.

23. What volume of oxygen at STP can be produced by 6.125 g of potassium chlorate according to the reaction,

$$2KClO_3 \longrightarrow 2KCl + 3O_2?$$

24. Calculate the number of gram of SO_2 which can be prepared by the treatment of 100 g of Na_2SO_3 with HCl.

25. A gold coloured metal object has a mass of 365 g and a volume of 22.12 cm^3. Is the object composed of pure gold?

Short Answer Type II Questions

3 Marks

26. (i) 0.5 mole each of H_2S and SO_2 mixed together in a reaction flask, react according to equation

$$2H_2S + SO_2 \longrightarrow 2H_2O + 3S$$

Calculate the number of moles of S formed.

(ii) Calculate the volume of 0.015 M HCl solution required to prepare 250 mL of a 8.25×10^{-5} M HCl solution.

27. Calculate the volume of 1.00 mol L^{-1} aqueous solution of sodium hydroxide that is neutralised by 200 mL of 2.00 mol L^{-1} aqueous hydrochloric acid and the mass of sodium chloride obtained. Neutralisation reaction is

$NaOH\,(aq) + HCl\,(aq) \longrightarrow NaCl\,(aq) + H_2O\,(l)$

28. Lithium oxide is used to remove water from air according to the reaction,

$$Li_2O(s) + H_2O\,(g) \longrightarrow 2\,LiOH\,(s)$$

If 72 kg of water is to be removed and 35 kg of Li_2O is available, then

(i) which reactant is limiting?

(ii) how many kg of excess reactant is left?

29. Weighing 3104 carats (1 carat = 200 mg), the Cullinan diamond was the largest natural diamond ever found. How many carbon atoms were present in the stone?

30. Commercially available concentrated hydrochloric acid contains 38% HCl by mass.

(i) What is the molarity of this solution? The density is 1.19 g cm^{-3}.

(ii) What volume of concentrated hydrochloric acid is required to make 1.00 L of 0.10 M HCl?

31. Calculate the percentage by mass of chromium in each of the following oxides.

(i) CrO (ii) Cr_2O_3 (iii) CrO_3

Long Answer Type Questions

5 Marks

32. (i) An element *X* forms four oxides having percentages of *X* equal to 77.4%, 63.2%, 69.9% and 72.0%. Verify law of multiple proportions.

(ii) A solution of glucose in water is labelled as 10% (w/W). The density of the solution is 1.20 g mL^{-1}. Calculate (a) molarity (b) molality

Answers

1. (i) Ampere

(ii) (a) same (b) proportion (c) weight (or mass).

(iii) gram molecular mass (gram molecule).

(iv) 22.4 L

(v) molarity

2. (i) (*c*) As the given sulphate, is isomorphous with $ZnSO_4.7H_2O$, its formula would be $MSO_4.7H_2O$. If m is the atomic weight of *M*, molecular weight of

$MSO_4.7H_2O = m + 32 + 64 + 126 = m + 222$

Hence, % of $M = \dfrac{m}{m+222} \times 100 = 9.87$ (given)

or $100m = 9.87\,m + 222 \times 9.87$

or $90.13m = 222 \times 9.87$

or $m = 24.3$

(ii) (*c*) H_3PO_2 disproportionates as

$$2H_3\overset{+1}{P}O_2 \longrightarrow \overset{-3}{P}H_3 + H_3\overset{+5}{P}O_4$$

Molecular wt. of $H_3PO_2 = 3 + 31 + 32 = 66$

$\therefore$ Eq. wt. $= \dfrac{66}{4} + \dfrac{66}{4} = 33$

(iii) (*c*) 1500 cm^3 of 0.10 N HCl

$= \dfrac{0.1}{1000} \times 1500 = 0.15$ g eq.

$= 0.15$g eq. of NaOH

$= 0.15 \times 40 = 6$ g NaOH

(iv) (*a*) Normality equation is,

$N_1V_1 + N_2V_2 + N_3V_3 = N_4(V_1 + V_2 + V_3)$

(HCl) (H_2SO_4) (HNO_3)

or $1 \times 5 + 20 \times \dfrac{1}{2} + 30 \times \dfrac{1}{3} = N_4(5 + 20 + 30)$

$\therefore$ Resulting normality $(N_4) = \dfrac{25}{55} = 0.45$

(v) (*d*) $3BaCl_2 + 2Na_3PO_4 \longrightarrow Ba_3(PO_4)_2 + 6NaCl$

Limiting reactant is Na_3PO_4

0.2 mol Na_3PO_4 will give

$Ba_3(PO_4)_2 = \dfrac{1}{2} \times 0.2 = 0.1$ mol

(vi) (*c*) Empirical formula mass of CH_2O

$= 12 + 2 \times 1 + 16 = 30$

$n = \dfrac{\text{Molecular mass}}{\text{Empirical formula mass}}$

$= \dfrac{180}{30} = 6$

$\therefore$ Molecular formula $= n \times$ empirical formula

$= 6 \times CH_2O = C_6H_{12}O_6$

3 (*c*) (A) $Zn + 2HCl \longrightarrow ZnCl_2 + H_2$

1 mole of Zn produces 2 g of H_2

0.5 mole of Zn will produce 1 g of H_2

(B) Molar mass of $C_{70}H_{22} = 862$

Mass of atoms $= \dfrac{862}{6.023 \times 10^{23}} = 1.43 \times 10^{-21}$ g

(C) 70 g of $Cl_2 = 6.023 \times 10^{23}$ moecules

35.5 g of $Cl_2 = 3.01 \times 10^{23}$ molecules

(D) Molar mass of $SO_2 = 64$ g = 1 mole

64 g or 1 mole of $SO_2 = 6.023 \times 10^{23}$ molecules

4. **Ans** Mass $= 3.22 \times 10^{-22}$ g

5. Number of moles $= 1.42$

6. Diamond is considered as an element because it is made up of pure carbon atoms.

7. (i) 38.2 (ii) 10.4

8. Law of definite proportions.

9. Empirical formula for given compounds:
(i) $C_6H_6 = CH$ (ii) Graphite = C
(iii) Magnesium chloride $= (MgCl_2)$

10. $$\underset{\text{(Red phosphorus)}}{P} + \underset{\text{(Conc. nitric acid)}}{5HNO_3} \xrightarrow{t^\circ C} \underset{\text{(Phosphoric acid)}}{H_3PO_4} + \underset{\text{(Nitrogen dioxide)}}{5NO_2} + \underset{\text{(Water)}}{H_2O}$$

11. **Ans** 2M, 7.64×10^{23} g

12. (c) (A) is correct and (R) is incorrect.
Correct Reason Zeros at the end or right of a number are significant.

13. (a) Both (A) and (R) are correct and (R) is the correct explanation of (A).

14. (c) (A) is correct, (R) is incorrect.
Equal moles of different substances contain same number of constituent particles but equal weights of different substances do not contain the same number of constituent particles.

15. (a) Both (A) and (R) are correct and (R) is the correct explanation of (A).

16. (d) (A) is incorrect and (R) is correct.
Correct Assertion Molarity of a solution represents its concentration.

17. (i) $CuSO_4 \cdot 5H_2O$ has 1 mole of Cu and 9 moles of oxygen atoms.
63.5 g of Cu $= 9 \times 16$ g of oxygen
$$\therefore 8.64 \text{ g of oxygen} = \frac{63.5}{9 \times 16} \times 8.64 = 3.81 \text{ g}$$
(ii) Equal volumes contain equal number of moles.
hence, molar ratio of He : $CH_4 = 1:1$
$\therefore$ Ratio by weight = 4 : 16 = 1 : 4
$$\therefore CH_4 \text{ present by weight} = \frac{4}{5} \times 100 = 80\%$$
(iii) 22.4 L of O_2 gas at STP = 1 gram molecule (1 mole)
$$5.6 \text{ L of } O_2 \text{ gas at STP} = \frac{1}{22.4} \times 5.6 \text{ of gram molecule}$$
$$= \frac{1}{4} \text{ gram molecule} = \frac{1}{4} \times 2 \text{ gram atoms}$$
$$= \frac{1}{2} \text{ gram atom}$$

18. (i) 1 L NH_3 will react with 1 L HCl to form NH_4Cl which has negligible volume.
Hence, final mixture will contain only 0.5 L HCl.
(ii) $$\underset{\substack{1\text{ mol}\\22.4\text{L}}}{H_2(g)} + \underset{\substack{1\text{ mol}\\22.4\text{ L}}}{Cl_2(g)} \longrightarrow \underset{\substack{2\text{ mol}\\2\times36.5\text{ g}}}{2HCl(g)}$$
For the formation of 3.65 g HCl, H_2 or Cl_2 required
$$= \frac{22.4}{2 \times 36.5} \times 3.65 = 1.12 \text{ L}$$
(iii) Equal volumes of gases contain equal number of moles.
Hence, molar ratio of He : $CH_4 = 1 : 1$
Ratio by weight $= 4 : 16 = 1 : 4$
$$\therefore CH_4 \text{ present by weight} = \frac{4}{5} \times 100 = 80\%$$

19. **Ans** 3.809 g/L

20. 112.6 g

21. Refer to text on page 10. (Topic-1, Laws of chemical combinations).

22. **Ans** $C_{10}H_8$

23. **Ans** 1.68 L

24. **Ans** 50.8 g

25. **Ans** No

26. **Ans** (i) 0.75 mol, (ii) 0.4 mL

27. **Ans** Volume of 1.00 M NaOH = 400 mL and mass of NaCl produced = 23.4 g

28. **Ans** (i) Li_2O, (ii) 43.36 kg

29. **Ans** 3.12×10^{25} atoms

30. **Ans** (i) 12.42 M, (ii) 8.1 mL

31. **Ans** (i) 76.47%, (ii) 68.42%, (iii) 52.00%

32. **Ans** (ii) (a) 0.67 M (b) 0.62 m

CHAPTER

02

Struture of Atom

TOPIC 01 Sub-atomic Particles and Some Atomic Models

In the previous chapter, you have read about the atom and Dalton's atomic theory that consider atoms as fundamental building of matter. Also, proposed that, matter was composed of extremely small particles called atoms which are structureless, possessed, fixed mass and were indivisible.

The discoveries of several scientists like Faraday, Thomson, Rutherford, etc. clearly revealed that the atom is divisible and composed of several smallest particles like electrons, protons, neutrons, etc. although atom is the smallest particles that take part in a chemical reaction.

- Sub-atomic Particles and Atomic Models
- Dual Nature, Heisenberg's Principle and Quantum Mechanical Model
- Quantum Numbers and Electronic Configuration

Subatomic Particles

At the end of 19th century, the discovery of radioactivity, Faraday's law of electrolysis and other observations proved that atom is divisible into three fundamental particles like electron, proton and neutron. These particles are collectively known as **subatomic particles.**

Discovery of Electron : Cathode Rays

Electron was discovered by **J J Thomson** by studying the electrical discharge through gases in partially evacuated glass tubes also known as **cathode ray tubes.**

The Experimental Setup

Cathode ray tubes were filled with neon (Ne) gas. The two electrodes of these tubes, i.e. anode (positive) and cathode (negative) were connected through a battery. The complete setup was operated at high voltage (around 10000 V) and low pressure (about 10^{-6} Pa).

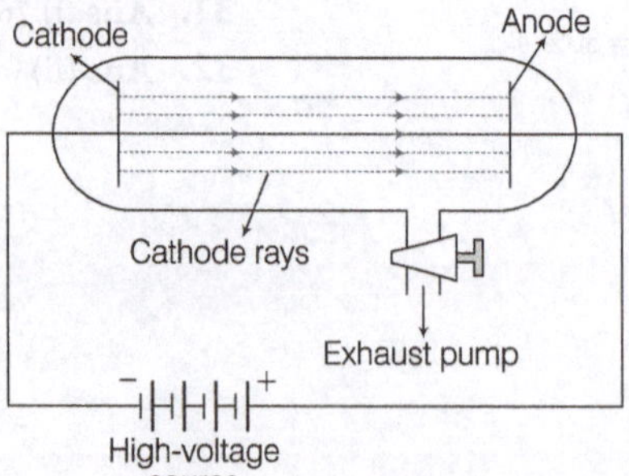

Cathode ray discharge tube

Note The low pressure inside these tubes is helpful in the acceleration of ions. This in turn ensures ejection of more electrons.

Observation

As soon as the circuit was complete, flow of particles was observed from cathode to anode. This stream of particles was called cathode rays.

To confirm the presence of cathode rays tiny holes were made in anode and wall of the tube behind anode was coated with phosphorescent material which is zinc sulphide. When these rays pass through holes of anode and strike the zinc sulphide coating a bright spot is developed, which confirmed the presence of rays. The name cathode rays was given as they start from cathode of discharge tube.

Properties of Cathode Rays

The cathode rays shows the following properties:

(i) These rays travel in straight path away from the cathode and cast sharp shadows of an object placed in their path.

(ii) These rays can penetrate through thin layers of matter.

(iii) They produce fluorescence when strike the glass wall of the discharge tube.

(iv) A small paddled mica wheel revolved when placed in the path of the cathode rays. The rays were thus shown to consists of particles whose kinetic energy was converted to mechanical energy of rotation of the wheel.

(v) The application of electric and magnetic fields deflected the rays in the discharge tube towards the cathode which indicates that these were consist of negatively charged particles which are called electrons.

(vi) Cathode rays produce X-rays when they strike a metallic target.

(vii) These rays cause ionisation of the gas through which they pass.

(viii) These rays can produce chemical changes and thus, affect photographic plates. Television picture tubes are cathode ray tubes and television pictures are the consequences of fluorescence on the television screen coated with certain fluorescent materials.

Discovery of Proton : Anode Rays

Later on, **Goldstein** in 1886 conducted experiment using perforated cathode and observed coloured rays produced from anode consisting of positively charged particles called anode rays or canal rays.

Properties of Anode Rays

(i) These rays travel in straight lines.

(ii) They are positively charged as they deflect towards negative plate of electric field in presence of electric field.

(iii) The mass of the positive particles is same as that of atomic mass of the gas taken in the discharge tube.

(iv) As the e/m ratio is found to be different for different gases thus, the properties of anode rays depends upon the nature of gas taken in a discharge tube.

(v) They produce green fluorescent on the glass wall behind the perforated cathode and causes zinc sulphide to glow.

Discovery of Neutron

Chadwick (1932) bombarded a thin sheet of beryllium(Be) by α-particles. He noticed that a electrically neutral particles having a mass slightly greater than that of the protons was emitted. He named these particles as neutrons.

$$\underset{}{{}^{9}_{4}\text{Be}} + \underset{\alpha\text{-particles}}{{}^{4}_{2}\text{He}} \longrightarrow {}^{12}_{6}\text{C} + \underset{\text{Neutron}}{{}^{1}_{0}n}$$

Neutron is, therefore having a mass 1.675×10^{-27} kg and no net charge. The density of neutron is 1.5×10^{14} g/cc. Isolated neutron is unstable and disintegrates into electron, proton and neutrino. Amongst all the sub-atomic particles, neutron is the heaviest and least stable particle.

Properties of Neutron

(i) Neutrons are electrically neutral particles having mass slightly higher than that of a proton.

(ii) Neutrons are highly penetrating but less than cosmic rays.

(iii) Neutrons are unable to ionise a gas. Therefore, they do not produce a track in a Wilson's cloud chamber.

Charge to Mass Ratio

Tiny charged particles just like subatomic particles are identified with the help of a specialised ratio called charge to mass ratio. For a particular subatomic particle, its value remains constant.

1. Charge to Mass Ratio of Electron

J J Thomson in 1897 studied the deflection of cathode rays under the simultaneous application of electric and magnetic fields. These fields were applied perpendicular to each other as well as to the path of electrons.

By measuring the amount of deflections of cathode rays in his experiments Thomson was able to calculate the value of e/m.

The complete setup is shown in the figure given below:

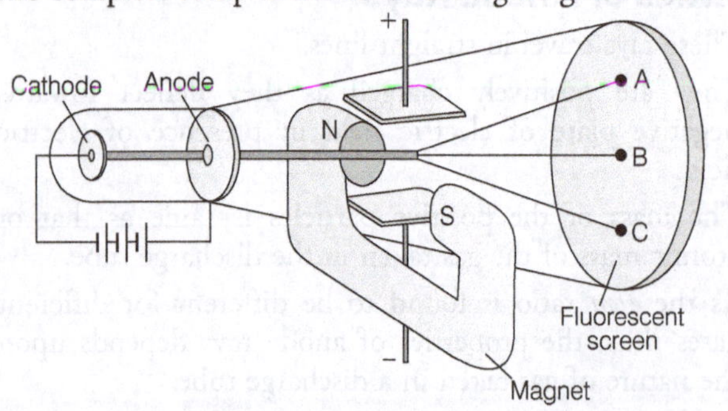

Apparatus to determine the charge to mass ratio of electron

When only electric field is applied, the electrons deviate from their paths and hit the cathode ray tube at point *A*. Similary, when only magnetic field is applied, the electrons strike the cathode ray tube at point *C*. In the absence of both fields, the cathode rays strike the fluorescent screen at the point *B*.

The accepted value of e/m for electron

$$= - 1.76 \times 10^{11} \text{C kg}^{-1}$$

where, m_e is the mass of the electron in kg and e is the magnitude of the charge on the electron in Coulomb (C).

(Because cathode rays carry a negative charge, the sign of the charge-to-mass ratio is also negative.)

Charge on the Electron : Millikan's Oil Drop Experiment

Through the oil-drop experiment performed by Millikan, the charge on the electron was found to be -1.6×10^{-19} C or 4.8×10^{-10}esu. This is the smallest measurable quantity of charge and is called **one unit**. Absolute value of charge on an electron was given by M. Faraday.

Mass of the Electron

Millikan using oil drop experiment determined the charge on the electron which is equal to 1.6022×10^{-19}C. Now, using Thomson's value of e/m and Millikan's value of e, the mass of the electron can be calculated as

$$m = \frac{e}{e/m} = \frac{1.6022 \times 10^{-19} \text{C}}{1.76 \times 10^{11} \text{C kg}^{-1}} = 9.1094 \times 10^{-31} \text{kg}$$

2. Charge to Mass Ratio of Proton

The specific charge of positive rays was found to vary with nature of gas. It is maximum in case of hydrogen.

The charge/mass ratio for the proton was found to be 9.57×10^7 C kg^{-1}.

(i) Charge on the proton is same as on the electron, i.e. 1.6×10^{-19} C.

(ii) Mass of the proton is equal to 1.673×10^{-27}kg.

$$\text{Thus, } \frac{m_p}{m_e} = \frac{1.673 \times 10^{-27}}{9.11 \times 10^{-31}} = 1836$$

i.e. the mass of the proton is 1836 times than the mass of the electron.

Properties of the Fundamental Particles

Properties	Proton (p)	Neutron (n)	Electron (e^-)
Mass	1.67262×10^{-27} kg	1.67495×10^{-27} kg	9.1094×10^{-31} kg
Charge	1.6022×10^{-19} C	03	1.6022×10^{-19} C
Mass relative to the electron	1836	1839	1
Charge relative to the proton	+1	0	–1
Discoverer	Goldstein	Chadwick	Thomson

Preliminary Atomic Models

To explain the distributions of various sub-atomic particles (i.e. electrons, protons and neutrons) in an atom several models have been proposed. These were called **atomic models**. Although some of these models were not able to explain the stability of atoms, two of these models, proposed by **JJ Thomson** and **Ernest Rutherford** are discussed below:

Thomson Model of Atom

It was proposed by JJ Thomson, in 1898. According to this model, an atom possesses a spherical shape (radius approximately 10^{-10} m) in which the positive charge is uniformly distributed. The electrons are embedded into it so that the most stable electrostatic arrangement is obtained.

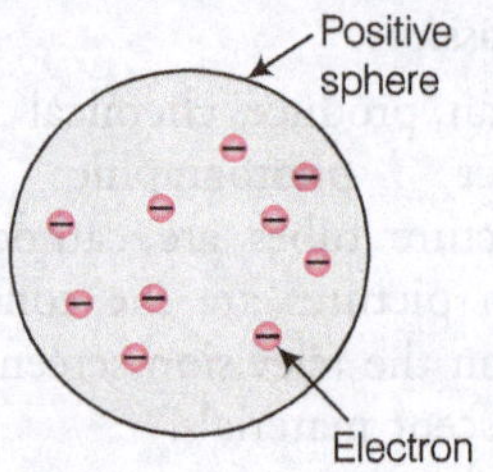

Thomson's model of atom

Limitations

It could not satisfactorily explain the results of some later experiments like gold foil scattering experiments of Rutherford.

Rutherford's Experiment

Rutherford and his students [Hans Geiger and Ernest Marsden] performed some scattering experiments in which they bombarded thin foils (nearly 100 nm thick) of heavy metals like gold, silver, platinum or copper with a beam of fast moving α-particles.

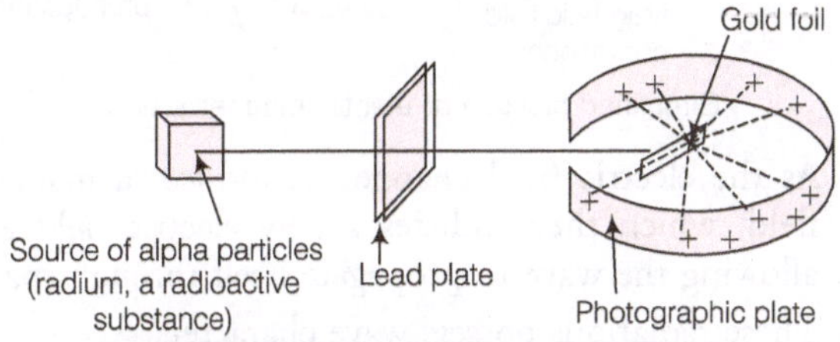

Rutherford's scattering experiment

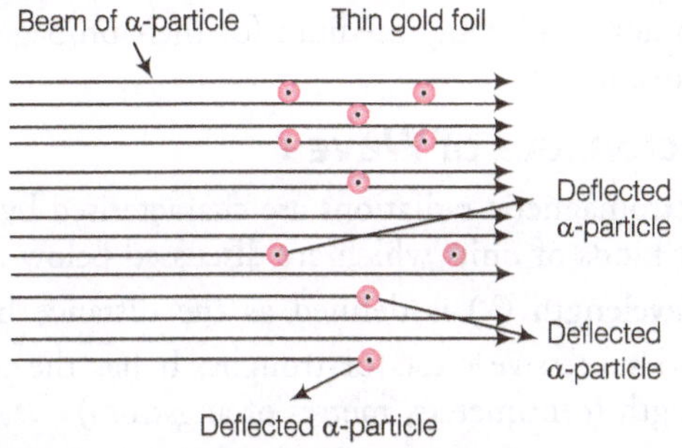

Schematic molecular view of the gold foil

Rutherford's Nuclear Model of Atom

On the basis of above observations and conclusions, Rutherford proposed the nuclear model of atom.

According to this model,

(i) The positive charge and most of the mass of the atom was densely concentrated in extremely small region, called the **nucleus** by Rutherford.

(ii) The nucleus is surrounded by electrons that move around the nucleus with a very high speed in circular paths, called **orbits.**

(iii) Electrons and the nucleus are held together by electrostatic forces of attraction.

Drawbacks or Demerits of Rutherford's Model

According to Rutherford model, electrons move around the nucleus in well defined orbits.

However, a body when moving in an orbit, undergoes acceleration (if its speed is constant, it must be accelerated by change in direction). So an electron in the nuclear model is under acceleration.

Maxwell electromagnetic theory suggested that charged particles when accelerated should emit electromagnetic radiation (It is not applicable for planets because these are uncharged).

Therefore, an electron in an orbit will emit radiation, the energy carried by radiation comes from electronic motion. The orbit will thus continue to shrink (calculations show that it should take an electron only 10^{-8} s to spiral into the nucleus). But this does not happen.

Thus, the Rutherford model **fails to explain the stability of an atom.**

If the electrons are considered to be stationary, electrostatic attraction between the dense nucleus and the electrons would pull the electrons toward the nucleus to form a miniature version of Thomson's model of atom.

Further, **this model says nothing about the electronic structure of atoms,** i.e. how the electrons are arranged around the nucleus and with what energies these are associated.

Atomic Number and Mass Number

The number of unit positive charge on the nucleus of an atom is called **atomic number.** It is numerically equal to the number of protons present in the nucleus of an atom.

Atomic number (Z) = nuclear charge or number of protons
= number of electrons (in neutral atom)

Total number of protons and neutrons in the nucleus is called **mass number** of the atom.

Mass number (A) = number of protons + neutrons
= atomic number + neutrons

Representation of an Atom

An atom is generally represented by its symbol for the element. Atomic number (Z) is written as the subscript of the symbol and the mass number (A) is written as the superscript.

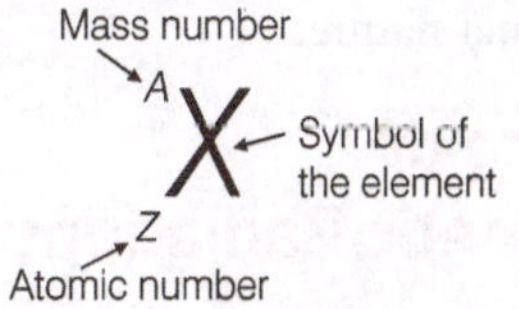

e.g. lithium with atomic number equal to 3 and mass number equal to 7 may be represented as ${}_3^7Li$.

Different Atomic Species

The atomic, species are of some following types:

(i) **Isotopes** These are the atoms of the same element which have the same atomic number but different mass numbers, e.g. protium $({}_1H^1)$, deuterium $({}_1D^2)$ and tritium $({}_1T^3)$ are three isotopes of H. ${}_6C^{12}$, ${}_6C^{13}$, ${}_6C^{14}$ are the isotopes of carbon.

(ii) **Isobars** These are the atoms of different elements which have same mass number but different atomic number, e.g. $_6C^{14}$ and $_7N^{14}$.

(iii) **Isotones** These are the species in which atomic number as well as mass number are different but number of neutrons are same, e.g. $_6C^{14}$, $_7N^{15}$ and $_8O^{16}$ as contain 8 neutrons.

(iv) **Isoelectronic** These are the species which contain same number of electrons, e.g. O^{2-}, F^-, Na^+ as they contain 10 electrons.

Developments Leading to the Bohr's Model of Atom

In 1913, **Neils Bohr** introduced his atomic model which tried to explain the drawbacks of Rutherford atomic models. Two developments played a major role in the development of Bohr's model. These are:

(i) **Dual Nature of Electromagnetic Radiation** The electromagnetic radiation has both wave and particle nature.

(ii) **Quantisation of Energy** Results of atomic spectra gave the evidence that energy is quantised.

Dual Nature of Electromagnetic Radiation

The two phenomenon, black body radiation and photoelectric effect confirmed the particle nature of light while the phenomenon like reflection, refraction, diffraction confirmed wave nature of light. Hence, light exhibits dual nature, i.e. waves as well as particle nature. Since, light is a kind of radiation, all radiations have both wave as well as particle characters. Therefore, all radiations have dual nature.

Wave Nature of Electromagnetic Radiations

Electromagnetic wave theory was put forward by **James Maxwell** in 1870. He suggested that when an electrically charged particle moves under acceleration, alternating electrical and magnetic fields are generated and transmitted in the form of waves called the **electromagnetic waves or electromagnetic radiations.**

Properties of Electromagnetic Radiation

(i) The oscillating electric and magnetic fields are perpendicular to each other and also to the direction of propagation of the wave.

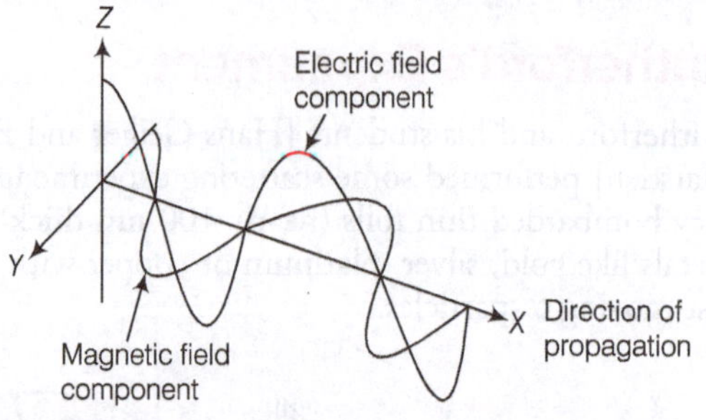

Simplified picture of electromagnetic wave

As the electric field changes, it induces a magnetic field, which then induces a new electric field etc., allowing the wave to propagate itself through space.

(ii) These radiations possess wave characters.

(iii) All these radiations travel with the speed of light and do not require any medium for their propagation or transmission.

Characteristics of Waves

The electromagnetic radiations are characterised by different kinds of units which are discussed below :

(i) **Wavelength** (λ) is defined as the distance between two successive crests or troughs. It has the units of length (centimeters, metres of angstrom)

$$1 \text{ Å} = 10^{-8} \text{ cm} = 10^{-10} \text{ m}, 1 \text{ nm} = 10^{-9} \text{ m}$$

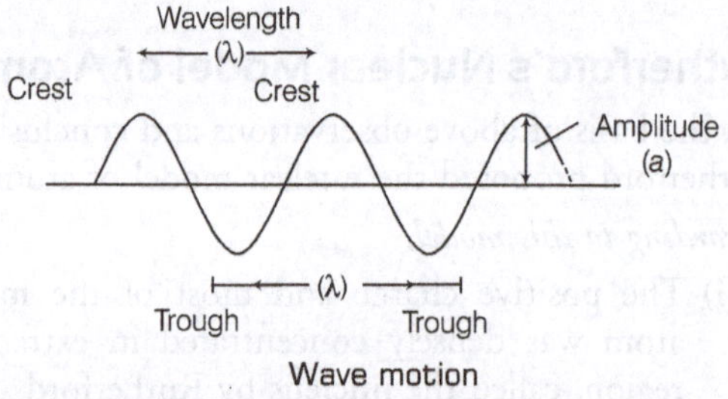

(ii) **Amplitude** The height of the crest or depth of the trough of a wave is called **amplitude** (*a*) which determines the intensity of the radiation.

(iii) **Frequency** (ν) is defined as the number of waves that pass through a given point in one second. Its SI unit is Hertz (Hz. s^{-1}). 1 Hz = 1 cycle per second

(iv) **Velocity** The distance travelled by a wave in one second is called the **velocity** (*c*) of the wave. Its unit is ms^{-1}. All the electromagnetic waves travel with the same velocity, i.e. $3 \times 10^8 \text{ ms}^{-1}$. The frequency (ν), wavelength (λ) and velocity of light (*c*) are related as $c = \nu\lambda$

(v) **Wave number** ($\bar{\nu}$) is defined as the number of wavelengths per unit length.

Its unit is cm^{-1} or m^{-1}

$$\bar{\nu} = \frac{1}{\lambda} = \frac{\nu}{c}$$

(vi) **Time period** Time taken by the wave for one complete cycle or vibration is called time period (T). It is expressed in second per cycle.

$$T = \frac{1}{\nu}$$

Representation of Wave Characteristics : Spectrum

A spectrum can be defined as, pictorial representation or arrangement of radiations in increasing order of wavelength or decreasing order of frequency.

1. Atomic Spectrum

The spectrum of atom is discontinuous and consists of sharp well defined lines or bands corresponding to definite frequencies. This is called line spectrum.

Depending upon the radiation absorbed or emitted, spectrum is classified as :

(i) **Emission Spectrum** The spectrum of radiation emitted by a substance that has absorbed energy (either by passing electric discharge through a gas at low pressure or by heating the substance to high temperature) is called an **emission spectrum.** Atoms, molecules or ions that have absorbed radiation are said to be in **excited state.**

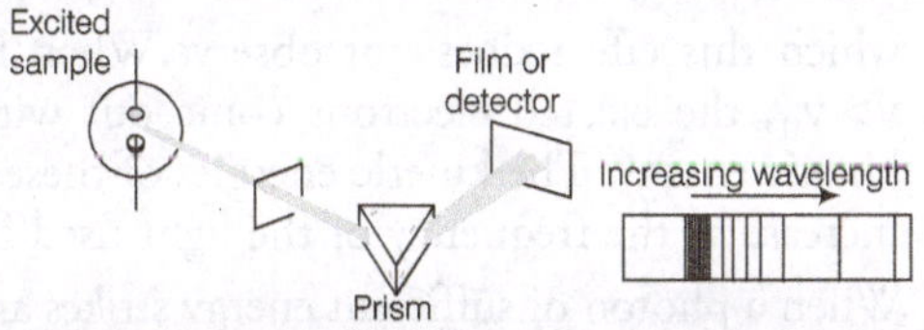

Representation of atomic emission spectrum

Note Spectroscope is an apparatus use to examine the spectra of an atom.

(ii) **Absorption Spectrum** It is like the photographic negative of an emission spectrum. To obtain an absorption spectra a continum of radiation is passed through a sample which absorbs radiation of certain wavelengths.

The missing wavelength which corresponds to the radiation absorbed by the matter, leave dark spaces in the bright continuous spectrum.

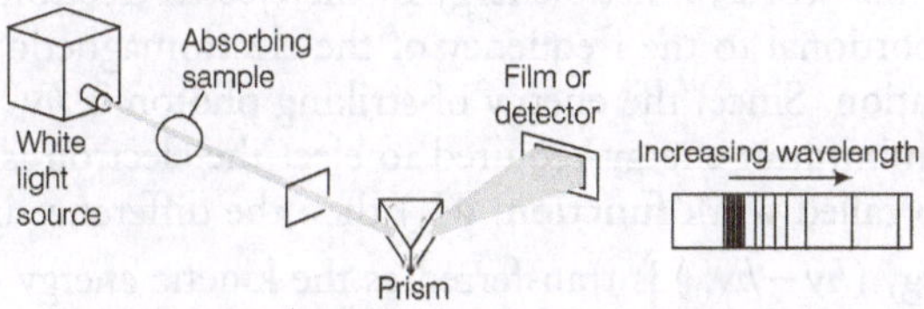

Representation of Absorption spectrum

Depending upon the pictorial characteristics, spectrum can be mainly classified as :

(i) **Continuous Spectrum** In this spectrum, visible radiations do not have a definite boundary, i.e. one radiation merge into other without any gap. Thus, this spectrum appear like a continuous band of radiations.

(ii) **Discontinuous Spectrum** In this spectrum, shape and well defined lines of a particular wavelength are visible. These are separated completely from other such lines to give a discontinuous appearance.

2. Electromagnetic Spectrum

There are many types of electromagnetic radiations which differ from one another in wavelength (λ) or frequency (ν). When the electromagnetic radiations are arranged in order of their increasing wavelength or decreasing frequencies, the complete spectrum obtained is called **electromagnetic spectrum.**

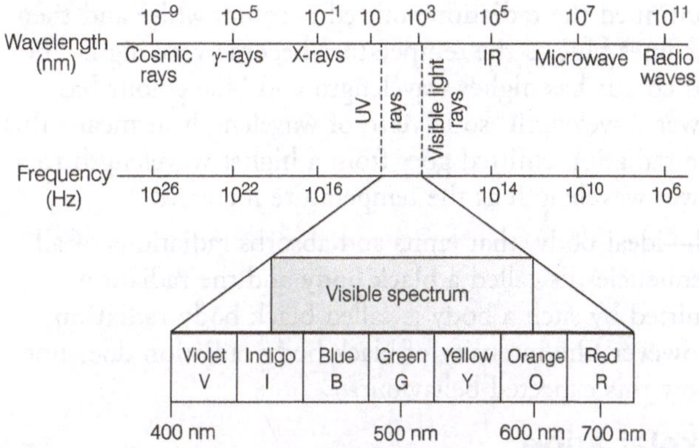

The spectrum of electromagnetic radiation and visible spectrum

As the speed of electromagnetic radiation is same as that of light, so Maxwell proposed that light itself is an electromagnetic radiations.

Particle Nature of Electromagnetic Radiation : Planck's Quantum Theory

To explain the phenomenon of black body radiation and photoelectric effect, Max Planck in 1900, proposed a theory known after his name as **Planck's quantum theory.** This theory was further extended by Einstein in 1905.

The main postulates of this theory are as follows:

(i) The radiant energy is emitted or absorbed not continuously, but discontinuously in the form of small discrete packets of energy, called a **quantum.** In case of light, the quantum of energy is known as **photon.**

(ii) The energy of each quantum is directly proportional to the frequency of the radiation,

i.e. $E \propto \nu$ or $E = h\nu$ ...(i)

where, h is the proportionality constant, called **Planck's constant.** Its value is approximately equal to 6.626×10^{-27} erg s or 6.626×10^{-34} joule sec.

(iii) The total amount of energy emitted or absorbed by a body will be some whole number quanta, i.e. energy is quantised.

Hence, $E = nh\nu$, where n is any integer. ...(ii)

Note The energy possessed by one mole of quanta (or photons), i.e. Avogadro's number (N_0) of quanta is called **one Einstein** of energy, i.e. 1 Einstein of energy (E) = $N_0 h\nu = N_0 h \frac{c}{\lambda}$

1. Phenomenon of Black Body Radiation

On heating a solid, its atoms start oscillating and they emit radiation over a wide range of wavelengths.

e.g. when an iron rod is heated in a furnace, it turns to dull red and then progressively becomes more and more red as the temperature increases. When heating is continued the radiation emitted becomes white and then becomes blue as the temperature become very high. The red colour has higher wavelength and blue colour has lower wavelength so in term of wavelength, it means that the radiation emitted goes from a higher wavelength to a lower wavelength as the temperature increases.

The ideal body, that emits and absorbs radiations of all frequencies, is called a **black body** and the radiation emitted by such a body is called **black body radiation.** However, the intensity of black body radiation does not show this expected behaviour.

Explanation

The exact wavelength distribution of the emitted radiation (i.e. intensity *versus* frequency curve of the radiation) from a black body depends only on its temperature. At a given temperature, intensity of radiation emitted increases with decrease of wavelength, reaches a maximum value at a given wavelength and then starts decreasing with further decrease of wavelength, as shown in graph given below:

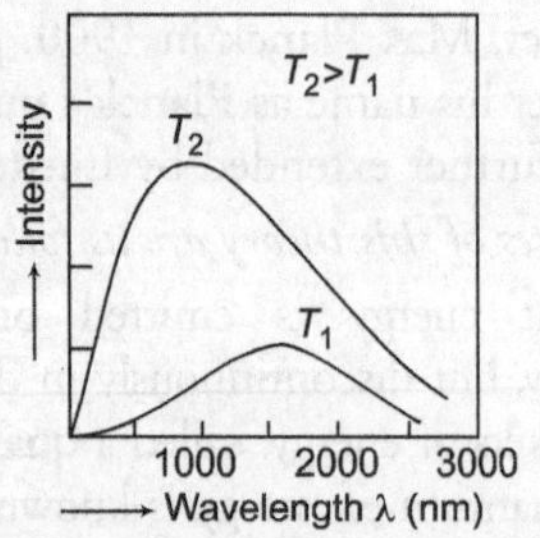

Emission of radiation from a black body at different temperatures (T_2 and T_1).

Note The variation given in above graph are from right to left.

2. Photoelectric Effect and Its Explanation

The phenomenon for ejection of electrons from the surface of a metal when light of suitable frequency falls on it, is called the **photoelectric effect** and the emitted electrons are called **photoelectrons.** In 1887, H. Hertz performed an experiment in which electrons (or electric current) were ejected when certain metals (e.g. potassium, rubidium, caesium etc.) were exposed to a beam of light as shown below in the figure. The ejected electrons are counted by a detector that measures their kinetic energy .

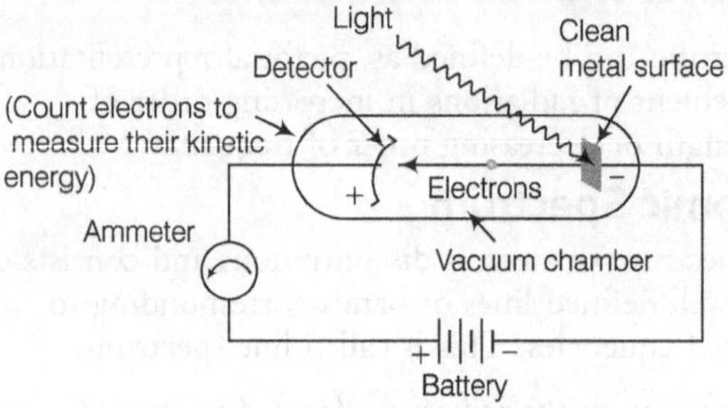

Equipment for studying the photoelectric effect

The result observed in this experiment were:

(i) The electrons are ejected from the metal surface as soon as the beam of light hits the surface.

(ii) The number of electrons ejected is proportional to the intensity or brightness of light.

(iii) For each metal, there is a characteristic minimum frequency, ν_0 (called the **threshold frequency**) below which this effect does not observe.When frequency $\nu > \nu_0$, the ejected electrons come out with certain kinetic energy. The kinetic energies of these electrons increase as the frequency of the light used increases. When a photon of sufficient energy strikes an electron in the atom of the metal, it transfers its energy instantaneously to the electron during the collision and the electron is ejected without any time lag or delay. Greater the energy possessed by the photon, greater will be the transfer of energy to the electron and kinetic energy of the ejected electron.

This may be expressed as:

Energy of striking photon = Binding energy + Kinetic energy of ejected electron

In other words, kinetic energy of the ejected electron is proportional to the frequency of the electromagnetic radiation. Since, the energy of striking photon is $h\nu$ and the minimum energy required to eject the electron is $h\nu_0$ (also called **work function,** W_0) then the difference in energy ($h\nu - h\nu_0$) is transferred as the kinetic energy of the photoelectron.

Following the law of conservation of energy, the kinetic energy of the ejected electron is given by the equation (iii).

$$h\nu = h\nu_0 + \frac{1}{2} m_e v^2 \quad \text{...(iii)}$$

where m_e is the mass of the electron moving with velocity, v. A more intense beam of light contains a larger number of photons, as a result the number of electrons ejected is also larger than that in an experiment in which a beam to weaker intensity of light is used.

Note The energy acquired by an electron when it is accelerated through a potential diffference of one volt is called one electron volt (1eV), 1 eV = 1.602×10^{-19} J.

Example 1 The threshold frequency (ν_0) for a metal is $7.0 \times 10^{14} s^{-1}$. Calculate the kinetic energy of an electron emitted when radiation of frequency (ν) = $1.0 \times 10^{15} s^{-1}$ hits the metal. **NCERT Textbook**

Sol. Given threshold frequency (ν_0) for metal $= 7 \times 10^{14} s^{-1}$

Frequency $(\nu) = 1.0 \times 10^{15} s^{-1}$

According to Einstein's equation, KE $= \frac{1}{2} mv^2 = h(\nu - \nu_0)$

$$= (6.626 \times 10^{-34} \text{ Js})(1.0 \times 10^{15} s^{-1} - 7.0 \times 10^{14} s^{-1})$$
$$= (6.626 \times 10^{-34} \text{ Js})(10.0 \times 10^{14} s^{-1} - 7.0 \times 10^{14} s^{-1})$$
$$= (6.626 \times 10^{-34} \text{ Js}) \times (3.0 \times 10^{14} s^{-1}) = 1.988 \times 10^{-19} \text{ J}$$

Limitations of Planck's Quantum Theory

Planck could not explain the **quantisation of energy**. He also remain unable to explain the distribution of intensity in radiation from a black body as a function of frequency at different temperatures with this assumption that energies are quantised.

Bohr's Model for Hydrogen Atom

In order to overcome the drawback of Rutherford's model of atom and to explain the line spectrum of hydrogen, Neils Bohr, a Danish physicist in 1913 proposed a new model of atom based upon Planck's quantum theory. This model is called **Bohr's atomic model**.

Postulates of Bohr's Atomic Model

The main postulates of this model are as follows :

(i) The electron in the hydrogen atom can move around the nucleus in a circular path of fixed radius and energy (i.e. energy of an electron is quantised). These paths are called **orbits, stationary states** or **allowed energy states.** These orbits are arranged concentrically around the nucleus. The stationary states for electron are numbered, $n = 1, 2, 3$ or $K, L, M....$ The integral numbers are known as **principal quantum number** .

(ii) The energy of an electron is certain in the orbit, i.e. it does not change with time. However, the energy is absorbed or emitted when electron jumps from lower to higher or higher to lower stationary states. The energy change does not take place in a continuous manner.

(iii) The frequency of radiation absorbed or emitted when transition occurs between two stationary states that differ in energy by ΔE is given by

$$\nu = \frac{\Delta E}{h} = \frac{E_2 - E_1}{h}$$

where E_1 and E_2 are the energies of the lower and higher allowed energy states, respectively. This expression is commonly known as Bohr's frequency rule.

(iv) The angular momentum (mvr) of an electron in a given stationary state can be expressed by the following equation,

$$m_e v r = n \cdot \frac{h}{2\pi} \qquad (n = 1, 2, 3 ...)$$

Thus, an electron can move only in those orbits for which its angular momentum is integral multiple of $h / 2\pi$ that's why only certain fixed orbits are allowed. This postulate, therefore, introduces the concept of **quantisation of angular momentum.**

Applications or Merits of Bohr's Model

This model is found useful to explain the following facts:

1. Stability of an Atom

Bohr suggested that an electron revolving in a particular orbit cannot radiate energy. Therefore, emission of radiation is not possible as long as the electron remains in one of its energy levels and hence, there is no cause of instability in his model.

2. Calculation of Bohr Radius

According to Bohr's model, radius of nth orbit is given by the expression

$$r_n = \frac{n^2 h^2}{4\pi^2 me^2 Z} \qquad \text{[For hydrogen atom } (Z = 1)]$$

$$r_n = a_0 n^2$$

where, $a_0 = 52.9$ pm

Thus, the radius of first stationary state is called the **Bohr radius** and has value 52.9 pm (or 0.0529 nm or 0.529 Å).

Thus, for H-atom, radius of first orbit is **52.9 pm.** Similarly, for hydrogen like species, the radii may be given by the expression :

$$r_n = \frac{a_0 n^2}{Z}$$

or $$r_n(\text{H-like}) = \frac{r_n(\text{H-atom})}{Z}$$

or $$r_n = \frac{52.9\, n^2}{Z}\ \text{pm} = \frac{0.0529\, n^2}{Z}\ \text{nm}$$

where Z is the nuclear charge. (Radius becomes smaller with increase of Z).

Example 2 Which state of the triple ionised beryllium (Be^{3+}) has the same orbit radius as that of the ground state of hydrogen atom?

Sol. For H-atom, radius of ground state is

$$r_1 = \frac{h^2}{4\pi^2 me^2} \quad \text{...(i)}$$

For hydrogen like atom,

$$r_n' = \frac{n^2 h^2}{4\pi^2 mZe^2} \quad \text{...(ii)}$$

Dividing Eq. (ii) by Eq. (i)

$$\frac{r_n'}{r_1} = \frac{n^2}{Z}$$

For Be^{3+} ion, $Z = 4$

$$\therefore \quad \frac{r_n'}{r_1} = \frac{n^2}{4}$$

Now, $$r_n' = r_1$$

$$\therefore \quad n^2 = 4 \quad \text{or} \quad n = 2$$

Thus, the second orbit of Be^{3+} has the same radius as the Bohr's radius of hydrogen atom.

3. Calculation of Energy of the Electron

Bohr on the basis of his postulates, derived a mathematical expression to calculate the energy of an electron moving in a particular orbit of hydrogen atom. He considered hydrogen atom as a system having single electron of mass m and negative charge electron, revolving in a circular orbit. The energy of the electron in the nth orbit has been found to be

$$E_n = -R_H\left(\frac{1}{n^2}\right) \quad (n = 1, 2, 3\ldots)$$

where R_H = Rydberg constant

$$= \frac{2\pi^2 me^4}{h^2} = 2.18 \times 10^{-18}\ \text{J}$$

So that, $$E_n = -\frac{2\pi^2 me^4}{n^2 h^2}$$

Therefore, the energy of the lowest state, also called as the **ground state**, is

$$E_1 = -2.18 \times 10^{-18}\left(\frac{1}{1^2}\right) = -2.18 \times 10^{-18}\ \text{J}$$

Similarly, for nth orbit,

$$E_n = -\frac{2.18 \times 10^{-18}}{n^2}\ \text{J per atom}$$

$$= -\frac{13.595\ \text{eV}}{n^2}\ \text{per atom}$$

$$[\because 1\text{eV} = 1.6022 \times 10^{-19}\ \text{J}]$$

$$= -\frac{1311.8}{n^2}\ \text{kJ mol}^{-1}$$

$$\approx \frac{1312}{n^2}\ \text{kJ mol}^{-1}$$

Thus, for each value of n, an energy level exists for the electron. With increase in the value of n the energy difference between successive energy levels decreases.

i.e. $E_2 - E_1 > E_3 - E_2 > E_4 - E_3$ and so on.

The energy of the electron in a hydrogen atom has a negative sign for all possible orbits.

This is because the energy of the electron in the atom is lower than the energy of a free electron at rest. A free electron at rest is an electron that is infinitely far away from the nucleus, i.e. free from the influence of nucleus and is assigned the energy value of zero. Mathematically, $n = \infty$ and thus, $E_\infty = 0$. In this state hydrogen atom is called ionised H-atom. As the electron gets closer to the nucleus (as n decreases), E_n becomes larger in absolute value and more and more negative. The most negative energy value is given by $n = 1$ which corresponds to the most stable orbit and called as ground state.

Similary, for hydrogen like species,

$$E_n = -\frac{2\pi^2 me^4 Z^2}{n^2 h^2}$$

$$= -2.18 \times 10^{-18}\left(\frac{Z^2}{n^2}\right)\ \text{J}$$

$$= -1311.8\left(\frac{Z^2}{n^2}\right)\ \text{kJ mol}^{-1}$$

where, Z is the nuclear charge which is equal to atomic number, e.g. for He^+, $Z = 2$, for Li^{2+}, $Z = 3$.

From the above equations, it is also evident that the value of energy becomes more negative as the n decreases. This means that electron will be tightly bound to the nucleus.

4. Calculation of Velocity of Electron in any Orbit

The velocity of electron in any orbit is given by the expression

$$v = \frac{nh}{2\pi mr}$$

On substituting the value of r, we get

$$v = \frac{2\pi e^2 Z}{nh}$$

$$= \frac{2.19 \times 10^6 Z}{n} \text{ ms}^{-1}$$

The velocities of the electrons in different orbits may be given as $v_n = v_0 \times Z/n$

where, v_0 is the velocity of the electron in the first orbit of hydrogen atom and has value 2.19×10^6 ms^{-1}.

Quantitatively, the magnitude of velocity of electron increases with increase of positive charge on the nucleus and decreases with increase in principal quantum number.

Line Spectrum of Hydrogen

On passing electric discharge through gaseous hydrogen, the H_2 molecules get dissociated to produce energetically excited hydrogen atoms that emit electromagnetic radiation of discrete frequencies.

Thus, the spectrum obtained is called **line spectrum** of hydrogen. This spectrum consists of several series of lines. Rydberg concluded that all series of lines could be described by the following expression,

$$\bar{\nu} = 109677 \left[\frac{1}{n_1^2} - \frac{1}{n_2^2}\right] \text{cm}^{-1}$$

(where, $n_1 = 1, 2..., n_2 = n_1 + 1, n_1 + 2...$)

The value 109677cm^{-1} is called the Rydberg constant for hydrogen and is represented by R_H. The first six series of lines that correspond to $n_1 = 1, 2, 3, 4, 5, 6$ are known as **Lyman, Balmer, Paschen, Brackett, Pfund and Humphrey** series, respectively.

Following series (in Table) of the hydrogen spectrum are obtained depending on the value of n_1 to which level electron falls from higher level n_2. The higher the value of n, smaller the energy difference between the successive levels (in given fig.)

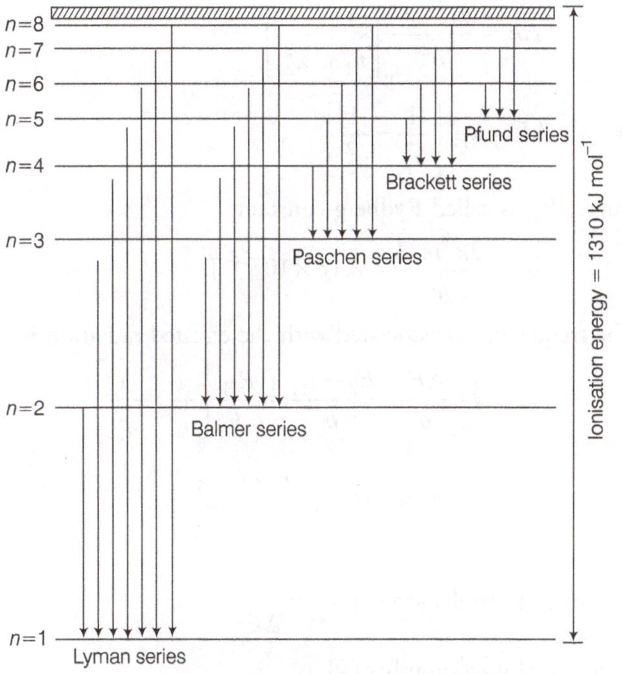

Spectrum lines in the hydrogen atom

Spectral Lines of Hydrogen Atom

Series	n_1	$n_2 > n_1$	$\bar{\nu} = \frac{1}{\lambda} = R_H\left[\frac{1}{n_1^2} - \frac{1}{n_2^2}\right]$	Region of spectrum
Lyman	1	2, 3, ...∞	$R_H\left[\frac{1}{1^2} - \frac{1}{n_2^2}\right]$	Ultraviolet
Balmer	2	3, 4, ... ∞	$R_H\left[\frac{1}{2^2} - \frac{1}{n_2^2}\right]$	Visible
Paschen	3	4, 5, ... ∞	$R_H\left[\frac{1}{3^2} - \frac{1}{n_2^2}\right]$	Infrared
Brackett	4	5, 6, ... ∞	$R_H\left[\frac{1}{4^2} - \frac{1}{n_2^2}\right]$	Infrared
Pfund	5	6, 7, ... ∞	$R_H\left[\frac{1}{5^2} - \frac{1}{n_2^2}\right]$	Infrared
Humphries (Discovered recently)	6	7, 8, ... ∞	$R_H\left[\frac{1}{6^2} - \frac{1}{n_2^2}\right]$	Far infrared

Explanation of Line Spectrum of Hydrogen

Bohr was successful in explaining the line spectrum of hydrogen. When an electron moves from a higher orbit, say n_2, to lower orbit, n_1, the radiations are emitted and appear in the form of lines called **spectrum.** Energy difference of n_2 and n_1 level is,

$$\Delta E = \frac{2\pi^2 me^4}{h^2}\left[\frac{1}{n_1^2} - \frac{1}{n_2^2}\right]$$

or $$\Delta E = R_H \left[\frac{1}{n_1^2} - \frac{1}{n_2^2}\right]$$

where, R_H is called Rydberg constant

$$R_H = \frac{2\pi^2 me^4}{h^2} = 2.18 \times 10^{-18} \text{ J}$$

The frequency (ν) associated with the emitted radiation is

$$\nu = \frac{\Delta E}{h} = \frac{E_2 - E_1}{h} = \frac{R_H}{h}\left[\frac{1}{n_1^2} - \frac{1}{n_2^2}\right]$$

$$\nu = 3.29 \times 10^{15} \text{ s}^{-1}\left(\frac{1}{n_1^2} - \frac{1}{n_2^2}\right)$$

In terms of wavelength $(\lambda) = \frac{c}{\nu} = \frac{hc}{\Delta E}$

In terms of wave number ($\bar{\nu}$),

$$\bar{\nu} = \frac{\nu}{c} = \frac{R_H}{hc}\left[\frac{1}{n_1^2} - \frac{1}{n_2^2}\right]$$

$$\bar{\nu} = \frac{3.29 \times 10^{15} \text{ s}^{-1}}{3.0 \times 10^8 \text{ ms}^{-1}}\left[\frac{1}{n_1^2} - \frac{1}{n_2^2}\right]$$

The numerical value of wave number,

$$\bar{\nu} = 1.09677 \times 10^7 \left[\frac{1}{n_1^2} - \frac{1}{n_2^2}\right] \text{m}^{-1}$$

where, $R_H = 1.09677 \times 10^7 \text{ m}^{-1}$

Thus, Bohr was able to quantitatively explain the line spectra of H-atoms because the expression for wave numbers given by Bohr was similar to the expression given by Johannes Rydberg for wave number.

He gave reasons for line spectrum because in the emission of spectra, each spectral line is due to a particular transition associated with a particular frequency or wavelength.

In large number of H-atoms, different possible transitions can be observed which leads to a large number of spectral lines.

(i) **Limiting Line** Each series of lines converges towards a limit beyond which the spectrum is continuous. This corresponds to the case when $n_2 = \infty$. This also gives spectral line of maximum wave number (minimum wavelength)

Thus, $$\bar{\nu}_{max} = \frac{1}{\lambda_{min}} = \frac{R_H Z^2}{n_1^2}$$

(ii) Minimum wave number is obtained for the case when $n_2 = (n_1 + 1)$. Thus,

$$\bar{\nu}_{min} = \frac{1}{\lambda_{max}} = R_H Z^2\left[\frac{1}{n_1^2} - \frac{1}{(n_1+1)^2}\right]$$

(iii) The number of emission lines when an electron jumps from n_2 level to n_1 level are given by

$$\frac{(n_2 - n_1)(n_2 - n_1 + 1)}{2}$$

Limitations or Defects of Bohr's Model

Bohr's model explains the stability and line spectra of hydrogen atom and hydrogen like species (such as He^+, Li^{2+}, etc). However, it was unable to explain the following facts:

(i) It could not explain spectrum of multielectron atoms.

(ii) Bohr's introduction of the concept of integers (n) in selecting the stable orbits for electrons was also arbitrary which merely fit experimental results. There was no theretical justification for it.

(iii) It could not explain the ability of atoms to form molecules by chemical bonds.

(iv) It could not explain about the dual nature of electron.

(v) It could not explain about Zeeman and Stark effect.

Note The splitting of spectral line in the magnetic field is called **Zeeman effect.** While the splitting of spectral line in electric field is called **Stark effect.**

(vi) It could not give explanation for de-Broglie hypothesis, Heisenberg's uncertainty principle.

(vii) It could not explain about the 3-D geometry of orbital and molecule.

Topic Practice 1

Very Short Answer Type Questions

I Mark

1 Fill in the Blanks

(i) The ...... charge and most of the mass of the atom was .... concentrated in extremely small region, called the ...... by Rutherford.

(ii) The distance between two adjacent ...... of .... is called wavelength.

(iii) Velocity is the distance travelled by a wave in one ....

(iv) The energy of each quantum is directly .... to the .... of the radiation.

2 Objective Type Questions

(i) The electrical discharge through the gases could be observed only at
  (a) very low pressure and very low voltage
  (b) very high pressure and very high voltage
  (c) very high pressure and very low voltage
  (d) very low pressure and very high voltage

(ii) Which of the following substances, shows the properties of phosphorescent?
  (a) Zinc sulphide
  (b) Zinc sulphate
  (c) Zinc nitrate
  (d) Zinc chloride

(iii) Many types of electromagnetic radiations, differ from one another in wavelength (or frequency) constitute a spectrum known as
  (a) electromagnetic spectrum
  (b) line spectrum
  (c) Both (a) and (b)
  (d) None of the above

(iv) What is/are correct about Hertz (Hz s^{-1})?
  (a) It is the SI unit of frequency (ν)
  (b) It is named after Heinrich Hertz
  (c) It is defined as the number of waves that pass through a given point in one second
  (d) All of the above

3 Match the following Columns and choose the correct option using the codes given below

Column I		Column II
A. X-rays	(i)	$\nu = 10^0 - 10^4$ Hz
B. Ultraviolet wave (UV)	(ii)	$\nu = 10^{10}$ Hz
C. Long radio waves	(III)	$\nu = 10^{16}$ Hz
D. Microwave	(iv)	$\nu = 10^{18}$ Hz

Codes

	A	B	C	D		A	B	C	D
(a)	(iv)	(iii)	(i)	(ii)	(b)	(iv)	(iii)	(i)	(ii)
(c)	(i)	(ii)	(iii)	(iv)	(d)	(ii)	(iii)	(iv)	(i)

4 What is the difference in the origin of cathode rays and anode rays?

5 In Millikan's experiment, static electric charge on the oil drops has been obtained by shining X-rays. If the static electric charge on the oil drop is -1.282×10^{-18} C, calculate the number of electrons present on it. **NCERT Textbook**

6 Which of the following will not show deflection from the path on passing through an electric field? Proton, cathode rays, electron, neutron.

7 Calculate the number of protons, neutrons and electrons in $^{80}_{35}Br$.

8 An atom having atomic mass number 13 has 7 neutrons. What is the atomic number of the atom? **NCERT Exemplar**

9 Name the element whose isotope has mass number 14 and 8 neutrons.

10 Arrange the following type of radiations in increasing order of frequency:
  (i) Radiation from microwave oven
  (ii) Amber light from traffic signal
  (iii) Radiation from FM radio
  (iv) Cosmic rays from outer space and
  (v) X-rays

11 What is the maximum number of emission lines when the excited electron of a H-atom in $n = 6$ drops to the ground state? **NCERT Textbook**

12 What is the experimental evidence in support of the idea that electronic energies in an atom are quantised?

13 Calculate the distance of separation between the second and third orbits of hydrogen atom.

14 Why are Bohr's orbits called stationary states?

Short Answer Type I Questions

(2 Marks)

15 Explain in detail the findings of Thomson's model of the atom. What was its shortcoming?

16 Why does the charge-to-mass ratio of positive rays depend on the residual gas in the discharge tube? Why is the charge-to-mass ratio of all cathode rays are same?

17 In Rutherford's experiment, generally the thin foil of heavy atoms, like gold, platinum, etc., have been used to be bombarded by the α-particles. If the thin foil of light atoms like aluminium, etc., is used, what difference would be observed from the above results? **NCERT Textbook**

18 Find energy of each of the photons which
(i) correspond to light of frequency 3×10^{15} Hz.
(ii) have wavelength of 0.50Å.

19 Chlorophyll present in green leaves of plants absorbs light at 4.620×10^{14} Hz. Calculate the wavelength of radiation in nanometer. Which part of the electromagnetic spectrum does it belong to? **NCERT Exemplar**

20 Wavelengths of different radiations are given below.
$\lambda(A) = 300$ nm, $\lambda(B) = 300$ µm, $\lambda(C) = 3$ nm, $\lambda(D) = 30$ Å
Arrange these radiations in the increasing order of their energies.

21 Calculate energy of one mole of photons of radiation whose frequency is 5×10^{14} Hz. **NCERT Textbook**

22 A 100 watt bulb emits monochromatic light of wavelength 400 nm. Calculate the number of photons emitted per second by the bulb.

23 Yellow light emitted from a sodium lamp has a wavelengh (λ) of 580 nm. Calculate the frequency (ν) and wave number ($\bar{\nu}$) of the yellow light.

24 The Vividh Bharati Station of All India Radio, Delhi, Broadcasts on a frequency of 1368 kHz (kilohertz). Calculate the wavelength of the electromagnetic radiation emitted by transmitter. Which part of the electromagnetic spectrum does it belong to?

25 What is the number of photons of light with a wavelength of 4000 pm that provide 1 J of energy? **NCERT Textbook**

26 Electromagnetic radiation of wavelength 242 nm is just sufficient to ionise the sodium atom. Calculate the ionisation energy of sodium in kJ mol^{-1}. **NCERT Textbook**

27 The mass of an electron is 9.1×10^{-31} kg. If its KE is 3×10^{-25} J, then calculate its wavelength.

28 What is photoelectric effect? How does particle nature of light explain this effect?

29 The work function (W_0) of some metals is listed below. Count the number of metals which will show photoelectric effect when light of 300 nm wavelength falls on the metal.

Metal	Li	Na	K	Mg	Cu	Ag	Fe	Pt	W
W_0 (eV)	2.4	2.3	2.2	3.7	4.8	4.3	4.7	6.3	4.75

30 Electrons are emitted with zero velocity from a metal surface when it is exposed to radiation of wavelength 6800 Å. Calculate threshold frequency (ν_0) and work function (W_0) of the metal. **NCERT Textbook**

31 What transition in the hydrogen spectrum would have the same wavelength as the Balmer transition $n = 4$ to $n = 2$ of He^+ spectrum?

32 What is the wavelength of light emitted when the electron in a hydrogen atom undergoes transition from an energy level with $n = 4$ to an energy level with $n = 2$? **NCERT Textbook**

33 Life times of the molecules in the excited states are often measured by using pulsed radiation source of duration nearly in the nanosecond range. If the radiation source has the duration of 2 ns and the number of photons emitted during the pulse source is 2.5×10^{15}, calculate the energy of the source.

34 A gas absorbs a photon of 355 nm and emits at two wavelengths. If one of the emissions is at 680 nm, at what place the other emission occur?

35 (i) The energy associated with the first orbit in the hydrogen atom is -2.18×10^{-18} J atom^{-1}. What is the energy associated with the fifth orbit?
(ii) Calculate the radius of Bohr's fifth orbit for hydrogen atom. **NCERT Textbook**

36 For a hydrogen like particle, derive the expression

$$v_n = \left(\frac{Ze^2}{mr_n}\right)^{1/2}$$

where v_n is the velocity of the electron at distance r_n from the nucleus, Z is the atomic number of the H-like particle, e and m are the charge and mass of the electron.

37 Nitrogen laser produces a radiation at a wavelength of 337.1 nm. If the number of photons emitted is 5.6×10^{24}, calculate the power of this laser. **NCERT Textbook**

38 When electromagnetic radiation of wavelength 300 nm falls on the surface of sodium, electrons are emitted with a kinetic energy of 1.68×10^5 J mol^{-1}. What is the minimum energy needed to remove an electron from sodium? What is the maximum wavelength that will cause a photoelectron to be emitted.

39 Calculate the energy associated with the first orbit of He^+. What is the radius of this orbit? **NCERT Intext**

Short Answer Type II Questions

3 Marks

40 An ion with mass number 56 contains 3 units of positive charge and 30.4% more neutrons than the electrons. Assign the symbol to this ion. **NCERT Textbook**

41 According to Rutherford's model of the atom, where is the positive charge concentrated? What does it predict about the relative size of the nucleus and the radius of the atom? What is the nucleus composed of according to his model?

42 Which of the following are isoelectronic species, i.e. those having the same number of electrons? Na^+, K^+, Mg^{2+}, Ca^{2+}, S^{2-}, Ar **NCERT Textbook**

43 Calculate the wavelength, frequency and wave number of a light wave whose period is 2.0×10^{-10} s. **NCERT Textbook**

44 What is an atomic spectrum? How does it differ from a continuous spectrum? What fundamental fact is implied by the existence of atomic spectra?

45 Neon gas is generally used in sign boards. If it emits strongly at 616 nm, calculate

(i) the frequency of emission.

(ii) distance travelled by this radiation is 30 s.

(iii) energy of quantum.

(iv) number of quanta present if it produces 2 J of energy. **NCERT Textbook**

46 How much energy is required to ionise a H atom if the electron occupies $n = 5$ orbit? Compare your answer with the ionisation enthalpy of H-atom (energy required to remove the electron from $n = 1$ orbit). **NCERT Textbook**

47 What is the energy in joules, required to shift the electron of the hydrogen atom from the first Bohr orbit to the fifth Bohr orbit and what is the wavelength of the light emitted when the electron returns to the ground state? The ground state electron energy is -2.18×10^{-11} erg.

48 The electron energy in hydrogen atom is given by $E_n = (-2.18 \times 10^{-18}) / n^2$J. Calculate the energy required to remove an electron completely from the $n = 2$ orbit. What is the longest wavelength of light in cm that can be used to cause this transition?

49 The longest wavelength doublet absorption transition is observed at 589 nm and 589.6 nm. Calculate the frequency of each transition and energy difference between two excited states.

50 The ejection of the photoelectron from the silver metal in the photoelectric effect experiment can be stopped by applying the voltage of 0.35 V when the radiation of 256.7 nm is used. Calculate the work function for silver metal. **NCERT Textbook**

51 If the photon of the wavelength 150 pm strikes an atom and one of its inner bound electrons is ejected out with a velocity of 1.5×10^7 m s^{-1}, calculate the energy with which it is bound to the nucleus.

52 Emission transitions in the Paschen series end at orbit $n = 3$ and start from orbit n and can be represented as $\nu = 3.29 \times 10^{15}$ (Hz) $\left[\frac{1}{3^2} - \frac{1}{n^2}\right]$. Calculate the value of n if the transition is observed at 1285 nm. Find the region of the spectrum. **NCERT Textbook**

53 The radius of first Bohr orbit of hydrogen atom is 0.529 Å. Calculate the radii of (i) the third orbit of He^+ ion and (ii) the second orbit of Li^{2+} ion.

54 (i) Name the first five series of lines that occur in the atomic spectrum of hydrogen and indicate the region in the electromagnetic spectrum where these series occur.

(ii) Give the general equation for the wave number applicable to all the series.

55 Calculate the wavelength of the spectral line obtained in the spectrum of Li^{2+} ion when the transition takes place between two levels whose sum is 4 and the difference is 2.

Long Answer Type Questions

5 Marks

56 (i) Calculate the total number of electrons present in one mole of methane.

(ii) Find (a) the total number and (b) the total mass of neutrons in 7 mg of ^{14}C. (Assume that, mass of a neutron = 1.675×10^{-27} kg)

(iii) Find (a) the total number and (b) the total mass of protons in 34 mg of NH_3 at STP. (Mass of 1 $p = 1.6726 \times 10^{-27}$ kg.)

Will the answer change, if the temperature and pressure are changed? **NCERT Textbook**

57 What observations in scattering experiment led Rutherford to make the following conclusions?

(i) The most of the space in an atom is empty.

(ii) The whole of the mass of the atom is present in the centre of the nucleus.

(iii) Nucleus has positive charge.

On the basis of scattering of α-particles by a thin metal foil, describe the Rutherford model of an atom. What are the drawbacks of this model?

58 What is photoelectric effect? State the result of photoelectric effect experiment that could not be explained on the basis of laws of classical physics. Explain this effect on the basis of quantum theory of electromagnetic radiations.

59 A photon of wavelength 4×10^{-7} m strikes on metal surface, the work function of the metal being 2.13 eV. Calculate:

(i) the energy of the photon (eV).

(ii) the kinetic energy of the emission.

(iii) the velocity of the photoelectron ($1 \text{ eV} = 1.6020 \times 10^{-19}$ J). **NCERT Textbook**

60 Following results are observed when sodium metal is irradiated with different wavelengths. Calculate

(i) threshold wavelength

(ii) Planck's constant

λ (nm)	500	450	400
$v \times 10^5 (ms^{-1})$	2.55	4.35	5.20

NCERT Textbook

61 When an electric discharge is passed through hydrogen gas, the hydrogen molecules dissociated to produce excited hydrogen atoms. These excited atoms emit electromagnetic radiation of discrete frequencies which can be given by the general formula

$$\bar{v} = 109677\left[\frac{1}{n_i^2} - \frac{1}{n_f^2}\right]$$

What points of Bohr's model of an atom can be used to arrive at this formula? Based on these points derive the above formula giving description of each step and each term. **NCERT Exemplar**

Hints & Solutions

1. (i) positive, densely, nucleus

(ii) crests, troughs

(iii) second

(iv) proportional, frequency.

2. (i)→(d), (ii)→(a), (iii)→(a), (iv)→(d)

3. (a) A → (iv) B → (iii) C → (i) D → (ii)

4. Cathode rays originate from the cathode whereas anode rays are not obtained from the anode. They are produced from the gaseous atoms by knock out of the electrons with high speed cathode rays.

5. Number of electrons, $n = \dfrac{\text{total charge in oil drop}}{\text{charge on 1 electron}}$

$$= \frac{-1.282 \times 10^{-18} \text{ C}}{-1.6022 \times 10^{-19} \text{ C}} = 0.800 \times 10 = 8.0 \text{ electrons}$$

6. Neutron is a neutral particle. Hence, it will not be deflected on passing through an electric field.

7. In given element $^{80}_{35}Br$, Z (atomic number) is 35 and atomic mass number (A) is 80. As, species are neutral, therefore, number of protons are equal to number of electrons, i.e. 35.

Number of neutrons = 80 − 35 = 45.

8. As $A = n + p$

$\therefore$ $p = A - n = 13 - 7 = 6$

Hence, atomic number, $Z = p = 6$

9. Atomic number = Mass number − Number of neutrons

Atomic number = 14 − 8 = 6, so the element is carbon.

10. The frequency of radiation increases in order FM radio < microwaves < amber light < X-rays < cosmic rays.

11. Number of lines produced when electron from nth shell drops to ground state = $\dfrac{n(n-1)}{2}$

When $n = 6$, number of lines produced

$$= \frac{6(6-1)}{2} = \frac{6 \times 5}{2} = 15$$

12. The line spectrum of any element has lines corresponding to definite wavelengths. Lines are obtained as a result of electronic transitions between the energy levels. Hence, the electrons in these levels have fixed energy, i.e. quantised values.

13. For H-atom, the radius of n th orbit is given by

$$r_n = 0.529 \times n^2 \text{ Å}$$

$$\therefore \quad r_3 - r_2 = 0.529(3^2 - 2^2)\text{ Å} = 0.529 \times 5 = 2.645 \text{ Å}$$

14. This is because the energies of the orbits in which the electrons revolve are fixed.

15. Refer to text on page 50 (Thomson model of atom).

16. In case of positive rays, the ions remaining after the loss of electrons might have the same magnitude of charge, but different masses. Hence, they will have different charge to-mass ratio. Cathode rays are made up of electrons and all electrons have same charge to-mass ratio. That's why charge to mass ratio of all cathode rays is same. [2]

17. Heavy atoms such as gold, platinum have heavy nucleus. Heavy nucleus contains large amount of positive charge. When a beam of a α -particles is shot at a thin gold foil, most of them pass through without much effect. [1]

Some however, are deflected back or deflected by small angles due to enormous repulsive force of heavy nucleus. If light aluminium foil is used, the number of α-particles deflected back or those deflected by small angles will be negligible. [1]

18. (i) Energy, $E = h\nu$

[h = Planck's constant = 6.626×10^{-34} J s

$\nu = 3 \times 10^{15}$ Hz $= 3 \times 10^{15}$ Cps]

Energy, $E = 6.626 \times 10^{-34} \text{ J s} \times 3 \times 10^{15} s^{-1}$ [1]

$$= 19.878 \times 10^{-19} \text{ J} = 1.9878 \times 10^{-18} \text{ J}$$

(ii) Energy, $E = \dfrac{hc}{\lambda}$

$$\lambda = 0.50 \text{ Å} = 0.50 \times 10^{-10} \text{ m}$$

$$E = \frac{6.626 \times 10^{-34} \text{ J s} \times 3 \times 10^8 \text{ ms}^{-1}}{0.50 \times 10^{-10} \text{ m}}$$

$$= 39.756 \times 10^{-16} \text{ J} = 3.975 \times 10^{-15} \text{ J}$$ [1]

19. As we know, $\lambda = \dfrac{c}{\nu} = \dfrac{3.0 \times 10^8 \text{ ms}^{-1}}{4.620 \times 10^{14} \text{ s}^{-1}} = 649.4$ nm

Thus, it lies in the visible light. [2]

20. (A) $\lambda = 300 \text{ nm} = 300 \times 10^{-9}$ m

(B) $\lambda = 300\ \mu\text{m} = 300 \times 10^{-6}$ m

(C) $\lambda = 3 \text{ nm} = 3 \times 10^{-9}$ m

(D) $\lambda = 30 \text{ Å} = 30 \times 10^{-10} \text{ m} = 3 \times 10^{-9}$ m

$\because$ Energy, $E = \dfrac{hc}{\lambda}$ or $E \propto \dfrac{1}{\lambda}$

$\therefore$ Increasing order of energy is $B < A < C = D$. [2]

21. Energy (E) of one photon is given by $E = h\nu$

$$h = 6.626 \times 10^{-34} \text{ Js}$$

$$\nu = 5 \times 10^{14}$$

$$E = 6.626 \times 10^{-34} \text{ Js} \times 5 \times 10^{14} \text{s}^{-1} = 3.313 \times 10^{-19} \text{ J}$$

Energy of 1 mole of photons

$$= 3.313 \times 10^{-19} \text{ J} \times 6.022 \times 10^{23} \text{ mol}^{-1} = 199.51 \text{ kJ mol}^{-1}$$ [2]

22. Power of the bulb = 100 watt = 100 J s^{-1}

$$E = h\nu = \frac{hc}{\lambda} = \frac{6.626 \times 10^{-34} \text{ J} \times 3 \times 10^8 \text{ ms}^{-1}}{400 \times 10^{-9} \text{ m}}$$

$$= 4.969 \times 10^{-19} \text{ J}$$ [1]

Number of photons emitted

$$= \frac{100 \text{J s}^{-1}}{4.969 \times 10^{-19}} = 2.012 \times 10^{20} \text{s}^{-1}$$ [1]

23. Frequency, $\nu = \dfrac{c}{\lambda}$

$\because$ 1 nm $= 10^{-9}$ m

$\therefore$ 580 nm $= 580 \times 10^{-9}$ m or 580×10^{-7} cm

$$\nu = \frac{3.0 \times 10^8 \text{ ms}^{-1}}{580 \times 10^{-9} \text{ m}} = 5.17 \times 10^{14} \text{ s}^{-1}$$ [1]

[c = Velocity of light $= 3 \times 10^8$ m s^{-1}]

Wave number, $\bar{\nu} = \dfrac{1}{\lambda} = \dfrac{1}{580 \times 10^{-7} \text{ cm}}$ [1]

$$= 1.724 \times 10^4 \text{ cm}^{-1}$$

24. Frequency, $\nu = \dfrac{c}{\lambda}$

$$1368 \times 10^3 \text{ Hz} = \frac{3 \times 10^8 \text{ ms}^{-1}}{\lambda}$$

or $\lambda = \dfrac{3 \times 10^8 \text{ m s}^{-1}}{1368 \times 10^3 \text{Hz}} = 219.3$ m, radiowave [2]

25.

> **Key Idea** Number of photons is calculated by dividing total energy by energy of 1 photon, so first calculate the energy of 1 photon by applying, $E = \dfrac{hc}{\lambda}$
>
> Then, calculate the number of photons by using the formula;
>
> $$N = \frac{\text{total energy}}{\text{energy of one photon}}$$

Energy of one photon,

$$E = \frac{hc}{\lambda} = \frac{6.626 \times 10^{-34} \text{ Js} \times 3.0 \times 10^8 \text{ ms}^{-1}}{4000 \times 10^{-12} \text{ m}}$$

[$\because$ 1 pm $= 10^{-12}$ m]

$$= 4.9695 \times 10^{-17} \text{ J}$$ [1]

Number of photons,

$$N = \frac{1 \text{ J}}{4.9695 \times 10^{-17} \text{ J}} = 2.0122 \times 10^{16} \text{ photons}$$ [1]

26. Given, wavelength, $\lambda = 242 \text{ nm} = 242 \times 10^{-9}$ m

Energy, $E = h\nu = \frac{hc}{\lambda}$

$$= \frac{6.626 \times 10^{-34} \text{ Js} \times 3.0 \times 10^8 \text{ ms}^{-1}}{242 \times 10^{-9} \text{ m}}$$

$$E = 0.0821 \times 10^{-17} \text{ J/atom}$$ [1]

This energy is sufficient for ionisation of one Na atom, so it is the ionisation energy of Na.

$$E = 6.023 \times 10^{23} \times 0.0821 \times 10^{-17} \text{ J/mol}$$

$$E = 4.945 \times 10^5 \text{ J/mol} = 4.945 \times 10^2 \text{ kJ/mol}$$ [1]

27. Wavelength depends upon the mass and velocity of electron. So first calculate the velocity of electron from the formula of kinetic energy (KE $= \frac{1}{2}mv^2$) then, calculate the wavelength by using the formula $\lambda = \frac{h}{mv}$

$$\text{KE} = \frac{1}{2}mv^2$$

$$v^2 = \frac{2\text{ KE}}{m} \text{ or } v = \sqrt{\frac{2\text{KE}}{m}}$$

$$v = \sqrt{\frac{2 \times 3.0 \times 10^{-25} \text{ J}}{9.1 \times 10^{-31} \text{ kg}}}$$ [1 J = 1 kg m²s⁻²]

$$v = \sqrt{0.6593 \times 10^6} = 0.8119 \times 10^3$$ [1]

$$= 812.0 \text{ ms}^{-1}$$

Wavelength, $\lambda = \frac{h}{mv} = \frac{6.626 \times 10^{-34} \text{ Js}}{9.1 \times 10^{-31} \text{ kg} \times 812.0 \text{ ms}^{-1}}$

$$\lambda = 0.0008967 \times 10^{-3} \text{ m}$$ [1]

$$\lambda = 8967 \text{ Å}$$

28. Refer to text on pages 54 and 55 (Photoelectric effect and its explanation).

29. Given that wavelength is

$\lambda = 300 \text{ nm} = 3 \times 10^{-7}$ m

Therefore, energy is

$$E = h\nu = \frac{hc}{\lambda} = \frac{6.626 \times 10^{-34} \times 3 \times 10^8}{3 \times 10^{-7} \times 1.6 \times 10^{-19}}$$

$$= 4.1 \text{ eV}$$ [1]

For a metal to show photoelectric effect, its work function has to be less than or equal to 4.1 eV. So, the number of metals having work function less than 4.1 eV or 4, i.e. Li, Na, K and Mg. [1]

30. Threshold wavelength,

$$\lambda_0 = 6800 \text{ Å} = 6800 \times 10^{-10} \text{ m}$$

Threshold frequency,

$$\nu_0 = \frac{c}{\lambda_0} = \frac{3.0 \times 10^8 \text{ ms}^{-1}}{6800 \times 10^{-10} \text{ m}} = 4.41 \times 10^{14} \text{ s}^{-1}$$ [1]

Work function, $W_0 = h\nu_0$

$$= 6.626 \times 10^{-34} \text{ Js} \times 4.41 \times 10^{14} \text{ s}^{-1}$$ [1]

$$= 2.922 \times 10^{-19} \text{ J}$$

Note For each metal, there is a characteristic minimum frequency, ν_0 which is also known as threshold frequency below which photoelectric effect is not observed.

31. Wave number, $\bar{\nu} = RZ^2\left(\frac{1}{n_1^2} - \frac{1}{n_2^2}\right)$ and $\bar{\nu} = \frac{1}{\lambda}$

For He^+ spectrum (for Balmer transition)

$$\bar{\nu} = R \times (2)^2\left(\frac{1}{2^2} - \frac{1}{4^2}\right) = R \times 4 \times \frac{3}{16} = \frac{3}{4}R \quad \text{...(i)}$$ [1]

For H-spectrum, $\bar{\nu} = R \times 1^2\left(\frac{1}{n_1^2} - \frac{1}{n_2^2}\right)$ ...(ii)

$$\frac{3}{4}R = R\left(\frac{1}{n_1^2} - \frac{1}{n_2^2}\right) \Rightarrow \frac{3}{4} = \frac{1}{n_1^2} - \frac{1}{n_2^2}$$ [1]

Hence, $n_1 = 1$ and $n_2 = 2$. In H-spectrum, the transition from $n = 2$ to $n = 1$ have same wavelength as the Balmer transition from $n = 3$ to $n = 2$ of He^+ spectrum.

32. Wave number, $\bar{\nu} = \frac{1}{\lambda} = R\left\{\frac{1}{n_1^2} - \frac{1}{n_2^2}\right\}$

[Rydberg constant, $R = 109677 \text{ cm}^{-1}$]

$$\frac{1}{\lambda} = 109677\left(\frac{1}{2^2} - \frac{1}{4^2}\right) \text{cm}^{-1}$$

$$= 109677\left(\frac{3}{16}\right) \text{cm}^{-1} = 20564.4 \text{ cm}^{-1}$$ [1]

$$\lambda = \frac{1}{20564.4} \text{ cm} = 486 \times 10^{-7} \text{ cm}$$

$$= 486 \times 10^{-9} \text{ m} = 486 \text{ nm}$$ [1]

33. Frequency, $\nu = \frac{1}{\text{Period}} = \frac{1}{2 \text{ ns}} = \frac{1}{2 \times 10^{-9}\text{s}}$

$$= 0.5 \times 10^9 \text{s}^{-1}$$ [1]

Energy of the source = Energy of 1 photon × number of photons produced

$$E_{\text{source}} = h\nu \times N$$

$$= 6.626 \times 10^{-34} \text{ Js} \times 0.5 \times 10^9 \text{s}^{-1} \times 2.5 \times 10^{15}$$

$$= 8.28 \times 10^{-10} \text{ J}$$ [1]

34. The wavelength of absorbed radiation is related to those of emitted radiation as,

$$\frac{1}{\lambda_{\text{absorbed}}} = \frac{1}{\lambda_1} + \frac{1}{\lambda_2}$$

Therefore, $\frac{1}{355} = \frac{1}{680} + \frac{1}{\lambda_2}$ [1]

$$\frac{1}{355} - \frac{1}{680} = \frac{1}{\lambda_2} \Rightarrow \frac{325}{241400} = \frac{1}{\lambda_2}$$

$$\lambda_2 = \frac{241400}{325} = 742.78 \text{ nm} \simeq 743 \text{ cm}$$ [1]

35. (i) Energy in nth orbit, $E_n = \frac{-2.18\times 10^{-18}}{n^2}$ J

Energy in fifth orbit,

$$E_5 = \frac{-2.18\times 10^{-18}}{5^2} \text{ J} = -8.72\times 10^{-20} \text{ J}$$ [1]

(ii) For H-atom, radius of nth orbit,

$$r_n = 0.529 \times n^2 \text{ Å}$$

∴ Radius of 5th Bohr orbit,

$$r_5 = 0.529 \times 5^2 = 13.225 \text{ Å} = 1.3225 \text{ nm}$$ [1]

36. For H-like particle, force of attraction between the electron and the nucleus = centrifugal force

i.e. $\frac{Ze^2}{r^2_n} = \frac{mv_n^2}{r_n}$ or $v_n^2 = \frac{Ze^2}{mr_n}$ or $v_n = \left(\frac{Ze^2}{mr_n}\right)^{1/2}$ [2]

37. If n photons are emitted by a laser, the total energy of the photons emitted is equal to the power of the laser.

Energy of 1 photon, $E = \frac{hc}{\lambda}$

$$= \frac{6.626\times 10^{-34} \text{ Js}\times 3.0\times 10^8 \text{ ms}^{-1}}{337.1\times 10^{-9} \text{ m}} \quad (1 \text{ nm} = 10^{-9} \text{ m})$$

$$= 0.05896\times 10^{-17} \text{ J}$$ [1]

Energy of 5.6×10^{24} photons

$$= 0.05896\times 10^{-17} \times 5.6\times 10^{24} \text{ J}$$

$$= 0.3302\times 10^7 \text{ J} = 3.302\times 10^6 \text{ J}$$ [1]

38. Energy of 300 nm photon $= h\nu = hc/\lambda$

$$= \frac{6.626\times 10^{-3} \text{ Js}\times 3.0\times 10^8 \text{ ms}^{-1}}{300\times 10^{-9} \text{ m}} = 6.626 \times 10^{-19} \text{ J}$$

The energy of one mole of photons

$$= 6.626 \times 10^{-19} \text{ J} \times 6.022 \times 10^{23} \text{ mol}^{-1}$$

$$= 3.99 \times 10^5 \text{ J mol}^{-1}$$

The minimum energy needed to remove one mole of electrons from sodium

$$= (3.99 - 1.68) \times 10^5 \text{ J mol}^{-1} = 2.31 \times 10^5 \text{ Jmol}^{-1}$$

The minimum energy for one electron

$$= \frac{2.31\times 10^5 \text{ Jmol}^{-1}}{6.022\times 10^{23} \text{ electrons mol}^{-1}}$$

$$= 3.84 \times 10^{-19} \text{ J}$$ [1]

This corresponds to the wavelength

$$\therefore \quad \lambda = \frac{hc}{E} = \frac{6.626\times 10^{-34} \text{ Js}\times 3.0\times 10^8 \text{ ms}^{-1}}{3.84\times 10^{-19} \text{ J}}$$

The maximum wavelength to emit a photoelectron = 517 nm [1]

39. $E_n = \frac{(-2.18\times 10^{-18} \text{ J})Z^2}{n^2}$ atom^{-1}

For He^+, $n = 1$, $Z = 2$

$$E_1 = \frac{(-2.18\times 10^{-18} \text{ J})(2^2)}{(1)^2} = -8.72\times 10^{-18} \text{ J}$$ [1]

The radius of the orbit is given by $r_n = \frac{(0.0529 \text{ nm})n^2}{Z}$

Since, $n = 1$ and $Z = 2$

$$r_n = \frac{(0.0529 \text{ nm})1^2}{2} = 0.02645 \text{ nm.}$$ [1]

40. Let the number of electrons in an ion = x

∴ Number of neutrons $= x + \frac{30.4}{100} x = 1.304\, x$

(∵ Number of neutrons are 30.4% more than the number of electrons).

In the netural atom, number of electrons = $x + 3$

(∵ The ion carries + 3 charge)

So, number of protons = $x + 3$

We know that, mass number = $n + p$

$$= 1.304\, x + x + 3 = 56$$

or $\quad 2.304\, x = 53,\; x = \frac{53}{2.304} = 23.003 \approx 23$

∴ Number of protons = 23 + 3 = 26 = Atomic number

Therefore, the symbol of the ion is $^{56}_{26}Fe^{3+}$.

41. According to Rutherford's model of atom, the positive charge is concentrated at the centre, that is, at the nucleus. Since, a small fraction of α-particles were deflected through small angle and also a few of them bounced back, it proved that the nucleus occupies a very small volume in the atom. The radius of the atom is about 10^{-10} m while of nucleus is 10^{-15} m. The nucleus is composed of protons and neutrons and is surrounded by revolving electrons.

42. Isoelectronic species have the same number of electrons but different atomic numbers. Number of positive charge shows the number of electrons lost and number of negative charges shows the number of electrons gained by an atom. Calculation of number of electrons have been shown below:

$_{11}Na^+ = 11 - 1 = 10\,e^-$, $_{19}K^+ = 19 - 1 = 18\,e^-$,

$_{12}Mg^{2+} = 12 - 2 = 10\,e^-$, $_{20}Ca^{2+} = 20 - 2 = 18\,e^-$,

$_{16}S^{2-} = 16 + 2 = 18\,e^-$, $_{18}Ar = 18\,e^-$

Hence, isoelectronic species are:

(i) Na^+ and Mg^{2+}

(ii) K^+, Ca^{2+}, S^{2-} and Ar

43. Given, time period of light = 2.0×10^{-10} s

Frequency, $\nu = \frac{1}{\text{time period}} = \frac{1}{2.0\times 10^{-10} \text{s}} = 5\times 10^9 \text{s}^{-1}$ [1]

Wavelength, $\lambda = \frac{c}{\nu} = \frac{3.0\times 10^8 \text{ ms}^{-1}}{5\times 10^9 \text{ s}^{-1}}$

$$= 0.6\times 10^{-1} \text{ m} = 6.0\times 10^{-2} \text{ m}$$ [1]

Wave number, $\overline{\nu} = \frac{1}{\lambda} = \frac{1}{6.0 \times 10^{-2}\ \text{m}} = 16.66\ \text{m}^{-1}$ [1]

44. Refer to text on page 53 (Atomic spectrum).

45. Given, wavelength (λ) of neon gas = 616 nm

$$= 616 \times 10^{-9}\ \text{m}$$

(i) Frequency, $\nu = \frac{c}{\lambda}$

$$\nu = \frac{3.0 \times 10^{8}\ \text{ms}^{-1}}{616 \times 10^{-9}\ \text{m}} = 4.870 \times 10^{14}\ \text{s}^{-1}$$ [1/2]

(ii) Distance travelled = speed × time

$$= 3.0 \times 10^{8}\ \text{ms}^{-1} \times 30\ \text{s}$$

$$= 9.0 \times 10^{9}\ \text{m}$$ [1/2]

(iii) Energy of quantum (or photon),

$$E = h\nu = 6.626 \times 10^{-34}\ \text{J s} \times 4.870 \times 10^{14}\ \text{s}^{-1}$$

$$= 32.268 \times 10^{-20}\ \text{J}$$ [1]

(iv) Number of quanta present

$$= \frac{\text{Total energy produced}}{\text{Energy of 1 quanta}}$$

$$= \frac{2\ \text{J}}{32.27 \times 10^{-20}\ \text{J}} \approx 6.2 \times 10^{18}\ \text{quanta}$$ [1]

46. **Key Idea** Find ΔE, when, $n_i = 5$ and $n_f = \infty$. Find, $\Delta E'$ when $n_i = 1$ and $n_f = \infty$ and compare them.

Energy change, $\Delta E = E_f - E_i$

$$\Delta E = 2.18 \times 10^{18}\ \text{J}\left(\frac{1}{n_i^2} - \frac{1}{n_f^2}\right)$$

When $n_i = 5$ and $n_f = \infty$,

$$\Delta E = 2.18 \times 10^{-18}\ \text{J}\left(\frac{1}{5^2} - \frac{1}{\infty}\right) = 0.0872 \times 10^{-18}\ \text{J}$$ [1]

When $n_i = 1$ and $n_f = \infty$,

$$\Delta E' = 2.18 \times 10^{-18}\ \text{J}\left(\frac{1}{1^2} - \frac{1}{\infty}\right)$$

$$\Delta E' = 2.18 \times 10^{-18}\ \text{J}$$

$$\frac{\Delta E'}{\Delta E} = \frac{2.18 \times 10^{-18}}{0.0872 \times 10^{-18}} = 25$$ [1]

Hence, energy required to remove an electron from first orbit is 25 times greater than that required to remove an electron from fifth orbit. [1]

47. $\Delta E = E_5 - E_1 = 2.18 \times 10^{-11}\left(\frac{1}{n_i^2} - \frac{1}{n_f^2}\right)$ erg

[$n_i = 1$ and $n_f = 5$]

$$\Delta E = 2.18 \times 10^{-11}\left(\frac{1}{1^2} - \frac{1}{5^2}\right)\ \text{erg}$$ [1]

$$\Delta E = 2.18 \times 10^{-11} \times \frac{24}{25} = 2.0928 \times 10^{-11}\ \text{erg}$$

$$= 2.0928 \times 10^{-18}\ \text{J} \qquad [\because 1\ \text{erg} = 10^{-7}\ \text{J}]$$ [1]

When electron returns to ground state, it emits energy equals to ΔE hence,

$$\Delta E = \frac{hc}{\lambda}$$

or $\lambda = \frac{hc}{\Delta E} = \frac{6.626 \times 10^{-34}\ \text{Js} \times 3.0 \times 10^{8}\ \text{ms}^{-1}}{2.0928 \times 10^{-18}\ \text{J}}$

$$= 9.498 \times 10^{-8}\ \text{m} = 949.8 \times 10^{-10}\ \text{m} = 949.8\ \text{Å}$$ [1]

48. Energy required to shift an electron from $n = 2$ to $n = \infty$.

$$\Delta E = E_\infty - E_2 = 0 - \left(-\frac{2.18 \times 10^{-18}\ \text{J atom}^{-1}}{2^2}\right)$$

$$= 5.45 \times 10^{-19}\ \text{J atom}^{-1}$$ [2]

Wavelength, $\lambda = \frac{hc}{\Delta E} = 3.647 \times 10^{-5}\ \text{cm}$ [1]

49. Given, wavelength

$$\lambda_1 = 589\ \text{nm} = 589 \times 10^{-9}\ \text{m}$$

$$\lambda_2 = 589.6\ \text{nm} = 589.6 \times 10^{-9}\ \text{m}$$

Frequency of wavelength 589 nm,

$$\nu_1 = \frac{c}{\lambda_1} = \frac{3.0 \times 10^{8}\ \text{ms}^{-1}}{589 \times 10^{-9}\ \text{m}} = 5.093 \times 10^{14}\ \text{s}^{-1}$$

Frequency of wavelength 589.6 nm,

$$\nu_2 = \frac{c}{\lambda_2} = \frac{3.0 \times 10^{8}\ \text{ms}^{-1}}{589.6 \times 10^{-9}\ \text{m}} = 5.088 \times 10^{14}\ \text{s}^{-1}$$ [2]

Energy difference between two excited states,

$$\Delta E = h\nu_1 - h\nu_2 = h(\nu_1 - \nu_2)$$

$$\Delta E = 6.626 \times 10^{-34}\ \text{Js}\ (5.093 \times 10^{14}\ \text{s}^{-1} - 5.088 \times 10^{14}\ \text{s}^{-1})$$

$$\Delta E = 6.626 \times 10^{-34}\ \text{Js} \times 0.005 \times 10^{14}\ \text{s}^{-1}$$ [1]

$$\Delta E = 3.31 \times 10^{-22}\ \text{J}$$

50. Energy of incident radiation, $h\nu = h\nu_0 + \text{KE}$

$$E = h\nu = \frac{hc}{\lambda} = \frac{6.626 \times 10^{-34}\ \text{Js} \times 3.0 \times 10^{8}\ \text{ms}^{-1}}{256.7 \times 10^{-9}\ \text{m}}$$

$$= 7.74 \times 10^{-19}\ \text{J}$$

Energy in eV $= \frac{7.74 \times 10^{-19}\ \text{eV}}{1.602 \times 10^{-19}} = 4.83\ \text{eV}$ [1]

Applied potential gives kinetic energy to the electron, i.e.

$$eV_0 = \frac{1}{2}mv_{max}^2 = \text{K.E}$$

$$\therefore \frac{1}{2}mv_{max}^2 = 1.6 \times 10^{-19} \times 0.35 = 0.56 \times 10^{19}\ \text{J}$$ [1]

Energy in eV $= \frac{0.56 \times 10^{19}}{1.602 \times 10^{-19}} = 0.35\ \text{eV}$

$\therefore$ KE = 0.35 eV

Work function, W_0 or

$h\nu_0 = h\nu - \text{KE} = 4.83\ \text{eV} - 0.35\ \text{eV} = 4.48\ \text{eV}$ [1]

51. **Key Idea** The energy ($h\nu_0$) with which an electron is bound to the nucleus is calculated by using the formula $h\nu = h\nu_0 + KE$, so first find $h\nu$ of incident radiation and K.E of electron by using the formula $KE = \frac{1}{2}mv^2$.

Then substitute the values of $h\nu$ and KE to find $h\nu_0$ (i.e. energy with which electron is bound to the nucleus).

Given, wavelength of upcoming photon = 150 pm
$= 150 \times 10^{-12}$ m

Velocity of ejected electron $= 1.5 \times 10^7$ ms^{-1}

Mass of the electron $= 9.11 \times 10^{-31}$ kg

Energy of incident radiation $h\nu = h\nu_0 + \frac{1}{2}mv^2$ [1]

$$E = h\nu = \frac{hc}{\lambda} = \frac{6.626 \times 10^{-34}\ \text{Js} \times 3.0 \times 10^8\ \text{ms}^{-1}}{150 \times 10^{-12}\ \text{m}}$$

$$E = 13.25 \times 10^{-16}\ \text{J}$$

$$\text{KE of ejected electron} = \frac{1}{2}mv^2$$

$$= \frac{1}{2} \times 9.11 \times 10^{-31}\ \text{kg} \times (1.5 \times 10^7\ \text{ms}^{-1})^2$$ [1]

$$\text{KE} = 1.025 \times 10^{-16}\ \text{J}$$

$$W_0 = h\nu_0 = h\nu - \frac{1}{2}mv^2$$

$$= 13.25 \times 10^{-16}\ \text{J} - 1.025 \times 10^{-16}\ \text{J} \quad [\because E = h\nu]$$

$$= 12.225 \times 10^{-16}\ \text{J}$$

$$= \frac{12.225 \times 10^{-16}}{1.602 \times 10^{-19}}\ \text{eV} = 7.63 \times 10^3\ \text{eV}$$ [1]

Note Energy with which the electron was bound to the nucleus = work function (W_0) for the metal.

52. Given, frequency, $\nu = \frac{c}{\lambda} = 3.29 \times 10^{15}\ \text{Hz}\left(\frac{1}{3^2} - \frac{1}{n^2}\right)$

$$\nu = \frac{3.0 \times 10^8\ \text{ms}^{-1}}{1285 \times 10^{-9}\ \text{m}} = 3.29 \times 10^{15}\ \text{Hz}\left(\frac{1}{9} - \frac{1}{n^2}\right)$$

$$\frac{3.0 \times 10^8\ \text{ms}^{-1}}{1285 \times 10^{-9}\ \text{m} \times 3.29 \times 10^{15}\ \text{Hz}} = \left(\frac{1}{9} - \frac{1}{n^2}\right)$$

$$7.096 \times 10^{-4} \times 10^2 = \left[0.111 - \frac{1}{n^2}\right]$$

$$7.096 \times 10^{-2} = \left[0.111 - \frac{1}{n^2}\right] = 0.0709 = \left[0.111 - \frac{1}{n^2}\right]$$

$$\frac{1}{n^2} = 0.1111 - 0.0709$$

$$\Rightarrow n^2 = 25 \text{ or } n = 5$$ [2]

$\therefore$ The electrons jump from $n = 5$ to $n = 3$, i.e. the transitions occurs in Paschen series and lies in infrared region.

Moreover, the radiation 1285 nm lies in the infrared region. [1]

53. Radius of nth Bohr orbit, $r_n = \frac{n^2h^2}{4\pi^2 m Ze^2}$

For hydrogen atom $Z = 1$, first orbit $n = 1$

$$r_1 = \frac{h^2}{4\pi^2 me^2} = 0.529\ \text{Å}$$

(i) For He^+ ion, $Z = 2$, third orbit, $n = 3$

$$r_3(He^+) = \frac{3^2h^2}{4\pi^2 m \times 2 \times e^2} = \frac{9}{2}\left[\frac{h^2}{4\pi^2 me^2}\right]$$

$$= \frac{9}{2} \times 0.529 = 2.380\ \text{Å}$$ [2]

(ii) For Li^{2+} ion, $Z = 3$, second orbit, $n = 2$

$$r_2(Li^{2+}) = \frac{2^2h^2}{4\pi^2 m \times 3 \times e^2} = \frac{4}{3}\left[\frac{h^2}{4\pi^2 me^2}\right]$$

$$= \frac{4}{3} \times 0.529 = 0.7053\ \text{Å}$$ [1]

54. Refer to text on pages 53 and (Electromagenetic spectrum) 57 (Line spectrum of hydrogen).

55. Suppose the transition takes place between levels n_1 and n_2. Then,

$n_1 + n_2 = 4$ and $n_2 - n_1 = 2$

By solving these equations, we get $n_1 = 1$, $n_2 = 3$

$$\therefore \quad \frac{1}{\lambda} = R\left(\frac{1}{n_1^2} - \frac{1}{n_2^2}\right)Z^2$$ [1]

For Li^{2+}, $Z = 3$

$$\therefore \quad \frac{1}{\lambda} = 109677\ \text{cm}^{-1}\left(\frac{1}{1^2} - \frac{1}{3^2}\right) \times 3^2$$

$$= 109677 \times \left(\frac{1}{1} - \frac{1}{9}\right) \times 9\ \text{cm}^{-1}$$

$$= 109677 \times 8\ \text{cm}^{-1}$$

$$\text{or} \quad \lambda = \frac{1}{109677 \times 8\ \text{cm}^{-1}} = 1.14 \times 10^{-6}\ \text{cm}$$ [2]

56. (i) 1 molecule of methane (CH_4) contains 10 electrons [6 from C and 1 from each H-atom]

$\therefore$ 1 mole molecule of methane will contain $6.022 \times 10^{23} \times 10 = 6.022 \times 10^{24}$ electrons

(ii) (a) 1 mole $^{14}C = 14\ \text{g} = 6.022 \times 10^{23}$ carbon atoms

Number of neutrons in 1 carbon atom
$= 14 - 6 = 8$ neutrons

$\because$ 6.022×10^{23} carbon atoms will contain $6.022 \times 10^{23} \times 8$ neutrons.

or 14 g C-14 have $6.022 \times 10^{23} \times 8$ neutrons

$\therefore$ 7 mg or 7×10^{-3} g carbon-14 will have

$$= \frac{7 \times 10^{-3} \times 6.022 \times 10^{23} \times 8}{14}\ \text{neutrons}$$

$$= 24.088 \times 10^{20}\ \text{neutrons}$$ [1]

$$= 2.4088 \times 10^{21}\ \text{neutrons}$$

(b) Mass of 1 neutron = 1.675×10^{-27} kg

Mass of 2.4088×10^{21} neutrons

$= 2.4088\times 10^{21} \times 1.675\times 10^{-27}$ kg

$= 4.0347\times 10^{-6}$ kg [1]

(iii) 1 mole of NH_3 = 10 moles of protons

$= 6.022\times 10^{23} \times 10$ protons

(a) 1 mole of NH_3 (or 17g) contains 6.022×10^{24} protons

$\therefore$ 34 mg or 34×10^{-3} g NH_3 will contain

$$= \frac{34\times 10^{-3} \times 6.022\times 10^{24}}{17}$$

$= 12.044\times 10^{21}$ protons

$= 1.2044\times 10^{22}$ protons

(b) Mass of 1 proton = 1.6726×10^{-27} kg

$\therefore$ Mass of 1.2044×10^{22} protons

$= 1.2044\times 10^{22} \times 1.6726\times 10^{-27}$ kg [1]

$= 2.01447\times 10^{-5}$ kg [1]

There is no effect of temperature and pressure change. The answer will remain the same. [1/2]

57. Refer to text on page 51 (Rutherford's Model).

58. Refer to text on pages 54 and 55 [Photoelectric effect and its explanation].

59. (i) Energy of a photon

$$E = \frac{hc}{\lambda} = \frac{6.626\times 10^{-34}\ \text{J-s}\times 3.0\times 10^{8}\ \text{ms}^{-1}}{4\times 10^{-7}\ \text{m}}$$

$E = 4.969 \times 10^{-19}$ J $\quad [\because 1.602 \times 10^{-19}\ \text{J} = 1\ \text{eV}]$

$$= \frac{4.969 \times 10^{-19}}{1.602 \times 10^{-19}} = 3.10\ \text{eV}$$ [1]

(ii) Kinetic energy of an ejected electron,

KE $= h\nu - h\nu_0$

$h\nu = 3.10$ eV (Energy of striking photon)

$h\nu_0 = W_0 = 2.13$ eV (Work function of the metal)

KE $= 3.10 - 2.13 = 0.97$ eV

(iii) KE $= \frac{1}{2} mv^2 = 0.97$ eV [1]

$\frac{1}{2} mv^2 = 0.97 \times 1.602 \times 10^{-19}$ J

$[\because 1\ \text{eV} = 1.602\times 10^{-19}\ \text{J}]$

$\frac{1}{2}\times 9.11\times 10^{-31}\ \text{kg}\times v^2 = 0.97 \times 1.602 \times 10^{-19}$ J

$[\because$ Mass of 1 $e^- = 9.11\times 10^{-31}$ kg $]$

$$v^2 = \frac{0.97 \times 1.602\times 10^{-19} \times 2\ \text{J}}{9.11 \times 10^{-31}\ \text{kg}} = 0.341\times 10^{12}$$

$v = 0.584 \times 10^{6} = 5.84 \times 10^{5}\ \text{ms}^{-1}$ [2]

Note Minimum energy required to eject the electron is $h\nu_0$. It is also called work function, W_0.

60. (i) Kinetic energy, KE $= h(\nu - \nu_0) = \frac{1}{2} mv^2$

On substituting the given results of the three experiments, we get

For 1st experiment

$$\nu = \frac{c}{\lambda} = \frac{3.0 \times 10^{8}\ \text{ms}^{-1}}{500 \times 10^{-9}\ \text{m}} = 6 \times 10^{14}\ \text{s}^{-1}$$

$h(6\times 10^{14}\ \text{s}^{-1} - \nu_0) = \frac{1}{2} m(2.55 \times 10^{5}\ \text{ms}^{-1})^2$ ...(i)

For 2nd experiment

$$\nu = \frac{c}{\lambda} = \frac{3.0 \times 10^{8}\ \text{ms}^{-1}}{450 \times 10^{-9}} = 6.67 \times 10^{14}\text{s}^{-1}$$

$h(6.67\times 10^{14}\text{s}^{-1} - \nu_0) = \frac{1}{2} m(4.35 \times 10^{5}\text{ms}^{-1})^2$ ...(ii)

For 3rd experiment

$$\nu = \frac{c}{\lambda} = \frac{3.0 \times 10^{8}\ \text{ms}^{-1}}{400 \times 10^{-9}\text{m}} = 7.5 \times 10^{14}\text{s}^{-1}$$

$h(7.5\times 10^{14}\ \text{s}^{-1} - \nu_0) = \frac{1}{2} m(5.20 \times 10^{5}\ \text{ms}^{-1})^2$ ...(iii) [2]

(ii) On dividing Eq. (ii) by Eq. (i), we get

$$\frac{6.67 \times 10^{14}\ \text{s}^{-1} - \nu_0}{6 \times 10^{14}\ \text{s}^{-1} - \nu_0} = \frac{(4.35)^2}{(2.55)^2} = 2.91$$

On solving, $\nu_0 = \frac{10.79 \times 10^{14}\text{s}^{-1}}{1.91} = 5.649\times 10^{14}\text{s}^{-1}$

(iii) $\lambda_0 = \frac{c}{\nu_0} = \frac{3.0 \times 10^{8}\ \text{ms}^{-1}}{5.649 \times 10^{14}\text{s}^{-1}} = 5.31\times 10^{-7}$ m [1]

(iv) On substituting the value of ν_0 in Eq. (iii), we get

$h(7.5\times 10^{14}\ \text{s}^{-1} - 5.649\times 10^{14}\text{s}^{-1})$

$= \frac{1}{2} \times 9.11\times 10^{-31}\ \text{kg} \times (5.20\times 10^{5}\text{ms}^{-1})^2$

$h(1.851\times 10^{14}\text{s}^{-1})\times 2 = 9.11\times 10^{-31}$ kg $\times (5.20 \times 10^{5}\text{ms}^{-1})^2$

On solving, $h = 6.6539\times 10^{-34}$ Js

$[\because 1\ \text{J} = 1\ \text{kg m}^2\text{s}^{-2}]$ [2]

61. The two important points of Bohr's model can be used to derive the given formula are as follows:

(i) Electrons revolve around the nucleus in a circular path of fixed radius and energy. These paths are called orbits, stationary states or allowed energy states. [2]

(ii) Energy is emitted or absorbed when an electron moves from higher stationary state to lower stationary state or from lower stationary state to higher stationary state respectively.

Derivation Refer to text on pages 55 and 56 (Application or Merits of Bohr's model). [3]

TOPIC 02 Dual Nature, Heisenberg's Principle and Quantum Mechanical Model

Towards Quantum Mechanical Model of the Atom

In order to overcome the drawbacks of the Bohr's model, several attempts were made to develop a more suitable and general model for atoms. The development of new model was mainly based on the following concepts:

(i) Dual behaviour of matter

(ii) Heisenberg's uncertainty principle

Dual Behaviour of Matter

It was the French physicist, de-Broglie, who in 1924 proposed that matter, like radiations, should also exhibit dual behaviour, i.e. it should exhibit particle as well as wave like properties.

It means that just like photon, electrons should also have momentum as well as wavelength.

The wave associated with a particle is called a **matter wave or de-Broglie wave.** de-Broglie suggested that the wavelength associated with a particle of mass m, moving with velocity v can be given as:

$$\boxed{\lambda = \frac{h}{mv} = \frac{\lambda}{P}}$$

where, h is Planck's constant, with value 6.626×10^{-34} Js and $P\ (=mv)$ is momentum of the particles moving with velocity, v. This equation is called **de-Broglie equation.**

1. Derivation of de-Broglie Equation

de-Broglie equation can be derived by combining the mass-energy relationships proposed by Max Planck and Einstein.

According to Max Planck, photon of light energy E is associated with a wave of frequency ν by the expression,

$$E = h\nu \quad \ldots\text{(i)}$$

Einstein suggested that mass and energy are related as

$$E = mc^2 \quad \ldots\text{(ii)}$$

where, c is the velocity of light.

From Eqs. (i) and (ii) we get,

$$h\nu = mc^2 \qquad \left[\because \nu = \frac{c}{\lambda}\right]$$

$$\therefore \quad \frac{hc}{\lambda} = mc^2 \text{ or } \frac{h}{\lambda} = mc \text{ or } \boxed{\lambda = \frac{h}{mc}}$$

This equation is applicable for a photon. de-Broglie suggested that by substituting the mass of the particle (m) and its velocity (v) in place of mass of electron, m and velocity of light (c), the equation can also be used for material particles. Since h is constant,

$$\therefore \quad \lambda \propto \frac{1}{\text{Momentum}}$$

This means that the wavelength of a particle in motion is inversely proportional to its momentum. It is called the **de-Broglie relationship.**

2. Significance of de-Broglie Equation

de-Broglie suggested that every object in motion have a wave character. But it is significant for microscopic bodies only. This is because the wavelengths associated with ordinary objects are too short due to their large masses that their wave properties cannot be detected. Therefore, practically these bodies are said to have no wavelengths. Whereas, the wavelength associated with electrons and other sub-atomic particles can be detected experimentally.

Example 1 If the velocity of the electron in Bohr's first orbit is $2.19\times 10^{6}\ \text{ms}^{-1}$, calculate the de-Broglie wavelength associated with it. **NCERT Textbook**

Sol. We know that, mass of electron $= 9.11\times 10^{-31}$ kg

$h = 6.626\times 10^{-34}$ J s

Wavelength,

$$\lambda = \frac{h}{mv} = \frac{6.626\times 10^{-34}\ \text{kg m}^2\text{s}^{-1}}{9.11\times 10^{-31}\ \text{kg}\times 2.19\times 10^{6}\ \text{ms}^{-1}}$$

$$\lambda = 3.32\times 10^{-10}\ \text{m} = 332\ \text{pm}$$

Heisenberg's Uncertainty Principle

This principle is a result of dual nature of matter and radiation. It is put forwarded by W Heisenberg a German physicist in 1927. According to this principle, it **is impossible to determine simultaneously, the exact position and exact momentum (or velocity) of an electron.**

Mathematically, it can be given as

$$\Delta x \times \Delta P_x \geq \frac{h}{4\pi} \quad \text{or} \quad \Delta x \times \Delta (mv_x) \geq \frac{h}{4\pi}$$

$$\text{or} \quad \Delta x \times \Delta v_x \geq \frac{h}{4\pi m}$$

where, Δx is the uncertainty in position and ΔP_x (or Δv_x) is the uncertainty in momentum (or velocity) of the particle. If we know the position of the electron with high degree of accuracy (Δx is small), then the uncertainty in the velocity of the electron (Δv_x) will be large and *vice-versa*.

Significance of Uncertainty Principle

This principle rules out the existence of definite paths or trajectories of electrons and other similar particles. However, the effect of this principle is significant only in case of microscopic objects and is negligible in case of macroscopic object.

For an electron of mass 9.11×10^{-31} kg.

$$\Delta v \cdot \Delta x = \frac{h}{4\pi m}$$

$$= \frac{6.626\times 10^{-34}\ \text{Js}}{4\times 3.1416\times 9.11\times 10^{-31}\ \text{kg}}$$

$$= 10^{-4}\ \text{m}^2\text{s}^{-1}$$

It means that, if we want to find the exact location of the electron, with an uncertainty of only 10^{-8} m, then the uncertainty Δv in velocity is given by

$$\frac{10^{-4}\ \text{m}^2\text{s}^{-1}}{10^{-8}\ \text{m}} = 10^4\ \text{ms}^{-1}$$

The value obtained is large enough so that the classical picture of electrons moving in Bohr's orbital (fixed) cannot hold good for it. Therefore, **it means that the precise statements of the position and momentum of electrons should be replaced by the statements of probability, that the electron possesses at a given position and momentum.** The quantum mechanical model of atom deals with this fact.

Example 2 A golf ball has a mass of 40 g and a speed of 45 m/s. If the speed can be measured within accuracy of 2%, calculate the uncertainty in the position.

NCERT Textbook

Sol. Uncertainty in velocity,

$$\Delta v = \frac{45\times 2}{100} = 0.9\ \text{ms}^{-1}$$

From Heisenberg's principle,

$$\Delta x = \frac{h}{4\pi m \cdot \Delta v}$$

$$= \frac{6.6\times 10^{-34}\ \text{kg m}^2\text{s}^{-1}}{4\times 3.14\times 40\times 10^{-3}\ \text{kg}\times 0.9} = 1.46\times 10^{-33}\ \text{m}$$

Reasons for the Failure of the Bohr's Model

Different reasons for failure of the Bohr's model are discussed below :

(i) Bohr model consider electron as a charged particle moving in well defined circular orbits about the nucleus. It did not take wave character of the electron into consideration, i.e. it did not consider the dual behaviour of matter.

(ii) Bohr considered that an orbit is a clearly defined path which can completely be defined only if both the position and the velocity of the electron are known exactly at the same time. But this is against the Heisenberg uncertainty principle.

(iii) Bohr model of the hydrogen atom, was not only against the dual behaviour of matter but it also contradicts Heisenberg uncertainty principle. Because of these weaknesses there was no point to extend Bohr model for other atoms.

(iv) Indeed there is a need for such theory which could account for wave-particle duality of matter and be consistent with Heisenberg uncertainty principle. Quantum mechanics is an alternative for dealing them.

Quantum Mechanical Model of Atom

The branch of science that deals with the dual behaviour of matter, i.e. wave as well as particle nature is called **quantum mechanics.** When quantum mechanical concept is applied to macroscopic objects (for which wave character is negligible) the results are the same as those from the classical mechanics. Quantum mechanical model of atom is the picture of the structure of atom. The fundamental equation of quantum mechanics was developed by Schrodinger equation.

Schrodinger Wave Equation

In 1926, Werner Heisenberg and Erwin Schrodinger developed quantum mechanics independently. On the basis of quantum mechanics, Schrodinger proposed a **quantum mechanical model** of an atom which considered both, the dual nature of matter and Heisenberg uncertainty principle. In 1927, Erwin Schrodinger gave following **Schrodinger wave equation** to describe the wave motion of the electron in three dimensional space around the nucleus.

$$\frac{\partial^2\psi}{\partial x^2} + \frac{\partial^2\psi}{\partial y^2} + \frac{\partial^2\psi}{\partial z^2} + \frac{8\pi^2 m}{h^2}(E-V)\psi = 0$$

where, ψ (psi) = a wave function of space coordinates x, y and z represent the amplitude of the electron wave.

h = the Planck's constant, (= 6.626×10^{-34} Js)

m = the mass of an electron.

E = the permissible total energy of the electron. The total energy of the system means the kinetic energies of all the sub-atomic particles (electrons, nuclei), attractive potential between the electrons and nuclei and repulsive potential among the electrons and nuclei individually.

V = the potential energy of the electron, $\frac{Ze^2}{r}$.

When this equation is solved for ψ three integers, n, l, m were obtained. These integers are called **quantum numbers.** [You will learn about the solutions of this equation for different systems in higher classes.] For systems like atoms or molecules energy of which does not change with time, the Schrodinger wave equation may be written as $\hat{H}\psi = E\psi$. Here $\hat{H}$ is a mathematical operator, called **Hamiltonian operator.** The values of E and ψ are obtained from the solutions of Schrodinger wave equation.

Hydrogen Atom and the Schrodinger Equation

With the help of solution of Schrodinger equation , all the discrepancies raised in Bohr's model were removed in the following ways:

- The solutions obtained by solving the Schrodinger wave equation for hydrogen atom, indicates the possible energy states (or energy levels) that an electron can occupy. The values showing the energy states are called **eigen values.** The corresponding values of wave functions (ψ) of the electron associated with these energy values are called **eigen functions.**
- Thus, the solutions of the Schrodinger wave equation result in quantised energy states and in corresponding wave functions that are characterised by a set of three quantum numbers, called the principal quantum number (n), azimuthal quantum number (l) and magnetic quantum number (m_l).
- The wave function is a mathematical function, value of which depends upon the coordinates of the electron in the atom and does not carry any physical meaning. Such wave functions of hydrogen or hydrogen like species with one electron are called **atomic orbitals.**
- In case of multielectron systems, the Schrodinger wave equation cannot be solved exactly, hence, approximate methods can be used to get solutions of reasonable accuracy. Such calculations can also be done with the help of modern computers. The results clearly reveals that the orbitals of atoms other than hydrogen do not differ from hydrogen in any radical way but they are some what contracted in size due to increased nuclear charge.
- Moreover, they also differ in energy as the energy in case of orbitals of hydrogen or hydrogen like species depends only upon principal quantum number (n) but in case of multielectron system, the energy of orbitals is decided by quantum numbers n and l (as discussed later).

Probability Picture of an Electron : Concept of Atomic Orbital

According to quantum mechanical approach, it is not possible to simply locate an electron at a particular point, but there are certain regions in space around the nucleus where the probability (chances) of finding the electron is maximum (90-95%).

These most probable regions in space are referred as orbitals. Thus, "**an orbital is a region in space around the nucleus where the probability of finding the electron is maximum**".

Difference between Orbit and Orbital

The main points of differences between orbit and orbital are tabulated below :

Orbit	Orbital
It is a well defined circular path around the nucleus in which the electrons revolve.	Its shows the three dimensional space around the nucleus within which the probability of finding an electron is maximum (upto 90%).
The concept of an orbit does not consider the wave character of electrons and uncertainty principle.	The concept of an orbital is in accordance with the wave character of electrons and uncertainty principle.
They do not have any directional characteristics.	Except s-orbitals, all orbitals have directional characteristics.
The maximum number of electrons that an orbit can have is given by $2n^2$ where n is the number of the orbit.	The maximum number of electrons that can be occupied by an orbital is always two.

Significance of ψ and ψ^2

In an atom the wave function ψ for an electron has no physical significance as such. However, its square i.e. ψ^2 at any point gives the intensity of the electron wave at that point.

In view of Heisenberg's uncertainty principle, it shows the probability of finding the electron at that point and therefore, termed as **probability density.**

Important Features of the Quantum Mechanical Model of Atom

The following are the important features of this model :

(i) The energy of electrons in atoms is quantised (i.e. can only have certain specific values).

(ii) The existence of quantised electronic energy levels is a direct consequence of the wave like properties of electrons and are allowed solutions of Schrodinger wave equation.

(iii) It is not possible to determine both the exact position and exact velocity of an electron in an atom simultaneously (Heisenberg uncertainty principle). Only the probability of finding the electron at different points in an atom is considered.

(iv) The wave function ψ for an electron in an atom shows the atomic orbital of that electron. In each orbital, the energy of electron is definite and an orbital can occupy a maximum of two electrons. In case of a multielectron atom, the electrons are filled in various orbitals in increasing order of energy.

(v) The probability of finding an electron at a point within an atom is proportional to the square of the orbital wave function i.e. $|\psi|^2$ at that point.

Topic Practice 2

Very Short Answer Type Questions

1 Mark

1 Fill in the Blanks

(i) The maximum number of electrons that an orbit can have is given by ...... where, n is the number of the orbit.

(ii) The energy of electrons in atom is ....

(iii) The probability of finding an electron at a point with an atom is .... to the .... of the orbital wave function, i.e. $|\psi|^2$ at that point.

(iv) An orbital is a region in space around the nucleus where the .... of finding the electron is ......

2 Objective Type Questions

(i) The energy required to break one mole of Cl—Cl bonds in Cl_2 is 243 kJ mol^{-1}. The largest wavelength of light capable of breaking a single Cl—Cl bond is

(a) 700 nm (b) 494 nm
(c) 596 nm (d) 640 nm

(ii) The number of wavelengths per unit length is called

(a) frequency (ν)
(b) wavelength (λ)
(c) wave number ($\bar{\nu}$)
(d) None of the abvoe

(iii) What is the number of photons of light with a wavelength of 4000 pm that provide 1J of energy?

(a) 2.145×10^{14} photons
(b) 2.0122×10^{16} photons
(c) 2.0012×10^{10} photons
(d) 2.0233×10^{8} photons

3 Match the principle in Column I with discoverer in Column II and choose the correct option using the codes given below..

	Column I (Principle)		Column II (Discoverer)
A.	Dual behaviour of matter	(i)	Hund
		(ii)	Heisenberg
B.	Uncertainty principle	(iii)	Einstein
C.	Quantum theory	(iv)	Planck
		(v)	de-Broglie

Codes

(a) A - (v), B - (ii), C - (iv)
(b) A - (v), B - (iv), C - (ii)
(c) A - (iv), B - (i), C - (v)
(d) A - (v), B - (i), C - (iv)

4 What will be the wavelength of a ball of mass 0.1 kg moving with a velocity of 10 ms^{-1}? **NCERT Intext**

5 Out of the electron and proton which one will have, a higher velocity to produce matter waves of the same wavelength? Explain it. **NCERT Exemplar**

6 Why does a car cannot seem to travel in the form of a wave although de-Broglie relation is applicable to it?

7 Can we apply Heisenberg's uncertainty principle to a stationary electron? Why or why not?

8 Explain, why the uncertainty principle is significant only for the motion of sub-atomic particles but is negligible for the macroscopic objects?

9 What physical meaning is attributed to the square of the absolute value of wave function, $|\psi|^2$?

Short Answer Type I Questions

2 Marks

10 Calculate the mass of a photon with wavelength 3.6 Å.

11 Calculate the wavelength of an electron moving with velocity of 2.05×10^7 ms^{-1}.

12 Dual behaviour of matter proposed by de-Broglie led to the discovery of electron microscope often used for the highly magnified images of biological molecules and other type of materials. If the velocity of the electron in this microscope is $1.6 \times 10^6 ms^{-1}$, calculate de-Broglie wavelength associated with this electron. **NCERT Textbook**

13 Similar to electron diffraction, neutron diffraction microscope is also used for the determination of the structure of molecules. If the wavelength used here is 800 pm, calculate the characteristic velocity associated with the neutron (mass of neutron $= 1.675 \times 10^{-27}$ kg). **NCERT Textbook**

14 A proton is moving with kinetic energy 5×10^{-27} J. What is the velocity of the proton?

15 What kind of information about an electron in an atom is obtained from its wave function?

16 In an atom, an electron is moving with a speed of 600 ms^{-1} with an accuracy of 0.005 %. Find the certainty with which the position of the electron can be located. ($h = 6.6 \times 10^{-34}$ kg $m^2 s^{-1}$, mass of electron, $m_e = 9.1 \times 10^{-31}$kg).

17 The velocity associated with a proton moving in a potential difference of 1000 V is 4.37×10^5 ms^{-1}. If the hockey ball of mass 0.1 kg is moving with this velocity, calculate the wavelength associated with this velocity. **NCERT Textbook**

18 A microscope using suitable photons is employed to locate an electron in an atom within a distance of 0.1 Å. What is the uncertainty involved in the measurement of its velocity?

19 Prove that if the uncertainty in position of a moving electron is equal to its de-Broglie wavelength then its velocity is completely uncertain.

20 The effect of uncertainty principle is significant only for motion of microscopic particles and is negligible for the macroscopic particles. Justify the statement with the help of a suitable example. **NCERT Exemplar**

21 How does the Bohr theory of the hydrogen atom differ from that of Schrodinger?

Short Answer Type II Questions

3 Marks

22 According to de-Broglie, matter should exhibit dual behaviour, that is both particle and wave like properties. However, a cricket ball of mass 100 g does not move like a wave when it is thrown by a bowler at a speed of 100 km/h. Calculate the wavelength of the ball and explain why it does not show wave nature? **NCERT Exemplar**

23 Find out the number of wave made by a Bohr electron in one complete revolution in its 3rd orbit.

24 State Heisenberg's uncertainty principle. Give its mathematical expression. Also give its significance.

Long Answer Type Questions

5 Marks

25 (i) Why was a change in the Bohr model of atom is required, due to which important development(s), concept of movement of an electron in an orbit was replaced by the concept of probability of finding electron in an orbital? What is the name given to the changed model of atom? **NCERT Exemplar**

(ii) A molecule of O_2 and that of SO_2 travel with the same velocity. What is the ratio of their wavelengths?

26 (i) A beam of helium atoms move with a velocity of 2.0×10^3 ms^{-1}. Find the wavelength of the particle constituting the beam ($h = 6.626 \times 10^{-34}$ Js).

(ii) An electron is moving with a kinetic energy of 2.275×10^{-25} J. Calculate its de-Broglie wavelength. (Mass of electron $= 9.1 \times 10^{-31}$kg, $h = 6.6 \times 10^{-34}$ Js)

Hints & Solutions

1. (i) $2n^2$
   (ii) quantised
   (iii) proportional, square
   (iv) probability, maximum
2. (i)→(b), (ii)→(c), (iii)→(b)
3. (a) A - (v), B - (ii), C - (iv)
4. Given, mass of ball = 0.1 kg

   velocity of moving ball = 10 ms^{-1}

   $$\lambda = \frac{h}{mv} = \frac{6.626 \times 10^{-34}\ \text{Js}}{(0.1\ \text{kg})\ (10\ \text{ms}^{-1})} = 6.626 \times 10^{-34}\ \text{m}$$

   $[\because \text{J} = \text{kgm}^2\text{s}^{-2}]$
5. From de-Broglie equation, wavelength, $\lambda = \frac{h}{mv}$. For same wavelength with two different particles, i.e. electron and proton $m_1v_1 = m_2v_2$ (h is constant). Lesser the mass of the particle, greater will be the velocity. Hence, electron will have higher velocity.
6. This is because in this case wavelength is negligible as the mass of car is very high and wavelength is inversely proportional to mass.
7. No, because velocity = 0 and thus, position can be measured accurately.
8. The energy of photon is sufficient to disturb a sub-atomic particle so that there is uncertainty in the measurement of position and momentum of the sub-atomic particle. However, the energy is insufficient to disturb a macroscopic object.
9. $|\psi|^2$ shows the probability of finding the electron at a point with coordinates (x, y, z).
10. Given $\lambda = 3.6\ \text{Å} = 3.6 \times 10^{-10}$ m

    Velocity of photon = Velocity of light

    $$m = \frac{h}{\lambda v} = \frac{6.626 \times 10^{-34}\ \text{Js}}{(3.6 \times 10^{-10}\text{m})\ (3 \times 10^8\ \text{m s}^{-1})}$$

    $$= 6.135 \times 10^{-29}\ \text{kg}$$ [2]
11. Given, velocity of moving electron = 2.05×10^7 m sec^{-1}

    We know that mass of an electron,

    $$m = 9.11 \times 10^{-31}\ \text{kg},$$

    Applying, $\lambda = \frac{h}{mv}$

    $$= \frac{6.626 \times 10^{-34}\ \text{Js}}{(9.11 \times 10^{-31}\ \text{kg})(2.05 \times 10^7\ \text{ms}^{-1})}$$

    $$= 3.5 \times 10^{-11}\ \text{m}$$ [2]
12. Given, velocity of electron = 1.6×10^6 m sec^{-1}

    Mass of electron = 9.11×10^{-31} kg

    Using de-Broglie wavelength, $\lambda = \frac{h}{mv}$

    $$= \frac{6.626 \times 10^{-34}}{9.11 \times 10^{-31} \times 1.6 \times 10^6} = 0.455 \times 10^{-9}\ \text{m}$$

    $$= 455 \times 10^{-12}\ \text{m}$$

    $\Rightarrow \quad \lambda = 455$ pm [2]
13. Given, velocity of neutron = 800 pm

    mass of neutron = 1.675×10^{-27} kg

    Wavelength, $\lambda = \frac{h}{mv}$

    or $$v = \frac{6.626 \times 10^{-34}\ \text{kg m}^2\text{s}^{-1}}{1.675 \times 10^{-27}\ \text{kg} \times 800 \times 10^{-12}\ \text{m}}$$

    $$= 0.494 \times 10^3\ \text{m s}^{-1} = 4.94 \times 10^2\ \text{m s}^{-1}$$ [2]
14. Mass of proton = $\frac{1.008 \times 10^{-3}}{6.02 \times 10^{23}}$ kg = 1.67×10^{-27} kg

    $$\text{KE} = \frac{1}{2}mv^2$$ [1]

    or $$v = \frac{2\text{KE}}{m} = \frac{2 \times 5 \times 10^{-27}}{1.67 \times 10^{-27}} = 5.98$$ [1]
15. The square of the amplitude of the electron wave, i.e. ψ^2 at any point gives probability of finding an electron at that point. Since, the region around the nucleus which represents the electron density at different points is called an orbital, hence the wave function for an electron in an atom is called orbital wave function. [2]
16. $\Delta v = 600 \times \frac{0.005}{100} = 0.03$ ms^{-1}

    Using Heisenberg's uncertainty principle,

    you get, $$\Delta x = \frac{6.6 \times 10^{-34}}{4 \times 3.14 \times 9.1 \times 10^{-31} \times 0.03}$$

    $$= 1.92 \times 10^{-3}\ \text{m}$$ [2]
17. Given, velocity of proton = 4.37×10^5 m sec^{-1}

    Potential difference = 1000 V

    Mass of hockey ball = 0.1 kg

    Wavelength associated with the velocity of hockey ball

    $$\lambda = \frac{h}{mv} = \frac{6.626 \times 10^{-34}\ \text{kg m}^2\text{s}^{-1}}{0.1\ \text{kg} \times 4.37 \times 10^5\ \text{m s}^{-1}}$$

    $$= 15.16 \times 10^{-39}\ \text{m} = 1.516 \times 10^{-38}\ \text{m}$$ [2]
18. Uncertainty in position, $(\Delta x) = 0.1$Å

    $$\Delta x \cdot \Delta P = \frac{h}{4\pi}, \quad \Delta x \cdot m\Delta v = \frac{h}{4\pi} \quad \text{or} \quad \Delta v = \frac{h}{4\pi\Delta xm}$$

    $$\Delta v = \frac{6.626 \times 10^{-34}\ \text{Js}}{4 \times 3.14 \times 0.1 \times 10^{-10}\ \text{m} \times 9.11 \times 10^{-31}\ \text{kg}}$$

    $$= 0.579 \times 10^7\ \text{ms}^{-1} \quad [\because 1\ \text{J} = 1\ \text{kg m}^2\text{s}^{-2}]$$

    $$= 5.79 \times 10^6\ \text{ms}^{-1}$$ [2]
19. Let the uncertainty in position be Δx.

    $\therefore \quad \Delta x = \lambda$ (de-Broglie wavelength)

    Using de-Broglie relationship, $\lambda = h/mv$.

Putting $\lambda = \Delta x$, we get

$$\Delta x = \frac{h}{mv} = \frac{h}{P}$$ [1]

According to Heisenberg's uncertainty principle,

$$\Delta x \cdot \Delta P \approx \frac{h}{4\pi}$$

$$\therefore \quad \frac{h}{P} \times \Delta P \approx \frac{h}{4\pi}$$

or $$\frac{\Delta P}{P} \approx \frac{1}{4\pi} \qquad [\because \Delta x = h/P]$$

Now, $P = m \times v$ ...(i)

and $\Delta P = m \times \Delta v$, so ...(ii)

By dividing equation (ii) by equation (i) we get

$$\frac{\Delta v}{v} \approx \frac{1}{4\pi} \Rightarrow \Delta v \approx \frac{v}{4\pi}$$

Thus, uncertainty in velocity is so large that its velocity is uncertain. [1]

20. If uncertainty principle is applied to an object of mass, say about a milligram (10^{-6}kg), then

$$\Delta v \cdot \Delta x = \frac{h}{4\pi m} \Rightarrow \Delta v \cdot \Delta x = \frac{6.626 \times 10^{-34} \text{ kg m}^2\text{s}^{-1}}{4 \times 3.14 \times 10^{-6} \text{ kg}}$$

$$= 0.52 \times 10^{-28} \text{m}^2\text{s}^{-1}$$

The value of $\Delta v \cdot \Delta x$ obtained is extremely small and is insignificant. Therefore, for milligram sized or heavier objects, the associated uncertainties are hardly of any real consequence. [2]

21. Bohr's theory does not consider the de-Broglie concept of dual nature of electron and also contradicts with the Heisenberg's uncertainty principle, while the Schrodinger equation is based on quantum mechanics which deals with the microscopic objects having both the particle as well as wave like character. [2]

22. Given, $m = 100$ g $= 0.1$ kg

$$v = 100 \text{ km/h} = \frac{100 \times 1000}{60 \times 60} = \frac{1000}{36} \text{ ms}^{-1}$$ [1]

From de-Broglie equation, wavelength,

$$\lambda = \frac{h}{mv} = \frac{6.626 \times 10^{-34} \text{ kgm}^2\text{s}^{-1}}{0.1 \text{ kg} \times \frac{1000}{36} \text{ ms}^{-1}} = 238.5 \times 10^{-36} \text{ m}$$

As the wavelength is very small so wave nature cannot be detected. [2]

23. In general, number of waves in any orbit is

$$\text{Number of waves} = \frac{\text{circumference of orbit}}{\text{wavelength}} = \frac{2\pi r}{\lambda}$$

But, $$\lambda = \frac{h}{mv}$$

$$\text{Number of waves} = \frac{2\pi r}{h/mv} = \frac{2\pi r \cdot mv}{h} = \frac{2\pi (mvr)}{h}$$ [2]

The angular momentum of Bohr's 3rd orbit is

$$mvr = \frac{3h}{2\pi}$$

$$\therefore \text{ Number of waves} = \frac{2\pi}{h} \times \frac{3h}{2\pi} = 3$$

Number of waves in Bohr's 3rd orbit = 3. [1]

24. Refer to text on pages 69 and 70 [Topic-2, Heisenberg's uncertainty principle].

25. (i) In Bohr model, an electron is regarded as a charged particle moving in well defined circular orbits about the nucleus. An orbit can completely be defined only if both the position and the velocity of the electron are known exactly at the same time. This is not possible according to the Heisenberg's uncertainty principle. Further, the wave character of the electron is not considered in Bohr model.

Therefore, concept of movement of an electron in an orbit was replaced by the concept of probability of finding electron in an orbital due to de-Broglie concept of dual nature of electron and Heisenberg's uncertainty principle.

The changed model is called quantum mechanical model of the atom. [3]

(ii) $\lambda_{O_2}/\lambda_{SO_2} = 2$ (because $\lambda = \frac{h}{mv}$, i.e. $\lambda \propto \frac{1}{m}$ and mass of SO_2 molecule *viz.* 64 u, is double than that of O_2 molecule *viz.* 32 u). [2]

26. (i) Given, velocity of beam of helium atoms

$$= 2.0 \times 10^3 \text{ m sec}^{-1}$$

$$\text{Mass of helium atom} = \frac{4}{6.022 \times 10^{23}}$$

$$= 6.64 \times 10^{-24} \text{ g} = 6.64 \times 10^{-27} \text{ kg}$$

According to de-Broglie equation, $\lambda = \frac{h}{mv}$

$$= \frac{6.626 \times 10^{-34} \text{ kg m}^2\text{ s}^{-1}}{(6.64 \times 10^{-27} \text{ kg}) \times (2.0 \times 10^3 \text{ ms}^{-1})}$$

$$= 4.99 \times 10^{-11} \text{ m} = 49.9 \text{ pm}$$ [2]

(ii) Kinetic energy of electron,

$$\frac{1}{2}mv^2 = 2.275 \times 10^{-25} \text{ J}$$

or $$v^2 = \frac{2 \times 2.275 \times 10^{-25}}{9.1 \times 10^{-31}}$$

$$v = 0.707 \times 10^3 \text{ ms}^{-1}$$

Now, $$\lambda = \frac{h}{mv}$$

$$= \frac{6.6 \times 10^{-34} \text{ kg m}^2\text{s}^{-1}}{(9.1 \times 10^{-31} \text{ kg}) \times (0.707 \times 10^3 \text{ m s}^{-1})}$$ [3]

$$= 1.029 \times 10^{-6} \text{ m} = 1029 \text{ nm}$$

TOPIC 03 Quantum Numbers and Electronic Configuration

Quantum Numbers

The characteristics of an orbital are expressed in terms of three numbers, called **principal (n), azimuthal (l)** and **magnetic quantum numbers (m_l)**. These numbers are obtained from the solutions of the Schrodinger wave equation. Further, to represent the spin (rotation) of the electron about its own axis, a fourth quantum number, called **spin quantum number** has been introduced.

Thus, a set of four numbers which give us complete information i.e. location, energy, the type of orbital occupied, shape and orientation of that orbital, etc., about all the electrons present in an atom, is called the **quantum numbers.**

The various quantum numbers are briefly discussed below :

Principal Quantum Number (n)

It determines the size and to a large extent the energy of the orbital.It is always a positive integer with value of $n=1, 2, 3 \ldots$ This quantum number also identifies **shell.** The shell with $n=1$ is called the **first shell.** The shell with $n=2$ is called the **second shell** and so on. The various shells are represented by the following letters :

$$\text{Shell} = K\ L\ M\ N \ldots$$
$$n = 1\ 2\ 3\ 4 \ldots$$

With the help of this quantum number the average distance of the electron from the nucleus can be determined. Distance of the electron from the nucleus, energy and size of orbital increase as the value of principal quantum number 'n' increases. Further with the increase in the value of 'n', the number of allowed orbital increases and are given by 'n^2'

Azimuthal Quantum Number (l)

It determines the angular momentum of the electron and is also known as **orbital angular momentum** or **subsidiary quantum number**. Moreover, it shows the three dimensional shape of the orbital. For a given value of n, the value of l can vary from 0 to $n-1$, i.e. for a given value of n, the possible value of l are $l = 0, 1, 2, \ldots\ldots (n-1)$. e.g. if $n=1$, value of l is only 0.

In each shell there are one or more **subshells** or **sub levels.** The number of subshells in a principal shell is equal to the value of principal quantum number, n.

Each subshell is assigned an azimuthal quantum number (l). Subshells corresponding to different values of l are indicated by the following symbols.

Value for l : 0 1 2 3 4 5…

Notation for subshell : $s\ p\ d\ f\ g\ h \ldots$

Angular momentum of the electron in an orbital

$$= \sqrt{l(l+1)}\ \frac{h}{2\pi} = \sqrt{l(l+1)}\ \hbar$$

The energies of the different subshells present within the same principal shell are found to be in order $s < p < d < f$ i.e. the energy of an electron present in the s-subshell is lower than that present in the p-subshell of the same principal shell. It will be proved later in this section that **In the s, p, d and f-subshells the maximum number of electrons are 2, 6, 10 and 14 respectively.**

Magnetic Quantum Number (m_l)

It shows the behaviour of electron in a magnetic field. It gives information related to the spatial orientation of the orbital with respect to standard set of coordinate axis.

For a given value of l (subshell), $2l+1$ values are possible for m_l. These values are given by

$m_l = -l, -(l-1), -(l-2) \ldots 0, 1 \ldots (l-2), (l-1), l.$

Thus, the value of m varies from $-l$ to $+l$ including zero. i.e. for s-subshell ($l=0$), $m=0$, i.e. only one orientation is possible which means s-subshell consists of only one orbital.

For p-subshell ($l=1$), $m = -1, 0, +1$, i.e. three different orientations (i.e. along X-axis, Y-axis and Z-axis) are possible in case of p-subshell which means that p-subshell contains three orbitals.

Likewise, d-subshell contains five orbitals and f-subshell contains seven orbitals.

Thus, it can also be said that the magnetic quantum number gives the number of orbitals present in a given subshell. The following chart gives the relation between the subshell and the number of orbitals present with in it.

Value of l	0	1	2	3	4	5
Subshell notation	s	p	d	f	g	h
Number of orbitals	1	3	5	7	9	11

Spin Quantum Number (s)

A fourth quantum number called the **electron spin quantum number** (m_s) is introduced to explain the line spectra of multielectron atoms. An electron spins around its own axis like earth spins around its own axis, thus, has intrinsic spin angular quantum number, which is a vector quantity and can have two orientations relative to the chosen axis.

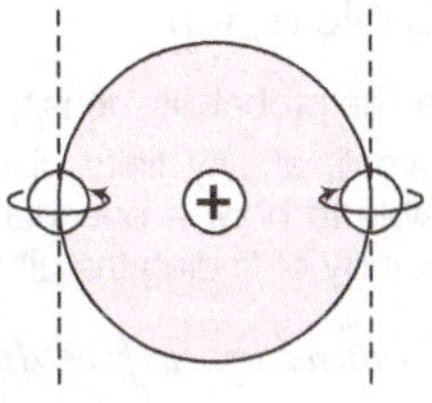

Spinning of electrons

To distinguish between these two orientations, two values $+1/2$ or $-1/2$ are assigned to the spin quantum number, m_s. These are known as the two spin states of the electron and are generally represented by two arrows, ↑ (spin up) and ↓ (spin down).

Two electrons having different m_s values (one $+1/2$ and the other $-1/2$) are said to have opposite spins. Thus, an orbital can hold a maximum of two electrons with opposite spins. The magnitude of spin angular momentum can be calculated from the following formula:

$$\text{Spin angular momentum} = \sqrt{s(s+1)}\,\frac{h}{2\pi}$$

Note • *Number of subshells in n^{th} shell = n*

- *Number of orbitals in a subshell = $2l + 1$,*
- *Maximum number of electrons in a subshell = $2(2l + 1)$*
- *Number of orbitals in n^{th} shell = n^2,*
- *Maximum number of electrons in n^{th} shell = $2n^2$.*

Example 1 Using *s, p, d, f* notations describe the orbital with the following quantum numbers : **NCERT Textbook**

(i) $n = 2, l = 1$, (ii) $n = 4, l = 0$, (iii) $n = 5, l = 3$, (iv) $n = 3, l = 2$

Sol.

	n	l	Orbital
(i)	2	1	$2p$
(ii)	4	0	$4s$
(iii)	5	3	$5f$
(iv)	3	2	$3d$

Orbital-wave Functions, Probability Distributions

An orbital wave functions (ψ) can be written as product of two functions, the **radial function** and the **angular function.** The radial function is function of distance only while the angular function of two angle variables.

$$\psi = R(r)\,A(\theta, \phi)$$

In other words, the complete wave function represents an orbital in which the radial part $R(r)$ depends upon quantum numbers n and l. It tells us about the size of orbital. Whereas, the angular part $A(\theta, \phi)$ depends upon quantum number l and m_l and tells about the shape of the orbital.

Radial Wave Functions

The shapes of orbitals can also be obtained from the variation of wave function ψ as a function of r (distance from the nucleus). It is also called **radial dependence** or **radial wave function.** This can be shown by just plotting a graph between wave function (ψ) and distance (r) from the nucleus.

These graphs for $1s$, $2s$ and $2p$-orbitals are shown in the figure given below. Figure (a) clearly reveals that wave function for $1s$ orbital continuously decreases as the value of r increases. However, in case of $2s$ orbital [figure (b)], the wave function first decreases, becomes zero at a particular distance and then becomes negative.

The wave function in case of $2p$-orbital [figure (c)] first increases to maximum and then decreases.

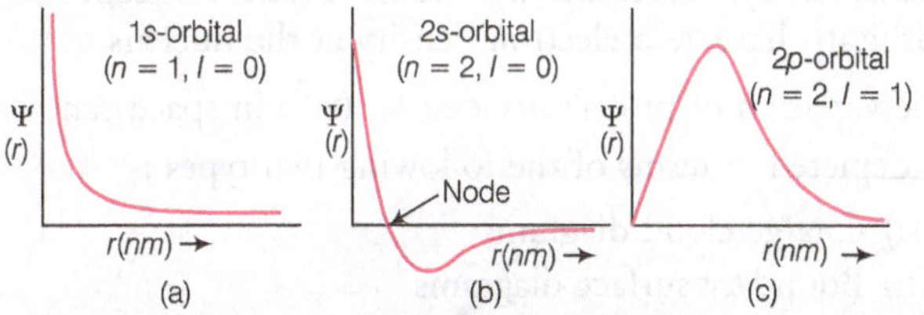

Plots of wave function (ψ) with distance from the nucleus for (a) 1s-orbital (b) 2s-orbital (c) 2p-orbital

In case of $2s$-orbital, the point, at which wave function becomes zero is called radial nodal surface or simply node. At this point, the value of wave function gets inverted, i.e. becomes negative from positive. In general, it has been found that there are $(n-1)$ nodes for ns orbitals, $(n-2)$ nodes for np orbitals and so on, e.g. the radial wave function of $2p$-orbital has no node as shown in the above figure.

It is also interesting to note that the value of $2s$ wave function can be positive or negative depending upon the distance from the nucleus. Here, **positive and negative signs refer to the sign of the wave function and are not related with the positive and negative charges.**

In all cases ψ approaches zero as r approaches infinity.

Probability Density (ψ^2) Graphs

German physicist, Max Born suggested that the probability density of the electron at any point is obtained by the square of the wave function (i.e. ψ^2) at that point. The variation of ψ^2 as a function of r for $1s$ and $2s$-orbitals is shown in figure below.

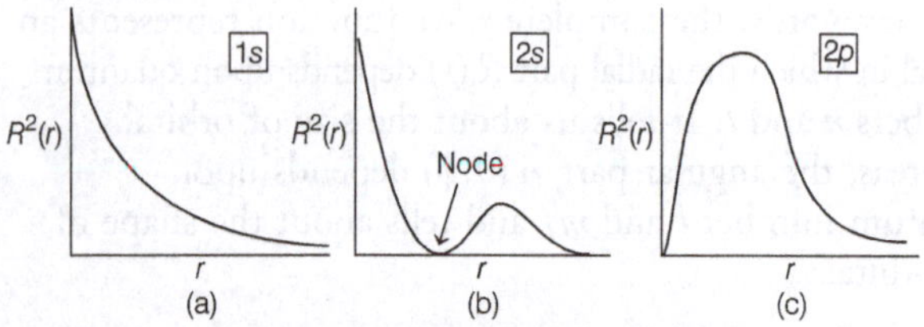

Variation of probability density Ψ^2 as a function of distance r of the electron from the nucleus.

Here again, the curves for 1*s* and 2*s*-orbitals are different. These graphs are known as **probability density graphs.**

From the graph (a), it is obvious that for 1*s*-orbital the probability density is maximum at the nucleus and then decreases sharply as the distance further increases. However, in case of 2*s*-orbital, it first decreases sharply upto zero and then again starts increasing. After reaching a small maxima, it decreases again and approaches zero as the value of *r* increases further. The region at which this probability density function reduced to zero is called **nodal surfaces or simply nodes.** Always remember that all the orbitals (except *s*-orbital) have zero electron density at the nucleus.

The variation of probability density (ψ^2) in space can be depicted in terms of the following two types :

(i) Charge cloud diagrams
(ii) Boundary surface diagrams

1. Charge Cloud Diagram

In charge cloud diagrams, the probability density (ψ^2) is shown as "collection of dots in such a way that density of dots represents the electron probability density in that region.

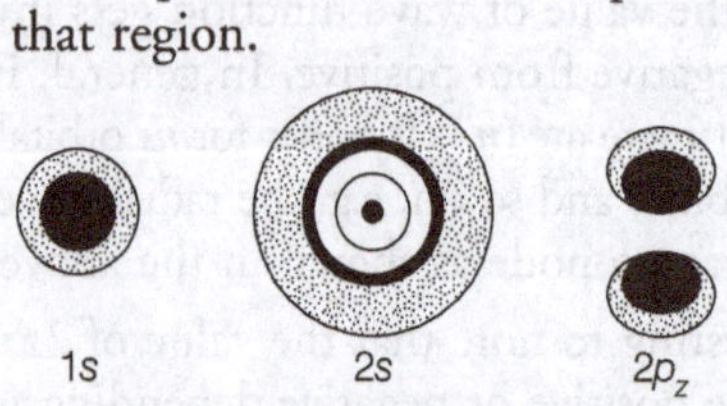

Charge cloud diagrams for 1s, 2s and $2p_z$ atomic orbitals

2. Boundary Surface Diagrams

In these diagrams, the density of the dots in a region shows the electron probability density in that region. Although several such boundary surface diagrams may be possible but the shape of an orbital is given by only that boundary surface diagram where the probability density is constant, i.e. which encloses a region or volume of about 90% probability of finding the electron. In other words, boundary surface diagrams shows the most probable region.

Note The probability density $|\psi|^2$ has always some value, however it may be, small, at any finite distance from the nucleus. It is therefore, not possible to draw a boundary surface diagram of a rigid size where the probability of finding the electron is 100%.

The boundary surface diagrams of some orbitals are discussed below :

(i) **Shapes of *s*-orbitals** Boundary surface diagram of a *s*-orbital is actually a sphere centred on the nucleus. In two dimensions, it looks like a circle which encloses a region where probability of finding the electron is about 90%.

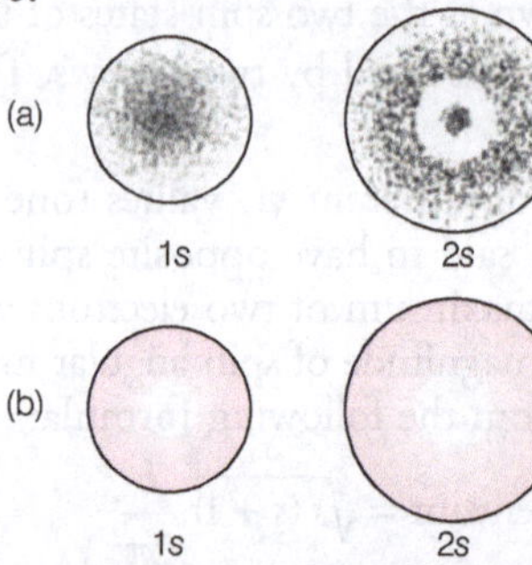

(a) probability density plots of 1s and 2s atomic orbitals
(b) boundary surface diagram for 1s and 2s orbitals

Thus, **the shape of all the *s*-orbitals are spherical,** i.e. there is equal probability of finding the electron at a given distance in all the directions further. It is also observed that the size of the *s*-orbital increases as the value of *n* increases. Thus, the order of size of *s*-orbital is $4s > 3s > 2s > 1s$.

(ii) **Shapes of *p*-orbitals** Boundary surface diagrams for three 2*p*-orbitals ($l = 1$) are given in the figure given below. In these diagrams, the nucleus is at the origin. Each *p*-orbital have two sections which are called its **lobes.**

These lobes lie on either side of the plane that passes through the nucleus. The probability density function is zero at the place where the two lobes touch each other.

These **three *p*-orbitals are identical in size, shape and energy but differ in orientation of lobes.** Since, the lobes may be considered to lie along the *x*, *y* or z-axis, they are represented by $2p_x, 2p_y$ and $2p_z$.

The size and energy of *p*-orbitals increases as the value of principal quantum number *n* increases.

Thus, the order of the energy and size of various *p*-orbitals is $4p > 3p > 2p$.

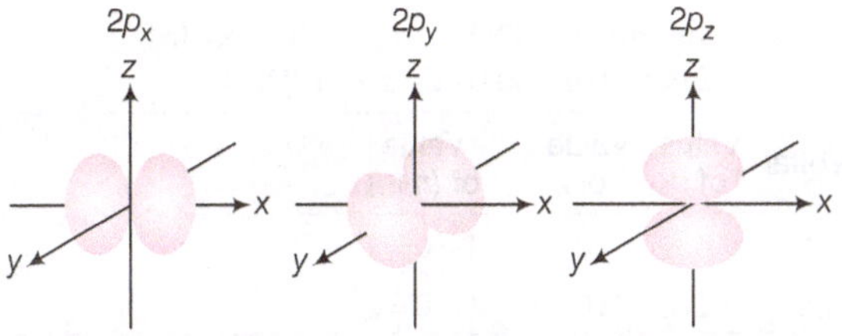

Boundary surface diagrams of the three 2p-orbitals

Further, like *s*-orbitals, the probability density functions for *p*-orbital also pass through value zero, besides at zero and infinite distance, as the distance from the nucleus increases.

(iii) **Shapes of *d*-orbitals** $l = 2$ shows *d*-orbital and the minimum value of principal quantum number (n) for which is 3. [This is because the value of l cannot be greater than $n-1$). For $l = 2$, m_l have five values($-2, -1, 0, +1$ and $+2$) thus, there are five *d*-orbitals. The boundary surface diagram of these five *d*-orbitals are given below:

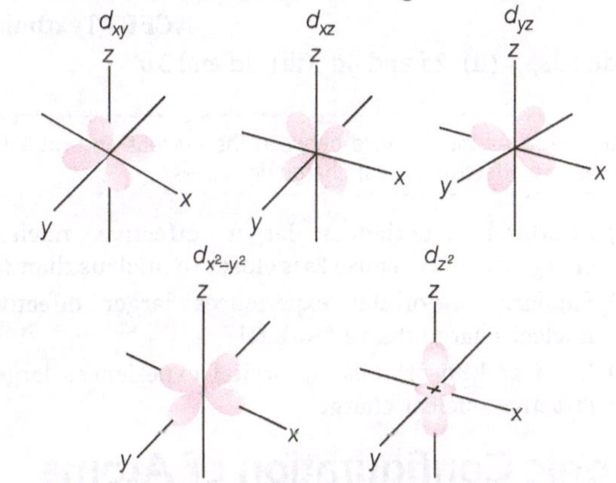

Boundary surface diagrams of the five 3d-orbitals.

The five *d*-orbitals are designated as d_{xy}, d_{yz}, d_{xz}, $d_{x^2-y^2}$ and d_{z^2} and are of equal energy, i.e. degenerate. The first four *d*-orbitals have similar shape but the shape of fifth one, i.e. d_{z^2} is different from that of the other. *d*-orbitals having higher value of *n*, i.e. ($4d, 5d$ ...) also have shapes similar to $3d$-orbital, but differ in energy and size.

Nodes and Nodal Planes

As we have discussed earlier, the place or point where radial wave function passes through zero are called **nodes or radial nodes.** Its value is obtained by the expression ($n - l - 1$)

e.g. $2s$ has one node ($2-0-1=1$), $3s$ has two nodes ($3-0-1=2$) and so on. In case of np and nd orbitals, the probability density functions are zero at the plane(s) passing through the nucleus (origin).

These nodes are called **angular nodes** e.g. for p_z-orbital, *xy*-plane is a nodal plane, for d_{xy}-orbital there are two nodal planes passing through the origin and bisecting the *xy*-plane containing *Z*-axis. The number of angular nodes are equal to 'l', i.e. one angular node for *p*-orbitals, two angular nodes for *d*-orbitals and so on.

In general, in an orbital Total number of nodes $= n - 1$

Number of angular nodes $= l$

Number of radial nodes $= n - l - 1$

Energies of Orbitals

Energies of different orbitals of hydrogen and hydrogen like particles depend only upon the value of principal quantum number (n) but in case of multielectron atoms it depends upon the principal quantum number (n) as well as on the azimuthal quantum number (l).

1. For H-Atom and H-like Atoms

The energy of an electron in a hydrogen atom is determined by the principal quantum number. Thus, the increasing order of energy of different orbitals is

$1s < 2s = 2p < 3s = 3p = 3d < 4s = 4p = 4d = 4f$. It is shown in figure below. Although the $2s$ and $2p$-orbitals differ in shapes, yet an electron present in these orbitals must possess the same energy.

The orbitals of the same subshell having the same energy are called **degenerate orbitals.**

In the case of hydrogen atom, there is only one electron and therefore, no shielding effect. The only electrical interaction present in hydrogen atom is the attraction between the negatively charged electron and the positively charged nucleus. As a consequence, the different orbitals (*s, p, d* and *f*) of the same energy level possess the same energies.

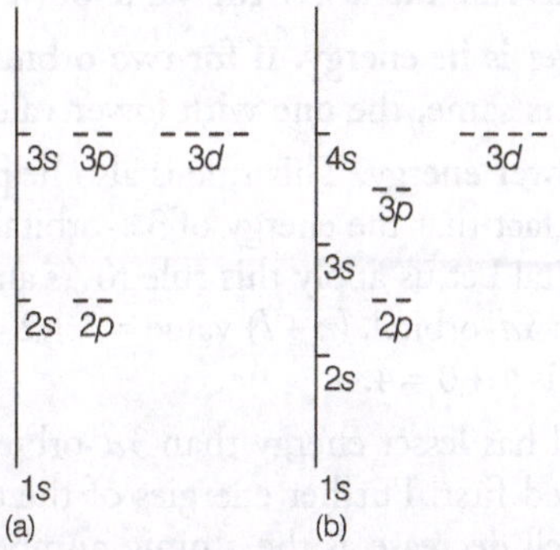

Energy level diagrams for the few electronic shells of [a] hydrogen atom and [b] multi-electronic atoms.

The 1s-orbital in a hydrogen atom corresponds to the most stable condition and is called the **ground state.** The electron residing in this orbital experience lowest energy and is most strongly held by the nucleus.

If the electron is present in the $2s, 2p$ or higher orbitals in a hydrogen atom, it is said to be in **excited state.** It is an unstable state which is not possible under ordinary conditions.

2. For Multielectron Atoms

In these atoms, for different subshells, the energy is different. The main reason for having different energies of the subshells is the mutual repulsion among the electrons.

In general, the energy of an electron in an orbital is affected by the nuclear charge, principle energy level and the presence of electrons in the lower energy levels.Thus, the shielding of the outer shell electrons from the nucleus by the inner shell electrons is called **shielding or screening effect.**

This effect is different in different type of orbitals. The net positive charge experienced by the electron from the nucleus is called **effective nuclear charge** (Z_{eff}) and decreases with increasing shielding effect. The order of shielding (also in case of orbitals of same shell) is $s > p > d > f$.

Thus, the electron present in a s-orbital will be more tightly bound to the nucleus as compared to that which is present in p-orbital. A p-orbital electron will be more tightly bound than the d-orbital electron. Hence, the energy of electrons in s-orbital will be lower (more negative) than that of the p-orbital electron which will be lower than that of d-orbital electron and so on.

$(n + l)$ Rule

According to this rule **the lower the value of $(n + l)$ for an orbital, the lower is its energy. If for two orbitals, the value of $(n + l)$ is same, the one with lower value of n will have the lower energy.** This rule is also helpful to account for the fact that the energy of 3d-orbital is higher than the 4s-orbital.Let us apply this rule to 4s and 3d-orbitals. For 3d-orbital, $(n + l)$ value $= 3 + 2 = 5$ while for 4s-orbital it is $4 + 0 = 4$.

Thus, 4s-orbital has lesser energy than 3d-orbital and, therefore, is filled first. Further energies of the orbitals in the same subshell decrease as the atomic number (Z) increases, e.g. energy of 2s-orbital of hydrogen atom is greater than that of 2s-orbital of lithium and that of lithium is greater than that of sodium and so on, i.e. $E_{2s}(\text{H}) > E_{2s}(\text{Li}) > E_{2s}(\text{Na}) > E_{2s}(\text{K})$.

Arrangement of Orbitals with Increasing Energy on the Basis of $(n+l)$ Rule

Orbital	Value of n	Value of l	Value of $(n+l)$	
1s	1	0	$1+0=1$	
2s	2	0	$2+0=2$	
2p	2	1	$2+1=3$	2p(n = 2) has lower energy than
3s	3	0	$3+0=3$	3s(n = 3)
3p	3	1	$3+1=4$	3p(n = 3) has lower energy than
4s	4	0	$4+0=4$	4s(n = 4)
3d	3	2	$3+2=5$	3d(n = 3) has lower energy than
4p	4	1	$4+1=5$	4p(n = 4)

Example 2 Among the following pairs of orbitals, which orbital will experience the larger effective nuclear charge? **NCERT Textbook**

(i) 2s and 3s, (ii) 2d and 4d (iii) 3d and 3p

Key Idea As the distance between the nucleus and orbital increases, effective nuclear charge decreases.

Sol. (i) 2s-orbital experiences larger effective nuclear charge than 3s because 2s is closer to nucleus than 3s.

(ii) Similarly, 4d-orbital experiences larger effective nuclear charge than 4f-orbital.

(iii) In 3d and 3p-orbitals, 3p-orbital experiences larger effective nuclear charge.

Electronic Configuration of Atoms

The distribution of electrons into orbitals of an atom is called its **electronic configuration.** The way to assign the electronic configuration of different atoms is as follows :

$s^a p^b d^c$ ... **notation** In it, the letter symbol shows subshell and the superscript such as a, b, c,... etc., shows, the number of electrons present in the subshell.

The similar subshell represented for different shells is differentiated by writing the principal quantum number before the respective subshell.

Alternatively, the electronic configuration of any orbital can be simply represented by the notation nl^x, where n = principal quantum number or number of the main or principal shell, l = symbol of the subshell or orbital, i.e. s, p, d, f and x = number of electrons present in that orbital.

Thus, $4p^1$ means that one electron is present in p-subshell of the 4th main shell.

Rules for Filling of Electrons in Different Orbitals

The filling of electrons in different orbitals is governed by the following rules :

1. Aufbau Principle

According to this principle, in the ground state of the atoms, the orbitals are filled in increasing order of energies, i.e. electrons first occupy the lowest energy orbital available to them and then enter into higher energy orbitals provided that the lower energy orbitals are completely occupied.

Hence, the order in which the orbitals are filled is $1s, 2s, 2p, 3s, 3p, 4s, 3d, 4p, 5s, 4d, 5p, 6s, 4f, 5d, 6p, 7s \ldots$.

You can also remember the above order by using the method given in the following figure. Starting from the top, the direction of the arrows shows the order of filling of orbitals, which is starting from right top to bottom left.

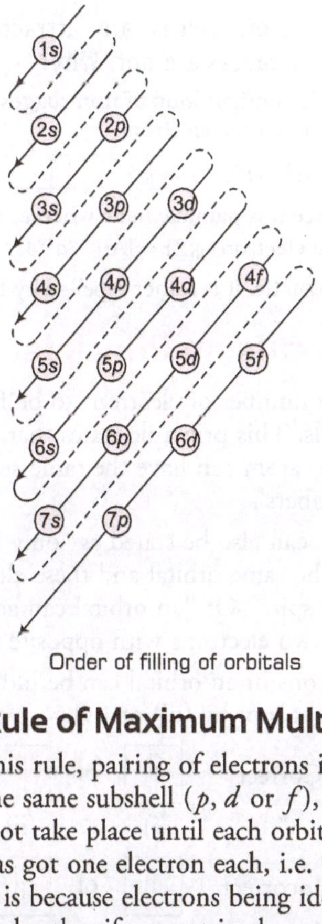

Order of filling of orbitals

2. Hund's Rule of Maximum Multiplicity

According to this rule, pairing of electrons in the orbitals belonging to the same subshell (p, d or f), i.e. degenerate orbitals, does not take place until each orbital belonging to that subshell has got one electron each, i.e. it is singly occupied. This is because electrons being identical in charge, repel each other if present in the same orbital. The repulsion can be minimised if two electrons move as far apart as possible by occupying different degenerate orbitals or if they have parallel spins (of course in different orbitals). e.g. the electronic configuration of nitrogen having atomic number 7 can be written as

(i) 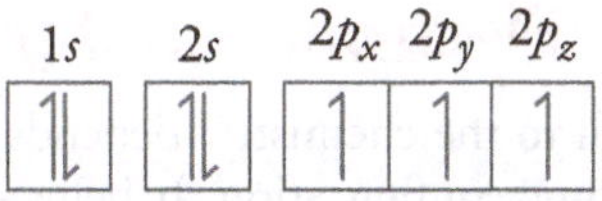

Total spin of unpaired electrons $= \frac{1}{2} + \frac{1}{2} + \frac{1}{2} = 1\frac{1}{2}$

(ii) 

Total spin of unpaired electrons $= +\frac{1}{2} - \frac{1}{2} + \frac{1}{2} = \frac{1}{2}$

(iii) 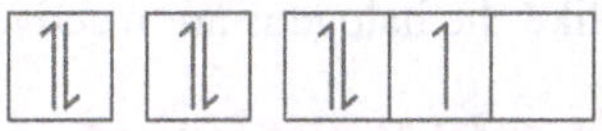

Total spin $= 1/2$

The term maximum multiplicity, means the total spin of unpaired electrons is maximum.

e.g. the total spin of the unpaired electrons in configurations (i), (ii), and (iii) are respectively $1\frac{1}{2}, \frac{1}{2}$ and $\frac{1}{2}$. Thus, configuration (i) with maximum multiplicity of $1\frac{1}{2}$ is correct according to Hund's rule of maximum multiplicity.

Example 3 Which of the following representation of electronic configuration is excluded by the Aufbau principle ? Which by the Pauli exclusion principle ? Which by Hund's rule ? Which is correct ? Explain how a principle or rule is violated in the others.

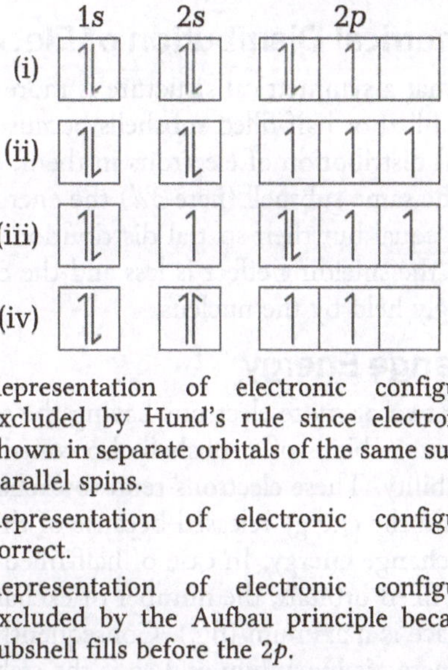

Sol. (i) Representation of electronic configuration is excluded by Hund's rule since electrons are not shown in separate orbitals of the same subshell with parallel spins.

(ii) Representation of electronic configuration is correct.

(iii) Representation of electronic configuration is excluded by the Aufbau principle because the $2s$ subshell fills before the $2p$.

(iv) Representation of electronic configuration is excluded by the Pauli exclusion principle since the two electrons in the $2s$-orbital cannot have the same spin.

Significance of Electronic Configuration

The modern approach to the chemistry, depends almost entirely on the electronic configuration. It helps us to answer the following questions:

(i) Why two or more atoms combine to form molecules?

(ii) Why some elements are metals while others are non-metals or metalloids?

(iii) Why elements like helium and argon are not reactive but elements like the halogens are reactive?

Stability of Completely Filled and Half-Filled Subshells

Most of the atoms follow the basic rules to write their electronic configuration. However, in certain elements like Cu, or Cr, in which the energy of two subshells (4*s* and 3*d*) is only slightly different, an electron shifts from a subshell of lower energy (4*s*) to a subshells of higher energy (3*d*), if such a shifting results in either completely filled or half-filled orbitals of the subshell of higher energy. The valence shell electronic configurations of Cr and Cu, therefore, are $3d^5, 4s^1$ and $3d^{10}, 4s^1$ respectively and not $3d^4, 4s^2$ and $3d^9 4s^1$. It has been found that these configurations are more stable as compared to the former one. The more stability of completely filled and completely half-filled subshells is because of the following reasons.

1. Symmetrical Distribution of Electrons

We know that a symmetrical structure is more stable. The completely filled or half-filled subshells because of the symmetrical distribution of electrons in them, are more stable. In the same subshell (here 3*d*) the energy of electrons is equal but their spatial distribution is different. As a result, the shielding effect is less and the electrons are more strongly held by the nucleus.

2. Exchange Energy

Presence of two or more electrons having the same spin in the degenerate orbitals of a subshell also contributes towards stability. These electrons tend to exchange their positions and the energy released because of this exchange is called **exchange energy**. In case of half-filled or completely filled orbitals, the number of exchanges that can take place is maximum (fig.). Consequently the exchange energy is maximum and so is the stability. Here it is also interesting to notify that exchange energy is based on Hund 's rule which states that electrons when enter in orbitals of equal energy have parallel spins as far as possible.

In other words, it can be said that the extra stability of half-filled and completely filled subshell is because of (i) relatively small shielding, (ii) smaller coulombic repulsion energy and (iii) larger exchange energy. [More details about the exchange energy you will read in higher classes.]

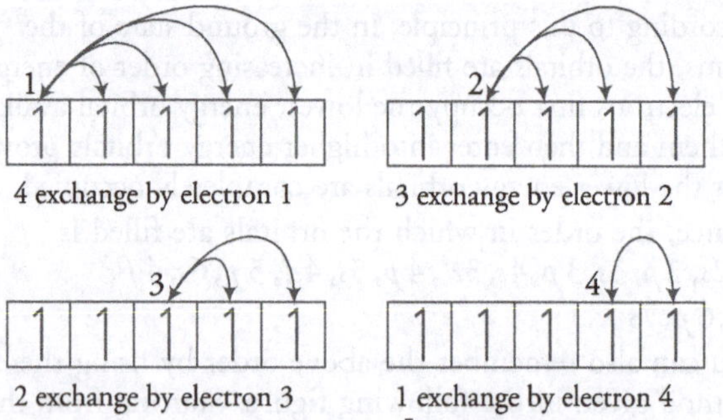

Possible exchanges for a d^5-configuration

Example 4 Iron pieces are attracted towards a magnet but zinc pieces are not. Why?

Sol. Electronic configuration of iron suggests that it contains unpaired electrons

$({}_{26}Fe = [Ar]^{18} 3d^6 4s^2) =$ 

and hence it is paramagnetic whereas zinc has no unpaired electron $({}_{30}Zn = [Ar]^{18} 3d^{10} 4s^2)$ and hence, it is diamagnetic. It is rather repelled by the magnet.

Pauli's Exclusion Principle

It restricts the number of electrons to be filled in various orbitals. This principle states that, 'No two electrons in an atom can have the same set of four quantum numbers'.

This principle can also be stated as "only two electrons may exist in the same orbital and these electrons must have opposite spin." Or "an orbital can accommodate a maximum of two electrons with opposite spins".

e.g. two electrons in an orbital can be indicated either by (i) or (ii) but, not by (iii) or (iv).

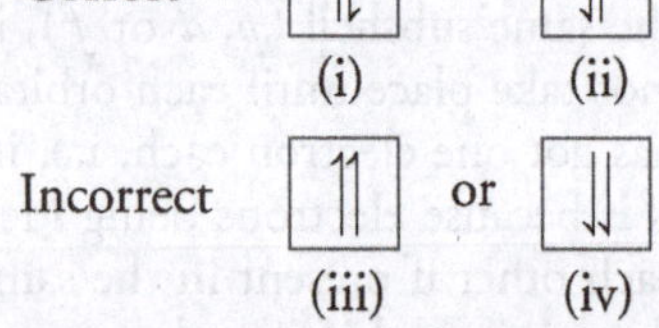

It means that, if for two electrons the three quantum numbers *n*, *l* and m_l, have same value, the value of fourth quantum number, i.e. spin quantum number is different, i.e. +1/2 for one and −1/2 for other.

This restriction in the filling of electrons in an orbital helps in calculating the capacity of electrons to be present in any subshell e.g. in 1*s* subshell there is only one orbital and hence, the maximum number of electrons present in 1*s* subshell are two.

Similarly, in *p* and *d* subshells with 3 and 5-orbitals respectively, the maximum number of electrons are 6 and 10 and so on. Thus, the rule can be summed up as "**the maximum number of electrons present in a shell with principal quantum number *n* is equal to $2n^2$.**"

The Electronic Configuration of the Elements

Atomic number	Symbol	Electronic configuration	Atomic number	Symbol	Electronic configuration
1	H	$1s^1$	19	K	$[Ar]\ 4s^1$
2	He	$1s^2$	20	Ca	$[Ar]\ 4s^2$
3	Li	$[He]2s^1$	21	Sc	$[Ar]\ 4s^2 3d^1$
4	Be	$[He]2s^2$	22	Ti	$[Ar]\ 4s^2 3d^2$
5	B	$[He]2s^2 2p^1$	23	V	$[Ar]\ 4s^2 3d^3$
6	C	$[He]2s^2 2p^2$	24	Cr	$[Ar]\ 4s^1 3d^5$
7	N	$[He]2s^2 2p^3$	25	Mn	$[Ar]\ 4s^2 3d^5$
8	O	$[He]2s^2 2p^4$	26	Fe	$[Ar]\ 4s^2 3d^6$
9	F	$[He]2s^2 2p^5$	27	Co	$[Ar]\ 4s^2 3d^7$
10	Ne	$[He]2s^2 2p^6$	28	Ni	$[Ar]\ 4s^2 3d^8$
11	Na	$[Ne]\ 3s^1$	29	Cu	$[Ar]\ 4s^1 3d^{10}$
12	Mg	$[Ne]\ 3s^2$	30	Zn	$[Ar]\ 4s^2 3d^{10}$
13	Al	$[Ne]\ 3s^2 3p^1$	31	Ga	$[Ar]\ 4s^2 3d^{10} 4p^1$
14	Si	$[Ne]\ 3s^2 3p^2$	32	Ge	$[Ar]\ 4s^2 3d^{10} 4p^2$
15	P	$[Ne]\ 3s^2 3p^3$	33	As	$[Ar]\ 4s^2 3d^{10} 4p^3$
16	S	$[Ne]\ 3s^2 3p^4$	34	Se	$[Ar]\ 4s^2 3d^{10} 4p^4$
17	Cl	$[Ne]\ 3s^2 3p^5$	35	Br	$[Ar]\ 4s^2 3d^{10} 4p^5$
18	Ar	$[Ne]\ 3s^2 3p^6$	36	Kr	$[Ar]\ 4s^2 3d^{10} 4p^6$

Electronic Configuration of Ions

The electronic configuration of the ions may also be written almost in the same manner as that for atoms. However, in case of negatively charged ions, the extra electrons equal to the charge are added to the outermost orbital after writing the electronic configuration of atom. e.g. Cl ($Z = 17$) :

$$1s^2\ 2s^2\ 2p^6\ 3s^2\ 3p_x^2\ 3p_y^2\ 3p_z^1$$

$$Cl^- (Z = 17 + 1 = 18) : 1s^2\ 2s^2\ 2p^6\ 3s^2\ 3p_x^2\ 3p_y^2\ 3p_z^2$$

In case of positively charged ions, the electrons equal to the charge on the ion are removed from the configuration of neutral atom. Here, remember that always remove the electrons having the highest value of *n* first. If there are more than one subshell of the valence shell, the one with the highest value of *l* loses the electron first.

e.g. $Mg\ (Z = 12)\ :\ 1s^2\ 2s^2, 2p^6 3s^2$

$Mg^{2+}\ (Z = 12) :\ 1s^2\ 2s^2, 2p^6$

$Fe (Z = 26)\ :$

$1s^2\ 2s^2, 2p^6, 3s^2, 3p^6, 3d^6, 4s^2$

$Fe^{2+}\ (Z = 26) :$

$1s^2\ 2s^2, 2p^6, 3s^2, 3p^6, 3d^6$

Thus, in case of Fe^{2+} ion, the electrons are removed from 4*s*-orbital first (highest value of *n*) and not from 3*d*-orbitals.

The electronic configuration of elements can also be represented by using **orbital diagram.** In this notation, box is used to represent each orbital of the subshell and an arrow [with positive (↑) or negative (↓) spins] represents the electron. e.g.

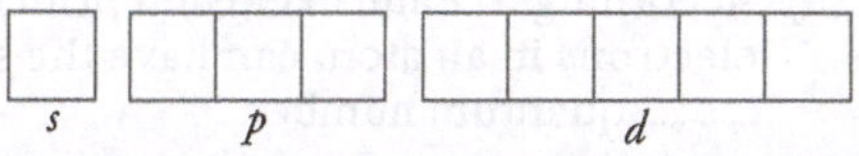

The advantage of this notation over the other is that it shows all the four quantum numbers. e.g. hydrogen atom contains only one electron which enters in the orbital with the lowest energy, namely 1*s*.

Thus, the electronic configuration of the hydrogen atom = $1s^1$. Helium (He) contains two electrons. The first electron enters in 1*s*-orbital like H-atom. The second electron can also occupy the 1*s*-orbital. Thus, its configuration = $1s^2$.

The orbital diagram for these two atoms are as

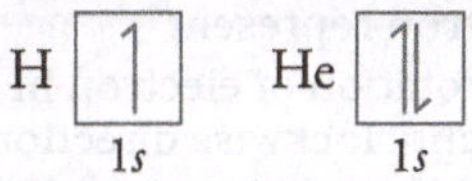

(As electrons must have opposite spin)

Nitrogen (Atomic number = 7) The seventh electron in case of nitrogen enters in $2p_z$ orbital.

N ($Z=7$) $1s^2\,2s^2\,2p_x^1\,2p_y^1\,2p_z^1$ or

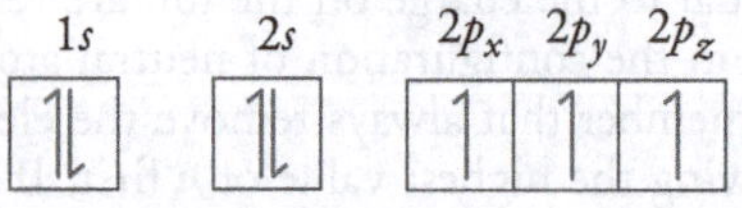

The electrons present in the completely filled shells are called **core electrons** and the electrons that are added to the electronic shell with the highest principal quantum number are called the **valence electrons**.e.g.
Na $=[\text{Ne}]\,3s^1 = 1s^2, 2s^2, 2p^6, 3s^1$.

The electrons present in Ne-atom (or $1s^2, 2s^2, 2p^6$) are the core electrons and the electrons present in 3rd shell are the valence electrons.

Topic Practice 3

Very Short Answer Type Questions

1 Mark

1 Fill in the Blanks

(i) Number of orbitals in a subshell is equal to ....

(ii) According to Pauli exclusion principle "no two electrons in an atom can have the same set of .... quantum number.

(iii) Spin quantum number refer to orientation of the electron, i.e. clockwise or ....

(iv) The region at which this probability density function reduced to .... is called nodal surfaces.

2 Objective Type Questions

(i) Among the following sets of quantum numbers, which one is incorrect for 4*d*-electron?

(a) $4, 3, 2, +\frac{1}{2}$ (b) $4, 2, 1, +\frac{1}{2}$

(c) $4, 2, -2, +\frac{1}{2}$ (d) $4, 2, 1, -\frac{1}{2}$

(ii) The spin quantum numbers $+\frac{1}{2}$ and $-\frac{1}{2}$ for an electron represent

(a) rotation of electron in clockwise and anticlockwise direction respectively

(b) rotation of electron in anticlockwise and clockwise direction respectively

(c) magnetic moment of electron pointing up and down respectively

(d) two quantum mechanical spin states which have no classical analogue

(iii) A Mo atom in its ground state has $4d^5, 5s^1$ configuration and a Ag atom has configuration. This is because a shell which is half-filled or completely filled is particularly

(a) strongly exchange stabilised

(b) weakly exchange stabilised

(c) weakly exchange destabilised

(d) strongly exchange destabilised

(iv) In a set of degenerate orbitals, the electrons distribute themselves to retain like spins as far as possible. This statement belongs to

(a) Pauli's exclusion principle

(b) Aufbau principle

(c) Hund's rule of maximum multiplicity

(d) Slater's rule

3 Matching the following rules with their statements and choose the correct option using the codes given below.

	Rules		Statements
A.	Hund's Rule	(i)	No two electrons in an atom can have the same set of four quantum numbers.
B.	Aufbau Principle	(ii)	Half-filled and completely filled orbitals have extra stability.
C.	Pauli Exclusion Principle	(iii)	Pairing of electrons in the orbitals belonging to the same subshell does not take place until each orbital is singly occupied.
D.	Heisenberg's Uncertainty Principle	(iv)	It is impossible to determine the exact position and exact momentum of a subatomic particle simultaneously.
		(v)	In the ground state of atoms, orbitals are filled in the order of their increasing energies.

Codes

	A	B	C	D		A	B	C	D
(a)	(i)	(iii)	(iv)	(ii)	(b)	(i)	(ii)	(iii)	(iv)
(c)	(iii)	(v)	(i)	(iv)	(d)	(v)	(i)	(iii)	(ii)

4 Calculate the total number of angular nodes and radial nodes present in 3*p*-orbital.
NCERT Exemplar

5 What is lowest value of *n* that allows *g* orbitals to exist?

6 Which of the following orbitals are degenerate?
$3d_{xy}, 4d_{xy}, 3d_{z^2}, 3d_{yz}, 4d_{yz}\ 4d_{z^2}$
NCERT Exemplar

7 Show the distribution of electrons in oxygen atom (atomic number 8) using orbital diagram. **NCERT Exemplar**

8 The bromine atom possesses 35 electrons. It contains 6 electrons in $2p$-orbital, 6 electrons in $3p$-orbital and 5 electrons in $4p$-orbital. Which of these electron experiences the lowest effective nuclear charge?

9 Arrange *s*, *p* and *d*-subshells of a shell in the increasing order of effective nuclear charge (Z_{eff}) experienced by the electron present in the nucleus.

10 Nickel atom can lose two electrons and form Ni^{2+} ion. The atomic number of Ni is 28. From which orbital will nickel lose two electrons? **NCERT Exemplar**

11 Write the values of the quantum number *n*, *l*, *m* and *s* for electron filling 21st place in the atom of element with atomic number 24.

12 In which atom, the outermost electron can have the following set of quantum numbers?
$n = 3, l = 0, m_l = 0, m_s = -1/2$

Short Answer Type I Questions

2 Marks

13 Using *s*, *p*, *d* notations, describe the orbital with the following quantum numbers :
(i) $n = 1, l = 0$ (ii) $n = 3, l = 1$
(iii) $n = 4, l = 2$ (iv) $n = 4, l = 3$. **NCERT Textbook**

14 Which orbital in each of the following pairs is lower in energy in a many electron atom?
(i) $2s, 2p$ (ii) $3p, 3d$ (iii) $3s, 4s$ (iv) $4d, 5f$

15 (i) How many subshells are associated with $n = 4$?
(ii) How many electrons will be present in the subshell having m_s value of $-1/2$ for $n = 4$?

16 Discuss the similarities and differences between 1s and 2s-orbitals.

17 Hydrogen atom has only one electron, so mutual repulsion between electrons is absent. However, in multielectron atoms mutual repulsion between the electrons is significant. How does this affect the energy of an electron in the orbitals of the same principal quantum number in multielectron atom?

18 An atom of an element contains 29 electrons and 35 neutrons. Deduce
(i) the number of protons. **NCERT Textbook**
(ii) the electronic configuration of the element.

19 Write the electronic configuration of $_9F^{19}$, $_{16}S^{32}$ and $_{18}Ar^{38}$ and then point out the element with
(i) maximum nuclear charge.
(ii) minimum number of neutrons.
(iii) maximum number of unpaired electrons.

20 The unpaired electrons in Al and Si are present in $3p$-orbital. Which electron will experience more effective nuclear charge from the nucleus?

21 The electronic configuration of valence shell of Cu is $3d^{10}4s^1$ and not $3d^9 4s^2$. How is this configuration explained? **NCERT Exemplar**

22 In each of the following pairs of salts, which one is more stable?
(i) Ferrous and ferric salts
(ii) Cuprous and cupric salts

Short Answer Type II Questions

3 Marks

23 Explain, giving reasons which of the following sets of quantum numbers are not possible? **NCERT Textbook**
(i) $n = 0, l = 0, m_l = 0, m_s = +1/2$
(ii) $n = 1, l = 0, m_l = 0, m_s = -\frac{1}{2}$
(iii) $n = 1, l = 1, m_l = 0, m_s = +\frac{1}{2}$
(iv) $n = 2, l = 1, m_l = 0, m_s = -\frac{1}{2}$
(v) $n = 3, l = 3, m_l = -3, m_s = +\frac{1}{2}$
(vi) $n = 3, l = 1, m_l = 0, m_s = +\frac{1}{2}$

24 The quantum numbers of six electrons are given below. Arrange them in order of increasing energies. If any of these combination(s) has/have the same energy lists.
(i) $n = 4, l = 2, m_l = -2, m_s = -\frac{1}{2}$ **NCERT Textbook**
(ii) $n = 3, l = 2, m_l = 1, m_s = +\frac{1}{2}$

(iii) $n = 4, l = 1, m_l = 0, m_s = +\frac{1}{2}$

(iv) $n = 3, l = 2, m_l = -2, m_s = -\frac{1}{2}$

(v) $n = 3, l = 1, m_l = -1, m_s = +\frac{1}{2}$

(vi) $n = 4, l = 1, m_l = 0, m_s = +\frac{1}{2}$

25 Write down the quantum numbers *n*, and *l* for the following orbitals.
(i) $3d_{x^2-y^2}$ (ii) $4d_{z^2}$ (iii) $3d_{xy}$
(iv) $4d_{xz}$ (v) $2p_z$ (vi) $3p_x$

26 (i) What is the common between d_{xy} and $d_{x^2-y^2}$ orbitals?
(ii) What is the difference between them?
(iii) What is the angle between the lobes of the above two orbitals?

27 The first shell may contain upto 2 electrons, the second shell upto 8, the third shell upto 18, and the fourth shell upto 32. Explain this arrangement in terms of quantum numbers.

28 Correct the following electronic configuration of the elements in the ground state.
(i) $1s^2 2s^1, 2p_x^2, 2p_y^2, 2p_z^2, 3s^2, 2p_x^1$
(ii) $1s^2 2s^1, 2p_x^1, 2p_y^1, 2p_z^1$
(iii) $1s^2 2s^1, 2p^6, 3s^2, 3p^6, 3d^5$
(iv) $1s^2 2s^2, 2p^6, 3s^2, 3p^6, 3d^4, 4s^2$

29 The arrangement of orbitals on the basis of energy is based upon their $(n + l)$ value. Lower the value of $(n + l)$, lower is the energy. For orbitals having same values of $(n + l)$, the orbitals with lower value of *n* will have lower energy.
(i) Based upon the above information, arrange the following orbitals in the increasing order of energy.
(a) 1s 2s, 3s, 2p (b) 4s, 3s, 3p, 4d
(c) 5p, 4d, 5d, 4f, 6s (d) 5f, 6d, 7s, 6p
(ii) Based upon the above information, solve the questions given below.
(a) Which of the following orbitals has the lowest energy? 4d, 4f, 5s, 5p
(b) Which of the following orbitals has the highest energy? 5p, 5d, 5f, 6s, 6p

NCERT Exemplar

30 Which of the following sets of orbitals are degenerate and why?
(i) 1s, 2s and 3s in Mg-atom.
(ii) $2p_x, 2p_y$ and $2p_z$ in C-atom.
(iii) 3s, $3p_x$ and 3d-orbitals in H-atom.

Long Answer Type Questions

5 Marks

31 What is an orbital? Draw the shapes of the $1s^2, 2s^2, 2p_x, 2p_y, 2p_z, 3d_{xy}, 3d_{xz}, 3d_{yz}, 3d_{x^2-y^2}$ and $3d_{z^2}$ orbitals.

32 (i) An atomic orbital has $n = 3$. What are the possible values of *l* and m_l?
(ii) List the quantum numbers (m_l and *l*) of electrons for 3d-orbital.
(iii) Which of the following orbitals are possible? 1p, 2s, 2p and 3f.

33 Indicate the number of unpaired electrons in (i) P (ii) Si (iii) Cr (iv) Fe (v) Kr

34 A neutral atom of an element has 2*K*, 8*L* and 5*M* electrons. Find out the following.
(i) Atomic number of the element
(ii) Total number of *s*-electrons
(iii) Total number of *p*-electrons
(iv) Number of protons in the nucleus
(v) Valency of the element

35 (i) Write the electronic configurations of the following ions.
(a) H^- (b) Na^+ (c) O^{2-} (d) F^-
(ii) What are the atomic numbers of elements whose outermost electrons are represented by
(a) $3s^2$ (b) $2p^3$ (c) $3p^5$?
(iii) Which atoms are indicated by the following configuration?
(a) [He] $2s^1$ (b) [Ne] $3s^2 3p^3$
(c) [Ar] $4s^2 3d^1$

NCERT Textbook

Hints & Solutions

1. (i) $2l+1$, (ii) four, (iii) anti-clockwise, (iv) zero

2. (i)→(a), (ii)→(a), (iii)→(a), (iv)→(c)

3. (c) A → (iii), B → (v), C → (i), D → (iv)

4. For 3*p*-orbital, principal quantum number, $n = 3$ and azimuthal quantum number, $l = 1$
Number of angular nodes $= l = 1$.
Number of radial nodes $= n - l - 1 = 3 - 1 - 1 = 1$

5. For *g* subshell, $l = 4$ and to have $l = 4$, minimum value of $n = 5$ [because the value of $l = 0$ to $(n-1)$].

6. The orbitals which belongs to same subshell and same shell are called degenerate orbitals. $(3d_{xy}, 3d_{z^2}, 3d_{yz})$ and $(4\,d_{xy}, 4\,d_{zy}, 4\,d_{z^2})$ are the two sets of degenerate orbitals.

7. $_8O = 1s^2\ 2s^2\ \ 2p^4$

$1s^2$	$2s^2$	$2p^4$		
↑↓	↑↓	↑↓	↑	↑

8. Effective nuclear charge decreases as the distance of the orbitals increases from the nucleus. Hence, 4*p* electrons experience the lowest effective nuclear charge.

9. *s*-orbital is spherical in shape, it shields the electrons from the nucleus more effectively than *p*-orbital which in turn shields more effectively than *d*-orbital. Therefore, the effective nuclear charge (Z_{eff}) experienced by electrons present in them is $d < p < s$.

10. $_{28}Ni = 1s^2, 2s^2, 2p^6, 3s^2, 3p^6, 3d^8, 4s^2$; Nickel will lose 2 electrons from 4*s* (outermost shell) to form Ni^{2+} ion.

11. Electronic configuration of element

$$= 1s^2, 2s^2, 2p^6, 3s^2, 3p^6, 4s^1, 3d^3$$

21st electron goes to 3*d*-orbital. Its quantum numbers are

$$n = 3,\ l = 2,\ s = +\frac{1}{2} \text{ or } -\frac{1}{2}$$

m can have any value out of $-2, -1, 0, +1, +2$.

12. $n = 3$ and $l = 0$ means the last electron enters in 3*s*-orbital. Thus, the complete configuration upto 3*s* is $1s^2, 2s^2, 2p^6, 3s^1$. Total number of electrons $= 2 + 2 + 6 + 1 = 11$. Thus, the element is sodium.

13.

> **Key Idea** *n* represents the main shell and 0, 1, 2, 3, ... values of *l* represent the *s*, *p*, *d*, *f* ... orbitals respectively.

	n	*l*	Subshell notation
(i)	1	0	1*s*
(ii)	3	1	3*p*
(iii)	4	2	4*d*
(iv)	4	3	4*f*

14. (i) $2s < 2p$ (ii) $3p < 3d$ (iii) $3s < 4s$ (iv) $4d < 5f$
This is because lower the value of $(n + l)$, lower is the energy and if $(n + l)$ are same, the orbital with lower value of *n* is of lower energy. **[2]**

15. (i) If $n = 4$ then $l = 0, 1, 2, 3$. Therefore, subshell in $n = 4$ are 4, i.e. 4*s*, 4*p*, 4*d* and 4*f*. **[1]**
(ii) Number of orbitals in 4th shell $= n^2, 4^2 = 16$
The maximum number of electrons present in any orbital is two and each orbital has one electrons with $m_s = -1/2$. Hence, there are 16 electrons with $m_s = -1/2$. **[1]**

16. *The similarities in 1s and 2s-orbitals are as follows :*
(i) Both have spherical shape.
(ii) Both have the same angular momentum.
The difference in between them are as follows.
(i) Size of 2*s*-orbital is larger than that of 1*s*-orbital.
(ii) Energy of 2*s*-orbital is greater than that of 1*s*-orbital.
(iii) 2*s*-orbital has one node while 1*s*-orbital has no node. **[2]**

17. In hydrogen atom, the energy of an electron is determined by the value of *n* and in multielectron atom, it is determined by $n + l$. Hence, for a given principal quantum, electrons of *s*, *p*, *d* and *f*-orbitals have different energy (for *s*, *p*, *d* and *f*, $l = 0, 1, 2$ and 3 respectively). **[2]**

18. (i) For a neutral atom,
Number of electrons = number of protons
29 electrons = 29 protons. **[1]**
(ii) $_{29}Z = 1s^2 2s^2, 2p^6, 3s^2, 3p^6, 3d^{10}, 4s^1$ **[1]**
(The element is copper (Cu))

19. $_9F^{19} = 1s^2\ 2s^2 2p_x^2 2p_y^2 2p_z^1,$

$_{16}S^{32} = 1s^2\ 2s^2 2p^6 3s^2 3p_x^2 3p_y^1 3p_z^1,$

$_{18}Ar^{38} = 1s^2 2s^2 2p^6 3s^2 3p^6$

(i) Maximum nuclear charge $= 18$ in $_{18}Ar^{38}$.
(ii) Minimum number of neutrons $= 10$ in $_9F^{19}$.
(iii) Maximum number of unpaired electrons = 2 in $_{16}S^{32}$.

20. $_{13}Al = 1s^2, 2s^2, 2p^6, 3s^2\ 3p^1$; $_{14}Si = 1s^2, 2s^2, 2p^6, 3s^2\ 3p^2$
Si (+ 4) has greater nuclear charge than aluminium (+ 3). Hence, 3*p* unpaired electrons of Si experience greater effective nuclear charge than Al. **[2]**

21. Configurations with completely filled and half-filled orbitals have extra stability. In $3d^{10}4s^1$, *d*-orbitals are completely filled and *s*-orbital is half-filled. Hence, it is a more stable configuration for Cu as compare to $3d^9 4s^2$. **[2]**

22. (i) **Ferrous and Ferric Salts** In ferrous salts Fe^{2+}, the configuration is $1s^2 2s^2, 2p^6, 3s^2, 3p^6, 3d^6$. In ferric salts Fe^{3+}, the configuration is $1s^2 2s^2, 2p^6, 3s^2, 3p^6, 3d^5$.
As half-filled $3d^5$ configuration is more stable therefore, ferric salts are more stable than ferrous salts. **[1]**

(ii) **Cuprous and Cupric Salts** In cuprous salts, the configuration of Cu^+ is $1s^2 2s^2 2p^6 3s^2 3p^6 3d^{10}$. In cupric salts, the configuration of Cu^{2+} is $1s^2 2s^2, 2p^6, 3s^2, 3p^6, 3d^9$. Although Cu^+ has completely filled d-orbital, yet cuprous salts are less stable. This is because the nuclear charge is not sufficient enough to hold 18 electrons of Cu^+ ion present in the outermost shell. [1]

23.

> **Key Idea** n always be a positive integer.

(i) is not possible as $n \neq 0$ (ii) is possible ($1s$)
(iii) is not possible because if $n=1$, $l=0$ only ($l \neq 1$)
(iv) is possible ($2p$)
(v) is not possible because if $n=3$, $l=0, 1$ and 2 ($l \neq 3$)
(vi) is possible ($3p$) [6 × 1/2]

24.

Quantum number	Subshell notation	$n+l$
(i) $n=4, l=2, m_l=-2, m_s=-\frac{1}{2}$	$4d$	$4+2=6$
(ii) $n=3, l=2, m_l=1, m_s=+\frac{1}{2}$	$3d$	$3+2=5$
(iii) $n=4, l=1, m_l=0, m_s=+\frac{1}{2}$	$4p$	$4+1=5$
(iv) $n=3, l=2, m_l=-2, m_s=-\frac{1}{2}$	$3d$	$3+2=5$
(v) $n=3, l=1, m_l=-1, m_s=+\frac{1}{2}$	$3p$	$3+1=4$
(vi) $n=4, l=1, m_l=0, m_s=+\frac{1}{2}$	$4p$	$4+1=5$

$\because$ (v) < (ii) = (iv) < (iii) = (vi) < (i)
$\therefore$ $3p < 3d = 3d < 4p = 4p < 4d$
(Arrangement of orbitals in order of their increasing energies). [3]

25. (i) $n=3, l=2$, (ii) $n=4, l=2$
(iii) $n=3, l=2$ (iv) $n=4, l=2$,
(v) $n=2, l=1$, (vi) $n=3, l=1$, [6 × 1/2]

26. (i) Both have identical shape, consisting of four lobes. [1]
(ii) Lobes of $d_{x^2-y^2}$ lie along the x and y-axes whereas those of d_{xy} lie between x and y-axes. [1]
(iii) 45°

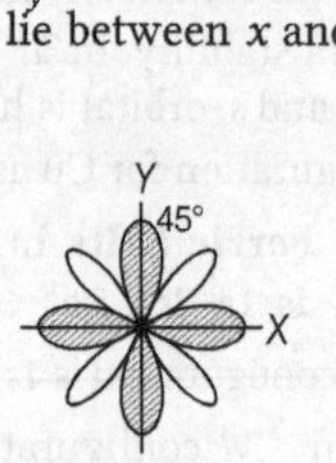

[1]

27. (a) For the first shell $n=1, l=0, m_l=0, m_s=+1/2$ and $-1/2$. It can have 2 electrons both with opposite spins.
(b) For $n=2$,
$l=0, m_l=0, m_s=+1/2, -1/2$,
$l=1, m_l=-1, 0, +1, m_s=+1/2, -1/2$.
Therefore, a total of $2+6=8$ electrons are present. [1]
(c) For $n=3$, when,
$l=0, m_l=0, m_s=+1/2, -1/2$
$l=1, m_l=-1, 0, +1, m_s=1/2, -1/2$
$l=2, m_l=-2, -1, 0, +1, +2, m_s=+1/2, -1/2$.
Therefore, a total of $2+6+10=18$ electrons are present. [1]
(d) For $n=4$, when,
$l=0, m_l=0, m_s=+1/2, -1/2$
$l=1, m_l=-1, 0, +1, m_s=+1/2, -1/2$
$l=2, m_l=-2, -1, 0, +1, +2, m_s=+1/2, -1/2$
$l=3, m_l=-3, -2, -1, 0, +1, +2, +3$,
$m_s=+1/2, -1/2$
Therefore, a total of $2+6+10+14=32$ electrons are present. [1]

28. (i) $1s^2 2s^2, 2p_x^2, 2p_y^2, 2p_z^2, 3s^2$
(ii) $1s^2 2s^2, 2p_x^1, 2p_y^1, 2p_z^0$
(iii) $1s^2 2s^2, 2p^6, 3s^2, 3p^6, 4s^2, 3d^2$
(iv) $1s^2 2s^2, 2p^6, 3s^2, 3p^6, 3d^5, 4s^1$

29. (i) (a) $(n+l)$ values are :
$1s=1+0=1$, $2s=2+0=2$,
$3s=3+0=3$, $2p=2+1=3$
Hence, increasing order of their energy is $1s < 2s < 2p < 3s$.
(b) $4s=4+0=4$, $3s=3+0=3$, $3p=3+1=4$,
$4d=4+2=6$.
Hence $3s < 3p < 4s < 4d$.
(c) $5p=5+1=6$, $4d=4+2=6$,
$5d=5+2=7$, $4f=4+3=7$, $6s=6+0=6$.
Hence, $4d < 5p < 6s < 4f < 5d$.
(d) $5f=5+3=8$, $6d=6+2=8$, $7s=7+0=7$,
$7p=7+1=8$.
Hence, $7s < 5f < 6d < 7p$. [2]
(ii) (a) $4d=4+2=6$, $4f=4+3=7$,
$5s=5+0=5$, $7p=7+1=8$.
Hence, $5s$ has the lowest energy.
(b) $5p=5+1=6$, $5d=5+2=7$,
$5f=5+3=8$, $6s=6+0=6$, $6p=6+1=7$
Hence, $5f$ has highest energy. [1]

30. (i) $1s$, $2s$ and $3s$-orbitals in Mg-atom are not degenerate because these have different values of n.
(ii) $2p_x$, $2p_y$ and $2p_z$-orbitals in C-atom are degenerate because these belong to same subshell.

(iii) 3s, $3p_x$ and 3d-orbitals in H-atom are degenerate because for H-atom, the subshells having same value of n have same energies. [3]

31. Refer to text on pages 78 and 79 [Boundary surface diagram].

32.

> **Key Idea** l has the values 0 to $(n-1)$
> m has the values $-l$ to $+l$
> The value of l never be equal to, or greater than n.

(i) For $n=3$,
$l=0, 1, 2, l=0, m_l=0$
$l=1, m_l=-1, 0, +1$
$l=2, m_l=-2, -1, 0, +1, +2$ [2]

(ii) For 3d-orbital, $n=3, l=2, m_l=-2, -1, 0, +1, +2$ [1]

(iii) $1p$ is not possible because if $n=1$ then $l=0$ only and for $p, l=1$
$2s$ is possible because if $n=2$ then $l=0$, 1 and for $s, l=0$
$2p$ is possible because if $n=2$ then $l=0$, 1 and for $p, l=1$
$3f$ is not possible because if $n=3$ then $l=0$, 1 and 2 for $f, l=3$ [2]

33. (i) ${}_{15}P=1s^2, 2s^2, 2p^6, 3s^2, 3p^3$
3 unpaired electrons

(ii) ${}_{14}Si=1s^2, 2s^2, 2p^6, 3s^2, 3p^2$
2 unpaired electrons

(iii) ${}_{24}Cr=1s^2, 2s^2, 2p^6, 3s^2, 3p^6, 3d^5, 4s^1$
6 unpaired electrons

(iv) ${}_{26}Fe=1s^2, 2s^2, 2p^6, 3s^2, 3p^6, 3d^6, 4s^2$
4 unpaired electrons

(v) ${}_{36}Kr=1s^2, 2s^2, 2p^6, 3s^2, 3p^6, 3d^{10}, 4s^2, 4p^6$
No unpaired electrons [5 × 1]

34. The electronic configuration of the element with 2K, 8L and 5M electrons will be

$$1s^2 2s^2 2p_x^2 2p_y^2 2p_z^2 3s^2 3p_x^1 3p_y^1 3p_z^1$$

(i) Total number of electrons $= 2+8+5 = 15$
$\therefore$ Atomic number of the element $= 15$

(ii) Total number of s-electrons $= 2+2+2 = 6$

(iii) Total number of p-electrons $= 6+3 = 9$

(iv) Since, the atom is neutral.
$\therefore$ Number of protons = Number of electrons
= Atomic number = 15

(v) Since, the element has only half-filled atomic orbitals, therefore, valency of the element = 3. [5 × 1]

35. (i) (a) ${}_1H = 1s^1$, $H^- = 1s^2$

(b) ${}_{11}Na = 1s^2 2s^2, 2p^6, 3s^1$, $Na^+ = 1s^2 2s^2 2p^6$

(c) ${}_8O = 1s^2 2s^2, 2p^4$, $O^{2-} = 1s^2 2s^2 2p^6$

(d) ${}_9F = 1s^2 2s^2, 2p^5$, $F^- = 1s^2 2s^2 2p^6$ [2]

(ii) To obtain atomic number of an element fill the orbitals in order of their increasing energies upto the given outer orbital configuration.

(a) $1s^2 2s^2, 2p^6, 3s^2 (Z=12)$

(b) $1s^2 2s^2, 2p^3 (Z=7)$

(c) $1s^2 2s^2, 2p^6, 3s^2, 3p^5 (Z=17)$. [2]

(iii) (a) [He] $2s^1$ represents ${}_3$Li (lithium).

(b) [Ne] $3s^2, 3p^3$ represents ${}_{15}$P (phosphorus).

(c) [Ar] $4s^2, 3d^1$ represents ${}_{21}$Sc (scandium). [1]

SUMMARY

- The smallest particle taking part in a chemical reaction is called atom.
- Electron is one of the fundamental constituent of an atom. (Charge $= -1.6 \times 10^{-19}$C and mass $= 9.1 \times 10^{-31}$ kg).
- Protons and neutrons are other fundamental particles of an atom. Proton (charge $= +1.6 \times 10^{-19}$C and mass $= 1.6 \times 10^{-31}$ kg). Neutron (charge $= 0$, mass $= 1.67 \times 10^{27}$ kg). These are present in the **nucleus** of an atom.
- An atom can be represented as $^{A}_{Z}X$, where, A = mass number, Z = atomic number
- An atom can be represented as $^{A}_{Z}X$, where, A = mass number, Z = atomic number. Atomic species can be classified as :
  (i) **Isotopes** Species having same atomic number but different mass number. These are chemically same.
  (ii) **Isoelectronic** Species having same number of electrons.
  (iii) **Isobars** Species with same mass number but different atomic number are called isobars.
  (iv) **Isotones** Species having same number of neutrons.
- Two preliminary models are :
  (i) Thomson's model assumed atom as a pudding of positive charge with electrons embedding in it.
  (ii) Rutherford's model assumed that protons and neutrons are present in the nucleus and electrons revolve around it.
- Wavelength (λ), frequency (ν), velocity (c) and wave number ($\bar{\nu}$) are related as $c = \nu . \lambda$ and $\bar{\nu} = \frac{1}{\lambda}$.
- EMR spectra is used to detect wavelengths. It shows increasing order of wavelengths.
- Bohr's model assumes electrons revolve only in stationary orbits of fixed energy.

  Bohr radius, $r_n = a_0 \cdot \frac{n^2}{Z}$ ($a_0 = 52.9$pm), Calculation of energy, $E = -2.18 \times 10^{-18} \left(\frac{Z^2}{n^2}\right) \cdot$ J

  Calculation of velocity, $v = 2.19 \times 10^6 \times \left(\frac{Z}{n}\right)$ms^{-1}, Calculation of spectral lines, $x = \frac{(n_2 - n_1) \cdot (n_2 - n_1 + 1)}{2}$
- **Line spectra** of hydrogen (H) can be expressed as $\bar{\nu} = 109677\left[\frac{1}{n_1^2} - \frac{1}{n_2^2}\right]$, where, $n_1 = 1, 2, 3, \ldots$ and $n_2 = n_1 + 1$; $n_1 = 1, 2, 3, 4$ and 5 are respectively series of **Lyman, Balmer, Paschen, Brackett** and **Pfund** lines.
- A set of four numbers gives the complete information about the electron. These are called quantum numbers.
  (i) Principal quantum number (n) (ii) Azimuthal Quantum number (l)
  (iii) Magnetic quantum number (m) (iv) Spin quantum number (s)
- Angular momentum of electron in $l = \sqrt{l+1} \cdot \frac{h}{2\pi}$.
- **Quantum Mechanical Model** Assume only the probability of finding an electron upto a distance.
- de-Broglie equation : $\lambda = \frac{h}{p}$ or $\lambda = \frac{h}{mv}$.
- Heisenberg uncertainty principle : $\left[\Delta x \times \Delta p \geq \frac{h}{4\pi} : \Delta x \cdot m \cdot \Delta v \geq \frac{h}{4\pi}\right]$,
- Orbital is the region of maximum electron density.
- **Electronic configuration is the** distribution of electrons in various orbitals.
- **Rules of Filling of Electrons**
  (i) **Aufbau principle** Electrons are filled in increasing order of energy.
  (ii) **Hund's rule of maximum multiplicity** Pairing of electrons occurs only when each orbital is single occupied.
  (iii) **Pauli exclusion principle** An orbital can accommodate a maximum of two electrons with opposite spins.

Chapter Practice

Very Short Answer Type Questions

1 Mark

1. Fill in the Blanks

(i) l describes the .... of the orbital occupied by the electron.

(ii) The wave function ψ describes properties of the orbital and the .... that occupies the orbital.

(iii) $|\psi|^2$ and ψ at any point is .... to the probability of finding that .... at that point

(iv) .... determined the charge on the electron.

2. Objective Type Questions

(i) Which of the following will violates Aufbau principle as well as Pauli's exclusion principle?

(a) 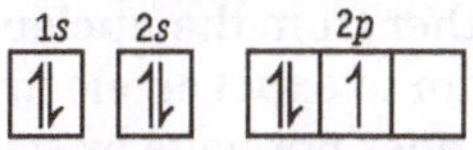
(b) 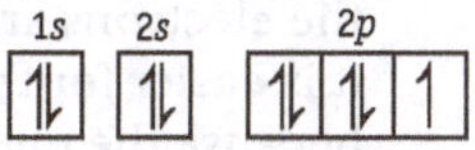
(c) 
(b) None of these

(ii) The atomic number of an element is 35 and its mass is 81. The number of electrons in its outermost shell is

(a) 3 (b) 5 (c) 7 (d) 9

(iii) Total number of orbitals associated with third shell will be **[NCERT Exemplar]**

(a) 2 (b) 4 (c) 9 (d) 3

(iv) Number of angular nodes for 4d orbital is **[NCERT Exemplar]**

(a) 4 (b) 3
(c) 2 (d) 1

3. Match the following Columns and choose the correct option using the codes given below.

Column I		Column II	
A.	Photon	(i)	Value is 4 for N-shell
B.	Electron	(ii)	Probability density
C.	ψ^2	(iii)	Always positive value
D.	Principal quantum number, n	(iv)	Exhibits both momentum and wavelength

Codes

	A	B	C	D
(a)	(i)	(iii, iv)	(ii)	(iii)
(b)	(iv)	(v)	(ii, iii)	(i, iii)
(c)	(i)	(ii)	(iii)	(iv)
(d)	(iv)	(iii, i)	(ii)	(i)

4. Calculate the amount of energy required to remove the only electron present in the hydrogen atom.

5. The minimum energy required to eject an electron from a metal is 4.34×10^{-19} J. What is the minimum frequency of light required for photoelectric effect in the metal?

6. Give the name and atomic number of the inert gas atom in which the total number of d-electrons is equal to the difference between the numbers of total s-electrons.

7. What is the difference between ground state and excited state?

8. Write the electronic configuration of a divalent ion of a coinage metal.

Assertion-Reason

Directions (Q. Nos. 9-13) In the following questions. an Assertion (A) is followed by a corresponding Reason (R) Use the following keys to choose the appropriate answer.

(a) Both (A) and (R) are correct and (R) is the correct explanation of (A).
(b) Both (A) and (R) are correct but (R) is not the correct explanation of (A).
(c) (A) is correct and (R) is incorrect.
(d) (A) is incorrect and (R) is correct.

9. Assertion (A) Cathode rays consist of negatively charged particles, called electrons.

Reason (R) In the presence of electrical/ magnetic field, the behaviour of cathode rays is similar to the negatively charged particles.

10. **Assertion** (A) *s*-orbital electron will be more tightly bound to the nucleus than *p*-orbital electron.

Reason (R) Z_{eff} experienced by the electron decreases with increase of azimuthal quantum number (l).

11. **Assertion** (A) For $n = 3$, l may be 0, 1 and 2 and m may be 0, ± 1 and ± 2.

Reason (R) For each value of n, there are 0 to $(n - 1)$ possible values of l, and for each value of l, there are 0 to $\pm l$ values of m.

12. **Assertion** (A) The radius of first orbit of hydrogen atom is 0.529 Å.

Reason (R) Radius for each circular orbital

$$(r_n) = 0.529\left(\frac{n^2}{Z}\right)$$

where, $n = 1, 2, 3$ and Z = atomic number.

13. **Assertion** (A) All isotopes of a given element show the same type of chemical behaviour.

Reason (R) The chemical properties of an atom are controlled by the number of electrons in the atom.

Case-Study

14. A total of four quantum numbers are used to describe completely the movement and trajectories of each electron within an atom. Each electron in an atom has a unique set of quantum numbers; according to the Pauli's exclusion principle, no two electrons can share the same combination of four quantum numbers. Quantum numbers are important because they can be used to determine the electron configuration of an atom and the probable location of the atom's electrons.

In atoms, there are a total of four quantum numbers; the principal quantum number (n), the orbital angular momentum quantum number (l), the magnetic quantum number (m_l), and the electron spin quantum number (m_s). The principal quantum number, (n), describes the energy of an electron and the most probable distance of the electron from the nucleus.

In other words, it refers to the size of the orbital and the energy level an electron is placed.

The number of subshells, or l, describes the shape of the orbital. It can also be used to determine the number of angular nodes. The magnetic quantum number, (m_l) describes the energy levels in a subshell, and (m_s) refers to the spin on the electron, which can either be up or down. The value of the principal quantum number n is the level of the principal electronic shell (principal level). All orbitals that have the same n value are in the same principal level.

The size of the atom and its atomic radius increases. Because the atomic radius increases, the electrons are farther from the nucleus. Thus, it is easier for the atom to expel an electron because the nucleus does not have as strong a pull on it, and the ionisation energy decreases. We can designate a principal quantum number, n, and a certain subshell by combining the value of n and the name of the subshell (which can be found using (l).

The *s*-orbital, because the value of m_l can only be 0, can only exist in one plane. The *p*-orbital, however, has three possible because the value of m_l and so it has three possible orientations of the orbitals, shown by p_x, p_y and p_z. The pattern continues, with the *d*-orbital containing 5 possible orbital orientations, and *f* has 7.

(i) Define Pauli's exclusion principle.

(ii) Discuss the use of principal quantum numbers to determine electric configuration of an atom.

(iii) What is the difference between orbit and orbitals?

15. The characteristics of an orbital are expressed in terms of three numbers, called principal (n), azimuthal (l) and magnetic quantum numbers (m_l).

These numbers are obtained from the solutions of the Schrodinger wave equation. Further, to represent the spin (rotation) of the electron about its own axis, a fourth quantum number, called spin quantum number has been introduced.

n defines the shell, determines the size of the orbital and also to a large extent the energy of orbitals. There are n subshells in the nth shell. 'l' identifies the subshell and determines the shape of the orbital. m_l designates the orientation of orbital. For a given value of l, m_l has $(2l+1)$ values, the same as the number of orbitals per subshell. m_s refers to orientation of the spin of the electron.

(i) For a given principal quantum number, s, p, d, f......, subshells, all have different energies. Why?

(ii) What is the number of nodes in 2s-orbitals?

(iii) Half-filled and fully-filled degenerate set of orbitals aquire extra stability. Why?

Short Answer Type I Questions

2 Marks

16. Show that ground state energy of electrons in hydrogen atom is equal to the first excited state energy of electron in He^+ ion, assuming that their Rydberg's constants are equal.

17. Two particles A and B are in motion. The momentum of particle B is the double of A. If the wavelength associated with the particle A is 5×10^{-8} m, calculate the wavelength associated with the particle B.

18. A certain radio station broadcasts on a frequency of 980 kHz (kilohertz). What is the wavelength of electromagnetic radiation broadcast by the radio station?

19. Calculate the wavelength of an electron moving with a velocity of 2.05×10^7 ms^{-1}. Also calculate the wave number of the electron.

20. What is the angular momentum of an electron in (i) 2s-orbital (ii) 4f-orbital?

21. List the values of n and l for the following orbitals.

(i) 3s (ii) 4p
(iii) 4f (iv) 3d

Short Answer Type II Questions

3 Marks

22. (i) State the principle that suggests the presence of only two electrons in an orbital.

(ii) Account for the following:

(a) Chromium has configuration $3d^5\ 4s^1$ and not $3d^4\ 4s^2$.

(b) Bohr's orbits are called stationary orbits or states.

23. A photon of wavelength 1.4 Å collides with a stationary electron. After collision, the wavelength of the photon is found to be 2.0 Å. Calculate the energy of the scattered electron.

24. Light of wavelength 1281.8 nm is emitted when an electron of H-atom drops from 5th to 3rd energy level.

Calculate the wavelength of the photon emitted when electron falls from third to ground level.

25. In the ultraviolet region of atomic spectrum of hydrogen, a line is obtained at 1050 Å. Calculate the energy of one million photons of this wavelength.

26. The wavelength of first spectral line in the Balmer series is 6561 Å. Calculate the wavelength of the second spectral line in Balmer series.

27. When a certain metal was irradiated with a light of frequency 3.2×10^{16} Hz, the photoelectrons had twice the kinetic energy as emitted when the same metal was irradiated with light of frequency 2.0×10^{16} Hz. Calculate the threshold frequency (ν_0) of the metal.

28. What is the energy in joules required to same electron of the hydrogen from the first Bohr orbit to the fifth Bohr orbit and what is the wavelength of the light emitted when the electron returns to the ground state? The ground state electron energy is -2.18×10^{-11} ergs.

Long Answer Type Questions

(5 Marks)

29. (i) The effect of uncertainty principle is significant only for motion of microscopic particles and is negligible for the macroscopic particle. Justify the statement with the help of a suitable example.

(ii) Calculate the velocity condition for the wavelength associated with a moving electron to be equal to the wavelength associated with a moving proton.

(Mass of electron $= 9.11\times10^{-28}$ g;

Mass of proton $= 1.67\times10^{-24}$ g;

$h = 6.6\times10^{-34}$ Js; J $\equiv$ kg m^2 s^{-2})

30. (i) Why is + 2 oxidation state of Mn (25) quite stable, while the same is not true for iron (26)?

(ii) What is meant by dual nature of electrons? Calculate the energy and wavelength of the photon emitted by hydrogen atom when electron makes a transition from $n=2$ to $n=1$.

Given that the ionisation potential is 13.6 eV ($1\text{ eV} = 1.6\times10^{-19}$ J).

Answers

1. (i) shape
(ii) electron
(iii) proportional, particle
(iv) Millikan

2. (i)→(c), (ii)→(c), (iii)→(c), (iv)→(c)

3. (b) A → (iv), B → (v), C → (ii, iii), D → (i, iii)

4. Refer to text on page 56 [Topic-1, Calculation of energy of the electron].

5. $E = h\nu$

6. Krypton

7. The main difference between ground state and excited state is that ground state is a state wereas electrons in a system are in the lowest possible energy levels.

Whereas excited state is any state of the system that has a higher energy than the ground state.

8. Refer to text on page 80 [Topic-3, Electronic configuration of atoms]

9. (*a*) Both (A) and (R) are correct and (R) is the correct explanation of (A).

10. (*a*) Both (A) and (R) are correct and (R) is the correct explanation of (A).

11. (*a*) Both (A) and (R) are correct and (R) is the correct explanation of (A).

12. (*a*) Both (A) and (R) are correct and (R) is the correct explanation of (A).

13. (*a*) Both (A) and (R) are correct and (R) is the correct explanation of (A). Isotopes have the same atomic number, i.e. same number of electrons which are responsible for their chemical behaviour.

Hence, these exhibit similar chemical properties.

14. (i) Pauli's exclusion principle states that "no two electrons in an atom can have the same set of four quantum numbers".

e.g. Two electrons in an orbital can be indicated either by (i) or (ii); not by (iii) or (iv).

$\uparrow\downarrow$ (i) Or $\downarrow\uparrow$ (ii) (Correct)

$\downarrow\downarrow$ (iii) Or $\uparrow\uparrow$ (iv) (Incorrect)

(ii) Principal quantum number (n) tells about the shell of an atom. If $n = 1, 2, 3$ ....

Shell = K, L, M, N ....

(iii) Orbit represents the circular path along which the electron moves but orbtials represents the three dimensional space around the nucleus within which the probability of finding the electron is maximum.

15. (i) For a given principal quantum number, s, p, d, f......, subshell, all have different energies because mutual repulsion exists among the electrons in multi-electrons atoms.

(ii) The number of nodes in 2*s*-orbitals are

$$(n-l-1) = (2-0-1) = 1$$

2*s*-orbital has one node.

(iii) Because of the presence of the symmetry or such orbitals. Half-filled and fully-filled degenerate set of orbitals aquire extra stability.

16. Refer to text on page 56 [Topic-1, Calculation of energy of the electron].

17. $\dfrac{\lambda_1}{\lambda_2} = \dfrac{P_2}{P_1}$

18. $c = \nu \times \lambda$

19. $n\lambda = 2\pi r,\ \bar{\nu} = \frac{1}{\lambda}$

20. Refer to text on page 76 [Topic-3, Quantum numbers].

21. Refer to text on page 76 [Topic-3, Qunatum numbers].

22. (i) Refer to text on page 82 [Topic-3, Pauli's exclusion principle].

(ii) (a) Refer to text on pages 80 and 81 [Topic-3, Electronic configuration of atoms].

(b) Refer to text on page 55 [Topic-1, Bohr's model for hydrogen atom].

23. $E = \frac{hc}{\lambda}$

24. $\frac{1}{\lambda} = R\left[\frac{1}{n_1^2} - \frac{1}{n_2^2}\right]$

25. $E = \frac{Nhc}{\lambda}$

26. $\frac{1}{\lambda} = R\left[\frac{1}{n_1^2} - \frac{1}{n_2^2}\right]$

27. $h\nu = h\nu_0 + \frac{1}{2}m_e v^2$

28. $E_n = -2.18 \times 10^{-18}\left(\frac{Z^2}{n^2}\right)$ J

29. (i) Refer to text on pages 69 and 70 [Topic-2, Heisenberg's uncertainty principle].

(ii) $\Delta x \cdot \Delta v = \frac{h}{4\pi m}$

30. (i) Refer to text on page 80 [Topic-3, Electronic configuration of atoms].

(ii) Refer to text on page 69 [Topic-2, Dual behaviour of matter].

CHAPTER

03

Classification of Elements and Periodicity in Properties

In the beginning of 18th century, only 31 elements were known but by 1865 the number had became more than double, i.e. 63. Till now 118 elements have been discovered and efforts to discover new elements are still on. With such a large number of elements, it is difficult to study the chemistry (or properties) of each element and their compounds. Therefore, to study the properties of each element scientists felt the need to classify the elements into various groups or families.

- Classification of Elements : Periodic Table
- Nomenclature and Relation between Electronic Configuration and Periodic Table
- Periodic Properties : Atomic Radii and Ionisation Enthalpy
- Electron Gain Enthalpy, Electronegativity and Periodic Trends in Chemical Properties

TOPIC 01 Classification of Elements: Periodic Table

Periodic table is an arrangement of elements with similar properties placed together. A number of scientists through their observations and experiments formulated various laws such as Dobereiner's law of triads, Newland's law of octanes and Lother Meyer curve.

Mendeleev's Periodic Table

The Russian chemist, **Dmitri Mendeleev** (1869) proposed that when elements are arranged in increasing order of their atomic weight, element having similar properties, reoccurs at regular intervals. On this basis he gave a law, called the Mendeleev's periodic law, which states that "**the physical and chemical properties of the element are the periodic function of their atomic weight**".

The repeatation of properties of elements after certain regular intervals is called **periodicity of properties.**

GROUPS OF ELEMENTS

S. No.	0	I	II	III	IV	V	VI	VII	VIII
1		Hydrogen H 1.008							
2	Helium He 4.0	Lithium Li 7.03	Beryllium Be 9.1	Boron B 11.0	Carbon C 12.0	Nitrogen N 14.04	Oxygen O 16.00	Fluorine F 19.0	
3	Neon Ne 19.9	Sodium Na 23.5	Magnesium Mg 24.3	Aluminium Al 27.0	Silicon Si 28.4	Phosphorus P 31.0	Sulphur S 32.06	Chlorine Cl 35.45	
4	Argon Ar 38	Potassium K 39.1	Calcium Ca 40.1	Scandium Sc 44.1	Titanium Ti 48.1	Vanadium V 51.4	Chromium Cr 52.1	Manganese Mn 55.0	Iron Fe 55.9; Cobalt Co 59; Nickel Ni (Cu) 59
5		Copper Cu 63.6	Zinc Zn 65.4	Gallium Ga 70.0	Germanium Ge 72.3	Arsenic As 75	Selenium Se 79	Bromine Br 79.95	
6	Krypton Kr 81.8	Rubidium Rb 85.4	Strontium Sr 87.6	Yttrium Y 89.0	Zirconium Zr 90.6	Niobium Nb 94.0	Molybdenum Mo 96.0		Ruthenium Ru 101.7; Rhodium Rh 103.0; Palladium Pd (Ag) 106.5
7		Silver Ag 107.9	Cadmium Cd 112.4	Indium In 114.0	Tin Sn 119.0	Antimony Sb 120.0	Tellurium Te 127.6	Iodine I 126.9	
8	Xenon Xe 128	Caesium Cs 132.9	Barium Ba 137.4	Lantanum La 139	Cerium Ce 140				
9									
10				Ytterbium Yb 173		Tantalum Ta 183	Tungsten W 184		Osmium Os 191; Iridium Ir 193; Platinum Pt (Au) 194.9
11		Gold Au 197.2	Mercury Hg 200.0	Thallium T 204.1	Lead Pb 206.9	Bismuth Bi 208			
12			Radium Ra 224		Thorium Th 232		Uranium U 239		
HIGHER SALINE OXIDES	R	R_2O	RO	R_2O_3	RO_2	R_2O_5	RO_3	R_2O_7	RO_4
HIGHER GASEOUS HYDROGEN COMPOUNDS					RH_4	RH_3	RH_2	RH	

Mendeleev's periodic table published earlier

Properties

(i) Among chemical properties, Mendeleev considered mainly the properties of compound of elements with oxygen and hydrogen (i.e. properties of their oxides and halides).

(ii) Reason for the selection of these compounds as the basis of classification are the high reactivity of hydrogen and oxygen and formation of large number of compounds by these elements.

(iii) Mendeleev arranged the elements then known in increasing order of their atomic weight and generated a table called **periodic table.**

Note At some place of periodic table, he had ignored the increasing order of atomic weight.

Characteristics of Mendeleev's Periodic Table

The periodic table, generated by Mendeleev's had the following features:

(i) In this periodic table, there were eight vertical columns, named as **groups.** These were represented by Roman numerals I to VIII. Each group is divided into sub-groups *A* and *B* except the VIII group which had nine elements arranged in three rows as triads, i.e. in the group of three.

(ii) In this table, there were six horizontal rows, named as **periods** which were further divided into 12 series.

Advantages of the Mendeleev's Periodic Table

The main advantages of the Mendeleev's periodic table are as follows:

(i) Atomic weights of elements were determined with the help of periodic table.

Atomic weight = Valency × Equivalent weight.

(ii) Atomic weight of elements were corrected. Atomic weight of Be was calculated to be $3\times 4.5 = 13.5$ by considering its valency 3 but, Mendeleev calculated it as $2\times 4.5 = 9$

(iii) In Mendeleev's periodic table two consecutive members differ by two or three units in the atomic weight. In some cases, where this gap was more, the gaps were left in the periodic table. This helped in discovering of new elements.

Limitations (Defects) of Mendeleev's Periodic Table

Following are the main limitations of the Mendeleev's periodic table:

(i) Position of hydrogen was uncertain. It has been placed in IA and VIIA groups because of its resemblance with elements of both the groups.

(ii) No separate positions were given for isotopes.

(iii) No separate group for lanthanoides and actinoides.

(iv) Although there is no resemblance except valency of subgroups *A* and *B*, they have been put in the same group.

(v) Order of increasing atomic weights is not strictly followed in the arrangement of elements in the periodic table. e.g. Te (At. wt. 127.5) is placed before I (127) and Ar (39.9) before K (39).

Modern Periodic Law and the Long Form of the Periodic Table

In 1913, **Henry Moseley**, the English physicist performed an experiment by bombarding high speed electrons on 38 different elements starting from aluminium and ending on gold in vacuum and generated X-rays. He observed that the square root of the frequency (ν) of the X-rays emitted by a metal is proportional to the atomic number and not to the atomic weight of the element of the electron i.e. $\sqrt{\nu} = a(Z - b)$ [where, a and b = constants]

Thus, when he plotted $\sqrt{\nu}$ with atomic number (Z), a straight line is obtained, but this is not true when $\sqrt{\nu}$ is plotted with atomic mass. He thereby shows that the atomic number is a more fundamental property of an element than its atomic mass. Thus, he modified the Mendeleev's periodic law and gave **modern periodic law**, which states that.

"**The physical and chemical properties of the elements are the periodic function of their atomic numbers,** i.e. when elements are arranged in increasing order of atomic numbers, the elements having similar properties are repeated after certain regular intervals."

Long Form of Periodic Table (Present form of the Periodic Table)

Several periodic tables have been proposed from time to time. Some were based on chemical reactions and valence electrons while the others were focused on the electronic configuration of elements. The most convenient and widely used version among them is called the **long form of periodic table.**

Representative elements (s-block elements) — GROUP NUMBER 1, 2

Transition elements (d-block elements) — GROUP NUMBER 3 to 12

Representative elements (p-block elements) — GROUP NUMBER 13 to 17; Noble gases — 18

Period Number	1 IA	2 IIA	3 IIIB	4 IVB	5 VB	6 VIB	7 VIIB	8 VIII	9 VIII	10 VIII	11 IB	12 IIB	13 IIIA	14 IVA	15 VA	16 VIA	17 VIIA	18 0
1	1 H $1s^1$																	2 He $1s^2$
2	3 Li $2s^1$	4 Be $2s^2$											5 B $2s^22p^1$	6 C $2s^22p^2$	7 N $2s^22p^3$	8 O $2s^22p^4$	9 F $2s^22p^5$	10 Ne $2s^22p^6$
3	11 Na $3s^1$	12 Mg $3s^2$											13 Al $3s^23p^1$	14 Si $3s^23p^2$	15 P $3s^23p^3$	16 S $3s^23p^4$	17 Cl $3s^23p^5$	18 Ar $3s^23p^6$
4	19 K $4s^1$	20 Ca $4s^2$	21 Sc $3d^14s^2$	22 Ti $3d^24s^2$	23 V $3d^34s^2$	24 Cr $3d^54s^1$	25 Mn $3d^54s^2$	26 Fe $3d^64s^2$	27 Co $3d^74s^2$	28 Ni $3d^84s^2$	29 Cu $3d^{10}4s^1$	30 Zn $3d^{10}4s^2$	31 Ga $4s^24p^1$	32 Ge $4s^24p^2$	33 As $4s^24p^3$	34 Se $4s^24p^4$	35 Br $4s^24p^5$	36 Kr $4s^24p^6$
5	37 Rb $5s^1$	38 Sr $5s^2$	39 Y $4d^15s^2$	40 Zr $4d^25s^2$	41 Nb $4d^45s^1$	42 Mo $4d^55s^1$	43 Tc $4d^55s^2$	44 Ru $4d^75s^1$	45 Rh $4d^85s^1$	46 Pd $4d^{10}$	47 Ag $4d^{10}5s^1$	48 Cd $4d^{10}5s^2$	49 In $5s^25p^1$	50 Sn $5s^25p^2$	51 Sb $5s^25p^3$	52 Te $5s^25p^4$	53 I $5s^25p^5$	54 Xe $5s^25p^6$
6	55 Cs $6s^1$	56 Ba $6s^2$	57 La* $5d^16s^2$	72 Hf $4f^{14}5d^26s^2$	73 Ta $5d^36s^2$	74 W $5d^46s^2$	75 Re $5d^56s^2$	76 Os $5d^66s^2$	77 Ir $5d^76s^2$	78 Pt $5d^96s^1$	79 Au $5d^{10}6s^1$	80 Hg $5d^{10}6s^2$	81 Tl $6s^26p^1$	82 Pb $6s^26p^2$	83 Bi $6s^26p^3$	84 Po $6s^26p^4$	85 At $6s^26p^5$	86 Rn $6s^26p^6$
7	87 Fr $7s^1$	88 Ra $7s^2$	89 Ac** $6d^17s^2$	104 Rf	105 Db	106 Sg	107 Bh	108 Hs	109 Mt	110 Ds	111 Rg	112 Cn	113 Nh	114 Fl	115 Mc	116 Lv	117 Ts	118 Og

Inner-transition elements (f-block elements)

*Lanthanoids $4f^n5d^{0-1}6s^2$	58 Ce $4f^25d^06s^2$	59 Pr $4f^35d^06s^2$	60 Nd $4f^45d^06s^2$	61 Pm $4f^55d^06s^2$	62 Sm $4f^65d^06s^2$	63 Eu $4f^75d^06s^2$	64 Gd $4f^75d^16s^2$	65 Tb $4f^95d^06s^2$	66 Dy $4f^{10}5d^16s^2$	67 Ho $4f^{11}5d^06s^2$	68 Er $4f^{12}5d^06s^2$	69 Tm $4f^{13}5d^06s^2$	70 Yb $4f^{14}5d^06s^2$	71 Lu $4f^{14}5d^16s^2$
**Actinoids $5f^n6d^{0-2}7s^2$	90 Th $5f^06d^27s^2$	91 Pa $5f^26d^17s^2$	92 U $5f^36d^17s^2$	93 Np $5f^46d^17s^2$	94 Pu $5f^66d^07s^2$	95 Am $5f^76d^07s^2$	96 Cm $5f^76d^17s^2$	97 Bk $5f^96d^07s^2$	98 Cf $5f^{10}6d^07s^2$	99 Es $5f^{11}6d^07s^2$	100 Fm $5f^{12}6d^07s^2$	101 Md $5f^{13}6d^07s^2$	102 No $5f^{14}6d^07s^2$	103 Lr $5f^{14}6d^17s^2$

Long form of the periodic table

Features of Long Form of Periodic Table

This table is based on the electronic configuration of the elements and is also called the **Bohr's table** as it follows the Bohr's scheme to arrange various electrons around the nucleus.

Salient features of this table are as follows :

(i) The table consist of 18 vertical columns called **groups** and 7 horizontal rows called **periods.** The groups are numbered from 1 to 18.

(ii) Elements with similar valence shell configuration [i.e. with same number of valence electrons] are arranged in same group.

(iii) Each period corresponds to the highest principal quantum number (n) of the elements in the period. First period contain 2 elements and subsequent periods contain 8, 8, 18, 18 and 32 elements.

(iv) Elements of groups 1 and 2 are called **alkali metals** and **alkaline earth metals** respectively.

(v) Elements of groups 3 to 12 are called **transition elements.**

(vi) The elements of 6th period [from $Z=58$ to $Z=71$] (i.e. elements after lanthanum) known as **lanthanides** and 14 elements of 7th period [from $Z=90$ to $Z=103$] (i.e. elements after actinium) known as **actinide**, are placed in separate rows below the periodic table. These are also known as **inner transition elements.**

Note The numbers 2, 8, 8, 18, 18, 32 are sometimes referred as magic numbers as the repetition in properties is observed after these number of elements in successive periods.

Advantages of Long Form of Periodic Table

This table is based on the atomic number which is the basic fundamental property of an atom and hence, it is found helpful in removing most of the anomalies of Mendeleev's periodic table. Some of its important merits are as follows:

(i) This table removed the anomalies of inversions that existed in the Mendeleev's periodic table. e.g. potassium with atomic number 19 is placed after argon with atomic number 18. Similarly, cobalt with atomic number 27 is placed before nickel with atomic number 28.

(ii) In this table same position is alloted to each isotope of an element as all the isotopes of an element have same atomic number.

(iii) Other anomalies of Mendeleev's periodic table like grouping of dissimilar elements together and similar elements separately has also been removed by this table.

(iv) It also explains the cause of periodicity on the basis of electronic configuration. Further it relates the position of an element in the periodic table with its electronic configuration.

(v) It provides an easier way to remember all the elements and their properties by just knowing their atomic numbers and electronic configurations.

Demerits of Long Form of the Periodic Table

Although this periodic table provided a systematic way to study the chemistry of elements and removed most of the anomalies of Mendeleev's and other modern periodic tables, yet it suffers from the following defects.

(i) In this periodic table also, the position of hydrogen is not clear, although it is placed in a separate box just above the group-I.

(ii) Lanthanoids and actinoids has not been merged within the main body of the periodic table.

Topic Practice 1

Very Short Answer Type Questions

1 Mark

1. Fill in the Blanks

(i) According to Mendeleev's periodic table, physical and chemical properties of the element are ...... function of their ....

(ii) Henry Moseley established the relation, that ...... of X-rays, emitted by a metal is ...... to the atomic number.

(iii) According to modern periodic law, the physical and chemical properties of the elements are periodic function of their ......

(iv) In long form of periodic table, we have ...... periods and ...... groups.

2. Objective Type Questions

(i) Periodic classification of elements can be done on the basis of electronic configuration and is used to examine the

(a) periodic trends in physical properties of elements
(b) periodic trends in chemical properties of elements
(c) Both (a) and (b)
(d) None of the above

(ii) Which of the following statements is incorrect?

(a) In 1800, only 31 elements were discovered
(b) The recently discovered elements are man-made
(c) At present 110 elements are known
(d) None of the above

(iii) Which of the following statements is incorrect?

(a) Mendeleev's arranged elements in horizontal rows and vertical columns
(b) Mendeleev's arranged elements in order of their increasing atomic number
(c) Mendeleev's system of classifying elements was more elaborate than that of Lothar Meyer
(d) None of the above

(iv) In Mendeleev's periodic table, iodine with lower atomic weight than that of tellurium was placed alongwith

(a) iron, cobalt and nickel
(b) fluorine, chlorine and bromine
(c) oxygen, sulphur and selenium
(d) carbon, silicon and germanium

(v) Mendeleev left the gap under aluminium and a gap under silicon having atomic weights 68 and 72 respectively. These elements respectively are

(a) Eka-aluminium and Eka-silicon
(b) aluminium and silicon
(c) Eka-germanium and Eka-silicon
(d) Eka-aluminium and Eka-germanium

(vi) Henry Moseley plotted a graph between $\sqrt{\nu}$ and Z, where ν was the frequency of X-ray emitted by an atom and Z was its atomic number. This graph showed that

(a) the atomic mass is fundamental properties of an element
(b) the atomic number is fundamental property of an element
(c) Both (a) and (b)
(d) The frequency (ν) was independent of atomic number

3. Match the Column I with Column II and select the correct option using the codes given below :

Column I (Number of periods)	Column II (Number of elements)
A. First period	(i) 14
B. Third period	(ii) 2
C. Lanthanoids	(iii) 8
D. Actinoids	(iv) 4

Codes

	A	B	C	D
(a)	(ii)	(iv)	(i)	(iii)
(b)	(ii)	(iii)	(i)	(i)
(c)	(iv)	(ii)	(i)	(iii)
(d)	(iv)	(ii)	(iii)	(iii)

4. What is the basic theme of organisation in the periodic table? **NCERT Textbook**

5. Which element do you think would have been named by
(i) Lawrence Berkeley laboratory
(ii) Seaborg's group **NCERT Textbook**

6. Which properties of the elements depend on the electronic configuration of the atoms and which do not?

7. Write the number designation of a group that has 2 electrons beyond a noble gas configuration.

Short Answer Type I Questions

2 Marks

8. What is the basic difference in approach between the Mendeleev's periodic law and the modern periodic law? **NCERT Textbook**

9. Which important property did Mendeleev use to classify the elements in his periodic table and did he stick to that? **NCERT Textbook**

Long Answer Type Questions

5 Marks

10. (i) Write the drawbacks in Mendeleev's periodic table that led to its modification.
(ii) In what manner is the long form of periodic table better than Mendeleev's periodic table? Explain with examples. **NCERT Exemplar**

11. What is modern periodic law? Discuss the main features of the long form of the periodic table. Give its important disadvantages.

Hints & Solutions

1. (i) periodic, atomic weight
(ii) square root frequency, proportional
(iii) atomic number (iv) seven, eighteen

2. (i) (*c*) Periodic classification of elements follows a logical consequence of electronic configuration of atoms, which is used to examine the physical and chemical properties of the elements.
(ii) (*c*) In 1800, only 31 elements were known. By 1865, the number of identified elements had more than doubled to 63. At present 118 elements are known. Of them, the recently discovered elements are man-made.
(iii) (*b*) Mendeleev's arranged elements in horizontal rows and vertical columns of table in the order of their increasing atomic weights in such a way that the elements with similar properties occupied the same vertical column or group. Mendeleev's system of classifying elements was more elaborate than that of Lothar Meyer's.
(iv) (*b*) Iodine with lower atomic weight than that of tellurium was placed in group-VII alongwith fluorine, chlorine, bromine because of similarities in properties.
(v) (*a*) Mendeleev left the gap under aluminium and a gap under silicon, are called as Eka-aluminium and Eka-silicon, respectively.
(vi) (*b*) Henry Moseley plot graph of $\sqrt{v}$ *vs* Z and showed that the atomic number is more fundamental property of an element than its atomic mass.

3. (b) A → (ii), B → (iii), C → (i), D → (i).
A. First period contains 2 elements.
B. Third period contains 8 elements.
C and D. 14 elements of both sixth and seventh periods are known as lanthanoids and actinoids respectively.

4. The basic theme of organisation in the periodic table is to simplify and systematise the study of physical and chemical properties of all the elements and their innumerable compounds.

5. (i) Lawrencium ($Z = 103$) and Berkelium ($Z = 97$)
(ii) Seaborgium ($Z = 106$)

6. Chemical and many physical properties of the elements depend on the electronic configuration of the atoms, whereas the nuclear properties do not.

7. The number designation of a group that has 2 electrons beyond a noble gas configuration will be 2 which means it will belong to group 2 of the periodic table.

8. **Mendeleev's periodic law** It states that the properties of the elements are a periodic function of their atomic weights. [1]
Modern periodic law It states that the properties of the elements are a periodic function of their atomic numbers. Thus, change in the base of classification of elements from atomic weight to atomic number is the basic difference between Mendeleev's periodic law and the modern periodic law. [1]

9. Mendeleev used atomic weight as the basis of classification of elements in the periodic table. He arranged 63 elements known at that time in the periodic table on the basis of the order of their increasing atomic weight. At some places he ignored the increasing order of atomic weights where the elements having similar properties are placed together. [2]

10. (i) Refer to text on page 98 (Limitations of Mendeleev's periodic table).
(ii) Refer to text on pages 98 and 99 (Merits of long form of periodic table).

11. Refer to text on pages 98 and 99 (Modern periodic law and the present form of periodic table and features of long form of periodic table).

TOPIC 02 Nomenclature, Relation between Electronic Configuration and Periodic Table

Nomenclature of Super Heavy Elements (Atomic Numbers > 100)

IUPAC appointed a Commission on Nomenclature of Inorganic Chemistry (CNIC) in 1994 to give a rational system of nomenclature for elements having atomic number greater than 100.

The basic rules to write the name of an element in accordance with the system of nomenclature are as follows :

(i) The elements name is derived directly from their atomic number by using the numerical root for 0 and numbers 1-9. These root names are listed below.

Digit	0	1	2	3	4	5	6	7	8	9
Root name	nil	un	bi	tri	quad	pent	hex	sept	oct	enn
Abbreviation	n	u	b	t	q	p	h	s	o	e

(ii) The roots are put together in order of digits which make the atomic number and at the end suffix-ium is added. If there is already an 'i' present in root name (like bi, tri) then 'i' is ignored while fixing the 'ium' suffix.

(iii) The symbol of these elements constitute abbreviation for each root names, with the first one being capital.

Elements with $Z > 100$ and their Names and Symbols are listed below

Atomic number	Name	Symbol	IUPAC official name	IUPAC symbol
101	Unnilunium	Unu	Mendelevium	Md
102	Unnilbium	Unb	Nobelium	No
103	Unniltrium	Unt	Lawrencium	Lr
104	Unnilquadium	Unq	Rutherfordium	Rf
105	Unnilpentium	Unp	Dubnium	Db
106	Unnilhexium	Unh	Seaborgium	Sg
107	Unnilseptium	Uns	Bohrium	Bh
108	Unniloctium	Uno	Hassium	Hs
109	Unnilennium	Une	Meitnerium	Mt
110	Ununnillium	Uun	Darmstadtium	Ds
111	Unununnium	Uuu	Rontgenium	Rg
112	Ununbium	Uub	Copernicium	Cn
113	Ununtrium	Uut	Nihonium	Nh
114	Ununquadium	Uuq	Flerovium	Fl
115	Ununpentium	Uup	Mosovium	Mc
116	Ununhexium	Uuh	Livermorium	Lv
117	Ununseptium	Uus	Tennessine	Ts
118	Ununoctium	Uuo	Oganesson	Og

Electronic Configuration of Elements and the Periodic Table

Long form of periodic table is completely based on the electronic configuration and with the help of electronic configuration, it is possible to find out the position (period and group) of an element in the periodic table.

Electronic Configurations in Periods

The period of an element is indicated by its principal quantum number (n) for the outermost or valence shell. Thus, each period begins with the filling of a new principal energy level and for successive periods in the periodic table, the electron enters in the next higher energy level (i.e. $n = 1, 2, \ldots$ etc). The number of elements present in any period is twice the number of atomic orbitals available in that energy level.

Its detailed explanation is given below :

1. Elements in First Period

First period corresponds to $n = 1$ (or K shell) which have only one orbital i.e. the lowest energy $1s$ orbital. Since an orbital can accommodate a maximum of two electrons therefore there are only two elements hydrogen (with $1s^1$ configuration) and helium (with $1s^2$ configuration), in this period.

2. Elements in Second Period

This period corresponds to $n=2$ (or L shell) which contains one $2s$ and three $2p$ orbitals with a capacity of 8 electrons. Therefore, eight elements are present in this period.

3. Elements in Third Period

This period corresponds to $n=3$ (or M shell), which contains one $3s$, three $3p$ and five $3d$ orbitals, i.e., total nine orbitals. But the energy of $3d$ orbital is somewhat larger than that of $4s$ orbital, so it is filled after filling of $4s$ orbital. Consequently, this period involves the filling of only four orbital, i.e. one $3s$ orbital and three $3p$-orbitals. Therefore, eight elements from sodium $(3s^1)$ to argon $(3s^2\,3p^6)$ are included in this period.

4. Elements of Fourth Period

This period corresponds to $n=4$, which contains one $4s$, three $4p$, five $4d$ and seven $4f$-orbitals or a total of 16 orbitals but the energy of later two orbitals (i.e. $4d$ and $4f$-orbitals) is higher than that of the $5s$ orbital, so these are filled only after the filling of $5s$ orbital (which corresponds to $n=5$).

However, the energy of $3d$ orbitals is comparable to that of $4s$ orbital but less than that of $4p$ orbitals. So after filling the $4s$ orbital, the electron enters in the $3d$ orbitals. Filling of $3d$ orbitals generate $3d$ transition series of elements which begins with scandium (electronic configuration $3d^1\,4s^2$).

The fourth period, however, ends with krypton in which the last electron enters in $4p$ orbitals (outer configuration $3d^{10}\,4s^2\,4p^6$). Thus, the period contains eighteen elements from potassium ($Z=19$) to krypton ($Z=36$).

5. Elements of Fifth Period

This period corresponds to $n=5$. Just like fourth period, it involves the filling of one $5s$, five $4d$ and three $5p$-orbitals and hence, total 18 electrons can be accommodated in these orbitals. Thus, this period also contains a total of eighteen elements from rubidium $(5s^1)$ to xenon $(5s^2\,5p^6)$.

Filling of $4d$-orbitals results in $4d$ transition series which begins with yttrium ($Z=39$, with outer configuration $4d^1, 5s^2$) and ends at cadmium ($Z=48$, with outer configuration $4d^{10}, 5s^2$).

6. Elements of Sixth Period

This period corresponds to $n=6$ i.e. sixth shell. Thus, one $6s$, seven $4f$, five $5d$ and three $6p$ orbitals i.e. total 16 orbitals are available for filling of electrons. Hence, number of elements present in this period is thirty two (32). This period begins with the filling of $6s$ orbital in caesium ($Z=55$ with outer configuration $6s^1$) and ends at radon ($Z=86$, with outer configuration $6s^2\,6p^6$). When $6s$ orbital filled up completely, the electron enters in $5d$ orbital rather than $4f$ orbital (which is against aufbau principle). This is because of high stability of xenon core. Since $5d$ orbital lie outside this core and have energy slightly higher than the $4f$ orbital, so it gets electron first.

Once an electron enters in the $5d$ orbital, the next electron goes in the inner $4f$ orbital (as in cerium with $Z=58$) due to greater nuclear charge. After that the electrons enter continuously in the $4f$ shell till it gets completed at lutetium ($Z=71$ with configuration $4f^{14}, 5d^1, 6s^2$). These fourteen elements from cerium to lutetium constitute the $4f$ or inner-transition series, which is also named as the **lanthanoid series** due to the resemblance of properties of these elements with lanthanum (d-block element with $Z=57$).

When $4f$-orbitals are filled completely, the electrons enter in $5d$-orbitals (to form $5d$ transition series) and finally in $6p$-orbitals.

7. Elements of Seventh Period

This period corresponds to $n=7$, i.e. seventh shell. Just like sixth period, it involves the filling of $7s, 5f, 6d$ and $7p$ (total 16) orbitals successively. However most of the elements of this period are **synthetic** or **man-made radioactive elements.**

Example 2 How would you justify the presence of elements in the 5th period of the periodic table?

NCERT Textbook

Sol. The 5th period begins with the filling of principal quantum number, $n=5$. When $n=5$, $l=0, 1, 2, 3$. But according to Aufbau principle, in 5th period, electrons can be filled only in 5s, 4d and 5p-subshells whose energies increases in the order $5s < 4d < 5p$ (the energies of 5d and 5f-subshells are higher than that of 6s-subshell but the energy of 4d-subshell is lower than that of 5p-subshell). Thus, the available orbitals are one 5s, five 4d and three 5p orbitals, i.e. total 9 orbitals which can accommodate a maximum of 18 electrons. Hence, this period contains 18 elements.

Groupwise Electronic Configurations

Elements of a group or same vertical column have the same number of electrons in the outermost shell (also called the **valence shell**) i.e. have same valence shell electronic configuration.

Since properties of an element mainly depends upon the number of valence shell electrons, so the elements having same valence shell electronic configuration also exhibit resemblance in their properties. That's why elements of a specific group of the periodic table has resemblance in their properties.

Example 3 Write down the outermost electronic configurations of alkali metals. How will you justify their placement in group 1 of the periodic table?

NCERT Exemplar

Sol. All the elements of group IA (or I) i.e. alkali metals have the similar outer electronic configuration i.e. ns^1 where n refers to the number of principle shells. Their electronic configurations are given below.

Atomic Number	Symbol	Electronic configuration
3	Li	$1s^2 2s^1$ (or) $[He]2s^1$
11	Na	$1s^2 2s^2 2p^6 3s^1$ (or) $[Ne]3s^1$
19	K	$1s^2 2s^2 2p^6 3s^2 3p^6 4s^1$ (or) $[Ar]4s^1$
37	Rb	$1s^2 2s^2 2p^6 3s^2 3p^6 4s^2 3d^{10} 4p^6 5s^1$ (or) $[Kr]5s^1$
55	Cs	$1s^2 2s^2 2p^6 3s^2 3p^6 3d^{10} 4s^2 4p^6 4d^{10} 5s^2 5p^6 6s^1$ or $[Xe]\ 6s^1$
87	Fr	$[Rn]7s^1$

Hence, placement of all these elements of group 1 of the periodic table because of similarity in electronic configuration and all the elements have similar properties. Thus, it is also evident that the physical and chemical properties of the elements depend on their atomic number and not on their atomic mass.

Thus, it is also evident that the physical and chemical properties of the elements depend on their atomic number and not on their atomic mass.

Divison of Periodic Table as *s*, *p*, *d* and *f*-Blocks

Depending upon the nature of atomic orbitals in which the last electron enters, the elements can be classified into four blocks *viz*, *s*-block, *p*-block, *d*-block and *f*-block.

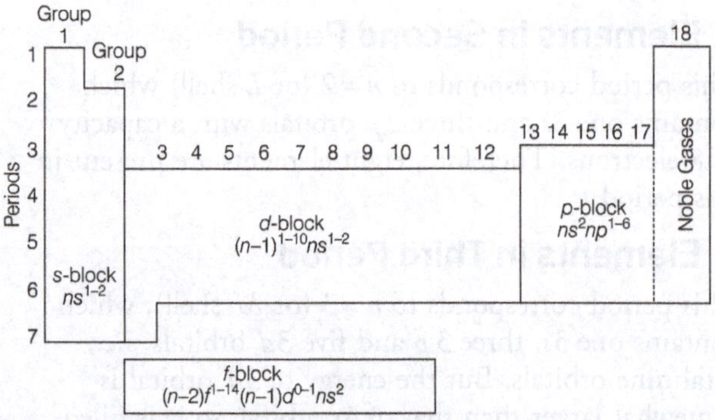

Division of periodic table into s, p, d and f-blocks

General characteristics of these blocks are described below. (During this discussion certain terms has been used, description of which has been provided later in this chapter).

The *s*-Block Elements

The elements in which the last electron enters in the *s*-orbital of their respective outermost shell are called the ***s*-block elements**. Since, *s*-subshell have only one orbital which can accommodate a maximum of two electrons, so only two group, i.e. group 1 (alkali metals) and group 2(i.e. alkaline earth metals) belong to this block. These groups lie on the extreme left of the periodic table.

General characteristics of elements of this block are:

(i) General electronic configuration of elements of this block is ns^{1-2} (where $n = 1, 2, \ldots$). Thus, the valence shell configuration of alkali metals is ns^1 and of alkaline earth metals is ns^2.

(ii) They are soft metals with low melting and boiling points.

(iii) Because of their lower ionisation enthalpy, these metals are highly reactive and hence, never found pure in nature. Reactivity of these metals increases on moving down the group as the distance between the valence electrons and nucleus increases.

(iv) They are electropositive and metallic elements. Their metallic character also increases on moving down the group.

(v) They are strong reducing agents.

Note Alkali metals like K, Rb and Cs are used in photoelectric cells due to their low ionisation enthalpy.

The *p*-Block Elements

The elements in which the last electron enters in any of the three *p*-orbitals of their respective outermost shell are called the ***p*-block elements**. Since a *p*-orbital can accommodate a maximum of 6 electrons, thus, six group, i.e. group 13 to 18 belong to this block. Elements of group 15, 16, 17 and 18 are respectively known as **pnictogens** (means Choking), **chalcogens, halogens** and **noble gases.** Group 13 to 18 are present on the extreme right of the periodic table.

General characteristics of elements of this block are as follows:

(i) The outermost electronic configurations of these elements varies from $ns^2\ np^1$ to $ns^2\ np^6$ in each period i.e. the general configuration for these elements can be written as $ns^2\ np^{1-6}$ (where $n = 1, 2, \ldots$).

(ii) They are generally non-metals but some metals and metalloids are also present. The non-metallic character increases from left to right along a period but metallic character increases on moving down a group of this block.

(iii) They have high electron gain enthalpy (negative) and ionisation energy. Both properties increases along a period from left to right and decreases on moving down a group.

(iv) Their oxidising character increases on moving from left to right along a period and reducing character increases from top to bottom in a group.

Note Elements of *s*-block and *p*-block are collectively known as representative elements.

The *d*-Block Elements (Transition Elements)

Elements in which the last electron enters in one of the inner *d*-orbital, are called ***d*-block elements.** Since there can be a maximum of ten electrons in a *d*-subshell, so ten groups, i.e. group 3, 4, 5, 6, 7, 8, 9, 10, 11, 12 belong to this block.

The properties of elements of these groups are midway between those of *s*-block and *p*-block elements, thus, they act as a bridge between the highly reactive metals of *s*-block and the less reactive elements of group 13 and 14, i.e. they show transition (change) in behaviour and hence, known as **transition elements.**

General characteristics of elements of this block are as follows :

(i) General electronic configuration of elements of this block is $(n-1)\ d^{1-10}\ ns^{(0-2)}$.

(ii) They all are metals with very high melting and boiling points.

(iii) Most of them form coloured ions because of the presence of partially filled *d*-orbitals.

(iv) They generally exhibit variable valency (oxidation states) because the 3*d* and 4*s* orbitals are of comparable energy and hence, take part in bonding.

(v) They generally show paramagnetism because of the presence of unpaired electrons in the *d* oribtals. (Higher the number of unpaired electrons, more is the paramagnetic character).

(vi) They are used as catalysts because of their variable valency and partially filled *d*-orbitals.

Note Zn, Cd and Hg because of the presence of completely filled *d*-orbitals (i.e. $(n-1)d^{10}\ ns^2$ configuration) these do not exhibit most of the properties of transition elements and hence, these are not considered as typical transition elements. [Typical transition elements have partially filled *d*-orbitals in any of their oxidation states.]

The *f*-Block Elements (Inner-Transition Elements)

The elements in which the last electron enters in *f*-orbital of anti-penultimate shells are called the ***f*-block elements.** These are also called inner-transition elements because of the filling of inner-penultimate or anti-penultimate shell by last electron.

This block contains two series of elements, called the 4*f* and 5*f* series, each of which contains 14 elements. The elements of 4*f* series [i.e. from atomic number 58 (Ce) to 71(Lu)] are called **lanthanoids** and the elements of 5*f* series [i.e. from atomic number = 90 (Th) to 103 (Lr)] are called **actinoids.**

These two series of elements are present at the bottom of the periodic table.

General characteristics exhibited by elements of this block are as follows:

(i) General outer electronic configuration for these elements is $(n-2)\ f^{1-14}\ (n-1)\ d^{0-1}\ ns^2$. Thus, the outer electronic configuration for lanthanoids and actinoids are

$$4f^{1-14}\ 5d^{0-1}\ 6s^2 \quad \text{and} \quad 5f^{1-14}\ 6d^{0-1}\ 7s^2$$

(ii) All of these are metals.

(iii) Actinoids exhibit a large number of oxidation states because of the comparable energy of 5*f*, 6*d* and 7*s* orbitals and hence, their chemistry is more complicated as compared to the corresponding lanthanoids. However, the most common oxidation state exhibited by *f*-block elements is +3.

(iv) All the actinoids are radioactive in nature. The first three elements i.e. thorium (Th), protoactinium (Pa) and uranium (U) are natural but the remaining i.e. from neptunium to Uub ($Z = 112$) are synthetic i.e. man made by nuclear reactions. The later are also called **transuranic** or **transuranium** elements as these follow uranium in the periodic table. Lanthanoids are also known as rare earth elements because they occur scarcely in the earth's crust.

Anomalies Associated with *s, p, d, f* Classification

Although the classification is very important and helpful for predicting the properties of an element or a group of elements, yet it is associated with certain anomalies which are as follows :

1. Position of Helium (He)

The electronic configuration of helium is $1s^2$, so it should be kept in *s*-block as the last electron enters in *s* orbital. But it is placed in *p*-block with elements of group 18, due to the presence of completely filled valence or outermost shell ($1s^2$) and hence, it shows similarity in properties with other noble gases.

2. Position of Hydrogen (H)

The electronic configuration of hydrogen is $1s^1$. Because of the presence of only one electron in *s* orbital, it can be placed in group 1 with alkali metals. But it can also accept an electron to achieve the electronic configuration of nearest inert gas (which is helium) like halogens (elements of group 17) so it can also be placed alongwith them. Because of its unique behaviour, hydrogen is placed at the top of the periodic table.

Algorithm for Predicting Position of an Element in the Periodic Table

In the prediction of position of an element in the periodic table, following steps are involved.

Step 1 First write the electronic configuration of the element, if not given.

Step 2 Find the principal quantum number of the valence shell, it shows the **period of the element**.

Step 3 Predict the orbital which receives the last electron. It shows the **block of the element**.

Step 4 **The group of an element is then predicted as**

(i) If the element belongs to *s*-block, its group number = Number of valence (or outermost shell) electrons.

(ii) If the element belongs to *p*-block, Group number = 10 + number of valence electrons $\Rightarrow$ 10 + *ns* electrons + *np* electrons (here *n* = outermost shell)

(iii) If the element belongs to *d*-block, Group number = number of electrons in $(n-1)d$ subshell + number of electron/s in *ns* shell.

(iv) If the element belongs to *f*-block, Group number = 3.

Example 4 The elements $Z = 117$ and 120 have not yet been discovered. In which family/group would you place these elements and also give the electronic configuration in each case. **[NCERT Textbook]**

Sol. ***Step* I** Electronic configuration of the given elements is

$$Z = 117 = [\text{Rn}]\ 5f^{14}\ 6d^{10}\ \underbrace{7s^2\ 7p^5}_{\text{Valence shell}}$$

$$Z = 120 = [\text{Uun}]\ \underbrace{8s^2}_{\text{Valence shell}}$$

***Step* II** (i) Principal quantum number of the valence shell is 7 for $Z = 117$, so it belongs to 7th period.

(ii) Principal quantum number of the valence shell is 8 for $Z = 120$, so it belongs to 8th period.

***Step* III** (i) Element with $Z = 117$ belongs to *p*-block.

(ii) Element with $Z = 120$ belongs to *s*-block.

***Step* IV** (i) Thus, for element with $Z = 117$

Group number $= 10 + 2 + 5 = 17$

i.e. it belongs to **halogen family**.

(ii) For element with $Z = 120$,

Group number = number of electrons in valence shell = 2

So, it belongs to **alkaline earth metals**.

Classification of Elements. Metals, Non-metals and Metalloids

In addition to *s, p, d, f* classification, elements can also be classified as metals, non-metals and metalloids.

1. Metals

These comprise more than 78% of all known elements and appear on the left side of the periodic table.

Some important properties of metals are as follows :

(i) They are generally solid at room temperature with an exception of mercury which is liquid at room temperature.

(ii) They have very high melting and boiling point except gallium and caesium (melting point of which are respectively 303 K and 302 K).

(iii) They are good conductors of heat and electricity.

(iv) They are malleable (i.e. can be flattened into thin sheets by hammering) and ductile (i.e. can be drawn into wires).

2. Non-Metals

These are present only in *p*-block and occupy the top right side of the periodic table. (Although *p*-block have some metals and metalloids also).

Some important properties exhibited by non-metals are as follows :

(i) They can be either solid or gas at room temperature with an exception of bromine (which is in liquid state at room temperature).

(ii) Their melting and boiling points are very low with exception of boron and carbon.

(iii) They are poor conductors of heat (except diamond) and electricity (except graphite).

(iv) They are generally brittle and are neither malleable nor-ductile.

3. Metalloids

These are very few in numbers and present in between metals and non-metals. They exhibit the properties of both metals and non-metals. That's why, they are called **semi-metals** or **metalloids**. e.g. silicon, germanium, arsenic, antimony, tellurium etc. In the periodic table, these elements form a *zig-zag* line and separate metals from non-metals. (see long form of periodic table).

Trends in Metallic and Non-Metallic Properties

The metals are present on the left hand side of periodic table. Thus, metallic character decreases from left to right along a period and on moving down the group, metallic character increases. Non-metallic character, on the other hand, increases from left to right along a period and decreases on moving down the group.

Example 5 Considering the atomic number and position in the periodic table, arrange the following elements in the increasing order of metallic character : Si, Be, Mg, Na, P. **NCERT Textbook**

Sol. Metallic character increases down a group and decreases along a period as we move from left to right. The position of these elements in the periodic table is as follows :

I	II	III	IV	V
	Be			
Na	Mg		Si	P

Thus, the order of increasing metallic character is

$$P < Si < Be < Mg < Na$$

Topic Practice 2

Very Short Answer Type Questions

1 Mark

1. Fill in the Blanks

(i) IUPAC name of the element with atomic number 110 is ....

(ii) The fourteen elements from cerium to lutetium are named as ....

(iii) General electronic configuration of *d*-block elements is ....

(iv) Elements of group-15 (nitrogen family) are also known as ....

2. Objective Type Questions

(i) An element *A* belongs to third period and fifteenth group of the periodic table. Which one of the following is true regarding the outer electronic configuration of *A*?

(a) It has completely filled *s*-orbital and *p*-orbital
(b) It has partially filled *d*-orbitals and completely filled *s*-orbital
(c) It has half-filled *d*-orbitals and completely filled *s*-orbitals
(d) It has completely filled *s*-orbital and half-filled *p*-orbitals

(ii) Successive filling of 3*s* and 3*p*-orbitals give rise to the third period. The number of elements present in this period are

(a) 2 (b) 4 (c) 6 (d) 8

(iii) 3*d*-transition series of elements start with scandium which has the electronic configuration

(a) $3d^1\ 4s^2$ (b) $3d^1\ 4s^1$
(c) $3d^2\ 4s^2$ (d) $3d^3\ 4s^2$

(iv) Which of the following statements is incorrect?

(a) The 4th period in the periodic table ends at krypton with the filling up of the 3*p*-orbitals
(b) The 5th period in the periodic table contains the 4*d*-transition series
(c) Starting element of 4*d*-transition series is yttrium
(d) Filling up of the 4*f*-orbitals begins with cerium

(v) All of the group-I elements have ns^1 valence shell electronic configuration and the properties of an element have

(a) periodic dependence upon its atomic mass
(b) periodic dependence upon its atomic number
(c) periodic dependence upon its atomic radius
(d) None of the above

(vi) Which of the following groups does helium belongs?

(a) *s*-block (b) *p*-block
(c) *d*-block (d) *f*-block

3. Matching Type Questions

(i) Match the Column I with Column II and select the correct answer using given codes.

Column I (Element types)		Column II (Electronic configuration)
A. Inert gas elements	(i)	$(n-1)d^{1-10}\ ns^{1-2}$
B. Transition elements	(ii)	ns^2 and ns^2np^6
C. Inner-transition elements	(iii)	$(n-2)f^{1-14}(n-1)d^{0-1}ns^2$

Codes

	A	B	C		A	B	C
(a)	(i)	(ii)	(iii)	(b)	(ii)	(i)	(iii)
(c)	(iii)	(ii)	(i)	(d)	(ii)	(iii)	(i)

(ii) Match the Column I with Column II and select the correct answer using given codes.

Column I		Column II
A. 3*d*-transition series	(i)	Cerium ($Z = 58$)
B. 4*d*-transition series	(ii)	Actinium ($Z = 89$)
C. 4*f*-inner transition series	(iii)	Scandium ($z = 21$)
D. 5*f*-inner transition series	(iv)	Yttrium ($Z = 39$)

Codes

	A	B	C	D
(a)	(i)	(ii)	(iii)	(iv)
(b)	(i)	(ii)	(iv)	(iii)
(c)	(iii)	(iv)	(ii)	(i)
(d)	(iii)	(iv)	(i)	(ii)

4. Why do elements in the same group have similar physical and chemical properties? **NCERT Textbook**

5. Write the atomic number of the element present in the third period and seventeenth group of the periodic table.

6. An element *X* belongs to the third period of *p*-block. It has 4 electrons in the outermost shell. Name the element.

7. In terms of period and group where would you locate the element with $Z = 114$?

8. In terms of electronic configuration, what does elements of a given period and a group have in common?

Short Answer Type I Questions

(2 Marks)

9. On the basis of quantum numbers, justify that sixth period of the periodic table should have 32 elements. **NCERT Textbook**

10. Write the general outer electronic configuration of *s*, *p*, *d* and *f*-block elements.

11. Write four characteristic properties of *p*-block elements.

12. All transition elements are *d*-block elements, but all *d*-block elements are not transition elements. Explain.

13. What are the major differences between metals and non-metals? **NCERT Textbook**

14. (i) How do the electronic configurations of the elements with $Z = 107$ to 109 differ from one another?

(ii) Rn ($Z = 86$) is the last noble gas discovered. Predict what will be the atomic number of the next noble gas to be discovered. Write its symbol.

15. How many elements can be accommodated in the present set up of the long form of the periodic table? Explain.

Short Answer Type II Questions

(3 Marks)

16. (i) Which orbitals are filled with electrons in third period?

(ii) Which of the lanthanoids is man-made element?

(iii) To which series do man-made elements belong?

17. Assign the position of the element having outer electronic configuration.

(i) $ns^2\ np^4$ for $n = 3$

(ii) $(n-1)\ d^2\ ns^2$ for $n = 4$ and

(iii) $(n-2)\ f^7\ (n-1)\ d^1\ ns^2$ for $n = 6$, in the periodic table. **NCERT Textbook**

18. Give the name and atomic number of the inert gas atom in which the total number of *d*-electrons is equal to the difference in numbers of total *p* and *s* electrons.

19. Can an element with atomic number 126, if discovered, be accommodated in the present set up of the long form of periodic table?

Long Answer Type Questions

5 Marks

20. Justify the given statement with suitable examples "the properties of the elements are a periodic function of their atomic numbers". **NCERT Exemplar**

21. Which elements have the following electronic configurations? (Use only the periodic table.)

(i) $1s^2, 2s^2, 2p^5$ (ii) [Ar] $4s^2, 3d^{10}, 4p^1$

(iii) [Xe] $6s^2$ (iv) [Xe] $6s^2, 5d^1, 4f^7$

(v) [Ar] $4s^1, 3d^{10}$ (exception to rules)

22. Use the periodic table to answer the following questions.

(i) Identify an element with five electrons in the outer subshell.

(ii) Identify an element that would tend to lose two electrons.

(iii) Identify an element that would tend to gain two electrons.

(iv) Identify the groups having metal, non-metal, that contains liquid as well as gas at the room temperature. **NCERT Textbook**

Hints & Solutions

1. (i) ununnillium (ii) lanthanoids

(iii) $(n-1)d^{(1-10)}ns^{(0-2)}$ (iv) pnictogens

2. (i) (d) The element *A* may be phosphorus (P) and its electronic configuration is

$$A(\text{P}) = 1s^2,\ 2s^2 2p^6,\ 3s^2 3p^3$$

So, element '*A*' has completely filled *s*-orbital and half-filled *p*-orbitals.

(ii) (*d*) Successive filling of $3s$ and $3p$-orbitals give rise to the third period of 8 elements from sodium to argon.

(iii) (*a*) Before the $4p$-orbital is filled, filling up of $3d$-orbitals becomes energetically favourable and we come across the so called $3d$ transition series of elements. This starts from scandium ($Z = 21$) which has electronic configuration-[Ar]$3d^1 4s^2$.

(iv) (*a*) The fourth period ends at krypton with the filling up of the $4p$-orbitals. Altogether 18 elements are present in this fourth period.

(v) (*b*) All group-1 elements have ns^1 valence shell electronic configuration and the properties of an element have periodic dependence upon its atomic number.

(vi) (*b*) Helium belongs to the *p*-block, inspite of differentiating electron occupy 1*s*-orbital, because it has a completely filled valence shell ($1s^2$) and exhibits characteristic properties of other noble gases.

3. (i) (*b*) A → (ii), B → (i), C → (iii)

A. Inert gas elements ⟶ ns^2 and ns^2np^6.

B. Transition elements ⟶ $(n-1)\,d^{1-10}\,ns^{1-2}$

C. Inner transition elements

⟶ $(n-2)f^{1-14}(n-1)d^{0-1}ns^2$

(ii) (*d*) A → (iii), B → (iv), C → (i), D, → (ii),

A. $3d$ transition series ⟶ Scandium to zinc (d^1 to d^{10})

B. $4d$ transition series ⟶ Yttrium to cadmium (39 to 48 atomic number)

C. $4f$-inner transition series ⟶ Cerium to lutetium (58 to 71 atomic number)

D. $5f$-inner transition series ⟶ Actinium (thorium to lawrencium) 90 to 103 atomic number.

4. Same group elements have similar valence shell electronic configuration. Therefore, have similar physical and chemical properties.

5. General configuration for 17th group elements is $ns^2\ np^5$. In the third period, the principal quantum number for valence shell is three, so the electronic configuration of valence shell for the given element is $3s^2, 3p^5$.

Third period starts from atomic number, $Z = 11$ and ends at $Z = 18$. Hence, the atomic number of the given element is $10 + 7 = 17$.

6. The outer configuration of the element is $3s^2\ 3p^2$ (as it has 4 elements in outermost shell). Thus, the complete configuration is $1s^2$, $2s^2\ 2p^6, 3s^2, 3p^2$. So the atomic number is $2 + 8 + 4 = 14$. Hence, the element is silicon.

7. First write electronic configuration of the given element. Highest value of *n* shows the period of element and group number = 10 + number of valence electrons in *ns* and *np* shells.

$${}_{114}Z = {}_{86}[\text{Rn}]\, 7s^2, 5f^{14}, 6d^{10}, 7p^2$$

In the periodic table, the element with $Z = 114$ is located in *p*-block (as last electron enters in *p*-subshell).

Period-7th (as $n = 7$ for valence shell)

Group-14th (for *p*-block elements, group number = 10 + number of electrons in valence shell).

8. In a period, all elements have equal number of shells whereas in a group, all elements have same number of electrons in the outermost shell.

9. In the modern periodic table, each period starts with the filling of a new principal energy level. Sixth period begins with filling of principal quantum number, $n = 6$. [1]

According to aufbau principle, in the ground state of the atoms, the orbitals are filled in order of their increasing energies. Therefore, in sixth period, electrons enter in $4f$, $5d$, $6s$ and $6p$ subshells. [1]

10. Refer to text on pages 104 and 105 [Division of periodic table as *s*, *p*, *d* and *f*-block].

11. Refer to text on pages 104 and 105 [*p*-block elements].

12. Elements in which the last electron enters in the d-orbitals, are called d-block elements or transition elements. These elements have the general outer electronic configuration $(n-1)\,d^{1-10}\,ns^{0-2}$. Zn, Cd and Hg having the electronic configuration, $(n-1)\,d^{10}\,ns^2$ do not show most of the properties of transition elements. The d-orbitals in these elements are completely filled in the ground state as well as in their common oxidation states.
Therefore, they are not regarded as transition elements. Thus, on the basis of properties, all transition elements are d-block elements but on the basis of electronic configuration, all d-block elements are not transition elements. [2]

13. Refer to text on pages 106 ans 107 [Metals, non-metal and metalloids].

14. (i) Element with $Z=107$ has five, $Z=108$ has six electrons while $Z=109$ has seven $6d$-electrons. Thus, these elements differ in the number of electrons in the $6d$-subshell. [1]
(ii) 118, Og (Organesson) [1]

15. In the present set up of the long form of the periodic table, we have eighteen groups, seven periods (i.e. principal quantum number, $n=7$) and four blocks (s, p, d and f-block elements). [1]
Therefore, the maximum number of elements which can be accommodated in the present set up of the long form of the periodic table in accordance with Aufbau principle is
$1s^2, 2s^2, 2p^6, 3s^2, 3p^6, 4s^2, 3d^{10}, 4p^6, 5s^2, 4d^{10}, 5p^6, 6s^2, 4f^{14}, 5d^{10}, 6p^6, 7s^2, 5f^{14}, 6d^{10}, 7p^6 = 118.$ [1]

16. (i) In third period, $3s$ and $3p$ orbitals are filled.
(ii) Promethium (Pm) with atomic number 61 is a man-made lanthanoid.
(iii) Actinoid series (f-block elements). [2]

17. (i) $ns^2\,np^4$ for $n=3$
$n=3$ means element belongs to third period. Since, last electron enters in the p-orbital, it belongs to p-block. For p-block elements, the group number $=10+$ valence shell electrons $=10+(2+4)=16$.
Hence, the element (sulphur) belongs to 16th group. [1]
(ii) $(n-1)\,d^2\,ns^2$ for $n=4$
$n=4$ means the element belongs to fourth period. Since, last electron enters in d-orbital, the given element belongs to d-block. For d-block elements, group number = number of d-electrons + number of ns electrons $=2+2=4$
Hence, the element (titanium) belongs to 4th group. [1]
(iii) $(n-2)\,f^7\,(n-1)\,d^1\,ns^2$ for $n=6$
$n=6$ means the element belongs to sixth period.Since, last electron enters in f-orbital, the given element belongs to f-block and all f-block elements are the members of third group. Hence, the element belongs to third group. [1]

18. The first inert gas which contains d electrons is krypton. Its atomic number is 36 and its electronic configuration is $1s^2, 2s^2, 2p^6, 3s^2, 3p^6, 3d^{10}, 4s^2, 4p^6$
Total number of d-electrons $=10$
Total number of p-electrons $=6+6+6=18$
Total number of s-electrons $=2+2+2+2=8$ [1]
$\therefore$ Difference in total number of p and s electrons
$=18-8=10$ [2]
Thus, the inert gas is krypton.

19. No, the maximum number of elements which can be accommodated in the present set up of the long form of the periodic table is 118. Thereafter, filling of $8s$-orbital shell begin which will accommodate only two electrons. After $8s$-orbitals, the filling of $5g$-orbitals will begin. Since we do not have any provision for g-block elements in the present set up of the long form of periodic table, therefore, an element with atomic number 126, if discovered, cannot be accommodated in the present set up of the long form of periodic table. [3]

20. There are numerous physical properties of elements such as melting points, boiling points, heats of fusion and vaporisation, energy of atomisation, etc., which show periodic variations. The cause of periodicity in properties is the repetition of similar outer electronic configuration after certain regular intervals. e.g. all the elements of 1s group (alkali metals) have similar outer electronic configuration, i.e. ns^1.
$_3Li = 1s^2, 2s^1$
$_{11}Na = 1s^2, 2s^2, 2p^6, 3s^1$
$_{19}K = 1s^2, 2s^2, 2p^6, 3s^2, 3p^6, 4s^1$ [2]
Therefore, due to similar outermost shell electronic configuration all alkali metals have similar properties. e.g., sodium and potassium both are soft and reactive metals. They all form basic oxides and their basic character increases down the group. They all form unipositive ion by the loss of one electron. Similarly, all the elements of 17th group (halogens) have similar outermost shell electronic configuration, i.e. $ns^2\,np^5$ and thus possess similar properties.
$_9F = 1s^2, 2s^2, 2p^5$
$_{17}Cl = 1s^2, 2s^2, 2p^6, 3s^2, 3p^5$
$_{35}Br = 1s^2, 2s^2, 2p^6, 3s^2, 3p^6, 3d^{10}, 4s^2, 4p^5$ [3]

21. (i) The outer electronic configuration of $1s^2, 2s^2, 2p^5$ is $2s^2, 2p^5$. Therefore, this element is a p-block element and belongs to the second period and group 17. Thus, the element is fluorine, F. [1]
(ii) The outer electronic configuration of [Ar] $4s^2, 3d^{10}, 4p^1$ is $4s^2\,4p^1$, therefore, it is a p-block element. It belongs to the fourth period and 13 group . Therefore, the element is gallium, Ga. [1]
(iii) The outer electronic configuration of [Xe] $6s^2$ is $6s^2$, therefore, it is a s-block element and belongs to the

sixth period and group 2 of the periodic table. Therefore, the element is barium, Ba. [1]

(iv) In the electronic configuration [Xe] $6s^2, 5d^1, 4f^7$ the electrons are in $4f$ shell, therefore, it is a f-block element and belongs to the sixth period and third group. Therefore, the element is gadolinium, Gd. [1]

(v) The outer electronic configuration of [Ar] $4s^1, 3d^{10}$ is $4s^1, 3d^{10}$, therefore, it is a d-block element and belongs to the fourth period and group 11. Therefore, the element is copper, Cu. [1]

22. (i) General electronic configuration of elements having five electrons in the outer subshell is $ns^2\ np^5$. This configuration belongs to halogen family, i.e. F, Cl, Br, I, At. [1]

(ii) Elements of second group are known as alkaline earth metals (Mg, Ca, Sr, Ba, etc.). Their general electronic configuration for valence shell is ns^2. These elements can form dipositive cations by the loss of two electrons easily. [1]

(iii) 16th group elements such as O, S, Se etc., have a tendency to accept two electrons because, by the gain of two electrons they attain noble gas configuration.

Their general electronic configuration for valence shell is ns^2np^4. [1]

(iv) Group 1 or 17 of the periodic table contains metal, non-metal, that are liquid as well as gas at the room temperature, e.g. H is a non-metal and present in gaseous state (H_2) at room temperature. All other elements of this group are metals. Cs is a liquid metal. Similarly, Br_2 is a liquid non-metal while other elements of this group are gaseous non-metals. Iodine can form I^+ so it has metallic properties also. [2]

TOPIC 03 Periodic Properties : Atomic Radii and Ionisation Enthalpy

Periodic Trends in Properties of Elements

Here, we will discuss the periodic trends in physical properties (like atomic and ionic radii, ionisation enthalpy, electron gain enthalpy and electronegativity) as well as in chemical properties (like valency, nature of oxides etc.,) one by one.

Atomic Radius

The **atomic radius,** is defined as **"the distance from the centre of the nucleus to the outermost shell (valence shell) containing electrons."**

The determination of exact radius of atom is not possible because of the very small size (~ 1.2 Å) of atom and its non-sharp boundary. Thus, atomic radius is generally estimated by knowing the distance between the atoms in the combined form.

Depending upon the nature of combining atoms, atomic radius can be of following types.

1. Covalent Radius

If the combining atoms are non-metals (except noble gases), their radius is called the **covalent radius.**

Covalent radius is defined as **"the one-half of the distance between the centres of nuclei of two covalently bonded atoms of the same element in a molecule,"**

For a diatomic molecule,

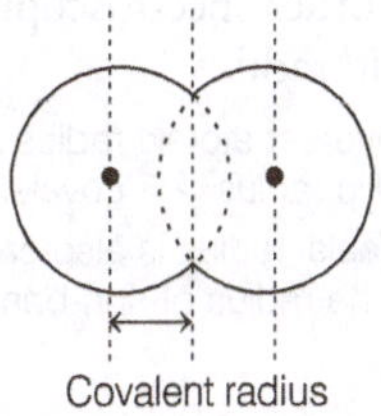

i.e. $r_{\text{covalent}} = \frac{1}{2}$

[Internuclear distance between two covalently bonded atoms with a single bond].

2. Metallic Radius or Crystal Radius

In case of metals, the atomic radius is called the metallic radius and is defined as "the one-half of the internuclear distance separating the metal cores in the metallic crystal."

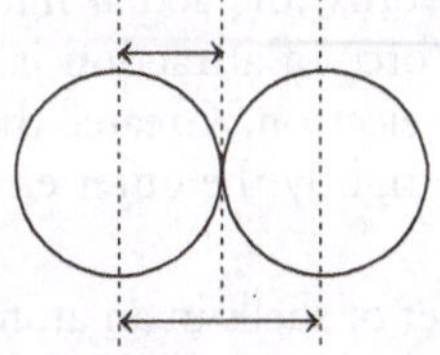

Note In metallic lattice, the electrons are mobile and hence, only weakly attracted by the kernels. But in covalent molecules, the electrons are strongly attracted by the nuclei of combining atoms. Thus, metallic radius is always larger than covalent radius.

3. van der Waals' Radius

In case of noble gases, the atomic radius is called the van der Waals' radius, which is defined as **"one-half of the distance between the nuclei of two identical non-bonded isolated atoms"**.

Since, the van der Waals' forces are very weak and hence, the internuclear distance between the atoms held by van der Waals' forces is much larger as compared to that between covalently bonded atoms. In other words, we can also say that the radius of a noble gas is largest in its period.

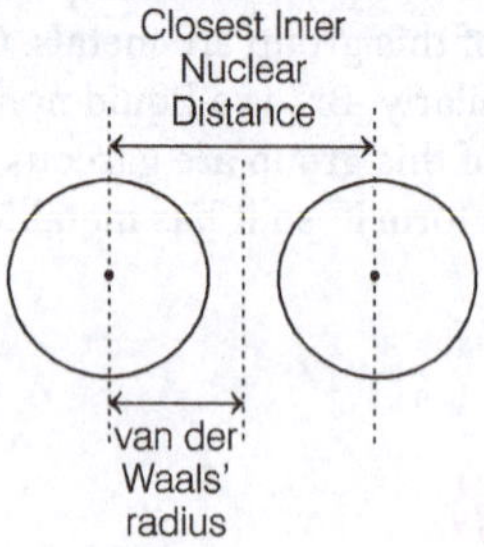

Closest approach of two atoms and van der Waals' radius

For the sake of convenience, we will use the term atomic radius for covalent, metallic and van der Waals' radii in this book. X-ray and other spectroscopic methods are used to measure the atomic radii.

Note
- The order of different atomic radius is van der Waals' radius > metallic radius >> covalent radius.
- The van der Waals' radius is also called the **non-bonded radius** as it is the radius of non-bonded atoms or molecules,

Factors Affecting Atomic Radii

(i) **Screening or Shielding Effect** The electrons of inner shells, also called the core electrons, shield or screen the outermost electron(s) from the attractive pull of the nucleus. This effect is therefore, called the shielding (or screening) effect. Atomic radii varies directly with shielding effect, i.e. greater the shielding effect, larger will be the atomic radii.

(ii) **Effective Nuclear Charge (Z^*)** It is defined as the net nuclear attraction towards the valence shell electrons or in other words ,the actual nuclear charge whose electrostatic force of attraction is being experienced by the outer electron. Greater the effective nuclear charge, more tightly the outer electrons are hold by nucleus.

(iii) As the number of shells in an atom increases, atomic radii increases. Atomic radii varies inversely with effective nuclear charge, i.e.

$$\text{Atomic radii} \propto \frac{1}{\text{Effective nuclear charge}}$$

Variation of Atomic Radii in the Periodic Table

1. Variation Along a Period

The atomic radius generally decreases from left to right along a period, as illustrated in the below graph for the elements of second period. This is because, with in a period, the electron is added to the same valence shell, due to which the effective nuclear charge increases and hence, the outer electron is held by the nucleus more tightly which results in decreased radii.

Here, it is important to note that the electrons of the same shell do not screen each other, hence the increased nuclear charge is not compensated by the screening effect and thus, results in decreased radii.

Exception

(i) Transition elements show a little variation in their atomic radii due to poor shielding effect of *d*-electrons.

(ii) Lanthanoid also exhibit a little variation in their atomic radii due to lanthanoid contraction.

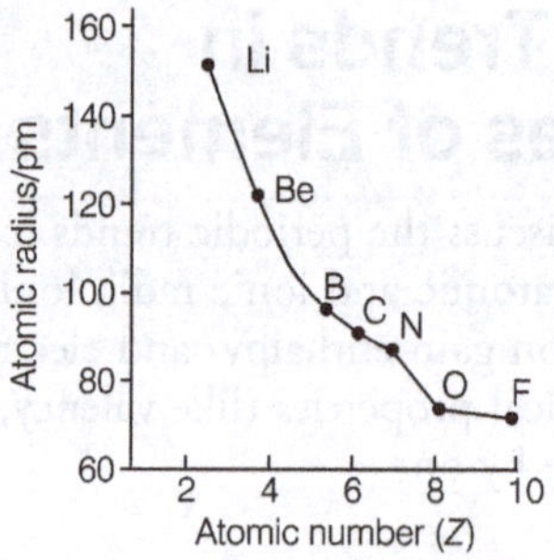

Variation of atomic radius with atomic number

(iii) In a period of the periodic table, generally the size of an atom decreases with increase in atomic number but at the end of each period, i.e. in noble gases, the atomic sizes increases abruptly. This is due to the fact that noble gases do not form covalent bonds. Their radius is calculated in terms of van der Waals' radius which is larger than the covalent radius of other atoms.

2. Variation in a Group

The atomic radius generally increases on moving down a group as illustrated in the following graph for alkali metals and halogens. This is because the electrons are added in the successive shells, i.e. principal quantum number (n) increases and thus, the electrons of inner shells shield the electrons of principal energy level from the pull of the nucleus, due to which the distance between the valence electron and the nucleus increases and hence, the atomic radius increases.

[Here, note that the shielding effect is more pronounced than the effect of increased nuclear charge].

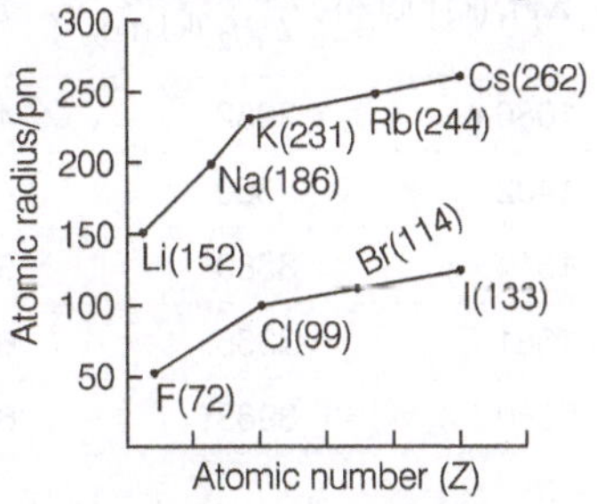

Variation of atomic radius with atomic number for alkali metals and halogens

Exception

Among d-block elements, the radii increases from member of first series to the corresponding member of second but the radius of members of second and third series are almost equal due to lanthanoid contraction.

Ionic Radius

In case of ions the radius is called **ionic radius** and is defined as **"the effective distance from the centre of the nucleus of an ion upto which it has an influence in the ionic bond "**.

The distance between the nuclei of cation and anion, i.e. internuclear distance in an ionic crystal can be measured by X-ray method. By knowing the internuclear distance the radius of one ion can be determined. Similarly, the radius of other ion can also be calculated.

Internuclear distance = radii of cation + radii of anion

Comparison of the Ionic Radii with Corresponding Atomic Radii

The study of ionic radii leads to following two generalisations :

(i) The size of cation is smaller than its parent atom. A cation is formed by the loss of electron, thus, has fewer electrons while its nuclear charge (i.e. number of protons) is same as that present in parent atom. Consequently, the nucleus binds the electrons more tightly (i.e. effective nuclear charge increases) and hence, the size of the atom decreases. e.g.

	Na	$\longrightarrow$	$Na^+ + e^-$
	$1s^2, 2s^2, 2p^6, 3s^1$} three shells		$1s^2, 2s^2, 2p^6$ } two shells
	11 protons 11 electrons		11 protons 10 electrons
Radii	186 pm (Atomic)		95 pm (Ionic)

(ii) **The size of anion is larger than its parent atom.** Anions are the result of addition of one or more electrons to an isolated gaseous atom. Due to addition of electrons, the number of electrons increases but nuclear charge (i.e. number of protons) remains the same. Thus, more electrons are held by the same nuclear charge, i.e. effective nuclear charge decreases. Further, addition of electron(s), also leads to the repulsion among the electrons, due to which the electron cloud gets expanded.

This effect decreases the effective nuclear charge and increased repulsion result in lesser force of attraction or more distance between the nucleus and the outermost electron(s), which in turn results in increased ionic radius. That's why the radius of an anion is always larger than its parent atom.

e.g.	F $+ e^-$	$\longrightarrow$	F^-
	Two {$1s^2, 2s^2, 2p^5$ shells		$1s^2, 2s^2, 2p^6$ } Two shells
	9 protons 9 electrons		9 protons 10 electrons
Radii	64 pm (atomic)		136 pm (ionic)

Note If number of $p^+ >$ number of e^-, effective nuclear charge increases and if number of $p^+ <$ number of e^-; effective nuclear charge decreases.

Variation of Ionic Radii

Ionic radii shows same trend in the periodic table as shown by the atomic radii, i.e. it decreases across a period and increases on moving down the group.

Isoelectronic Species and their Radii

(i) Species (atoms or ions) having the same number of electrons are called the **isoelectronic species.**

(ii) In case of isoelectronic species, as the magnitude of nuclear charge increases, force of attraction by the nucleus on the electrons increases and hence, ionic radius decreases. In short,

$$\text{Ionic radius} \propto \frac{1}{\text{nuclear charge}}$$

(iii) In case of O^{2-}, F^-, Na^+ and Mg^{2+}, the nuclear charge are respectively, + 8, + 9, + 11, + 12, thus, the order of their radii is $Mg^{2+} < Na^+ < F^- < O^{2-}$.

Ionisation Enthalpy (IE)

The minimum amount of energy required to remove an electron from an isolated gaseous atom (X) in its ground state is called the ionisation enthalpy.

$$X(g) \longrightarrow X^{+}(g) + e^{-}; \Delta_i H = +\text{ve}$$

or $$X(g) + \Delta_i H \longrightarrow X^{+}(g) + e^{-}$$

It is actually the quantitative measure of the tendency of an element to lose electron. The ionisation enthalpy can be expressed in kJ mol^{-1} or kcal mol^{-1} or eV $atom^{-1}$.

$$1 \text{ eV/atom} = 96.49 \text{ kJ mol}^{-1}$$

Thus, one electron volt is the energy acquired by an electron when it is moving under a potential difference of one volt.

Successive Ionisation Enthalpies

The energy require to remove the most loosely bound electron from an isolated gaseous atom is called the **first ionisation enthalpy** and is represented by $\Delta_i H_1$,

e.g. $X(g) \longrightarrow X^{+}(g) + e^{-}$; $\Delta_i H_1 = +\text{ve}$

Similarly, the energies required to remove the second, third or successive electrons from the positive ion, are called the **second, third** and **successive ionisation energies** respectively.

e.g. $$X^{+}(g) + \Delta_i H_2 \longrightarrow X^{2+}(g) + e^{-}(g)$$

$$X^{2+}(g) + \Delta_i H_3 \longrightarrow X^{3+}(g) + e^{-}(g)$$

where, $\Delta_i H_2$ and $\Delta_i H_3$ are the second and third ionisation enthalpies respectively.The second ionisation enthalpy is always higher than the first one. Similarly, the third ionisation enthalpy is higher than the second one and so on. This is because, the positive ion has more effective nuclear charge which holds the remaining electrons more firmly and hence, a large amount of energy is required to remove the electron from it as compared to a neutral atom.

Similarly, a bipositive ion holds the electrons more firmly and hence, the required energy is higher than that required in case of unipositive ion. Thus, the order of successive ionisation enthalpies is

$$\Delta H_3 > \Delta H_2 > \Delta H_1$$

The first, second and third ionisation enthalpies of some elements are given in the following table :

Elements and its Electronic Configuration	First Ionisation Energy IE_1 or $\Delta_i H_1$ (kJ mol^{-1})	Second Ionisation Energy IE_2 or $\Delta_i H_2$ (kJ mol^{-1})	Third Ionisation Energy IE_3 or $\Delta_i H_3$ (kJ mol^{-1})
H($1s^1$)	1312.0	—	—
He($1s^2$)	2372.6	5246.7	—
Li($1s^2 2s^1$)	520.3	7297	11810
Be($1s^2 2s^2$)	899.5	1757	14850
B($1s^2 2s^2 2p^1$)	800.6	2427	3650
C($1s^2 2s^2 2p^2$)	1086.4	2352	4619
N($1s^2 2s^2 2p^3$)	1402	2860	4577
O($1s^2 2s^2 2p^4$)	1314	3389	5301
F($1s^2 2s^2 2p^5$)	1681	3366	6066
Ne($1s^2 2s^2 2p^6$)	2080	3963	6192

It is also interesting to note that the ionisation enthalpies are always positive. This is because energy is always required to remove an electron from an atom/ion.

Note If the difference in ionisation enthalpies of two successive oxidation states is approx equal to 965 -1450 kJ mol^{-1} or less, the lower oxidation state is not stable. However, if the difference is more than 1450 kJ mol^{-1}, the lower oxidation state is more stable.

Factors Affecting Ionisation Enthalpy

Ionisation enthalpy depends upon the several factors, which are discussed below :

1. Screening or Shielding Effect

In general, greater the screening (shielding) effect, easier is the removal of loosely bound electron and lesser is the ionisation enthalpy.Shielding effect is most effective when the orbitals of inner shells are completely filled, as present in case of alkali metals.

2. Nuclear Charge

The ionisation enthalpy increases as the nuclear charge increases. This is because nucleus with greater nuclear charge, bound the electron more firmly and hence, large amount of energy is required to remove the electron from the atom. e.g. the ionisation enthalpy increases across a period from left to right due to increased nuclear charge.

3. Penetration Effect of the Electrons

In case of multielectron atoms the order of penetrating power of different electrons of the same shell (i.e. having same value of n) follows the order $s > p > d > f$. If penetration power is more, electron will be closer to the nucleus and held more firmly, thus, a large amount of energy is required to remove the electron, i.e. energy is higher.

4. Electronic Configuration

Since, the configuration with half-filled or fully filled orbitals is more stable, so in case of atoms having such a configuration, ionisation energy is high because a large amount of energy is required to remove the electron.

Variation of Ionisation Enthalpy in the Periodic Table

1. Variation Along a Period

On moving along a period from left to right, the successive addition of one electron results in increased nuclear charge but since the electrons are added to the orbitals of same principal quantum number, the shielding effect remains the same and is not enough to compensate for the increased nuclear charge (i.e. increased attraction of the electron to the nucleus). Thus, increased nuclear charge outweighs the shielding effect across a period. As a result, the outermost electrons are held more and more firmly and hence, ionisation enthalpy increases across a period.

Note Ionisation enthalpy is maximum (highest) for noble gases and lowest for alkali metals in a period.

2. Variation in a Group

On moving down a group, the ionisation enthalpy decreases. On moving down a group, nuclear charge increases due to addition of electrons but since the electrons are added to the new energy levels, i.e. distance between the valence electron(s) and nucleus increases, the shielding effect on the outermost electron(s) increases due to increase in the number of inner electrons.

The increased shielding effect outweighs the increasing nuclear charge and thus, a less amount of energy is required to remove the outermost electrons.

Exception

(i) **First ionisation energy of group 2 (IIA) elements is greater than the corresponding elements of group-13 (IIIA).** It is due to the presence of fully filled s-orbitals in case of group 2 elements (their outermost electronic configuration is ns^2). It is always difficult to pull out electron from stable configuration.

(ii) **First ionisation energies of group 15(VA) elements is greater than the corresponding elements of group 16(VIA).** It is due to presence of stable half-filled electronic configuration in group 15 elements. (Their outermost electronic configuration is ns^2np^3).

(iii) In case of transition elements opposite trends are observed. Thus, $(IE)_1$ of the corresponding elements of 3*d* and 4*d*-series are almost similar but these are smaller than the $(IE)_1$ of the 5*d*-series elements. Certainly the higher values of ionisation energies of the 5*d*-transition elements are consistent with the relatively small size of the atoms.

Topic Practice 3

Very Short Answer Type Questions

(1 Mark)

1. Fill in the Blanks

(i) If the combining atoms are non-metals (except noble gases), their radius is called ....

(ii) van der Waals' radius is defined as 'one-half' of the distance between the nuclei of two identical .... isolated atoms.

(iii) Species having same electrons are called .... species.

(iv) The energy required to remove the most loosely bonded electron from an isolated gaseous atom is called .... of that atom.

(v) In case of multielectron atoms, the order of penetrating power of different electrons of the same main shell is ....

2. Objective Type Questions

(i) Atomic radii of fluorine and neon (in Å) are respectively given by

(a) 0.72, 1.60 (b) 1.60, 1.60
(c) 0.72, 0.72 (d) None of these

(ii) Which one of the following is smallest in size?

(a) N^{3-} (b) O^{2-}
(c) F^- (d) Na^+

(iii) The correct order of radii is

(a) N < Be < B
(b) $F^- < O^{2-} < N^{3-}$
(c) N < Li < K
(d) $Fe^{3+} < Fe^{2+} < Fe^{4+}$

(iv) Chloride ion and potassium ion are isoelectronic, then

(a) their sizes are same
(b) Cl^- ion is bigger than K^+ ion
(c) K^+ ion is relatively bigger
(d) their sizes depend on other cation and anion

(v) The first ionisation potential of Na, Mg, Al and Si are in the order

(a) Na < Mg > Al < Si (b) Na > Mg > Al > Si
(c) Na < Mg < Al > Si (d) Na < Mg > Al < Si

(vi) The correct order of second ionisation potential of carbon, nitrogen, oxygen and fluorine is

(a) C > N > O > F (b) O > N > F > C
(c) O > F > N > C (d) F > O > N > C

3. Match Column (I) with (II) and choose the correct option using the codes given below:

Column I	Column II
A. $Li^+ < Mg^{2+}$	(i) Higher first ionisation energy between metals.
B. $Li < K$	(ii) More atomic size
C. $F > Cl$	(iii) Higher first ionisation energy between non-metals.
D. Na^+ and F^-	(iv) isoelectronic species.

Codes

	A	B	C	D		A	B	C	D
(a)	(i)	(ii)	(iii)	(iv)	(b)	(iv)	(iii)	(ii)	(i)
(c)	(ii)	(i)	(iii)	(iv)	(d)	(i)	(ii)	(iv)	(iii)

4. In group 1 of the periodic table, three elements *X*, *Y* and *Z* have ionic radii 133 pm, 95 pm, 60 pm respectively. Giving a reason, arrange these elements in the order of increasing atomic number in the group.

5. Atomic radii of fluorine is 72 pm where as atomic radii of neon is 160 pm. Why?

6. Which of the following species will have the largest and the smallest size? Mg, Mg^{2+}, Al, Al^{3+}.

7. Out of Na and Mg, which has higher second ionisation energy?

8. Four elements have the following first ionisation enthalpies (in kJ mol^{-1}); 869, 941, 1191 and 1142. The elements, in random order, are Se, Br, Te and I. Which of the above elements has an ionisation enthalpy of 869 kJ mol^{-1} and 1142 kJmol^{-1} respectively?

9. Would you expect the first ionisation enthalpies for two isotopes of the same element to be the same or different? Justify your answer. **NCERT Textbook**

Short Answer Type I Questions

2 Marks

10. Match the correct atomic radius with the element. **NCERT Exemplar**

Element	Atomic radius (pm)
Be	74
C	88
O	111
B	77
N	66

11. List the factors that can influence the ionic radius of an element.

12. Describe the theory associated with the radius of an atom as it **NCERT Textbook**
    (i) gains an electron
    (ii) loses an electron

Or

Compare the size of
(i) Cl atom with Cl^- ion.
(ii) Na atom with Na^+ ion.

13. Explain, why cations are smaller and anions are larger in radii than their parent atoms?

14. What are the various factors due to which the ionisation enthalpy of the main group elements tends to decrease down a group?

15. Which of the elements Na, Mg, Si and P would have the greatest difference between the first and second ionisation enthalpies. Briefly explain your answer.

16. How would you explain the fact that the first ionisation enthalpy of sodium is lower than that of magnesium but its second ionisation enthalpy is higher than that of magnesium?

Note The species having exactly half-filled or fully filled orbitals have very high ionisation enthalpies.

17. Energy of an electron in the ground state of the hydrogen atom is -2.18×10^{-18}J. Calculate the ionisation enthalpy of atomic hydrogen in terms of J mol^{-1}. **NCERT Textbook**

18. Among the elements B, Al, C and Si,
    (i) which element has the highest first ionisation enthalpy?
    (ii) which element has the most metallic character? Justify your answer in each case.

19. The first ionisation enthalpy ($\Delta_i H$) values of the third period elements, Na, Mg and Si are respectively 496, 737 and 786 kJ mol^{-1}. Predict whether the first $\Delta_i H$ value for Al will be more close to 575 or 760 kJ mol^{-1}? Justify your answer.

Short Answer Type II Questions

3 Marks

20. What does atomic radius and ionic radius mean to you? **NCERT Textbook**

21. What do you understand by isoelectronic species? Name a species that will be isoelectronic with each of the following atoms or ions.
(i) F^- (ii) Ar (iii) Mg^{2+} (iv) Rb^+

22. Consider the following species
N^{3-}, O^{2-}, F^-, Na^+, Mg^{2+} and Al^{3+}
(i) What is common in them?
(ii) Arrange them in the order of increasing ionic radii.

23. Arrange the elements N, P, O and S in the order of
(i) increasing first ionisation enthalpy.
(ii) increasing non-metallic character.
Give reason for the arrangement assigned. **NCERT Exemplar**

24. Among the second period elements the actual ionisation enthalpies are in the order.
Li < B < Be < C < O < N < F < Ne
Explain why?
(i) Be has higher $\Delta_i H$ than B?
(ii) O has lower $\Delta_i H$ than N and F? **NCERT Textbook**

25. The first ionisation enthalpy values (in kJ mol^{-1}) of group 13 elements are

B	Al	Ga	In	Tl
801	577	579	558	589

How would you explain this deviation from the general trend? **NCERT Textbook**

Long Answer Type Questions

5 Marks

26. Ionisation enthalpies of elements of second period are given below.
Ionisation enthalpy/kcal mol^{-1} : 520, 899, 801, 1086, 1402, 1314, 1681, 2080.

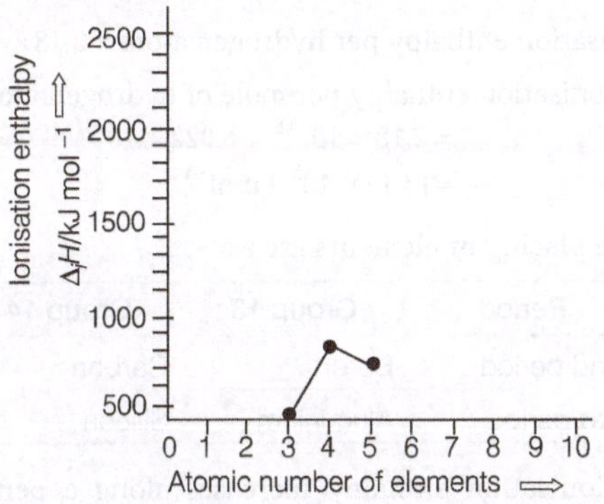

Match the correct enthalpy with the elements and complete the graph given in figure. Also write symbols of elements with their atomic number. **NCERT Exemplar**

27. Define ionisation enthalpy. Discuss the factors affecting ionisation enthalpy of the elements and its trends in the periodic table. **NCERT Exemplar**

Hints & Solutions

1. (i) covalent radius (ii) non-bonded
(iii) isoelectronic
(iv) ionisation-energy (enthalpy)
(v) $s > p > d > f$

2. (i) (a) Atomic radii of neon being van der Waals' radius is higher than that of fluorine which is covalent radius.
(ii) (d) As the nuclear charge increases, atomic size decreases (in case of isoelectronic species).
(iii) (b) Among the isoelectronic species, the size increases as the negative charge increases.
(iv) (b) In isoelectronic species, anion is larger in size than the cation.
(v) (d) IE_1 of Mg is higher than that of Na because of increased nuclear charge and also that of Al because in Mg, a 3s electron (more stable) has to be removed while in Al it is the 3p-electron.
The IE_1 of Si is, however, higher than those of Mg and Al because of increased nuclear charge. Thus, the overall order is Na < Mg > Al < Si.
(vi) (c) After the removal of an electron from C, N, O and F, their electronic configurations are :
$C^+(1s^2, 2s^2 2p_x^1)$
$N^+(1s^2, 2s^2 2p_x^1 2p_y^1)$
$O^+(1s^2, 2s^2 2p_x^1 2p_y^1 2p_z^1)$
and $F^+(1s^2, 2s^2 2p_x^2 2p_y^1 2p_z^1)$
Since O^+ gives a stable electronic configuration with exactly half-filled 2p-subshell.
∴ IE_2 of O is higher than that of F. The IE_2 of C because of the larger size is lower than that of N. Thus, the overall order is: O > F > N > C.

3. (a) A → (i), B → (ii), (C) → (iii), (D) → (iv)

4. Ionic radii increases with increase in atomic number. Thus, the increasing order of atomic number is $Z < Y < X$.

5. Atomic radius of F is expressed in terms of covalent radius while, atomic radius of neon is usually expressed in terms of van der Waals' radius. van der Waals' radius of an element is always larger than its covalent radius. Therefore, atomic radius of F is smaller than atomic radius of Ne(F = 72 pm, Ne = 160 pm).

6. Mg and Al belongs to same period (i.e. third period) and along a period, atomic radii decreases. Thus, the order of size of Mg and Al is Al < Mg

Further, the size of a cation is always smaller than its parent atom and in case of isoelectronic species, size decreases as the nuclear charge increases.

Thus, the size of $Mg^{2+} > Al^{3+}$

$\therefore$ The correct order of size is $Al^{3+} < Al < Mg^{2+} < Mg$.

Thus, Mg is the largest atom and Al^{3+} is the smallest ion.

7. Electronic configuration of Na and Mg are

$Na = 1s^2, 2s^2, 2p^6, 3s^1$ and $Mg = 1s^2, 2s^2, 2p^6, 3s^2$.

Second ionisation energy of Na is higher because it acquires nearest noble gas configuration after losing one electron and second electron is thus, to be removed from the noble gas configuration.

8. Se and Te belong to 16 group and fourth and fifth period respectively whereas Br and I belong to 17 group and fourth and fifth period respectively. In a period ionisation energy increases but along a group, it decreases. Thus, the order of ionisation enthalpy is Te < I < Se < Br. i.e. Te has IE of 869 and Se has IE of 1142 kJ mol^{-1}.

9. First ionisation enthalpies of two isotopes of the same element are expected to be same because ionisation enthalpy depends upon the electronic configuration and effective nuclear charge. Isotopes of an element have same electronic configuration and thus, have the same nuclear charge.

10. All the given elements are of same period and along a period, atomic radii decreases because effective nuclear charge increases. Thus, the order of atomic radii is O < N < C < B < Be or, Be = 111 pm, O = 66 pm, C = 77 pm, B = 88 pm, N = 74 pm. [2]

11. Ionic radius is affected by following factors

(i) **Effective nuclear charge** As the effective nuclear charge increases, ionic radius decreases. [1]

(ii) **Shielding effect** As the shielding effect increases, ionic radius increases. [1]

12. Refer to text on page 113 (Ionic radius : Comparison of the ionic radii with corresponding atomic radii).

13. Refer to text on page 113 (Comparison of the ionic radii with corresponding atomic radii).

14. The ionisation enthalpy of the main group elements decreases regularly on moving down the group due to *the following two factors.*

(i) **Atomic size** On moving down the group, atomic size increases due to the addition of new higher energy shell. As a result of this, forces of attraction of nucleus for valence electrons decreases and ionisation enthalpy also decreases. [1]

(ii) **Screening effect** On moving down the group, screening effect or shielding effect increases, so ionisation enthalpy decreases (because forces of attraction between nucleus and electron decreases). [1]

15. Among the given elements Na being alkali metal has only one electron in the valence shell, therefore has very low $\Delta_i H_1$. However, after the removal of one electron, it acquires nearest inert gas or neon gas configuration, i.e. Na^+ $(1s^2, 2s^2, 2p^6)$. Therefore, its $\Delta_i H_2$ is expected to be very high. Consequently, the difference in first and second ionisation enthalpies would be greatest in case of Na. [1]

However, it may be noted here that in case of Mg, Si and P, although their $\Delta_i H_1$ will be much higher than that of Na but their $\Delta_i H_2$ will be much lower than that of Na. As a result, the difference in their respective, $\Delta_i H_1$ and $\Delta_i H_2$ would be much lower than that of Na. [1]

16. First ionisation enthalpy of sodium $(Na = 1s^2, 2s^2, 2p^6, 3s^1)$ is lower than that of magnesium $(Mg = 1s^2, 2s^2\ 2p^6, 3s^2)$ because the electron to be removed in both the cases is from 3s-orbital but the nuclear charge is lower in the Na than that of magnesium $\left(\because \text{IE} \propto \dfrac{1}{\text{atomic size}}\right)$. [1]

After the removal of first electron, Na^+ acquires inert gas (Ne) configuration $(Na^+ = 1s^2, 2s^2, 2p^6)$ and hence, removal of second electron from sodium ion is difficult. While in case of magnesium, after the removal of first electron, the electronic configuration of Mg^+ is $1s^2, 2s^2, 2p^6, 3s^1$. In this case, $3s^1$ electron is easy to remove in comparison with removal of an electron from inert gas configuration. Therefore, IE_2 of Na is higher than that of Mg. [1]

Note The species having exactly half-filled or fully filled orbitals have very high ionisation enthalpies.

17. Ionisation energy is the amount of energy required to remove the electron from the ground state (E_1) to infinity (E_∞). [1]

$$E_1 = -2.18 \times 10^{-18}\ \text{J};\ E_\infty = 0;$$

$$\Delta E = E_\infty - E_1 = 0 - (-2.18 \times 10^{-18}\ \text{J}) = 2.18 \times 10^{-18}\ \text{J}$$

Ionisation enthalpy per hydrogen atom $= 2.18 \times 10^{-18}$ J

$\therefore$ Ionisation enthalpy per mole of hydrogen atoms

$$= 2.18 \times 10^{-18} \times 6.022 \times 10^{23}$$

$$= 13.12 \times 10^5\ \text{J mol}^{-1}$$ [1]

18. The placing of elements are as

Period	Group 13	Group 14
2nd period	Boron	Carbon
3rd period	Aluminium	Silicon

(i) Ionisation enthalpy increases along a period (as we move from left to right in a period) with decrease in atomic size and decreases down the group with increase in atomic size. Hence, carbon has the highest first ionisation enthalpy. [1]

(ii) Metallic character decreases across a period but increases on moving down the group. Hence, aluminium has the most metallic character. [1]

19. We know that the first ionisation enthalpy generally increases from left to right along a period but the ionisation enthalpy of elements of group 2 (i.e. Mg) is higher than that of the corresponding element of group 13 (i.e., Al) due to the more penetrating power and less shielding of *ns*-electron. Thus, the correct order of ionisation enthalpy is [1]

Na < Mg < Si

We know, 496 < 737 < 786

Therefore, from the above discussion it is clear that ionisation enthalpy of Al must be lower than that of the Mg, so its value will be close to 575 (which is less than 737). [1]

20. Refer to text on pages 111 and 113 (Atomic radius and ionic radius).

21. Isoelectronic species have the same number of electrons but different nuclear charges.

In case of isoelectronic species, as the nuclear charge increases, their size decreases.

(i) F^- has 10 electrons (9 + 1).

(ii) Ar has 18 electrons.

(iii) Mg^{2+} has 10 electrons (12–2) and

(iv) Rb^+ has 36 electrons (37–1). [1]

N^{3-}, O^{2-}, Ne, Na^+ and Al^{3+} are some species which are isoelectronic with F^- and Mg^{2+}.

P^{3-}, S^{2-}, Cl^-, K^+ and Ca^{2+} are some species which are isoelectronic to Ar.

Similarly, Br^-, Kr and Sr^{2+} are isoelectronic with Rb^+. [2]

22. (i) All the given species have same number of electrons ($10e^-$). Therefore, all are isoelectronic species. [1]

(ii) The ionic radii of isoelectronic species decreases with increase in atomic number (as magnitude of the nuclear charge increases with increase in atomic number). Also, it general anions have larger ionic radius than cation.

Therefore, their ionic radii increases in the order

$$\underset{Z=13}{Al^{3+}} < \underset{12}{Mg^{2+}} < \underset{11}{Na^+} < \underset{9}{F^-} < \underset{8}{O^{2-}} < \underset{7}{N^{3-}}$$ [2]

23.

	Group 15	Group 16
2nd period	N	O
3rd period	P	S

[1]

(i) Ionisation enthalpy of nitrogen ($_7N = 1s^2, 2s^2, 2p^3$) is greater than oxygen ($_8O = 1s^2, 2s^2, 2p^4$) due to extra stable half-filled 2*p*-orbitals. Similarly, ionisation enthalpy of phosphorus ($_{15}P = 1s^2, 2s^2, 2p^6, 3s^2, 3p^3$) is greater than sulphur ($_{16}S = 1s^2, 2s^2, 2p^6, 3s^2, 3p^4$). On moving down the group, ionisation enthalpy decreases with increasing atomic size. So, the increasing order of first ionisation enthalpy is S < P < O < N. [1]

(ii) Non-metallic character across a period (left to right) increases but on moving down the group it decreases. So, the increasing order of non-metallic character is P < S < N < O. [1]

24. (i) Be has higher $\Delta_i H$ (ionisation enthalpy) than boron. In both the cases, the electron need to be removed from the same principal shell. In $_4Be = (1s^2, 2s^2)$, it is 2*s*-electron while in boron $_5B = (1s^2, 2s^2, 2p^1)$ it is 2*p*-electron. The penetration of a 2*s*-electron to the nucleus is more than that of a 2*p*-electron. It means 2*s*-electrons are more strongly attracted by the nucleus than 2*p*-electrons. Therefore, higher amount of energy is required to remove 2*s*-electron than a 2*p*-electron. Hence, Be has higher $\Delta_i H$ than B. [1]

(ii) O has lower $\Delta_i H$ than N and F.

$$_7N = 1s^2, 2s^2, 2p_x^1, 2p_y^1, 2p_z^1$$
$$_8O = 1s^2, 2s^2, 2p_x^2, 2p_y^1, 2p_z^1$$
$$_9F = 1s^2, 2s^2, 2p_x^2, 2p_y^2, 2p_z^1$$

Across a period, ionisation enthalpy increases as we move from left to right due to decrease in atomic size. But $\Delta_i H$ of nitrogen is greater than oxygen. It is because of the more stable electronic configuration (exactly half-filled orbitals are more stable) of nitrogen, so it is difficult to remove an electron from nitrogen than from oxygen and fluorine. That's why oxygen has lower ionisation enthalpy than nitrogen and fluorine. [2]

25. In general, on moving down the group (13th group) from B to Al, the ionisation enthalpy decreases with increase in atomic size and screening effect as expected. But IE_1 of Ga is slightly higher (only 2 kJ mol^{-1}) than IE_1 of Al. It is due to imperfect shielding of the valence electrons by 3*d*-electrons. As a result of this, effective nuclear charge in Ga is slightly more than that of Al. That's why (IE_1) $\Delta_i H_1$ of Ga is slightly more than that of Al. On moving from In to Tl, $\Delta_i H_1$ of Tl is larger than that of In. It is due to the fact that effective nuclear charge outweighs the shielding effect of all the electrons present in 4*f* and 5*d*-electrons. [3]

Note *d*-and *f*-electrons shield the valence shell electrons from nucleus less effectively than *s* and *p*-electrons.

26. As on moving from left to right across a period, the ionisation enthalpy keeps on increasing due to increased nuclear charge and simultaneous decrease in atomic radius. However, there are some exceptions also.

(i) Inspite of increased nuclear charge, the first ionisation enthalpy of B is lower than that of Be. This is due to the reason that in case of Be, the outermost electron lies in the 2*s*-orbital but in case of B, it is present in a 2*p*-orbital. Since, the electrons in 2*s*-orbital are more tightly held by the nucleus than those present in 2*p*-orbital, therefore, ionisation enthalpy of B is lower than that of Be. [1]3

(ii) The first ionisation enthalpy of N is higher than that of O though the nuclear charge of O is higher than that of N. This is due to the reason that in case of N, ($1s^2\ 2s^2\ 2p_x^1\ 2p_y^1\ 2p_z^1$) the electron is to be removed from a more stable exactly half-filled electronic configuration but in case of O ($1s^2\ 2s^2\ 2p_x^2\ 2p_y^2\ 2p_z^2$), it is not so.

Therefore, the first ionisation enthalpy of N is higher than that of O. The symbols of elements along with their atomic numbers are given in the graph. [2]

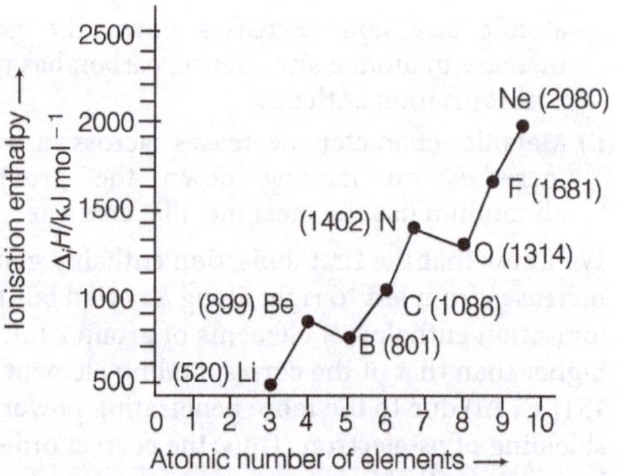

27. Refer to text on pages 113 and 114 (Ionisation enthalpy).

TOPIC 04 Electron Gain Enthalpy, Electronegativity and Periodic Trends in Chemical Properties

Electron Gain Enthalpy ($\Delta e_g H$)

When an electron is added to an isolated gaseous atom in its ground state to convert it into a negative ion, the enthalpy change accompanying the process is called the electron gain enthalpy ($\Delta_{eg} H$). It is a direct measure of the ease with which an atom attracts an electron to form anion.

$$X(g) + e^- \longrightarrow X^-(g); \quad \Delta H = \Delta e_g H$$

The most stable state of an atom is the ground state. If an isolated gaseous atom is in excited state, comparatively lesser energy will be released on adding an electron. So, electron gain enthalpies of gaseous atoms must be determined in their ground states. Therefore, the terms ground state and isolated gaseous atom has been also included in the definition of electron gain enthalpy. Like ionisation enthalpy, electron gain enthalpy is measure either in electron volts per atom or kJ per mole. [To see the significance of term isolated gaseous atom, see topic ionisation enthalpy]

Units The values of electron gain enthalpy are expressed either in electron volt per atom or kilo joules per mole of atoms e.g. electron affinity of chlorine is -348 kJ mol^{-1}.

Nature of Electron Gain Enthalpy The electron gain enthalpy can be **positive** (i.e. endothermic process) **or negative** (i.e. exothermic process) depending upon the nature of element to which electron is to be added. However, for most of the elements, it is generally negative, i.e. energy is released when an electron is added to an isolated gaseous atom. e.g. the general electronic configuration for halogen family is $ns^2 np^5$. Thus to attain the stable noble gas electronic configuration, they have very high tendency to attract an electron. Hence, their electron gain enthalpy is highly negative.

Electron Gain Enthalpy of Noble Gases

If we see the electronic configuration of noble gases, we find that their valence shell is completely filled, i.e. they have $ns^2\ np^6$ configuration, and hence, there is no need to add and remove electrons in this configuration.

But if still we add an electron to this configuration, the electron enters in the next higher principal quantum level leading to a highly unstable configuration and for this a large amount of energy is required. That's why electron gain enthalpy of noble gases has large positive value.

The **energy released** when an electron is added to an isolated gaseous atom is called the **electron affinity** (A_e).

It is positive when energy is released on adding an electron to an atom (contrary to thermodynamic convention) and is negative if energy is required for adding an electron to an atom. It is defined at absolute zero and is related to electron gain enthalpy by the relation.

$$\Delta_{eg}H = -A_e - \frac{5}{2}RT$$

At 298 K, the value of $\frac{5}{2}RT$ is only 2.477 kJ mol^{-1} and this small value can be ignored, thus, the two terms (i.e. electron gain enthalpy and electron affinity) are indistinguishable with the only difference that the former is just the negative of later, *i.e.* the two quantities have opposite signs.

Successive Electron Gain Enthalpies

The enthalpy changes occurring when second, third,... electrons are added to the uninegative ion, are referred as second, third .... electron gain enthalpies. We found that the magnitude of first electron gain enthalpy is generally negative. However, when an electron is added to a negative ion, there is a repulsion between the electron and negative charge. To overcome this repulsion, energy has to be supplied.
Thus, the second and further electron gain enthalpies are generally positive i.e. the process is endothermic. e.g. let us study the addition of electrons to oxygen atom.
First electron gain enthalpy of O-atom

$$O(g) + e^- \longrightarrow O^-(g)\ ;\ \Delta_{eg}H_1 = -141\text{ kJ}$$
(energy is released)

Second electron gain enthalpy of O-atom

$$O^-(g) + e^- \longrightarrow O^{2-}(g);\ \Delta_{eg}H_2 = +780\text{ kJ}$$
(energy is absorbed)

Factors Affecting Electron Gain Enthalpies

Electron gain enthalpy depends upon the following factors :

1. Atomic Size

As the atomic size increases, i.e. distance between the nucleus and outermost shell increases, the force of attraction between them decreases. Hence, the electron gain enthalpy becomes less negative.

2. Nuclear Charge

As the nuclear charge increases, force of attraction between the nucleus and incoming electron increases and hence, the electron gain enthalpy becomes more negative.

3. Electronic Configuration

In case of elements having half-filled or fully-filled outer shell, because of their higher stability, energy has to be supplied to add an electron. i.e. the value of electron gain enthalpy is positive e.g. noble gases, elements of group 15 etc.

Variation of Electron Gain Enthalpy in the Periodic Table

The variation of electron gain enthalpy is not as regular as that of ionisation enthalpy. The variation of electron gain enthalpy in the periodic table is shown as

1. Variation Along a Period

On moving from left to right across a period, effective nuclear charge increases and hence size decreases, thus, the added electron on an average would be closer to the nucleus, i.e. strongly attracted by the nucleus. Thus, the value of electron gain enthalpy becomes more negative as we move from left to right along a period.

Exception

Electron gain enthalpies of elements of group 2 and 15 is low because of their stable fully filled and half-filled configuration respectively but that of elements of group 18 is positive because of their complete valence shell.

2. Variation Along a Group

On moving down a group, the size of atom increases and hence, the distance between the nucleus and incoming electron increases or force of attraction between the nucleus and incoming electron decreases, thus, the value of electron gain enthalpy becomes less negative.

Exception

The electron gain enthalpy of elements of second period (N, O, F) is less negative than the succeeding elements (P, S, Cl) of third period. This is because in case of elements of second period, the incoming electron enters in the smaller $n = 2$ quantum level and hence, experience greater force of repulsion by the other electrons present in the level whereas in elements of third period, it enters in larger $n = 3$ quantum level and hence, the force of repulsion is much lesser as compared to that in case of elements of second period.
Thus, chlorine has the highest negative electron gain enthalpy in the periodic table.

Example 3 Which of the following will have the most negative electron gain enthalpy and which is the least negative? (P, S, Cl, F) Explain your answer. **NCERT Textbook**

Sol. As we know the negative value of electron gain enthalpy increases along a period and decreases on moving down the group but the elements of second period like F have lesser electron gain enthalpy than the corresponding element of third period.

This is because of the smaller size and hence greater repulsion in case of F as compared to Cl. Thus, the order of electron gain enthalpy is P < S < F < Cl. i.e, the electron gain enthalpy is most negative for chlorine and less negative for phosphorus.

Electronegativity

A qualitative measure of the ability of an atom to attract the shared pair of electrons towards itself in a covalent bond is called electronegativity of that atom. Unlike other properties such as electron gain enthalpy and ionisation enthalpy, which are related to the isolated state of atom, electronegativity is related to the combined or bonded state of atom.

In general, greater the electronegativity, higher is its tendency to attract the shared pair of electron. Since, this tendency is highest in **fluorine, so it is the most electronegative element.** Further, noble gases because of their stable outermost electronic arrangement do not exhibit electronegativity. Electronegativity is not a constant property. It depends upon the nature of other elements bound to the particular atom, e.g. the electronegativity of C in CH_4, CCl_3, C_2H_4, CF_3 is respectively 2.48, 3.30, 2.75 and 3.35.

Different Scales for Calculating Electronegativity

Electronegativity is not a measureable quantity, so several numerical scales of electronegativity have been developed. *These scales are as follows* :

1. Pauling Scale

It is the most widely used scale and was proposed by **Linus Pauling**, an American scientist, in 1922. He arbitrarily assigned a value of 4.0 to the most electronegative element fluorine and calculate the electronegativity of other elements with respect to it by using the formula $X_A - X_B = 0.1017\sqrt{\Delta}$

(if bond dissociation enthalpies are in kJ mol^{-1})

Or

$$X_A - X_B = 0.208\sqrt{\Delta}$$

(if bond dissociation enthalpies are in kcal mol^{-1})

where, $\Delta = E_{A—B} - \sqrt{E_{A—A} \times E_{B—B}}$

$X_A - X_B$ = electronegativity difference between two atoms A and B

$E_{A—B}$, $E_{A—A}$ and $E_{B—B}$ = bond energies of the molecules AB, A_2 and B_2 respectively.

The electronegativity values of some elements on the Pauling scale are shown in the following table.

Electronegativities of Representative Elements
(on the Pauling Scale)

Group	1	2	13	14	15	16	17
Period I	H						
Electronegativity	2.1						
Period II	Li	Be	B	C	N	O	F
Electronegativity	1.0	1.5	2.0	2.5	3.0	3.5	4.0
Period III	Na	Mg	Al	Si	P	S	Cl
Electronegativity	0.9	1.2	1.5	1.8	2.1	2.5	3.0
Period IV	K	Ca	Ga	Ge	As	Se	Br
Electronegativity	0.8	1.0	1.6	1.8	2.0	2.4	2.8
Period V	Rb	Sr	In	Sn	Sb	Te	I
Electronegativity	0.8	1.0	1.7	1.8	1.9	2.01	2.5
Period VI	Cs	Ba	Tl	Pb	Bi	Po	At
Electronegativity	0.7	0.9	1.8	1.9	1.9	1.76	2.2

The main disadvantage associated with this scale is that for many elements, the bond enthalpies are not known with good degree of accuracy and hence, the electronegativity values are only the relative values.

Example 4 Calculate the electronegativity of carbon if $E_{H—H} = 104.2$ kcal mol^{-1}, $E_{C—C} = 83.1$ kcal mol^{-1}, $E_{C—H} = 98.8$ kcal mol^{-1}, $X_H = 2.1$.

Sol. We know that, $X_C - X_H = 0.208\sqrt{\Delta}$

$$\Delta = E_{C—H} - \sqrt{E_{C—C} \times E_{H—H}}$$

$$= 98.8 - \sqrt{83.1 \times 104.2}$$

$$= 98.8 - 93.05 = 5.74$$

$$\therefore \quad X_C - X_H = 0.208\sqrt{5.74} = 0.498$$

$$X_C = 0.498 + X_H = 0.498 + 2.1 = 2.59 \approx 2.6$$

2. Mulliken-Jaffe Scale

Mulliken suggested that the value of electronegativity is the average of the ionisation enthalpy and electron gain enthalpy. On this scale electronegativity is denoted by word chi (χ) which can be calculated as $\chi = \dfrac{IE + A_e}{2}$

(i) If IE and A_e are determined in eV then $\chi = \dfrac{(IE + A_e)}{5.6 \text{ eV}}$

(ii) If IE and A_e are determined in kJ/g-atom then $\chi = (IE + A_e) / 125$ kcal / g-atom.

(iii) If IE and A_e are in kJ/mol then
$\chi = (\text{IE} + A_e) / 544 \text{ kJ/mol}$.
Mulliken's values were about 208 times larger than the Pauling's values.

Factors Affecting the Magnitude of Electronegativity

Various factors which affect the magnitude of electronegativity are as follows :

1. Atomic Radius

As the atomic radius of the elements increases, the electronegativity value decreases, i.e.

$$\text{Electronegativity} \propto \frac{1}{\text{Atomic radius}}$$

2. Effective Nuclear Charge

The electronegativity value increases as the effective nuclear charge on the atomic nucleus increases.

Electronegativity $\propto$ Effective nuclear charge (Z_{eff})

3. Oxidation State

The electronegativity increases as the oxidation state (i.e. the number of positive charge) of the atom increases.

4. Hybridisation

If the *s*-character in the hybridisation state of the atom increases, electronegativity also increases because *s*-electrons are comparatively close to the nucleus e.g. the electronegativity values of C-atom in various hybridisation states are as under

Hybridisation	sp^3	sp^2	sp
s-character	25%	33.33%	50%
Electronegativity	2.48	2.75	3.25

(*s*-character is increasing, so, the electronegativity value is also increasing.)

5. Nature of Substituents Attached

The electronegativity of a group also varies with the nature of the substituents. This is due to the inductive effect of the substituent group

e.g. $CH_3 = 2.30$,
$CCl_3 = 3.30$, $CF_3 = 3.35$

The electronegativity of carbon is adjusted by the presence of substituents (3H, 3Cl or 3F-atoms).

Variation of Electronegativity in the Periodic Table

The variation of electronegativity in the periodic table is shown as follows:

1. Variation Along a Period

On moving from left to right across a period, the effective nuclear charge increases and size decreases, the value of electronegativity increases due to increase in the attraction between the outer (or valence) electrons and the nucleus.

2. Variation Along a Group

On moving down a group, as the atomic size increases, the force of attraction between the outer (valence) electron and the nucleus decreases and hence, the electronegativity decreases.

Applications of Electronegativity

Some important applications of electronegativity are:

1. Nature of Bond

If the difference between the electronegativities of two atoms (bonded together) is less than 1.9, the bond formed between them is predominantly covalent and if this difference is more than 1.9, the bond is predominantly ionic, but if the difference is 1.9, the bond is 50% ionic and 50% covalent. [Electronegativity also helps in predicting the polar and non-polar bonds in molecules which has been discussed in chapter 4].

2. Metallic and Non-metallic Character

Non-metals have strong tendency to attract the electrons, so these are more electronegative. On the other hand, metals, because of their very less tendency to attract the electrons, generally have low electronegativity.

Thus, electronegativity is directly related to the non-metallic character but inversely related to the metallic character.

Hence, as the electronegativity increases across a period, the non-metallic character also increases (but metallic character decreases). Similarly, the electronegativity decreases down a group and the non-metallic character decreases (but metallic character increases down a group).

Difference between electron gain enthalpy and electronegativity

S.No.	Electron gain enthalpy	Electronegativity
1.	Electron gain enthalpy is the tendency of an isolated gaseous atom to attract an electron.	Electronegativity is the tendency of an atom in a molecule to attract the shared pair of electrons.
2.	It is the absolute electron attracting power of an atom.	It is the relative attracting power of an atom.
3.	It is the property of isolated atoms	It is the property of a bonded atom.
4.	It can be experimentally measured	It is only a relative number, cannot be measured experimentally.
5.	Electron gain enthalpy value for an atom is constant.	Electronegativity of an atom is not constant. However, it depends upon the oxidation state of an atom, hybridisation state of the atom and the nature of substituent attached to it.

The periodic trends of different periodic properties of elements in the periodic table are shown below :

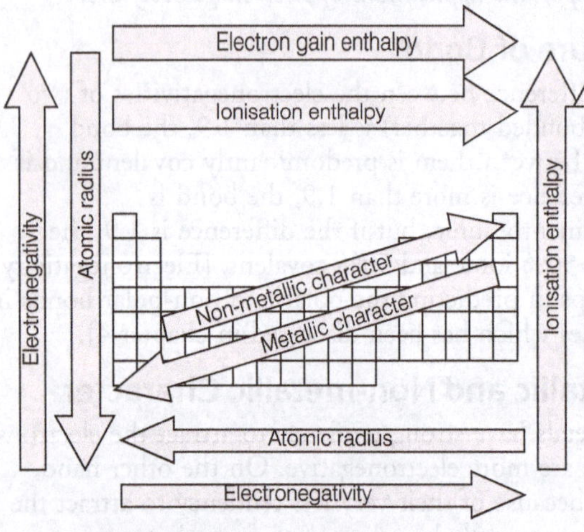

Periodic Trends in Chemical Properties

From the above discussion, it is clear that the periodic properties play a key role in the study of chemistry of different elements and their compounds. Moreover, these properties also affect the chemical behaviour of the elements to a larger extent. However, most of trends in chemical properties like diagonal relationship, inert pair effect, lanthanoid contraction and its effect will be discussed later along with the study of chemistry of different blocks. Here, we will discuss only some of the chemical properties.

These are as follows :

Periodicity of Valency or Oxidation States

Valency is the most important characteristic property of an element and is defined as

'the number of hydrogen or halogen atoms or double the number of oxygen atoms that combine(s) with an atom of the element.' It is infact the combining capacity of an element and can never be zero (except for noble gases). For representative elements (*s* and *p*-blocks elements), it is generally equal to the number of electrons present in the outermost (or valence shell) and/or equal to eight minus the number of electrons present in the outermost shell.

Valency (valencies) of representative elements is shown in the following table.

Valency of Representative Elements

Group	1	2	13	14	15	16	17	18
Number of valence electrons	1	2	3	4	5	6	7	8
Valency	1	2	3	4	3, 5	2, 6	1, 7	0, 8
	s-block		*p*-block					

However, now a days the term **oxidation state** is more in use as compared to valency. It is defined as **"the charge acquired by an atom on the basis of electronegativities of other atoms in the molecule."** e.g. in the two oxygen compound, OF_2 and Na_2O, the order of electronegativity of the elements is F > O > Na. In OF_2, each fluorine atom with outer electronic configuration $2s^2\,2p^5$ share its one electron with the oxygen. Being most electronegative, F has an oxidation state of –1. Oxygen with outer electronic configuration $2s^2\,2p^4$, shares two electrons with two fluorine atoms and acquires two positive charge, i.e. its oxidation state in OF_2 is +2. Further, in Na_2O, oxygen being more electronegative accepts two electrons from two Na atoms (one from each Na atom) and hence, shows the oxidation state –2 whereas Na with outer electronic configuration $3s^1$, loses this electrons to oxygen and thus, exhibits an oxidation state +1. The above discussion also shows that oxidation state of an element can be zero, positive or negative.

Note
- Higher *p*-block elements show more stability for lower oxidation state because of inert pair effect (i.e. reluctance of *s*-electron of the valence shell to take part in bonding) e.g. Pb^{4+} is less stable than Pb^{2+}.
- For *d*-block elements, maximum oxidation state $= (n-1)d\,e^-$ (unpaired) $+\, ns\,e^-$.

Variation of Valency in the Periodic Table

(i) On moving from left to right along a period, the number of valence electrons increases from 1 to 8, the valency of the elements with respect to hydrogen and chlorine increases from 1 to 4 and then decreases to zero. It can be better understood by taking examples of different elements of second period.

Variation of valency of elements of second period

Group	1	2	13	14	15	16	17
Second period	Li	Be	B	C	N	O	F
Valence with respect to H	LiH (1)	BeH_2 (2)	BH_3 or B_2H_6 (6)	CH_4 (4)	NH_3 (3)	H_2O (2)	HF (1)
Valence with respect to Cl	LiCl (1)	$BeCl_2$ (2)	BCl_3 (3)	CCl_4 (4)	NCl_3 (3)	Cl_2O (2)	ClF (1)

(ii) In a group, all the elements have same valency as, the number of valence electrons are same in all.

Note Transition elements and actinoids also exhibit variable valency which we shall study later.

Prediction of the Formula of a Compound from Valency

From the valencies of the elements, it is possible to predict the formula of the compound formed by them e.g. if we have element beryllium and chlorine and want to know the formula of the compound formed by these elements, then first of all, we have to find their valency. Beryllium belongs to group second (2) and has 2 valence electrons, chlorine however, belongs to halogen with the valence of 1. When these two combine, the formula of the compound obtained would be $BeCl_2$.

Anomalous Properties of Second Period Elements

The first member of each group of the representative elements [i.e. group 1 (lithium), 2 (beryllium) and groups 13 to 17 (boron to fluorine)] differ from the other members of their respective groups. This anomalous behaviour is because of (*i*) their small size (*ii*) large charge/radius ratio (*iii*) high electronegativity (*iv*) absence of *d*-orbitals. *Some of the anomalous properties are as follows.*

1. Diagonal Relationship

Some elements of second period like lithium, beryllium and boron resemble in their properties with the corresponding element of third period placed diagonally to them.

This similarity in properties of elements placed diagonally to each other is called the **diagonal relationship** in the periodic properties. e.g.

Group 1	Group 2	Group 13	Group 14
Li	Be	B	C
Na	Mg	Al	Si

(Li → Mg, Be → Al, B → Si)

2. Nature of Compounds

The nature of compounds formed by lithium, beryllium and boron is generally covalent but other members of their respective groups predominantly form ionic compounds. e.g. LiCl is covalent but NaCl is purely ionic.

3. Maximum Covalency

In the first member of each group, only four valence orbitals (i.e. one 2*s* and three 2*p* orbitals) are available for bonding whereas for the second members, the number of available valence orbitals is nine (i.e. one 3*s*, three 3*p* and five 3*d*). Thus, the maximum covalency exhibited by first member of each group is 4 [e.g. boron can only form $[BF_4^-]$ but not $[BF_6^-]$] whereas the other members of the group can expand their valence shell to show a covalency of 6. e.g. aluminium generally form $[AlF_6]^{3-}$. [This is because of the presence of empty *d*-orbital in it].

4. $p\pi$-$p\pi$ Multiple Bonding

Because of their smaller size and higher electronegativity, the first member of each group of *p*-block shows a higher tendency to form $p\pi$-$p\pi$ multiple bonds with its own atoms (like C=C, C≡C, N≡N etc.) and with the other elements of second period (like C=O, C=N, C≡N, N=O) as compared to the subsequent members of the same group.

Periodic Trends and Chemical Reactivity

The ionisation enthalpy is least for the alkali metals (because of their larger size in the respective period) which occupy the left corner of the periodic table. Thus, these elements have high tendency to lose an electron to form cation and this tendency increases on moving down the group. **Thus, alkali metals are highly reactive metals and their reactivity increases on moving down the group.**

Further, the halogen which occupy the right extreme in the periodic table because of their highest negative electron gain enthalpy have high tendency to accept an electron to form an anion and this tendency decreases on moving down the group.

Thus, **halogens are highly reactive non-metals and their reactivity decreases on moving down the group**. Thus, it is obvious that the **chemical reactivity is highest at two extremes and lowest in the centre.**

Trends of some other chemical properties are as follows :

1. Electropositive Character or Metallic Character

It is the tendency of an atom to lose its outermost electron to form cation. It generally increases as the ionisation enthalpy decreases. Thus, it is highest for alkali metals and lowest for halogens.

On moving down the group, electropositive character or metallic character increases due to decrease in ionisation enthalpy. Transition elements, however, are less electropositive than group 1 and 2 metals because of their lower ionisation enthalpy.

2. Electronegative Character or Non-metallic Character

It is the tendency of an element to accept electrons to form anion. It generally increases along a period from left to right and decreases on moving down a group.

3. Oxidising and Reducing Property

Reducing property depends upon the tendency to lose electron, i.e. electropositive or metallic character whereas oxidising property depends upon the tendency to gain electron i.e. electronegative or non-metallic character.

In the periodic table, reducing property increases down the group whereas oxidising property decreases. Alkali metals are strong reducing agents while halogens are strong oxidising agents.

The increasing order of reducing character of alkali metal is Na < K < Rb < Cs. The increasing order of oxidising character of halogens is $I_2 < Br_2 < Cl_2 < F_2$.

4. Acidic and Basic Nature of Oxides

Metal oxides are basic, i.e. form alkaline solutions when dissolved in water. Similarly, non-metal oxides are acidic while semi-metal oxides are amphoteric in nature. Thus, the basic character of oxides shows following trend in the periodic table.

→ Decreases (across the period)
→ Increases (down the group)

Similarly, acidic nature of oxides shows the following trend

→ Increases (across the period)
→ Decreases (down the group)

The oxides CO, N_2O, NO and H_2O are neutral in nature. The oxides of Al, Zn, Sn, As and Sb along with metalloids are amphoteric in nature.

The acidic character of the oxides of a non-metal increases with increase in oxygen content in it, e.g. $N_2O_3 < N_2O_5$; $SO_2 < SO_3$; $Cl_2O < Cl_2O_3 < Cl_2O_7$.

Non-metal oxides when dissolved in water form oxy-acids, thus they are called anhydrides of the acid formed.

Topic Practice 4

Very Short Answer Type Questions

1 Mark

1 Fill in the Blanks

(i) Electron gain enthalpy is highest for the element ....

(ii) .... is the most electronegative element in the periodic table.

(iii) In long form of periodic table, electronegativity .... as we move left to right in a period.

(iv) Electronegativity .... as positive oxidation state of element increases.

2 Objective Type Questions

(i) Among halogens, the correct order of amount of energy released in gaining of electron (electron gain enthalpy) is

(a) F > Cl > Br > I (b) F > Cl < Br < I
(c) F < Cl > Br > I (d) F < Cl < Br < I

(ii) Which one of the following arrangement represents the correct order of electron gain enthalpy of the given atomic species?

(a) Cl < F < S < O
(b) O < S < F < Cl
(c) S < O < Cl < F
(d) F < Cl < O < S

(iii) Which of the following statements is/are incorrect?

(a) Electron gain enthalpy becomes more negative with increase in atomic number across a period

(b) Effective nuclear charge increases from left to right across period

(c) Electron gain enthalpy becomes less negative as we go up in a group
(d) All of the above statements are incorrect

(iv) The ability of an atom in a chemical compound to attract shared electron is termed as
(a) electron affinity (b) ionisation enthalpy
(c) atomic attraction (d) electronegativity

(v) The correct order of electronegativity of Na, O and F is
(a) Na > O > F (b) O > F > Na
(c) O > Na > F (d) F > O > Na

3. Match the trend given in Columns (I) with the periodic property given in Column (II) and choose the correct option using the codes given below :

Column I	Column II
A. Cl > F > Br > I	(i) Electron gain enthalpy in a period.
B. F > Cl > Br > I	(ii) Reducing character in a group.
C. Na < K < Rb < Cs	(iii) Electronegativity in a group.
D. Si < P < S < Cl	(iv) Electro gain enthalpy in a group.

Codes

	A	B	C	D		A	B	C	D
(a)	(iii)	(iv)	(i)	(ii)	(b)	(iv)	(iii)	(i)	(ii)
(c)	(i)	(ii)	(iii)	(iv)	(d)	(iv)	(iii)	(ii)	(i)

4. Electron gain enthalpy usually becomes less negative from top to bottom in a group. Is there any exception to this generalisation? Comment.

5. Which of the following atoms would most likely to form an anion (i) Be, (ii) Al, (iii) Ga, (iv) I?

6. Why are electron gain enthalpies of Be and Mg positive?

7. Explain, why chlorine can be converted into chloride ion more easily as compared to fluoride ion from fluorine?

8. How would you react to the statement that the electronegativity of N on Pauling scale is 3.0 in all the nitrogen compounds? **NCERT Textbook**

9. Among alkali metals which element do you expect to be least electronegative and why? **NCERT Exemplar**

10. What is the basic difference between the terms electron gain enthalpy and electronegativity?

11. Are the oxidation state and covalency of Al in $[AlCl(H_2O)_5]^{2+}$ same?

Short Answer Type I Questions

2 Marks

12 Electronic configuration of some elements is given in Column I and their electron gain enthalpies are given in Column II. Match the electronic configuration with electron gain enthalpy.

	Column I (Electronic configuration)		Column II (Electron gain enthalpy / kJ mol^{-1})
A.	$1s^2 2s^2 2p^6$	(i)	– 53
B.	$1s^2 2s^2 2p^6 3s^1$	(ii)	– 328
C.	$1s^2 2s^2 2p^5$	(iii)	– 141
D.	$1s^2 2s^2 2p^4$	(iv)	+ 48

NCERT Exemplar

13 Give reason for the following statements :
(i) Halogens act as good oxidising agents.
(ii) Electron gain enthalpy of noble gases is almost zero.

14 Would you expect the second electron gain enthalpy of O as positive, more negative or less negative than the first? Justify your answer.

15 Using the periodic table, predict the formulae of compounds which might be formed by the following pairs of elements; (i) silicon and bromine (ii) aluminium and sulphur.

16 Show by a chemical reaction with water that Na_2O is a basic oxide and Cl_2O_7 is an acidic oxide.

17 Which of the following pairs of elements would have a more negative electron gain enthalpy?
(i) O or F (ii) F or Cl **NCERT Textbook**

18 Arrange the elements with the following electronic configurations in order of increasing electron gain enthalpy.
(i) $1s^2 2s^2 2p^5$ (ii) $1s^2 2s^2 2p^4$
(iii) $1s^2 2s^2 2p^3$ (iv) $1s^2 2s^2 2p^6 3s^2 3p^4$

Short Answer Type II Questions

3 Marks

19 What is the significance of the terms – 'isolated gaseous atom' and 'ground state' while defining the ionisation enthalpy and electron gain enthalpy? **NCERT Textbook**

20 Which one (atom/ion) in the following pairs has higher electron gain enthalpy?
(i) O^-, S (ii) O, S^- (iii) O^-, S^- (iv) N^-, P

21. Match the correct ionisation enthalpies and electron gain enthalpies of the following elements.

	Elements		ΔH_1	ΔH_2	$\Delta_{eg}H$
(i)	Most reactive non-metal	A.	419	3051	–48
(ii)	Most reactive metal	B.	1681	3374	–328
(iii)	Least reactive element	C.	738	1451	–40
(iv)	Metal forming binary halide	D.	2372	5251	+48

22 Nitrogen has positive electron gain enthalpy whereas oxygen has negative. However, oxygen has lower ionisation enthalpy than nitrogen. Explain. **NCERT Exemplar**

23 The increasing order of reactivity among group 1 elements is Li < Na < K < Rb < Cs whereas that among group 17 elements is F > Cl > Br > I. Explain. **NCERT Textbook**

24 First member of each group of representative elements (i.e. *s* and *p*-block elements) shows anomalous behaviour. Illustrate with two examples. **NCERT Exemplar**

25 Arrange the following as stated.
(i) Increasing order of bond dissociation energy of N_2, O_2, F_2, Cl_2.
(ii) Decreasing order of electropositive character of Cu, Fe, Mg.
(iii) Increasing order of valency of nitrogen in HNO_3, HNO_2, NO_2.

26 How does the metallic and non-metallic character vary on moving from left to right in a period?

Long Answer Type Questions

5 Marks

27 Discuss the factors affecting electron gain enthalpy and the trend in its variation in the periodic table.

28 *p*-block elements form acidic, basic and amphoteric oxides. Explain each property by giving two examples and also write the reactions of these oxides with water.

29 Predict the formulae of the stable binary compounds that would be formed by the combination of the following pairs of elements.
(i) Lithium and oxygen
(ii) Magnesium and nitrogen
(iii) Aluminium and iodine
(iv) Silicon and oxygen
(v) Phosphorus and fluorine
(vi) Element with Z = 71 and fluorine
NCERT Textbook

Hints & Solutions

1. (i) chlorine (ii) fluorine
(iii) increases (iv) increases

2. (i) (*c*) F < Cl > Br > I
(Electron gain enthalpy) = –328 –349 –325 – 295

This irregular trend is due to small size and *e/m* ratio of F-atom in comparison to other halogens. The extra added electron experiences more force of repulsion in F-atom.

(ii) (*b*) In periodic table, chlorine has more electron gain enthalpy than F. Generally electron gain enthalpy increases from left to right across the period. So, order of electron gain enthalpy is O < S < F < Cl.

(iii) (*c*) Generally electron gain enthalpy becomes more negative as we go up a group. Because the size of the atom decreases and the added electron would be nearer to the nucleus.

(iv) (*d*) A qualitative measure of the ability of an atom in a chemical compound to attract shared electrons to itself is called electronegativity.

(v) (*d*) The order of EN of Na, O and F is F > O > Na.

3. (b) A → (iv), B → (iii), (C) → (ii), (D) → (i)

4. **Exception** The $\Delta_{e_g} H$ of N is positive while the $\Delta_{e_g} H$ of other elements of group 15 becomes more and more negative down the group from P to Bi.

5. I, because of high electron gain enthalpy, it can accept an electron readily to form an anion.

6. Be and Mg have fully filled *s*-orbitals and hence have no tendency to accept an additional electron. Consequently, energy has to be supplied if an extra electron has to be added to the much higher energy *p*-orbitals of the valence shell. That is why electron gain enthalpies of Be and Mg are positive.

7. This is because of higher electron gain enthalpy of Cl than that of F.

8. The statement that electronegativity of N on Pauling scale is 3.0 in all the nitrogen compounds is wrong because electronegativity of any given element is not constant.

It varies depending on the element to which it is bound. It increases as the oxidation state of the element increases or percentage of *s*-character of hybrid orbital increases.

9. On moving down the group, electronegativity decreases because atomic size increases. Fr has the largest size, therefore it is least electronegative.

10. Refer to text on page 124 (Electron gain enthalpy, electronegativity and periodic trends in chemical properties; Difference between electron gain enthalpy and electronegativity).

11. No, the oxidation state of Al is +3 and the covalency is 6.

12. A. → (iv), B. → (i), C. → (ii), D. → (iii)

A. This electronic configuration corresponds to the noble gas i.e. neon. Since, noble gases have $+\Delta_{eg} H$ values, therefore, electronic configuration (*A*) corresponds to the $\Delta_{eg} H = +48 \text{ kJ mol}^{-1}$.

B. This electronic configuration corresponds to the alkali metal i.e. potassium. Alkali metals have small negative $\Delta_{eg} H$ values, hence, electronic configuration (*B*) corresponds to $\Delta_{eg} H = -53 \text{ kJ mol}^{-1}$.

C. This electronic configuration corresponds to the halogen i.e. fluorine. Since, halogens have high negative $\Delta_{eg} H$ values, therefore, electronic configuration (*C*) corresponds to $\Delta_{eg} H = -328 \text{ kJ mol}^{-1}$.

D. This electronic configuration corresponds to the chalcogen i.e. oxygen. Since, chalcogens have $\Delta_{eg} H$ values less negative than those of halogens, therefore, electronic configuration (*D*) corresponds to $\Delta_{eg} H = -141 \text{kJ mol}^{-1}$. [4 × 1/2]

13. (i) Due to highly negative electron gain enthalpy they act as good oxidising agents as they can gain electrons easily. [1]

(ii) Electronic configuration of noble gases is such that all subshells are completely filled. Hence, their electron gain enthalpy is almost zero.

14. $$O(g) + e^- \longrightarrow O^-(g); \Delta_{eg} H = -141 \text{ kJ mol}^{-1}$$

$$O(g) + e^- \longrightarrow O^{2-}(g); \Delta_{eg} H = +780 \text{ kJ mol}^{-1}$$

When an electron is added to oxygen atom to form ion, energy is released. Hence, first electron gain enthalpy of oxygen is negative. [1]

But when another electron is added to O^- ion to form O^{2-} ion, it feels stronger electrostatic repulsion.

Hence, addition of second electron takes place with absorption of energy. That's why the second electron gain enthalpy of oxygen is positive. [1]

15. (i) Silicon (Si) being a member of group 14 have four valence electrons, i.e. its valency is 4. Bromine is a member of halogen family and hence, its valency is 1.

When these combine, the formula of the compound formed would be Si (4) ⤫ Br (1) or $SiBr_4$. [1]

(ii) Aluminium being a member of group 13 contains three valence electrons so its valency is 3. Sulphur, on the other hand, belongs to group 16 and has 6 valence electrons, so its valency is $8-6=2$. When these combine, the formula of the compound formed would be = Al (3) ⤫ S (2) or Al_2S_3. [1]

16. When Na_2O is treated with water, it forms NaOH (sodium hydroxide) which is a strong base. [Its basic nature can be tested by using a red litmus paper, which turns blue]

$$Na_2O + H_2O \longrightarrow 2\,NaOH$$

Further, when Cl_2O_7 is treated with water, it forms $HClO_4$, which is a strong acid (as it turns blue litmus paper red).

$$Cl_2O_7 + H_2O \longrightarrow 2\,HClO_4$$ [2]

17. (i) Oxygen and fluorine both belong to second period. Electron gain enthalpy generally becomes more negative across a period as we move from left to right. On moving from oxygen to fluorine, the effective nuclear charge increases and atomic size decreases with increase in atomic number.

Due to this, forces of attraction of the nucleus increases for the incoming electron. That's why electron gain enthalpy becomes more negative for fluorine than that of oxygen. Furthermore, fluorine attains stable gas configuration by picking up an electron.

$$\underset{2,7}{F(g)} + e^- \longrightarrow \underset{2,8}{F^-(g)}$$

Therefore, electron gain enthalpy of fluorine is much more negative (-328 kJ mol^{-1}) than that of oxygen (-141 kJ mol^{-1}). [1]

(ii) Within a group, electron gain enthalpy becomes less negative down a group. But electron gain enthalpy of chlorine is more negative (-349 kJ mol^{-1}) than that of the fluorine (-328 kJ mol^{-1}).

This is due to small size of fluorine as the electron-electron repulsions in relatively compact 2*p*-orbital is greater than that in the larger 3*p*-orbital and hence, the incoming electron feels greater repulsion in fluorine than in the chlorine. That's why chlorine have more negative electron gain enthalpy than that of fluorine. [1]

18. Out of F ($1s^2\ 2s^2\ 2p^5$), O ($1s^2\ 2s^2\ 2p^4$), N ($1s^2\ 2s^2\ 2p^3$) and S ($1s^2\ 2s^2\ 2p^6 3s^2\ 3p^4$), only N has positive electron gain enthalpy because of its stable (exactly half-filled electronic configuration) while all others have negative electron gain enthalpies. Since, F needs only one more electron to acquire the nearest inert gas configuration, therefore, it has the most negative electron gain enthalpy.

Out of O and S, O has less negative electron gain enthalpy than S because of electron-electron repulsions present in its small compact $2p$-orbital. Thus, overall order of increasing electron gain enthalpy is :
(i) < (iv) < (ii) < (iii). [2]

19. Ionisation enthalpy It is the minimum amount of energy required to remove an electron from an isolated gaseous atom (X) in its ground state.

$$X(g) \longrightarrow X^+(g) + e^-$$

The force by which an electron is attracted by nucleus is also affected by the presence of other atoms within its molecule or in the neighbourhood. Therefore, ionisation enthalpy is determined in gaseous state because in gaseous state interatomic distances are larger and interatomic forces of attraction are minimum. Further more, ionisation enthalpy is determined at a low pressure because it is not possible to isolate a single atom but interatomic attractions can be further reduced by reducing pressure. Due to these reasons, the term isolated gaseous atom in ground state has been included in definition of ionisation enthalpy. [2]

Electron gain enthalpy It is the energy released when an isolated gaseous atom (X) in ground state gains an electron to form gaseous anion.

$$X(g) + e^- \longrightarrow X^-(g)$$

The most stable state of an atom is ground state. If isolated gaseous atom is in excited state, comparatively lesser energy will be released on addition of an electron. So, electron gain enthalpies of gaseous atoms must be determined in their ground states. Therefore, the terms ground state and isolated gaseous atom (explained above) has been also included in the definition of electron gain enthalpy. [1]

20. (i) Due to repulsion between the electrons on O^- and the additional incoming electron, the electron gain enthalpy of O^- is positive while that of S is negative.

(ii) On similar grounds, the electron gain enthalpy of S^- is positive while that of O is negative. [1]

(iii) Due to small size, repulsions between O^- and the incoming electron is much more than in S^-. Therefore, electron gain enthalpy of O^- is more positive than that of S^-. [1]

(iv) Due to repulsions between N^- and the incoming electron, electron gain enthalpy of N^- is positive while that of P is negative. [1]

21. (i) Most reactive non-metal has high $\Delta_i H_1$ and $\Delta_i H_2$ and most negative $\Delta_{eg} H$. Therefore, the element is B.

(ii) Most reactive metal has low $\Delta_i H_1$ and high $\Delta_i H_2$ (because the second electron has to be lost from noble gas configuration) and has small negative $\Delta_{eg} H$. Therefore, the element is A. [1]

(iii) Noble gases are the least reactive elements. They have very high $\Delta_i H_1$ and $\Delta_i H_2$ and have positive $\Delta_{eg} H$ values. Thus, the element is D. [1]

(iv) Metal forming binary halides are alkaline earth metals. They have $\Delta_i H_1$ value little higher than those of most reactive metals (such as A) and have comparatively slightly less negative $\Delta_{eg} H$ values. Thus, the element is C. [1]

22. Electronic configuration of $_7N$

$$= 1s^2, 2s^2, 2p_x^1, 2p_y^1, 2p_z^1.$$

Nitrogen has stable configuration because $2p$-orbital is half-filled. Therefore, addition of extra electron to any of the p-orbital requires large amount of energy.

Electronic configuration of $_8O$ [1]

$$= 1s^2, 2s^2, 2p_x^2, 2p_y^1, 2p_z^1.$$

Oxygen has $2p^4$ electrons, so process of adding an electron to the p-orbital is exothermic.

Oxygen has lower ionisation enthalpy than nitrogen because by removing one electron from $2p$-orbital, oxygen acquires stable configuration, *i.e.*, $2p^3$. On the other hand, in case of nitrogen it is not easy to remove one of the three $2p$-electrons due to its stable configuration. [1]

23. Chemical reactivity of alkali metals is exhibited by the loss of an electron leading to the formation of cation. The tendency of an element to lose an electron depends upon the ionisation enthalpy that decreases down the group. Hence, the reactivity increases down the group (Li < Na < K < Rb < Cs). [1]

On the other hand, chemical reactivity of halogens is shown by the gain of an electron leading to the formation of anion. The tendency to gain an electron to form an anion is related to electron gain enthalpy. [1]

Electron gain enthalpy becomes less and less negative as we move from chlorine to iodine. Hence, reactivity decreases from chlorine to iodine. Fluorine has less electron gain enthalpy but it is the most reactive due to its low bond dissociation enthalpy.

Group-17	F	Cl	Br	I	At
$\Delta_{eg} H$ (kJ mol^{-1})	−328	−349	−325	−295	−270

⟶ Reactivity decreases ⟶ [1]

24. First member of each group of representative elements (i.e. s and p-block elements) shows anomalous behaviour due to (i) small size (ii) high ionisation enthalpy (iii) high electronegativity and (iv) absence of d- orbitals.

For example in s-block elements, lithium shows anomalous behaviour from rest of the alkali metals.

(i) Compounds of lithium have significant covalent character. While compounds of other alkali metals are predominantly ionic. [1]

(ii) Lithium reacts with nitrogen to form lithium nitride while other alkali metals do not form nitrides. [1]

In p-block elements, first member of each group has four orbitals, one $2s$-and three $2p$-orbitals in their valence shell. So, these elements show a maximum covalency of four while other members of the same group or different group show a maximum covalency beyond four due to availability of vacant *d*- orbitals. [1]

25. (i) In general, as the size of atom or multiplicity of bond increases, bond dissociation energy increases but bond dissociation energy of F_2 is less than that of Cl_2 because of the small size of F.

Thus, the correct order of bond dissociation energy in (kJ/mol) is

F_2	<	Cl_2	<	O_2	<	N_2
155		242		494		941

[1]

(ii) Electropositive character means tendency to give an electron to form cation. It varies directly with atomic radii. Thus, the correct order is Mg > Fe > Cu. [1]

(iii) In HNO_3, N is in contact with three electronegative O atoms each of which share two electrons and hence acquire −2 charge. [1]

Therefore, N acquire +6 charge but charge of one O is used to make bond with H. So in actual, the charge or valency of N in HNO_3 is +5.

Similarly, its valency in HNO_2 is +3 and in NO_2 is +4.

The order of valency of N is $HNO_2 < NO_2 < HNO_3$. [1]

26. As we move from left to right in a period, the number of valence electrons increases by one at each succeeding element but the number of shells remains same. Due to this, effective nuclear charge increases. [1]

More is the effective nuclear charge, more is the attraction between nuclei and electron. [1]

Hence, the tendency of the element to lose electrons decreases, this results in decrease in metallic character. Furthermore, the tendency of an element to gain electrons increases with increase in effective nuclear charge, so non-metallic character increases on moving from left to right in a period. [1]

27. Refer to text on pages 121 (Factors affecting electron gain enthalpy, variation of electron gain enthalpy in the periodic table).

28. In *p*-block, when we move from left to right in a period, the acidic character of the oxides increases due to increase in electronegativity. e.g.

(i) **2nd period**

$B_2O_3 < CO_2 < N_2O_3$: Acidic character increases. [1]

(ii) **3rd period**

$Al_2O_3 < SiO_2 < P_4O_{10} < SO_3 < Cl_2O_7$: Acidic character increases. [1]

On moving down the group, acidic character decreases and basic character increases. e.g.

(a) **Nature of oxides of 13 group elements**

B_2O_3	Al_2O_3	Ga_2O_3	In_2O_3	Tl_2O
Weakly acidic	Amphoteric	Amphoteric	Basic	Strongly basic

[1]

(b) **Nature of oxides of 15 group elements**

N_2O_5	P_4O_{10}	As_4O_{10}	Sb_4O_{10}	Bi_2O_3
Strongly acidic	Moderately acidic	Amphoteric	Amphoteric	Basic

Among the oxides of same element, higher the oxidation state of the element, stronger is the acid. e.g. SO_3 is a stronger acid than SO_2.

Reaction of the oxides of *p*-block elements showing their acidic, basic and amphoteric behaviour. B_2O_3 is weakly acidic and on dissolution in water, it forms orthoboric acid. Orthoboric acid does not act as a protonic acid (it does not ionise) but acts as a weak Lewis acid.

$$\underset{\text{Boron trioxide}}{B_2O_3} + 3H_2O \rightleftharpoons \underset{\text{Orthoboric acid}}{2H_3BO_3}$$

$$B(OH)_3 + H{-}OH \longrightarrow [B(OH)_4]^- + H^+$$

Al_2O_3 is amphoteric in nature. It is insoluble in water but dissolves in alkalies and react with acids.

$$\underset{\text{Aluminium trioxide}}{Al_2O_3} + 2NaOH \xrightarrow{\Delta} \underset{\text{Sodium meta aluminate}}{2NaAlO_2} + H_2O$$

$$Al_2O_3 + 6HCl \xrightarrow{\Delta} \underset{\text{Aluminium chloride}}{2AlCl_3} + 3H_2O$$

Tl_2O is as basic as NaOH due to its lower oxidation state (+1). [1]

$$Tl_2O + 2HCl \longrightarrow 2TlCl + H_2O$$

P_4O_{10} on reaction with water gives orthophosphoric acid.

$$\underset{\text{Phosphorus pentoxide}}{P_4O_{10}} + 6H_2O \longrightarrow \underset{\text{Orthophosphoric acid}}{4H_3PO_4}$$

Cl_2O_7 is strongly acidic in nature and on dissolution in water, it gives perchloric acid.

$$\underset{\text{Dichlorine heptoxide}}{Cl_2O_7} + H_2O \longrightarrow \underset{\text{Perchloric acid}}{2HClO_4}$$ [1]

29.

S.No.	Element	Group number	Electrons in valence shell	Valency	Formulae of binary compound
(i)	Lithium	Group 1	1	1	Li_2O
	Oxygen	Group 16	6	8 – 6 = 2	
(ii)	Magnesium	Group 2	2	2	Mg_3N_2
	Nitrogen	Group 15	5	8 – 5 = 3	
(iii)	Aluminium	Group 13	3	3	AlI_3
	Iodine	Group 17	7	8 – 7 = 1	
(iv)	Silicon	Group 14	4	4	SiO_2
	Oxygen	Group 16	6	8 – 6 = 2	
(v)	Phosphorus	Group 15	5	3 or 5	PF_3 or PF_5
	Fluorine	Group 17	7	8 – 7 = 1	
(vi)	Element with Z = 71 (Lutetium)	Group 3	3	3	LuF_3
	Fluorine	Group 17	7	8 – 7 = 1	

Note

(i) In case of *s* and *p*-block elements (representative elements), the valency of an atom is generally equal to either the number of valence electrons or equal to eight minus the number of valence electrons.

(ii) In case of lanthanoids (inner-transition elements), there is involvement of *d* and *f*-electrons with valence shell electrons in bond formation. Common valence for lanthanoids is 3.

(iii) Electronic configuration of $_{71}Lu$ = [Xe] $4f^{14}$, $5d^1$, $6s^2$; (Valency = 3).

SUMMARY

- Periodic table is an arrangement of elements on the basis of similarity and dissimilarity in properties to systematise the study of element.
- **Mendeleev's periodic table** is based on Mendeleev's periodic law, which states that the properties of the elements are the periodic function of their atomic weights. This table contains 9 groups and 12 series (or 6 periods).
- **Long form of periodic table** is based on modern periodic law which states the properties of the elements are the periodic function of their atomic numbers. This table contains 18 groups and 7 periods. The elements present in 1, 2, 3, 4, 5, 6 and 7 periods are respectively 2, 8, 8, 18, 18, 32 and 32.
- **Position of elements in the periodic table**

  Period Principal quantum number of valence shell.

  Block Orbital receiving last electrons.

  Group Number of valence electrons (for *s* and *p*-block) = $(n-1)de^- + nse^-$ (for *d*-block) = 3 (for *f*-block)
- **Nomenclature of elements with atomic number > 100** : Root word of each number + ium, e.g. 112 = ununbium.
- ***s*-block** General configuration ns^{1-2} (includes group 1 and 2).
- ***p*-block** General configuration $ns^2 \cdot np^{1-6}$, (includes mainly non-metals).
- ***d*-block** General configuration $(n-1)d^{1-10} \cdot ns^{0-2}$, also called transition elements. Show paramagnetism and variable valancy.
- ***f*-block** General configuration $(n-2)f^{1-14} \cdot (n-1)d^{0-1} \cdot ns^2$.
- **Periodic Properties** Properties showing regular gradation along the period and group.
  These can be physical properties (atomic radius, ionic radius, ionisation energy, electron gain enthalpy and electronegativity) or chemical properties (metallic or non-metallic character, nature of oxides, valency etc.)
- **Periodic trends in Physical Properties**
  - (i) **Atomic Radius** It may be covalent, metallic or van der Waals' radii. It decreases along a period but increases on moving down the group.
  - (ii) **Ionic Radius** It also follow the same trend as atomic radius. A cation is smaller than its parent atom but an anion is larger than its parent atom.
  - (iii) **Ionisation Energy** (I.E) It is the energy required to remove an electron from isolated gaseous atom. It decreases in the group and increases along a period from left to right.
  - (iv) **Electron Gain Enthalpy** It is the energy change occurring during the conversion of an isolated gaseous atom into anion. It also follow the same trend as I.E.
  - (v) **Electronegativity** It is the tendency of an atom to attract the shared pair of electrons towards itself in a covalent bond. It also follows the same trend as I.E.
- **Periodic trends in Chemical Properties**
  - (i) **Metallic and Non-metallic Character** Metallic character increases on moving down the group and decreases along a period. Reverse is true for non-metallic character.
  - (ii) **Nature of Oxides** Acidic nature of oxides increases along a period from left to right but decreases on moving down the group. Reverse is true for basic nature.
  - (iii) **Valency** It increases from 1 to 7 along a period w.r.t oxygen (O) but with respect to hydrogen (H), it first increases from 1 to 4 and then decreases to zero.
  - (iv) **Oxidising and Reducing Property** In *s*-block elements, the reducing property increases but oxidising property decreases down the group. In case of *p*-block, the order is reverse.

Chapter Practice

Very Short Answer Type Questions

1 Mark

1. Fill in the Blanks

(i) Elements of group (1), (2) and (13) to (17) are main groups. These are also called .... elements.

(ii) The period number represents the highest .... quantum number of the element.

(iii) Most of the 5*f*-elements are radioactive, the element upto uranium are natural and rest of the elements are synthetic. Therefore, these are also called .... elements.

(iv) Ca^{2+} has a smaller ionic radius than K^+ because it has............ .

(v) The energy released when an electron is added to a neutral gaseous atom is called ....

(vi) Second electron gain enthalpy is always ....

(vii) On Mulliken scale, the average of ionisation potential and electron affinity is known as......... .

(viii) For elements of second period, the maximum possible covalency is ....

(ix) For *s*-block elements, the basic nature of oxides, ... as we move down the group.

2. Objective Type Questions

(i) Which of the following statements regarding modern periodic law is incorrect?

(a) Henry Moseley observed regularities in the characteristics X-ray spectra of elements

(b) A plot of frequency of X-rays emitted against atomic number (*Z*) give a straight line

(c) The atomic number of an element is equal to the number of neutron(s) in a neutral atom

(d) Electronic configuration of an atom determine the physical and chemical properties

(ii) 4*f* inner-transition series and 5*f* inner-transition series of elements are termed as, respectively

(a) actinoid and 3*d*- series

(b) lanthanoid and actinoid series

(c) cerium and 3*d*- series

(d) None of the above

(iii) Which of the following is correct?

(a) *p*-block elements has highly negative electron gain enthalpies

(b) The two groups of *p*-block elements have highly negative electron gain enthalpies

(c) Group -17 is known as halogen family

(d) Both (b) and (c)

(iv) The first ionisation potential of Na is 5.1 eV. The value of electron gain enthalpy of Na^+ will be

(a) −2.55 eV (b) −5.1 eV

(c) −10.2 eV (d) +2.55 eV

(v) Which of the following is/are general characteristics of an atom with high electronegativity?

(a) Tendency to form positive ions

(b) Small atomic size

(c) High effective nuclear charge

(d) Both (b) and (c)

(vi) The oxide formed by the element on extreme right and in the left of periodic table are generally

(a) acidic, amphoteric respectively

(b) acidic, basic respectively

(c) neutral, amphoteric respectively

(d) basic, neutral respectively

3. Matching Type Questions

(i) Match the Column I with Column II and select the correct answer using given codes.

Column I (Atomic number)	Column II (Position in the periodic table)
A. 52	(i) *s*-block
B. 56	(ii) *p*-block
C. 57	(iii) *d*-block
D. 60	(iv) *f*-block

Codes

	A	B	C	D		A	B	C	D
(a)	(ii)	(i)	(iii)	(iv)	(b)	(ii)	(i)	(iv)	(iii)
(c)	(i)	(ii)	(iii)	(iv)	(d)	(i)	(ii)	(iv)	(iii)

(ii) Match Column I with Column II and select the correct answer using given codes.

Column I (Elements)	Column II (Properties)
A. He	(i) Highest electronegativity
B. F	(ii) Most electropositive
C. Rb	(iii) Strongest reducing agent
D. Li	(iv) Highest ionisation energy

Codes

	A	B	C	D		A	B	C	D
(a)	(iv)	(ii)	(iii)	(i)	(b)	(i)	(iv)	(ii)	(iii)
(c)	(iv)	(i)	(iii)	(ii)	(d)	(iv)	(i)	(ii)	(iii)

4. Give the general electronic configurations of
   (i) *p*-block element (ii) actinoids

5. The element with Z = 118 is newly discovered. What is its IUPAC name and symbol?

6. Which has the largest ionic radius among Ca^{2+}, Mg^{2+}, Ba^{2+}?

Or Arrange the following ions in the order of increasing size

$$Be^{2+}, Cl^-, S^{2-}, Na^+, Mg^{2+}, Br^-$$

7. The radius of Na^+ cation is less than that of Na atom. Give reason.

8. Noble gases have positive electron gain enthalpy. Why?

9. Elements in the same group have equal valency. Comment on it.

Assertion-Reason

Directions (Q. Nos. 10-14) In the following questions an Assertion (A) is followed by a corresponding Reason (R). Use the following keys to choose the appropriate answer.

(a) Both (A) and (R) are correct and (R) is the correct explanation of (A).
(b) Both (A) and (R) are correct but (R) is not the correct explanation of (A).
(c) (A) is correct and (R) is incorrect.
(d) (A) is incorrect and (R) is correct.

10. **Assertion** (A) Noble gases are highly reactive.
    Reason (R) Noble gases have stable closed shell electronic configuration.

11. **Assertion** (A) Na^+ and Al^{3+} are isoelectronic.
    Reason (R) Na belongs to *s*-block, while Al belongs to *p*-block.

12. **Assertion** (A) First ionisation enthalpy for nitrogen is lower than that of oxygen.
    Reason (R) Across a period, effective nuclear charge increases.

13. **Assertion** (A) The elements having $1s^2, 2s^2, 2p^6, 3s^2$ and $1s^2, 2s^2$ electronic configuration belong to same period.
    Reason (R) Both have same outermost electronic configuration.

14. **Assertion** (A) Isoelectronic species have same radii.
    Reason (R) They contain same number of electrons.

Case-Study

15. When an electron is added to a gaseous atom in its ground state to convert into a negative ion, the enthalpy change accompanying the process is called the electron gain enthalpy ($\Delta_{eg}H$). It is a direct measure of the ease with which an atom attracts an electron to form anion.

$$X(g) + e^- \longrightarrow X^-(g);\ \Delta H = \Delta_{eg}H$$

The most stable state of an atom is the ground state. If an isolated gaseous atom is in excited state, comparatively lesser energy will be released on adding an electron. So, electron gain enthalpies of gaseous atoms must be determined in their ground states.

Therefore, the terms ground state and isolated gaseous atom has been also included in the definition of electron gain enthalpy. Like ionisation enthalpy, electron gain enthalpy is measure either in electron volts per atom or kJ per mole.

(i) Why noble gases have positive electron gain enthalpy.
(ii) The electron gain enthalpy of O or F is less than that of S or Cl. Give reason.
(iii) Why beryllium has higher ionisation enthalpy than boron?

16. In the modern periodic table, elements are arranged in order of increasing atomic numbers which is related to the electronic configuration.

Depending upon the type of orbitals receiving the last electron, the elements in the periodic table have been divided into four blocks, *viz*, *s*, *p*, *d* and *f*.

The modern periodic table consists of 7 periods and 18 group. Each period begins with the filling of a new energy shell. In accordance with the Aufbau principle, the seven periods (1 to 7) have 2, 8, 8, 18, 18, 32, and 32 elements respectively.

The seventh period is still incomplete. To avoid the periodic table being too long, the two series of *f*-block elements, called lanthanoids and actinoids are placed to the bottom of the main body of the periodic table.

(i) Write the outermost electronic configuration of last element of p-block in 6th period.

(ii) Which element cannot be accompandated in the present setup of the long form of the periodic table?

(iii) Write the electronic configuration of element which is just above the element with the atomic number 43 in the same group.

Short Answer Type I Questions

2 Marks

17. What are transition elements? Which of the following are not transition elements?
Cu (Z = 29), S (Z = 16), Ga (Z = 31), Pd (Z = 46) and U (Z = 92).

18. Locate each of the following elements on the periodic table and identify each of them.
(i) [Ar] $3d^7 4s^2$ (ii) [Ar]$3d^5 4s^1$
(iii) [Kr]$4d^2 5s^2$ (iv) [Xe] $4f^3 6s^2$

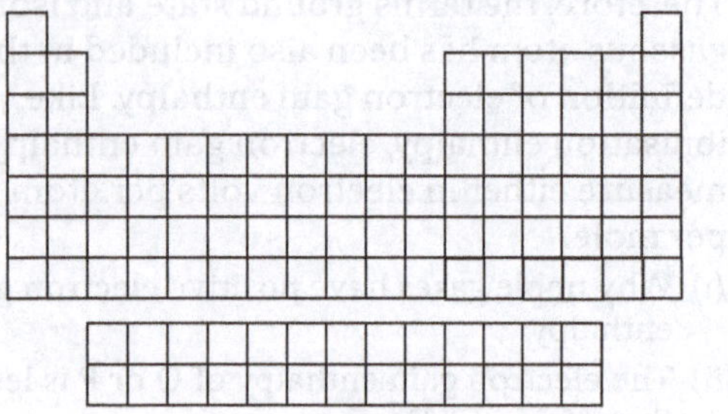

19. Write the name and deduce the atomic numbers of the following atoms.
(i) The fourth alkali metal
(ii) Second transition element
(iii) The fourth noble gas
(iv) Fourth element in the second period

20. In a period of the periodic table, generally the size of an atom decreases with increase in atomic number but at the end of each period in noble gases, the atomic size increases abruptly. Explain.

21. Why is the first ionisation energy of the transition elements reasonably constant?

22. What is the significance of the large increase in the third ionisation energy of Ca and fifth ionisation energy of Si?

23. The first ionisation enthalpy of carbon atom is greater than that of boron whereas the reverse is true for the second ionisation enthalpy. Explain.

24. Which of the following pairs of elements would you expect to have lower first ionisation enthalpy? Explain.
(i) Cl or F (ii) Cl or S
(iii) K or Ar (iv) Kr or Xe

25. Among the elements K, Mg, C and N, which would show the greatest difference in first and second ionisation enthalpies?

26. Predict the formulas of stable compounds that would be formed by following pairs of elements.
(i) Aluminium and bromine
(ii) Calcium and iodine
(iii) Element with $z = 114$ 114 and fluorine
(iv) Element with $z = 120$ and oxygen

27. (i) Explain the variation in acidic and basic character of oxides of second row elements.
(ii) Account for the variation in metallic or non-metallic character in third row elements.

28. Name the properties of the elements which,
(i) increases in going from left to right in a period.
(ii) decreases in going from left to right in a period.
(iii) increases in going from top to bottom in a group.
(iv) decreases in going from top to bottom in a group.

Short Answer Type II Questions

3 Marks

29. (i) Name the most metallic element and most non-metallic element in second period.
(ii) Name the element with (a) largest atomic radius, (b) smallest radius in third period.
(iii) Name the element having general electronic configuration $ns^2\ np^4$ in fourth period.

30. Consider the ground state electronic configuration given below.
(A) $1s^2\ 2s^2\ 2p^6$ (B) $1s^2\ 2s^2\ 2p^4$
(C) $1s^2\ 2s^2\ 2p^6\ 3s^2$ (D) $1s^2\ 2s^2\ 2p^6\ 3s^1$
(E) $1s^2\ 2s^2\ 2p^5$
(i) Identify the configuration which is associated with the lowest and the highest ionisation enthalpy?
(ii) Arrange the above configurations in order of increasing negative electron gain enthalpy.

31. What is the cause of periodicity in the properties of elements? How do the following properties vary in a (a) group, (b) period?
(i) Atomic size
(iii) Electronegativity
(ii) Ionisation energy

32. Given below is a part of the periodic table
Arrange the given elements.

H																	He
Li	Br											B	C	N	O	F	Ne
Na																	
K																	
Rb																	
Cs																	

(i) In the order of decreasing size in the period ......
(ii) In the order of increasing metallic character in the group ......
(iii) In the order of increasing electronegativity in the period ......

33. Arrange the following as stated :
(i) Increasing order of basic character ; MgO, SrO, K_2O, NiO, Cs_2O
(ii) Increasing the first ionisation energy; Mg, Al, Si, Na
(iii) Increasing acidic proeprty ; ZnO, Na_2O_2, P_2O_5, MgO

Long Answer Type Question

5 Marks

34. Explain what is meant by the ionisation energy of an element. How does this vary between hydrogen and neon in the periodic table? Discuss how the variation can be related to the electronic structure of the atoms.

Hints & Solutions

1. (i) representative (typical) (ii) principal
(iii) transuranic (iv) more positive charge
(v) electron gain enthalpy (vi) positive
(vii) electronegativity (viii) four
(ix) increases

2. (i) (*c*) The atomic number of an element is equal to the number of electrons/number of protons in a neutral atom. Atomic number $(Z) =$ Number of e^- or p^+
(ii) (*b*) 4*f* inner-transition series is lanthanoid series, whereas 5*f* inner-transition is known as actinoid series.
(iii) (*d*) The two groups such as 16th and 17th groups have highly negative electron gain enthalpies. Group 17 is known as halogen family.
(iv) (*b*) $Na \rightarrow Na^+ + e^-$, first IE
$Na^+ + e^- \rightarrow Na$
Electron gain enthalpy of Na^+ is reverse of (IE)
Because reaction is reverse so $\Delta H(\text{eq}) = -5.1$ eV
(v) (*d*) Electronegativity $\propto$ high effective nuclear charge
$\propto \dfrac{1}{\text{atomic size}}$
(vi) (*b*) Oxides formed by the element on extreme right of the periodic table is acidic. The oxides formed by the element in the left of the periodic table are basic.

3. (i) (*a*) A $\rightarrow$ (ii), B $\rightarrow$ (i), C $\rightarrow$ (iii), D $\rightarrow$ (iv)
A. 52 $\longrightarrow 5s^2 5p^4$ (*p*-block)
B. 56 $\longrightarrow 6s^2$ (*s*-block)
C. 57 $\longrightarrow 5d^1 6s^2$ (*d*-block)
D. 60 $\longrightarrow 4f^4 5d^0 6s^2$ (*f*-block)
(ii) (*d*) A $\rightarrow$ (iv), B $\rightarrow$ (i), C $\rightarrow$ (ii), D $\rightarrow$ (iii),
Helium (He) $1s^2$ $\longrightarrow$ Highest ionisation energy due to noble gas in nature.
Fluorine (F) $1s^2$, $2s^2 2p^5$ $\longrightarrow$ High electronegativity in nature due to small size and -1 oxidation state.
Rubidium (Rb) $\longrightarrow$ Most electropositive element due to large atomic size.
Lithium (Li) $\longrightarrow$ Strongest reducing agent due to small size and positive oxidation state (+1).

4. (i) $ns^2 np^{1-6}$ (ii) $5f^{1-14} 6d^{0-1} 7s^2$

5. IUPAC name Oganesson, symbol : Og

6. Refer to text on page 113 (Topic-3, Variation of ionic radii).
Or
Order of increasing size :
$Be^{2+} < Mg^{2+} < Na^+ < Cl^- < S^{2-} < Br^-$

7. Refer to text on page 113 (Topic-3, Comparison of ionic radii with corresponding atomic radii).

8. Refer to text on pages 120 and 121 (Topic-4, Electron gain enthalpy of noble gases).

9. Refer to text on page 125 (Topic-4, Variation of valency in periodic table).

10. (*d*) (A) incorrect and (R) is correct.
Noble gases are very less reactive due to stable closed shell electronic configuration like $ns^2 np^6$ or ns^2. They are reluctant to share electrons from their filled outer electron shells, noble gases are generally considered unreactive.

11. (*b*) Both (A) and (R) are correct but (R) is not the correct explanation of (A). The ions or atoms having same number of electrons are called isoelectronic species. Both Na^+ and Al^{3+} are isoelectronic due to presence of 10 electrons.

12. (*d*) In a period from left to right, effective nuclear charge increases and size decreases as a result ionisation energy increases. But element of II A and IA group on the account of their half-filled and completely filled orbitals have high IE than the elements of III A and VI A group, respectively.
Thus, (A) is incorrect and (R) is correct.

13. (*a*) Both (A) and (R) are correct and (R) is the correct explanation of (A).

14. (*d*) (A) is incorrect and (R) is correct.
Isoelectronic species have same number of electrons.

15. (i) Due to stable configuration noble gas do not accept an electron and hence they have positive electron gain enthalpy.
(ii) There is more repulsion for the incoming electron when the size of atom is small. When an electron is added to O or F, it goes to a smaller ($n = 2$) level and suffers more repulsion than the electron in S or Cl in larger ($n = 3$) level.
(iii) It is easier to remove electron from 2*p*-orbital as compared to 2*s*-orbital due to more penetration of *s*-electrons.

16. (i) Each period starts with the filling of electrons in a new principal energy shell. Therefore, 6th period starts with the filling of 6*s*-orbital and ends when 6*p*-orbitals are completely filled.
In between, $4f$ and 5*d*-orbitals are filled in accordance with Aufbau principle. Thus, the outermost electronic configuration of the last element of the *p*-block in the 6th period is

$$6s^2 4f^{14} 5d^{10} 6p^6 \text{ or } 4f^{14} 5d^{10} 6s^2 6p^6.$$

(ii) The long form of the periodic table contain element with atomic number 1 to 118. The fifth period begins with Rb($Z = 37$) and ends at Xe ($Z = 54$).
(iii) Thus, the element with $Z = 43$ lies in the 5th period. Since, the 4th period has 18 elements, therefore, the atomic number of the element which lies just above the element with atomic number 43 is $43 - 18 = 25$.
Now, the electronic configuration of element with $Z = 25$ is

$$1s^2 2s^2 2p^6 3s^2 3p^5 3d^5 4s^2 \text{ (i.e. Mn)}.$$

17. Refer to text on page 105 (Topic-2, The *d*-block elements : Transition elements).

18. Refer to text on page 106 (Topic-2, Algorithm for predicting position of an element in the periodic table).

19. Refer to text on page 97 (Topic-1, Periodic Table)

20. Refer to text on page 115 [Topic-3, Variation along a period (exceptions)].

21. Refer to text on page 115 [Topic-3, Variation of ionisation enthalpy in the periodic table (exception)].

22. Refer to text on page 114 (Topic-3, Successive ionisation enthalpies).

23. The size of carbon atom is smaller than boron. So the valence electrons of carbon experiences greater nuclear charge. Hence, the first I.E. of carbon is higher than that of boron. After loosing one electron boron acquires fully filled as compared to carbon which has partially filled orbitals. So, greater amount of energy will be needed to remove second electron from boron. Hence, second I.E. of boron is greater than that of carbon.

24. Refer to text on page 115 (Topic-3, Variation of ionisation enthalpy in the periodic table).

25. Refer to solution no. 31 on page 113 (Topic-3).

26. Refer to text on page 124 (Topic-4, Prediction of the formula of a compound from valency).

27. (i) Refer to text on page 126 (Topic-4, Acidic and basic nature of oxides).
(ii) Refer to text on page 107 (Topic-2, Trends in metallic and non-metallic properties).

28. (i) Electronegativity (ii) Atomic size
(iii) Atomic size (iv) Ionisation enthalpy

29. (i) Most metallic element is lithium and most non-metallic element is fluorine in the second period.
(ii) Largest atomic radius : Sodium
Smallest radius : Chlorine
(iii) In fourth period, selenium has general electronic configuration ns^2np^4 where n (principal quantum number) $= 4$.

30. (i) Refer to text on page 115 (Topic-3, Variation of ionisation enthalpy in the periodic table).
(ii) Refer to text on page 121 (Topic-4, Variation of electron gain enthalpy in the periodic table).

31. The main cause of periodicity in properties is the repetition of similar electronic configuration at regular intervals.
(i) Refer to text on page 112 (Topic-3, Variation of atomic radii in the periodic table).
(ii) Refer to text on page 115 (Topic-3, Variation of ionisation enthalpy in the periodic table).
(iii) Refer to text on page 121 (Topic-4, Variation of electron gain enthalpy in the periodic table).

32. (i) Refer to text on page 112 (Topic-3, Variation of atomic radius along a period).
(ii) Refer to text on page 107 (Topic-2, Trends in metallic and non-metallic properties).
(iii) Refer to text on page 123 (Topic-4, Variation of electronegativity along a period).

33. (i) Refer to text on page 126 (Topic-4, Acidic and basic nature of oxides).
(ii) Refer to text on page 115 (Topic-3, Variation of ionisation enthalpy in the periodic table).
(iii) Refer to text on page 126 (Topic-4, Acidic and basic nature of oxides).

34. Refer to text on pages 113 and 114 (Topic-3, Ionisation enthalpy).

CHAPTER

04

Chemical Bonding and Molecular Structure

We have studied that matter is made up of atoms and also that atoms other than noble gases do not exist independently under normal conditions. However, a group of atoms behaving like a single species called **molecule** do exist independently. So, obviously there must be some force which holds the constituent atoms in a molecule together. Such force is called a **chemical bond.**

TOPIC 01 General Introduction to Bonding: Ionic, Covalent Bond and Coordinate Bond

- General Introduction to Bonding: Ionic, Covalent Bond and Coordinate Bond
- Resonance and VSEPR Theory
- Valence Bond Theory and Hybridisation
- Molecular Orbital Theory and Hydrogen Bonding

Chemical Bonding

A chemical bond is a kind of attraction which holds two or more constituents (atoms, molecules or ions) together. The process of their combination is called **chemical bonding.**

For an element, bond formation is valency dependent phenomenon. The valency is defined as **"the combining capacity of an element"**. In simpler words, the number of bonds formed by an element with the other similar species is called the valency of that element.

The formation of a chemical bond is always accompanied by decrease in energy. As a matter of fact all the attractive forces constituting a chemical bond are electrostatic in nature. Depending upon different situation, different names are assigned to them.

The chemical bonds can be classified as below :

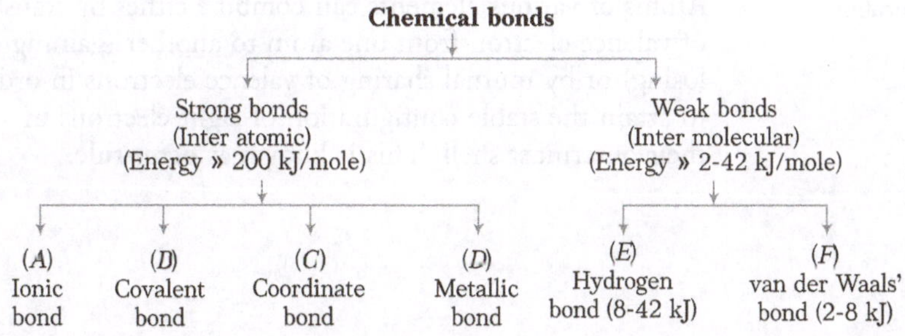

Lewis Symbols

The simple notations to represent the valence electrons of an atom are called **Lewis symbols**. These were introduced by an American chemist, G N Lewis.

In these symbols, the valence electrons are represented by placing dots (·) or crosses (×) around the symbol, e.g. the Lewis symbols for the atoms of second period are

Significance of Lewis Symbols

The Lewis symbols indicate the number of outermost or valence electrons, which helps to calculate the common or group valency of the element. The group valency of the elements is generally either equal to the number of dots in Lewis symbols or 8 minus the number of dots or valence electrons, e.g. in case of Na, Mg, Al, the group valence is equal to the number of dots, i.e. 1, 2 and 3 respectively but in case of N, O, F and Ne, it is equal to 8 – number of dots in Lewis symbol, i.e. $(8-5)=3, (8-6)=2, (8-7)=1$ and $(8-8)=0$ respectively.

Kossel-Lewis Approach to Chemical Bonding

In 1916 **Kossel** and **Lewis** succeeded independently to give first successful explanation about the cause of combination between atoms which was based upon the understanding of electronic configuration of noble gases. Since, this theory was based on the electronic concept of atom, so it is also referred as **electronic theory of valency.**

The main postulates of this theory are as follows:

(i) Lewis pictured the atom in terms of a positively charged 'Kernel' (the nucleus plus the inner electrons) and the outer shell, which is called the **valence shell.** The electrons present in this shell are called the **valence electrons** and are responsible for the reactivity of atoms.

(ii) The electronic configurations of the noble gases are as:

Noble gas	Atomic number	Electronic configuration
Helium	2	2
Neon	10	2, 8
Argon	18	2, 8, 8

The study of electronic configurations of the noble gases, clearly reveals that they have 8 electrons in their outermost orbit except in case of helium which has 2. These eight electrons occupy all the corners of a cube which surround the 'Kernel'. This octet of electrons shows a particularly stable electronic arrangement. Thus, are chemically inert.

(iii) Lewis postulated that atoms achieve the stable octet (or duplet in case of H, He and Li etc.) when they are joined through chemical bonds. Atoms join together either by transfer of valence electrons from one atom to another (gaining or losing) or by sharing of valence electrons in order to complete their octet.
In this process each atom attains a stable outer octet of electrons.

To explain chemical bonding, Kossel drew attention to the following facts :

(i) In the periodic table, noble gases separate the highly electronegative halogens from the highly electropositive alkali metals.

(ii) The formation of a negative ion from a halogen atom is associated with the gain of an electron and the formation of a positive ion from an alkali metal atom is associated with the loss of an electron.

(iii) The negative and positive ions thus obtained achieve stable noble gas electronic configurations. The noble gases (with the exception of helium which has duplet of electrons) have a particularly stable outer shell configuration of eight (octet) electrons, ns^2np^6.

(iv) The negative and positive ions are bind together by electrostatic forces of attraction.

(v) Such type of electrostatic forces of attraction results in **electrovalent bond.**

The above postulates provide a base to develop the modern concept about the ion formation by electron transfer and the formation of ionic crystalline compounds.

Octet Rule

Atoms of various elements can combine either by transfer of valence electron from one atom to another (gaining or losing) or by mutual sharing of valence electrons in order to attain the stable configuration of eight electrons in their outermost shell. This is known as **octet rule.**

Ionic or Electrovalent Bond

The bond formed as a result of electrostatic force of attraction between two oppositely charged ions i.e. positive and negative ions together is termed as the **electrovalent** or **ionic bond.** It is formed by complete transfer of electrons from one atom to another, so that all the combining atoms complete their octet (or duplet in case of H, He, Li etc.).

It is generally formed between a non-metal and a metal atom, so that they get converted into an anion and cation respectively. The number of unit charge(s) present on the ion is the **electrovalence** of that ion.

e.g. formation of sodium chloride.

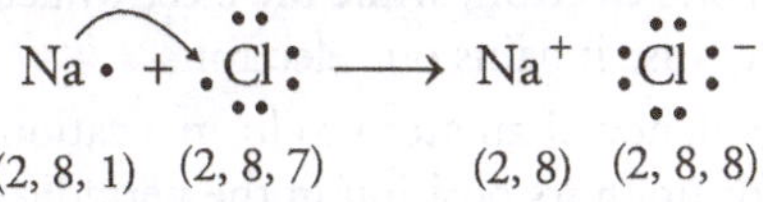

Lewis Structures of Some Ionic Compounds

(i) Formation of lithium oxide (Li_2O)

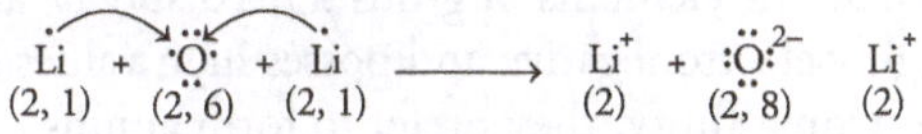

(ii) Formation of magnesium oxide (MgO)

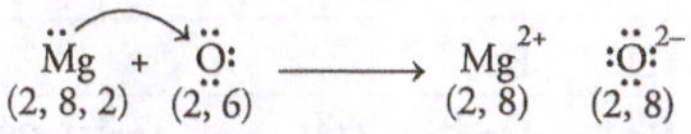

(iii) Formation of magnesium fluoride (MgF_2)

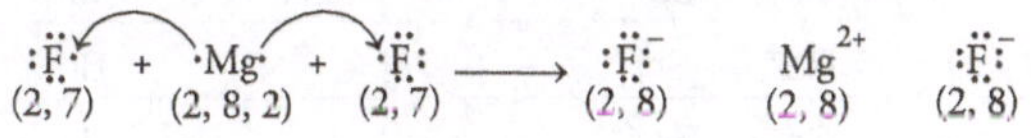

(iv) Formation of calcium oxide (CaO)

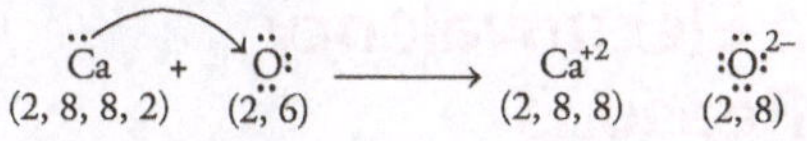

(v) Formation of Na_2S

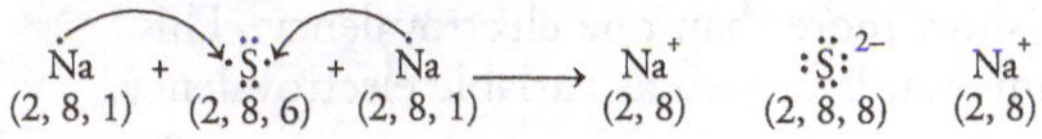

Conditions for the Formation of Ionic Bond

(i) **Low Ionisation Energy of Metal atom** Ionisation energy is the amount of energy required to remove the most loosely bond electron from an isolated gaseous atom to form a positive ion.

So, lesser the ionisation energy of metal atom, greater is the case of losing the valence electron and hence greater is the tendency to form ionic bonds.

(ii) **High Electron Gain Enthalpy of Non-metal Atom** The electron gain enthalpy is the amount of energy released when an electron is added to an isolated gaseous atom to form a negative ion.

So, higher the value of negative electron gain enthalpy, greater will be the case of formation of anion and hence greater is the tendency to form ionic compounds.

(iii) **Electronegativity Difference Between the Reacting Atoms** There should be large difference between the electronegativities of the reacting atoms. Higher is the difference between the electronegativity of atoms, greater is the ease of formation of ionic bond.

(iv) **Lattice Enthalpy** Lattice enthalpy of an ionic solid may be defined as the amount of energy required to completely separate one mole of a solid ionic compound into gaseous consituitent ions. A qualitative measure of the stability of an ionic compound is provided by its enthalpy of lattice formation and not simply by achieving octet of electrons around the ionic species in the gaseous state. Higher the value of lattice energy, higher is the ease of formation of ionic compound.

The value of lattice enthalpy depends upon the following factors :

(i) **Charge on the Ions** Higher the charge on the ions, greater is the force of attraction and hence larger is the amount of energy released. e.g. Lattice enthalpies of some ionic compounds are in the order

$$\overset{+\ -}{NaCl} < \overset{2+\ -1}{CaCl_2} < \overset{2+\ 2-}{MgO}$$

(− 758) (Uni-univalent) < (− 2254) (Bi-univalent) < (− 3932) kJ mol^{-1} (Bi-bivalent)

(ii) **Size of the Ions** Larger the size of ions, higher is the internuclear distance and lesser will be the force of attraction and hence lesser will be the lattice energy.

e.g. Lattice enthalpies of some ionic compounds follow the order

$$\underset{(-758)}{NaCl} > \underset{(-752)}{NaBr} \qquad \underset{(-1033)}{LiF} > \underset{(-140)}{LiI}$$

[Lattice enthalpy is calculated with the help of **Born Haber cycle** which will be discussed in chapter 6 (Thermodynamics).]

Note If Lattice enthalpy + Electron gain enthalpy > Ionisation enthalpy, the net effect will be the release of energy and hence results in the formation of an ionic bond.

Characteristics of Ionic Compounds

The compounds in which ionic bonds are present, are called **ionic compounds.**

The characteristic properties exhibited by these compounds are :

1. Physical State

These compounds generally exist as crystalline solids, known as **crystal lattice**, which consist of orderly three dimensional arrangements of cations and anions held together by coulombic interaction.

2. Melting and Boiling Points

In ionic compounds, the ions are tightly held together by strong electrostatic forces of attraction and hence a huge amount of energy is required to break the crystal lattice, thus they possess high melting and boiling points.

3. Solubility

These compounds are soluble in solvents like water having high polarity and high dielectric constant.

It is because of the fact that the polar solvent interacts with the ions of the crystals and further the high dielectric constant of the solvent cuts off the force of attraction between these ions.

Furthermore, the ions may combine with the solvent to liberate energy called the **hydration enthalpy** which is adequate to overcome the attractive forces between the ions.

Non-polar solvents such as carbon tetrachloride, benzene etc., having low dielectric constant are not capable to dissolve ionic solids.

4. Electrical Conductivity

Ionic compounds are good conductors of electricity in the aqueous solution or in their molten states, because of the presence of free ions in these states. However, these do not conduct electricity in their solid state because of the absence of free ions as strong electrostatic forces of attraction bind the ions.

5. Ionic Reactions

These compounds split up into oppositely charged ions when dissolved in water. Thus, the chemical reactions of these compounds are characteristic of their constituent ions and are known as **ionic reactions.** These reactions are almost instantaneous. e.g.

$$Na^+Cl^-(aq) + Ag^+NO_3^-(aq) \longrightarrow AgCl(s) + NaNO_3(aq)$$

6. Non-Directional Character

The ionic bond is non-directional. This is because, each ion is surrounded by oppositely charged ions uniformly distributed all around the ion. The formula of an ionic compound can easily be written by knowing the valency of combining atoms or charges of ions. e.g. the formula of barium chloride is

$$\underset{+2}{Ba} \times \underset{-1}{Cl} = BaCl_2$$

Elements and their Ions in Periodic Table

(i) The number of electrons that an atom gains or loses during the formation of an ionic bond is called its electrovalency.

(ii) The electrovalency is the charge present on the ion. **For example**, the electrovalency of Na is +1 because it loses one electron, while the electrovalency of Cl is −1 because it gains one electron.

(iii) The tendency of an atom to form a cation or anion depends upon its position in the periodic table.

(iv) The elements of group 1 and 2 are highly electropositive and have very low ionisation energies, these elements prefer to form cations. While, the elements of grous 15, 16 and 17 are highly electronegative and posses high values of electron affinity, they prefer to form anions.

Group	1	2	13	14	15	16	17
	Li^+	Be^{2+}					
	Na^+	Mg^{2+}	Al^{3+}		N^{3-}	O^{2-}	F^-
	K^+	Ca^{2+}			P^{3-}	S^{2-}	Cl^-
	Rb^+	Sr^{2+}					Br^-
	Cs^+	Ba^{2+}					I^-

Variable Electrovalency and Its Reasons

There are several elements present in the periodic table which show more than one electrovalency. This phenomenon is known as variable electrovalency.

e.g. Copper forms Cu^+ ion (cuprous) and Cu^{2+} ion (cupric).

Elements exhibit variable electrovalency mainly due to the following reasons:

1. Inert Electron Pair Effect

Some *p*-block elements having electronic configuration of valence shell as ns^2np^{1-4}, e.g. Ga, In, Tl, Ge, Sn, Pb, As, Sb, Bi, Te, Po etc. show variable electrovalency due to inert electron pair effect which may be defined as follows:

The reluctance of ns^2-electron pair to get excited and to take part in bond formation is called inert electron pair effect.

For example,

$Sn\,(Z=50);\ 1s^2 2s^2 2p^6 3s^2 3p^6 3d^{10} 4s^2 4p^6 4d^{10} 5s^2 5p^2$

It has 4 valence electrons and can form Sn^{4+} ions by losing them. Thus, Sn^{4+} ion will have the following electronic configuration.

$$Sn^{4+} = 1s^2 2s^2 2p^6 3s^2 3p^6 3d^{10} 4s^2 4p^6 4d^{10}$$

Due to large energy gap between 5*s* and 5*p* orbitals, the excitation of $5s^2$ electron pair is not always possible and $5s^2$ electron pair shows reluctance to get excited. Therefore, Sn would be able to lose only $5p^2$ electrons. This is why, it would prefer to form Sn^{2+} ion.

$$Sn^{2+} = 1s^2 2s^2 2p^6 3s^2 3p^6 3d^{10} 4s^2 4p^6 4d^{10} 5s^2$$

Thus, Sn can show both the valency +4 and +2 but it prefers +2.

2. Unstable Nature of the Core or Kernel

When an atom loses one or more valence electrons to form a cation, the remaining part of atom left is known as core or kernel of atom. For Example : Lithium $(1s^2 2s^1)$ loses its 2*s* electron to form a kernel Li^+. Thus, core of lithium consists of lithium nucleus and $1s^2$ electrons.

$$\underset{1s^2 2s^1}{Li} \longrightarrow \underset{\substack{1s^2 \\ \text{Core}}}{Li^+} + e^-$$

However, in some element if the core formed is unstable, it may be compelled to lose some more electrons in order to acquire greater stability. This gives rise to the phenomenon of variable electrovalency.

e.g. Iron shows two electrovalency +2 and +3.

$$\underset{\substack{(1s^2 2s^2 2p^6 \\ 3s^2 3p^6 3d^6 4s^2)}}{Fe} \longrightarrow \underset{\substack{(1s^2 2s^2 2p^6 \\ 3s^2 3p^6 3d^6)}}{Fe^{2+}} + 2e^-$$

$$\underset{\substack{1s^2 2s^2 2p^6 \\ 3s^2 3p^6 3d^6}}{Fe^{2+}} \longrightarrow \underset{\substack{1s^2 2s^2 2p^6 \\ 3s^2 3p^6 3d^5}}{Fe^{3+}} + e^-$$

Covalent Bond

The bond formed by mutual sharing of electrons between the combining atoms of the same or different elements is called the **covalent bond.** This bond is generally formed between two electronegative, i.e. non-metallic elements.

The number of electrons shared by an atom in order to complete its octet is called the **covalency** of that atom.

e.g. Consider the formation of chlorine molecule, Cl_2. The electronic configuration of Cl atom is [Ne] $3s^2 3p^5$. It has one electron less than the stable noble gas configuration. Cl_2 molecule can be formed by sharing two electrons between two chlorine atoms, each chlorine atom contributing one electron to the shared pair so that both chlorine atoms attain the outer shell octet of nearest noble gas (i.e. argon).

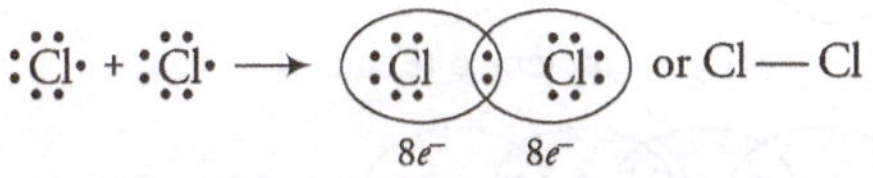

Covalent bond between two Cl atoms

Since, both the Cl atoms share one electron, the covalency of chlorine atom is 1. Similarly, in formation of HCl molecule, hydrogen atom attains a duplet of electrons and Cl, the octet.

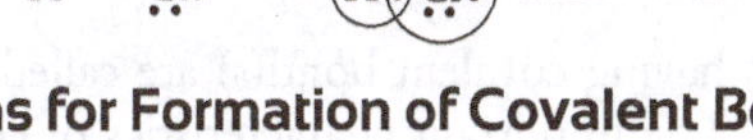

Conditions for Formation of Covalent Bonds

(i) **High Ionisation Energy** For the formation of covalent bonds, the ionisation energy of atoms should be high, so that they are not able to transfer their valence electrons and form ionic bonds.

(ii) **Equal Electron Gain Enthalpy** The combining atoms for covalent bond should have equal electron gain enthalpy.

(iii) **Equal Electronegativity** The combining atoms should have equal electronegativity, so that no transfer of electrons takes place and the bond formed is covalent.

Types of Covalent Bonds

Depending upon the number of electrons 2, 4 or 6 shared between two atoms, a covalent bond is called **single, double or triple bond** respectively. e.g

(i) H•+•H⟶H: H or H—H (H_2 molecule)
Single bond

(ii) 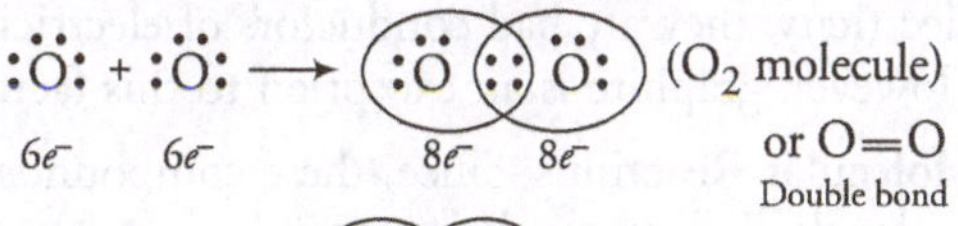

(iii) 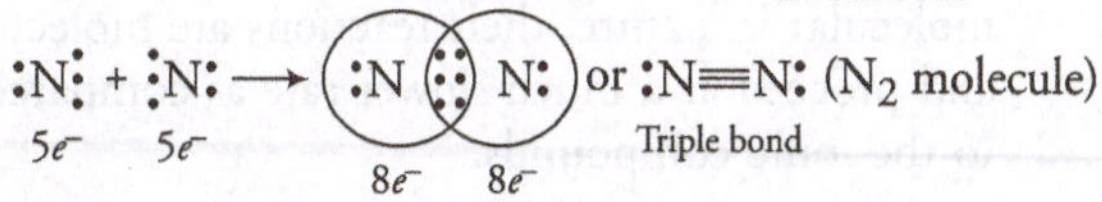

- **Formation of Ethane, Ethene and Ethyne**

(i) 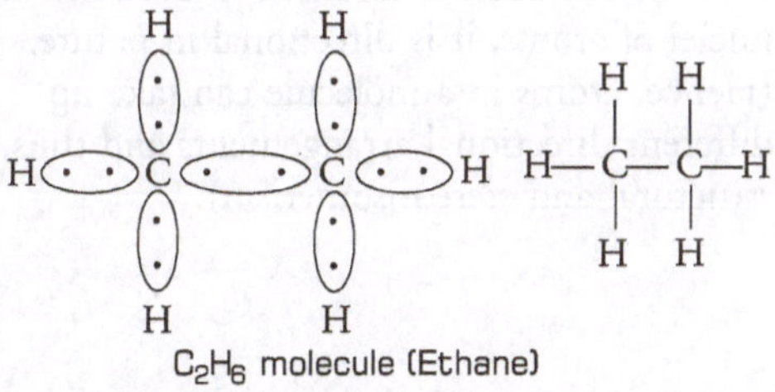

C_2H_6 molecule (Ethane)

(ii) 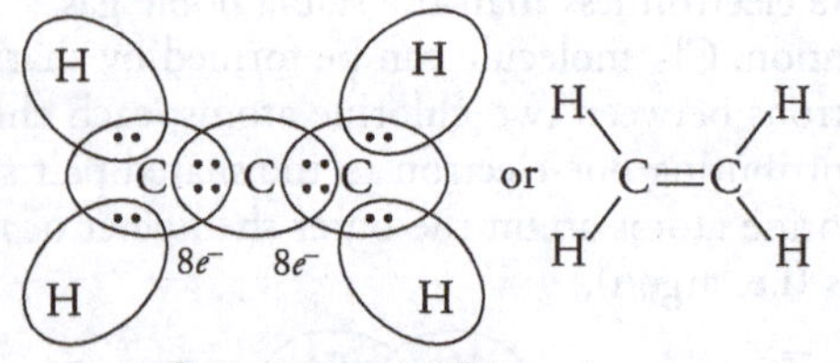

C_2H_4 molecule [Ethene]

(iii) 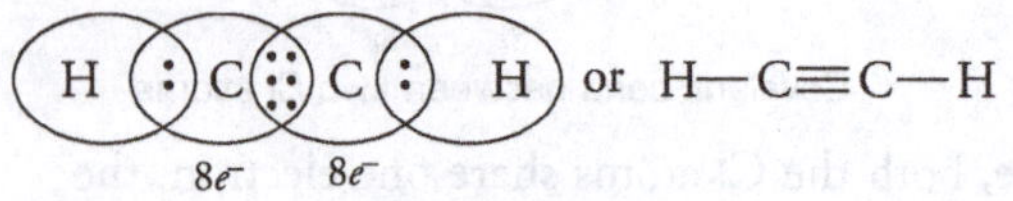

C_2H_2 molecule [Ethyne]

Characteristics of Covalent Compounds

Compounds having covalent bond(s) are called covalent compounds. The important characteristics of covalent compounds are as follows:

(i) **Physical State** The covalent compounds exist in all the three states *viz* solid, liquid and gas. They usually contain molecules rather than ions.

(ii) **Low Melting and Boiling Points** These compounds have low melting and boiling points because of the presence of weak forces of attraction between the molecules which are easily overcome at low temperatures.

Note However covalent compounds having H-bonding can be dissolved in water.

(iii) **Solubility** Being non-polar these are generally insoluble or less soluble in water and in other polar solvents. However, these are soluble in non-polar solvents such as benzene, carbon tetrachloride, etc. (like dissolves like).

(iv) **Electrical Conductivity** Since, there are no free ions in covalent compounds to conduct electricity, they are bad conductors of electricity. However, graphite is an exception to this fact.

(v) **Molecular Reactions** Since, these compounds are molecular in nature, their reactions are molecular and proceed at a much slower rate as compared to the ionic compounds.

(vi) **Directional Characteristics and Isomerism** Since, the covalent bond is localised in between the nuclei of atoms, it is directional in nature. (Hence, atoms in a molecule can take up different directional arrangements and thus, show structural and stereo-isomerism).

Classification of Covalent Bonds Based on Electronegativity of Atom

Depending upon the electronegative character of combining atoms, the covalent bonds can be of two types :

1. Non-polar Covalent Bond

When a covalent bond is formed between two atoms having almost same electronegativity, then the shared pair of electrons are equally shared by the two atoms and situated exactly between the two identical nuclei or in other words in between the two homonuclear atoms. This type of covalent bond is called non-polar covalent bonds. This type of bond is usually found between to similar atoms, e.g. $H_2, O_2, Cl_2,\ F_2, Br_2$ etc.

2. Polar Covalent Bond

When a covalent bond is formed between two atoms having significant difference in their electronegativities, then the shared pair of the electrons slightly shift towards the more electronegative atom and the bond thus formed attain partial ionic character. This type of covalent bond is called polar covalent bond. This type of bond is usually found between two dissimilar (or heteronuclear) atoms, e.g.

$$H^{\delta+}—Cl^{\delta-}, H^{\delta+}—F^{\delta-}, H^{\delta+}—O^{\delta-}—H^{\delta+} \text{ etc.}$$

Lewis Representation of Simple Molecules (The Lewis Structures)

The structures that provide a picture of bonding in molecules and ions in terms of the shared pairs of electrons and the octet rule, are called the **Lewis dot structures.** Although these structures do not explain the bonding and behaviour of a molecule completely, yet they are helpful to understand the properties and formation of molecules to a greater extent.

Molecule/Ion	Lewis representation
H_2 (Hydrogen)	H:H or H—H
O_3 (Ozone)	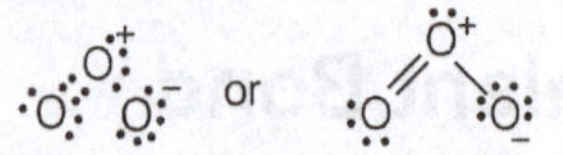
CH_4 (Methane)	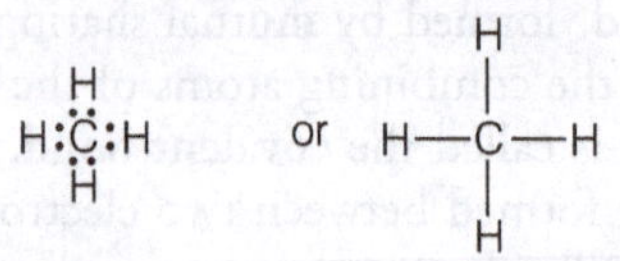
NF_3 (Nitrogen trifluoride)	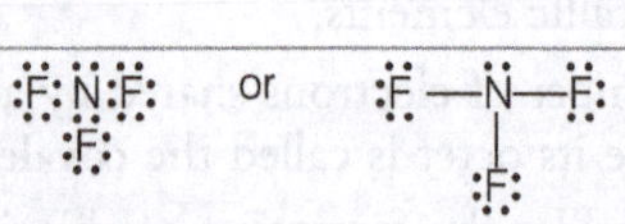

Molecule/Ion	Lewis representation
NH_3 (Ammonia)	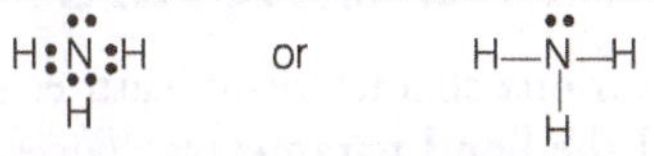
OF_2 (Oxygen difluoride)	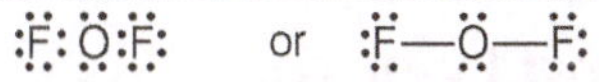
H_2O (Water)	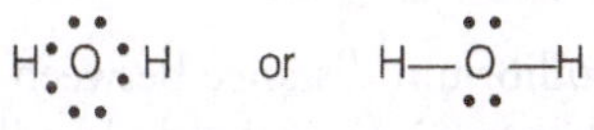
$SiCl_4$ (Silicon tetrachloride)	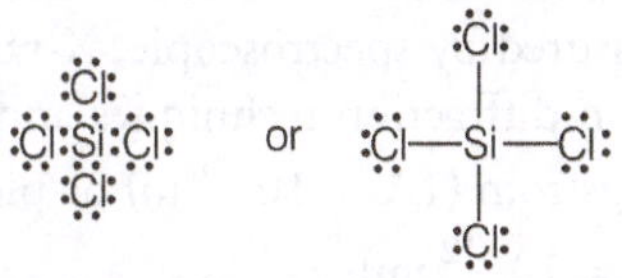
HNO_2 (Nitrous acid)	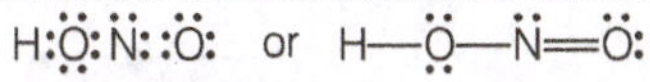
HNO_3 (Nitric acid)	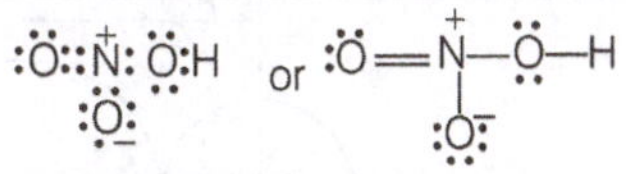
CO_2 (Carbon dioxide)	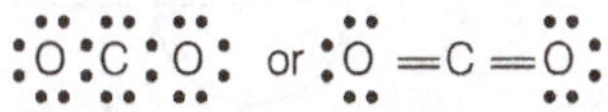

Example 1 Write the Lewis structure of the nitrite ion. **NCERT Textbook**

Sol.

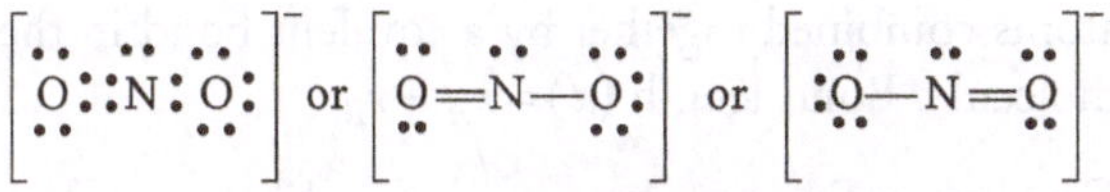

Variable Covalency and Its Reason

(i) Covalency is defined as the number of valence electrons shared by an atom of an element with electrons of other atoms of same or different elements to form covalent bond.

(ii) The number of covalencies of an element depends upon the number of unpaired electrons present in its outermost shell, i.e. upon the number of half filled orbitals.

(iii) Certain elements possess vacant orbitals in their outermost shell and are capable of promoting the paired electron of outer shell to them. The state of the atom obtained by such promotion of electrons is known as **excited state of the atom.**

(iv) In the excited state, the number of unpaired electrons is greater than ground state. The number of electrons which get excited depends upon the energy available for excitation.

(v) Thus, in the excited state, an atom has a greater probability of sharing its unpaired electrons with those of other atoms.

(vi) Such an atom can thus show more than one covalency depending upon the availability of unpaired electrons. This phenomenon is known as variable covalency. e.g.

- Phosphorus
  $P(Z = 15) 1s^2 2s^2, 2p^6 3s^2 3p_x^1 3p_y^1 3p_z^1$
  Phosphorus shows two covalencies 3 and 5.
- Sulphur $S(Z = 16) 1s^2 2s^2 2p^6 3s^2 3p_x^2 3p_y^1 3p_z^1$
  Sulphur shows three covalencies 2, 4 and 6.
- Chlorine $Cl(Z = 17) 1s^2 2s^2 2p^6 3s^2 3p_x^2 3p_y^2 3p_z^1$

Chlorine shows four covalencies 1, 3, 5 and 7.

Formal Charge

It is a factor which is based on a pure covalent view of bonding in which electron pairs are shared equally by neighbouring atoms. In case of a polyatomic molecule or ion, the formal charge of an atom may be defined as the difference between the number of valence electrons of that atom in an isolated or free state and the number of electrons assigned to that atom in the Lewis structure.

$$FC = V - L - \frac{1}{2}S$$

where, FC = Formal charge on an atom in a Lewis structure

V = Total number of valence electrons in the free atom.

L = Total number of non-bonding (lone pair) electrons.

S = Total number of bonding (shared) electrons.

Formal charge do not indicate the real charge separation within the molecule but it only helps in keeping track of the valence electrons in the molecule.

Moreover, it also helps to select the lowest energy structures from a number of possible Lewis structures for a given species. Generally the structure having the smallest formal charges on the atoms is of lowest energy.

Note
- The sum of the formal charges in a molecule is zero.
- When several Lewis structures are possible, the one with formal charges closest to zero is the most stable and is preferred.

Example 2 Calculate formal charge on each O-atom of O_3 molecule.

Sol. *The Lewis structure of O_3 may be drawn as:*

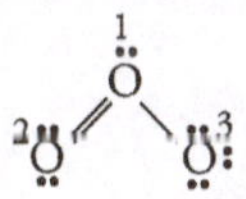

The oxygen atoms have been numbered as 1, 2 and 3. The formal charge on

(i) the central O-atom marked as $1 = V - L - \frac{1}{2}S$

$= 6 - 2 - \frac{1}{2}(6) = +1$

(ii) the end O-atom marked as $2 = V - L - \frac{1}{2}S$

$= 6 - 4 - \frac{1}{2}(4) = 0$

(iii) the end O-atom marked as $3 = V - L - \frac{1}{2}S$

$= 6 - 6 - \frac{1}{2}(2) = -1$

Hence, the O_3 molecule along with the formal charges can be represented as follows:

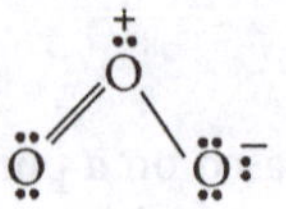

Example 3 Calculate the formal charge on each atoms of

(i) carbonate ion and (ii) SO_2 molecule

Sol. (i) Lewis structure of CO_3^{2-} ion is

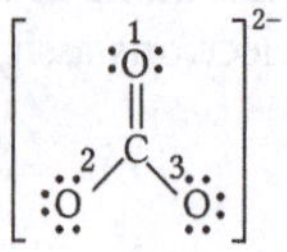

The formal charge on

(a) the carbon atom $= V - L - \frac{1}{2}S$

$= 4 - 0 - \frac{1}{2}(8) = 0$

(b) the oxygen atom marked as $(1) = V - L - \frac{1}{2}S$

$= 6 - 4 - \frac{1}{2}(4) = 0$

(c) the oxygen atoms marked as (2) and $(3) = V - L - \frac{1}{2}S$

$= 6 - 6 - \frac{1}{2}(2) = -1$

(ii) Lewis structure of SO_2 molecule is

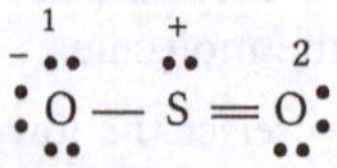

The formal charge on

(a) the sulphur atom $= V - L - \frac{1}{2}S$

$= 6 - 2 - \frac{1}{2}(6) = +1$

(b) the oxygen atom marked as $(1) = V - L - \frac{1}{2}S$

$= 6 - 6 - \frac{1}{2}(2) = -1$

(c) the oxygen atom marked as $(2) = V - L - \frac{1}{2}S$

$= 6 - 4 - \frac{1}{2}(4) = 0$

Bond Parameters

The various characteristic features shown by a bond are called the **bond parameters**. *These are as follows :*

1. Bond Length

The equilibrium distance between the nuclei of two bonded atoms in a molecule is called the **bond length.** It is measured by spectroscopic, X-ray diffraction and electron diffraction techniques and is expressed in terms of Angstrom ($1Å = 10^{-10}$ m) or picometer ($1 \text{ pm} = 10^{-12}$ m).

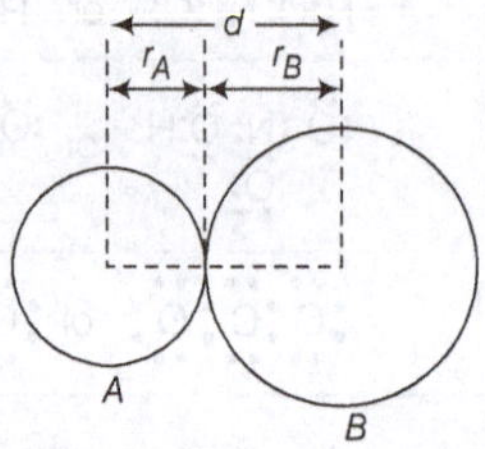

The bond length (d) in a covalent molecule *AB*

In a covalent bond, it is called the **covalent radius** and is defined as the half of the distance between two similar atoms combined together by a covalent bond in the same molecule. Bond length $(d) = r_A + r_B$

Covalent radius $= r_A = r_B = \frac{d}{2}$ [if $r_A = r_B$]

Here, r_A and r_B are the covalent radii of two atoms *A* and *B* respectively. Covalent and van der Waals' radii of chlorine are shown in the figure.

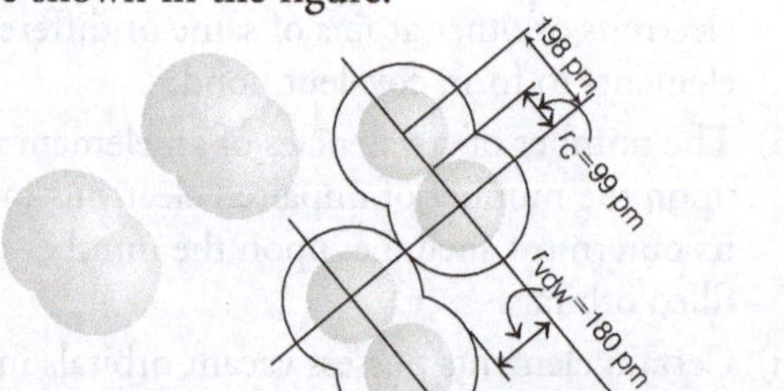

Covalent and van der Waals' radii in a chlorine molecule. The inner circles correspond to the size of the chlorine atom (r_{vdw} and r_c are van der Waals' and covalent radii.

The various factor that affect bond length are as follows:

(i) **Size of the Atoms** The bond length increases with increase in the size of the atoms. Thus, the order of bond length of H—*X* bond is

HF < HCl < HBr < H—I

Similarly, C—C < Si—Si < Ge—Ge

(ii) **Bond Multiplicity** The bond length decreases as the multiplicity of the bond increases. Thus, the carbon-carbon bond lengths follows the order

$$C\equiv C < C=C < C-C$$

Note Bond length also increases as the p-character increases i.e.

$$\underset{\text{more } p\text{-character}}{sp^3} > sp^2 > sp.$$

2. Bond Angle

The angle between the orbitals containing bonding electron pairs around central atom in a molecule/complex ion is called the **bond angle.** It is expressed in degree which can be experimentally determined by spectroscopic methods.

Bond angle gives some idea about the distribution of orbital around the central atom in a molecule and hence, helps in determining the shape of the molecule and about the lone pairs of electrons, as **more the number of lone pairs of electrons, lesser is the bond angle.**

e.g. H—C—H bond angle in CH_4, H—N—H bond angle in NH_3, H—O—H bond angle in H_2O and F—B—F bond angle in BF_3 are shown below:

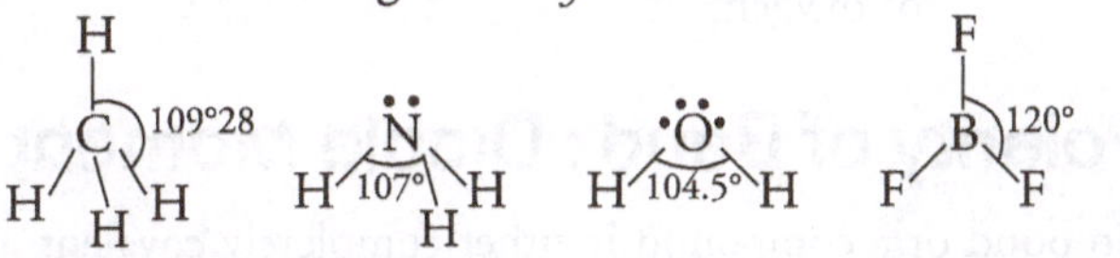

Tetrahedral (no lone pair) | One lone pair so less than (tetrahedral) | Two lone pairs | No lone pair (trigonal planar)

Example 5 Predict all the bond angles in these molecules

(i) CH_4 and (ii) $CH_2=CH_2$

Sol. (i) The Lewis structure for CH_4 is

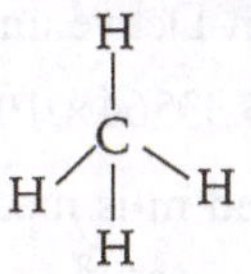

Tetrahedral

Because here only four bonding domain are present, i.e. the carbon is surrounded by four groups through single bond, the bond angle should be equal to 109°28′.

(ii) The Lewis structure for $CH_2=CH_2$ is

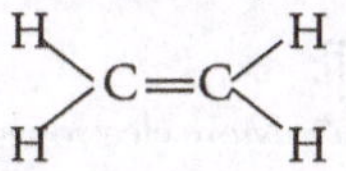

Here, the central carbon surrounded by three bonding domain.

Thus, the bond angle is 120°.

3. Bond Enthalpy

It is the amount of energy required to break one mole of bonds of a particular type between two atoms in gaseous state. The unit of bond enthalpy is kJ mol^{-1}. e.g. The H—H bond enthalpy in hydrogen molecule is 435.8 kJ mol^{-1}.

$$H_2(g) \longrightarrow H(g)+H(g); \; \Delta_a H^\ominus = 435.8 \text{ kJ mol}^{-1}$$

Note Larger the bond dissociation enthalpy, stronger will be the bond in the molecule.

In case of **diatomic molecules** such as H_2, O_2, N_2, HCl etc., the bond enthalpies are equal to their dissociation enthalpies and hence, have fixed values but in case of **polyatomic molecules,** a particular type of bond is present in different molecules (e.g. O—H bond in H—O—H or CH_3O—H etc.) or even in the same molecule (e.g. four C—H bonds in CH_4) do not possess the same bond enthalpy (due to different electronic environment), hence, bond enthalpies are usually the average values and are called **mean** or **average bond enthalpy,** e.g. in H_2O, first

O—H bond enthalpy = 502 kJ mol^{-1}

and second bond enthalpy = 427 kJ mol^{-1}.

$$\text{Hence, average bond enthalpy} = \frac{502+427}{2} = 464.5 \text{ kJ mol}^{-1}$$

Several factors that affect the bond enthalpy are :

(i) **Size of the Atoms** Greater the size of the atom, greater is the bond length and hence, lesser is the bond dissociation enthalpy, i.e. lesser is the bond strength.

(ii) **Bond Multiplicity** Greater the multiplicity of the bond, greater is the bond dissociation enthalpy. This is firstly because atoms come closer and secondly, the number of bonds to be broken is more, e.g. bond dissociation enthalpies of H_2, O_2 and N_2 follow the order H—H < O=O < N≡N.

(iii) **Number of Lone Pairs of Electrons** Greater the number of lone pairs of electrons present on the bonded atoms, greater is the repulsion between the atoms and hence, lesser is the bond dissociation enthalpy.

(iv) **Extent of Overlapping** Higher the extent of overlapping, stronger is the bond and higher the bond strength.

4. Bond Order

In the Lewis description of covalent bond, the number of bonds formed between the two atoms in a molecule is called the **bond order.** e.g. The bond orders of a few molecules are given below.

Molecule	H—H	O=O	N≡N	C≡O
Bond order	1	2	3	3

In case of odd electron molecules, the three electron bonds are considered as equivalent to half covalent bond thus, bond order can be fractional also. e.g.

Lewis structure of NO is $:\dot{N}=\ddot{O}:$.

Therefore, the bond order $= 2\frac{1}{2}$

In case of **isoelectronic molecules** and ions, the bond orders may be identical. e.g. F_2 and O_2^{2-} have bond order 1. N_2, CO and NO^+ have bond order 3.

Note With increase in bond order, bond enthalpy increases and bond length decreases.

i.e. Bond order $\propto$ Bond enthalpy $\propto \frac{1}{\text{Bond length}}$

Limitations of Deviation from the Octet Rule

Although octet rule can explain the formation of a large number of compounds but it has many exceptions also, *which are discussed below :*

(i) **Electron Deficient Molecules** (incomplete octet of the central atom) There are some molecules in which the central atom is surrounded by less than eight electrons, i.e. their octet is incomplete. Elements having less than four valence electrons generally form molecules of this category.

e.g. $BeCl_2$, BF_3, $AlCl_3$, LiCl, BeH_2 etc.

(ii) **Odd Electron Molecules** Molecules like NO, NO_2, O_2 etc., are examples of such molecules in which bonded atoms have odd number of electron(s) (usually 3) in between them. That's why these are called **odd electron molecules.**

In case of these molecules, the octet rule is not satisfied for all the atoms, e.g. nitric oxide

$$(NO) = :\dot{N}::\ddot{O}: \text{ or } \dot{N}=\ddot{O}$$

Species with one unpaired electron are called **free radicals.** These are paramagnetic and most of them are generally unstable.

(iii) **Electron Rich Molecules** Elements of the third and higher periods of the periodic table, which have the availability of *d*-orbitals can expand their covalency and can accommodate more than eight valence electrons around the central atom.

This is referred as **expanded octet.**

Here, also the octet rule is not applicable. e.g. PF_5 (10 electrons around P-atom),

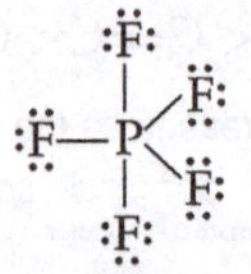

PF_5

Compounds having expanded octet are also termed as **hypervalent compounds.**

(iv) **Other Drawbacks** Some other drawbacks of this theory are as follows :

(a) Octet rule is based on the inertness of noble gases but some noble gases like xenon and krypton form several compounds with oxygen and fluorine like XeF_2, XeF_4, XeF_6, $XeOF_4$, XeO_2F_2, KrF_2 etc.

(b) It does not tell anything about the shapes of molecules and their relative stabilities.

(c) It fails to explain the paramagnetic behaviour of oxygen.

Polarity of Bond : Dipole Moment

No bond or a compound is either completely covalent or ionic. **Dipole moment is the measure of degree of polarity and is defined as the product of the magnitude of the charge and the distance between the centres of positive and negative charge.** It is usually represented by a Greek letter μ (mu).

Mathematically, it is expressed as:

Dipole moment (μ) = charge (Q) × distance of separation (r)

It is usually expressed in Debye units (D).

$$1 \text{ D} = 3.33564 \times 10^{-30} \text{ C m}$$

where, C is coulomb and m is metre.

or $$1 \text{ D} = 1 \times 10^{-18} \text{ esu (or, stat C cm)}$$

Here, esu = electrostatic unit

stat C-cm = static coulomb · centimeter

It is a vector quantity and is represented by the crossed arrow (⟶ with cross) pointing towards the more electronegative atom.

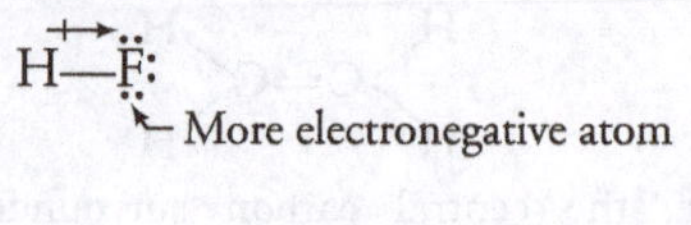

Dipole Moment of Molecular Structures

1. Dipole Moment in Case of Diatomic Molecule

In diatomic molecules, the dipole moment of the polar bond gives the dipole moment of the molecule.

e.g. dipole moment of H — Cl bond is 1.03 D, which is same for dipole moment of HCl molecule.

The degree of polarity of such molecules is also affected by the magnitude of electronegativity difference. Greater the difference in the electronegativites of the combining atoms, greater will be the charge separation and hence, greater will be the polarity of the molecule.

2. Dipole Moment of Polyatomic Molecule

In polyatomic molecules, the dipole moment not only depends upon individual dipole moments of bonds (called bond dipoles) but also on the spatial arrangement of various bonds in the molecule.

In such cases, the resultant dipole moment is the vector summation of the vector dipole moments of various bonds. Symmetrical molecules like CO_2, BF_3, CH_4, CCl_4 without lone pair of e^- will have $\mu = 0$ as their μ cancels out that lies in opposite direction.

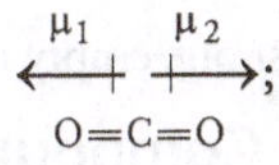

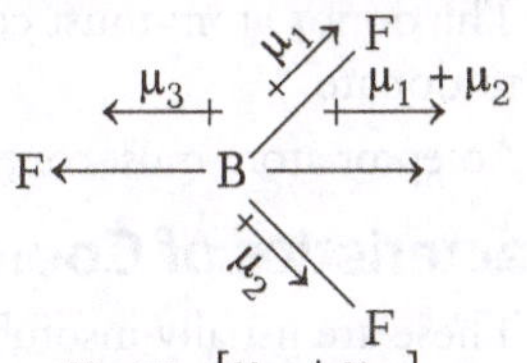

$\mu_1 = -\mu_2$ $\qquad\qquad$ $\mu_3 = -[\mu_1 + \mu_2]$

$\mu_{net} = \mu_1 + \mu_2 = 0$ $\qquad$ $\therefore \mu_{net} = 0$

Unsymmetrical molecules with lone pair of electrons have some dipole moment as lone pair of e^- also possesses some dipole moment.

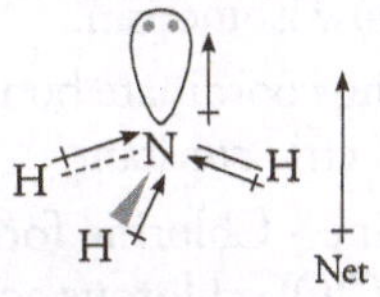

Ammonia (μ = 1.47 D)

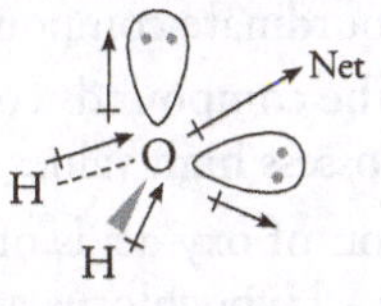

Water (μ = 1.85 D)

Dipole moment of NH_3 is greater than that of NF_3. This is because, in case of NH_3, the orbital dipole of lone pair is in the same direction as the resultant dipole moment of the N—H bonds whereas in NF_3, the orbital dipole is in the direction opposite to the resultant dipole moment of the three N — F bonds and, hence cancel the resultant dipole moment.

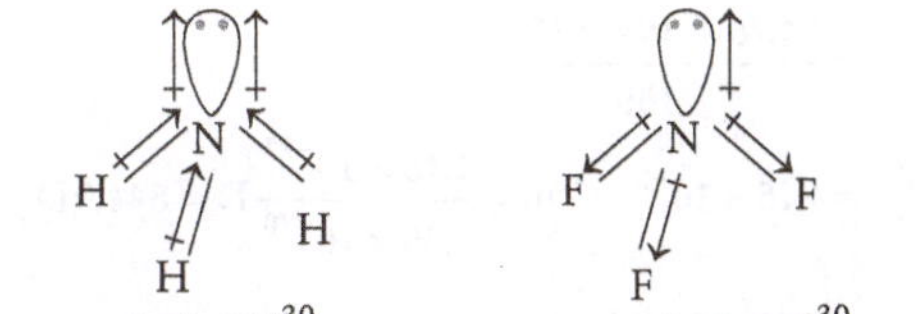

$\mu_{net} = 4.90 \times 10^{-30}$ cm $\qquad$ $\mu_{net} = 0.80 \times 10^{-30}$ cm

By using dipole moment, the percentage ionic character of a polar bond (A—B) can be calculated as:

% ionic character in a molecule

$$= \frac{\text{observed value of } \mu}{\text{theoretical value of } \mu} \times 100$$

% ionic character of $\underset{39.4\%}{\text{HF}} > \underset{16.0\%}{\text{HCl}} > \underset{10.8\%}{\text{HBr}} > \underset{4.7\%}{\text{HI}}$

Molecule HX is 50% ionic of electronegativity difference of H and X 151.7 eV. A comparison of three types of compounds is summarised in given table.

Dipole moments of some of the molecules are tabulated below.

Type of molecule	Example	Dipole moment, μ(D)	Geometry
Molecule (AB)	H_2	0	linear
	HF	1.78	linear
	HCl	1.07	linear
	HBr	0.79	linear
	HI	0.38	linear
Molecule (AB_2)	CO_2	0	linear
	H_2O	1.85	bent
	H_2S	0.95	bent
Molecule (AB_3)	BF_3	0	trigonal-planar
	NH_3	1.47	trigonal-pyramidal
	NF_3	0.23	trigonal-pyramidal
Molecule (AB_4)	CH_4	0	tetrahedral
	CCl_4	0	tetrahedral
	$CHCl_3$	1.04	tetrahedral

Example 7 The percentage ionic character in certain bond A—B is 54.76% and the bond length A—B is given as 246 Å. What is the dipole moment of AB molecule?

Sol. If the molecule is 100% ionic, then

$$\mu_{\text{calculated for 100\% ionic}} = q \times d$$
$$= 1.602 \times 10^{-19} \text{ (C)} \times 246 \times 10^{-10} \text{ (m)}$$
$$= 3.94 \times 10^{-27} \text{ C m}$$

$$\text{\% ionic character} = \frac{\mu_{observed}}{\mu_{calculated}} \times 100$$

$$\mu_{observed} = \frac{\text{\% ionic character} \times \mu_{calculated}}{100}$$

$$= \frac{54.76 \times 3.94 \times 10^{-27}}{100}$$

$$= 2.15 \times 10^{-27}\ C\ m = \frac{2.15 \times 10^{-27}}{3.35 \times 10^{-30}} D = 644.0 D$$

Covalent Character in Ionic Bonding : Fajan's Rule

Just as all the covalent bonds have some partial ionic character, the ionic bonds also have some partial covalent character. The partial covalent character of ionic bonds was discussed by Fajans' in terms of the following rules, called the **Fajans' rules.**

1. Small Size of Cation

The small sized cations because of their high electron density tend to distort or polarise the electron cloud of the anion to a greater extent. Hence, **the compounds containing small cations will have more covalent character.** e.g. LiCl is more covalent than NaCl and KCl due to smaller size of Li^+ ion as compared to Na^+ and K^+.

2. Large Size of the Anion

Larger the anion, greater is its polarisability. This is because in case of larger anion the hold on the electron cloud by the nucleus decreases. Because of this fact the covalent character of lithium halides is in the order LiI > LiBr > LiCl > LiF

and hence, their melting points are in the order

LiI	<	LiBr	<	LiCl	<	LiF
(446°C)		(547° C)		(613°C)		(870° C)

3. High Charge on the Cation or Anion

Higher the charge on the cation, greater is its polarising power (because the cation attracts the electron cloud of the anion more easily and strongly). Hence, covalent character increases. That's why the covalent character of the chlorides follow the order $Na^+Cl^- < Mg^{2+}Cl_2 < Al^{3+}Cl_3$. Similarly, greater the charge on the anion, more easily it gets polarised.

4. Electronic Configuration of the Cation

In case of two cations having the same size and charge, the one with pseudo noble gas configuration (with 18 electrons in the outermost shell) has greater polarising power as compared to the other with noble gas configuration (with 8 electrons in the outermost shell).

Note According to Fajan's rules, the covalent character will be favoured by
(i) small size of cation.
(ii) large size of anion.
(iii) high charge on cation or anion.
(iv) the cation having 18-electrons shell.

Coordinate Bond

As a special case of covalent bonds, this type of bonds was proposed by Perkins in 1912.

In a covalent bond when both the shared electrons are contributed by one of the bonded atom, the covalent bond is known as **coordinate or dative bond.**

The atom which contributes the pair of electrons (lone pair) is known as donor (Lewis base) and the atom which accepts these electrons is called acceptor (Lewis acid).

The coordinate bond is usually represented by an arrow pointing towards an acceptor.

e.g. 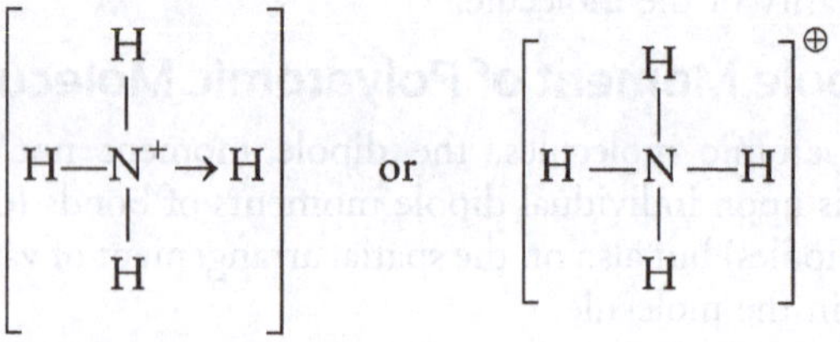

Other examples are, SO_3, SO_2, O_3, H_3O^+, NH_4^-, NO_3^-, HNO_3 etc.

Conditions for the Formation of Coordinate Bond

(i) The donor atom must contain lone pair of electrons to donate.
(ii) Acceptor atom must contain at least one empty orbital.

Characteristics of Coordinate Compounds

(i) These are usually insoluble in water but soluble in organic solvents.
(ii) The melting and boiling points of these compounds are higher than pure covalent compounds. They are bad conductors of electricity.
(iii) The coordinate bond is rigid and directional, thus coordinate compounds show isomerism.
(iv) The compounds containing coordinate bond possess high values of dielectric constant.

Formation of oxy acids of chlorine - Chlorine forms four oxyacids - Hypochlorus acid (HClO), chlorous acid ($HClO_2$), chloric acid ($HClO_3$) and perchloric acid ($HClO_4$).

All these acids contain one — OH group attached to the central Cl - atom. The hypochlorous acid is a covalent compound and possesses no coordinate linkage remaining possesses one, two and three coordinate bonds respectively.

(a) Formation of chloric acid ($HClO_2$)

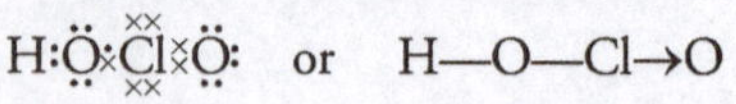

(b) Formation of chloric acid ($HClO_3$)

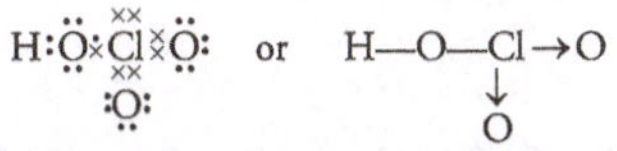

(c) Formation of perchloric acid ($HClO_4$)

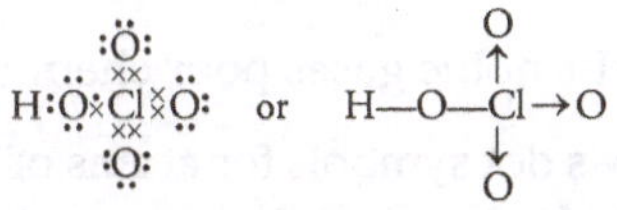

(d) Formation of ozone (O_3)

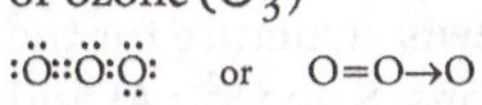

(e) Formation of ammonium ion (NH_4^+)

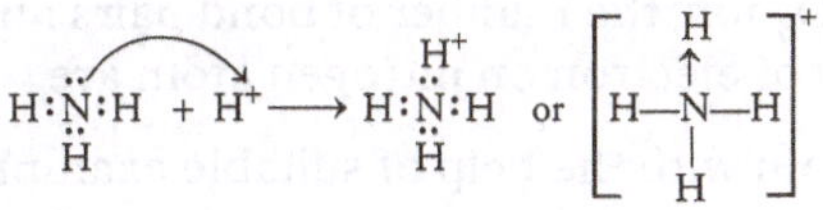

(f) Formation of hydronium ion (H_3O^+)

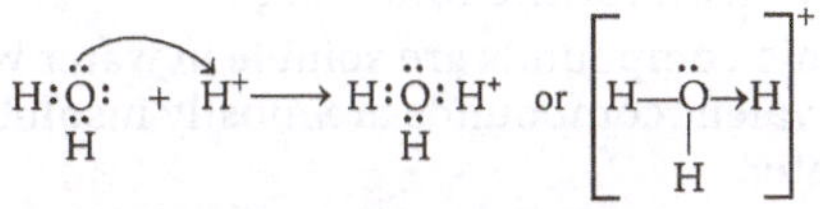

(g) Formation of nitric acid (HNO_3)

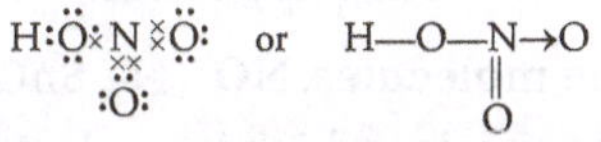

Comparison of Ionic, Covalent and Coordinate Compounds

	Properties	Ionic	Covalent	Coordinate
(i)	Binding force	Between ions (strong coulombic)	Between molecules smaller (van der Waals')	In between
(ii)	Melting point/ boiling point	High	Less than ionic	In between
(iii)	Conduction	Conductor of electricity in fused state and in aqueous solution	Bad conductor	Greater than covalent
(iv)	Solubility in polar solvent (H_2O)	High	Less	In between
(v)	Solubility in non-polar solvents (ether)	Low	High	In between
(vi)	Physical state	Generally solid	Liquid and gas	Solid, liquid, gas

Topic Practice 1

Very Short Answer Type Questions

(1 Mark)

1. Fill in the Blanks

(i) Lewis postulated that atoms achieve the stable octet when they are linked by ...... bonds.

(ii) Lewis has pictured that atom in terms of kernel and the outermost shell that could accommodate a maximum of .... electrons.

(iii) .... under normal conditions exist as an independent atoms in nature.

2. Objective Type Questions

(i) In the formation of a molecule, only the outer shell electrons take part in chemical combination and are known as

(a) valence electrons (b) inner electrons
(c) inert electrons (d) reactive electrons

(ii) In case of bond formation between sodium and chlorine, the electron transfer takes place from

(a) sodium to chlorine (b) chlorine to sodium
(c) Both (a) and (b) (d) None of these

(iii) The bond formed as a result of the electrostatic attraction between the positive and negative ions was termed as

(a) electrovalent bond (b) covalent bond
(c) coordinate bond (d) None of these

(iv) In PO_4^{3-} ion formal charge on the oxygen atom of P—O bond is **NCERT Exemplar**

(a) +1 (b) −1 (c) −0.75 (d) +0.75

3. In the following Lewis structure of HNO_3

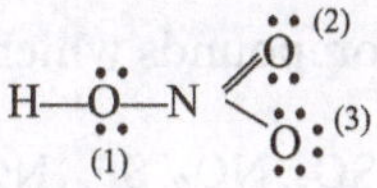

Match the following molecule given in Column I with their formal charges given in Column II and choose the correct option using the codes given below :

	Column I		Column II
A.	$O_{(1)}$	(i)	Zero
B.	$O_{(2)}$	(ii)	−1
C.	$O_{(3)}$	(iii)	+1

Codes

	A	B	C		A	B	C
(a)	(i)	(ii)	(iii)	(b)	(ii)	(i)	(ii)
(c)	(i)	(i)	(ii)	(d)	(iii)	(ii)	(i)

4. The skeletal structure of CH_3COOH as shown below is correct, but some of the bonds are shown incorrectly. Write the correct Lewis structure for acetic acid. **NCERT Textbook**

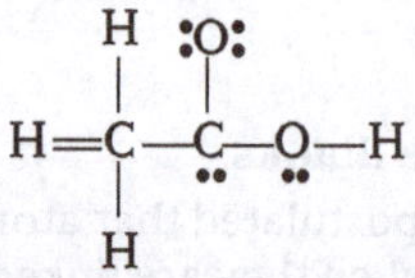

5. Given is the electron dot structure for carbon suboxide, C_3O_2. Write its structural formula.

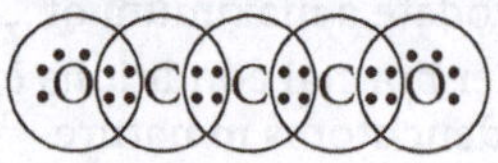

6. Write Lewis dot symbols for the following atoms and ions.
   (i) O^{2-} (ii) P^{3-}
   (iii) N^{3-} (iv) Xenon
7. Why is NaCl harder than sodium metal?
8. Which of the following has highest lattice energy and why?
   CsF, CsCl, CsBr, CsI
9. If the electronic configuration of an element is $1s^2\,2s^2\,2p^6\,3s^2\,3p^6\,3d^2\,4s^2$, the four electrons involved in chemical bond formation will be?
10. Explain the following : HCl is a covalent compound but it ionises in the solution.
11. Define the bond length. **NCERT Textbook**
12. How do you express the bond strength in terms of bond order? **NCERT Textbook**
13. Identify the compounds which do not follow octet rule.
    PCl_3, SO_2, SO_3, NO_2, SF_4, NO, BF_3, H_2S, SF_6.
14. Which of the following molecules show super octet?
    CO_2, ClF_3, SO_2, IF_5
15. Indicate whether the following statement is true or false. Justify your answer in not more than three lines. The dipole moment of CH_3F is greater than that of CH_3Cl.
16. Explain why BeH_2 molecule has a zero dipole moment although the Be—H bonds are polar? **NCERT Textbook**
17. Why AlF_3 is a high melting solid whereas SiF_4 is a gas?

Short Answer Type I Questions

(2 Marks)

18. Explain the formation of a chemical bond. **NCERT Textbook**
19. Why are the noble gases poor chemical reactants?
20. Write Lewis dot symbols for atoms of the following elements Mg, Na, B, O, N, Br. **NCERT Textbook**
21. Write the Lewis structure for the following atoms and ions: S and S^{2-}; Al and Al^{3+}; H and H^- **NCERT Textbook**
22. In NO_3^- ion, the number of bond pairs and lone pairs of electron on nitrogen atom are
23. Explain with the help of suitable example polar covalent bond. **NCERT Textbook**
24. Give reason for the following :
    (i) Ionic compounds are soluble in water whereas covalent compounds are mostly insoluble in water.
    (ii) Ionic compounds have higher melting points than the covalent compounds.
25. Among the molecules, NO^+, N_2, $SnCl_2$ and NO_2^-, identify the species which is isoelectronic with CO.
26. Predict the dipole moment of
    (i) a molecule of the type AX_2 having a linear geometry.
    (ii) a molecule of the type AX_4 having tetrahedral geometry.
    (iii) a molecule of the type AX_2 having angular geometry.
    (iv) a molecule of the type AX_4 having square planar geometry.
27. Which is more polar : CO_2 or N_2O? Give reason.
28. Although both CO_2 and H_2O are triatomic molecules, the shape of the H_2O molecule is bent while that of CO_2 linear. Explain this on the basis of dipole moment. **NCERT Textbook**
29. Which out of NH_3 and NF_3 has higher dipole moment and why?
30. Arrange the bonds in order of increasing ionic character in the molecules; LiF, K_2O, N_2, SO_2 and ClF_3. **NCERT Textbook**
31. Arrange the following bonds in order of increasing ionic character giving reason.
    N—H, F—H, C—H and O—H **NCERT Exemplar**
32. Aluminium forms the ion Al^{3+}, but not Al^{4+} why?

Short Answer Type II Questions

(3 Marks)

33. Write lewis structure of the following compounds and show formal charge each atom.
HNO_3, NO_2, H_2SO_4 **NCERT Exemplar**

34. Use Lewis symbols to show electron transfer between the following atoms to form cations and anions.
(i) K and S (ii) Ca and O (iii) Al and N

35. Define electronegativity. How does it differ from electron gain enthalpy?

36. Write the favourable factors for the formation of ionic bond. **NCERT Textbook**

37. Explain the terms bond enthalpy and bond angle.

38. What is meant by the term average bond enthalpy? Why is there difference in bond enthalpy of O—H bond in ethanol (C_2H_5OH) and water?

39. Give reasons for the following :
(i) Covalent bonds are directional bond while ionic bonds are non-directional.
(ii) Water molecule has bent structure whereas carbon dioxide molecule is linear.
(iii) Ethyne molecule is linear.

40. (i) X, Y and Z elements have 4,5 and 7 valence electrons. Draw the structure of XH_4, YH_5, YH_3 and H—Z.
(ii) Which of these compounds has the highest dipole moment? **NCERT Exemplar**

41. The dipole moment of a molecule AB is 0.54D and the bond distance is 1.41 Å. Calculate the fractional change δ on A and B atom in AB molecule (electronic charge, $e = 4.8 \times 10^{-10}$ esu).

42. In each of the following pairs of compounds, which one is more covalent and why?
(i) AgCl, AgI (ii) $BeCl_2$, $MgCl_2$
(iii) $SnCl_2$, $SnCl_4$ (iv) CuO, CuS

Long Answer Type Questions

(5 Marks)

43. Define octet rule. Write its significance and limitations. **NCERT Textbook**

44. Draw the Lewis structures for the following molecule and ions.
H_2S, $SiCl_4$, BeF_2, CO_3^{2-}, HCOOH

45. What is an ionic bond? With two suitable examples the difference between an ionic and a covalent bond? **NCERT Exempalr**

46. (i) What factors favours the formation of ionic bond. Explain with examples.
(ii) Arrange the following in increasing order of ionic character and also give the reason.
NaCl, $CaCl_2$, $MgCl_2$, MgO.

47. Why are some covalent bonds polar? What is a dipole? How can a molecule that has polar bonds be non-polar molecule? How do dipole moments of molecules of CO_2, CH_4, H_2O and NH_3 help in ascertaining their structure?

48. (i) Discuss the significance/applications of dipole moment.
(ii) Represent diagrammatically the bond moments and the resultant dipole moment in CO_2, NF_3 and $CHCl_3$.

Hints & Solutions

1. (i) chemical (ii) eight
(iii) Noble gases

2. (i) → a (ii) → a (iii) → a (iv) → c

3. (c) A → (i), B → (i), C → (ii)

4. The correct Lewis structure for acetic acid is

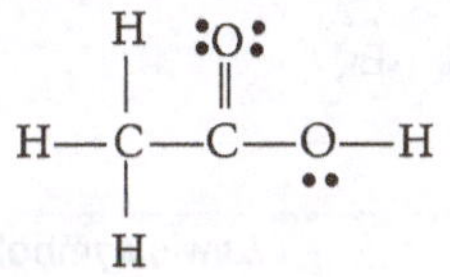

5. O=C=C=C=O

6. (i) $:\ddot{O}:^{2-}$ (ii) $:\ddot{P}:^{3-}$ (iii) $:\ddot{N}:^{3-}$ (iv) $:\ddot{Xe}:$

7. This is because in NaCl, there is strong ionic bond between Na^+ and Cl^- whereas in Na metal, there is weak metallic bond.

8. CsF has highest lattice energy because 'F' is smallest in size and is more electronegative, therefore, it has maximum ionic character and maximum force of attraction, hence, highest lattice energy.

9. The given electronic configuration shows that the element is vanadium ($Z = 22$). It belongs to d-block of the periodic table. In transition elements, i.e. d-block elements, electrons of ns and $(n-1)\,d$ subshell, take part in bond formation.

10. This is because of the large difference in the electronegativity of H and Cl-atoms. Due to which polarity is generated which is responsible for separation of ions.

11. Refer to text on page 146 [Topic-1 Bond parameters (bond length)].

12. With increase in bond order, bond enthalpy increase. Therefore, greater the bond order, higher is the bond strength, i.e. bond strength $\propto$ bond order.

13. SF_4, NO_2, NO, BF_3, SF_6 do not follow octet rule.

14. ClF_3 and IF_5 are super octet molecules.

15. True, this is because C—F bond is more polar than C—Cl bond due to larger electronegativity of F than Cl. As a result, the resultant dipole moment of CH_3F is more.

16. BeH_2 molecule is linear. The two equal bond dipoles point in opposite directions and cancel the effect of each other. That's why its net dipole moment is zero.

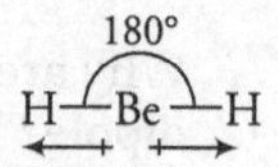

BeH_2 molecule, $\mu = 0$

17. AlF_3 is an ionic compound whereas SiF_4 is a non-polar covalent compound. Hence, interparticle forces in AlF_3 are much stronger than in SiF_4 that's why it is a high melting solid.

18. Refer to text on page 139 (Chemical bonding).

19. Refer to text on page 140 (Kossel-Lewis approach to chemical bond).

20.

Ions	Lewis symbol
$_{12}Mg = 2, 8, 2$	$\ddot{Mg}$
$_{11}Na = 2, 8, 1$	$\dot{Na}$
$_{5}B = 2, 3$	$\cdot\dot{B}\cdot$
$_{8}O = 2, 6$	$:\ddot{O}\cdot$
$_{35}Br = 2, 8, 18, 7$	$\cdot\ddot{\underset{..}{Br}}:$

21.

Element	Lewis symbol
$_{16}S = 2, 8, 6$	$:\ddot{S}\cdot$
$S^{2-} = (16 + 2)$ electrons	$[:\ddot{\underset{..}{S}}:]^{2-}$
$_{13}Al = 2, 8, 3$	$\dot{Al}\cdot$
$Al^{3+} = (13 - 3) = 10$ electrons	$[Al]^{3+}$
$_{1}H = 1$	$\dot{H}$
$H^{-} = (1 + 1) = 2$ electrons	$[\ddot{H}]^{-}$

[2]

22. **Key Idea** To solve this question, we must know the structure of NO_3^- ion. i.e.

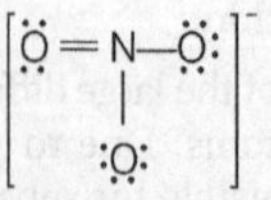

Then, count the bond pairs and lone pairs of electron on nitrogen

In N-atom, number of valence electrons = 5

Due to the presence of one negative charge, number of valence electrons = 5 + 1 = 6. one O-atom forms two bond (= bond) and two O-atom shared with two electrons of N-atom. [1]

Thus, 3 O-atoms shared with 8 electrons of N-atom.

$\therefore$ Number of bond pairs (or shared pairs) = 4

Number of lone pairs = 0 [1]

23. Refer to text on page 144, (Classification of covalent bonds, based on electronegativity of atom).

24. (i) Being polar in nature ionic compounds are soluble in water but covalent compounds are generally non-polar so they are insoluble in water (like dissolves like). [1]

(ii) Because of the presence of strong electrostatic forces of attraction melting points of ionic compounds are higher than that of covalent compounds. [1]

25. Isoelectronic species are those species have same number of electrons but different nuclear charge.

Electrons present in CO = 6 + 8 = 14

Then, In $NO^+ = 7 + 8 - 1 = 14$

In $N_2 = 7 + 7 = 14$ [1]

In $SnCl_2 = 50 + 17 \times 2 = 50 + 34 = 84$

In $NO_2^- = 7 + 16 + 1 = 24$ [1]

26. (i) Zero

$X \rightleftharpoons A \rightleftharpoons X$ [1/2]

(ii) Zero

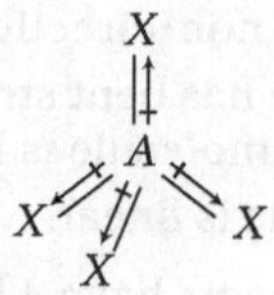

[1/2]

(iii) Appreciable dipole moment

(Resultant dipole moment) [1/2]

(iv) Zero

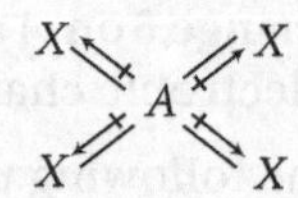

[1/2]

27. N_2O is more polar than CO_2. This is because CO_2 is linear and symmetrical. Its net dipole moment is zero ($O \leftrightarrows C \leftrightarrows O$). N_2O on the other hand, is linear but unsymmetrical. It is considered as a resonance hybrid of the following two structures

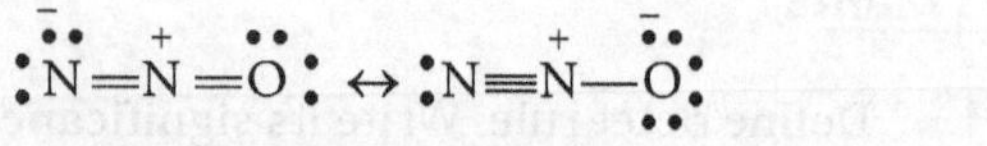

It has a net dipole moment of 0.116 D. [2]

28. **Key Idea** For symmetrical or regular structures dipole moment is zero. Unsymmetrical structures have some dipole moment.

The net dipole moment of CO_2 is zero. This is because the two equal bond dipoles ($\overset{\delta^+}{C}$—$\overset{\delta^-}{O}$) point in opposite directions and cancel the effect of each other. Hence, CO_2 is linear. On the other hand, H_2O molecule is found to have a net dipole moment (1.84 D) which suggests that the two O–H dipoles are not in a straight line opposing each other, i.e. H_2O does not have linear structure, but they (O–H) must be inclined to each other at certain angle. Thus, H_2O molecule has a bent structure in which the two O–H bonds are oriented at an angle of 104.5°. [1]

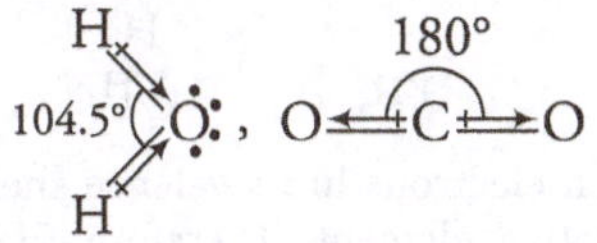

29. Refer to text on page 149, (Dipole moment of molecular structures).

30. Ionic character ∝ lattice energy

$$\propto \frac{1}{\text{size of ion}} \propto \text{charge on ion,}$$ [1]

A non-polar molecule like N_2 has almost negligible ionic character.

∴ The order of ionic character is

$$N_2 < SO_2 < ClF_3 < K_2O < LiF$$ [1]

31. Greater is the electronegativity difference between the two bonded atoms, greater is the ionic character.

	N—H	F—H	C—H	O—H
Electronegativity difference	(3.0 − 2.1) = 0.9	(4.0 − 2.1) = 1.9	(2.5 − 2.1) = 0.4	(3.5 − 2.1) = 1.4

Therefore, increasing order of ionic character of the given bonds is as follows:

$$C—H < N—H < O—H < F—H$$ [1]

32. Aluminium ($[Ne]^{3s^2}3p^1$) can achieve the electronic configuration of the nearest noble gas (Ne) by losing only three electrons. : $Al^{3+} = 1s^2 2s^2 2p^6$. Aluminium with not form the Al^{4+} ion because an extremely high amount of energy would be required to remove an electron from the stable noble gas configuration. [2]

33. HNO_3

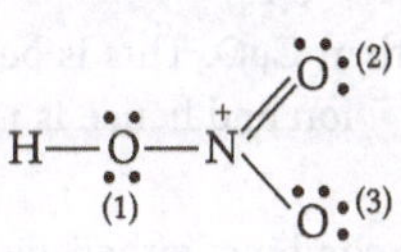

Formal charge on an atom in a Lewis structure

= [total number of valence electrons in free atom]

− [total number of non-bonding (lone pairs) electrons]

$-\frac{1}{2}$ [total number of bonding or shared electrons]

Formal charge on H $= 1 - 0 - \frac{1}{2} \times 2 = 0$

Formal charge on N $= 5 - 0 - \frac{1}{2} \times 8 = 1$

Formal charge on O (1) $= 6 - 4 - \frac{1}{2} \times 4 = 0$

Formal charge on O (2) $= 6 - 4 - \frac{1}{2} \times 4 = 0$

Formal charge on O (3) $= 6 - 6 - \frac{1}{2} \times 2 = -1$ [1]

NO_2

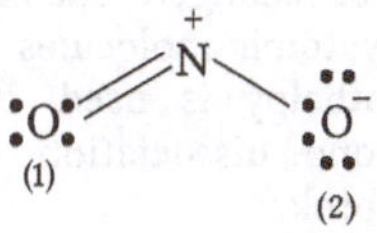

Similarly on solving we get, formal charges on O(1), N and O(2) as 0, +1 and −1 respectively. [1]

H_2SO_4

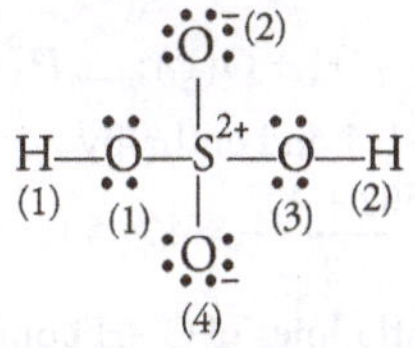

Similarly, on solving we get formal charge charges on H(1), H(2), O(1), O(2), O(3), O(4) and S, as 0, 0, 0, −1, 0, −1 and +2 respectively. [1]

34. **Hint** Metals lose electrons to complete their octet while non-metals gain electrons to complete octet.

So, write the Lewis symbol, i.e. symbols with valence electrons to show the transfer of electron from metal to non-metal.

(i) $\underset{2,8,8,1}{K^{\bullet}} + \underset{2,8,6}{:\ddot{S}:} \longrightarrow 2K^+ [:\ddot{S}:]^{2-}$; K_2S [1]

(ii) $\underset{2,8,8,2}{Ca:} + \underset{2,6}{\ddot{O}:} \longrightarrow Ca^{2+} [:\ddot{O}:]^{2-}$; CaO [1]

(iii) $Al\dot{:} + \dot{N}: \longrightarrow Al^{3+} [:\ddot{N}:]^{3-}$; AlN [1]

35. Electronegativity of an element is the tendency of its atom to attract the shared pair of electrons towards itself in a covalent bond. Electron gain enthalpy of an element may be defined as the energy released when a neutral isolated gaseous atom accepts an extra electron to form the gaseous negative ion, i.e. anion.

$$\underset{\text{Neutral gaseous atom}}{X(g)} + e^- \longrightarrow \underset{\text{Anion}}{X^-(g)}\ ;\ \Delta H = \Delta_{eg}H$$ [1]

Greater the amount of energy released in the above process, higher is the electron gain enthalpy of the element. Electronegativity differs from electron gain enthalpy because electronegativity is a property of an atom in the bonded state while electron gain enthalpy relates to atoms in their isolated gaseous states. [For details see chapter 3] [2]

36. Refer to text on page 141 (Conditions for the formation of ionic bond).

37. Refer to text on pages 146 and 147 (Bond parameters, bond enthalpy and bond angle).

38. All the similar bonds in a polyatomic molecule do not have the same bond enthalpies. e.g. in H_2O (H—O—H) molecule after the breaking of first O–H bond, the second O–H bond undergoes some change because of changed chemical environment. Therefore, in polyatomic molecules the term mean or average bond enthalpy is used. It is obtained by dividing total bond dissociation enthalpy by the number of bonds broken. **[1]**

e.g. $H_2O(g) \longrightarrow H(g) + OH(g);$

$$\Delta_a H_1^\circ = 502 \text{ kJ mol}^{-1}$$

$$OH(g) \longrightarrow H + O(g);\ \Delta_a H_2^\circ = 427 \text{ kJ mol}^{-1}$$

Average O–H bond enthalpy

$$= \frac{502 + 427}{2} = 464.5 \text{ kJ mol}^{-1}$$ **[1]**

The bond enthalpies of O–H bond in C_2H_5OH and H_2O are different because of the different chemical (electronic) environment around oxygen atom.

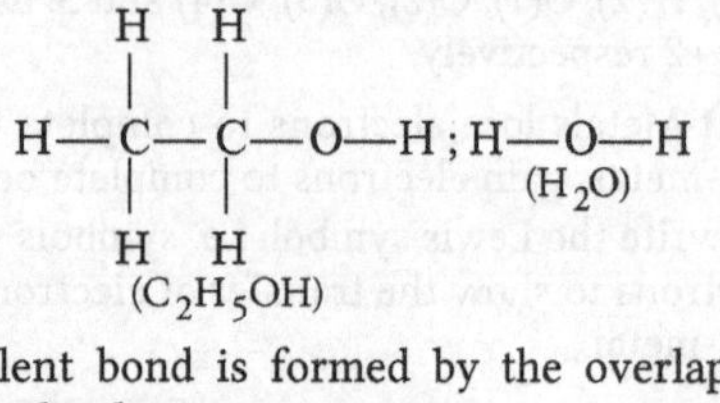

[1]

39. (i) A covalent bond is formed by the overlapping of atomic orbitals.

The direction of overlapping gives the direction of bond. In ionic bond, the electrostatic field of an ion is non-directional. Each positive ion is surrounded by a number of anions in any direction depending upon its size and *vice-versa.*

That's why covalent bonds are directional bonds while ionic bonds are non-directional. **[1]**

(ii) In H_2O, oxygen atom is sp^3 hybridised with two lone pairs. The four sp^3 hybridised orbitals acquire a tetrahedral geometry with two corners occupied by hydrogen atoms while other two by the lone pairs. The bond angle is reduced to 104.5° from 109.5° due to greater repulsive forces between *lp-lp* and the molecule thus acquires a V-shape or bent structure (angular structure).

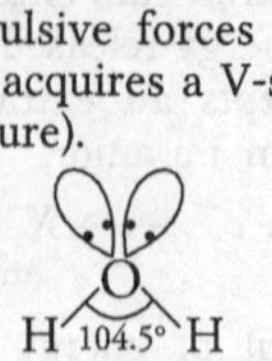

In CO_2 molecule, carbon atom is *sp*-hybridised. The two *sp* hybrid orbitals are oriented in opposite directions forming an angle of 180° $O \overset{\pi}{\underset{\sigma}{=}} C \overset{\pi}{\underset{\sigma}{=}} O$. **[1]**

That's why H_2O molecule has bent structure whereas CO_2 molecule is linear.

(iii) In ethyne molecule, both the carbon atoms are *sp* hybridised having two unhybridised orbitals, i.e. $2p_x$ and $2p_y$. The two *sp* hybrid orbitals of both the carbon atoms are oriented in opposite direction forming an angle of 180°.

$$H— \overset{\sigma}{C \equiv C} —H$$
$$2\pi\text{-bond}$$

That's why ethyne molecule is linear. **[1]**

40. (i)

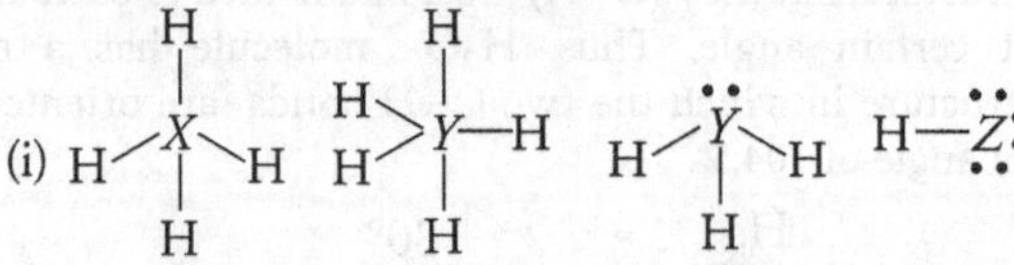

XH_4 YH_5 YH_3 HZ **[1]**

(ii) Z has seven electrons in its valence shell. It is the most electronegative element. Therefore, HZ will have the highest dipole moment. **[2]**

41. Dipole moment, $\mu = q \times d$

$$\mu = 0.54 \Rightarrow D = 0.54 \times 10^{-18} \text{ stat C cm}$$

$$\delta = 1.41 \times 10^{-8} \text{ cm}$$

$$\therefore\ q = \frac{0.54 \times 10^{-18} \text{ stat C cm}}{1.41 \times 10^{-8} \text{ cm}} = 0.38 \times 10^{-10} \text{ stat}$$

Now, fraction of charge $= \frac{\text{Charge present}}{\text{Electronic charge}}$

$$= \frac{0.38 \times 10^{-10}}{4.8 \times 10^{-10}} = 0.08$$

$$\therefore\ \delta_A = 0.08,\ \delta_B = -0.08$$ **[2]**

42. Applying Fajans' rules, the result can be obtained in each case as follows:

(i) AgI is more covalent that AgCl. This is because I^- ion is larger in size than Cl^- ion and hence, is more polarised than Cl^- ion.

(ii) $BeCl_2$ is more covalent than $MgCl_2$. This is because Be^{2+} ion is smaller in size than Mg^{2+} ion and hence has the greater polarising power. **[1]**

(iii) $SnCl_4$ is more covalent than $SnCl_2$. This is because Sn^{4+} ion has greater charge and smaller size than Sn^{2+} ion and hence has greater polarising power. **[1]**

(iv) CuS is more covalent than CuO. This is because S^{2-} ion has larger size than O^{2-} ion and hence is more polarised than O^{2-} ion. **[1]**

43. Octet rule Atoms can combine either by transfer of valence electrons from one atom to another (gaining or losing) or by sharing of valence electrons in order to have a complete octet in their valence shell. **[2]**

Significance of octet rule It help to explain why different atom combine with each other to form ionic or covalent compounds. **[1]**

Limitations of octet rule Refer to text on page 148 (limitations of the octet rule). **[2]**

44. In Lewis structures, all the elements (except H) have 8 electrons in their outer shell. H has only 2 electrons.

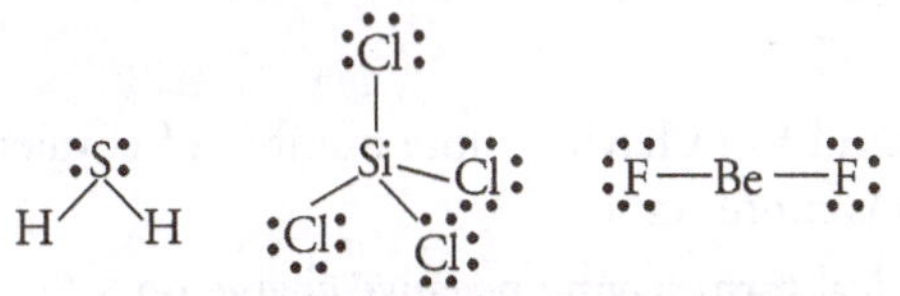

H_2S $SiCl_4$ BeF_2 [2]

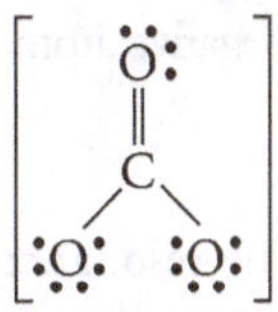

CO_3^{2-}

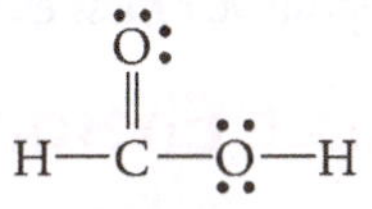

HCOOH [3]

45. Ionic bond The bond formed, as a result of the electrostatic attraction between the positive and negative ions was termed as the electrovalent bond or ionic bond. e.g. The formation of NaCl from sodium and chlorine can be explained as :

$$\underset{[Ne]\,3s^1}{Na} \longrightarrow \underset{[Ne]}{Na^+} + e^-$$

$$\underset{[Ne]\,3s^2\,3p^5}{Cl} + e^- \longrightarrow \underset{[Ne]\,3s^2\,3p^6 \text{ or } [Ar]}{Cl^-}$$

$$Na^+ + Cl^- \longrightarrow NaCl \text{ or } Na^+Cl^-$$ [1]

Similarly, the formation of CaF_2 may be shown as :

$$\underset{[Ar]4s^2}{Ca} \longrightarrow \underset{[Ar]}{Ca^{2+}} + 2e^-$$

$$\underset{[He]\;2s^2\,2p^5}{F} + e^- \longrightarrow \underset{[He]\;2s^2\,2p^6 \text{ or } [Ne]}{F^-}$$

$$Ca^{2+} + 2F^- \longrightarrow CaF_2 \text{ or } Ca^{2+}(F^-)_2$$ [2]

The melting and boiling point of such ionic compounds are very high and they are soluble in polar solvents .

Covalent bond The bond formed between the two atoms by mutual sharing of electrons between them is called covalent bond, e.g. the formation of chlorine molecule can be explained as :

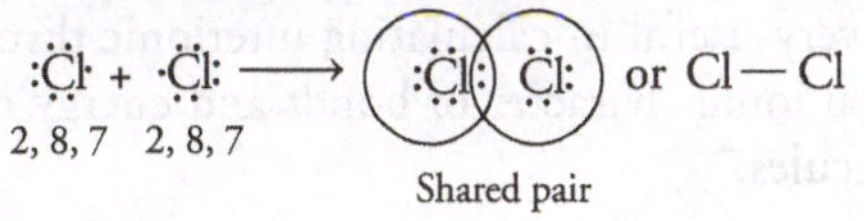

Similarly, in the formation of HCl

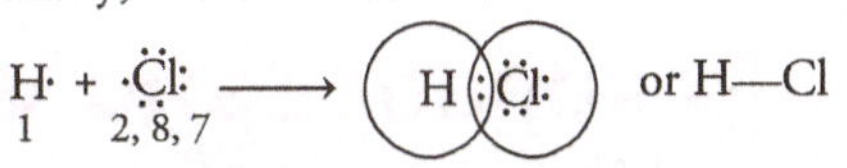

[2]

The melting and boiling point of such covalent compounds is less and are almost insoluble in polar solvents.

46. (i) Refer to text on page 141 (Ionic or electrovalent bond).

(ii) Ionic character ∝ Lattice enthalpy and lattice enthalpy ∝ 1/size of cation. Thus, the order of ionic character is $CaCl_2 < MgCl_2 < MgO < NaCl$.

47. Refer to text on pages 148 and 149, (Polarity of bond, dipole moment of molecular structure).

48. (i) The applications of dipole moment are :

(a) The dipole moment helps to predict whether a molecule is polar or non-polar. As $\mu = q \times d$, greater is the magnitude of dipole moment, higher will be the polarity of the bond. For non-polar molecules, the dipole moment is zero.

(b) The percentage of ionic character can be calculated as

Percentage of ionic character

$$= \frac{\mu_{\text{observed}}}{\mu_{\text{calculated}}} \times 100$$

(c) Symmetrical molecules have zero dipole moment although they have two or more polar bonds. (In determination of symmetry).

(d) It helps to distinguish between *cis* and *trans*-isomers. Usually *cis*-isomer has higher dipole moment than *trans*-isomer.

(e) It helps to distinguish between *ortho*, *meta* and *para*-isomers. Dipole moment of *para*-isomer is zero. Dipole moment of *ortho*-isomer is greater than that of *meta* isomer. [3]

(ii)

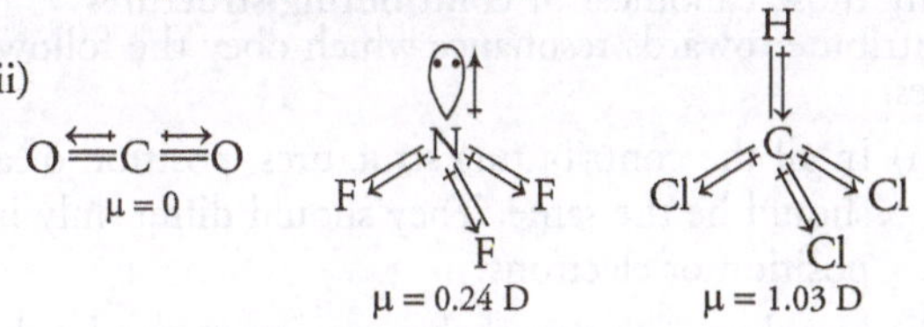

[2]

TOPIC 02 Resonance and VSEPR Theory

Resonance

The phenomenon of resonance was put forward by **Heisenberg.** According to this concept, whenever, a single Lewis structure cannot describe all the properties of a molecule, a number of structures with similar energy, positions of nuclei, bonding and non-bonding pairs of electrons are written to describe all the properties. The actual structure is in between all these contributing structures and is known as the **resonance hybrid** and the different individual structures are termed as **resonating structures** or canonical forms. This phenomenon is called **resonance.**

Double headed arrows are used in between canonical structures to separate them as shown below.

Experimentally determined oxygen-oxygen bond lengths in the O_3 molecule are same (128 pm) which is not represented by either structure 'a' or 'b'. Thus, the oxygen-oxygen bond in O_3 molecule are intermediate between a double and a single bond and is represented by resonance hybrid (structure 'c').

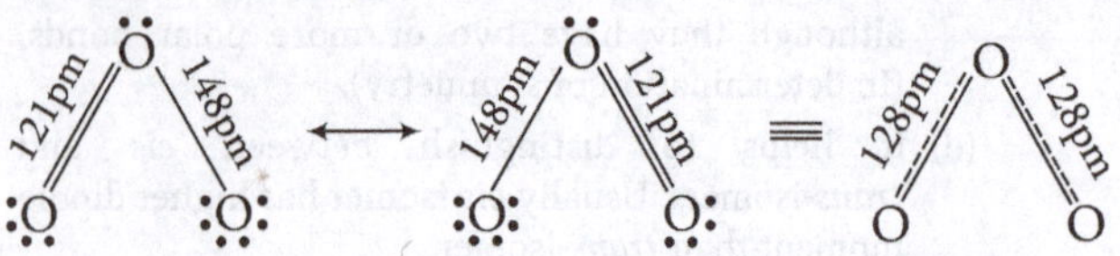

(a) (b) (c)

Rules for Writing Resonating Structures

Only those canonical or contributing structures contribute towards resonance which obey the following rules.

(i) In all the contributing structures, position of atoms should be the same. They should differ only in the position of electrons.

(ii) Number of unpaired electrons must also be the same in all the contributing structures.

(iii) The energy of contributing structures should be nearly the same.

Stability of a Resonance Hybrid

In order to find the most stable hybrid form, follow the following rules.

(i) Non-polar molecules are always more stable as compared to polar (charged) molecules.

(ii) Canonical form having more number of covalent bonds is more stable.

(iii) Canonical form having negative charge on electronegative atom and positive charge on electropositive or less electronegative atom is more stable.

Resonance Energy

The difference in the energy of the resonance hybrid and the most stable contributing structure (having least energy) is called **resonance energy,** e.g. benzene has resonance energy 150.3 kJ mol^{-1} or 36 kcal mol^{-1}.

Resonance in Inorganic Molecules

(i) **Carbon dioxide** (CO_2)

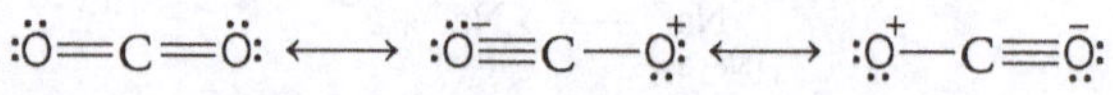

(ii) **Nitrate ion** (NO_3^-)

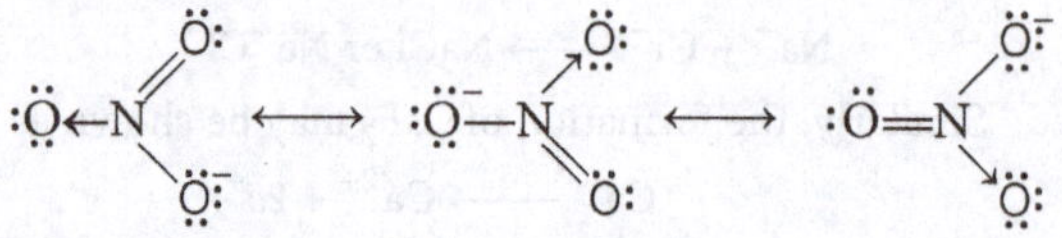

(iii) **Carbonate ion** (CO_3^{2-})

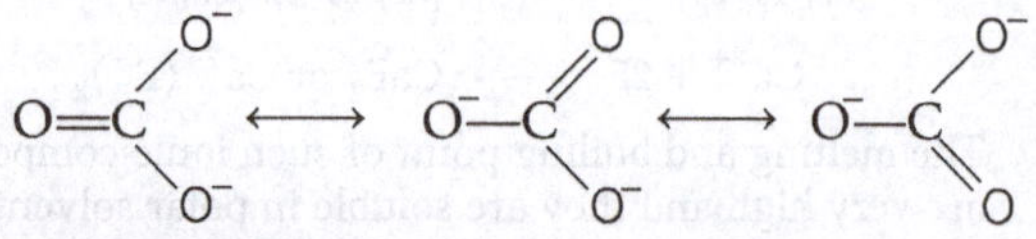

Applications

The important applications of resonance are as follows:

(i) It is very useful in calculating interionic distance, partial ionic character of bonds and energy of the molecules.

(ii) With the help of resonance we can explain the mechanism of serveral chemical reactions.

(iii) It explains the existence of odd electron bonds.

(iv) With the help of resonance energy, the relative electronegativity of the atoms can be determined.

Relative electronegativity $= 0.208\sqrt{\text{Resonance energy}}$

Example 1 All the chlorine-oxygen bond distance in ClO_4^- are 144 pm. What explanation can be given for this?

Sol. ClO_4^- ion is a resonance hybrid of the following structures I, II, III and IV.

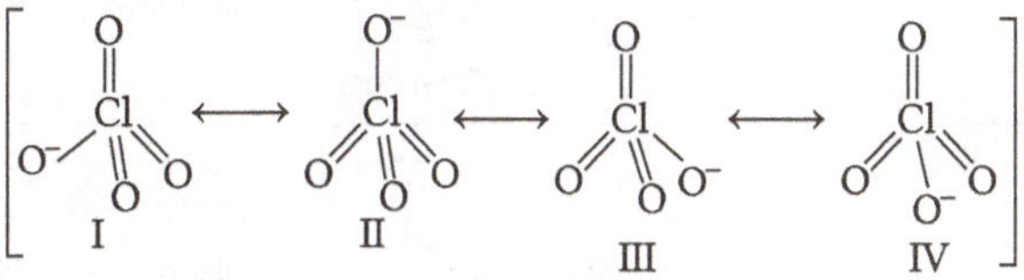

The probable hybrid structure is

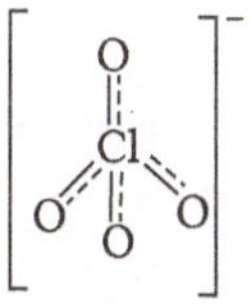

Thus, all the Cl—O bonds are equivalent having bond order = 1.75 and all the chlorine oxygen bond distances are 144 pm.

Valence Shell Electron Pair Repulsion (VSEPR) Theory

Lewis concept although explains the structure of several molecules but in many cases it is found unable to explain the shapes of molecules. In order to explain the shapes of these molecules adequately, **Sidgwick** and **Powell** in 1940 proposed a valence shell electron pair repulsion theory based on the repulsive interaction of the electron pairs in the valence shell of the atoms. **Nyholm** and **Gillespie** (1950) further developed and redefined the concept. The main postulates of this theory are as follows:

(i) The number of valence shell electron pairs (bonded or non-bonded) present around the central atom decides the shape of the molecules. (The shared electron pairs are called bond pairs and unshared or non-bonding electrons are called lone pairs).

(ii) Electron pairs of valence shell repel one another because their electron clouds are negatively charged.

(iii) These electron pairs arrange themselves in such a way so that there is minimum repulsion and maximum distance in between them.

(iv) The valence shell is considered as a sphere in which the electron pairs are localised on the spherical surface at maximum distance from one another.

(v) A multiple bond is treated as if it is a single electron pair and the two or three electron pairs of a multiple bond are treated as a single super pair.

(vi) If a molecule has several resonating structures, the VSEPR model is applicable to any such structure.

(vii) A lone pair occupies more space than a bonding pair, since it lies closer to the central atom.
This means that the repulsion between the different electron pairs follow the order
Lone pair-lone pair > lone pair-bond pair > bond pair – bond pair

$$(lp - lp) > (lp - bp) > (bp - bp)$$

(viii) Repulsive forces decrease sharply as the angle between the electron pairs increases. They are strong at 90°, weaker at 120° and weakest at 180°.

Nyholm and Gillespie (1957) improved the VSEPR model by explaining the important difference between the lone pairs and bond pairs of electrons.

The **lone pairs** of electrons are localised on the central atom, whereas bond pairs are shared between two atoms. Consequently, the lone pair of electrons in a molecule occupy more space as compared to the bond pairs.

Thus, there is greater repulsion between lone pairs of electrons as compared to the lone pair-bond pair and bond pair-bond pair repulsions. The effects of these repulsions are deviations from idealised shapes and alterations in bond angles in molecules.

Shapes of Molecules on the Basis of VSEPR Theory

The geometry of a molecule depends upon the total number of electron pairs (*lps* + *bps*) **present around the central atom of a molecule.**

It is convinient to divide molecules into two categories as :

(i) **Geometry of molecules in which the central atom has no lone pair of electrons,** e.g. if there are only two bond pairs and no lone pairs around the central atom, the only way to keep them as far apart as possible is to arrange them at an angle of 180° to each other. The molecule in such a case will adopt **linear** geometry.

Number of electron pairs	Arrangement of electron pairs	Molecular geometry	Examples
2	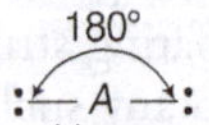 Linear	B—A—B Linear	$BeCl_2$, $HgCl_2$, $ZnCl_2$
3	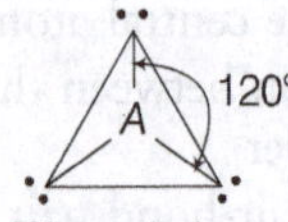 Trigonal planar	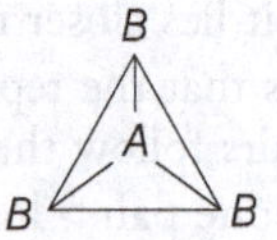 Trigonal planar	BF_3, AlF_3
4	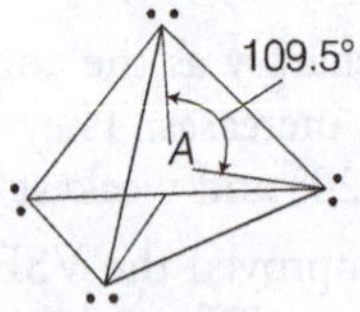 Tetrahedral	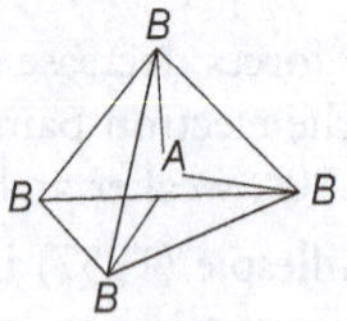 Tetrahedral	CH_4, NH_4^+, CCl_4
5	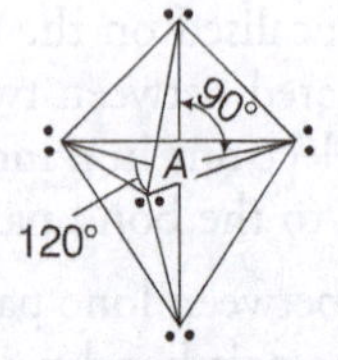 Trigonal bipyramidal	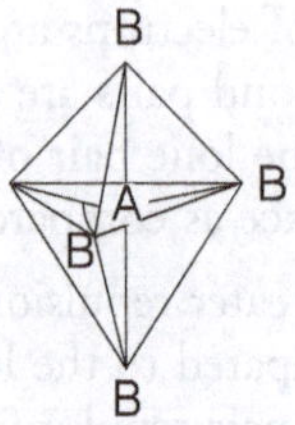 Trigonal bipyramidal	PCl_5
6	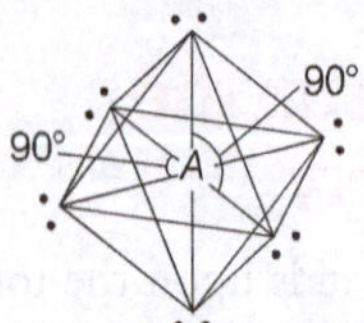	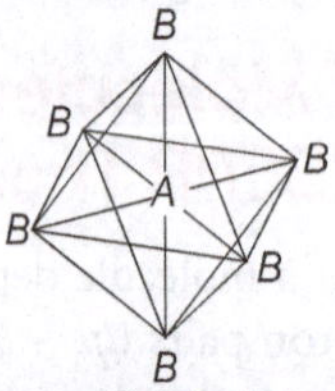 Octahedral	SF_6

(ii) **Shape (Geometry) of some simple molecules/ions with central ions having one or more lone pairs of electrons (*e*) :** In the molecule type given below, '*A*' is the central atom, '*B*' the side atom and '*E*' is the lone pair of electrons.

Molecule type	No. of bonding pairs	No. of lone pairs	Arrangement of electron pairs	Shape	Examples
AB_2E	2	1	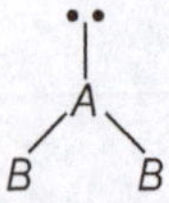 Trigonal planar	Bent	SO_2, O_3
AB_3E	3	1	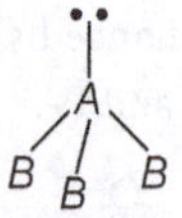 Tetrahedral	Trigonal pyramidal	NH_3, PCl_3
AB_2E_2	2	2	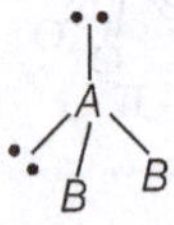 Tetrahedral	Bent	H_2O
AB_4E	4	1	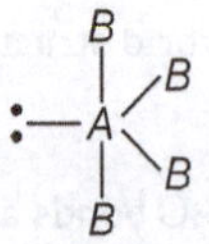 Trigonal bipyramidal	*See-saw*	SF_4
AB_3E_2	3	2	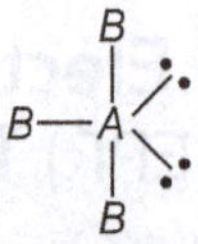 Trigonal bipyramidal	T-shape	ClF_3
AB_5E	5	1	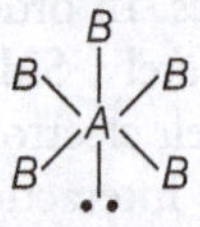 Octahedral	Square pyramidal	BrF_5
AB_4E_2	4	2	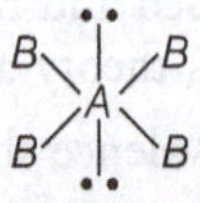 Octahedral	Square planar	XeF_4

Example 2 On the basis of VSEPR theory, predict the shapes of the following:

(i) NH_2^- (ii) O_3

Sol. (i) **Shape of NH_2^-**

Number of valence electrons on central N-atom = 5 + 1 (due to one unit negative charge) = 6

Number of atoms linked to it = 2

$\therefore$ Total number of electron pairs around N $= \frac{6+2}{2} = 4$

and number of bond pairs = 2

$\therefore$ Number of lone pairs = 4 − 2 = 2. Thus, the ion is of the type AB_2E_2. Hence, it has **bent** shape (V-shape).

(ii) **Shape of O_3**

While predicting geometry of molecules containing the double (or multiple) bond is considered as one electron pair, e.g. in case of ozone, its two resonating structures are :

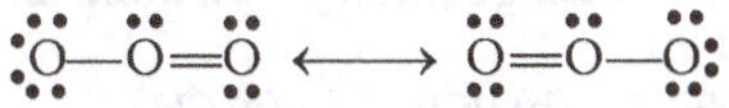

Thus, the central O-atom is considered to have two bond pairs and one lone pair, i.e. it is of the type AB_2E. Hence, it is a **bent molecule**. Thus, the two resonating structures will be

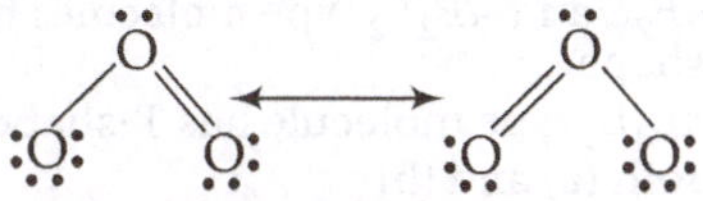

Explanation of the Geometry of Molecules having Lone Pairs

1. Shape of NH_3 Molecule

In NH_3, N is the central atom ($1s^2 2s^2 2p^3$) with five valence electrons. The three hydrogen atoms form single bond with N-atom and therefore the molecule contains 3 bond pairs. The two electrons remain localise as non-bonded pair on nitrogen atom.

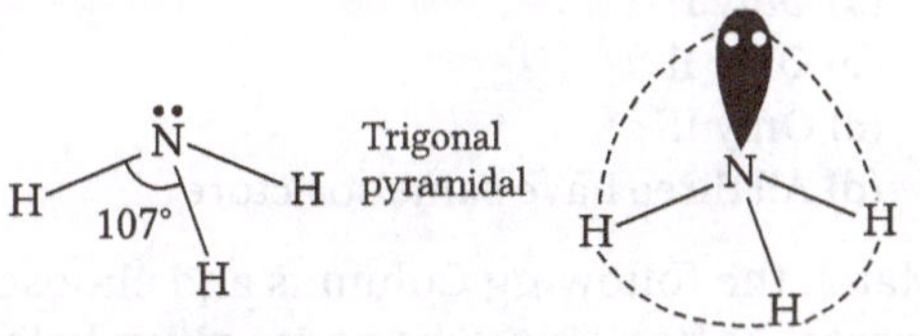

Had there been a *bp* in place of *lp* the shape would have been tetrahedral but one lone pair is present and due to the repulsion between *lp-bp* (which is more than *bp-bp* repulsion) the angle between bond pairs is reduced to 107° from 109.5°.

2. Shape of H_2O Molecule

In H_2O, O is the central atom ($1s^2\ 2s^2\ 2p^4$) with valence electrons. The two hydrogen atoms form single bond with O-atom and therefore the molecule contains 2 bond pairs. The four electrons remain localised as two lone pairs on oxygen atom.

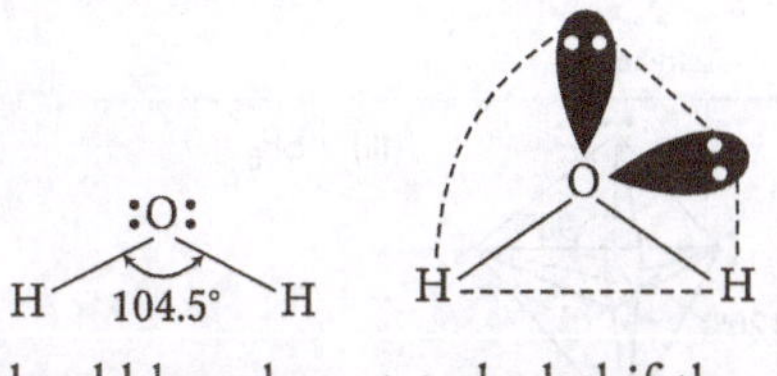

The shape should have been tetrahedral if there were all *bp* but two *lp* are present so the shape is distorted tetrahedral or angular. The reason is *lp-lp* repulsion is more than *lp-bp* which is more than *bp-bp* repulsion. Thus, the angle is reduced to 104.5° from 109.5°.

3. Shape of Sulphur Tetrafluoride (SF_4) Molecule

In this molecule, S is the central atom with six valence electrons. Out of which four are involved in bonding with four F-atoms and the remaining two behave as a lone pair. The possible arrangement of these pairs are as follows:

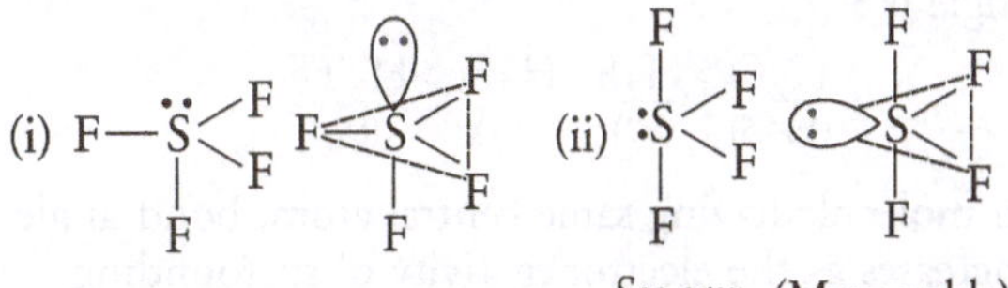

See-saw (More stable)

In (i) the *lp* occupy axial position so there are three *lp-bp* repulsions at 90°. In (ii) the *lp* occupy an equatorial position, and hence there are two *lp-bp* repulsions. Hence, arrangement (ii) is more stable. The shape shown in structure (ii) is a distorted tetrahedron, a folded square or a *see-saw*.

4. Shape of Chlorine Trifluoride (ClF_3)

Here Cl is the central atom with 7 valence electrons, out of which three are involved in bonding with three F atoms and the remaining four act as two lone pairs. These 5 electron pairs (3*bp* + 2*lp*) arrange them in trigonal bipyramidal geometry in the following manner.

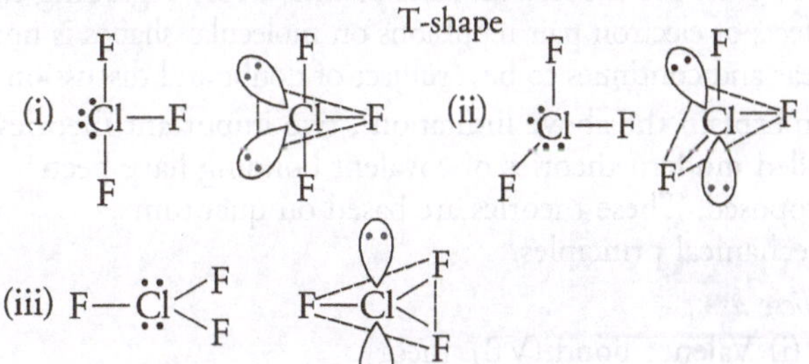

In structure (*i*) the lone pairs occupy equatorial positions so there are less *lp-bp* repulsions as compared to others in which the lone pairs occupy axial positions. So, structure (*i*) T-shaped is most stable.

Variation of Bond Angle

For molecules or ions having regular geometry, the change in the electronegativity of the central atom or the surrounding atom has no effect on the bond angle. e.g. BF_3, BCl_3, $AlCl_3$ etc., all have the same bond angle, *viz*, 120°. Similarly, CH_4, CCl_4, NH_4^+ etc., all have the same bond angle, viz. 109°28'.

If the molecules or ions do not possess regular geometry then

(i) As the number of lone pair of electrons increases, the bond angle decreases.
The order of bond angle is

$$\underset{(109°28)}{CH_4} > \underset{(106°51)}{NH_3} > \underset{(104°31)}{H_2O}$$

(ii) Bond angle increases as the electronegativity of the central atom increases.
e.g. In hydrides of oxygen family, order of bond angle is :

$$\underset{(104.5)}{H_2O} > \underset{(92)}{H_2S} > \underset{(91)}{H_2Se} > \underset{(89)}{H_2Te}$$

(iii) In molecule having same central atom, bond angle increases as the electronegativity of surrounding atom decreases.
e.g. The order of bond angle of following molecules is

$$\underset{(102)}{PI_3} > \underset{(101.5)}{PBr_3} > \underset{(100)}{PCl_3}$$

Limitations of VSEPR Theory

The VSEPR theory is found useful for predicting the geometry of a large number of molecules, especially the compounds of *p*-block elements accurately. This theory is also successful in determining the geometry quite-accurately even when the energy difference between possible structures is very small.
However, the theoretical basis of this theory regarding the effects of electron pair repulsions on molecular shapes is not clear and continues to be a subject of doubt and discussion.
To explain the above limitations, two important theories, called modern theories of covalent bonding have been proposed. These theories are based on quantum mechanical principles.

These are :

(i) Valence bond (VB) theory
(ii) Molecular orbital (MO) theory

Topic Practice 2

Very Short Answer Type Questions

(1 Mark)

1. Fill in the Blanks

(i) The structure of IF_7 is..........
(ii) Due to..........the deviations occurs from idea-lised shape of H_2O and NH_3 molecules
(iii) The structure that represents the molecular structure more accurately is called.......... .

2. Objective Type Questions

(i) Resonance structures can be written for
(a) O_3 (b) NH_3 (c) CH_4 (d) H_2O

(ii) Which of the molecules has trigonal bipyramidal geometry with bond angles 120° and 90°?
(a) SF_6 (b) PCl_5 (c) CH_4 (d) BF_3

(iii) Bent shape is observed in AB_2E, AB_2E_2 and AB_3E_2 type of molecule. Choose the correct option.
E = number of lone pair
(a) AB_2E and AB_2E_2 type molecules have bent shape
(b) AB_3E_2 type molecule has T-shape
(c) Both (a) and (b)
(d) None of the above

(iv) Which of the following structures is most stable?

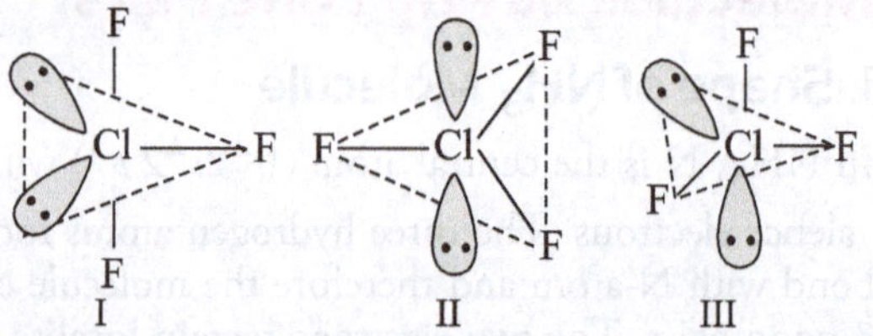

Choose the correct option.
(a) Only I
(b) Only II
(c) Only III
(d) All three have same structure

3. Match the following Columns and choose the correct option using the codes given below:

Column I	Column II
A. 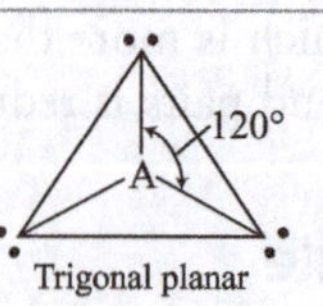 Trigonal planar	(i) PCl_5
B. 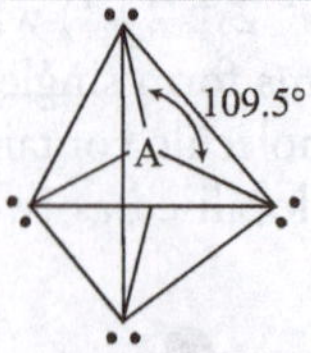 Tetrahedral	(ii) NH_4^+
C. 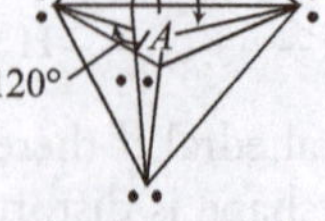 Trigonal bipyramidal	(iii) SF_6

Column I	Column II
D. 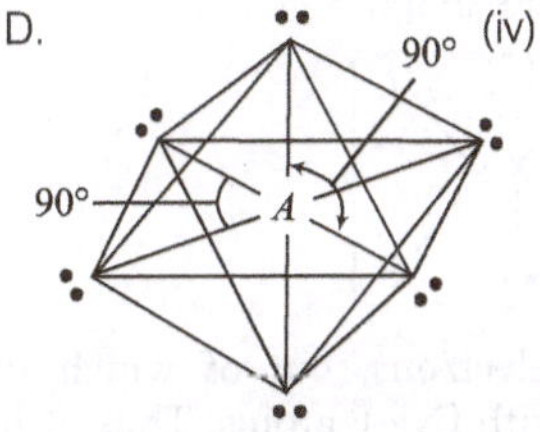 (iv) Octahedral	BF_3

Codes

	A	B	C	D		A	B	C	D
(a)	(i)	(ii)	(iii)	(iv)	(b)	(iv)	(iii)	(ii)	(i)
(c)	(iv)	(ii)	(i)	(iii)	(d)	(i)	(i)	(ii)	(iv)

4. H_3PO_3 can be represented by structures 1 and 2 shown below. Can these two structures be taken as the canonical forms of the resonance hybrid representing H_3PO_3? If not give reasons for the same. **NCERT Textbook**

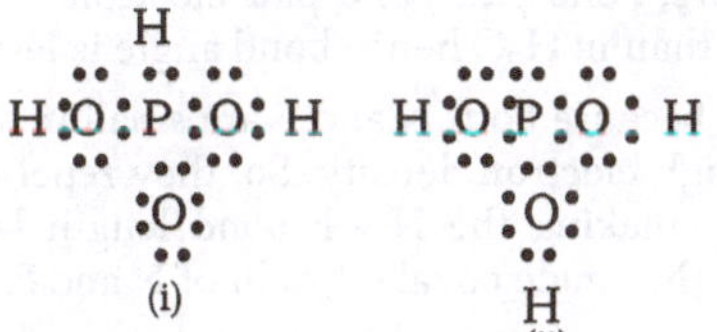

(i) (ii)

5. Explain giving reasons whether BH_4^- and H_3O^+ will have same or different shape.
6. Predict the shape of XeF_4 molecule.
7. Calculate the number of bond pairs and lone pairs in IF_5 molecule.
8. Why NF_3 is pyramidal but BF_3 is triangular planar?
9. The H—S—H bond angle in H_2S is 92.2° whereas the H—O—H bond angle in H_2O is 104.5°, why?
10. Account for the following :
The experimentally determined N—F bond length in NF_3 is greater than the sum of the single covalent radii of N and F.

Short Answer Type I Questions

2 Marks

11. All the C—O bonds in carbonate ion (CO_3^{2-}) are equal in length. Explain.
12. How do you account for equal bond lengths in ozone molecule?
13. What do you understand by bond pairs and lone pairs of electrons? Illustrate by giving one example of each type. **NCERT Textbook**
14. Explain the structure of CO_2 molecule. **NCERT**
15. Why are lone pair-lone pair repulsions stronger than the lone pair-bond pair repulsion?
16. Which of the following has larger bond angle in each pair?
(i) CO_2, BF_3 (ii) NH_3, CH_4
(iii) H_2O, H_2S (iv) SiF_4, C_2H_2
17. Arrange the following in order of decreasing bond angle, giving reason NO_2, NO_2^+, NO_2^-.
18. Explain the shape of BrF_5. **NCERT Exemplar**
19. Although geometries of NH_3 and H_2O molecules are distorted tetrahedral, bond angle in water is less than that of ammonia. Discuss.
20. Group the given molecules as linear and non-linear molecules. **NCERT Exemplar**
$H_2O, HOCl, BeCl_2, Cl_2O$

Short Answer Type II Questions

3 Marks

21. What is resonance? What are the guidelines for writing resonating structures. Out of the following four resonance structures for the CO_2 molecule, which are important for describing the bonding in the molecules and why?

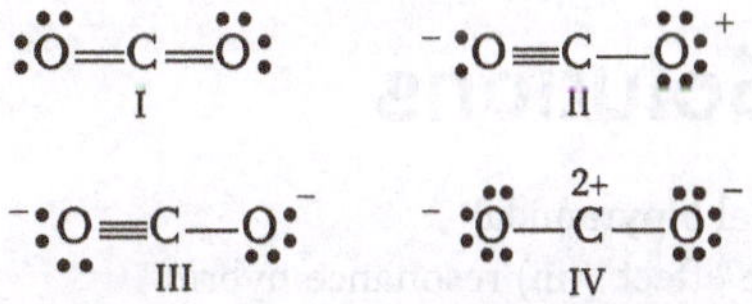

22. Explain the important aspects of resonance with reference to the CO_3^{2-} ion. **NCERT Exemplar**
23. Write the resonance structures for SO_3, NO_2 and NO_3^-.
24. Draw the resonating structure of
(i) ozone molecule
(ii) nitrate ion
25. Explain, why CO_3^{2-} ion cannot be represented by a single Lewis structure. How can it be represented?
26. Explain the non-linear shape of H_2S and non-planar shape of PCl_3 using valence shell electron pair repulsion theory. **NCERT Exemplar**

27. Give example each of the molecules which have the following geometries.
(i) Linear (ii) Trigonal planar
(iii) Tetrahedral (iv) Trigonal bipyramidal
(v) Octahedral (vi) Bent

28. Arrange the following sets of molecules in the decreasing order of bond angle.
(i) SF_6, CCl_4, H_2O, NH_3 (ii) CH_4, NH_3, H_2O, BF_3
(iii) $AlCl_3, H_2O, BeH_2, H_2S$

29. BeF_2 molecule is linear while SF_2 is angular though both are triatomic?

Long Answer Type Questions

5 Marks

30. What are the main postulates of valence shell electron pair repulsion (VSEPR) theory? What improvement was made by Nyholm and Gillespie?

31. Discuss the shape of the following molecules using VSEPR model **NCERT Textbook**

$BeCl_2, BCl_3, SiCl_4, AsF_5, H_2S, PH_3$

32. (i) Sketch the following molecular shapes and give the various bond angles in the structure linear, triangular planar, tetrahedral and octahedral.
(ii) What are the shapes of $PCl_5, NH_3, BCl_3, SF_6, H_2O, CCl_4, SF_4, ClF_3, [BrF_5]^-, XeF_4, XeF_2$?

Hints & Solutions

1. (i) pentagonal bipyramidal
(ii) repulsive effect (iii) resonance hybrid

2. (i) → a, (ii) → b, (iii) → c, (iv) → a

3. (c) A → (iv), B → (ii), C → (i), D → (iii)

4. **Hint** Resonating structures or canonical forms differ only in the arrangement of electrons, but not in the positions of atoms. So, these two structures cannot be taken as the canonical forms of the resonance hybrid because position of the H-atom has been changed in the two structures.

5. In BH_4^- ion, there are 4*bps* and 0*lp* whereas in H_3O^+, there are 3*bps* and 1*lp*, so there shapes will be different. BH_4^- ion will have tetrahedral geometry whereas H_3O^+ will have pyramidal shape.

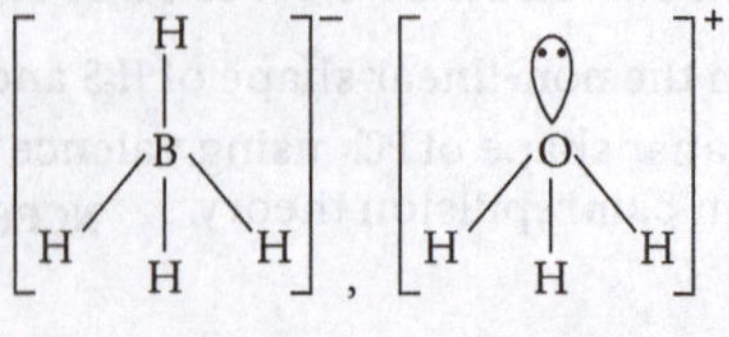

6. $XeF_4 = 4bp + 2lp$ (This is because Xe contains 8 valence electrons) = square planar shape.

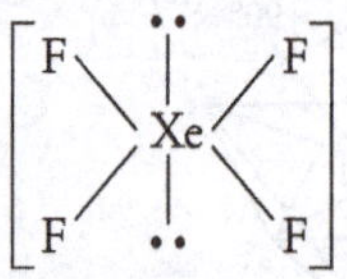

7. I contains 7 valence electrons, out of which five are utilised to form bond with five F atoms. Thus, it has five bond pairs. Number of lone pairs = valence e^- − bond pairs = 7 − 5 = 2 electrons or 1 lone pair.

8. In NF_3, N is surrounded by three F atoms and a lone pair thus, have *lp-bp* repulsion along with *bp-bp* repulsion. Thus, its shape is **pyramidal**.
In BF_3, B is surrounded by only three F atoms, i.e. have no lone pairs, so only repulsion present in it is *bp-bp*. Thus, its shape is triangular planar.

9. In H_2S, there is less polarity as compared to H_2O because sulphur is bigger in size and less electronegative, therefore, bond pair-bond pair electrons repulsion is less in H_2S than in H_2O hence bond angle is less.

10. This is because both N and F are small in size and hence, have high electron density. So, they repel the bond pairs thereby making the N—F bond length larger than the sum of the single covalent radii of N and F.

11. **Key Idea** To explain the reason of equal in length of C—O bonds, we should keep in mind about the resonance. As a result of resonance, the bond length in a molecule become equal.
Carbonate ion (CO_3^{2-}) = 3 bond pair + 1 lone pair
⇒ trigonal planar

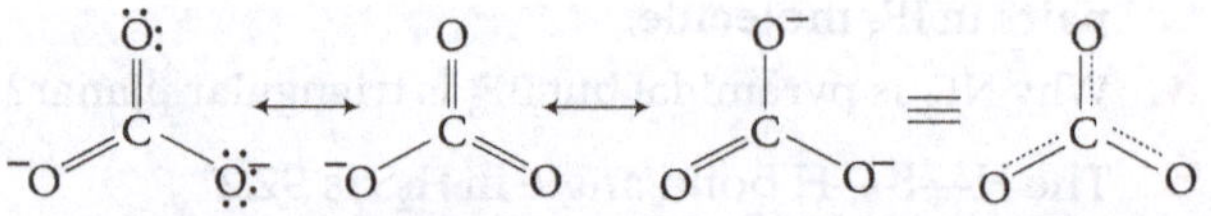

Due to resonance all C—O bond length are equal. [2]

12. Refer to text on page 158 (Resonance).

13. Covalent bond is formed by mutual sharing of electrons. The shared pair of electrons present between the bonded atoms are called bond pairs of electrons and unshared pair (non-bonding) electrons are called the lone pairs of electrons, e.g. ammonia, NH_3 contains 3 bond pairs and 1 lone pair of electrons, whereas CH_4 contains only 4 bond pairs.

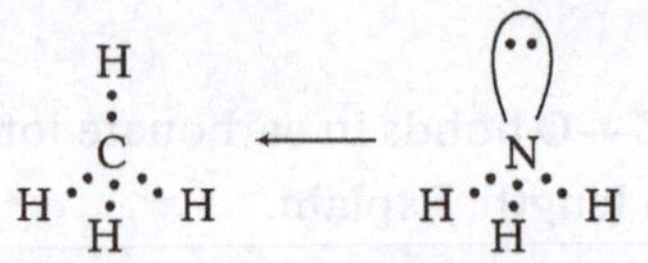

[2]

14. :Ö :C: :Ö: If we consider only structure I for CO_2
I
molecule, there should be two carbon to oxygen double bonds. The bond length of normal C=O double bond is 121 pm. However, experimentally, each carbon to oxygen

bond length in CO_2 is found to be 115 pm which is in between that of C=O double bond (121 pm) and C≡O triple bond (110 pm). Hence, CO_2 is considered as a resonance hybrid of the following three Lewis structures.

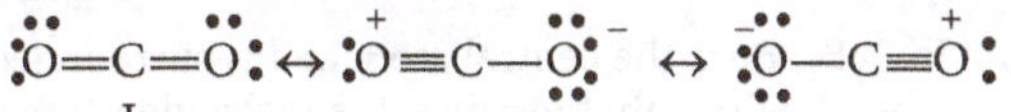

I II III [2]

15. Refer to the text on page 159 (VSEPR Theory).

16. (i) CO_2 (ii) CH_4
(iii) H_2O (iv) C_2H_2 [4 × 1/2]

17. $NO_2^+ > NO_2 > NO_2^-$. This is because NO_2^+ has no lone pair of electrons (i.e. has only bond pairs on two sides) and hence, it is linear.

NO_2 has one unshared electron while NO_2^- has one unshared electron pair. This exerts a greater repulsion than the single electron in NO_2, so the O—N—O angle is reduced further. [1]

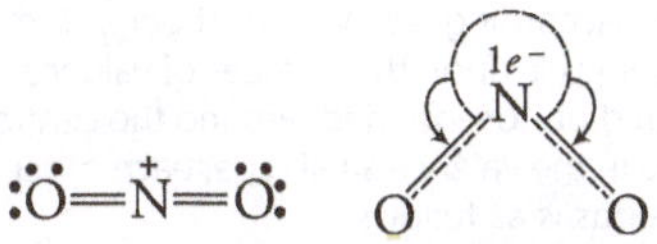

Bond angle = 180° Bond angle = 132°

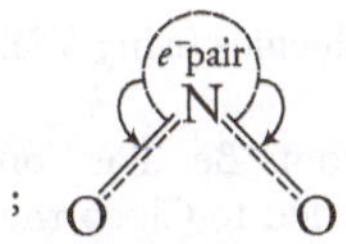

Curved arrows represent repulsions on bond pairs

Bond angle = 115°

[1]

18. The central atom Br has seven electrons in the valence shell. Five of these will form bonds with five fluorine atoms and the remaining two electrons are present as one lone pair. Hence, total pairs of electrons are six (5 bond pairs and 1 lone pair).

To minimize repulsion between lone pairs and bond pairs, the shape becomes square pyramidal.

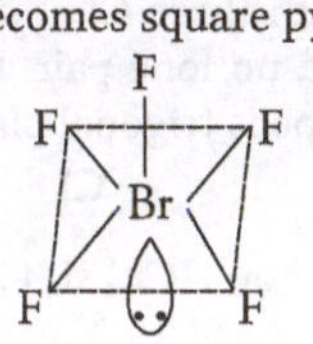

[2]

19.

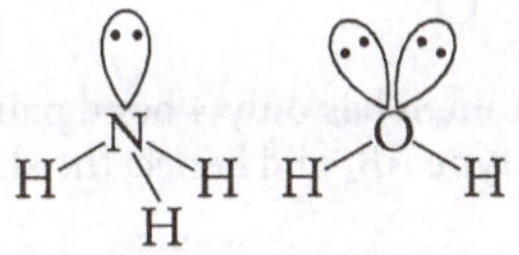

NH_3 $bp = 3$ $lp = 1$

H_2O $bp = 2$ $lp = 2$

[1]

In H_2O molecule, there is lone pair-lone pair repulsion due the presence of two lone pairs of electrons while in NH_3 molecule, there is only lone pair-bond pair repulsion.

According to VSEPR theory, the former one is more stronger and hence, the bond angle in water is less than that of ammonia (NH_3). [1]

20.

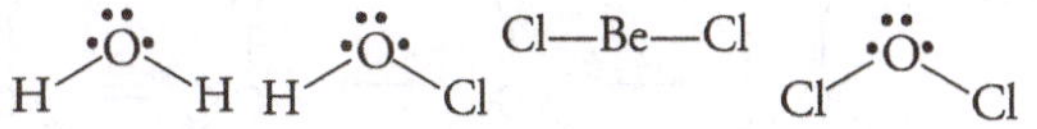

Therefore, only $BeCl_2$ is linear and rest of the molecules are non-linear. [2]

21. **Resonance** Refer to text on page 158 (Resonance). I and II are more important as the I is non-polar and (II) has more number of covalent bonds and negative charge on more electronegative atom.

22. When a single Lewis structure of a molecule cannot describe its all properties, a number of structures, called canonical structures, are written.

The actual structure, known as resonance hybrid, is in between of all these canonical forms. This phenomenon is called resonance.

According to experimental findings, all carbon to oxygen bonds in CO_3^{2-} are equivalent, while in a single Lewis structure, there are two single bonds and one double bond between carbon and oxygen. So, a single Lewis structure is inadequate for the representation of CO_3^{2-} ion. The carbonate ion is best described as a hybrid of the canonical or resonance forms I, II and III. [1]

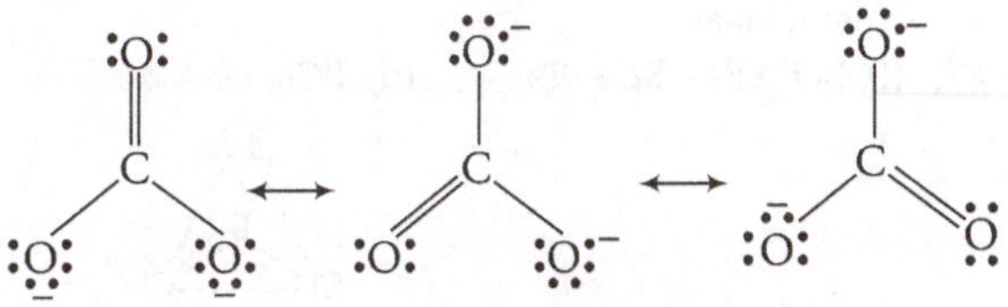

I II III

Resonance in CO_3^{2-} ion

All canonical forms have similar energy, same positions of atoms and same number of bonded and non-bonded pairs of electrons. Thus, in CO_3^{2-} all the C—O bonds are equivalent. [2]

23. **Sulphur trioxide**, SO_3

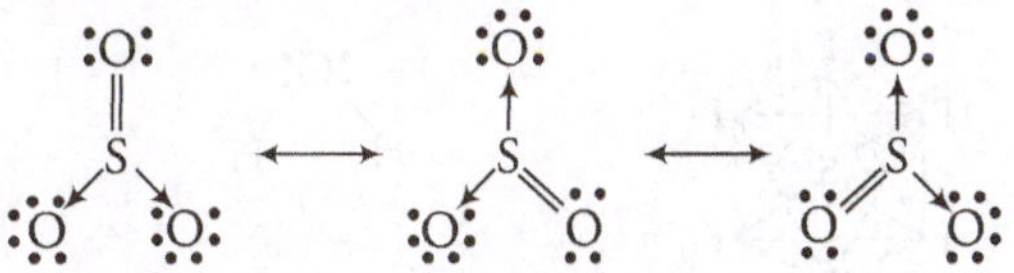

[1]

Nitrogen dioxide, NO_2

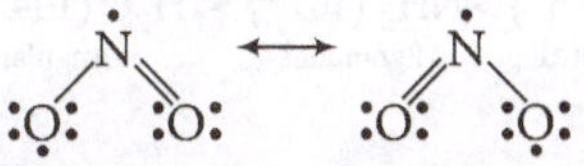

[1]

Nitrate ion, NO_3^- Refer to text on page 158 (Resonance in inorganic molecules).

24. (i) Refer to text on page 158 (Resonance) (ii) Refer to text on page 158 (Resonance in inorganic molecule).

25. A single Lewis structure of CO_3^{2-} ion cannot explain all the properties of this ion. It can be represented as a resonance hybrid of the following structures:

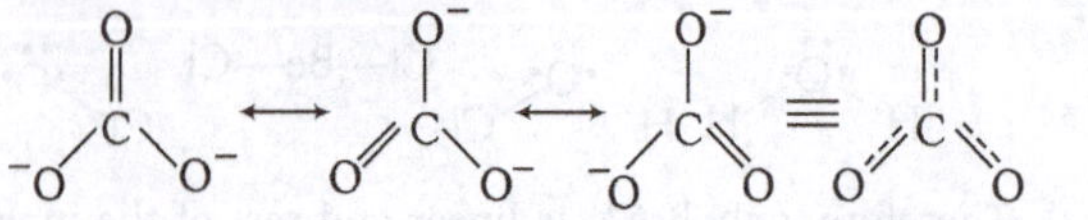

I II III Resonance hybrid [1]

If, it were represented only by one structure, there should be two types of bonds, i.e. C=O double bond and C—O single bonds but actually all bonds are found to be identical with same bond length and same bond strength. [2]

26. **H_2S** In it, the central atom is sulphur. There are 6 electrons in its valence shell ($_{16}S = 2, 8, 6$). Two electrons are shared with two H-atoms and the remaining four electrons are present as two lone pairs. Hence, total pairs of electrons are four (2 bond pairs and 2 lone pairs). [1]

Due to the presence of 2 lone pairs the shape becomes distorted tetrahedral or angular or bent (non-linear). [1]

PCl_3 In it, the central atom is phosphorus. There are 5 electrons in its valence shell ($_{15}P = 2, 8, 5$). Three electrons are shared with three Cl-atoms and the remaining two electrons are present as one lone pair. Hence, total pairs of electrons are four (1 lone pair and 3 bond pairs). Due to the presence of one lone pair, the shape becomes pyramidal (non-planar). [1]

27. (i) BeF_2; F—Be—F :

(ii) BCl_3 :

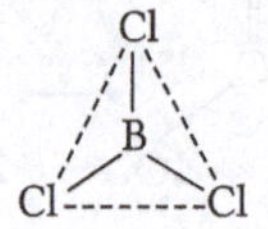

(iii) $SiCl_4$:

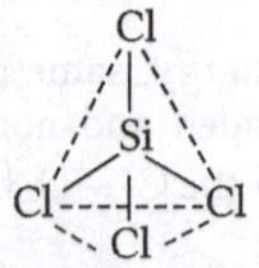

(iv) PF_5 :

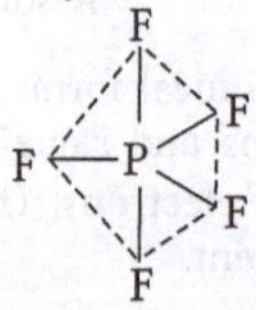

(v) SF_6 :

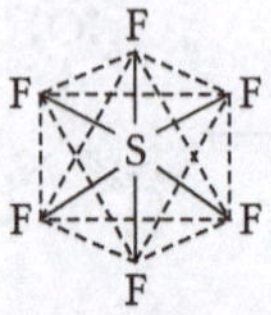

(vi) H_2O

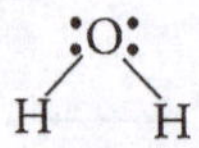

[½ × 6]

28. (i) $CCl_4(109.5°) > NH_3\ (107°) > H_2O\ (104.5°) > SF_6\ (90°)$
Tetrahedral, Pyramidal, Angular, Octahedral [1]

(ii) $BF_3(120°) > CH_4\ (109.5°) > NH_3\ (107°) > H_2O\ (104.5°)$
Planar, Tetrahedral, Pyramidal, Angular [1]

(iii) $BeH_2(180°) > AlCl_3\ (120°) > H_2O\ (104.5°) > H_2S\ (100°)$
Linear, Planar, Angular, Angular but S is less electronegative than O [1]

29. In BeF_2, Be is the central atom and is surrounded by 2 bond pairs only therefore, the molecule is linear. On the other hand, in SF_2, the central atom S is surrounded by 2 bond pairs and 2 lone pairs. Since SF_2 is surrounded by 4 electron pairs, the geometry is angular with two positions occupied by lone pairs.

F—Be—F
2 bond pairs
(Linear)

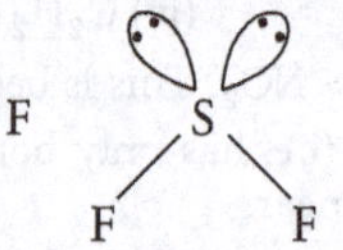

2 bond pairs, 2 lone pairs
(Angular)

30. Refer to text on pages 159 (VSEPR theory).

31. **Key Idea** According to VSEPR theory, the shape of a molecule depends upon the number of valence shell electron pairs (bonded or non-bonded) around the central atom. Pairs of electrons in the valence shell repel each other. The order of their repulsions is as follows

$$lp - lp > lp - bp > bp - bp$$

The shape of the given molecules using VSEPR model are shown below.

(i) **$BeCl_2$** The central atom Be has only 2 valence electrons which are bonded to Cl, so there are only 2 bond pairs and no lone pairs. It is of the type AB_2 and hence, the shape is linear. [1/2]

Cl—Be—Cl or Cl : Be : Cl

(ii) BCl_3

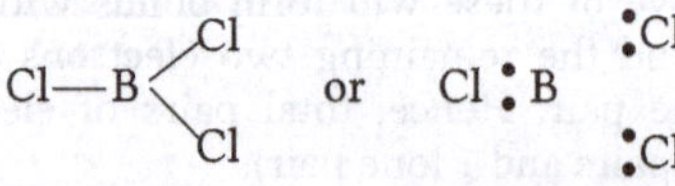

The central atom B has only 3 valence electrons which are bonded with three Cl atoms, so it contains only 3 bond pairs and no lone pair. It is of the type AB_3 and hence, the shape is trigonal planar. [1/2]

(iii) $SiCl_4$

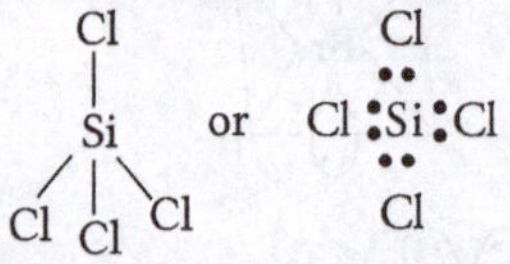

Similarly, the central atom Si has only 4 bond pairs and no lone pair. It is of the type AB_4 and hence, the shape is tetrahedral. [1]

(iv) AsF_5

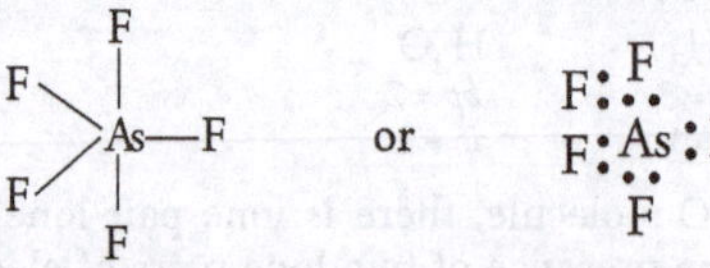

The central atom As has only 5 bond pairs and no lone pair. It is of the type AB_5 and hence, the shape is trigonal bipyramidal. [1]

(v) H_2S

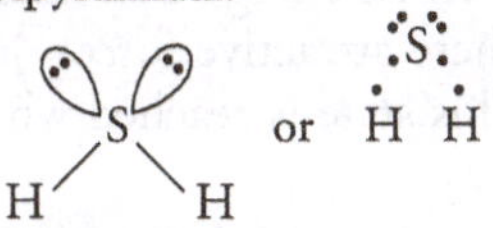

The central atom S has 6 valence electrons. Out of these only two are used in bond formation with two H-atoms while four (two pairs) remains as non-bonding electrons (i.e. lone pairs). So, it contains 2 bond pairs and 2 lone pairs. It is of the type AB_2E_2 and hence, the shape is bent or V- shaped. [1]

(vi) PH_3

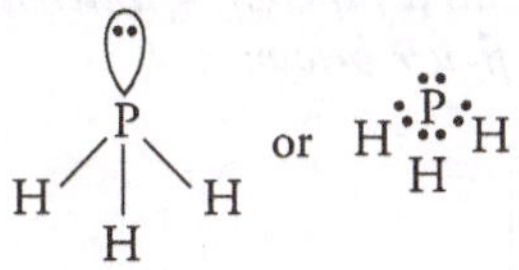

The central atom P has 5 valence electrons. Out of which three are utilised in bonding with H atoms and one pair remains as lone pair.

So, it contains 3 bond pairs and one lone pair. It is of the type AB_3E and hence the shape is pyramidal. [1]

32. (i)

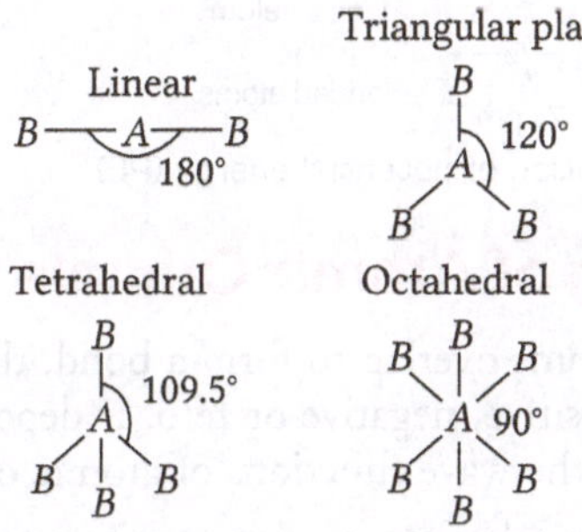

[2]

(ii) The shape of the molecules are given below:

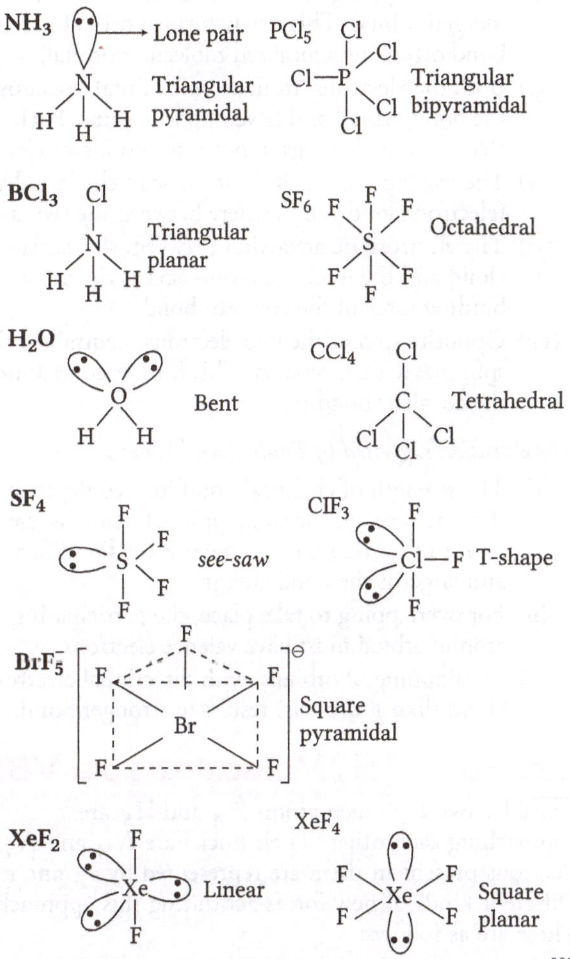

[3]

TOPIC 03 Valence Bond Theory and Hybridisation

Valence Bond Theory (VBT)

This theory was introduced by **Heitler and London** in 1927 and further improved by **Pauling and Slater** in 1931. It is based on the knowledge of atomic orbitals, electronic configurations of elements, the criteria of overlapping of atomic orbitals and the hybridisation of atomic orbitals and the principles of variation and superposition.

Postulates

The postulates of VBT are as follows :

(i) Overlapping of two distinct atomic orbital, each having an unpaired electron, results in formation of covalent bond.

(ii) This process of overlapping completes with release in energy. This makes the resulting bond stable. Hence, overlapping results decrease in energy.

(iii) The overlapping of two atomic orbitals form a single merged orbital. This newly formed orbital is called bond orbital or a localised molecular orbital.
(iv) Both the electrons, from atomic orbitals, occupy the bond orbital and have opposite spins. Each electron now belongs to both the atomic nuclei.
(v) The overlapping results in increase in electron density, (electron cloud), somewhere between the two atoms.
(vi) The electrostatic attraction between, the electron cloud and the nuclei of atoms acts as the major binding force of the covalent bond.
(vii) Opposite spin of the two electrons, neutralises their spin magnetic moments. This further contributes to the covalent bonding.

The extension suggested by Pauling and Slater are:

(i) The strength of chemical bond formed depends on the extent of atomic overlapping. Greater is the extent of overlapping, stronger is the bond formed and larger is the bond energy.
(ii) For overlapping to take place, the participating atomic orbital must have valence electrons.
(iii) Overlapping of orbitals, with directional electron cloud (like *p*-orbitals) results in stronger bond.

Structure of H_2 Molecule as per VBT

Consider two hydrogen atoms H_A and H_B are approaching each other. Their nuclei are N_A and N_B and electrons present in them are represented by e_A and e_B. Different kinds of new forces act during this approach. These are as follows:

(i) **Attractive forces** are between Nucleus of one atom and its own electrons, i.e. $N_A - e_A$ and $N_B - e_B$ or between nucleus of one atom and electron of other atom, i.e. $N_A - e_B$ and $N_B - e_A$
(ii) **Repulsive forces are between**
- Electron e_A and electron e_B
- Nucleus N_A and nucleus N_B

Attractive forces tend to bring the combining atoms close to each other. On the other hand, repulsive forces tend to push them apart.

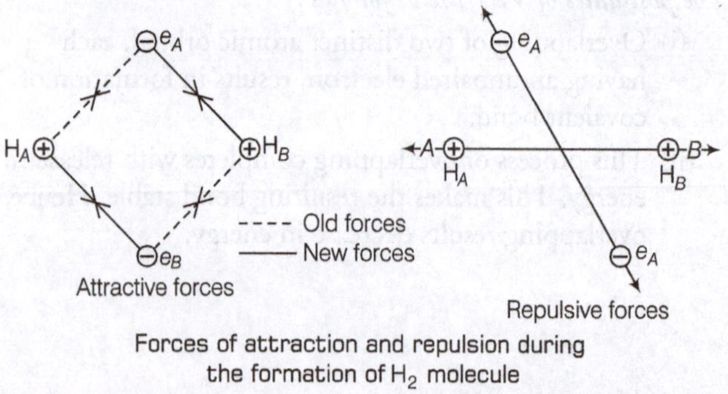

Forces of attraction and repulsion during the formation of H_2 molecule

The magnitude of new attractive forces is more than the new repulsive forces. As a result, two atoms approach each other and potential energy decreases. Ultimately, a stage is reached where attractive forces, just balance the repulsive forces. This state is reached when the atoms are at critical distance r_0.

At a distance greater than r_0, the attractive forces are dominant whereas at a distance smaller than r_0, the repulsive forces are dominant over the attractive forces which leads to increase of potential energy. Maximum lowering of energy takes place at critical distance r_0.

The lowering of PE as a function of inter-nuclear distance has been shown in figure below:

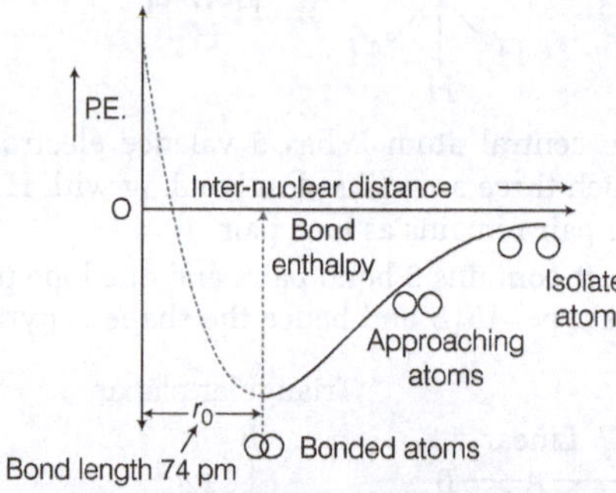

Variation of potential energy (PE)

Overlapping of Atomic Orbitals

Orbitals of two atoms overlap to form a bond, their overlap may be positive, negative or zero. It depends upon the sign for the wave functions of atomic orbitals.

e.g. positive overlap takes place when two $2p_z$-orbitals overlap along the internuclear axis with the lobes of same sign.

On the other hand, when two $2p_z$-orbitals overlap along the internuclear axis with the lobes of opposite sign, it results in negative overlap. This is because lobes of opposite sign cannot combine.

The different arrangements of *s* and *p*-orbitals resulting in positive, negative and zero overlaps are given below:

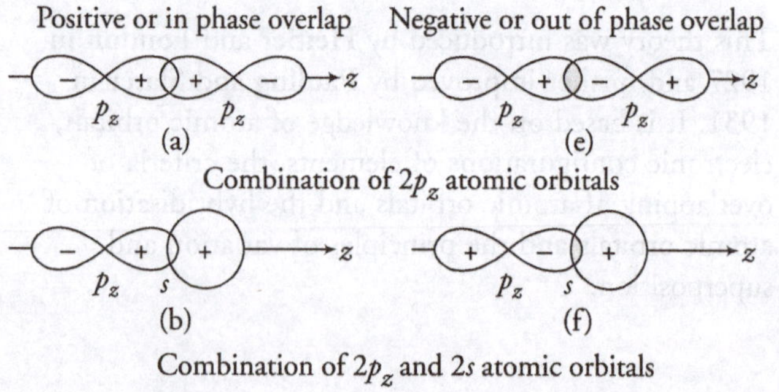

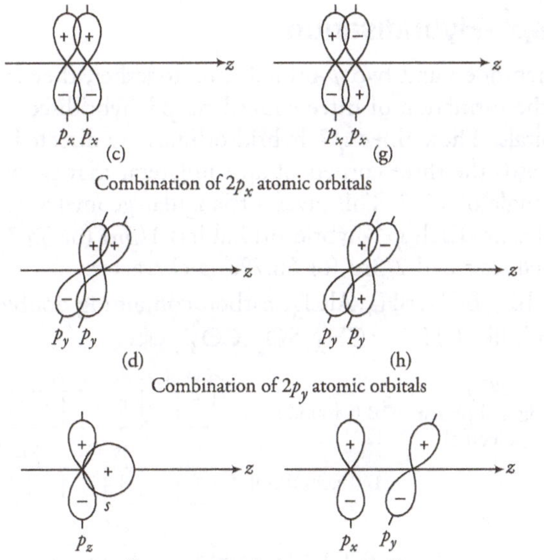

Positive, negative and zero overlaps of *s* and *p* atomic orbitals

Types of Overlapping and Nature of Covalent Bonds

Depending upon the types of overlapping, the covalent bond may be classified into two types :

(i) **Sigma (σ) Bond** This type of bond is formed by the end to end (head-on) overlap of bonding orbitals along the internuclear axis. It is also known as **head on overlap** or **axial overlap.** This bond is stronger due to a large overlapping of atomic orbitals. This can be formed by any one of the following types of combinations of atomic orbitals.

- ***s-s* Overlapping** In it, there is overlap of two half-filled *s*-orbitals along the internuclear axis as shown below.

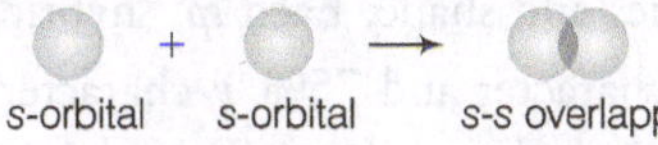

- ***s-p* Overlapping** This type of overlap takes place between half-filled *s*-orbitals of one atom and half-filled *p*-orbitals of another atom.

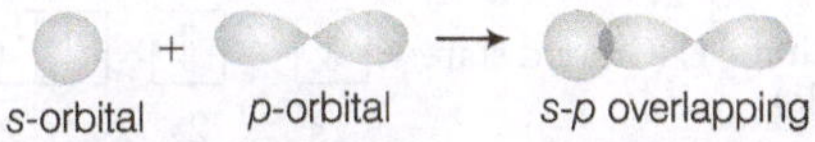

- ***p-p* Overlapping** It occurs between half-filled *p*-orbitals of the two atoms and overlap along their axis.

Note If *Z*-axis is chosen as the internuclear axis, then no overlapping can take place between *s* and p_x or p_y orbital, or p_x and p_y orbitals, i.e. there is zero overlap.

(ii) **pi (π) Bond** When the atomic orbitals overlap in such a way that their axis remain parallel to each other and perpendicular to the internuclear axis, the bond formed is called **π-bond.**

The orbitals formed as a result of sidewise overlapping contains two saucer type charged clouds above and below the plane of the participating atoms.

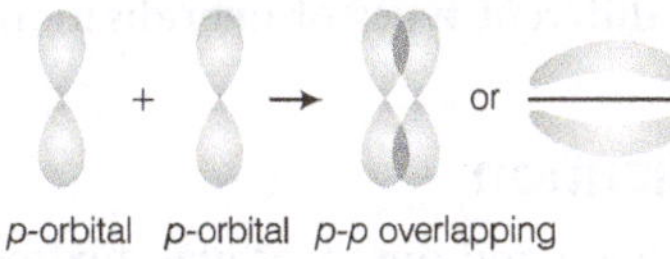

Hybridisation

This concept was put forward by **Pauling.** He suggested that the atomic orbitals mix together to generate a new set of equivalent orbitals, called the **hybrid orbitals** or **hybridised orbitals.** These orbitals are used in bond formation. The phenomenon is called **hybridisation.**

It can be defined as the process of intermixing of the orbitals of slightly different energies so as to redistribute their energies, to generate a new set of orbitals of equivalent energies and shape, e.g. when one 2*s* and three 2*p*-orbitals of carbon hybridise, they result in the formation of four new sp^3 hybrid orbitals.

Salient Features of Hybridisation

The main features of hybridisation are as follows :

(i) The number of hybrid orbitals generated is equal to the number of the atomic orbitals that can be hybridised.

(ii) The hybridised orbitals are always equivalent in energy and shape.

(iii) The hybrid orbitals are more effective in forming stable bonds than the pure atomic orbitals.

(iv) These hybrid orbitals arrange themselves in space in such a direction so that there is minimum repulsion between electron pairs and thus a stable arrangement is obtained. Therefore, the type of hybridisation indicates the geometry of the molecules.

Important Conditions for Hybridisation

(i) Only valence shell orbitals of an atom take part in hybridisation.

(ii) The orbitals undergoing hybridisation should have almost equal energy.

(iii) Promotion of electron is not essential condition prior to hybridisation.

(iv) It is not necessary that only half-filled orbitals are involved in the hybridisation. In some cases, even filled orbitals of valence shell can also be involved in hybridisation.

Types of Hybridisation

There are many types of hybridisation involving *s*, *p* and *d*-orbitals. The different types of hybridisations are as follows:

1. *sp*-Hybridisation

It occurs when one *s* and one *p*-orbital mix together and result in the formation of two equivalent *sp*-hybrid orbitals. Each *sp* hybrid orbital is associated with 50% *s*-character and 50% *p*-character. Such a molecule in which the atom is *sp*-hybridised and linked directly to two other atoms have linear geometry. This hybridisation is also known as **diagonal hybridisation.**

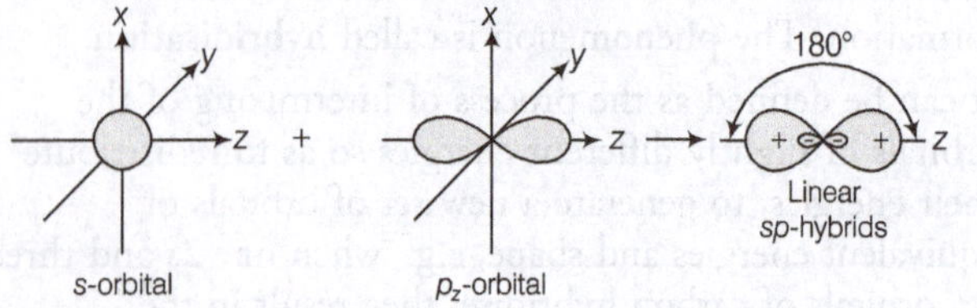

e.g.

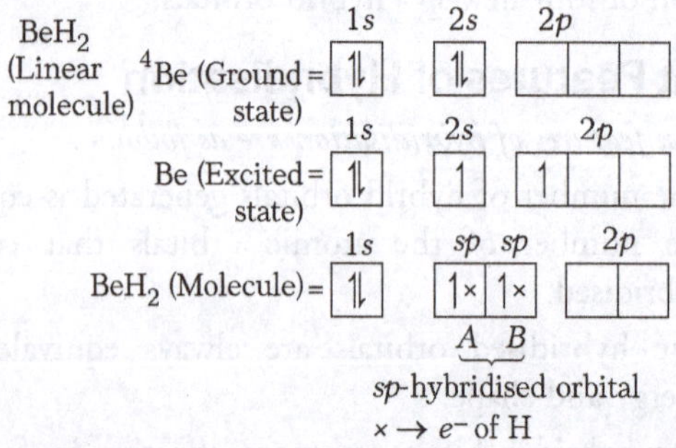

The two half-filled *A* and *B* *sp*-hybrid orbitals form σ-bonds with half-filled *s*-orbitals of two H-atoms by (*sp* - *s*) overlap thus, forming two Be — H bonds.

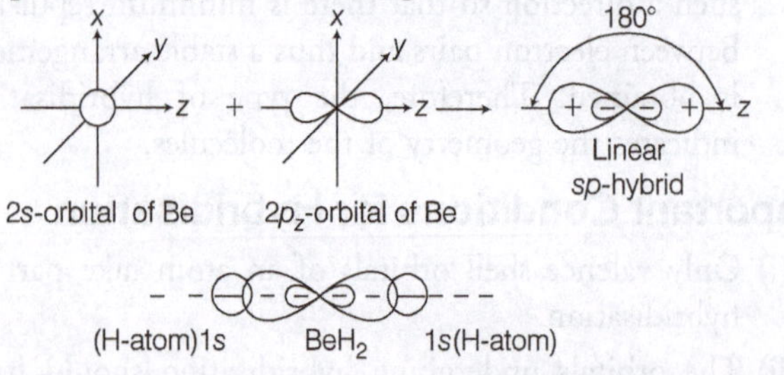

(Linear shape, *sp*-hybridisation)

2. sp^2-Hybridisation

When one *s* and two *p*-orbitals mix together, they result in the formation of three equivalent sp^2 hybridised orbitals. These three sp^2-hybrid orbitals are directed towards the three corners of an equilateral triangle with an angle of 120°. This gives a triangular geometry to the molecule. Each sp^2-hybrid orbital has 1/3rd (or 33.33%) s-character and 2/3rd (or 66.7%) *p*-character.

e.g. $BF_3, BCl_3, BH_3, AlCl_3$, carbon containing double bond, like $CH_2 = CH_2, SO_2, CO_3^{2-}$ etc.

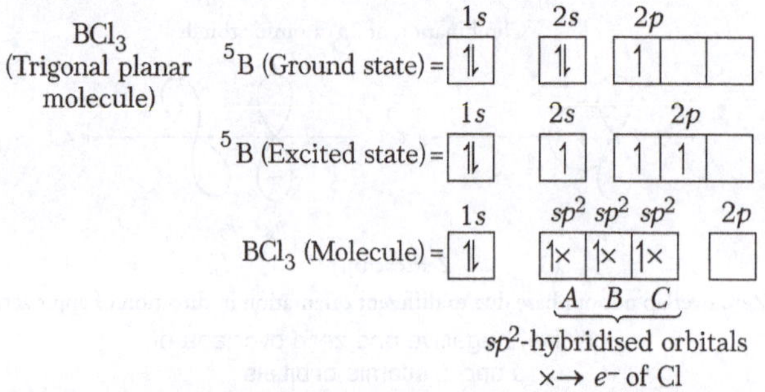

The three half-filled *A*, *B* and *C* sp^2-hybrid orbitals form σ-bonds with half-filled *p*-orbitals of three Cl-atoms by (sp^2 – *p*) overlap and give trigonal planar geometry.

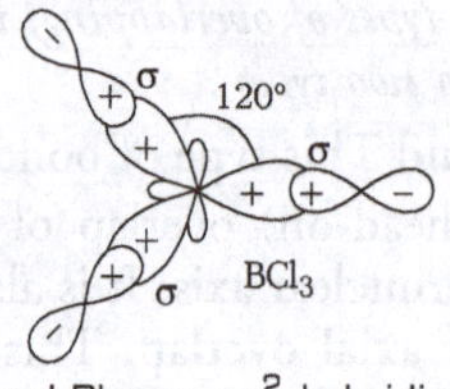

(Trigonal Planar, sp^2-hybridisation)

3. sp^3-Hybridisation

In this hybridisation, one *s* and three *p*-orbitals of the valence shell intermix to form four sp^3 hybrid orbitals of equivalent energies and shape. Each sp^3 hybrid orbital contains 25% *s*-character and 75% *p*-character. The four sp^3 hybrid orbital so obtained are directed towards the four corners of a regular tetrahedron. The angle between sp^3 hybrid orbitals is 109.5°. e.g.

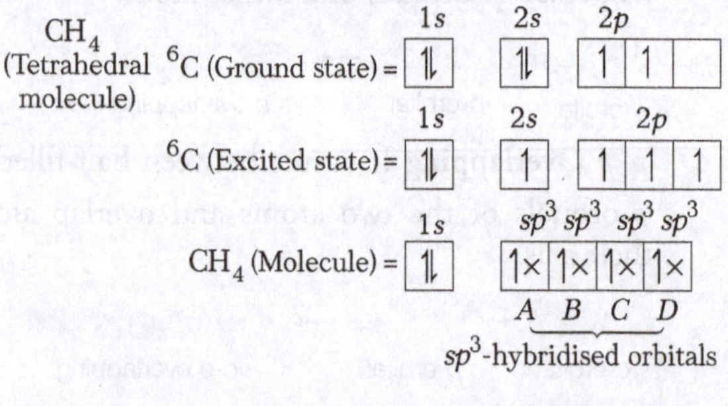

The four half-filled A, B, C and D sp^3-hybrid orbitals form σ-bonds with half-filled s-orbitals of four H-atoms by $(sp^3 - s)$ overlap and gives tetrahedral geometery.

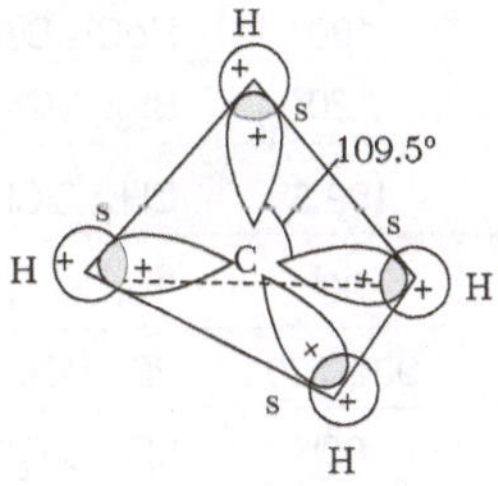

CH_4
(Tetrahedral, sp^3-hybridisation)

Note The size of different hybrid orbitals increases as : $sp < sp^2 < sp^3$.

4. Hybridisation of Elements Involving *d*-Orbitals

Elements of third period have d-orbitals also along with s and p-orbitals, which are also involved in hybridisation. This is because the energy of the $3d$-orbitals are comparable to the energy of the $3s$ and $3p$-orbitals.

The energy of $3d$-orbitals are also comparable to those of $4s$ and $4p$-orbitals, consequently the hybridisation involving either $3s, 3p$ and $3d$ or $3d, 4s$ and $4p$ is possible. Because of the more difference in the energies of $3p$ and $4s$-orbitals no hybridisation involving $3p, 3d$ and $4s$-orbitals is possible.

The most common examples involving hybridisation of d-orbitals are as follows:

1. Formation of PCl_5 (sp^3d-Hybridisation)

The ground state and the excited state electronic configurations of the central atom, i.e. phosphorus ($Z = 15$) are given below :

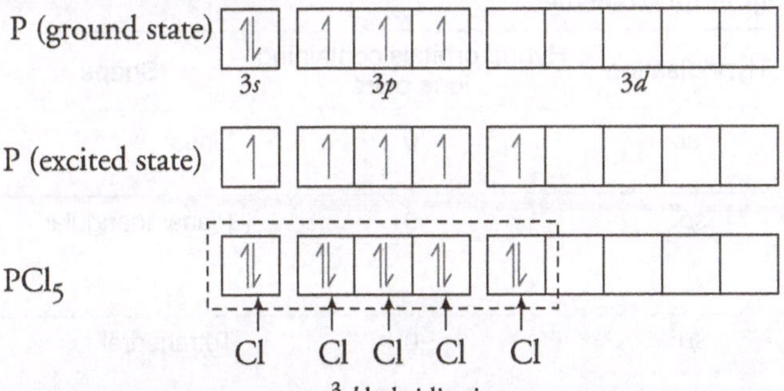

sp^3d-hybridisation

Thus, the five orbitals (i.e. one s, three p and one d-orbitals) undergo hybridisation and give a set of five sp^3d hybrid orbitals which are directed towards the five corners of a trigonal bipyramidal as shown in the figure.

In PCl_5, the five sp^3d orbitals of phosphorus overlap with the singly occupied p-orbitals of chlorine atoms to form five P—Cl σ-bonds out of which three P—Cl bonds lie in one plane at an angle of 120° with each other and are termed as **equatorial bond.**

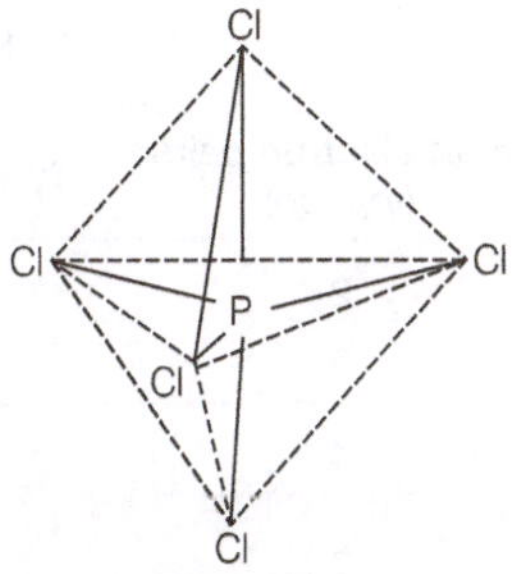

Trigonal bipyramidal geometry of PCl_5 molecule

Out of the remaining two P—Cl bonds, one lie above and the other lie below the equatorial plane, making an angle of 90° with the plane. These bonds are called **axial bonds.** It has been found that axial bond pair suffers greater repulsion than equatorial bond pairs and therefore, the axial bonds have been found to be slightly longer and hence, slightly weaker than the equatorial bonds. Thus PCl_5 molecule is more reactive than PCl_3 and hence, it readily split into PCl_3 and Cl_2.

$$PCl_5 \longrightarrow PCl_3 + Cl_2$$

2. Formation of SF_6 (sp^3d^2-Hybridisation)

In SF_6, sulphur is the central atom with outer electronic configuration $3s^2 3p^4$. In the exited state, the available six orbitals, i.e. $1s$, $3p$ and $2d$ are singly occupied by electrons and hybridise to form six new sp^3d^2 hybrid orbitals, that are projected towards the six corners of a regular octahedron in SF_6. These six sp^3d^2 hybrid orbitals overlap with singly occupied orbitals of fluorine atoms to form six S—F σ-bonds. Thus, SF_6 molecule has a regular octahedral geometry.

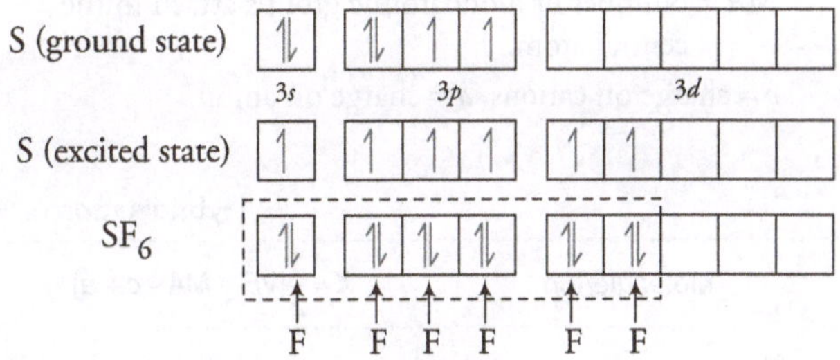

sp^3d^2-hybridisation

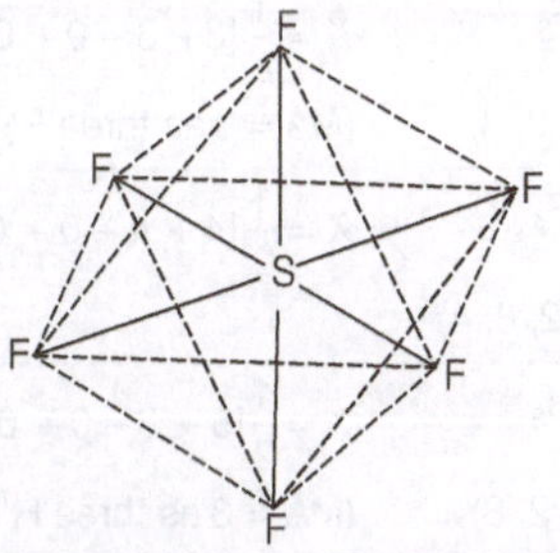

Octahedral geometry of SF_6 molecule

Hybrid Orbitals and Molecular Shapes of Molecules involving s, p and d-orbitals

No. of electron pairs (lp + bp)	Type of hybridisation	Atomic orbital	Shape	Bond angle	Examples
2	sp	$s + p$	Linear	180°	$HgCl_2$, $BeCl_2$, C_2H_2
3	sp^2	$s + 2(p)$	Trigonal planar	120°	BF_3, $AlCl_3$, C_2H_4, CO_3^{2-}, NO_3^-
4	sp^3	$s + 3(p)$	Tetrahedral	109.5°	CH_4, $SiCl_4$, NH_4^+, ClO_4^-
4	dsp^2	$d + s + 2(p)$	Square planar	90°	$[Ni(CN)_4]^{2-}$, $[PtCl_4]^{2-}$
5	sp^3d	$s + 3(p) + d$	Trigonal bipyramidal	90°, 120°	PF_5, PCl_5
6	sp^3d^2 or d^2sp^3 or sp^3d^2	$s + 3(p) + 2(d)$ or $2(d) + s + 3(p)$ or $s + 3(p) + 2(d)$	Octahedral Square pyramidal	90° 90°	SF_6, CrF_6^{3-} $[Co(NH_3)_6]^{3+}$ BrF_5
7	sp^3d^3 (d are d_{xy}, d_{yz}, d_{zx})	$s + 3(p) + 3(d)$	Pentagonal bipyramidal	90° 72°	IF_7

Method for Predicting the Hybridisation and Shapes of Molecules

Predicting Hybridisation

Follow the following steps to predict the hybridisation of a molecule.

Step 1 Find the value of X with the help of following formula

$$X = \frac{1}{2}[VE + MA - c + a]$$

X = No. of hybrid orbitals.

where, VE = Number of valence electrons present in central atom.

MA = Number of monoatomic groups attach to the central atom.

c = charge on cations, a = charge on anion.

Step 2 After knowing the value of X, predict the hybridisation with the help of following table :

Value of X	2	3	4	5	6	7
Type of hybridisation	sp	sp^2	sp^3	sp^3d	sp^3d^2	sp^3d^3

Predicting Shape

If number of hybrid orbitals are equal to the number of surrounding atoms/groups (monovalent or divalent etc.) the molecule/ion has a regular geometry and the shape is same as that predicted by hybridisation.

However, if number of surrounding atoms/groups is less than the number of hybrid orbitals, the difference gives the number of lone pairs present on the central atom and the species are said to have irregular geometry and the shape is predicted by leaving the hybrid orbitals containing the lone pairs.

Hybridisation of Some Important Molecules

	Molecule/Ion	$X = \frac{1}{2}[VE + MA - c + a]$	Hybridisation	Hybrid orbitals containing lone pairs	Shape
(i)	CO_2 ($_6C = 2, 4$)	$X = \frac{1}{2}[4 + 0 - 0 + 0] = 2$	sp	0	Linear
(ii)	BF_3 ($_5B = 2, 3$)	$X = \frac{1}{2}[3 + 3 - 0 + 0] = 3$ (MA = 3 as three F's are monovalent)	sp^2	0	Planar triangular
(iii)	SiF_4 ($_{14}Si = 2, 8, 4$)	$X = \frac{1}{2}[4 + 4 - 0 + 0] = 4$	sp^3	0	Tetrahedral
(iv)	NH_3 ($_7N = 2, 8$)	$X = \frac{1}{2}[5 + 3 - 0 + 0] = 4$ (MA = 3 as three H's are monovalent)	sp^3	1	Pyramidal

	Molecule/Ion	$X=\frac{1}{2}[VE+MA-c+a]$	Hybridisation	Hybrid orbitals containing lone pairs	Shape
(v)	IF_7	$X=\frac{1}{2}[7+7-0+0]=7$	sp^3d^3	0	Pentagonal bipyramidal
(vi)	H_2O ($_8O=2, 6$)	$X=\frac{1}{2}[6+2-0+0]=4$	sp^3	2	Bent (V-shaped)
(vii)	NH_4^+ ($_7N=2, 5$)	$X=\frac{1}{2}[5+4-1+0]=4$ ($c=1$ as charge on cation $=1$)	sp^3	0	Tetrahedral
(viii)	H_3O^+ ($_8O=2, 6$)	$X=\frac{1}{2}[6+3-1+0]=4$	sp^3	1	Pyramidal
(ix)	CH_3^+ (Carbocation)	$X=\frac{1}{2}[4+3-1+0]=3$	sp^2	0	Triangular planar
(x)	NO_3^- ($_7N=2, 5$)	$X=\frac{1}{2}[5+0-0+1]=3$ ($a=1$ as charge on anion $=1$)	sp^2	0	Triangular planar
(xi)	CO_3^{2-} ($_6C=2, 4$)	$X=\frac{1}{2}[4+0-0+2]=0$ ($a=2$ as charge on anion $=2$)	sp^2	0	Triangular planar
(xii)	SO_4^{2-} ($_{16}S=2, 8, 6$)	$X=\frac{1}{2}[6+0-0+2]=4$ (MA $=0$ as oxygen is divalent)	sp^3	0	Tetrahedral
(xiii)	ClO_4^- (Perchlorate ion)	$X=\frac{1}{2}[7+0-0+1]=4$	sp^3	0	Tetrahedral

Topic Practice 3

Short Answer Type Questions

1 Mark

1. Fill in the Blanks

(i) According to Pauling, the atomic orbitals combine to form new set of equivalent atomic orbitals known as ....

(ii) Diagonal hybridisation is the another name of ....

(iii) Shape of molecule having sp^3d^3-hybridisation is ......

2. Objective Type Questions

(i) The multiple of hydrogen atom is formed due to the overlapping of orbitals of two hydrogen atoms. Which of the following types of overlapping takes place in the formation of H_2 molecules?

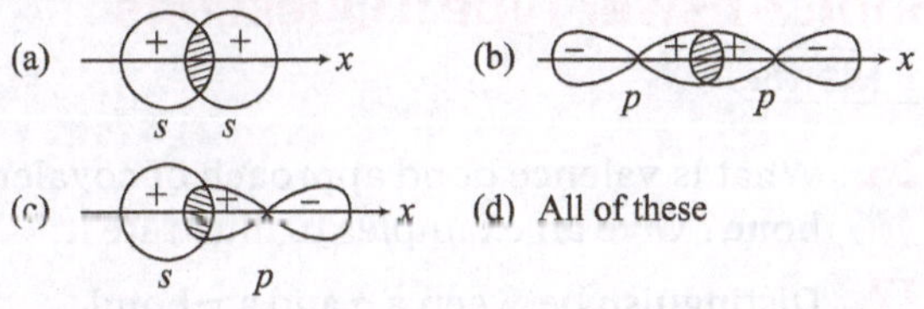

(ii) Which of the following does not represent positive overlap?

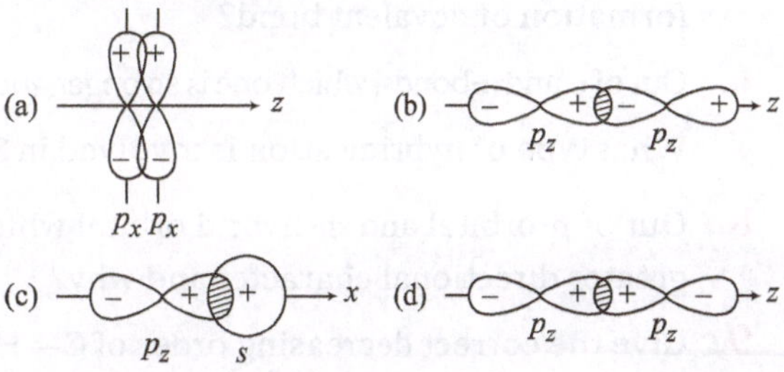

(iii) Which of the following species contains equal number of σ and π-bonds?

(a) HCO_3^-

(b) XeO_4

(c) $(CN)_2$

(d) $CH_2(CN)_2$

(iv) Which of the two ions from the list given below have the same hybridisation of orbitals, $NO_2^-, NO_3^-, NH_2^-, NH_4^+$?

(a) NO_2^- and NH_2^-

(b) NO_2^- and NO_3^-

(c) NH_4^+ and NO_3^-

(d) NO_2^- and NH_2^-

3. Match the species in Column I with the geometry/shape in Column II and choose the correct option using the codes given below.

Column I	Column II
A. H_3O^+	(i) Linear
B. $HC \equiv CH$	(ii) Angular
C. ClO_2^-	(iii) Tetrahedral
D. NH_4^+	(iv) Trigonal bipyramidal
	(v) Pyramidal

Codes

	A	B	C	D
(a)	(v)	(i)	(ii)	(iii)
(b)	(i)	(iii)	(v)	(iv)
(c)	(ii)	(i)	(ii)	(v)
(d)	(iv)	(ii)	(i)	(iii)

4. Why does the type of overlap given in the following figure not result in bond formation? **NCERT Exemplar**

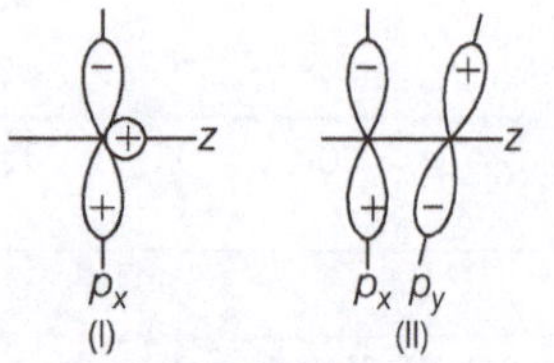

5. What is valence bond approach for the formation of covalent bond?

6. Out of σ and π-bonds, which one is stronger and why?

7. What type of hybridisation is involved in SF_6?

8. Out of *p*-orbital and *sp*-hybrid orbital which has greater directional character and why?

9. Give the correct decreasing order of C—H bond, lengths in the molecule C_2H_6, C_2H_4 and C_2H_2.

10. What type of hybridisation is present in C-atoms of C_{60} allotrope called fullerene?

11. BH_4^- and NH_4^+ are iso structural. Explain.

12. Why axial bonds of PCl_5 are longer than equatorial bonds?

Short Answer Type I Questions

(2 Marks)

13. What is the total number of σ and π-bonds in the following molecules? **NCERT Textbook**
(i) C_2H_2 (ii) C_2H_4

14. Explain how the strength of a bond is related to (i) extent of overlapping (ii) shape of the orbital.

15. What is the total number of sigma and pi bond in the following molecules?
(i) C_2H_3Cl (ii) $C_4H_4Cl_2$
(iii) $H_3C—C(H)=C(H)—C\equiv C—H$

16. Arrange the following in order of decreasing bond angles.
(i) CH_4, NH_3, H_2O, BF_3, C_2H_2
(ii) NH_3, NH_2^-, NH_4^+

17. Which of the species have similar shape and why? NO_2^-, NO_2^+, CO_2, O_3

18. Using valence bond theory, draw the molecular structures of OSF_4 and XeF_4 indicating the location of lone pairs(s) of electrons and hybridisation of central atoms.

19. Explain, why PCl_5 is trigonal bipyramidal, whereas IF_5 is square pyramidal?

20. Explain the shape of I_3^- ion.

21. Explain, why carbon has a valency of four and not two and why are the four C—H bonds in methane identical.

22. Draw diagram showing the formation of a double bond and a triple bond between the C-atoms in C_2H_4 and C_2H_2. **NCERT Textbook**

23. In both water and dimethyl ether $\left(CH_3—\ddot{\underset{\cdot\cdot}{O}}—CH_3\right)$, oxygen atom is central atom and has the same hybridisation, yet they have different bond angles. Which one has the greater bond angle? Give reason.

24. Describe the change in hybridisation (if any) of the Al-atom in the following reaction.
$$AlCl_3 + Cl^- \longrightarrow AlCl_4^-$$

25. Is there any change in the hybridisation of B and N-atoms as a result of the reaction?
$$BF_3 + NH_3 \longrightarrow F_3B \cdot NH_3$$

Short Answer Type II Questions

(3 Marks)

26. What is valence bond approach of covalent bond? Give an examples to illustrate it.

27. Distinguish between a σ and a π-bond.

28. Explain the following on the basis of valence bond theory.
(i) BF_3 is planar but NH_3 is not.
(ii) CCl_4 and $SiCl_4$ are tetrahedral.
(iii) The HSH bond angle is H_2S is closer to 90° than HOH bond angle in H_2O.

29. Predict the hybridisation of each carbon in the molecule of organic compound give below. Also indicate the total number of σ and π-bonds in this molecule. **NCERT Exemplar**

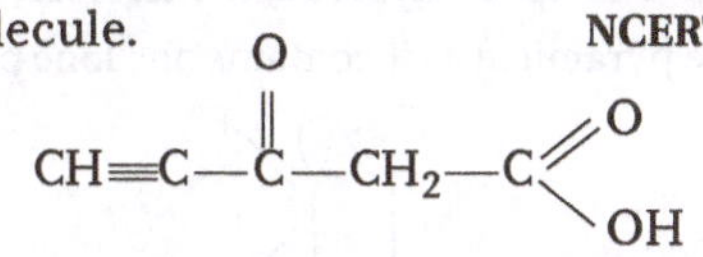

30. Apart from tetrahedral geometry, another possible geometry for CH_4 is square planar with the four H-atoms at the corners of the square and the C-atom at its centre. Explain, why CH_4 is not square planar? **NCERT Textbook**

31. Draw the shape of the following hybrid orbitals *sp*, sp^2 and sp^3.

32. Indicate the type of bonds present in NH_4NO_3 and state the mode of hybridisation of two N-atoms in it.

33. Discuss the hybridisation of Be in gaseous state and solid state.

Long answer Type Questions

5 Marks

34. Explain the formation of H_2 molecule on the basis of valence bond theory. **NCERT Textbook**

35. What is meant by hybridisation of atomic orbitals. Describe the shapes of *sp*, sp^2 and sp^3 hybrid orbitals. **NCERT Textbook**

36. Which hybrid orbitals are used by C-atoms in the following molecules?
(i) $CH_3—CH_3$ (ii) $CH_3CH{=}CH_2$
(iii) CH_3CH_2OH (iv) CH_3CHO
(v) CH_3COOH **NCERT Textbook**

37. (i) Discuss the concept of hybridisation. What are its different types in a C-atom?
(ii) What is the type of hybridisation of carbon atoms marked with star?

(a) 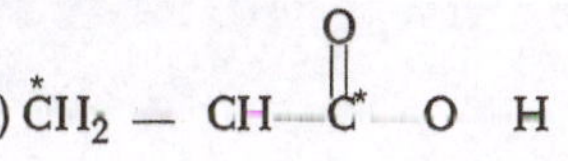

(b) $CH_3—\overset{*}{C}H_2—OH$

(c) $CH_3—CH_2—\overset{*}{C}(=O)—H$

(d) $\overset{*}{C}H_3—CH{=}CH—CH_3$

(e) $CH_3—\overset{*}{C}{\equiv}CH$ **NCERT Exemplar**

38. Describe hybridisation in the case of PCl_5 and SF_6. The axial bonds are longer as compared to equatorial bonds in PCl_5 whereas in SF_6 both axial bonds and equatorial bonds have the same bond length. Explain. **NCERT Exemplar**

Hints & Solutions

1. (i) hybrid orbitals (ii) *sp*-hybridisation (iii) pentagonal bipyramidal.

2. (i) → a, (ii) → d, (iii) → b, (iv) → b

3. (a) A → (v), B → (i), C → (ii), D → (iii)

4. In the figure I area of ++ overlap is equal to + − overlap, so net overlap is zero, while in the figure II there is no overlap due to different symmetry.

5. A covalent bond is formed by the overlap of half-filled atomic orbitals.

6. σ-bond is stronger. This is because σ-bond is formed by head-on overlapping of atomic orbitals and therefore, the overlapping is large. π-bond is formed by sideways overlapping which is small.

7. SF_6, S is the central atom with six valence electrons.

$$\therefore \text{Number of hybrid orbitals} = \frac{1}{2}[6+6-0+0] = 6$$

Hence, the hybridisation involved in sp^3d^2.

8. *sp*-orbital has greater directional character than *p*-orbital. This is because *p*-orbital has equal sized lobes, with equal electron density in both the lobes whereas *sp*-hybrid orbital has greater electron density on one side.

9. 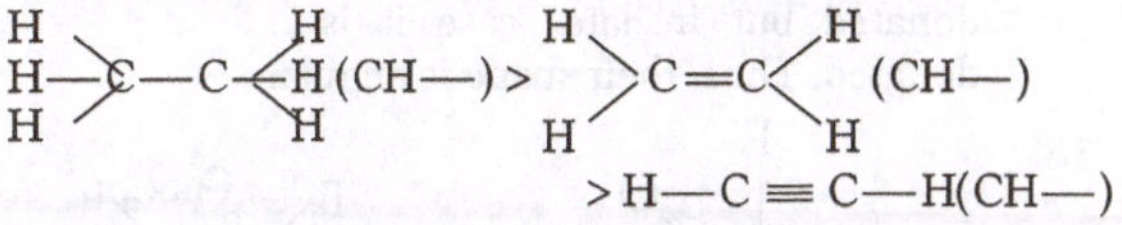

This is because hybrid orbitals of carbon involved in overlapping with 1s-orbital of hydrogen are sp^3, sp^2 and *sp* respectively and their sizes are in the order $sp^3 > sp^2 > sp$.

10. sp^2, each C-atom is linked to two other C-atoms.

11. Both have tetrahedral shape, i.e. four lobes of sp^3 hybridised orbitals so called iso structural.

12. This is due to greater repulsion on the axial bond pairs by the equatorial bond pairs of electrons.

13. (i) C_2H_2

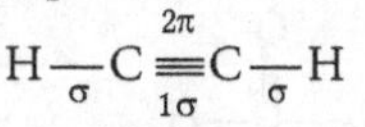

(3 σ and 2π) [1]

(ii) C_2H_4

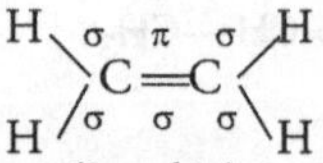

(5σ and 1π) [1]

14. Refer to test on pages 168 and 169 (Overlapping of atomic orbitals).

15. (i) is

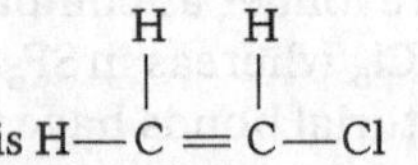

(5 σ-bonds, one π-bonds) [1/2]

(ii) is

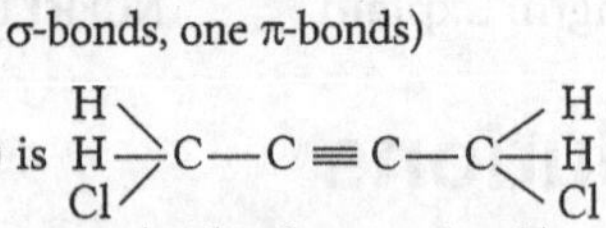

(9 σ-bonds, two π-bonds) [1/2]

(iii) is

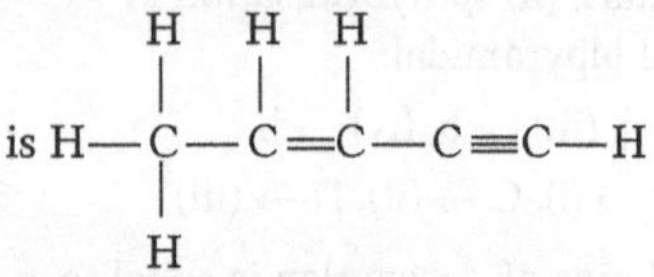

(10 σ-bonds, 3 π-bonds) [1]

16. (i) $C_2H_2(180°) > CH_4\ (109°28') > BF_3\ (120°) > NH_3(107)° > H_2O > (104.5°)$ [1]

(ii) $NH_4^+ > NH_3 > NH_2^-$

This is because all of them involve sp^3-hybridisation but have different lone pairs. The number of lone pair of electrons present on N-atom are 0, 1 and 2 respectively. Greater the number of lone pairs, greater is the repulsion and lesser is the bond angle. [1]

17. NO_2^+ and CO_2 are *sp* hybridised, therefore, they have linear shape.

$O{=}\overset{+}{N}{=}O$, $O{=}C{=}O$

Linear Linear [1]

NO_2^- and O_3 are sp^2-hybridised. Both have lone pair of electrons but in former case it is not donated but in later case it is donated. Thus, their shape is angular. [1]

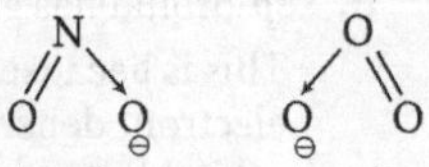

Angular Angular

18.

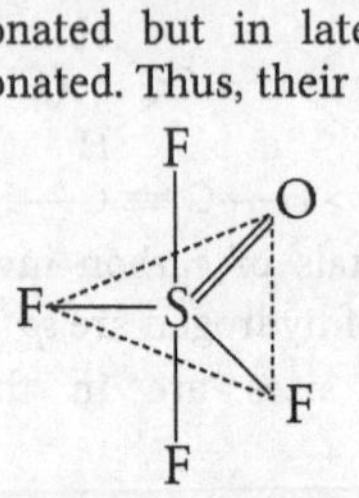

Trigonal bipyramidal (sp^3d-hybridisation)

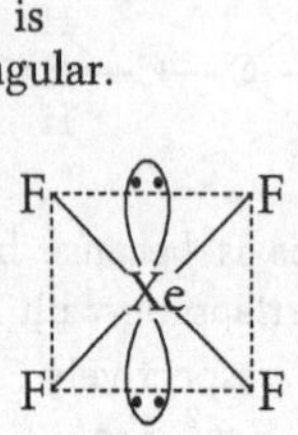

Square planar (sp^3d^2-hybridisation) [2]

19. PCl_5 Refer to text on page 171 (Formation of PCl_5)

IF_5 The ground state and the excited state outer electronic configurations of iodine ($Z = 53$) are represented below :

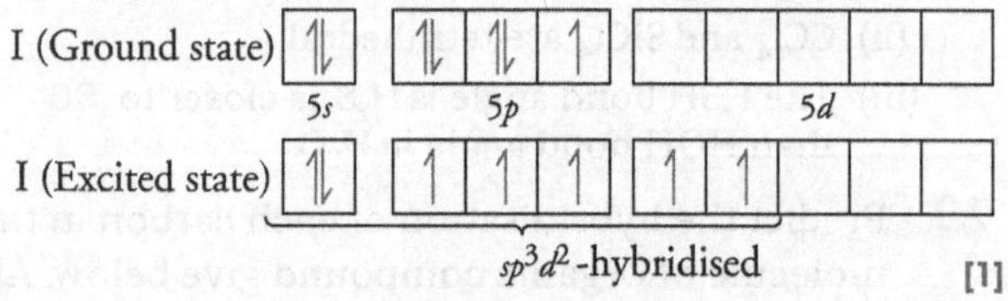

[1]

In IF_5, I is sp^3d^2-hybridised therefore, shape of IF_5 is square pyramidal as it contains one lone pair of electrons.

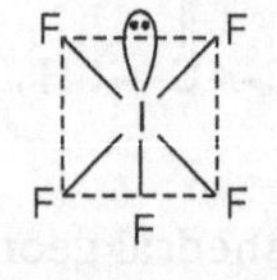

[1]

20. The central I-atom has the outer shell electronic configuration in the ground state as $5s^2 5p_x^2 5p_y^2 5p_z^1 5d^0$. It undergoes sp^3d hybridisation. Out of the five sp^3d hybrid orbitals, one is half-filled, one is empty and the remaining three are fully-filled. The half-filled orbital forms covalent bond with iodine atom. [1]

The empty orbital accepts electron pair from I^- ion to form a coordinate bond. The remaining three fully-filled orbitals occupy equatorial positions. Thus, the geometry of three lone pairs and two bond pairs is trigonal bipyramidal and the shape of I_3^- is linear as shown in the figure. [1]

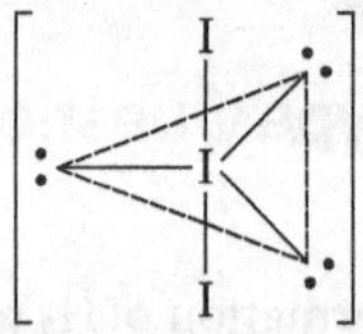

The triiodide ion

21. The ground state electronic configuration of carbon is $1s^2, 2s^2, 2p^2$. But carbon forms bond with other atoms in excited state. The electronic configuration in excited state $1s^2, 2s^1, 2p_x^1\ 2p_y^1, 2p_z^1$. [1]

The one *s*-orbital and three *p*-orbitals of the valence shell intermix to form four sp^3 hybrid obitals of equivalent energies and shape.

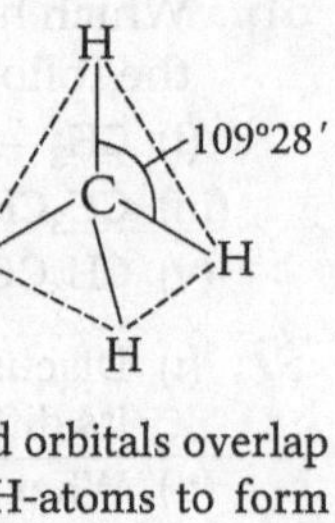

These hybrid orbitals are arranged tetrahedrally at an angle of 109° 28′ to each other. The four sp^3 hybrid orbitals overlap with the half-filled 1*s* orbitals of four H-atoms to form CH_4 as shown. [1]

22.

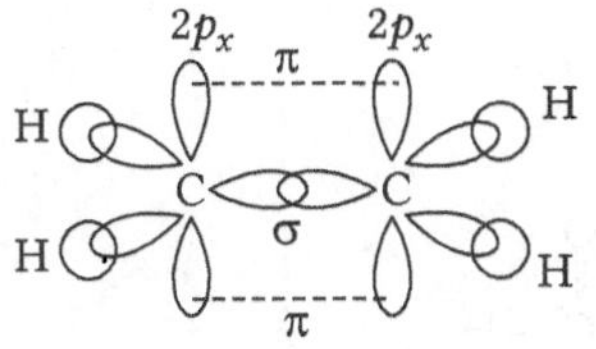

Formation of C_2H_4

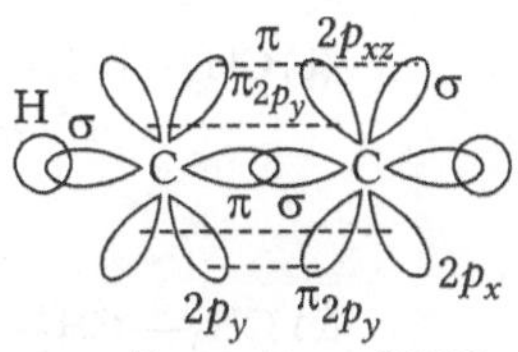

Formation of C_2H_2

[2]

23. Dimethyl ether has greater bond angle than that of water, however in both the molecules central atom oxygen is sp^3 hybridised with two lone pairs. In dimethyl ether, bond angle is greater (111.7°) due to the greater repulsive interaction between the two bulky alkyl (methyl) groups than that between two H-atoms.

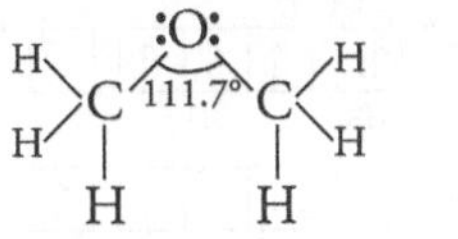

Dimethyl ether

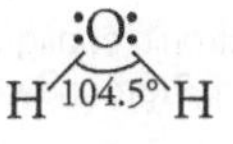

Water

Actually C of CH_3 group is attached to three H-atoms through σ-bonds. These three C—H bond pair of electrons increases the electronic charge density on C-atom.

24. Electronic configuration of Al

In ground state $_{13}Al = 1s^2, 2s^2, 2p^6, 3s^2, 3p_x^1$

In excited state $= 1s^2, 2s^2, 2p^6, 3s^1, 3p_x^1, 3p_y^1$

In the formation of $AlCl_3$, Al undergoes sp^2-hybridisation and it is trigonal planar in shape. While in the formation of $AlCl_4^-$, Al undergoes sp^3-hybridisation. It means empty $3p_z$-orbital also involved in hybridisation. Thus, the shape of $AlCl_4^-$ ion is tetrahedral. [2]

25. In BF_3, there are 3 bond pairs 0 lone pair, so boron is sp^2 hybridised and in NH_3, there are 3 bond pairs and 1 lone pair, so nitrogen is sp^3 hybridised. After the reaction hybridisation of boron changes to sp^3 but hybridisation of nitrogen remains the same because N shares its lone pair with electron deficient B. [2]

26. Refer to text on pages 167 and 168 (VBT postulates and structure of H_2 molecule).

27. Refer to pages 168 and 169, [Types of overlapping and nature of covalent bonds (σ and X bond)].

28. (i) In BF_3, B-atom undergoes sp^2-hybridisation. Hence, BF_3 is triangular planar. In NH_3, N-atom undergoes sp^3-hybridisation. Hence, NH_3 has pyramidal shape with one lone pair on N-atom. [1]

(ii) Both C in CCl_4 and Si and $SiCl_4$ undergo sp^3-hybridisation. Hence, they are tetrahedral. [1]

(iii) This is because of lower electronegativity of S as compared to O. [1]

29.

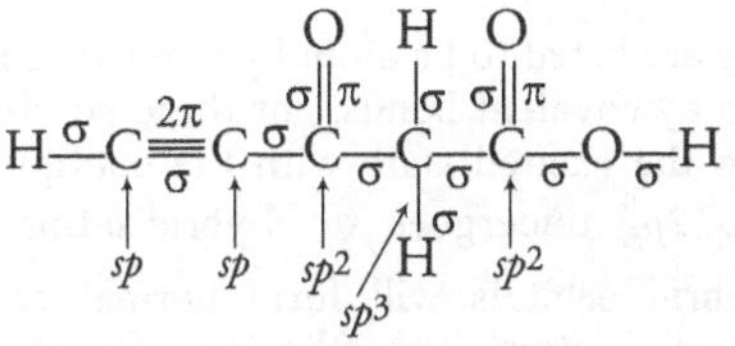

σ-bonds = 11

π-bonds = 4

[3]

30. Electronic configuration of carbon

In ground state $_6C = 1s^2, 2s^2, 2p_x^1, 2p_y^1$

In excited state $1s^2, \underbrace{2s^1, 2p_x^1, 2p_y^1, 2p_z^1}_{sp^3\text{-hybridised}}$ [1]

In CH_4 molecule, carbon is sp^3 hybridised, so it is tetrahedral in shape. For square planar, dsp^2 hybridisation is required which is not possible in carbon due to the absence of *d*-orbitals. Furthermore according to VSEPR theory, the four bonded electron pairs around C - atom arranged themselves in a regular tetrahedral geometry. For tetahedral structure, the bond angle is 109°,28′ while is square planar structure, the bond angle in 90°. Therefore, in tetrahedral structure repulsions between bonded electron pairs is less than that of the square planar. [1]

31.

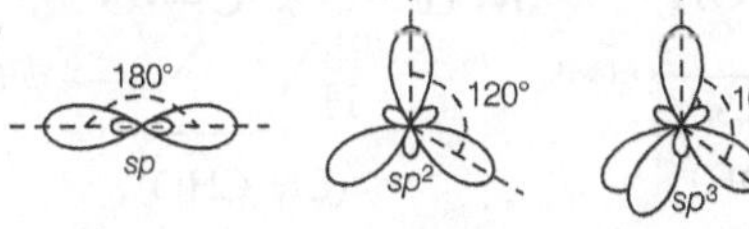

[1]

All the hybrid orbitals have same shape. However, their sizes are in the order : $sp < sp^2 < sp^3$.

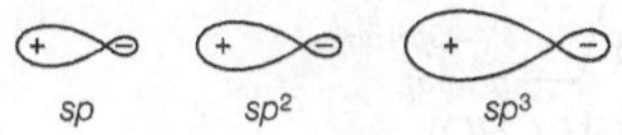

[2]

32.

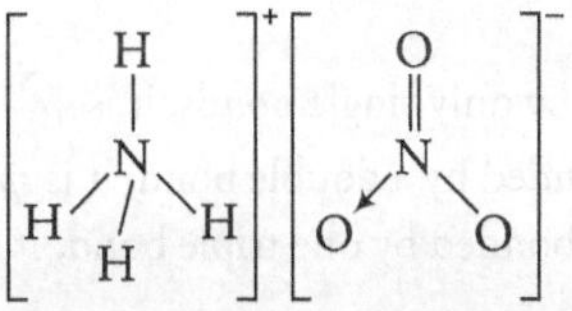

[1]

NH_4^+ ion contains covalent and dative bonds. (It is formed by donation of lone pair of electrons on N in NH_3 to H^+ ion). NO_3^- ion also contains covalent and dative bonds. Bond between NH_4^+ and NO_3^- ions is ionic.

N of NH_4^+ ion is sp^3 hybridised and is tetrahedral.

N of NO_3^- ion is sp^2 hybridised and is planar. [2]

33. In gaseous state at high temperature, $BeCl_2$ exists as linear molecule, Cl—Be—Cl, thus the hybridisation of the central atoms is *sp*.

Cl—Be —Cl

Structure of BeCl in gaseous state

[1]

In solid state, it has a polymeric stucture with chlorine bridges as follows :

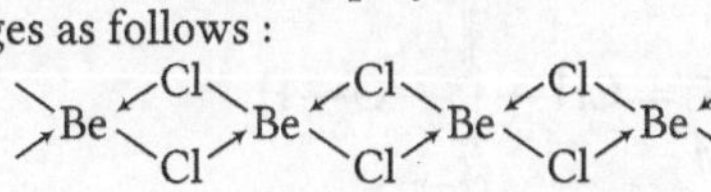

Two Cl-atoms are listed to be atom by two coordination bond and two by covalent bonds. For these bonds to be formed, Be in the excited state with the configuration $1s^2\ 2s^1\ 2p_x^1 2p_y^0 2p_z^0$ undergoes sp^3 hybridisation. Two half-filled hybrid orbitals will form normal covalent bonds with two Cl-atom. The other two Cl-atoms are coordinated to Be-atom by donating electron pairs into the empty hybrid orbtitals. [2]

34. Refer to text on pages 167 and 168 (VBT, Structure of H_2 molecule).

35. Refer to text on pages 169 and 170 (Hybridisation, Types of hybridisation)

36.

(i) 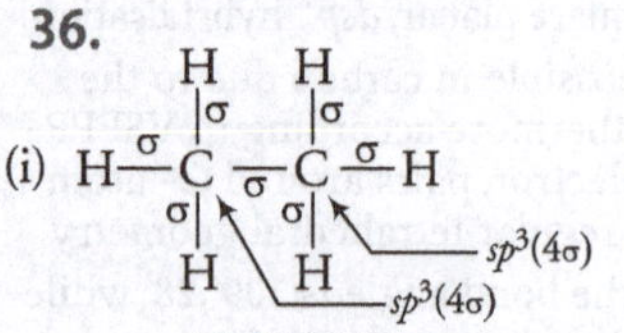

(C_2H_6) (4σ)

(ii) 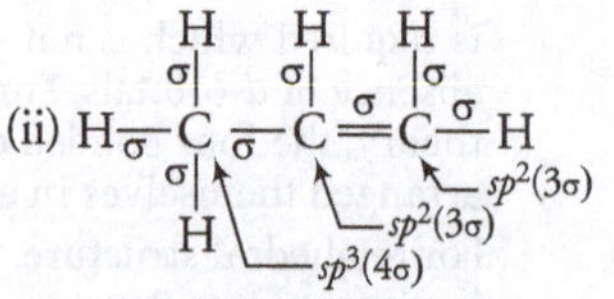

($CH_3CH{=}CH_2$)

(iii) 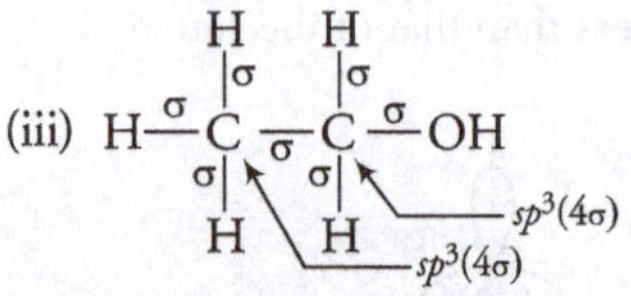

(CH_3CH_2OH)

(iv) 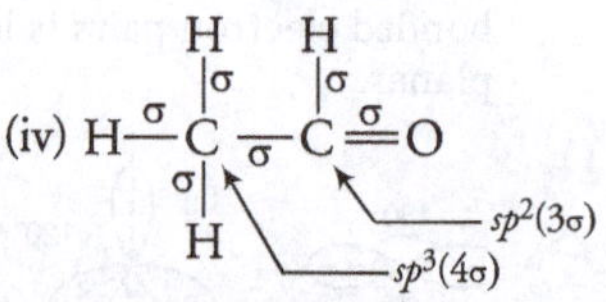

(CH_3CHO)

(v) 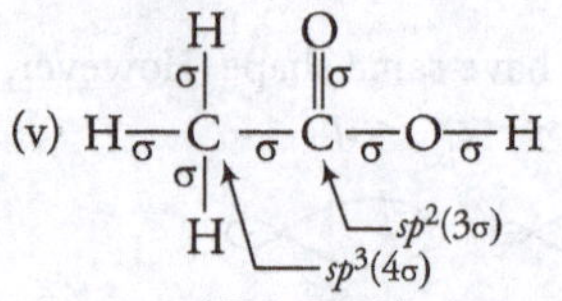

(CH_3CHO)

If a C-atom is bonded by only single bonds, it is sp^3 hybridised and if is bonded by a double bond, it is sp^2 hybridised and if it is bonded by one triple bond, it is sp hybridised. [5 × 1]

37. Hybridisation Refer to text on page 169 (Hybridisation)

Types of hybridisation in carbon atom.

(i) (a) **Digonal or sp-hybridisation** All compounds of carbon containing C≡C triple bond like ethyne (C_2H_2).

(b) **Trigonal or sp^2-hybridisation** All compounds of carbon containing C=C (double bond) like ethene (C_2H_4).

(c) **Tetrahedral or sp^3-hybridisation** All compounds of carbon containing C–C single bonds only like ethane (C_2H_6). [2]

(ii) (a) $\overset{*}{C}H_2{=}CH{-}\overset{*}{C}({=}O){-}O{-}H$ — sp^2 (3σ), sp^2 (3σ)

(b) $CH_3{-}\overset{*}{C}H_2{-}OH$ — sp^3 (4σ)

(c) $CH_3{-}CH_2{-}\overset{*}{C}({=}O){-}H$ — sp^2 (3σ)

(d) $\overset{*}{C}H_3{-}CH{=}CH{-}CH_3$ — sp^3 (4σ)

(e) $CH_3{-}\overset{*}{C}{\equiv}CH$ — sp (2σ) [3]

38. Formation of PCl_5

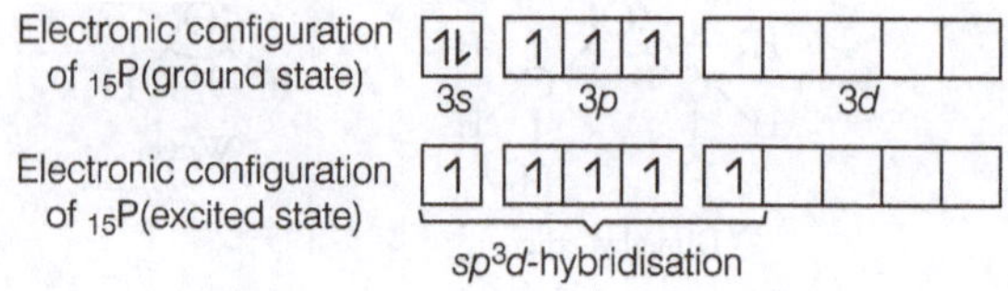

In PCl_5, phosphorus is sp^3d-hybridised to produce a set of five sp^3d hybrid orbitals which are directed towards the five corners of a trigonal bipyramidal. These five sp^3d hybrid orbitals overlap with singly occupied p-orbitals of Cl-atoms to form five P–Cl σ-bonds.

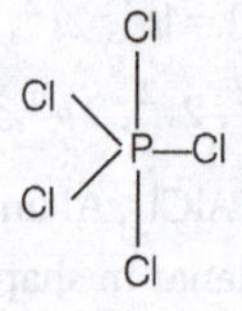

(Trigonal bipyramidal)
PCl_5

Three P–Cl bonds lie in one plane and make an angle of 120° with each other. These bonds are called equatorial bonds. The remaining two P–Cl bonds one lying above and other lying below, the plane make an angle of 90° with the equatorial plane.

These bonds are called axial bonds. Axial bonds are slightly longer than equatorial bonds because axial bond pairs suffer more repulsive interaction from the equatorial bond pairs. [3]

Formation of SF_6

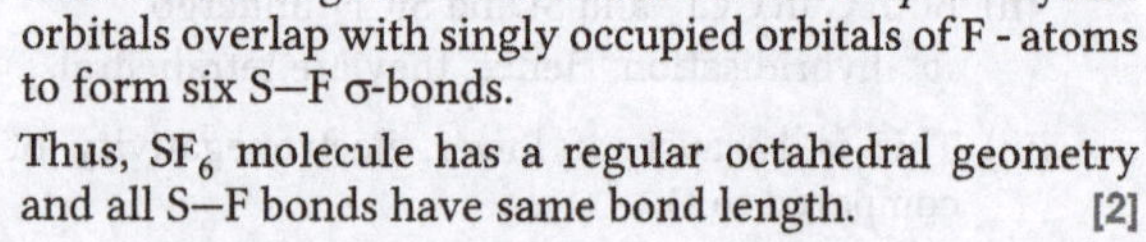

In SF_6, sulphur is sp^3d^2 hybridised to produce a set of six sp^3d^2 hybrid orbitals which are directed towards the six corners of a regular octahedron. These six sp^3d^2 hybrid orbitals overlap with singly occupied orbitals of F - atoms to form six S–F σ-bonds.

Thus, SF_6 molecule has a regular octahedral geometry and all S–F bonds have same bond length. [2]

TOPIC 04

Molecular Orbital Theory and Hydrogen Bonding

Molecular Orbital Theory (MOT)

This theory was given by **F Hund** and **R S Mulliken** in 1932, in order to explain the characteristics of molecules like their relative bond strengths, magnetic nature etc.

Salient Features of MOT

The main features of this theory are as follows:

(i) The electrons in a molecule occupy various molecular orbitals just like the electrons of atoms are present in various atomic orbitals.

(ii) Molecular orbitals are obtained when atomic orbitals of comparable energies and proper symmetry combine together.

(iii) In an atomic orbital an electron is under the influence of one nucleus, while in a molecular orbital it is under the influence of two or more nuclei depending upon the number of atoms in the molecule. Thus, an atomic orbital is called **monocentric**, while a molecular orbital is termed as **polycentric.**

(iv) The number of molecular orbitals obtained is always equal to the number of combining atomic orbitals. When two atomic orbitals combine, two types of molecular orbitals are obtained. One is known as **bonding molecular orbital,** while the other is known as **antibonding molecular orbital.**

(v) The bonding molecular orbital because of their lower energy have greater stability than the corresponding antibonding molecular orbital.

(vi) A molecular orbital shows the electron probability distribution around a group of nuclei in a molecule.

(vii) Just like atomic orbitals, the molecular orbitals are filled in accordance with the Aufbau principle obeying the Pauli's exclusion principle and the Hund's rule.

Formation of Molecular Orbitals : Linear Combination of Atomic Orbitals (LCAO)

According to this method, the molecular orbitals are formed by the linear combination of atomic orbitals that can take place by addition and by subtraction of wave functions of individual atomic orbitals.

Consider there are two hydrogen atoms A and B in a hydrogen molecule, each of which in its ground state contains one electron in $1s$-orbital. The atomic orbitals of these atoms may be represented by the wave functions ψ_A and ψ_B respectively.

Then, these atomic orbitals combine by the addition and subtraction of wave functions of individual atomic orbitals as shown below.

$$\psi_{MO} = \psi_A \pm \psi_B$$

Therefore, the two molecular orbitals σ and σ^* are formed as $\sigma = \psi_A + \psi_B$; $\overset{*}{\sigma} = \psi_A - \psi_B$

Bonding Molecular Orbitals

The molecular orbitals obtained by the addition of atomic orbitals are called **bonding molecular orbitals** (BMOs) and are represented by σ and π. In the formation of these orbitals, the two electron waves of the bonding atoms reinforce each other due to constructive interference. In these orbitals, the electron density is located between the nuclei of the bonded atoms because of which the repulsion between the nuclei is very less.

Electrons present in a bonding molecular orbital tend to hold the nuclei together and stabilise a molecule. Therefore, a bonding molecular orbital always possesses lower energy than either of the atomic orbitals that have joined to form it.

Antibonding Molecular Orbitals

The molecular orbitals obtained by the subtraction of atomic orbitals are called **antibonding molecular orbitals** (AMOs) and are represented by $\overset{*}{\sigma}$ and $\overset{*}{\pi}$. In the formation of AMOs, the electron waves cancel each other due to destructive interference.

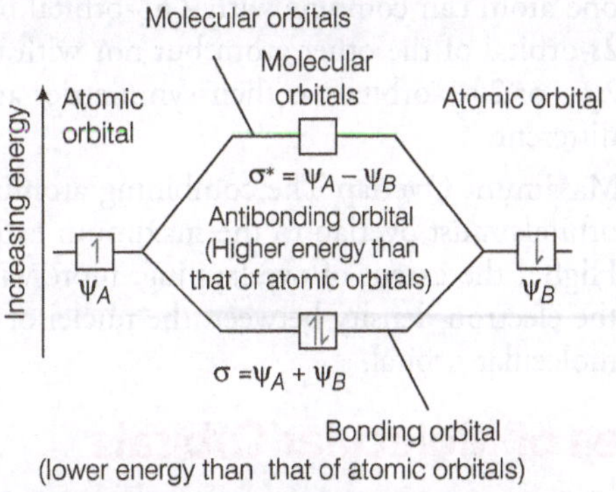

Formation of bonding (σ) and antibonding (σ^*) molecular orbitals

In these orbitals, most of the electron density is located away from the space in between the nuclei.

Infact, they have a nodal plane (in which the electron density is zero) in between the nuclei and hence, the repulsion between the nuclei is high.

In contrast to the bonding molecular orbitals, the electrons placed in these orbitals destabilise the molecule because of more mutual repulsion of the electrons in this orbital as compared to the attraction between the electrons and the nuclei, which cause a net increase in energy.

Note The energy of the antibonding orbitals is more than the energy of combined atomic orbitals, whereas the energy of the bonding orbitals is lower than the parent orbitals. However, the total energy of two molecular orbitals remain same as that of two original atomic orbitals.

Conditions for the Combination of Atomic Orbitals

The linear combination of atomic orbitals to form molecular orbitals is possible only when they satisfy the following conditions.

(i) **Similar Energy of Combining Atomic Orbitals** The combining atomic orbitals must possess the same or nearly the same energy. It means that 1*s*-orbital can combine with another 1*s*-orbital but not with 2*s*-orbital because the energy of 2*s*-orbital is appreciably higher than that of 1*s*-orbital. However, it is not true in case of very different atoms.

(ii) **Similar Symmetry of Combining Atomic Orbitals** The combining atomic orbitals must possess the same symmetry about the molecular axis along with the same energy. If the orbitals have same energy but their symmetry is not same, they will not combine. e.g. $2p_z$-orbital of one atom can combine with $2p_z$-orbital or 2*s*-orbital of the other atom but not with the $2p_x$ or $2p_y$-orbitals as their symmetries are different.

(iii) **Maximum Overlap** The combining atomic orbitals must overlap to the maximum extent. Higher the extent of overlapping, more will be the electron-density between the nuclei of a molecular orbital.

Types of Molecular Orbitals

In case of diatomic molecules, molecular orbitals are designated as σ (sigma), π (pi), δ (delta) etc. If the molecular orbital is symmetrical about the internuclear axis (or bond axis) it is called **σ-molecular orbital** and if it is not symmetrical about the internuclear axis, it is called a π **molecular orbital.**

Representing the orbitals in terms of signs of the wave function, as *s*-orbitals are spherically symmetrical, the sign of their wave function is same in all the directions.

In case of *p*-orbitals, one lobe has '+' sign and the other '–' sign. Overlapping of '+' part of the electron cloud of one atom with '+' part of the electron cloud of the second atom shows addition of atomic orbitals and lead to the formation of the bonding molecular orbital.

The overlap of '+' part of the electron cloud of one atom with '–' part of the electron cloud of the second atom shows the subtraction of the atomic orbitals and lead to the formation of anti-bonding molecular orbital. A few simple cases of the combination of atomic orbitals are shown below:

(i) **Combination of *s* Atomic Orbitals** The linear combination of 1*s*-orbitals centered on two nuclei gives two molecular orbitals that are symmetrical around the bond-axis. Such molecular orbitals are of the σ type and are designated as σ 1*s* and $\overset{*}{\sigma}$ 1*s*.

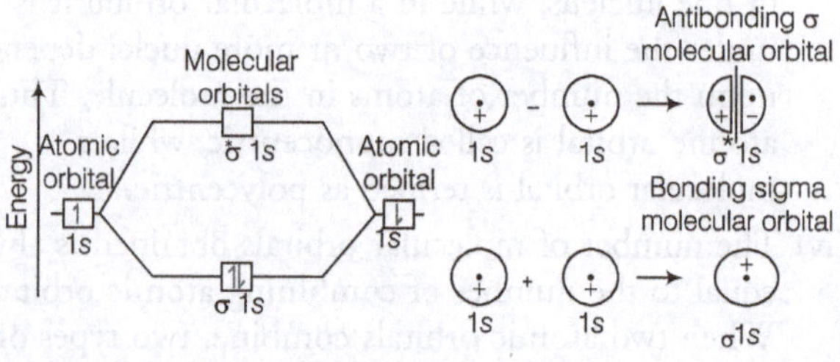

Similarly, 2*s* atomic orbitals combine to give σ 2*s* and $\overset{*}{\sigma}$ 2*s*-orbitals.

(ii) **Combination of 2 *p*-Atomic Orbitals** The three *p*-orbitals namely $2p_x, 2p_y$ and $2p_z$ are directed in space along the *x*, *y* and *z* coordinate axes respectively. If *Z*-axis is the internuclear axis, the *X* and *Y*-axis would then be perpendicular to it. The combination of 2 *p*-orbitals results in two types of MOs, *viz.*, sigma (σ) MOs and pi (π) MOs.

- **Formation of σ-Molecular Orbitals** It is the result of head on overlapping of two $2p_z$ orbitals, along the internuclear axis. Thus, two $2p_z$ atomic orbitals combine to give two molecular orbitals, i.e. a bonding MO ($\sigma 2p_z$) and antibonding MO ($\overset{*}{\sigma} 2p_z$).
- **Formation of π-Molecular Orbitals** These are obtained by sidewise overlap of $2p_x$ or $2p_y$ orbitals which are not symmetrical around the bond axis because of the presence of positive lobes above and negative lobes below the molecular plane. The molecular orbitals obtained are designated π and π*. A π-bonding MO has larger electron density above and below the internuclear axis. The π*-antibonding MO has a node in between the nuclei.

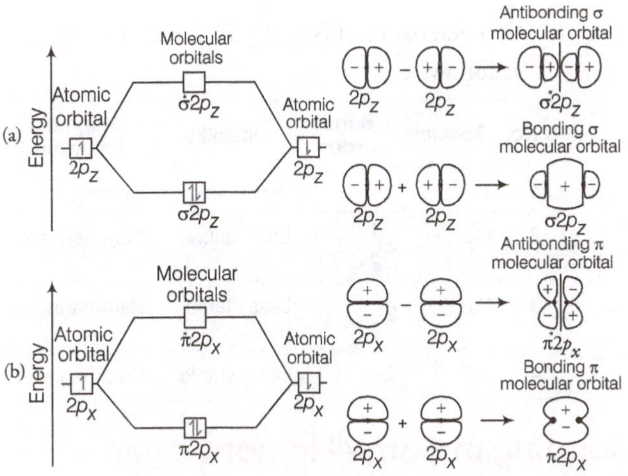

Contours and energies of bonding and antibonding molecular orbitals formed through combinations of atomic orbitals

Note $\pi 2p_x$ or $\pi 2p_y$ contains one nodal plane, whereas $\overset{*}{\pi}2p_x$ or $\overset{*}{\pi}2p_y$ contains two nodal planes.

Example 1 Label the molecular orbitals formed by the following combinations of atomic orbitals (assume Z-axis as internuclear axis).

(*i*) $2s + 2s$ (*ii*) $2p_x - 2p_x$ (*iii*) $2p_z + 2p_z$

(*iv*) $2p_y + 2p_y$

Sol. The MOs formed are

(i) $2s + 2s = \sigma 2s$ and $\overset{*}{\sigma}2s$ (ii) $2p_x - 2p_x = \pi 2p_x$ and $\overset{*}{\pi}2p_x$

(iii) $2p_z + 2p_z = \sigma 2p_z$ and $\overset{*}{\sigma}2p_z$

(*v*) $2p_y + 2p_y = \pi 2p_y$ and $\overset{*}{\pi}2p_y$

Energy Level Diagram for Molecular Orbitals

You have studied that 1*s* atomic orbitals form two molecular orbitals designated as σ 1*s* and $\overset{*}{\sigma}$ 1*s*. Similarly, 2*s* and 2*p* atomic orbitals (eight atomic orbitals of two atoms) combine to give following eight molecular orbitals.

Antibonding MOs $\overset{*}{\sigma}2s$ $\overset{*}{\sigma}2p_z$ $\overset{*}{\pi}2p_x$ $\overset{*}{\pi}2p_y$

Bonding MOs $\sigma 2s$ $\sigma 2p_z$ $\pi 2p_x$ $\pi 2p_y$

The energy levels of these orbitals have been determined experimentally from spectroscopic data for homonuclear diatomic molecules of second row elements of the periodic table. In the case of O_2 and F_2, the increasing order of energies of various molecular orbitals follow the order

$$\sigma 1s < \overset{*}{\sigma}1s < \sigma 2s < \overset{*}{\sigma}2s < \sigma 2p_z < (\pi 2p_x \approx \pi 2p_y) < (\overset{*}{\pi}2p_x \approx \overset{*}{\pi}2p_y) < \overset{*}{\sigma}2p_z$$

However, the above sequence of energy levels is not true in case of remaining molecules like Li_2, Be_2, B_2, C_2, N_2.

For these molecules the increasing order of energies of various molecular orbitals is:

$$\sigma 1s < \overset{*}{\sigma}1s < \sigma 2s < \overset{*}{\sigma}2s < \pi 2p_x \approx \pi 2p_y < \sigma 2p_z < \overset{*}{\pi}2p_x \approx \overset{*}{\pi}2p_y < \overset{*}{\sigma}2p_z$$

The important characteristic feature of this order is that the energy of $\sigma 2p_z$ molecular orbital is higher than that of $\pi 2p_x$ and $\pi 2p_y$ molecular orbitals.

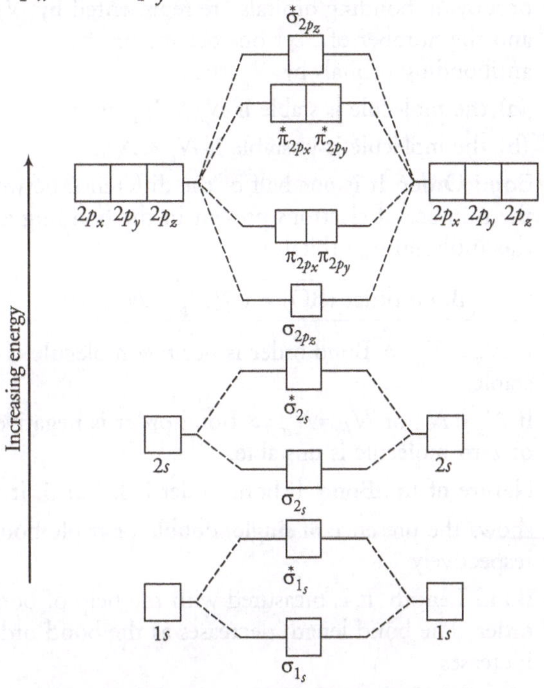

Molecular orbital energy level diagram for O_2, and F_2

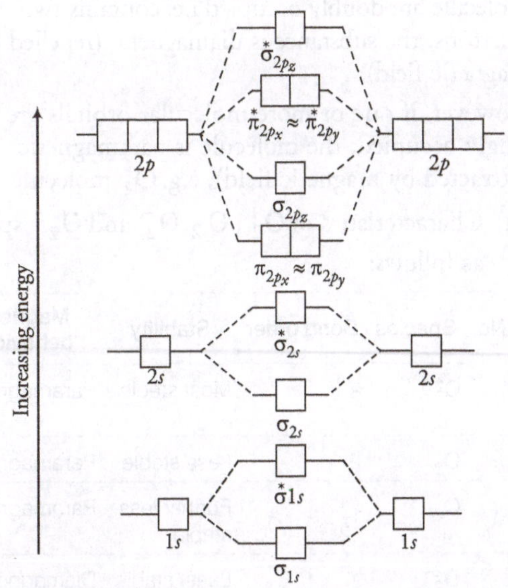

Molecular orbital energy level diagram for Li_2, Be_2, B_2, C_2 and N_2 molecules

Electronic Configuration and Molecular Behaviour

The distribution of electrons in various molecular orbitals is called **the electronic configuration of the molecule.** Electronic configuration gives the following information:

(i) **Stability of Molecules** If the number of electrons occupying bonding orbitals are represented by N_b and the number of electrons occupying the antibonding orbitals by N_a then

(a) the molecule is stable if $N_b > N_a$ and

(b) the molecule is unstable if $N_b < N_a$.

(ii) **Bond Order** It is one half of the difference between the number of electrons present in the bonding and the antibonding orbitals i.e.

$$\boxed{\text{Bond order (BO)} = 1/2(N_b - N_a)}$$

If $N_b > N_a \Rightarrow$ Bond order is positive molecule is stable.

If $N_b < N_a$ or $N_b = N_a \Rightarrow$ Bond order is negative or zero molecule is unstable.

(iii) **Nature of the Bond** If bond order is 1, 2 or 3, it shows the presence of single, double or triple bonds respectively.

(iv) **Bond Length** It is measured with the help of bond order. The bond length decreases as the bond order increases.

(v) **Magnetic Nature** If all the molecular orbitals in a molecule are doubly occupied i.e. contains two electrons, the substance is diamagnetic (repelled by magnetic field).

However, if one or more molecular orbitals are singly occupied, the molecule is paramagnetic (attracted by magnetic field), e.g. O_2 molecule.

(a) Characteristics of O_2^+, O_2, O_2^- and O_2^{2-} species as follows:

S.No.	Species	Bond order	Stability	Magnetic behaviour
1.	O_2^+	$2\frac{1}{2}$	Most stable	Paramagnetic
2.	O_2	2	Less stable	Paramagnetic
3.	O_2^-	$1\frac{1}{2}$	Further less stable	Paramagnetic
4.	O_2^{2-}	1	Least stable	Diamagnetic

Stability order : $O_2^+ > O_2 > O_2^- > O_2^{2-}$

(b) Characteristics of N_2, N_2^+, N_2^- and N_2^{2-} species as follows :

S.No.	Species	Bond order	Stability	Magnetic behaviour
1.	N_2	3	Very stable	Diamagnetic
2.	N_2^+	$2\frac{1}{2}$	Less stable	Paramagnetic
3.	N_2^-	$2\frac{1}{2}$	Less stable	Paramagnetic
4.	N_2^{2-}	2	Least stable	Paramagnetic

Bonding in Some Homonuclear Diatomic Molecules

Here the term homonuclear means that there is only one type of nucleus, i.e. one element is present and diatomic means that the molecule is composed of two atoms.

Example of some such molecules are given below :

1. Hydrogen Molecule (H_2)

It is formed when two hydrogen atoms combine together.

Number of electrons in one H-atom = 1

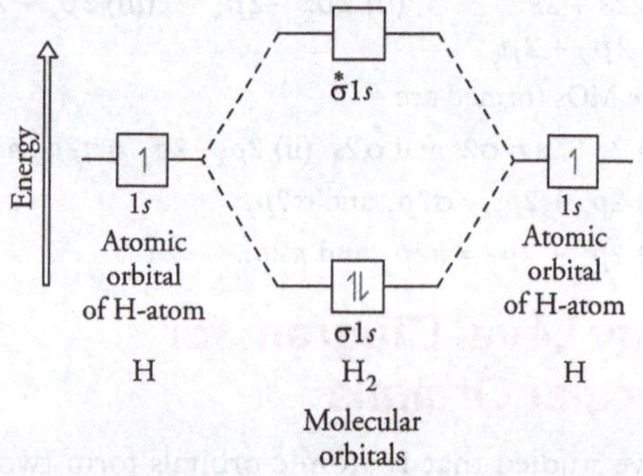

Molecular orbital energy level diagram for H_2 molecule

$\therefore$ Number of electrons in H_2 molecule = 1 + 1 = 2.

MO configuration of $H_2 = \sigma\, 1s^2$

Here, $N_b = 2$

and $N_a = 0$

$\therefore$ Bond order $= \frac{N_b - N_a}{2} = \frac{2-0}{2} = 1$

Bond order = 1 means that the two hydrogen atoms are bonded together by a single covalent bond. The bond dissociation energy of hydrogen molecule has been found to be 438 kJ mol^{-1} and bond length equal to 74 pm.

Since, there is no unpaired electron in the hydrogen molecule, so it is diamagnetic.

2. Hydrogen Molecular Positive ion (H_2^+)

It is the simplest molecular species containing one electron only. Thus, the MO configuration of H_2^+ $= \sigma\, 1s^1$

Here, $N_b = 1, N_a = 0$

$\therefore$ Bond order $= \dfrac{(N_b - N_a)}{2} = \dfrac{1}{2}(1-0) = \dfrac{1}{2}$

The bond order is positive. Hence, H_2^+ ion should be stable. Since, one unpaired electron is present, hence, H_2^+ ion should be paramagnetic. In terms of energy level diagram, it may be represented as:

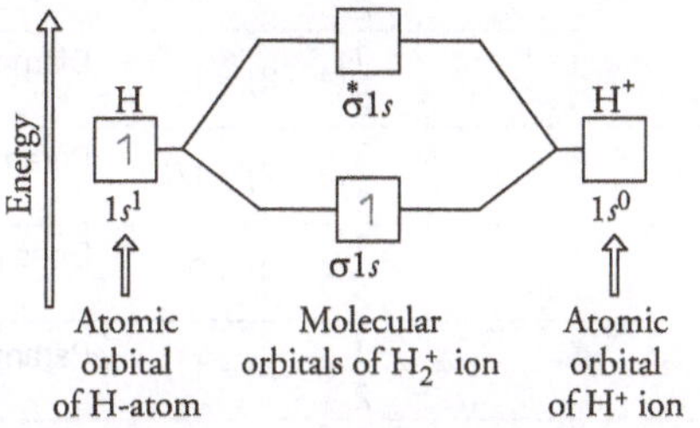

Molecular orbital energy level diagram for H_2^+ ion

3. Hydrogen Molecular Negative Ion (H_2^-)

Number of electrons in H_2 molecule $= 1 + 1 = 2$

$\therefore$ Number of electrons in H_2^- ion $= 2 + 1 = 3$

[Negative charge means addition of electron]

The electronic configuration of H_2^- ion is $\sigma\, 1s^2\, \overset{*}{\sigma}\, 1s^1$.

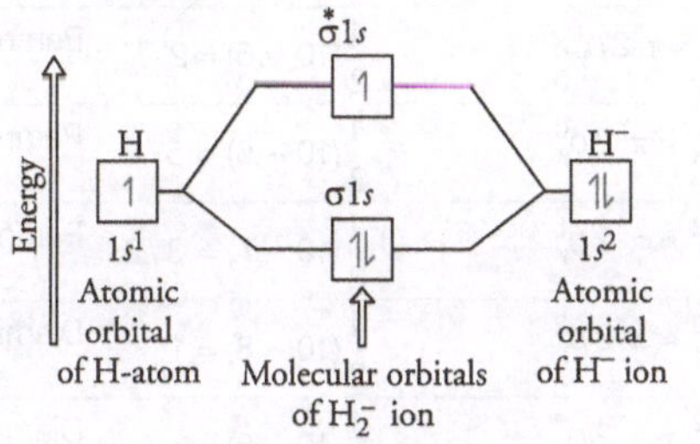

Molecular orbital energy level diagram for H_2^- molecule

$$\text{Bond order} = \frac{(N_b - N_a)}{2} = \frac{1}{2}(2-1) = \frac{1}{2}$$

Smaller positive value of bond order indicates that it is somewhat stable. Since, it has one electron in $\overset{*}{\sigma}$ (1s) orbital, it is paramagnetic.

Note H_2^+ and H_2^- have the same bond order, i.e. $\frac{1}{2}$, yet H_2^- is slightly less stable than H_2^+. This is because H_2^- contains one electron in the antibonding orbital which results in repulsion and decreases the stability. On the other hand H_2^+ does not contain any electron in the antibonding molecular orbital.

4. Oxygen Molecule (O_2)

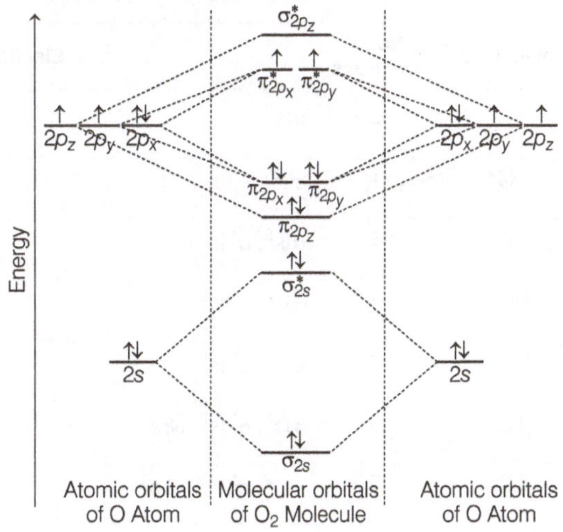

Molecular orbital diagram of O_2 molecule

Oxygen molecule (O_2) is formed by the combination of two oxygen atoms. The configuration of each 'O' atom is $1s^2 2s^2 2p_x^2 2p_y^1 2p_z^1$ so, each atom has eight electrons. So, the O_2 molecule has a total of 16 electrons, out of which four electrons of K shell are non-bonding. Thus, O_2 molecule possesses a total of 12 bonding electrons.

Configuration of O_2 molecule

$$\Rightarrow (\sigma 1s)^2 (\sigma^* 1s)^2 (\sigma 2s)^2 (\sigma^* 2s)^2 (\sigma 2p_z^2)\, \pi 2p_x^2 = (\pi 2p_y^2)$$
$$(\pi^* 2p_x{}^1 = \sigma^* 2p_y)^1$$

When two oxygen atoms combine together, their atomic orbitals overlap together to form four bonding and four antibonding molecular orbitals. It is to be noted that in O_2 molecule, the $\sigma 2p_z$ orbital lies below $\pi 2p_x$ and $\pi 2p_y$ orbitals.

Oxygen molecule thus contains 8 e^-s in bonding and 4 in antibonding molecular orbitals, i.e $N_b = 8$ and $N_a = 4$

Hence, bond order $= \dfrac{N_b - N_a}{2} = \dfrac{8-4}{2} = 2$

Magnetic Nature of O_2 Molecule

From MO diagram of O_2, it is clear that Aufbau's order of filling of molecular orbitals leave two unpaired electrons, one each in $\pi^* 2p_x$ and $\pi^* 2p_y$ molecular orbitals.

Thus, O_2 molecule possesses two unpaired electrons even in the ground state, these unpaired electrons impart paramagnetic character to oxygen molecule. So, O_2 molecule is paramagnetic in nature.

The electronic configuration of some diatomic molecules are given in the following table.

Bond Order and Magnetic Property of Some Homonuclear and Heteronuclear Molecules and their Ions

S. No.	Molecule/Ion	No. of electrons	Electronic configuration	Bond order $1/2(N_b - N_a)$	Magnetic property
1.	H_2	2	$\sigma 1s^2$	$\frac{1}{2}(2-0)=1$	Diamagnetic
2.	H_2^+	1	$\sigma 2s^1$	$\frac{1}{2}(1-0)=1/2$	Paramagnetic
3.	H_2^-	3	$\sigma 1s^2, \sigma^* 1s^1$	$\frac{1}{2}(2-1)=1/2$	Paramagnetic
4.	He_2	4	$\sigma 1s^2, \sigma^* 1s^2$	$\frac{1}{2}(2-2)=0$	Does not exist
5.	He_2^+	3	$\sigma 1s^2, \sigma^* 1s^1$	$\frac{1}{2}(2-1)=1/2$	Paramagnetic
6.	Li_2	6	$\sigma 1s^2, \sigma^* 1s^2, \sigma 2s^2$	$\frac{1}{2}(4-2)=1$	Diamagnetic
7.	Li_2^+	5	$\sigma 1s^2, \sigma^* 1s^2, \sigma 2s^1$	$\frac{1}{2}(3-2)=1/2$	Paramagnetic
8.	Be_2	8	$\sigma 1s^2, \sigma^* 1s^2, \sigma 2s^2, \sigma^* 2s^2$	$\frac{1}{2}(4-4)=0$	Does not exist
9.	B_2	10	$\sigma 1s^2, \sigma^* 1s^2, \sigma 2s^2, \sigma^* 2s^2, \pi 2p_x^1 \approx \pi 2p_y^1$	$\frac{1}{2}(6-4)=1$	Paramagnetic
10.	C_2	12	$\sigma 1s^2, \sigma^* 1s^2\ \sigma 2s^2, \sigma^* 2s^2, \pi 2p_x^2 \approx \pi 2p_y^2$	$\frac{1}{2}(8-4)=2$	Diamagnetic
11.	C_2^+	11	$\sigma 1s^2, \sigma^* 1s^2, \sigma 2s^2, \sigma^* 2s^2, \pi 2p_x^2 \approx \pi 2p_y^1$	$\frac{1}{2}(7-4)=3/2$	Paramagnetic
12.	C_2^-	13	$\sigma 1s^2, \sigma^* 1s^2, \sigma 2s^2, \sigma^* 2s^2, \pi 2p_x^2 \approx \pi 2p_y, \sigma 2p_z^1$	$\frac{1}{2}(9-4)=5/2$	Paramagnetic
13.	N_2	14	$\sigma 1s^2, \sigma^* 1s^2, \sigma 2s^2, \sigma^* 2s^2, \pi 2p_x^2 \approx \pi 2p_y, \sigma 2p_z^2$	$\frac{1}{2}(10-4)=3$	Diamagnetic
14.	N_2^+	13	$\sigma 1s^2, \sigma^* 1s^2, \sigma 2s^2, \sigma^* 2s^2, \pi 2p_x^2 \approx \pi 2p_y^2, \sigma 2p_z^1$	$\frac{1}{2}(9-4)=5/2$	Paramagnetic
15.	O_2	16	$\sigma 1s^2, \sigma^* 1s^2, \sigma 2s^2, \sigma^* 2s^2, \sigma 2p_z^2, \pi 2p_x^2 \approx \pi 2p_y^2, \pi^* 2p_x^1 \approx \pi^* 2p_y^1$	$\frac{1}{2}(10-6)=2$	Paramagnetic
16.	O_2^+	15	$\sigma 1s^2, \sigma^* 1s^2, \sigma 2s^2, \sigma^* 2s^2, \sigma 2p_z^2, \pi 2p_x^2 \approx \pi 2p_y^2, \pi^* 2p_x^1 \approx \pi^* 2p_y^0$	$\frac{1}{2}(10-5)=5/2$	Paramagnetic
17.	O_2^-	17	$\sigma 1s^2, \sigma^* 1s^2, \sigma 2s^2, \sigma^* 2s^2, \sigma 2p_z^2, \pi 2p_x^2 \approx \pi 2p_y^2, \pi^* 2p_x^2 \approx \pi^* 2p_y^1$	$\frac{1}{2}(10-7)=3/2$	Paramagnetic
18.	O_2^{2-}	18	$\sigma 1s^2, \sigma^* 1s^2, \sigma 2s^2, \sigma^* 2s^2, \sigma 2p_z^2, \pi 2p_x^2 \approx \pi 2p_y^2, \pi^* 2p_x^2 \approx \pi^* 2p_y^2$	$\frac{1}{2}(10-8)=1$	Diamagnetic
19.	F_2	18	$\sigma 1s^2, \sigma^* 1s^2, \sigma 2s^2, \sigma^* 2s^2, \sigma 2p_z^2, \pi 2p_x^2 \approx \pi 2p_y^2, \pi^* 2p_x^2 \approx \pi^* 2p_y^2$	$\frac{1}{2}(10-8)=1$	Diamagnetic
20.	F_2^+	17	$\sigma 1s^2, \sigma^* 1s^2, \sigma 2s^2, \sigma^* 2s^2, \sigma 2p_z^2, \pi 2p_x^2 \approx \pi 2p_y^2, \pi^* 2p_x^2 \approx \pi^* 2p_y^1$	$\frac{1}{2}(10-7)=3/2$	Paramagnetic
21.	F_2^-	19	$\sigma 1s^2, \sigma^* 1s^2, \sigma 2s^2, \sigma^* 2s^2, \sigma 2p_z^2, \pi 2p_x^2 \approx \pi 2p_y^2, \pi^* 2p_x^2 \approx \pi^* 2p_y^2, \sigma^* 2p_z^1$	$\frac{1}{2}(10-9)=1/2$	Paramagnetic
22.	Ne_2	20	$\sigma 1s^2, \sigma^* 1s^2, \sigma 2s^2, \sigma^* 2s^2, \sigma 2p_z^2, \pi 2p_x^2 \approx \pi 2p_y^2, \pi^* 2p_x^2 \approx \pi^* 2p_y^2, \sigma^* 2p_z^2$	$\frac{1}{2}(10-10)=0$	Does not exist
23.	Ne_2^+	19	$\sigma 1s^2, \sigma^* 1s^2, \sigma 2s^2, \sigma^* 2s^2, \sigma 2p_z^2, \pi 2p_x^2 \approx \pi 2p_y^2, \pi^* 2p_x^2 \approx \pi^* 2p_y^2, \sigma^* 2p_z^1$	$\frac{1}{2}(10-9)=1/2$	Paramagnetic
24.	NO	15	$\sigma 1s^2, \sigma^* 1s^2, \sigma 2s^2, \sigma^* 2s^2\ \sigma 2p_z^2, \pi 2p_x^2 \approx \pi 2p_y^2, \pi^* 2p_x^1 \approx \pi^* 2p_y^0$	$\frac{1}{2}(10-5)=5/2$	Paramagnetic
25.	$(NO)^+$	14	$\sigma 1s^2, \sigma^* 1s^2, \sigma 2s^2, \sigma^* 2s^2, \sigma 2p_z^2, \pi 2p_x^2 \approx \pi 2p_y^2$	$\frac{1}{2}(10-4)=3$	Diamagnetic
26.	CO	14	$\sigma 1s^2, \sigma^* 1s^2, \sigma 2s^2, \sigma^* 2s^2, \sigma 2p_z^2, \pi 2p_x^2 \approx \pi 2p_y^2$	$\frac{1}{2}(10-4)=3$	Diamagnetic

Example 19 It is possible to isolate compounds containing the O_2^+ cation, the O_2^- (superoxide) anion or the O_2^{2-} (peroxide) anion. By considering their molecular orbital energy level diagrams, place these ions in order of increasing O—O bond length.

> **Key Idea** To predict the relative values of the bond lengths, first calculate the bond orders for the different ions. Use the molecular orbital configuration to calculate bond order.

Sol. O_2^+ $(8+8-1=15)=$

$$\sigma 1s^2, \overset{*}{\sigma}1s^2, \sigma 2s^2, \overset{*}{\sigma}2s^2, \sigma 2p_z^2, \pi 2p_x^2 \approx \pi 2p_y^2, \overset{*}{\pi}2p_x^1$$

$$\therefore \text{ Bond order } = \frac{N_b - N_a}{2} = \frac{10-5}{2} = 2.5$$

O_2^- $(8+8+1=17)=$ $\sigma 1s^2, \overset{*}{\sigma}1s^2, \sigma 2s^2, \overset{*}{\sigma}2s^2, \sigma 2p_z^2, \pi 2p_x^2 \approx \pi 2p_y^2, \overset{*}{\pi}2p_x^2 \approx \overset{*}{\pi}2p_y^1$

$$BO = \frac{10-7}{2} = 1.5$$

O_2^{2-} $(8+8+2=18)=\sigma 1s^2, \overset{*}{\sigma}1s^2, \sigma 2s^2, \overset{*}{\sigma}2s^2, \sigma 2p_z^2, \pi 2p_x^2 \approx \pi 2p_y^2, \overset{*}{\pi}2p_x^2 \approx \overset{*}{\pi}2p_y^2$

$$BO = \frac{10-8}{2} = 1$$

$$\therefore \quad \text{Bond length} \propto \frac{1}{\text{Bond order (BO)}}$$

$\therefore$ The order of increasing bond length is

$$O_2^+ < O_2^- < O_2^{2-}.$$

Hydrogen Bonding

The attractive force which binds hydrogen atom of one molecule with the highly electronegative atom (F, O or N) of the same or another molecule is called **hydrogen bonding**. It is represented by a dotted line.

e.g. in case of HF molecule, the hydrogen bond exists between hydrogen atom of one molecule and fluorine atom of another molecule as shown below :

$$\ldots H^{\delta+}—F^{\delta-}\ldots\ldots H^{\delta+}—F^{\delta-}\ldots\ldots H^{\delta+}—F^{\delta-}$$

Here, hydrogen bond behaves like a bridge between two atoms that holds one atom by covalent bond and the other by hydrogen bond.

Cause of Formation of Hydrogen Bond

If hydrogen is bonded to a highly electronegative element X, the shared pair of electrons moves far away from hydrogen atom. Consequently, the hydrogen atom becomes highly electropositive with respect to the other atom X.

Since, there is displacement of electrons towards X, the hydrogen acquires partial positive charge (δ^+), while X gains partial negative charge (δ^-). It results in the formation of a polar molecule with electrostatic force of attraction as shown below.

$$H^{\delta+}—X^{\delta-}\ldots H^{\delta+}—X^{\delta-}\ldots H^{\delta+}—X^{\delta-}$$

The magnitude of H-bonding also depends on the physical state of the compound. In case of solid, it is maximum and for gases, it is minimum. Thus, the hydrogen bonds have great influence on the structure and physical properties of the compounds.

Conditions for Hydrogen Bonding

A hydrogen bond is formed when the following conditions are satisfied.

(i) **High Electronegativity of Atom Combining with Hydrogen** The molecule must have an atom of high electronegativity such as F, O or N directly bonded to hydrogen atom as present in HF, H_2O and NH_3.

(ii) **Small Size of the Electronegative Atom** The size of the electronegative atom should be quite small because a smaller atom attracts the bonded electron pair strongly.

Types of H-Bonds

There are two types of H-bonds :

1. Intermolecular Hydrogen Bond

Such bond exists between two different molecules of the same or different compounds, e.g. H-bond in case of HF molecule, alcohol or water molecules etc. It results in association of two molecules and hence results in increased melting point, boiling points and solubility.

(i)

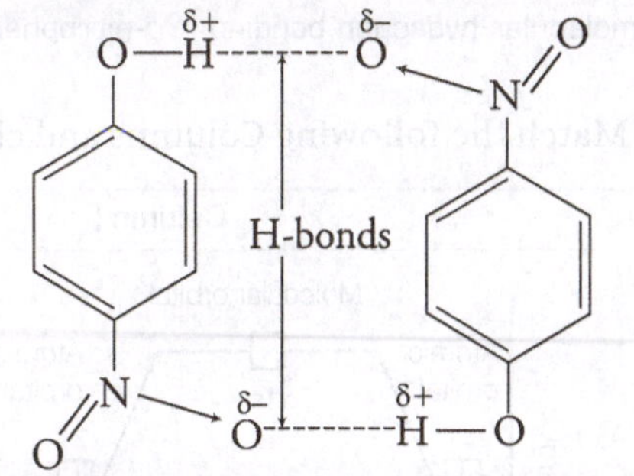

Intermolecular hydrogen bonding in *p*-nitrophenol

(ii)

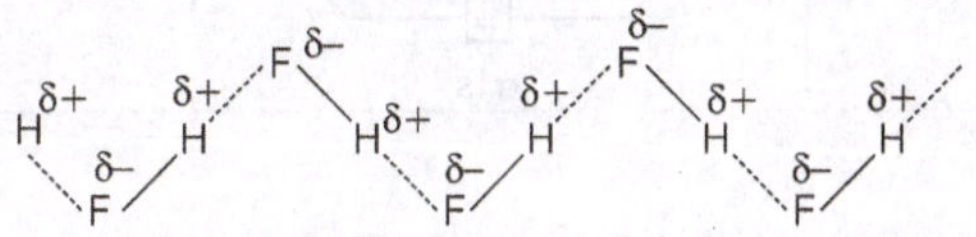

Intermolecular hydrogen bonding in Hydrogen Fluoride

(iii) 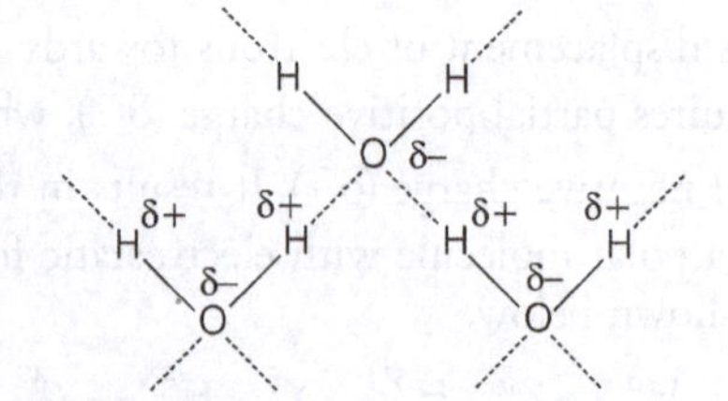

Intermolecular hydrogen bonding between water molecule

(d) 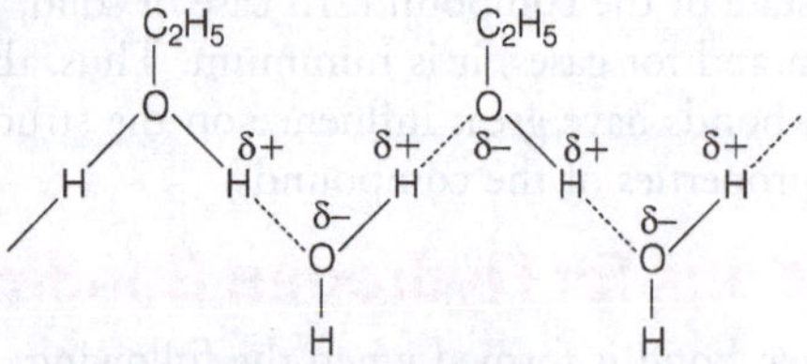

Intermolecular hydrogen bonding between alcohol and water

2. Intramolecular Hydrogen Bond

Such bond exists when hydrogen atom is in between the two highly electronegative (F, O, N) atoms present within the same molecule. e.g. in *o*-nitrophenol, the hydrogen is in between the two oxygen atoms.

This bonding prevents the association of molecules, making the molecule more shielded in comparison of molecules where intermolecular hydrogen bonding occurs. Hence, it decreases melting point, boiling point, and solubility, e.g. *o*-nitrophenol has lower boiling point that *p*-nitrophenol.

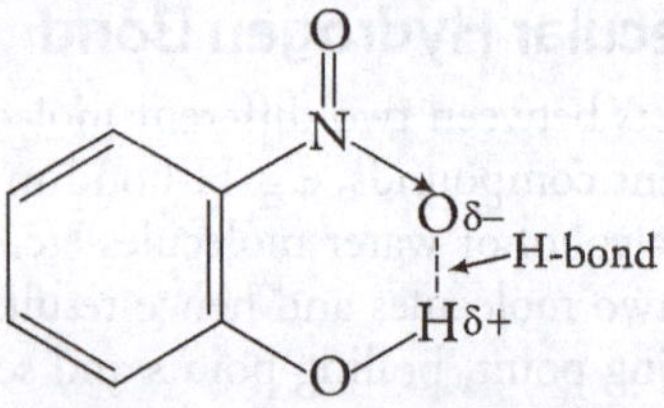

Intramolecular hydrogen bonding in *o*-nitrophenol molecule

Topic Practice 4

Very Short Answer Type Questions

1 Mark

1. Fill in the Blanks

(i) Molecules having no unpaired electrons gives rise to .... character.

(ii) Molecules having unpaired electrons gives rise to .... character.

(iii) The boiling point of a substance increases with increase in .... hydrogen bonding.

2. Objective Type Questions

(i) The correct bond order in the following species is

(a) $O_2^{2+} > O_2^+ > O_2^-$ (b) $O_2^{2+} < O_2^- < O_2^+$

(c) $O_2^+ > O_2^- < O_2^{2+}$ (d) $O_2^- < O_2^+ > O_2^{2+}$

(ii) Four diatomic species are listed below. Identify the correct order in which the bond order is increasing in them

(a) $NO < O_2^- < C_2^{2-} < He_2^+$

(b) $O_2^- < NO < C_2^{2-} < He_2^+$

(c) $C_2^{2-} < He_2^+ < O_2^- < NO$

(d) $He_2^+ < O_2^- < NO < C_2^{2-}$

(iii) Which one of the following molecules is expected to exhibit diamagnetic behaviour?

(a) C_2 (b) N_2^+

(c) O_2 (d) S_2

(iv) Which of the following molecule does not show hydrogen bonding?

(a) HF (b) H_2O

(c) NH_3 (d) H_2S

3. Match the following Columns and choose the correct option using the codes given below :

Column I		Column II
A. 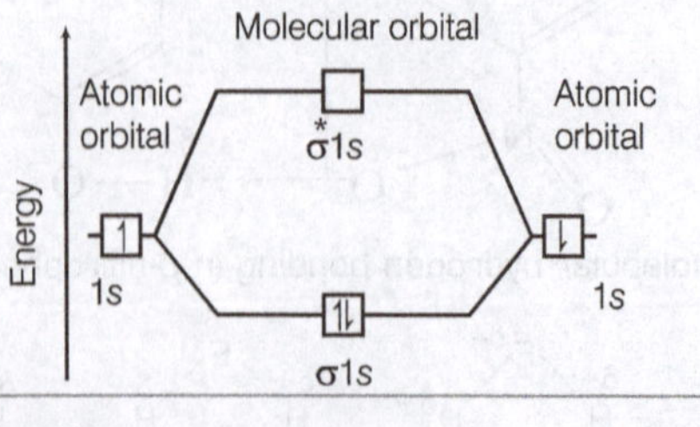	(i)	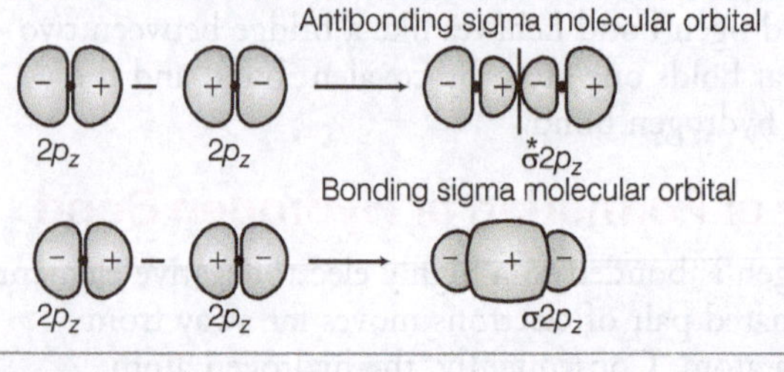

Column I	Column II

B.

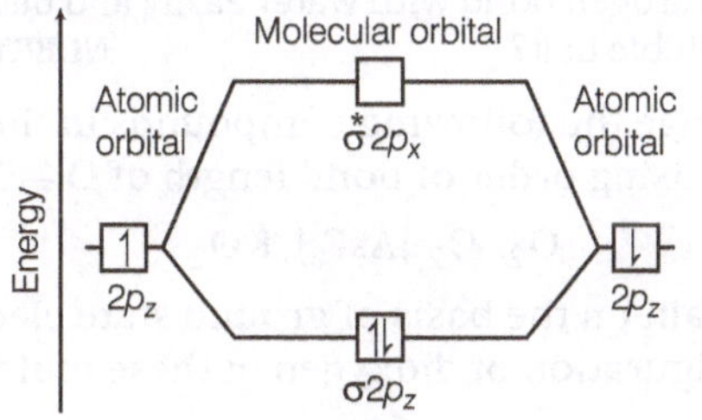

(ii)

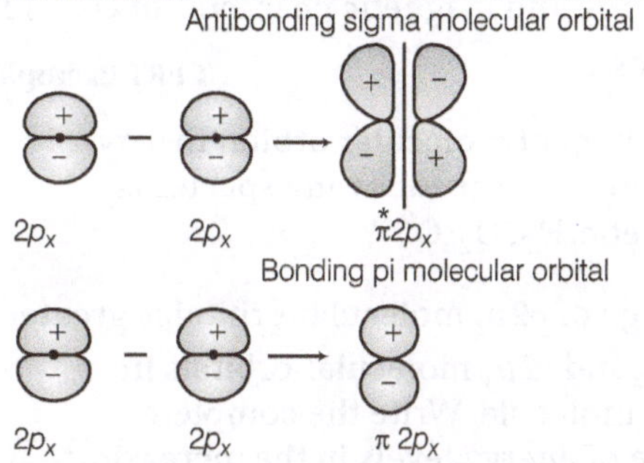

C.

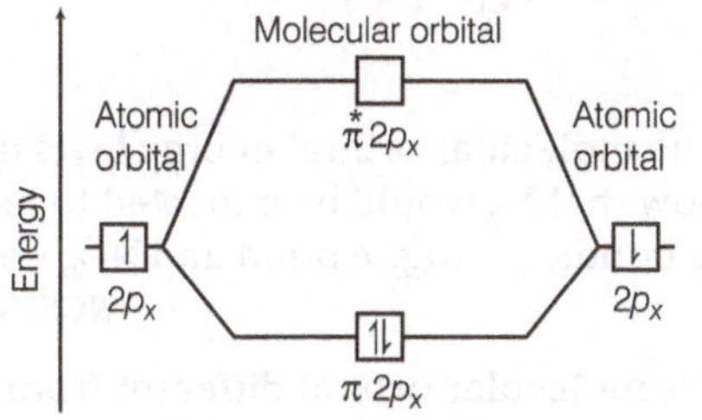

(iii)

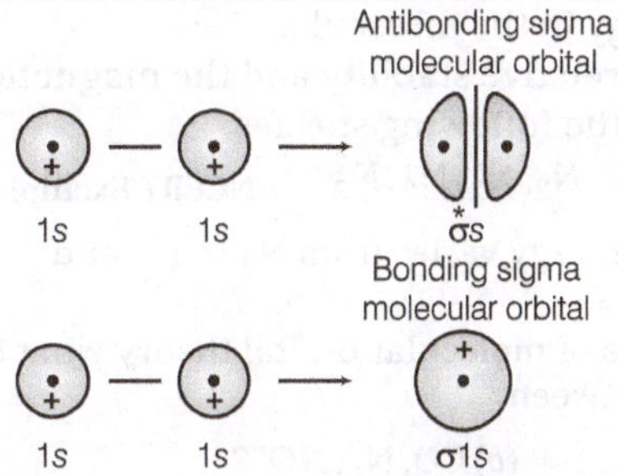

Codes

	A	B	C		A	B	C
(a)	(iii)	(i)	(ii)	(b)	(i)	(iii)	(ii)
(c)	(i)	(ii)	(iii)	(d)	(ii)	(iii)	(i)

4. Write the significance of a plus and a minus sign shown in representing the orbitals. **NCERT Textbook**

5. What type of atomic orbitals can overlap to form molecular orbitals?

6. Can we have a diatomic molecule with its ground state molecular orbitals full with electrons? Give a reason for your answer.

7. Use molecular orbital theory to explain why the Be_2 molecule does not exist? **NCERT Textbook**

8. Why is the energy of $\pi 2p_x$ and $\pi 2p_y$ molecular orbital lower than $\sigma 2p_z$ molecular orbital in N_2 molecule?

9. Is it correct to say that bond order always increases when an electron is lost?

10. Why KHF_2 exists but $KHCl_2$ does not?

11. How many nodal planes are present in $\pi(2p_x)$ and $\pi^*(2p_x)$ molecular orbitals?

12. What is the magnetic character of the anion of KO_2?

Short Answer Type I Questions

(2 Marks)

13. Out of H and H_2, the latter has higher first ionisation energy while out of O and O_2, the former has higher first ionisation energy. Explain why?

14. Compare the relative stability of the following species and indicate their magnetic properties.

$$O_2^{2-} > O_2 > O_2^+ > O_2^-$$

15. Compare the relative stabilities of O_2^- and N_2^+ and comment on their magnetic (paramagnetic or diamagnetic) behaviour.

16. What is the effect of following process on the bond order in N_2 and O_2?

(i) $N_2 \longrightarrow N_2^+ + e^-$ (ii) $O_2 \longrightarrow O_2^+ + e^-$

17. Why does formic acid exist as dimer? What is its one consequence?

18. Explain, why HF is less viscous than H_2O?

Short Answer Type II Questions

(3 Marks)

19. Write the important conditions required for the linear combination of atomic orbitals to form molecular orbitals. **NCERT Textbook**

20. Using molecular orbital theory, compare the bond energy and magnetic character of O_2^+ and O_2^- species. **NCERT Exemplar**

21. With the help of molecular orbital theory, predict which of the following species is diamagnetic H_2^+, O_2, O_2^{2+}?

22. The energy of $\sigma 2p_z$ molecular orbital is greater than $\pi 2p_x$ and $\pi 2p_y$ molecular orbitals in nitrogen molecule. Write the complete sequence of energy levels in the increasing order of energy in the molecule.
Compare the relative stability and the magnetic behaviour of the following species.
$N_2, N_2^+, N_2^-, N_2^{2+}$ **NCERT Exemplar**

23. (i) How bond energy varies from N_2^- to N_2^+ and why?
(ii) On the basis of molecular orbital theory what is similarly between
(a) F_2, O_2^{2-} (b) CO, N_2, NO^+?

24. What is meant by the term bond order? Calculate the bond order of N_2, O_2, O_2^+ and O_2^-.

25. Which of the following species has the shortest bond length?
NO, NO^+, NO^{2+}, NO^-

26. Arrange the following species in order of increasing stability.
Li_2, Li_2^+ and Li_2^-
Justify your choice with a molecular orbital configuration.

27. Structures of molecules of two compounds are given below.
(i) Which of the two compounds will have intermolecular hydrogen bonding and which compound is expected to show intramolecular hydrogen bonding?

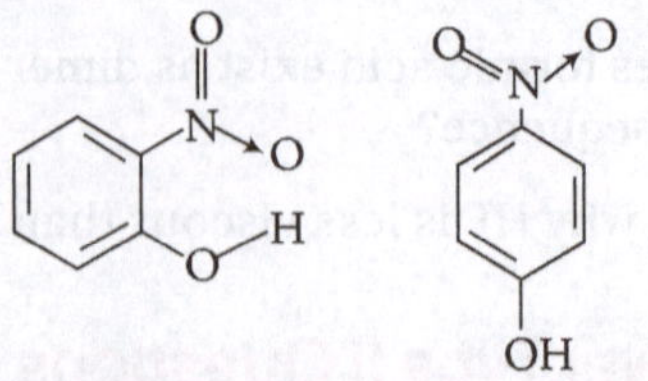

I II

(ii) The melting point of a compound depends on the extent of hydrogen bonding among many other things. On this basis, explain which of the above two compounds will show higher melting point?
(iii) Solubility of compounds in water depends on power to form hydrogen bonds with water. Which of the above compounds will form hydrogen bond with water easily and be more soluble in it? **NCERT Exemplar**

28. Arrange the following compounds in the increasing order of bond length of O—O bond:
O_2, $O_2\,[AsF_6]$, KO_2
Explain on the basis of ground state electronic configuration of dioxygen in these molecules.

Long Answer Type Questions

5 Marks

29. Use the molecular orbital energy level diagram to show that N_2 would be expected to have a triple bond; F_2 a single bond and Ne_2, no bond. **NCERT EXemplar**

30. How is molecular orbital different from atomic orbital? Give electronic configuration of (i) H_2^+ (ii) Li_2, (iii) B_2 and (iv) C_2. Calculate their bond order and predict their paramagnetic behaviour.

Hints & Solutions

1. (i) diamagnetic (ii) paramagnetic
(iii) intermolecular
2. (i) → a (ii) → d (iii) → a (iv) → d
3. (a) (A)→ (iii), (B)→ (i), (C)→ (ii)
4. Orbitals are represented by wave functions. A plus sign in an orbital represents a positive wave function and a minus sign represents a negative wave function. Combination of two wave function having similar sign give bonding molecular orbitals, while that having opposite sign give antibonding molecular orbitals.
5. Atomic orbitals with comparable energies and proper orientation overlap to form molecular orbitals.
6. No, because bond order becomes zero, e.g. in case of He_2, Be_2, Ne_2 etc. Note that in H_2, $\sigma 1s$ molecular orbital is full but $\overset{*}{\sigma}1s$ is empty.
7. Electronic configuration of Be_2 molecule $(4+4=8)$,
$\sigma 1s^2, \overset{*}{\sigma}1s^2, \sigma 2s^2, \overset{*}{\sigma}2s^2$
$$\text{Bond order} = \frac{1}{2}[N_b - N_a] = \frac{1}{2}(4-4) = 0$$
Since, bond order is zero, so Be_2 does not exist.
8. This is because of intermixing of 2s and $2p_z$ orbitals because of their close proximity. Due to intermixing, $\sigma 2p_z$ molecular orbital becomes higher in energy than $\pi\, 2p_x$ and $\pi\, 2p_y$ molecular orbitals.

9. Bond order may increase or decrease, when an electron is lost depending upon whether the electron is lost from bonding or antibonding molecular orbital.

10. Due to H-bonding in HF, we have

H—F...... H—F...... H—F......

This can dissociate to give HF_2^- ion and hence, KHF_2 exists but there is no H-bonding in H–Cl. So, HCl_2^- ion does not exist and hence, $KHCl_2$ also does not exist.

11. One and two respectively.

12. Anion of KO_2 is O_2^- (superoxide ion) which has one unpaired electron and hence is paramagnetic.

13. In H_2, first electron has to be removed from bonding orbital, $\sigma(1s)$ which has lower energy (more stable) than H-atom. In O_2, first electron has to be removed from antibonding orbital $\overset{*}{\pi}(2p_x)$ or $\overset{*}{\pi}(2p_y)$ orbital which has higher energy than $2p$-orbital of O-atom. [2]

14. First Calculate the bond order of given species as shown in table on page 182 and bond order $\propto$ stability.

Thus, relative stability of the above species in decreasing order is :

$$O_2^+ > O_2 > O_2^- > O_2^{2-}$$ [2]

15. Calculate bond order as shown in table on page 182.

As bond order of $N_2^+ >$ bond order of O_2^-, therefoe, N_2^+ is more stable than O_2^-. Each of them contains unpaired electron, hence both are paramagnetic. [1]

16. According to molecular orbital theory, the electronic configurations and bond order of N_2, N_2^+, O_2 and O_2^+ species are as follows :

$$N_2\,(14e^-) = \sigma 1s^2, \overset{*}{\sigma}1s^2, \sigma 2s^2, \overset{*}{\sigma}2s^2, (\pi 2p_x^2 \approx \pi 2p_y^2), \sigma 2p_z^2$$

$$\text{Bond order} = \frac{1}{2}[N_b - N_a] = \frac{1}{2}(10-4) = 3$$

$$N_2^+\,(13e^-) = \sigma 1s^2, \overset{*}{\sigma}1s^2, \sigma 2s^2, \overset{*}{\sigma}2s^2, (\pi 2p_x^2 \approx \pi 2p_y^2)\, \sigma 2p_z^1$$

$$\text{Bond order} = \frac{1}{2}[N_b - N_a] = \frac{1}{2}(9-4) = 2.5$$

$$O_2\,(16e^-) = \sigma 1s^2, \overset{*}{\sigma}1s^2, \sigma 2s^2, \overset{*}{\sigma}2s^2, \sigma 2p_z^2, (\pi 2p_x^2 \approx \pi 2p_y^2), (\overset{*}{\pi}2p_x^1 \approx \overset{*}{\pi}2p_y^1)$$

$$\text{Bond order} = \frac{1}{2}[N_b - N_a] = \frac{1}{2}(10-6) = 2$$

$$O_2^+\,(15e^-) = \sigma 1s^2, \overset{*}{\sigma}1s^2, \sigma 2s^2, \overset{*}{\sigma}2s^2, \sigma 2p_z^2, (\pi 2p_x^2 \approx \pi 2p_y^2), (\overset{*}{\pi}2p_x^1 \approx \overset{*}{\pi}2p_y^0)$$

$$\text{Bond order} = \frac{1}{2}[N_b - N_a] = \frac{1}{2}(10-5) = 2.5$$ [1]

(i) $\underset{BO = 3}{N_2} \longrightarrow \underset{BO = 2.5}{N_2^+} + e^-$ [1/2]

Thus, bond order decreases.

(ii) $\underset{BO = 2}{O_2} \longrightarrow \underset{BO = 2.5}{O_2^+} + e^-$ [1/2]

Thus, bond order increases.

17. Formic acid exists as dimer because of intermolecular hydrogen bonding.

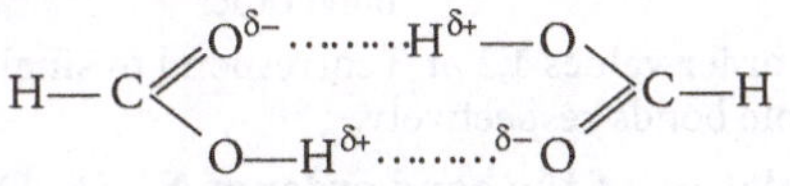

Because of intermolecular hydrogen bonding, its boiling and melting point increases. [2]

18. There is greater intermolecular hydrogen bonding in H_2O than that in HF as each H_2O molecule forms four H-bonds with other water molecules, whereas HF forms only two H-bonds with other HF molecules. Greater the intermolecular H-bonding, greater is the viscosity. Hence, HF is less viscous than H_2O. [2]

19. Refer to text on page 180 (Conditions for the combination of atomic orbitals).

20. Calculate bond order of O_2^+ and O_2^- according to table given on page 184.

Higher bond order of O_2^+ shows that it is more stable than O_2^-. Both the species have unpaired electrons. So both are paramagnetic in nature.

21. The damagnetic species are those which contain only paired electrons. This can be predicted from the molecular orbital electronic configurations as given below. [1]

$H_2^+ : \sigma 1s^1$

$$O_2 : \sigma 1s^2, \overset{*}{\sigma}1s^2, \sigma 2s^2, \overset{*}{\sigma}2s^2, \sigma 2p_z^2, \pi 2p_x^2 = \pi 2p_y^2, \overset{*}{\pi}2p_y^1 \approx \overset{*}{\pi}2p_x^1$$

$$O_2^{2+} : \sigma 1s^2, \overset{*}{\sigma}1s^2, \sigma 2s^2, \overset{*}{\sigma}2s^2, \sigma 2p_z^2, \pi 2p_x^2, \pi 2p_y^2$$

Since, O_2^{2+} contain all paired electrons, it will be diamagnetic. [2]

22. Refer to text on page 182 (Electronic configuration and molecular behaviour : Magnetic nature)

23. (i) Bond energy of N_2^+ = Bond energy of N_2^-. This is because they have the same bond order.

(Strictly speaking, N_2^- is slightly less stable and hence, has less bond energy then N_2^+ due to presence of greater number of electrons in the antibonding molecular orbitals). [1]

(ii) (a) Same bond order and bond length. [1]

(b) Same bond order and bond length. [1]

24. **Bond order** is defined as one half the difference between the number of electrons present in the bonding and anti-bonding orbitals, i.e.

$$\text{Bond order (BO)} = \frac{1}{2}(N_b - N_a)$$

A positive bond order means a stable molecule while a negative or zero bond order means an unstable molecule.

$$\text{Stability of a molecule} \propto \text{bond order}$$

$$\text{Bond length} \propto \frac{1}{\text{bond order}}$$

Bond order values 1,2 or 3 correspond to single, double or triple bonds respectively. [1]

Calculation of the bond order of N_2, O_2, O_2^+ and O_2^-

Electronic configuration of N_2 (14 electrons)

$\sigma 1s^2, \overset{*}{\sigma}1s^2, \sigma 2s^2, \overset{*}{\sigma}2s^2, (\pi 2p_x^2 \approx \pi 2p_y^2), \sigma 2p_z^2$

$$\text{Bond order} = \frac{1}{2}[N_b - N_a] = \frac{1}{2} \times (10-4) = 3$$

EC of O_2 (16 electrons)

$= \sigma 1s^2, \overset{*}{\sigma}1s^2, \sigma 2s^2, \overset{*}{\sigma}2s^2, \sigma 2p_z^2,$

$(\pi 2p_x^2 \approx \pi 2p_y^2), (\overset{*}{\pi}2p_x^1 \approx \overset{*}{\pi}2p_y^1)$

$$\text{Bond order} = \frac{1}{2}(N_b - N_a) = \frac{1}{2}(10-6) = 2$$

EC of O_2^+ (15 electrons) $= \sigma 1s^2, \overset{*}{\sigma}1s^2, \sigma 2s^2, \overset{*}{\sigma}2s^2, \sigma 2p_z^2,$

$(\pi 2p_x^2 \approx \pi 2p_y^2), (\overset{*}{\pi}2p_x^1 \approx \overset{*}{\pi}2p_y)$

$$\text{Bond order} = \frac{1}{2}(N_b - N_a) = \frac{1}{2}(10-5) = 2.5$$

EC of O_2^- (17 electrons)

$= \sigma 1s^2, \overset{*}{\sigma}1s^2, \sigma 2s^2, \overset{*}{\sigma}2s^2, \sigma 2p_z^2,$

$(\pi 2p_x^2 \approx \pi 2p_y^2), (\overset{*}{\pi}2p_x^2 \approx \overset{*}{\pi}2p_y^1)$

$$\text{Bond order} = \frac{1}{2}(N_b - N_a) = \frac{1}{2}(10-7) = 1.5$$

[2]

25. Calculate the bond order of given species as shown in table on page 184.

$$\text{As bond length} \propto \frac{1}{\text{bond order}}.$$

Since, NO^+ has the highest bond order and therefore, the shortest bond length.

26. Calculate bond order of given species in the same way as given in table on page 184.

As stability ∝ bond order

The order of stability is $Li_2 > Li_2^+ > Li_2^-$.

27. (i) Compound (I) will form intramolecular H-bonding. Intramolecular H-bonding is formed when H-atom, in between the two highly electronegativity atoms, is present within the same molecule. In *ortho*-nitrophenol (compound I), H-atom is in between the two oxygen atoms.

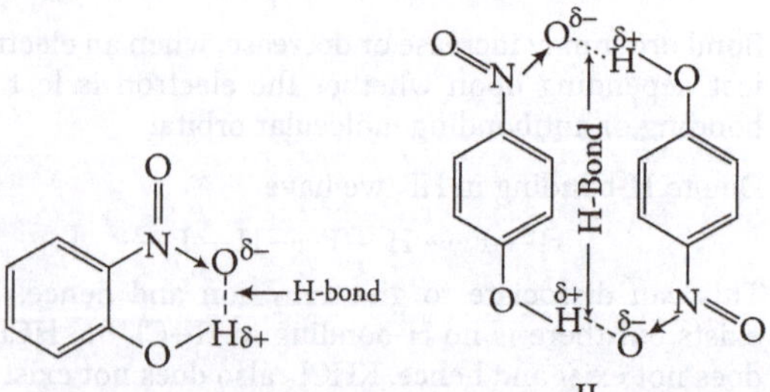

I II

[1]

Compound II forms intermolecular H-bonding. In *para*-nitrophenol II there is a gap between NO_2 and OH group. So, H-bond exists between H-atom of one molecule and O-atom of another molecule as depicted in given fig. I and II.

(ii) Compound II will have higher melting point because it has intermolecular H-bonding which increases melting point. [1]

(iii) Due to intramolecular H-bonding compound I is not able to form H-bond with water, so it is less soluble in water. While molecules of compound II form intermolecular H-bonding with H_2O easily, so it is soluble in water. [1]

28. $O_2[AsF_6]$ has O_2^+ ion, while KO_2 has O_2^- ion.

Calculate bond order of O_2, O_2^+ and O_2^- as shown in the table on 184. Higher the bond order, smaller is the bond length. Hence, order of O—O bond length is

$O_2[AsF_6] < O_2 < KO_2$. [1]

29. Formation of N_2 molecule

${}_7N = 1s^2, 2s^2, 2p_x^1, 2p_y^1, 2p_z^1$

$N_2 = \sigma 1s^2, \overset{*}{\sigma}1s^2, \sigma 2s^2, \overset{*}{\sigma}2s^2, \pi 2p_x^2 \approx \pi 2p_y^2, \sigma 2p_z^2$

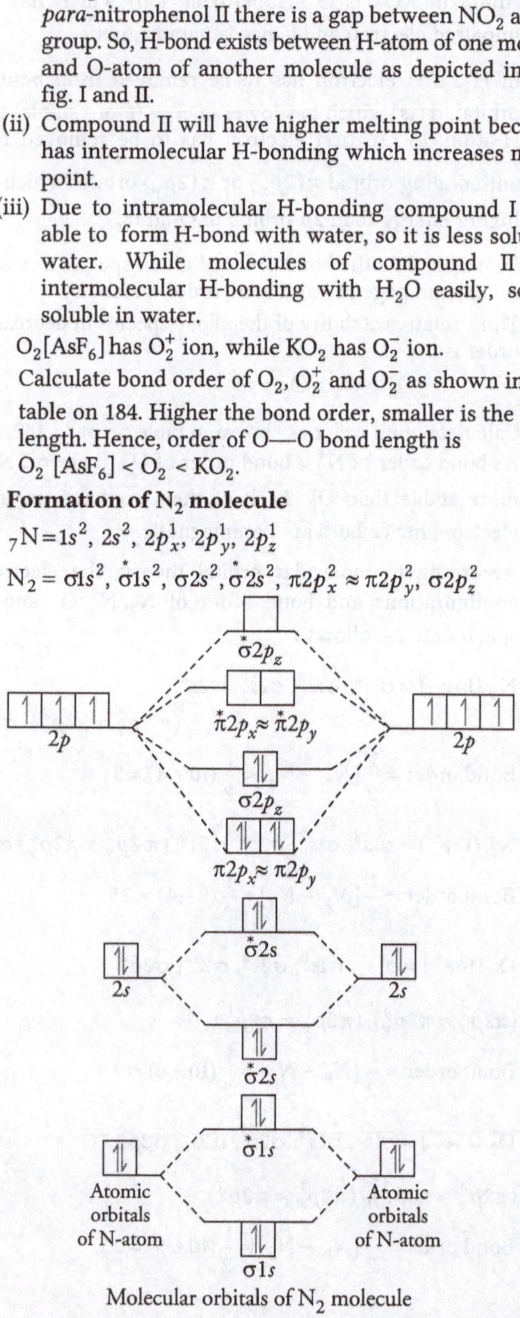

Molecular orbitals of N_2 molecule

Bond order $= \frac{1}{2}[N_b - N_a] = \frac{1}{2}(10-4) = 3$

Bond order value of 3 means that N_2 contains a triple bond.

Formation of F_2 molecule ${}_9F = 1s^2, 2s^2, 2p_x^2, 2p_y^2, 2p_z^1$ [1½]

$F_2 = \sigma 1s^2, \overset{*}{\sigma}1s^2, \sigma 2s^2, \overset{*}{\sigma}2s^2, \sigma 2p_z^2, \pi 2p_x^2 \approx \pi 2p_y^2,$
$\overset{*}{\pi}2p_x^2 \approx \overset{*}{\pi}2p_y^2$

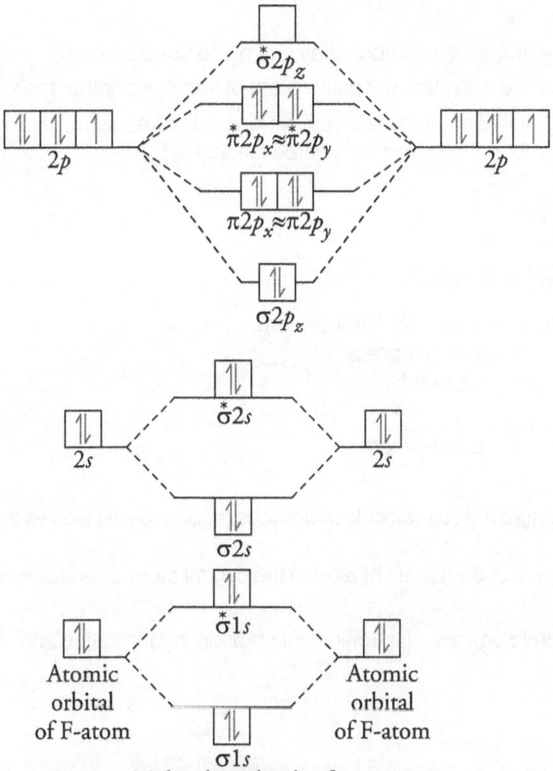

Molecular orbitals of F_2 molecule

Bond order $= \frac{1}{2}[N_b - N_a] = \frac{1}{2}(10-8) = 1$

Bond order value 1 means that F_2 contains single bond [1½]

Formation of Ne_2 molecule

${}_{10}Ne = 1s^2, 2s^2, 2p_x^2, 2p_y^2, 2p_z^2$

$Ne_2 = \sigma 1s^2, \overset{*}{\sigma}1s^2, \sigma 2s^2, \overset{*}{\sigma}2s^2, \sigma 2p_z^2, \pi 2p_x^2 \approx \pi 2p_y^2,$
$\overset{*}{\pi}2p_x^2 \approx \overset{*}{\pi}2p_y^2, \overset{*}{\sigma}2p_z^2$

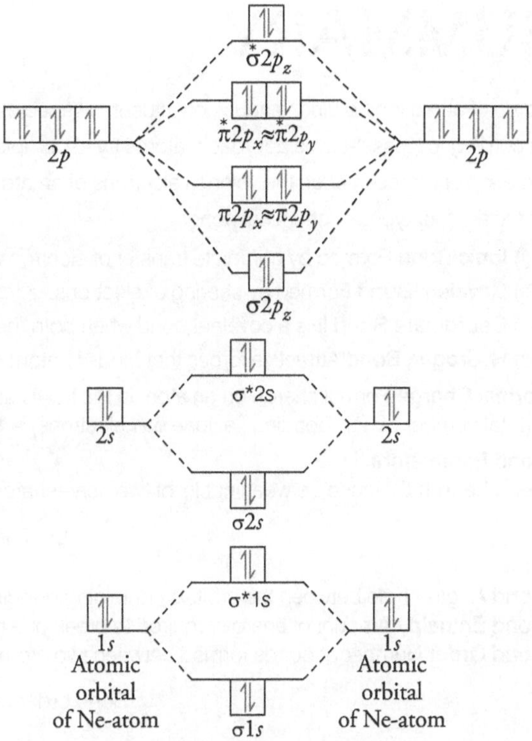

Molecular orbital of Ne_2 molecule

Bond order $= \frac{1}{2}[N_b - N_a] = \frac{1}{2}(10-10) = 0$

Bond order value zero means that there is no formation of bond between two Ne atoms. Hence, Ne_2 molecule does not exist. [2]

30. Difference between molecular and atomic orbitals.

Refer to text on page 179 (Formation of molecular orbitals).

(i) $H_2^+ (1) = (\sigma 1s)^1$

$\Rightarrow$ Bond order $= 1/2(1-0) = 1/2$, paramagnetic [1]

(ii) $Li_2 (6) = (\sigma 1s)^2 (\overset{*}{\sigma}1s)^2 (\sigma 2s)^2$

$\Rightarrow$ Bond order $= \frac{1}{2}(4-2) = \frac{2}{2} = 1$, diamagnetic [1]

(iii) $B_2(10) = (\sigma 1s)^2 (\overset{*}{\sigma}1s)^2 (\sigma 2s)^2 (\overset{*}{\sigma}2s)^2 (\pi 2p_x^1 \approx \pi 2p_y^1)$

$\Rightarrow$ Bond order $= \frac{1}{2}(6-4) = 1$, paramagnetic [1]

(iv) $C_2 (12) = (\sigma 1s)^2 (\overset{*}{\sigma}1s)^2 (\sigma 2s)^2 (\overset{*}{\sigma}2s)^2 (\pi 2p_x^2 \approx \pi 2p_y^2)$

$\Rightarrow$ Bond order $= \frac{1}{2}(8-4) = 2$, diamagnetic [1]

SUMMARY

- Force of attraction holding various constituents of species is called **chemical bond.**
- According to Kossel-Lewis approach, atoms try to complete their octet (except H which complete its duplet).
- Notation or representation the valence electrons of an atom is called Lewis symbol.
- There are four types of chemical bonds :
  (i) **Ionic Bond** Formed by complete transfer of electrons.
  (ii) **Covalent Bond** Formed by sharing of electrons.
  (iii) **Coordinate Bond** It is a covalent bond when both the shared electrons are contributed by one of the bonded atom.
  (iii) **Hydrogen Bond** Attractive forces that binds H-atom of one molecule with electronegative atom of same or another molecule.
- **Formal Charge** Formal charge on an atom in the Lewis structure = [(total number of valence electrons in the free atom) – (total number of non-bonding i.e. lone pair electrons) – 1/2 (total number of bonding, i.e. shared electrons)]
- **Bond Parameters**
  Bond Length Distance between nuclei of two nearest atoms.

$$\text{Bond length} \propto \frac{1}{\text{bond multiplicity}}.$$

  Bond Angle Angle between the orbitals containing bonding electron pairs around the central atom.
  Bond Enthalpy Amount of energy required to break one mole of bonds in gaseous phase.
  Bond Order Number of bonds formed between two atoms in a covalent compound.

$$\text{Bond order} \propto \text{bond enthalpy} \propto \frac{1}{\text{bond-length}}$$

- **Theories of Covalent Bonding**
  Resonance When all the properties cannot be shown by a single structure then a molecule undergoes resonance. It involves transfer of only π or one pair of electrons, not of atoms.
  VSEPR Theory Number of valence shell electron pairs (bonded or non-bonded) present around the central atom decides the shape of a molecule.
- **Valence Bond Theory** This theory is based on the knowledge of atomic orbitals, electronic configuration, hybridisation and criteria of overlapping of atomic orbital.

Related Concepts to Valence Bond Theory

- **Orbital Overlapping** created by sigma and pi-bonds.
  Hybridisation Phenomenon of intermixing of orbitals having slightly different energies and shapes to generated orbitals of same energy and shape. Its important types are sp, sp^2, sp^3.
- **Polar Character** species can be non-polar or polar.
  Covalent bond formed between two similar atoms, **non polar covalent bond,** e.g. H_2, O_2 etc.
  Covalent bond formed between two dissimilar atoms, called **polar covalent bond,** e.g. HCl, HF. It is expressed in terms of dipole moment. Dipole-moment (μ) μ = charge (Q) $\times$ distance of separation (r) unit = Debye (D).

Molecular Orbital Theory

- According to molecular orbital theory, molecular orbitals (bonding and anti-bonding) are combination of atomic orbitals of comparable energies and proper symmetry.
- Stability of molecule: If $N_b > N_a$, the molecule is stable and if $N_b \le N_a$, molecule is unstable.
- Bond order (On basis of M.O.T) $= \dfrac{N_b - N_a}{2}$.
- All molecular orbitals which are doubly occupied is called diamagnetic substance and if, one molecular orbital is singly occupied is called paramagnetic substance.

Chapter Practice

Very Short Answer Type Questions

1 Mark

1. Fill in the Blanks

(i) The combining capacity of different constituents is called their......... .

(ii) According to Fajan's rule,............cation and ....anion form ionic bond.

(iii) The net dipole moment of symmetrical molecule is............ .

(iv) For sp^2-hybridisation, the geometry is generally............ .

(v) In NH_3, nitrogen has............lone pair of electrons.

(vi) In carbide ion, two carbon atoms are joined by......... .

2. Objective Type Questions

(i) The molecule of hydrogen atom is formed due to the overlapping of orbitals of two hydrogen atoms. Which of the following types of overlapping takes place in the formation of H_2 molecule?

(a) 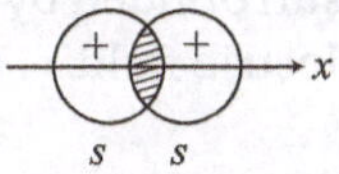

(b) 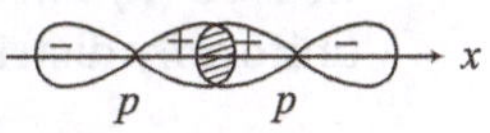

(c) 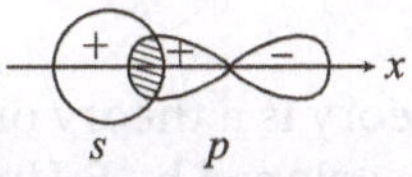

(d) All of these

(ii) The valence bond theory explains the shape, the formation and directional properties of bonds in polyatomic molecules like CH_4, NH_3 and H_2O etc, in terms of

(a) overlapping of atomic orbitals
(b) hybridisation of atomic orbitals
(c) Both (a) and (b)
(d) None of the above

(iii) Lewis approach helps in writing the structure of molecules but it fails to explain

(a) the formation of chemical bond
(b) the reason for the difference in bond dissociation enthalpies and bond lengths in molecule like H_2, F_2 etc
(c) the idea about the shapes of polyatomic molecules
(d) All of the above

(iv) Which of the following has minimum bond length?

(a) O_2 (b) O_2^+ (c) O_2^- (d) O_2^{2-}

(v) In which of the following pairs of molecules/ions both the species are not likely to exist?

(a) H_2^+, He_2^{2-} (b) H_2^-, He_2^{2-} (c) H_2^+, He_2 (d) H_2^-, He_2^{2+}

(vi) The pair of species with the same bond order is

(a) O_2^{2-}, B_2 (b) O_2^+, NO^+ (c) NO, CO (d) N_2, O_2

(vii) Nitrogen, oxygen and fluorine are the highly electronegative elements. When they are attached to a hydrogen atom to form covalent bond, the electrons of the covalent bond are shifted towards the more electronegative atom. This partially positively charged hydrogen atom forms a bond with the other more electronegative atom. This bond is known as

(a) hydrogen bond (b) σ-bond
(c) π-bond (d) covalent bond

3. Matching Type Questions

(i) Match the following Columns and choose the correct option using the codes given below:

Column I	Column II
A. 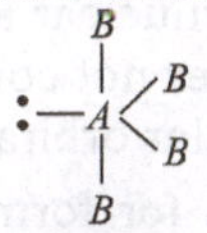 Trigonal bipyramidal	(i) Square planar
B. 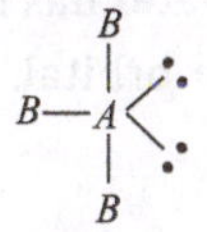 Trigonal bipyramidal	(ii) T-shaped
C. 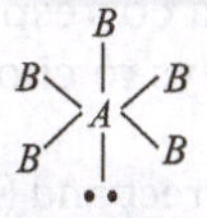 Octahedral	(iii) Square pyramidal
D. 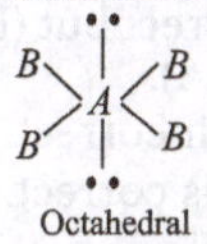 Octahedral	(iv) see-saw

Codes

	A	B	C	D		A	B	C	D
(a)	(i)	(iii)	(ii)	(iv)	(b)	(iv)	(ii)	(iii)	(i)
(c)	(iii)	(ii)	(iv)	(i)	(d)	(ii)	(i)	(iii)	(iv)

(ii) Match the species in Column I with the type of hybrid orbitals in Column II and choose the correct option using the codes given below:

Column I		Column II
A. SF_4	(i)	sp^3d^2
B. IF_5	(ii)	d^2sp^3
C. NO_2^+	(iii)	sp^3d
D. NH_4^+	(iv)	sp^3
	(v)	sp

Codes

	A	B	C	D		A	B	C	D
(a)	(i)	(iv)	(ii)	(iii)	(b)	(iii)	(i)	(v)	(iv)
(c)	(ii)	(v)	(iii)	(i)	(d)	(iv)	(ii)	(iv)	(i)

4. Choose the compounds containing ionic, covalent and coordinate bonds out of the following $MgCl_2$, CH_4, CaO, HCl, NH_4^+, O_3.
5. Calculate the bond order of He_2^+ molecular ion.
6. Which of the two : KCl or Cl_2 has higher boiling point and why?
7. Which of the following has maximum bond angle? H_2O, CO_2, NH_3, CH_4
8. Write the state of hybridisation of boron in BF_3.
9. Taking Z-axis as the internuclear axis, explain why $2p_x$ or $2p_y$ orbital does not combine with 2s-orbital to form molecular orbitals?
10. List two main conditions for forming hydrogen bonds.
11. Which of the two: ice or water has lower density?
12. Define bonding molecular orbital.

Assertion-Reason

Directions (Q. Nos. 13-17) In the following questions. an Assertion (A) is followed by a corresponding Reason (R) Use the following keys to choose the appropriate answer.

(a) Both (A) and (R) are correct and (R) is the correct explanation of (A).
(b) Both (A) and (R) are correct but (R) is not the correct explanation of (A).
(c) (A) is correct and (R) is incorrect.
(d) (A) is incorrect and (R) is correct.

13. **Assertion** (A) SF_4 molecule has two types of structure,

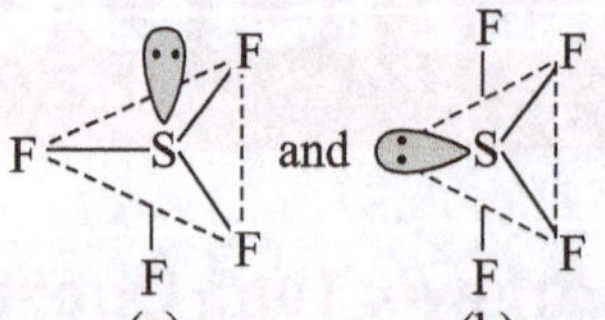

(a) (b)

where structure (b) is more stable than (a).

Reason (R) *lp-bp* repulsions decide the greater stability of structure (b).

14. **Assertion** (A) PCl_5 molecule has trigonal bipyramidal structure.

Reason (R) PCl_5 contains 5 electron pairs and its hybridisation is sp^3d.

15. **Assertion** (A) The values of dipole moment of CO_2 molecule is zero.

Reason (R) CO_2 molecule is linear.

16. **Assertion** (A) NO^+ and CN^- both have same bond order and magnetism.

Reason (R) NO^+ and CN^- are isoelectronic species.

17. **Assertion** (A) Ionic bond is non-directional.

Reason (R) Each ion is surrounded by a uniformly distributed electric field.

Case-Study

18. Molecular orbital theory is a theory on chemical bonding, developed by F. Hund and R.S Mulliken to describe the structure and properties of different molecules. The valence bond theory failed to explain how certain molecules contains two or more equivalent bonds whose bond orders lie between that of a single bond and double bond, such as the bonds in resonance stabilised molecules. This is where the molecular orbital theory proved to be more powerful.

In simple terms, the molecular orbital theory states that each atom tends to combine together and form molecular orbitals. As a result of such arrangement electrons are found in various atomic orbitals and they are usually associated with different nuclei.

(i) When O_2 changes to O_2^- ion, then electrons are add in which orbital?
(ii) What is the bond order and magnetic characteristic of CN^-?
(iii) Addition of electrons in antibonding molecular orbital destabilises the molecule. Why?

19. Chemical bonding, involves interactions that account for the association of atoms into molecules, ions, crystals, and other stable species that make up the familiar substances of the everyday world. When atoms approach one another, their nuclei and electrons interact and tend to distribute themselves in space in such a way that the total energy is lower than it would be in any alternative arrangement. If the total energy of a group of atoms is lower than the sum of the energies of the component atoms, then bond together and the energy lowering is the bonding energy.

The ideas that helped to establish the nature of chemical bonding came during early 20th century, after the electron had been discovered and quantum mechanics had provided a language for the description of the behaviour of electrons in atoms. However, even though chemists need quantum mechanics to attain a detailed quantitative understanding of bond formation, much of their pragmatic understanding of bonds is expressed in simple intuitive models. These models treat bonds as primarily of two kinds-namely, ionic and covalent.

The type of bond that is most likely to occur between two atoms can be predicted on the basis of the location of the elements in the periodic table, and to some extent the properties of the substances so formed can be related to the type of bonding.

A key concept in a discussion of chemical bonding is that of the molecule. Molecules are the smallest unit of compounds that can exist. One feature of molecules that can be predicted with reasonable success is their shape. Molecular shapes are of considerable importance for understanding the reactions that compounds can undergo, and so the link between chemical bonding and chemical reactivity is discussed briefly here.

(i) According to molecular orbital theory, H_2^{2-} molecule does not exist, why?
(ii) In PO_4^{3-}, calculate formal charge on each oxygen atom and P—O bond order.
(iii) Acetophenone has higher dipole moment than ethanol. Explain?

Short Answer Type I Questions

2 Marks

20. Give correct reason for the following.
(i) BF_3 has a zero dipole moment although the B—F bonds are polar.
(ii) All carbon to oxygen bonds in CO_3^{2-} are equivalent.

21. Give shapes of :
(i) NH_4^+ (ii) CO_3^{2-}
(iii) BeF_3^- (iv) SO_4^{2-}

22. Presence of lone pairs distorts the geometry of a molecule. Explain with example.

23. CO_2 and H_2O both are triatomic molecules but there is a large difference in their dipole moment values. Explain.

24. Each carbon-oxygen bond in carbon dioxide molecule is a polar but the molecule itself is non-polar. Explain.

Short Answer Type II Questions

3 Marks

25. Give reason for the following. The molecule of $MgCl_2$ is linear while that of stannous chloride is angular.

26. What is the effect of the following ionisation processes on the bond order in C_2 and O_2?
(i) $C_2 \longrightarrow C_2^+ + e^-$
(ii) $O_2 \longrightarrow O_2^+ + e^-$

27. Arrange the following according to bond length giving reasons
(i) H—F, H—Cl, H—Br, H—I
(ii) C—C, C=C, C≡C
(iii) C—H bond length in CH_4, C_2H_4 and C_2H_2

28. (i) What are the important characteristics of ionic compounds?
(ii) Which one is most ionic? Explain with reason $MgCl_2$, $CaCl_2$, CaO, PCl_5

29. Which of the following species have same shape /same bond order? NO_2^+, NO_2^-, CO_2, O_3
Also draw their structures.

30. Which bond do you expect to be stronger in each of the following cases and why?
(i) H—H, Cl—Cl (ii) O_2, N_2
(iii) F—F, Cl—Cl

31. Write shortnotes on (i) resonance (ii) σ and π−bonds, (iii) covalent bond.

Long Answer Type Questions

5 Marks

32. Define Lattice energy. On what factors does it depends? How does it help to predict the stability of the ionic compound formed?

33. Draw the molecular structure of (i) XeF_2, (ii) $XeOF_2$ (iii) XeF_4
Also find the hybridisation of central atom and bond angles in the structures.

34. What are the main points of similarity and difference between valence bond theory and molecular orbital theory.

35. Arrange the given dicarbon species in order of their bond length giving reasons C_2, C_2^-, C_2^{2-}.

36. Which two of H_2^+, H_2^- and H_2^{2-} have the same bond order?

37. In each of the following pairs, predict which has higher value of the property mentioned and why?
(i) HF, HCl Polar character
(ii) $NH_3 H_2O$ Bond angle
(iii) KCl, KF Lattice enrhalpy
(iv) NF_3, NH_3 Dipole moment
(v) C_2H_2, C_2H_4 s-character in the hydridisation of carbon

Answers

1. (i) valency,
(ii) largest, smallest,
(iii) zero
(iv) triangular planar
(v) one
(vi) triple bond.

2. (i) → a, (ii) → c, (iii) → d, (iv) → b, (v) → c, (vi) → a, (vii) → a

3. (i) b, (ii) b

4. The compounds containing ionic bonds-$MgCl_2$, CaO, Covalent bonds-HCl, CH_4 and coordinate bonds-NH_4^+ and O_3.

5. The bond order of He_2^+ molecular ion is 0.5.

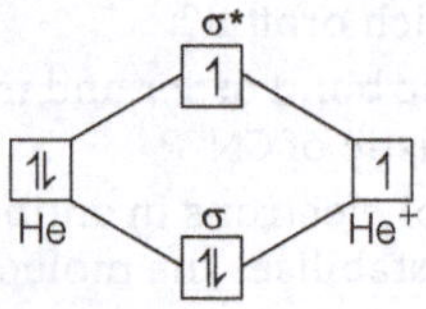

$$\text{Bond order} = \frac{N_b - N_a}{2}$$
$$= \frac{2-1}{2} = \frac{1}{2} = 0.5$$

6. KCl has higher boiling point than Cl_2 because Cl_2 is a gas and the ionic bond is present between potassium and chlorine atoms of KCl. So, KCl is solid at room temperature.

7. Bond angle of the following compounds as below :
$H_2O = 104.5°$ $CO_2 = 180°$
$NH_3 = 109.5°$ $CH_4 = 109.5°$
Hence, CO_2 has maximum bond angle.

8. The state of hybridisation of boron in BF_3 is sp^2
BF_3 (Trigonal planar molecule).

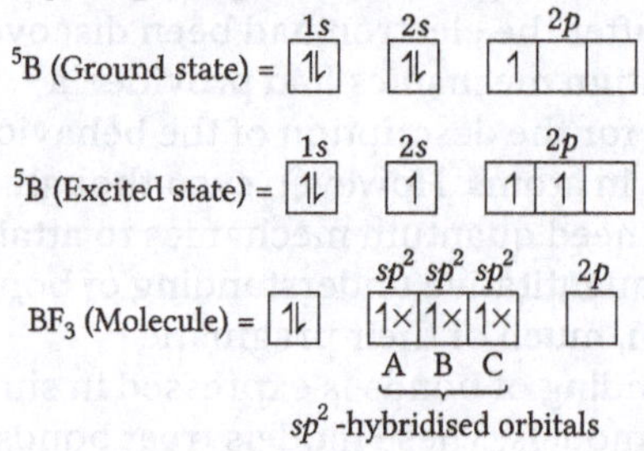

So, boron would be sp^2-hybridised in BF_3.

9. $2p_x$ and $2p_y$-orbitals have different symmetry and energies as compared to 2s-orbital. Thus, they can't overlap with 2s-orbital to form molecular orbitals.

10. Refer to text on page 185 (Topic-4, Conditions for hydrogen bonding).

11. Ice is less dense than water because the orientation of hydrogen bonds causes molecules to push farther apart, which lower the density.
When water freezes, water molecules form a crystalline structure maintained by H - bonding. So, (solid water) ice is less dense then liquid water.

12. Refer to text on page 179 (Topic-4, LCAO, Bonding molecular orbital).

13. (a) Both (A) and (R) are correct and (R) is the correct explanation of (A).

14. (a) Both (A) and (R) are correct and (R) is the correct explanation of (A).

15. (*a*) Both (A) and (R) are correct and (R) is the correct explanation of (A).

16. (*a*) Both (A) and (R) are correct and (R) is the correct explanation of (A).

17. (*a*) Both (A) and (R) are correct and (R) is the correct explanation of (A).

18. (i) During change of O_2 to O_2^-, the electron adds on π^* orbital. i.e. Electronic configuration of O_2 $(16e^-)$ is

$\sigma 1s^2 \sigma^* 1s^2 \sigma 2s^2 \sigma^* 2s^2 \sigma 2p_z^2 \pi 2p_x^2 \approx \pi 2p_y^2 \pi^*(2p_x^1)$

$\approx \pi(2p_y^1)$ and configuration $O_2^-(17e^-)$ is

$\sigma 1s^2 \sigma^* 1s^2 \sigma 2s^1 \sigma^* 2s^2 \sigma^* 2p_z^2 \pi 2p_x^2 \approx \pi 2p_y^2 \pi^* 2p_x^1 \approx \pi 2p_y^1$

(ii) CN^- has 14 electrons (6 from C, 7 from N and 1 from negative charge).

It has $10e^-$ in bonding orbital and $4e^-$ in antibonding orbital.

Thus, bond order $= \dfrac{10-7}{2} = 3$

Since, it does not have any unpaired e^-, thus it is diamagnetic.

(iii) Electrons placed in *ABMO* destabilises the molecule because the neutral repulsion of the e^- in this orbital is more than the attraction between the e^- and nuclei, that causes increase in energy.

19. (i) Generally, if bond order of any species is zero, then that molecule does not exist.

Bond order of $H_2^{2-} = \sigma 1s^2, \sigma^* 1s^2 = \dfrac{2-2}{2} = 0$

(ii) In PO_4^{3-}, the formal charge on each O-atom

$= -\dfrac{3}{4} = -0.75$

P—O bond order in PO_4^{3-}

$= \dfrac{\text{no. of bonds}}{\text{no. of resonating structures}}$

$= \dfrac{5}{4} = 1.25$

(iii) The dipole moment of acetophenones is 3 Debye which is higher than ethanol as it has strong electron withdrawing group.

20. (i) Refer to text on page 149 (Topic-1, Dipole moment of molecular structure).

(ii) If structure of carbonate ion (CO_3^{2-}) is considered, there should be two C—O single bonds and one C=O double bond. But experimentally, it is observed that carbon oxygen bonds have same bond length which is in between that of C—O single bond and C=O double bond. Thus is because of resonance.

This can be explained by the following resonance structures:

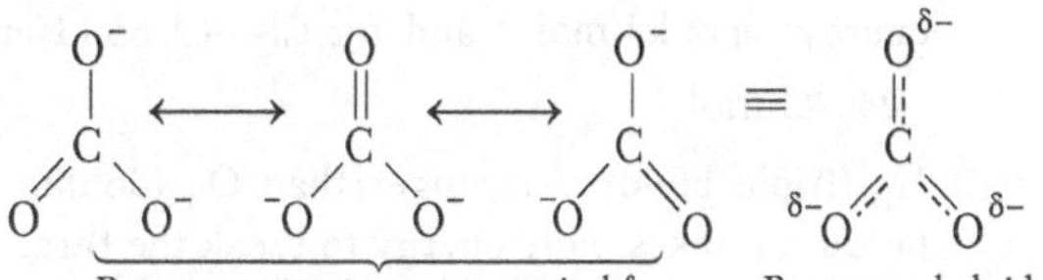

Resonance structures or canonical forms   Resonance hybrid

21. Shapes of

(i) NH_4^+ = tetrahedral   (ii) CO_3^{2-} = trigonal planar

(iii) BeF_3^- = trigonal planar (iv) SO_4^{2-} = tetrahedral

22. Refer to text on page 160, (Topic-2, Shape of some simple molecules/ions with central ions having are or more lone pair).

23. CO_2 is symmetrical and has dipole moment zero. Therefore, it will have a linear shape with bond angle 180° but H_2O is a unsymmetrical molecule and bent geometry, the geometry has specific dipole moment 1.84 D because the bond polarities do not cancel each other. Therefore, H_2O will have a bent structure with bond angle 104°.

24. CO_2 is non-polar because it has a linear, symmetrical structure, with 2 oxygen atoms of equal electronegativity pulling the electron density from carbon at an angle of 180° from either direction.

25. In case of $MgCl_2$, Mg is *sp*-hybridesed with a bond angle of 180° and hence is linear, whereas in the case of stannous chloride ($SnCl_2$), Sn is sp^2-hybridised with the bond angle of 120° and hence, the molecule is angular.

26. (i) $C_2 \longrightarrow C_2^+ + e^-$

As the bond order changes from 2 to 1.5, the bond length increases. Also, with the loss of e^-, C_2^+ becomes paramagnetic in nature.

(ii) $O_2 \longrightarrow O_2^+ + e^-$

As the bond order changes from 2 to 2.5, the bond length decreases. There is no change in magnetic character in this case.

27. (i) Refer to text on page 146 (Topic-1, Bond length, various factors that affect bond length, (i)]

(ii) Refer to text on page 146 (Topic-1, Bond length, various factors that affect bond length, (ii)]

(iii) $C_2H_2 < C_2H_4 < CH_4$

28. (i) Refer to text on page 142 (Topic-1, Characteristics of ionic compounds).

(ii) Refer to text on pages 141 (Topic-1, Lattice enthalpy)

29. NO_2^-, O_3 NO_2^+ have triangular shape whereas CO_2 has linear shape.

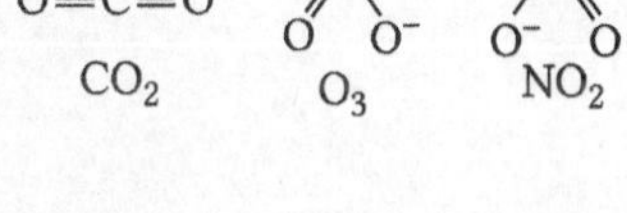

CO_2 O_3 NO_2

30. (i) H—H bond is more stronger than Cl— Cl bond. Both molecule have one covalent bond but H—H bond energy =432 kJ mol^{-1} and for Cl—Cl bond energy =240 kJ mol^{-1}

(ii) N_2 (triple bond) is stronger than O_2 (double bond because it takes more energy to break the three bond of nitrogen, than the two bonds of oxygen.

(iii) F—F, Cl—Cl

The bond Cl—Cl is stronger than F—F because bond disociation energy of fluorine is however, lower than chlorine due to its small size, its inter electronic repulsion is very high.

31. Refer to text on page no.

(i) 158 (Topic-3, Resonance).

(ii) 169, (Topic-3, Nature of covalent bonds).

(iii) 143, (Topic-1, Covalent bond).

32. Refer to text on page 141 (Topic-1, Lattice enthalpy).

33. (i) XeF_2 - Linear, *sp* hybridisation

(ii) XeF_2 - T-shaped, sp^3d-hybridisation

(iii) $XeOF_4$ - Square planar, dsp^2-hybridisation

34. Similarities

(i) Both the theory include the sharing of electrons by the nuclei.

(ii) According to both the theories the energy of overlapping orbitals must be comparable and the symmetry must be similar.

Dissimilarities

(i) Resonance plays an important role in VBT whereas there is no such place for resonance in MOT.

(ii) There is no explanation of paramagnetic character of oxygen by VBT whereas paramagnetic charater is satisfactory explained by MOT.

35. The bond order results show that the C_2^- has the highest number of valence electrons and highest bond energy. Therefore C_2^- has the shortest bond length, C_2^+ has lesser bond energy than C_2 therefore C_2^+, has longer bond length than C_2. Hence, dicarbon species in order of decreasing bond length,

$$C_2^+ > C_2 > C_2^-$$

36. Refer to text on pages 182 and 183 (Topic-4, Bonding in some homonuclear diatomic molecule).

37. (i) As the electronegativity of F is more than Cl. ∴ HF is more polar than HCl.

(ii) Refer to text on page 147 (Topic-1, Bond parameter, bond angle).

(iii) Refer to text on page 141 [Topic-1, Lattice enthalpy, (ii)]

(iv) Refer to text on page 149 (Topic-1, Dipole moment of molecular structures).

(v) As C_2H_2 has *sp* hybridisation and C_2H_4 has sp^2-hybridisation. Thus, C_2H_2 has more character.

CHAPTER

05

Thermodynamics

Thermodynamics is the branch of science that deals with different forms of energy. It also interrelates these energy forms from quantitative point of view. Thermodynamics is derived from Greek word (*thermos* = heat and *dynamics* =flow). It is mainly based on four generalisations, these are called the **zeroth first, second** and **third** laws of thermodynamics.
The branch of science that deals with different forms of energy and their quantitative inter-relationships is known as **thermodynamics.**

- General Introduction, Work, Heat First Law of Thermodynamics and Enthalpy
- Different Types of Enthalpics
- Spontaneity, Entropy and Gibbss Free Energy

TOPIC 01 General Introduction, Work, Heat First Law of Thermodynamics and Enthalpy

Thermodynamics is an important branch of science as it helps us to

(i) predict the feasibility of a reaction, i.e. whether certain reaction is possible under given conditions of temperatures and pressures or not.

(ii) predict the extent of chemical reaction.

(iii) predict the force that drives chemical (reaction) process.

(iv) deduce some important laws like distribution law, law of chemical equilibrium etc.

Thermodynamic Terms

Some terms related to thermodynamics are given below:

System and Surroundings

The part of the universe that is under thermodynamic observations is called the **system**, while the remaining part of the universe that can interact with the system is called **surroundings**. System and surroundings together constitute the universe, i.e.

Universe = system + surroundings

The real or imaginary surfaces or lines separating two or more systems or a system from its surroundings is called the **boundary**. The boundary may be **diathermic** (i.e. allow passage of heat) or **adiabatic** (i.e. does not allow passage of heat).

It helps us to control and keep track of all movements of matter and energy in or out of the system.

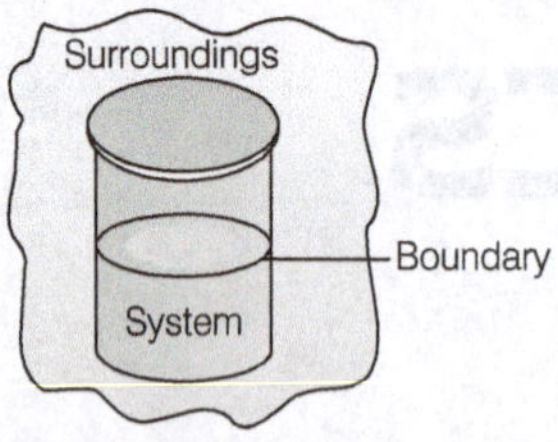

System, surroundings and boundary

Types of the System

Depending upon the movement of matter or energy in or out of the systems, the systems can be of following types :

1. Open System

An open system can exchange matter as well as energy with its surroundings. The boundary here is not sealed and non-insulated thermally i.e. it is generally imaginary. e.g. presence of reactants in an open beaker, reactions occurring in all living systems, car engines, etc.

For such a system, $\Delta m \neq 0, \Delta E \neq 0$ i.e. change in mass and energy is not zero.

2. Closed System

A closed system does not exchange matter with its surroundings but can exchange energy in the form of heat, work or radiations, i.e. here the boundary is sealed but not insulated, e.g. hot water kept in a closed container.

For such a system, $\Delta m = 0, \Delta E \neq 0$.

3. Isolated System

An isolated system exchanges neither matter nor energy with its surroundings i.e. here the boundary is sealed as well as insulated, e.g. thermos flask.

For such a system, $\Delta m = 0, \Delta E = 0$.

Example 1 Which of the following are open, closed or isolated systems?

(i) Human being (ii) The earth

(iii) Can of tomato soup (iv) Ice cube tray filled with water

(v) Coffee in a thermos flask and

(vi) Helium filled in balloon

Sol.

Open system	Closed system	Isolated system
Human being	Can of tomato soup	Coffee in a thermos flask
The earth	Helium filled in balloon	
Ice cube tray filled with water		

Thermodynamic Properties

The physical quantities that are used to define the state of a system are called **properties.** Thermodynamics deals with matter in bulk (i.e. in large excess) and the properties arises because of bulk behaviour of matter are called **macroscopic properties or bulk properties of the system.**

These properties are further of two types:

1. Intensive Properties

The properties which do not depend upon the quantity or size of matter are called **intensive properties,** e.g. pressure, temperature, density, concentration, surface tension, viscosity, refractive index etc.

2. Extensive Properties

The properties which depend upon the quantity or size of matter are called **extensive properties,** e.g. volume (V), Gibbs energy (G), number of moles (n), enthalpy (H), entropy (S), mass, work, internal energy (E or U), heat capacity (C_p or C_V), etc.

It may be noted that the **ratio of the two extensive properties becomes intensive in nature.**If x is any extensive property of n moles of system, the molar property of the system, x_m is intensive because it refers to the property of 1 mole of the system and is independent of the quantity of matter

$$\boxed{x_m = x/n}$$

Similarly, molar volume (V_m) and molar heat capacity (C_m) are intensive properties.

State of the System

A set of conditions in which physical and chemical properties are fixed and specific is called the thermodynamic state of the system. In other words, a particular state when all measurable properties of system have fixed values then the state of system is called thermodynamic state of the system.

The property of a system whose value depends only upon the states of the system (i.e., initial and final states) and is independent of the path or manner by which the state is reached is called the **state function** or **state variables.**

e.g. pressure, volume internal energy (U), enthalpy (H), entropy (S), Gibbs free energy (G), temperature (T), etc. However, the variables, values of which is affected by the path followed, are called **path functions** e.g. work (W), heat (q) etc.

Thermodynamic Equilibrium

It is an equilibrium that involves following three equilibria :

(i) Mechanical equilibrium, i.e. when no work is done on the system or by the system.

(ii) Thermal equlibrium, i.e. temperature remains constant through out the system including the surroundings.

(iii) Chemical equilibrium, i.e. composition of the system remains constant and definite.

Types of Processes

The state of a variable can be changed via thermodynamic process. These processes are of the following types:

(i) **Adiabatic Process** In adiabatic process, the system does not exchange heat with its surroundings, i.e. no heat can flow in or out of the system.

In this process, the wall separating the system and the surroundings is called the **adiabatic wall.**

For an adiabatic process, $dq = 0$

(ii) **Isothermal Process** The isothermal process is carried out at constant temperature, i.e. it is the process in which temperature remains fixed.

For an isothermal process, $dT = 0$ and thus, $dE = 0$

(iii) **Isobaric Process** In isobaric process, change of state is brought about at constant pressure, i.e. $dp = 0$

(iv) **Isochoric Process** In an isochoric process, volume of the system remains constant, i.e. $dV = 0$.

The above four basic thermodynamic processes can be represented in a graph as:

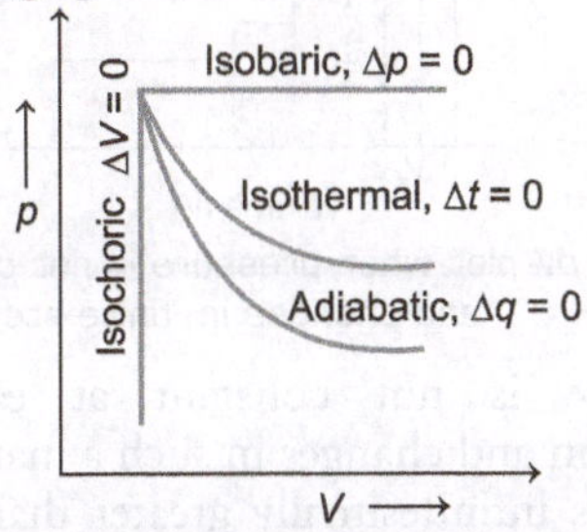

p versus V graph for various thermodynamic processes

(v) **Cyclic Process** When a system has undergone a number of different changes and finally returns to its initial state, the process is called **cyclic.**

For such a process, change in internal energy (dE or dU) and enthalpy (dH) are zero, i.e.

$$dE \text{ or } dU = 0 \text{ and } dH = 0$$

(vi) **Reversible Process** A reversible process can be defined as a process which is carried out infinitesimally slowly in such away that each step remains in equilibrium with the previous step and the process can be reversed at any state.

(vii) **Irreversible Process** In an irreversible process, the direction of process cannot be reversed by small change in variables. A irreversible process involves only a single step to transit the system from the initial state to the final state.

All natural processes are generally irreversible and the net work done in an irreversible process is somewhat less than that in reversible process, i.e. $W_{irr} < W_{rev}$. (This will be proved later in this chapter).

Example 2 Identify the steps involved in the following cyclic process. Temperature at A, B and F is T_1 and at C, D and E is T_2. Given $T_1 > T_2$

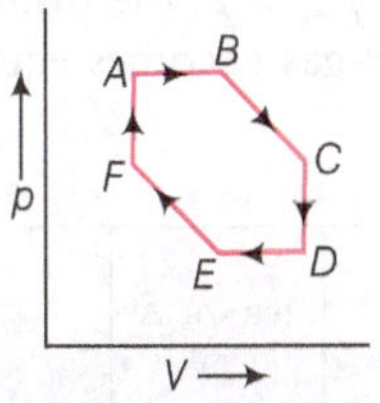

Sol. (i) $A \rightarrow B$ (Temperature and pressure are constant).

$\therefore$ It is isothermal and isobaric process.

(ii) $B \rightarrow C$ It is adiabatic expansion in which temperature falls from T_1 to T_2.

(iii) $C \rightarrow D$ (Temperature and volume are constant.)

$\therefore$ This process is isothermal and isochoric.

(iv) $D \rightarrow E$ (Temperature and pressure are constant.)

$\therefore$ It is isothermal and isobaric contraction.

(v) $E \rightarrow F$ (It is adiabatic compression in which temperature increases from T_2 to T_1.)

(vi) $F \rightarrow A$ (Temperature and volume are constant.)

$\therefore$ It is isothermal and isochoric process.

Work

It is defined as a mode of transfer of energy when system and surroundings differ in pressure, till their pressures become equal.

If an object is displaced through a distance dx by a force F, the amount of work done is given by

$$\boxed{W = F \times dx}$$

i.e. *it is the product of two factors*

(i) Intensity factor, F (ii) Capacity factor, dx

If intensity factor is pressure and capacity factor is volume, the work is called **mechanical work** or **pressure volume work** (pV work). Work done is a path function, as it depends upon the path followed. Work done on the system increases the energy of the system and is taken as positive while work done by the system is taken as negative. i.e.

Work done by the system = – ve

Work done on the system = + ve

Or

In other words, if a system loses energy, work is done by the system and if it gains energy, work is done on the system.

Mechanical (Pressure-Volume) Work Done by a System

Consider a cylinder, having one mole of an ideal gas fitted with a frictionless piston. Let the total volume and pressure of the gas are respectively, V_t and p. If p_{ex} is the external pressure and $p_{ex} > p$, the piston moves inward till the pressure of the gas becomes equal to external pressure (i.e. $p = p_{ex}$)

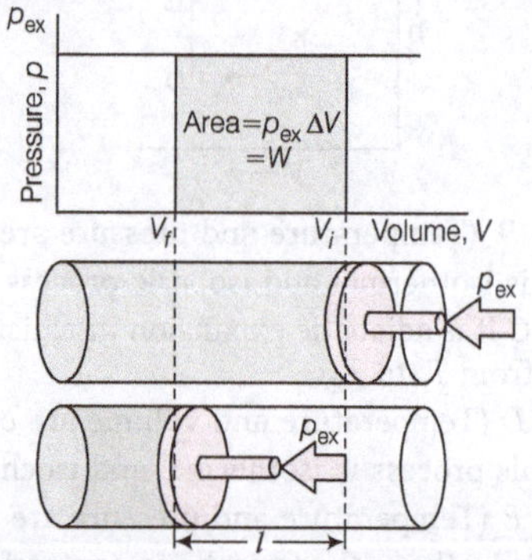

Work done on an ideal gas in a cylinder when it is compressed by a constant external pressure. p_{ex} (in single stop) is equal to the shaded area.

The condition of $p = p_{ex}$ can be achieved by following two ways :

1. If it is Achieved in a Single Step (i.e. Irreversible Process)

Let final volume of the gas is V_f if the change is carried out in a single step. Suppose during compression, the piston moves a distance l and the area of cross-section of the piston is A. Then, volume change

$$= l \times A = \Delta V = (V_f - V_i)$$

As we know, pressure $= \dfrac{\text{force}}{\text{area}}$

$\therefore$ Force on the piston $= p_{ex} \cdot A$

If W is the work done on the system by movement of the piston then

$$W = \text{force} \times \text{distance} = p_{ex} \cdot A \cdot l$$
$$= p_{ex} \cdot (-\Delta V) = -\, p_{ex} \Delta V$$

$$\boxed{W = -\, p_{ex}(V_f - V_i)}$$

Significance of Negative Sign in the Expression of Work

The negative sign in the expression of work is a conventional sign, which represents that work is done by the system, as in case of expansion. In case of compression, work is done on the system, so the sign of W should be positive. It is achieved by multiplying the negative value of $(V_f - V_i)$ with negative sign.

Example 3 Two litres of an ideal gas at a pressure of 10 atm expands isothermally against a constant external pressure of 1 atm, until its total volume is 10 L. How much work is done during the expansion? **[NCERT Textbook]**

Sol. $W = -p_{ex}(\Delta V) = -1(10 - 2) = -1(8) = -8$ L atm

2. If it is Achieved in a Number of Steps (i.e. Reversible Process)

(i) If pressure is not constant at every stage of compression, i.e. it changes in number of finite steps, then work done on the gas is sum of work done in all the steps involved and is given by the expression

$$\boxed{W = -\Sigma p \Delta V}$$

This work in the p *vs* V plot can be represented by the shaded area as shown below.

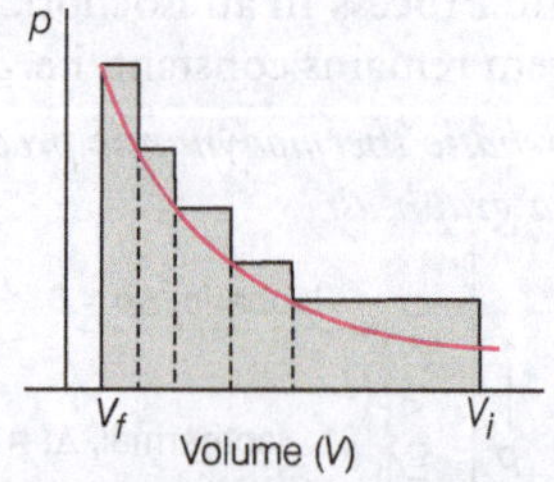

pV-plot when pressure is not constant and changes in finite steps

(ii) If pressure is not constant at each stage of compression and changes in such a manner such that it is always infinitesimally greater than the pressure of the gas and the volume during the process decreases by an infinitesimal amount dV, then work done is given by the expression

$$\boxed{W = -\int_{V_i}^{V_f} p_{ex}\, dV}$$

In case of compression, $p_{ex} = p_{in} + dp$ (i.e. external pressure is greater than the pressure of the gas) and in case of expansion, $p_{ex} = p_{in} - dp$ (i.e. external pressure is less than the pressure of the gas).

In general, $p_{ex} = (p_{in} \pm dp)$

$$\therefore \quad W_{rev} = -\int_{V_i}^{V_f} (p_{in} \pm dp)\, dV$$

The above expression shows that work is done during reversible conditions. Since, $dp \times dV$ is very small in comparison to $p_{in}\, dV$, so

$$W_{rev} = -\int_{V_i}^{V_f} p_{in}\, dV$$

In terms of volume, from ideal gas equation $(pV = nRT)$ for n moles of an ideal gas.

$$p_{in} \quad \text{or} \quad p = nRT/V$$

$\therefore$ At constant temperature (isothermal process),

$$W_{rev} = -\int_{V_i}^{V_f} nRT \frac{dV}{V} = -nRT \ln \frac{V_f}{V_i}$$

$$\boxed{W_{rev} = -2.303\, nRT \log \frac{V_f}{V_i}}$$

[where, V_i = initial volume, V_f = final volume, n = number of moles, R = gas constant and T = absolute temperature (in K)]. In case of infinitesimal changes in pressure, the work done in the p vs V plot is shown by the area of the plot (as shown in the following figure.)

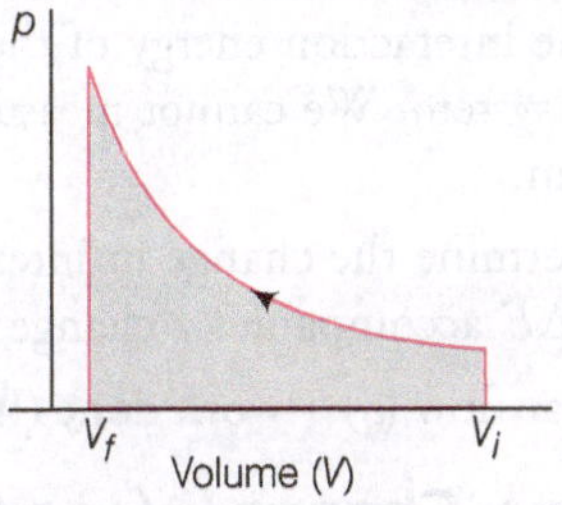

pV-plot when pressure is not constant and changes in infinite steps (reversible conditions)

W_{rev} is Maximum Work

Work done during isothermal expansion of an ideal gas is given by the equation,

$$W = -p_{ex} \Delta V$$

Now, for given change of volume (ΔV), W can be maximum if p_{ex} is maximum. But for expansion, p_{ex} has to be smaller than p_{in}. This means that for getting maximum work, the external pressure has to be infinitesimally smaller than the internal pressure of the gas.

These conditions are nearly close to reversibility. Thus, for a given change of volume

$$W_{rev} = W_{max}$$

Work in Case of Free Expansion

When a gas expands under vacuum, i.e. no external pressure works on it $(p_{ex} = 0)$, its expansion is called **free expansion**. Since, $p_{ex} = 0$, W is also 0 in case of free expansion of an ideal gas, i.e. no work is done, whether the process is reversible or irreversible.

Example 4

(i) 5.2 mol of ideal gas at 3 atm and 25° C expands isothermally to 3 times of its original volume against the external pressure of 1 atm. Calculate work done.

(ii) If the same gas expands isothermally in a reversible manner, then what will be the value of work done?

Sol. (i) $w = -p_{ex}(V_2 - V_1)$

Now initial volume $(V_1) = \frac{nRT}{p}$

$$= \frac{5.2 \times 0.082 \times 298}{3} = 42.35\ \text{L}$$

Final volume $(V_2) = 42.35 \times 3 = 127.05$ L

Now, $W = -1(127.05 - 42.35)$

$= 84.7$ L atm

$= -84.7 \times 101.325$ J $= -8582.22$ J

(ii) For isothermal reversible expansion of ideal gas

$$W_{rev} = -2.303\, nRT \log \frac{V_2}{V_1}$$

$$= -2.303 \times 5.2 \times 8.314 \times 298 \log\left(\frac{127.05}{42.35}\right)$$

$= 14156.38$ J

Heat

Temperature is the measure of degree of hotness or coldness and the quantity of energy which flows between system and surroundings on account of temperature difference is called **heat**, q. It is also a path function, i.e. depends upon the path followed.

q is positive, when heat is transferred from the surroundings to the system and q is negative when heat is transferred from system to the surroundings.

If change in temperature is ΔT, then heat transferred, q = coefficient $\times \Delta T$. The magnitude of the coefficient depends upon the size, composition and nature of the system.

Heat Capacity

The quantity of heat required to raise the temperature of a system by 1° is called heat capacity of that system. In other words, if the magnitude of heat capacity is large, there is only a small rise in temperature by a given amount of heat, e.g. heat capacity of H_2O is large. Thus, a large amount of heat is required to raise its temperature.

As we know that heat flow is dependent on temperature difference therefore, mathematically,

$$q \propto \Delta T \quad \text{or} \quad q = C \cdot \Delta T$$

Here, the constant C represents the heat capacity.

Types of Heat Capacity Based on the Quantity

There are two types of heat capacity based on the amount of a body or system under consideration.

These are as follows:

(i) **Specific Heat Capacity (C_S)** It is defined as "the heat required to raise the temperature of one unit mass by 1 degree".

Mathematically, $q = C_s \times m \times \Delta T$

where,

q = heat required to raise the temperature by 1°C or 1 K

C_s = specific heat capacity, m = mass

ΔT = temperature change (in °C or K)

(ii) **Molar Heat Capacity** It is defined as "the heat required to raise the temperature of one mole of a body by one degree.

Mathematically, $q = C_m \times n \times \Delta T$

where, n = number of moles and C_m = molar heat capacity

Note Relation among C, C_s and C_m

$$C_s = \frac{C}{m} \;;\; C_m = \frac{C}{n}$$

Types of Heat Capacity Based on Conditions

Based on the conditions, such as volume and pressure, there are two types of heat capacity (specifically molar heat capacity) which are discussed as follow:

(i) **Heat Capacity at Constant Volume (C_V)** It is defined as the amount of heat required to raise the temperature of one mole of a gas by one degree, when volume of the gas is kept constant.

$$\text{Mathematically, } C_V = \left(\frac{q}{\Delta T}\right)_V$$

(ii) **Heat Capacity at Constant Pressure (C_p)** It is defined as the amount of heat required to raise the temperature of one mole of a gas by one degree, when pressure of the gas is kept constant.

$$\text{Mathematically}, C_p = \left(\frac{q}{\Delta T}\right)_p$$

Note Heat capacity at constant pressure (C_p) is always greater than heat capacity at constant volume (C_V).

C_p / C_V Ratio

The ratio of molar heat capacities at constant pressure and constant volume is represented by γ. The value of γ gives information about the atomicity of gases. The value of γ is 1.67, 1.40 and 1.33 for monoatomic, diatomic and triatomic gases, respectively.

Internal Energy

The internal energy of the system, E, (or U) is simply the sum of all the possible kinds of energy associated with substance in that system. Every substance is associated with a definite amount of internal energy which depends on its chemical nature as well as on its temperature, pressure and volume.

Internal energy is made up of **kinetic energy** and **potential energy** of the constituent particles. The kinetic energy arises due to motion of the particles (which can be translation, rotation or vibration).

The potential energy arises from different types of interaction between particles. This can be the interaction between the electrons and the nuclei in atoms or molecules and the interaction energy of the constituent molecules in the system. We cannot measure the internal energy of a system.

We can only determine the change in internal energy, i.e. ΔE. ΔE accompanies a change in the system.

$$\Delta E = \text{heat flow } (q) + \text{work done } (W)$$

Internal Energy Change (ΔU or ΔE)

The internal energy of a system is a state function, i.e. it depends upon the state of the system and not upon how the system attains that state. This means that a change in the internal energy (represented as ΔU or ΔE) depends only upon the initial and final states of the system and not upon the intermediate states.

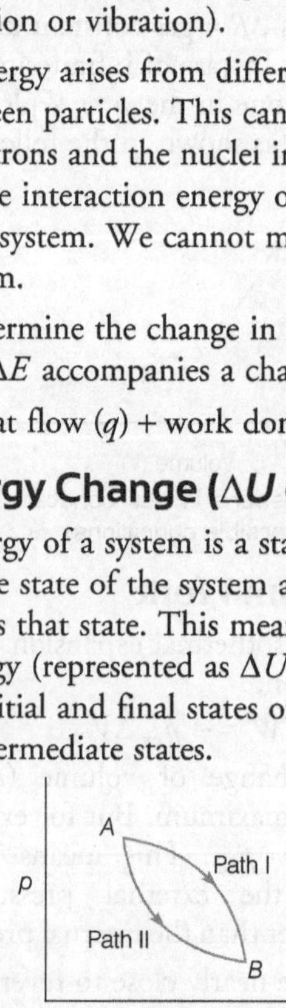

p-V curve

ΔE_1 = change in internal energy by path I
ΔE_2 = change in internal energy by path II
then, $\Delta E = \Delta E_1 = \Delta E_2 = E_B = E_A$

Therefore, while determining the value of ΔU, we are not concerned with the path or the way by which a system transits from one state to another. **The change in internal energy (ΔU or ΔE) is defined as the difference in the internal energies of the system in the final and the initial states.**

Thus, $\Delta U = U_{\text{final state}} - U_{\text{initial state}}$

The value of ΔU or ΔE is positive when energy is transferred from the surroundings to the system and it is negative when energy is transferred from the system to the surroundings.

When, a chemical reaction occurs, the internal energy of the system before the reaction is usually different from the internal energy after the reaction. This is because the nature of the molecules of products obtained in the reaction is different from that of the molecules of reactants. The change in internal energy in a chemical reaction is given by

$$\Delta U = U_{\text{products}} - U_{\text{reactants}} \quad \text{or} \quad \Delta U = U_P - U_R$$

where, U_P represents the internal energy of products while U_R that of reactants.It is to be noted that the absolute value of internal energy of a substance cannot be determined accurately. However, the change in internal energy, i.e. ΔU can easily be measured with the help of first law of the thermodynamics as discussed in the forthcoming subsections.

Relationship between C_V and ΔU

C_V can be represented as, $C_V = \dfrac{q_V}{dT}$

where, q_V = infinitesimally small amount of heat absorbed by the system at constant volume to raise its temperature (dT). Also, $q_v = \Delta U$

$$\therefore \; C_V = \left(\frac{\Delta U}{dT}\right)_{\text{at constant volume}}, \; C_V = \left(\frac{\partial U}{\partial T}\right)_V$$

Thus, **heat capacity at constant volume (C_V) may be defined as the rate of change of internal energy with temperature at constant volume.**

Zeroth Law of Thermodynamics

Zeroth law of thermodynamics was put forward much after the establishment of the first and second law of thermodynamics and states that "if two objects is in thermal equilibrium with a third object then they are also in thermal equilibrium with each other." It is also called law of temperature or law of thermal equilibrium.

First Law of Thermodynamics

This law states that energy can neither be created nor be destroyed, although it can be transformed from one form to another. In other words, the total energy of the universe remains constant or the energy of a system that is isolated from its surroundings is constant. This is also called as the **law of conservation of energy.**

Mathematical Formulation of First Law of Thermodynamics

Suppose a system consumes heat (q) and work (W) is done on the system. In this process, the internal energy changes from U_1 to U_2 then

$$\boxed{\Delta U = q + W}$$

where, $\Delta U = (U_2 - U_1) = \Delta E$

It is the **mathematical expression of first law of the thermodynamics.**

The first law of thermodynamics under different cases are discussed below:

(i) When a system undergoes isothermal change $\Delta U = 0$, i.e. there is no increase or decrease in the internal energy of the system then the first law of thermodynamics reduces to

$$0 = q + W \quad \text{or} \quad q = -W$$

- In case of isothermal reversible change.

$$W_{\text{rev}} = -2.303\, nRT \ln \frac{V_f}{V_i}$$

$$q = -W = 2.303\, nRT \log \frac{V_f}{V_i}$$

- In case of isothermal irreversible change

$$q = -W = p_{\text{ex}}(V_f - V_i)$$

- In case the process is carried out at constant volume (i.e. $\Delta V = 0$), work done will also be zero, thus the first law reduces to

$$\boxed{\Delta U = q_V}$$

i.e. increase in internal energy of the system is equal to the heat absorbed by the system or decrease in internal energy of the system is equal to heat lost by the system. Here, subscript V in q_V indicates that heat is given at constant volume.

(ii) When a system undergoes adiabatic change $q = 0$, i.e. there is no exchange of heat between system and surrounding, the first law reduces to

$$\boxed{\Delta U = W}$$

i.e. work is done at the expense of internal energy.

(iii) **In case of gaseous system,** if a gas expands against the constant external pressure, p, let the volume change be ΔV, the mechanical work done by the gas is equal to $-p \times \Delta V$.
Substituting the value in $\Delta U = q + W$, we get
$$\Delta U = q - p\Delta V \quad \ldots\text{(i)}$$
(iv) **If change is cyclic** Here, $\Delta U = 0$, as the system in a cyclic process returns to it original state.
Thus, equation (i) becomes
$$q = -W \text{ or } q = p\Delta V$$

Application of First Law of Thermodynamics

There are several applications of the first law of thermodynamics. Among these, Joule-Thomson effect is highly significant.

Joule-Thomson Effect

The phenomenon of change of temperature produced when a gas is made to expand adiabatically from a region of high pressure to a region of extremely low pressure is called **Joule-Thomson effect.**

This effect is zero in case of an ideal gas in which van der Waals' forces of attraction are negligible.

Thus, there is no expenditure of energy in overcoming these forces of attraction. Joule-Thomson coefficient, μ_{JT} is given by

$$\boxed{\mu_{JT} = \frac{dT}{dp} = \frac{1}{C_p}\left[\frac{2a}{RT} - b\right]}$$

The temperature below which a gas becomes cooler on expansion is known as the **inversion temperature** (T_i). At this, μ_{JT} changes its sign.

Hence, $\mu_{JT} = 0,\ T_i = \dfrac{2a}{Rb}$

where, a and b are called van der Waals' constants.

Limitations of First Law of Thermodynamics

This law fails to explain:

(i) the extent and direction of the convertibility of one form of energy into another.
(ii) amount of heat energy transferred from one system to another.
(iii) whether a process is feasible or not.
(iv) why it is not possible to convert heat energy completely into an equivalent amount of work.

According to the first law of thermodynamics, the energy of one form can be converted into an equivalent amount of energy of some other form. But, according to our common experience, it is not possible to convert heat into an equivalent amount of work. The first law has no explanation for this anomaly.

Thus, we need another law of thermodynamics which is free from the above limitations. Hence, another law known as **Second law of thermodynamics** was introduced. The law is discussed later in detail.

Example 5 Express the change in internal energy of a system when

(i) No heat is absorbed by the system from the surroundings, but work (W) is done on the system. What type of wall does the system have?
(ii) No work is done on the system, but q amount of heat is taken out from the system and given to the surroundings. What type of wall does the system have?
(iii) W amount of work is done by the system and q amount of heat is supplied to the system. What type of system would it be? **NCERT Textbook**

Sol. (i) If heat absorbed is zero, i.e. $q = 0$ or the process is adiabatic, the first law reduces to $\Delta U = W_{ad}$
In such a system adiabatic or insulated wall is used.
(ii) If work done is zero, the first law reduced to $\Delta U = -q$. For such a system, the walls must be thermally conducting.
(iii) If $W \neq 0$ and $q \neq 0$, then from first law of thermodynamics, $\Delta U = q - W$ (as work is done by the system). Thus, it is a closed system.

Example 6 Two litre of an ideal gas at a pressure of 10 atm expands isothermally into a vacuum until its total volume is 10 L. How much heat is absorbed and how much work is done in the expansion? **NCERT Textbook**

Sol. For isothermal process, $\Delta U = 0$, so from first law of thermodynamics, $0 = q + W$
or $$q = -W = p_{ex}(10-2) = 0(8) = 0$$
Thus, no work is done; and hence, no heat is absorbed.

Enthalpy

The total heat content of a system at constant pressure is called the enthalpy of the system. Indeed, it is the sum of internal energy and the product of pressure-volume work. It is an extensive quantity and represented by the symbol H. Like internal energy, it is also a state function.

$$\therefore \quad H = U + p\Delta V \quad \ldots\text{(i)}$$

Its units are kcal or kJ/mol. Suppose a system absorbs heat, q_p at constant pressure and its volume changes from V_1 to V_2. The work done by the system,

$$(W) = -p(V_2 - V_1) = -p\Delta V$$

Now, applying the first law of thermodynamics,

$$\Delta U = q_p - p(V_2 - V_1) \text{ or, } (U_2 - U_1) = q_p - p(V_2 - V_1)$$

or $$(U_2 + pV_2) - (U_1 + pV_1) = q_p \quad \text{...(ii)}$$

We know that,

$$U + pV = H \quad \text{(i.e. enthalpy of the system)}$$

Thus, $(U_2 + pV_2) = H_2$ and $(U_1 + pV_1) = H_1$

By putting these values in Eq. (ii), we get

$$H_2 - H_1 = q_p \text{ or } \Delta H = q_p$$

Now in the equation,

$$\boxed{\Delta U + p\Delta V = \Delta H}$$

ΔH is negative for exothermic reaction which evolve heat during the reaction and ΔH is positive for endothermic reactions which absorb heat from the surroundings.

If $\Delta V = 0$, $\Delta H = \Delta E$ and as $\Delta H = q_p$

Hence, $\Delta E = q_V$

Here, q_V = heat supplied at constant volume

Thus, we can say that "**heat supplied at constant pressure is the measure of enthalpy change, while the heat supplied at constant volume is the measure of internal energy change.**"

Relationship between ΔH and ΔU

The difference in ΔH and ΔU is insignificant in case of solids and liquids, however, for gases , if pressure and temperature remain constant and V_A be the total volume of the gaseous reactants, V_B is the total volume of the gaseous products, n_A is the total number of moles of gaseous reactants and n_B is the total number of moles of gaseous products, then from ideal gas equation,

For reactants $$pV_A = n_A RT$$

and for products $$pV_B = n_B RT$$

Thus, $$pV_B - pV_A = n_B RT - n_A RT$$

or $$p(V_B - V_A) = (n_B - n_A)RT$$

or $$p\Delta V = \Delta n_g RT$$

Here, Δn_g refers to the total number of moles of gaseous products minus the total number of moles of gaseous reactants.

i.e. $$\Delta n_g = n_P - n_R$$

Substituting the value of $p\Delta V$ in the expression of enthalpy change, (i.e. $\Delta H = \Delta U + p\Delta V$), we get

$$\Delta H = \Delta U + \Delta n_g RT$$

This equation is helpful for calculating ΔH from ΔU and *vice-versa.*

If, *Case* I $\Delta n_g = 0$ then $\Delta H = \Delta U$

Case II $\Delta n_g < 0$ then $\Delta H < \Delta U$

Case III $\Delta n_g > 0$ then $\Delta H > \Delta U$

Example 7 The reaction of cyanamide, $NH_2CN(s)$, with dioxygen was carried out in a bomb colorimeter, and ΔU was found to be $-742.7\ \text{kJ mol}^{-1}$ at 298 K. Calculate the enthalpy change for the reaction at 298 K ($R = 8.314 \times 10^{-3}\ \text{kJ K}^{-1}\ \text{mol}^{-1}$).

$$NH_2CN(s) + \frac{3}{2}O_2(g) \rightarrow N_2(g) + CO_2(g) + H_2O\ (l)$$

NCERT Textbook

Sol. Use the following steps to solve such problems :

Step I Write the balanced equation

$$NH_2CN(s) + \frac{3}{2}O_2(g) \longrightarrow N_2(g) + CO_2(g) + H_2O(l)$$

Step II Calculate Δn_g

Difference of moles of gaseous products and reactants, $\Delta n_g = n_p - n_r = 2 - \frac{3}{2} = \frac{1}{2} = 0.5$ mol

Step III Calculate ΔH by using the formula

$$\Delta H = \Delta U + \Delta n_g RT$$

$$\Delta H = -742.7\ \text{kJ mol}^{-1} + (0.5\ \text{mol} \times 8.314 \times 10^{-3}\ \text{kJ mol}^{-1} \times 298\ \text{K})$$

$$= -741.46\ \text{kJ mol}^{-1}$$

Note
- During calculation always remember the units of different quantities, i.e. ΔH, ΔU and R must be the same.
- In a laboratory most of the reactions are carried out at constant pressure, so ΔH is more significant than ΔU.

Relationship between C_p and C_V from the Expression of Enthalpy Change

If q is the amount of heat involved in a system then at constant volume, $q = q_V = C_V \Delta T = \Delta U$

and at constant pressure, $q = q_p = C_p \Delta T = \Delta H$

For a mole (n = 1) of an ideal gas, enthalpy change

$$\Delta H = \Delta U + \Delta(pV) = \Delta U + \Delta(RT)$$
$$= \Delta U + R\Delta T$$

$$\therefore \quad \Delta H = \Delta U + R\Delta T$$

On substituting the values of ΔH and ΔU, we get

$$C_p \Delta T = C_V \Delta T + R\Delta T$$

or $$C_p = C_V + R \text{ or } C_p - C_V = R$$

If number of moles is n then

$$\boxed{C_p - C_V = nR}$$

Topic Practice 1

Very Short Answer Type Questions

1 Mark

1 Fill in the Blanks

(i) The ratio of the two extensive properties becomes.............in nature.

(ii) In isobaric process, change of state is brought about at constant............

(iii) Work done during............expansion of an ideal gas is given by, $W = -p_{ex}\Delta V$.

(iv) Heat capacity is defined as the quantitiy of............required to raise the ....of a system by 1°.

2 Objective Type Questions

(i) Thermodynamics deals mainly with
- (a) the study of different forms of energy and the quantitative relationship between them
- (b) rate of reaction
- (c) physical and chemical properties of the system
- (d) All of the above

(ii) In thermodynamics, the part of universe in which observations are made and remaining universe are respectively called
- (a) system and surrounding
- (b) surrounding and system
- (c) system and open system
- (d) surrounding and open system

(iii) Which one of the following is correct option for free expansion of an ideal gas under adiabatic condition?
- (a) $q \neq 0, \Delta T = 0; W = 0$
- (b) $q = 0, \Delta T = 0; W = 0$
- (c) $q = 0, \Delta T < 0; W \neq 0$
- (d) $q = 0, \Delta T \neq 0; W = 0$

(iv) When heat is absorbed by the system at constant pressure then
- (a) $\Delta H = q_V$
- (b) $\Delta U = q_p$
- (c) $\Delta H = q_p$
- (d) $\Delta U = q_V$

3 Match the following diagram given in Column I with their system given in Column II and choose the correct option using the codes given below:

Column I	Column II
A. 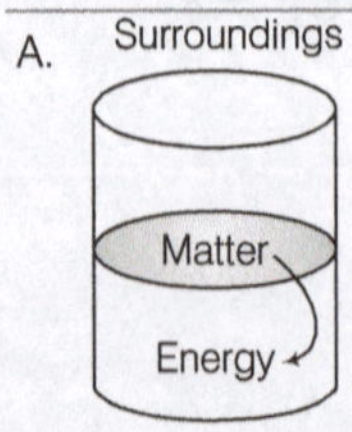	(i) open system
B. 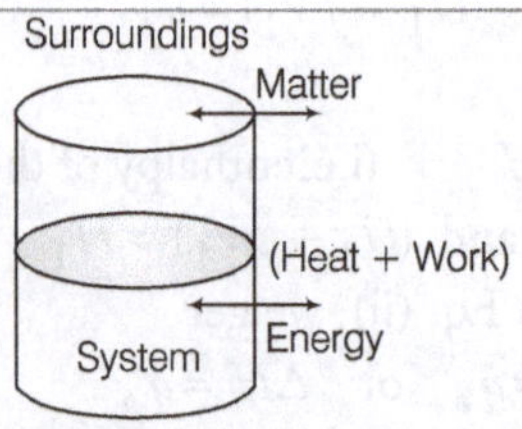	(ii) Isolated system
C. 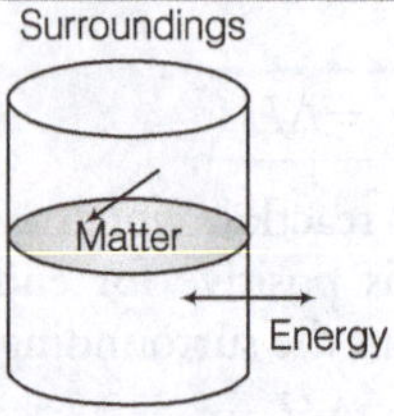	(iii) Closed system

Codes

	A	B	C		A	B	C
(a)	(ii)	(i)	(iii)	(b)	(iii)	(i)	(i)
(c)	(ii)	(iii)	(i)	(d)	(i)	(ii)	(iii)

4 Identify the state functions and path functions out of the following. Enthalpy, entropy, heat, temperature, work, free energy. **NCERT Exemplar**

5 Neither q nor W is a state function but $q + W$ is state function. Explain why?

6 Heat capacity (C_p) is an extensive property but specific heat (C) is an intensive property. What will be the relation between C_p and C for 1mole of water?

7 A sample of 1.0 mole of a monoatomic ideal gas is taken through a cyclic process of expansion and compression as shown in the figure. What will be the value of ΔH for the cycle as a whole?

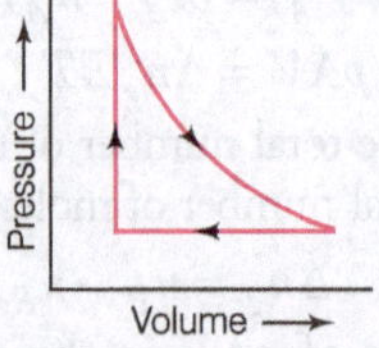

8 Predict the change in internal energy for an isolated system at constant volume

9 If the combustion of 1 g of graphite produces 20.7 kJ of heat, what will be molar enthalpy change? Give the significance of sign also.

Short Answer Type I Questions

(2 Marks)

10 How will you calculate the work done on an ideal gas in a compression, when change in pressure is carried out in infinite steps? **NCERT Exemplar**

11 Carbon monoxide is allowed to expand isothermally and reversibly from 10 m^3 to 20 m^3 at 300 K and work obtained is 4.754 kJ. Calculate the number of moles of carbon monoxide.

12 An ideal gas is allowed to expand against a constant pressure of 2 bar from 10 L to 50 L in one step. Calculate the amount of work done by the gas. If the same expansion were carried out reversibly, will the work done be higher or lower than the earlier case (given that 1 L bar = 100 J)?

13 Calculate the number of kJ of heat necessary to raise the temperature of 60.0 g of aluminium from 35°C to 55°C. Molar heat capacity of Al is 24 J mol^{-1} K^{-1}. Molar mass of Al = 27 g mol^{-1}

14 Expansion of a gas in vacuum is called free expansion. Calculate the work done and the change in internal energy when 1 L of ideal gas expands isothermally into vacuum until its total volume becomes 5 L? **NCERT Exemplar**

15 Although heat is path function but heat absorbed by the system under certain specific conditions is independent of path. What are those conditions? Explain. **NCERT Exemplar**

16 6.72 dm^3 of an unknown gas at STP requires 113.35 J of heat to raise its temperature by 15°C at constant volume. Calculate C_V, C_p and atomicity of the gas.

17 Determine the value of ΔH and ΔU for the reversible isothermal evaporation of 90.0 g of water at 100°C. Assume that water vapour behave as an ideal gas and heat of evaporation of water is 540 cal ($R = 2.0$ cal mol^{-1} K^{-1}).

18 Establish a relationship between ΔH and ΔU in Haber's process of synthesis of ammonia assuming that gaseous reactants and products are ideal.

19 The enthalpy change for the reaction, $Zn(s) + 2H^+(aq) \longrightarrow Zn^{2+}(aq) + H_2(g)$, is 154.40 kJ mol^{-1}. The formation of 2 g of hydrogen expands the system by 22.4 L at 1 atm pressure. What is the internal energy change of the reaction?

20 Show that for an isothermal expansion of an ideal gas (i) $\Delta U = 0$ and (ii) $\Delta H = 0$.

Short Answer Type II Questions

(3 Marks)

21 Give main differences between a reversible process and an irreversible process.

22 Extensive properties depend on the quantity of matter but intensive properties do not. Explain whether the following properties are extensive or intensive. Mass, internal energy, pressure, heat capacity, molar heat capacity, density, mole fraction, specific heat, temperature and molarity. **NCERT Exemplar**

23 1 mole of an ideal gas undergoes reversible isothermal expansion from an initial volume of V_1 to a final volume of 10 V_1 and does 10 kJ of work. The initial pressure was 1×10^7 Pa.

(i) Calculate V_1

(ii) If there were 2 moles of gas, what must its temperature have been?

24 1.0 mole of a monoatomic ideal gas is expanded from state (1) to state (2) as shown in figure.

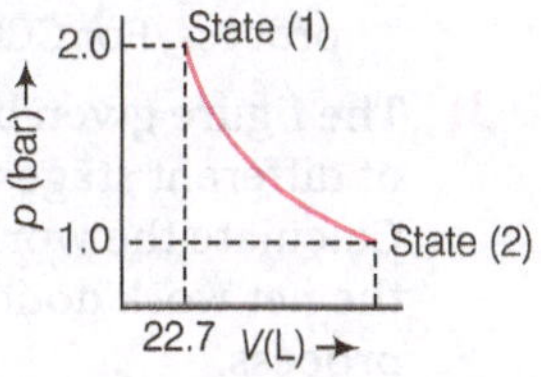

Calculate the work done for the expansion of gas from state (1) to state (2) at 298 K. **NCERT Exemplar**

25 Calculate the work done when 11.2 g of iron dissolves in hydrochloric acid in

(i) a closed vessel

(ii) an open beaker at 25°C (Atomic mass of Fe = 56 u)

26 Two moles of an ideal gas initially at 27°C and one atmospheric pressure are compressed isothermally and reversibly till the final pressure of the gas is 10 atm. Calculate q, W and ΔU for the process.

27 100 mL of a liquid is contained in an insulated container at a pressure of 1 bar. The pressure is steeply increased to 100 bar. The volume of the liquid is decreased by 1 mL at this constant pressure. Find ΔH and ΔU.

28 10 g of argon is compressed isothermally and reversibly at a temperature of 27°C from 10 L to 5 L. Calculate q, W, ΔU and ΔH for this process. $R = 2.0 \text{ cal K}^{-1} \text{ mol}^{-1}$, $\log 2 = 0.30$, atomic weight of Ar = 40.

29 10 moles of an ideal gas expand isothermally and reversibly from a pressure of 5 atm to 1 atm at 300 K. What is the largest mass that can be lifted through a height of 1 m by this expansion?

Long Answer Type Questions

5 Marks

30 (i) When 20.0 g of ammonium nitrate (NH_4NO_3) is dissolved in 125 g of water in a coffee cup calorimeter, the temperature falls from 296.5 K to 286.4 K. Find the value of q for the calorimeter. (Take heat capacity of water as the heat capacity of the calorimeter and its contents).

(ii) A chemist while studying the properties of gaseous CCl_2F_2, a chlorofluorocarbon refrigerant, cooled a 1.25 g sample at constant atmospheric pressure of 1.0 atm from 320 K to 293 K. During cooling, the sample volume decreased from 274 to 248 mL. Calculate ΔH and ΔU for the chlorofluorocarbon for this process. For CCl_2F_2, $C_p = 80.7 \text{ J/(mol K)}$.

31 The figure given below represents pV diagram of different stages of a thermodynamic process. Calculate the work done in each stage and also the net work done in the complete cyclic process.

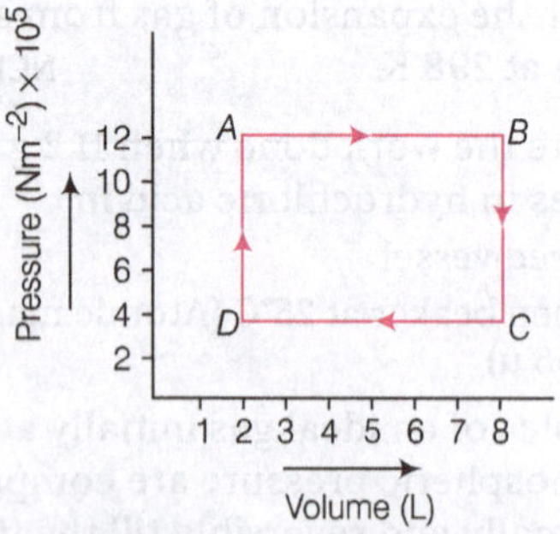

Hints & Solutions

1 (i) intensive (ii) pressure, $dp = 0$ (iii) isothermal (iv) heat, temperature

2. (i) → a, (ii) → a, (iii) → d, (iv) → c

3. (a) A → (ii), B → (i), C → (iii)

4. State function Enthalpy, entropy, temperature, free energy.
Path function Heat, work

5. Both q and W are not state functions but $q + W$ is equal to ΔU which is a state function.

6. For water, molar heat capacity, $C_p = 18 \times$ specific heat, C

Specific heat, $C = 4.18 \text{ Jg}^{-1}\text{K}^{-1}$ (for water)

Heat capacity, $C_p = 18 \times 4.18 \text{ JK}^{-1} = 75.24 \text{ JK}^{-1}$

7. The net enthalpy change, ΔH for a cyclic process is zero as enthalpy change is a state function.

8. For isolated system, there is no transfer of energy as heat or work, so according to the first law of thermodynamics,

$$\Delta U = q + W \Rightarrow \Delta U = 0 + 0 = 0$$

9. Molar enthalpy change for the combustion of graphite, ΔH = enthalpy of combustion of 1 g graphite × molar mass

$$\Delta H = -20.7 \text{ kJ g}^{-1} \times 12 \text{ g mol}^{-1}$$
$$= -2.48 \times 10^2 \text{ kJ mol}^{-1}$$

Negative sign in the value of ΔH indicates that the reaction is exothermic.

10. When compression is carried out in infinite steps with change in pressure, it is a reversible process. Work done on the gas is represented by the shaded area

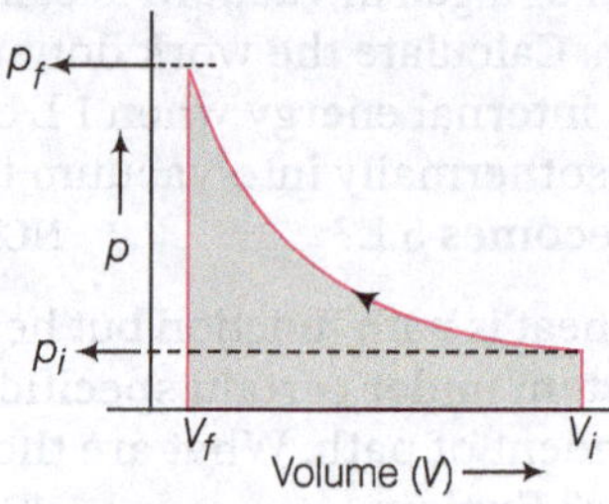

[2]

11. $W = -2.303\, nRT \log \frac{V_2}{V_1}$

$$-4754 = -2.303 \times n \times 8.314 \times 300 \times \log \frac{20}{10}$$

On solving, $n = 2.75$ mol [2]

12. In the first case, as the expansion is against constant external pressure,

$$W = -p_{ext}(V_2 - V_1) \quad [1/2]$$
$$= -2 \text{ bar} \times (50 - 10) \text{ L}$$
$$= -80 \text{ L bar} = -80 \times 100 \text{ J}$$
$$= -8 \text{ kJ} \quad (\because 1 \text{ L bar} = 100 \text{ J})$$

If the above expansion were carried out reversibly, the internal pressure of the gas should be infinitesimally greater than the external pressure at every stage. Hence, the work done will be more. [2]

13. Given, mass of Al = 60.0 g

Molar mass of Al = 27 g mol^{-1}

Molar heat capacity, $C = 24 \text{ J mol}^{-1} \text{ K}^{-1}$

$$\Delta T = 55°C - 35°C = 20°C \text{ or } 20K$$

Heat, $q = n \cdot C \cdot \Delta T$

$$q = \frac{60}{27} \times 24\,\text{J mol}^{-1}\,\text{K}^{-1} \times 20\,\text{K} \left(n = \frac{60}{27}\,\text{mol}\right)$$

$$= 1066.66\,\text{J} = 1.067\,\text{kJ}$$ [2]

14. Work done, $W = -p_{ext}(V_2 - V_1)$

As $p_{ext} = 0$, so $W = -0(5-1) = 0$ [1]

For isothermal expansion,

$\Delta U = 0$ as $\Delta T = 0$ [1]

15. The two conditions under which heat becomes independent of path are

(i) when volume remains constant [1]

(ii) when pressure remains constant

(a) **At constant volume** By first law of thermodynamics, $\Delta U = q + W$ or $q = \Delta U - W$. But $W = -p\Delta V$. Hence, $q = \Delta U + p\Delta V$. But as volume remains constant, $\Delta V = 0$.

$\therefore q_V = \Delta U$ and ΔU is state function. Hence, q_V is state function.

(b) **At constant pressure** $q_p = \Delta U + p\Delta V$.

But $\Delta U + p\Delta V = \Delta H$.

$\therefore q_p = \Delta H$. As ΔH is a state function, therefore, q_p is a state function. [1]

16 22.4 dm^3 of a gas at STP = 1 mol

$\therefore 6.72\,dm^3$ of the gas at STP $= \frac{1}{22.4} \times 6.72 = 0.3$ mol

Thus, for 15° rise, 0.3 mol of the gas at constant volume require heat = 113.35 J

$\therefore$ For 1° rise, 1 mole of the gas at constant volume will require heat $= \frac{113.35}{15 \times 0.3}\,\text{J} = 25.19\,\text{J}$ [1]

$\therefore \quad C_V = 25.19\,\text{JK}^{-1}\text{mol}^{-1}$

Now, $C_p = C_V + R = 25.19\,\text{JK}^{-1}\,\text{mol}^{-1} + 8.314\,\text{JK}^{-1}\,\text{mol}^{-1}$

$$= 33.5\,\text{JK}^{-1}\,\text{mol}^{-1};\ \therefore \gamma = \frac{C_p}{C_V} = \frac{33.5}{25.19} = 1.33.$$

Hence, the gas is triatomic. [1]

17. $\Delta H = 90.0 \times 540 = 48600$ cal [1/2]

$T = 100°\text{C} = 273 + 100 = 373\,\text{K}$

$\Delta H = \Delta U + p\Delta V = \Delta U + p(V_{vap} - V_{liq})$

Volume of liquid is negligible as compared to volume of vapour.

$\Delta H = \Delta U + pV_{vap}$ [1/2]

$\Delta H = \Delta U + nRT$ or $\Delta U = \Delta H - nRT$

$$= 48600 - \frac{90}{18} \times 2 \times 373 \left(n = \frac{90}{18}\right)$$ [1/2]

$\therefore \quad \Delta U = 48600 - 3730 = 44870$ cal [1/2]

18. Haber's process for synthesis of ammonia is

$$N_2(g) + 3H_2(g) \longrightarrow 2NH_3(g)$$

$\Delta n_g = 2 - (1+3) = -2$ [1]

But $\Delta H = \Delta U + \Delta n_g RT$

$\therefore \quad \Delta H = \Delta U - 2RT$ [1]

19. Taking the initial volume as negligible (as no gaseous reactant is present), change in volume during expansion $(\Delta V) = 22.4$ L, External pressure $(p_{ext}) = 1$ atm

$\Delta H = \Delta U + p\Delta V$

or $\Delta U = \Delta H - p\Delta V$ [1]

$p\Delta V = 1\,\text{atm} \times 22.4\,\text{L}$

$= 22.4$ L atm

$= 22.4 \times 101.3$ J

$= 2307\,\text{J} = 2.31$ kJ

$\therefore \quad \Delta U = -154.4 - 2.31 = -156.71$ kJ [1]

20. (i) For one mole of an ideal gas, $C_V = \left(\frac{\Delta U}{\Delta T}\right)_V$

or $\Delta U = C_V \Delta T$

For an isothermal process, T is constant so that $\Delta T = 0$

$\therefore \quad \Delta U = 0$ [1]

(ii) $\Delta H = \Delta U + \Delta(pV)$

For an ideal gas, $pV = RT$

$\therefore \quad \Delta H = \Delta U + \Delta(RT) = \Delta U + R\Delta T$

Since T is constant, $\Delta T = 0$

$\therefore \quad \Delta H = 0$ [1]

21. Refer to text on page 228 (Types of processes).

22. **Extensive properties** are those properties whose value depends on the quantity or size of matter present in the system, e.g. mass, internal energy, heat capacity.

Intensive properties are those properties which do not depend on the quantity or size of matter present, e.g. pressure, molar heat capacity, density, mole fraction, specific heat, temperature and molarity.Mole fraction or molarity of a solution is same whether we take a small amount of the solution or large amount of the solution. Ratio of two extensive properties is always intensive.

$$\frac{\text{Extensive}}{\text{Extensive}} = \text{Intensive}$$ [2]

So, mole fraction and molarity are intensive properties.

e.g. Mole fraction (Intensive)

$$= \frac{\text{Moles of the component}}{\text{Total number of moles}} = \frac{\text{Extensive}}{\text{Extensive}}$$

and molarity (Intensive) $= \frac{\text{Mole}}{\text{Volume}} = \frac{\text{Extensive}}{\text{Extensive}}$

Intensive properties cannot be added or subtracted directly. Only extensive properties can be added or subtracted. [1]

23. (i) We know that, $W = -2.303\,nRT \log \frac{V_2}{V_1}$

$$10 \times 10^3\,\text{J} = 2.303 \times 1 \times 8.314 \times T \times \log \frac{10V_1}{V_1}$$

or $T = 522.3$ K

For initial conditions, $p_1 V_1 = n_1 RT$,

i.e. $(10^7\,\text{Pa})V_1 = 1 \times 8.314 \times 522.3$

or $V_1 = 4.342 \times 10^{-4}\,\text{m}^3 = 4.342 \times 10^2\,\text{cm}^3$

$= 434.2\,\text{cm}^3$

We cannot apply the formula, $W = p\Delta V$ because expansion is not against constant pressure. [2]

(ii) If there were 2 moles of the gas, applying $p_1V_1 = n_1RT$, we get $(10^7 \text{ Pa})(4.342\times 10^{-4} \text{ m}^3) = 2\times 8.314\times T$

or $T = 261.1$ K, i.e. half of the first value. [1]

24. The given diagram represents that the process is carried out in infinite steps, hence, it is isothermal reversible expansion of the ideal gas from pressure 2.0 atm to 1.0 atm at 298 K. [1]

$$W = -2.303\, nRT \log\frac{p_1}{p_2}$$

$$W = -2.303\times 1 \text{ mol}\times 8.314 \text{ JK}^{-1}\text{mol}^{-1} \times 298 \text{ K} \log 2 \quad \left(\because \frac{p_1}{p_2} = \frac{2}{1}\right)$$

$W = -1717.63$ J [2]

25. Iron reacts with hydrochloric acid to produce H_2 gas as

$$Fe(s) + 2HCl(aq) \longrightarrow FeCl_2(aq) + H_2(g)$$

Thus, 1 mole of Fe, i.e. 56 g Fe produces H_2 gas = 1 mol.

$\therefore$ 11.2 g Fe will produce H_2 gas $= \frac{1}{56}\times 11.2 = 0.2$ mol

(i) If the reaction is carried out in closed vessel, $\Delta V = 0$

$\therefore \quad W = -p_{ext}\Delta V = 0$ [1]

(ii) If the reaction is carried out in open beaker (external pressure being 1 atm)

Initial volume = 0 (because no gas is present)

Final volume occupied by 0.2 mole of H_2 at 25°C and 1 atm pressure can be calculated as follows, $pV = nRT$

$$\therefore V = \frac{nRT}{p} = \frac{0.2 \text{ mol}\times 0.0821 \text{ L atm K}^{-1}\text{mol}^{-1}\times 298 \text{ K}}{1 \text{ atm}}$$

$= 4.89$ L

$\therefore \Delta V = V_{final} - V_{initial} = 4.89$ L

$W = -p_{ext}\Delta V = -1 \text{ atm}\times 4.89$ L

$= -4.89$ L atm $= -4.89\times 101.3$ J $= -495.4$ J [2]

26. Here, $n = 2$ moles, $T = 27°C = 300$ K, $p_1 = 1$ atm, $p_2 = 10$ atm

$$W = 2.303\, n\, RT \log\frac{p_2}{p_1} = 2.303\times 2\times 8.314 \text{ JK}^{-1} \text{ mol}^{-1} \times 300 \text{ K}\times \log\frac{10}{1} = 11488.28 \text{ J}$$ [1]

For isothermal compression of ideal gas, $\Delta U = 0$ [1]

Further, $\Delta U = q + W$

$\therefore \quad q = -W = -11488$ J [1]

27. $p_1 = 1$ bar, $p_2 = 100$ bar, $V_1 = 100$ mL, $V_2 = 99$ mL

For adiabatic process, $q = 0$, $\Delta U = q + W$

$\Delta U = W$

$W = -p\Delta V = -100(99-100) = 100$ bar mL [1]

$\Delta H = \Delta U + \Delta pV = 100 + p_2V_2 - p_1V_1$

$= 100 + (100\times 99) - (1\times 100)$

$= 100 + 9900 - 100 = 9900$ bar mL [2]

28. For reversible isothermal system,

$$q = 2.303\, nRT\log\frac{V_2}{V_1} = 2.303\times\frac{10}{40}\times 300\times\log\frac{5}{10}$$

$= -103.635$ cal

For isothermal expansion, $\Delta U = 0$ [1]

$W = \Delta U - q = 0 - (-103.635)$ [1/2]

$= +103.635$ cal [1/2]

Also, when temperature is constant,

$p_1V_1 = p_2V_2$ or $pV = $ constant

$\Delta H = \Delta E + \Delta(pV) = 0 + 0 = 0$ [1]

29. $W_{exp} = -2.303\, nRT \log\frac{p_1}{p_2}$

$= -2.303\,(10)\times(8.314)(300)\log\frac{5}{1} = -40.15\times 10^3$ J [1]

If M is the mass that can be lifted by this work through a height of 1 m, then work done = Mgh

$40.15\times 10^3 \text{ J} = M\times 9.81\times \text{m s}^{-1}\times 1$ m

or $M = \frac{40.15\times 10^3 \text{ kg m}^2\text{s}^{-2}}{9.81 \text{ m s}^{-2}\times 1 \text{ m}}$ $(\because \text{J} = \text{kg m}^2\text{ s}^{-2})$

$= 4092.76$ kg [2]

30. (i) As heat capacity of water = heat capacity of calorimeter, the heat gained by water = heat lost by calorimeter $= 125\times(296.5 - 286.4)\times 4.184$ J

$= 5282$ J $= 5.282$ kJ [2]

(ii) $\Delta H = q_p$ and C_p is heat evolved or absorbed per mole for 1° fall or rise in temperature. Here, fall in temperature $320 - 293 = 27$ K. [1/2]

Molar mass of $CCl_2F_2 = 12 + 2\times 35.5 + 2\times 19$

$= 121 \text{ g mol}^{-1}$ [1/2]

$\therefore$ Heat evolved from 1.25 g of the sample on being cooled from 320 K to 293 K at constant pressure

$= \frac{80.7}{121}\times 1.25\times 27 \text{ J} = 22.51$ J [1/2]

Further, $\Delta H = \Delta U + p\Delta V = -22.51$ J

$[\because p\Delta V = 1 \text{ atm}\times\frac{(248-274)}{1000} \text{ L} = -0.026 \text{ L atm}$

$= -0.026\times 101.325 \text{ J} = -2.63$ J [1/2]

$\therefore \quad -22.51 = \Delta U - 2.63$ J [1/2]

or $\quad \Delta U = -22.51 + 2.63 \text{ J} = -19.88$ J [1/2]

31. Process $A \longrightarrow B$ (expansion),

$p = 12\times 10^5 \text{ Nm}^{-2}$, $\Delta V = 8 - 2 = 6 \text{ L} = 6\times 10^{-3} \text{ m}^3$

$\therefore$ Work done $= -p\Delta V$

$= -(12\times 10^5)\times(6\times 10^{-3})$ J $= -7200$ J [1]

Process $B \longrightarrow C$, No change in volume, i.e. $\Delta V = 0$ [1]

$\therefore$ Work done = 0

Process $C \longrightarrow D$ (contraction)

$\Delta V = 8 - 2 = 6\text{L} = 6\times 10^{-3} \text{ m}^3$, $p = 4\times 10^5 \text{Nm}^{-2}$

$\therefore$ Work done $p\Delta V = (4\times 10^5)(6\times 10^{-3}) = 2400$ J [1]

Process $D \rightarrow A$, No change in volume, i.e. $\Delta V = 0$

$\therefore$ Work done = 0 [1]

$\therefore$ Net work done in the complete cyclic process

$= -7200 + 2400 \text{ J} = -4800$ J [1]

Minus sign shows that net work has been done by the gas.

TOPIC 02 Different Types of Enthalpies

Enthalpy Change, $\Delta_r H$ of a Reaction (Heat of Reaction)

It is the enthalpy change accompanying a chemical reaction or it may also be defined as the enthalpy change when the quantities (moles) of reactants have reacted completely as indicated by balanced chemical equation

e.g. $2H_2(g)+O_2(g) \longrightarrow 2H_2O(l)$; $\Delta H=-572$ kJ

Enthalpy change of a reaction can also be calculated by the following expression.

$\Delta_r H$ = sum of enthalpies of products − sum of enthalpies of reactants

$$\boxed{\Delta_r H=\sum_i x_i H_P-\sum_i y_i H_R}$$

where, x_i and y_i = stoichiometric coefficients of products and reactants respectively in a balanced equation.

Σ = sigma, used for summation.

H_P = enthalpy of products

H_R = enthalpy of reactants

e.g. For the reaction,

$$CH_4(g)+2O_2(g) \longrightarrow CO_2(g)+2H_2O(l)$$

$\Delta_r H$ is written as

$$\Delta_r H=[H_{(CO_2,g)}+2\times H_{(H_2O,l)}]-[H_{(CH_4,g)}+2\times H_{(O_2,g)}]$$

Note • If H_P is lesser than H_R, the reaction occur with the evolution of heat, i.e. the reaction is exothermic and ΔH is negative.
• If H_R is lesser than H_P, the reaction occur with the absorption of heat, i.e. the reaction is endothermic and ΔH is positive.

Factors Affecting Enthalpy of Reaction

The factors that affect the magnitude of the enthalpy of reaction are :

(i) **Physical States of the Reactants and Products** An appreciable change in heat energy is involved on changing a substance from one physical state (solid, liquid, gas or vapour) to another,

e.g. $H_2(g)+\frac{1}{2}O_2(g) \longrightarrow H_2O(l)$; $\Delta H°=-285.9$ kJ mol^{-1}

$H_2(g)+\frac{1}{2}O_2(g) \longrightarrow H_2O(g)$; $\Delta H°=-241.8$ kJ mol^{-1}

The difference in two $\Delta H°$ values arises due to different physical states of water.

Thus, $H_2O(l) \longrightarrow H_2O(g)$, $\Delta H°=44.1$ kJ mol^{-1}

It represents **molar enthalpy of vaporisation of water.**

(ii) **Allotropic Forms of the Element** Enthalpy also varies when an element reacts in different allotropic forms within the same reaction.

C (graphite) + $O_2(g) \longrightarrow CO_2(g)$ $\Delta H°=-393.5$ kJ mol^{-1}

C (diamond) + $O_2(g) \longrightarrow CO_2(g)$ $\Delta H°=-380.4$ kJ mol^{-1}

The difference in two $\Delta H°$ values arises due to the involvement of different allotropes of carbon in above reactions.

Thus, C (diamond) $\longrightarrow$ C (graphite); $\Delta H°=13.1$ kJ mol^{-1}

Note It represents **molar enthalpies** of transition of carbon.

(iii) **Reactions Conditions** Reaction conditions also affect the enthalpy of a reaction because heat change associated with a chemical reaction occurring at constant pressure is called **enthalpy change** (ΔH) while heat change at constant volume is called **internal energy** (ΔE) change.

(iv) **Effect of Temperature** Heat of reaction depends upon the temperature at which reaction is occurring. The variation of the heat of reaction with temperature at constant pressure or constant volume which is given as

$$\Delta H_2=\Delta H_1+\Delta C_p(T_2-T_1)$$

where, ΔH_1 and ΔH_2 are change in heat enthalpies at temperature T_1 and T_2, respectively.

Similarly, at constant volume

$$\Delta E_2=\Delta E_1+\Delta C_V(T_2-T_1)$$

where, ΔE_1 and ΔE_2 are change in internal energy at temperatures T_1 and T_2, respectively.

$$\Delta C_p=\Sigma C_p(\text{products})-\Sigma C_p(\text{reactants})$$

$$\Delta C_V=\Sigma C_V(\text{products})-\Sigma C_V(\text{reactants})$$

(v) **Quantities of Reaction** The amount of heat evolved or absorbed depends upon the amounts of reactants.

Standard Enthalpy of Reaction

The enthalpy change occurring during a reaction when all the involved substances are in their standard states, is called the **standard enthalpy of the reaction.**

The purest and most stable form of a substance at 1 bar and at a specified temperature is called its standard state. e.g. the standard state of solid iron at 500 K is pure iron at 1 bar. The standard enthalpy change is represented by writing the superscript $\ominus$ to the symbol ΔH, i.e. by $\Delta H^{\ominus}$.

Enthalpies for Different Types of Reactions

Depending upon the type of reactions, the enthalpies can be of following types :

Enthalpy Change During Phase Transformations

We know that energy is required to convert a substance from one phase (say solid) to another phase (say liquid). The process of conversion of solid into liquid is called **melting**, the process of conversion of liquid into gas is called **vaporisation** and the process of conversion of solid directly into gases is called **sublimation.** These processes are collectivly known as **phase transformations** and they involve energy changes.

Depending upon the type of process, enthalpy change further can be of following types :

1. Enthalpy of Fusion, $\Delta_{fus}H$

The enthalpy change when 1 mole of a solid substance melts completely into its liquid form is called molar enthalpy of fusion, $\Delta_{fus}H$. This enthalpy change under standard condition is called standard enthalpy of fusion, $\Delta_{fus}H°$. This enthalpy change under standard condition is called **standard enthalpy of fusion,** $\Delta_{fus}H°$. e.g.

$$H_2O(s) \longrightarrow H_2O(l); \quad \Delta_{fus}H^{\ominus} = 6.00 \text{ kJ mol}^{-1}$$

(Endothermic process)

If water freezes, i.e. the above process is reversed, equal amount of heat is given off to the surroundings. So, $\Delta_{freezing}H$ is negative, i.e. the process is exothermic.

2. Enthalpy of Vaporisation

The enthalpy change when one mole of a liquid is converted into vapours at its boiling temperature and under standard pressure (1 bar) is called enthalpy of vaporisation ($\Delta_{vap}H$) or molar enthalpy of vaporisation.

e.g.

$$H_2O(l) \longrightarrow H_2O(g); \ \Delta_{vap}H^{\ominus} = +40.79 \text{ kJ mol}^{-1}$$

Here, $\Delta_{vap}H^{\ominus}$ is the standard enthalpy of vaporisation.

3. Enthalpy of Sublimation

The process of conversion of a solid into its vapours without coming in the liquid state is called **sublimation.** The enthalpy change when one mole of a solid substance sublimes, i.e. converted into its vapours without melting at a temperature below its melting point (and at 1 bar pressure) is called the enthalpy of sublimation or molar enthalpy of sublimation and under standard condition, this enthalpy change is called standard enthalpy of sublimation, $\Delta_{sub}H^{\ominus}$. e.g.

$$I_2(s) \xrightarrow{\Delta} I_2(v); \ \Delta_{sub}H^{\ominus}(I_2) = 62.4 \text{ kJ mol}^{-1}$$

$$\underset{\text{Dry ice}}{CO_2(s)} \xrightarrow[195\text{ K}]{\Delta} CO_2(v); \ \Delta_{sub}H^{\ominus} = 25.2 \text{ kJ mol}^{-1}$$

As sublimation is, infact, combination of both fusion and vaporisation, so we can write as

$$\Delta_{sub}H^{\ominus} = \Delta_{fus}H^{\ominus} + \Delta_{vap}H^{\ominus}$$

Factors Affecting Enthalpy of Phase Transformation

The magnitude of enthalpy change depends upon the strength of intermolecular forces working on the substances that undergo phase transformations. e.g. in between water molecules, strong hydrogen bonds exist which are strong enough for keeping water in liquid phase. Further, the organic liquids like acetone have weak intermolecular forces (i.e. dipole-dipole interactions) so less amount of heat is required to vapourise 1 mole of acetone as compared to that required for the vaporisation of 1 mole of water. In general, the order of enthalpy of vaporisation is ionic liquid > > polar liquids > non-polar liquids.

Example 1 When 1g of liquid naphthalene ($C_{10}H_8$) solidifies, 149 J of heat is evolved. Calculate the heat of fusion of naphthalene.

Sol. Molecular mass of naphthalene,

$$C_{10}H_8 = 10 \times 12 + 8 \times 1 = 128 \text{ g mol}^{-1}$$

For the solidification reaction,

$$C_{10}H_8(l) \longrightarrow C_{10}H_8(s)$$

Heat evolved when 1 g of naphthalene solidifies = 149 J

Heat evolved when 128 g of naphthalene solidify

$$= 149 \times 128 = 19072 \text{ J}$$

As solidification is reverse of fusion, therefore enthalpy of fusion will have same magnitude as that of enthalpy of solidification but with opposite sign.

i.e. $C_{10}H_8(s) \longrightarrow C_{10}H_8(l); \Delta_{fus}H^\ominus = -19072\text{ J}$

Enthalpy of Formation

The enthalpy change accompanying the formation of one mole of a compound from its constituent elements, when they are in their most stable states or reference states, is called **enthalpy (heat) of formation,** $\Delta_f H^\ominus$.

Standard Enthalpy of Formation, ($\Delta_f H$)

The enthalpy change at standard condition is called standard enthalpy of formation. It is denoted by $\Delta_f H°$.

e.g. $H_2(g) + \frac{1}{2}O_2(g) \longrightarrow H_2O(l);$

$$\Delta_f H^\ominus = -285.8\text{ kJ mol}^{-1}$$

$C(\text{graphite}, s) + 2H_2(g) \longrightarrow CH_4(g);$

$$\Delta_f H^\ominus = -74.81\text{ kJ mol}^{-1}$$

$2C(\text{graphite}, s) + 3H_2(g) + \frac{1}{2}O_2(g) \rightarrow C_2H_5OH(l);$

$$\Delta_f H^\ominus = -277.7\text{ kJ mol}^{-1}$$

The most stable state of aggregation of an element at 25°C and 1 bar pressure is called its **reference state.** e.g. H_2 gas is the reference state of dihydrogen. Similarly, O_2 gas, C_{graphite}, Br_2 liquid and S_{rhombic} are the reference states of dioxygen, carbon, bromine and sulphur respectively. By convention, the standard enthalpy of formation, $\Delta_f H^\ominus$ of an element in its reference or most stable state of aggregation is taken as zero.

Special Case of Enthalpy Change of a Reaction

It should be noted that enthalpy, changes for all reactions are not enthalpy of formation. e.g. the following reaction shows the formation of calcium carbonate from calcium oxide and carbon dioxide.

$CaO(s) + CO_2(g) \longrightarrow CaCO_3(s);$

$$\Delta_r H° = -178.3\text{ kJmol}^{-1}.$$

Here, the $\Delta_r H°$ is not equal to enthalpy of formation, $\Delta_f H^\ominus$ of calcium carbonate because calcium carbonate has been formed from other compounds and not from its constituent elements. Similarly in the reaction,

$H_2(g) + Br_2(g) \longrightarrow 2HBr(g); \Delta_r H° = -72.8\text{ kJmol}^{-1}$

The enthalpy change for the reaction is not standard enthalpy of formation; $\Delta_f H^\ominus$ for HBr because here two moles of product are formed instead of one from the reference state.

Therefore, if we divide all coefficients in the balanced chemical equation by 2. The enthalpy of formation may be written as

$\frac{1}{2}H_2(g) + \frac{1}{2}Br_2(g) \longrightarrow HBr(g);$

$$\Delta_f H^\ominus = -36.4\text{ kJmol}^{-1}$$

The standard heat of reaction is equal to the difference of standard heat of formation of products and the standard heat of formation of reactants.

$$\Delta_r H° = \Sigma H_f^\circ(\text{products}) - \Sigma H_f^\circ(\text{reactants})$$

Enthalpy of Combustion, $\Delta_c H$

The amount of heat evolved when one mole of the substance is burnt completely in oxygen or air is called the **enthalpy of combustion.** This enthalpy change under standard conditions is called standard enthalpy of combustion.

e.g. $C_4H_{10}(g) + \frac{13}{2}O_2(g) \longrightarrow 4CO_2(g) + 5H_2O(l);$

$$\Delta_c H^\ominus = -2658.0\text{ kJ mol}^{-1}$$

$C_6H_{12}O_6(g) + 6O_2(g) \longrightarrow 6CO_2(g) + 6H_2O(l);$

$$\Delta_c H^\ominus = -2802.0\text{ kJ mol}^{-1}$$

Combustion is an exothermic process, so enthalpy of combustion is always negative.

Note Our body also generates energy from food by the same above process of combustion, although the final products are produced after a series of complex biochemical reactions involving enzymes.

Calorific Value of Foods and Fuels

The grading of food articles and various fuels can be done on the basis of the values of enthalpies of combustion.

If enthalpy of combustion is measured in k cal/g or kJ/g (i.e. calculated for one gram of a substance), it is called the **calorific value.** In other words, the amount of heat produced in calorie or joule when one gram of a substance (food or fuel) is completely burnt or oxidised is called calorific value. Mathematically,

$$\text{Calorific value} = \frac{\Delta_c H}{\text{Mass}}$$

Example 2 The combustion of one mole of benzene takes place at 298 K and 1 atm. After combustion, $CO_2(g)$ and $H_2O(l)$ are produced and 3267.0 kJ of heat is liberated. Calculate the standard enthalpy of formation, $\Delta_f H^\ominus$ of benzene. Standard enthalpies of formation of $CO_2(g)$ and $H_2O(l)$ are -393.5 kJ mol^{-1} and -285.83 kJ mol^{-1} respectively. **NCERT Textbook**

Sol. The reaction for the formation of benzene is given by

$$6C\,(\text{graphite}) + 3H_2(g) \longrightarrow C_6H_6(l);\ \Delta_f H^\ominus = ? \quad \text{...(i)}$$

The enthalpy of combustion of 1 mole of benzene is

$$C_6H_6(l) + \frac{15}{2}O_2 \longrightarrow 6CO_2(g) + 3H_2O(l);$$
$$\Delta_c H^\ominus = -3265\text{ kJ mol}^{-1} \quad \text{...(ii)}$$

The enthalpy of formation of 1 mole of CO_2 (g).

$$C\,(\text{graphite}) + O_2(g) \longrightarrow CO_2(g);$$
$$\Delta_f H^\ominus = -393.5\text{ kJ mol}^{-1} \quad \text{...(iii)}$$

The enthalpy of formation of 1 mole of $H_2O(l)$ is

$$H_2(g) + \frac{1}{2}O_2(g) \longrightarrow H_2O(l);$$
$$\Delta_f H^\ominus = -285.83\text{ kJ mol}^{-1} \quad \text{...(iv)}$$

On multiplying Eq. (iii) by 6 and Eq. (iv) by 3 we get

$$6C\,(\text{graphite}) + 6O_2(g) \longrightarrow 6CO_2(g);$$
$$\Delta_f H^\ominus = -2361\text{ kJ mol}^{-1} \quad \text{...(v)}$$

$$3H_2(g) + \frac{3}{2}O_2(g) \longrightarrow 3H_2O(l);$$
$$\Delta_f H^\ominus = -857.49\text{ kJ mol}^{-1} \quad \text{...(vi)}$$

On adding Eqs. (v) and (vi), we get

$$6C\,(\text{graphite}) + 3H_2(g) + \frac{15}{2}O_2(g) \rightarrow 6CO_2(g) + 3H_2O(l)$$
$$\Delta_f H^\ominus = -3218.49\text{ kJ mol}^{-1} \quad \text{...(vii)}$$

On reversing Eqs (ii);

$$6CO_2(g) + 3H_2O\,(l) \longrightarrow C_6H_6(l) + \frac{15}{2}O_2;$$
$$\Delta_f H^\ominus = 3267.0\text{ kJ mol}^{-1} \quad \text{...(viii)}$$

Adding Eqs. (vii) and (viii), we get

$$6C\,(\text{graphite}) + 3H_2(g) \longrightarrow C_6H_6(1);$$
$$\Delta_f H^\ominus = 48.51\text{ kJ mol}^{-1}$$

Enthalpy of Atomisation, $\Delta_a H$

The enthalpy change on breaking one mole of bonds completely to obtain atoms in the gas phase is called the **enthalpy of atomisation** e.g.

(i) $CH_4(g) \longrightarrow C(g) + 4H(g);$

$$\Delta_a H = 1665\text{ kJ mol}^{-1}$$

(ii) $Na(s) \longrightarrow Na(g);\ \Delta_a H = 108.4\text{ kJ mol}^{-1}$

(In this case, enthalpy of atomisation is same as that of sublimation.)

(iii) $H_2(g) \longrightarrow 2H(g);\ \Delta_a H = 435.0\text{ kJ mol}^{-1}$

(Here, enthalpy of atomisation is same as the bond dissociation enthalpy.)

Hence, it can be concluded that in case of diatomic molecule, $\Delta_a H$ = bond dissociation enthalpy and in case of monoatomic element, $\Delta_a H$ is equal to sublimation enthalpy.

Enthalpy of Neutralisation, $\Delta_n H$

The heat change (usually the heat evolved) that takes place when one equivalent of an acid is neutralised by one equivalent of a base in a fairly dilute solution is called enthalpy of neutralisation ($\Delta_n H$)

For Strong Acids and Strong Bases (Constancy in Heat of Neutralisation)

It should be noted that, $\Delta_n H^-$ of strong acid-strong base is always **constant and is numerically equal to −57.1 kJ.**

e.g. $H^+(aq) + OH^-(aq) \longrightarrow H_2O(l);\ \Delta_n H^\ominus = -57.1$ kJ

The value of enthalpy of neutralisation of weak acid/strong base or strong acid/ weak base is numerically less than 57.1 kJ. Neutralisation reactions are always exothermic, thus, it always has a negative sign.

The heat of neutralisation of an acid or base can be easily determined in the laboratory with the help of polythene or polystyrene bottle. In this experiment, bottle is fitted with rubber cork through which a thermometer and a stirrer are fitted as shown in the fig. below. 100 mL each of acid and alkali of equal normality are taken in separate bottles. The temperature of each solution is regularly recorded. When constant temperature is attained, the alkali solution is added to the acid solution. The mixture is quickly stirred and the maximum temperature attained is noted.

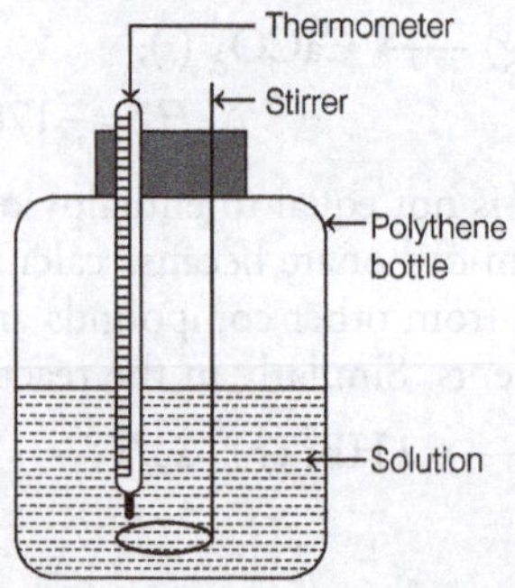

Determination of heat of neutralisation

Calculations

Suppose, the initial temperature of acid base $= T_1$

Final temperature of solution after mixing $= T_2$

Rise in temperature $= T_2 - T_1$

For the purpose of simplicity, the heat capacity of the bottle may be neglected as it is very small in comparison to that of solution. The specific heat capacity of the solution is assumed to be the same as that of water.

Q = Heat change in reaction or heat evolved by the neutralisation.

= Mass of solution × specific heat × $(T_2 - T_1)$

Therefore, the enthalpy of neutralisation $= \frac{Q}{100} \times 1000 \times \frac{1}{x}$

where, x = normality of the acid or base.

Lattice Enthalpy, $\Delta_{\text{lattice}}H$

The enthalpy change when one mole of an ionic compound dissociates completely into its constituent ions in gaseous state is called the **lattice enthalpy** of the ionic compound e.g.

$$Na^+Cl^-(s) \longrightarrow Na^+(g) + Cl^-(g);$$

$$\Delta_{\text{lattice}} H^\ominus = +788 \text{ kJ mol}^{-1}$$

Higher the lattice enthalpy, lesser the dissolution of an ionic compound in water. It is impossible to determine lattice enthalpies directly by experiment, therefore, lattice enthalpy is calculated, indirectly by using **Born-Haber cycle** (which has also been described in chapter 4).

The steps involved in Born-Haber cycle (in case of NaCl) are as follows:

(i) $Na(s) \longrightarrow Na(g)$, sublimation of sodium metal,

$$\Delta_{\text{sub}} H^\ominus = 108.4 \text{ kJ mol}^{-1}$$

(ii) $Na(g) \longrightarrow Na^+(g) + e^-(g)$, the ionisation of sodium atoms, (ionisation enthalpy)

$$\Delta_i H^\ominus = 496 \text{ kJ mol}^{-1}$$

(iii) $\frac{1}{2} Cl_2(g) \longrightarrow Cl(g)$, the dissociation of chlorine, the reaction enthalpy is half of the bond dissociation enthalpy.

$$\frac{1}{2} \Delta_{\text{bond}} H^\ominus = 121 \text{ kJ mol}^{-1}$$

(iv) $Cl(g) + e^-(g) \longrightarrow Cl^-(g)$, electron gained by chlorine atoms. (electron gain enthalpy,)

$$\Delta_{\text{eg}} H^\ominus = -348.6 \text{ kJ mol}^{-1}$$

(v) $Na^+(g) + Cl^-(g) \longrightarrow Na^+Cl^-(s); \; \Delta_{\text{lattice}} H^\ominus = ?$

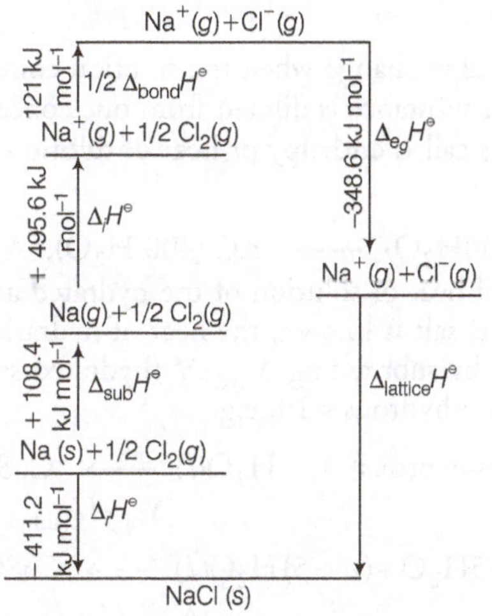

Enthalpy diagram for lattice enthalpy of NaCl

Applying Hess's law, (discussed later) we get

$\Delta_{\text{lattice}} H^\ominus = 411.2 + 108.4 + 121 + 495.6 - 348.6;$

$\Delta_{\text{lattice}} H^\ominus = +788$ kJ

If $\Delta_{\text{hyd}} H^\ominus$ is -784 kJ mol^{-1} for NaCl

then $\Delta_{\text{sol}} H^\ominus = +788 \text{ kJ mol}^{-1} - 784 \text{ kJ mol}^{-1}$

$= +4 \text{ kJ mol}^{-1}$

Note
- Ionisation enthalpy and electron gain enthalpy (about which you have read before) are defined at absolute zero. At any other temperature, only heat capacities are considered.

$$\Delta_r H^\ominus(T) = \Delta_r H^\ominus(0) + \int_0^T \Delta_r C_p^\ominus \, dT$$

and $\Delta_r C_p^\ominus = +\frac{5}{2} R$ (for ionisation)

$\Delta_r C_p^\ominus = -(5/2) R$ (for electron gain)

- Therefore, $\Delta_r H^\ominus$ (ionisation enthalpy) $= \text{IE} + (5/2) RT$
- $\Delta_r H^\ominus$ (electron gain enthalpy) $= -\text{EA} - (5/2) RT$

Enthalphy of Hydration, $\Delta_{\text{hyd}}H$

The enthalpy change can be defined as **enthalpy** or **heat of hydration** when one mole of anhydrous or partially hydrated salt combines with required number of moles of water to form a specific hydrate. Its symbol is $\Delta_{\text{hyd}} H$, e.g.

$$CuSO_4(s) + 5H_2O(l) \longrightarrow CuSO_4 \cdot 5H_2O(s);$$

$$\Delta_{\text{hyd}} H = 78.22 \text{ kJ}$$

In general cases, hydration is an exothermic process but there are some cases also where hydration is an endothermic process.

Enthalpy of Dilution, $\Delta_{dil}H$

The enthalpy change when the solution containing one mole of a substance is diluted from one concentration to another is called **enthalpy** or **heat of dilution.**

e.g.,

$$\text{KCl }(200H_2O) \longrightarrow \text{KCl}(300\ H_2O);\ \Delta_{dil} H = x \text{ kJ}$$

If integral heat of solution of the hydrated and anhydrous salt is known, the heat of hydration is obtained by subtracting $\Delta_{hyd} H$ (hydrated salt) from $\Delta_{hyd} H$ (anhydrous salt). e.g.

$$CuSO_4(\text{anhydrous}) + a\ H_2O(l) \longrightarrow CuSO_4 \cdot aH_2O \quad \Delta_{hyd} H_{(anhy)} = -66.50 \text{ kJ}$$

$$CuSO_4 \cdot 5H_2O + (a-5)H_2O(l) \longrightarrow CuSO_4 \cdot a\,H_2O \quad \Delta_{hyd} H_{(Hydrated)} = 11.71 \text{ kJ}$$

Thus, $\Delta_{hyd} H$ of solution

$$= \Delta_{hyd} H(\text{anhy.}) - \Delta_{hyd} H\ (\text{hydrated})$$

Enthalpy of Solution, $\Delta_{sol}H$

The enthalpy change when one mole of solute is dissolved completely in specified amount of solvent or water is called **enthalpy of solution.**

If solvent is in excess i.e. the interactions between the ions (or solute molecules) are negligible, the enthalpy change is called **enthalpy of solution at infinite dilution.**

The enthalpy of solution is also given as,

$$\Delta_{sol} H^\ominus = \Delta_{lattice} H^\ominus + \Delta_{hyd} H^\ominus$$

$\Delta_{sol} H^\ominus$ is generally positive for most of the ionic compounds i.e. the dissolution is an endothermic process and their solubility increases with rise in temperature.

Enthalpy of Ionisation, $\Delta_{ion}H$

The enthalpy change when one mole of a weak acid or a weak base is completely ionised into its constituents, is called the **enthalpy** or **heat of ionisation.** It is represented by $\Delta_{ion} H$, e.g.

$$CH_3COOH(aq) \rightleftharpoons CH_3COO^-(aq) + H^+(aq); \quad \Delta_{ion} H = -55.43 \text{ kJ mol}^{-1}$$

Heat of ionisation can also be obtained by subtracting the heat of neutralisation of weak acid or a weak base from the heat of neutralisation of strong acid and strong base (i.e. –13.7 kcal or –57.32 kJ)

Since, heat is required for ionisation process, the enthalpy of ionisation is usually negative.

Example 3 Use the following data to calculate $\Delta_{lattice} H^\ominus$ for NaBr. $\Delta_{sub} H^\ominus$ for sodium metal $= 108.4$ kJ mol^{-1}, ionisation enthalpy of sodium $= 496$ kJ mol^{-1}, electron gain enthalpy of bromine $= -325$ kJ mol^{-1}, bond dissociation enthalpy of bromine $= 192$ kJ mol^{-1}, $\Delta_f H^\ominus$ for $NaBr(s) = -360.1$ kJ mol^{-1}

> This question is based upon the concept of Born-Haber cycle as well as Hess's law. Following steps are used to solve this problem.
> - $Na(s) \rightarrow Na(g); \Delta_{sub} H^\ominus$
> - $Na(g) \rightarrow Na^+(g) + e^-(g)$; IE
> - $\frac{1}{2} Br_2(g) \rightarrow Br(g); \Delta_{diss} H^\ominus$
> - $Br(g) + e^-(g) \rightarrow Br^-(g); \Delta_{eg} H^\ominus$
> - Applying Hess's law
>
> $\Delta_f H^\ominus = \Delta_{sub} H^\ominus + \text{IE} + \Delta_{diss} H^\ominus + \Delta_{eg} H^\ominus + U$

Sol. Given that, $\Delta_{sub} H^\ominus$ for Na metal $= 108.4$ kJ mol^{-1}

IE of Na $= 496$ kJ mol^{-1}, $\Delta_{eg} H^\ominus$ of

Br $= -325$ kJ mol^{-1}, $\Delta_{diss} H^\ominus$ of Br $= 192$ kJ mol^{-1},

$\Delta_f H^\ominus$ for NaBr $= -360.1$ kJ mol^{-1}

Born-Haber cycle for the formation of NaBr is as

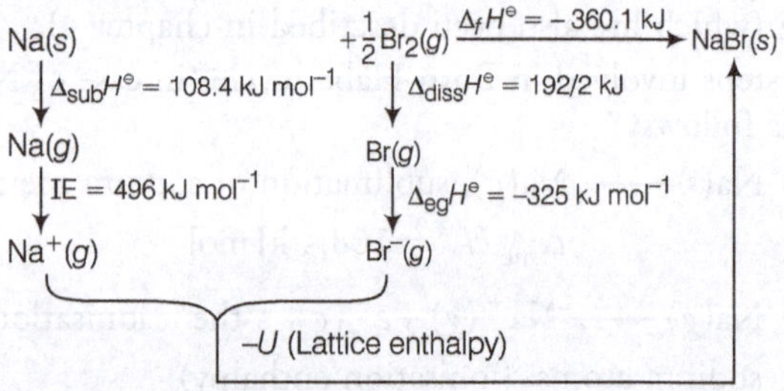

By applying Hess's law,

$$\Delta_f H^\ominus = \Delta_{sub} H^\ominus + \text{IE} + \Delta_{diss} H^\ominus + \Delta_{eg} H^\ominus + U$$

$$-360.1 = 108.4 + 496 + 96 + (-325) - U$$

$$U = +735.5 \text{ kJ mol}^{-1}$$

Bond Enthalpy, $\Delta_{bond}H$

In chemical reactions, there is simultaneous making and breaking of bonds. In bond breaking, energy is required and in bond making, energy is released. Thus, enthalpy change is related to the types of bonds formed or broken.

In general, bond is defined in two terms.

(i) In terms of bond dissociation enthalpy (for diatomic molecules).

(ii) In terms of mean bond enthalpy (for polyatomic molecules).

1. Bond Dissociation Enthalpy

The enthalpy change accompanying the breaking of one mole of covalent bonds of a gaseous covalent compound to give products in the gas phase, is called the bond dissociation enthalpy. e.g.

$$H_2(g) \longrightarrow 2H(g);\ \Delta_{H-H}H^\ominus = 435.0\ \text{kJ mol}^{-1}$$

The bond dissociation enthalpy of dihydrogen, i.e. $\Delta_{H-H}H^\ominus$ is the same as its enthalpy of atomisation. This is true for all diatomic molecules. e.g.

$$Cl_2(g) \longrightarrow 2Cl(g);\ \Delta_{Cl-Cl}H^\ominus = 242\ \text{kJ mol}^{-1}$$

$$O_2(g) \longrightarrow 2O(g);\ \Delta_{O=O}H^\ominus = 428\ \text{kJ mol}^{-1}$$

2. Mean (Average) Bond Enthalpy

In case of polyatomic molecules, all the bonds between similar atoms are identical in bond length and energy but they differ in their strength. i.e. different amounts of energy is required to break each individual bond. So in case of these molecules, the mean of bond dissociation enthalpies of all the bonds present in the compound is taken. Thus, in such cases bond enthalpy is called the **mean bond enthalpy** e.g. the enthalpy of atomisation for methane is given as

$$CH_4(g) \longrightarrow \dot{C}H_3(g) + \dot{H}(g);\ \Delta_{bond}H^\ominus = +427\ \text{kJ mol}^{-1}$$

$$\dot{C}H_3(g) \longrightarrow \dot{\underset{\cdot}{C}}H_2(g) + \dot{H}(g);\ \Delta_{bond}H^\ominus = +439\ \text{kJ mol}^{-1}$$

$$\dot{C}H_2(g) \longrightarrow \bullet\dot{\underset{\cdot}{C}}H(g) + \dot{H}(g);\ \Delta_{bond}H^\ominus = +452\ \text{kJ mol}^{-1}$$

$$\bullet\dot{C}H(g) \longrightarrow \bullet\dot{\underset{\cdot}{C}}\bullet(g) + \dot{H}(g);\ \Delta_{bond}H^\ominus = +347\ \text{kJ mol}^{-1}$$

Therefore, $CH_4(g) \longrightarrow \bullet\dot{\underset{\cdot}{C}}\bullet(g) + 4\dot{H}(g);$

$$\Delta_a H^\ominus = 1665\ \text{kJ mol}^{-1}$$

Thus, in CH_4, $\Delta_{C-H}H^\ominus$ is calculated as

$$\Delta_{C-H}H^\ominus = \frac{1}{4}(\Delta_a H^\ominus) = \frac{1}{4}(1665\ \text{kJ mol}^{-1})$$

$$= 416\ \text{kJ mol}^{-1}$$

The mean bond enthalpy vary slightly from compound to compound but it does not differ in a great deal.

The net enthalpy change of a reaction is the amount of energy required to break all the bonds in the reactant molecules minus the amount of energy required to break all the bonds in the product molecules.

$$\Delta_r H = \Sigma BE_{\text{Reactants}} - \Sigma BE_{\text{Products}}$$

The above relations are valid only when the reactants and products are in gaseous state.

Note
- Bond dissociation enthalpy and mean bond enthalpy have the same symbol.
- As the bond multiplicity increases, bond enthalpy increases.

  e.g., $C-C < C=C < C\equiv C$ (order of bond enthalpy)

  414 611 837
- In case of monoatomic species, bond enthalpy is replaced by heat of atomisation.

Example 4 Calculate the enthalpy change (ΔH) of the following reaction.

$$C_2H_2(g) + \frac{5}{2}O_2(g) \longrightarrow 2CO_2(g) + H_2O(g)$$

Given average bond enthalpies of various bonds. i.e. C—H, C≡C, O=O, C=O, O—H as 414, 810, 499, 724 and 460 kJ mol^{-1} respectively.

Sol. The equation representing various substances involved in chemical reaction is

$$(H-C\equiv C-H) + \frac{5}{2}(O=O) \longrightarrow 2(O=C=O) + (H-O-H)$$

The reaction involves the breaking of 2C—H bonds, C≡C bonds, $\frac{5}{2}$ O=O bonds and formation of 4C=O bonds and 2O—H bonds.

$$\Delta_r H^\ominus = \begin{bmatrix}\text{Sum of bond enthalpies}\\ \text{of reactants}\end{bmatrix} - \begin{bmatrix}\text{Sum of bond enthalpies}\\ \text{of products}\end{bmatrix}$$

$$= [2\Delta_{C-H}H^\ominus + \Delta_{C\equiv C}H^\ominus + \frac{5}{2}\Delta_{O=O}H^\ominus] - [4\Delta_{C=O}H^\ominus + 2\Delta_{O-H}H^\ominus]$$

$$= (2\times 414 + 810 + \frac{5}{2}\times 499) - (4\times 724 + 2\times 460)$$

$$= 2885.5 - 3816 = -930.5\ \text{kJ}$$

Hess's Law of Constant Heat Summation

According to this law, "the total heat change (ΔH) accompanying a chemical reaction is the same whether the reaction takes place in one step or more than in one steps".

If a reaction takes place in several steps then its standard reaction enthalpy is the sum of the standard enthalpies of the intermediate reactions into which the overall reaction may be divided at the same temperature.

Suppose, enthalpy change for direct conversion, $A \longrightarrow B$ is ΔH, B can also be prepared from A through intermediates C and D, for which enthalpy changes are $\Delta H_1, \Delta H_2$ and ΔH_3 respectively as shown in the below figure :

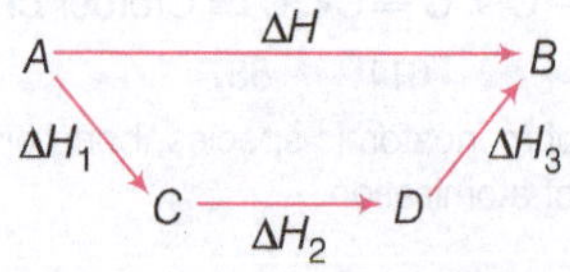

Then according to Hess's law, $\Delta H = \Delta H_1 + \Delta H_2 + \Delta H_3$

It clearly indicates that when chemical equations are added, subtracted or multiplied, the heat changes can also be added, substracted or multiplied accordingly.

Applications of Hess's Law

(i) For the determination of enthalpies of formation of compounds.

(ii) For the determination of enthalpies of extremely slow reactions.

(iii) For the determination of enthalpies of transformation of one allotropic form into another.

(iv) For the determination of bond energies

$\Delta H_{\text{reaction}} = \Sigma$ bond energies of reactants $- \Sigma$ bond energies of products.

(v) For the determination of resonance energy.

$\therefore$ Resonance energy = experimental or actual heat of formation − calculated heat of formation.

Example 5 Enthalpy is an extensive property. In general, if enthalpy of an overall reaction, $A \rightarrow B$ along one route is $\Delta_r H$ and $\Delta_r H_1, \Delta_r H_2, \Delta_r H_3 \ldots$ represent enthalpies of intermediate reactions leading to product B. What will be the relation between $\Delta_r H$ (overall reaction) and $\Delta_r H_1, \Delta_r H_2 \ldots$ etc., for intermediate reactions.

NCERT Exemplar

Sol. In general, if enthalpy of an overall reaction, $A \rightarrow B$ along one route is $\Delta_r H$ and $\Delta_r H_1, \Delta_r H_2, \Delta_r H_3 \ldots$ representing enthalpies of reaction leading to same product B along another route, then we have

$$\Delta_r H = \Delta_r H_1 + \Delta_r H_2 + \Delta_r H_3 + \ldots$$

Topic Practice 2

Very Short Answer Type Questions

1 Mark

1 Fill in the Blanks

(i) The unit of enthalpy change is..........

(ii) The process of conversion of a solid into its vapours without coming in the the liquid state is called..........

(iii) According to Hess's law, the total..........accompanying a chemical reaction, is same whether the reaction takes place in one or..........steps.

(iv) Hess's law is used for the determination of..........of extremely..........reaction.

2 Multiple Choice Questions

(i) The bond dissociation energies of H_2, Cl_2 and HCl are 104, 58 and 103 kcal mol^{-1} respectively. The enthalpy of formation of HCl would be

(a) −22 kcal mol^{-1} (b) − 44 kcal mol^{-1}

(c) +44 kcal mol^{-1} (d) +22 kcal mol^{-1}

(ii) Calculate the bond enthalpy of Xe—F bond as given in the equation,

$XeF_4(g) \longrightarrow Xe^+(g) + F^-(g) + F_2(g) + F(g)$;

$\Delta_r H = 292$ kcal mol^{-1}

Ionisation energy of Xe = 279 kcal/mol

Bond energy (F—F) = 38 kcal/mol

Electron affinity of F = 85 kcal/mol

(a) 8.5 kcal/mol

(b) 34 kcal/mol

(c) 24 kcal/mol

(d) None of these

(iii) Enthalpy change for the reaction,

$4H(g) \longrightarrow 2H_2(g)$ is −869.6 kJ

The dissociation energy of H—H bond is

(a) −869.6 kJ (b) +434.8 KJ

(c) +217.4 kJ (d) −434.8 kJ

(iv) Enthalpy change when one mole of covalent bonds of a gaseous covalent compound is broken to form products in the gas phase. It is called

(a) bond association enthalpy

(b) bond dissociation enthalpy

(c) mean bond dissociation enthalpy

(d) mean bond association enthalpy

3 Match the following enthalpies with their example and choose the correct option using the codes given below:

Enthalpies	Example
A. Enthalpy of Fusion	(i) $I_2(s) \xrightarrow{\Delta} I_2(v)$
B. Enthalpy of vaporisation	(ii) $H_2O(s) \longrightarrow H_2O(l)$
C. Enthalpy of sublimation	(iii) $H_2O(l) \longrightarrow H_2O(g)$
D. Enthalpy of formation	(iv) $H_2(s) + \frac{1}{2}O_2(s) \longrightarrow H_2O(l)$

Codes

	A	B	C	D
(a)	(i)	(ii)	(iii)	(iv)
(b)	(ii)	(iii)	(i)	(iv)
(c)	(ii)	(i)	(iii)	(iv)
(d)	(iii)	(i)	(ii)	(iv)

4 The enthalpy of reaction for the reaction $2H_2(g) + O_2(g) \longrightarrow 2H_2O(l)$ is

$$\Delta_r H^\ominus = -572 \text{ kJ mol}^{-1}$$

What will be standard enthalpy of formation of $H_2O(l)$?

5. The molar enthalpy of vaporisation of acetone is less than that of water. Why? **NCERT Exemplar**

6 Enthalpy of combustion of carbon to CO_2 is -393.5 kJ mol^{-1}. Calculate the heat released upon formation of 35.2 g of CO_2 from carbon and dioxygen gas. (Molar mass of CO_2 = 44 g mol^{-1}). **NCERT Textbook**

7 The enthalpy of atomisation for the reaction,

$$CH_4(g) \longrightarrow C(g) + 4H(g)$$

is 1665 kJ mol^{-1}. What is the bond energy of C–H bond ?

Short Answer Type I Questions

2 Marks

8. Given, $N_2(g) + 3H_2(g) \longrightarrow 2NH_3(g)$;

$$\Delta_r H^\circ = -92.4 \text{ kJ mol}^{-1}$$

What is the standard enthalpy of formation of NH_3 gas ? **NCERT TextBook**

9. The value of $\Delta_f H^\ominus$ for NH_3 is -91.8 kJ mol^{-1}. Calculate enthalpy change for the following reaction.

$$2NH_3(g) \longrightarrow N_2(g) + 3H_2(g)$$

10 Enthalpies of formation of $CO(g)$, $CO_2(g)$, $N_2O(g)$ and $N_2O_4(g)$ are -110, -393, 81 and 9.7 kJ mol^{-1} respectively. Find the value of $\Delta_r H$ for the reaction.

$$N_2O_4(g) + 3CO(g) \longrightarrow N_2O(g) + 3CO_2(g)$$

NCERT Textbook

11 Standard molar enthalpy of formation, $\Delta_f H^\circ$ is just a special case of enthalpy of reaction, $\Delta_r H^\circ$. Is the $\Delta_r H^\circ$ for the following reaction same as $\Delta_f H^\circ$? Give reason for your answer.

$$CaO(s) + CO_2(g) \longrightarrow CaCO_3(s);$$
$$\Delta_f H^\circ = -178.3 \text{ kJ mol}^{-1}$$

NCERT Exemplar

12 The enthalpy of formation of carbon monoxide and steam are -110.5 and -243.0 kJ respectively. Calculate the heat of the reaction when steam is passed over coke as

$$C(s) + H_2O(g) \longrightarrow CO(g) + H_2(g)$$

13 The standard heat of formation of $CH_4(g)$, $CO_2(g)$ and $H_2O(g)$ are -76.2, -394.8 and -241.6 kJ mol^{-1} respectively. Calculate the amount of heat evolved by burning 1 m^3 of methane measured at NTP.

14 Given that the enthalpy of formation of H_2O is -68 kcal/mol. Calculate the enthalpy of formation of OH^- ions.

15 18.0 g water completely vaporises at 100°C and 1 bar pressure and the enthalpy change in the process is 40.79 kJ mol^{-1}. What will be the enthalpy change for vaporising two moles of water under the same conditions? What is the standard enthalpy of vaporisation for water ? **NCERT Exemplar**

16 The enthalpy of a vaporisation of CCl_4 is 30.5 kJ mol^{-1}. Calculate the heat required for the vaporisation of 284 g of CCl_4 at constant pressure (molar mass of CCl_4 = 154 g mol^{-1})

17 Standard vaporisation enthalpy of benzene at boiling point is 30.8 kJ mol^{-1}. For how long would 100 W electric heater have to operate in order to vaporise a 100 g sample at that temperature
(power= energy/time and 1 W = 1 Js^{-1})?

18 A swimmer coming out from a pool is covered with a film of water weighing about 18 g. How much heat must be supplied to evaporate this water at 298 K? Calculate the internal energy of vaporisation at 100°C ?

$\Delta_{vap} H^\ominus$ for water at 373 K = 40.66 kJ mol^{-1}

19 Acetic acid (ethanoic acid) and hydrochloric acid react with KOH solution. The enthalpy of neutralisation of ethanoic acid is – 55.8 kJ mol^{-1} while that of hydrochloric acid is – 57.3 kJ mol^{-1}. Can you think of why are these different?

20 An average healthy man needs about 10000 kJ of energy per day. How much carbohydrates (in mass) he will have to consume assuming that all this energy needs are met only by carbohydrates in the form of glucose? The enthalpy of combustion of glucose is 2816 kJ mol^{-1}.

21 Calculate $\Delta_r H°$ for the reaction,

$$H—\underset{H}{\underset{|}{C}}=\underset{H}{\underset{|}{C}}—H + 3O=O \longrightarrow 2O=C=O + 2H—O—H$$

The average bond enthalpies of various bonds are as follows.

Bond	Bond enthalpy (kJ mol^{-1})
C—H	414
O=O	499
C=O	724
O—H	460
C=C	619

22 The net enthalpy change of a reaction is the energy required to break all the bonds in reactant molecules minus amount of energy required to form all the bonds in the product molecules. What will be the enthalpy change for the following reaction. **NCERT Exemplar**

$$H_2(g) + Br_2(g) \longrightarrow 2HBr(g)$$

Given that bond energy of H_2, Br_2 and HBr is 435 kJ mol^{-1}, 192 kJ mol^{-1} and 368 kJ mol^{-1} respectively.

Short Answer Type II Questions

(3 Marks)

23 Give the appropriate reason :

(i) It is preferable to determine the change in enthalpy rather than the change in internal energy.

(ii) It is necessary to define the 'standard state'.

(iii) It is necessary to specify the phases of the reactants and products in a thermochemical equation.

24 Calculate the standard enthalpy of formation of $CH_3OH(l)$ from the following data **NCERT Textbook**

(i) $CH_3OH(l) + \frac{3}{2}O_2(g) \longrightarrow CO_2(g) + 2H_2O(l)$;
$\Delta_r H° = -726$ kJ mol^{-1}

(ii) $C_{(graphite)} + O_2(g) \longrightarrow CO_2(g)$;
$\Delta_c H° = -393$ kJ mol^{-1}

(iii) $H_2(g) + \frac{1}{2}O_2(g) \longrightarrow H_2O(l)$;
$\Delta_f H° = -286$ kJ mol^{-1}

25 Calculate the enthalpy change for the process,

$$CCl_4(g) \longrightarrow C(g) + 4Cl(g)$$

and calculate the bond enthalpy of C–Cl in $CCl_4(g)$

$\Delta_{vap}H°(CCl_4) = 30.5$ kJ mol^{-1}

$\Delta_f H°(CCl_4) = -135.5$ kJ mol^{-1}

$\Delta_a H°(C) = 715.0$ kJ mol^{-1}

where, $\Delta_a H°$ is enthalpy of atomisation,

$\Delta_a H°(Cl_2) = 242$ kJ mol^{-1} **NCERT Textbook**

26 The standard molar enthalpies of formation of cyclohexane (*l*) and benzene (*l*) at 25°C are – 156 and + 49 kJ mol^{-1} respectively. The standard enthalpy of hydrogenation of cyclohexene(*l*) at 25°C is – 119 kJ mol^{-1}. Use these data to estimate the magnitude of the resonance energy of benzene.

27 Using the data (all values are in kilocalories per mole at 25°C) given below, calculate the bond energy of C–C and C–H bonds.

$\Delta H°$ combustion (ethane) = – 372.0

$\Delta H°$ combustion (propane) = – 530.0

$\Delta H°$ for C (graphite) → C(g) = 172.0

Bond energy of H–H = 104.0

$\Delta_f H°$ of H_2O (*l*) = – 68.0

$\Delta H°$ for $CO_2(g)$ = – 94.0

28 Use the following data to calculate, $\Delta_{lattice}H°$ for NaBr. $\Delta_{sub}H°$ for sodium metal = 108.4 kJ mol^{-1}

Ionisation enthalpy of sodium = 496 mol^{-1}

Electron gain enthalpy of bromine = – 325 kJ mol^{-1}

Bond dissociation enthalpy of bromine = 192 kJ mol^{-1}, $\Delta_f H°$ for NaBr(s) = – 360.1 kJ mol^{-1} **NCERT Exemplar**

29 A man takes a diet equivalent to 10000 kJ per day and does work, in expending his energy in all forms equivalent to 12500 kJ per day. What is change in internal energy per day? If the energy lost was stored as sucrose (1632 kJ per 100 g), how many days should it take to lose 2 kg of his weight? (Ignore water loss)

30 Calculate the enthalpy change on freezing of 1.0 mole of water at 10.0°C to ice at – 10.0°C. $\Delta_{fus}H = 6.03$ kJ mol^{-1} at 0°C. **NCERT Textbook**

$C_p[H_2O(l)] = 75.3$ J $mol^{-1}K^{-1}$;

$C_p[H_2O(s)] = 36.8$ J $mol^{-1}K^{-1}$

Long Answer Type Questions

5 Marks

31 (i) An athlete is given 100 g of glucose of energy equivalent to 1560 kJ. He utilises 50% of this gained energy in the event. In order to avoid storage of energy in the body, calculate the weight of water that would need to perspire. The enthalpy of vaporisation of water is 44 kJ mol^{-1}.

(ii) Compound with carbon-carbon double bond, such as ethylene, C_2H_4, add hydrogen in a reaction called hydrogenation,

$$C_2H_4(g) + H_2(g) \longrightarrow C_2H_6(g)$$

Calculate enthalpy change for the reaction, using the following combustion data

$$C_2H_4(g) + 3\,O_2(g) \longrightarrow 2\,CO_2(g) + 2\,H_2O(l); \quad \Delta_c H° = -1401 \text{ kJ mol}^{-1} \text{...(i)}$$

$$C_2H_6(g) + \frac{7}{2}O_2(g) \longrightarrow 2\,CO_2(g) + 3\,H_2O\,(l) \quad \Delta_c H° = -1550 \text{ kJ mol}^{-1} \text{...(ii)}$$

$$H_2(g) + \frac{1}{2}O_2(g) \rightarrow H_2O\,(l); \quad \Delta_c H° = -286.0 \text{ kJ mol}^{-1} \text{...(iii)}$$

Hints & Solutions

1. (i) kJ mol^{-1} (ii) sublimation, (iii) heat change, more (iv) enthalpies, slow

2. (i) $\rightarrow$ a, (ii) $\rightarrow$ b, (iii) $\rightarrow$ b, (iv) $\rightarrow$ b

3. (b) A $\rightarrow$ (ii), B $\rightarrow$ (iii), C $\rightarrow$ (i), D $\rightarrow$ (iv)

4. Enthalpy of formation is the enthalpy change of the reaction when 1 mole of the compound is formed from its elements,

$$H_2(g) + \frac{1}{2}O_2(g) \longrightarrow H_2O(l), \Delta_r H° = ?$$

This can be obtained by dividing the given equation by 2.

$$\text{Hence,} \quad \Delta_f H°(H_2O) = \frac{-572 \text{ kJ mol}^{-1}}{2} = -286 \text{ kJ mol}^{-1}$$

5. Enthalpy of vaporisation of acetone is less than that of water because there is strong hydrogen bonding in H_2O molecules.

6. The reaction for the combustion of carbon into CO_2 is

$$C(s) + O_2(g) \longrightarrow \underset{44\,g}{CO_2(g)}; \quad \Delta H = -393.5 \text{ kJ mol}^{-1}$$

Heat released in the formation of 44 g CO_2 = 393.5 kJ

∴ Heat released in the formation of 35.2 g CO_2

$$= \frac{393.5 \text{ kJ} \times 35.2 \text{ g}}{44 \text{ g}} = 314.8 \text{ kJ}$$

7. In CH_4, there are four C—H bonds. The enthalpy of atomisation of 1 mole of CH_4 means dissociation of four moles of C—H bond.

$$\therefore \text{C—H bond energy per mol} = \frac{1665 \text{ kJ}}{4 \text{ mol}} = 416.25 \text{ kJ mol}^{-1}$$

8. Firstly, standard enthalpy of formation means heat released in the formation of 1 mole of substance.

Given, $N_2(g) + 3H_2(g) \longrightarrow 2NH_3(g)$;

$\Delta_r H° = -92.4$ kJ mol^{-1} [1]

Chemical reaction for the enthalpy of formation of $NH_3(g)$ is as follows :

$$\frac{1}{2}N_2(g) + \frac{3}{2}H_2(g) \longrightarrow NH_3(g)$$

Therefore, $\Delta_f H° = \dfrac{-92.4}{2} = -46.2$ kJ mol^{-1} [1]

9. Given, $\frac{1}{2}N_2(g) + \frac{3}{2}H_2(g) \rightarrow NH_3(g)$;

$\Delta_f H^{\ominus} = -91.8$ kJ mol^{-1}

($\Delta_f H^{\ominus}$ means enthalpy of formation of 1 mole of NH_3)

∴ Enthalpy change for the formation of 2 moles of NH_3

$N_2(g) + 3H_2(g) \rightarrow 2NH_3(g)$;

$\Delta_f H^{\ominus} = 2\times -91.8 = -183.6$ kJ mol^{-1} [1]

and for the reverse reaction,

$2NH_3(g) \rightarrow N_2(g) + 3H_2(g); \Delta_f H^{\ominus} = +183.6$ kJ mol^{-1}

Hence, the value of $\Delta_f H^{\ominus}$ for NH_3 is +183.6 kJ mol^{-1}. [1]

10. Heat of reaction,

$\Delta_r H° = \Sigma\Delta_f H°_{products} - \Sigma\Delta_f H°_{reactants}$ [1]

$= [\Delta_f H°(N_2O) + 3\Delta_f H°(CO_2)] - [\Delta_f H°(N_2O_4) + 3\Delta_f H°(CO)]$

$= [81 + (3\times -393)] - [9.7 + (3\times -110)]$ kJ

$= -777.7$ kJ ≈ -778 kJ [1]

11. The standard enthalpy change for the formation of one mole of a compound from its elements in their most stable states (reference states) is called standard molar enthalpy of formation, $\Delta_f H°$.

$$Ca(s) + C(s) + \frac{3}{2}O_2(g) \longrightarrow CaCO_3(s); \Delta_f H°$$

This reaction is different from the given reaction.

Hence, $\Delta_r H° \neq \Delta_f H°$ [2]

12. We are given,

(i) $C(s) + \frac{1}{2}O_2(g) \longrightarrow CO(g); \; \Delta H = -110.5$ kJ [1]

(ii) $H_2(g) + \frac{1}{2}O_2(g) \longrightarrow H_2O(g); \; \Delta H = -243.0$ kJ

Subtracting Eq. (ii) from Eq. (i), we get

$C(s) + H_2O(g) \longrightarrow CO(g) + H_2(g)$;

$\Delta H = +132.5$ kJ [1]

13. The burning of methane may be expressed as

$$CH_4(g) + 2O_2(g) \longrightarrow CO_2(g) + 2H_2O(g)$$

$$\Delta_f H° = [\Delta_f H°(CO_2) + 2\Delta_f H°(H_2O)] - [\Delta_f H°(CH_4) + 2\Delta_f H°(O_2)]$$

$$= [-394.8 + 2\times(-241.6)] - [-76.2 + 2\times(0)]$$

$$= -801.8 \text{ kJ}$$ [1]

1 mole or 22.4 L of CH_4 evolve heat = 801.8 kJ

1 m^3 or 1000 L of CH_4 evolve heat $= \frac{801.8\times 1000}{22.4}$

$= 35794.6 \text{ kJ}$ [1]

14. For neutralisation reaction, we know that

$$H^+ + OH^- \longrightarrow H_2O; \Delta_r H° = -13.7 \text{ kcal}$$

$$\therefore \Delta_r H° = \Delta_f H°(H_2O) - [\Delta_f H°(H^+) + \Delta_f H°(OH^-)]$$

i.e. $-13.7 = -68 - [0 + \Delta_f H°(OH^-)]$ $[\because + \Delta_f H°(H^+) = 0]$

or $\Delta_f H°(OH^-) = -68 + 13.7 = -54.3 \text{ kcal mol}^{-1}$ [2]

15. 18.0 g H_2O = 1 mol H_2O

Enthalpy change for vaporising 1 mole of H_2O = 40.79 kJ

$\therefore$ Enthalpy change for vaporising 2 moles of H_2O

$= 2\times 40.79 \text{ kJ} = 81.58 \text{ kJ}$ [1]

Standard enthalpy of vaporisation at 100°C and 1 bar pressure, $\Delta_{vap}H° = +40.79 \text{ kJ mol}^{-1}$ [1]

16. 1 mole of CCl_4 = 154 g

Heat required for vaporising 154 g CCl_4 = 30.5 kJ [1]

$\therefore$ Heat required for vaporising 284 g of CCl_4

$= \frac{30.5\times 284}{154} \text{ kJ} = 56.25 \text{ kJ}$ [1]

17. $\Delta_{vap}H°(\text{benzene}) = 30.8 \text{ kJ mol}^{-1}$

Molar mass of benzene,

$C_6H_6 = (6\times 12 + 6\times 1) \text{ g mol}^{-1} = 78 \text{ g mol}^{-1}$

Energy needed to vaporise benzene

$= 30.8 \text{ kJ mol}^{-1} \times \frac{100 \text{ g}}{78 \text{ g mol}^{-1}} = 39.49 \text{ kJ}$ [1]

So Time $= \frac{\text{energy}}{\text{power}} = \frac{39.49 \text{ kJ}}{100 \text{ W}} = \frac{39.49\times 10^3 \text{ J}}{100 \text{ Js}^{-1}}$ [1]

$= 394.9 \text{ s} = 6.6 \text{ min}$

18 The process of evaporation can be represented as

$$18 \text{ g } H_2O(l) \xrightarrow{\text{Vaporisation}} 18 \text{ g } H_2O(g)$$

Number of moles in 18 g $H_2O(l) = \frac{18 \text{ g}}{18 \text{ g mol}^{-1}} = 1 \text{ mol}$ [1]

and $\Delta_{vap}H^\ominus$ is the amount of heat required to vaporise 1 mole of a substance. Thus, 40.66 kJ mol^{-1} heat is required for evaporation of 18 g of water.

Further, we know that

$$\Delta_{vap}U = \Delta_{vap}H^\ominus - p\Delta V \Rightarrow \Delta_{vap}H^\ominus - \Delta n_g RT$$

(assuming steam behaving as an ideal gas).

$\therefore \Delta_{vap}U = 40.66 \text{ kJ mol}^{-1} - (1)(8.314 \text{ JK}^{-1} \text{ mol}^{-1})(373 \text{ K})(10^{-3})$

$\Delta_{vap}U^\ominus = 40.66 \text{ kJ mol}^{-1} - 3.10 \text{ kJ mol}^{-1} = 37.56 \text{ kJ mol}^{-1}$ [1]

19. The thermochemical equations for the neutralisation of acetic acid and hydrochloric acids are,

$$CH_3COOH(aq) + KOH(aq) \longrightarrow CH_3COOK(aq) + H_2O(l); \Delta_n H° = -55.8 \text{ kJ mol}^{-1}$$

and $$HCl(aq) + KOH(aq) \longrightarrow KCl(aq) + H_2O(l); \Delta_n H° = -57.3 \text{ kJ mol}^{-1}$$

In dilute solution, HCl is completely ionised into H^+ and Cl^-, whereas CH_3COOH is ionised to very small extent. This difference between the enthalpy of neutralisation of the two acids is due to the endothermic nature of the reaction involving the ionisation of acetic acid, i.e.

$$CH_3COOH(aq) \rightleftharpoons CH_3COO^-(aq) + H^+(aq)$$

$$\Delta_{ion}H° = -55.8 - (-57.3) \text{ kJ mol}^{-1} = 1.5 \text{ kJ mol}^{-1}$$ [2]

20. Enthalpy of combustion of glucose = 2816 kJ mol^{-1}

Molecular mass of glucose $(C_6H_{12}O_6)$

$= 6\times 12 + 12\times 1 + 6\times 16 = 180 \text{ g mol}^{-1}$ [1]

2816 kJ of energy is evolved from glucose = 180 g

10000 kJ of energy will be evolved from glucose

$= \frac{180}{2816}\times 10000 = 639.20 \text{ g}$ [1]

21. In this reaction, four C—H bonds, one C═C bond and three O═O bonds are broken and four C═O bonds and four O—H bonds are formed. Thus,

$\Delta H° = [4 \times$ (bond enthalpy of C—H) + (bond enthalpy of C═C) + 3× bond enthalpy of O═O] − [(4× bond enthalpy of C═O) + 4 (bond enthalpy of O—H)]

$$\Delta H = (4\times 414 + 619 + 3\times 499) - (4\times 724 + 4\times 460)$$

$$= -964 \text{ kJ mol}^{-1}$$ [2]

22. $H_2(g) + Br_2(g) \longrightarrow 2HBr(g)$

$\Delta_r H° = \Sigma \text{BE (reactants)} - \Sigma\text{BE (products)}$

$= BE(H_2) + BE(Br_2) - 2\,BE(HBr)$

$= 435 + 192 - (2\times 368) \text{ kJ mol}^{-1} = -109 \text{ kJ mol}^{-1}$ [2]

23. (i) Because it is easier to make measurement under constant pressure than under constant volume conditions. [1]

(ii) Enthalpy change depends upon the conditions in which a reaction is carried out. For making the comparison of results obtained by different people meaningful, the reaction conditions must be well-defined. [1]

(iii) Because enthalpy depends upon the phase of reactants and products. [1]

24.

> **Key Idea** Firstly write the required chemical equation for the formation of 1 mole of methanol (l) and then calculate $\Delta_f H°$ for the formation of methanol by adding all the equation in such a way so that it give the required equation (i.e. apply Hess's Law).

Required reaction for the formation of methanol is as follows.

$C(s) + 2H_2(g) + \frac{1}{2}O_2(g) \longrightarrow CH_3OH(l);\ \Delta_f H° = ?$

Multiplying Eq. (iii) by 2, we have

(iv) $2H_2(g) + O_2(g) \longrightarrow 2H_2O(l);$

$\Delta_f H° = -572\ \text{kJ mol}^{-1}$ [1]

Summing up the Eqs. (ii) and (iv), we get

(v) $C(s) + 2H_2(g) + 2O_2(g) \longrightarrow CO_2(g) + 2H_2O(l);$

$\Delta_f H° = -965\ \text{kJ mol}^{-1}$ [1]

Reversing Eq. (i), we get

(vi) $CO_2(g) + 2H_2O(g) \longrightarrow CH_3OH(l) + \frac{3}{2}O_2(g);$

$\Delta_r H° = +726\ \text{kJ mol}^{-1}$

Adding Eqs. (v) and (vi) we get the required equation

$C(s) + 2H_2(g) + \frac{1}{2}O_2(g) \longrightarrow CH_3OH(l);$

$\Delta_f H° = -965 + 726 = -239\ \text{kJ mol}^{-1}$ [1]

25. Given,

(i) $CCl_4(l) \longrightarrow CCl_4(g);\ \Delta_{vap} H° = +30.5\ \text{kJ mol}^{-1}$

(ii) $C(s) + 2Cl_2(g) \longrightarrow CCl_4(l);\ \Delta_f H° = -135.5\ \text{kJ mol}^{-1}$

(iii) $C(s) \longrightarrow C(g);\ \Delta_a H° = 715.0\ \text{kJ mol}^{-1}$ [1]

(iv) $Cl_2(g) \longrightarrow 2Cl(g);\ \Delta_a H° = 242\ \text{kJ mol}^{-1}$

Multiplying Eq. (iv) by 2, we get

(v) $2Cl_2(g) \longrightarrow 4Cl(g);\ \Delta_a H° = 484.0\ \text{kJ mol}^{-1}$

Adding Eqs. (iii) and (v), we get

(vi) $C(s) + 2Cl_2(g) \longrightarrow C(g) + 4Cl(g);\ \Delta H = 1199\ \text{kJ mol}^{-1}$

Reversing Eqs. (i) and (ii), we get

(vii) $CCl_4(g) \longrightarrow CCl_4(l);\ \Delta H = -30.5\ \text{kJ mol}^{-1}$ [1]

(viii) $CCl_4(l) \longrightarrow C(s) + 2Cl_2(g);\ \Delta H = +135.5\ \text{kJ mol}^{-1}$

Adding Eqs. (vi), (vii) and (viii), we get

$CCl_4(g) \longrightarrow C(g) + 4Cl(g);\ \Delta H = 1304\ \text{kJ mol}^{-1}$

Bond enthalpy of C—Cl bond in

$CCl_4 = \frac{1304}{4} = 326\ \text{kJ mol}^{-1}$

(∵ There are four C—Cl bonds in CCl_4, Cl—C(Cl)(Cl)—Cl.) [1]

26. Standard enthalpy of hydrogenation of cyclohexene $= -119\ \text{kJ mol}^{-1}$. This is the observed enthalpy of hydrogenation of one double bond (present in cyclohexene).

If benzene is considered as cyclohexatriene, the observed enthalpy of the reaction,

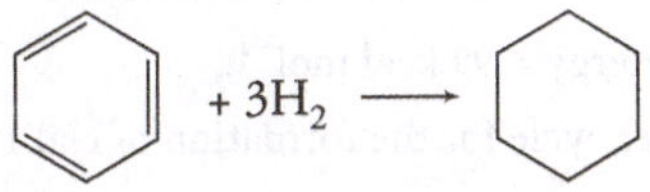

would be $= 3 \times (-119) = -357\ \text{kJ mol}^{-1}$ [1]

Calculated enthalpy of the above reaction is

$\Delta_r H = \Delta H_f^°(C_6H_{14}) - [\Delta H_f^°(C_6H_6) + 3\,\Delta H_f^°(H_2)]$

$= -156 - (49 + 0) = -205\ \text{kJ mol}^{-1}$ [1]

∴ Resonance energy = Observed $\Delta_r H°$ − calculated $\Delta_r H°$

$= (-357) - (-205)\ \text{kJ mol}^{-1}$

$= -152\ \text{kJ mol}^{-1}$ [1]

27. We are given,

(i) $C_2H_6(g) + \frac{7}{2}O_2(g) \longrightarrow 2CO_2(g) + 3H_2O;$

$\Delta H° = -372.0\ \text{kcal}$

(ii) $C_3H_8(g) + 5O_2(g) \longrightarrow 3CO_2(g) + 4H_2O;$

$\Delta H° = -530.0\ \text{kcal}$

(iii) $C(s) \longrightarrow C(g);\quad \Delta H° = 172.0\ \text{kcal}$

(iv) $H_2(g) \longrightarrow 2H(g);\quad \Delta H° = 104.0\ \text{kcal}$

(v) $H_2(g) + \frac{1}{2}O_2(g) \longrightarrow H_2O(l);\ \Delta H° = -68.0\ \text{kcal}$

(vi) $C(g) + O_2(g) \longrightarrow CO_2(g);\quad \Delta H° = -94.0\ \text{kcal}$

Suppose the bond energy of C—C bond = x kcal mol^{-1} and that of C—H bond = y kcal mol^{-1}. Then for $C_2H_6(g)$,

i.e. $H_3C—CH_3 \longrightarrow 2C(g) + 6H;$

$\Delta H = x + 6y$ ...(vii)

and for $C_3H_8(g)$; i.e.

$H_3C—CH_2—CH_3 \longrightarrow 3C(g) + 8H(g);$

$\Delta H = 2x + 8y$ ...(viii)

To get Eq. (vii), operate, Eq. (i) + 2 × Eq. (iii) + 3 × Eq. (iv) − 3 × Eq. (v) − 2 × Eq. (vi).

It gives $\Delta H = 676$ kcal

To get Eq. (viii) operate, Eq. (ii) + Eq. (iii) + 4 × Eq (iv) − 4 × Eq. (v) − 3 × Eq (vi)

It gives $\Delta H = 956$ kcal

Thus, $x + 6y = 676,\quad 2x + 8y = 956$

On solving these equations, we get $x = 82$, $y = 99$
Hence, C—C bond energy = 82 kcal mol^{-1} and C—H bond energy = 99 kcal mol^{-1}. [3]

28. Born-Haber cycle for the formation of NaBr is as

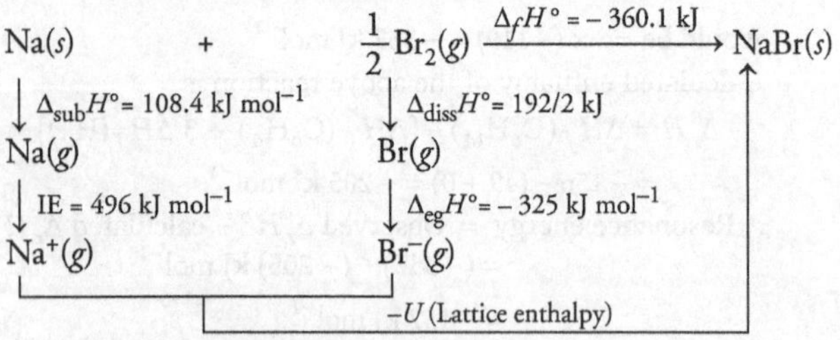

By applying Hess's law,

$$\Delta_f H° = \Delta_{sub}H° + IE + \Delta_{diss}H° + \Delta_{eg}H° + U$$

$$-360.1 = 108.4 + 496 + 96 + (-325) - U; U = +735.5 \text{ kJ mol}^{-1}$$ [3]

29. Energy taken by a man = 10000 kJ. Change in internal energy per day = 12500 − 10000 = 2500 kJ. The energy is lost by the man as he expends more energy than he takes. Now 100 g of sugar corresponds to energy = 1632 kJ loss in energy.

2000 g of sugar corresponds to energy $= \frac{1632 \times 2000}{100}$
$= 32640$ kJ [2]

∴Number of days required to lose 2000 g of weight or 32640 kJ of energy $= \frac{32640}{2500} = 13$ days [1]

30. **Key Idea** Conversion of 1 mole of water at 10°C to ice at −10°C involves the following steps

1 mol $H_2O(l)$ at 10° C ⟶ 1 mol $H_2O(l)$ at 0° C
$\Delta H_1 = C_{pH_2O(l)} \times \Delta T$

1 mol $H_2O(l)$ at 0° C ⟶ 1 mol $H_2O(s)$ at 0° C
$\Delta H_2 = \Delta H_{freezing}$

1 mol $H_2O(s)$ at 0° C ⟶ 1 mol $H_2O(s)$ at − 10° C
$\Delta H_3 = C_{pH_2O(s)} \times \Delta T$;

$\Delta T = 10$ K and we know that according to Hess's law, total enthalpy change, $\Delta H = H_1 + H_2 + H_3$ so first calculate ΔH_1, ΔH_2, ΔH_3 and then ΔH.

Enthalpy change for the conversion of 1 mole of liquid water at 10°C into 1 mole liquid water at 0°C,

$$\Delta H_1 = C_{p\,H_2O(l)} \times \Delta T = -75.3 \text{ J mol}^{-1} \text{ K}^{-1} \times 10 \text{ K}$$
$$= -753 \text{ J mol}^{-1} = -0.753 \text{ kJmol}^{-1}$$

Enthalpy of fusion, $\Delta H_2 = \Delta H_{freezing} = -\Delta H_{fusion}$
$= -6.03$ kJ mol^{-1} [1]

Enthalpy change for the conversion of 1 mole of ice at 0°C to 1 mole of ice at 10°C,

$$\Delta H_3 = C_{p\,H_2O(s)} \times \Delta T$$
$$= -36.8 \text{ J mol}^{-1} \text{ K}^{-1} \times 10\text{K}$$
$$= -368 \text{ J mol}^{-1} = -0.368 \text{ kJmol}^{-1}$$ [1]

$$\Delta H_{total} = -(0.753 + 6{\cdot}03 + 0.368) \text{ kJ mol}^{-1}$$
$$= -7.151 \text{ kJ mol}^{-1}$$ [1]

Note Heat is evolved in the process of cooling (freezing) so each step will have a negative sign with ΔH.

31. (i) 100 g of glucose is equivalent to 1560 kJ of energy

Energy utilised in the event $= \frac{1560 \times 50}{100}$
$= 780$ kJ [1/2]

Energy left unutilised = 1560 − 780 = 780 kJ [1/2]

Enthalpy of vaporisation of water = 44 kJ/mol
$= \frac{44}{18}$ kJ/g [1/2]

∴Water needed to perspire $= \frac{44}{18} \times 780$
$= 1906.66$ g [1/2]

(ii) Adding Eqs. (i) and (iii) and substract Eq. (ii),

$$C_2H_4(g) + 3\,O_2(g) + H_2(g) + \frac{1}{2}\,O_2(g) - C_2H_6(g)$$
$$-\frac{7}{2}\,O_2(g) \longrightarrow 2\,CO_2(g) + 2\,H_2O\,(l) + H_2O(l)$$
$$-2\,CO_2\,(g) - 3\,H_2O(l)$$ [1]

and $\Delta_r H° = -1401 \text{ kJ mol}^{-1} - 286.0 \text{ kJ mol}^{-1} - (-1550 \text{ kJ mol}^{-1})$ [1]

These equations give,

$$C_2H_2(g) + H_2(g) \longrightarrow C_2H_6(g);$$
$$\Delta_r H° = -137 \text{ kJ mol}^{-1}$$ [1]

TOPIC 03 Spontaneity, Entropy and Gibbs Free Energy

Spontaneity

A physical or chemical change that occurs by its own, i.e. without the assistance of external source, is called **spontaneous process** or **natural process** or **feasible process** or **probable process.**

Or

A spontaneous process is an irreversible process and may only be reversed by some external agency, e.g. rolling ball, heat flow, gas flow etc. There are also some processes which require some initiation before they proceed spontaneously. These processes are also considered as spontaneous processes.

Thus, we can say that spontaneous processes are of two types.

(i) Spontaneous processes which do not require initiation, e.g. dissolution of sugar in water, evaporation of water from river, ponds etc.

(ii) Spontaneous processes where initiation is required, e.g.

$$2H_2(g) + O_2(g) \xrightarrow[\text{spark}]{\text{Electric}} 2H_2O(l)$$

Here, the reaction is initiated by electric spark and then proceeds spontaneously.

$$CH_4(g) + 2O_2(g) \longrightarrow CO_2(g) + 2H_2O(g)$$

Here, CH_4 burns spontaneously when ignited initially. Rest of the other processes which require a continuous supply of energy from outside the system are called **non-spontaneous processes.**

Decrease in Enthalpy as a Criterion for Spontaneity

All the spontaneous process have a tendency to acquire the state of minimum energy. Further, in case of exothermic reactions, the enthalpy (energy) of the system (reaction) decreases, thus these reactions are considered as spontaneous processes. e.g.

$$\frac{1}{2}N_2(g) + \frac{3}{2}H_2(g) \rightleftharpoons NH_3(g); \Delta_r H^\ominus = -46.1 \text{ kJ mol}^{-1}$$

$$\frac{1}{2}H_2(g) + \frac{1}{2}Cl_2(g) \rightleftharpoons HCl(g); \Delta_r H^\ominus = -92.32 \text{ kJ mol}^{-1}$$

Thus, it can be concluded that a tendency to attain the minimum energy, i.e. decrease in energy is responsible for the spontaneity or feasibility of a reaction. The enthalpy diagram, for an exothermic reaction, showing the decrease in enthalpy when reactants are converted into products is shown below.

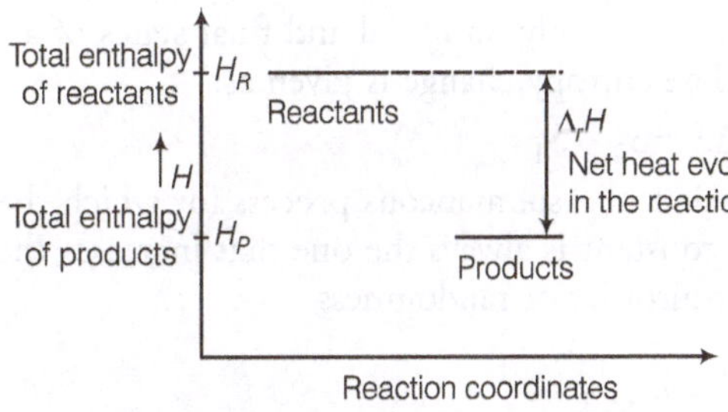

Limitations of the Criterion of Decrease in Energy (Enthalpy)

The above criterion fails to explain the following facts :

(i) In case of endothermic reaction, ΔH is positive, i.e. enthalpy (or energy) of the system increases, but there are several endothermic reactions that are spontaneous. e.g. $\frac{1}{2}N_2(g) + O_2(g) \longrightarrow NO_2(g);$

$$\Delta_r H^\ominus = +33.2 \text{ kJmol}^{-1}$$

The enthalpy diagram for such reactions is shown below.

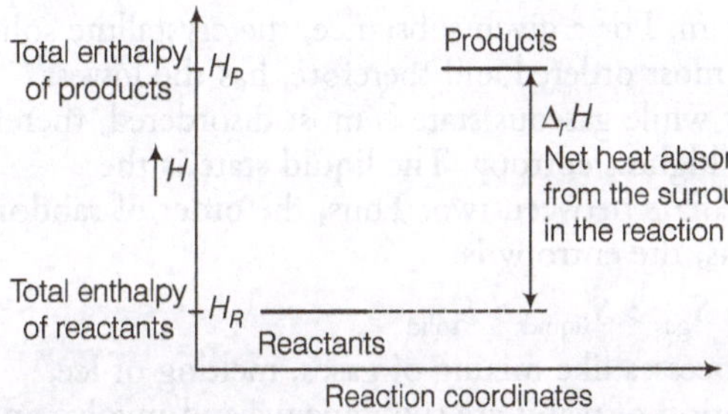

(ii) Several such reactions are also spontaneous for which ΔH is zero. e.g.

$$CH_3COOH(l) + C_2H_5OH(l) \longrightarrow \underset{\text{Ethyl acetate}}{CH_3COOC_2H_5(l)} + H_2O(l)$$

(iii) Even those reactions for which ΔH is negative, rarely proceed to completion even though ΔH remains negative throughout.

(iv) Reversible reaction, e.g. the reactions that occur in forward as well as reverse direction, are also spontaneous in both the directions.From the above discussion, it is obvious that although decrease in enthalpy may be a criteria for spontaneity but it is not true for all the processes.

Entropy

The thermodynamic property that measures the amount of molecular disorder is called the **entropy.** It is denoted by *S*. The entropy is a state function. It means that entropy depends only on initial and final states of a system. The entropy change is given as:

$$\Delta S = S_2 - S_1$$

The direction of a spontaneous process for which the energy is constant is always the one that increases the molecular disorder or randomness.

(a) (b)

Note If similar amount of heat is given to a system at lower temperature and a system at higher temperature, the randomness is more in the system having lower temperature than the system having higher temperature. It shows that entropy change varies inversely with temperature.

Physical Significance of Entropy

Entropy is a measure of randomness or disorder of a system. Greater the randomness, higher is the entropy of the system. For a given substance, the crystalline solid state is most ordered and therefore, has the lowest entropy while gaseous state is most disordered, therefore, has the highest entropy. The liquid state is the intermediate between two. Thus, the order of randomness and thus, the entropy is

$$S_{gas} > S_{liquid} > S_{solid}$$

The processes like mixing of gases, melting of ice, evaporation of water are spontaneous and involve an increase in the disorder of randomness of the system. Therefore, all such processes are accompanied by an increase in the entropy of the system.

Entropy Change in Reversible Process

Consider an isothermal reversible process in which system absorbs q amount of heat from surroundings at temperature, T. The increase in the entropy of the system will be

$$\Delta S_{system} = + \frac{q_{sys,\, rev}}{T}$$

On the other hand, surroundings loose the same amount of heat at the same temperature. The decrease in the entropy of the surroundings will be

$$\Delta S_{surroundings} = - \frac{q_{surroundings,\, rev}}{T}$$

Total change in entropy of the process = entropy change in system + entropy change in surroundings

$\Delta S_{universe}$ (Rev. process) or

$$\Delta S_{total} = \Delta S_{system} + \Delta S_{surroundings} = \frac{q}{T} - \frac{q}{T} = 0$$

When the reversible process is adiabatic, there will be no heat exchange between system and surroundings, i.e. $q = 0$

$$\therefore \quad \Delta S_{system} = 0$$

$$\Delta S_{surroundings} = 0$$

$$\Delta S_{total} = \Delta S_{system} + \Delta S_{surroundings} = 0$$

Entropy Change in Irreversible Processes

Consider a system at higher temperature T_1 and its surroundings at lower temperature T_2. q amount of heat goes irreversibly from system to surroundings.

$$\therefore \quad \Delta S_{system} = -\frac{q}{T_1}; \quad \Delta S_{surroundings} = +\frac{q}{T_2}$$

$$\Delta S_{total} = \Delta S_{system} + \Delta S_{surroundings}$$

$$= -\frac{q}{T_1} + \frac{q}{T_2} = q\left[\frac{T_1 - T_2}{T_1 T_2}\right]$$

But $T_1 > T_2$

$$\therefore \quad T_1 - T_2 = +\text{ve} \text{ or } \Delta S_{total} > 0$$

Hence, entropy increases in an irreversible process.

Note Most of the natural phenomenon are irreversible in nature as most of the systems have a natural tendency to move towards more randomness.

Entropy Change in Isothermal Expansion

The internal energy, $\Delta U = 0$ for the isothermal reversible expansion of a gas. Thus, from first law of thermodynamics,

$$\Delta U = q + W$$

$$\therefore \quad q = -W$$

The work done in the expansion of n moles of gas from volume (V_1) to volume (V_2) at constant temperature (T) is given by $w = -2.303nRT \log V_2 / V_1$

$$\therefore \quad \Delta S = \frac{q}{T} = -\frac{W}{T} = \frac{2.303nRT \log V_2 / V_1}{T}$$

$$\therefore \quad \Delta S = 2.303\, nR \log V_2 / V_1$$

Entropy Change During Phase Transition

The change of matter from one state to another is called **phase transition.** The entropy changes at the time of phase change can be summarised as

$$\Delta S_{melting} = S_{liq} - S_{sol} = \frac{\Delta H_{fusion}}{T_m}$$

where, T_m = melting point of substance, S_{liquid} = molar entropy of the liquid, S_{solid} = molar entropy of the solid

$$\Delta S_{vaporisation} = S_{vap} - S_{liq} = \frac{\Delta H_{vaporisation}}{T_b}$$

where T_b = boiling point of substance

Similarly, $\Delta S_{sublimation} = S_{vap} - S_{sol} = \frac{\Delta H_{sublimation}}{T_{sub}}$

where, T_{sub} = sublimation temperature.

Example 1 For oxidation of iron, $4Fe(s) + 3O_2(g) \longrightarrow 2Fe_2O_3(s)$ entropy change is $-549.4\ JK^{-1}mol^{-1}$ at 298 K. Inspite of negative entropy change of this reaction, why is the reaction spontaneous? ($\Delta_r H^\ominus$ for this reaction is $-1648 \times 10^3 J\ mol^{-1}$)

NCERT Textbook

Sol. The spontaneity of the reaction is decided by considering $\Delta S_{total} (\Delta S_{sys} + \Delta S_{surr})$. At temperature T, entropy change of the surroundings is given by

$$\Delta S_{surr} = \frac{\Delta_r H^\ominus}{T} \quad \text{(at constant pressure)}$$

$$= -\frac{(-1648 \times 10^3\ Jmol^{-1})}{298\ K} = 5530.20\ JK^{-1}mol^{-1}$$

Thus, total entropy change for this reaction

$$\Delta S_{total} = 5530\ JK^{-1}mol^{-1} + (-549.4\ JK^{-1}mol^{-1})$$

$$= 4980.8\ JK^{-1}mol^{-1}$$

Positive value of ΔS_{total} shows that the above reaction is spontaneous.

Second Law of Thermodynamics

The second law of thermodynamics came as a rescue for the limitations of the first law of thermodynamics.

It introduced the concept of entropy (S) and spontaneity.

The second law of thermodynamics can be stated as:

(i) Whenever a spontaneous process takes place, it is always accompanied by an increase in total entropy of the universe.

(ii) It is impossible to take heat from a hotter reservoir. Further, it is also impossible to convert the taken heat into work by a cyclic process without transferring a part of heat to a cooler reservoir. This statement of second law is called **Kelvin's statement.**

(iii) It is impossible for a cyclic process to transfer heat from a body at lower temperature to one at a higher temperature without converting some heat to work. This statement of the second law of thermodynamics is known as **Clausius statement.** The above statements of the second law, in simplified form, can be stated as "for a spontaneous process in an isolated system, the change in entropy is positive."

Thermal Death

This is predicted by second law of thermodynamics. As time passes the entropy of universe keeps on increasing trying to reach a maximum all the time. As this happens, all forms of energy in the universe keep getting transformed into the single form of heat. When finally, the universe reaches a temperature so high, that everything is equally illuminated, there is no way of distinguishing anything from anyother. Entropy reaches its maximum, temperature reaches maximum, pressure and volume of the universe reach their maxima and the universe reaches the state of death. Such a state of affairs will correspond to the thermal death of the inhabitants of the universe.

Helmholtz Free Energy (Work Function)

A thermodynamic energy that measures the amount of useful work obtained from a closed system at constant pressure is called **work function** or **Helmholtz free energy** (A).

Mathematically, it is given as

$$A = E - TS$$

and $\quad \Delta A = \Delta E - T\Delta S$

$$= \Delta E - q \quad \text{(by first law)}$$

$\therefore \quad -\Delta A = W = 2.303\ nRT \log \frac{V_2}{V_1}$

Thus, decrease in A, $(-\Delta A)$, is equal to work involved.

Gibbs Energy and Spontaneity

The maximum amount of energy available to a system, during a process, that can be converted into useful work is called **free energy** or **Gibbs free energy** or **Gibbs energy.** It was called Gibbs free energy in early literature but in accordance with IUPAC recommendations we shall use the term **free energy** for it. Free energy is denoted by G and mathematically expressed as

$$\boxed{G = H - TS}$$

where, H = enthalpy of system, S = entropy of system

T = absolute temperature

Gibbs function, G is an extensive property and state function.

The change in Gibbs energy for the system, ΔG_{sys} can be written as, $\Delta G_{sys} = \Delta H_{sys} - T\Delta S_{sys} - S_{sys}\Delta T$

At constant temperature, $\Delta T = 0$

$\therefore \quad \Delta G_{sys} = \Delta H_{sys} - T\Delta S_{sys}$

Usually the subscript 'sys' (for system) is dropped and the equation simply can be represented as

$$\Delta G = \Delta H - T\Delta S$$

The above equation is called **Gibbs Helmholtz** equation or simply **Gibbs equation.** In this equation,

ΔG = change in free energy

ΔH = enthalpy change, ΔS = change in entropy

T = absolute temperature

The units of ΔG is same as that of units of energy because ΔH and $T\Delta S$ ($\because T\Delta S = \text{kJK}^{-1}$) both are energy terms.

Gibbs Free Energy as a Criterion of Spontaneity

We know that, $\Delta S_{total} = \Delta S_{sys} + \Delta S_{surr}$

At the state of thermal equilibrium,

Increase in enthalpy of the surroundings = Decrease in the enthalpy of the system.

Entropy change of surroundings,

$$\Delta S_{surr} = \frac{\Delta H_{surr}}{T} = -\frac{\Delta H_{sys}}{T}$$

$$\Delta S_{total} = \Delta S_{sys} + \left(-\frac{\Delta H_{sys}}{T}\right)$$

Rearranging the above equation.

$$T\Delta S_{total} = T\Delta S_{sys} - \Delta H_{sys}$$

For spontaneous process, $\Delta S_{total} > 0$, so

$$T\Delta S_{sys} - \Delta H_{sys} > 0$$

$$\Rightarrow -(\Delta H_{sys} - T\Delta S_{sys}) > 0$$

Using equation, $\Delta G = \Delta H - T\Delta S$, the above equation can be written as:

$$-\Delta G > 0$$

or $\Delta G = \Delta H - T\Delta S < 0$

Here, ΔH_{sys} = enthalpy change of the reaction.

$T\Delta S_{sys}$ = energy which is unavailable for doing useful work.

ΔG = net energy available for doing useful work, so it is the measure of free energy.

At a given temperature and pressure :

(i) If ΔG is negative, (< 0) the process is spontaneous.

(ii) If ΔG is positive (> 0), the process is non-spontaneous.

(iii) If ΔG is zero, the process is in equilibrium state.

The various conditions in which a reaction occur spontaneously are tabulated below :

Effect of Temperature on Spontaneity of Reactions

$\Delta_r H^\ominus$	$\Delta_r S^\ominus$	$\Delta_r G^\ominus$	Description
–	+	– (at all T)	Reaction is spontaneous at all temperature.
–	–	– (at low T)	Reaction is spontaneous at low temperature.
–	–	+ (at high T)	Reaction is non-spontaneous at high temperature.
+	+	+ (at low T)	Reaction is non-spontaneous at low temperature.
+	+	– (at high T)	Reaction is spontaneous at high temperature.
+	–	+ (at all T)	Reaction is non-spontaneous at all temperature.

Note The term low temperature and high temperature are relative. For a particular reaction, high temperature could even mean room temperature.

From the above table, it is obvious that an endothermic reaction moves spontaneously towards more randomness at a higher temperature as for this $\Delta H = +\text{ve}$, $\Delta S = +\text{ve}$ and T is high enough so that $T\Delta S > \Delta H$ and hence, $\Delta G = \Delta H - T\Delta S < 0$ and thus, reaction is spontaneous.

Standard Free Energy Change

The free energy change for a process at 298 K and 1 atm pressure in which the reactants in their standard state, are converted into products in their standard state is called **standard free energy change.** It is denoted by $\Delta G°$.

$$\Delta_r G° = \left[\begin{array}{l}\text{Sum of the standard free energy}\\ \text{of formation of products}\end{array}\right] - \left[\begin{array}{l}\text{Sum of the standard free energy}\\ \text{formation of reactants}\end{array}\right]$$

$$= \sum \Delta_f G°(\text{product}) - \sum \Delta_r G° \text{ (reactant)}$$

Standard Free Energy of Formation

Free energy change when 1 mole of the compound is made from its elements in their standard states is called **standard molar free energy of formation of a compound.** For an element, it is taken as zero by convention. Standard free energy for formation of H^+ (*aq*) is zero.

In a fuel cell, it is found that the heat evolved (ΔH) is not completely converted into energy, i.e. useful work (given by ΔG). The ratio $\Delta G / \Delta H$ is called the **efficiency** of the fuel cell. Thus, efficiency of a fuel cell $= \dfrac{\Delta G}{\Delta H}$

Note
- Process with negative ΔG is called exo-ergonic and with positive ΔG is called endo-ergonic.
- $\Delta_f H^\circ$ and ΔG° of an element is taken as zero but ΔS° of an element never be equal to zero.

Relationship between Gibbs Free Energy and Helmholtz Energy

Gibbs free energy change is given by

$$\Delta G = \Delta H - T\Delta S \quad \ldots(i)$$

Enthalpy change at constant pressure is given by

$$\Delta H = \Delta U + p\Delta V$$

On substituting the value of ΔH in Eq. (i), we get

$$\Delta G = \Delta U + p\Delta V - T\Delta S$$

Now, change in Helmholtz free energy is given

$$\Delta A = \Delta U - T\Delta S$$

$$\therefore \quad \Delta G = \Delta A + p\Delta V$$

The above equation represents relationship between free energy change and Helmholtz free energy change.

Relation between Gibbs Free Energy and Equilibrium Constant

$$\Delta G = \Delta G^\circ + RT \ln Q$$

At equilibrium, $\Delta G = 0$ and $Q = K$

where, Q = reaction quotient and K = equilibrium constant

On putting the values we get

$$0 = \Delta G^\circ + RT \ln K \text{ or } \Delta G^\circ = -RT \ln K$$

Thus, the standard free energy (ΔG°) is related to equilibrium constant K as

$$\Delta G^\circ = -RT \ln K, \text{ i.e. } \Delta G^\circ = -2.303RT \log K$$

Also, $\Delta G^\circ = \Delta H^\circ - T\Delta S^\circ = -RT\ln K$

The above equation is helpful in the following ways.

(i) It is possible to obtain an estimate of $\Delta G^\ominus$ from the measurement of $\Delta H^\ominus$ and $\Delta S^\ominus$, and then calculate K at any temperature for economic yields of the products.

(ii) If K is measured directly in the laboratory, value of ΔG° at any other temperature can be calculated.

Relationship between the Standard Free Energy Change and the Equilibrium Constant

ΔG°	$\log K$	K	Comment
$\Delta G^\circ = 0$	$\log K = 0$	1	The equilibrium mixture contains comparable amounts of reactants and products (K=1 for 1M concentrations and 1 atm partial pressures).
$\Delta G^\circ < 0$	$\log K > 0$	$K > 1$	The equilibrium mixture is mainly composed of products.
$\Delta G^\circ > 0$	$\log K < 0$	$K < 1$	The equilibrium mixture is mainly composed of reactants.

Relation between Gibbs Free Energy and EMF of a cell

The free energy change (ΔG) is related to the electrical work done in the cell as

$$\boxed{\Delta G = -n FE_{\text{cell}}}$$

where, E_{cell} = emf of the cell

n = number of moles of electrons involved

F = Faraday's constant i.e. 96500 C

If reactions and products are in their standard state,

$$\Delta G^\circ = -nFE^\circ$$

where, E° = standard cell potential

Third Law of Thermodynamics

This law was proposed by German chemist Walther Nernst. According to this law, "The entropy of a perfectly crystalline substance approaches zero as the absolute zero of temperature is approached".

It forms the basis from which entropies at other temperatures can be measured.

$$\lim_{T \to 0} S = 0$$

In case of CO and NO molecules in solid state, there is randomness even at 0 K due to their dipole moment hence entropy in such cases is not zero even at 0 K.

Note The entropy possessed by a substance at absolute zero is called its **residual entropy**.

☑ Topic Practice 3

Very Short Answer Type Questions

(1 Mark)

1 Fill in the Blanks

(i) Spontaneons process does not require............in some cases.

(ii) Stretching of rubber band results in......... of entropy.

(iii) In case of atoms or molecules belonging to different elements, the one with............mass have greater entropy.

(iv) Process with............ΔG is called exo-ergonic and with............ΔG is called endo-ergonic

2 Multiple Choice Questions

(i) Which of the following properties is the measure of the degree of randomness or disorder in the system?

(a) Entropy (b) Enthalpy

(c) Internal energy (d) None of these

(ii) Which of the following process is an irreversible process and may only be reversed by some external agency?

(a) Spontaneous (b) Non-spontaneous

(c) Atomisation (d) None of these

(iii) The exothermic reaction is spontaneous, because

(a) increase in energy has taken place

(b) decrease in energy has taken place

(c) energy remains same during reaction

(d) Both (a) and (c)

(iv) $C(\text{graphite}, s) + 2S(l) \longrightarrow CS_2(l);\ \Delta_r H^\circ = +128.5\ \text{kJ mol}^{-1}$

The above reaction is

(a) exothermic and spontaneous

(b) exothermic and non-spontaneous

(c) endothermic and spontaneous

(d) endothermic and non-spontaneous

3 Match the following parameters with description for spontaneity and choose the correct option using the codes given below :

	$\Delta_r H^\circ$ $\Delta_r S^\circ$ $\Delta_r G^\circ$		Description
A.	− + −	(i)	Reaction is non-spontaneous at high temperature
B.	− − −	(ii)	Reaction is spontaneous at all temperature
C.	− − + (at high T)	(iii)	Reaction is spontaneous at low temperature

Codes

	A	B	C
(a)	(ii)	(iii)	(i)
(b)	(iii)	(ii)	(i)
(c)	(i)	(ii)	(iii)
(d)	(iii)	(i)	(ii)

4 Heat has randomising influence on a system and temperature is the measure of average chaotic motion of particles in the system. Write the mathematical relation which relates these three parameters. **NCERT Exemplar**

5 How can you say that universe is going towards chaos?

6 Increase in enthalpy of the surroundings is equal to decrease in enthalpy of the system. Will the temperature of system and surroundings be the same when they are in thermal equilibrium?

7 For the reaction, $2\ Cl(g) \longrightarrow Cl_2(g)$, what are the signs of ΔH and ΔS? **NCERT Textbook**

8 Given that $\Delta H = 0$ for mixing of two gases. Explain whether the diffusion of these gases into each other in a closed container is a spontaneous process or not? **NCERT Exemplar**

9 Why for predicting the spontaneity of a reaction, free energy criteria is better than the entropy criteria?

10 At 298 K, K_p for the reaction, $N_2O_4(g) \rightleftharpoons 2NO_2(g)$ is 0.98. Predict whether the reaction is spontaneous or not.

11 Water can be lifted into the water tank at the top of the house with the help of a pump. Then why is it not considered to be spontaneous?

12 Under what condition, the heat evolved or absorbed in a reaction is equal to its free energy change?

13 Air contains about 99% of N_2 and O_2 gases. Why do not they combine to form NO under the standard conditions? Standard Gibbs energy of formation of NO (g) is 86.7 kJ mol^{-1}.

Short Answer Type I Questions

2 Marks

14 For an isolated system, $\Delta U = 0$, what will be ΔS? **NCERT Textbook**

15 Calculate the entropy change in surroundings when 1.00 mole of $H_2O(l)$ is formed under standard conditions. ($\Delta_f H° = -286$ kJ mol^{-1}).

16 Predict in which of the following, entropy increases/decreases.

(i) A liquid crystallises into a solid.

(ii) Temperature of a crystalline solid is raised from 0 K to 115 K.

(iii) $2NaHCO_3(s) \longrightarrow Na_2CO_3(s) + CO_2(g) + H_2O(g)$

(iv) $H_2(g) \longrightarrow 2H(g)$

17 Calculate $\Delta_r G°$ for conversion of oxygen to ozone, $(3/2)\, O_2(g) \longrightarrow O_3(g)$ at 298 K, if K_p for this conversion is 2.47×10^{-29}. **NCERT TextBook**

18 Find out the value of equilibrium constant for the following reaction at 298 K.

$2\,NH_3(g) + CO_2(g) \rightleftharpoons NH_2CONH_2(aq) + H_2O(l)$

Standard Gibbs energy change, $\Delta G^{\ominus}$ at the given temperature is -13.6 kJ mol^{-1}.

19 At 60°C, dinitrogen tetroxide is fifty per cent dissociated. Calculate the standard free energy change at this temperature and at one atmosphere. **NCERT Exemplar**

20 Represent the potential energy/enthalpy change in the following processes graphically

(i) Throwing a stone from the ground to roof.

(ii) $\frac{1}{2}H_2(g) + \frac{1}{2}Cl_2(g) \rightleftharpoons HCl(g)$;

$\Delta_r H^{\ominus} = -92.32$ kJ mol^{-1}

In which of the above processes potential energy/enthalpy change is contributing factor to the spontaneity?

21 Taking a specific example, show that ΔS_{total} is a criterion for the spontaneity of a change.

22 For the reaction at 298 K, $2A + B \longrightarrow C$

$\Delta H = 400$ kJ mol^{-1} and $\Delta S = 0.2$ kJ K^{-1} mol^{-1}

At what temperature will the reaction become spontaneous considering ΔH and ΔS to be constant over the temperature range? **NCERT Textbook**

23 At 0°C, ice and water are in equilibrium and $\Delta H = 6.06$ kJ mol^{-1} for the process,

$$H_2O(s) \longrightarrow H_2O(l)$$

What will be ΔS and ΔG for the conversion of ice into liquid water?

24 The equilibirum constant for a reaction is 10. What will be the value of $\Delta G°$? $R = 8.314$ J K^{-1}mol^{-1}, $T = 300$ K. **NCERT Textbook**

25 Why standard entropy of an elementary substance is not zero whereas standard enthalpy of formation is taken as zero?

26 Starting with the thermodynamic relationship $G = H - TS$, derive the following relationship

$\Delta G = -T\Delta S_{total}$

27 Calculate the free energy change when 1 mole of NaCl is dissolved in water at 298 K. (Given, lattice energy of NaCl $= -777.8$ kJ mol^{-1}, hydration energy $= -774.1$ kJ mol^{-1} and $\Delta S = 0.043$ kJ K^{-1}mol^{-1} at 298 K).

Short Answer Type II Questions

3 Marks

28 The enthalpy of vaporisation of liquid diethyl ether $(C_2H_5)_2O$ is 26.0 kJ mol^{-1} at its boiling point (35.0°C). Calculate $\Delta S°$ for the conversion of

(i) liquid to vapour and

(ii) vapour to liquid at 35°C.

29 Calculate the standard Gibbs energy change for the formation of propane at 298 K.

$3\,C\,(\text{graphite}) + 4H_2(g) \longrightarrow C_3H_8(g)$

$\Delta_f H°$ for propane, $C_3H_8(g)$ is -103.8 kJ mol^{-1}

Given, $S^{\circ}_m[C_3H_8(g)] = 270.2$ JK^{-1}mol^{-1}

$S^{\circ}_m[C^-\,(\text{graphite})] = 5.70$ JK^{-1}mol^{-1}

and $S^{\circ}_m[H_2(g)] = 130.7$ JK^{-1}mol^{-1}

30 Calculate the equilibrium constant for the following reaction at 298 K and 1 atm pressure

$$NO(g) + \frac{1}{2}O_2(g) \rightleftharpoons NO_2(g)$$

Given ΔH°_f at 298 K are $NO(g) = 90.4$ kJ mol^{-1} and $NO_2(g) = 33.8$ kJ mol^{-1}, $\Delta S°$ at 298 K for the reaction $= -70.0$ JK^{-1}mol^{-1}, $R = 8.31$ JK^{-1}mol^{-1}.

31 For the reaction, $2A(g) + B(g) \longrightarrow 2D(g)$;
$\Delta U° = -10.5$ kJ and $\Delta S° = -44.1\ JK^{-1}$.

Calculate $\Delta G°$ for the reaction and predict whether the reaction may occur spontaneously. ($R = 8.314 \times 10^{-3}$ kJ $K^{-1} mol^{-1}$, $T = 298K$)

NCERT Textbook

32 Justify the following statements.

(i) Reactions with $\Delta G° < 0$ always have an equilibrium constant greater than 1.

(ii) Many thermodynamically feasible reactions do not occur under ordinary conditions.

(iii) At low temperatures, enthalpy change dominates the ΔG expression and at high temperatures, it is the entropy which dominates the value of ΔG.

Long Answer Type Questions

5 Marks

33 The standard Gibbs energy change for the reaction, $N_2(g) + 3H_2(g) \rightleftharpoons 2NH_3(g)$

is $-33.2\ kJ\ mol^{-1}$ at 298 K.

(i) Calculate the equilibrium constant for the above reaction.

(ii) What would be the equilibrium constant if the reaction is written as

$$\frac{1}{2}N_2(g) + \frac{3}{2}H_2(g) \rightleftharpoons NH_3(g)$$

(iii) What will be the equilibrium constant if the reaction is

$$NH_3(g) \rightleftharpoons \frac{1}{2}N_2(g) + \frac{3}{2}H_2(g)$$

34 Sodium carbonate, Na_2CO_3 can be obtained by heating sodium hydrogen carbonate, $NaHCO_3$ as
$2NaHCO_3(s) \longrightarrow Na_2CO_3(s) + H_2O(g) + CO_2(g)$.
The essential data are

	$NaHCO_3(s)$	$Na_2CO_3(s)$	$CO_2(g)$	$H_2O(g)$
$\Delta_f H°$ ($kJ\ mol^{-1}$)	−947.7	−1130.9	−393.51	−241.82
$S°_m$ ($J\ mol^{-1}$)	102.1	136	188.83	213.74

Calculate the temperature above which $NaHCO_3$ decomposes to give products at 1 bar.

Hints & Solutions

1. (i) intiation, (ii) increase, (iii) higher, (iv) negative, positive

2. (ii) → a, (iii) → a, (iv) → b, (i) → c

3. (a) A→(ii), B→(iii), C→(i)

4. Heat has randomising influence on a system and temperature is the measure of average chaotic motion of particles in the system. The mathematical relation which relates these three parameters is $\Delta S = \frac{q_{rev}}{T}$

Here, ΔS = change in entropy
q_{rev} = heat of reversible reaction
T = temperature

5. Most of the naturally occurring processes are accompanied by increase of randomness. Hence, randomness of the universe is continuously increasing. Thus, we are going towards chaos.

6. *Yes*, the temperature of system and surroundings be the same when they are in thermal equilibrium.

Note Thermal equilibrium is defined as when two physical systems are brought into a connection that does not allow transfer of matter and energy between them, such a connection is said to permit transfer of energy as heat and is called diathermal. If a diathermal connection is made between two physical systems and the making of the connection is followed by no change of state of either, then the two systems are said to be in relation of thermal equilibrium. It obeys zeroth law of thermodynamics.

7. In the given reaction, a molecule of Cl_2 is formed from its two gaseous atoms and the energy is released with the formation of bond. Hence, ΔH is −ve. In this reaction, randomness (entropy) also decreases because 2 mole atoms of Cl have more randomness than one mole molecule of chlorine. Hence, ΔS is −ve.

8. It is a spontaneous process because although $\Delta H = 0$, i.e. energy factor has no role to play but randomness or entropy increases, i.e. randomness factor favours the process.
∴ From, $\Delta G = \Delta H - T\Delta S$
As $\Delta H = 0$ and ΔS = +ve
Thus, ΔG is negative which indicates that diffusion of these gases into each other is a spontaneous process.

9. Criteria of free energy change is better because it requires free energy change of the system only whereas the entropy change requires the total entropy change of the system and the surroundings.

10. $\Delta_r G° = -2.303\ RT \log K_p$
Here, $K_p = 0.98$, i.e. $K_p < 1$ and $\log K_p < 0$ therefore, $\Delta_r G°$ is positive. Hence, the reaction is non-spontaneous.

11. A spontaneous process should occur continuously by itself after initiation. But this is not so in the given case because water will go up as long as the pump is working.

12. As $\Delta G = \Delta H - T\Delta S$. Thus, $\Delta G = \Delta H$ only when either the reaction is carried out at 0 K or the reaction is not accompanied by any entropy change, i.e. $\Delta S = 0$.

13. For the combination of N_2 and O_2 to form NO, the standard Gibbs energy of formation, is +ve

$$\frac{1}{2}N_2(g)+\frac{1}{2}O_2(g)\longrightarrow NO(g)\ (\Delta_f G^\circ_{NO}=+\ 86.7\ \text{kJ mol}^{-1})$$

Therefore, this reaction is non-spontaneous under the standard conditions and hence N_2 and O_2 do not combine to form NO.

14. For an isolated system, $\Delta U=0$ and for a spontaneous process, total entropy change must be positive. For example, consider the diffusion of two gases A and B into each other in a closed container which is isolated from the surroundings. The two gases A and B are separated by a movable partition. When partition is removed, the gases begin to diffuse into each other and the system becomes more disordered. It shows that $\Delta S>0$ and $\Delta U=0$ for this process. [1]

Moreover, $\Delta S=\frac{q_{rev}}{T}=\frac{\Delta H}{T}$

$$\Delta S=\frac{\Delta U+p\Delta V}{T}=\frac{p\Delta V}{T}\qquad(\because \Delta U=0)$$

[1]

15. Enthalpy change for the formation of 1 mole of $H_2O(l)$,

$$H_2(g)+\frac{1}{2}O_2(g)\longrightarrow H_2O(l);\ \Delta_f H^\circ=-\ 286\ \text{kJ mol}^{-1}$$

Energy released in the above reaction, is absorbed by the surroundings. [1]

$$\therefore\quad q_{surr}=+\ 286\ \text{kJ mol}^{-1}$$

Also, $\Delta S=\frac{q_{surr}}{T}=\frac{+\ 286\ \text{kJ mol}^{-1}}{298\ \text{K}}$

$=0.9597\ \text{kJ K}^{-1}\text{mol}^{-1}=959.7\ \text{JK}^{-1}\text{mol}^{-1}$. [1]

16 (i) Solids have more ordered arrangement of constituents particles as compared to liquids, thus entropy decreases when a liquid crystallises into a solid. [1/2]

(ii) On raising temperature, the oscillation of constituent particles about their equilibrium positions in the lattice increases, thus the system becomes more disordered and hence, the entropy increases. [1/2]

(iii) At reactant side only solid $NaHCO_3$ is present whereas at product side Na_2CO_3, CO_2 and H_2O are present. CO_2 and H_2O are in gaseous state and gases because of more randomness of constituent particles have more entropy. Thus, in this reaction entropy of the system increases. [1/2]

(iv) At reactant side, there is only one gaseous molecule and at product side there are two gaseous atoms. Thus, randomness is more towards product side, i.e. entropy of two moles of H-atoms is higher than one mole of dihydrogen molecule. [1/2]

17. $\Delta_r G^\ominus=-\ 2.303\ RT\log K_p$

$$\therefore\ \Delta_r G^\ominus=-\ 2.303\ (8.314\ \text{JK}^{-1}\text{mol}^{-1})\times(298\ \text{K})(\log 2.47\times10^{-29})$$

$=163000\ \text{J mol}^{-1}=163\ \text{kJ mol}^{-1}$ [2]

18. $\log K=\frac{-\Delta_r G^\ominus}{2.303\ RT}=\frac{-(-\ 13.6)}{2.303\times 8.314\times 298}=2.38$

Hence, $K=$ antilog $2.38=2.4\times10^2$ [2]

19 $N_2O_4(g)\rightleftharpoons 2\ NO_2(g)$

If N_2O_4 is 50% dissociated,

$$x_{N_2O_4}=\frac{1-0.5}{1+0.5}\Rightarrow x_{NO_2}=\frac{2\times0.5}{1+0.5}$$

$$p_{N_2O_4}=\frac{0.5}{1.5}\times 1\ \text{atm},\ p_{NO_2}=\frac{1}{1.5}\times1\ \text{atm}.$$

The equilibrium constant K_p is given by

$$K_p=\frac{(p_{NO_2})^2}{p_{N_2O_4}}=\frac{1.5}{(1.5)^2\ (0.5)}=1.33\ \text{atm}$$ [1]

Since, $\Delta_r G^\ominus=-\ RT\ln K_p$

$$\Delta_r G^\ominus=(-\ 8.314\ \text{JK}^{-1}\ \text{mol}^{-1})\times(333\ \text{K})\times(2.303)\times(0.1239)$$

$=-\ 763.8\ \text{kJ mol}^{-1}$ [1]

20.

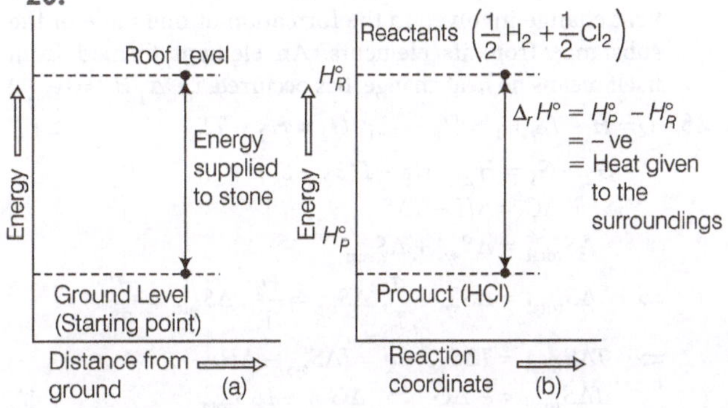

Energy increases in (a) and it decreases in (b). Hence, in process (b), enthalpy change is the contributing factor to the spontaneity. [2]

21. For spontaneous process, ΔS_{total} must be positive,

i.e. $\Delta S_{total}=\Delta S_{system}+\Delta S_{surroundings}>0$.

Consider the freezing of water at 272 K and 1 atm pressure.

For this process, $\Delta S_{system}=-\ 21.85\ \text{J K}^{-1}\text{mol}^{-1}$

$$\Delta S_{surroundings}=+\ 21.93\ \text{J K}^{-1}\text{mol}^{-1}$$ [1]

$$\therefore\ \Delta S_{total}=-\ 21.85+(21.93)=+\ 0.08\ \text{J K}^{-1}\text{mol}^{-1}$$

As ΔS_{total} is positive, the freezing of water at 272 K and 1 atm pressure is spontaneous. [1]

22. For a reaction to be spontaneous, $\Delta G\leq 0$. So, calculate the temperature at which $\Delta G=0$ by using the relation,

$$\Delta G=\Delta H-T\Delta S$$

Gibbs free energy, $\Delta G=\Delta H-T\Delta S$

$0=400\ \text{kJ mol}^{-1}-T\times0.2\ \text{kJ K}^{-1}\text{mol}^{-1}$

Temperature, $T=\frac{400\ \text{kJ mol}^{-1}}{0.2\ \text{kJ K}^{-1}\text{mol}^{-1}}=2000\ \text{K}$

Therefore, above 2000 K, the reaction will become spontaneous. [2]

Note If $\Delta G < 0$, the process is spontaneous and if $\Delta G > 0$, the process is non-spontaneous.

23. For equilibrium reaction,

$$H_2O(s) \rightleftharpoons H_2O(l)$$

$$\Delta G = 0 \Rightarrow \Delta G = \Delta H - T\Delta S$$

$$\Rightarrow \quad 0 = \Delta H - T\Delta S$$

or $$\Delta S = \frac{\Delta H}{T} = \frac{6.06 \text{ kJ mol}^{-1}}{273}$$

$$= 0.02219 \text{ kJ K}^{-1}\text{mol}^{-1} = 22.2 \text{ J K}^{-1}\text{mol}^{-1}$$ [2]

24. $$\Delta G° = -2.303\, RT \log K_c$$

Given, $R = 8.314 \text{ JK}^{-1}\text{mol}^{-1}$, $T = 300$ K, $K_c = 10$

$$\Delta G° = -2.303 \times 8.314 \text{ JK}^{-1}\text{mol}^{-1} \times 300 \text{ K} \times \log 10$$

$$= -5744.14 \text{ J mol}^{-1} \quad [\because \log 10 = 1]$$

25. A substance has a perfectly ordered arrangement of its constituent particles only at absolute zero. Hence, entropy is zero only at absolute zero. Enthalpy of formation is the heat change involved in the formation of one mole of the substance from its elements. An element formed from itself means no heat change, has occurred, i.e. $\Delta_f H° = 0$. [2]

26. $G = H - TS$, $G_1 = H_1 - TS_1$, $G_2 = H_2 - TS_2$

$$G_2 - G_1 = H_2 - H_1 - T(S_2 - S_1)$$

$$\Delta G = \Delta H - T\Delta S$$

$$\Delta S_{total} = \Delta S_{sys} + \Delta S_{surr}$$

$$\Rightarrow \quad \Delta S_{total} = \Delta S_{sys} - \frac{q}{T},\ \Delta S_{sys} = \frac{+q}{T},\ \Delta S_{surr} = \frac{-q}{T}$$

$$\Rightarrow \quad T\Delta S_{total} = T\Delta S_{sys} - q = T\Delta S_{sys} - \Delta H$$

$$T\Delta S_{total} = -\Delta G \Rightarrow \Delta G = -T\Delta S_{total}$$ [2]

27. ΔH = hydration energy − lattice energy

$$\Delta H = -774.1 \text{kJ mol}^{-1} - (-777.8 \text{ kJ mol}^{-1}) = 3.7 \text{ kJ mol}^{-1}$$

$$\Delta G = \Delta H - T\Delta S = +3.7 - 298 \times 0.043 = +3.7 - 12.81$$

$$\Delta G = -9.11 \text{ kJ mol}^{-1}$$ [2]

28. (i) For vaporisation of diethyl ether

$$\therefore \quad \Delta_{vap}S° = \frac{\Delta_{vap}H°}{T}$$

$$\Delta_{vap}H° = 26.0 \text{ kJ mol}^{-1},\ T = 273 + 35 = 308\text{K}$$

$$\Delta_{vap}S° = \frac{26.0 \times 10^3 \text{ J mol}^{-1}}{308 \text{ K}} = 84.4 \text{ JK}^{-1}\text{mol}^{-1}$$ [1]

(ii) The conversion of vapour into liquid is condensation. The enthalpy of condensation is negative of enthalpy of vaporisation.

$$\Delta_{vap}H° = -\Delta_{cond}H°$$

$\therefore$ For condensation of diethyl ether (*i.e.*, conversion of vapour to liquid)

$$\Delta_{cond}S° = \frac{\Delta_{cond}H°}{T} = \frac{-26.0 \times 10^3 \text{ mol}^{-1}}{308}$$

$$= -84.4 \text{ JK}^{-1}\text{mol}^{-1}$$ [2]

29. $$3C(\text{graphite}) + 4H_2(g) \longrightarrow C_3H_8(g)$$

$$\Delta_r S = \Sigma S°_m (\text{products}) - S°_m (\text{reactants})$$

$$\Delta_r S = S°_m[C_3H_8(g)] - [3S°_m[C\ (\text{graphite})] + 4S°_m[H_2]]$$

$$= (270.2 - 3 \times 5.70 - 4 \times 130.7) \text{ JK}^{-1}\text{mol}^{-1}$$

$$= (270.2 - 17.10 - 522.80) \text{ JK}^{-1}\text{mol}^{-1}$$

$$= (270.2 - 539.90) = -269.7 \text{ JK}^{-1}\text{mol}^{-1}$$ [1]

$$\Delta_r H° = \Delta_f H°(\text{products}) - \Delta_f H°(\text{reactants})$$

$$\Delta_r H° = \Delta_f H°(C_3H_8) - 4\Delta_f H°[H_2(g)] - 3\Delta_f H°[C\ (\text{graphite})]$$

$$\Delta_r H° = -103.8 \text{ kJ mol}^{-1}$$

$$\Delta_r G° = \Delta_r H° - T\Delta_r S°$$

$$= \left(-103.8 - \frac{298 \times (-269.7)}{1000}\right) \text{kJ mol}^{-1}$$

$$= (-103.80 + 80.370) \text{ kJmol}^{-1}$$

$$= -23.43 \text{ kJ mol}^{-1}$$ [2]

30. Enthalpy change for the reaction,

$$\Delta H° = \Sigma\Delta_f H°_{(\text{products})} - \Sigma\Delta_f H°_{(\text{reactants})}$$

$$\Delta H° = [\Delta_f H° NO_2(g)] - [\Delta_f H° NO(g) + \frac{1}{2}\Delta_f H° O_2(g)]$$

$$= [33.8] - \left[90.4 + \frac{1}{2} \times 0\right] = -56.6 \text{ kJ mol}^{-1}$$

$$\Delta S° = -70 \text{ JK}^{-1}\text{mol}^{-1}$$ [1]

Now, $\Delta G° = \Delta H° - T\Delta S°$, $T = 298$ K

$$\therefore \quad \Delta G° = -56600 - 298 \times (-70)$$

$$= -35740 \text{ J mol}^{-1}$$

$$\log K = -\frac{\Delta G}{2.303\, RT}$$

or $$\log K = -\frac{-35740}{2.303 \times 8.31 \times 298} = 6.267$$

$$\therefore \quad K = \text{Antilog}\ (6.267)$$

$$= 1.85 \times 10^6$$ [2]

31. We know that $\Delta G° = \Delta H° - T\Delta S°$, so first find $\Delta H°$ by using the formula, $\Delta H = \Delta U + \Delta n_g RT$ and then $\Delta G°$ by putting the values of $\Delta H°$, T and $\Delta S°$.

For a spontaneous reaction, $\Delta G \leq 0$.

$$2A(g) + B(g) \longrightarrow 2D(g);$$

$$\Delta n_g = \Sigma n_p - \Sigma n_r = 2 - 3 = -1$$

$$\Delta H° = \Delta U° + \Delta n_g RT$$

$$\Delta H° = -10.5 \text{ kJ} + (-1 \times 8.314 \times 10^{-3} \text{ kJ K}^{-1}\text{mol}^{-1} \times 298 \text{ K})$$

$$= -12.977 \text{ kJ mol}^{-1}$$ [1]

$$\Delta G° = \Delta H° - T\Delta S°$$

$$\Delta G° = -12.977 \text{ kJ mol}^{-1} - (298 \text{ K} \times -44.1 \times 10^{-3} \text{ kJ K}^{-1}\text{mol}^{-1}) = +0.1165 \text{ kJmol}^{-1}$$

The reaction will not occur spontaneously because $\Delta G°$ is positive. [2]

32. (i) $\Delta G = -2.303\ RT \log K$. Thus, when $\Delta G° < 0$, $K > 1$). [1]

(ii) Under ordinary conditions, the average energy of the reactants may be less than threshold energy. They require some activation energy to initiate the reaction. [1]

(iii) $\Delta G = \Delta H - T\Delta S$. At low temperature, $T\Delta S$ is small. Hence, ΔH dominates ΔG value. At high temperature, $T\Delta S$ is large, i.e. ΔS dominates the value of ΔG. [1]

33. (i) $\log K = -\dfrac{\Delta G}{2.303\ RT}$

$$\therefore\ \log K = -\frac{-33.2\times 10^3\ \text{J mol}^{-1}}{2.303\times(8.314\ \text{JK}^{-1}\text{mol}^{-1})\times(298\ \text{K})}$$

$= 5.82$ or $K = 6.6\times 10^5$ [2]

(ii) For the given reaction,

$$\Delta G° = \frac{1}{2}\times -33.2 = -16.6\ \text{kJ mol}^{-1}$$

or $\log K = -\dfrac{-16.6\times 10^3\ \text{J mol}^{-1}}{2.303\times(8.314\ \text{JK}^{-1}\ \text{mol}^{-1})\times(298\ \text{K})} = 2.91$

or $K = 8.1\times 10^2$ [1]

(iii) For the given reaction,

$$NH_3(g) \longrightarrow \frac{1}{2}N_2(g) + \frac{3}{2}H_2(g)$$

$$\Delta G° = -[-16.6\ \text{kJ mol}^{-1}] = 16.6\ \text{kJ mol}^{-1}$$

$$\log K = -\frac{16.6\times 10^3\ \text{JK}^{-1}\ \text{mol}^{-1}}{2.303\times(8.314\ \text{JK}^{-1}\ \text{mol}^{-1})\times(298\ \text{K})}$$

$= -2.91$ or $K = 1.23\times 10^{-3}$ [2]

34. $2NaHCO_3(s) \longrightarrow Na_2CO_3(s) + CO_2(g) + H_2O(g)$

$\Delta_r H° = \Delta_f H°(Na_2CO_3) + \Delta_f H°(CO_2) + \Delta_r H°(H_2O) - 2\Delta_f H°(NaHCO_3)$

$= -1130.9 + (-393.51) + (-241.82) - 2\times(-947.7)$

$= -1766.23 + 1895.4 = 129.17\ \text{kJ mol}^{-1}$ [2]

$\Delta_r S° = \Delta_r S°_m(Na_2CO_3) + S°_m(CO_2) + S°_m(H_2O) - 2S°_m(NaHCO_3)$

$= 136.0 + 188.83 + 213.74 - 2\times 102.1$

$= 538.57 - 204.2 = 334.37\ \text{J K}^{-1}\text{mol}^{-1}$ [2]

From second law of thermodynamics $\Delta_r S° = \dfrac{\Delta_r H°}{T}$

$$\therefore\ T = \frac{\Delta_r H°}{\Delta_r S°} = \frac{129.17}{334.37\times 10^{-3}} = 386.3\ \text{K}$$

$\therefore$ Reaction will be spontaneous above 386.3 K. [1]

SUMMARY

- Thermodynamics is the branch of science which deals with different forms of energies and their inter-relationship.
- System is the part that is under thermodynamic studies.
  - (i) Open system $\Delta m \neq 0$, $\Delta E \neq 0$, where Δm and ΔE are change in mass and energy.
  - (ii) Close system $\Delta m = 0, \Delta E \neq 0$
  - (iii) Isolated system $\Delta m = 0, \Delta E = 0$
- State functions are the variables that depends only on the initial and final states of a system. Their value is zero for reversible process.
- Intensive properties do not depend upon quantity of matter.
- Extensive properties depend upon quantity of matter.
- Thermodynamic process
  - (i) If $dq = 0$, process is adiabatic
  - (ii) If $dT = 0$ and $dE = 0$, the process is isothermal.
  - (iii) If $dV = 0$, process is isochoric.
  - (iv) If, $dp = 0$, process is isobaric.
- Heat (q) is a path function, $q = C\Delta T$, where, C = specific heat and $C_p - C_V = n.R$
- Work (W) is the mode of transfer of energy and is a path function.
- $W = -p_{ex}(V_f - V_i)$ [for irreversible process];

  $W = -2.303\, nRT \log \frac{V_f}{V_i}$ [for reversible process]

  In vacuum $p_{ex} = 0$, so $W = 0$.
  Work done by the system = (–)ve ; Work done on the system = (+)ve
- **First law of thermodynamics**
  Change in internal energy, $\Delta U = q + w$
  for adiabatic process, $q = 0$, $\Delta U = W_{(ad)}$
  Similarly for isochoric process,
  $\Delta V = 0, W = p\Delta V = 0, \Delta U = q$
- Enthalpy (H) is the total heat content of a system at constant pressure, $\Delta H = \Delta U + \Delta n_g \cdot RT$
  where, $\Delta n_g = n_p - n_R$, i.e. number of moles of gaseous product – number of moles of gaseous reactant.
- Enthalpy change of a reaction is the enthalpy change when a given reactant reacts completely, $\Delta H = \Sigma H_p - \Sigma H_R$.
- Standard enthalpy of formation is the enthalpy change occurring during the formation of 1 mole of a substance from its constituents.
- Enthalpies for different process
  - (i) Enthalpy change occurring during the conversion of 1 mole of a substance from one state to another is called enthalpy change during phase transformation.
  - (ii) Standard enthalpy of combustion ($\Delta_C H^\circ$) is the enthalpy change when one mole of a substance burnt completely in air.
  - (iii) Enthalpy of solution $\Delta H^\circ_{sol} = \Delta H^\circ_{lattice} + \Delta H^\circ_{hyd}$,
    where $\Delta H^\circ_{lattice} = S + I + \frac{1}{2}D - \Delta_{eg}H + \Delta H$
  - (iv) Enthalpy of atomisation is the enthalpy change during the breaking of one of bonds to get one mole of gaseous atoms.
  - (v) Bond enthalpy is the enthalpy change accompanying the breaking of one mole of covalent bonds (of same type)
- Resonance energy (RE) = Experimental or actual heat of formation – calculated heat of formation.
- Hess law of constant heat summation
  $\Delta H = \Delta H_1 + \Delta H_2 + \Delta H_3$
- **Second Law of Thermodynamics** It states, in a spontaneous process, total energy of the universe increases.
- **Entropy** (S) is the measure of randomness, $\Delta S = \frac{\Delta H}{T}$
- For reversible process, $\Delta S_{total} = 0$ and for irreversible process, $\Delta S_{total} > 0$
- **Gibbs energy** (G) is the measure of useful work. It is given by $\Delta G = \Delta H - T\Delta S$
- For spontaneous process, ΔG must be (–)ve and if $\Delta G = 0$, process is at equilibrium. Also, $\Delta G = -nFE_{(cell)}$ and $\Delta G^\circ = -RT \ln k$.

Chapter Practice

Very Short Answer Type Questions

(1 Mark)

1. Fill in the Blanks

(i) Work is not a .... but is path .... quantity.

(ii) All natural processes are spontaneous and ....

(iii) For a spontaneous reaction, ΔG must be .... then zero.

(iv) Maximum work is done in .... process.

2. Objective Type Questions

(i) In the given equation,

$$4Fe(s) + 3O_2(g) \longrightarrow 2Fe_2O_3(s)$$

The entropy change is $-549.4 \text{ JK}^{-1}\text{ mol}^{-1}$ at 298 K. ($\Delta_r H° = -1648 \times 10^3 \text{ J mol}^{-1}$). The above reaction is

(a) spontaneous

(b) non-spontaneous

(c) non-spontaneous at 500 K

(d) None of the above

(ii) Select the incorrect expression from the following.

(a) $\Delta S_{total} = \Delta S_{system} + \Delta S_{surr}$

(b) $\Delta S_{surr} = \dfrac{\Delta H_{surr}}{T} = \dfrac{\Delta H_{system}}{T}$

(c) $\Delta S_{total} < 0$ (spontaneous process)

(d) $\Delta G = \Delta H - T\Delta S$

(iii) The sign of ΔG for a spontaneous and non-spontaneous process respectively are

(a) positive and negative

(b) negative and positive

(c) zero and positive

(d) positive and zero

(iv) In which of the following reactions, standard reaction entropy change ($\Delta S°$) is positive and standard Gibbs energy change ($\Delta G°$) decreases sharply with increasing temperature?

(a) $C \text{ (graphite)} + \frac{1}{2}O_2(g) \longrightarrow CO(g)$

(b) $CO(g) + \frac{1}{2}O_2(g) \longrightarrow CO_2(g)$

(c) $Mg(s) + \frac{1}{2}O_2(g) \longrightarrow MgO(s)$

(d) $\frac{1}{2}C\text{(graphite)} + \frac{1}{2}O_2(g) \longrightarrow \frac{1}{2}CO_2(g)$

3. Match the following process given in Column I with changes take place given in Column II and choose the correct option using the codes given below.

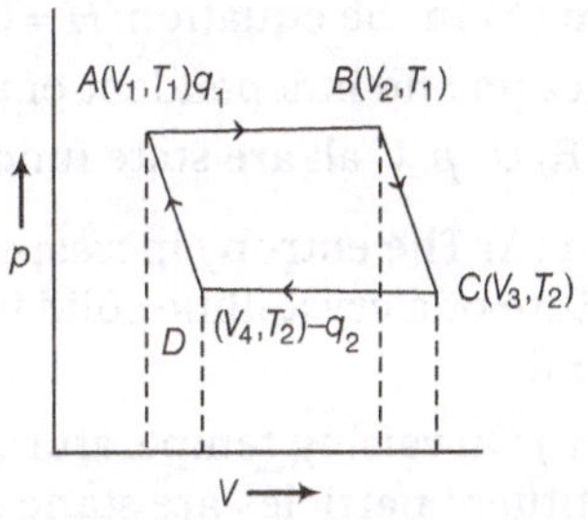

Column I (Process)	Column II (Type)
A. $A \to B$	(i) Adiabatic contraction, temperature increases to T_1.
B. $B \to C$	(ii) Isothermal expansion at T_1.
C. $C \to D$	(iii) Isothermal compression at T_2.
D. $D \to A$	(iv) Adiabatic expansion, temperature falls to T_2.
	(v) Isochoric and isothermal (pressure increases).

Codes

	A	B	C	D
(a)	(i)	(ii)	(iii)	(v)
(b)	(ii)	(iv)	(iii)	(i)
(c)	(ii)	(iii)	(i)	(iv)
(d)	(iii)	(ii)	(v)	(iv)

4. One kilogram of graphite is burnt in a closed vessel. The same amount of graphite is burnt in an open vessel. Will the heat evolved in two cases be same or different.

5. Do you expect ΔS to be + ve, – ve or zero for the reaction

$$H_2(g) + I_2(g) \rightleftharpoons 2HI(g)$$

6. What is the basic of Hess's law of heat summation?

7. Give two examples of state functions

8. Will the change in enthalpy of the system be zero in an adiabatic process?

Assertion-Reason

Directions (Q. Nos. 9-13) In the following questions, a statement of Assertion (A) is followed by a corresponding statements of Reason (R) of the following statements, choose the correct one.

(a) Both (A) and (R) are correct and (R) is the correct explanation of (A).
(b) Both (A) and (R) are correct but (R) is not the correct explanation of (A).
(c) (A) is correct and (R) is incorrect.
(d) (A) is incorrect and (R) is correct.

9. **Assertion** (A) In the equation, $H = U + pV$, H is a state function and independent of path.

Reason (R) U, p, V all are state functions.

10. **Assertion** (A) The entropy increase when the temperature of a crystalline solid is raised from 0 K to 115 K.

Reason (R) On raising temperature 0 K to 115 K, the constituent particles are static and entropy is maximum.

11. **Assertion** (A) The variables like q, V, T are called state functions.

Reason (R) The values of state function depend only on the state of the system.

12. **Assertion** (A) For a reaction,

$$2NH_3(g) \longrightarrow N_2(g) + 3H_2(g), \Delta H > \Delta U$$

Reason (R) Enthalpy change in always greater than internal energy change.

13. **Assertion** (A) Internal energy is a state function and extensive property.

Reason (R) Internal energy of a substance depends upon the gravitational force of attraction.

Case-Study

14. Every system is associated with a definite amount of energy, called the **internal energy** (U or E) of the system. It is the sum of chemical, electrical, mechanical or any other form of energy that anyone may think of. However, gravitational energy is generally neglected.

(i) heat flows into or out of the system,
(ii) work is done on or by the system,
(iii) matter enters or leaves the system.

The absolute value of internal energy possessed by a substance cannot be calculated because it is not possible to predict the exact values of different forms of energy. Thus, we can just calculate the change in internal energy, which is achieved by changing the state of a system.

First law of thermodynamics was proposed by Helmholtz and Robert-Mayer who stated that the energy of an isolated system is constant, i.e. energy can neither be created nor be destroyed but can converted from one form to another. That's why also called law fo conservation of energy.

(i) Out of mass and density, which is an intensive property and why?
(ii) Explain thermodynamically how is the heat absorbed by system is used in doing work at constant temperature and pressure.
(iii) What is the change in the energy of system if 500 cal of heat energy are added to a system and system does 350 cal of work on the surroundings?

15. Thermodynamics is the study of the relationship between heat and work. The change in the enthalpy of the system during a chemical reaction is defined as the change in its internal energy plus the change in the product of the pressure times the volume of the system. Chemical reactions can be exothermic and endothermic. Entropy denoted by the symbol 'S'.

Entropy is the measure of the number of possible microscopic configurations of the atoms and molecules or accordance with the microscopic state of the system.

Gibbs free energy is used to measure the amount of available energy that a chemical reaction provides.

(i) Draw enthalpy diagram for endothermic reaction.
(ii) Are all exothermic reaction spontaneous?
(iii) Why is molar entropy of vaporisation for water more than ethanol?

Short Answer Type I Questions

2 Marks

16. Calculate the enthalpy of formation of methane from the following data.

$$C(s) + O_2(g) \longrightarrow CO_2(g); \Delta_r H^\circ = -393.5 \text{ kJ}$$

$$2H_2(g) + O_2(g) \longrightarrow 2H_2O(l); \Delta_r H^\circ = -571.8 \text{ kJ}$$

$$CH_4(g) + 2O_2(g) \longrightarrow CO_2(g) + 2H_2O(l);$$

$$\Delta_r H^\circ = -890.3 \text{ kJ}$$

17. How does Hess's law help in calculating the enthalpy change for the conversion of diamond to graphite?

18. The enthalpy of formation of CH_4, C_2H_6 and C_4H_{10} are – 74.8, – 84.7 and – 126.1 kJ mol^{-1} respectively. Arrange them in the order of their efficiency as fuel per gram (enthalpy of formation of $CO_2(g)$ and $H_2O(l)$ are – 393.5 and – 285.8 kJ mol^{-1} respectively).

19. When 0.532 g of benzene (C_6H_6), boiling point 353 K, is burnt with excess of oxygen in a constant volume system, 22.3 kJ of heat is given out. Calculate ΔH for the combustion process ($R = 8.31$ J K^{-1} mol^{-1}).

20. Is it possible for any process to have $\Delta H = \Delta E$? If yes, state under what conditions? If no, state why not?

21. Calculate the work done when 1.0 mole of water at 373 K vaporises against an atmospheric pressure of 1.0 atmosphere. Assume ideal gas behaviour.

22. Which of the following are state functions and why?
(i) Height of a hill
(ii) Distance travelled in climbing the hill
(iii) Energy consumed in climbing the hill

Short answer Type II Questions

(3 Marks)

23. Calculate the enthalpy of formation of carbon disulphide given that the enthalpy of combustion of carbon disulphide is 110.2 kJ mol^{-1} and those of sulphur and carbon are 297.4 kJ and 394.5 kJ/g atom respectively.

24. Calculate the enthalpy of formation of acetic acid (CH_3COOH) if its enthalpy of combustion is – 867 kJ mol^{-1}. The enthalpies of formation of $CO_2(g)$ and $H_2O(l)$ are – 393.5 and – 285.9 kJ mol^{-1} respectively.

25. Define heat capacity, specific heat capacity and molar heat capacity. How are they related?

26. A 5 L cylinder contained 10 moles of oxygen gas at 27°C. Due to sudden leakage through the hole, all the gas escaped into the atmosphere and the cylinder got empty. If the atmospheric pressure is 1.0 atmosphere, calculate the work done by the gas. (1 L atm = 101.3 J)

27. Neither the enthalpy change nor the entropy change alone can be used to explain the spontaneity of a reaction. Explain.

28. It is planned to carry the reaction, $CaCO_3(s) \rightleftharpoons CaO(s) + CO_2(g)$ at 1273 K and 1 bar
(i) Is this reaction spontaneous at this temperature and pressure?
(ii) Calculate the value of
(a) K_p at 1273 K for the reaction and
(b) partial pressure of CO_2 at equilibrium.

Given, $\Delta_f H°$ values (kJ mol^{-1}): $CaCO_3(s) = -1206.9$, $CaO(s) = -635.1$, $CO_2(g) = -393.5$
$\Delta S°$ values (J $K^{-1}mol^{-1}$),
$CaCO_3(s) = 92.9$, $CaO(s) = 39.8$, $CO_2(g) = 213.7$

Long Answer Type Questions

(5 Marks)

29. State the law of thermodynamics that was first formulated by Nernst in 1906. What is the utility of this law? The equilibrium constant for the reaction $A \rightleftharpoons B$ is 1.8×10^{-7} at 298 K.

Calculate the value of $\Delta G°$ for the reaction [$R = 8.314$ J K^{-1} mol^{-1}]. Predict the feasibility of the reaction under standard states.

30. Two moles of a perfect gas undergo the following processes :
(i) a reversible isobaric expansion from (1.0 atm, 20.0 L) to (1.0 atm, 40.0 L)
(ii) a reversible isochoric change of state from (1.0 atm, 40.0 L) to (0.5 atm, 40.0 L)
(iii) a reversible isothermal compression from (0.5 atm, 40.0 L) to (1.0 atm, 20.0 L)

Answer the following questions related to the above processes.
(a) Sketch with labels each of the processes on the same *p*-*V* diagram.
(b) Calculate the total work (*W*) and the total heat change (*q*) involved in the above processes.
(c) What will be the value of ΔU, ΔH and ΔS for the overall process?

Hints & Solutions

1. (i) state function, dependent (ii) irreversible (iii) less (iv) reversible isothermal

2. (i) → (a), (ii) → (c), (iii) → (b), (iv) → (a)

3. (*b*) A → (ii), B → (iv), C → (iii), D → (i)

4. Yes, the heat evolved in both the process will be same. Because heat of the reaction depends upon the number of moles not the volume of the surroundings.

5. ΔS should be negative because two different molecules (H_2 and I_2) would have more randomnes than two same molecules.

6. Refer to text on pages 219 and 220.

7. Pressure and volume.

8. As in adiabatic process, the temperature is held constant, therefore change in energy is zero. So, the heat absorbed by the gas equals the work done by the ideal gas on its surroundings. Enthalpy change is also equal to zero, because change in energy is zero and the pressure and volume is constant.

9. (*a*) Both (A) and (R) are correct and (R) is the correct explanation of (A).

10. (*a*) Both (A) and (R) are correct and (R) is the correct explanation of (A). The entropy increase when the temperature of a crystalline solid is raised (from 0 to 115 K) as randomness increases.

11. (*d*) (A) is incorrect while (R) is correct. Among the given variable functions, q is not the state function, it is the path function.

12. (*c*) (A) is correct and (R) is incorrect.

For the reaction,

$$2NH_3(g) \longrightarrow N_2(g) + 3H_2(g)$$

$$\Delta H = \Delta U + \Delta nRT$$

$$\Delta n = 4 - 2 = 2$$

$$\Delta H > \Delta U$$

Both enthalpy change is not always greater than internal energy change.

13. (*c*) (A) is correct and (R) is incorrect. The correct Reason is internal energy does not depend on gravitational force of attraction.

14. (i) Density is an intensive property as it is characteristic of a material and does not change with amount whereas mass does change.

(ii) $\Delta U = q + W$ (From 1st law of thermodynamics)

$0 = q + W$ ($\Delta U = 0$, at constant temperature)

$0 = q - pdV$

$q = -W$

∴ Heat absorbed is used to do work by the system.

(iii) According to the first law of thermodynamics,

$$\Delta E = q + W = 500 + (-350) = +150 \text{ cal}$$

15. (i) Chemical reactions that absorb energy is endothermic reaction.

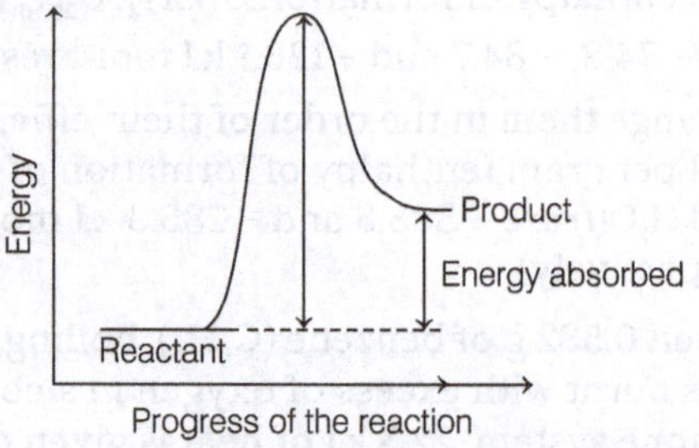

(ii) Thermodynamically an exothermic reaction is sometimes not spontaneous.

(iii) The molar enthalpy of vaporisation for water is more than ethanol. It is due to the pressure of hydrogen bonding present in water molecule.

16. [**Ans.** –75.0 kJ] Refer to text on pages 219 and 220 (Topic-2, Hess's law of constant heat summation).

17. **Ans.** –75.0 kJ

18. Refer to text on pages 219 and 220 (Topic-2, Hess's law of constant heat summation)

19. [**Ans.** $\Delta H = -3269$ kJ] Refer to text on pages 215 and 216, (Topic-2, Enthalpy of combustion)

20. [**Ans.** $\Delta H = -3269$K]

21. [**Ans.** 3097.3 J] Refer to text on page 207 (Topic-1, Relationship between ΔH and ΔU)

22. Refer to text on page 228 (Topic-3, Entropy)

23. [**Ans.** –879.1 kJ mol^{-1}] Refer to text on page 204 (Topic-1, Heat capacity)

24. [**Ans.** –419.8 kJ mol^{-1}]

25. Ans. –879.1 kJ mol^{-1}

26. [**Ans.** –24443.7 J]

27. Refer to text on page 230 (Topic-3, Gibbs free energy as a criterion of spontaneity)

28. (i) Refer to text on page 230 (Topic-3, Gibbs free energy as a criterion of spontaneity)

(ii) Refer to text on page 231 (Topic-3, Relationship between Gibbs free energy and equilibrium constant)

29. [**Ans.** $\Delta_r G = 10{,}195.82$ J] Refer to text on page 231 (Topic-3, Relationship between Gibbs free energy and equilibrium constant)

30. (a) Refer to text on page 201 (Topic-1, *p versus V* graph for various thermodynamic processes)

(b) $q = -W = +620.77$ J

(c) $\Delta U = 0$; $\Delta H = 0$; $\Delta S = 0$

CHAPTER

06

Equilibrium

- Physical and Chemical Equilibria
- Ionic Equilibrium : Acids and Bases and their Ionisation
- Salt Hydrolysis, Buffer Solutions and Solubility Product

Most of the chemical reactions occurring around us are irreversible in nature, i.e. proceed only in one direction and go to completion, but there are certain reactions that proceed in forward as well as in reverse direction and never go to completion.

The state of a process/reaction, at which the rates of forward and backward processes/reactions become equal is called the **equilibrium state**.

TOPIC 01 Physical and Chemical Equilibria

Equilibrium in Physical Processes

The equilibrium developing between different phases or physical properties of a substance is termed as **physical equilibria**.

As there are three physical states of matter, solid, liquid and gas, therefore three types of physical equilibrium exist as:

solid (s) $\rightleftharpoons$ liquid (l); liquid (l) $\rightleftharpoons$ gas (g); solid (s) $\rightleftharpoons$ gas (g)

Here, the symbol ($\rightleftharpoons$) repesents a reversible process.

General Characteristics of Equilibria Involving Physical Processes

For the physical processes following characteristics are common to the system at equilibrium.

(i) At equilibrium, all the measurable properties of the system remain constant.

(ii) Equilibrium is attained only in a closed system at a given temperature.

(iii) Equilibrium is dynamic in nature, i.e. the opposing processes do not stop but take place simultaneously and with the same rate.

(iv) The physical equilibrium is characterised by constant value of one of its parameter (such as melting point, concentration of solute, ratio of product to reactant etc.,) at a given temperature.

(v) The magnitude of these parameters at any stage shows the extent of physical process upto which it has proceeded before reaching equilibrium.

Some examples of equilibrium existing between physical states of a substance are as follows:

1. Solid-Liquid Equilibrium

When ice (solid) and water (liquid) are kept in a perfectly insulated thermos flask at 273 K and 1 atmospheric pressure, they are in a state of equilibrium,

i.e. $H_2O(s) \rightleftharpoons H_2O(l)$.

At this condition their mass and the temperature of the reaction mixture remain constant. This is because the rates of transfer of ice into water and of water into ice are equal at 273 K or at a particular temperature and 1 atmospheric pressure, i.e. equilibrium between a solid and liquid appears only at particular temperature and pressure.

The temperature at which the solid and liquid phases of a pure substance at one atmospheric pressure are at equilibrium is called the normal melting point or normal freezing point of the substance.

Note When ice melts, its volume decreases from 1.09 mL to 1.01 mL per gram.

2. Liquid-Vapour Equilibrium

When a watch glass containing water is placed in a dry transparent box fitted with U-tube filled with mercury (manometer), the level of the mercury in the right limb of the manometer increases slowly and then attains a constant value. It shows that the pressure inside the box initially increases and then attains a constant value.

Also the volume of water placed in the watch glass decreases and of water vapours inside the box increases. This is due to constant evaporation of water and finally, a stage is reached at which there appears no evaporation as the rate of evaporation becomes equal to the rate of condensation. This is called the **state of equilibrium.**

$$H_2O(l) \underset{\text{Rate of condensation}}{\overset{\text{Rate of evaporation}}{\rightleftharpoons}} H_2O(\text{vap.})$$

At equilibrium, Rate of evaporation = Rate of condensation

(**Remember !** in an open system the equilibrium is not set up as the rate of condensation is much less than the rate of evaporation due to availability of large volume for vapours).

3. Solid-Vapour Equilibrium

Such equilibrium exists only in case of substances which undergo sublimation i.e. solid directly converts into vapour without liquefication e.g. if a sublimate like solid iodine is placed in a closed vessel, after sometime the vessel gets filled up with violet vapours and the intensity of colour increases with time.

After sometime, the intensity of colour becomes constant and at this stage the rate of sublimation of solid iodine to iodine vapours becomes equal to the rate of condensation of iodine vapours into solid. This stage is referred to the equilibrium state, i.e.

$$I_2(s) \rightleftharpoons I_2(\text{vap.})$$

Other examples showing solid vapour equilibrium are:

$$\text{Camphor (solid)} \rightleftharpoons \text{camphor (vapour)}$$

$$NH_4Cl\text{(solid)} \rightleftharpoons NH_4Cl \text{ (vapour)}$$

4. Equilibrium Involving Dissolution of Solid or Gases in Liquids

(i) **Solids in Liquids** In a saturated solution (the solution having much amount of solute than it can hold), there is an equilibrium between the solid solute and its solution (i.e. solute solution), as the rate of dissolution of solute becomes equal to the rate of crystallisation of solute. e.g.

$$\text{Sugar (solution)} \rightleftharpoons \text{Sugar (solid)}$$

The dynamic nature of the equilibrium has been confirmed with the help of radioactive sugar. If we place some radioactive sugar into saturated solution of non-radioactive sugar, then with time radioactivity is observed both in the solution and in the solid sugar and the ratio of the radioactive to non-radioactive molecules in the solution increases till it attains a constant value.

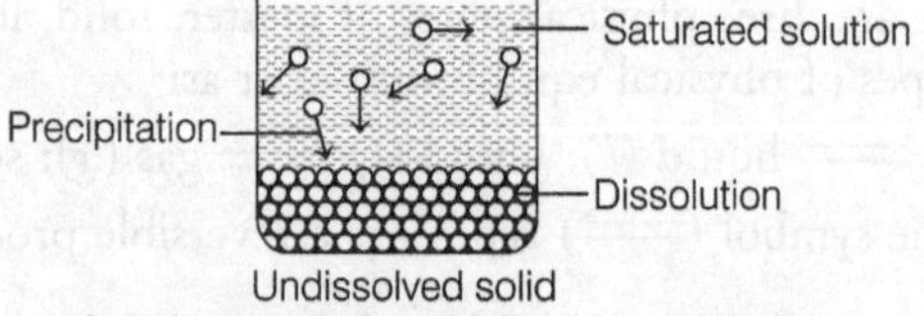

Attainment of solid-liquid equilibrium

(ii) **Gases in Liquids** When a gas is dissolved in water, an equilibrium is developed between the gaseous molecules and dissolved molecules of the gas under pressure. e.g. dissolution of CO_2 under pressure.

$$CO_2(g) \rightleftharpoons CO_2\text{(solution)}$$

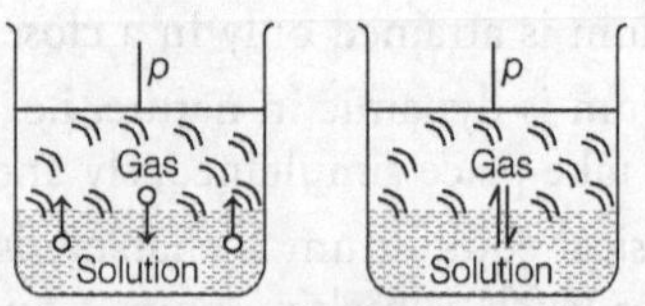

Attainment of gas-liquid equilibrium

Such equilibrium is governed by Henry's law, according to which, "**the mass of a gas dissolved in a given mass of a solvent at any temperature** (i.e. extent of solubility) **is directly proportional to the pressure of the gas above the solvent**', i.e.

$$m \propto p \quad \text{or} \quad m = K_H p$$

where, K_H is the proportionality constant, called the **Henry's law constant** and depends upon the temperature. Thus, on increasing the temperature or decreasing the pressure, the amount of dissolved gas decreases. Because of solubility of dinitrogen into blood at high pressure, a mixture of helium and dioxygen is used by deep sea divers for breathing.

Helium is very less soluble in blood even at high pressure, which prevents a painful medical condition in divers, called **bend**.

Different Physical Equilibria at a Glance

Process	Conclusion
Liquid-vapour equilibria. $H_2O(l) \rightleftharpoons H_2O(g)$	Pressure or vapour pressure is constant at a given temperature.
Solid-liquid equilibria. $H_2O(s) \rightleftharpoons H_2O(l)$	Melting point or freezing point is constant at a given temperature.
Solute (s) $\rightleftharpoons$ Solute (solution) Sugar (s) $\rightleftharpoons$ Sugar (solution)	Concentration of solute in the solution is constant at a given temperature.
Gas$(g) \rightleftharpoons$ Gas (aq) $CO_2(g) \rightleftharpoons CO_2(aq)$	[Gas (aq)]/ [gas (g)] is constant at a given temperature [CO_2 (aq)]/[CO_2 (g)] is constant at a given temperature.

Equilibrium in Chemical Processes

The equilibrium that involves only chemical change, is called chemical equilibrium. Chemical equilibrium is attained in the chemical systems involving reversible reactions carried in closed vessels.

e.g.
$$PCl_5(g) \rightleftharpoons PCl_3(g) + Cl_2(g)$$
$$N_2(g) + 3H_2(g) \rightleftharpoons 2NH_3(g)$$
$$H_2(g) + I_2(g) \rightleftharpoons 2HI(g)$$

At equilibrium , the rate at which reactants converted to products is equal to the rate at which product converted into reactants and hence, the concentration of reactants and products do not change with time.

Dynamic Nature of Chemical Equilibrium

Chemical equilibrium is also defined as "the stage at which rate of forward reaction (R_f) is equal to rate of backward reaction (R_b)". At equilibrium forward and backward reactions continue with equal rate. That's why chemical equilibrium is also called as **dynamic equilibrium.**

The variation of concentration of reactants and products in a reversible reaction can be represented as :

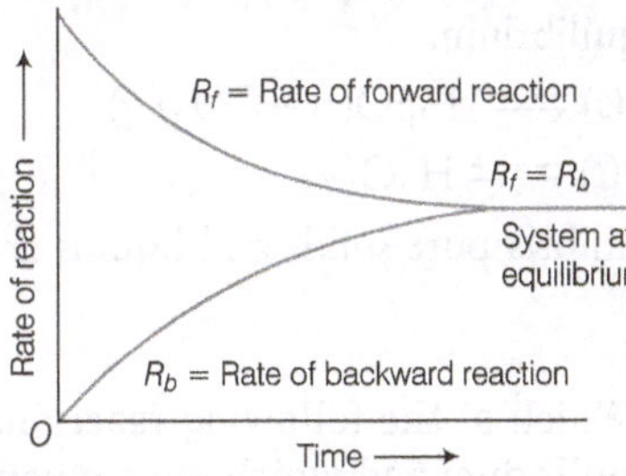

Variation of the concentration of the reactants and products

Characteristics of Chemical Equilibrium

The important characteristics of chemical equilibrium are as follows:

(i) In chemical equilibrium, at a given temperature, the measurable properties like pressure, concentration, density or colour remain constant.

(ii) Chemical equilibrium can be attained from either side.

(iii) Chemical equilibrium remains unaffected if the reaction occurs in the presence of a catalyst. However, equilibrium can be attained in a lesser time by the use of a catalyst.

(iv) Chemical equilibrium is dynamic in nature (i.e. the reaction does not stop but continues in both the directions with same speed).

(v) The chemical equilibrium will continue indefinitely if the conditions such as temperature and concentration are not changed.

(vi) The magnitude of such quantities at any stage indicates the extent to which the reaction has proceeded before reaching equilibrium.

Types of Chemical Equilibrium

Depending upon the number of phases, chemical equilibrium can be of following two types:

1. Homogeneous Equilibrium

If all the reactants and products of an equilibrium reaction are in the same phase, the equilibrium is called homogeneous equilibrium.

e.g. $H_2(g) + I_2(g) \rightleftharpoons 2HI(g)$

$Fe^{3+}(aq) + SCN^-(aq) \rightleftharpoons [Fe(SCN)]^{2+}(aq)$

$CH_3COOH(l) + C_2H_5OH(l) \rightleftharpoons CH_3COOC_2H_5(l) + H_2O(l)$

2. Heterogeneous Equilibrium

If all the reactants and products of an equilibrium reaction are not in the same phase, i.e. they are present in two or more phases then the equilibrium is called heterogeneous equilibrium.

e.g. $MgCO_3(s) \rightleftharpoons MgO(s) + CO_2(g)$

$H_2O(l) \rightleftharpoons H_2O(g)$

Thus, in this equilibria pure solids and liquids are also involved.

Example 1 Which of the following reactions involve homogeneous equilibrium and which ones involve heterogeneous equilibrium ?

(i) $2N_2O(g) \rightleftharpoons 2N_2(g) + O_2(g)$

(ii) $2NH_3(g) \rightleftharpoons N_2(g) + 3H_2(g)$

(iii) $2Cu(NO_3)_2(s) \rightleftharpoons 2CuO(s) + 4NO_2(g) + O_2(g)$

(iv) $CaCO_3(s) \rightleftharpoons CaO(s) + CO_2(g)$

(v) $Fe^{3+}(aq) + 3OH^-(aq) \rightleftharpoons Fe(OH)_3(s)$

Sol. (i) Homogeneous equilibrium

(ii) Homogeneous equilibrium

(iii) Heterogeneous equilibrium

(iv) Heterogeneous equilibrium

(v) Heterogeneous equilibrium

Law of Mass Action

This law was proposed by two Norwegian chemists **Cato Maximillian Guldberg and Peter Waage in 1864.**

According to this law, 'the rate at which a substance reacts is proportional to its active mass and hence the rate of a chemical reaction is proportional to the product of the active masses of the reactants'.

The term active mass means the molar concentration, i.e. number of moles per litre. It is expressed by enclosing the formula of substance in square brackets.

e.g. active mass of H_2 is represented as $[H_2]$.

Note Active masses of pure solids and liquids are taken as unity because their concentration (or density) remain same throughout the reaction. This is because Gibbs' function for pure solid and liquid are defined at stipulated pressure of 1.00 bar and as the pressure of system changes, Gibbs function remain constant.

Law of Chemical Equilibrium and Equilibrium Constant

Consider a homogeneous reversible reaction,

$$aA + bB \rightleftharpoons cC + dD$$

According to law of mass action,

Rate of forward reaction,

$$R_f \propto [A]^a [B]^b \quad \text{or} \quad R_f = k_f [A]^a [B]^b$$

Rate of backward reaction,

$$R_b \propto [C]^c [D]^d \quad \text{or} \quad R_b = k_b [C]^c [D]^d$$

where, k_f and k_b are the rate constants for forward and backward reactions respectively. At equilibrium,

rate of forward reaction = rate of backward reaction

i.e. $$k_f [A]^a_{eq} [B]^b_{eq} = k_b [C]^c_{eq} [D]^d_{eq}$$

[Generally the subscript 'eq' which is used to show state of equilibrium is omitted from the concentration terms].

$$\therefore \quad \frac{k_f}{k_b} = \frac{[C]^c [D]^d}{[A]^a [B]^b} \quad \text{or} \quad K_c = \frac{[C]^c [D]^d}{[A]^a [B]^b}$$

Here subscript '*c*' shows that K_c is expressed in concentration of mol L^{-1}. K_c is known as **equilibrium constant.**

Thus, at a given temperature, the value obtained by dividing the product of concentrations of reaction products raised to the respective stoichiometric coefficient in the balanced chemical equation by the product of concentrations of reactants raised to their individual stoichiometric coefficients is constant. This is called law of chemical equilibrium or equilibrium law and the obtained value is called equilibrium constant.

e.g. equilibrium constant for the reaction,

$4NH_3(g) + 5O_2(g) \rightleftharpoons 4NO(g) + 6H_2O(g)$ is written as

$$K_c = \frac{[NO]^4 [H_2O]^6}{[NH_3]^4 [O_2]^5}$$

Example 2 PCl_5, PCl_3 and Cl_2 are at equilibrium at 500 K in a closed container and their concentrations are $0 \cdot 8 \times 10^{-3}$ mol L^{-1}, 1.2×10^{-3} mol L^{-1} and 1.2×10^{-3} mol L^{-1}, respectively. Calculate the value of K_c for the reaction

$PCl_5(g) \rightleftharpoons PCl_3(g) + Cl_2(g)$ will be **NCERT Exemplar**

Sol. For the reaction, $PCl_5 \rightleftharpoons PCl_3 + Cl_2$

At 500 K in a closed container,

$$[PCl_5] = 0.8\times 10^{-3} \text{ mol L}^{-1}$$

$$[PCl_3] = 1.2\times 10^{-3} \text{ mol L}^{-1}$$

$$[Cl_2] = 1.2\times 10^{-3} \text{ mol L}^{-1}$$

$$K_c = \frac{[PCl_3]\,[Cl_2]}{[PCl_5]}$$

$$= \frac{(1.2\times 10^{-3})\times(1.2\times 10^{-3})}{(0.8\times 10^{-3})} = 1.8\times 10^{-3}$$

Characteristics of Equilibrium Constant

(i) The equilibrium constant has a definite value for every chemical reaction at a particular temperature. The value of equilibrium constant is independent of initial concentrations of the reacting species. The value of equilibrium constant, K changes with change in temperature only.

(ii) If an equation is divide by a factor 'n', the new equilibrium constant is nth root of the previous value.

i.e. $$K' = (K)^{1/n}$$

(iii) If the equation is multiplied by a factor 'n', the new equilibrium constant is nth power of the previous value.

i.e. $$K' = (K)^n$$

(iv) If the equation representing equilibrium constant is reversed, the new equilibrium constant is inverse of the first value.

i.e. $$K' = \frac{1}{K}$$

(v) If two equations are added, their equilibrium constants are multiplied and if they are subtracted, their equilibrium constants are divided (always remember, equilibrium constants are never added or subtracted).

(vii) The value of the equilibrium constant is not affected by the addition of a catalyst to the reaction. This is because the catalyst increases the speed of the forward reaction and the backward reaction to the same extent.

(viii) The value of equilibrium constant changes with change to temperature. If K_1 and K_2 be the equilibrium constants of a reaction at absolute temperatures T_1 and T_2 and ΔH is the heat change of reaction at constant pressure then

$$\log K_2 - \log K_1 = -\frac{1}{2.303R}\left[\frac{1}{T_2} - \frac{1}{T_1}\right]\Delta H$$

or $$\log \frac{K_2}{K_1} = \frac{\Delta H}{2.303R}\left[\frac{1}{T_1} - \frac{1}{T_2}\right]$$

Example 3 At 500 K, equilibrium constant, K_c, for the following reaction is 5.

$$\frac{1}{2}H_2(g) + \frac{1}{2}I_2(g) \rightleftharpoons HI(g)$$

What would be the equilibrium constant K_c for the reaction?

$$2HI(g) \rightleftharpoons H_2(g) + I_2(g)$$

Sol. For the reaction, $\frac{1}{2}H_2(g) + \frac{1}{2}I_2(g) \rightleftharpoons HI(g)$

$$K_c = \frac{[HI]}{[H_2]^{1/2}\,[I_2]^{1/2}} = 5$$

Thus, for the reaction, $2HI(g) \rightleftharpoons H_2(g) + I_2(g)$

$$K_{c_1} = \frac{[H_2]\,[I_2]}{[HI]^2} = \left(\frac{1}{K_c}\right)^2 = \left(\frac{1}{5}\right)^2 = \frac{1}{25} = 0.04$$

Example 4 K_{a_1}, K_{a_2} and K_{a_3} are the respective ionisation constants for the following reactions:

$$H_2S \rightleftharpoons H^+ + HS^-$$
$$HS^- \rightleftharpoons H^+ + S^{2-}$$
$$H_2S \rightleftharpoons 2H^+ + S^{2-}$$

Write the correct relationship between $K_{a_1}, K_{a_2}, K_{a_3}$.

Sol.

> **Key Idea** To find out the correct relationship between three ionisation constants (K_{a_1}, K_{a_2} and K_{a_3}) this must be keep in mind that when two reactions are added, their equilibrium constants are multiplied.

For the reaction, $H_2S \rightleftharpoons H^+ + HS^-$

$$K_{a_1} = \frac{[H^+]\,[HS^-]}{[H_2S]}$$

For the reaction, $HS^- \rightleftharpoons H^+ + S^{2-}$

$$K_{a_2} = \frac{[H^+]\,[S^{2-}]}{[HS^-]}$$

When, the above two reactions are added, their equilibrium constants are multiplied, thus

$$K_{a_3} = \frac{[H^+]^2\,[S^{2-}]}{[H_2S]} = K_{a_1}\times K_{a_2}$$

Hence, $$K_{a_3} = K_{a_1}\times K_{a_2}$$

Equilibrium Constant in Gaseous Systems

When all the reactants and products of a reaction are in gaseous state, their concentration is expressed in term of partial pressures. If in the following reaction

$$aA + bB \rightleftharpoons cC + dD,$$

The partial pressure of A, B, C and D are p_A, p_B, p_C and p_D respectively, then, the expression of equilibrium constant, K_p is given as $K_p = \frac{p_C^c \cdot p_D^d}{p_A^c \cdot p_B^b}$

Relation between K_p and K_c

Consider a gaseous phase reaction,

$$n_1 A + n_2 B \rightleftharpoons m_1 C + m_2 D$$

According to law of mass action,

$$K_p = \frac{p_C^{m_1} \, p_D^{m_2}}{p_A^{n_1} \, p_B^{n_2}} \quad \ldots(i)$$

In terms of molar concentration,

$$K_c = \frac{[C]^{m_1}[D]^{m_2}}{[A]^{n_1}[B]^{n_2}} \quad \ldots(ii)$$

Since for gases, the ideal gas equation is written as,

$$pV = nRT$$

or $$p = \frac{n}{V} RT = CRT \quad [C = \text{concentration}]$$

$\therefore$ $$p_A = C_A RT, \quad p_B = C_B RT$$
$$p_C = C_C RT, \quad p_D = C_D RT$$

Using these expressions in Eq. (i), we get

$$K_p = \frac{(C_C RT)^{m_1} (C_D RT)^{m_2}}{(C_A RT)^{n_1} (C_B RT)^{n_2}}$$

or $$K_p = \frac{C_C^{m_1} C_D^{m_2}}{C_A^{n_1} C_B^{n_2}} (RT)^{(m_1 + m_2) - (n_1 + n_2)}$$

or $$K_p = \frac{C_C^{m_1} C_D^{m_2}}{C_A^{n_1} C_B^{n_2}} (RT)^{\Delta n_g}$$

$$= \frac{[C]^{m_1}[D]^{m_2}}{[A]^{n_1}[B]^{n_2}} \quad \ldots(iii)$$

[$\because$ $\Delta n_g = (m_1 + m_2) - (n_1 + n_2)$ or Δn_g = moles of gaseous products – moles of gaseous reactants]

From Eqs. (i) and (iii)

$$K_p = K_c (RT)^{\Delta n_g}$$

If, $\Delta n_g = 0$ then $K_p = K_c$

If, $\Delta n_g = +\text{ve}$ then $K_p > K_c$

If, $\Delta n_g = -\text{ve}$ then $K_p < K_c$

Note While calculating the value of K_p, pressure should be expressed in bar because standard state of pressure is 1 bar. We know from unit 1 that, 1 pascal, Pa = 1 Nm^{-2}, and 1 bar = 10^5 Pa

Equilibrium Constant for Different Chemical Equilibria

The equilibrium constants for the two types of equilibria viz homogeneous and heterogeneous equilibria are discussed below:

1. Equilibrium Constant for Homogeneous Equilibrium

For homogeneous equilibrium, the equilibrium constant is written as the ratio of the product of molar concentration or partial pressure, divided by the product of the molar concentrations or partial pressures of the reactants. Here each concentration term is raised to the power equal to its stoichiometric coefficients if any. Consider the following example,

(i) $PCl_5(g) \rightleftharpoons PCl_3(g) + Cl_2(g)$

$$K_C = \frac{[PCl_3(g)][Cl_2(g)]}{[PCl_5(g)]}$$

$$K_p = \frac{p_{PCl_3} \times p_{Cl_2}}{p_{PCl_5}}$$

(ii) $NH_3(aq) + H_2O(l) \rightleftharpoons NH_4^+(aq) + OH^-(aq)$

$$K = \frac{[NH_4^+(aq)][OH^-(aq)]}{[NH_3(aq)][H_2O(l)]}$$

As H_2O is always present in excess, therefore, H_2O is constant.

Thus, $$K = \frac{[NH_4^+(aq)][OH^-(aq)]}{[NH_3(aq)]}$$

2. Equilibrium Constant of Heterogeneous System

Heterogeneous equilibria often involve pure solids or liquids but the concentration of a pure solid or liquid is constant (i.e. independent of the amount present). Therefore we can simplify equilibrium expression for the heterogeneous equilibria by taking the concentrations of pure solids and liquids as unity. e.g. equilibrium constant of the following heterogeneous equilibria is given as

$$CaCO_3(s) \overset{\Delta}{\rightleftharpoons} CaO(s) + CO_2(g)$$

$$K_c = [CO_2], \quad K_p = p_{CO_2}$$

Since, $[CaCO_3(s)]$ and $[CaO(s)]$ are both constant.

Example 5 Write the expression for the equilibrium constant, K_c for each of the following reactions.

(i) $2NOCl(g) \rightleftharpoons 2NO(g) + Cl_2(g)$

(ii) $2Cu(NO_3)_2(s) \rightleftharpoons 2CuO(s) + 4NO_2(g) + O_2(g)$

(iii) $CH_3COOC_2H_5(aq) + H_2O(l) \rightleftharpoons CH_3COOH(aq) + C_2H_5OH(aq)$

(iv) $Fe^{3+}(aq) + 3OH^-(aq) \rightleftharpoons Fe(OH)_3(s)$

(v) $I_2(s) + 5F_2(g) \rightleftharpoons 2IF_5(g)$ **NCERT Textbook**

Sol. (i) $K_c = \dfrac{[NO]^2[Cl_2]}{[NOCl]^2}$

(ii) $K_c = [NO_2]^4\,[O_2]$

(because molar concentrations of pure solids are constant)

(iii) $K_c = \dfrac{[CH_3COOH][C_2H_5OH]}{[CH_3COOC_2H_5]\,[H_2O(l)]}$

(iv) $K_c = \dfrac{1}{[Fe^{3+}]\cdot[OH^-]^3}$ because $[Fe(OH)_3\ (s) = 1]$

(v) $K_c = \dfrac{[IF_5]^2}{[F_2]^5}$ $[I_2(s) = 1]$

Example 6 We know that the relationship between K_c and K_p is $K_p = K_c\,(RT)^{\Delta n_g}$

What would be the value of Δn for the reaction?

$$NH_4Cl(s) \rightleftharpoons NH_3(g) + HI(g)$$

Sol. The relationship between K_p and K_c is

$$K_p = K_c\,(RT)^{\Delta n_g}$$

where, Δn_g = (number of moles of gaseous products) − (number of moles of gaseous reactants)

For the reaction,

$NH_4Cl\ (s) \rightleftharpoons NH_3(g) + HCl\ (g)$

$\therefore \quad \Delta n_g = 2 - 0 = 2$

Units of Equilibrium Constant

The units of K_p and K_c also depend upon the value of Δn_g. If number of moles of reactants and products are equal (i.e. $\Delta n_g = 0$) e.g. $2NO(g) \rightleftharpoons N_2(g) + O_2(g)$ then, K_p as well as K_c have no units.

If a reaction proceeds with increase or decrease in number of moles then, unit of K_p is $(\text{atmosphere})^{\Delta n_g}$ and unit of K_c is $(\text{mol per litre})^{\Delta n_g}$.

Applications of Equilibrium Constants

Equilibrium constant is helpful

(i) in predicting the extent of a reaction on the basis of its magnitude.

(ii) in predicting the direction of the reaction and

(iii) in calculating the equilibrium concentrations and pressure.

1. Predicting the Extent of a Reaction

The numerical values of equilibrium constant helps us to predict the extent of a reaction. If the value of K is greater than 10^3, products predominates i.e. reaction go to nearly completion; if value of K is less than 10^{-3}, reactant predominates i.e. the reaction occurs rarely; if it is in between 10^3 to 10^{-3}, considerable amounts of both reactant and product are present.

The above generalisation is shown in the following figure.

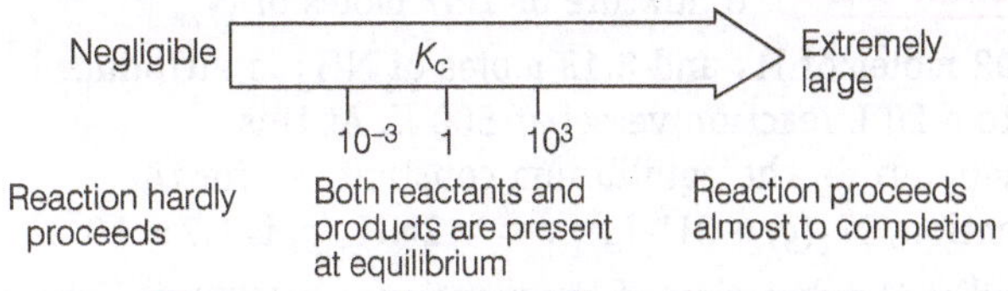

Dependence of extent of reaction on K_c

Note Higher value of K_c shows the reaction will go in the forward direction and products are more stable than the reactants.

2. Predicting the Direction of the Reaction

Equilibrium constant is also found useful for predicting the direction in which a reaction will progress at any stage. For this a new term, reaction quotient is introduced.

Reaction quotient is the ratio of the molar concentration or partial pressure of the product species to that of reactant species at any stage in the reaction not necessarily at equilibrium.

For a reaction, $aA + bB \rightleftharpoons cC + dD$

$$Q_c = \frac{[C]^c[D]^d}{[A]^a[B]^b}$$

Reaction quotient, Q is denoted as Q_c or Q_p depending upon whether the concentration is taken in terms of moles per litre or partial pressure respectively.

With the help of reaction quotient we can predict the direction of reaction.

(i) If $Q_c = K_c$ or $Q_p = K_p$; the reaction is in equilibrium i.e. no net reaction occurs.

(ii) If $Q_c > K_c$ or $Q_p > K_p$; the reaction moves from right to left, (i.e. in backward direction or in the direction of reactants).

(iii) If $Q_c < K_c$ or $Q_p < K_p$; the reaction moves from left to right (i.e. in forward direction or in the direction of products).

Example 7 The value of K_c for the reaction $2A \rightleftharpoons B + C$ is 2×10^{-3}. At a given time, the composition of reaction mixture is $[A] = [B] = [C] = 3 \times 10^{-4}$ M. In which direction the reaction well proceed? **NCERT Textbook**

Sol. For the reaction the reaction quotient,

$$Q_c = [B]\,[C] / [A]^2$$

as $[A] = [B] = [C] = 3 \times 10^{-4}$ M

$$Q_c = (3 \times 10^{-4})\,(3 \times 10^{-4}) / (3 \times 10^{-4})^2 = 1$$

As $Q_c > K_c$ so the reaction will proceed in the reverse direction.

Example 8 A mixture of 1.57 moles of N_2, 1.92 moles of H_2 and 8.13 moles of NH_3 is introduced into a 20 L reaction vessel at 500 K. At this temperature, the equilibrium constant, K_c for the reaction, $N_2(g) + 3H_2(g) \rightleftharpoons 2NH_3(g)$ is 1.7×10^2. Predict the direction of the reaction. **NCERT Textbook**

Sol. $N_2(g) + 3H_2(g) \rightleftharpoons 2NH_3(g)$

$$Q_c = \frac{[NH_3]^2}{[N_2][H_2]^3}$$

Given, $[NH_3] = \frac{8.13}{20}$ M $= 0.4065$ M

$[N_2] = \frac{1.57}{20}$ M $= 0.0785$ M;

$[H_2] = \frac{1.92}{20}$ M $= 0.096$ M

$$Q_c = \frac{[0.4065\text{ M}]^2}{[0.0785\text{ M}][0.096\text{ M}]^3} = 2.379 \times 10^3\ \text{M}^{-2}$$

$Q_c \neq K_c$, so the reaction mixture is not in equilibrium.

$Q_c > K_c$, it indicates that the reaction will proceed in the direction of reactants i.e. the reverse direction.

3. Calculating Equilibrium Concentration

The value of equilibrium constant also helps us in calculating the equilibrium concentration of various substances taking part in a reaction.

Algorithm for Calculating Equilibrium Concentration

The following steps are involved for calculating equilibrium concentration of various substances from the value of equilibrium constant.

Step I Write the balanced equation for the given reaction.

Step II Assume 'X' as the amount of the reactant reacted on as the product formed.

Step III Calculate the equilibrium concentration of each reactant and product from the stoichiometry of equation.

Step IV Write the expression for K_c or K_p or K_χ.

Step V Substitute the values of equilibrium concentration and equilibrium constant in the expression of equilibrium constant for the given reaction and solve the equation to get the value of x.

[If a quadratic equation of the type $ax^2 + bx + c = 0$, $a \neq 0$ is formed, solve it by using the formula $x = \frac{-b \pm \sqrt{b^2 - 4ac}}{2a}$]

Step VI From the value of x, calculate the equilibrium concentrations of different substances.

Step VII Check your results by substituting the equilibrium concentration into the equilibrium equation.

Example 9 The value of K_p for the reaction,

$$CO_2\,(g) + C\,(s) \rightleftharpoons 2CO(g)$$

is 3.0 at 1000 K. If initially p_{CO_2} = 0.48 bar and $p_{CO} = 0$ bar and pure graphite is present, calculate the equilibrium partial pressures of CO and CO_2. **NCERT Textbook**

Sol. For the reaction, let 'x' be the decrease in pressure of CO_2, then

	$CO_2(g)$ + C (s)	$\rightleftharpoons$ 2CO(g)
Initial pressure	0.48 bar	0
At equilibrium	(0.48 − x) bar	$2x$ bar

$$K_p = \frac{p^2_{CO}}{p_{CO_2}} \Rightarrow K_p = \frac{(2x)^2}{(0.48 - x)} = 3$$

$$4x^2 = 3\,(0.48 - x) \text{ or } 4x^2 + 3x - 1.44 = 0$$

$$a = 4,\ b = 3,\ c = -1.44$$

By applying $x = \frac{\left(-b \pm \sqrt{b^2 - 4ac}\right)}{2a}$

$$x = 2.66/8 = 0.33$$

The equilibrium partial pressures are,

$$p_{CO} = 2x = 2 \times 0.33 = 0.66 \text{ bar}$$

$$p_{CO_2} = 0.48 - x = 0.48 - 0.33 = 0.15 \text{ bar}$$

Relationship between Equilibrium Constant (K), Reaction Quotient (Q) and Gibbs Energy (G)

Gibbs free energy change and reaction quotient are related as:

$$\Delta G = \Delta G° + 2.303RT \log Q_c$$

where $\Delta G°$ = Standard Gibbs energy

At equilibrium $\Delta G = 0$ and $Q_c = K_c$

On substituting values, $\Delta G° = -2.303RT \log K_c$

Similarly, $\Delta G° = -RT \ln K_p$ (for ideal gases)

$$\therefore \qquad \ln K = -\frac{\Delta G^\circ}{RT}$$

Taking antilog on both sides, we get

$$K = e^{-\Delta G^\circ / RT}$$

The above equation is helpful in predicting the spontaneity of the reaction. e.g.

(i) If $\Delta G^\circ < 0$, $-\Delta G^\circ / RT = +$ve and $e^{-\Delta G^\circ / RT} > 1$ and hence, $K > 1$. It means that the reaction occurs spontaneously in the forward direction or products predominate over reactants.

(ii) If $\Delta G^\circ > 0$; $-\Delta G^\circ / RT = -$ve and $e^{-\Delta G^\circ / RT} < 1$ and hence, $K < 1$. It means that the reaction is non-spontaneous in forward direction (i.e. product side) but spontaneous in reverse direction (i.e. reactants predominate over products or the reaction occurs rarely.

Example 10 Hydrolysis of sucrose gives,

$$\text{Sucrose} + H_2O \rightleftharpoons \text{Glucose} + \text{Fructose}$$

Equilibrium constant K_c for the reaction is 2×10^{13} at 300 K. Calculate $\Delta G^\ominus$ at 300 K. **NCERT Textbook**

Sol. $\Delta G^\ominus = -RT \ln K_c$

$$\Delta G^\ominus = -8.314 \text{ J mol}^{-1}\text{K}^{-1} \times 300 \text{ K} \ln (2 \times 10^{13})$$

$$\Delta G^\ominus = -7.64 \times 10^4 \text{ J mol}^{-1}$$

Example 11 Calculate (i) ΔG° and (ii) the equilibrium constant for the formation of the NO_2 from NO and O_2 at 298 K. **NCERT Textbook**

$$NO(g) + \frac{1}{2} O_2(g) \rightleftharpoons NO_2(g)$$

where, $\Delta_f G^\circ(NO_2) = 52.0$ kJ/mol,

$$\Delta_f G^\circ(NO) = 87.0 \text{kJ/mol}, \Delta_f G^\circ(O_2) = 0 \text{kJ/mol}$$

Note
- Calculate the $\Delta_r G^\circ$ by using the formula $\Delta_r G^\circ = \Sigma \Delta_f G^\circ_p - \Sigma \Delta_f G^\circ_r$ (p = products and r = reactants.)
- Calculate the equilibrium constant, K_c by using the formula, $\Delta G^\circ = -2.303 RT \log K_c$.

Sol. (i) $NO(g) + \frac{1}{2} O_2(g) \rightleftharpoons NO_2(g)$;

$$\Delta_r G^\circ = \Sigma \Delta_f G^\circ_{\text{products}} - \Sigma \Delta_f G^\circ_{\text{reactants}}$$

$$\Delta_r G^\circ = \Delta_f G^\circ(NO_2) - \left(\Delta_f G^\circ(NO) + \frac{1}{2} \Delta_f G^\circ(O_2)\right)$$

$$\Delta_r G^\circ = 52.0 - \left(87.0 + \frac{1}{2} \times 0\right) \text{ kJ mol}^{-1}$$

$$\Delta_r G^\circ = -35.0 \text{ kJ mol}^{-1}$$

(ii) $\Delta_r G^\circ = -2.303\, RT \log K_c$ $-35000 \text{ J mol}^{-1}$

$$= -2.303 \times 8.314 \text{ J mol}^{-1} \text{ K}^{-1} \times 298 \text{ K} \times \log K_c$$

$$\log K_c = \frac{35000}{5705.85} = 6.134$$

$$K_c = \text{antilog } 6.134$$

$$K_c = 1.361 \times 10^6$$

Factors Affecting of Equilibria and Le-Chatelier's Principle

Thus, the factors from which the state of equilibrium is affected are:

(i) Change in concentration of reactants or products.
(ii) Change in temperature.
(iii) Change in pressure.
(iv) Addition of inert gas (at constant pressure).
(v) Addition of catalyst.

Effect of change in all the above mentioned factors on an equilibrium, is decided by using Le-Chatelier's principle, which is described in the next section.

Le-Chatelier's Principle

According to this principle, 'if any of the factors that determine the equilibrium condition, of a system (like temperature, pressure, concentration etc.,) is changed, the system will move in such a direction so that effect of the change is reduced or nullified.' This law is true for almost all physical and chemical equilibria.Thus, the effects of various factors on the state of equilibrium according to Le-Chatelier's principle are as follows

1. Effect of Concentration Change

According to Le-Chatelier's principle,

(i) The concentration stress due to the addition of reactant/product is relieved by shifting of the net reaction in that direction where the added substance is consumed.

(ii) The concentration stress due to the removal of reaction/product is relieved by shifting of the net reaction in that direction where the removed substance is replenished or in other words, "change in the concentration of either reactant(s) or product(s) shift the reaction in such a direction in which the effect of the change is minimised or nullified."

2. Effect of Pressure Change

Pressure change, that is achieved by changing the volume of the system, generally affect the gaseous reactions having different number of moles of gaseous reactants and products. It has no effect on solids/liquids as the volume (and concentration) of liquids is nearly independent of pressure. In general, **increase in pressure shifts the equilibrium in that direction where the number of moles of the gas or pressure decreases and *vice-versa*.** This is because, with increase in pressure, volume of the system (products) decreases and hence, the value of Q_c decreases (i.e. $Q_c << K_c$).

Thus, in order to reachieve the equilibrium, the reaction proceeds in the forward direction.

Quick Trick

Calculate Δn_g for the given reaction. If $\Delta n_g = 0$, pressure change has no effect on the state of equilibrium. If $\Delta n_g < 0$, increased pressure favours forward reaction and if $\Delta n_g > 0$, increased pressure favours backward reaction or decreased pressure favours forward reaction. e.g.

$$\underset{0}{C(s)} + \underset{1}{CO_2(g)} \longrightarrow \underset{2}{2\,CO(g)};\ \Delta n_g = 2 - 1 = 1$$

Since, $\Delta n_g > 0$, increased pressure favours the backward reaction or formation of CO is favoured by low pressure.

3. Effect of Inert Gas Addition

Inert gas can be added to an equilibrium mixture, under two conditions.

(i) **At Constant Volume** Since inert gas does not take part in the reaction, so the equilibrium remains unaffected if volume is kept constant. This is because at constant volume, the partial pressures or the molar concentrations of the substance involved in the reaction remain unchanged.

(ii) **At Constant Pressure** If an inert gas is added to an equilibrium process at constant pressure, the volume of the process will increase.

Hence, the equilibrium will shift in a direction in which there is an increase in the number of moles of the gases.

4. Effect of Temperature Change

Temperature directly affects the value of equilibrium constant, K_c and rate of reactions. Increased temperature shifts the equilibrium in such a direction where heat is absorbed and decreased temperature shift the equilibrium in such direction where heat is released. *Thus, in general :*

(i) In case of an exothermic reaction ($\Delta H = -$ ve), the equilibrium constant decreases with rise in temperature and hence, to make it constant the reaction proceeds in backward direction.

(ii) In case of an endothermic reaction ($\Delta H = +$ ve), the equilibrium constant increases with rise in temperature and hence, the reaction moves in forward direction.

5. Effect of Catalyst

A catalyst alters the rate of a reaction by providing a new pathway of lower activation energy. It affects the rate of forward and backward reactions to the same extent. Hence, it has no effect on the state of equilibrium. However, in the presence of a catalyst, the equilibrium is achieved in lesser time.

A catalyst has no effect on the equilibrium composition of the mixture. Further, it is not shown in the balanced chemical equation or in the expression of equilibrium constant.

Effect of Varying Conditions of the Equilibrium, $aA + bB \rightleftharpoons cC + dD, \Delta n_g = (c + d) - (a + b)$

S.No.	Change imposed on the system in equilibrium	Equilibrium position moves	Equilibrium constant	Any other points
1.	Conc. of *A* and/or *B* increased	To right	No change	No change
2.	Conc. of *C* and/or *D* increased	To left	No change	No change
3.	Pressure increased	To right if $(c + d) < (a + b)$, i.e. $\Delta n_g = -$ ve To left if $(c + d) > (a + b)$, i.e. $\Delta n_g = +$ ve No change if $(c + d) = (a + b)$, i.e. $\Delta n_g = 0$	No change No change No change	Very little effect if any on reactions in liquid solution
4.	Temperature increased	To left if $\Delta H = -$ve (exothermic) To right if $\Delta H = +$ ve (endothermic)	Value decreased Value decreased	Equilibrium achieved faster
5.	Addition of catalyst	No change	No change	Equilibrium achieved faster
6.	Addition of inert gas			
	(i) At constant *p*	To the direction of increasing gaseous moles	No change	No change
	(ii) At constant *V*	No effect	No change	No change

Applications of Le-Chatelier's Principle

Some of its applications are mentioned below:

1. Haber's Process of Synthesis of Ammonia

$$N_2(g) + 3H_2(g) \rightleftharpoons 2NH_3(g); \Delta H = -22.4 \text{ kcal}$$

The favourable conditions are:

(i) high concentration of N_2 or/and H_2.
(ii) high pressure (as $\Delta n_g = -2$).
(iii) low temperature (as the reaction is exothermic).

Although the low temperature favour the formation of NH_3, yet an optimum temperature is set, as the rate of reaction is very slow at low temperature. A temperature of 500°C is selected and a pressure of 200 atm is applied in practice. To enhance the rate of reaction, catalyst, finely divided iron containing molybdenum (acts as promoter) is used.

2. Manufacture of Sulphuric Acid by Contact Process

The first step of the process is the conversion of SO_2 into SO_3.

$$2SO_2(g) + O_2(g) \longrightarrow 2SO_3(g); K_c = 1.7 \times 10^{26}$$

But the process is very slow so its speed is increased by using catalyst like platinum or divanadium pentaoxide, V_2O_5. Other conditions favouring this process are:

(i) increase in pressure (as $\Delta n_g = -1$).
(ii) high concentration of SO_2 and O_2.
(iii) low concentration of SO_3.
(iv) low temperature as the reaction is exothermic.

3. Hydrolysis of Simple Esters

$$\underset{\text{Ethyl acetate}}{CH_3COOC_2H_5} + H_2O \overset{H^+}{\rightleftharpoons} \underset{\text{Ethyl alcohol}}{C_2H_5OH} + \underset{\text{Acetic acid}}{CH_3COOH}$$

The factors favouring formation of C_2H_5OH and CH_3COOH.

(i) Increase in concentration of ethyl acetate.
(ii) Unaffected by pressure change (as $\Delta n_g = 0$)

It is a homogeneous liquid system, there will be no effect of changing pressure on this system and an increase in the concentration of ethyl acetate will favour the formation of ethyl alcohol and acetic acid.

4. Dissociation of Dinitrogen Tetraoxide

$$\underset{\text{Dinitrogen tetraoxide}}{N_2O_4} \rightleftharpoons \underset{\text{Nitrogen dioxide}}{2NO_2}$$

The favourable conditions for forward reaction are :

(i) An increase in the concentration of NO_2 will suppress the dissociation of N_2O_4.
(ii) The dissociation of N_2O_4 increases with a decrease in pressure.
(iii) Equilibrium is shifted to the N_2O_4 side upon a decrease in temperature.

5. Manufacture of Nitric Acid (Birkeland-Eyde Process)

$$N_2(g) + O_2(g) \rightleftharpoons 2NO(g); \Delta H = +43.2 \text{ kcal}$$

The factors favouring formation of NO are

(i) increase in concentration of N_2 and O_2.
(ii) unaffected by pressure change (as $\Delta n_g = 0$).
(iii) increase in temperature (as the reaction is endothermic).

Topic Practice 1

Very Short Answer Type Questions

1 Mark

1. Fill in the Blanks

(i) .... reactions do not proceed to completion.
(ii) A mixture of reactants and products in the equilibrium state is called ....
(iii) .... will not affect the concentration of NH_3 at equilibrium.

2. Objective Type Questions

(i) Ice and water kept in a perfectly insulated thermos flask at 273K and the atmospheric pressure are in equilibrium state then the system shows
(a) liquid - liquid equilibrium
(b) liquid - vapour equilibrium
(c) solid - liquid equilibrium
(d) solid - gas equilibrium

(ii) Which of the following reactions is correct regarding homogeneous equilibria?
(a) $N_2(g) + 3H_2(g) \rightleftharpoons 2NH_3(g)$
(b) $CH_3COOC_2H_5(aq) + H_2O(l) \rightleftharpoons CH_3COOH(aq) + C_2H_5OH(aq)$
(c) $Fe^{3+}(aq) + SCN^-(aq) \rightleftharpoons [Fe(SCN)]^{2+}(aq)$
(d) All of the above

(iii) For the reaction, $SO_2(g) + \frac{1}{2}O_2(g) \rightleftharpoons SO_3(g)$ if $K_p = K_C(RT)^x$ where, the symbols have usual meaning, then the value of x is (assuming ideality)
(a) -1 (b) $-\frac{1}{2}$ (c) $\frac{1}{2}$ (d) 1

(iv) The correct equation of equilibrium constant in terms of Gibbs energy is

(a) $K = e^{-\Delta G^\circ/RT}$ (b) $K = e^{-\Delta G/RT}$

(c) $K = e^{\Delta G^\circ/RT}$ (d) $K = e^{\Delta G/RT}$

3. For the reaction, $N_2(g) + 3H_2(g) \rightleftharpoons 2NH_3(g)$

Equilibrium constant, $K_c = \frac{[NH_3]^2}{[N_2][H_2]^3}$

Some reactions are written below in Column I and their equilibrium constants in terms of K_c are written in Column II. Match the following reactions with the corresponding equilibrium constant.

Column I (Reaction)	Column II (Equilibrium constant)
A. $2N_2(g) + 6H_2(g) \rightleftharpoons 4NH_3(g)$	(i) $2K_c$
B. $2NH_3(g) \rightleftharpoons 2N_2(g) + 3H_2(g)$	(ii) $K_c^{1/2}$
C. $\frac{1}{2}N_2(g) + \frac{3}{2}H_2(g) \rightleftharpoons NH_3(g)$	(iii) $\frac{1}{K_c}$
	(iv) K_c^2

Codes

	A	B	C		A	B	C
(a)	(iv)	(iii)	(ii)	(b)	(i)	(ii)	(iv)
(c)	(i)	(iii)	(ii)	(d)	(ii)	(iv)	(iii)

4. A tank is full of water. Water is coming in as well as going out at same rate. What will happen to level of water in a tank ? What is name given to such a state?

5. Explain, why pure liquids and solids can be ignored while writing the equilibrium constant expression? **NCERT Textbook**

6. The equilibrium constant expression for a gas reaction is,

$$K_c = \frac{[NH_3]^4 [O_2]^5}{[NO]^4 [H_2O]^6}$$

Write the balanced chemical equation corresponding to this expression. **NCERT Textbook**

7. For an exothermic reaction, what happens to the equilibrium constant if temperature is increased?

8. Predict which of the following reaction will have appreciable concentration of reactants and products?

(i) $Cl_2(g) \rightleftharpoons 2Cl(g); K_c = 5 \times 10^{-39}$

(ii) $Cl_2(g) + 2NO(g) \rightleftharpoons 2NOCl(g); K_c = 3.7 \times 10^{-8}$

(iii) $Cl_2(g) + 2NO_2(g) \rightleftharpoons 2NO_2Cl(g); K_c = 1.8$

NCERT Textbook

9. What is the effect of reducing volume on the following system ?

$$2C(s) + O_2(g) \rightleftharpoons 2CO(g)$$

10. For the reaction, $H_2(g) + I_2(g) \rightleftharpoons 2HI(g)$, the standard free energy is $\Delta G^\ominus > 0$. How is the equilibrium constant affected? **NCERT Exemplar**

11. At 0°C, ice and water are present in equilibrium.

What will happen on increasing the pressure?

12. Ice melts slowly at higher altitudes. Explain why?

Short Answer Type I Questions

2 Marks

13. Which of the following reactions involve homogeneous equilibrium and which involve heterogeneous equilibrium ?

(i) $Ag_2O(s) + 2HNO_3(aq) \rightleftharpoons 2AgNO_3(aq) + H_2O(l)$

(ii) $C(s) + CO_2(g) \rightleftharpoons 2CO(g)$

(iii) $CH_3COOC_2H_5(aq) + H_2O(l) \rightleftharpoons CH_3COOH(aq) + C_2H_5OH(aq)$

(iv) $2SO_2(g) + O_2(g) \rightleftharpoons 2SO_3(g)$

14. What is K_c for the following equilibrium when the equilibrium concentration of each substance is $[SO_2] = 0.60$ M, $[O_2] = 0.82$ M and $[SO_3] = 1.90$ M ?

$2SO_2(g) + O_2(g) \rightleftharpoons 2SO_3(g)$ **NCERT Textbook**

15. The value of K_c for the reaction, $3O_2(g) \rightleftharpoons 2O_3(g)$ is 2.0×10^{-50} at 25°C. If the equilibrium concentration of O_2 in air at 25°C is 1.6×10^{-2}, what is the concentration of O_3?

16. For the following equilibrium,

$K_c = 6.3 \times 10^{14}$ at 1000 K

$$NO(g) + O_3(g) \rightleftharpoons NO_2(g) + O_2(g)$$

Both the forward and reverse reactions in the equilibrium are elementary bimolecular reactions. What is K_c for the reverse reaction?

17. The reaction,

$CO(g) + 3H_2(g) \rightleftharpoons CH_4(g) + H_2O(g)$

is at equilibrium at 1300 K in a 1L flask. It also contains 0.30 mole of CO, 0.10 mole of H_2 and 0.02 mole of H_2O and an unknown amount of CH_4 in the flask.

Determine the concentration of CH_4 in the mixture. The equilibrium constant, K_c for the reaction at the given temperature is 3.90.
NCERT Textbook

18. At 450 K, $K_p = 2.0 \times 10^{10}$/bar for the given reaction at equilibrium,

$$2SO_2(g) + O_2(g) \rightleftharpoons 2SO_3(g)$$

What is K_c at this temperature?

19. At a certain temperature and total pressure of 10^5 Pa, iodine vapour contains 40% by volume of I atoms.

$$I_2(g) \rightleftharpoons 2I(g)$$

Calculate K_p for the equilibrium.
NCERT Textbook

20. For the reaction, $N_2(g) + 3H_2(g) \rightleftharpoons 2NH_3(g)$, the partial pressures of N_2 and H_2 are 0.80 and 0.40 atmosphere respectively at equilibrium. The total pressure of the system is 2.80 atmosphere. What is K_p for the above reaction?

21. One mole of H_2O and one mole of CO are taken in 10 L vessel and heated to 725 K. At equilibrium, 40% of water (by mass) reacts with CO according to the equation,

$$H_2O(g) + CO(g) \rightleftharpoons H_2(g) + CO_2(g)$$

Calculate the equilibrium constant for the reaction.

22. A sample of pure PCl_5 was introduced into an evacuated vessel at 473 K. After equilibrium was attained, concentration of PCl_5 was found to be 0.5×10^{-1} mol L^{-1}. If value of K_c is 8.3×10^{-3}, what are the concentration of PCl_3 and Cl_2 at equilibrium ?

23. What is the equilibrium concentration of each of the substances in the equilibrium when the initial concentration of ICl was 0.78 M ?

$$2ICl(g) \rightleftharpoons I_2(g) + Cl_2(g) ; K_c = 0.14$$

NCERT Textbook

24. A sample of HI(*g*) is placed in flask at a pressure of 0.2 atm. At equilibrium, the partial pressure of HI(*g*) is 0.04 atm. What is K_p for the given equilibrium?

$$2HI(g) \rightleftharpoons H_2(g) + I_2(g)$$

NCERT Textbook

25. Dihydrogen gas used in Haber's process is produced by reacting methane from natural gas with high temperature steam. The first stage of two stage reaction involves the formation of CO and H_2.

In second stage, CO formed in first stage is reacted with more steam in water gas shift reaction, $CO(g) + H_2O(g) \rightleftharpoons CO_2(g) + H_2(g)$

If a reaction vessel at 400°C is charged with an equimolar mixture of CO and steam such that $p_{CO} = p_{H_2O} = 4.0$ bar, what will be the partial pressure of H_2 at equilibrium? $K_p = 10.1$ at 400°C.
NCERT Textbook

26. $2NO(g) + O_2(g) \rightleftharpoons 2NO_2(g); \Delta H = -117$ kJ

(i) Predict the effect of an increase in concentration of NO on the equilibrium concentration of NO_2.

(ii) Predict the effect of decrease in pressure as a result of increased volume on the equilibrium concentration of NO_2.

27. When hydrochloric acid is added to cobalt nitrate solution at room temperature, the following reaction takes place and the reaction mixture becomes blue. On cooling the mixture it becomes pink. On the basis of this information. What would you infer about the enthalpy of the reaction?

$$\underset{\text{(Pink)}}{[Co(H_2O_6)]^{3+}}(aq) + 4Cl^-(aq) \rightleftharpoons \underset{\text{(Blue)}}{[CoCl_4]^{2-}}(aq) + 6H_2O(l)$$

NCERT Exemplar

28. Following data is given for the reaction,

$$CaCO_3(s) \rightleftharpoons CaO(s) + CO_2(s)$$

$$\Delta_f H°[CaO(s)] = -635.1 \text{ kJ mol}^{-1}$$
$$\Delta_f H°[CO_2(g)] = -393.5 \text{ kJ mol}^{-1}$$
$$\Delta_f H°[CaCO_3(s)] = -1206.9 \text{ kJ mol}^{-1}$$

Predict the effect of temperature on the equilibrium constant of the above reaction.
NCERT Exemplar

Short Answer Type II Questions

3 Marks

29. A liquid is in equilibrium with its vapour in a sealed container at a fixed temperature. The volume of the container is suddenly increased.

(i) What is the initial effect of change on vapour pressure?

(ii) How do rates of evaporation and condensation change initially?

(iii) What happens when equilibrium is restored finally and what will be the final vapour pressure?
NCERT Textbook

30. At 700 K, equilibrium constant for the reaction, $H_2(g) + I_2(g) \rightleftharpoons 2HI(g)$ is 54.8. If 0.5 mol L^{-1} of HI(g) is present at equilibrium at 700 K, what are the concentration of $H_2(g)$ and $I_2(g)$ assuming that we initially started with HI(g) and allowed it to reach equilibrium at 700 K? **NCERT Textbook**

31. The value of K_c for the reaction

$2HI(g) \rightleftharpoons H_2(g) + I_2(g)$ is 1×10^{-4}.

At a given time, the composition of reaction mixture is $[HI] = 2 \times 10^{-5}$ mol, $[H_2] = 1 \times 10^{-5}$ mol and $[I_2] = 1 \times 10^{-5}$ mol. In which direction will the reaction proceed? **NCERT Exemplar**

32. Find out the value of K_c for each of the following equilibria from the value of K_p

(i) $2NOCl\ (g) \rightleftharpoons 2NO\ (g) + Cl_2\ (g)$; $K_p = 1.8 \times 10^{-2}$ at 500 K

(ii) $CaCO_3\ (s) \rightleftharpoons CaO\ (s) + CO_2\ (g)$; $K_p = 167$ at 1073 K **NCERT Textbook**

33. Nitric oxide reacts with Br_2 and gives nitrosyl bromide as per reaction given below

$2NO(g) + Br_2(g) \rightleftharpoons 2NOBr(g)$

When 0.087 mole of NO and 0.0437 mole of Br_2 are mixed in a closed container at constant temperature, 0.0518 mole of NOBr is obtained at equilibrium. Calculate the equilibrium amount of NO and Br_2.

34. 50.0 g of $CaCO_3$ are heated to 1073 K in a 5 L vessel. What per cent of the $CaCO_3$ would decompose at equilibrium? K_p for the reaction. $CaCO_3(s) \rightleftharpoons CaO(s) + CO_2(g)$ is 1.15 atm at 1073 K.

35. One of the reaction that takes place in producing steel from iron ore is the reduction of iron(II) oxide by carbon monoxide to give iron metal and CO_2.

$FeO\ (s) + CO\ (g) \rightleftharpoons Fe\ (s) + CO_2\ (g)$; $K_p = 0.265$ atm at 1050 K

What are the equilibrium partial pressures of CO and CO_2 at 1050 K if the initial partial pressures are, $p_{CO} = 1.4$ atm and $p_{CO_2} = 0.80$ atm?

36. The equilibrium constant for the following reaction is 1.6×10^5 at 1024 K

$H_2(g) + Br_2(g) \rightleftharpoons 2HBr(g)$

Find the equilibrium pressure of all gases if 10.0 bar of HBr is introduced into a sealed container at 1024 K.

37. An equilibrium mixture at 300 K contains N_2O_4 and NO_2 at 0.28 and 1.1 atm pressure respectively. If the volume of the container is doubled, calculate the new equilibrium pressure of two gases.

38. Bromine monochloride, BrCl decomposes into bromine and chlorine and reaches the equilibrium, $2BrCl(g) \rightleftharpoons Br_2(g) + Cl_2(g)$ for which $K_c = 32$ at 500 K. If initially pure BrCl is present at a concentration of 3.3×10^{-3} mol L^{-1}, what is its molar concentration in the mixture at equilibrium? **NCERT Textbook**

39. At 473 K, equilibrium constant K_c for decomposition of phosphorus pentachloride, PCl_5 is 8.3×10^{-3}. If decomposition is depicted as,

$PCl_5(g) \rightleftharpoons PCl_3(g) + Cl_2(g)$; $\Delta H° = 124.0$ kJ mol^{-1}

(i) Write an expression for K_c for the reaction.

(ii) What is the value of K_c for the reverse reaction at the same temperature?

(iii) What would be the effect on K_c if (a) more PCl_5 is added (b) pressure is increased (c) the temperature is increased ?

40. How can you predict the following stages of a reaction by comparing the value of K_c and Q_c?

(i) Net reaction proceeds in the forward direction.

(ii) Net reaction proceeds in the backward direction.

(iii) No net reaction occurs. **NCERT Exemplar**

41. Equilibrium constant, K_c for the reaction, $N_2(g) + 3H_2(g) \rightleftharpoons 2NH_3\ (g)$ at 500 K is 0.061. At a particular time, the analysis shows that composition of the reaction mixture is 3.0 mol L^{-1} N_2, 2.0 mol L^{-1} H_2 and 0.5 mol L^{-1} NH_3. Is the reaction at equilibrium? If not, in which direction does the reaction tend to proceed to reach equilibrium? **NCERT Textbook**

42. Some processes are given below. What happens to the process if it is subjected to a change given in the brackets?

(i) Ice $\xrightleftharpoons{\text{Melting point}}$ water (Pressure is increased)

(ii) Dissolution of NaOH in water (Temperature is increased)

(iii) $N_2(g) + O_2(g) \rightleftharpoons 2NO(g) - 180.7$ kJ (Pressure is increased and temperature is decreased.)

43. Does the number of moles of reaction products increase, decrease or remain same when each of the following equilibria is subjected to a decrease in pressure by increasing the volume?
(i) $PCl_5(g) \rightleftharpoons PCl_3(g) + Cl_2(g)$ **NCERT Textbook**
(ii) $CaO(s) + CO_2(g) \rightleftharpoons CaCO_3(s)$
(iii) $3Fe(s) + 4H_2O(g) \rightleftharpoons Fe_3O_4(s) + 4H_2(g)$

44. At 1127 K and 1 atm pressure, a gaseous mixture of CO and CO_2, in equilibrium with solid carbon has 90.55% CO by mass.
$$C(s) + CO_2(g) \rightleftharpoons 2CO(g)$$
Calculate K_c for this reaction at the above temperature.

45. Reaction between N_2 and O_2 takes place as follows
$$2N_2(g) + O_2(g) \rightleftharpoons 2N_2O(g)$$
If a mixture of 0.482 mole N_2 and 0.933 mole O_2 is placed in a 10 L reaction vessel and allowed to form N_2O at a temperature for which $K_c = 2.0 \times 10^{-37}$, determine the composition of equilibrium mixture. **NCERT Textbook**

Long Answer Type Questions

5 Marks

46. Ethyl acetate is formed by the reaction between ethanol and acetic acid and the equilibrium is represented as
$$CH_3COOH\,(l) + C_2H_5OH\,(l) \rightleftharpoons CH_3COOC_2H_5\,(l) + H_2O\,(l)$$
(i) Write the concentration ratio (reaction quotient), Q_c, for this reaction (**Note** Water is not in excess and is not a solvent in this reaction).
(ii) At 293 K, if one starts with 1.00 mole of acetic acid and 0.18 mole of ethanol, there is 0.171 mole of ethyl acetate in the final equilibrium mixture. Calculate the equilibrium constant.
(iii) Starting with 0.5 mole of ethanol and 1.0 mole of acetic acid and maintaining it at 293 K, 0.214 mole of ethyl acetate is found after sometime. Has equilibrium been reached? **NCERT Textbook**

47. $K_p = 0.04$ atm at 899 K for the equilibrium shown below. What is the equilibrium concentration of C_2H_6 when it is placed in a flask at 4.0 atm pressure and allowed to come to equilibrium?
$$C_2H_6(g) \rightleftharpoons C_2H_4(g) + H_2(g)$$

48. Write a relation between ΔG and Q and define the meaning of each term and answer the following:
(i) Why a reaction proceeds forward when $Q < K$ and no net reaction occurs when $Q = K$?
(ii) Explain the effect of increase in pressure in terms of reaction quotient Q for the reaction,
$$CO(g) + 3H_2(g) \rightleftharpoons CH_4(g) + H_2O(g)$$

49 On the basis of Le-Chatelier principle explain how temperature and pressure can be adjusted to increase the yield of ammonia in the following reaction.
$$N_2(g) + 3H_2(g) \rightleftharpoons 2NH_3(g) \quad \Delta H = -92.38 \text{ kJ mol}^{-1}$$
What will be the effect of addition of argon to the above reaction mixture at constant volume? **NCERT Exemplar**

50 (i) Describe the effect of
(a) addition of H_2
(b) addition of CH_3OH
(c) removal of CO
(d) removal of CH_3OH on the equilibrium of the reaction,
$$2H_2(g) + CO(g) \rightleftharpoons CH_3OH(g)$$
(ii) What happens to an equilibrium in a reversible reaction if a catalyst is added to it? **NCERT Textbook**

51 Which of the following reactions will get affected by increasing the pressure? Also, mention whether change will cause the reaction to go into forward or backward direction.
(i) $COCl_2(g) \rightleftharpoons CO(g) + Cl_2(g)$
(ii) $CH_4(g) + 2S_2(g) \rightleftharpoons CS_2(g) + 2H_2S(g)$
(iii) $CO_2(g) + C(s) \rightleftharpoons 2CO(g)$
(iv) $2H_2(g) + CO(g) \rightleftharpoons CH_3OH(g)$
(v) $CaCO_3(s) \rightleftharpoons CaO(s) + CO_2(g)$
(vi) $4NH_3(g) + 5O_2(g) \rightleftharpoons 4NO(g) + 6H_2O(g)$

52 Dihydrogen gas is obtained from natural gas by partial oxidation with steam as per following endothermic reaction,
$$CH_4(g) + H_2O(g) \rightleftharpoons CO(g) + 3H_2(g)$$
(i) Write an expression of K_p for the above reaction.
(ii) How will the values of K_p and composition of equilibrium mixture be affected by
(a) increasing the pressure
(b) increasing the temperature
(c) using a catalyst?

Hints & Solutions

1. (i) reversible
(ii) equilibrium mixture
(iii) addition of catalyst

2. (i) (c), (ii) (d), (iii) (b), (iv) (a)

3. (a) A → (iv), B → (iii), C → (ii)

For the reaction, $N_2(g) + 3H_2(g) \rightleftharpoons 2NH_3(g)$

Equilibrium constant $K_c = \dfrac{[NH_3]^2}{[N_2]\,[H_2]^3}$

A. The given reaction $[2N_2(g) + 6H_2(g) \rightleftharpoons 4NH_3(g)]$ is twice the above reaction.

Hence, $K = K_c^2$

B. The reaction $[2NH_3(g) \rightleftharpoons N_2(g) + 3H_2(g)]$ is reverse of the above reaction.

C. The reaction $\left[\frac{1}{2}N_2(g) + \frac{3}{2}H_2(g) \rightleftharpoons NH_3(g)\right]$ is half of the above reaction.

Hence, $K = \sqrt{K_c} = K_c^{\frac{1}{2}}$.

4. It will remain the same because rate of inflow is equal to rate of outflow. The state is called state of 'equilibrium'.

5. Molar concentration of a pure solid or liquid (if in excess) is constant (i.e. independent of the amount present). That's why pure liquids and solids can be ignored while writing the equilibrium constant expression.

6. The expression shows that 4NO and 6 H_2O molecules are reactants and 4 NH_3 and 5O_2 molecules are products. Thus, the balanced chemical equation is

$$4\,NO + 6\,H_2O \rightleftharpoons 4\,NH_3 + 5O_2$$

7. $K = \dfrac{k_f}{k_b}$.

In exothermic reaction, with increase of temperature, k_b increases much more than k_f. Hence, K decreases.

8. For the reaction (iii) equilibrium constant, K_c is neither high nor very low so the reactants and products will be present in appreciable concentrations.

9. On reducing volume, pressure will increase. According to Le-Chatelier principle, equilibrium will shift to the side where number of moles of gas can be increased. In the above reaction, equilibrium will shift in forward direction.

10. $\Delta G^{\ominus}$ and K are related as :

$$\Delta G^{\ominus} = -RT \ln K_c$$

when $\Delta G^{\ominus} > 0$ means ΔG° is positive. This can be only if $\ln K_c$ is negative, i.e. $K_c < 1$.

11. On increasing the pressure, ice melts to form water (because water has lesser volume than ice).

12. Ice $(s) \longrightarrow$ Water (l)

The melting of ice is favoured at high pressure because there is decrease in volume in the forward reaction. Since at high altitudes, atmospheric pressure is low and therefore, ice melts slowly.

13. (i) Heterogeneous equilibrium [1/2]
(ii) Heterogeneous equilibrium [1/2]
(iii) Homogeneous equilibrium [1/2]
(iv) Homogeneous equilibrium [1/2]

14. Equilibrium constant,

$$K_c = \frac{[SO_3]^2}{[SO_2]^2 \cdot [O_2]} = \frac{(1.90\ M)^2}{(0.60\ M)^2\ (0.82\ M)} \approx 12.23\ M^{-1}$$ [2]

15. $3O_2(g) \rightleftharpoons 2O_3(g)\ K_c = \dfrac{[O_3]^2}{[O_2]^3}$

or $O_3 = \sqrt{K_c[O_2]^3} = \sqrt{(2.0\times10^{-50})(1.6\times10^{-2})^3}$

$[O_3] = 2.86 \times 10^{-28}\ \text{mol L}^{-1}$ [2]

16. For the reaction,

$$NO(g) + O_3(g) \rightleftharpoons NO_2(g) + O_2(g)$$

($K_c = 6.3\times 10^{14}$ at 1000 K)

$$K_c = \frac{[NO_2][O_2]}{[NO][O_3]} = 6.3\times10^{14} \quad ...(i)$$

For reverse reaction,

$$NO_2(g) + O_2(g) \rightleftharpoons NO\ (g) + O_3(g)$$

$$K_c' = \frac{[NO][O_3]}{[NO_2][O_2]} \quad ...(ii)$$ [1]

From Eqs. (i) and (ii), we get

$$K_c' = \frac{1}{K_c} = \frac{1}{6.3\times 10^{14}} = 1.587\times 10^{-15}$$ [1]

17. $CO(g) + 3H_2(g) \rightleftharpoons CH_4(g) + H_2O(g)$

$K_c = 3.90$ at 1300 K.

$$K_c = \frac{[CH_4]\cdot[H_2O]}{[CO]\,[H_2]^3}$$

$$\Rightarrow \quad 3.90 = \frac{[CH_4]\ [0.02]}{[0.30]\ [0.10]^3}$$ [1]

(Molar concentration means number of moles present in 1 L and volume of the flask is 1 L.)

$$[CH_4] = \frac{3.90\times 0.30\times (0.10)^3}{0.02} = 0.0585\ M$$

$$[CH_4]_{eq} = 5.85\times 10^{-2} M$$ [1]

18. $2SO_2(g) + O_2(g) \rightleftharpoons 2SO_3(g)$

$\therefore \quad \Delta n_g = 2 - 3 = -1$

$$K_c = \frac{K_p}{(RT)^{\Delta n_g}} = \frac{K_p}{(RT)^{-1}}$$

$$K_c = K_p \times RT = 2.0\times 10^{10} \times 0.0831 \times 450$$

$$= 7.479\times 10^{11}\ \text{L mol}^{-1}$$ [2]

19. **Key Idea** *K_p depends upon the partial pressures of reactants and products so find their partial pressures from the percentage given and then, calculate K_p.*

Given, $I_2(g) \rightleftharpoons 2I(g)$

I atoms in iodine vapours = 40% by volume

So, iodine vapours of I_2 molecules = 60% by volume

Partial pressure of iodine atoms, $p_1 = \frac{40}{100} \times 10^5$

$= 0.40 \times 10^5$ Pa

Similarly, partial pressure of iodine molecules (I_2),

$$p_2 = \frac{60}{100} \times 10^5 = 0.60 \times 10^5 \text{ Pa}$$ [1]

According to equation,

$$K_p = \frac{p_I^2}{p_2} = \frac{(0.40 \times 10^5 \text{ Pa})^2}{(0.60 \times 10^5 \text{ Pa})}$$

$$= 0.2666 \times 10^5 \text{ Pa}$$

$$\approx 2.67 \times 10^4 \text{ Pa}$$ [1]

20. $N_2(g) + 3H_2(g) \rightleftharpoons 2NH_3(g)$

Given, at equilibrium, $p_{N_2} = 0.80$ atmosphere,

$p_{H_2} = 0.40$ atmosphere

$p_{N_2} + p_{H_2} + p_{NH_3} = 2.80$ atmosphere

$\therefore \quad p_{NH_3} = 2.80 - (0.80 + 0.40) = 1.60$ atmosphere [1]

From, $K_p = \frac{p_{NH_3}^2}{p_{N_2} \times p_{H_2}^3} = \frac{(1.60)^2}{0.80 \times (0.40)^3} = 50.0 \text{ atm}^{-2}$ [1]

21. $H_2O(g) + CO(g) \rightleftharpoons H_2(g) + CO_2(g)$

Initial conc.	1	1	0	0
Equili. conc.	$(1-x)$	$(1-x)$	x	x

H_2O reacted = 40% of 1 mole of H_2O = 0.4 mol

$\therefore \quad x = 0.4$ mol

$(1-x) = 1 - 0.4 = 0.6$ mol

$$K_c = \frac{[H_2]\,[CO_2]}{[H_2O]\,[CO]} = \frac{0.4 \times 0.4}{0.6 \times 0.6} = 0.444$$ [2]

22. $PCl_5(g) \rightleftharpoons PCl_3(g) + Cl_2(g)$

At equili. 0.5×10^{-1} M $\quad x \quad x$

$$\therefore \quad K_c = \frac{[PCl_3]\,[Cl_2]}{[PCl_5]}$$ [1]

$$8.3 \times 10^{-3} = \frac{x^2}{0.05} \quad (\because [PCl_3] = [Cl_2])$$

or $\quad x^2 = 0.415 \times 10^{-3} = 4.15 \times 10^{-4}$

$x \approx 2.04 \times 10^{-2}$ mol L^{-1}

Hence, $\quad [PCl_3] = [Cl_2] = 2.04 \times 10^{-2}$ mol L^{-1} [1]

23. $2ICl(g) \rightleftharpoons I_2(g) + Cl_2(g)$

Initial conc.	0.78 M	0	0
Equili conc.	$0.78 - 2x$	x	x

$$K_c = \frac{[I_2]\,[Cl_2]}{[ICl]^2} = \frac{x \cdot x}{(0.78 - 2x)^2} = 0.14 \Rightarrow \frac{x^2}{(0.78 - 2x)^2} = 0.14$$

or $\quad \frac{x}{(0.78 - 2x)} = \sqrt{0.14} = 0.374$ [1]

or $\quad x = 0.29172 - 0.748x$

or $\quad 1.748x = 0.29172$ or $x = \frac{0.29172}{1.748} = 0.1668$

$[I_2]_{equiv} = [Cl_2]_{equiv} = 0.1668$

$[ICl]_{equili} = 0.45$ [1]

24. $2HI(g) \rightleftharpoons H_2(g) + I_2(g)$

Initial pressure	0.2 atm	0	0
Equili. pressure	0.04 atm	0.08 atm	0.08 atm

(Decrease in pressure of HI = 0.2 − 0.04 = 0.16 atm; so equilibrium pressure of H_2 is $\frac{0.16}{2} = 0.08$ atm, and for I_2 is $\frac{0.16}{2} = 0.08$ atm as two moles of HI on dissociation gives 1 mole H_2 and 1 mole I_2) [1]

$$K_p = \frac{p_{H_2} \times p_{I_2}}{p_{HI}^2} = \frac{0.08 \times 0.08}{(0.04)^2} = 4.0$$ [1]

25. $CO(g) + H_2O(g) \rightleftharpoons CO_2(g) + H_2(g)$

Initial pressure	4.0	4.0	0	0
At equili.	$(4.0 - p)$	$(4.0 - p)$	p	p

$$K_p = \frac{p_{CO_2} \cdot p_{H_2}}{p_{CO} \cdot p_{H_2O}} = \frac{p \cdot p}{(4 - p) \cdot (4 - p)}$$

$$10.1 = \frac{p^2}{(4-p)^2}$$ [1]

On solving, $\quad p = \frac{12.71}{4.17} = 3.04$ bar

Hence, $\quad p_{H_2} = 3.04$ bar [1]

26. $2NO(g) + O_2(g) \rightleftharpoons 2NO_2(g);\ \Delta H = -117$ kJ

(i) If we increase the concentration of NO, the rate of forward reaction will increase, i.e. more NO_2 will be formed. [1]

(ii) Decrease in pressure will favour backward reaction, i.e. less NO_2 will be formed. [1]

27. In the reaction,

$$\underset{\text{(Pink)}}{[Co(H_2O)_6]^{3+}(aq)} + 4Cl^-(aq) \rightleftharpoons \underset{\text{(Blue)}}{[CoCl_4]^{2-}(aq)} + 6H_2O(l)$$

On cooling, the equilibrium shifts in backward direction or on heating, the equilibrium shifts forward direction. Hence, reaction is endothermic. i.e. $\Delta H > 0$. [2]

28. $CaCO_3(s) \rightleftharpoons CaO(s) + CO_2(g)$

$$\Delta_f H° = [\Delta_f H°[CaO(s)] + \Delta_f H°[CO_2(g)]] - \Delta_f H°[CaCO_3(s)]$$

$$\Delta_f H° = [-635.1 + (-393.5)] - (-1206.9) = +178.3 \text{ kJ mol}^{-1}$$

Because ΔH value is positive, so the reaction is endothermic. Hence, according to Le-Chatelier's principle, reaction will proceed in forward direction on increasing temperature. [2]

29. $A(l) \longrightarrow A(g)$

Low pressure High pressure

If volume is increased at constant temperature, pressure decreases, since, $p \propto 1/V$ at constant temperature.

(i) Decrease in pressure shift the equilibrium in the direction of high pressure i.e. more vapours are formed hence vapour pressure increases. [1]

(ii) Rate of evaporation increases and rate of condensation decreases. [1]

(iii) When equilibrium is restored finally the rate of evaporation again becomes equal to the rate of condensation and the final vapour pressure becomes equal to the vapour pressure that was before the sudden increase in the volume of the container. [1]

30. As we started the reaction with HI, so equilibrium constant for the dissociation of HI ($2HI \rightleftharpoons H_2 + I_2$) is required. Thus, calculate equilibrium constant for backward reaction (K_c') $\left(K'_c = \frac{1}{K_c}\right)$ and then calculate $[H_2]$ and $[I_2]$.

$$H_2(g) + I_2(g) \rightleftharpoons 2HI(g)\ ;\ K_c = 54.8$$

$$2HI(g) \rightleftharpoons H_2(g) + I_2(g);\ K_c' = \frac{1}{K_c} = \frac{1}{54.8}$$

Again, $K_c' = \frac{[H_2][I_2]}{[HI]^2} = \frac{1}{54.8}$ [1]

Given, $[HI] = 0.5 \text{ mol L}^{-1}$

According to equation, $[H_2] = [I_2] = [x]$

$$\frac{x \cdot x}{[0.5]^2} = \frac{1}{54.8} \text{ or } x^2 = \frac{[0.5]^2}{54.8} = 0.00456$$

$$x = 0.0675 \text{ M}$$

Hence, $[H_2] = [I_2] = x = 0.0675$ M [2]

31. Given that, $[HI] = 2 \times 10^{-5}$ mol; $[H_2] = 1 \times 10^{-5}$ mol

$[I_2] = 1 \times 10^{-5}$ mol [1]

At a given time, the reaction quotient Q for the reaction will be given by the expression

$$Q = \frac{[H_2][I_2]}{[HI]^2} = \frac{1 \times 10^{-5} \times 1 \times 10^{-5}}{(2 \times 10^{-5})^2} = \frac{1}{4} = 0.25 = 2.5 \times 10^{-1}$$

As the value of reaction quotient is greater than the value of K_c, i.e. 1×10^{-4} the reaction will proceed in the reverse direction. [2]

32. **Key idea** First, find Δn_g by subtracting the moles of gaseous reactants from the moles of gaseous products for each equation, as K_p and K_c are related as $K_p = K_c (RT)^{\Delta n_g}$. Then, calculate K_c in each case.

(i) $2NOCl(g) \rightleftharpoons 2NO(g) + Cl_2(g)$;

$K_p = 1.8 \times 10^{-2}$ at 500 K

$\Delta n_g = n_P - n_R = 3 - 2 = 1$

$$K_c = \frac{K_p}{(RT)^{\Delta n_g}} = \frac{1.8 \times 10^{-2}}{0.0821 \times 500} = 4.38 \times 10^{-4}$$ [1]

(ii) $CaCO_3(s) \rightleftharpoons CaO(s) + CO_2(g)$;

$K_p = 167$ at 1073 K

$\Delta n_g = n_P - n_R = 1$

$$K_c = \frac{K_p}{(RT)^{\Delta n_g}} = \frac{167}{0.0821 \times 1073} = 1.89$$ [2]

33. In order to solve such problems, following steps are involved.:

Step I Set up a balance sheet using symbols for the expected equilibrium amounts of reactants and products. [Remember! multiply the value of x with the stoichiometric coefficient of the molecule].

Step II Compare with the given information

Given: equilibrium moles of NOBr = 0.0518

$\therefore\ 2x = 0.0518$ and $x = \frac{0.0518}{2} = 0.0259$ [1]

Step III Put the value of x to obtained equilibrium concentration of other species.

Moles of NO at equilibrium $= (0.087 - 2x)$

$= 0.087 - 0.0518 = 0.0352$ mol

Moles of Br_2 at equilibrium $= (0.0437 - x)$

$= 0.0437 - 0.0259 = 0.0178$ mol [2]

34. $CaCO_3(s) \rightleftharpoons CaO(s) + CO_2(g)$

$K_p = p_{CO_2} = 1.15$ atm, $pV = nRT$

$$n_{CO_2} = \frac{p_{CO_2} V}{RT} = \frac{115 \times 5}{0.082 \times 1073} = 0.065 \text{ mol}$$ [1]

1 mole of CO_2 is obtained by decomposition of 1 mole $CaCO_3$. Therefore, moles of $CaCO_3$ decomposed is equal to the moles of $CO_2 = 0.065$ mol.

Moles of $CaCO_3$ initially present $= \frac{50}{100} = 0.5$ mol

[Molecular mass of $CaCO_3 = 100$]

Per cent of $CaCO_3$ decomposed

$$= \frac{0.065}{0.5} \times 100 = 13\%$$ [2]

35. First find Q_p by the given initial partial pressures of [CO] and [CO_2]. Compare Q_p and K_c to find the equilibrium partial pressure of [CO] and [CO_2].

$$FeO(s) + CO(g) \rightleftharpoons Fe(s) + CO_2(g);$$

Initial pressure: CO 1.4 atm, CO_2 0.80 atm

($K_p = 0.265$ at 1050 K)

$$Q_p = \frac{p_{CO_2}}{p_{CO}} = \frac{0.80}{1.4} = 0.571$$ [$\because$ Fe and FeO are solids]

$\because Q_p > K_p$, the reaction will go in reverse direction. Due to this, pressure of CO_2 will decrease and that of CO will increase to attain equilibrium. [1]

Suppose p is the decrease in pressure of CO_2 and p is the increase in pressure of CO. Hence, $p_{CO_2} = (0.80 - p)$ and $p_{CO} = (1.4 + p)$.

Now, from $K_p = \frac{p_{CO_2}}{p_{CO}} \Rightarrow 0.265 = \frac{(0.80 - p)}{(1.4 + p)}$

$$p = \frac{0.429}{1.265} = 0.339 \text{ atm}$$

Hence, at equilibrium, $p_{CO_2} = 0.80 - 0.339 = 0.461$ atm

and $p_{CO} = 1.4 + 0.339 = 1.739$ atm [2]

36. $H_2(g) + Br_2(g) \rightleftharpoons 2HBr(g)$;

$K_p = 1.6 \times 10^5$ at 1024 K

$\therefore$ $2HBr(g) \rightleftharpoons H_2(g) + Br_2(g)$;

Initial pressure	10.0 bar	0	0
Equili. pressure	$(10 - x)$	$\frac{x}{2}$	$\frac{x}{2}$

$$K'_p = \frac{1}{1.6 \times 10^5} \text{ at 1024 K}$$

or $$K'_p = \frac{p_{H_2} \cdot p_{Br_2}}{p^2_{HBr}} = \frac{\frac{x}{2} \cdot \frac{x}{2}}{(10 - x)^2}$$

$$\frac{1}{1.6 \times 10^5} = 0.625 \times 10^{-5} = \frac{\frac{x}{2} \cdot \frac{x}{2}}{10 \times 10}$$ [1]

[$(10 - x) \approx 10$ because magnitude of K_p is small.)]

$$2 \times 2 \times 10 \times 10 \times 0.625 \times 10^{-5} = x^2 \text{ or } x = 0.050$$

$$p_{H_2} = p_{Br_2} = \frac{x}{2} = \frac{0.050}{2} = 0.025 \text{ bar} = 2.5 \times 10^{-2} \text{ bar}$$ [1]

$$p_{HBr} = 10 - 0.050 = 9.95 \approx 10 \text{ bar}$$ [1]

37. $N_2O_4(g) \rightleftharpoons 2NO_2(g)$

Pressure at equilibrium 0.28 1.1

$$K_p = \frac{p(NO_2)^2}{p(N_2O_4)} = \frac{(1.1)^2}{(0.28)} = 4.32 \text{ atm}$$

If volume of the container is doubled, the pressure will be reduced to half.

$N_2O_4 \rightleftharpoons 2NO_2$

New pressure $\left(\frac{0.28}{2} - p\right)$ $\left(\frac{1.1}{2} + 2p\right)$

$$K_p = \frac{\left(\frac{1.1}{2} + 2p\right)^2}{\left(\frac{0.28}{2} - p\right)} = 4.32 \text{ atm}$$ [1]

On solving,

$$p = 0.045$$

$\therefore$ $p(N_2O_4) = 0.14 - 0.045 = 0.095$ atm

$p(NO_2) = 0.55 + 0.045 = 0.64$ atm [2]

38. First, find equilibrium concentration for all reactants and products given in the equation by assuming x mole of BrCl decomposes.

Find x by the expression of K_c and then find $[BrCl]_{equilibrium}$.

	$2BrCl(g)$	$\rightleftharpoons Br_2(g)$	$+ Cl_2(g)$
Initial conc.	3.30×10^{-3}	0	0
Equili. conc.	$(3.30 \times 10^{-3} - x)$	$x/2$	$x/2$

$(K_c = 32$ at 500 K)

$$K_c = \frac{[Br_2][Cl_2]}{[BrCl]^2} = \frac{\frac{x}{2} \times \frac{x}{2}}{(3.30 \times 10^{-3} - x)^2} = 32$$

$$\frac{x}{2(3.30 \times 10^{-3} - x)} = 5.65$$ [1]

or $$x = \frac{0.03732}{12.312} = 3.032 \times 10^{-3} \text{ mol L}^{-1}$$

$$[BrCl]_{eqm.} = (3.30 \times 10^{-3} - 3.032 \times 10^{-3}) \text{ mol L}^{-1}$$

$$= 2.68 \times 10^{-4} \text{ mol L}^{-1}$$ [2]

39. $PCl_5(g) \rightleftharpoons PCl_3(g) + Cl_2(g)$; $K_c = 8.3 \times 10^{-3}$

(i) $K_c = \frac{[PCl_3][Cl_2]}{[PCl_5]}$ [1]

(ii) For the reverse reaction,

$$K_c' = \frac{1}{K_c} = \frac{1}{8.3 \times 10^{-3}} = 120.48$$ [1]

(iii) (a) Addition of PCl_5 has no effect on K_c because K_c is constant at constant temperature.

(b) K_c does not change with pressure.

(c) The given reaction is endothermic, hence on increasing the temperature, K_f will increase, this results in increase in K_c $\left(K_c = \frac{K_f}{K_b}\right)$. [1]

40. Prediction of the following stages of a reaction by comparing the value of K_c and Q_c are

(i) If $Q_c < K_c$, the reaction will proceed in the direction of the products (forward reaction). [1]

(ii) If $Q_c > K_c$, the reaction will proceed in the direction of reactants (reverse reaction). [1]

(iii) If $Q_c = K_c$, the reaction mixture is already at equilibrium. [1]

41. Find Q_c and compare it with K_c. If $Q_c = K_c$, the reaction is in equilibrium, if $Q_c < K_c$, the reaction will go in forward direction and if $Q_c > K_c$, the reaction will go in backward direction.

$N_2(g) + 3H_2(g) \rightleftharpoons 2NH_3(g)$; $K_c = 0.061$ at 500K

Given, $[N_2] = 3.0$ mol L^{-1}, $[H_2] = 2.0$ mol L^{-1}

and $[NH_3] = 0.5$ mol L^{-1} at time t

so, $$Q = \frac{[NH_3]^2}{[N_2][H_2]^3} = \frac{[0.5]^2}{[3.0][2.0]^3}$$

$$Q_c = 0.0104$$

Because $Q \neq K_c$, equilibrium has not been attained.

Also, because $Q_c < K_c$ (0.0,104 < 000.061), the reaction will proceed from left to right, i.e. towards formation of more products.

42. (i) Equilibrium will shift in the forward direction, i.e. more of ice will melt. [1]

(ii) Solubility will decrease because it is an exothermic process. [1]

(iii) Pressure has no effect. Decrease of temperature will shift the equilibrium in the backward direction. [1]

43. According to Le-Chatelier's principle, on decreasing pressure equilibrium shifts in that direction where pressure increases (i.e. number of moles in gaseous state are more). Therefore, number of moles of reaction products in (i) increases ($\because \Delta n_g = 1$) (ii) decreases ($\because \Delta n_g = -1$) (iii) remains the same. (If $\Delta n_g = 0$, there is no effect of change in pressure). **[3]**

44. Since, the percentage by mass is given, so calculate the number of moles of CO and CO_2 to calculate their mole fractions. Then, calculate the partial pressures of CO and CO_2 by using the formula $p_A = x_A \cdot p_{total}$

Calculate K_p by using the formula, $K_p = \dfrac{p_{CO_2}}{p_{CO_2}}$ and

K_c by using the formula, $K_p = K_c(RT)^{\Delta n_g}$.

90.55% CO by mass means 90.55 g CO and 9.45 g CO_2 are present in 100 g mixture.

Number of moles of CO, $n_{CO} = \dfrac{90.55}{28} = 3.234$ mol

(Molar mass of CO = 28 g mol^{-1})

Number of moles of CO_2, $n_{CO_2} = \dfrac{9.45}{44} = 0.215$ mol

(Molar mass of CO_2 = 44 g mol^{-1})

Partial pressure of CO, $p_{CO} = x_{CO} \cdot p_{total}$

$$= \frac{3.234}{3.234 + 0.215} \times 1$$

$$p_{CO} = 0.938 \times 1 = 0.938 \text{ atm}$$ **[1]**

Similarly, $p_{CO_2} = x_{CO_2} \cdot p_{total} = \dfrac{0.215}{3.234 + 0.215} \times 1$

$$p_{CO_2} = 0.062 \times 1 = 0.062 \text{ atm}$$

$$C(s) + CO_2(g) \rightleftharpoons 2CO(g)$$

$$K_p = \frac{p^2_{CO}}{p_{CO_2}} = \frac{(0.938)^2}{0.062} = 14.11$$ **[1]**

$$\Delta n_g = 2 - 1 = 1$$

$$K_p = K_c(RT)^{\Delta n_g}$$

$$\Rightarrow \quad K_c = \frac{K_p}{RT} \quad (\because \Delta n_g = 1)$$

$$K_c = \frac{14.11}{0.0821 \times 1127}$$

$$= 0.15336 \approx 0.153$$ **[1]**

45. Find the equilibrium concentrations of reactants and products in the given equation by assuming $2x$ mole of N_2 and x mole of O_2 are disappeared and $2x$ mole of N_2O are appeared.

Find the value of x to determine the concentration of reaction mixture.

	$2N_2(g)$ +	$O_2(g)$ $\rightleftharpoons$	$2N_2O(g)$
Initial conc.	0.482	0.933	0
Equilibrium conc.	$(0.482 - 2x)$	$(0.933 - x)$	$2x$
Active mass	$\left(\dfrac{0.482 - 2x}{10}\right)$	$\left(\dfrac{0.933 - x}{10}\right)$	$\left(\dfrac{2x}{10}\right)$

K_c is very small, which means negligible amounts of N_2 and O_2 react.

$$[N_2]_{eq} = \frac{0.482 - 2x}{10} = \frac{0.482}{10} = 0.0482$$ **[1]**

Similarly, $[O_2]_{eq} = \dfrac{0.933 - x}{10} = \dfrac{0.933}{10} = 0.0933$

$$K_c = \frac{[N_2O]^2}{[N_2]^2\,[O_2]} = 2.0 \times 10^{-37} = \frac{\left[\dfrac{4x^2}{100}\right]}{(0.0482)^2\,(0.0933)}$$ **[1]**

or $x^2 = 10.837 \times 10^{-40}$ or $x = 3.292 \times 10^{-20}$

$$[N_2O] = \frac{2x}{10} = \frac{2 \times 3.292 \times 10^{-20}}{10} = 6.58 \times 10^{-21} \text{ mol L}^{-1}$$

$$[N_2] = 0.0482 \text{ mol L}^{-1}$$

$$[O_2] = 0.0933 \text{ mol L}^{-1}$$ **[1]**

46. $CH_3COOH(l) + C_2H_5OH(l) \rightleftharpoons CH_3COOC_2H_5(l) + H_2O(l)$

(i) $Q_c = \dfrac{[CH_3COOC_2H_5]\,[H_2O]}{[CH_3COOH]\,[C_2H_5OH]}$

Here, H_2O is not in excess that's why its concentration is not constant. **[1]**

(ii)

	$CH_3COOH(l)$ +	C_2H_5OH $\rightleftharpoons$	$CH_3COOC_2H_5(l)$ +	$H_2O(l)$
Initial conc	1.00 mol	0.180 mol	0	0
Equili. conc.	$(1 - x)$	$(0.180 - x)$	x	x

Given, $[CH_3COOC_2H_5]_{equili} = 0.171 \text{ mol} = x$

$$\therefore \quad K_c = \frac{[CH_3COOC_2H_5]\,[H_2O]}{[CH_3COOH]\,[C_2H_5OH]}$$

or $K_c = \dfrac{0.171 \times 0.171}{(1 - 0.171) \times (0.180 - 0.171)}$

$$= \frac{0.171 \times 0.171}{0.829 \times 0.009} = 3.919 \approx 3.92$$ **[2]**

(iii)

	$CH_3COOH(l)$ +	$C_2H_5OH(l)$ $\rightleftharpoons$	$CH_3COOC_2H_5(l)$ +	$H_2O(l)$
Initial conc.	1.0 mol	0.5 mol	0	0
After t conc.	$(1.0 - 0.214)$ = 0.786 mol	$(0.5 - 0.214)$ = 0.286 mol	0.214	0.214

$$Q_c = \frac{[CH_3COOC_2H_5]\,[H_2O]}{[CH_3COOH]\,[C_2H_5OH]}$$

$$Q_c = \frac{0.214 \times 0.214}{0.786 \times 0.286} = 0.2037 \approx 0.204$$

$Q_c \neq K_c$, hence equilibrium has not been reached. **[2]**

47.

	$C_2H_6(g)$ $\rightleftharpoons$	$C_2H_4(g)$ +	$H_2(g)$
Initial pressure	4.0 atm	0	0
Equili. pressure	$(4.0 - p)$ atm	p	p

$$K_p = \frac{p_{C_2H_4} \cdot p_{H_2}}{p_{C_2H_6}} = \frac{p \times p}{4.0 - p}$$ [1]

$$0.04 = \frac{p^2}{4.0 - p} \quad \text{or} \quad 0.16 - 0.04p = p^2$$ [2]

$$p^2 + 0.04p - 0.16 = 0$$

$$(a = 1,\ b = 0.04,\ c = -0.16)$$

$$\therefore \quad p = -0.04 \pm \frac{\sqrt{0.0016 - 4(-0.16)}}{2}$$

$$p = \frac{-0.04 \pm 0.80}{2} \Rightarrow p = 0.38$$

(by taking positive value)

Hence, $p_{C_2H_6} = 4.0 - 0.38 = 3.62$ atm [2]

48. The relation between ΔG and Q is

$$\Delta G = \Delta G^\ominus + RT \ln Q$$

ΔG = change in free energy as the reaction proceeds

$\Delta G^\ominus$ = standard free energy

Q = reaction quotient

R = gas constant

T = absolute temperature in K

(i) Since, $\Delta G^\ominus = -RT \ln K$

$$\therefore \Delta G = -RT \ln K + RT \ln Q; \Delta G = RT \ln \frac{Q}{K}$$

If $Q < K$, ΔG will be negative and the reaction proceeds in the forward direction. If $Q = K$, $\Delta G = 0$ reaction is in equilibrium and there is no net reaction. [2]

(ii) $CO(g) + 3H_2(g) \rightleftharpoons CH_4(g) + H_2O(g)$

$$K_c = \frac{[CH_4]\,[H_2O]}{[CO]\,[H_2]^3}$$

On increasing pressure, volume decreases. If we doubled the pressure, volume will be halved but the molar concentrations will be doubled. Then,

$$\frac{2[CH_4] \cdot 2[H_2O]}{2[CO]\,\{2[H_2]\}^3} = \frac{1}{4}\,\frac{[CH_4]\,[H_2O]}{[CO]\,[H_2]^3} = \frac{1}{4} K_c$$

Therefore, Q_c is less than K_c, so Q_c will tend to increase to re-establish equilibrium and the reaction will go in forward direction.

49. $N_2(g) + 3H_2(g) \rightleftharpoons 2NH_3(g); \Delta H = -92.38 \text{ kJ mol}^{-1}$

It is an exothermic process as ΔH is negative.

Effect of temperature According to Le-Chatelier's principle, low temperature is favourable for high yield of ammonia, but practically very low temperatures slow down the reaction. So, optimum temperature 700 K is favourable in attainment of equilibrium. [2]

Effect of pressure Similarly, high pressure about 200 atm is favourable for high yield of ammonia.

On increasing pressure, reaction goes in the forward direction because the number of moles decreases in the forward direction. [2]

Addition of argon At constant volume addition of argon (an inert gas) does not affect the equilibrium because it does not change the partial pressures of the reactants or products involved in the reaction and the equilibrium remains undisturbed. [1]

50. (i) $2H_2(g) + CO(g) \rightleftharpoons CH_3OH(g)$

According to Le-Chatelier's principle,

(a) addition of H_2 (increase in concentration of reactants) shifts the equilibrium in forward direction (more product is formed).

(b) addition of CH_3OH (increase in concentration of product) shifts the equilibrium in backward direction.

(c) removal of CO also shifts the equilibrium in backward direction.

(d) removal of CH_3OH shifts the equilibrium in forward direction. [3]

(ii) When catalyst is added, the state of equilibrium is not disturbed but equilibrium is attained quickly. This is because the catalyst increases the rate of forward and backward reaction to the same extent. [2]

51. According to Le-Chatelier's principle, increase in pressure shifts the equilibrium in the direction where pressure decreases (i.e. number of moles are less). Furthermore, if $n_p \neq n_r$, the change in pressure affects the equilibrium.

(i) $n_p > n_r$, the reaction will go in backward direction.

(ii) $n_p = n_r$, the reaction will not be affected by increasing pressure.

(iii) $n_p > n_r$, the reaction will go in backward direction.

(iv) $n_p < n_r$, the reaction will go in forward direction.

(v) $n_p > n_r$, the reaction will go in backward direction.

(vi) $n_p > n_r$, the reaction will go in backward direction.

52. $CH_4(g) + H_2O(g) \rightleftharpoons CO(g) + 3H_2(g)$

(i) $$K_p = \frac{p_{CO} \cdot p^3_{H_2}}{p_{CH_4} \cdot p_{H_2O}}$$ [2]

(ii) (a) Increase in pressure shifts the equilibrium in the direction where pressure decreases (i.e. number of moles are less). This is backward direction. K_p remains unaffected from pressure change.

(b) Since, ΔH = +ve (endothermic reaction), reaction takes place with absorption of heat. Hence, increase in temperature shifts the equilibrium in the direction where heat is absorbed (i.e. forward). It also increases the value of K_p.

(c) No effect, since catalyst affects rate of both directions equally. [3]

TOPIC 02 Ionic Equilibrium : Acids and Bases and their Ionisation

Ionic Equilibrium in Solution

Equilibria that involves ions only are studied under different class called **ionic equilibrium**. e.g. following equilibrium establish between iron (II) thiocyanate and its constituent ion when it is dissolved in water.

$$[Fe(SCN)]^{2+}(aq) \rightleftharpoons Fe^{3+}(aq) + SCN^-(aq)$$

Such equilibrium reactions are known as ionic equilibrium. But it is well known that all substances do not dissociate into their constituent ions when dissolved in water such as sugar, glucose etc. The substances which dissociate into their constituent ions conduct electricity in aqueous or molten state. On this basis, Michael Faraday classified the substances into following two categories.

Non-Electrolytes

A solution of substances like urea, glucose, etc. that does not dissociate into ions when dissolved in water and hence they are a bad conductor of electricity. Such substances are termed as **non-electrolytes.**

Electrolytes

The substance that dissociate into ions when dissolved in water, are called **electrolytes.** Such substance conduct electricity in aqueous solution. Depending upon the extent of ionisation, the electrolytes are further classified into two classes by Faraday.

1. Strong Electrolytes

These are dissociated largely or almost completely 100 % in solution and the solution consequently becomes very good conductor of electricity. e.g. aqueous solution of common salt (NaCl) contains mainly sodium ions and chloride ions. Other example of strong electrolytes are HCl, H_2SO_4, HNO_3, NaOH, KOH, KCl, KNO_3, NH_4Cl etc.

2. Weak Electrolytes

These get never completely dissociated. In ordinary conditions, weak electrolytes dissociate in solution to a small extent (~5%) and the solution, consequently, is a poor conductor of electricity. e.g. aqueous solution of acetic acid contains mainly unionised acetic acid molecules, and only some acetate ions and hydronium ions.

Other examples of such electrolytes are

H_3PO_4, H_3BO_3, NH_4OH, $(NH_4)_2CO_3$, HCN etc.

Ionisation of Weak Electrolytes: Ostwald's Dilution Law

Before discussing the ionisation of weak electrolytes given by Ostwald dilution law, let us discuss the concept of degree of dissociation related to the law.

Degree of Dissociation (Ionisation)

In the solutions of weak electrolytes, an equilibrium is established between the ions and unionised electrolytes. e.g. an electrolyte *AB* ionises as

$$AB \rightleftharpoons A^+ + B^-$$

The equilibrium established between *AB* and A^+ and B^- is called ionic equilibrium. The fraction of total number of molecules that undergo ionisation or dissociation is called the **degree of ionisation** or **dissociation** (α). Thus,

$$\alpha = \frac{\text{number of molecules of electrolyte ionised as ions}}{\text{total number of molecules of electrolyte dissolved}}$$

or $$\alpha = \frac{\text{amount of electrolyte ionised}}{\text{initial amount}}$$

Degree of ionisation (α) increases with dilution and reaches to maximum limit (unity) at infinite dilution for weak electrolytes. The extent of ionisation also depends upon the strength of the bond and the extent of solvation of ions obtained.

Ostwald's Dilution Law

Ostwald applied 'law of mass action' to ionic equilibrium. This is called as **Ostwald's dilution law.** This law is applicable only to weak electrolytes. Thus, according to Ostwald dilution law

	$HA + H_2O \rightleftharpoons$	A^-	$+ H_3O^+$
Initially (mol L^{-1})	C	0	0
At equilibrium	$C(1-\alpha)$	$C\alpha$	$C\alpha$

where, α = degree of ionisation

Dissociation constant of weak acids (K_a)

$$K_a = \frac{[A^-][H_3O^+]}{[HA]} = \frac{C^2\alpha^2}{C(1-\alpha)} = \frac{C\alpha^2}{(1-\alpha)}$$

For weak electrolytes, So $\alpha << 1$

$$K_a = C\alpha^2 \text{ or } \alpha = \sqrt{\frac{K_a}{C}}$$

That means, $\alpha \propto \sqrt{\frac{1}{C}} \propto \sqrt{V}$ $\left[\text{as } C \propto \frac{1}{V}\right]$

where, V = dilution of solution,

concentration of anion $= C\alpha = \sqrt{K_a C}$

Also, $[H_3O^+] = C\alpha = \sqrt{K_a C}$

In case of a weak electrolytes, at a given temperature, the degree of ionisation is inverslely proportional to the square root of the molar concentration or directly proportional to square root of the volume of the solution. Relative strength of two weak acids in terms of degree or ionisation.

$$\frac{\alpha_1}{\alpha_2} = \sqrt{\frac{K_1 C_2}{K_2 C_1}}$$

If $C_1 = C_2$, $\frac{\alpha_1}{\alpha_2} = \sqrt{\frac{K_1}{K_2}}$

Similarly, for weak base

K_b (ionisation constant of weak base) $= \frac{C\alpha^2}{(1-\alpha)} \approx C\alpha^2$

$\therefore$ $\alpha = \sqrt{\frac{K_b}{C}}$

$$[OH^-] = C\alpha = \sqrt{K_b C}$$

Relative strength of two weak bases in terms of degree of ionisation

$$\frac{\alpha_1}{\alpha_2} = \sqrt{\frac{K_1 C_2}{K_2 C_1}}$$

If $C_1 = C_2$, $\frac{\alpha_1}{\alpha_2} = \sqrt{\frac{K_1}{K_2}}$

Note In terms of $[H^+]$ for two weak acids, $\frac{[H^+]_1}{[H^+]_2} = \sqrt{\frac{K_1 C_1}{K_2 C_2}}$

Acids, Bases and Salts

The earlier criteria for classification of acids and bases were the experimentally observed properties of aqueous solutions. The word acid has been derived from a Latin word *acidus* meaning sour. Thus, the substance that have sour taste, turns blue litmus red, liberates hydrogen with some metals and neutralises base, is termed as an **acid.**

On the other hand, the substance having bitter taste, turns red litmus blue, feel soapy and neutralises acids is termed as a **base.** When acid and base react together, they neutralise each other and result in the formation of **salt** alongwith water.

Although the above mentioned concepts of acids and bases are not applicable for all the substances. Hence, many scientist have been proposed the revised definitions of acids and bases from time to time.

Few such definitions are discussed below:

Arrhenius Concept of Acids and Bases

According to this concept, all substances, that give hydrogen ions, H^+ (*aq*) in their aqueous solutions are called acids, while that, which furnish hydroxyl ions, OH^- (*aq*) in water are called bases.

e.g. $HA(aq) \rightleftharpoons H^+(aq) + A^-(aq)$ (Acid)

Or $HA(aq) + H_2O(l) \longrightarrow H_3O^+(aq) + A^-(aq)$ (Acid)

Similarly, $BOH(aq) \longrightarrow B^+(aq) + OH^-(aq)$ (Base)

Number of H^+ ions delivered by an acid in its aqueous solution is called **basicity** or **protocity** of the acid. The acids are referred as monobasic, dibasic, tribasic etc., according to the number of protons given in aqueous solution as one, two or three. Similarly, the number of OH^- furnished by the base in its aqueous solution is called its **acidity.** The substance that furnish both $H^+(aq)$ and $OH^-(aq)$ are called **amphoteric substance** , e.g. water

$$\underset{}{H_2O(l)} \rightleftharpoons \underset{\text{Hydrogen ion}}{H^+(aq)} + \underset{\text{Hydroxyl ion}}{OH^-(aq)}$$

Limitations of Arrhenius Theory

(i) Free H^+ and OH^- ions, because of their high reactivity do not exist in water.

(ii) This concept is limited to aqueous solutions only.

(iii) The acidic character of certain salts like, $AlCl_3, BF_3$ and basic character of NH_3, PH_3 cannot be explained with the help of this concept.

(iv) It is not applicable to the compounds which do not contain free H^+ or OH^- ions.

Bronsted-Lowry Concept of Acids and Bases

This concept was proposed by the Danish chemist, **Johannes Bronsted** and the English chemist, **Thomas M. Lowry.**

According to this concept, an acid is a substance (molecule or ion) which can donate H^+ to a base and a base is a substance which can accept a proton from an acid.

Thus, an acid is a proton donor (**protogenic**) and a base is a proton acceptor (**protophilic**).

- **The acid-base pair, which differ by a proton, are said to form a conjugate acid-base pair.**

Add proton

$$\underset{\text{Base}}{NH_3\,(aq)} + \underset{\text{Acid}}{H_2O(l)} \rightleftharpoons \underset{\text{Conjugate acid}}{NH_4^+\,(aq)} + \underset{\text{Conjugate base}}{OH^-\,(aq)}$$

Loses proton

Thus, the acid-base pair in the above example are :

$$NH_3 \underset{-H^+}{\overset{+H^+}{\rightleftharpoons}} NH_4^+ \text{ and } H_2O(l) \underset{+H^+}{\overset{-H^+}{\rightleftharpoons}} OH^-$$

The general form of such reactions is

Add proton

$$\text{Acid} + \text{Base} \rightleftharpoons \text{Conjugate base} + \text{Conjugate acid}$$

Loses proton

Or

$$\text{Acid}_1 + \text{Base}_2 \rightleftharpoons \text{Base}_1 + \text{Acid}_2$$

- **If bronsted acid is a strong acid then its conjugate base is a weak base and *vice-versa*.**

It is also interesting to note that some substances exhibit dual behaviour. i.e. they have the tendency of accepting as well as donating the H^+ ion or in other words, they behave as an acid and a base both.

Such substances are called **amphoteric** or **amphiprotic substances.**

e.g. NH_3, H_2O, CH_3COOH etc.

$$\underset{\text{Acid}}{H_2O} + \underset{\text{Base}}{H_2O} \rightleftharpoons \underset{\text{Conjugate acid}}{H_3O^+} + \underset{\text{Conjugate base}}{OH^-}$$

$$NH_3 + NH_3 \rightleftharpoons NH_4^+ + NH_2^-$$

$$CH_3COOH + CH_3COOH \rightleftharpoons CH_3CO\overset{+}{O}H_2 + CH_3COO^-$$

Limitations of Bronsted-Lowry Concept

(i) This definition is unable to explain the reactions occurring in the non-protonic solvents such as $COCl_2, SO_2, N_2O_4$ etc.

(ii) It cannot explain the reactions between some acidic oxides (such as CO_2, SO_2, SO_3) and basic oxides (such as CaO, BaO, MgO) which take place even in the absence of the solvent, e.g. $CaO + SO_3 \longrightarrow CaSO_4$

(iii) $BF_3, AlCl_3$ etc., do not have any hydrogen and hence, cannot give a proton but are known to behave as acids.

Example 1 The ionisation of hydrochloric acid in water is given below.

$$HCl\,(aq) + H_2O\,(l) \rightleftharpoons H_3O^+\,(aq) + Cl^-\,(aq)$$

Label two conjugate acid-base pairs in this ionisation.

NCERT Exemplar

Sol.

Adds proton

$$\underset{\text{Acid}}{HCl\,(aq)} + \underset{\text{Base}}{H_2O(l)} \rightleftharpoons \underset{\text{Conjugate acid}}{H_3O^+(aq)} + \underset{\text{Conjugate base}}{Cl^-(aq)}$$

Loses proton

Note If Bronsted acid is a strong acid then its conjugate base is a weak base and *vice-versa*. Generally, the conjugate acid has one extra proton and each conjugate base has one less proton.

Example 2 The species H_2O, HCO_3^-, HSO_4^- and NH_3 can act both as Bronsted acids and bases. For each case give the corresponding conjugate acid and conjugate base.

NCERT Textbook

Sol. A conjugate acid is obtained by adding a proton to the species and a conjugate base is obtained by removing a proton from the given species. Thus, the corresponding conjugate acid and base for the given species are as follows.

Species	Conjugate acid	Conjugate base
H_2O	H_3O^+	OH^-
HCO_3^-	H_2CO_3	CO_3^{2-}
HSO_4^-	H_2SO_4	SO_4^{2-}
NH_3	NH_4^+	NH_2^-

Lewis Concept of Acids and Bases

According to this concept, a **base** is a substance that has a tendency to donate an electron pair to form a coordinate bond and an **acid** is a substance that accepts the electron pair donated by the Lewis base.

Thus, a Lewis acid is an electrophile or electron deficient species. e.g. $AlCl_3, Co^{3+}, Mg^{2+}$ etc., whereas a Lewis base is a nucleophile or electron rich species

e.g. H_2O, NH_3, OH^-, NO, CO etc.

According to Lewis, a general acid-base reaction can be expressed in the following manner.

$$A + :B \longrightarrow A \leftarrow B$$

Examples of some acid-base reactions,

$$\text{Acid} + \text{Base} \longrightarrow \text{Complex}$$

$$H^+ + :OH^- \longrightarrow H \leftarrow OH$$

$$BF_3 + :NH_3 \longrightarrow H_3N \rightarrow BF_3$$

It is also interesting to notify that **all Bronsted-Lowry bases also act as Lewis bases** because of the presence of lone pairs on all the bases. But **all Bronsted-Lowry acids do not behave as Lewis acids** because of the absence of proton, as in BF_3 .

It acts as Lewis acid because of its electron deficiency but not a Bronsted acid due to absence of proton.

Limitations of Lewis Concept

(i) The strength of Lewis acids and bases is found to depend on the type of reaction, it is not possible to arrange them in any order of their relative strength.

(ii) It does not explain the behaviour of protonic acids such as HNO_3, HCl, H_2SO_4 etc.

(iii) Catalytic activity of Lewis acid can't be explained because the catalytic activity of many acids is due to their tendency to furnish H^+. Lewis acid does not do so.

Example 3 A reaction between ammonia and boron trifluoride is given below : $NH_3 + BF_3 \longrightarrow H_3N:BF_3$ Identify the acid and base in this reaction. Which theory explains it? What is the hybridisation of B and N in the reactants? **NCERT Exemplar**

Sol. Although BF_3 does not have a proton but acts as Lewis acid as it is an electron deficient compound. It reacts with NH_3 by accepting the lone pair of electrons from NH_3 and complete its octet. The reaction can be represented by

$$BF_3 + :NH_3 \longrightarrow BF_3 \leftarrow NH_3$$

Lewis electronic theory of acids and bases can explain it. Boron in BF_3 is sp^2 hybridised where N in NH_3 is sp^3 hybridised.

Example 4 Classify the following species into Lewis acids and Lewis bases and show how these act as such

(i) HO^- (ii) F^- (iii) H^+ (iv) BCl_3

NCERT Textbook

Sol. (i) Hydroxyl ion acts as a Lewis base because has a tendency to donate a lone pair of electrons (OH^-).

(ii) Flouride ion acts as a Lewis base because it has a tendency to donate anyone of its four lone pairs of electrons.

(iii) A proton behaves as a Lewis acid because it can accept a lone pair of electrons from bases like hydroxyl ion and fluoride ion.

(iv) BCl_3 behaves as a Lewis acid because it can accept a lone pair of electrons from species like ammonia or amine molecules.

Strengths of Acids and Bases

The strengths of acids and bases are as follows:

1. According to Arrhenius Concept

According to this concept the acids that dissociate almost completely into their constituent ions in an aqueous medium and thus, readily provide a proton are called **strong acids.** e.g. perchloric acid ($HClO_4$), hydrochloric acid (HCl), hydroiodic acid (HI), nitric acid (HNO_3), sulphuric acid (H_2SO_4) etc.

Similarly, the base that dissociate almost completely into their constituent ions in an aqueous medium and thus, readily provides a hydroxyl ion, are called **strong bases** e.g. alkali metal hydroxides (NaOH, LiOH, KOH, CsOH), barium hydroxide etc.

2. According to Bronsted- Lowry Concept

According to this concept, between the two acids, the acid having higher tendency to give a proton is termed as the **stronger acid** and in such a condition, the equilibrium reaction goes in the direction of weaker acid. e.g. in the reaction,

$$\underset{\text{Acid}}{HA(aq)} + \underset{\text{Base}}{H_2O(l)} \rightleftharpoons \underset{\text{Conjugate acid}}{H_3O^+(aq)} + \underset{\text{Conjugate base}}{A^-(aq)}$$

If HA is a stronger acid than H_3O^+ it readily gives its proton to H_2O and the reaction shifts in the forward direction i.e. the solution will mainly contain A^- and H_3O^+ ions. The H_3O^+ and A^- both are weaker as strong acid gives its proton to a strong base.

It means that **the conjugate base obtained from a strong acid is weak and that obtained from a weak acid is strong.** e.g. $ClO_4^-, Cl^-, Br^-, I^-, NO_3^-$, and HSO_4^- that are the conjugate base of strong acids are much weaker bases than water. Whereas, NO_2, F^-, CH_3COO^- the conjugate base of weak acids are stronger than water. Similarly, **a conjugate acid obtained from a strong base is weak and that obtained from a weak base is strong.** e.g. NH_2^-, O^{2-} and H^- being good acceptor are stronger base as compared to water.

Note Water soluble organic compounds such as phenophthalein and bromothymol blue are weak acids and have different colour in their acid (HIn) and conjugate base (In^-) forms, so these are widely used as indicators in acid- base titrations.

$$\underset{\text{Acid}}{HIn(aq)} + \underset{\text{Base}}{H_2O(l)} \rightleftharpoons \underset{\text{Conjugate acid}}{H_3O^+(aq)} + \underset{\text{Conjugate base}}{In^-(aq)}$$

Ionisation Constant of Water and Its Ionic Product

It is well known now that the water acts as an acid as well as base. In pure water, one water molecule acts as an acid by donating its proton while the other acts as a base by accepting the proton at the same time. Thus, the following equilibrium exists in the water.

$$\underset{\text{Acid}}{H_2O(l)} + \underset{\text{Base}}{H_2O(l)} \rightleftharpoons \underset{\text{Conjugate acid}}{H_3O^+(aq)} + \underset{\text{Conjugate base}}{OH^-(aq)}$$

Applying law of mass action, the dissociation constant,

$$K = \frac{[H_3O^+][OH^-]}{[H_2O]^2}$$

Since, water is a pure liquid, so its concentration remains constant. Hence, $[H_2O]^2$ is incorporated with K and a new constant, K_w is used in place of $K[H_2O]^2$.

i.e. $K_w = [H_3O^+][OH^-]$ or $K_w = [H^+][OH^-]$

$[\because [H_3O^+]$ and $[H^+]$ are same$]$

K_w is called the **ionic product of water.**

From the experiments, it is found that at 298 K,

$$[H^+] = [H_3O^+] = 1.0 \times 10^{-7} \text{ M}$$

Since, water produces $[H_3O^+]$ and $[OH^-]$ in equal numbers, so $[H_3O^+] = [OH^-] = 1.0 \times 10^{-7}$ M

On substituting the values, we get

$$K_w = (1 \times 10^{-7})^2 = 1 \times 10^{-14} \text{ M}^2 \quad \text{(at 298 K)}$$

- $K_w = [H^+][OH^-]$ (at 298 K)
- If $[H^+] = [OH^-]$, solution is neutral.
- If $[H^+] > [OH^-]$, solution is acidic. and if $[H^+] < [OH^-]$, solution is basic.

Example 5 At 363 K, pure water has $[H_3O^+] = 10^{-6}$ M. Calculate the value of K_w at this temperature.

Sol. Given, $[H_3O^+] = [OH^-] = 10^{-6}$ M

From $K_w = [H_3O^+][OH^-] = 10^{-12}$ M

Example 6 Calculate the value of H_3O^+ and OH^- ion concentrations at 25°C in

(i) 0.02 N HNO_3 solution (ii) 0.005 N KOH solution

Sol. (i) HNO_3 completely ionises as

$$HNO_3 + H_2O \longrightarrow H_3O^+ + NO_3^-$$

$\therefore [H_3O^+] = [HNO_3] = 0.02$ N (Given)

$= 0.02$ M $\quad (\because HNO_3$ is monobasic$)$

$= 2 \times 10^{-2}$ M

Now, as $[H_3O^+][OH^-] = K_w = 10^{-14}$

$$\therefore [OH^-] = \frac{K_w}{[H_3O^+]} = \frac{10^{-14}}{2 \times 10^{-2}} = 5 \times 10^{-13} \text{ M}$$

(ii) KOH completely ionises as $KOH \longrightarrow K^+ + OH^-$

$\therefore [OH^-] = [KOH] = 0.005$ N (Given)

$= 5 \times 10^{-3}$ M $\quad (\because$ KOH is monoacidic$)$

Now, as $[H_3O^+][OH^-] = K_w = 10^{-14}$

$$\therefore [H_3O^+] = \frac{K_w}{[OH^-]} = \frac{10^{-14}}{5 \times 10^{-3}} = 2 \times 10^{-12} \text{ M}$$

The pH Scale

In order to represent the hydronium ion concentration more conveniently in terms of molarity, Sorensen introduced a logarithmic scale, called the **pH scale**. The pH of a solution is defined as

"the negative logarithm to base 10 of the activity of hydrogen ion (a_{H^+}). If the solution is very dilute (i.e. < 0.01M), the activity of hydrogen ion becomes equal to its molarity, i.e.

$$a_{H^+} = \frac{[H^+]}{\text{mol L}^{-1}} \quad (a_{H^+} \text{ is a dimensionless quantity})$$

From the definition of pH,

$$pH = -\log a_{H^+} = (-\log H^+ / \text{mol L}^{-1})$$

or $$pH = -\log [H^+] = \log \frac{1}{H^+}$$

e.g. pH of acidic solution of HCl of concentration 10^{-2}M is 2, and a basic solution of NaOH having $[\overline{OH}] = 10^{-4}$ M and $[H_3O^+] = 10^{-10}$ M is 10.

Also, at 25°C the hydrogen ion concentration of water = 10^{-7} M. Hence, pH of pure water is given as

$$pH = -\log(10^{-7}) = 7$$

Acidic solution has pH < 7

Basic solution has pH > 7

Neutral solution has pH = 7

Since, pH scale is a logarithmic scale, so a decrease of a single pH unit corresponds to ten folds increase in acidic nature. That's why change in pH with temperature is often ignored.

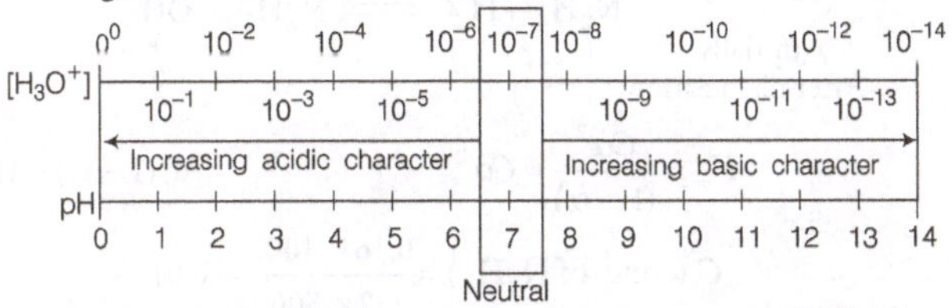

pH scale and $[H_3O^+]$ at room temperature (298 K)

Example 7 The concentration of hydrogen ion in a sample of soft drink is 3.8×10^{-3} M. What is its pH?

Sol. $pH = -\log[H^+] = -\log[3.8\times 10^{-3}]$ **NCERT Exemplar**

$$= -[\log[3.8] + \log[10^{-3}]]$$
$$= -[(0.58) + (-3.0)] = -[-2.42] = 2.42$$

Therefore, the pH of the soft drink is 2.42.

Measurement of pH

pH of a solution is generally measured by using pH paper, which gives different colours with the solutions of different pH. The pH in the range of 1-14 can be determined with an accuracy of ~0.5 by using pH papers. The pH paper consists of strips which show different colours with different pH value. The pH value can be as certain by matching the strip with a reference colour chart provided with it.

The more accurate value of pH is determined by using pH meter, a device that measures the pH dependent electrical potential of the test solution within 0.001 precision. Very small sized pH meters are also available in the market.

pH of some common substances are tabulated below:

The pH of Some Common Substances

Name of the fluid	pH	Name of the fluid	pH
		Black coffee	5.0
0.1 M NaOH solution	13	Tomato juice	~ 4.2
Lime water	10.5	Soft drinks and vinegar	~ 3.0
Milk of magnesia	10	Lemon juice	~2.2
Egg white, sea water	7.8	Gastric juice	~1.2
Human blood	7.4	1 M HCl solution	~0
Milk	6.8	Concentrated HCl	~1.0
Human saliva	6.4		

pOH value

As pH indicates H^+ ion concentration, pOH represents the OH^- ion concentration.

$$pOH = -\log_{10}[OH^-] = \log\frac{1}{[OH^-]}$$

As the solution becomes more basic, its $[OH^-]$ increases and its pOH decreases.

Example 8 Calculate the pH of N/1000 sodium hydroxide solution assumming complete ionisation ($K_w = 1.0\times 10^{-14}$).

Sol. NaOH completely ionises as $NaOH \longrightarrow Na^+ + OH^-$

$$\therefore [OH^-] = [NaOH] = \frac{N}{1000} = 10^{-3}\,N \Rightarrow 10^{-3}\,M$$

[Equivalent mass = Molecular mass in case of NaOH]

Now, as $[H_3O^+][OH^-] = 10^{-14}$

$$\because\ [H_3O^-] = \frac{10^{-14}}{[OH^-]} = \frac{10^{-14}}{[OH^-]} = \frac{10^{-14}}{10^{-3}} = 10^{-11}$$

$$\therefore\quad pH = -\log[H_3O^+] = -\log 10^{-11} = 11$$

Limitations of pH Scale

(i) pH values of the solutions do not give us immediate idea of the relative strengths of the solutions.

(ii) pH value of 1 N solution of strong acid is obtained zero. But in case when the concentration is 2 N, 3N, 10 N etc., the respective pH values are negative.

(iii) A solution of an acid having very low concentration say 10^{-8} N shows pH value less than 7 and not 8 shown by pH formula.

Example 9 Calculate the pH of 10^{-8} M HCl Solution.

Sol. $\because pH = -\log[H^+] = -\log 10^{-8} = 8$

But this is not true because an acidic solution cannot have pH greater than 7. In this condition, $[H^+]$ of water cannot be neglected.

Therefore, $[H^+]_{total} = [H^+]_{HCl} + [H^+]_{H_2O} = 10^{-8} + 10^{-7}$

$$= 10^{-8}(1+10) = 11\times 10^{-8}$$

Now from, $pH = -\log[H^+] = -\log(11\times 10^{-8})$

$$= -\log 11 - \log 10^{-8} = 6.958$$

Ionisation Constants of Weak Acids and Bases

The dissociation of weak acids or weak bases in water can be represented as an equilibrium process, e.g.

$$CH_3COOH + H_2O \rightleftharpoons CH_3COO^- + H_3O^+$$

Applying the law of chemical equilibrium, the expression for equilibrium constant will be

$$K = \frac{[A^-][H_3O^+]}{[HA][H_2O]}$$

The concentration of water is very large and remains almost constant. So, the equilibrium constant becomes

$$K_a = \frac{[CH_3COO^-][H_3O^+]}{[CH_3COOH]}$$

K_a is called **acid ionisation constant.** At a given temperature, K_a is a measure of the strength of the acid, i.e. larger the value of K_a, stronger is the acid. Similar, for a weak base, K_b is called **base ionisation constant.**

$$NH_4OH \rightleftharpoons NH_4^+ + OH^-$$

$$K_b = \frac{[NH_4^+][OH^-]}{[NH_4OH]}$$

Relation between K_a and K_b

K_a and K_b are related as :

or $K_b = \frac{K_w}{K_a}$ or $K_a = \frac{K_w}{K_b}$

$$K_a \times K_b = K_w$$

Example 10 The ionisation constant of phenol is 1.0×10^{-10}. What is the concentration of phenolate ion in 0.05 M solution of phenol? What will be its degree of ionisation if the solution is also 0.01 M in sodium phenolate? **NCERT Textbook**

Sol. The equation of the dissociation of phenol is as

$$C_6H_5OH \rightleftharpoons C_6H_5O^- + H^+ \text{ or } (H_3O^+)$$

By Ostwald dilution law, $[C_6H_5O^-] = [H_3O^+]$

$$= \sqrt{K_a \cdot C} = \sqrt{1.10 \times 10^{-1} \times 0.05} = 2.24 \times 10^{-6} \text{ M}$$

When mixture contains 0.05 M phenol and 0.01 M phenolate ion (from sodium phenolate) then

$$K_a = \frac{[C_6H_5O^-][H_3O^+]}{[C_6H_5OH]}$$

$$1.0 \times 10^{-10} = \frac{[0.01] \times [H_3O^+]}{[0.05]}$$

$$[H_3O^+] = \frac{0.05 \times 1.0 \times 10^{-10}}{0.01} = 5 \times 10^{-10} \text{ M}$$

$$[H_3O^+] = C \cdot \alpha = 5 \times 10^{-10}$$

or $\alpha = \frac{5 \times 10^{-10}}{C} = \frac{5 \times 10^{-10}}{0.05} = 1 \times 10^{-8}$

Example 11 0.16 g N_2H_4 is dissolved in water and the total volume is made upto 500 mL. Calculate the percentage of N_2H_4 that has reacted with water in this solution. K_b for N_2H_4 is 4.0×10^{-6} M.

Sol. N_2H_4 ionises in the following manner

	$N_2H_4 + H_2O \rightleftharpoons$	$N_2H_5^+$	$+ OH^-$
Initially	1	0	0
After dissociation	$1-\alpha$	α	α

$$K_b = \frac{C\alpha^2}{(1-\alpha)} = C\alpha^2 \quad [\text{if, } (1-\alpha) \approx 1]$$

$$C \text{ (conc. of } N_2H_4) = \frac{0.16 \times 1000}{32 \times 500} = 0.01$$

$$K_b = 4 \times 10^{-6} \text{ M}$$

$$\alpha = \sqrt{\frac{4 \times 10^{-6}}{0.01}} = 0.02 \text{ or } 2\%$$

pK Value

p stands for negative logarithm. Thus, p*K* is the negative logarithm of dissociation constant.

$\therefore$ $pK_a = -\log K_a$ and $pK_b = -\log K_b$

Weak acids have higher pK_a values. Similarly weak bases have higher pK_b values.

For any conjugate acid-base pair in aqueous solution, we know that,

$$K_a \times K_b = K_w \Rightarrow 1 \times 10^{-14} \text{ (at 298 K)}$$

Taking logarithm on both sides, we have

$$\log (K_a \times K_b) = \log (1 \times 10^{-14})$$

or $\log K_a + \log K_b = -14$

or $(-\log K_a) + (-\log K_b) = 14$

or $pK_a + pK_b = 14$ (at 298 K)

Example 12 The ionisation constant of HF is 3.2×10^{-4}. Calculate the degree of dissociation of HF in its 0.02 M solution. Calculate the concentration of all species present (H_3O^+, F^- and HF) in the solution and its pH. **NCERT Textbook**

Sol. ***Step* I** HF is a Bronsted acid and water is a base here.

***Step* II** The following proton transfer reactions are possible

(i) $HF + H_2O \rightleftharpoons H_3O^+ + F^-$; $K_a = 3.2 \times 10^{-4}$

(ii) $H_2O + H_2O \rightleftharpoons H_3O^+ + OH^-$; $K_w = 1.0 \times 10^{-14}$

***Step* III** As $K_a >> K_w$, $\therefore$ (i) is the principle reaction.

***Step* IV**

	$HF + H_2O \rightleftharpoons$	H_3O^+	$+ F^-$
Initial conc. (M)	0.02	0	0
Change in conc. to reach equilibrium (M)	$-0.02\,\alpha$	$+0.02\alpha$	$+0.02\,\alpha$
Equili. conc. (M)	$0.02 - 0.02\,\alpha$	$0.02\,\alpha$	$0.02\,\alpha$

Step **V** Equilibrium constant,

$$K_a = \frac{(0.02\,\alpha)^2}{(0.02 - 0.02\alpha)} = \frac{0.02\,\alpha^2}{(1-\alpha)} = 3.2\times 10^{-4}$$

or $\alpha^2 + 1.6\times 10^{-2}\,\alpha - 1.6\times 10^{-2} = 0 \quad [\because 1 >>> \alpha]$

using, $x = \dfrac{-b \pm \sqrt{b^2 - 4ac}}{2a}$

we get, $\alpha = +0.12$ and -0.12

The negative root is not acceptable and hence, $\alpha = 0.12$

Step **VI** $\therefore [H_3O^+] = [F^-] = C\alpha = 0.02\times 0.12 = 2.4\times 10^{-3}$ M

$[HF] = C(1-\alpha) = 0.02\,(1 - 0.12) = 17.6\times 10^{-3}$ M

*Step***VII** $pH = -\log[H^+] = -\log(2.4\times 10^{-3}) = 2.62$

Example 13 Calculate the pH of 0.08 M solution of hypochlorous acid, HOCl. The ionisation constant of the acid is 2.5×10^{-5}. Determine the percent dissociation of HOCl. **NCERT Textbook**

Sol. The ionisation equation of HOCl is as follows :

	$HOCl(aq)$ + $H_2O(l)$	$\rightleftharpoons H_3O^+(aq)$	+ $ClO^-(aq)$
Initial conc. (M)	0.08	0	0
Change in conc. to reach equili. (M)	$-x$	$+x$	$+x$
Equili conc. (M)	$0.08 - x$	x	x

$$\therefore \quad K_a = \frac{[H_3O^+][ClO^-]}{[HOCl]} = \frac{x^2}{(0.08 - x)}$$

$\because \quad x << 0.08,$

$\therefore \quad 0.08 - x \simeq 0.08$

$x^2 = 2.0\times 10^{-6}$ or $x = 1.41\times 10^{-3}$

$[H^+] = 1.41\times 10^{-3}$ M

$$\text{Per cent dissociation} = \frac{[HOCl]_{dissociated}}{[HOCl]_{initial}}\times 100$$

$$= \frac{1.41\times 10^{-3}}{0.08} = 1.76\%$$

$pH = -\log[H^+] = -\log(1.41\times 10^{-3}) = 2.85$

Di- and Polybasic Acids, Di- and Polyacidic Bases

Acids having more than one ionisable proton per molecule of acids are known as **polybasic** or **polyprotic acids**, e.g. oxalic acid (HOOC—COOH), sulphuric acid (H_2SO_4), phosphoric acid (H_3PO_4) etc.

The ionisation reactions for a dibasic acid, H_2X *involve following two steps as shown below.*

$$H_2X(aq) \rightleftharpoons H^{\oplus}(aq) + HX^{\ominus}(aq)$$

$$HX^{\ominus}(aq) \rightleftharpoons H^{\oplus}(aq) + X^{2-}(aq)$$

The equilibrium constants for the above two reaction are as follows:

$$K_{a_1} = \frac{[H^{\oplus}][HX^{\ominus}]}{[H_2X]} \text{ and } K_{a_2} = \frac{[H^{\oplus}][X^{2-}]}{[HX^{\ominus}]}$$

(K_{a_1} and K_{a_2} are the first and second ionisation constants, respectively, of the acid H_2X).

Thus, the solution of a diprotic acid contains H_2X, HX^- and X^{2-}. The H^+ ions mainly obtained from the first ionisation step. Similarly, in case of a tribasic acids such as H_3PO_4, there are three ionisation constants. It is found that K_{a_1} of polyprotic acid is greater than K_{a_2} or K_{a_3} (i.e. $K_{a_1} > K_{a_2} > K_{a_3}$), because it is more difficult to remove a positively charged proton from a negative ion due to electrostatic forces. Similarly, it is more difficult to remove a proton from a doubly charged anion as compared to single charged anion.

Example 14 K_1 and K_2 for dissociation of H_2S are 4×10^{-3} and 1×10^{-5}. Calculate sulphide ion concentration in 0.1 M H_2S Solution.

Sol. The first step of the dissociation of H_2S is

$$H_2S \rightleftharpoons H^{\oplus} + HS^{\ominus}$$

$$K_1 = \frac{[H^{\oplus}][HS^{\ominus}]}{[H_2S]} = 4\times 10^{-3}$$

$\because \quad [H^{\oplus}] = C\alpha, [HS^{\ominus}] = C\alpha, [H_2S] = C(1-\alpha)$

$$\therefore \quad 4\times 10^{-3} = \frac{C\alpha\cdot C\alpha}{C(1-\alpha)} = \frac{C\alpha^2}{(1-\alpha)}$$

$$4\times 10^{-3} = \frac{0.1\times\alpha^2}{(1-\alpha)} \quad (1-\alpha \text{ should not be neglected})$$

or $\quad \alpha = 0.18,$

$\therefore \quad [H^{\oplus}] = C\alpha = 0.1\times 0.18 = 0.018$ M

$[HS^{\ominus}] = C\alpha = 0.1\times 0.18 = 0.018$ M

$[H_2S] = C(1-\alpha) = 0.1\,(1 - 0.18) = 0.082$ M

Now, $HS^{\ominus}$ further dissociates to $H^{\oplus}$ and S^{2-}

$C_1 = [HS^{\ominus}] = 0.018$ M

	$HS^{\ominus}$	$\rightleftharpoons H^{\oplus}$	+ S^{2-}
	1	0	0
	$(1-\alpha_1)$	α_1	α_1

$$\therefore \quad K_2 = 1\times 10^{-5} = \frac{[H^{\oplus}][S^{2-}]}{[HS^{\ominus}]}$$

Because $[H^{\oplus}]$ already in solution = 0.018 and thus, dissociation of $HS^{\ominus}$ further suppresses due to common ion effect and $1-\alpha \approx 1$.

$$\therefore \quad 1\times 10^{-5} = \frac{0.018\times C_1\alpha_1}{C_1(1-\alpha_1)} = 0.018\times\alpha_1$$

$$\therefore \quad \alpha_1 = \frac{1\times 10^{-5}}{0.018} = 5.55\times 10^{-4}$$

$$\therefore \quad [S^{2-}] = C_1\alpha_1 = 0.018\times 5.55\times 10^{-4} = 0.099\times 10^{-4}$$

Common Ion Effect in the Ionisation of Acids and Bases

The degree of dissociation of an electrolyte or weak acid or weak base is suppressed by the addition of another electrolyte containing a common ion. This phenomenon is termed as **common ion effect.** e.g. HAC is a weak acid and ionises in the following manner.

$$HAC\,(aq) \rightleftharpoons H^+(aq) + AC^-(aq);\; K_a = \frac{[H^+][AC^-]}{[HAC]}$$

If an another electrolyte that furnish either H^+ or AC^- is added to the above equilibrium, it will increase the concentration of H^+ or AC^- ions and in order to keep K_a constant, the concentration of HAC must increase, i.e. the equilibrium shifts towards undissociated acid.

Example 15 Calculate the pH of a 0.10M ammonia solution. Also, calculate the pH when 50.0 mL of this solution has treated with 25.0 mL of 0.10M HCl. The dissociation constant of ammonia, $K_b = 1.77 \times 10^{-5}$.

Sol. $NH_3 + H_2O \rightleftharpoons NH_4^+ + OH^-$

$$K_b = [NH_4^+]\,[OH^-]/[NH_3] = 1.77 \times 10^{-5}$$

Before neutralisation.

or $\quad K_b = \dfrac{x.x}{(0.10 - x)}$

$(\because [NH_4^+] = [OH^-] = x)$

$[NH_3] = 0.10 - x \approx 0.10$

$x^2/0.10 = 1.77 \times 10^{-5}$

Thus, $\quad x = 1.33 \times 10^{-3} = [OH^-]$

Therefore, $[H^+] = K_w/[OH^-] = 10^{-14}/(1.33 \times 10^{-3})$

$= 7.51 \times 10^{-12}$

$pH = -\log(7.5 \times 10^{-12}) = 11.12$

On addition of 25 mL of 0.1 M HCl solution (i.e. 2.5 mol of HCl) to 50 mL of 0.1 M ammonia solution (i.e. 5 mol of NH_3) 2.5 mmol of ammonia molecules get neutralised the resulting 75 mL solution contains the remaining unneutralised 2.5 m mol of NH_3 molecules and 2.5 mmol of NH_4^+.

	NH_3	+ HCl	$\longrightarrow$ NH_4^+	+ Cl^-
Initially	2.5	2.5	0	0
At equilibrium	0	0	2.5	2.5

The resulting 75 mL of solution contains 2.5 mmol of NH_4^+ ions. (i.e. 0.033 M) and 2.5 mmol (i.e. 0.33 M) of unneutralised NH_3 molecules. This NH_3 exists in the following equilibrium.

$$\underset{0.033\,M - y}{NH_4OH} \rightleftharpoons \underset{y}{NH_4^+} + \underset{y}{OH^-}$$

where, $y = [OH^-] = [NH_4^+]$

The final 75 mL solution after neutralisation already contains 2.5 m mol NH_4^+ ions (i.e. 0.033 M), thus total concentration of NH_4^+ ions is given as :

$$[NH_4^+] = 0.033 + yM$$

As y is small, $[NH_4OH] \approx 0.033$ M and $[NH_4^+] \approx 0.033$ M.

We know, $K_b = \dfrac{[NH_4^+][OH^-]}{[NH_4OH]} \Rightarrow \dfrac{y\,(0.033)}{(0.033)} = 1.77 \times 10^{-5}$ M

Thus, $\quad y = 1.77 \times 10^{-5} = [OH^-]$

$[H^+] = \dfrac{10^{-14}}{1.77 \times 10^{-5}} = 0.56 \times 10^{-9}$

Hence, $\quad pH = 9.25$

Topic Practice 2

Very Short Answer Type Questions

1 Mark

1 Fill in the Blanks

(i) The degree of ionisation of a compound depends nature of .... molecules.

(ii) Electron deficient species behaves as ....

(iii) Addition of NH_4Cl to NH_4OH decreases the ionisation of NH_4Cl due to ....

2 Objective Type Questions

(i) According to Arrhenius theory, acids are substances that dissociate in water to give X ions and bases are substances that produce Y ions. X and Y respectively are

(a) hydronilium and hydroxyl
(b) hydroxyl and hydrogen
(c) hydrogen and hydroxyl
(d) hydroxyl and hydronium

(ii) Choose the correct one, which is the weakest acid.

(a) HCl (b) HF
(c) H_2SO_4 (d) HNO_3

(iii) In the reaction,

Adds proton (from NH_3 to H_2O)

$$\underset{X}{NH_3(aq)} + \underset{Y}{H_2O(l)} \rightleftharpoons \underset{\text{Conjugate acid}}{NH_4^+(aq)} + \underset{\text{Conjugate base}}{\bar{O}H(aq)}$$

Loses proton (from H_2O to $\bar{O}H$)

X and Y respectively are

(a) neutral and acid (b) acid and base
(c) base and acid (d) base and neutral

3 Match the Column I with Column II and choose the correct option using the codes given below:

Column I	Column II
A. Acidic oxide	(i) H_2SO_4
B. Basic oxide	(ii) SO_3
C. Strong electrolyte	(iii) HCN
D. Weak electrolyte	(iv) CaO

Codes

	A	B	C	D
(a)	(ii)	(iv)	(iii)	(i)
(b)	(i)	(iii)	(iv)	(ii)
(c)	(ii)	(iv)	(i)	(iii)
(d)	(i)	(ii)	(iii)	(iv)

4 Why solution of sugar in water does not conduct electricity whereas that of common salt in water does?

5 What will be the conjugate bases for the following Bronsted acids HF, H_2SO_4 and H_2CO_3? **NCERT Textbook**

6 Write the conjugate acids for the following Bronsted bases NH_2^-, NH_3 and $HCOO^-$.

7 Why is ammonia termed as a base though it does not contain OH^- ions?

8 Which of the following are Lewis acids?
H_2O, BF_3, H^+, NH_4^+ **NCERT Textbook**

9 BF_3 does not have proton but still acts as an acid and reacts with $\ddot{N}H_3$. Why is it so? What type of bond is formed between the two? **NCERT Exemplar**

10 K_b for NH_4OH is 1.8×10^{-5} and for CH_3NH_2 is 4.4×10^{-4}. Which of them is strongest base and why?

11 What happens to ionic product of water if some acid is added to it ?

12 pK_a value of acids *A*, *B*, *C*, *D* are 1.5, 3.5, 2.0 and 5.0. Which of them is strongest acid ?

13 How does common ion effect affects the solubility of electrolyte?

Short Answer Type I Questions

(2 Marks)

14 The aqueous solution of sugar does not conduct electricity. However, when sodium chloride is added to water, it conducts electricity. How will you explain this statement on the basis of ionisation and how is it affected by concentration of sodium chloride? **NCERT Exemplar**

15 Glycine is an α-amino acid. It exists in the form of Zwitter ion as $^+NH_3CH_2COO^-$.

Write the formula of its (i) conjugate acid (ii) conjugate base.

16 Ionisation constant of a weak base *M*OH ,is given by the expression $K_b = \frac{[M^+][OH^-]}{[MOH]}$

Values of ionisation constant of some weak bases at a particular temperature are given below.

Base	Dimethyl amine	Urea	Pyridine	Ammonia
K_b	5.4×10^{-4}	1.3×10^{-14}	1.77×10^{-9}	1.77×10^{-5}

Arrange the bases in decreasing order of the extent of their ionisation at equilibrium. Which of the above base is the strongest? **NCERT Exemplar**

17 Calculate:

(i) Dissociation constant of conjugate base of HF, $K_a = 6.8 \times 10^{-4}$.

(ii) Dissociation constant of conjugate acid of CO_3^{2-}, $K_b = 2.1 \times 10^{-4}$.

18 The concentration of hydrogen ion in a sample of soft drink is 3.8×10^{-3} M. What is its pH?

19 The pH of a sample of vinegar is 3.76. Calculate the concentration of hydrogen ion in it. **NCERT Textbook**

20 Urine has a pH of 6.0. If a patient eliminates 1300 mL of urine per day, how many gram equivalents of the acid he eliminates per day ?

21 Calculate the pH of a solution formed by mixing equal volumes of two solutions, *A* and *B* of a strong acid having pH = 6 and pH = 4 respectively.

22 pH of a solution of a strong acid is 5.0. What will be the pH of the solution obtained after diluting the given solution 100 times? **NCERT Exemplar**

23 One millilitre solution of 0.01 M HCl is added to 1 L of sodium chloride solution. What will be the pH of the resulting solutions?

24 Calculate the pH of the solution, if 2g of NaOH is dissolved in water to make 1 L solution.

25 Ionic product of water at 310 K is 2.7×10^{-14}. What is the pH of neutral water at this temperature?

26 pH of 0.08 mol dm^{-3} HOCl solution is 2.85. Calculate its ionisation constant.

27 Calculate the pH of a solution containing 0.1 M acetic acid and 0.1 M benzoic acid, K_a for CH_3COOH and C_6H_5COOH are 1.8×10^{-5} and 6.5×10^{-5} respectively.

28 (i) Sulphuric acid is a very strong acid, yet it can also act as base in some reactions. Explain how?
(ii) All Bronsted acids are not Lewis acids. Explain.

29 Neutral solutions have pH = 7 at 298 K. A sample of pure water is found to have pH < 7. Does it mean that it is acidic ? Explain.

Short Answer Type II Questions

3 Marks

30 What do you meant by the conjugate acid-base pair? Find the conjugate acid/base for the following species.
$HNO_2, CN^-, HClO_4, F^-, OH^-, CO_3^{2-}$ and S^{2-}
NCERT Textbook

31 Classify the following species into Lewis acids and Lewis bases and show how these act as Lewis acid/base?
(i) OH^- (ii) F^- (iii) H^+ (iv) BCl_3

32 The ionisation constant of HF, HCOOH and HCN at 298 K are 6.8×10^{-4}, 1.8×10^{-4} and 4.8×10^{-9} respectively. Calculate the ionisation constants of the corresponding conjugate base.

33 The average concentration of SO_2 in atmosphere over a city on a certain day is 10 ppm, when the average temperature is 298 K. Given that the solubility of SO_2 in water at 298 K is 1.3653 mol/L and the pK_a of H_2SO_3 is 1.92, estimate the pH of acid rain on that day.

34 The pH of 0.005 M codeine ($C_{18}H_{21}NO_3$) solution is 9.95. Calculate its ionisation constant and pK_b.

35 It has been found that the pH of a 0.01 M solution of an organic acid is 4.15. Calculate the concentration of the anion, the ionisation constant of the acid and its pK_a. **NCERT Textbook**

36 If 0.561 g of KOH is dissolved in water to give 200 mL of solution at 298 K, calculate the concentrations of potassium, hydrogen and hydroxyl ions. What is its pH?

37 Calculate the pH of the resultant mixtures
(i) 10 mL of 0.2 M $Ca(OH)_2$ + 25 mL of 0.1 M HCl
(ii) 10 mL of 0.01 M H_2SO_4 + 10 mL of 0.01 M $Ca(OH)_2$
(iii) 10 mL of 0.1 M H_2SO_4 + 10 mL of 0.1 M KOH
NCERT Textbook

38 The ionisation constant of acetic acid is 1.74×10^{-5}. Calculate the degree of dissociation of acetic acid in its 0.05 M solution. Calculate the concentration of acetate ion in the solution and its pH.

39 The degree of ionisation of a 0.1 M bromoacetic acid solution is 0.132. Calculate the pH of the solution and the pK_a of bromoacetic acid.

40 The pH of 0.1M solution of cyanic acid (HCNO) is 2.34. Calculate the ionisation constant of the acid and its degree of ionisation in the solution.

41 The ionisation constant of dimethylamine is 5.4×10^{-4}. Calculate its degree of ionisation in its 0.02 M solution. What percentage of dimethylamine is ionised if the solution is also 0.1 M in NaOH? **NCERT Textbook**

Long Answer Type Questions

5 Marks

42. The pH of milk, black coffee, tomato juice, lemon juice and egg white are 6.8, 5.0, 4.2, 2.2 and 7.8 respectively. Calculate the corresponding hydrogen ion concentration in each.
NCERT Textbook

43. Calculate the pH of the following solutions:
(i) 2 g of TlOH dissolved in water to give 2 L of solution.
(ii) 0.3 g of $Ca(OH)_2$ dissolved in water to give 500 mL solution.
(iii) 0.3 g of NaOH dissolved in water to give 200 mL of solution.
(iv) 1 mL of 13.6 M HCl is diluted with water to give 1 L of solution. **NCERT Textbook**

44 Calculate the degree of ionisation of 0.05 M acetic acid if its pK_a value is 4.74. How is the degree of dissociation affected when its solution also contains (i) 0.01 M (ii) 0.1 M in HCl?
NCERT Textbook

45 What is the pH of 0.001 M aniline solution? The ionisation constant of aniline is 4.27×10^{-10}. Calculate the degree of ionisation of aniline in the solution. Also calculate the ionisation constant of the conjugate acid of aniline. **NCERT Textbook**

46. The first ionisation constant of H_2S is 9.1×10^{-8}. Calculate the concentration of HS^- ion in its 0.1 M solution. How will this concentration be affected if the solution is 0.1 M in HCl also? If the second dissociation constant of H_2S is 1.2×10^{-13}, calculate the concentration of S^{2-} under both conditions.

47. The ionisation constant of propanoic acid is 1.32×10^{-5}. Calculate the degree of ionisation of the acid in its 0.05 M solution and also its pH. What will be its degree of ionisation if the solution is 0.01 M in HCl also? **NCERT Textbook**

Hints & Solutions

1. (i) solute (ii) Lewis acid (iii) common-ion effect
2. (i) (c), (ii) (b), (iii) (c)
3. (c) A → (ii), B → (iv), C → (i), D → (iii)
4. Common salt (NaCl) is an electrolyte which in the aqueous solution gives Na^+ and Cl^- ions. Hence, it conducts electricity. Sugar is sucrose ($C_{12}H_{22}O_{11}$) which is a non-electrolyte and does not give ions in the solution. Hence, it does not conduct electricity.
5. Acid $\rightleftharpoons$ Conjugate base + H^+
The conjugate bases-should have one proton less in each case and therefore the corresponding conjugate bases are F^-, HSO_4^- and HCO_3^- respectively.
6. Base + $H^+ \rightleftharpoons$ Conjugate acid
The conjugate acid should have one extra proton in each case and therefore the corresponding conjugate acid are NH_3, NH_4^+ and HCOOH respectively.
7. The basic nature of ammonia is due to its tendency to donate electron pair. Therefore, it is a Lewis base.
8. Lewis acids have a tendency to accept electrons. Electron deficient or positively charged species have such tendency.
BF_3, H^+ and NH_4^+ act as Lewis acids.
9. BF_3 is an electron deficient compound and hence acts as Lewis acid. $\ddot{N}H_3$ has one lone pair which it can donate to BF_3 and form a coordinate bond. Hence, NH_3 acts as a Lewis base.

$$H_3N\!:\longrightarrow BF_3$$
Coordinate bond

10. CH_3NH_2 is strongest base because it has high value of base dissociation constant.
11. Ionic product will remain unchanged.
12. Acid *A* with $pK_a = 1.5$ is strongest acid
($\because$ lower the value of pK_a stronger will be the acid).
13. Solubility of electroyte decreases due to common-ion effect.
14. Explanation for the given statement on the basis of ionisation and effect upon the concentration of sodium chloride is given below:
(i) Sugar being a non-electrolyte does not ionise in water whereas NaCl ionises completely in water and produces Na^+ and Cl^- ion which help in the conduction of electricity. [1]
(ii) When concentration of NaCl is increased, more Na^+ and Cl^- ions will be produced. Hence, conductance or conductivity of the solution increases. [1]
15. Conjugate acid $^+NH_3CH_2COOH$. [1]
Conjugate base $NH_2CH_2COO^-$. [1]
16. Greater the ionisation constant (K_b) of a base, greater is its ionisation. The decreasing order of the extent of ionisation at equilibrium is : Dimethylamine > Urea > pyridine > ammonia.
Hence, dimethyl amine is the strongest base. [2]
17. (i) $HF \rightleftharpoons H^+ + F^-$

$$K_a\,(HF)\times K_b\,(F^-) = 1.0\times 10^{-14}$$

$$K_b(F^-) = \frac{1.0\times 10^{-14}}{6.8\times 10^{-4}} = 1.47\times 10^{-11}$$ [1]

(ii) $CO_3^{2-} + H^+ \rightleftharpoons HCO_3^-$

$$K_b(CO_3^{2-})\times K_a(HCO_3^-) = 1\times 10^{-14}$$

$$K_a(HCO_3^-) = \frac{1\times 10^{-14}}{2.1\times 10^{-4}} = 4.76\times 10^{-11}$$ [1]

18. $\because$ $pH = -\log[H^+] = -\log[3.8\times 10^{-3}]$ [1]
$\therefore$ $pH = -0.57 + 3 = 2.43$ [1]
19. $pH = -\log[H^+] = 3.76$
$\log[H^+] = -3.76$ [1]
[Before taking antilog add −1 in characteristic (−3) and +1 in mantissa (0.76), i.e. $-3.76 - 1 + 1 = \bar{4}.24$]
$\log[H^+] = \bar{4}.24$ or $[H^+]$ = antilog $\bar{4}.24$
$[H^+]$ = antilog(3.76) = 1.738×10^{-4} M [1]
20. $\because$ pH = 6.0
$\therefore$ $[H_3O^+] = 10^{-6}$ M,
i.e. $[Acid] = 10^{-6}\,M = 10^{-6}\,N$ [1]
Thus, 1000 mL (1 L) of the urine contain acid $= 10^{-6}$ g eq.
$\therefore$ 1300 mL (1.3 L) of the urine will contain acid $= 1.3\times 10^{-6}$ g eq. [1]

21. Since, pH of solution $A = 6$. Hence, $[H^+] = 10^{-6}$ mol L^{-1}

pH of solution $B = 4$. Hence, $[H^+] = 10^{-4}$ mol L^{-1}

On mixing 1 L of each solution, molar concentration of total $[H^+]$ is halved. [1]

Total, $[H^+] = \dfrac{10^{-6} + 10^{-4}}{2}$ mol L^{-1}

or $[H^+] = 5.05 \times 10^{-5}$ mol L^{-1}

$\because$ $pH = -\log [H^+]$

$\therefore$ $pH = -\log (5.0 \times 10^{-5}) = 4.2967 \approx 4.3$ [1]

22. Since, pH = 5, hence, $[H^+] = 10^{-5}$ mol L^{-1}

On diluting the solution 100 times,

$[H^+] = \dfrac{10^{-5}}{100} = 10^{-7}$ mol L^{-1} [1]

Total H^+ ion concentration = H^+ ions from acid + H^+ ion from water

i.e. $[H^+] = 10^{-7} + 10^{-7} = 2 \times 10^{-7}$ M

$pH = -\log [2 \times 10^{-7}] = 6.699$ [1]

23. NaCl is neutral, it simply dilutes the HCl solution from 1 mL to 1000 mL so that

$[H^+] = \dfrac{0.01}{1000} = 10^{-5}$ M [1]

$pH = -\log (10^{-5}) = 5$ [1]

24. Weight of NaOH dissolved = 2g

$\therefore$ Equivalent of NaOH dissolved $= \dfrac{2}{40}$

$\therefore$ $N_{NaOH} = \dfrac{2}{40} = 0.05$

$\therefore$ $[OH^-] = 0.05 = 5 \times 10^{-2}$

or $pOH = -\log[OH^-] = -\log(5 \times 10^{-2})$

$= 1.3010$ (1)

$pH + pOH = 14$

$\therefore$ $pH = 14 - pOH$

$= 14 - 1.3010 = 12.699$ (1)

25. $K_w = [H_3O^+] \cdot [OH^-] = 2.7 \times 10^{-14}$ at 310 K

$H_2O + H_2O \rightleftharpoons [H_3O^+][OH^-]$

As $[H_3O^+] = [OH^-]$

$\therefore$ $K_w = [H_3O^+]^2$ or $\sqrt{K_w} = [H_3O^+]$

Thus, $[H_3O^+] = \sqrt{2.7 \times 10^{-14}} = 1.643 \times 10^{-7}$ M [1]

$pH = -\log [H_3O^+] = -\log 1.643 \times 10^{-7}$

$pH = 7 + (-0.2156) = 6.7844$ [1]

26. To solve this problem, we use two steps.

Step **I** Find out the concentration of hydrogen ion $[H^+]$ through the formula $-pH = \log [H^+]$.

Step **II** Afterward, calculate the K_a of HOCl which is weak monobasic acid by using the formula $K_a = \dfrac{[H^+]^2}{C}$. where, C is concentration of the solution.

pH of HOCl = 2.85

But, $-pH = \log [H^+]$;

$\therefore$ $-2.85 = \log [H^+]$

$\Rightarrow$ $[H^+] = 1.413 \times 10^{-3}$ [1]

For weak monobasic acid $[H^+] = \sqrt{K_a \times C}$

$\Rightarrow$ $K_a = \dfrac{[H^+]^2}{C} = \dfrac{(1.413 \times 10^{-3})^2}{0.08}$

$= 24.957 \times 10^{-6} = 2.4957 \times 10^{-5}$ [1]

27. $[H_3O^+] = \sqrt{K_{a_1} C_1 + K_{a_2} C_2}$

$= \sqrt{(1.8 \times 10^{-5})(0.1) + (6.5 \times 10^{-5})(0.1)}$

$= \sqrt{1.8 \times 10^{-6} + 6.5 \times 10^{-6}}$

$= \sqrt{8.3 \times 10^{-6}} = 2.88 \times 10^{-3}$ M [1]

$pH = -\log [H_3O^+] = -\log (2.88 \times 10^{-3})$

$= 3 - 0.4594 = 2.5406$ [1]

28. (i) Sulphuric acid (H_2SO_4) is weaker acid with respect to perchloric acid ($HClO_4$). H_2SO_4 can take up a proton from $HClO_4$ to form $H_3SO_4^+$. Hence, it acts as a base in this reaction. [1]

(ii) Bronsted acids can donate H^+ easily but they may not be able to accept electrons, e.g. HCl, H_2SO_4, HNO_3 etc. Therefore, all Bronsted acids are not Lewis acids. [1]

29. pH < 7 for pure H_2O shows that water is at a temperature higher than 298 K. It is neutral at all temperatures. At higher temperature, H_2O dissociates more to give large concentrations of H^+ ions and OH^- ions. Hence, pH < 7. However, $[H^+] = [OH^-]$ at all temperatures. [2]

30. Acid $- H^+ \longrightarrow$ Conjugate base

Base $+ H^+ \longrightarrow$ Conjugate acid

An acid-base pair differ by a proton is known as conjugate acid-base pair. Conjugate bases for HNO_2, $HClO_4$ and OH^- are NO_2^-, ClO_4^- and O^{2-} respectively, conjugate acids for CN^-, F^-, OH^-, CO_3^{2-} and S^{2-} are HCN, HF, H_2O, HCO_3^- and HS^- respectively. [3]

31. Lewis acids have a tendency to accept electrons and Lewis bases have a tendency to donate electrons.

OH^- and F^- are electron rich species and can donate electron pair. Hence, these act as Lewis base.

$:\ddot{O}H^- + H^+ \longrightarrow H_2O$

$:\ddot{F}:^- + BF_3 \longrightarrow [BF_4^-]$

$[1\frac{1}{2}]$

H^+ and BCl_3 are electron deficient species and can accept electron pair. Hence, these act as Lewis acid.

$$H_3N\!:\; + H^+ \longrightarrow NH_4^+$$

$$H_3N\!:\; + BCl_3 \longrightarrow H_3N \rightarrow BCl_3$$ [1 ½]

32. To find K_b of a conjugate base, use the formula

$$K_a \cdot K_b = K_w = 1\times 10^{-14}.$$

Conjugate bases of HF, HCOOH and HCN are F^-, $HCOO^-$ and CN^- respectively.

If K_a is the ionisation constant of a weak acid (HA) and K_b is the ionisation constant of its conjugate base (A^-) then $K_a \cdot K_b = K_w$

$$K_b\,(F^-) = \frac{K_w}{K_a\,(HF)} = \frac{1\times 10^{-14}}{6.8\times 10^{-4}} = 1.47\times 10^{-11}$$ [1]

$$K_b\,(HCOO^-) = \frac{K_w}{K_a\,(HCOOH)} = \frac{1\times 10^{-14}}{1.8\times 10^{-4}}$$

$$= 5.56\times 10^{-11}$$ [1]

$$K_b\,(CN^-) = \frac{K_w}{K_a\,(HCN)} = \frac{1\times 10^{-14}}{4.8\times 10^{-9}} = 2.08\times 10^{-6}$$ [1]

33. Amount of SO_2 (in atmosphere) $= 10$ ppm $= \frac{10}{10^6} = 10^{-5}$

Molar conc. of SO_2 in pressure of water

$=$ amount of $SO_2 \times$ solubility of SO_2 in water

H_2SO_3 dissociates as $= 1.3653\times 10^{-5}$

	$H_2SO_3 \rightleftharpoons$	H^+ +	HSO_3^-
Initial conc.	1.3653×10^{-5}	0	0
Molar conc. of equiv.	$(1.3653\times 10^{-5} - x)$	x	x

$$K_a = \frac{x^2}{(1.3653\times 10^{-5} - x)}$$

$\because$ $pK_a = 1.92$ [1]

$\therefore$ $-\log K_a = 1.92$

or $K_a = 1.2\times 10^{-2}$

Substituting $1.2\times 10^{-2} = \frac{x^2}{(1.3653\times 10^{-5} - x)}$

or $x^2 = 1.2\times 10^{-2}\,(1.3653\times 10^{-5} - x)$ [1]

On solving, we get $x = 1.3664\times 10^{-5}$

$\therefore$ $pH = -\log(1.364\times 10^{-5}) = 4.865$ [1]

34. • As codeine is a weak base, its ionisation constant is related to OH^- as $K_b = \frac{[OH^-]^2}{[Codeine]}$

• Calculate $[OH^-]$ from pOH with the help of the formula

$$pOH = -\log[OH^-]$$

$$pK_b = -\log K_b$$

$$\text{Codeine}\,(C_{18}H_{21}NO_3) + H_2O \rightleftharpoons \text{Codeine}\,H^+ + OH^+$$

$\because$ $pH = 9.95$

$\therefore$ $pOH = 14 - 9.95 = 4.05$

Again, from $pOH = -\log[OH^-]$

$\log[OH^-] = -4.05 = \bar{5}.95$

$[OH^-] = \text{antilog}\,\bar{5}.95 = 8.913\times 10^{-5}$

$$K_b = \frac{[\text{codeine}\,H^+]\,[OH^-]}{[\text{codeine}]} = \frac{[OH^-]^2}{[\text{codeine}]}$$ [1]

(because $[\text{codeine}\,H^+] = [OH^-]$)

$$K_b = \frac{(8.913\times 10^{-5})^2}{0.005} = 1.588\times 10^{-6}$$

From, $pK_b = -\log[K_b] = -\log[1.588\times 10^{-6}]$ [1]

$pK_b = 6 + (-0.2009) = 5.7991 \approx 5.80$ [1]

35. • Organic acids are weak acids, so dissociate as $HA \rightleftharpoons H^+ + A^-$ and their K_a is calculated as,

$$K_a = \frac{[H^+][A^-]}{[HA]}.$$

• To calculate K_a, $[H^+]$ and $[A^-]$ are required. Calculate $[H^+]$ by using the formula, $pH = -\log[H^+]$ and calculate $[A^-]$ by using the equation $HA \rightleftharpoons H^+ + A^-$.

• Then, calculate K_a by using the formula,

$$K_a = \frac{[H^+][A^-]}{[HA]}.$$

• Calculate pK_a by using the formula $pK_a = -\log K_a$.

$$HA \rightleftharpoons H^+ + A^-$$

$pH = -\log[H^+] = 4.15$

$\log[H^+] = -4.15$

$\log[H^+] = \bar{5}.85$ or $[H^+] = \text{antilog}\,\bar{5}.85 = 7.079\times 10^{-5}$

$[H^+] = [A^-] = 7.079\times 10^{-5}$ M [1]

Thus, $K_a = \frac{[H^+]\,[A^-]}{[HA]} = \frac{(7.079\times 10^{-5})\,(7.079\times 10^{-5})}{0.01}$

$= 5011.22\times 10^{-10} = 5.0\times 10^{-7}$ [1]

From, $pK_a = -\log K_a = -\log[5.0\times 10^{-7}]$

$= -0.699 + 7 = 6.301$ [1]

36. Molar mass of KOH $= 39 + 16 + 1 = 56\text{ g mol}^{-1}$

Molarity of KOH,

$$M = \frac{\text{mass of KOH (g)}\times 1000}{\text{molar mass (KOH)}\times\text{volume of solution (in mL)}}$$

$$\Rightarrow M = \frac{0.561\times 1000}{56\times 200} = 0.05 \;\Rightarrow M = 0.05\text{ mol L}^{-1}$$

$$KOH \rightleftharpoons K^+ + OH^-$$

$\therefore$ $[K^+] = 0.05$ M and $[OH^-] = 0.05$ M

From, $[H^+]\cdot[OH^-]=K_w=1.0\times10^{-14}$ [1]

$$[H^+]=\frac{1.0\times10^{-14}}{0.05}=20\times10^{-14}\ M=2.0\times10^{-13}M$$ [1]

$pH=-\log[H^+]=-\log[2.0\times10^{-13}]=-0.3010+13=12.7$ [1]

37. (i) Millimoles of base, $Ca(OH)_2=M_1V_1=2\times0.2\times10=4$
Millimoles of acid, $HCl=M_2V_2=0.1\times25=2.5$
i.e. $M_1V_1>M_2V_2$ hence, solution is basic.

$$\therefore [OH^-]=\frac{M_1V_1-M_2V_2}{V_1+V_2}=\frac{4-2.5}{10+25}=0.043\ M$$

$\therefore pOH=-\log[4.3\times10^{-2}]=-0.6335+2=1.3665$

$pH=14-pOH=14-1.3665=12.6335$ [1]
≈ 12.63

(ii) Millimoles of acid, $H_2SO_4=M_1V_1=2\times0.01\times10=0.2$
Millimoles of base, $Ca(OH_2)=M_2V_2$
$=2\times0.01\times10=0.2$
$\because$ $M_1V_1=M_2V_2$, hence solution is neutral.
$\therefore$ $pH=7$ [1]

(iii) Millimoles of acid, $H_2SO_4=M_1V_1=2\times0.1\times10=2$
Millimoles of base, $KOH=M_2V_2=0.1\times10=1$
i.e. $M_1V_1>M_2V_2$, hence solution is acidic,

$$[H^+]=\frac{M_1V_1-M_2V_2}{V_1+V_2}=\frac{(0.2\times10)-(0.1\times10)}{10+10}$$

$$=\frac{2-1}{20}=0.05\ M$$

$pH=-\log[0.05]=-\log[5.0\times10^{-2}]=1.301\approx1.30$ [1]

38. $CH_3COOH+H_2O \rightleftharpoons CH_3COO^-+H_3O^+$

	CH_3COOH		CH_3COO^-	H_3O^+
Initially	C		0	0
At time t	$C-C\alpha$		$C\alpha$	$C\alpha$

$$\because \quad K_a=\frac{[CH_3COO^-][H_3O^+]}{[CH_3COOH]}$$

$\because [CH_3COO^-]=[H_3O^+]$

$\therefore [CH_3COO^-]=[H_3O^+]\Rightarrow\sqrt{K_a\cdot[CH_3COOH]}$

Given, $K_a=1.74\times10^{-5}$, $[CH_3COOH]=0.05\ M$

$\therefore [CH_3COO^-]=[H_3O^+]\Rightarrow\sqrt{1.74\times10^{-5}\times0.05}$

$[CH_3COO^-]=[H_3O^+]=\sqrt{17.4\times10^{-6}\times5.0\times10^{-2}}$
$=9.33\times10^{-4}\ M$ [1]

Again, from $[CH_3COO^-]=[H_3O^+]=C\cdot\alpha$

$$\text{Degree of dissociation, } \alpha=\frac{[H_3O^+]}{C}=\frac{9.33\times10^{-4}}{0.05}$$

$=1.86\times10^{-2}$ [1]

$pH=-\log[H_3O^+]$
$pH=-\log[9.33\times10^{-4}]$
$=4-0.9699=3.0301$ [1]

39. • Find K_a by using the formula $K_a=C\cdot\alpha^2$ (for weak acid).
• Find pK_a by using the formula $pK_a=-\log K_a$.
• To find pH of the solution, find $[H_3O^+]$ concentration, by using the relation $[H_3O^+]=C\alpha$.

$CH_2(Br)COOH+H_2O \rightleftharpoons CH_2(Br)COO^-+H_3O^+$

	$CH_2(Br)COOH$	$CH_2(Br)COO^-$	H_3O^+
Initial conc.	C	0	0
Equili. conc.	$C-C\alpha$	$C\alpha$	$C\alpha$

$C(1-\alpha)$

$$K_a=\frac{[CH_2(Br)COO^-][H_3O^+]}{[CH_2(Br)COOH]}$$

$$=\frac{C\alpha\cdot C\alpha}{C(1-\alpha)}=\frac{C\alpha^2}{(1-\alpha)}$$

$K_a=C\alpha^2$ [For weak acid $(1-\alpha)\approx1$]

$K_a=0.1\times(0.132)^2=0.00174$ [1]
$\approx1.74\times10^{-3}$

From $pK_a=-\log K_a$
$pK_a=-\log[1.74\times10^{-3}]$
$=-0.2405+3=2.7595$ [1]

From $[H_3O^+]=C\alpha=0.1\times0.132=0.0132$

$\because$ $pH=-\log[H_3O^+]$
$\therefore$ $pH=-\log[1.32\times10^{-2}]$
$pH=-0.1206+2=1.8794\approx1.88$ [1]

40. As we have pH, find $[H_3O^+]$ to calculate K_a and α.

$$\alpha=\frac{[H_3O^+]}{C}$$

$HCNO+H_2O \rightleftharpoons H_3O^++CNO^-$

$pH=-\log[H_3O^+]=2.34$

$\therefore$ $\log[H_3O^+]=-2.34=\bar{3}.66$

$[H_3O^+]=\text{antilog}\ \bar{3}.66=4.571\times10^{-3}M$ [1]

$$\text{Ionisation constant, } K_a=\frac{[H_3O^+][CNO^-]}{[HCNO]}$$

$$=\frac{4.571\times10^{-3}\times4.571\times10^{-3}}{0.1}=2.089\times10^{-4}$$ [1]

$$\because \text{Degree of ionisation, } \alpha=\frac{[H_3O^+]}{C}=\frac{4.571\times10^{-3}}{0.1}$$

$\alpha=4.571\times10^{-2}$ [1]

41. Given, K_b for dimethylamine $=5.4\times10^{-4}$,
C for dimethylamine $=0.02$ M

$$\alpha=\sqrt{K_b/C}=\sqrt{\frac{5.4\times10^{-4}}{0.02}}$$

$=1.64\times10^{-1}=0.164$

In the presence of 0.1 M NaOH,

$$(CH_3)_2NH + H_2O \rightleftharpoons (CH_3)_2\overset{+}{N}H_2 + OH^-$$

Initial conc.	0.02 M	0	0
Equili. conc.	$(0.02 - C\alpha)$ ≈ 0.02	$C\alpha$	$C\alpha + 0.1$ ≈ 0.1 (0.1from 0.1 M NaOH)

$$K_b = \frac{[(CH_3)_2\overset{+}{N}H_2]\,[OH^-]}{[(CH_3)_2NH]}$$ [1]

$$\therefore 5.4 \times 10^{-4} = \frac{0.02\,\alpha \times 01}{0.02}$$ [1]

$$\alpha = \frac{5.4\times 10^{-4} \times 0.02}{0.02\times 0.1} = 54\times 10^{-4} = 5.4\times 10^{-3}$$

$$\alpha = 0.54\%$$ [1]

42. (i) pH of milk $= 6.8$

$$\log [H^+] = -6.8 = \bar{7}.20$$

$$[H^+] = \text{antilog } \bar{7}.20 = 1.585\times 10^{-7} M$$ [1]

(ii) pH of black coffee $= 5.0$

$$\log [H^+] = -5.0$$

$$[H^+] = 10^{-5} M$$ [1]

(iii) pH of lemon juice $= 2.2$

$$\log [H^+] = -2.2 = \bar{3}.8$$

$$[H^+] = \text{antilog } \bar{3}.8 = 6.310\times 10^{-3} M$$ [1]

(iv) pH of tomato juice $= 4.2$

$$\log [H^+] = -4.2 = \bar{5}.80$$

$$[H^+] = \text{antilog } \bar{5}.80 = 6.310\times 10^{-5} M$$ [1]

(v) pH of egg white $= 7.8$

$$\log [H^+] = -7.8 = \bar{8}.20$$

$$[H^+] = \text{antilog } \bar{8}.20 = 1.585\times 10^{-8} M$$ [1]

43. To find pH of the given solution, first find concentration of solution in mol L^{-1}.

To find pH of the given acidic solution, use the formula, $pH = -\log [H_3O^+]$.

To find pH of the given basic solution, first find pOH of the solution by using the formula $pOH = -\log [OH^-]$ and then find pH by using the formula $pH + pOH = 14$.

(i) Molecular mass of TlOH $= 204 + 16 + 1 = 221$ g mol^{-1}

$$\text{Conc. in mol L}^{-1}\text{ (molarity)} = \frac{\text{mass of TlOH (g)}}{\text{molar mass of TlOH} \times \text{volume of solution (L)}}$$

$$= \frac{2}{221\times 2} = 0.00452 = 4.52\times 10^{-3} M$$

$$\because pOH = -\log [OH^-] = -\log [4.52\times 10^{-3}] = 2.344$$

From, $pH + pOH = 14$

$$pH = 14 - 2.334 = 11.656 \approx 11.66$$ [1]

(ii) Molecular mass of $Ca(OH)_2$

$$= 40 + [(16+1)\times 2] = 74 \text{ g mol}^{-1}$$

Molarity, M

$$= \frac{\text{mass of } Ca(OH)_2 (g) \times 1000}{\text{molar mass of } Ca(OH)_2 \times \text{volume of solution (in mL)}}$$

$$M = \frac{0.3\times 1000}{74\times 500} = 0.0081$$

One mole of $Ca(OH)_2$ gives 2 moles of OH^-.

So, $[OH^-] = 2\times 0.0081 = 0.0162$ M

$$pOH = -\log [OH^-] = -\log [0.0162]$$

$$= 1.7905 \approx 1.79$$

From, $pH + pOH = 14$ or $pH = 14 - 1.79 = 12.21$ [2]

(iii) Molecular mass of NaOH $= 23 + 16 + 1 = 40$ g mol^{-1}

$$M = \frac{\text{mass of NaOH (g)} \times 1000}{\text{molar mass of NaOH} \times \text{volume of solution (mL)}}$$

$$= \frac{0.3\times 1000}{40\times 200} = 0.0375$$

$$pOH = -\log [0.0375] = -\log [3.75\times 10^{-2}]$$

$$= 1.426 \approx 1.43$$

From, $pH + pOH = 14$

$$pH = 14 - 1.43 = 12.57$$ [1]

(iv) In case of dilution, $M_1V_1 = M_2V_2$

$$13.6\times 1 = M_2 \times 1000$$

$$M_2 = \frac{13.6\times 1}{1000} = 0.0136 = 1.36\times 10^{-2} \text{ M}$$

$$pH = -\log [1.36\times 10^{-2}] = -0.1335 + 2$$

$$= 1.8665 \quad pH = 1.87$$ [1]

44.
- α is related to K_a as $\alpha = \sqrt{K_a / C}$, so first find K_a from pK_a as $pK_a = -\log (K_a)$ and then calculate α.
- To find α in the presence of 0.01 M HCl or 0.1 M HCl, calculate $C\alpha$ for acetate ions by taking $[H^+]$ ion concentrations 0.01 M or 0.1 M.

$\because \quad pK_a = -\log K_a,$

$\therefore \quad 4.74 = -\log K_a$ or $K_a = \text{antilog } \bar{5}.26 = 1.82\times 10^{-5}$

From, $\alpha = \sqrt{K_a / C}$

$$\alpha = \sqrt{\frac{1.82\times 10^{-5}}{0.05}} = \sqrt{0.364\times 10^{-3}} = \sqrt{3.64\times 10^{-4}}$$

$$\alpha = 1.908\times 10^{-2}$$ [1]

(i) In the presence of 0.01 M H^+

$$CH_3COOH \rightleftharpoons CH_3COO^- + H^+$$

Initiaconc.	0.05M	0	0
Equili. conc.	$0.05 - C\alpha$ ≈ 0.05	$C\alpha$	$(C\alpha + 0.01)$ ≈ 0.01

[CH_3COOH is a weak acid and HCl is a strong acid, so we can assume that $(C\alpha + 0.01) \approx 0.01$]

$$\because \quad K_a = \frac{[CH_3COO^-]\,[H^+]}{[CH_3COOH]}$$

$$\therefore 1.82\times 10^{-5} = \frac{C\alpha \times 0.01}{0.05}$$

or $C\alpha = \frac{1.82\times 10^{-5}\times 0.05}{0.01}$ or $0.05\times\alpha = 9.1\times 10^{-5}$

$\alpha = \frac{9.1\times 10^{-5}}{0.05} = 1.82\times 10^{-3}$ [2]

(ii) In the presence of 0.1 M HCl

Similarly, $K_a = \frac{[CH_3COO^-][H^+]}{[CH_3COOH]}$

$1.82\times 10^{-5} = \frac{C\alpha \times 0.1}{0.05}$

$[H^+] = (C\alpha + 0.1\text{ M}) \approx 0.1\text{ M}$

(because 0.1M HCl = 0.1M H^+ ions)

$C\alpha = \frac{1.82\times 10^{-5}\times 0.05}{0.1} = 0.91\times 10^{-5}$

$\alpha = \frac{0.91\times 10^{-5}}{0.05} = 1.82\times 10^{-4}$ [2]

In the presence of strong acid, dissociation of weak acid i.e. CH_3COOH decreases due to common ion effect.

45. **Key Idea**

- Find $[OH^-]$ ion concentration by using the formula $[OH^-] = \sqrt{K_bC}$.
- To find pH of the solution first find pOH and then pH from pH + pOH = 14.
- Find α by using the formula $\alpha = \sqrt{K_b/C}$ (for weak base).
- Find K_a by using the formula $K_a\cdot K_b = K_w = 10^{-14}$.

$$C_6H_5NH_2 + H_2O \rightleftharpoons C_6H_5NH_3^+ + OH^-$$

$$K_b = \frac{[C_6H_5NH_3^+][OH^-]}{[C_6H_5NH_2]} = \frac{[OH^-]^2}{[C_6H_5NH_2]}$$

$$[OH^-] = \sqrt{K_b\cdot C} = \sqrt{4.27\times 10^{-10}\times 0.001}$$

$$[OH^-] = 6.534\times 10^{-7}$$

$$pOH = -\log[OH^-] = -\log[6.534\times 10^{-7}]$$

$$pOH = -0.8152 + 7 = 6.18$$

From, pH + pOH = 14

$pH = 14 - 6.18 = 7.82$ [1]

	$C_6H_5NH_2 + H_2O \rightleftharpoons$	$C_6H_5NH_3^+$	$+ OH^-$
Initial conc.	C	0	0
Equili. conc.	$C - C\alpha$	$C\alpha$	$C\alpha$

$K_b = \frac{C\alpha\cdot C\alpha}{C(1-\alpha)}$ $[(1-\alpha)\approx 1$ for weak base$]$

$K_b = C\alpha^2$ or $\alpha = \sqrt{K_b/C}$ [2]

Degree of ionisation,

$$\alpha = \sqrt{\frac{4.27\times 10^{-10}}{0.001}} = 6.53\times 10^{-4}$$

K_a of conjugate acid of aniline,

$K_a = \frac{K_w}{K_b} = \frac{10^{-14}}{4.27\times 10^{-10}} = 2.34\times 10^{-5}$ [2]

46.

- H_2S being a weak acid, dissociates a
  $H_2S + H_2O \rightleftharpoons H_3O^+ + HS^-$
  ∴ $K_a = \frac{[H_3O^+][HS^-]}{[H_2S]}$.
- HCl being a strong acid dissociates completely, so calculate $[HS^-]$ in the presence of 0.1 M HCl by taking $[H^+]$ concentration as 0.1 M.
- Calculate $[S^{2-}]$ ion concentration by using the equation, $HS^- + H_2O \rightleftharpoons H_3O^+ + S^{2-}$
- Calculate $[S^{2-}]$ ion concentration in the presence of 0.1 M HCl.

(i) $H_2S + H_2O \rightleftharpoons H_3O^+ + HS^-$

$$K_{a_1} = \frac{[H_3O^+][HS^-]}{[H_2S]}$$

$$[H_3O^+] = [HS^-] \Rightarrow \sqrt{K_{a_1}\cdot C}$$

$$= \sqrt{9.1\times 10^{-8}\times 0.1}$$

$= 9.54\times 10^{-5}$ M [1]

(ii) In the presence of 0.1 M HCl

$$[H_3O^+] = 0.1\text{ M}$$

$$K_{a_1} = \frac{[H_3O^+][HS^-]}{[H_2S]}$$

$$9.1\times 10^{-8} = \frac{[0.1][HS^-]}{[0.1]} \Rightarrow [HS^-] = 9.1\times 10^{-8}\text{ M}$$

Hence, concentration of $[HS^-]$ is decreased in the presence of 0.1 M HCl due to common ion effect. [1]

(iii) For second dissociation constant,

$HS^- + H_2O \rightleftharpoons H_3O^+ + S^{2-}$ (In absence of HCl)

$$[HS^-][H_3O^+] = 9.54\times 10^{-5}\text{ M}$$

Now, $K_{a_2} = \frac{[H_3O^+][S^{2-}]}{[HS^-]}$

$$[H_3O^+] = [S^{2-}] = \sqrt{K_{a_2}\cdot C}$$

$$= \sqrt{1.2\times 10^{-13}\times 9.54\times 10^{-5}}$$

$= 3.38\times 10^{-9}$ M [1]

(iv) In the presence of 0.1 M HCl,

$$K_{a_2} = \frac{[H_3O^+][S^{2-}]}{[HS^-]} = \frac{[0.1][S^{2-}]}{[9.1\times 10^{-8}]}$$

$[S^{2-}] = 1.092\times 10^{-19}$ M [2]

47. $CH_3CH_2COOH + H_2O \rightleftharpoons CH_3CH_2COO^- + H_3O^+$;

Propanoic acid $(0.05 - C\alpha)$ $C\alpha$ $C\alpha$

From Ostwald's dilution law,

$$\alpha = \sqrt{K_a/C}$$

$= \sqrt{\frac{1.32\times 10^{-5}}{0.05}} = 0.016248$ [1]

$$[H_3O^+] = C\alpha = 0.05 \times 0.016248$$
$$= 0.0008124 = 8.124 \times 10^{-4}$$

From, $pH = -\log [H_3O^+] = -\log (8.124 \times 10^{-4})$
$$= 3.0902 \approx 3.09$$

When the solution contains 0.01 M HCl

$$K_a = \frac{[CH_3CH_2COO^-][H_3O^+]}{[CH_3CH_2COOH]}$$

$$1.32 \times 10^{-5} = \frac{C\alpha \times 0.01}{(0.05 - C\alpha)}$$

($[H_3O^+] = 0.01$ M from HCl. In the presence of 0.01 M HCl, dissociation of propanoic acid decreases).

$$C\alpha = \frac{1.32 \times 10^{-5} \times (0.05 - C\alpha)}{0.01}$$

$$= \frac{1.32 \times 10^{-5} \times 0.05}{0.01} \quad [\text{as } (0.05 - C\alpha) \approx 0.05]$$

or $\quad 0.05 \times \alpha = 6.60 \times 10^{-5}$

$$\alpha = \frac{6.60 \times 10^{-5}}{0.05} = 1.32 \times 10^{-3}$$ [2]

TOPIC 03 Salt Hydrolysis, Buffer Solutions and Solubility Product

Hydrolysis of Salts and the pH of their Solutions

Salts are the result of interaction of acids and bases and such reactions are called **neutralisation reactions.** The process of interaction of cation or anion or both provided by salt with water is called **hydrolysis** or **salt hydrolysis.** This process also affects the pH of the solutions. Depending upon the nature of acid and base from which a salt is obtained, the salts are categorised into four categories.

Salts of Strong Acid and Strong Base

The cations obtained from strong bases (like alkali metal ions and alkaline earth metal ions i.e. Ba^{2+}, Ca^{2+}) and anions obtained from strong acids (like Cl^-, Br^-, NO_3^-, ClO_4^- etc.,) do not hydrolyse. It involves only ionisation of water and no hydrolysis. Thus, the salt formed by these ions like NaCl, $NaNO_3$, $BaCl_2$ etc., are not hydrolysed by water and hence, the solutions of such salts remain neutral with pH 7. e.g.

$$NaCl + H_2O \longrightarrow NaOH + HCl$$

or $$Na^+ + Cl^- + H_2O \longrightarrow Na^+ + OH^- + H^+Cl^-$$

or $$H_2O \longrightarrow H^+ + OH^-$$

Salts of Weak Acids and Strong Bases

Salts of sodium and potassium other than halides, sulphates and nitrates fall in this category. Such a salt, *BA* *in aqueous medium exhibits following equilibrium.*

$$BA \longrightarrow B^+ + A^-$$
$$B^+ + A^- + H_2O \rightleftharpoons HA + BOH^-$$

or $$A^- + H_2O \rightleftharpoons HA + \bar{O}H$$

Thus, this process is called **anionic hydrolysis.** (BOH being a strong base remains dissociated completely). Thus, for this reaction,

Equilibrium constant, $$K = \frac{[HA][OH^-]}{[A^-][H_2O]}$$

As $K \times [H_2O]$ is regarded as constant, hence, we may write a new constant, K_h

$$\therefore \quad K_h = \frac{[HA][OH^-]}{[A^-]}$$

K_h is called **hydrolysis constant.**

A brief discussion of the quantitative aspect of hydrolysis of this type of salt is given below :

1. Degree of Hydrolysis

It is defined as the fraction of total salt that has undergone hydrolysis on attainment of equilibrium. It is denoted by *h*. Let *C* be the concentration of salt and *h* be its degree of hydrolysis.

$$\underset{C-Ch}{A^\ominus} + H_2O \rightleftharpoons \underset{Ch}{\overset{\ominus}{O}H} + \underset{Ch}{HA} \quad \text{(equation of hydrolysis)}$$

$$K_h = \frac{[\overset{\ominus}{O}H][HA]}{[A^\ominus]} = \frac{(Ch)(Ch)}{C - Ch} = \frac{Ch^2}{1-h}$$

$$\therefore \quad K_h = Ch^2 \quad [\text{assuming } h << 1]$$

$$h = \sqrt{\frac{K_h}{C}}$$

Now, considering the dissociations of weak acid, HA and H_2O.

$$HA \rightleftharpoons H^{\oplus} + A^{\ominus}; \quad K_a = \frac{[H^{\oplus}][A^{\ominus}]}{[HA]} \quad \ldots(i)$$

$$H_2O \rightleftharpoons H^{\oplus} + \overset{\ominus}{O}H, \quad K_w = [H^{\oplus}][\overset{\ominus}{O}H] \quad \ldots(ii)$$

$$K_h = \frac{K_w}{K_a}$$

(Subtracting Eq. (i) from Eq. (ii), we get the equation of hydrolysis)

Now substituting the value of K_h in expression of h.

$$h = \sqrt{\frac{K_w}{K_a C}}$$

Note Weaker is the acid, greatest is the hydrolysis constant. The degree of hydrolysis increases when C decreases, i.e. with dilution.

2. pH of Solution

pH of a basic solution is given as :

$$pH + pOH = 14 \Rightarrow pH = 14 - pOH$$

$$pH = 14 + \log(\overset{\ominus}{O}H)$$

and $\quad [\overset{\ominus}{O}H] = Ch = \sqrt{K_h C}$

Substituting for K_h, we get $[\overset{\ominus}{O}H] = \sqrt{\frac{K_w C}{K_a}}$

$$\Rightarrow \quad pH = 14 + \log\sqrt{\frac{K_w C}{K_a}}$$

$$\Rightarrow \quad pH = pK_w + \frac{1}{2}[\log(K_w) + \log C - \log K_a]$$

$$[\because K_w = 1 \times 10^{-14} \Rightarrow pK_w = 14]$$

$$= pK_w - \frac{1}{2}pK_w + \frac{1}{2}[pK_a + \log C]$$

$$= \frac{1}{2}pK_w + \frac{1}{2}[pK_a + \log C]$$

$$= 7 + \frac{1}{2}(pK_a + \log C) \text{ at } 25°C$$

Clearly, $\quad pH > 7$

Salts of Strong Acids and Weak Bases

Halides, sulphates and nitrates of metals other than sodium, potassium fall in this category. The aqueous solution of such a salt BA, exhibits following equilibrium.

$$BA \longrightarrow B^+ + A^-$$

$$B^+ + A^- + H_2O \rightleftharpoons BOH + HA$$

or $\quad B^+ + H_2O \rightleftharpoons BOH + H^+$

Since, B^+ ion undergoes hydrolysis, so this process is called **cationic hydrolysis**. Because of the generation of H^+ ions the solution becomes acidic. [as the acid HA is strong]

The hydrolysis constant is given by,

$$K_h = \frac{[H^+][BOH]}{[B^+]}$$

1. Degree of Hydrolysis

The net reaction of hydrolysis is

$$\underset{C-Ch}{B^{\oplus}} + H_2O \rightleftharpoons \underset{Ch}{BOH(aq)} + \underset{Ch}{H^{\oplus}(aq)}$$

$$K_h = \frac{[BOH][H^{\oplus}]}{[B^{\oplus}]} = \frac{(Ch)(Ch)}{C - Ch} = \frac{Ch^2}{1-h} = Ch^2$$

$$\therefore \quad h = \sqrt{\frac{K_h}{C}} \quad (h << 1)$$

Considering ionisation of weak base BOH and H_2O

$$BOH \rightleftharpoons B^{\oplus} + \overset{\ominus}{O}H; \quad K_b = \frac{[B^{\oplus}][\overset{\ominus}{O}H]}{[BOH]} \quad \ldots(i)$$

$$H_2O \rightleftharpoons H^{\oplus} + \overset{\ominus}{O}H; \quad K_w = [H^{\oplus}][\overset{\ominus}{O}H] \quad \ldots(ii)$$

Relation between K_w, K_b and K_h can be written as:

$$\boxed{\frac{K_w}{K_b} = K_h}$$

Thus, the hydrolysis constant K_h, varies inversely with the dissociation constant, K_b of the weak base.

As in the above case, the degree of dissociation,

$$h = \sqrt{\frac{K_w}{K_b}V} = \sqrt{\frac{K_w}{K_b C}}$$

2. pH of Solution

Now,

$$pH = -\log[H^{\oplus}] \text{ and } [H^{\oplus}] = Ch = C\sqrt{\frac{K_h}{C}} = \sqrt{K_h C}$$

$$\Rightarrow \quad [H^{\oplus}] = \sqrt{\frac{K_w C}{K_b}} \Rightarrow pH = -\log\sqrt{\frac{K_w C}{K_b}}$$

$$\Rightarrow \quad pH = \frac{1}{2}(pK_w - pK_b - \log C)$$

$$= 7 - \frac{1}{2}(pK_b + \log C) \text{ at } 25°C$$

Clearly, $\quad pH < 7$

Salts of Weak Acids and Weak Bases

The salts other than halides, sulphates, nitrates of metals (other than sodium, potassium) fall in this category. In aqueous solution such a salt BA exhibits following equilibrium

$$B^+ + A^- + H_2O \rightleftharpoons BOH + HA$$

Here cation and anion both undergo hydrolysis.

The hydrolysis constant is given by,

$$K_h = \frac{[BOH][HA]}{[B^+][A^-]}$$

1. Degree of Hydrolysis

$$B^+ + A^{\ominus} + H_2O \rightleftharpoons \underset{\text{(Weak base)}}{BOH(aq)} + \underset{\text{(Weak acid)}}{HA(aq)}$$

Initially	C	C	0	0
At equili.	$C - Ch$	$C - Ch$	Ch	Ch

$$\Rightarrow \quad K_h = \frac{[BOH][HA]}{[B^{\oplus}][A^{\ominus}]} = \frac{(Ch)(Ch)}{(C-Ch)^2}$$

$\Rightarrow \quad K_h = \dfrac{h^2}{(1-h)^2}$; taking square root on both sides to get

$$h = \frac{\sqrt{K_h}}{1+\sqrt{K_h}} \quad \text{(Here, } 1-h \neq 1\text{)}$$

(**Remember !** that the degree of hydrolysis of such salts is independent of the concentration of salt solution).

Now, considering the dissociation of both weak base and acid.

$$HA \rightleftharpoons H^{\oplus} + A^{\ominus}; K_a = \frac{[H^{\oplus}][A^{\ominus}]}{[HA]}$$

$$BOH \rightleftharpoons B^{\oplus} + \overset{\ominus}{O}H; K_b = \frac{[B^{\oplus}][\overset{\ominus}{O}H]}{[BOH]}$$

$$H_2O \rightleftharpoons H^{\oplus} + \overset{\ominus}{O}H; K_w = [H^{\oplus}][\overset{\ominus}{O}H]$$

Combining K_h, K_b, K_a and K_w, we have $K_h = \dfrac{K_w}{K_a \cdot K_b}$

Also, $K_h = \dfrac{h^2}{(1-h)^2}$

$$\sqrt{K_h} = \frac{h}{1-h} \text{ (if } h \text{ is not neglected compared to 1).}$$

$$h = \sqrt{K_h} = \sqrt{\frac{K_w}{K_a K_b}} \quad (\text{if } h << 1)$$

2. pH of Solution

Consider, $K_a = \dfrac{[H^{\oplus}][A^{\ominus}]}{[HA]} \Rightarrow [H^{\oplus}] = K_a \dfrac{[HA]}{[A^{\ominus}]}$

Since, bases and acids are weaker, hence

$$[BOH] = [HA] \Rightarrow [B^{\oplus}] = [A^{\ominus}]$$

$$\Rightarrow \quad K_h = \frac{[BOH][HA]}{[B^{\oplus}][A^{\ominus}]} = \frac{[HA]^2}{[A^{\ominus}]}$$

$$\Rightarrow \quad [H^{\oplus}] = K_a\sqrt{K_h} = \sqrt{\frac{K_w K_a}{K_b}}$$

$$pH = -\log [H^{\oplus}] = -\log\sqrt{\frac{K_w K_a}{K_b}}$$

$$\Rightarrow \quad pH = \frac{1}{2}(pK_w + pK_a - pK_b)$$

$$\text{(at 25°C)} = 7 + \frac{1}{2}(pK_a - pK_b)$$

If $pK_a = pK_b$, i.e. the dissociation constants of acid and base are equal, then pH = 7. Thus, the solution will be neutral, despite the fact that hydrolysis has taken place.

***Case* I** If $pK_a > pK_b$ or $K_a < K_b$, i.e. base is relatively stronger than pH > 7

***Case* II** If $pK_a < pK_b$ or $K_a > K_b$, i.e. acid is relatively stronger than pH < 7.

Summary of Salt Hydrolysis

S. No.	Salt	Nature	Degree of hydrolysis	pH
1.	NaCl (strong acid + strong base)	Neutral	No hydrolysis	—
2.	CH_3COONa (weak acid + strong base)	Basic	$h = \sqrt{\dfrac{K_w}{CK_a}}$	$pH = \dfrac{1}{2}[pK_w + pK_a + \log C]$
3.	NH_4Cl (strong acid + weak base)	Acidic	$h = \sqrt{\dfrac{K_w}{CK_b}}$	$pH = \dfrac{1}{2}[pK_w - pK_b - \log C]$
4.	CH_3COONH_4 (weak acid + weak base)	*	$h = \sqrt{\dfrac{K_w}{K_a \times K_b}}$	$pH = \dfrac{1}{2}[pK_w + pK_a - pK_b]$

Indicators

An indicator is a substance, which is used to determine the end point in a titration. These compounds have the ability to produce a characteristic colour change with the change in medium.

Acid-base Indicators/pH Indicator

It is a substance which possesses one colour in acid solution and altogether different colour in alkaline medium. In other words, a substance whose colour changes with change in pH, is acid-base indicator.

Indicators in acid-base titrations

Acid-base titrations	Indicators
1. Strong acid *vs* strong base	bromothymol blue, phenolphthalein
2. Strong acid *vs* weak base	methyl orange, methyl red, bromocresol green
3. Weak acid *vs* strong base	phenolphthalein, thymophthalein
4. Weak acid *vs* weak base	phenol red

In acid-base titrations, organic substances are generally used as indicators. They change within a certain pH range. The colour change and the pH range of some common indicators are tabulated below:

Colour change of indicators with pH

Indicator	pH range	Colour in	
		Acid solution	Alkaline solution
Thymol blue (acid)	1.2-2.8	Red	Yellow
Bromophenol blue	3.1- 4.6	Yellow	Purple
Methyl orange	3.1- 4.5	Red/orange	Yellow
Methyl red	4.2-6.3	Red	Yellow
Bromothymol blue	6.0-7.5	Orange	Blue
Phenol red	6.4-8.2	Yellow	Red
Thymol blue (base)	8.1-9.6	Yellow	Blue
Phenolphthalein	8.0-9.8	Colourless	Pink
Thymolphthalein	9.3-10.5	Colourless	Blue
Alizarin yellow *R*	10.1-12.1	Yellow	Lilac

Example 1 The pK_a of acetic acid and pK_b of ammonium hydroxide are 4.76 and 4.75 respectively. Calculate the pH of ammonium acetate solution.

NCERT Textbook

Sol. Ammonium acetate is a salt of weak acid and weak base and for such salts,

$$pH = 7 + \frac{1}{2}[pK_a - pK_b] = 7 + \frac{1}{2}[4.76 - 4.75]$$

$$= 7 + \frac{1}{2}[0.01] = 7 + 0.005 = 7.005$$

Buffer Solutions

The solutions that resist change in their pH on dilution or on addition of small amounts of acids or alkalies are called **buffer solutions** and the ability of a buffer solution to resist changes in pH on adding acids or base is called buffer action.

Buffer solutions are generally of three types:

1. Natural Buffer

It is a salt of weak acid and weak base e.g. CH_3COONH_4, $[(NH_4)_2CO_3]$.

2. Acidic Buffer

It is a mixture of a weak acid and its conjugate base (or salt with strong base).

(i) $CH_3COOH + CH_3COONa$ (pH = 4.75)

(ii) Boric acid + Borax

(iii) Phthalic acid + Potassium acid phthalate

pH of such buffer are always less than 7.

e.g. pH of an acidic buffer is given by **Henderson-Hasselbalch equation or Henderson equation** which is as,

$$pH = pK_a + \log\frac{[Salt]}{[Acid]}$$

where, K_a is dissociation constant of the acid.

Mechanism of Buffer Action

Consider a solution containing CH_3COOH and CH_3COONa, *which dissociate as follows:*

$$CH_3COOH \rightleftharpoons CH_3COO^- + H^+ \text{ (Feebly ionised)}$$

$$CH_3COONa \longrightarrow CH_3COO^- + Na^+ \text{ (Completely ionised)}$$

$$H_2O \rightleftharpoons H^+ + OH^- \text{ (Much weakly ionised)}$$

***Case* I** Now suppose we add a drop of conc. HCl (a strong electrolyte) to the above solution. HCl immediately ionises as $HCl \rightleftharpoons H^+ + Cl^-$. These H^+ ions combine with CH_3COO^- ions present in the solution to form CH_3COOH, which ionises to a slight extent. This means that CH_3COO^- and H^+ ions cannot exist together in solution to a large extent. Hence, even addition of HCl, a strong electrolyte does not produce any appreciable change in H^+ ion concentration of pH of the solution.

Case II When a drop of NaOH is added to it, the OH^- ions react with undissociated acid to form H_2O molecules.

$$CH_3COOH + OH^- \longrightarrow CH_3COO^- + H_2O$$

Again pH remains unchanged.

3. Basic Buffer

It is a mixture of weak base and its conjugate acid (or its salt with strong acid).

e.g. (i) $NH_4OH + NH_4Cl$ (pH = 9.25)

(ii) Glycine + glycine hydrochloride

pH of basic buffer is calculated through **Henderson-Hasselbalch equation or Henderson equation** and can be given as

$$pOH = pK_a + \log \frac{[Salt]}{[Base]} \text{ and } pH = 14 - pOH$$

Mechanism of Buffer Action

Consider a solution containing weak base (NH_4OH) and one of its salt (NH_4Cl). The NH_4OH is slightly ionised hence, the solution contains a very small concentration of OH^- ions. Moreover common NH_4^+ ions from highly ionised NH_4Cl which further suppresses the ionisation of weak electrolyte, NH_4OH.

$$NH_4OH \rightleftharpoons NH_4^+ + OH^- \text{ (Feebly ionised)}$$

$$NH_4Cl \rightleftharpoons NH_4^+Cl^- \text{ (Completely ionised)}$$

Case I When a drop of NaOH is added to it, the OH^- ions from it, combined with NH_4^+ ions present in the solution to form NH_4OH which is a weak base. Thus, even the addition of NaOH (a strong electrolyte) does not produce a market change in the pH of the solution.

Case II Now, suppose we add a drop of conc. HCl to the above solutions. HCl immediately ionises as:

$$HCl \rightleftharpoons H^+ + Cl^-$$

The H^+ ions react with undissociated base to from H_2O molecules, as $NH_4OH + H^+ \longrightarrow NH_4^+ + H_2O$

Again, pH remains unchanged.

Buffer Capacity

Buffer capacity is quantitatively defined as the number of moles of acid or base added in 1 L of solution to change the pH by unity.

$$\text{Buffer capacity } (\phi) = \frac{\text{Number of moles of acid or base added to 1 L of buffer}}{\text{Change in pH}}$$

Applications of Buffer Solutions

(i) Normal blood has pH of 7.4. This pH is maintained by buffer action of following two buffers.

(a) Buffer of carbonic acid (H_2CO_3 and $NaHCO_3$)

(b) Buffer of phosphoric acid ($H_2PO_4^-, HPO_4^{2-}$)

(ii) $NH_4Cl + NH_4OH$ buffer is used for the precipitation of hydroxides of third group of qualitative analysis.

(iii) Buffers find numerous applications in industrial processes, like manufacture of paper, drugs, dyes, inks, paints etc.

(iv) Buffer solutions are applied for digestion process of food.

(v) These are used as preservatives of foods and fruits.

(vi) Buffer can be used for preservation of many dairy and agricultural products.

Example 2 A weak acid HA after treatment with 1.2 mL of 0.1 M strong base has a pH of 5. At the end point, the volume of same base required is 26.6 mL calculate the value of K_a.

Sol. For complete neutralisation,

Total millieq. of acid = millieq. of base

$$= 26.6 \times 0.1 = 2.66$$

For partial neutralisation,

	HA	+ BOH	⟶ BA	+ H_2O
Before reaction	2.66	1.2	0	0
After reaction	1.46	0	1.2	1.2

The resultant mixture has HA and BA and thus acts as buffer.

$$pH = -\log K_a + \log \frac{[Salt]}{[Acid]}$$

$$\Rightarrow \quad 5 = -\log K_a + \log \frac{1.2}{1.46} \quad \text{or} \quad K_a = 8.31 \times 10^{-6}$$

Solubility Equilibria of Sparingly Soluble Salts

Lattice enthalpy and solvation enthalpy play a key role in deciding the solubility of the salts in a particular solvent. For a salt to be able to dissolve in a particular solvent, its solvation enthalpy must be higher than its lattice enthalpy. i.e. ion solvent interaction must be higher than the interaction between the ions. Non-polar solvent have very small solvation enthalpy which is not sufficient to overcome the lattice enthalpy of the salt. Hence, salts are generally insoluble in non-polar solvents.

Depending upon their solubility, the salts are categories into three groups:

Category I	Soluble	Solubility > 0.1 M
Category II	Slightly soluble	0.01 M < Solubility < 0.1 M
Category III	Sparingly soluble	Solubility < 0.01 M

Solubility Product Constant

The concentration of substance in a saturated solution is defined as its solubility (S). Its value depends upon the nature of solvent and the temperature. Consider saturated solution of sparingly soluble electrolyte, AB.

$$\underset{\text{Solid}}{AB} \rightleftharpoons \underset{\text{Unionised dissolved}}{AB} \rightleftharpoons \underbrace{A^+ + B^-}_{\text{Ions}}$$

Applying the law of mass action, $K = \dfrac{[A^+][B^-]}{[AB]}$. Since, the solution is saturated, the concentration of unionised molecules of the electrolyte will be constant at a particular temperature, i.e. $[AB] = \text{constant} = K'$ (say). Hence, $[A^+][B^-] = KK' = K_{sp}$ (constant)

This new constant K_{sp} is called **solubility product** and is defined as the product of the concentration of ions in a saturated solution of an electrolyte at a given temperature. Consider, in general, the electrolyte of the type A_xB_y, which is dissociated as:

$$A_xB_y \rightleftharpoons xA^{y+} + yB^{x-};\ K_{sp} = [A^{y+}]^x[B^{x-}]^y$$

Thus, solubility product may be defined as the product of concentrations of the ions raised to a power equal to the number of times the ions occur in the equation representing the dissociation of the electrolyte at a given temperature when the solution is saturated.

Example 3 Calculate the solubility of A_2X_3 in pure water, assuming that neither kind of ion reacts with water. The solubility product of A_2X_3 is $K_{sp} = 1.1 \times 10^{-23}$.

Sol. $\underset{S}{A_2X_3} \rightleftharpoons \underset{2S}{2A^{3+}} + \underset{3S}{3X^{2-}}$;

$$K_{sp} = [A^{3+}]^2[X^{2-}]^3 = 1.1 \times 10^{-23}$$

$$\therefore \quad K_{sp} = (2S)^2(3S)^3 = 108S^5 = 1.1 \times 10^{-23}$$

or $\quad S^5 = 1 \times 10^{-25} \Rightarrow S = 1.0 \times 10^{-5}$ mol / L.

Example 4 The values of K_{sp} of two sparingly soluble salts $Ni(OH)_2$ and AgCN are 2.0×10^{-15} and 6×10^{-17} respectively. Which salt is more soluble? Explain.

Sol. $AgCN \rightleftharpoons Ag^+ + CN^-$

$$K_{sp} = [Ag^+][CN^-] = 6 \times 10^{-17}$$

$$Ni(OH)_2 \rightleftharpoons Ni^{2+} + 2OH^-$$

$$K_{sp} = [Ni^{2+}][OH^-]^2 = 2 \times 10^{-15}$$

Let $[Ag^+] = S_1$, then $[CN^-] = S_1$

Let $[Ni^{2+}] = S_2$ then $[OH^-] = 2S_2$

$$S_1^2 = 6 \times 10^{-17}, S_1 = 7.8 \times 10^{-9}$$

$$(S_2)(2S_2)^2 = 2 \times 10^{-15}, S_2 = 7.9 \times 10^{-6}$$

Thus, $Ni(OH)_2$ is more soluble than AgCN.

Applications of Solubility Product

1. Predicting Precipitate Formation from K_{sp}

At the state of equilibrium, the value of K_{sp} is equal to the value of Q_{sp} but if the concentration of anyone ion is not in equilibrium, $Q_{sp} \neq K_{sp}$. In order to make, $Q_{sp} = K_{sp}$, the reaction moves in the required direction.

The value of Q (ionic product) and K_{sp} are also helpful for predicting whether a precipitate is formed or not. In general,

If $Q > K_{sp}$, then precipitation will take place.

If $Q < K_{sp}$, then no precipitation will occur.

If $Q = K_{sp}$, the reaction is at equilibrium.

Example 5 The solubility product of $BaSO_4$ at 25°C is 1.0×10^{-9}. What would be the concentration of H_2SO_4 necessary to precipitate $BaSO_4$ from a solution of 0.01 M Ba^{2+} ions?

Sol. Precipitation will take place when Ionic product > Solubility product

$$BaSO_4 \rightleftharpoons \underset{0.01}{Ba^{2+}} + \underset{S}{SO_4^{2-}}$$

$$\because \quad K_{sp} = [Ba^{2+}][SO_4^{2-}]$$

$$\therefore \quad S = \frac{1.0 \times 10^{-9}}{0.01} = 10^{-7} \text{mol/L}$$

Example 6 A sparingly soluble salt gets precipitated only when the product of concentration of its ions in the solution (Q_{sp}) becomes greater than its solubility product. If the solubility of $BaSO_4$ in water is 8×10^{-4} mol dm^{-3}. Calculate its solubility in 0.01 mol dm^{-3} of H_2SO_4.

NCERT Exemplar

Sol. $BaSO_4(s) \rightleftharpoons Ba^{2+}(aq) + SO_4^{2-}(aq)$

$$K_{sp} \text{ for } BaSO_4 = [Ba^{2+}][SO_4^{2-}] = S \times S = S^2$$

But $\quad S = 8 \times 10^{-4}$ mol dm^{-3}

$$\therefore \quad K_{sp} = (8 \times 10^{-4})^2 = 64 \times 10^{-8}$$

In the presence of 0.01 M H_2SO_4, the expression for K_{sp} will be

$$K_{sp} = [Ba^{2+}][SO_4^{2-}]$$

$$K_{sp} = (S)\cdot(S + 0.01)$$

(0.01 M SO_4^{2-} ions from 0.01 M H_2SO_4)

$$\Rightarrow \quad 64 \times 10^{-8} = S \cdot (S + 0.01)$$

$$\Rightarrow S^2 + 0.01S - 64 \times 10^{-8} = 0$$

$$\therefore \quad S = \frac{-0.01 \pm \sqrt{(0.01)^2 + (4 \times 64 \times 10^{-8})}}{2}$$

$$= \frac{-0.01 \pm \sqrt{10^{-4} + (256 \times 10^{-8})}}{2}$$

$$= \frac{-0.01 \pm \sqrt{10^{-4}(1 + 256 \times 10^{-4})}}{2}$$

$$= \frac{-0.01 \pm 10^{-2}\sqrt{1 + 0.0256}}{2} = \frac{10^{-2}(-1 \pm 1.012719)}{2}$$

$$= 5 \times 10^{-3}(-1 + 1.012719) = 6.4 \times 10^{-5} \text{ mol dm}^{-3}$$

Note $S <<< 0.01$, so $S + 0.01 \approx 0.01$ and $64 \times 10^{-8} = S \times 0.01$

$$S = \frac{64 \times 10^{-8}}{0.01} = 6.4 \times 10^{-5}$$

2. Calculation of Solubility in Presence of Common Ion

Solubility of a sparingly soluble salt is decreased by the addition of a common ion, e.g. solubility of $AgNO_3$ decreases the solubility of Ag_2CrO_4 as:

Let S is the solubility of silver chromate,

$$Ag_2CrO_4 \rightleftharpoons 2Ag^+ + CrO_4^{2-}$$

The solubility product of

$$Ag_2CrO_4 \text{ is } K_{sp} = (2S)^2 \times S = 4S^2 \quad \ldots\text{(i)}$$

Now suppose that x mol/L of $AgNO_3$ is added and in this solution, the solubility of Ag_2CrO_4 is S', then

$$[Ag^+] = 2S' + x \text{ and } [CrO_4^{2-}] = S'$$

$$\therefore \quad K_{sp} = (2S' + x)(S') \quad \ldots\text{(ii)}$$

Eqs. (i) and (ii) can be used to find S'. If K_{sp} is very small, we may neglect $2S'$ against x in Eq. (ii) and it becomes

$$K_{sp} = xS'$$

Example 7 Calculate the molar solubility of $Ni(OH)_2$ in 0.10 M NaOH. The ionic product of $Ni(OH)_2$ is 2.0×10^{-15}. **NCERT Textbook**

Sol. $Ni(OH)_2 \rightleftharpoons Ni^{2+} + 2OH^-$

S mol/L $\quad S$ mol/L $\quad 2S$ mol/L

$NaOH \longrightarrow Na^+ + OH^-$

0.10 M $\quad$ 0.10 M $\quad$ 0.10 M

$$[OH^-]_{total} = (2S + 0.10)$$

$$K_{sp} = 2.0 \times 10^{-15}$$

$$\Rightarrow [Ni^{2+}][OH^-]^2 = (S)(0.10 + 2S)^2$$

As K_{sp} is small, $2S << 0.10$, thus $(0.10 + 2S) \approx 0.10$

$$\therefore \quad 2.0 \times 10^{-15} = S(0.10)^2$$

$$\Rightarrow \quad S = 2.0 \times 10^{-13} \text{ M} = [Ni^{2+}]$$

3. In Qualitative Analysis of Salt

Cationic qualitative analysis is largely based on the principle of solubility product and common ion effect.

Cations are separated into following groups depending on the solubility of their salts :

Group II ($Hg^{2+}, Bi^{3+}, Cu^2, Cd^{2+}, Sn^{4+}$) These ions are precipitated as their sulphides by adding H_2S in the presence of HCl. The K_{sp} of their sulphides are low, thus lower concentration of S^{2-} is required. This is obtained by adding HCl which suppresses the ionisation of H_2S due to common ion effect.

Common ion

$$H_2S \rightleftharpoons 2H^+ + S^{2-}$$

$$HCl \rightleftharpoons H^+ + Cl^-$$

Group III ($Fe^{3+}, Cr^{3+}, Al^{3+}$) These ions are precipitated as their hydroxide by adding NH_4OH in the presence of NH_4Cl. The K_{sp} of their hydroxides are low, thus lower concentration of OH^- is required. This is obtained by adding NH_4Cl followed by NH_4OH.

Common ion

$$NH_4Cl \rightleftharpoons NH_4^+ + Cl^-$$

$$NH_4OH \rightleftharpoons NH_4^+ + OH^-$$

The ions of group IV and group VI have high K_{sp} of their hydroxide hence, does not precipitated.

Group IV ($Mn^{2+}, Zn^{2+}, Ni^{2+}, Co^{2+}$) These ion are also precipitated as their sulphides by adding H_2S in the presence of NH_4OH. The K_{sp} of their sulphides are high.

Topic Practice 3

Very Short Answer Type Questions

1 Mark

1 Fill in the Blanks

(i) A buffer solution is a solution, whose pH value on keeping in the air............ .

(ii) The process of interaction of cation or anion or both provided by salt with water is called............ .

(iii) A buffer solution shows little change in pH on adding small amount of............or............ .

2 Objective Type Questions

(i) The solutions which resist change in pH on dilution or with the addition of small amounts of acid or alkali are called

(a) homogeneous solutions
(b) heterogeneous solutions
(c) ionic solutions
(d) buffer solutions

(ii) Which of the following is correct regarding buffer solution?

(a) It contains a weak acid and its conjugate base
(b) It contains a weak base and its conjugate acid
(c) It shows little change in pH on adding small amount of acid or base
(d) None of the above

(iii) The pK_a of HCN is 9.30. The pH of a solution prepared by mixing 2.5 moles of KCN and 2.5 moles of HCN in water and making up the total volume of 500 mL is

(a) 9.30 (b) 7.30
(c) 10.30 (d) 8.30

3 Match the Column I with Column II and choose the correct option using the codes gives below:

Column I (Hydrolysis of the salts)	Column II (Example)
A. Weak acid and strong base	(i) NH_4Cl
B. Strong acid and weak base	(ii) CH_3COONH_4
C. Weak acid and weak base	(iii) CH_3COONa

Codes

	A	B	C		A	B	C
(a)	(iii)	(ii)	(i)	(b)	(i)	(ii)	(iii)
(c)	(ii)	(iii)	(i)	(d)	(iii)	(i)	(ii)

4 What will be the pH of 1M Na_2SO_4 solution?

5 What is the expression for K_{sp} of Ag_2CrO_4?

6 Under what conditions is a substance precipitated from its solution?

7 Is it possible to get precipitate of $Fe(OH)_3$ at pH = 2 ? Give reason.

8 Will AgCl be more soluble in aqueous solution or NaCl solution and why?

9 Why pH of our blood remains almost constant at 7.4 though we quite often eat spicy food?

Short Answer Type I Questions

2 Marks

10 What will be the pH of 0.1 M ammonium acetate solution? $pK_a = pK_b = 4.74$.

11 The ionisation constant of formic acid is 1.8×10^{-4}. Calculate the ratio of sodium formate and formic acid in a buffer of pH 4.25.

12 A 0.02 M solution of pyridinium hydrochloride has pH = 3.44. Calculate the ionisation constant of pyridine. **NCERT Textbook**

13 A certain buffer is made by mixing sodium formate and formic acid in water. With the help of equations explain how this buffer neutralises addition of a small amount of an acid or a base?

14 The solubility of silver chloride (AgCl) in water at 25°C is 1.06×10^{-5} mol L^{-1}. Calculate the solubility product of AgCl at this temperature.

15 The molar solubility of lead iodate, $Pb(IO_3)_2$ is 4.0×10^{-5} mol/L at 25°C. Calculate its K_{sp}.

$$Pb(IO_3)_2 \rightleftharpoons Pb^{2+} + 2IO_3$$

16 The solubility product of $Fe(OH)_3$ is 1×10^{-36}. What is the minimum concentration of OH^- ions required to precipitate $Fe(OH)_3$ from a 0.001 M solution of $FeCl_3$?

17 The K_{sp} values of two slightly soluble salts AB and PQ_2 are each equal to 4.0×10^{-18}. Which salt is more soluble?

18 What is the maximum concentration of equimolar solutions of ferrous sulphate and sodium sulphide so that when mixed in equal volumes, there is no precipitation of iron sulphide? (For iron sulphide, $K_{sp} = 6.3 \times 10^{-18}$) **NCERT Textbook**

19 A sparingly soluble salt having general formula $A_x^{p+} B_y^{q-}$ and molar solubility S is in equilibrium with its saturated solution. Derive a relationship between the solubility and solubility product for such salt.

Short Answer Type II Questions

(3 Marks)

20 Arrange the following in increasing order of pH. **NCERT Exemplar**

$KNO_3(aq)$, $CH_3COONa(aq)$, $NH_4Cl(aq)$, $C_6H_5COONH_4(aq)$

21 Predict if the solutions of the following salts are neutral, acidic or basic

NaCl, KBr, NaCN, NH_4NO_3, $NaNO_2$ and KF

22 The solubility product of $Al(OH)_3$ is 2.7×10^{-11}. Calculate its solubility (in g L^{-1}) and also find out pH of this solution. (Atomic mass of Al = 27 u)

23 The ionisation constant of nitrous acid is 4.5×10^{-4}. Calculate the pH of 0.04 M sodium nitrite solution and also its degree of hydrolysis. **NCERT Textbook**

24 The solubility product of AgCl is 1.5×10^{-10}. Predict whether there will be any precipitation by mixing 50 mL of 0.01 M NaCl and 50 mL of 0.01 M $AgNO_3$ solution.

25 The ionisation constant of chloroacetic acid is 1.35×10^{-3}. What will be the pH of 0.1 M acid and its 0.1 M sodium salt solution?

26 The concentration of sulphide ion in 0.1 M HCl solution saturated with hydrogen sulphide is 1.0×10^{-19} M. If 10 mL of this is added to 5 mL of 0.04 M solution of the following $FeSO_4$, $MnCl_2$, $ZnCl_2$ and $CdCl_2$, in which of these solutions precipitation will take place? (Given, K_{sp} of FeS $= 6.3 \times 10^{-18}$, K_{sp} of MnS $= 2.5 \times 10^{-13}$ K_{sp} of ZnS $= 1.6 \times 10^{-24}$, K_{sp} of CdS $= 8.0 \times 10^{-27}$) **NCERT Textbook**

27 Equal volumes of 0.002 M solutions of sodium iodate and cupric chlorate are mixed together. Will it lead to the precipitation of copper iodate? (For cupric iodate, $K_{sp} = 7.4 \times 10^{-8}$) **NCERT Textbook**

28 The buffers of X and Y of pH 4.0 and 6.0 respectively are prepared from acid HA and the salt NA. Both the buffers are 0.50 M in HA. What would be the pH of the solution obtained by mixing equal volumes of the two buffers? ($K_{HA} = 1.0 \times 10^{-5}$)

29 How much volume of 0.1 M CH_3COOH should be added to 50 mL of 0.2 M CH_3COONa solution to prepare a buffer solution of pH 4.91. (pK_a of AcH is 4.76).

30 The ionisation constant of benzoic acid is 6.46×10^{-5} and K_{sp} for silver benzonate is 2.5×10^{-13}.

How many times is silver benzoate more soluble in a buffer of pH 3.19 compared to its solubility in pure water?

31 The solubility product of lead bromide is 8×10^{-5} at 298 K. If the salt is 80% dissociated in saturated solution, calculate the solubility of the salt (in g/L).

32 Calculate the volume of water required to dissolve 0.1 g lead (II) chloride to get a saturated solution (K_{sp} of $PbCl_2 = 3.2 \times 10^{-8}$, atomic mass of Pb = 207 u). **NCERT Exemplar**

33 The solubility product of Ag_2CrO_4 and AgBr are 1.1×10^{-12} and 5.0×10^{-13} respectively. Calculate the ratio of the molarities of their saturated solutions. **NCERT Textbook**

34 What is the minimum volume of water required to dissolve 1g of calcium sulphate at 298 K? (For calcium sulphate, K_{sp} is 9.1×10^{-6}).

Long Answer Type Questions

(5 Marks)

35 Calculate the pH of a buffer which is 0.1 M in acetic acid and 0.15 M in sodium acetate. Given that the ionisation constant of acetic acid is 1.75×10^{-5}. Also calculate the change in pH of the buffer if, to 1 L of the buffer (i) 1 cc of 1 M NaOH are added. (ii) 1 cc of 1 M HCl are added. Assume that the change in volume is negligible. (iii) What will be the buffer index of the above buffer?

36 Determine the solubilities of silver chromate, barium chromate, ferric hydroxide, lead chloride and mercurous iodide at 298 K from their solubility product constants.

(i) $K_{sp}(Ag_2CrO_4) = 1.1 \times 10^{-12}$,

(ii) $K_{sp}(BaCrO_4) = 1.2 \times 10^{-10}$,

(iii) $K_{sp}[Fe(OH)_3] = 1.0 \times 10^{-38}$,

Also, determine the molarities of individual ions. **NCERT Textbook**

Hints & Solutions

1. (i) does not change (ii) hydrolysis (iii) acid, base

2. (i) d (ii) c

(iii) (a) As, [salt] = [acid] pH = pK_a= 9.30

3. (d)

4. Na_2SO_4 is salt of strong acid and strong base, thus its aqueous solution will be neutral. Therefore, its pH will be 7.

5. $Ag_2CrO_4(s) \rightleftharpoons \underset{2S}{2Ag^+(aq)} + \underset{S}{CrO_4^{2-}(aq)}$;
$\underset{S}{}$

$$K_{sp} = [Ag^+]^2 [CrO_4^{2-}]$$
$$= (2S)^2(S) = 4S^3$$

6. Precipitation takes place, when ionic product exceeds the solubility product.

7. No, because $Fe(OH)_3$ will dissolve in strongly acidic medium.

8. In NaCl solution, the Cl^- ions will increase. Since solubility product, $K_{sp} = [Ag^+][Cl^-]$ remains constant.

$[Ag^+]$ will decrease. Therefore, solubility of AgCl will be less in NaCl solution than in water.

9. Blood is a buffer containing carbonic acid (H_2CO_3) and bicarbonate ions (HCO_3^-). Small amounts of the acid or base produced from the spicy food does not disturb its pH.

10. For a salt of ammonium acetate,

$$pH = \frac{1}{2} pK_w + \frac{1}{2} pK_a - \frac{1}{2} pK_b$$
$$= \frac{1}{2}(14) + \frac{1}{2}(4.74) - \frac{1}{2}(4.74) = 7$$

[2]

11. $pK_a = -\log(1.8 \times 10^{-4}) = 3.74$

$$\log \frac{[Salt]}{[Acid]} = pH - pK_a = 4.25 - 3.74 = 0.51$$ [1]

or $\frac{[Salt]}{[Acid]}$ = Antilog 0.51 = 3.24 [1]

12. Key Idea

- *Pyridinium hydrochloride is a salt of weak base (pyridine) and strong acid (hydrochloric acid). Therefore, to calculate K_b, first calculate pK_b by using the formula,*
- $$pH = 7 - \frac{pK_b}{2} - \frac{\log C}{2}$$
- *Calculate K_b, by using the formula $pK_b = -\log K_b$*

$C_6H_5N^+HCl^- + H_2O \rightleftharpoons C_6H_5N^+HOH^- + HCl$

(Solution is acidic due to hydrolysis)

$$pH = 7 - \frac{pK_b}{2} - \frac{\log C}{2};\ 3.44 = 7 - \frac{pK_b}{2} - \frac{\log 0.02}{2}$$ [1]

$$pK_b = 8.82;$$
$$pK_b = 8.82$$

$$\Rightarrow \quad -\log K_b$$
$$\log K_b = -8.82 = \bar{9}.18$$
$$K_b = \text{antilog } \bar{9}.18 = 1.5 \times 10^{-9}$$ [1]

Alternatively,

(i) Find $[H_3O^+]$ ion conc. by using the formula
$$pH = -\log[H_3O^+]$$

(ii) Calculate K_a by using the formula,
$$K_a = \frac{[C_6H_5N^+Cl^-][H_3O^+]}{[C_6H_5N \cdot HCl]}.$$

(iii) Calculate pK_a from K_a and then pK_b by using the formula $pK_a + pK_b = 14$. [1]

(iv) Calculate K_b from pK_b.

$$C_6H_5N \cdot HCl + H_2O \rightleftharpoons C_6H_5N^+Cl^- + H_3O^+$$
$$K_a = \frac{[C_6H_5N^+Cl^-][H_3O^+]}{[C_6H_5N \cdot HCl]}$$
$$pH = 3.44 = -\log[H_3O^+]$$
$$\log[H_3O^+] = -3.44 = \bar{4}.56$$
$$[H_3O^+] = \text{antilog } \bar{4}.56 = 3.63 \times 10^{-4} M$$
$$[H_3O^+] = [C_6H_5N^+Cl^-] = 3.63 \times 10^{-4}$$

Hence, $K_a = \dfrac{3.63 \times 10^{-4} \times 3.63 \times 10^{-4}}{0.02} = 6.588 \times 10^{-6}$

$$pK_a = -\log K_a = -\log 6.588 \times 10^{-6}$$
$$pK_a = 6 + (-0.8187) = 5.18$$
$$pK_a + pK_b = 14;\ pK_b = 14 - 5.18 = 8.82$$
$$-\log K_b = -8.82 \text{ or } \log K_b = -8.82 = \bar{9}.18$$
$$K_b = \text{antilog } \bar{9}.18 = 1.5 \times 10^{-9}$$ [1]

13. $HCOONa \longrightarrow HCOO^- + Na^+$

$HCOOH \rightleftharpoons HCOO^- + H^+$ [1]

$HCOO^-$ is common ion in the above acidic buffer. When small amount of H^+ ions is added, these H^+ ions combine with $HCOO^-$ which are in excess to form HCOOH back and $[H^+]$ remains practically same, so pH remains constant. When small amount of OH^- ions are added, OH^- ions will take up H^+ and association of HCOOH will increase so as to maintain concentration of H^+ ions. So, pH is not affected. [1]

14. The solubility of AgCl at equilibrium is

$$AgCl(s) \rightleftharpoons Ag^+(aq) + Cl^-(aq)$$

One mole of AgCl in solution gives 1 mole of Ag^+ ions and 1 mole of Cl^- ions. Since, the solubility of AgCl is 1.06×10^{-5} mol L^{-1}, it will give 1.06×10^{-5} mol L^{-1} of Ag^+ ions and 1.06×10^{-5} mol L^{-1} of Cl^- ions. Therefore, $[Ag^+] = 1.06 \times 10^{-5}$ mol L^{-1}, $[Cl^-] = 1.06 \times 10^{-5}$ mol L^{-1}

Now, $K_{sp} = [Ag^+][Cl^-] = (1.06 \times 10^{-5}) \times (1.06 \times 10^{-5})$

$$= 1.12 \times 10^{-10}$$

[2]

15. $\therefore K_{sp} = [Pb^{2+}][IO_3^-]^2$

$\because$ The molar solubility of $Pb(IO_3)_2$ is 4.0×10^{-5} mol L^{-1}

$\therefore$ $[Pb^{2+}] = 4.0 \times 10^{-5}$ mol L^{-1}

$[IO_3^-] = 2 \times 4.0 \times 10^{-5}$ mol L^{-1}

$\therefore$ $K_{sp} = (4.0 \times 10^{-5})(8.0 \times 10^{-5})^2 = 2.56 \times 10^{-13}$ [2]

16. K_{sp} for $Fe(OH)_3$ is $K_{sp} = [Fe^{3+}][OH^-]^3$

Precipitation will occur when ionic product, $[Fe^{3+}][OH^-]^3$ becomes greater than K_{sp}.

$$[Fe^{3+}] = [FeCl_3] = 0.001\text{ M}$$ [1]

The concentration of OH^- ions required to start the precipitation is

$$[OH^-]^3 = \frac{K_{sp}}{[Fe^{3+}]} = \frac{1 \times 10^{-36}}{0.001} = 1 \times 10^{-33}$$

$\therefore$ $[OH^-] = (1 \times 10^{-33})^{1/3} = 1 \times 10^{-11}$ mol L^{-1}

Thus, concentration of OH^- required to start precipitation of $Fe(OH)_3 = 1 \times 10^{-11}$ mol L^{-1} [1]

17. For AB salt, $K_{sp} = [A^+][B^-]$. If x is the solubility, then

$$x^2 = 4.0 \times 10^{-18}$$

or $x = 2.0 \times 10^{-9}$ [1]

For PQ_2 salt, $K_{sp} = [P^{2+}][Q^-]^2$

If y is the solubility, then

$$4y^3 = K_{sp} = 4.0 \times 10^{-18} \text{ or } y = 1.0 \times 10^{-6}$$

Since y is more than x, PQ_2 salt has more solubility. [1]

18. FeS is at the point of precipitation when

$$[Fe^{2+}][S^{2-}] = K_{sp}$$

$[Fe^{2+}] = [S^{2-}] = \sqrt{K_{sp}}$ ($\because$Given, $[Fe^{2+}] = [S^{2-}]$)

$= \sqrt{6.3 \times 10^{-18}}$

$[Fe^{2+}] = [S^{2-}]$

$= 2.51 \times 10^{-9}$ M [1]

Since, equimolar solutions are to be mixed, hence on mixing concentration is halved. Thus, in original solution

$[FeSO_4] = [Na_2S] = 2 \times 2.51 \times 10^{-9}$; $M = 5.02 \times 10^{-9}$M [1]

19. A sparingly soluble salt having general formula $A_x^{p+} B_y^{q-}$. Its molar solubility is S mol L^{-1}.

Then, $A_x^{p+} B_y^{q-} \rightleftharpoons \underset{xS}{xA^{p+}(aq)} + \underset{yS}{yB^{q-}(aq)}$ [1]

S moles of A_xB_y dissolve to give x moles of A^{P+} and y moles of B^{q-}. Therefore, solubility product

$$(K_{sp}) = [A^{P+}]^x [B^{q-}]^y$$

$$-[xS]^x [yS]^y = x^x y^y S^{x+y}$$ [1]

20. (i) KNO_3 is a salt of strong acid (HNO_3) and strong base (KOH), hence, its aqueous solution is neutral; pH = 7.

(ii) CH_3COONa is a salt of weak acid (CH_3COOH) and strong base (NaOH), hence, its aqueous solution is basic; pH > 7. [1]

(iii) NH_4Cl is a salt of strong acid (HCl) and weak base (NH_4OH), hence its aqueous solution is acidic; pH < 7. [1]

(iv) $C_6H_5COONH_4$ is a salt of weak acid, C_6H_5COOH and weak base, NH_4OH. But NH_4OH is slightly stronger than C_6H_5COOH. Hence, pH is slightly > 7.

Therefore, increasing order of pH of the given salts is,

$NH_4Cl < KNO_3 < C_6H_5COONH_4 < CH_3COONa$ [1]

21. The solution of a salt of strong acid and strong base is neutral while that of weak acid and strong base is basic. A solution of salt of strong acid and weak base is acidic.

	Salt	Acid	Base	Hydrolysis reaction	Nature of solution
(i)	NaCl	HCl	NaOH	No hydrolysis	Neutral
(ii)	KBr	HBr	KOH	No hydrolysis	Neutral
(iii)	NaCN	HCN	NaOH	$CN^- + H_2O \rightleftharpoons HCN + OH^-$	Basic
(iv)	NH_4NO_3	HNO_3	NH_4OH	$NH_4^+ + H_2O \rightleftharpoons NH_4OH + H^+$	Acidic
(v)	$NaNO_2$	HNO_2	NaOH	$NO_2^- + H_2O \rightleftharpoons HNO_2 + OH^-$	Basic
(vi)	KF	HF	KOH	$F^- + H_2O \rightleftharpoons HF + OH^-$	Basic

22. Let S be the solubility of $Al(OH)_3$.

$$Al(OH)_3 \rightleftharpoons Al^{3+}(aq) + 3OH^-(aq)$$

	$Al(OH)_3$	Al^{3+}	$3OH^-$
Concentration of species at $t = 0$	1	0	0
Concentration of various species at equilibrium	$1-S$	S	$3S$

$K_{sp} = [Al^{3+}][OH^-]^3 = (S)(3S)^3 = 27S^4$

$$S^4 = \frac{K_{sp}}{27} = \frac{2.7 \times 10^{-11}}{27} = 1 \times 10^{-12};$$

$S = 1 \times 10^{-3}$ mol L^{-1} [1]

(i) Solubility of $Al(OH)_3$

Molar mass of $Al(OH)_3$ is 78 g. Therefore,

Solubility of $Al(OH)_3$ in g L^{-1}

$= 1 \times 10^{-3} \times 78$ g $L^{-1} = 78 \times 10^{-3}$ g L^{-1}

$= 7.8 \times 10^{-2}$ g L^{-1} [1]

(ii) pH of the solution $S = 1 \times 10^{-3}$ mol L^{-1}

$[OH^-] = 3S = 3 \times 1 \times 10^{-3} = 3 \times 10^{-3}$

pOH = 3 − log 3

pH = 14 − pOH = 11 + log 3 = 11.4771 [1]

23. **Key Idea**

- Sodium nitrite is a salt of weak acid and strong base. Hence, to calculate pH of its aqueous solution use the formula $pH = 7 + \frac{pK_a + \log C}{2}$,
- Degree of hydrolysis, $h = \sqrt{\frac{K_W}{K_a C}}$

Given, $[NaNO_2] = 0.04$ M

K_a of $HNO_2 = 4.5 \times 10^{-4}$

$\therefore \quad pK_a = -\log K_a = -\log(4.5 \times 10^{-4})$

$pK_a = 4 - 0.6532 = 3.3468 \approx 3.35$

From $pH = 7 + \frac{pK_a + \log C}{2} = 7 + \frac{3.35 + \log 0.04}{2} = 7.97$ [1]

Degree of hydrolysis, $h = \sqrt{\frac{K_W}{K_a \cdot C}}$

$= \sqrt{\frac{10^{-14}}{4.5 \times 10^{-4} \times 0.04}}$

$h = 2.36 \times 10^{-5}$ [2]

24. On mixing 50 mL of 0.01 M NaCl and 50 mL of 0.01 M $AgNO_3$, the total volume becomes 100 mL. Therefore,

Conc. of NaCl in 100 mL $= \frac{0.01 \times 50}{100} = 0.005$ M

Conc. of $AgNO_3$ in 100 mL $= \frac{0.01 \times 50}{100} = 0.005$ M [1]

Now $\quad NaCl(aq) \rightarrow Na^+(aq) + Cl^-(aq)$

and $\quad AgNO_3(aq) \rightarrow Ag^+(aq) + NO_3^-(aq)$

$[Cl^-] = [NaCl] = 0.005$ M

$[Ag^+] = [AgNO_3] = 0.005$ M [1]

$\therefore$ Ionic product of $[Ag^+][Cl^-] = 0.005 \times 0.005 = 2.5 \times 10^{-5}$

Since ionic product is greater than its solubility product, precipitation will occur. [1]

25.
- To calculate pH of the solution first find $[H_3O^+]$ ion concentration by using the formula, $[H_3O^+] = \sqrt{K_a C}$
- Calculate pH by using the formula, $pH = -\log[H_3O^+]$.
- Sodium chloroacetate is a salt of strong base and weak acid therefore, $pH = 7 + \frac{pK_a + \log C}{2}$.

$$CH_2ClCOOH + H_2O \rightleftharpoons CH_2ClCOO^- + H_3O^+$$

$K_a = 1.35 \times 10^{-3}$ (given)

$pK_a = -\log K_a = -\log[1.35 \times 10^{-3}]$

$= 3 - 0.13 = 2.87$ [1]

By Ostwald's dilution law,

$[H_3O^+] = \sqrt{K_a \cdot C} = \sqrt{1.35 \times 10^{-3} \times 0.1}$

$[H_3O^+] = 1.16 \times 10^{-2}$M

pH of acid $= -\log[H_3O^+]$

$= -\log(1.16 \times 10^{-2})$ M

$pH = 2 - 0.06 = 1.94$ [1]

0.1 M $CH_2ClCOONa$ (sod. chloroacetate) is basic due to hydrolysis.

$$CH_2ClCOO^- + H_2O \rightleftharpoons CH_2ClCOOH + OH^-$$

For a salt of strong base + weak acid,

$pH = 7 + \frac{pK_a + \log C}{2} = 7 + \frac{2.87 + \log 0.1}{2}$

$pH = 7 + \frac{2.87 + (-1)}{2} = 7 + \frac{1.87}{2} = 7 + 0.935 \approx 7.94$

$pH = 7.94$ [1]

Alternatively

To find pH of 0.1 M sodium salt solution use the formula,

$pH = -\frac{1}{2}[\log K_w + \log K_a - \log C]$ [1]

$pH = -\frac{1}{2}[\log 10^{-14} + \log(1.35 \times 10^{-3}) - \log 0.1]$

$pH = -\frac{1}{2}[-14 + (-3 + 0.1303) - (-1)]$ [1]

$pH = -\frac{1}{2}[-15.8697] = 7.93485 \approx 7.94$ [1]

26. For precipitation, ionic product > solubility product, so calculate ionic product of each salt and compare it with solubility product.

$[S^{2-}] = 1 \times 10^{-19}$ M

10 mL of S^{2-} is mixed with 5 mL of 0.04 M solution of different solutes so that final volume of solution is 15 mL.

$\therefore \quad [S^{2-}]_{mix} = \frac{10 \times 10^{-19}}{15} = 6.67 \times 10^{-20}$ M

[Use, $M_1V_1 = M_2V_2$] [1]

$[M^{2+}] = \frac{5 \times 0.04}{15} = 1.33 \times 10^{-2}$ M

where, $[M^{2+}] = Fe^{2+}, Mn^{2+}, Zn^{2+}$ or Cd^{2+}

$[M^{2+}][S^{2-}] = 1.33 \times 10^{-2} \times 6.67 \times 10^{-20}$ [1]

i.e. ionic product of $[M^{2+}][S^{2-}] = 8.87 \times 10^{-22}$

Since, ionic product of $[M^{2+}][S^{2-}] > K_{sp}$ of ZnS and CdS.

So, these ($CdCl_2$ and $ZnCl_2$) are precipitated as CdS and ZnS. [1]

27. For precipitation, ionic product > K_{sp}, so first find concentration, (mol L^{-1}) of Cu^{2+} ions and IO_3^- ions in mixture and then ionic product of $[Cu^{2+}]$ and $[IO_3^-]$.
If ionic product > K_{sp}, precipitation of $Cu(IO_3)_2$ will take place, otherwise not.

$$2NaIO_3 + Cu(ClO_3)_2 \longrightarrow 2NaClO_3 + \underset{\text{Copper iodate}}{Cu(IO_3)_2}$$

$$[Cu^{2+}]_{mix} = \frac{0.002}{2} = 0.001\ M$$

$$[IO_3^-]_{mix} = \frac{0.002}{2} = 0.001\ M \quad [1]$$

(Due to mixing of equal volumes, molar concentrations of each species is halved.)

$$Cu(IO_3)_2 \rightleftharpoons Cu^{2+} + 2\,IO_3^-$$

$Cu(IO_3)_2$ is precipitated if $[Cu^{2+}]\cdot[IO_3^-]^2 > K_{sp}$ [1]

$$[Cu^{2+}][IO_3^-]^2 = (1.0\times 10^{-3})\times(1.0\times 10^{-3})^2 = 1\times 10^{-9}$$

∵ Ionic product < K_{sp}

∴ There will be no precipitation. [1]

28. $K_{HA} = 1.0\times 10^{-5}$ ∴ $pK_a = -\log(1.0\times 10^{-5}) = 5.0$

Determination of conc. of salt in buffer *X*.

$$pH = pK_a + \log\frac{[Salt]}{[Acid]};\ 4.0 = 5.0 + \log\frac{[Salt]}{0.5}$$

$$\log\frac{[Salt]}{0.5} = -1 \Rightarrow \frac{[Salt]}{0.5} = 10^{-1}$$

$$[Salt] = 0.5\times 10^{-1} = 0.05\ M \quad [1]$$

Determination of conc. of salt in buffer *Y*

$$6.0 = 5.0 + \log\frac{[Salt]}{0.5}$$

$$\log\frac{[Salt]}{0.5} = 1.0 \Rightarrow \frac{[Salt]}{0.5} = 10$$

$$[Salt] = 10\times 0.5 = 5.0$$

Conc. of salt in the mixture,

$$[Salt]_{mix} = \frac{0.5+5}{2} = 2.75\ M \quad [1]$$

$$pH = pK_a + \log\frac{[Salt]}{[Acid]} = 5.0 + \log\frac{2.75}{0.5}$$

$$= 5.0 + 0.74 = 5.74 \quad [1]$$

29. According to Henderson's equation

$$pH = pK_a + \log\frac{[Salt]}{[Acid]};\ pH = 4.91,\ pK_a = 4.76$$

$$4.91 = 4.76 + \log\frac{[Salt]}{[Acid]}$$

$$\log\frac{[NaAc]}{[AcH]} = 4.91 - 4.76 = 0.15$$

$$\frac{[NaAc]}{[AcH]} = \text{antilog}(0.15) = 1.41 \quad [1]$$

If *V* is the volume of 0.1 M AcH required

$$\frac{[NaAc]}{[AcH]} = \frac{\frac{0.2\times 50}{1000}}{\frac{0.1\times V}{1000}} = 1.41$$

$$= \frac{0.2\times 50}{0.15\times V} = 1.41 \quad [1]$$

or $$V = \frac{0.2\times 50}{0.1\times 1.41} = 70.92\ mL$$

Volume of 0.1 M acetic acid required

$$= 70.92\ mL \quad [1]$$

30.
- In order to find the hydrolysis constant of silver benzoate, first write the equation of ionisation of benzoic acid and ionisation of silver benzoate and find a relation of K_3 (hydrolysis constant) with K_1 (K_{sp}) and K_a.
- Find $[H^+]$ concentration to find *S* (solubility of silver benzoate) in buffer.
- Find solubility of silver benzoate in aqueous solution and compare them.

$$C_6H_5COOAg(s) \rightleftharpoons C_6H_5COO^- + Ag;$$

$$C_6H_5COOAg(s) \rightleftharpoons C_6H_5COO^- + Ag;\ K_1 = K_{sp}$$

$$C_6H_5COO^- + H^+ \rightleftharpoons C_6H_5COOH;\ K_2 = \frac{1}{K_a}$$

$$C_6H_5COOAg(s) + H^+ \rightleftharpoons C_6H_5COOH + Ag^+$$

$$\because\ K_3 = \frac{K_{sp}}{K_a}$$

$$\therefore\ K_3 = \frac{[C_6H_5COOH][Ag^+]}{[H^+]} = \frac{S\cdot S}{[H^+]} = \frac{S^2}{[H^+]} = \frac{K_{sp}}{K_a}$$

where, *s* is the solubility of C_6H_5COOAg. [1]

In a buffer of pH = 3.19,

$$\log[H^+] = -3.19 = \bar{4}.81$$

$$\Rightarrow\ [H^+] = \text{antilog}\,\bar{4}.81 = 6.46\times 10^{-4}$$

$$\frac{S^2}{[H^+]} = \frac{K_{sp}}{K_a}\ \text{or}\ S^2 = \frac{K_{sp}\times[H^+]}{K_a}$$

$$S = \sqrt{\frac{2.5\times 10^{-13}\times 6.46\times 10^{-4}}{6.46\times 10^{-5}}}$$

$$S = \sqrt{2.5 \times 10^{-13} \times 10}$$

$\Rightarrow$ $S = 1.6 \times 10^{-6}$ M (in buffer) [1]

In aqueous solution, solubility of C_6H_5COOAg

$$K_{sp} = [C_6H_5COO^-][Ag^+] = S \cdot S = S^2$$

$$S = \sqrt{K_{sp}} = \sqrt{2.5 \times 10^{-13}} = 5 \times 10^{-7} \text{ M}$$

$$\frac{S_{(C_6H_5COOAg)} \text{ in buffer}}{S_{(C_6H_5COOAg)} \text{ in aqueous solution}} = \frac{1.6 \times 10^{-6}}{5.0 \times 10^{-7}} = 3.2$$ [1]

31. The solubility equilibrium is

$$PbBr_2(s) \rightleftharpoons Pb^{2+}(aq) + 2Br^-(aq)$$

Suppose the solubility of $PbBr_2$ is S moles per litre. Then, the concentrations of various species at equilibrium are

$$[Pb^{2+}] = S, [Br^-] = 2S$$

Now, $K_{sp} = [Pb^{2+}][Br^-]^2$

$$8 \times 10^{-5} = (S) \times (2S)^2$$

$$8 \times 10^{-5} = 4S^3 \text{ or } S^3 = \frac{8 \times 10^{-5}}{4} = 2 \times 10^{-5}$$ [1]

$$S = (2.0 \times 10^{-5})^{1/3} = 2.714 \times 10^{-2} \text{ mol L}^{-1}$$

This is the solubility of $PbBr_2$ if it is 100% dissociated. [1]

Solubility of $PbBr_2$ if it is 80% dissociated

$$= \frac{2.714 \times 10^{-2} \times 80}{100} = 2.172 \times 10^{-2} \text{ mol L}^{-1}$$

Molecular weight of $PbBr_2 = 207 + 2 \times 80 = 367$ g mol^{-1}

Solubility of $PbBr_2 = 2.172 \times 10^{-2} \times 367 = 7.97$ g L^{-1} [1]

32. Suppose solubility of $PbCl_2$ in water is S mol L^{-1}.

$$\underset{(1-S)}{PbCl_2(s)} \rightleftharpoons \underset{S}{Pb^{2+}(aq)} + \underset{2S}{2Cl^-(aq)}$$

$$K_{sp} = [Pb^{2+}] \cdot [Cl^-]^2$$

$$K_{sp} = [S][2S]^2 = 4S^3; 3.2 \times 10^{-8} = 4S^3$$

$$S^3 = \frac{3.2 \times 10^{-8}}{4} = 0.8 \times 10^{-8}; S^3 = 8.0 \times 10^{-9}$$ [1]

Solubility of $PbCl_2$, $S = 2 \times 10^{-3}$ mol L^{-1} [1]

Solubility of $PbCl_2$ in g L^{-1} $= 278 \times 2 \times 10^{-3} = 0.556$ g L^{-1}

($\because$ Molar mass of $PbCl_2 = 207 + (2 \times 35.5) = 278$)

$\because$ 0.556 g of $PbCl_2$ dissolve in = 1 L

$\therefore$ 0.1 g of $PbCl_2$ will dissolve in $= \frac{1 \times 0.1}{0.556}$

$= 0.1798$ L $= 179.8$ mL [1]

33. $$\underset{S}{Ag_2CrO_4} \rightleftharpoons \underset{2S}{2Ag^+} + \underset{S}{CrO_4^{2-}}; K_{sp} = 1.1 \times 10^{-12}$$

(Solubility of Ag_2CrO_4 is S mol L^{-1})

$$K_{sp} = [Ag^+]^2[CrO_4^{2-}]$$

$$K_{sp} = (2S)^2 \cdot S = 4S^3$$

or $$S^3 = \frac{K_{sp}}{4} = \frac{1.1 \times 10^{-12}}{4} = 0.275 \times 10^{-12}$$

$$S^3 = 2.75 \times 10^{-13} = 6.503 \times 10^{-5} \text{ M}$$ [1]

Thus, solubility of $[Ag_2CrO_4] = 6.503 \times 10^{-5}$ M

$$\underset{S}{AgBr} \rightleftharpoons \underset{S}{Ag^+} + \underset{S}{Br^-}; K_{sp} = 5.0 \times 10^{-13}$$

(Solubility of AgBr is S mol L^{-1})

$$K_{sp} = [Ag^+][Br^-] = S \cdot S = S^2$$

or $$S = \sqrt{K_{sp}} = \sqrt{5.0 \times 10^{-13}} = \sqrt{50 \times 10^{-14}}$$

$$S = 7.07 \times 10^{-7} \text{ M}$$ [1]

Ratio of their solubilities

$$\frac{S\,(Ag_2CrO_4)}{S\,(AgBr)} = \frac{6.50 \times 10^{-5} \text{ M}}{7.07 \times 10^{-7} \text{ M}} = 91.93 \approx 92$$ [1]

34. $$\underset{S}{CaSO_4} \rightleftharpoons \underset{S}{Ca^{2+}} + \underset{S}{SO_4^{2-}}; K_{sp} = 9.1 \times 10^{-6}$$

where s is the solubility of $CaSO_4$

$$K_{sp} = [Ca^{2+}][SO_4^{2-}] = S \cdot S = S^2$$

$$S = \sqrt{K_{sp}} = \sqrt{9.1 \times 10^{-6}}$$

$\Rightarrow$ $S = 3.017 \times 10^{-3}$ M [1]

$\therefore$ Solubility of $CaSO_4 = 3.017 \times 10^{-3}$ mol L^{-1}

$= 3.017 \times 10^{-3} \times 136$ g L^{-1}

(Molar mass of $CaSO_4 = 136$ g mol^{-1})

$= 410.3 \times 10^{-3}$ gL^{-1} [1]

$\because$ 410.3×10^{-3} g $CaSO_4$ is dissolved in = 1 L

$\therefore$ 1g $CaSO_4$ is dissolved in $= \frac{1 \times 1}{410.3 \times 10^{-3}} = 2.437$ L [1]

35. $$pH = pK_a + \log\frac{[Salt]}{[Acid]} = -\log(1.75 \times 10^{-5}) + \log\frac{0.15}{0.10}$$

$$= (5 - 0.2430) + 0.1761 = 4.757 + 0.1761 = 4.933.$$

(i) 1 cc of 1 M NaOH contains NaOH $= 10^{-3}$ mol. This will convent 10^{-3} mol of acetic acid into the salt so that salt formed $= 10^{-3}$ mol.

Now, [Acid] $= 0.10 - 0.001 = 0.099$ M

[Salt] $= 0.15 + 0.001 = 0.151$ M

$$pH = 4.757 + \log\frac{0.151}{0.099}$$

$$= 4.757 + 0.183 = 4.940$$

$\therefore$ Increase in $pH = 4.940 - 4.933 = 0.007$ which is negligible. [2]

(ii) 1 cc of 1 M HCl contains $HCl = 10^{-3}$ mol. This will convert 10^{-3} mol CH_3COONa into CH_3COOH.

$\therefore$ Now, [Acid] $= 0.10 + 0.001 = 0.101$ M

[Salt] $= 0.15 - 0.001 = 0.149$ M

$$\therefore \quad pH = 4.757 + \log\frac{0.149}{0.101}$$

$$= 4.757 + 0.169$$

$$= 4.925$$

$\therefore$ Decrease in pH $= 4.933 = 0.007$ which is again negligible. [2]

(iii) **Calculation of buffer index**

No. of moles of HCl or NaOH added $= 0.001$ mol

Change in $pH = 0.007$

$$\text{Hence, buffer index} = \frac{dn}{dpH} = \frac{0.001}{0.007}$$

$$= \frac{1}{7} = 0.143$$ [1]

36. (i) $\underset{S}{Ag_2CrO_4} \rightleftharpoons \underset{2S}{2Ag^+} + \underset{S}{CrO_4^{2-}}$; $K_{sp} = 1.1 \times 10^{-12}$

$$K_{sp} = [Ag^+]^2 \cdot [CrO_4^{2-}]$$

$$K_{sp} = [2S]^2 \cdot [S] = 4S^3, \; S^3 = \frac{K_{sp}}{4}$$

$$\therefore \quad S^3 = \frac{1.1 \times 10^{-12}}{4} = 0.275 \times 10^{-12}$$

On solving $S = 6.503 \times 10^{-5}$ M

$$[Ag^+] = 2S = 2 \times 6.503 \times 10^{-5}$$

$$= 13.006 \times 10^{-5} \approx 1.3 \times 10^{-4} \text{ M}$$

and $[CrO_4^{2-}] = S = 6.503 \times 10^{-5}$ M [2]

(ii) $\underset{S}{BaCrO_4} \rightleftharpoons \underset{S}{Ba^{2+}} + \underset{S}{CrO_4^{2-}}$; $K_{sp} = 1.2 \times 10^{-10}$

(Solubility of $BaCrO_4$ is S mol L^{-1})

$$K_{sp} = 1.2 \times 10^{-10} = [Ba^{2+}] \cdot [CrO_4^{2-}] = S^2$$

$$S = \sqrt{1.2 \times 10^{-10}} = 1.1 \times 10^{-5} \text{M}$$

$$[Ba^{2+}] = [CrO_4^{2-}] = 1.1 \times 10^{-5} \text{ M}$$ [1]

(iii) $\underset{S}{Fe(OH)_3} \rightleftharpoons \underset{S}{Fe^{3+}} + \underset{3S}{3\,OH^-}$; $K_{sp} = 1.0 \times 10^{-38}$

(Solubility of $Fe(OH)_3$ is S mol L^{-1})

$$K_{sp} = [Fe^{3+}]\,[OH^-]^3$$

$$K_{sp} = S \cdot (3S)^3 = 27S^4 \quad \text{or} \quad S^4 = \frac{K_{sp}}{27}$$

$$S^4 = \frac{1.0 \times 10^{-38}}{27} = 0.037 \times 10^{-38}$$

$$S = 1.387 \times 10^{-10}, \; S \approx 1.39 \times 10^{-10}$$

$$[Fe^{3+}] = 1.39 \times 10^{-10} \text{ M}$$

$$[OH^-] = 3S = 3 \times 1.39 \times 10^{-10} = 4.17 \times 10^{-10} \text{ M}$$ [2]

SUMMARY

- The state at which rate of forward reaction becomes equal to the rate of backward reaction is called equilibrium state.
- Equilibrium can be classified as :

  (i) Chemical equilibrium (ii) Ionic equilibrium
- Chemical equilibrium established between two opposite reactions or processes.
- Equilibrium in physical processes involves :

  (i) Solid-liquid equilibria (ii) Liquid-vapour equilibria

  (iii) Solid-vapour equilibria (vi) Gas-liquid equilibria
- Equilibrium in chemical processes exists between reactants and products.
- Types of chemical equilibrium

  (i) Homogeneous equilibrium exists when all the species of the reaction are in same phase.

  (ii) Hetrogeneous equilibrium exists when phases of all the species of the reaction are not same.
- Equilibrium constant is the ratio of concentration of products to that of the reactants with each concentration term is raised to their stoichiometric coefficient, e.g. for reaction $aA \longrightarrow bB + cC$.

$$K_C = \frac{[B]^b \cdot [C]^c}{[A]^a} \text{ and } K_p = K_C (RT)^{\Delta n_g}$$

  Units $K_C = (\text{mol}/\text{L})^{\Delta n_g}$, $K_p = (\text{atm})^{\Delta n_g}$
- **Characteristics** (i) If a reaction is multiplied by n, K (new) $= K^n$.

  (ii) If reaction is divided by n, K (new) $= n\sqrt{K}$

  (iii) If two reactions are added having $K = K_1$ and K_2 respectively. New equilibrium constant becomes $= K_1 \times K_2$
- **Applications of Equilibrium**

  (i) Extent of reaction

  (a) $K_C > 10^3$, product predominates (b) $K_C < 10^{-3}$, reactant predominates

  (c) $10^{-3} > K_C > 10^3$ both reactants and products are present.

  (ii) Direction of reaction

  (a) If $Q = K$, equilibrium. (b) If $Q > K$, backward reaction

  (c) If $Q < K$, forward reaction (where, Q = reaction quotient)
- **Le-Chatelier's Principle**

  (i) If $[P]$ is removed or $[R]$ is added, reaction moves in forward direction.

  (ii) If $\Delta n_g = 0$, no effect of pressure. If $n_P > n_R$, high pressure favours reverse reaction.

  (iii) For endothermic reaction, high temperature favours forward reaction and for exothermic reaction, it favours backward reaction. (Here, P = product and R = reactant.)
- The equilibrium established between ionised and un-ionised forms of substance is called ionic equilibrium.
- Electrolytes are the substance which provide ions when dissolved in water.
- Acids are sour and turns blue litmus red while bases turns red litmus blue.
- **Salts** is the neutralisation product of acid and base.
- **Arrhenius Concept** Acids are H^+ donor while bases are OH^- donor.
- **Bronsted-Lowry Concept** Acids are H^+ donor but bases are H^+ acceptor.
- **Conjugate Acid-Base Pair** is the pair that differ by a proton, e.g. NH_3 and NH_4^+.
- **Lewis Concept** Acids are electron pair acceptor while bases are electron pair donor.
- Ionisation constant is the ratio of ionised and unionised forms.

(i) Ionisation of water, $K_w = [H^+][OH^-] = 10^{-14} \cdot M^2$

(ii) Ionisation of weak acid/base K_a or $K_b = C \cdot \alpha^2 \Rightarrow K_a \cdot K_b = K_w$

(where, α = degree of dissociation and C = concentration of solution)

- **pH scale**

(i) pH $= -\log[H^+]$, (ii) pOH $= -\log[OH^-]$, (iii) pH + pOH = 14, (iv) If pH>>, 7 solution is basic, (v) If pH <7, solution is acidic,

(vi) If pH = 7, solution is neutral.

Common ion effect is the reduction in dissociation of weak electrolyte in the presence of common ion.

- **Salt hydrolysis** is the process of interaction of ions of salt with water. If cation react with water, it is called cationic hydrolysis and if anion reacts with water, it is called anionic hydrolysis.

(i) Salt of strong acid and strong base, e.g. KCl, NaCl, Na_2SO_4. They do not hydrolyse. pH of their solution is always 7.

(ii) Salt of weak acid and strong base, e.g. CH_3COONa. $pH = 7 + \frac{1}{7}[pK_a + \log C]$, $h = \sqrt{\frac{K_w}{K_a \cdot C}}$

(iii) Salt of weak base and strong acid, e.g. NH_4Cl. $pH = 7 + \frac{1}{2}[pK_b + \log C]$, $h = \sqrt{\frac{K_w}{K_b \cdot C}}$

(iv) Salt of weak base and weak acid, $pH = 7 + \frac{1}{2}[(pK_a - pK_b)]$, $h = \sqrt{\frac{K_w}{K_a \cdot K_b}}$

- **Buffer solutions** These solution resist their pH.

(i) Acidic buffer is a mixture of weak acid and its conjugate base $pH = pK_a + \log \frac{[salt]}{[acid]}$

(ii) Basic buffer is a mixture of weak base and its conjugate acid $pOH = pK_b + \log \frac{[salt]}{[base]}$ and pH = 14 − pOH

- Solubility product $(K_{sp}) K_{sp} = x^x \cdot y^y \cdot S^{x+y}$ where, S = solubility, x and y = number of ions and solubility decreases with the increase in pH.
- If $Q > K_{sp}$, precipitate will form.

Chapter Practice

Very Short Answer Type Questions

(1 Mark)

1. Fill in the Blanks

(i) At equilibrium, ΔG will be ....

(ii) According to Bronsted and Lowry, an acid is a .... while a base is ....

(iii) Salts of weak acids and strong bases hydrolyse in water to form ...... solutions.

(iv) At equilibrium the concentrations of all ......and .... are equal.

(v) The aqueous solution of $CuSO_4$ is .... in nature.

(vi) The conjugate acid of PO_4^{3-} is ....

2. Objective Types Questions

(i) The solid-vapour equilibrium can be represented as:

(a) I_2 (solid) $\rightleftharpoons$ I_2 (vapour)

(b) Camphor (solid) $\rightleftharpoons$ Camphor (vapour)

(c) NH_4Cl (solid) $\rightleftharpoons$ NH_4Cl (vapour)

(d) All of the above

(ii) Which of the following is the example of a reversible reaction?

(a) $Pb(NO_3)_2(aq) + 2NaI(aq) \longrightarrow PbI_2(s) + 2NaNO_3(aq)$

(b) $2Na(s) + 2H_2O(l) \longrightarrow 2NaOH(aq) + H_2(g)$

(c) $AgNO_3(aq) + HCl(aq) \longrightarrow AgCl(s) + HNO_3(aq)$

(d) $KNO_3(aq) + NaCl(aq) \longrightarrow KCl(aq) + NaNO_3(aq)$

(iii) For reaction in equilibrium,

$H_2(g) + I_2(g) \rightleftharpoons 2HI(g)$

Choose the correct option.

(a) $K_C = \dfrac{[HI(g)]^2}{[H_2(g)]\,[I_2(g)]}$

(b) $K_p = \dfrac{[HI(g)]^2\,[RT]^2}{[H_2(g)]RT \cdot [I_2(g)]RT}$

(c) In this reaction, $K_p = K_C$, i.e. both equilibrium constants are equal

(d) All of the above

(iv) K_C for the reaction,

$N_2(g) + O_2(g) \rightleftharpoons 2NO(g)$

at 300 K is 4.0×10^{-6}. K_p for the above reaction will be ($R = 2$ cal $mol^{-1}K^{-1}$).

(a) 2.4×10^{-3} (b) 4×10^{-6}

(c) $4 \times 10^{-6}\,(RT)^2$ (d) 16×10^{-12}

(v) Production of ammonia according to the reaction,

$N_2(g) + 3H_2(g) \rightleftharpoons 2NH_3(g)$; $\Delta H = -92.38$ kJ mol^{-1}

is an exothermic process. At low temperature, the reaction shifts in

(a) forward direction

(b) backward direction

(c) either forward or backward direction

(d) None of the above

(vi) Which of the following will not change the concentration of ammonia in the equilibrium?

$4NH_3(g) + 5O_2(g) \rightleftharpoons 4NO(g) + 6H_2O(l)$; $\Delta H = +$ ve

(a) Increase of pressure

(b) Increase of volume

(c) Addition of catalyst

(d) Decrease of temperature

3. Matching Type Questions

(i) Match the Column I with Column II and choose the correct option using the codes given below:

Column I (Process)		Column II (Conclusion)
A. Liquid $\rightleftharpoons$ vapour	(i)	Concentration of solute in solution is constant at a given temperature.
B. Solid $\rightleftharpoons$ liquid	(ii)	[Gas (aq)]/ [gas (g)] is constant at a given temperature.
C. Solute (s) $\rightleftharpoons$ solute (solution)	(iii)	p_{H_2O} constant at given temperature.
D. Gas (g) $\rightleftharpoons$ Gas (aq)	(iv)	Melting point is fixed at constant pressure.

Codes

	A	B	C	D
(a)	(ii)	(iii)	(iv)	(i)
(b)	(i)	(ii)	(iii)	(iv)
(c)	(iv)	(iii)	(ii)	(i)
(d)	(iii)	(iv)	(i)	(ii)

(ii) Match the Column I (molecules/ions) with Column II (acid/base) and choose the correct option using the codes given below :

Column I	Column II
A. Mg^{2+}	1. Hard acid
B. H_2O	2. Soft acid
C. R_3P	3. Hard base
D. Ag^+	4. Soft base

Codes

	A	B	C	D		A	B	C	D
(a)	(i)	(iii)	(iv)	(ii)	(b)	(iv)	(ii)	(i)	(iii)
(c)	(i)	(ii)	(iv)	(iii)	(d)	(iv)	(iii)	(i)	(ii)

4. State Le-Chatelier's principle.

5. In the reaction equilibrium, $A+B \rightleftharpoons C+D$, what will happen to concentration of A, B, and D, if the concentration of C is increased?

6. The formation of NH_3 is exothermic. What is the effect of lower down the temperature of the system?

7. Which of the following is strongest Lewis acid?
$CCl_4, AlCl_3, NCl_3, PCl_3$

8. Will the pH of an aqueous solution of NH_4Cl greater, equal or less than 7?

Assertion-Reason

Directions (Q. Nos. 9-13) In the following questions, a statement of assertion is followed by a corresponding statements of reason of the following statements, choose the correct one.

(a) Both (A) and (R) are correct and (R) is the correct explanation of (A).
(b) Both (A) and (R) are correct but (R) is not the correct explanation of (A).
(c) (A) is correct and (R) is incorrect.
(d) (A) is incorrect and (R) is correct.

9. **Assertion** (A) A mixture of the solutions of a weak acid and its sodium salt acts as a good buffer.

Reason (R) The ratio of the salt to the acid in the mixture does not change substantially when small amount of acid and base is added to the buffer.

10. **Assertion** (A) If pK_a of an acid (HA) is x then pK_b of a conjugate base A^- is $(14 - x)$.

Reason (R) At 298K, in aqueous solution,
$$[H_3O^+]\,[OH^-] = 1\times10^{-14} = K_w$$

11. **Assertion** (A) For the reaction,
$$N_2(g) + 3H_2(g) \rightleftharpoons 2NH_3(g)$$
K_p is not equal to K_C.

Reason (R) Concentration of gaseous reactants and products is taken as unity.

12. **Assertion** (A) K_p can be less than, greater than or equal to K_C.

Reason (R) Relation between K_p and K_C depends on the change in number of moles of gaseous reactants and products (Δn).

13. **Assertion** (A) $N_2O_4(g) \rightleftharpoons 2NO_2(g)$ is the example of homogeneous equilibria.

Reason (R) The reactants and products are present in the same phase.

Case-Study

14. Equilibrium represents the state of a process in which properties like temperature, pressure, concentration of a system do not show any change. Any reaction at equilibrium can be represented as
$$aA + bB \rightleftharpoons cC + dD$$
Equilibrium is characterised by equilibrium constant K_C (reactant in solution) or K_p (reactants as gases). This constant is the ratio of concentration of products to reactant raised to the power of their stoichiometric quotient. This same ratio at condition other than equilibrium is known as reaction quotient and their difference shows if the reaction goes forward or backward.

(i) Write the expression for the equilibrium constant, K_C for the following reactions.
$$2Cu(NO_3)_2(s) \rightleftharpoons 2CuO(s) + 4NO_2(g) + O_2(g)$$

(ii) What is the unit of K_p and K_C for the reaction
$$2NO(g) \rightleftharpoons N_2(g) + O_2(g)$$

(iii) For the equilibrium
$$2NOCl(g) \rightleftharpoons 2NO(g) + Cl_2(g)$$
the value of the equilibrium constant, K_C is 3.17×10^{-6} at 1069 K.
Calculate the K_p for the reaction at this temperature.

15. According to Le-Chatelier's principle, "if any of the factors that determine the equilibrium condition' of a system (like temperature, pressure, concentration etc.,) is changed, the

system will move in such a direction so that effect of the change is reduced or nullified".

According to Le-Chatelier's principle, the concentration stress due to the addition of reactant/product is relieved by shifting of the net reaction in that direction where the added substance is consumed.

The concentration stress due to the removal of reaction/product is relieved by shifting of the net reaction in that direction where the removed substance is replenished or in other words, "change in the concentration of either reactant(s) or product(s) shift the reaction in such a direction in which the effect of the change is minimised or nullified".

Pressure change, that is achieved by changing the volume of the system, generally affect the gaseous reactions having different number of moles of gaseous reactants and products. It has no effect on solids/liquids as the volume (and concentration) of liquids is nearly independent of pressure.

In general, increase in pressure shifts the equilibrium in that direction where the number of moles of the gas or pressure decreases and *vice-versa*.

(i) What happens to the following reaction on increasing pressure?

$$\text{Ice} \rightleftharpoons \text{Water}$$

(ii) For the reactions,

$$SO_2(g)+\frac{1}{2}O_2(g) \rightleftharpoons SO_3(g)+\text{Heat}$$

What happens when temerature of reaction mixture is increased?

(iii) What is the effect of reducing volume on the following system?

$$2C(s)+O_2(g) \rightleftharpoons 2CO(g)$$

Short Answer Type I Questions

(2 Marks)

16. Can equilibrium be achieved between water and its vapours in an open vessel? Explain.

17. Explain the effect of temperature on a system at equilibrium..

18. Write expressions for K_p and K_c for the decomposition reaction of calcium carbonate.

19. Comment on the statement , "Even acids solution contains OH^- ions and even a basic solution contains H^+ ions".

20. 0.049 g of H_2SO_4 is dissolved per litre of the given solution. Calculate the pH of the solution

21. (i) Write the conjugate acid for NH_2^- and NH_3.
    (ii) What is the relationship between pK_a and pK_b values?

22. The value of K_w is 9.55×10^{-14} at a certain temperature. Calculate the pH of water of this temperature. How is the value of K_w affected with change in temperature?

23. Calculate the pH of 0.1 M ammonium acetate at 25°C. $K_a=K_b=1.8\times10^{-5}$.

24. Two moles of PCl_5 were heated to 327°C in a closed two litre vessel and when equilibrium was achieved, PCl_5 was found to be 40% dissociated into PCl_3 and Cl_2. Calculate the equilibrium constant for this reaction.

25. Show that the degree of dissociation (α) for the dissociation of PCl_5 into PCl_3 and Cl_2 in pressure p is given by $\alpha=\left(\frac{K_p}{p+K_p}\right)^{1/2}$.

26. When sulphur in the form of S_8 is heated at 900 K, the initial pressure of 1 atm falls by 29% at equilibrium. This is because of conversion of S_8 to S_2. Calculate the equilibrium constant for the reaction.

27. An equilibrium system for the reaction between hydrogen and iodine to give hydrogen iodide at 670 K in a 5 L flask contains 0.4 mole of hydrogen, 0.4 mole of iodine and 2.4 moles of hydrogen iodide. Calculate equilibrium constant.

28. The pH of a solution obtained by dissolving 0.025 mole of an acid (H*A*) in 250 mL of the aqueous solution was found to be 4.0. Calculate the dissociation constant of H*A*. **[Ans.10^{-7}]**

29. 0.16 g of N_2H_4 are dissolved in water and total volume made upto 500 mL. Calculate the percentage of N_2H_4 that has reacted with water in this solution. The K_b for N_2H_4 is 4.0×10^{-16} M.

30. For the reaction, $2\,NO(g) \rightleftharpoons N_2(g) + O_2(g)$; $\Delta H = -$ve; $K = 2.5 \times 10^{20}$ at 298 K. What will happen to concentration of N_2 if
(i) concentration of NO is increased?
(ii) temperature is decreased to 273 K?
(iii) pressure is reduced also explain your answer?

Short Answer Type II Questions

3 Marks

31. Calculate degree of hydrolysis and pH of 0.25 M NaCN solution at 25°C. $K_a = 4.8 \times 10^{-10}$.

32. Show that the degree of hydrolysis of a salt of weak acid and weak base is independent of concentration of the salt.

33. (i) Hydrolysis of sucrose give
$$\text{Sucrose} + H_2O \rightleftharpoons \text{Glucose} + \text{fructose}$$
Equilibrium constant K_c for the reaction is 2×10^{13} at 300 K. Calculate $\Delta G°$ at 300 K. ($\log 2 = 0.3010$)
(ii) The concentration of hydrogen in two samples of soft drinks *A* and *B* are 4.0×10^{-7} and 3.2×10^{-6} respectively. Which of these two soft drinks has higher pH?

34. The solubility of $Sr(OH)_2$ at 298 K is 19.23 g/L of solution. Calculate the concentrations of strontium and hydroxyl ions and the pH of the solution. **NCERT Textbook**

35. Explain solubility product and common ion effect? Discuss their applications in qualitative analysis.

36. 50 mL 0.04 M calcium nitrate solution is added to 150 mL of 0.08 M ammonium sulphate. Will a precipitate of calcium sulphate form or not? ($K_{sp} = 0.4 \times 10^{-5}$)

Long Answer Type Questions

5 Marks

37. (i) Which of the following are Lewis acids?
$$H_2O, BF_3, H^+ \text{ and } NH_4^+$$
(ii) The pH of a solution of lemon juice is 2.32. Calculate the concentration of hydrogen ion in it.
(iii) What is common ion effect?

38. (i) Define buffer solution. Give the application of buffer in daily life.
(ii) The value of K_c in the reaction, $2A \rightleftharpoons B + C$ is 2×10^{-3}. At a given time, the composition of reaction mixture is $A = B = C = 3 \times 10^{-4}$ M. In which direction the reaction will proceed?
(iii) The solubility product of $PbBr_2$ is 10.8×10^{-5}. It is 70% dissociated in saturated solution. Calculate the solubility of the salt.

Answers

1. (i) zero, (ii) proton donor, proton acceptor (iii) alkaline, (iv) reactants, products, (v) acidic (vi) HPO_4^{2-}
2. (i) → (d), (ii) → (d), (iii) → (d), (iv) → (b), (v) → (a), (vi) → (c),
3. (i) (d) A → (iii), B → (iv), C → (i), D → (ii)
(ii) (a) A → (i), B → (iii), C → (iv), D → (ii)
4. Refer to text on page 251 (Topic-1, Le-Chatelier's principle).
5. According to Le - Chatelier's principle when the concentration of a product is increased, the equilibrium shifts towards left in order to decrease the amount of

the added substances, so concentration of A and B will be increased and concentration of D will be decreased.

6. The low temperature favour the formation of NH_3 because the formation of NH_3 is exothermic.

$N_2(g) + 3H_2(g) \rightleftharpoons 2NH_3(g)$; $\Delta H = -22.4$ kcal

7. $AlCl_3$ is strongest Lewis acid.

8. NH_4Cl is a acidic salt of strong acid (HCl) and weak base (NH_4OH). So, its pH value is less than 7.

9. (a) Both (A) and and (R) are correct and (R) is the correct explanation of (A).

10. (a) Both (A) and (R) are correct and (R) is the correct explanation of (A).

11. (c) (A) is correct, (R) is incorrect.

II. The concentration of pure solid and liquid are taken as unity.

12. (a) Both (A) and (R) are correct, (R) is the correct explanation of (A).

13. (a) Both (A) and (R) are correct and (R) is the correct explanation of (A).

14. (i) $K_C = [NO_2]^4[O_2]$

(because molar concentrations of pure solids are constant)

(ii) Number of moles of reactants and products are equal (i.e. $\Delta n_g = 0$).

$$2NO(g) \rightleftharpoons N_2(g) + O_2(g)$$

then, K_p as well as K_C have no units.

(iii) We know that, $K_p = K_C(RT)^{\Delta n_g}$

For the above reaction,

$$\Delta n_g = (2+1) - 2 = 1$$

$$K_p = 3.17 \times 10^{-6}(0.0831 \times 1069)$$

$$K_p = 3.33 \times 10^{-4}$$

15. (i) Increase in pressure favours melting of ice into water because at higher pressure melting point ice is lowered.

(ii) As reaction is exothermic, low temperature favours forward reaction. High pressure favours forward reaction as it is accompanied by decrease in the number of moles.

(iii) On reducing volume, pressure will increase. According to Le-Chatelier's principle, equilibrium will shift to the side where number of moles of gas can be increased. In the above reaction, equilibrium will shift in forward direction.

16. Equilibrium cannot be achieved in an open vessel because in the case of an open vessel, water vapours will keep on escaping into atmosphese and reverse process, i.e condensation of vapours back to water cannot take place.

17. Refer to text on page 252 (Topic-1, Effect of temperature change).

18. $CaCO_3(s)0 \overset{\Delta}{\rightleftharpoons} CaO(s) + CO_2(g)$

$K_C = [CO_2]$, $K_p = p_{CO_2}$

19. A solution contains both H^+ and OH^- ions whether it is acidic or basic solution. But if the concentration of H^+ ion is higher then it is termed as acidic solution and when the concentration of OH^- ion is higher then it is termed as basic solution.

20. [Ans = 3.3]

21. (i) Conjugate acid for $NH_2^- \longrightarrow NH_3$

and for $NH_3 \longrightarrow NH_4^+$

(ii) $pK_a + pK_b = 14$

22. [Ans pH = 6.52]

23. [Ans = 7.0]

24. [Ans = 0.267]

25.

	PCl_5	$\rightleftharpoons$	PCl_3	+	Cl_2
Initial moles	1		0		0
Moles after diss.	$1-\alpha$		α		α

$$\therefore \quad p_{PCl_5} = \frac{1-\alpha}{1+\alpha} \times p, \; p_{PCl_3} = \frac{\alpha}{1+\alpha} \times p, \; (\text{Total} = 1+\alpha)$$

$$p_{Cl_2} = \frac{\alpha}{1+\alpha} \times p,$$

$$K_p = \frac{p_{PCl_3} \times p_{Cl_2}}{p_{PCl_5}} = \frac{\left(\frac{\alpha}{1+\alpha}p\right)\left(\frac{\alpha}{1+\alpha}p\right)}{\left(\frac{1-\alpha}{1+\alpha}p\right)} = \frac{\alpha^2 p}{1-\alpha^2}$$

or $(1-\alpha^2)K_p = \alpha^2 p$ or $(p + K_p)\alpha^2 = K_p$

$$\text{or} \quad \alpha = \left(\frac{K_p}{p + K_p}\right)^{1/2}$$

26. [Ans = 2.55 atm^3]

27. [Ans = 36.0]

28. [Ans = 10^{-7}]

29. [Ans = 2%]

30. **Ans.** Refer to text on pages 251 and 252 (Topic-1, Effect of concentration change, effect of pressure change, effect of temperature change).

31. **Ans.** 9.13×10^{-3} and 11.36 respectively

32. Refer to text on page 283 (Topic-3, Salts of weak acid and weak base).

33. (i) [Ans = -7.64×10^4 J/mol]

(ii) For soft drink $A = (H_3O^+) = 4.0 \times 10^{-7}$

$$pH = -\log(H_3O^+) = -\log(4.0 \times 10^{-7})$$

$$= -(\log 4.0 - 7\log 10) = -\log 4.0 + 7$$

$$= -0.6020 + 7 = 6.398$$

For soft drink B,

$(H_3O^+) = 3.2 \times 10^{-6}$

$pH = -\log(H_3O^+) = -\log(3.2 \times 10^{-6})$

$= -(\log 3.2 \times 6 \log 10) = -\log 3.2 + 6$

$= 0.505 + 6 = 5.495$

So, we can say that soft drink A has higher pH.

34. [**Ans** =13.5]

35. Refer to text on pages 272, 281 and 287 (Topic : 2, 3 Common ion effect, Solubility product, Application of solubility product in qualitative analysis of salt).

36. Refer to text on page 289; Q 24 (Topic-3).

37. (i) BF_3 and H^+

(ii) [**Ans** $= 4.786 \times 10^{-3}$ mol/L]

(iii) Refer to text on page 272 (Topic-2, Common ion effect in ionisation of weak acids and bases).

38. (i) Refer to text on pages 284 and 285 (Topic-3, Buffer solutions, Applications of buffer solutions).

(ii) For the given reaction, the reaction quotient,

$$Q_c = \frac{[B][C]}{[A]^2} = \frac{[3\times10^{-4}]\times[3\times10^{-4}]}{[3\times10^{-4}]}$$

The value of $K_c = 2 \times 10^{-3}$

Since $O_c > K_c$, the direction of reaction is backward.

CHAPTER 07

Redox Reactions

TOPIC 01 Redox Reactions and Oxidation Number

- Redox Reactions and Oxidation Number
- Redox Reactions : Types, Balancing and Applications

Redox reactions are very important as they play important role in governing a number of **natural processes** (corrosion, combustion), **biological processes** (respiration) and **chemical processes** (functioning of electrochemical and electrolytic cells). Development of ozone hole and environmental issues such as hydrogen economy (use of liquid hydrogen as fuel) are the latest examples of redox reactions. Redox reactions involve both oxidation and reduction simultaneously. Transformation of matter from one form to other takes place through several different chemical reactions that involve simultaneous making and breaking of bonds. Redox reactions are not only one of the most important category of reactions but include a large number of reactions. It is used in several areas like physical, biological, pharmaceutical, industrial, metallurgical, agricultural etc.

Concept of Redox Reactions

To understand the concept of redox reactions, it is essential to become aware of the oxidation and reduction processes. So, we will first discuss these processes and then redox reactions.

Oxidation

According to classical concept, oxidation is defined as the process that involves:

(i) **Addition of Oxygen**

e.g. $$2\,Mg(s) + O_2(g) \longrightarrow 2\,MgO(s)$$

All the combustion processes are examples of oxidation reactions, e.g. combustion of methane to produce CO_2 and water.

$$CH_4(g) + 2O_2(g) \longrightarrow CO_2(g) + 2H_2O(l)$$

(ii) **Addition of Electronegative Elements**

e.g. $$Mg(s) + \underset{\text{Electronegative element}}{Cl_2(g)} \longrightarrow MgCl_2(s)$$

(iii) **Removal of Hydrogen**

e.g. $2H_2S(g) + O_2(g) \longrightarrow 2S(s) + 2H_2O(l)$

(iv) **Removal of Other Electropositive Elements**

e.g. $2K_4[Fe(CN)_6](aq) + H_2O_2(aq) \longrightarrow 2K_3[Fe(CN)_6](aq) + 2KOH(aq)$

Reduction

According to classical and modern concept, reduction is defined as a process that involves:

(i) **Addition of Hydrogen**

e.g.

$$\underset{\text{Ethene}}{CH_2{=}CH_2(g)} + H_2(g) \longrightarrow \underset{\text{Ethane}}{CH_3{-}CH_3(g)}$$

(ii) **Addition of Other Electropositive Element**

e.g.

$$2HgCl_2(aq) + SnCl_2(aq) \longrightarrow Hg_2Cl_2(s) + SnCl_4(aq)$$

(iii) **Removal of Oxygen**

e.g.

$$2HgO(s) \xrightarrow{\Delta} 2Hg(l) + O_2(g)$$

(iv) **Removal of Other Electronegative Element**

e.g.

$$2FeCl_3(aq) + H_2(g) \longrightarrow 2FeCl_2(aq) + 2HCl(aq)$$

Redox Reactions

The reactions that involve oxidation and reduction as its two half reactions are called **redox reactions.**

Or

In other words, redox reactions are the reactions in which oxidation and reduction processes occurs simultaneously. e.g. if we consider the following reaction.

(i)

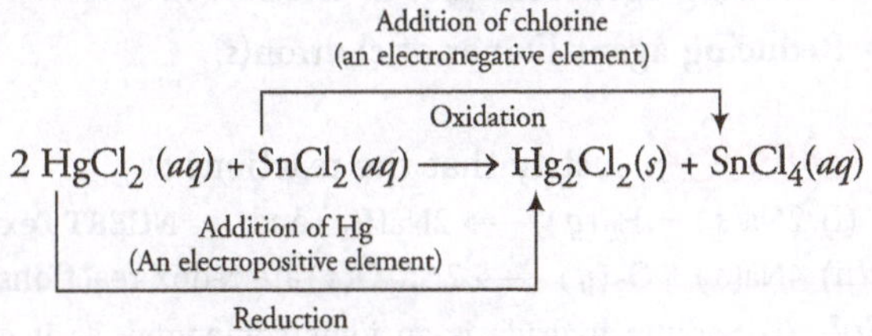

(ii)

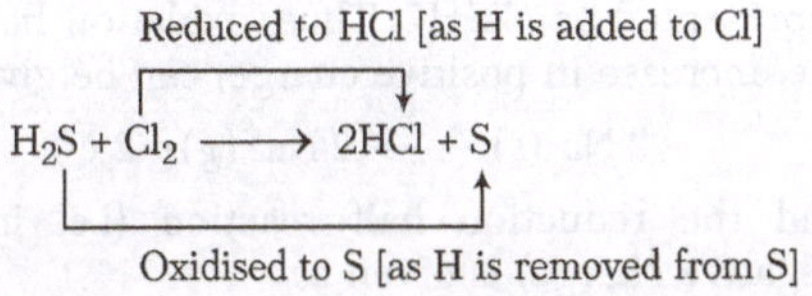

Since, in the above reactions oxidation and reduction occurs simultaneously, so they are examples of redox reaction.

Oxidising and Reducing Agents

In a reaction, the substance which oxidises the other or which itself undergoes reduction is called the **oxidising agent** or oxidant and the substance that reduces the other and itself undergoes oxidation is called the **reducing agent** or reductant.

Thus, in the below given example, Cl_2 is an oxidising agent (as it reduces) and Na is a reducing agent (as it oxidises).

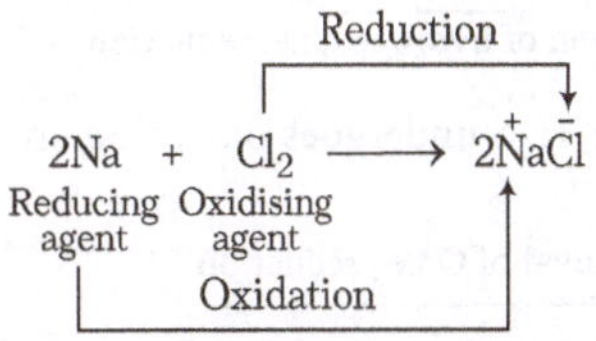

Redox Reactions in Terms of Electron Transfer Reactions

Electronic concept is the modern concept used to define redox reactions. It defines oxidation and reduction in terms of transfer of electrons as follows :

Oxidation in Terms of Electron Transfer

According to electronic concept, oxidation is the process which involves loss of electron(s). The species that undergoes oxidation becomes more positive (i.e. acquires more positive charge) or less negative (i.e. reduces negative charge)

e.g.

$Na \longrightarrow Na^+ + e^-$ (positive charge increases on Na)

$2Cl^- \longrightarrow Cl_2 + 2e^-$ (negative charge decreases on Cl)

Because of the loss of electrons, the oxidation process can also be named as **de-electronation.**

Reduction in Terms of Electron Transfer

Electronic concept also suggested that reduction is the process that involves gain of electron(s). The species undergoing reduction becomes more negative (i.e. acquires more negative charge) or less positive (i.e. reduces positive charge). e.g.

$Cl_2 + 2e^- \longrightarrow 2Cl^-$ (negative charge increases on Cl)

$Fe^{3+} + e^- \longrightarrow Fe^{2+}$ (positive charge reduces on Fe^{3+})

Because of the gain of electrons, reduction process is also called **electronation.**

Example 1 In the reactions given below, identify the species undergoing oxidation and reduction.

(i) $H_2S(g) + Cl_2(g) \longrightarrow 2HCl(g) + S(s)$

(ii) $3Fe_3O_4(s) + 8\,Al(s) \longrightarrow 9\,Fe(s) + 4Al_2O_3(s)$

(iii) $2Na\,(s) + H_2(g) \longrightarrow 2NaH(s)$ **NCERT Textbook**

Sol.

Removal of hydrogen, i.e. oxidation

(i) $H_2S(g) + Cl_2(g) \longrightarrow 2HCl(g) + S(s)$

Addition of hydrogen, i.e. reduction

Thus, here, H_2S undergoes oxidation and Cl_2 undergoes reduction.

Removal of O i.e., reduction

(ii) $3Fe_3O_4(s) + 8Al(s) \longrightarrow 9Fe(s) + 4Al_2O_3(s)$

Addition of O, i.e. oxidation

Thus, here Fe_3O_4 undergoes reduction and Al undergoes oxidation.

(iii) $2\,Na\,(s) + H_2(g) \longrightarrow 2\,NaH(s)$

Since, Na is more electropositive than H so, correct representation of NaH on the basis of electronegativity is Na^+H^-. It shows that here sodium is oxidised (although here it appears that hydrogen is added to it) and hydrogen is reduced.

Redox Reaction in Terms of Electron Transfer

The electron lost in an oxidation reaction is simultaneously gained in a reduction reaction. Because of simultaneous loss and gain of electrons in oxidation-reduction processes, the **redox reactions**, (or the oxidation-reduction reactions) are also called **electron transfer reactions.** e.g. The reaction between sodium and chlorine to give sodium chloride is a redox reaction as shown below.

Loss of $2e^-$ (oxidation half reaction)

$$2Na\,(s) + Cl_2\,(g) \longrightarrow 2\overset{+}{Na}\,\overset{-}{Cl}\,(s)$$

Gain of $2e^-$ (reduction half reaction)

The two half reactions can be written as :

Oxidation half reaction $2Na\,(s) \longrightarrow 2Na^+\,(g) + 2e^-$

Reduction half reaction $Cl_2\,(g) + 2e^- \longrightarrow 2Cl(g)$

Similarly, the following two redox reactions can also be illustrated in terms of loss and gain of electrons.

Loss of $2e^-$ (Oxidation half reaction)

$$4Na\,(s) + O_2\,(g) \longrightarrow 2(\overset{+}{Na})_2\overset{2-}{O}\,(s)$$

Gain of $2e^-$ (Reduction half reaction)

Loss of $2e^-$ (Oxidation half reaction)

$$2Na\,(s) + S\,(s) \longrightarrow (\overset{+}{Na})_2\,S^{2-}\,(s)$$

Gain of $2e^-$ (Reduction half reaction)

Oxidising and Reducing Agents in Terms of Electron Transfer

In a reaction, species that gains electrons is called **oxidising agent or oxidant** and the one that loses or donate the electrons to the interacting element is called the **reducing agent** or **reductant.** e.g.

Increase in positive charge, i.e. oxidation or loss of electrons

$$Zn(s) + Cu^{2+}\,(aq) \longrightarrow Cu(s) + Zn^{2+}(aq)$$

Decrease in positive charge, i.e. reduction or gain of electrons

Thus, here Zn acts as reducing agent as it reduces Cu^{2+} by providing it two electrons and Cu^{2+} acts as oxidising agent, as it gains (or accepts) two electrons from Zn.

- **Oxidation** Loss of electron(s) by any species.
- **Reduction** Gain of electron(s) by any species.
- **Oxidising agent** Acceptor of electron(s).
- **Reducing agent** Donor of electron(s).

Example 2 Justify that the reactions :

(i) $2Na(s) + H_2(g) \longrightarrow 2NaH(s)$ and **NCERT Textbook**

(ii) $4Na(s) + O_2(g) \longrightarrow 2Na_2O(s)$ are redox reactions.

Sol. (i) Sodium hydride is an ionic compound, so it can be represented as Na^+H^-. Thus, oxidation half reaction (i.e. increase in positive charge) can be given as

$$2\,Na\,(s) \longrightarrow 2\,Na^+(g) + 2\,e^- \quad \text{...(i)}$$

and the reduction half reaction (i.e. increase in negative charge) is given as

$$H_2(g) + 2e^- \longrightarrow 2H^-\,(g) \quad \text{...(ii)}$$

The sum of above two reactions give the overall reaction.

[while adding two reactions, remember that the number of electron lost must be equal to the number of electrons gained. If these two are not equal, make them equal by multiplying with a suitable integer as done in case of reaction (ii).]

Thus, $2\,Na(s) + H_2(g) \longrightarrow 2Na^+(aq) + 2H^-(aq)$

or $\quad 2Na(s) + H_2(g) \longrightarrow 2NaH(s)$

Since, this reaction involve oxidation and reduction as its two half reaction, it is a redox reaction.

(ii) Like NaH, sodium oxide is also an ionic compound and have the formula $(Na^+)_2O^{2-}$. Thus, oxidation and reduction half reactions can be written as

I. $2\,Na(s) \xrightarrow[\text{Loss of } 2e^-]{} 2\,Na^+(g) + 2e^-$ ...(i)

(Oxidation half reaction)

II. $O_2(g) + 4\,e^- \xrightarrow[\text{Gain of } 4e^-]{} 2O^{2-}(g)$ ...(ii)

(Reduction half reaction)

To equalise number of electrons, equation (i) is multiplied with 2, and hence, we get

III. $\quad 4\,Na(s) \longrightarrow 4\,Na^+(g) + 4\,e^-$

On adding equations II and III, we get

$$4\,Na(s) + O_2(g) \longrightarrow 4\,Na^+ + 2\,O^{2-}$$

Or

$$4Na\,(s) + O_2(g) \longrightarrow 2\,(Na^+)_2O^{2-}(s)$$

Since, the above reaction involve oxidation and reduction as its two half reactions, so it is a redox reaction.

Note NaCl and Na_2S being ionic compounds can also be represented as Na^+Cl^- and $(Na^+)_2S^{2-}$.

Example 3 Identify the oxidant and reductant in each of the following reactions.

(i) $MnO_4^-(aq) + C_2H_5OH(aq) \longrightarrow Mn^{2+}(aq) + CH_3COOH(aq)$

(ii) $Zn(s) + 2H^+(aq) \longrightarrow Zn^{2+}(aq) + H_2(g)$

(iii) $PbO(s) + C(s) \longrightarrow Pb(s) + CO(g)$

Sol. (i) MnO_4^- loses oxygen, therefore it is an oxidant while C_2H_5OH gains oxygen, therefore it is a reductant.

(ii) Zn is reductant while hydrogen (H) is oxidant.

(iii) PbO is oxidant while C is reductant.

Example 4 Write the half-reactions for the following redox reactions.

(i) $Al(s) + 3Ag^+(aq) \longrightarrow Al^{3+}(aq) + 3Ag(s)$

(ii) $2K(s) + Cl_2(g) \longrightarrow 2KCl(s)$

Sol. (i) $Al(s) \longrightarrow Al^{3+}(aq) + 3e^-$ (oxidation half reaction)

$3Ag^+(aq) + 3e^- \longrightarrow 3Ag(s)$ (reduction half reaction)

(ii) $2K \longrightarrow 2K^+ + 2e^-$ (oxidation half reaction)

$Cl_2 + 2e^- \longrightarrow 2Cl^-$ (reduction half reaction)

Oxidation Number

The concept of electron transfer is found unable to explain the redox changes or electron shift in case of covalent compounds. To explain these changes a new concept, called **oxidation number** is introduced. Oxidation number is defined **as the charge that an atom of the element has in its ion or appear to have when present in the combined state with other atoms.**

Or

In other words, **"it is also defined as the charge that an atom appear to have in a compound when all other atoms are removed as ions from the compound."**

Rules for Calculating Oxidation Number

Comparison between the electronegativities of two combining atoms is not an easy task in case of polyatomic molecules. That's why a set of rules has been given to calculate the oxidation number of an element in a given compound or ion.

These rules are given below:

Rule I. The oxidation number of an atom in its free or elementary state or in any of its allotropes is zero. e.g. The oxidation of H in H_2, S in S_8, P in P_4, O in O_2 or O_3, C in diamond is zero.

Rule II. In case of ions having only one kind of atoms, the oxidation number of each atom is equal to charge present on the ion. e.g. In case of Na^+, Mg^{2+}, Fe^{3+}, Cl^- and O^{2-}, the oxidation states are respectively +1, +2, +3, −1, −2.

Rule III. The oxidation state of alkali metals in all of their compounds is always +1. Similarly, in case of alkaline earth metals, it is always +2. For aluminium, oxidation state is always +3.

Rule IV. The oxidation state (OS) of oxygen in most of its compounds is −2, with an exception of peroxides and superoxides in which the oxidation state of oxygen is respectively −1 and −1/2. e.g. In H_2O_2 (hydrogen peroxide), oxidation state of O is −1 [peroxide linkage is — O— O—] and in KO_2 (potassium superoxide), oxidation state of O is −1/2.

Rule V. The oxidation state of hydrogen is generally +1 with an exception of metallic hydrides like NaH, CaH_2 etc. In these hydrides, oxidation state of hydrogen is −1.

Rule VI. The oxidation state of fluorine in all of its compounds is always −1. Other halogens (i.e. chlorine, bromine and iodine) also exhibit −1 oxidation state but it is not always true. In case of oxoacids and oxoanions, halogens (except fluorine) exhibit positive oxidation state.

Rule VII. The algebraic sum of the oxidation numbers of all the atoms present in a compound must be equal to zero.

Rule VIII. In case of polyatomic ions, the algebraic sum of oxidation number of all the atoms present in the ion must be equal to the charge on the ion. e.g. In case of carbonate ion (CO_3^{2-}) it is equal to −2.

Note Metals generally exhibit positive oxidation states whereas in case of non-metals it may be positive or negative. Moreover, transition elements exhibit variable oxidation states.

Highest oxidation state for first two groups
= group number

Highest oxidation state for other groups
= group number − 10

[Here, group number is in accordance with long form of periodic table]. e.g. In SF_6, highest oxidation state of S = 16 − 10 = 6. The highest oxidation state exhibited by an element generally increases along a period of the periodic table.

In third period, it increases from 1 to 7 as given in below table.

Group	1	2	13	14	15	16	17
Element	Na	Mg	Al	Si	P	S	Cl
Compound	NaCl	$MgSO_4$	AlF_3	$SiCl_4$	P_4O_{10}	SF_6	$HClO_4$
Highest oxidation number state of the group element	+1	+2	+3	+4	+5	+6	+7

Examples

(i) $K_2Cr_2O_7$ Suppose the oxidation state or oxidation number of Cr in $K_2Cr_2O_7$ is x. The oxidation number of each K atom is +1 and that of O atom is −2, since $K_2Cr_2O_7$ is a neutral molecule.

Therefore, $(+1)\times 2+(x)\times 2+(-2)\times 7=0$

$2x=+14-2=+12$

$x=+6$

So, the oxidation number of each Cr atom in $K_2Cr_2O_7$ is +6.

(ii) $S_2O_3^{2-}$ Suppose the oxidation state or oxidation number of each S atom in this ion be x.

The sum of oxidation numbers of all the atoms present must be equal to the charge present on this ion, i.e. equal to −2.

Therefore, $(x)\times 2+(-2)\times 3=-2$

$$2x=-2+6 \Rightarrow x=\frac{-2+6}{2}=+2$$

So, the oxidation number of Cr in $Cr_2O_7^{2-}$ is +6.

Example 4 Calculate the oxidation state of (*i*) Mn in $KMn0_4$ and (*ii*) N in NO_3^-.

Sol. (i) Let the oxidation number of Mn in $KMnO_4$ be x. Writing the oxidation number of each atom above its symbol

$$\overset{+1}{K}\,\overset{x}{Mn}\,\overset{-2}{O_4}$$

$$[1\times(+1)+(1\times x)+4\times(-2)]$$

$$1+x+(-8)=0$$

$$1+x-8=0$$

$$x-7=0$$

$$\therefore \quad x=+7$$

Hence, the oxidation number of Mn in $KMnO_4$ is + 7.

(ii) **N in NO_3^-.**

Let the oxidation number of N in NO_3^- be x. Writing the oxidation number of each atom above its symbol.

$$\overset{x}{N}\overset{-2}{O_3^-}$$

∴ Sum of the oxidation number of all the atoms in $NO_3^- = x+3(-2)=x-6$

But the sum of oxidation numbers of all the atoms in NO_3^- ion is equal to the charge present on it, i.e. −1

∴ $x-6=-1$ or $x=+5$

Thus, the oxidation number of N in NO_3^- is +5.

Note The oxidation state of O_2^+ and O_2^- are + 1/2 and − 1/2 respectively, i.e. fractional.

Applications of Oxidation Number

The important applications of oxidation numbers are as follows :

1. Stock Notation

In AuCl (aurous chloride), the oxidation state of Au is +1 and in $AuCl_3$ (auric chloride), the oxidation state of Au is +3. Thus, they can be distinguished as Au (I) Cl and Au (III) Cl or gold (I) chloride and gold (III) chloride. This system of nomenclature was introduced by **Alfred Stock**, a German chemist and is called the **Stock notations.**

With the help of Stock notations, it is possible to predict whether the species is present in oxidised form or reduced form.

Stock Notation of Some Important Compounds

Compound/Formula	Oxidation state of metal	Stock notation
$SnCl_2$ (Stannous chloride)	+ 2	Sn (II) Cl_2
$SnCl_4$ (Stannic chloride)	+ 4	Sn(IV) Cl_4
$FeSO_4$ (Ferrous sulphate)	+ 2	Fe (II) SO_4
V_2O_5 (Vanadium pentoxide)	+ 5	V_2(V)O_5
Cr_2O_3 (Chromium trioxide)	+ 3	Cr_2(III)O_3

- PCl_3 and PCl_5 can never be represented by Stock notations because non-metallic elements shows variable valencies.

Example 6 Using Stock notation, represent the following compounds $HAuCl_4$, Tl_2O, FeO, Fe_2O_3, CuI, CuO, MnO and MnO_2. **NCERT Textbook**

Sol. $HAuCl_4$

Let the oxidation state of Au is x.

$$\overset{+1}{\underset{(+1)}{H}}\quad \overset{x\ \ -1}{\underset{x\ \ 4(-1)}{Au\,Cl_4}}$$

$$(+1)+x+4(-1)=0 \text{ or } x-3=0 \text{ or } x=+3$$

Thus, the Stock notation for the compound is H Au (III) Cl_4. Find the Stock notations of other compounds in the same manner as shown above. You will get the answer Tl_2(II) O, Fe_2 (II) O, Fe_2(III) O_3, Cu (I) I, Cu (II) O, Mn (II) O, Mn (IV) O_2.

2. Oxidation and Reduction in Terms of Oxidation Number

(i) **Prediction of Oxidation-Reduction Reactions** In term of the concept of oxidation number, **oxidation is defined as the process in which the oxidation number of an element increases whereas reduction is the process in which the oxidation number of an element decreases**, e.g. consider the following reaction.

$$\overset{0}{Zn} + 2\,\overset{+1\,-1}{HCl} \longrightarrow \overset{+2\,-1}{ZnCl_2} + \overset{0}{H_2}$$

(Oxidation: Zn → $ZnCl_2$; Reduction: HCl → H_2)

In the above reaction, oxidation number of Zn increases from 0 to +2 but of H decreases from +1 to 0. Thus, here Zn is oxidised whereas HCl is reduced. Hence, it is a redox reaction. Thus, it is also concluded that the reactions in which the oxidation states of interacting species changes (i.e. increases and decreases, simultaneously) are called the **redox reactions.**

(ii) **Prediction of Oxidising and Reducing Agents** In term of concept of oxidation number (ON), an oxidising agent or **oxidant** is the substance, oxidation number of which decreases in the chemical reaction. It is the substance that itself undergoes reduction whereas **reducing agent** or **reductant** is the substance, oxidation number of which increases in the chemical reaction. Thus, it is the substance that itself undergoes oxidation, e.g. consider the following reaction.

$$\underset{\text{Oxidant}}{\overset{0}{Cl_2}}\,(g) + \underset{\text{Reductant}}{2\overset{-1}{Br^-}}\,(aq) \longrightarrow 2\overset{-1}{Cl^-}\,(aq) + \overset{0}{Br_2}\,(aq)$$

(Increase in ON, oxidation: Br^- → Br_2; Decrease in ON, reduction: Cl_2 → Cl^-)

Here, oxidation number of Br increases from −1 to 0, so it behaves as a **reductant** whereas the oxidation number of Cl decreases from 0 to −1, so it behaves as an **oxidant**.

Identification of Oxidant and Reductant

- A substance behaves as an oxidant only when any one of its elements is present in its highest oxidation state, e.g. $KMnO_4$.
- A substance behaves as a reductant only, when any one of its element is present in its lowest possible oxidation state, e.g. H_2S
- Substance having an element in its intermediate oxidation state can behave as oxidant as well as reductant, e.g. H_2O_2.

Example 7 Justify that the reaction,

$$2Cu_2O\,(s) + Cu_2S\,(s) \longrightarrow 6\,Cu\,(s) + SO_2(g)$$

is a redox reaction. Identify the species oxidised/reduced, which acts as an oxidant and which acts as a reductant. **NCERT Textbook**

Sol.

Step I Write the oxidation number of each element above it in the given reaction.

$$\text{e.g. } 2\,\overset{+1}{Cu_2}\,\overset{-2}{O}\,(s) + \overset{+1}{Cu_2}\,\overset{-2}{S}\,(s) \longrightarrow 6\overset{0}{Cu}(s) + \overset{+4\,-2}{SO_2}(g)$$

Step II Mark arrow to show the increase and decrease in oxidation number. Also mention it over the arrow.

$$2\,\overset{+1\ \ -2}{Cu_2O}\,(s) + \overset{+1\,-2}{Cu_2S}\,(s) \longrightarrow 6\,\overset{0}{Cu}(s) + \overset{+4}{SO_2}(g)$$

(Increase in oxidation number: S in Cu_2S → SO_2; Decrease in oxidation number: Cu in Cu_2O → Cu)

Step III If the reaction involves increase as well as decrease in the oxidation number of certain elements, then it is called redox reaction.

Since, in the above reaction oxidation state decreases as well as increases, so it is a redox reaction (proved).

Step IV Increase in oxidation number shows oxidation whereas decrease in oxidation number shows reduction.

Here oxidation number of S increases from −2 to +4, so Cu_2S is oxidised here. Further, oxidation number of Cu decreases for +1 to 0, so Cu_2O is reduced.

Thus, here Cu_2S is oxidised and Cu_2O is reduced .

Step V Further predict oxidant and reductant on the basis of the fact that oxidation number in case of oxidant decreases but in case of reductant increases. Thus, here Cu_2O is oxidant and Cu_2S is reductant.

Note

- The equivalent weight of oxidising/reducing agent

$$= \frac{\text{molecular weight of the reagent}}{\text{change in oxidation number}}$$

- Equivalent weight of $KMnO_4$ is calculated as follows: The reaction in acidic medium is

$$\overset{+7}{MnO_4^-} + 8H^+ + 5e^- \longrightarrow Mn^{2+} + 4H_2O$$

Change in oxidation number = 7−2 = 5

Thus, equivalent weight of

$$KMnO_4 = \frac{\text{molecular weight of } KMnO_4}{\text{change in oxidation number}}$$

$$= \frac{39 + 55 + 4 \times 16}{5} = 31.6$$

Topic Practice 1

Very Short Answer Type Questions

(1 Mark)

1. Fill in the Blanks

(i) Redox reactions involve both ...... and ...... simultaneously.

(ii) The substance that reduces the other and itself undergoes oxidation is called ....

(iii) The substance which oxidises the other and itself undergoes reduction is called ....

2. Objective Type Questions

(i) Which of the following processes takes place in reduction?
(a) Removal of oxygen
(b) Addition of hydrogen
(c) Removal of hydrogen
(d) Both (a) and (b)

(ii) In the reaction,

$$CH_2{=}CH_2 + H_2 \longrightarrow H_3C{-}CH_3$$

Which of the following process is occuring?
(a) Oxidation of ethylene
(b) Reduction of ethylene
(c) Both (a) and (b)
(d) None of the above

(iii) In the reaction, $2KClO_3 \longrightarrow 2KCl + 3O_2$, the elements which have been oxidised and reduced respectively are
(a) chlorine and oxygen
(b) oxygen and chlorine
(c) potassium and oxygen
(d) oxygen and potassium

(iv) In the reaction, $2Na + Cl_2 \longrightarrow 2Na^+Cl^-$ the half-reaction $2Na(s) \longrightarrow 2Na^+(g) + 2e^-$ is called
(a) oxidation half-reaction
(b) reduction half-reaction
(c) redox half-reaction
(d) None of the above

(v) For monoatomic ions, the oxidation number is equal to
(a) charge on the ion (b) zero
(c) more than 1 (d) less than 1

(vi) In which of the following compounds nitrogen exhibits highest oxidation state?
(a) N_2H_2 (b) NH_3 (c) N_3H (d) NH_2OH

3. Match the Column I (Reaction with underlined species) with Column II (Type of change shown by underlined species) and choose the correct option using the codes given below:

Column I	Column II
A. $\underline{2Mg} + O_2 \longrightarrow 2MgO$	(i) Removal of hydrogen
B. $\underline{Mg} + Cl_2 \longrightarrow MgCl_2$	(ii) Removal of electropositive element
C. $\underline{2H_2S} + O_2 \longrightarrow 2S + 2H_2O$	(iii) Addition of oxygen
D. $\underline{2KI} + H_2O + O_3 \longrightarrow 2KOH + I_2 + O_2$	(iv) Addition of electronegative element

Codes

	A	B	C	D
(a)	(i)	(iii)	(iv)	(i)
(b)	(iii)	(iv)	(i)	(ii)
(c)	(iii)	(iv)	(ii)	(i)
(d)	(iii)	(ii)	(i)	(iv)

4. Identify the substance that get reduced in the following reaction.

$$Fe_2O_3(s) + 3CO(g) \longrightarrow 2Fe(s) + 3CO_2(g)$$

5. Does the oxidation number of an element in any molecule or any polyatomic ion represent the actual charge on it?

6. The compound AgF_2 is unstable compound. However, if formed, the compound acts as a very strong oxidising agent. Why? **NCERT Textbook**

7. Zn rod is immersed in $CuSO_4$ solution. What will you observe after an hour? Explain your observation in terms of redox reaction.

8. If the following reaction can

$$Cr_2O_7^{2-} + H_2O \rightleftharpoons 2CrO_4^{2-} + 2H^+$$

be regarded as a redox reaction?

9. Assign oxidation number to the underlined elements in each of the following species. **NCERT Textbook**

(i) $NaH_2\underline{P}O_4$ (ii) $NaH\underline{S}O_4$ (iii) $H_4\underline{P}_2O_7$
(iv) $K_2\underline{Mn}O_4$ (v) $Ca\underline{O}_2$ (vi) $NaBH_4$
(vii) $H_2S_2O_7$ (viii) $KAl(\underline{S}O_4)_2 \cdot 12H_2O$
(ix) $\underline{Cr}_2O_7^{2-}$ (x) $\underline{S}_2O_3^{2-}$

10. The compound $YBa_2Cu_3O_7$, which shows superconductivity, has copper in x oxidation state. Assume that the rare earth element yttrium is in its usual +3 oxidation state. Predict the value of *x*.

Short Answer Type I Questions

2 Marks

11. In the below given reaction which substance is getting oxidised and which substance is getting reduced? Name reducing agent and oxidising agent.

$$2\,Cu_2S + 3O_2 \longrightarrow 2\,Cu_2O + 2\,SO_2$$

12. Calculate the oxidation number of phosphorus in the following species. **NCERT Exemplar**

(i) HPO_3^{2-} (ii) PO_4^{3-}

13. Nitric acid acts only as an oxidising agent while nitrous acid acts both as an oxidising as well as reducing agent. Explain.

14. Why does the following reaction occur?

$$XeO_6^{4-}(aq) + 2F^-(aq) + 6H^+(aq) \longrightarrow XeO_3(g) + F_2(g) + 3H_2O\,(l)$$

What conclusion about the compound Na_4XeO_6 (of which XeO_6^{4-} is a part) can be drawn from the reaction? **NCERT Textbook**

15. Consider the elements : Cs, Ne, I and F.
(i) Identify the element that exhibits only negative oxidation state.
(ii) Identify the element that exhibits only positive oxidation state.
(iii) Identify the element that exhibits both positive and negative oxidation states.
(iv) Identify the element which exhibits neither the negative nor does the positive oxidation state.

16. Consider the reactions,

$$2S_2O_3^{2-}(aq) + I_2\,(s) \longrightarrow S_4O_6^{2-}(aq) + 2I^-(aq)$$

$$S_2O_3^{2-}(aq) + 2Br_2(l) + 5H_2O\,(l) \longrightarrow 2SO_4^{2-}(aq) + 4Br^-(aq) + 10H^+(aq)$$

Why does the same reductant, thiosulphate react differently with iodine and bromine? **NCERT Textbook**

17. Fluorine reacts with ice and results in the change.

$$H_2O\,(s) + F_2(g) \longrightarrow HF(g) + HOF\,(g)$$

Justify that this reaction is a redox reaction. **NCERT Textbook**

18. The reaction

$$Cl_2(g) + 2OH^-(aq) \rightarrow ClO^-(aq) + Cl^-(aq) + H_2O(l)$$

represents the process of bleaching. Identify and name of the species that bleaches the substances due to its oxidising action. **NCERT Exemplar**

19. Nitric acid is an oxidising agent and reacts with PbO but it does not react with PbO_2. Explain why?

20. Consider the reactions,

(i) $H_3PO_2(aq) + 4AgNO_3(aq) + 2H_2O\,(l) \longrightarrow H_3PO_4(aq) + 4\,Ag\,(s) + 4HNO_3(aq)$

(ii) $H_3PO_2(aq) + 2\,CuSO_4(aq) + 2H_2O\,(l) \longrightarrow H_3PO_4(aq) + 2Cu\,(s) + H_2SO_4(aq)$

(iii) $C_6H_5CHO\,(l) + 2\,[Ag(NH_3)_2]^+(aq) + 3OH^-(aq) \longrightarrow C_6H_5COO^-(aq) + 2Ag\,(s) + 4\,NH_3(aq) + 2H_2O\,(l)$

(iv) $C_6H_5CHO\,(l) + 2Cu^{2+}(aq) + 5OH^-\,(aq) \longrightarrow$ No change observed

What inference do you draw about the behaviour of Ag^+ and Cu^{2+} from these reactions? **NCERT Textbook**

Short Answer Type II Questions

3 Marks

21. Calculate the oxidation number of each sulphur atom in the following compounds.
(i) $Na_2S_2O_3$ (ii) $Na_2S_4O_6$
(iii) Na_2SO_3 (iv) Na_2SO_4

22. Suggest a list of the substances where carbon can exhibit oxidation states from – 4 to + 4 and nitrogen from – 3 to + 5.

23. Calculate the oxidation number of sulphur, chromium and nitrogen in H_2SO_5, $Cr_2O_7^{2-}$ and NO_3^-. Suggest the structure of these compounds. Count for the fallacy.

24. Write formulae for the following compounds.
(i) Mercury (II) chloride (ii) Nickel(II) sulphate
(iii) Tin (IV) oxide (iv) Thallium (I) sulphate
(v) Iron (III) sulphate
(vi) Chromium (III) oxide **NCERT Textbook**

25. One mole of N_2H_4 loses 10 moles electrons to form a new compound Y. Assuming that all the nitrogen appears in the new compound, what is the oxidation number of N in Y? There is no change in oxidation state of H.

26. Whenever a reaction between an oxidising agent and a reducing agent is carried out, a compound of lower oxidation state is formed if the reducing agent is in excess and a compound of higher oxidation state is formed if the oxidising agent is in excess. Justify this statement giving three illustrations. **NCERT Textbook**

27. How does Cu_2O act as both oxidant and reductant? Explain with proper reactions showing the change of oxidation numbers in each example.

28. Why do the following reactions proceed differently?

$Pb_3O_4 + 8\,HCl \longrightarrow 3\,PbCl_2 + Cl_2 + 4H_2O$ and

$Pb_3O_4 + 4\,HNO_3 \longrightarrow 2Pb(NO_3)_2 + PbO_2 + 2H_2O$

29. Decide whether each of the following reaction involves oxidation-reduction reaction or not. If it does, identify which species is oxidised and which gets reduced?

(i) $4\,CH_3\overset{\overset{\displaystyle O}{\|}}{C}CH_3 + LiAlH_4 + 4H_2O \rightleftharpoons 4\,CH_3\overset{\overset{\displaystyle OH}{|}}{C}HCH_3 + LiOH + Al(OH)_3$

(ii) $CH_3CH_2OH \xrightarrow{H_2SO_4} CH_2{=}CH_2 + H_2O$

(iii) $CH_3\overset{\overset{\displaystyle O}{\|}}{C}OH + CH_3NH_2 \rightleftharpoons CH_3\overset{\overset{\displaystyle O}{\|}}{C}O^- + CH_3NH_3^+$

30. While sulphur dioxide and hydrogen peroxide can act as oxidising as well as reducing agents in their reactions, ozone and nitric acid act only as oxidants. Why? **NCERT Textbook**

Long Answer Type Questions

5 Marks

31. What do you understand by the term oxidation and reduction? Classify the following substances into oxidising and reducing agents.

(i) Carbon (ii) Ozone
(iii) Nascent hydrogen (iv) Nitric acid
(v) Chlorine

32. Using electron transfer concept, identify the oxidant and reductant in the following redox reactions.

(i) $Zn(s) + 2H^+(aq) \longrightarrow Zn^{2+}(aq) + H_2(g)$

(ii) $2[Fe(CN)_6]^{4-}(aq) + H_2O_2(aq) + 2H^+(aq) \longrightarrow 2[Fe(CN)_6]^{3-}(aq) + 2H_2O\,(l)$

(iii) $2[Fe(CN)_6]^{3-}(aq) + 2OH^-(aq) + H_2O_2(aq) \longrightarrow 2[Fe(CN)_6]^{4-}(aq) + O_2(g) + 2H_2O\,(l)$

(iv) $BrO_3^-(aq) + F_2(g) + 2OH^-(aq) \longrightarrow BrO_4^-(aq) + 2F^-(aq) + H_2O(l)$

(v) $2NaClO_3(aq) + I_2(aq) \longrightarrow 2NaIO_3(aq) + Cl_2(g)$

33. What are the oxidation numbers of the underlined elements in each of the following and how do you rationalise your results?

(i) $K\underline{I}_3$ (ii) $H_2\underline{S}_4O_6$
(iii) $\underline{Fe}_3O_4$ (iv) $\underline{C}H_3CH_2OH$
(v) $CH_3\underline{C}\,OOH$ **NCERT Textbook**

34. Identify the substance oxidised, reduced, oxidising agent and reducing agent for each of the following reactions.

(i) $2AgBr(s) + C_6H_6O_2(aq) \longrightarrow 2Ag(s) + 2HBr(aq) + C_6H_4O_2(aq)$

(ii) $HCHO(l) + 2\,[Ag(NH_3)_2]^+(aq) + 3OH^-(aq) \longrightarrow 2Ag\,(s) + HCOO^-(aq) + 4NH_3(aq) + 2H_2O\,(l)$

(iii) $HCHO\,(l) + 2Cu^{2+}(aq) + 5OH^-(aq) \longrightarrow Cu_2O\,(s) + HCOO^-(aq) + 3H_2O\,(l)$

(iv) $N_2H_4(l) + 2H_2O_2(l) \longrightarrow N_2(g) + 4H_2O\,(l)$

(v) $Pb\,(s) + PbO_2(s) + 2H_2SO_4(aq) \longrightarrow 2PbSO_4(s) + 2H_2O(l)$

35. Justify that the following reactions are redox reactions.

(i) $CuO(s) + H_2(g) \longrightarrow Cu(s) + H_2O(g)$

(ii) $Fe_2O_3(s) + 3CO(g) \longrightarrow 2Fe(s) + 3CO_2(g)$

(iii) $4BCl_3(g) + 3LiAlH_4(s) \longrightarrow 2\,B_2H_6(g) + 3LiCl(s) + 3AlCl_3(s)$

(iv) $2\,K(s) + F_2(g) \longrightarrow 2K^+F^-(s)$

(v) $4\,NH_3(g) + 5O_2(g) \longrightarrow 4NO\,(g) + 6H_2O\,(g)$

Hints & Solutions

1. (i) oxidation, reduction (ii) reducing agent
(iii) oxidising agent

2. (i) → (d), (ii) → (b), (iii) → (b), (iv) → (a), (v) → (a), (vi) → (b)

3. (b) A $\rightarrow$ (iii), B $\rightarrow$ (iv), C $\rightarrow$ (i), D $\rightarrow$ (ii)

4. In the reaction, Fe_2O_3 loses oxygen and thus, it is reduced to Fe.

5. No, the oxidation number of an element in any species is an apparent charge on the atom which it appears to have acquired when all other atoms in the species are removed as ions.

6. **Key Idea** Due to the presence of completely filled configuration Ag^+ is more stable than Ag^{2+}.An oxidising agent has a great tendency of accepting electron.

In AgF_2, Ag is in + 2 oxidation state. It is highly unstable so it readily accepts an electron to attain + 1 oxidation state which is more stable.

$$Ag^{2+} + e^- \longrightarrow Ag^+$$

That's why AgF_2 acts as a strong oxidising agent.

7. The blue colour of $CuSO_4$ solution will get discharged and reddish brown copper metal will be deposited on Zn rod. This is because blue colour Cu^{2+} (in $CuSO_4$) gets reduced to Cu by accepting two electrons from Zn, which gets oxidised to colourless $ZnSO_4$.

Reduction

$$\overset{0}{Zn}(s) + \overset{2+}{Cu}SO_4(aq) \longrightarrow \overset{2+}{Zn}SO_4^{2-}(aq) + \overset{0}{Cu}(s)$$

Oxidation

8. In this reaction, oxidation number of Cr in $Cr_2O_7^{2-}$ is + 6 and oxidation number of Cr in CrO_4^{2-} is + 6. Since, during the reaction, the oxidation number of Cr has neither decreased nor increased, therefore, the above reaction is not a redox reaction.

9. NaH_2PO_4

Let the oxidation number of P be x. Writing the oxidation number of each atom above its symbol, we get $\overset{+1}{Na}\overset{+1}{H_2}\overset{x}{P}\overset{-2}{O_4}$. In neutral compounds, the sum of the oxidation numbers of all the atoms is zero.

$$1(+1) + 2(+1) + x + 4(-2) = 0$$
$$3 + x + (-8) = 0$$
$$x = 8 - 3 = +5$$

Hence, the oxidation number of P in NaH_2PO_4 is + 5.

Calculate oxidation number of other elements in the same way as shown in (i). You will get oxidation number of S, P, Mn, O, B, S, S Cr, S in the given compound as +6, + 5, + 6, −1, + 3, + 6, + 6, + 6, + 2 respectively.

Note H_2O is a neutral molecule, therefore sum of oxidation numbers of all atoms in H_2O is zero. Hence, the oxidation number of S in $KAl(SO_4)_2 \cdot 12H_2O$ is + 6.

10. $1 \times (+3) + 2 \times (+2) + 3x + 7 \times (-2) = 0$

or $3 + 4 + 3x - 14 = 0$ or $3x = 7$; $x = \frac{7}{3}$

11. Since, oxygen is being added to Cu, therefore Cu_2S is oxidised to Cu_2O and the other reactant, i.e. O_2 is getting reduced. Hence, Cu_2S is a reducing agent and O_2 is an oxidising agent. [2]

12. (i) Suppose that the oxidation number of P in HPO_3^{2-} be x.

Then, $1 + x + 3(-2) = -2$

or $x + 1 - 6 = -2$ or $x = +3$ [1]

(ii) Suppose that the oxidation number of P in PO_4^{3-} be x.

Then, $x + 4(-2) = -3$ or $x - 8 = -3$ or $x = +5$ [1]

13. (i) HNO_3

Oxidation number of N in HNO_3 is + 5.

Maximum oxidation number of N is + 5 because it has five electrons in the valence shell ($2s^2 2p^3$).

Minimum oxidation number of N is − 3 because it can accept 3 more electrons to get noble gas configuration. Since, oxidation number of N in HNO_3 is maximum, therefore, it can only decrease. Thus, HNO_3 can act as an oxidising agent. [1]

(ii) HNO_2, Oxidation number of N = + 3

Maximum oxidation number of N = + 5

Minimum oxidation number of N = − 3

Therefore, the oxidation number of N can increase by losing electrons or can decrease by accepting electrons. Thus, HNO_2 can act both as an oxidising as well as a reducing agent. [1]

14. $\overset{+8}{Xe}O_6^{4-}(aq) + 2\overset{-1}{F}^-(aq) + 6H^+(aq) \longrightarrow \overset{+6}{Xe}O_3(g) + \overset{0}{F_2} + 3H_2O(l)$

In the above reaction, oxidation number of Xe in XeO_6^{4-} decreases from + 8 to + 6 in XeO_3 and oxidation number of F increases from −1 (in F^-) to zero (in F_2). [1]

Hence XeO_6^{4-} or Na_4XeO_6 is reduced and F^- is oxidised. This reaction occur because Na_4XeO_6 or XeO_6^{4-} is a stronger oxidising agent than fluorine. [1]

15. (i) F exhibits only negative oxidation state because it is the most electronegative element. [1/2]

(ii) Cs exhibits only positive oxidation state because it is the most electropositive element. [1/2]

(iii) I exhibits both positive and negative oxidation states. Iodine exhibits − 1, 0, + 1, +3, + 5 and + 7 oxidation states (+ 3, + 5 and + 7 oxidation states are exhibited by I due to the presence of vacant d-orbitals). [1/2]

(iv) Ne is an inert gas, so it neither exhibits negative nor positive oxidation states. [1/2]

16. Bromine is a stronger oxidising agent than iodine.

$$2\overset{+2}{S_2}\overset{-2}{O_3^{2-}}(aq) + \overset{0}{I_2}(s) \longrightarrow \overset{2.5}{S_4}\overset{-2}{O_6^{2-}}(aq) + 2I^-(aq)$$

$$\overset{+2}{S_2}\overset{-2}{O_3^{2-}}(aq) + 2\overset{0}{Br_2}(l) + 5H_2O(l) \longrightarrow 2\overset{+6}{S}\overset{-2}{O_4^{2-}}(aq) + 4Br^-(aq) + 10H^+(aq)$$

Bromine is a stronger oxidising agent in comparison to I_2. It oxidises S of $S_2O_3^{2-}$ to a higher oxidation state + 6 in SO_4^{2-}. While I_2 oxidises S of $S_2O_3^{2-}$ to oxidation state 2.5 in $S_4O_6^{2-}$. That's why same reductant, thiosulphate react differently with bromine and iodine. [2]

17. Redox reactions involve oxidation and reduction as its two half reactions. So, find the oxidation state of each element given in the equation to find which substance is oxidising and which is reducing, then check, if the given reaction is redox reaction.

$$\overset{+1\ -2}{H_2O}(s)+\overset{0}{F_2}(g) \longrightarrow \overset{+1\ -1}{HF}(g) + \overset{+1\ -2\ -1}{HOF}(g) \longrightarrow \overset{+1\ -1}{HF} + \overset{+1\ -2}{H_2O} + \overset{+2\ +1}{OF_2}$$

Oxidation number of F decreases from zero (in F_2) to −1 (in HF) and of O increases from − 2 to + 2 (in OF_2). This shows that F_2 is reduced. It is not a disproportionation reaction, but only a redox reaction.

In a disproportionation reaction, an element in one oxidation state is simultaneously reduced and oxidised. **[2]**

18. Write the oxidation number of each element above its symbol and then identify the bleaching reagent by observing the change in oxidation number.

$$\overset{0}{Cl_2}(g) + 2\overset{-2\ +1}{OH^-}(aq) \rightarrow \overset{+1\ -2}{ClO^-}(aq) + \overset{-1}{Cl^-}(aq) + \overset{+1\ -2}{H_2O}(l)$$

In this reaction, oxidation number of Cl increases from 0 (in Cl_2) to 1 (in ClO^-) as well as decreases from 0 (in Cl_2) to −1 (in Cl^-). So, it acts as both reducing as well as oxidising agent. This is an example of disproportionation reaction. In this reaction, ClO^- species bleaches the substances due to its oxidising action.

Note Disproportionation reactions are a special type of redox reactions in which an element in one oxidation state is simultaneously oxidised and reduced.

19. PbO is a base. It reacts with nitric acid and forms soluble lead nitrate.

$$\underset{\text{(Acid - base reaction)}}{PbO + 2HNO_3} \longrightarrow \underset{\text{Soluble}}{Pb(NO_3)_2} + H_2O$$

Nitric acid does not reacts with PbO_2. Both of them are strong oxidising agents. In HNO_3, nitrogen is in its maximum oxidation state (+ 5) and in PbO_2, lead is in its maximum oxidation state (+ 4). Therefore, no reaction takes place. **[2]**

20. To find the behaviour of Ag^+ and Cu^{2+} in the given reactions, find whether there is addition of oxygen or any other electronegative element and addition of hydrogen or any other electropositive element. If there is addition of O to a reactant then other reactant acts as reducing agent (or reductant) and if there is addition of hydrogen, they act as oxidant.

In, (*i*) and (*ii*) reactions, $AgNO_3$ and $CuSO_4$ act as oxidising agents respectively. They oxidise H_3PO_2, hypophosphorous acid to orthophosphoric acid. In reaction (*iii*), $[Ag(NH_3)_2]^+(aq)$ oxidises benzaldehyde to benzoic acid but in reaction (*iv*), Cu^{2+} does not oxidise benzaldehyde (C_6H_5CHO) to benzoic acid. This indicates that Ag^+ is a stronger oxidising agent than Cu^{2+}. **[2]**

21. (i) Let us consider the structure of $Na_2S_2O_3$.

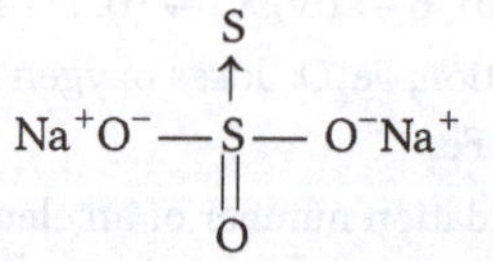

There is a coordinate bond between two sulphur atoms. The oxidation number of acceptor S-atom is − 2. Let the oxidation number of other S-atom be x.

$$\underset{\text{For Na}}{2(+1)} + \underset{\text{For O-atoms}}{3\times(-2)} + x + \underset{\text{For coordinate bonded S-atom}}{1(-2)} = 0$$

$$x = +6$$

Therefore, the two sulphur atoms in $Na_2S_2O_3$ have − 2 and + 6 oxidation number. The average oxidation number of two S-atom $= \frac{-2+6}{2} = +2$ **[1]**

(ii) Let us consider the structure of $Na_2S_4O_6$.

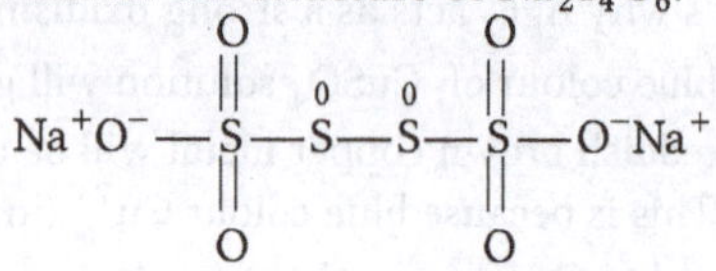

In this structure, two central sulphur atoms have zero oxidation number because electron pair forming the S—S bond remain in the centre. Let the oxidation number of S-atom (remaining) be x.

$$\underset{\text{For Na}}{2(+1)} + \underset{\text{For O}}{6(-2)} + 2x + 2(0) = 0$$

$$2 - 12 + 2x = 0 \text{ or } x = +\frac{10}{2} = +5$$

Therefore, the two central S-atoms have zero oxidation state and two terminal S-atoms have + 5 oxidation state each.

The average oxidation number of four S-atom **[1]**

$$= \frac{5+5+0+0}{4} = \frac{5}{2}$$

(iii) Na_2SO_3

Let the oxidation number of S in Na_2SO_3 be x.

$$2(+1) + x + 3(-2) = 0 \text{ or } x = +4$$ **[1/2]**

(iv) Na_2SO_4

Let the oxidation number of S be x.

$$2(+1) + x + 4(-2) = 0 \text{ or } x = +6$$ **[1/2]**

22.

Substance	ON of C	Substance	ON of N
CH_4	− 4	NH_3	− 3
C_2H_6	− 3	N_2H_4	− 2
C_2H_4 or CH_3Cl	− 2	N_2H_2	− 1
C_2H_2	− 1	N_2	0
CH_2Cl_2 or $C_6H_{12}O_6$	0	N_2O	+ 1
C_6Cl_6 or C_2Cl_2	+ 1	NO	+ 2
$CHCl_3$ or CO	+ 2	N_2O_3	+ 3
$(COOH)_2$	+ 3	N_2O_4	+ 4
CCl_4 or CO_2	+ 4	N_2O_5	+ 5

23. (i) Oxidation number of S in H_2SO_5 is

$$2(+1)+x+5(-2)=0 \quad \text{or} \quad x=+8$$

But oxidation number of S cannot be more than 6 because S has only 6 valence electrons. This fallacy is removed by calculating oxidation number of S by chemical bonding method.

Let us consider the structure of H_2SO_5,

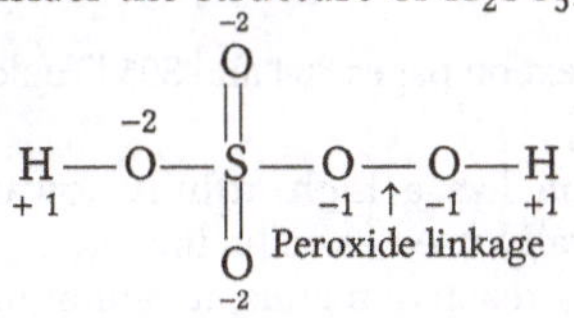

In H_2SO_5, two oxygen atoms are in −1 oxidation state.

Let the oxidation number of S be x.

$$\underset{\text{For H}}{2(+1)}+\underset{\text{For three O}}{3(-2)}+x+\underset{\text{For O—O}}{2(-1)}=0$$

$$2+(-6)+x+(-2)=0$$

$$x=+6$$

Therefore, the oxidation number of S in H_2SO_5 is + 6. [1]

(ii) Oxidation number of Cr in $Cr_2O_7^{2-}$ is

$$2x+(-2)7=-2$$

$$2x=+12$$

$$x=+6$$

Let us consider the structure of $Cr_2O_7^{2-}$ ion

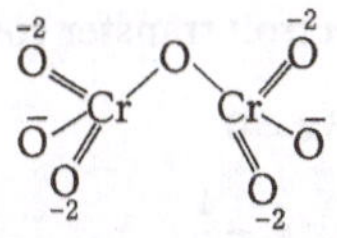

Let the oxidation number of each Cr-atom be x.

$$4(-2)+(-2)+1(-2)+2x=0$$

$$-8-2-2+2x=0$$

$$2x=+12$$

$$x=+6$$

Oxidation number of Cr in $Cr_2O_7^{2-}$ is same, i.e. + 6 whether it is calculated by conventional method or by chemical bonding method. Hence, there is no fallacy. [1]

(iii) Oxidation number of N in NO_3^- be x.

$$[x+3(-2)=-1 \quad \text{or} \quad x=+5]$$

Let us consider the structure of NO_3^- ion.

Let the oxidation number of N be x.

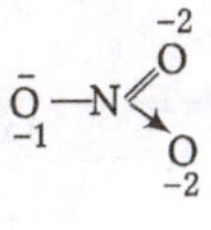

$$\underset{\text{For O}^-}{1(-1)}+x+\underset{\text{For (= O)}}{1(-2)}+\underset{\text{For (→ O)}}{1(-2)}=0$$

$$x=+5$$

Oxidation number of N in NO_3^- ion is same, i.e. + 5 whether it is calculated by conventional method or by chemical bonding method.

Hence, there is no fallacy. [1]

24. While writing the formula of a compound, oxidation state (or valency) of cation is written as the subscript of anion and valency of anion is written as the subscript of cation. Valency of chloride (Cl^-), sulphate (SO_4^{2-}) and oxide (O^{2-}) are −1, − 2 and − 2 respectively. Valencies of metals are given in brackets.

(i) Hg (II) Cl_2 (ii) Ni (II) SO_4

(iii) Sn (IV) O_2 (iv) Th_2(I) SO_4

(v) Fe_2(III)$(SO_4)_3$ (vi) Cr_2(III) O_3 [6 × 1/2]

25. Suppose the oxidation number of N in Y is x

$$(N^{2-})_2 \longrightarrow (2N)^x + 10e^-$$

$$(\text{as } N_2H_4 \longrightarrow Y + 10e^-)$$

Therefore, $2x-10=-4$, which gives $x=+3$. Hence, oxidation number of N in $Y=3$. [3]

26. (i) P_4 is a reducing agent and Cl_2 is an oxidising agent.

(a) $\underset{\text{Excess}}{\overset{0}{P_4}}(s)+6\,Cl_2(g) \longrightarrow \underset{\text{Lower oxidation state of P}}{4\overset{+3}{P}Cl_3}$

(b) $\overset{0}{P_4}(2)+\underset{\text{Excess}}{10\,Cl_2} \longrightarrow \underset{\text{Higher oxidation state of P}}{4\overset{+5}{P}Cl_5}$

Therefore, when P_4 (reducing agent) is in excess, PCl_3 is formed in which oxidation state of P is + 3 and if Cl_2 (oxidising agent) is in excess, PCl_5 is formed in which oxidation state of P is + 5.

Other two examples are: [1]

(ii) C is a reducing agent while O_2 is an oxidising agent.

(a) $\underset{\text{Excess}}{2\overset{0}{C}(s)}+O_2(g) \longrightarrow 2\overset{+2}{C}O(g)$

(b) $\overset{0}{C}(s)+\underset{\text{Excess}}{O_2} \longrightarrow \overset{+4}{C}O_2(g)$

When reducing agent C is in excess, a compound CO of lower oxidation state is formed, if oxidising agent O_2 is in excess, a compound CO_2 of higher oxidation state is formed. [1]

(iii) Na is a reducing agent while O_2 is an oxidising agent.

(a) $\underset{\text{Excess}}{4\,Na}(s)+\overset{0}{O_2}(g) \longrightarrow \underset{\text{(Lower oxidation state)}}{Na_2\overset{-2}{O}(s)}$

(b) $2\,Na(s)+\underset{\text{Excess}}{2O_2}(g) \longrightarrow \underset{\text{(Higher oxidation state)}}{Na_2\overset{-1}{O_2}(s)}$ [1]

27. Cu^+ undergoes disproportionation to form Cu^{2+} and Cu.

$$2\,Cu^+(aq) \longrightarrow Cu^{2+}(aq)+Cu\,(s)$$

Thus, Cu^+ or Cu_2O acts both as an oxidant as well as reductant.

(i) When heated in air, Cu_2O is oxidised to CuO.

$$\overset{+1}{Cu_2}\overset{-2}{O}+\frac{1}{2}\overset{0}{O_2} \longrightarrow 2\overset{+2}{Cu}\overset{-2}{O}$$

i.e. Cu_2O acts as a reductant and reduces O_2 to O^{2-}. [1]

(ii) When heated with Cu_2S, it oxidises S^{2-} to SO_2 and hence, Cu_2O acts as an oxidant.

$$2\overset{+1}{Cu_2}\overset{-2}{O}+\overset{+1}{Cu_2}\overset{-2}{S} \longrightarrow 6\overset{0}{Cu}+\overset{+4}{S}O_2 \quad [2]$$

28. Pb_3O_4 is actually a stoichiometric mixture of 2 moles of PbO and 1 mole of PbO_2, i.e. $(2\,PbO\cdot PbO_2)$. In PbO_2, lead is present in + 4 oxidation state, whereas the stable oxidation state of lead in PbO is + 2. PbO_2 thus can act as an oxidant (oxidising agent) and therefore, can oxidise Cl^- ion of HCl into chlorine. We may also keep in mind that PbO is a basic oxide. Therefore, the reaction

$$Pb_3O_4 + 8HCl \longrightarrow 3PbCl_2 + Cl_2 + 4H_2O \quad [1]$$

can be splitted into two reactions namely

$$\underset{\text{Base}}{2\,PbO}+\underset{\text{Acid}}{4\,HCl} \longrightarrow 2\,PbCl_2 + 2H_2O \quad \text{(acid-base reaction)}$$

$$\overset{+4}{Pb}O_2 + 4H\overset{-1}{Cl} \longrightarrow \overset{+2}{Pb}Cl_2 + \overset{0}{Cl_2} + 2H_2O \quad \text{(redox reaction)}$$

Since, HNO_3 itself is an oxidising agent, therefore it is unlikely that the reaction may occur between PbO_2 and HNO_3. However, the acid-base reaction occurs between PbO and HNO_3 as

$$2\,PbO + 4\,HNO_3 \longrightarrow 2Pb(NO_3)_2 + 2H_2O \quad [1]$$

It is the passive nature of PbO_2 against HNO_3 that makes the reaction different from the one that follows with HCl. [1]

29. (i) In this redox reaction, H in $LiAlH_4$ gets oxidised because of the addition of oxygen atom that leads to the formation of OH^-. Propanone (CH_3COCH_3) gets reduced because of addition of hydrogen atom to give propan-2-ol $(CH_3CH(OH)CH_3)$. [1]

(ii) This is not a redox reaction as oxidation number of elements (C, H or O) is same on both, reactant as well product side. [1]

(iii) This is not a redox reaction as oxidation number of elements (C, H or O) is same on both, reactant as well product side. [1]

30. An element, in its lowest oxidation state, can behave only as reductant while in its highest oxidation state can behave only as oxidants. In intermediate oxidation states, elements can behave as oxidant as well as reductant.

(i) In SO_2, S is in + 4 oxidation state. It can have minimum oxidation number − 2 and maximum oxidation number is + 6. Therefore, S in SO_2 can either decrease or increase its oxidation number. So, SO_2 can act both as oxidising as well as reducing agent. [1]

(ii) In H_2O_2, O is in −1 oxidation state. It can have minimum oxidation number − 2 and maximum oxidation number zero (+1 and + 2 also possible in O_2F_2 and OF_2 respectively). Therefore, O in H_2O_2 can either decrease or increase its oxidation number. So, H_2O_2 can act both as oxidising as well as reducing agent. [1]

(iii) In O_3, O is in zero oxidation state. It cannot increase its oxidation number, it can only decrease its oxidation number from zero to −1 or −2. So, ozone can act only as an oxidising agent. [1/2]

(iv) In HNO_3, the oxidation number of N is + 5. It is maximum. So, N in HNO_3 can only decrease its oxidation number. So, it can act as an oxidising agent only. [1/2]

31. Refer to text on pages 304 and 305 [Topic-1, Concept of redox reactions].

(i) Carbon has a high affinity towards oxygen so it is generally used as reducing agent. However, in case of highly reactive metals, it cannot be used as a reducing agent.

(ii) Ozone being a source of oxygen generally behaves as an oxidising agent.

(iii) As, we know addition of hydrogen is called reduction. So, nascent hydrogen behaves as a reducing agent.

(iv) Nitric acid is a good oxidant, i.e. oxidising agent as it readily provides oxygen.

(v) Chlorine can behave as oxidant as well as reductant depending upon the nature of other reactant. [5 × 1]

32. **Oxidants** (i) H^+ (ii) H_2O_2 (iii) $[Fe(CN)_6]^{3-}$ (iv) F_2 (v) $NaClO_3$

Reductants (i) Zn (ii) $[Fe(CN)_6]^{4-}$ (iii) H_2O_2 (iv) BrO_3^- (v) $2I_2$

(For details see electron transfer concept). [5 × 1]

33. (i) $\overset{+1}{K}\overset{x}{I_3}$; $1(+1)+3x=0$

or $x=-\frac{1}{3}$

Therefore, the average oxidation number of I is $-\frac{1}{3}$.

It is wrong because oxidation number can never be fractional. Let us consider the structure of KI_3.

$\overset{+1}{K}(I-I\leftarrow I)^{-1}$, in this structure, coordinate bond is formed between I_2 molecule and I^- ion. Hence, the oxidation number of three I-atoms in KI_3 are 0,0 (in I_2) and −1 respectively. [1]

(ii) Let the oxidation number of S in $H_2S_4O_6$ be x.

$$\overset{+1}{H_2}\overset{x}{S_4}\overset{-2}{O_6}$$

$$2(+1)+4x+6(-2)=0$$

$$4x=+10 \text{ or } x=+\frac{10}{4}=+2.5$$

Let us consider the structure of $H_2S_4O_6$

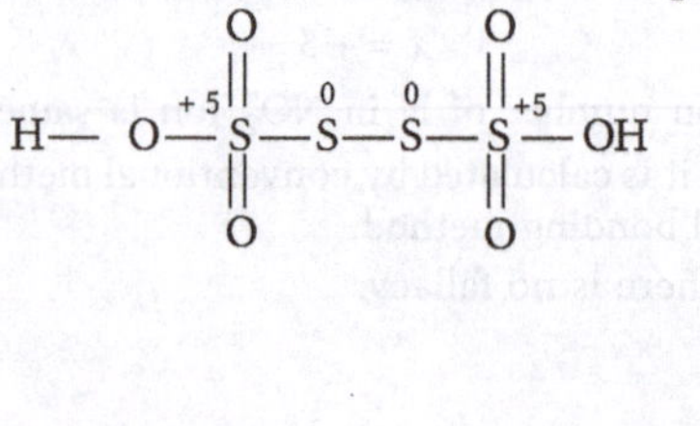

In $H_2S_4O_6$, the oxidation number of each of two S-atoms which are linked with each other by a single bond (in the centre) is zero and each of remaining two S-atoms is + 5. Hence, the oxidation number of 4 S-atoms in $H_2S_4O_6$ from left to right are + 5, 0, 0 and + 5 respectively. [1]

(iii) Let the oxidation number of Fe be x.

$$\overset{x}{Fe_3}\overset{-2}{O_4}$$

$$3x + 4(-2) = 0 \quad \text{or} \quad x = \frac{+8}{3}$$

Therefore, the average oxidation number of Fe is $\frac{8}{3}$.

But stoichiometrically, Fe_3O_4 is an equimolar mixture of FeO and Fe_2O_3. The oxidation number of Fe in $Fe_3O_4 (\equiv FeO.Fe_2O_3)$ is +2 and +3, respectively.

(iv) $CH_3\underline{C}H_2OH$

$$\overset{x}{C_2}\overset{+1}{H_6}\overset{-2}{O}$$

$$2x + 6(+1) + 1(-2) = 0$$

$$2x = -4 \quad \text{or} \quad x = -2$$

Therefore, the average oxidation number of C is – 2.

Let us consider the structure of CH_3CH_2OH.

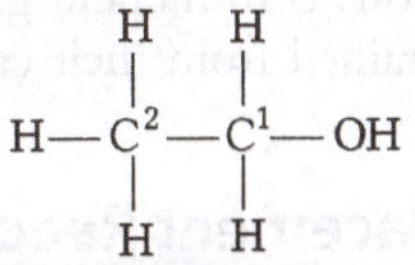

Oxidation number of C_1-atom

$$= 1(+1) + 2(+1) + x + 1(-1) = 0$$

[C_1-atom is attached to one CH_3 group (oxidation number = +1), two H atoms and one — OH group (oxidation number = –1)]

$\therefore \quad x = -2$

Oxidation number of C_2-atom

$$= 3(+1) + x + 1(-1) = 0$$

[C_2-atom is attached to three H-atoms and one — CH_2OH group (oxidation number = –1)]

$x = -2$ [1]

(v) $CH_3\underline{C}OOH$

$$\overset{x}{C_2}\overset{+1}{H_4}\overset{-2}{O_2}$$

$$2x + 4(+1) + 2(-2) = 0$$

$$2x + 4 + (-4) = 0 \text{ or } x = 0$$

Therefore, the average oxidation number of C is zero.

Let us consider the structure of CH_3COOH.

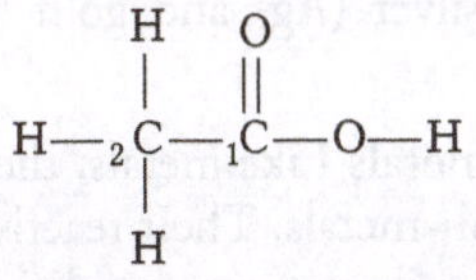

Oxidation number of C_1-atom

$$= 1(+1) + x + 1(-2) + 1(-1) = 0$$

[C_1-atom is attached to one — CH_3 group (oxidation number = +1), one oxygen atom and one — OH group (oxidation number = –1)] $x = +2$

Similarly, oxidation number of C_2-atom

$3(+1) + x + 1(-1) = 0 \Rightarrow x = -2$ [1]

34. To identify which substance is oxidised, reduced or act as oxidant or reductant, find the oxidation state of each element. The substance in which oxidation state of an element is increasing, gets oxidised, i.e. acts as reducing agent while that in which oxidation state decreases, gets reduced, i.e. acts as oxidising agent.

	Substance oxidised (Reducing agent)	Substance reduced (Oxidising agent)
(i)	$C_6H_6O_2(aq)$	AgBr(s)
(ii)	HCHO (*l*)	$[Ag(NH_3)_2]^+(aq)$
(iii)	HCHO(*l*)	$Cu^{2+}(aq)$
(iv)	$N_2H_4(l)$	$H_2O_2(l)$
(v)	Pb(s)	$PbO_2(s)$

[5 × 1]

35. (i) $CuO(s) + H_2(g) \longrightarrow Cu(s) + H_2O(g)$

Assign oxidation numbers of each atom above its symbol.

$$\overset{+2\,-2}{CuO}(s) + \overset{0}{H_2}(g) \longrightarrow \overset{0}{Cu}(s) + \overset{+1\,-2}{H_2O}(g)$$

Oxidation number of Cu in CuO is + 2. It decreases from + 2 to zero in Cu. While oxidation number of hydrogen increases from 0 (in H_2) to +1 (in H_2O). This shows that CuO is reduced to Cu but H_2 is oxidised to H_2O. Hence, it is an example of redox reaction. [1]

(ii) $$\overset{+3\,-2}{Fe_2O_3}(s) + 3\overset{+2\,-2}{CO}(g) \longrightarrow 2\overset{0}{Fe}(s) + \overset{+4\,-2}{CO_2}(g)$$

Oxidation number of Fe decreases from + 3 (in Fe_2O_3) to zero (in Fe) and oxidation number of C increases from + 2 (in CO) to + 4 (in CO_2). This shows that Fe_2O_3 is reduced to Fe and CO is oxidised to CO_2. Hence, it is a redox reaction. [1]

(iii) $$4\overset{+3\,-1}{BCl_3}(g) + 3\overset{+1\,+3\,-1}{LiAlH_4}(s) \longrightarrow 2\overset{-3\,+1}{B_2H_6}(g) + 3\overset{+1\,-1}{LiCl}(s) + 3\overset{+3\,-1}{AlCl_3}(s)$$

Oxidation number of B decreases from + 3 (in BCl_3) to – 3 (in B_2H_6) and oxidation number of H increases from –1 (in $LiAlH_4$) to +1 (in B_2H_6). This shows that BCl_3 is reduced to B_2H_6 and $LiAlH_4$ is oxidised. Hence, it is redox reaction. [1]

(iv) $$2\overset{0}{K}(s) + \overset{0}{F_2} \longrightarrow 2\overset{+1\,-1}{KF}(s)$$

Oxidation number of K increases from zero (in K) to + 1 (in KF) and oxidation number of F reduces from zero (in F_2) to –1 (in KF). This shows that K is oxidised and F_2 is reduced. Hence, it is a redox reaction.

(v) $$4\overset{-3\,+1}{NH_3}(g) + 5\overset{0}{O_2}(g) \longrightarrow 4\overset{+2\,-2}{NO}(g) + 6\overset{+1\,-2}{H_2O}(g)$$ [1]

Oxidation number of N increases from – 3 (in NH_3) to + 2 (in NO) and oxidation number of O decreases from zero (in O_2) to – 2 (in NO and H_2O). This shows that NH_3 is oxidised and O_2 is reduced. Hence, it is a redox reaction. [1]

TOPIC 02

Redox Reactions : Types, Balancing and Applications

Types of Redox Reactions

The redox reactions can be classified into following types :

Combination Reactions

The reactions in which two or more atoms or molecules combine together to give only a single compound are called **combination reactions.** All combustion reactions are included in this category,

e.g. $\overset{0}{2Mg}(s) + \overset{0}{O_2}(g) \longrightarrow 2\overset{+2\;-2}{MgO}(s)$

For a combination reaction to be a redox reaction, atleast one of its reactant must be in its elemental form. All combustion reactions, which make use of elemental dioxygen, as well as other reactions involving elements other than dioxygen are called redox reaction.

$$\overset{0}{C}(s) + \overset{0}{O_2}(g) \xrightarrow{\Delta} \overset{+4\;-2}{CO_2}(g)$$

$$2\overset{0}{Mg}(s) + \overset{0}{N_2}(g) \xrightarrow{\Delta} \overset{+2\;\;-3}{Mg_3N_2}(g)$$

Decomposition Reactions

These are just opposite to the combination reactions, i.e. in these reactions, one compound split into two or more simpler compounds, atleast one of which must be in elemental form. e.g.

e.g. $2\overset{+1\;-1}{NaH}(s) \xrightarrow{\Delta} 2\overset{0}{Na}(s) + \overset{0}{H_2}(g)$

$$\overset{+2\;+4\;-2}{CaCO_3}(s) \xrightarrow{\Delta} \overset{+2\;-2}{CaO}(s) + \overset{+4\;-2}{CO_2}(g)$$

The former reaction involves change in oxidation states. So, it is considered as redox reaction. The latter reaction, i.e. the decomposition of calcium carbonate is not a redox reaction as there is no change in the oxidation states of the elements involving in the reaction. It suggests that **all the decomposition reactions are not the redox reactions.**

Displacement Reactions

The reactions in which an atom (or ion) replaces the ion (or atom) of another element from a compound, are known as **displacement reactions.** These reactions can be represented as :

$$X + YZ \longrightarrow XZ + Y$$

Depending upon the nature of element displaced, these reactions can be classified into two categories.

1. Metal Displacement Reactions

When a free metal displaces another metal from its compounds, the reaction is known as **metal displacement reactions.** In general, a more reactive metal displaces the less reactive one from its compound.

e.g. $\overset{+2\;+6\;-2}{CuSO_4}(aq) + \overset{0}{Zn}(s) \longrightarrow \overset{0}{Cu}(s) + \overset{+2\;+6\;-2}{ZnSO_4}(aq)$

$$\overset{+5\;-2}{V_2O_5}(s) + 5\overset{0}{Ca}(s) \xrightarrow{\Delta} 2\overset{0}{V}(s) + 5\overset{+2\;-2}{CaO}(s)$$

In the above reactions, the metal which displaces the other from their salt is a good reducing agent, i.e. have more tendency to lose electrons as compared to the one that is displaced or reduced.

Above reactions also reveals that the metal displacement reactions are generally redox reactions. An important application of these reactions is in metallurgical processes where pure metals are obtained from their compounds in ores.

2. Non-metal Displacement Reactions

When some of the non-metal is displaced by a metallic or a non-metallic element, the reaction is said to be **non-metal displacement reaction.** In these reactions, generally the hydrogen is displaced but in some reactions, displacement of oxygen or halogen has also been observed.

e.g. $2Na(s) + 2H_2O(l) \longrightarrow 2NaOH(aq) + H_2(g)$

$$Mg(s) + 2H_2O(g) \longrightarrow Mg(OH)_2(aq) + H_2(g)$$

$$Zn(s) + 2HCl(aq) \longrightarrow ZnCl_2(aq) + H_2(g)$$

These displacement reactions help in estimating the reactivity of metals and non-metals as discussed below :

(i) **Reactivity of Metals** The rate of evolution of H_2 by metals from water and protonating solutions can be used to determine the order of reactivity of metals, e.g. sodium (Na) reacts with water at the fastest rate, magnesium (Mg) reacts slowly, iron (Fe) reacts at the slowest rate while silver (Ag) and gold (Au) do not reacts at all.

(ii) **Reactivity of Non-metals** Like metals, there is also an activity series for non-metals. Their reactivity depends upon their oxidising power, e.g. oxidising power of halogens decreases as we move down the group 17 from F to I. Fluorine is the strongest oxidising agent. It can displace other halogen ions from their aqueous solutions.

The generalised equation of these displacement reactions is given below.

$$2X^-(aq) + F_2(aq) \longrightarrow X_2(g) + 2F^-(aq)$$

(where, $X^- = Cl^-, Br^-, I^-$)

In fact, fluorine is so reactive that it even attacks water and displaces the oxygen of water.

$$2H_2O(l) + 2F_2(g) \longrightarrow 4HF(aq) + O_2(g)$$

Disproportionation Reactions

These are a special kind of redox reactions in which the same element undergoes oxidation as well as reduction. In hydrogen peroxides, oxygen undergoes disproportionation reaction.

$$2\overset{+1}{H_2}\overset{-1}{O_2}(aq) \longrightarrow 2\overset{+1}{H_2}\overset{-2}{O}(l) + \overset{0}{O_2}(g)$$

(Reduction: $-1 \rightarrow -2$; Oxidation: $-1 \rightarrow 0$)

Similarly, chlorine, sulphur and phosphorous undergo disproportionation in the alkaline medium as shown below.

$$\overset{0}{Cl_2}(g) + 2OH^-(aq) \longrightarrow \overset{+1}{Cl}O^-(aq) + \overset{-1}{Cl^-}(aq) + H_2O(l)$$

$$\overset{0}{S_8}(s) + 12OH^-(aq) \longrightarrow 4S^{2-}(aq) + 2\overset{+2}{S_2}O_3^{2-}(aq) + 6H_2O(l)$$

$$\overset{0}{P_4}(s) + 3OH^-(aq) + 3H_2O(l) \longrightarrow \overset{-3}{P}H_3(g) + 3H_2\overset{+1}{P}O_2^-(aq)$$

With an exception of ClO_4^- (in which Cl is present in highest oxidation state, so its further oxidation is not possible), all other oxoanions of chlorine undergo disproportionation reaction as shown below.

$$3\overset{+1}{Cl}O^- \longrightarrow 2\overset{-1}{Cl^-} + \overset{+5}{Cl}O_3^-$$

$$6\overset{+3}{Cl}O_2^- \xrightarrow{h\nu} 4\overset{+5}{Cl}O_3^- + 2\overset{-1}{Cl^-}$$

$$4\overset{+5}{Cl}O_3^- \longrightarrow \overset{-1}{Cl^-} + 3\overset{+7}{Cl}O_4^-$$

Example 1 Suggest a scheme of classification of the following redox reactions.

(i) $N_2(g) + O_2(g) \longrightarrow 2NO(g)$

(ii) $2Pb(NO_3)_2(s) \longrightarrow 2PbO(s) + 2NO_2(g) + \frac{1}{2}O_2(g)$

(iii) $NaH(s) + H_2O(l) \longrightarrow NaOH(aq) + H_2(g)$

(iv) $2NO_2(g) + 2OH^-(aq) \longrightarrow NO_2^-(aq) + NO_3^-(aq) + H_2O(l)$

NCERT Textbook

Sol. (i) Since, the two molecules are combining to give a single product, so it is an example of **combination reaction.**

(ii) Since, the compound splits up into several simpler substances, out of which O_2 is in the elemental form, thus, it is an example of **decomposition redox reaction.**

(iii) $NaH(s) + H_2O(l) \longrightarrow NaOH(aq) + H_2(g)$

The ionic form of the reaction is

$H^-(s) + H_2O(l) \longrightarrow OH^-(aq) + H_2(g)$

Here, H^-(hydride ion) displaces hydrogen from water molecule, so it is an example of **displacement redox reaction.**

(iv) $2\overset{+4}{N}O_2(g) + 2OH^-(aq) \longrightarrow \overset{+3}{N}O_2^-(aq) + \overset{+5}{N}O_3^-(aq) + H_2O(l)$

(Oxidation: $+4 \rightarrow +5$; Reduction: $+4 \rightarrow +3$)

Since, in the above reaction, the same element undergoes oxidation as well as reduction, so it is an example of **disproportionation reaction.**

Example 2 Which of the following species, do not show disproportionation reaction and why?

ClO^-, ClO_2^-, ClO_3^- and ClO_4^-

Also write reaction for each of the species that disproportionates. **NCERT Textbook**

Sol. Disproportionation reaction is shown by the species in which the element exhibit intermediate oxidation state. Among the oxoanions of chlorine listed above, ClO_4^- does not disproportionate because in the oxoanion, chlorine is present in its highest oxidation state that is +7. The disproportionation reactions for the other three oxoanions of chlorine are as follows:

$$3\overset{+1}{Cl}O^- \longrightarrow 2\overset{-1}{Cl^-} + \overset{+5}{Cl}O_3^-$$

$$6\overset{+3}{Cl}O_2^- \xrightarrow{h\nu} 4\overset{+5}{Cl}O_3^- + 2\overset{-1}{Cl^-}$$

$$4\overset{+5}{Cl}O_3^- \longrightarrow \overset{-1}{Cl^-} + 3\overset{+7}{Cl}O_4^-$$

Balancing of Redox Reactions

In order to satisfy the law of conservation of mass (which states that matter or mass can neither be created nor destroyed), the chemical reactions are balanced, i.e. the number of atoms of each element equalise on both sides of the chemical equation.

Several methods can be used to balance a redox reaction. *These methods are :*

(i) Oxidation number method

(ii) Half equation method or ion-electron method.

Oxidation Number Method

This method is based on the change in the oxidation number of oxidant and reductant and involves the following steps.

Step I **Writing skeleton ionic equation** Write the correct formula for each reactant and product and draw an arrow in between them. Convert it into skeleton ionic equation by removing the spectator ion, the ion which is not involve in the reaction.

Step II **Assigning Oxidation state to each element and balancing atoms other than H and O** Write the oxidation number of each element above its symbol and balance all the atoms other than H and O.

Step III **Finding change in oxidation number and equalise it** Calculate the decrease or increase in the oxidation number per atom and for the entire molecule/ion in which it is present. If the decrease and increase in oxidation number is not equal, then equalise them by multiplying with a suitable number.

Step IV **Balancing ionic charge by adding H^+ or OH^-** In case of reactions occurring in water, add H^+ or OH^- ions on the appropriate side to balance the charges of reactants and products. If medium is acidic, use H^+ ions and if medium is basic, use OH^- ions on the appropriate side.

Step V **Balancing H and O atoms** In order to equalise the number of hydrogen atoms, add water (H_2O) molecules on appropriate side. Now, check the number of oxygen atoms on both the sides. If these are found equal, then the equation is a balanced chemical equation.

Example 3 Write the net ionic equation for the reaction of potassium dichromate (VI), $K_2Cr_2O_7$ with sodium sulphite, Na_2SO_3, in an acid solution to give chromium (III) ion and the sulphate ion. **NCERT Textbook**

Sol.*Step* I Following steps are involved in order to solve such problems. Writing skeleton ionic equation.

e.g.

$$Cr_2O_7^{2-}(aq) + SO_3^{2-}(aq) \longrightarrow Cr^{3+}(aq) + SO_4^{2-}(aq)$$

Step II Assigning oxidation number to each element and balancing atoms other than H and O.

$$\overset{+6}{Cr_2}\,\overset{-2}{O_7^{2-}}(aq) + \overset{+4}{S}\overset{-2}{O_3^{2-}}(aq) \longrightarrow \overset{+3}{Cr^{3+}}(aq) + \overset{+6}{S}\,\overset{-2}{O_4^{2-}}(aq)$$

Step III Finding change in oxidation number and equalise it

Change in ON = 6 − 4 = 2] × 3

$$\overset{+6}{Cr_2}\,\overset{-2}{O_7^{2-}}(aq) + 3\overset{+4}{S}\,\overset{-2}{O_3^{2-}}(aq) \longrightarrow 2\overset{+3}{Cr^{3+}}(aq) + 3\overset{+6}{S}\,\overset{-2}{O_4^{2-}}(aq)$$

To balance number of Cr atoms

Change in ON = 6 − 3 = 3 per atom

or 3 × 2 = 6 net change (as two Cr atoms are involving)

To equalise the increase in oxidation state of S with decrease in oxidation state of Cr, we have to multiply it with 3, thus we have to multiply SO_3^{2-} and SO_4^{2-} with 3.

Step IV *Balancing ionic charge*

Since, the medium is acidic, so we can use only H^+ ions to balance the ionic charges.

$$Cr_2O_7^{2-}(aq) + 3SO_3^{2-}(aq) \longrightarrow 2Cr^{3+}(aq) + 3\,SO_4^{2-}(aq)$$

$(-2) + (-2 \times 3) = -8$; $= (2 \times +3) + (-2 \times 3) = 0$

So, to balance −8 charge, we have to add $8H^+$ ions at the reactant side. Thus, the reaction becomes

$$Cr_2O_7^{2-}(aq) + 3SO_3^{2-}(aq) + 8H^+(aq) \longrightarrow 2Cr^{3+}(aq) + 3\,SO_4^{2-}(aq)$$

Step V Balancing of H and O-atoms.

Now count the total number of H atoms on both the sides and add H_2O molecules to equalise them.

In the above reaction, there are 8H atoms towards the reactant side, so in order to balance them, we add $4H_2O$ towards the product side.

$$Cr_2O_7^{2-}(aq) + 3SO_3^{2-}(aq) + 8H^+(aq) \longrightarrow 2Cr^{3+}(aq) + 3\,SO_4^{2-}(aq) + 4\,H_2O$$

Now, we check the number of O atoms. Since, the number of O atoms are already balanced, so the equation is a balanced chemical equation.

Half Reaction Method or Ion Electron Method

This method is based upon the splitting of a redox reaction into two half reactions (one is oxidation half reaction and the other is reduction half reaction) and includes the following steps:

Step I **Converting unbalanced equation into ionic form** Break all the ionic compounds involved in the reaction into their constituent ions and cancel out the spectator ion to convert a molecular reaction into ionic form.

Step II **Splitting the equation into two halves** Separate the equation into oxidation half and reduction half reactions.

Step III **Balancing all elements except H and O** Balance all other elements except H and O in each half reaction individually.

Step IV **Balancing H and O-atoms** In acidic medium, add H_2O to balance O-atoms and H^+ to balance hydrogen atoms. However, if the medium is basic, add OH^- equal to number of H^+ ions on both the sides of the equation.

Step V **Balancing the charge**

(i) Balance the charge in each half equation by adding electrons toward the side having more positive charge (The number of electrons added should be equal to the excess in positive charge).

(ii) Now multiply the half equations by suitable integer so that the number of electrons (charge) become equal in both the half equations.

Step VI **Adding the half equations** Add the two half equations and cancel the electrons on each side to get the overall ionic equation.

Step VII **Verification of balanced equation** Check the correctness of equation by comparing the number of atoms of each element on both the sides and also by comparing the total charges of both the sides.

Step VIII **Conversion of ionic equation into molecular form** Convert the obtained equation into molecular form by adding spectator ions. (If mentioned in the question).

Example 4 In acidic medium, dichromate ions oxidise ferrous sulphate to ferric sulphate and itself gets reduced to Cr^{3+} ions. Write a balanced equation to represent this redox reaction. (Use ion electron method).

NCERT Textbook

Sol. The equation for the given reaction is

$$Cr_2O_7^{2-}(aq) + FeSO_4 + \underset{\text{Shows acidic medium}}{H^+} \longrightarrow Cr^{3+} + Fe_2(SO_4)_3$$

Balancing of this equation by ion electron method involves the following steps:

Step I **Converting unbalanced equation into ionic form** It can be achieved by splitting the ionic compounds into constituent ions and by cancelling spectator ions.

$$Cr_2O_7^{2-}(aq) + Fe^{2+}(aq) + SO_4^{2-}(aq) + H^+(aq) \longrightarrow Cr^{3+}(aq) + Fe^{3+}(aq) + SO_4^{2-}(aq)$$

Here, SO_4^{2-} is the spectator ion so after leaving it, the reaction becomes

Oxidation

$$\overset{+6}{Cr_2O_7^{2-}}(ag) + Fe^{2+}(ag) + H^+(aq) \longrightarrow Cr^{3+}(ag) + Fe^{3+}$$

Reduction

Step II **Splitting the equation into two halves**

Oxidation half equation $\overset{+2}{Fe^{2+}}(aq) \longrightarrow \overset{+3}{Fe^{3+}}(aq)$

Reduction half equation $\overset{+6\ -2}{Cr_2O_7^{2-}}(aq) \longrightarrow \overset{+3}{Cr^{3+}}(aq)$

Step III **Balancing all elements other than H and O** Here, oxidation half reaction is already balanced with respect to Fe atoms but to balance reduction half reaction, we have to multiply the Cr^{3+} by 2.

$$Cr_2O_7^{2-}(aq) \longrightarrow 2Cr^{3+}(aq)$$

Step IV **Balancing H and O-atoms** In oxidation half reaction, there is no need to balance H and O atoms, as in it these are not present. In reduction half reaction, we have to add $7H_2O$ towards product side to balance O-atoms and then add $14H^+$ towards reactant side to balance H-atoms.

$$Cr_2O_7^{2-} + \underset{\text{To balance H-atoms}}{14H^+} \longrightarrow 2\,Cr^{3+} + \underset{\text{To balance O-atoms}}{7H_2O}$$

Step V **Balancing of charge**

(i) $\underset{+2}{Fe^{2+}} \longrightarrow \underset{+3}{Fe^{3+}}$

So, we have to add one electron towards Fe^{3+} side.

Thus, $Fe^{2+} \longrightarrow Fe^{3+} + e^-$

Similarly, $Cr_2O_7^{2-} + 14H^+ \longrightarrow 2\,Cr^{3+} + 7\,H_2O$

$$-2 + 14 \qquad\qquad 2 \times (+3)$$
$$+12 \qquad\qquad +6$$
$$+6 \qquad\qquad 0$$

So, we have to add $6e^-$ towards the reactant side.

$$Cr_2O_7^{2-} + 14\,H^+ + 6\,e^- \longrightarrow 2Cr^{3+} + 7H_2O$$

(ii) $[Fe^{2+} \longrightarrow Fe^{3+} + e^-] \times 6$ to equalise number of electrons.

Step VI **Adding the half reactions** On adding the half reaction, we get the overall balanced equation.

$$6\,Fe^{2+}(aq) + Cr_2O_7^{2-}(aq) + 14H^+(aq) \longrightarrow 6\,Fe^{3+}(aq) + 2\,Cr^{3+}(aq) + 7\,H_2O(l)$$

Step VII **Verification of balanced equation** Since, the number of atoms of each element are equal on both the sides, so it is a balanced chemical equation.

Further; $6\,Fe^{2+}(aq) + Cr_2O_7^{2-}(aq) + 14\,H^+(aq) \longrightarrow 6\,Fe^{3+}(aq) + 2\,Cr^{3+}(aq) + 7\,H_2O\,(l)$

$$6 \times (+2) + (-2) + 14\,(+1) \equiv 6 \times (+3) + 2 \times (+3)$$

$$12 - 2 + 14 \equiv 18 + 6 \Rightarrow 24 = 24$$

Thus, the equation is also balanced with respect to charge.

Step VIII **Conversion of ionic equation into molecular form** As we know SO_4^{2-} is the spectator ion, and there are 6 Fe^{2+}(which require 6 SO_4^{2-} ions) and $14H^+$ ions (that require 7 SO_4^{2-} ions), so, we have to add 13 SO_4^{2-} ions on both the sides.

$$6\,Fe^{2+}(aq) + 6\,SO_4^{2-}(aq) + Cr_2O_7^{2-}(aq) + 14H^+(aq) + 7SO_4^{2-}(aq) \longrightarrow 6\,Fe^{3+}(aq) + 9\,SO_4^{2-}(aq) + 2Cr^{3+} + 3\,SO_4^{2-}(aq) + 7\,H_2O + SO_4^{2-}$$

or $$6\,FeSO_4 + Cr_2O_7^{2-}(aq) + 7H_2SO_4 \longrightarrow 3\,Fe_2(SO_4)_3 + Cr_2(SO_4)_3 + 7H_2O + SO_4^{2-}$$

Applications of Redox Reactions in Various Types of Chemical Reactions

1. Use of Redox Reaction in Titration

In redox titrations, the strength of a reductant/oxidant is determined by titrating it with standard solution of oxidant/reductant using a redox sensitive indicator.The indicators used for redox titrations depend upon the nature of redox reaction or reagent and product involved. Some examples of indicators used in different conditions of redox titrations are given below.

(i) **When One of the Reagents is Intensely Coloured** In redox titrations, if one of the reagents is intensely coloured, then it itself behaves as an indicator. Such an indicator is called **self** or **auto-indicator** e.g. permanganate ion (MnO_4^-).

Reactions involved in these titrations are:

$$MnO_4^- + 8H^+ + 5e^- \longrightarrow Mn^{2+} + 4H_2O$$
$$[Fe^{2+} \longrightarrow Fe^{3+} + e^-] \times 5$$
$$MnO_4^- + 8H^+ + 5Fe^{2+} \longrightarrow 5Fe^{3+} + Mn^{2+} + 4H_2O$$

(ii) **When One of the Reagents Oxidises the Indicator** These are the substances that get oxidised immediately after the consumption of last drop of reductant and produce a dramatic colour change. It is generally the case of potassium dichromate ($K_2Cr_2O_7$) titrations.

The indicators used in its titrations are of two types:

(a) **External indicators** These indicators are not added inside the reaction mixture but after the equivalence point, drops of indicator is placed over few drops of reaction mixture taken in watch glass with the help of glass rod to produce an intense blue colour, thus indicating the end point. Potassium ferricyanide is an example of such indicator.

(b) **Internal indicators** These are added directly into the solution or titration flask before the process of titration. Diphenylamine (which produces intense blue colour at the end point) and N-phenylanthranilic acid (which produces violet-red colour at the end point) are the examples of such indicators.

(iii) **When the Reagent can Oxidise Iodide Ion into Iodine or Iodine to Iodide Ion** In such reactions starch acts as the indicator as it produces violet or intense blue colour with the molecular iodine, so helps in detection of end point.

(a) Titration in which the liberated iodine from an oxidising agent is titrated with standard solution of sodium thiosulphate is called **iodometric titration.**

Reactions involved in this titration are:

$$2Cu^{2+}(aq) + 4I^-(aq) \longrightarrow Cu_2I_2(s) + \underset{\text{In presence of starch turns blue}}{I_2(aq)}$$

$$2Na_2S_2O_3(aq) + \underset{\text{Blue colour}}{I_2(aq)} \longrightarrow \underset{\text{Blue colour disappear}}{2NaI} + Na_2S_4O_6(aq)$$

(b) When iodine is titrated directly against a reducing agent such as sodium thiosulphate, the titration is known as iodimetric titration.

$$\underset{\text{Blue with starch}}{I_2(aq)} + 2S_2O_3^{2-}(aq) \longrightarrow \underset{\text{Blue colour disappear}}{2I^-(aq)} + \underset{\text{Tetrathionate ion}}{S_4O_6^{2-}(aq)}$$

2. Use of Redox Reaction in Converting Chemical Energy into Electrical Energy

The redox reactions in which the oxidation and reduction half reactions occur in the same vessel are called the **direct redox reactions**, e.g. placing a zinc strip inside the copper sulphate solution, where Zn is oxidised to Zn^{2+} and copper sulphate is reduced to metallic copper.

The redox reactions in which the oxidation and reduction half reactions are carried out into separate vessels, are called **indirect redox reactions.** In these reactions, the reaction occurs in both the vessels as well as at the interface of the metal. These reactions form the basis of **electrochemical cell** where indirect redox reaction is used as a source of energy and **electrolytic cell**, where a non-spontaneous reaction is carried out with the help of energy.

Terminology Used in Electrode Processes

Before discussing the role of redox reactions in the electrode processes, it is essential to become aware from the following terms.

(i) **Electrodes** A metal rod or strip dipped in its own salt solution is called an **electrode**, e.g. when copper rod is dipped in the copper sulphate solution, then term electrode is used for the rod.

(ii) **Anode** The electrode at which oxidation, i.e. loss of electrons from the metal takes place is called the **anode.** It is negative pole in case of an electrochemical cell but a positive pole in case of an electrolytic cell.

(iii) **Cathode** It is the electrode at which reduction, i.e. gain of electron by the metal ion occurs. It is the positive pole of an electrochemical cell whereas negative pole of an electrolytic cell.

(iv) **Redox Couple** The combination of the oxidised and reduced forms of a substance taking part in an oxidation or reduction half reaction is called the **redox couple**, e.g. Zn is the reduced form of Zn^{2+} and Zn^{2+} is the oxidised form of Zn. When these two are present together, they show a redox couple.

A redox couple is represented by separating the oxidised and reduced forms with the help of a vertical line or a slash which shows the interface, e.g. the redox couple of Zn and Zn^{2+} is represented as Zn^{2+}/Zn.

Always remember that in a redox couple, the oxidised form is placed before the reduced form. Just like zinc couple, the redox couple for copper is represented as Cu^{2+}/Cu.

(v) **Electrode Potential** The potential associated with an electrode is known as the electrode potential. It is represented by the symbol E.

(vi) **Standard Electrode Potential** The potential of an electrode in which the concentration of each species taking part in the electrode reaction is unity (if any gas is involved in the electrode reaction, its pressure is taken as 1 atmosphere) and temperature is maintained at 298 K is called the standard electrode potential.

It is represented by $E°$. Standard electrode potential of an electrode is indeed the direct measure of its tendency to remain in the oxidised/reduced form.

The negative value of $E°$ shows that the electrode has a higher tendency to lose electrons, i.e. acts as a stronger reducing agent as compared to a H^+/H_2 couple.Similarly, a positive value of $E°$ shows its higher tendency to gain electrons, i.e. to act as a stronger oxidising agent or a weaker reducing agent as compared to H^+/H_2 couple.

Electrochemical Cell

It is a technique which is used to convert chemical energy into electrical energy. Daniell or voltaic cell is an important example of this cell. In order to construct a Daniell cell, zinc rod is placed in 1M solution of zinc sulphate and copper rod is placed in 1M solution of copper sulphate. The beakers containing these two solutions are put side by side and connected through a **salt-bridge.**

The metallic rods are connected through a wire having provision for an ammeter and a switch. The set up is shown in the following figure.

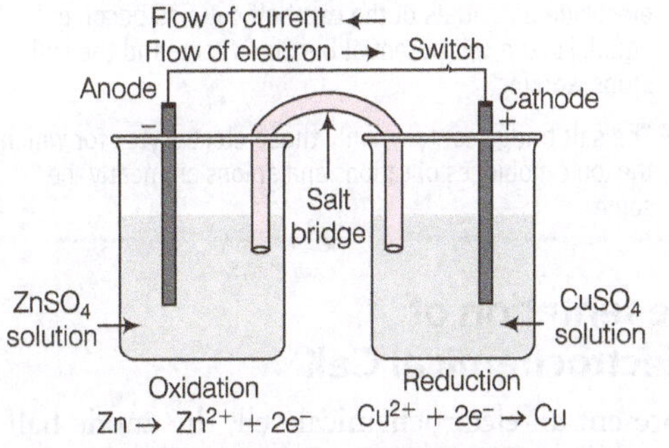

The set up for Daniell cell

When the switch is in off position, there is no reaction in either of the beakers and no current flows through the metallic wire. When switch is turned on

(i) The electrons generated at the anode and reach at the cathode

(ii) The electricity flows from the solution of one beaker to the solution of other beaker through the salt bridge. The current flows because the potentials of two redox couples are different. The difference between the potentials of two redox couple is called the **cell potential.** It is calculated by using the expression,

$$E^\circ_{cell} = E^\circ_{cathode} - E^\circ_{anode} = E^\circ_{reduction} + E^\circ_{oxidation}$$

For a cell reaction to be feasible, the E°_{cell} must be positive.

Functions of Salt-Bridge

The main functions of the salt bridge are as follows :

(i) It completes the cell circuit by connecting the solutions of two half cells, without allowing them to mix with each other.

(ii) It maintains the electrical neutrality of the solutions in the two half cells because of the flow of ions.

If salt bridge is removed, the cell potential drops to zero, i.e. there is no current flow. This is because of the accumulation of positive ions around the anode and negative ions (that are obtained after the reduction of metal ion) around the cathode, which results in the development of charges in the solution and hence, the current stops flowing.

- An electrochemical cell stops working after some time. This is because, as cell works, the concentration of metal ion towards the anode increases which results in increased electrode potential. At the same time, the concentration of metal ions towards the cathode decreases which results in decrease of electrode potential. Ultimately, a stage is reached at which the electrode potentials of the two half couples become equal, i.e. the cell potential becomes zero, and the cell stops working.
- The salt bridge contains only those electrolytes for which the ionic mobilities of cations and anions are nearly the same.

Representation of an Electrochemical Cell

To represent an electrochemical cell, the anode half reaction or electrode is written at the left and cathode half reaction or electrode is written at the right. These two are separated by two vertical lines representing the salt bridge.

Thus, a Daniell cell can be represented as

Anode half reaction (oxidation)

$$Zn \longrightarrow Zn^{2+} + 2e^-$$

Cathode half reaction (reduction)

$$Cu^{2+} + 2e^- \longrightarrow Cu$$

Thus, the Daniell cell is represented as :

$$\underbrace{Zn|Zn^{2+}}_{\text{Anode}}\ \underbrace{||}_{\text{Salt bridge}}\ \underbrace{Cu^{2+}|Cu}_{\text{Cathode}}$$

Topic Practice 2

Very Short Answer Type Questions

(1 Mark)

1. Fill in the Blanks

(i) The reactions in which two or more atoms or molecules combine together to give only a single compound are called ....

(ii) The reactions in which an atom replace with another atom of another element from a compound, are known as ....

(iii) .... is sensitive substance, used to find the end point of titration.

2. Objective Type Questions

(i) If a reaction is carried out in acidic medium then which is used to balance the equation?

(a) H^+ ions (b) OH^- ions
(c) H^- ions (d) O^{2-} ions

(ii) In acidic medium, H_2O_2 changes $Cr_2O_7^{2-}$ to CrO_5 which has two (— O —O —) bonds. Oxidation state of Cr in CrO_5 is

(a) + 5 (b) + 3 (c) + 6 (d) – 10

3. Match the Column I with Column II and select the correct option from the codes given below.

Column I (Compounds)	Column II (Oxidation number of nitrogen)
A. N_2O_3	(i) – 3
B. HNO_3	(ii) +5
C. NO	(iii) +3
D. NH_4OH	(iv) +2

Codes

	A	B	C	D		A	B	C	D
(a)	(ii)	(iii)	(iv)	(i)	(b)	(i)	(ii)	(iii)	(iv)
(c)	(iv)	(i)	(ii)	(iii)	(d)	(iii)	(ii)	(iv)	(i)

4. What is the most essential conditions that must be satisfied in a redox reaction?

5. Write the oxidation and reduction half reactions from the following redox reaction.

$$2Fe + 2H_2O + O_2 \longrightarrow 2Fe(OH)_2$$

6. Find the value of n in
$MnO_4^- + 8H^+ + ne^- \longrightarrow Mn^{2+} + 4H_2O$

7. What are spectator ions? Give one example.

8. Following cell is set up between copper and silver electrodes.

$$Cu \mid Cu^{2+}(aq) \parallel Ag^+(aq) \mid Ag$$

If its two half cells work under standard conditions, calculate the emf of the cell.
[Given $E^\circ_{Cu^{2+}/Cu} = +0.34$ V, $E^\circ_{Ag^+/Ag} = +0.80$ V]

9. What would happen if no salt bridge were used in the electrochemical cell (e.g. Zn -Cu cell)?

10. Why is anode called oxidation electrode, whereas cathode is called reduction electrode?

11. Can we use KCl as electrolyte in the salt bridge of the cell, $Cu(s) \mid Cu^{2+}(aq) \parallel Ag^+(aq) \mid Ag(s)$?

Short Answer Type I Questions

2 Marks

12. Why does fluorine not show disproportionation reaction? **NCERT Exemplar**

13. How would you know whether a redox reaction is taking place in an acidic, alkaline or neutral medium?

14. What are the net charges on the left and right side of the following equations? Add electrons as necessary to make each of them balanced half reactions.
(i) $NO_3^- + 10H^+ \longrightarrow NH_4^+ + 3H_2O$
(ii) $Cl_2 + 4H_2O \longrightarrow 2ClO_2^- + 8H^+$

15. The Mn^{3+} ion is unstable in solution and undergoes disproportionation to give Mn^{2+}, MnO_2 and H^+ ions. Write a balanced ionic equation for the reaction. [2]

16. Consider the reactions :
(i) $6CO_2(g) + 6H_2O(l) \longrightarrow C_6H_{12}O_6(aq) + 6O_2(g)$
(ii) $O_3(g) + H_2O_2(l) \longrightarrow H_2O(l) + 2O_2(g)$
Why it is more appropriate to write these reactions as
(a) $6CO_2(g) + 12H_2O(l) \longrightarrow C_6H_{12}O_6(aq) + 6H_2O + 6O_2(g)$
(b) $O_3(g) + H_2O_2(l) \longrightarrow H_2O(l) + O_2(g) + O_2(g)$
Also suggest a technique to investigate the path of the above (i) and (ii) redox reactions. **NCERT Textbook**

17. What sorts of informations can you draw from the following reaction? **NCERT Textbook**
$(CN)_2(g) + 2OH^-(aq) \longrightarrow CN^-(aq) + CNO^-(aq) + H_2O(l)$ [1]

18. Chlorine is used to purify drinking water. Excess of chlorine is harmful. The excess of chlorine is removed by treating with sulphur dioxide. Present a balanced equation for this redox change taking place in water. **NCERT Textbook**

19. How many millimoles of potassium dichromate is required to oxidise 24 mL of 0.5 M Mohr's salt solution in acidic medium?

20. MnO_4^{2-} undergoes disproportionation reaction in acidic medium but MnO_4^- does not. Give reason. **NCERT Textbook**

Short Answer Type II Questions

3 Marks

21. Identify the type of redox reaction taking place in the following.
(i) $3\overset{0}{Mg}(s) + \overset{0}{N_2}(g) \longrightarrow \overset{+2\,-3}{Mg_3N_2}(s)$
(ii) $\overset{+5\,-2}{V_2O_5}(s) + 5\overset{0}{Ca}(s) \longrightarrow 2\overset{0}{V}(s) + 5\overset{+2\,-2}{CaO}(s)$
(iii) $2\overset{+1\,+5\,-2}{KClO_3}(s) \longrightarrow 2\overset{+1\,-1}{KCl}(s) + 3\overset{0}{O_2}(g)$
(iv) $\overset{0}{Ca}(s) + 2\overset{+1\,-2}{H_2O}(l) \longrightarrow \overset{+2\,-2\,+1}{Ca(OH)_2}(aq) + \overset{0}{H_2}(g)$
(v) $\overset{0}{Br_2}(l) + 2\overset{-1}{I^-}(aq) \longrightarrow 2\overset{-1}{Br^-}(aq) + \overset{0}{I_2}(s)$
(vi) $\overset{0}{Cl_2}(g) + 2OH^-(aq) \longrightarrow \overset{+1}{ClO^-}(aq) + \overset{0}{Cl}(aq) + H_2O\ (l)$

22. Refer to the periodic table given in your book and answer the following questions.
(i) Select the possible non-metals that can show disproportionation reaction.
(ii) Select three metals that can show disproportionation reaction. **NCERT Textbook**

23. Write balanced chemical equation for the following reactions.
(i) Permanganate ion (MnO_4^-) reacts with sulphur dioxide gas in acidic medium to produce Mn^{2+} and hydrogen sulphate ion. (Balance by ion electron method)
(ii) Reaction of liquid hydrazine (N_2H_4) with chlorate ion (ClO_3^-) in basic medium produces nitric oxide gas and chloride ion in gaseous state. (Balance by oxidation number method)

(iii) Dichlorine heptaoxide (Cl_2O_7) in gaseous state combines with an aqueous solution of hydrogen peroxide in acidic medium of give chlorite ion (ClO_2^-) and oxygen gas. (Balance by ion electron method)

24. Write the anode reaction, the cathode reaction and the net cell reaction in the following cells. Which electrode would be positive terminal in each cell ?

(i) $Zn(s) \mid Zn^{2+} \parallel Br_2 \mid Br^- \mid Pt(s)$

(ii) $Cr(s) \mid Cr^{3+} \parallel I_2 \mid I^- \mid Pt(s)$

(iii) $Pt(s) \mid H_2(g) \mid H^+(aq) \parallel Cu^{2+} \mid Cu(s)$

25. Depict the galvanic cell in which the reaction,

$$Zn(s) + 2Ag^+(aq) \longrightarrow Zn^{2+}(aq) + 2Ag(s)$$

takes place, further show **NCERT Textbook**

(i) which of the electrode is negatively charged?

(ii) the carriers of the current in the cell.

(iii) individual reaction at each electrode.

Long Answer Type Questions

5 Marks

26. Write correctly the balanced equations for the following redox reactions using half reactions.

(i) $H_2S + Fe^{3+} \longrightarrow Fe^{2+} + S + H^+$

(ii) $I^- + IO_3^- + H^+ \longrightarrow I_2 + H_2O$

(iii) $Bi(s) + NO_3^- + H^+ \longrightarrow NO_2 + Bi^{3+} + H_2O$

(iv) $I^- + O_2(g) + H_2O \longrightarrow I_2 + OH^-$

Identify in each of the above reaction, which is getting oxidised and which is getting reduced?

27. Balance the following redox reactions by ion-electron method.

(i) $MnO_4^-(aq) + I^-(aq) \longrightarrow MnO_2(s) + I_2(s)$ (in basic medium)

(ii) $MnO_4^-(aq) + SO_2(g) \longrightarrow Mn^{2+}(aq) + HSO_4^-(aq)$ (in acidic solution)

(iii) $H_2O_2(aq) + Fe^{2+}(aq) \longrightarrow Fe^{3+}(aq) + H_2O(l)$ (in acidic solution)

(iv) $Cr_2O_7^{2-}(aq) + SO_2(g) \longrightarrow Cr^{3+}(aq) + SO_4^{2-}(aq)$ (in acidic solution)

NCERT Textbook

28. Balance the following equations in basic medium by ion electron and oxidation number methods and identify the oxidising agent and the reducing agent.

(i) $P_4(s) + OH^-(aq) \longrightarrow PH_3(g) + H_2PO_2^-(aq)$

(ii) $N_2H_4(l) + ClO_3^-(aq) \longrightarrow NO(g) + Cl^-(g)$

(iii) $Cl_2O_7(g) + H_2O_2(aq) \longrightarrow ClO_2^-(aq) + O_2(g)$

NCERT Textbook

29. How do you account for the following observations?

(i) Though alkaline potassium permanganate and acidic potassium permanganate both are used as oxidants, yet in the manufacture of benzoic acid from toluene, we use alcoholic potassium permanganate as an oxidant. Why? Write a balance redox equation for the reaction.

(ii) When concentrated sulphuric acid is added to an inorganic mixture containing chloride, we get colourless pungent smelling gas HCl, but if the mixture contains bromide, then we get red vapour of bromine. Why? **NCERT Textbook**

Hints & Solutions

1. (i) combination reactions (ii) displacement reactions (iii) indicators

2. (i) → (a), (ii) → (c)

3. (d) A → (iii), B → (ii), C → (iv), D → (i)

4. In a redox reaction, the total number of electrons lost by the reducing agent must be equal to the number of electrons gained by the oxidising agent.

5. $Fe \longrightarrow Fe^{2+} + 2e^-$ (Oxidation)

$\frac{1}{2}O_2 + H_2O + 2e^- \longrightarrow 2OH^-$ (Reduction)

6. $MnO_4^- + 8H^+ + ne^- \longrightarrow Mn^{2+} + 4H_2O$

$$-1 + 8 + n = +2$$
$$-1 - 2 + 8 + n = 0$$
$$n = -5 \text{ or } 5e^-$$

7. Spectator ions are ions that remains unaffected during a chemical reaction. They appear both as reactant and as product in an ionic equation, e.g. in the following ionic equation, the sodium and nitrate ions are spectator ions.

$$Ag^+(aq) + NO_3^-(aq) + Na^+(aq) + Cl^-(aq) \longrightarrow AgCl(s) + Na^+(aq) + NO_3^-(aq)$$

8. $E^\circ_{cell} = E^\circ_{cathode} - E^\circ_{anode}$

$= E^\circ_{Ag^+/Ag} - E^\circ_{Cu^{2+}/Cu} = +0.80 - (+0.34) = 0.46$ V

9. If no salt bridge is used, the positive ions (i.e. Zn^{2+}) formed by loss of electrons will accumulate around the zinc electrode and negative ions (i.e. SO_4^{2-}) left after reduction of Cu^{2+} ions will accumulate around the copper electrode. Thus, the solution will develop charges. Further, since the inner circuit is not complete, the current stops flowing.

10. At anode, loss of electrons takes place, i.e. oxidation takes place, whereas at cathode, gain of electrons takes place, i.e. reduction takes place. Therefore, cathode is called reduction electrode and anode is called oxidation electrode.

11. KCl cannot be used as electrolyte in the salt bridge because Cl^- ions will combine with Ag^+ ions to form white precipitates of AgCl.

12. In a disproportionation reaction, the same species simultaneously get oxidised as well as reduced. Therefore, for such a redox reaction to occur, the reacting species must contain an element which has atleast three oxidation states. The element, in reacting species, is present in an intermediate state while lower and higher oxidation states are available for reduction and oxidation to occur (respectively). Fluorine is the strongest oxidising agent. It does not show positive oxidation state. That's why fluorine does not show disproportionation reaction. [2]

13. If H^+ or any acid appears on either side of the chemical equation, the reaction takes place in the acidic solution. If OH^-, or any base, appears on either side of the chemical equation, the solution is basic. If neither H^+, OH^- nor any acid or base is present in the chemical equation, the solution is neutral. [2]

14. (i) +9 charge on the left, +1 charge on the right; add 8 electrons to the left side. [1]

(ii) 0 charge on the left, +6 charge on the right; add 6 electrons on the right side. [1]

15. The skeletal equation is,

$$Mn^{3+}(aq) \longrightarrow Mn^{2+}(aq) + MnO_2(s) + H^+(aq)$$

On solving similar to Example 3 [page 345]

$$2\,Mn^{3+}(aq) + 2H_2O(l) \longrightarrow Mn^{2+} + MnO_2(s) + 4\,H^+(aq)$$ [2]

16. (i) Mechanism of photosynthesis

Step I $\quad 12H_2O(l) \longrightarrow 12H_2(g) + 6O_2(g)$ (Decomposition of water)

Step II $\quad 6CO_2(g) + 12H_2(g) \longrightarrow C_6H_{12}O_6(s) + 6H_2O(l)$

(H_2 formed in step first reduces CO_2 to $C_6H_{12}O_6$ in second step). Hence, it is more appropriate to write the equation for photosynthesis as follows. (By adding step I and step II.) [1]

$$6CO_2(g) + 12H_2O(l) \longrightarrow C_6H_{12}O_6(s) + 6H_2O(l) + 6O_2(g)$$

Actually in the process of photosynthesis, $12H_2O$ are used up in first step and $6H_2O$ are formed per molecule of glucose (carbohydrate).

(ii) Mechanism of reaction of ozone with H_2O_2

Step I $\quad O_3(g) \longrightarrow O_2(g) + O(g)$

Step II $\quad H_2O_2(g) + O(g) \longrightarrow H_2O(l) + O_2(g)$

In first step, ozone liberates nascent oxygen, it oxidises H_2O_2 in step II.

Therefore, overall reaction is as follows

$$H_2O_2(l) + O_3(g) \longrightarrow H_2O\,(l) + O_2(g) + O_2(g)$$

In overall reaction, O_2 is written by two times because it is released in each of the two steps. [1]

17. $(CN)_2(g) + 2OH^-(aq) \longrightarrow CN^-(aq) + CNO^-(aq) + H_2O(l)$

(i) Let the oxidation number of C in $(CN)_2$ be x.

$$2x + 2(-3) = 0 \quad \text{or} \quad x = +3$$

(ii) Let the oxidation number of C in CN^- be x.

$$x + (-3) = -1 \quad \text{or} \quad x = +2$$

(iii) Let the oxidation number of C in CNO^- be x.

$$x + (-3) + (-2) = -1 \quad \text{or} \quad x = +4$$

$$\overset{+3}{(CN)_2}(g) + 2OH^-(aq) \longrightarrow \overset{+2}{CN^-}(aq) + \overset{+4}{CNO^-}(aq) + H_2O(l)$$

O.N. decreases ($(CN)_2 \to CN^-$)

O.N. increases ($(CN)_2 \to CNO^-$)

[1]

The following information we can drawn from the above reaction.

(i) Decomposition of cyanogen in the cyanide ion (CN^-) and cyanate ion (CNO^-) occurs in basic medium.

(ii) Cyanogen $(CN)_2$ acts as both reducing agent as well as oxidising agent.

(iii) The reaction is an example of disproportionation reaction (a special type of redox reaction).

(iv) Cyanogen $(CN)_2$ is called pseudohalogen while CN^-, CNO^- ions are called pseudohalide ions. [1]

18. $\overset{0}{Cl_2}(aq) + \overset{+4}{SO_2}(aq) + H_2O(l) \longrightarrow \overset{-1}{Cl^-}(aq) + \overset{+6\ 2-}{SO_4}(aq)$

ON decreases by 1 per Cl-atom

ON increases by 2 per S-atom

Multiply Cl^- by 2 because in Cl_2, there are two chlorine atoms. [1]

$$Cl_2(aq) + SO_2(aq) + H_2O(l) \rightarrow 2\,Cl^-(aq) + SO_4^{2-}(aq)$$

Balance firstly the charge by adding $4H^+$ to RHS and then multiply H_2O by 2.

$$Cl_2(aq) + SO_2(aq) + 2H_2O(l) \longrightarrow 2Cl^-(aq) + SO_4^{2-} + 4H^+$$

This represents the balanced redox reaction. [1]

19. Number of millimoles of $K_2Cr_2O_7$ present in 24 mL of 0.5 M solution = 24 × 0.5 = 12

The balanced chemical equation for the redox reaction is

$$K_2Cr_2O_7 + 6\,(NH_4)_2\,SO_4 \cdot FeSO_4 \cdot 6H_2O + 7H_2SO_4 \longrightarrow K_2SO_4 + 6\,(NH_4)_2\,SO_4 + 3\,Fe_2(SO_4)_3 + Cr_2(SO_4)_3 + 43\,H_2O$$ [1]

From the balanced equation, 6 moles Mohr's salt are oxidised by 1 mole of $K_2Cr_2O_7$.

$\therefore$ 12 millimoles of Mohr's salt will be oxidised by

$= \frac{1}{6} \times 12 = 2$ millimoles $K_2Cr_2O_7$ [1]

20. In MnO_4^{2-}, the oxidation number of Mn is +6. It can increase its oxidation number (to + 7) or decrease its oxidation number to + 4, + 3, + 2, 0. [1]

Hence, it undergoes disproportionation reaction in acidic medium.

$$\overset{+6}{3MnO_4^{2-}} + 4H^+ \longrightarrow \overset{+7}{3MnO_4^-} + \overset{+4}{MnO_2} + 2H_2O$$

O.N. increases by 1 per atom (oxidation)

O.N. decreases by 2 per atom (reduction) [1]

In MnO_4^-, Mn is in its highest oxidation state, i.e. +7. It can only decrease its oxidation number. Hence, it cannot undergo disproportionation reaction.

Note O.N. is used for oxidation number.

21. (i) Combination reaction

(ii) Displacement reaction

(iii) Decomposition reaction

(iv) Metal displacement reaction

(v) Non-metal displacement reaction

(vi) Disproportionation reaction [6 × 1/2]

22. (i) Phosphorus, chlorine and sulphur are the non-metals that can show disproportionation reaction. [1]

(a) $P_4(s) + 3OH^-(aq) + 3H_2O(l) \longrightarrow PH_3(g) + 3H_2PO_2^-(aq)$

(b) $Cl_2(g) + 2OH^-(aq) \longrightarrow Cl^-(aq) + ClO^-(aq) + H_2O(l)$ (cold)

$3Cl_2(g) + 6OH^-(aq) \longrightarrow 5Cl^-(aq) + ClO_3^-(aq) + 3H_2O(l)$ (hot)

(c) $S_8(s) + 12OH^- \longrightarrow 4S^{2-}(aq) + 2S_2O_3^{2-}(aq) + 6H_2O(l)$ [1]

(ii) Manganese, copper, gallium and indium are the metals that can show disproportionation reaction.

(a) $2Mn^{3+}(aq) + 2H_2O(l) \longrightarrow \overset{4+}{Mn}O_2(s) + Mn^{2+}(aq) + 4H^+$

(b) $2Cu^+(aq) \longrightarrow Cu^{2+}(aq) + \overset{0}{Cu}(s)$

(c) $3Ga^+(aq) \longrightarrow Ga^{3+}(aq) + 2\overset{0}{Ga}(s)$

(d) $3In^+(aq) \longrightarrow In^{3+}(aq) + 2\overset{0}{In}(s)$ [1]

23. (i) The skeleton equation for the given reaction is as

$MnO_4^-(aq) + SO_2(g) \longrightarrow Mn^{2+}(aq) + HSO_4^-(aq)$

On solving similar to example 4 on page 321, we get following balanced equation.

$2MnO_4^-(aq) + 5SO_2(g) + 2H_2O(l) + H^+(aq) \longrightarrow 2Mn^{2-}(aq) + 5HSO_4^-(aq)$

This represents the final balanced redox equation. [1]

(ii) Refer to example 3 on page 320. [1]

(iii) Refer to example 4 on page 321. [1]

24. (i) At anode $\quad Zn \longrightarrow Zn^{2+} + 2e^-$

At cathode $\quad Br_2 + 2e^- \longrightarrow 2Br^-$

$Zn + Br_2 \longrightarrow Zn^{2+} + 2Br^-$ [1]

(ii) At anode $\quad [Cr \longrightarrow Cr^{3+} + 3e^-] \times 2$

At cathode $\quad [I_2 + 2e^- \longrightarrow 2I^-] \times 3$

$2Cr + 3I_2 \longrightarrow 6I^- + 2Cr^{3+}$ [1]

(iii) At anode $\quad H_2(g) \longrightarrow 2H^+(aq) + 2e^-$

At cathode

$Cu^{2+}(aq) + 2e^- \longrightarrow Cu(s)$

$H_2(g) + Cu^{2+}(aq) \longrightarrow Cu(s) + 2H^+(aq)$ [1]

Cathode will be positive terminal in each cell.

25. The given redox reaction for the galvanic cell is

$Zn(s) + 2Ag^+(aq) \longrightarrow Zn^{2+}(aq) + 2Ag(s)$

At anode, Zn is oxidised to Zn^{2+} ions and at cathode, Ag^+ ions are reduced to Ag metal. Thus, galvanic cell for the above redox reaction may be depicted as

$Zns \mid Zn^{2+}(aq) \parallel Ag^+(aq) \mid Ag(s)$

(i) Zn electrode is negatively charged because of the oxidation of Zn to Zn^{2+} ions, electrons are accumulated on zinc electrode. [1]

(ii) The ions carry current in the cell. Current flows from Ag electrode to Zn electrode. While electrons flow from Zn electrode to Ag electrode. [1]

(iii) Individual reaction at each electrode

Anode $\quad Zn \longrightarrow Zn^{2+} + 2e^-$

Cathode $\quad Ag^+(aq) + e^- \longrightarrow Ag(s)$ [1]

26. (i) $H_2S + Fe^{3+} \longrightarrow Fe^{2+} + S + H^+$

Reduction ($Fe^{3+} \to Fe^{2+}$); Oxidation ($H_2S \to S$)

Here, H_2S is oxidised to sulphur (S), and Fe^{3+} is reduced to Fe^{2+}.

$2Fe^{3+} + H_2S \longrightarrow 2Fe^{2+} + S + 2H^+$ [1]

(ii) $I^- + IO_3^- + H^+ \longrightarrow I_2 + H_2O$

Reduction ($IO_3^- \to I_2$); Oxidation ($I^- \to I_2$)

Here, I^- is oxidised to I_2 and IO_3^- is reduced to I_2.

On solving, we get the following balanced equations

$2IO_3^- + 12I^- + 12H^+ \longrightarrow 7I_2 + 6H_2O$ [1]

Reduction

(iii) $Bi(s) + NO_3^- + H^+ \longrightarrow NO_2 + Bi^{3+} + H_2O$

Oxidation

Here, $Bi(s)$ is oxidised to Bi^{3+}, while NO_3^- is reduced to NO_2

$$Bi(s) + 3NO_3^- + 6H^+ \longrightarrow 3NO_2 + Bi^{3+} + 3H_2O \quad [1]$$

Reduction

(iv) $I^- + O_2(g) + H_2O \longrightarrow I_2 + OH^-$

Oxidation

Here, I^- is oxidised to I_2 and $O_2(g)$ is reduced to OH^-.

$$4I^- + O_2(g) + 2H_2O \longrightarrow 4OH^- + 2I_2 \quad [2]$$

27. (i) $\overset{+7}{Mn}O_4^-(aq) + I^-(aq) \longrightarrow \overset{+4}{Mn}O_2(s) + \overset{0}{I_2}(s)$

(In basic medium)

(a) Separate the equation into oxidation half reaction and reduction half reaction.

Oxidation half reaction,

$$I^-(aq) \longrightarrow I_2(s) \quad ...(i)$$

Reduction half reaction,

$$MnO_4^-(aq) \longrightarrow MnO_2(s) \quad ...(ii)$$

(b) To balance I-atoms in the oxidation half reaction, we write it as

$$2I^-(aq) \longrightarrow I_2(s) \quad ...(iii)$$

and to balance oxidation number add $2e^-$ to RHS

$$2I^-(aq) \longrightarrow I_2 + 2e^- \quad ...(iv)$$

There is no need to balance the charge (charge on either side of equation is balanced).

(c) To balance reduction half reaction, first balance oxidation number by writing required number of electrons to LHS and then balance charge by adding OH^- ions because reaction occurs in basic medium.

$$MnO_4^-(aq) + 3e^- \longrightarrow MnO_2(s) \quad ...(v)$$

$$MnO_4^-(aq) + 3e^- \longrightarrow MnO_2 + 4\,OH^- \quad ...(vi)$$

(d) Balance oxygen atoms by adding H_2O

$$MnO_4^- + 3e^- + 2H_2O \longrightarrow MnO_2 + 4\,OH^- \quad ...(vii)$$

By doing so, H atoms are automatically balanced.

(e) Now to equalise number of electrons we multiply oxidation half reaction (iv) by 3 and reduction half reaction (vii) by 2 respectively.

$$6I^-(aq) \longrightarrow 3\,I_2(s) + 6\,e^- \quad ...(viii)$$

$$2\,MnO_4^-(aq) + 6e^- + 4H_2O(l) \longrightarrow 2MnO_2(s) + 8OH^-(aq) \quad ...(ix)$$

(f) Add two half reactions to obtain net reactions after cancelling electrons on both sides.

$$2\,MnO_4^-(aq) + 6I^-(aq) + 4\,H_2O(l) \longrightarrow 2\,MnO_2(s) + 3\,I_2(s) + 8OH^-(aq)$$

This represents the final balanced redox reaction. [2]

(ii) $MnO_4^-(aq) + SO_2(g) \longrightarrow Mn^{2+}(aq) + HSO_4^-$

(in acidic medium)

Reduction half reaction

$$MnO_4^-(aq) + 8H^+(aq) + 5e^- \longrightarrow Mn^{2+}(aq) + 4H_2O(l) \quad ...(i)$$

Oxidation half reaction

$$SO_2(g) + 2H_2O(l) \longrightarrow HSO_4^-(aq) + 3H^+(aq) + 2e^- \quad ...(ii)$$

(Balance the oxidation number as in reaction (*i*). After balancing the oxidation number, charge is balanced on either side of equation by adding H^+ions because the reaction occurs in acidic medium).

Multiply equation (i) by 2 and equation (ii) by 5 and add, we get

$$2MnO_4^-(aq) + H^+(aq) + 5SO_2(g) + 2H_2O(l) \longrightarrow 2Mn^{2+}(aq) + 5HSO_4^-(aq) \quad [1]$$

(iii) By following the steps discussed in (i), we get

$$H_2O_2(aq) + 2\,Fe^{2+}(aq) + 2H^+\,(aq) \longrightarrow 2\,H_2O\,(l) + 2\,Fe^{3+}(aq) \quad [1]$$

(iv) By following the steps discussed in (i), we get

$$Cr_2O_7^{2-}\,(aq) + 2H^+(aq) + 3\,SO_2(g) \longrightarrow 2\,Cr^{3+}(aq) + 3\,SO_4^{2-}(aq) + H_2O\,(l) \quad [1]$$

28. (i) $P_4(s) + OH^-(aq) \longrightarrow PH_3(g) + H_2PO_2^-(aq)$

Ion electron method

Reduction half reaction

$$\overset{0}{P_4}(s) \longrightarrow \overset{-3}{P}H_3(g) \quad ...(i)$$

Balance P atom

$$P_4(s) \longrightarrow 4PH_3(g) \quad ...(ii)$$

Balance oxidation number by adding electrons,

$$P_4(s) + 12e^- \longrightarrow 4PH_3(g) \quad ...(iii)$$

Balance charge by adding OH^- ions,

$$P_4(s) + 12e^- \longrightarrow 4PH_3(g) + 12OH^-(aq) \quad ...(iv)$$

Balance 'O' atoms by adding H_2O

$$12H_2O + P_4(s) + 12e^- \longrightarrow 4PH_3(g) + 12OH^-(aq) \quad ...(v)$$

Oxidation half reaction

$$P_4(s) \longrightarrow H_2PO_2^-(aq) \quad ...(vi)$$

Balance P atoms,

$$\overset{0}{P_4}(s) \longrightarrow 4H_2\overset{+1}{P}O_2^-(aq) \quad ...(vii)$$

Balance oxidation number by adding electrons,

$$P_4(s) \longrightarrow 4H_2PO_2^-(aq) + 4e^- \quad ...(viii)$$

Balance charge by adding OH^- ions

$$P_4(s) + 8OH^-(aq) \longrightarrow 4H_2PO_2^-(aq) + 4e^- \quad ...(ix)$$

Oxygen and hydrogen are balanced automatically.

First multiply equation (ix) by 3 to equalise number of electrons gain and lose and add it to equation (v), we get,

$$4P_4(s) + 12OH^-(aq) + 12H_2O(l) \longrightarrow 4PH_3(g) + 12H_2PO_2^-(aq)$$

or $P_4(s) + 3OH^-(aq) + 3H_2O(l) \longrightarrow PH_3(g) + 3H_2PO_2^-(aq)$

Oxidation number method

$$\overset{0}{P_4}(s) + OH^-(aq) \longrightarrow \overset{-3\,+1}{PH_3}(g) + \overset{+1\,+1\,-2}{H_2PO_2^-}(aq)$$

O.N. decreases by 3 per P atom (3 electron gain)

O.N. increases by 1 per P atom (1 electron loss)

In a balanced chemical reaction loss of electrons = gain of electrons so multiply $H_2PO_2^-$ by 3 and we get

$$P_4(s) + OH^-(aq) \longrightarrow PH_3(g) + 3H_2PO_2^-$$

Multiply OH^- by 3 to balance the charge

$$P_4(s) + 3OH^-(aq) \longrightarrow PH_3(g) + 3H_2PO_2^-(aq)$$

Balance H by adding $3H_2O$ to LHS

$$P_4(s) + 3H_2O(l) + 3OH^-(aq) \longrightarrow PH_3(g) + 3H_2PO_2^-(aq)$$

In this equation, P_4 acts both as an oxidising agent as well as a reducing agent. **[3]**

(ii) $3N_2H_4(l) + 4ClO_3^-(aq) \longrightarrow 6NO(g) + 4Cl^-(aq) + 6H_2O(l)$

In this reaction, N_2H_4 acts as a reducing agent and ClO_3^- acts as an oxidising agent. **[1]**

(iii) $Cl_2O_7(g) + 4H_2O_2(aq) + 2OH^-(aq) \longrightarrow 2ClO_2^-(aq) + 5H_2O(l) + 4O_2(g)$

In this reaction, Cl_2O_7 acts as an oxidising agent and H_2O_2 as reducing agent. **[1]**

29. **Key Idea** Like dissolves like, i.e. benzoic acid and toluene being covalent readily dissolve in alcohol and form homogeneous solution.

HBr is a stonger reducing agent than HCl, so reduces H_2SO_4 to SO_2.

(i) Oxidation of toluene to benzoic acid in acidic medium.

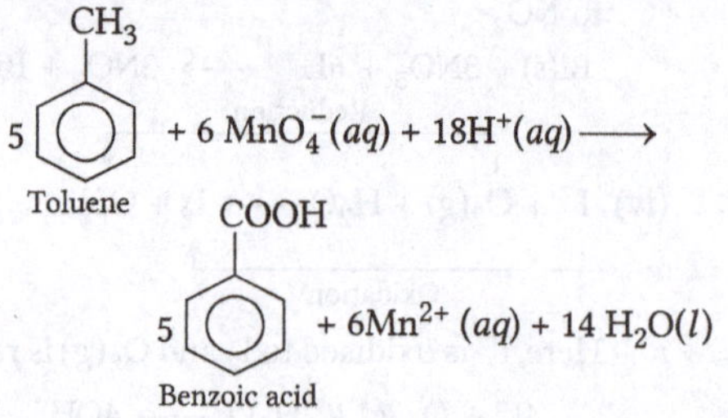

Oxidation of toluene to benzoic acid in basic and neutral medium.

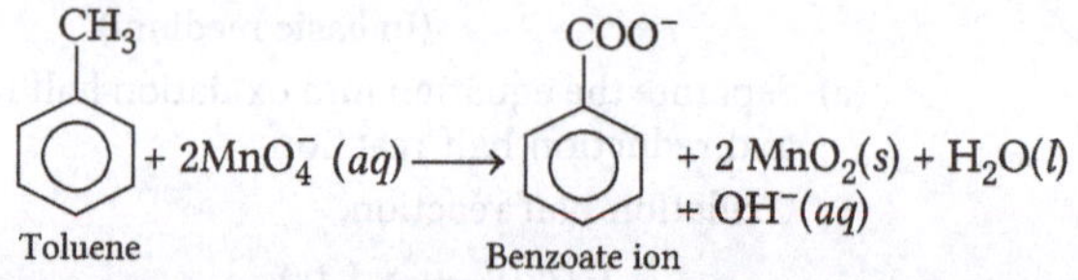

On industrial scale, alcoholic potassium permanganate is preferred to acidic or alkaline potassium permanganate because in the presence of alcohol, both the reactants $KMnO_4$ and $C_6H_5CH_3$ are mixed very well and form homogeneous solution. In homogeneous medium, reaction takes place faster than in heterogeneous medium. Furthermore, in neutral medium, OH^- ions are produced in the reaction itself. **[2]**

(ii) $\underset{\text{Sodium chloride (from inorganic mixture)}}{2NaCl} + 2H_2SO_4 \longrightarrow 2NaHSO_4 + 2HCl$

HCl is a weak reducing agent. It cannot reduce H_2SO_4 to SO_2, that's why pungent smelling gas HCl is obtained.

$\underset{\text{Sodium bromide (from inorganic mixture)}}{2NaBr} + 2H_2SO_4 \longrightarrow 2NaHSO_4 + 2HBr$

$$2HBr + H_2SO_4 \longrightarrow \underset{\text{Red vapours}}{Br_2\uparrow} + SO_2\uparrow + 2H_2O$$

HBr is a strong reducing agent, it reduces H_2SO_4 to SO_2 and is itself oxidised to Br_2. That's why we get red vapours of bromine when conc. H_2SO_4 reacts with inorganic mixture containing bromide salt. **[3]**

SUMMARY

- The reactions involving oxidation and reduction as their two half-reactions are known as **redox reactions**.
- **Oxidation** involves addition of oxygen or other electronegative element, removal of H or other electropositive element, loss of electron and increase in oxidation number.
- **Reduction** is just opposite of oxidation i.e. involves addition of H or other electropositive element, gain of electron etc.
- **Oxidising agent** is the species, which reduces, i.e. undergoes reduction.
- **Reducing agent** undergoes oxidation.
- Oxidation number (ON) is the charge that an atom appear to have in a compound when all other atoms are removed.
  It is zero for free elements (i.e. as exist in nature) e.g. P_4, O_2, S_8 etc.
  It is equal to group number for elements of group 1 and 2.
  Algebric sum of oxidation numbers= 0 (for compounds)= charge (for ions).
- Stock notation = cation + (oxidation number in roman numerals) + anion. e.g., Au(I)Cl.
- Types of redox reactions
  (i) **Combination reactions** involve combination of two or more atoms to give a single product.
  (ii) **Decomposition reactions** These involve splitting of a compound into two or more simpler products. However, all decomposition reactions are not the redox reactions.
  (iii) **Displacement reactions** involve displacement of one atom (or ion) by other.
  I. Metal displacement reactions; Here, one metal displaces the other metal.
  II. Non-metal displacement reactions; Here, non-metal is displaced by metal or non-metal.
  (iv) **Disproportionation reactions** In these reactions, the same element is oxidised as well as reduced.
  e.g. $2H_2O_2 \longrightarrow 2H_2O + O_2$
- **Balancing of Redox Reactions**
  (i) **Oxidation Number Method** First write ionic equation then assign oxidation number. Balance all other atoms except H and O, then predict change in oxidation number, balance charge and finally balance H and O.
  (ii) **Ion Electron Method** First write ionic equation and split it into two halves. Balance all other atoms except H and O, (in both halves), balance charge (in both halves) and add both half equations, verify balanced equation and convert ionic equation into molecular form.
- The titration involving redox reactions are called redox-titrations.
- **Terminology Used in Electrode Processes :**
  (i) A metal rod dipped in its salt solution is called Electrode.
  (ii) The electrode at which oxidation occurs is called Anode.
  (iii) The electrode at which reduction occurs is called cathode.
  (iv) Redox couple is the combination of oxidised and reduced forms. e.g. Zn^{3+} / Zn.
  (v) Electrode potential is the potential associated with an electrode.
- Electrochemical cell converts chemical energy into electrical energy, e.g. Daniell cell etc.
- Salt bridge completes the circuit and maintain electrical neutrality.

Chapter Practice

Very Short Answer Type Questions

1 Mark

1. Fill in the Blanks

(i) Electrons are gained in ...... reactions.

(ii) Addition of oxygen takes place in ...... processes.

(iii) The oxidation state of cobalt in $Co_2(CO)_8$ is ....

(iv) The oxidation number of oxygen in F_2O and H_2O_2 are .... and ...... respectively.

(v) The oxidation number of P in KH_2PO_3 is ....

(vi) Oxidation is the process which involves ...... of electrons and is accompanied by an .... in the oxidation number of the substance.

2. Objective Type Questions

(i) In the following reaction,

$$2Mg(s) + O_2(g) \longrightarrow 2MgO(s),$$

with respect to Mg, the process is called

(a) oxidation (b) reduction

(c) redox reaction (d) None of these

(ii) For the reaction given below,

$$2Na(s) + H_2(g) \longrightarrow 2NaH(s)$$

choose the correct option from the following.

(a) Na is reduced and hydrogen is oxidised

(b) Na is oxidised and hydrogen is reduced

(c) Na undergoes oxidation and hydrogen undergoes reduction

(d) Both (b) and (c)

(iii) In the given reaction,

Loss of $2e^-$

$$Cu(s) + 2Ag^+(aq) \longrightarrow Cu^{2+}(aq) + Ag(s)$$

Gain of $2e^-$

Copper metal, Cu(s), is oxidised to $Cu^{2+}(aq)$, while $Ag^+(aq)$ is reduced to silver metal, Ag (s), then the equilibrium greatly lies in favour of

(a) $Ag^+(s)$ and $Cu^{2+}(aq)$ (b) $Ag^+(aq)$ and $Cu^{2+}(s)$

(c) $Ag(s)$ and $Cu^{2+}(aq)$ (d) $Cu^{2+}(aq)$ and $Ag(s)$

(iv) An element if present in the free or in the uncombined state, its each atom bears an oxidation number

(a) more than 1 (b) less than 1

(c) more than 2 (d) zero

(v) Which is the best description of behaviour of bromine in the given equation?

$$H_2O + Br_2 \longrightarrow HBr + HOBr$$

(a) Proton acceptor

(b) Both oxidised and reduced

(c) Only oxidised

(d) Only reduced

(vi) The oxidation number of sulphur, chromium and nitrogen in H_2SO_5, $Cr_2O_7^{2-}$ and NO_3^- respectively are

(a) + 8, + 6 and + 5 (b) +6, −6 and +8

(c) + 6, + 6 and + 5 (d) +8, +6 and +7

3. Matching Type Questions

(i) Match the Column I with Column II and select the correct answer for oxidation number of iron, nickel, nitrogen and xenon from given codes.

Column I	Column II
A. $K_3[\underline{Fe}(CN)_6]$	(i) −3, +5
B. $[\underline{Ni}(CN)_4]^{2-}$	(ii) +8
C. $\underline{N}H_4\underline{N}O_3$	(iii) +3
D. $Ba_2\underline{Xe}O_6$	(iv) +2

Codes

	A	B	C	D		A	B	C	D
(a)	(iii)	(iv)	(i)	(ii)	(b)	(iii)	(iv)	(ii)	(i)
(c)	(ii)	(iii)	(i)	(iv)	(d)	(i)	(ii)	(iv)	(iii)

(ii) Match the items in Column I with relevant item given in Column II and choose the correct option using the codes given below:

Column I	Column II
A. Ions having positive charge	(i) +7
B. The sum of oxidation number of all atoms in a neutral molecule.	(ii) −1
C. Oxidation number of hydrogen ion	(iii) +1
D. Oxidation number of fluorine in NaF	(iv) 0
E. Ions having negative charge	(v) Cation
	(vi) Anion

Codes

	A	B	C	D	E
(a)	(v)	(iv)	(iii)	(ii)	(vi)
(b)	(i)	(iv)	(iii)	(v)	(vi)
(c)	(ii)	(i)	(iii)	(iv)	(v)
(d)	(vi)	(ii)	(iii)	(iv)	(v)

4. When magnesium ribbon is burnt in air, two products are formed, magnesium oxide and magnesium nitride. Point out the oxidising and reducing agents.

5. For the galvanic cell in which the following reaction takes place,
$Zn\,(s) + 2Ag^{+2}(aq) \longrightarrow Zn^{2+}(aq) + 2Ag\,(s)$,
write individual reaction at each electrode.

6. Calculate $E°$ for the cell
$Al \mid Al^{3+}(1\,M) \parallel Cu^{2+}(1\,M) \mid Cu$
Given, $E^{\circ}_{Al^{3+}/Al}$ and $E^{\circ}_{Cu^{2+}/Cu}$ are – 1.66 V and + 0.34 V respectively.

7. What is the relationship between direction of current and flow of electrons in a cell by convention?

Assertion-Reason

Directions (Q. Nos. 8-12) In the following questions. an Assertion (A) is followed by a corresponding Reason (R) Use the following keys to choose the appropriate answer.

(a) Both (A) and (R) are correct and (R) is the correct explanation of (A).
(b) Both (A) and (R) are correct but (R) is not the correct explanation of (A).
(c) (A) is correct and (R) is incorrect.
(d) (A) is incorrect and (R) is correct.

8. **Assertion** (A) Lithium ion is a poor oxidising agent.
Reason (R) Lithium ion has the lowest electrode potential.

9. **Assertion** (A) Bromide ion acts as a reducing agent in given following reaction.
$$2MnO_4^-(aq) + Br^-(aq) + H_2O(l) \longrightarrow MnO_2(aq) + BrO_3^-(aq) + 2OH^-(aq)$$
Reason (R) Oxidation number of Br increases from –1 to +5.

10. **Assertion** (A) In the representation $E^{\ominus}_{Fe^{3+}/Fe^{2+}}$ and $E^{\ominus}_{Cu^{3+}/Cu}$ are redox couples.
Reason (R) Redox couple is the combination of oxidised and reduced form of a substance involved in an oxidation or reduction half-cell.

11. **Assertion** (A) Among halogens, fluorine is the best oxidant.
Reason (R) Fluorine is the most electronegative atom.

12. **Assertion** (A) Fe reacts with HCl to produce H_2 gas.
Reason (R) Fe is a better oxidising agent thant H_2.

Case-Study

13. The oxidation state of an individual atom in its free state is 0. The total oxidation state of all atoms in a neutral species is 0 and in an ions is equal to the charge. Group 1 metals have an oxidation state of +1 and group 2 an oxidation state of +2.

The oxidation state of fluorine is –1 in compounds. Hydrogen generally has an oxidation state of +1 in compounds.

Oxygen generally has an oxidation state of –2 in compounds.

In binary metal compounds, group 17 elements have an oxidation state of –1, group 16 elements of –2, and group 15 element of –3. The sum of the oxidation states is equal to zero for neutral compounds and equal to the charge for polyatomic ion species.

(i) How many moles of I_2 is liberated when one mole of acidified $K_2Cr_2O_7$ is reacted with excess KI?
(ii) How many moles of H_2O_2 are oxidised by mole of ClO_2 when ClO_2 oxidises H_2O_2 to O_2 in alkaline medium?
(iii) What is the change occur in oxidation state during reduction and oxidation ?

14. The concept of the electron transfer is found unable to explain the redox changes or electron shift in case of covalent compounds.

To explain these changes a new concept, called oxidation number is introduced.

The oxidation state is the simplest attribute of an element in a compound. It is taught early in the chemistry curriculum as convenient electron-counting scheme for redox reactions. Its applications range from descriptive chemistry of elements to nomenclature and electrochemistry, or as an independent variable in plots and databases of bonded-atom properties.

The history of the oxidation state goes back about 200 years when it described the stepwise increase in the amount of oxygen bound by elements that form more than one oxide. In his 1835 texbook *Unorganische chemie*, Wöheler speaks of such an "oxydationsstufe". This expression remains in use for oxidation state in several languages. The equivalent term oxidation number is also common; in English this refers more to redox balancing than to the chemical systematics of an element.

(i) Name the compund of Mn in which it shows highest oxidation state.

(ii) Name the element which generally show negative oxidation state?

(iii) What is the oxidation state of Fe in brown ring complex?

Short Answer Type I Questions

2 Marks

15. Balance the following equation,

$Br_2 + H_2O_2 \longrightarrow BrO_3^- + H_2O$ (in acidic medium)

16. What is the oxidation number of S in the reactants and the products?

$2\,Na_2S_2O_3 + I_2 \longrightarrow Na_2S_4O_6 + 2\,NaI$

17. Write the cell reaction and calculate the standard $E°$ of the cell.

$Zn \mid Zn^{2+}(1\,M) \parallel Cd^{2+}(1\,M) \mid Cd$

Given, $E°_{Zn/Zn^{2+}} = 0.763$; $E°_{Cd/Cd^{2+}} = 0.403$ V

18. Arrange the following species in the increasing order of oxidation states of S.

$(NH_2)_2SO_4, HSO_3^-, S_2O_4^{2-}, S_2O_7^{2-}$

Short Answer Type II Questions

3 Marks

19. What is the oxidation number of nitrogen in

(i) nitric acid (ii) nitrous acid (iii) nitric oxide (iv) nitrous oxide (v) ammonia (vi) N_2

20. The standard electrode potentials at 298 K are given below

$E°_{Zn^{2+}/Zn} = -0.76$ V, $E°_{Fe^{2+}/Fe} = -0.44$ V,

$E°_{H^+/H_2} = 0.0$ V, $E°_{Cu^{2+}/Cu} = +0.34$ V

Which of the two electrodes should be combined to form a cell having highest emf? Identify the cathode and the anode and write the cell reaction.

21. Balance the following equations by the oxidation number method.

(i) $Fe^{2+} + H^+ + Cr_2O_7^{2-} \longrightarrow Cr^{3+} + Fe^{3+} + H_2O$

(ii) $I_2 + NO_3^- \longrightarrow NO_2 + IO_3^-$

(iii) $I_2 + S_2O_3^{2-} \longrightarrow I^- + S_4O_6^{2-}$

(iv) $MnO_2 + C_2O_4^{2-} \longrightarrow Mn^{2+} + CO_2$

Long Answer Type Questions

5 Marks

22. (i) Write short notes on

(a) electrochemical cell

(b) redox titrations

(c) oxidation and reduction in terms of oxidation number.

(ii) Calculate the oxidation number of sulphur in $S_2O_8^{2-}$ ion.

23. Iodate ion reacts with sulphite ion to give sulphate ion and iodide ion.

(i) Write a balanced net ionic equation for the reaction.

(ii) How many grams of sodium sulphite are needed to react with 5.00 g of sodium iodate?

24. Balance the following ionic equations by oxidation number method

(i) $Fe^{2+} + H_2O_2 \longrightarrow Fe^{3+} + H_2O$ (acidic medium)

(ii) $Zn + NO_3 \longrightarrow Zn^{2+} + NH_4^+$ (basic medium)

(iii) $H_2S + MnO_4^- \longrightarrow S + Mn^{2+} + H_2O$ (acidic medium)

(iv) $Cu + NO_3^- + H^+ \longrightarrow NO_2 + Cu^{2+}$ (acidic medium)

(v) $MnO_4^- + H_2C_2O_4 \longrightarrow Mn^{2+} + CO_2 + H_2O$ (acidic medium)

Answers

1. (i) reduction (ii) oxidation
(iii) zero (iv) +1 / 2, −1
(v) + 3 (vi) loss, increase

2. (i) → (a), (ii) → (d), (iii) → (d), (iv) → (d), (v) → (b), (vi) → (c)

3. (i) (a) A → (iii), B → (iv), C → (i), D → (ii)
(ii) (a) A → (v), B → (iv), C → (iii), D → (ii), E → (vi)

4. $2\overset{0}{Mg}(s) + O_2(g) \xrightarrow{\Delta} 2\overset{+2}{Mg}\overset{-2}{O}(s)$

$2\overset{0}{Mg}(s) + N_2(g) \xrightarrow{\Delta} \overset{+2}{Mg}\,\overset{-3}{N_2}(g)$

Oxidising agent → Oxygen and nitrogen
Reducing agent → Mg (magnesium)

5. Reaction at anode, (Oxidation half-reaction)

$$Zn \longrightarrow Zn^{+2} + 2e^-$$

Reaction at cathode, (Reduction half reaction)

$$Ag^{+2} + 2e^- \longrightarrow Ag$$

6. $E^\circ_{Al^{+3}/Al} = -1.66\ V$

$E^\circ_{Cu^{2+}/Cu} = +\,0.34\ V$

Here, Al/Al^{+3} couple is anode and Cu^{+2}/Cu is cathode.
Calculate the cell potential or emf using the expression

$$E^\circ_{red} = E^\circ_{cathode} - E^\circ_{anode}$$
$$E^\circ_{cell} = +\,0.34 - (-1.66)$$
$$E^\circ_{cell} = 0.34 + 1.66$$
$$E^\circ_{cell} = 2.00\ V$$

7. Electrons flow from the negative terminal to the positive.Conventional, current flows from the positive terminal to the negative.

8. (*a*) Both (A) and (R) are correct and (R) is the correct explanation of (A).

9. (*a*) Both (A) and (R) are correct and (R) is the correct explanation of (A).

10. (*a*) Both (A) and (R) are correct and (R) is the correct explanation of (A).

11. (*b*) Fluorine has the maximum E° value among the halogens, hence it reduces first than other halogen and acts as best oxidant. Fluorine is most electronegative atom due to its small size. Thus, both statement are correct but (R) is not the correct explanation of (A).

12. (*c*) (A) is correct while (R) is incorrect. Correct (R) is Fe is a better reducing agent than H_2.

13. (i) The balanced chemical equation is

$$K_2Cr_2O_7 + 6KI + 12H_2SO_4 \longrightarrow K_2SO_4 + Cr_2(SO_4)_3 + H_2O + 3I_2 + 6KOH$$

Hence, 3 moles of iodine will be liberated.

(ii) In alkaline medium balanced equation is

$$2ClO_2 + 5H_2O_2 + 2OH^- \longrightarrow 2Cl^- + 5O_2 + 6H_2O$$

2 moles of ClO_2 oxidise 5 moles of H_2O_2

1 mole of ClO_2 will oxidise $= \frac{5}{2} \times 1 = 2.5$ mol

(iii) In oxidation → oxidation state increases.
In reduction → oxidation state decreases.

14. (i) $KMnO_4$ is the compound of manganese which has highest oxidation state.

$$KMnO_4 (+1) + x + 4(-2) = 0$$
$$x = +7$$

(ii) Fluorine is the most electronegative element. Hence, does not possess positive oxidation number in any of its compound.

(iii) The brown ring complex is $[Fe(H_2O)_5NO]SO_4$. In this oxidation number of Fe is +3.

15. Balanced chemical equation :

$$Br_2 + 5H_2O_2 \longrightarrow 2BrO_3^- + 4H_2O + 2H^+$$

16. The oxidation number of S in $S_2O_3^{-2} = 2$ and the average oxidation number of S in $S_4O_6^{-2} = 5/2$.

17. The cell reaction,

$$Zn(s) + Cd^{2+}(aq) \longrightarrow Zn^{2+}(aq) + Cd(s)$$

Calculate the standard (E°)

$$E^\circ_{red} = E^\circ_{cathode} - E^\circ_{anode}$$
$$= -0.403 - (-0.763)$$
$$= -\,0.403 + 0.763$$
$$= +\,0.360\ V$$

18. Refer to text on pages 307 and 308 (Topic-1, Oxidation number).

19. Refer to text on pages 307 and 308 (Topic-1, Oxidation number).

20. **At anode** $Zn \longrightarrow Zn^{+2} + 2e^-\ (E^\circ_{Zn^{+2}/Zn)} = -0.76\ V)$

At cathode $Fe^{2+} + 2e^- \longrightarrow Fe\ (E^\circ_{Fe^{+2}/Fe)} = -0.44\ V)$

Cell reaction,

$$Fe^{+2} + Zn \longrightarrow Zn^{+2} + Fe$$
$$E^\circ_{red} = E^\circ_{cathode} - E^\circ_{anode}$$
$$= (-0.44) - (-0.76)$$
$$= -0.44 + 0.76 = -0.32\ V$$

Second cell

At anode $H_2 \longrightarrow H^+ + e^-\ [E^\circ_{H^+/H_2} = 0.0\ V]$

At cathode $Cu^{2+} + 2e^- \longrightarrow Cu\ [E^\circ_{Cu^{2+}/Cu} = +0.34\ V]$

Cell reaction,

$$Cu^{+2} + H_2 \longrightarrow H^+ + Cu$$

$$E^\circ_{red} = E^\circ_{cathode} - E^\circ_{anode}$$

$$= (0.34\ V) - (0.0) = +0.34\ V$$

Second cell having highest emf.

21. (i) $6Fe^{2+} + 14H^+ + Cr_2O_7^{2-} \longrightarrow 2Cr^{3+} + 6Fe^{3+} + 7H_2O$

(ii) $I_2 + 10NO_3^- + 8H^+ \longrightarrow 10NO_2 + 2IO_3^- + 4H_2O$

(iii) $I_2 + 2S_2O_3^{2-} \longrightarrow 2I^- + S_4O_6^{2-}$

(iv) $MnO_2 + C_2O_4^{2-} + 4H^+ \longrightarrow Mn^{2+} + 2CO_2 + 2H_2O$

22. (i) (a) Refer to text on pages 323 and 324. (Topic-2, Electrochemical cell).

(b) Refer to text on pages 322 and 323 (Topic-2, Applications of redox reactions in various types of chemical reactions).

(c) Refer to text on pages 309 (Topic-2, Oxidation and reduction in terms of oxidation number).

(ii) This is the thiosulphate ion in which sulphur (S) shows +6 oxidation number.

23. (i) $IO_3^- + 3SO_3^{-2} \longrightarrow I^- + 3SO_4^{-2}$

(ii) Balanced equation

$NaIO_3 + 3Na_2SO_3 \longrightarrow 3Na_2SO_4 + NaI$

9.55 g of sodium iodate is needed to react with 6.00 g of sodium sulphite.

24. Refer to text on pages 320 and 321 (Topic-2, Balancing of redox reactions).

CHAPTER

08

Organic Chemistry : Some Basic Principles and Techniques

In the previous chapter, you have studied about **catenation** (the property of self linking) and also about the fact that carbon possesses this property to maximum extent. Further, carbon is also capable to form compounds with other atoms like H, O, N, S, P and X (halogens). These compounds are called **organic compounds** and studied separately in a branch, called **organic chemistry**.

- General Introduction and Classification of Organic Compounds
- Nomenclature of Organic Compounds
- Fundamental Concepts in Organic Reaction Mechanism
- Purification and Characterisation of Organic Compounds
- Qualitative Analysis of Organic Compounds

TOPIC 01 General Introduction and Classification of Organic Compounds

In earlier days, the branch of chemistry, is deviated to the study of carbon compounds, whose source was related to the living system, was termed as **organic chemistry.** Essentially, all the chemical reactions that take place in the living organism are organic reactions. This is because the molecules of life such as proteins, vitamins, lipids, carbohydrates, chlorophyll, haemoglobin, nucleic acid and so on contain carbon. Infact, our dependency on nature of food, clothing (cotton, wool and silk) and energy (natural gas and petroleum) is basically the dependency of organic compounds.

Main reasons for the study of organic compounds in a separate branch of chemistry are as follows:

(i) Organic compounds exist in very large numbers so these cannot be included in inorganic chemistry (to avoid any disbalance).

(ii) Organic compounds are mainly made up of only three elements, i.e. C,H and O. Whereas inorganic compounds are formed from more than 110 elements.

(iii) Organic compounds have very complex structure whereas inorganic compounds are simple and possess low molecular weights.
(iv) Presence of functional group in organic compound decides its properties. No such behaviour is shown by inorganic compounds.
(v) Organic compounds possess low boiling and melting point. These are insoluble in water but soluble in non-polar solvents, whereas inorganic compounds possess high melting and boiling point. They are soluble in non-polar solvents.

Vital Force Theory (VFT)

Earlier it was thought that organic compound had never been synthesized from inorganic substances and chemists had no explanation for the complexities of organic compound. So, Berzelius proposed that these compounds were formed by a "vital force". The **vital force theory** proposed that organic substances could originate only from living material. In 1828, the results of a simple experiment by chemist Friedrich wohler (1800-1882) proved to be the end of this theory. In his experiment, he attempted to prepare ammonium cyanate (NH_4CNO) by heating cyanic acid (HCNO) and ammonia (NH_3). In the end of his experiment, he identified it as urea (H_2NCONH_2).

$$\underset{\text{Ammonium cyanate}}{NH_4CNO} \longrightarrow NH_3 + HNCO \longrightarrow \underset{\text{Urea}}{NH_2CONH_2}$$

With wohler's work, it was apparent that no vital force other than skill and knowledge was needed to synthesise organic compounds in the laboratory.

Further, synthesis of acetic acid by Kolbe and methane by Berthelot proved that synthesis of organic compounds from inorganic compounds was possible. After that, a detailed study of organic compounds reveal that they are either hydrocarbons or their derivatives. Therefore, the modified definition of organic chemistry can be defined as follows:

"The branch of chemistry that involves the chemistry of hydrocarbons and their derivatives".

In today's date, the number of organic compounds exceeds five million. The existence of such a large number of compounds is due to some unique properties of carbon.

Characteristics of Carbon Atoms (Tetravalency)

Carbon belongs to group 14 of the periodic table. Its atomic number is 6 and the electronic configuration is 2, 4. Thus, it has four electrons in the outermost shell. Hence, its valency is four, i.e. it is capable of bonding or pairing with four other carbon atoms or with the atoms of some other monovalent elements like hydrogen, halogen (chlorine, bromine) etc.

The ground state electronic configuration of carbon is 2, 4 or $1s^2, 2s^2, 2p^2$. Due to the presence of only two half-filled p-orbitals, carbon is expected to exhibit a valency of two. But in all of its known stable compounds, carbon is tetravalent. The tetravalency of carbon can be explained by the excited state concept, i.e. by exciting one of the paired $2s$ electrons to empty $2p$ orbital by absorbing energy from the system (according to classical concept of bonding).

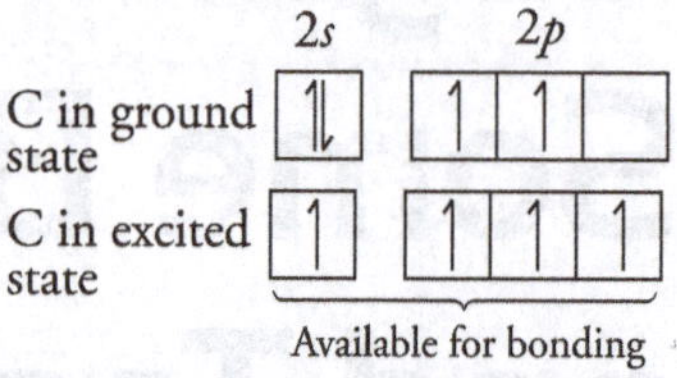

However, 4 equivalent C—H bonds in CH_4 is explained on the basis of concept of **hybridisation** (according to modern concept of bonding).

Carbon shares these electrons with other elements to form covalent compounds. From chapter 4, we know that in methane (CH_4), ethene (C_2H_4) and ethyne or acetylene (C_2H_2), the carbon is respectively sp^3, sp^2 and sp hybridised and hybridisation influences the bond characteristics.

The effect of hybridisation on different bond characteristics is tabulated below.

Hybridisation and Bond Characteristics

Bond	Hybridisation	Number of σ bonds formed by hybrid orbital	Geometry	s-character, p-character	C—C bond length (pm)	C—H bond length (pm)
Single (—)	sp^3	4	Tetrahedral	25%, 75%	154	111
Double (=)	sp^2	3	Trigonal planar	33.3%, 66.7%	134	110
Triple (≡)	sp	2	Linear	50%, 50%	120	108

From the table, it can be concluded that sp hybrid orbitals have maximum s-character, so it is closer to the nucleus and forms shorter and stronger bond as compared to sp^2 and sp^3 hybrid orbitals which has more p-character that result in the formation of longer and weaker bonds.

Since, s-character $\propto$ electronegativity

Therefore, sp hybrid orbitals are more electronegative among the three.

Reason for Large Number of Organic compounds

Various reasons for the existence of large number of organic compounds are as follows:

1. Catenation

The property of self linking of elements mainly carbon atoms through covalent bonds to form long, straight or branched chains and rings of different sizes is called catenation. Carbon shows maximum catenation in the periodic table due to its small size and high strength of C — C bonds.

A large number of carbon atoms can join together to form straight chain, branched chain or rings as shown below:

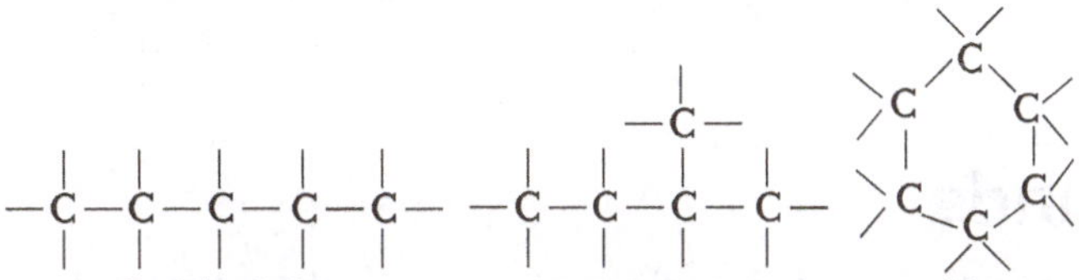

Straight chain Branched chain Ring

Note Elements other than carbon like sulphur, silicon also have a tendency to show the property of self linking, i.e. catenation but to a much lesser extent due to less *E*—*E*(*E* = element) bond energy or strength.

2. Tendency to Form Multiple Bonds

Due to its small size carbon has a strong tendency to form multiple bonds (double and triple bonds) by sharing more than one electron pair with its own atoms or with the atoms of elements like oxygen, nitrogen, sulphur etc. As a result, it can form a variety of compounds. e.g.

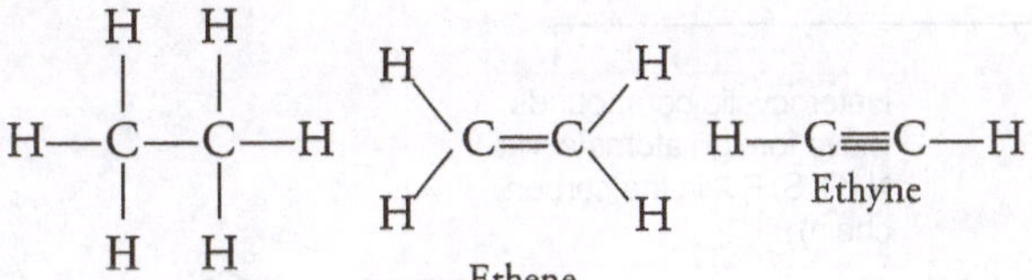

Ethane Ethene Ethyne

3. Isomerism

The phenomenon of isomerism helps carbon to increase the compounds. Isomerism is shown by those compounds that have same molecular formula but possess different structures or different arrangement of atoms in space, e.g. C_4H_{10} have two structural isomers.

These are as follows:

$CH_3CH_2CH_2CH_3$ (*n*-butane), $CH_3—\underset{\underset{CH_3}{|}}{CH}—CH_3$ (Isobutane)

Structural Representations of Organic Compounds

There are several ways to represent the organic compounds.

Three important representations are as follows :

1. Dash Structure or Complete Structure

If in the Lewis structure of an organic compound, all the bond pairs are replaced by a dash (—) then the obtained structure is called **dash structure** or **complete structure.**

e.g. the Lewis dot structure and dash structure of ethane are:

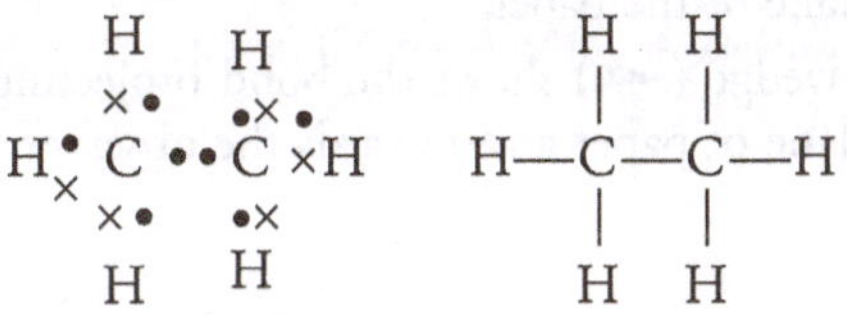

2. Condensed Structure

When all the bonds (except double and triple bonds) are omitted and the number of identical groups attached to an atom is represented by a subscript, the obtained structure is called **condensed structure** or **condensed structural formula.**

Thus, ethane, ethene, ethyne and methanol in their condensed form can be written as

CH_3CH_3	$H_2C{=}CH_2$	$HC{\equiv}CH$	CH_3OH
Ethane	Ethene	Ethyne	Methanol

Similarly, $CH_3CH_2CH_2CH_2CH_2CH_3$ can be further condensed to $CH_3(CH_2)_4CH_3$.

3. Bond Line Structure

In these structures, the carbon-carbon bonds are represented by *zig-zag* lines and the terminals denote methyl ($—CH_3$) groups unless stated otherwise by a functional group. e.g. the bond line and condensed structures of 3-methyloctane are,

$$\overset{1}{C}H_3\overset{2}{C}H_2\underset{\underset{CH_3}{|}}{\overset{3}{C}H}\overset{4}{C}H_2\overset{5}{C}H_2\overset{6}{C}H_2\overset{7}{C}H_2\overset{8}{C}H_3$$

The only atoms specifically written in the structure are oxygen, nitrogen, sulphur, chlorine etc.

So, draw 7 lines in *zig-zag* manner.

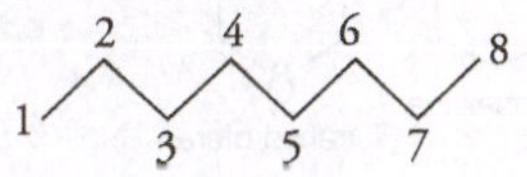

Attach 1 vertical line at carbon-3.

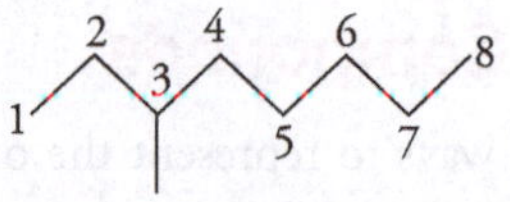

Note Terminals represent methyl group.

Three-Dimensional Representation of Organic Molecules

To represent an organic molecule three-dimensionally (3-D), following conventions should be kept in mind.

(i) Normal lines (—) always show the groups lying in the plane of the paper.

(ii) Solid-wedge (◄) shows the bond projecting out of the plane of paper and towards the observer.

(iii) Dashed-wedge (⫶⫶⫶) also shows the bond projecting out of the plane of paper but it is away from the observer.

(iv) The broad end of the wedge (both solid-wedge and dashed-wedge) is towards the observer. Keeping the above conventions in mind, the 3-D structure (wedge and dash representation) of methane (CH_4) can be represented as:

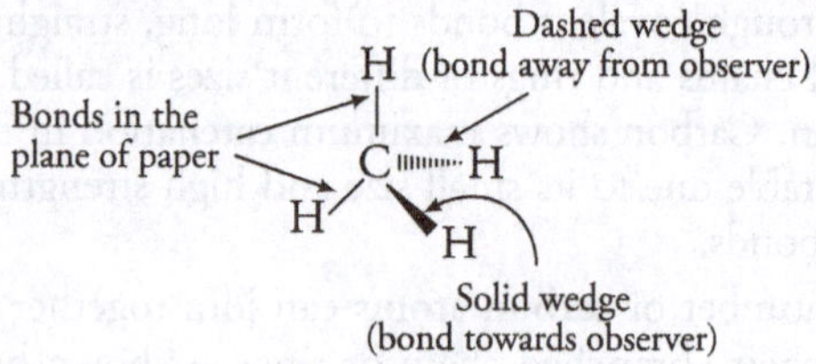

Classification of Organic Compounds

Due to its unique catenation power (power of self linking), carbon forms millions of organic compounds and to study these compounds conveniently, it is necessary to classify them. The organic compounds are classified as follows:

Classification Based on Carbon Skeleton

On this basis, organic compounds are classified into following manner.

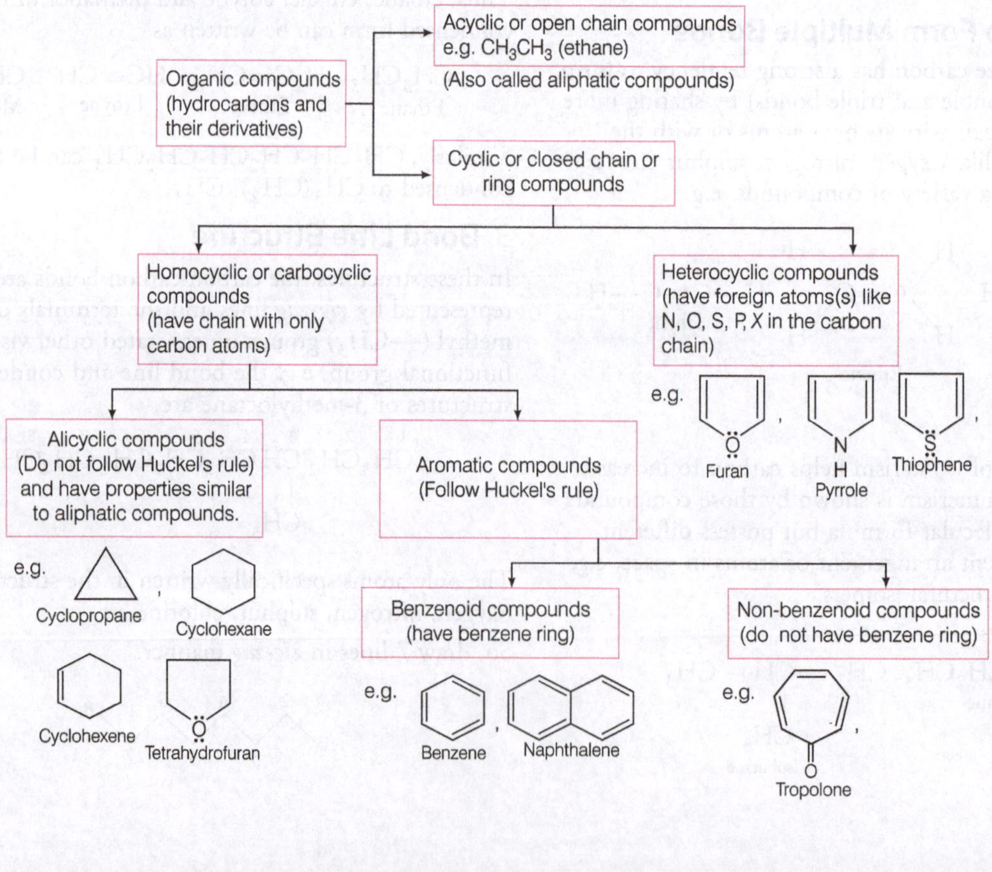

Classification of Organic Compounds Based on Functional Groups

Before discussing this type of classification, it is important to know about the functional group and homologous series.

1. Functional Group

An atom or a group of atom present in an organic compound, which is responsible for the chemical properties of the compound is called the **functional group**. e.g. hydroxyl group (—OH) etc.

2. Homologous Series

The group or series of compound having characteristic functional group is called the **homologous series** and the members of the series are called **homologous**, e.g. the homologous series of alkanes is as follows:

CH_4 (Methane), C_3H_8 (Propane), C_2H_6 (Ethane), C_4H_{10} Butane

The general characteristics of a homologous series are:

(i) All the members of a series contain same elements and the functional group.

(ii) All the members can be represented by a single general formula, e.g. C_nH_{2n+2} is the general formula for alkanes.

(iii) The molecular formula of each homologue differs from its previous and successive member by $—CH_2$ unit, i.e. their molecular mass differs by 14 units.

(iv) All members of a series can be prepared by almost similar methods and have almost similar chemical properties.

On the basis of functional groups, organic compounds are classified into following families or homologous series.

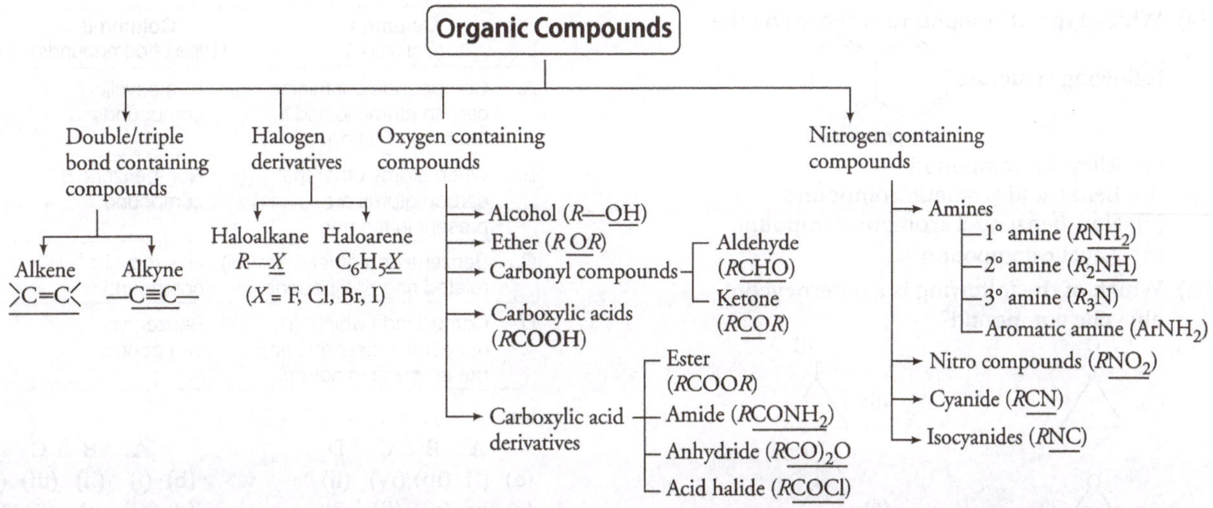

(Underlined groups are the functional groups of respective series). An organic molecule that contain more than one functional group is said to be **poly-functional**. In poly-functional compounds, properties of each functional group may be modified by the presence of the other.

Topic Practice 1

Very Short Answer Type Questions

(1 Mark)

1 Fill in the Blanks

(i) Presence of .... in organic compound decides its properties.

(ii) .... proved the synthesis of organic compound from an inorganic compound.

(iii) Methane is .... hybridised.

(iv) Furan is a .... compound.

2 Objective Type Questions

(i) Consider the following reaction,

$$\underset{\text{Ammonium cyanate}}{NH_4CNO} \xrightarrow{\text{Heat}} A$$

Here, A refers to

(a) NH_2COCl

(b) NH_2COOH

(c) NH_2COCH_3

(d) NH_2CONH_2

(ii) σ_{C-C} : 4; σ_{C-H} : 6; $\pi_{C=C}$: 1; $\pi_{C\equiv C}$: 2. These number of σ and π-bonds are present in which of the following molecule?
(a) $CH\equiv C-CH=CH-CH_3$
(b) $CH_2=C=CH-CH_3$
(c) $CH_2=CH-CH=CH-CH_3$
(d) None of the above

(iii) Catenation is the unique property of an element due to which it forms covalent bonds with other atoms of the same element ? Identify the element
(a) carbon (b) hydrogen
(c) neon (d) aluminium

(iv) Which group is denoted at the terminals in bond-line structural representations?
(a) Methyl group (CH_3—) or a functional group
(b) Ethyl group (CH_3CH_2—)
(c) No group
(d) Free-radical group

(v) Which type of compound is shown by the following structure 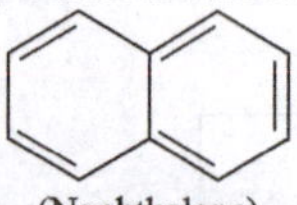 ?
(Naphthalene)
(a) Alicyclic compound
(b) Benzenoid aromatic compound
(c) Non-benzenoid aromatic compound
(d) Acyclic compound

(vi) Which of the following is a heterocyclic alicyclic compound?
(a) 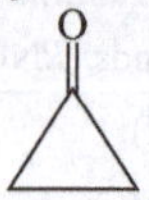
(b) 
(c) 
(d) 

(vii) Which one of the following statements is not correct for a homologous series?
(a) All members have a general formula
(b) All members have same chemical properties
(c) All members have same molecular mass
(d) All members have same functional group

(viii) Which of the following best describe the given statement "an atom or group of atoms joined in a specific manner which is responsible for the characteristic chemical properties of the organic compounds?
(a) Hetero atom
(b) Functional group
(c) Aromatic group
(d) Non-aromatic group

3 Matching Type Questions

(i) Match the terms of Column I with Column II and choose the correct option using the codes given below:

Column I (Structure of compound)	Column II (Hybridisation of carbon)
A. CH_3Cl	(i) sp^3 and sp^2
B. $(CH_3)_2CO$	(ii) sp^2
C. CH_3CN	(iii) sp^3
D. $HCONH_2$	(iv) sp^3 and sp

Codes

	A	B	C	D		A	B	C	D
(a)	(iii)	(i)	(iv)	(ii)	(b)	(iv)	(iii)	(ii)	(i)
(c)	(iii)	(i)	(iv)	(ii)	(d)	(i)	(ii)	(iii)	(iv)

(ii) Match the terms of Column I with Column II and choose the correct option using the codes given below:

Column I (Definition)	Column II (Type of compounds)
A. Compounds containing carbon atoms joined in the form of a ring.	(i) Homocyclic compounds
B. When atoms other than carbon atoms are present in the ring	(ii) Non-benzenoid compound
C. Benzene and other related ring compounds	(iii) Heterocyclic compound
D. Compounds which do not contain benzene ring but aromatic in nature.	(iv) Benzenoid compound

Codes

	A	B	C	D		A	B	C	D
(a)	(i)	(iii)	(iv)	(ii)	(b)	(i)	(ii)	(iii)	(iv)
(c)	(iv)	(iii)	(ii)	(i)	(d)	(iii)	(i)	(ii)	(iv)

Very Short Answer Type I Questions

1 Mark

4 How many σ bonds and π bonds are present in the second member of the alkene series?

5 What is the hybridisation of each carbon in $H_2C=C=CH_2$? **NCERT Exemplar**

6 Name the pair of hybridised orbitals involved in the formation of C_2-C_3 bond in the given compound $CH_2=CH-CH_2-CH_2-C\equiv CH$

7 Arrange the following in increasing order of C—C bond length : C_2H_6, C_2H_4, C_2H_2.

Short Answer Type I Questions

2 Marks

8 What are the possible structures for a carboxylic acid with a molecular formula $C_4H_8O_2$ and label each C atom as sp, sp^2 and sp^3?

9 What is the type of hybridisation of each carbon in the following compounds?

(i) CH_3Cl, (ii) $(CH_3)_2CO$,
(iii) CH_3CN, (iv) $HCONH_2$,
(v) $CH_3CH{=}CHCN$ **NCERT Textbook**

10 How many σ and π bonds are present in each of the following molecules?

(i) $CH_3CH_2C{\equiv}N$
(ii) $CH_3{-}CH{=}CH{-}CH_2{-}C{\equiv}CH$
(iii) $CH_2{=}C{=}CH_2$

11 Write the state of hybridisation of central carbon atom in the following compounds and shapes of each of the molecules.

(i) $CH_3{-}\overset{\overset{\displaystyle O}{\|}}{C}{-}CH_3$ (ii) $(CH_3)_3CCl$
(iii) $HC{\equiv}N$

12 For each of the following compounds, write a condensed formula and also their bond-line formula.

(i) $HOCH_2CH_2CH_2CH(CH_3)CH(CH_3)CH_3$

(ii) $N{\equiv}C{-}\overset{\overset{\displaystyle OH}{|}}{C}H{-}C{\equiv}N$ **NCERT Textbook**

13 Draw polygon formula having the molecular formula C_5H_{10}.

14 Expand each of the following bond line formula to show all the atoms including carbon and hydrogen.

(i) 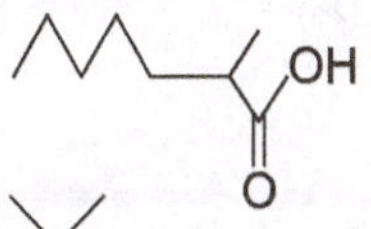

(ii) 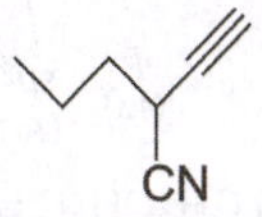

(iii) 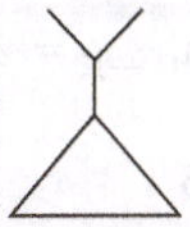

Short Answer Type II Questions

3 Marks

15 Indicate the σ and π bonds in the following molecules, C_6H_6, C_6H_{12}, CH_2Cl_2, $CH_2{=}C{=}CH_2$, CH_3NO_2, $HCONHCH_3$ **NCERT Textbook**

16 Identify the functional groups in the following compounds:

(i) 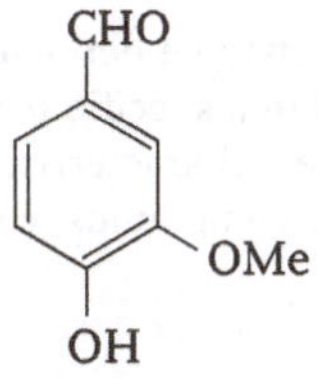

(ii) 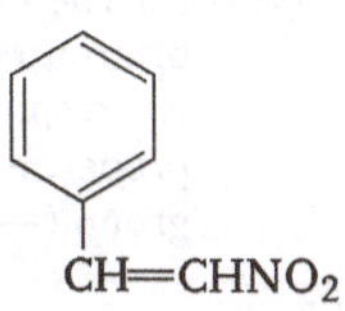

(iii) 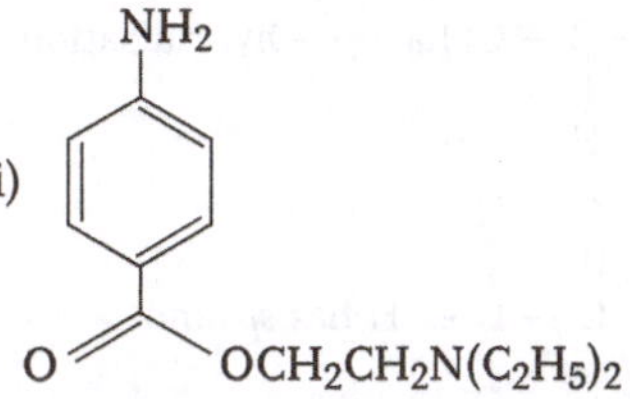

17 What are hybridisation states of each carbon atom in the following compounds?

$CH_2{=}C{=}O$, $CH_3CH{=}CH_2$, $(CH_3)_2CO$, $CH_2{=}CHCN$, C_6H_6 **NCERT Textbook**

Hints & Solutions

1. (i) functional group (ii) Friedrich wohler
(iii) sp^3 (iv) heterocyclic

2. (i) (*d*) $\underset{\text{Ammonium cyanate}}{NH_4CNO} \xrightarrow[\text{(Rearrangement)}]{\Delta} \underset{\text{Urea}}{NH_2CONH_2}$

(ii) (*a*) $H{-}C{\equiv}C{-}\overset{\overset{\displaystyle H}{|}}{C}{=}\overset{\overset{\displaystyle H}{|}}{C}{-}\underset{\underset{\displaystyle H}{|}}{\overset{\overset{\displaystyle H}{|}}{C}}{-}H$

$\sigma_{C-C} \Rightarrow 4$
$\sigma_{C-H} \Rightarrow 6$
$\pi_{C=C} \Rightarrow 1$
$\pi_{C\equiv C} \Rightarrow 2$

(iii) (*a*) The term catenation refers to chemical linkage into chains having atoms of same element. The property is visible only in those elements which have the ability to form atleast two covalent bonds. The property is predominant among carbon atoms, significant among sulphur and silicon atoms and slightly present among germanium, nitrogen, selenium and tellurium atom.

(iv) (*a*) The terminals denote methyl ($-CH_3$) groups (unless indicated otherwise by a functional group).

(v) (*b*) Since, the given compounds contain benzene nucleus, so naphthalene is a benzenoid aromatic compound.

(vi) (*c*) The heterocyclic alicyclic compound is 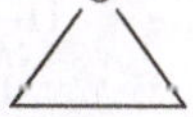

Heterocyclic alicyclic compounds are the compounds in which any hetero atom is present in the ring.

(vii) (*c*) The successive members of homologous series differ from each other by a mass of 14, i.e. they have different molecular mass.

(viii) (*b*) The functional group may be defined as an atom or group of atoms joined in a specific manner which is responsible for the characteristic chemical properties of the organic compounds. e.g., hydroxyl group (—OH).

3. (i) (*a*) 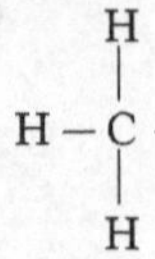 has sp^3- hybridisation.

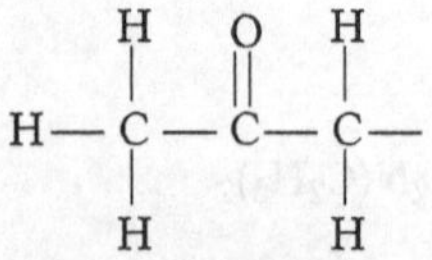 has sp^3 and sp^2-hybridisation.

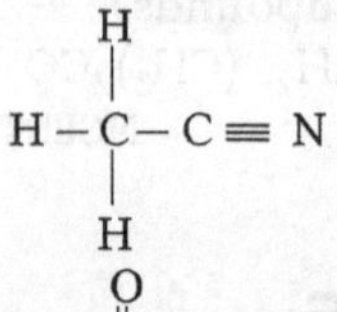 has sp^3 and *sp*-hybridisation

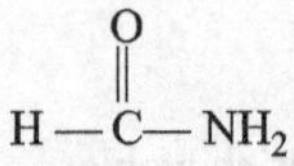 has sp^2- hybridisation.

(ii) (*a*) A. Compounds containing carbon atoms joined in the form of a ring are called homocyclic compounds.

e.g. 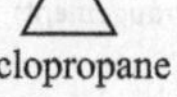

Cyclopropane

B. When atoms other than carbon atoms are present in the ring, they are heterocyclic in nature.

e.g. 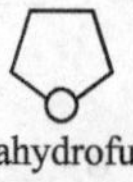

Tetrahydrofuran

C. Benzene and other related ring compounds are called benzenoid compounds.

Benzene

D. Compounds which do not contain benzene ring but aromatic in nature are called non-benzenoid compound.

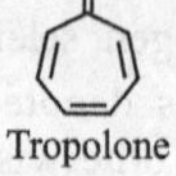

Tropolone

4. The second member of the alkene series is propene. The structural formula of the propene is

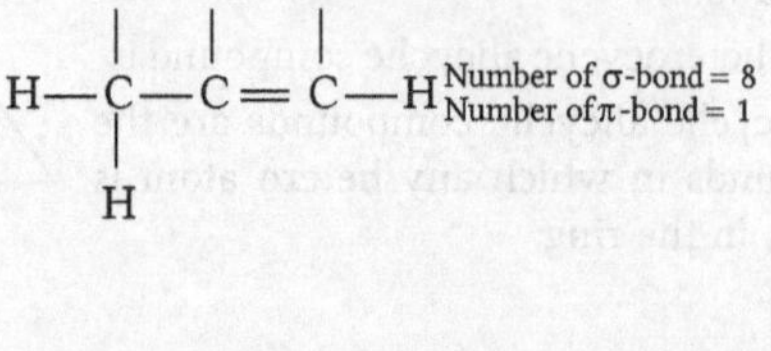

5. 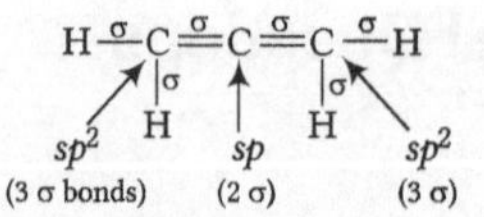

6. When double and triple bonds are present at equivalent positions, then preference is given to double bond while numbering the carbon chain. Thus,

$$\overset{1}{C}H_2 = \overset{2}{C}H - \overset{3}{C}H_2 - \overset{4}{C}H_2 - \overset{5}{C} \equiv \overset{6}{C}H$$
$$sp^2 \quad sp^2 \quad sp^3 \quad sp^3 \quad sp \quad sp$$

$\therefore C_2 - C_3$ bond is formed by overlap of sp^2 and sp^3 orbitals.

7. $C_2H_2(120\text{ pm}) < C_2H_4(134\text{ pm}) < C_2H_6(154\text{ pm})$.

8. The possible structures for a carboxylic acid are :

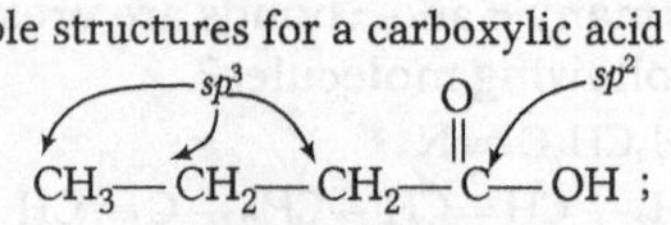

Butanoic acid

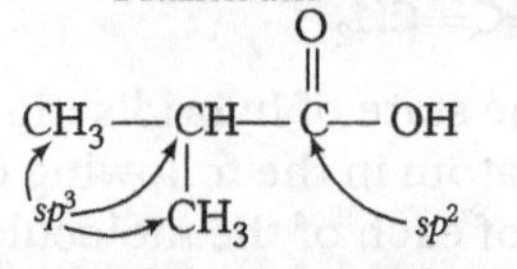

2-methyl propanoic acid

9. (i) 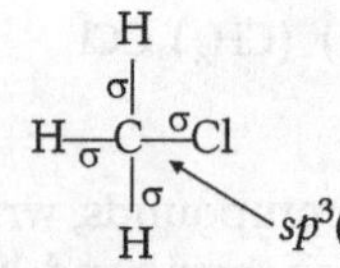

(4σ bonds, so sp^3-hybridised)

(ii) 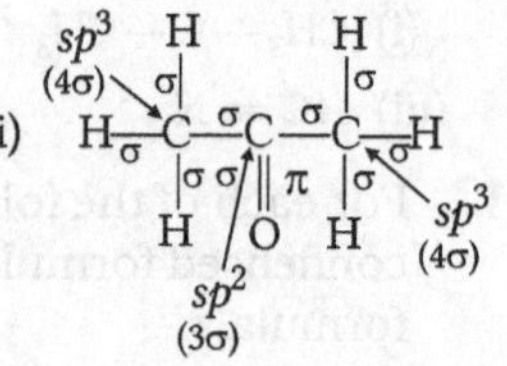

(iii) 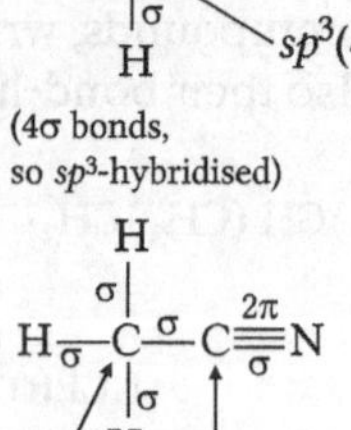

(iv) 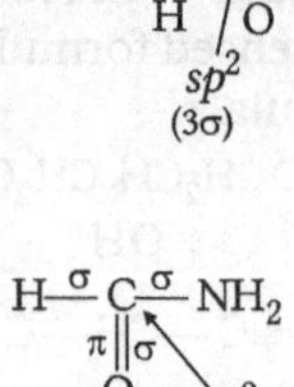

(v) 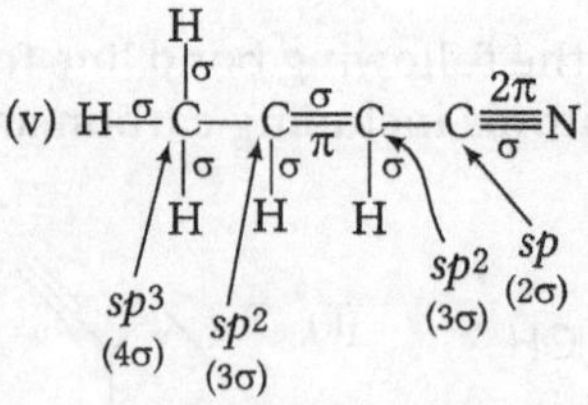

10. (i) $CH_3CH_2C \equiv N$

$\sigma_{C-C} = 2, \sigma_{C-H} = 5, \sigma_{C-N} = 1, \pi_{C-N} = 2$ [1/2]

(ii) $CH_3CH = CHCH_2C \equiv CH$

$\sigma_{C-C} = 5, \sigma_{C-H} = 8, \pi_{C-C} = 3$ [1½]

(iii) $CH_2 = C = CH_2$

$\sigma_{C-C} = 2, \sigma_{C-H} = 4, \pi_{C-H} = 2$ [1]

11. (i) sp^2-hybridised, trigonal planar

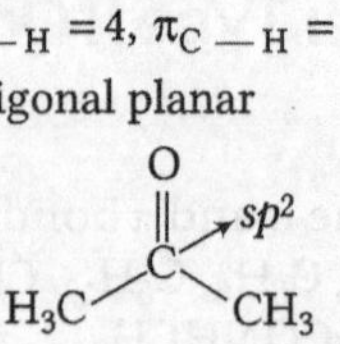

(ii) sp^3-hybridised, tetrahedral

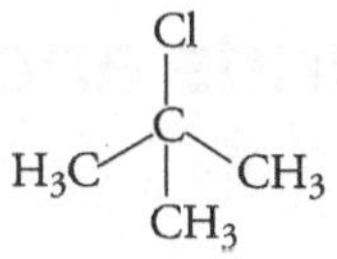

(iii) sp-hybridised, linear

$$H—C\equiv N$$ [2]

12. Condensed formulae for the given compounds are:

(i) $HO(CH_2)_3CH(CH_3)CH(CH_3)_2$

(ii) $HOCH(CN)_2$

Bond-line formula of the given compounds can be represented as:

(a)

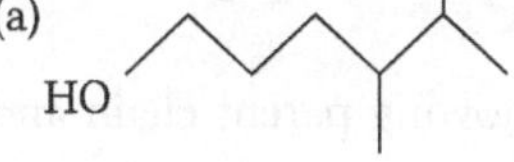

(b)

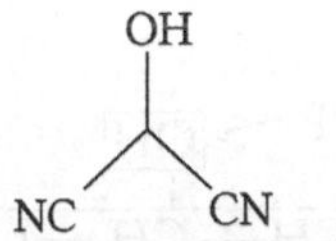

[2]

13. The different polygon formula of the compound having molecular formula C_5H_{10} are :

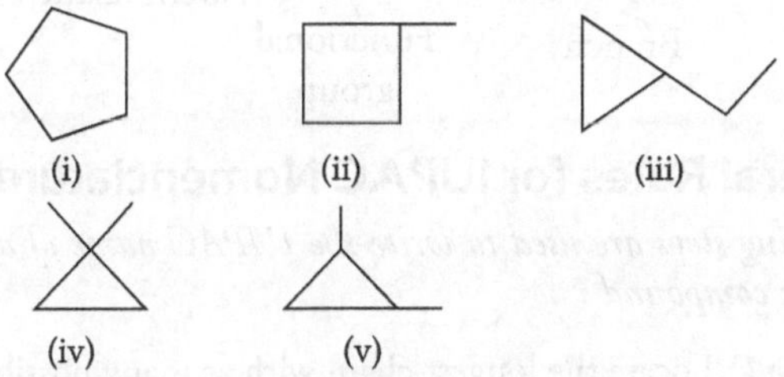

14.

(i)

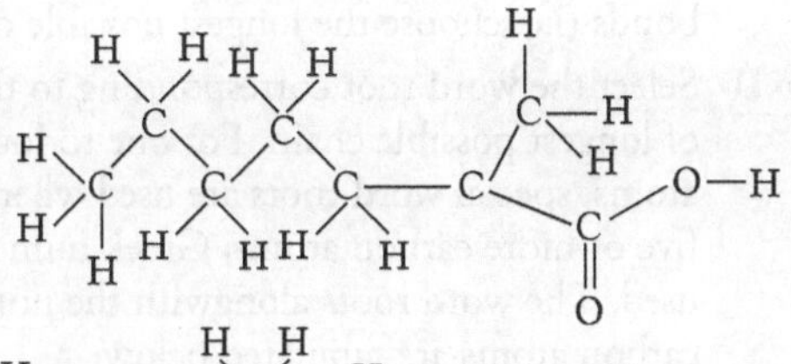

(ii)

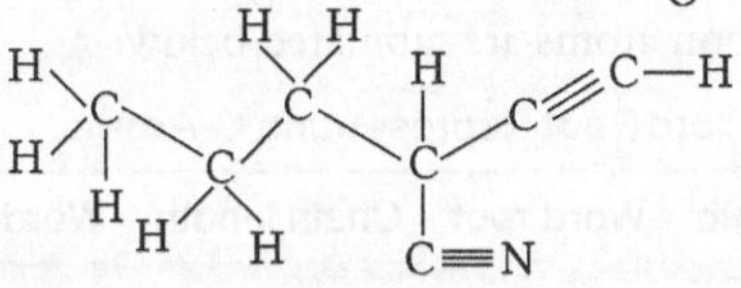

(iii)

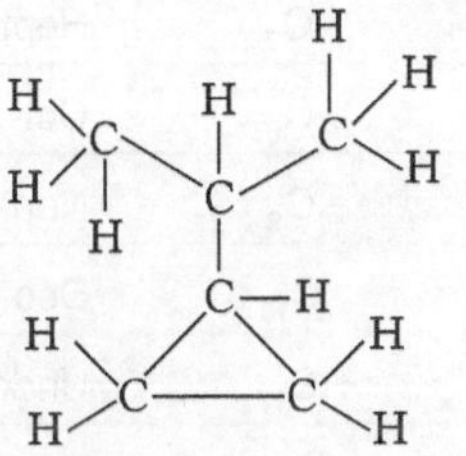

15.

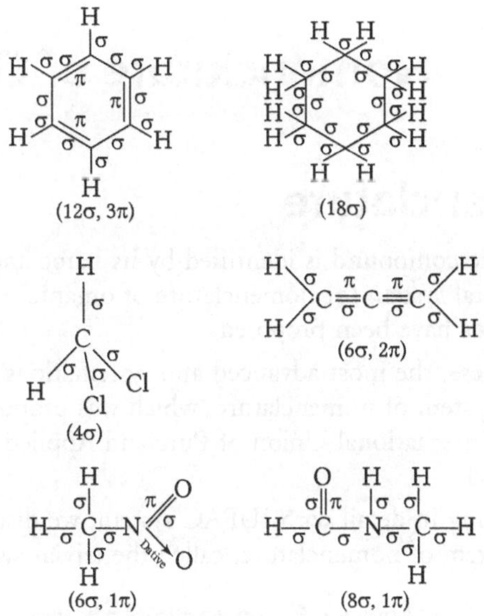

16. (i)

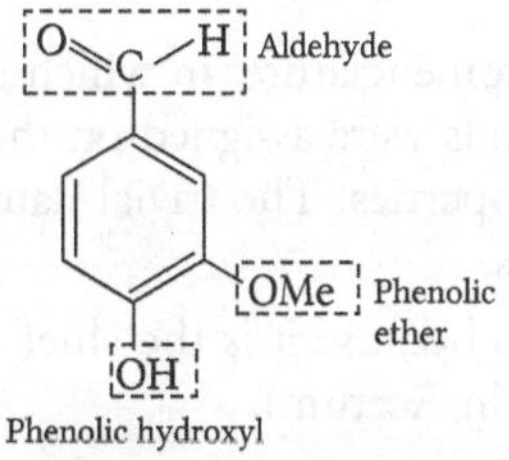

(ii)

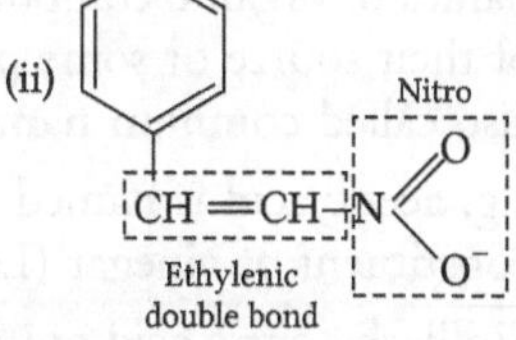

(iii)

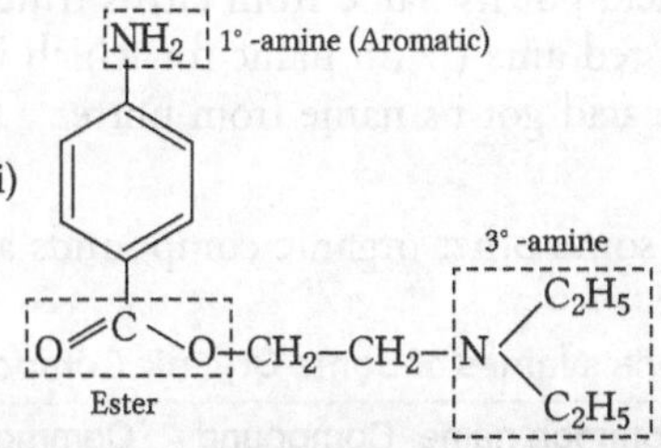

17. Hybridisation depends upon the number of σ bond formed by an atom. If number of σ bonds is 2, hybridisation is sp, if 3 then sp^2, if 4 then sp^3 and so on. So, count the number of σ bonds and find the hybridisation.

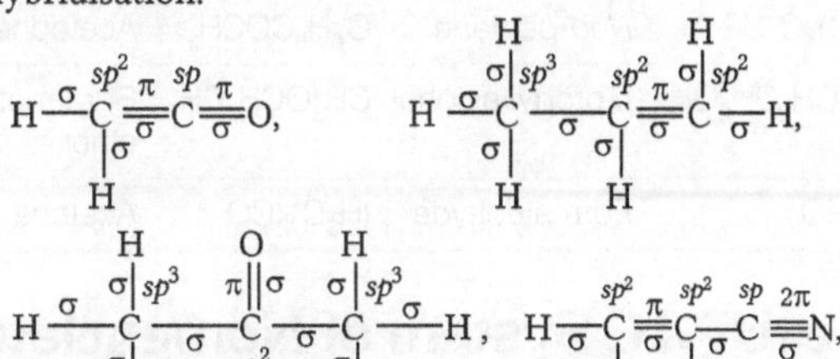

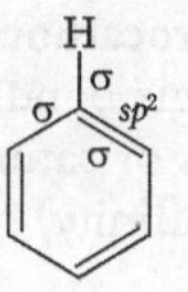

In benzene, each C is sp^2-hybridised.

TOPIC 02 Nomenclature of Organic Compounds and Isomerism

Nomenclature

An organic compound is identified by its name and till now, several system for nomenclature of organic compounds have been proposed.

Out of these, the most advanced and systematic is the **IUPAC system** of nomenclature, which was proposed by IUPAC (International Union of Pure and Applied Chemistry).

Before going in detail with IUPAC system, we discuss the oldest system of nomenclature, called the **trivial system.**

Trivial System of Nomenclature

It is the oldest system of nomenclature, in which the names of organic compounds were assigned on the basis of their source or some properties. The trivial names are also called **common names.**

e.g. acetic acid is named so because it is the chief constituent of vinegar (Latin Acetum).

Similarly, citric acid got its name from citrus fruits and formic acid from red ants (Latin name for which is formica). Butyric acid got its name from butter (butyrum).

Trivial names of some other organic compounds are tabulated below :

Common or Trivial Names of Some Organic Compounds

Compound	Common name	Compound	Common name
CH_4	Methane	$CHCl_3$	Chloroform
$H_3CCH_2CH_2CH_3$	*n*-butane	C_6H_6	Benzene
$(H_3C)_2CHCH_3$	*Iso*-butane	$C_6H_5OCH_3$	Anisole
$(H_3C)_4C$	*Neo*-pentane	$C_6H_5COCH_3$	Acetophenone
$H_3CCH_2CH_2OH$	*n*-propyl alcohol	$CH_3OCH_2CH_3$	Ethyl methyl ether
HCHO	Formaldehyde	$(H_3C)_2CO$	Acetone

The IUPAC System of Nomenclature

The simplest organic compounds are made up of only carbon and hydrogen and are called **hydrocarbons.** If all the carbon atoms are linked through single bonds in a hydrocarbon then they are called **alkanes or saturated hydrocarbons** or **paraffin** (Latin : little affinity) because of their inert nature.

However, if multiple bonds (= or ≡) are present between two or more carbon atoms, the hydrocarbon are called **unsaturated hydrocarbons.** To write the name of an organic compound in accordance with IUPAC system, firstly we have to identify the parent hydrocarbon (or alkane) and the functional groups attached to it.

After that, the name of parent hydrocarbon is modified by using suitable prefixes and suffixes to get the actual name of the compound.

An example of a molecule showing parent chain and functional group is given below.

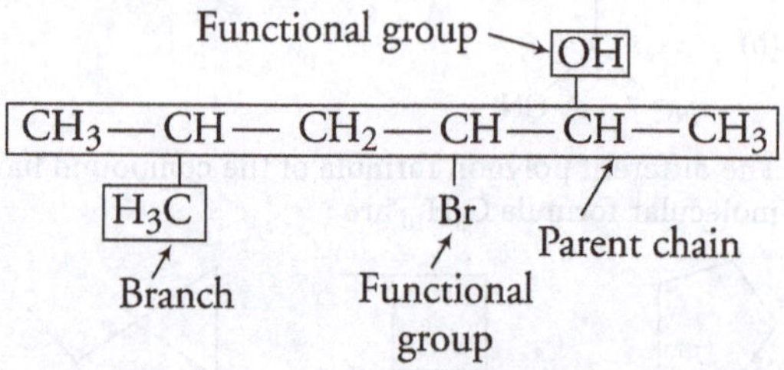

General Rules for IUPAC Nomenclature

Following steps are used to write the IUPAC name of an organic compound :

Step I Locate the longest chain with as many possible secondary functional groups alongwith multiple bonds (i.e. choose the longest possible chain).

Step II Select the word root corresponding to the length of longest possible chain. For one to four carbon atoms, special word roots are used whereas, for five or more carbon atoms, Greek numericals are used. The word roots alongwith the number of carbon atoms are tabulated below.

Word Root Representing C-Atoms

Chain length	Word root	Chain length	Word root
C_1	Meth–	C_7	Hept–
C_2	Eth–	C_8	Oct–
C_3	Prop–	C_9	Non–
C_4	But–	C_{10}	Dec–
C_5	Pent–	C_{11}	Undec–
C_6	Hex–	C_{12}	Dodec–

Word Root of Higher Members

C_{11}	Undec	C_{12}	Dodec
C_{13}	Tridec	C_{14}	Tetradec
C_{15}	Pentadec	C_{16}	Hexadec
C_{17}	Heptadec	C_{18}	Octadec
C_{19}	Nonadec	C_{20}	Icos
C_{21}	Henicos	C_{22}	Docos
C_{30}	Tricont	C_{40}	Tetracont

Step III Number the longest possible chain (according to the rules) to give an identification number to each C-atom of longest possible chain.

Step IV Add suitable **prefixes** and **suffixes** alongwith numerals to indicate the number and position of each side chain, substituent or functional group present in compound.

Prefix

It is used to indicate the substituents and is of the following two types :

(i) **Primary prefixes** are those prefixes which are usually used to distinguish between cyclic and acyclic compounds just like cyclo, bicyclo etc., or the prefixes used to tell us about the number of substituents present just like bi, di, tri, tetra, tris, tetrakis, ter, quater etc.

(ii) **Secondary prefixes** are infact the names of those groups to which IUPAC consider as substituents or branch either always (e.g. halogens) or under certain conditions i.e, whenever principal functional group is present alongwith the substituents in polyfunctional compounds. These prefixes are always written immediately before the root word. Some of these prefixes are given below.

Prefixes for Substituents

Substituent	Prefix	Substituent	Prefix
—F	Fluoro	—N═N—	diazo
—Cl	Chloro	—N═O	nitroso
—Br	Bromo	$—NO_2$	nitro

Note The prefix used for functional group are given later alongwith their suffix.

Suffix

It is used to indicate the functional group. The suffix also may be of two types :

(i) **Primary suffixes** are those words which tells us about the saturation or unsaturation of longest possible chain. The three basic primary suffixes are:

—**ane** for saturated chain,

—**ene** for unsaturated chain with a double bond,

—**yne** for unsaturated chain with a triple bond.

(ii) **Secondary suffixes** are infact the names of principal functional groups either in monofunctional or in polyfunctional compounds. These are given in the following table.

Prefix and Suffix of Various Functional Groups (in priority order) (as given under the 1993 recommendations of IUPAC)

S. No.	Class	Formula	Prefix	Suffix
1.	Carboxylic acids	—COOH	carboxy-	-carboxylic acid
		—(C)OOH	—	-oic acid
2.	Sulphonic acids	$—SO_3H$	sulpho-	-sulphonic acid
3.	Esters (of carboxylic acids)	—COOR*	(R*)-oxy-carbonyl	(R*)... carboxylate
		—(C)OOR*	(R*)-oxycarbonyl	(R*)...oate
4.	Acid halides	—C(═O)—X,	halocarbonyl –	-carbonyl halide
		—(C)(═O)—X where, X = halogen	—	-oyl halide
5.	Amides	$—CO—NH_2$	carbamoyl–	-carboxamide
		$—(C)O—NH_2$	—	-amide
6.	Nitriles	—C≡N	cyano–	-carbonitrile
		—(C)≡N	—	-nitrile
7.	Aldehydes	—CHO	formyl–	-carbaldehyde
		—(C)HO	—	-al
8.	Ketones	>C═O	oxo	-one
9.	Alcohols, Phenols	—OH	hydroxy–	-ol
10.	Thiols	—SH	sulphanyl-	-thiol
11.	Amines	$—NH_2$	amino–	-amine
12.	Imines	═NH	imino–	-imine
		═NR*	(R*) - imino	
13.	Ethers	—OR*	(R*) - oxy	-

In the above table R designates any alkyl group and C-atom in ( ) means when it is included in the main chain while C-atom without ( ) means it is not included in the main chain.

Hence, with the help of steps given above the IUPAC name of a compound can be written as :

Prefixes	+	Root word	+	Suffixes
Tells us about the branches or substituents except in the case of multiple bonds		Tells us about the length of longest possible chain		Tells us about the principal functional groups mostly except in the case of halogens

OR

Primary prefix + Secondary prefix + Root word + Primary suffix + Secondary suffix

IUPAC Nomenclature of Alkanes or Saturated Hydrocarbons

(i) **Nomenclature of Straight Chain Hydrocarbons (or Parent Hydrocarbon)** To write the name of straight chain hydrocarbon, first we write the '**word root**' or '**prefix**' that indicates the number of carbon atoms present in that chain with the help of following table. After writing the word root or prefix, we add suffix 'ane' to it to get the name of the hydrocarbon.

e.g. CH_4 contains one carbon atom so word root for it is meth and after adding suffix 'ane' we get its name methane. Thus, the name of an alkane can be written as

Word root + ane ⟶ Alkane

(ii) **Naming Alkyl Group** The group obtained by removing one H-atom from the saturated hydrocarbon (or alkane) is called the **alkyl group.** These groups are named by replacing 'ane' of alkane by 'yl'.

Alkane − ane + yl ⟶ alkyl

e.g. $\underset{\text{Methane}}{CH_4} \xrightarrow{-H^+} \underset{\text{Methyl group}}{—CH_3}$

Some alkyl groups are listed in the table given below:

Alkane		Alkyl group	
Molecular formula	Name of alkane	Structural formula	Name of alkyl group
CH_4	Methane	$—CH_3$	Methyl
C_2H_6	Ethane	$—CH_2CH_3$	Ethyl
C_3H_8	Propane	$—CH_2CH_2CH_3$	Propyl
C_4H_{10}	Butane	$—CH_2CH_2CH_2CH_3$	Butyl
$C_{10}H_{22}$	Decane	$—CH_2(CH_2)_8CH_3$	Decyl

Some alkyl group can also be represented by their abbreviation. e.g. methyl ($—CH_3$) is abbreviated as Me, ethyl ($—C_2H_5$) as Et, propyl ($—C_3H_7$) as Pr and butyl ($—C_4H_9$) as Bu.

Some alkyl groups are found in branched form. e.g.

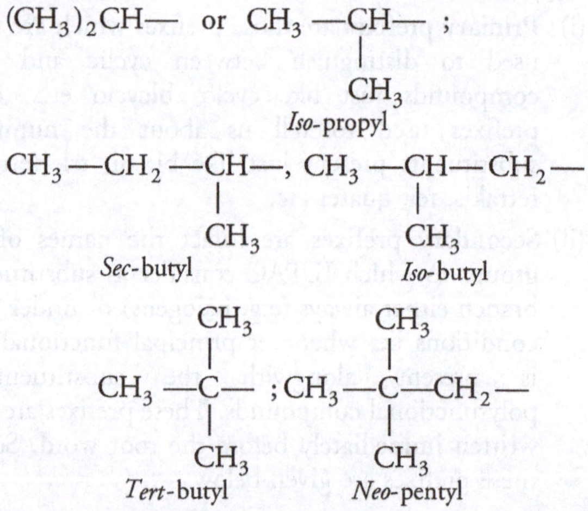

(iii) **Nomenclature of Branched Chain Alkanes or Hydrocarbons** The hydrocarbons in which small chains of carbon atoms are attached at one or more carbon atoms of the parent chain are called the branched chain hydrocarbons. The small chains (or branches) represent the alkyl group. e.g.

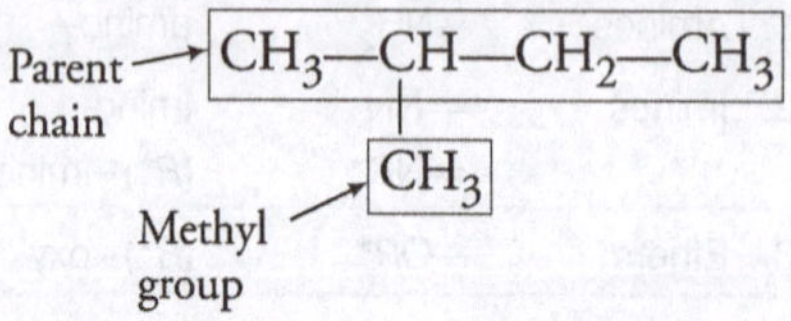

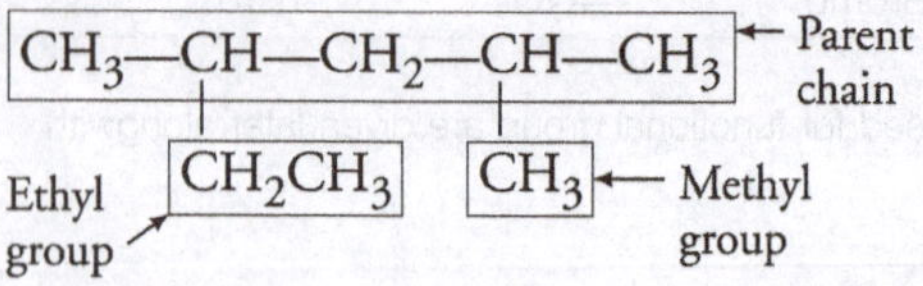

To write the name of such compound, the following rules have to be followed:

(i) Select the longest chain of carbon atoms and consider it as parent or root chain. e.g.

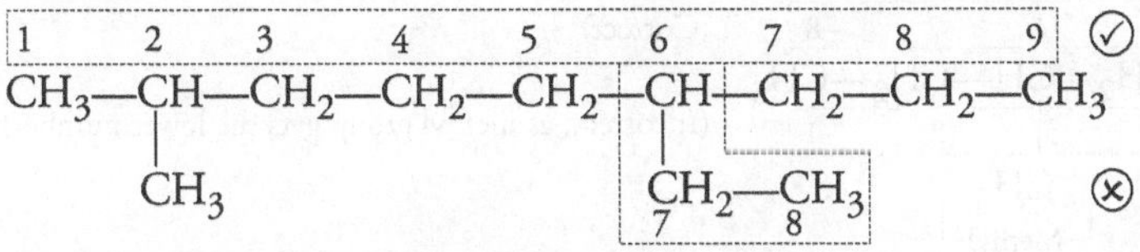

✓ (Correct way, as the longest chain has 9C-atoms)

⊗ (Incorrect way, as the longest chain has only 8C-atoms)

(ii) Number the longest possible chain to give an identification number to each C-atom of the longest chain in such a way that the branched carbon atoms (or alkyl groups) get the lowest possible numbers.

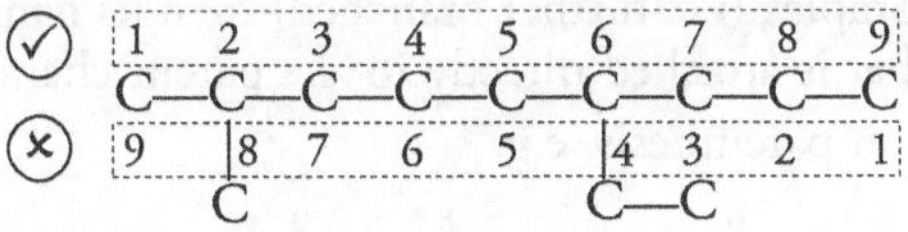

✓ (∵Position of branch = 2 and 6)

⊗ (∵Position of branch = 4 and 8)

Note Numbering is done in the parent chain to identify the parent alkane and to locate the position of branch.

(iii) The branches (or small chains) are named by adding the prefix of the alkyl group to the parent chain and their location is indicated by appropriate numbers. e.g.

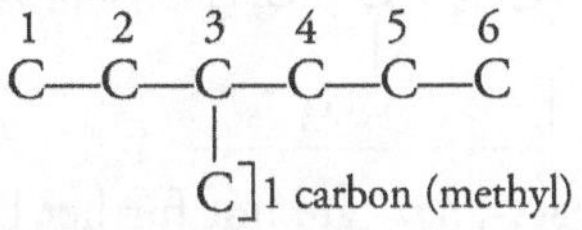

3-methylhexane

However, if the hydrocarbon have several branches (or alkyl groups), they are named alphabetically. e.g.

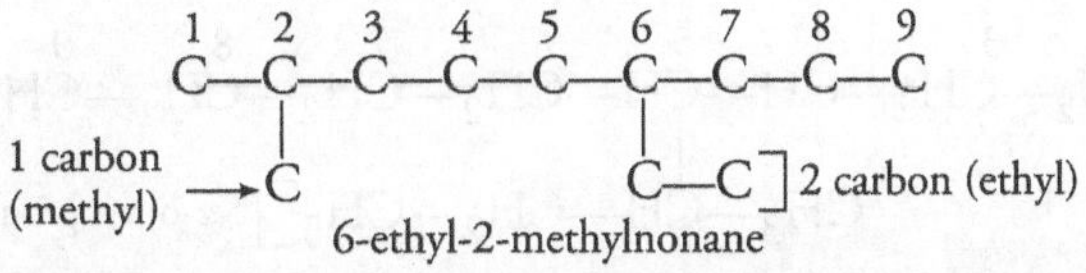

6-ethyl-2-methylnonane

Hyphens are used to separate number from the name of the alkyl group. No gap is present between the names of alkyl group and alkane (in the above case between methyl and nonane).

(iv) If the parent chain contains two or more identical branches or alkyl groups (or substituents), they are named by adding prefixes like di (for 2), tri (for 3), tetra (for 4), penta (for 5), hexa (for 6), hepta (for 7) etc. Alongwith their locations separated by comma before their names. e.g.

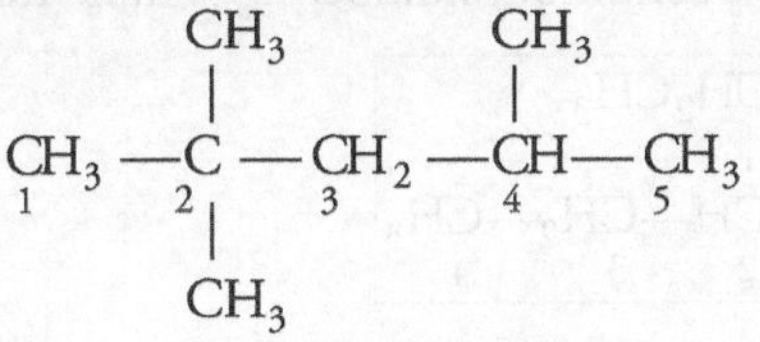

(∵Three Me groups are present at 2, 2 and 4 positions)

2,2,4-trimethylpentane

However, while writing the names of alkyl groups (or substituents) alphabetically, these prefixes are not considered. e.g.

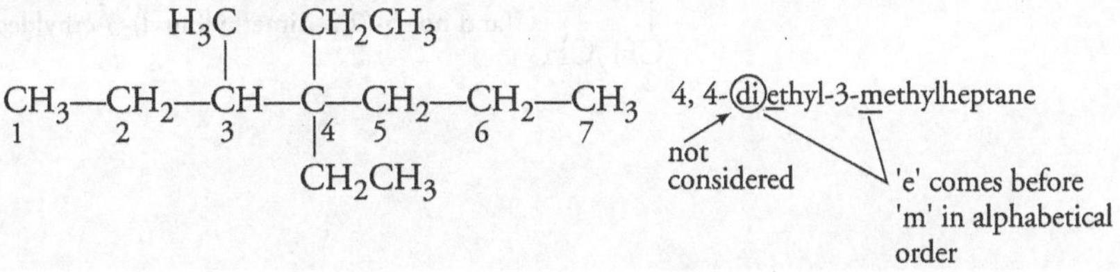

(v) If two different alkyl groups occupy equivalent positions in the parent chain then numbering is done from the side which gives lower number to the group coming first in alphabetical order. e.g.

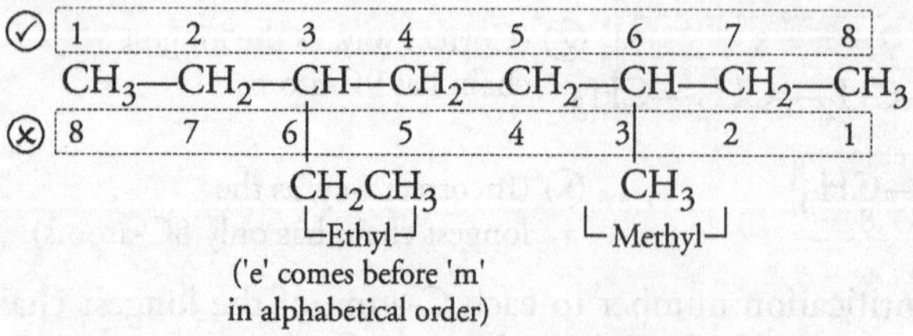

(Correct)

(Incorrect, as methyl group gets the lower number)

(vi) If the alkyl group attached to the parent chain is complex (i.e. further branched) then its name is given in the similar manner as of alkane. However, here, the carbon that is attached directly to the parent chain is numbered 1. The name of such alkyl groups are always written in parenthesis. e.g.

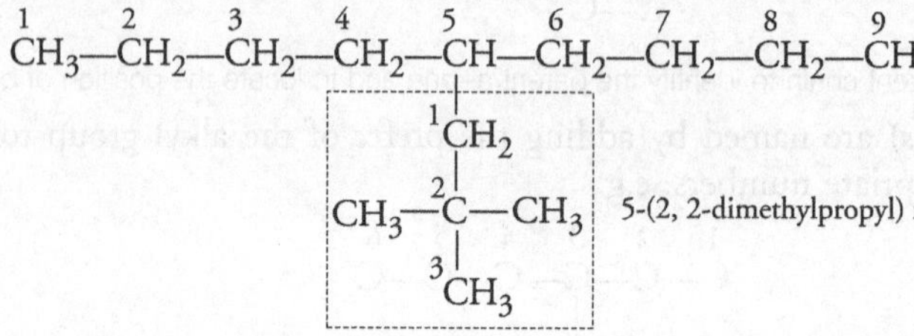

5-(2, 2-dimethylpropyl) nonane

(vii) If the branched alkyl groups like *iso-*, *neo-*, *sec-*, *tert-* are not further branched (or substituted) then they can also be written in IUPAC nomenclature. e.g.

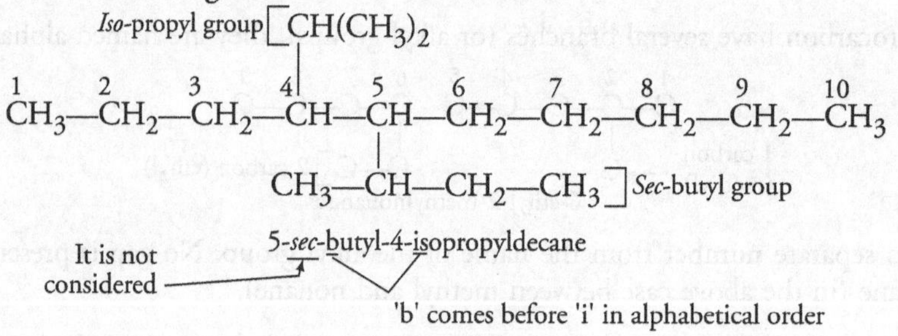

Here, it is important to note that while naming alphabetically, the prefix *iso* and *neo* are considered but *sec-* and *tert-* are not,

(viii) If there are two chains of equal length, then that chain is selected as parent (or root) chain which is more branched. i.e. have more number of substituent or alkyl groups. In such a condition, numbering is done from the side that is closer to substituent or alkyl chain. e.g.

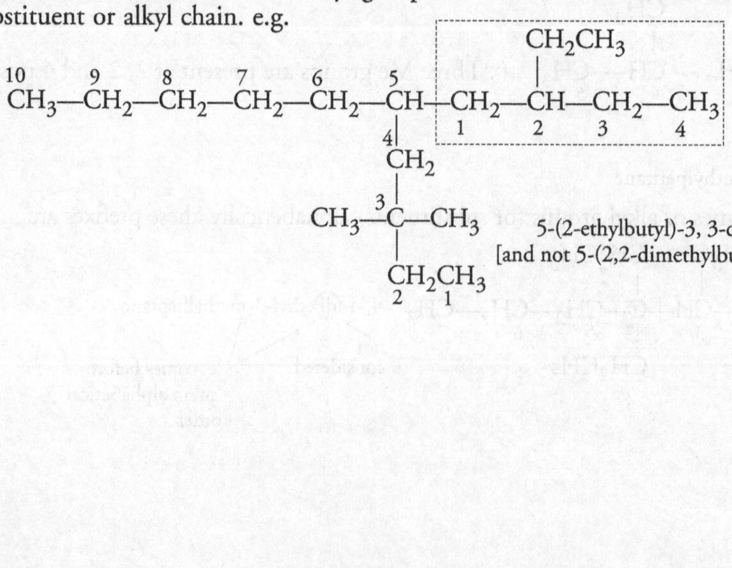

5-(2-ethylbutyl)-3, 3-dimethyldecane
[and not 5-(2,2-dimethylbutyl)-3-ethyldecane]

Nomenclature of Cyclic (Monocyclic) Hydrocarbons

To write the name of monocyclic hydrocarbons, following rules are followed:

(i) Prefix 'cyclo' is added to the name of corresponding straight chain alkane, if the hydrocarbon is unsubstituted (or unbranched). e.g.

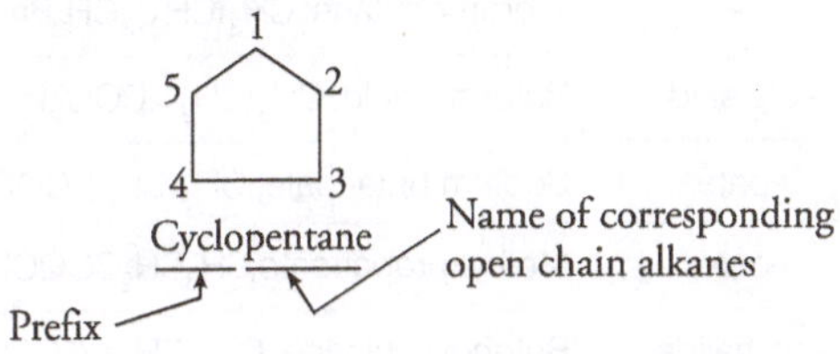

(ii) If the cyclic hydrocarbon is substituted, then

(a) Number the chain in such a manner that lower number is given to the group that comes first in alphabetical order. e.g.

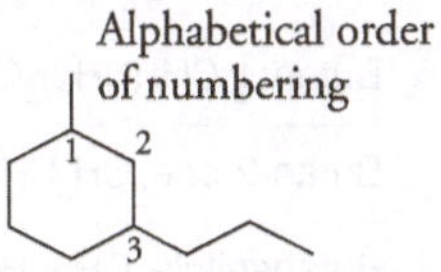

1-methyl-3-propylcyclohexane

(b) Number the chain in such a manner that more branched carbon gets the lower number

e.g.

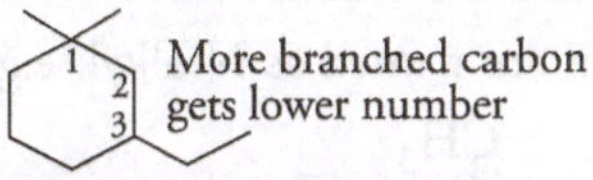

3-ethyl-1, 1-dimethylcyclohexane
(not 1-ethyl-3, 3-dimethylcyclohexane)

(iii) If the side chain have more number of carbon atoms than that present in the ring, then the ring or cycle is treated as substituent. e.g.

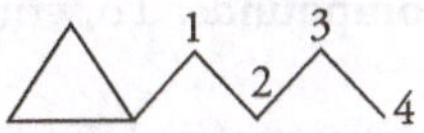

(1-cyclopropyl) butane

Example 1 Structures and IUPAC names of some hydrocarbons are given below. Explain why the names given in the parentheses are incorrect.

(i) $CH_3—CH(CH_3)—CH_2—CH_2—CH(CH_3)—CH(CH_3)—CH_2—CH_3$

2,5,6-trimethyloctane
[and not 3,4,7-trimethyloctane]

(ii) $CH_3—CH_2—CH(CH_2CH_3)—CH_2—CH(CH_3)—CH_2—CH_3$

3-ethyl-5-methylheptane
[and not 5-ethyl-3-methylheptane] **NCERT Textbook**

Sol. (i) Because locant number, 2, 5, 6 is lower than 3, 4, 7,

(ii) $\overset{1}{C}H_3\overset{2}{C}H_2\overset{3}{C}H(CH_2CH_3)—\overset{4}{C}H_2\overset{5}{C}H(CH_3)—\overset{6}{C}H_2\overset{7}{C}H_3$ (Correct)

Numbering 7, 6, 5, 4, 3, 2, 1 (Incorrect)

Since, substituents are in equivalent position so lower number is given to ethyl which comes first in the name according to alphabetical order.

IUPAC Nomenclature of Organic Compounds having Functional Groups

Nomenclature of Monofunctional Compounds

The compounds having only one functional group are called monofunctional compounds. To write name of such compounds, following rules have to be followed.

(i) Choose the longest carbon chain that contains functional group. e.g.

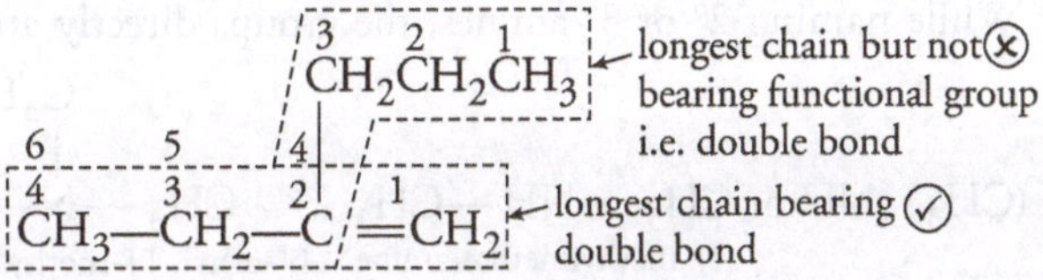

(ii) Number the chain in such a way that the functional group gets the lowest possible number in the chain.

(iii) Write the suffix of the functional group after the name of the parent hydrocarbon by omitting its 'e'.

Class of compounds	Functional group structure	IUPAC group prefix	IUPAC group suffix	Example
Alkanes	—	—	-ane	Propane, $CH_3(CH_2)CH_3$
Alkenes	$\rangle C{=}C\langle$	—	-ene	But-1-ene, $CH_2{=}CHCH_2CH_3$
Alkynes	$—C{\equiv}C—$	—	-yne	But-1-yne, $CH{\equiv}CCH_2CH_3$
Arenes	—	phenyl	—	Benzene, 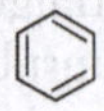
Halides	$-X$ (X = F, Cl, Br, I)	halo-	—	1-bromobutane, $CH_3(CH_2)_2CH_2Br$
Carboxylic acids	—COOH	carboxy	-oic acid	Butanoic acid, $CH_3(CH_2)_2COOH$
Carboxylate ions	$—COO^-$	—	-oate	Sodium butanoate, $CH_3(CH_2)_2COO^-Na^+$
Esters	—COOR	alkoxycarbonyl	-oate	Methyl propanoate, $CH_3CH_2COOCH_3$
Acyl halides	—COX (X = F, Cl, Br, I)	halocarbonyl	-oyl halide	Butanoyl chloride, $CH_3(CH_2)_2COCl$
Amines	$—NH_2$, $\rangle NH$, $\rangle N—$	amino–	-amine	Butan-2-amine, $CH_3CHNH_2CH_2CH_3$
Amides	$—CONH_2$, $—CONHR$, $—CONR_2$	-carbamoyl	-amide	Butanamide, $CH_3(CH_2)_2CONH_2$
Alcohols	—OH	hydroxy–	-ol	Butan-2-ol, $CH_2CH_2CH(OH)CH_3$
Aldehydes	—CHO	formyl or oxo	-al	Butanal, $CH_3(CH_2)_2CHO$
Ketones	$C{=}O$	oxo–	-one	Butan-2-one, $CH_3CH_2COCH_3$
Nitriles	$—C{\equiv}N$	cyano	nitrile	Butanenitrile, $CH_3CH_2CH_2CN$
Ethers	$R—O—R$	alkoxy–	—	Methoxyethane $CH_3CH_2OCH_3$
Nitro compounds	$—NO_2$	nitro	—	1-Nitrobutane, $CH_3(CH_2)_3NO_2$
Sulphonic acids	$—SO_3H$	sulpho	sulphonic acid	Methylsulphonic acid, CH_3SO_3H

* While naming 2° or 3° amines, the groups directly attached to the N atom are named as N-alkyl. e.g.

$(CH_3)_2NH$ or $CH_3—NH—CH_3$; N-methylmethanamine

$CH_3—N(C_3H_7)—C_2H_5$ (C_3H_7] longest) ; N-ethyl, N-methylpropanamine

$CH_3—N(CH_3)—CH_3$] identical groups are present. N, N-dimethylmethanamine

Nomenclature of Polyfunctional Compounds

The compounds having more than one functional group are called **polyfunctional compounds.** To write name of such compounds, following rules have to be followed:

(i) The first step to write the name of such compound is the selection of principal functional group on the basis of priority order. The order ofdecreasing priority for some functional groups is

$—COOH, —SO_3H, —COOR$ (R = alkyl group), $—COCl, —CONH_2, —CN, HC{=}O, \rangle C{=}O, —OH, —NH_2, \rangle C{=}C\langle, C{\equiv}C—$,

e.g. If in a compound —OH and —CHO both groups are present then —CHO is the principal functional group. The $—R$, $C_6H_5—$, halogens (—F, —Cl, —Br, —I), $—NO_2$, alkoxy (—OR) etc., are always prefix substituents.

(ii) Choose the longest chain that have principal functional group as well as double or triple bond.
e.g.

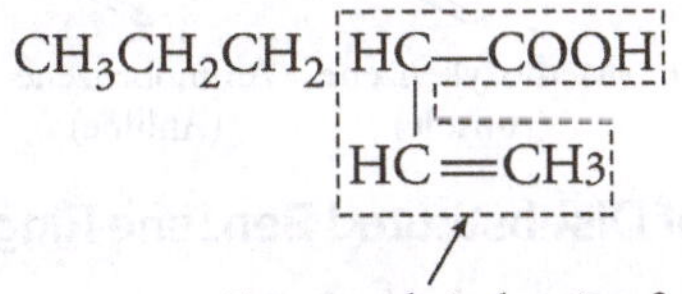

Longest chain bearing functional group as well as double bond

(iii) Number the chain in such a manner that the principal functional group gets the lowest possible number.

(iv) Now, write the prefix for functional groups other than the principal functional group before the name of the parent alkane and add suffix for the principal functional group by omitting 'e' of the alkane.

e.g. $\overset{7}{HOCH_2}\overset{4,5,6}{(CH_2)_3}\overset{3}{CH_2}\overset{2}{CO}\overset{1}{CH_3}$

∵ Priority order $>C=O > —OH$

Prefix for —OH is 'hydroxy', suffix for $>C=O$ is 'one'. There are 7 carbon atoms, so alkane is heptane. Therefore, its IUPAC name is 7-hydroxyheptan-2-one.

Similarly, $\overset{3}{Br CH_2}\overset{2}{CH}=\overset{1}{CH_2}$
3-bromoprop-1-ene

(v) If more than one functional group of the same type are present, their number is indicated by adding di, tri, etc. before the class suffix.
In such cases, the full name of the parent alkane is written before the class suffix.
e.g.

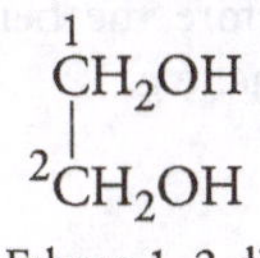

$CH_2=CH—CH=CH_2$
Buta-1, 3-diene

Ethane-1, 2-diol
'e' of alkane is not omitted.

Example 2 Write the IUPAC names of the compounds (i)-(iv) from their structures.

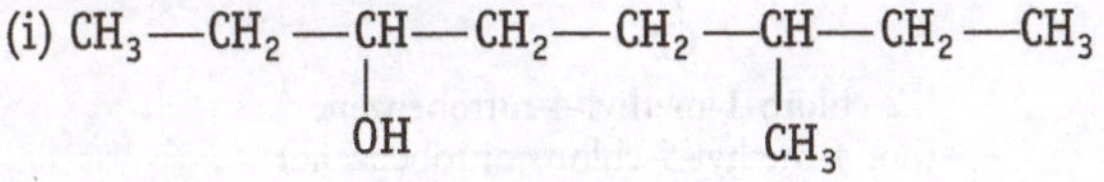

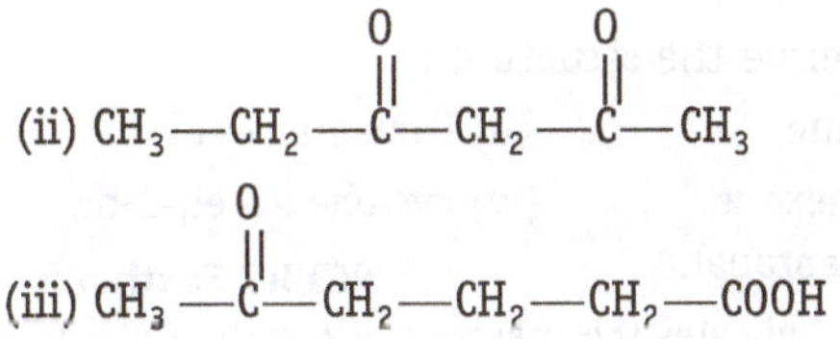

(iv) $CH\equiv C—CH=CH—CH=CH_2$ **NCERT Textbook**

Sol. Follow the given steps to solve out such problems.

Step **I** Predicting the principal functional group and suffix for the functional group

$—OH$ (i)(ol), $>C=O$ (ii)(-one), $—COOH$ (iii)(oicacid), $>C=C<$ (iv)(ene)

Step **II** Predicing substituent and their prefix

$—CH_3$ (i)(methyl), × (ii), $>C=O$ (iii)(oxo), $\equiv$ (iv)
(suffix-yne as it has no prefix).

Step **III** Number of C- atoms and parent alkane.
(i) 8 carbon (octane), (ii) 6 carbon (hexane), (iii) 6 carbon (hexane), (iv) 6 carbon (hexane)

Step **IV** Substituent location
(i) 6, (ii), (iii) 5, (iv) 5

Step **V** IUPAC name
(i) 6-methyl octan-3-ol, (ii) Hexane-2,4-dione, (iii) 5-oxohexanoic acid, (iv) Hexa-1, 3-dien-5-yne

Writing Structural Formula from the Name of the Compound

To write the structure of an organic compound from its name, the following steps are involved :

(i) Write a straight chain of carbon atoms according to the number of carbon atoms in the parent compound. At this stage, do not attach any hydrogen atoms to the carbon

C—C—C—C—C—C

(ii) Number the chain of carbon atoms from any end

$\overset{1}{C}—\overset{2}{C}—\overset{3}{C}—\overset{4}{C}—\overset{5}{C}—\overset{6}{C}$

(iii) In case, the name of the compound contains -ene or -yne, then draw double or triple bond at indicated locations.

(iv) Attach substituents and functional groups at the specified location.

(v) Make each carbon tetravalent by attaching a suitable number of hydrogen atoms.

Example 3 Derive the structure :

(i) 2-chlorohexane, (ii) Pent-4-en-2-ol,
(iii) 3-nitrocyclohexene, (iv) cyclohex-2-en-1-ol,
(v) 6-hydroxy-heptanal.

NCERT Textbook

Sol. (i) 'Hexane' indicates the presence of 6 carbon atoms in the chain. The functional group chloro is present at carbon 2. Hence, the structure of the compound is $CH_3CH_2CH_2CH_2CH(Cl)CH_3$.

(ii) 'Pent' indicates that parent hydrocarbon contains 5 carbon atoms in the chain. 'en' and 'ol' correspond to the functional groups C=C and –OH at carbon atoms 4 and 2 respectively. Thus, the structure is

$$CH_2 = CHCH_2CH(OH)CH_3.$$

(iii) As the name indicates, the compound is cyclic with a double bond.

The prefix 3-nitro means that a nitro group is present on C – 3 . Numbering is done from the carbon atom bearing double dond.

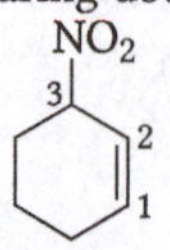

(iv) Again the compound is cyclic with a double bond. Here '1—ol' means that — OH group bears 1-position because it comes before double bond in priority order series of functional group.

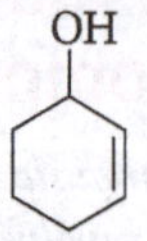

(iv) "Heptanal" indicates the compound to be an aldehyde containing 7 carbon atoms in the parent chain. '6-hydroxy' indicates that — OH group is present at carbon 6.

Thus,

$$\overset{7}{C}H_3\overset{6}{C}H(OH)\overset{5}{C}H_2\overset{4}{C}H_2\overset{3}{C}H_2\overset{2}{C}H_2\overset{1}{C}HO$$

Remember that carbon atom of — CHO group is included while numbering the carbon chain.

Nomenclature of Substituted Benzene Compounds

1. Nomenclature of Monosubstituted Benzene Ring

Such compounds are named by adding prefix of the substituent before the name benzene.

However, trivial or common names of the these compounds (given in bracket) are also widely used. e.g.

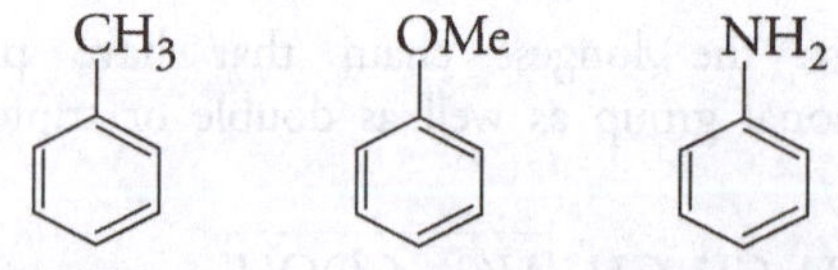

Methylbenzene (Toluene) Methoxybenzene (Anisole) Aminobenzene (Aniline)

2. Nomenclature of Disubstituted Benzene Ring

In case of these compounds, the first step is the numbering of the carbon atoms of the ring in such a manner that the substituents get the lowest possible numbers. Now write the name as in the previous case but with locations of the substituents. If both the substituents are same, add the prefix 'di' before the name of the substituents. e.g.

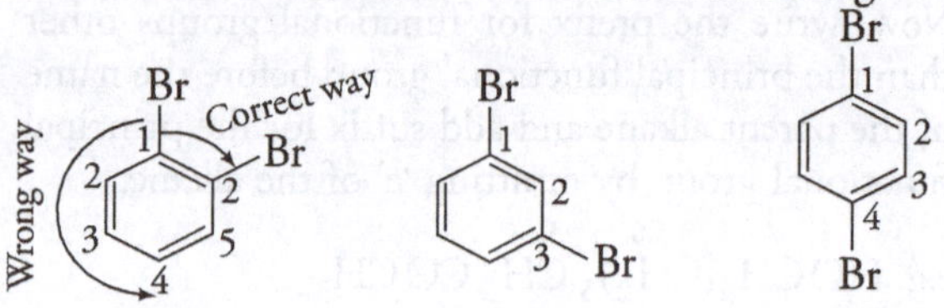

(a) 1,2-dibromobenzene not 1,6-dibromobenzene

(b) 1, 3-dibromobenzene

(c) 1, 4-dibromobenzene

In trivial system of nomenclature the position 1,2; 1,3; 1,4; are also called *ortho* (*o*), *meta* (*m*) and *para* (*p*) positions, so, the above compounds can also be named as *ortho* dibromobenzene, *meta* (or *m*-) dibromobenzene and *para* (or *p*-) dibromobenzene respectively.

3. Nomenclature of Tri-or Higher Substituted Benzene

For naming these compounds, following rules have to be followed :

(i) Number the carbon atoms of the ring in such a manner that the higher priority group gets the lowest possible number.

(ii) Write the prefix of the substituents in alphabetical order alongwith the locations before the benzene or trivial name of substituted benzene. e.g.

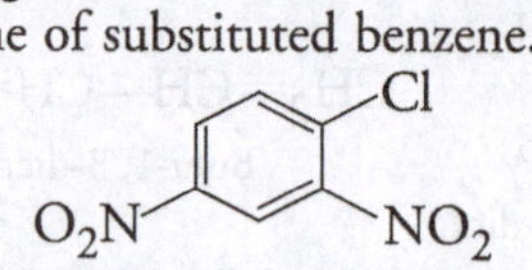

1-chloro-2, 4-dinitrobenzene
(not 4-chloro, 1, 3-dinitrobenzene)

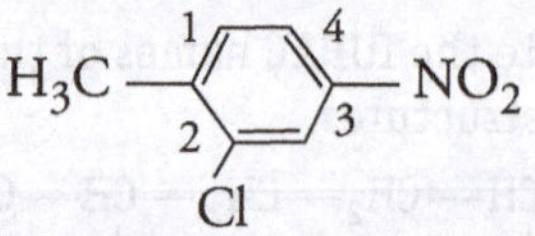

2-chloro-1-methyl-4-nitrobenzene
(not 4-methyl-5-chloro-nitrobenzene)

If benzene ring is attached to a chain that contains functional group, then it is considered as the substituent and named as phenyl (Ph).

Example 4 Write the structural formula of

(i) *o*-ethylanisole (ii) *p*-nitroaniline (iii) 2, 3-dibromo-1-phenylpentane

(iv) 4-ethyl-1-fluoro-2-nitrobenzene **NCERT Textbook**

Sol.

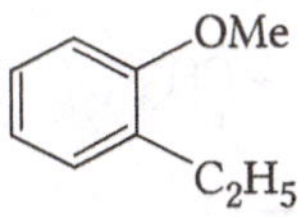

(i)

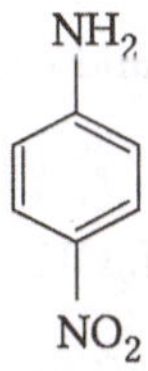

(ii)

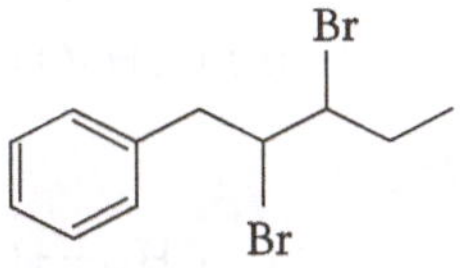

(iii)

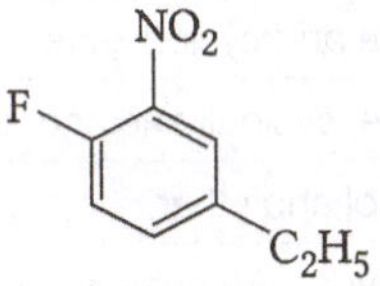

(iv)

Isomerism

Compounds having the same molecular formula but different properties such as physical and chemical properties or spatial arrangement are called **isomers** and the phenomenon is called **isomerism.**

Types of Isomerism

The different types of isomerism are shown in the following flow chart.

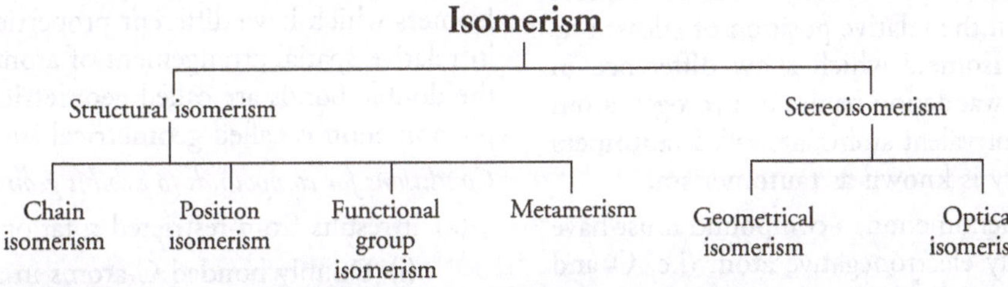

1. Structural Isomerism

Compounds having same molecular formula but different structural formula (i.e. way of linking) are called structural isomers and this phenomenon is called structural isomerism. It is also called constitutional isomerism and further classified into following sub-types.

(i) **Chain Isomerism** Two or more compounds that have same molecular formula but different carbon skeleton are called **chain or nuclear isomers** and this phenomenon is called **chain isomerism.** e.g. the chain isomers for C_5H_{12} are as follows:

$$\underset{\text{Pentane}}{CH_3CH_2CH_2CH_2CH_3}\ ; \quad \underset{\substack{\textit{Iso}\text{-pentane} \\ \text{(2-methylbutane)}}}{CH_3-\overset{\overset{\large CH_3}{|}}{C}HCH_2CH_3}$$

$$\underset{\substack{\textit{Neo}\text{-pentane} \\ \text{(2,2-dimethylpropane)}}}{CH_3-\overset{\overset{\large CH_3}{|}}{\underset{\underset{\large CH_3}{|}}{C}}-CH_3}$$

Note Only alkanes having atleast 4 carbon atoms can exhibit chain isomerism.

(ii) **Position Isomerism** It arises due to difference in the position of substituent atom or functional group on the carbon skeleton. Such compounds are called **position isomers.** e.g. The two isomers are possible for the molecular formula C_4H_8.

$$\underset{\text{But-1-ene}}{CH_3-CH_2-CH{=}CH_2}\ ,$$

$$\underset{\text{But-2-ene}}{CH_3-CH{=}CH-CH_3}$$

(iii) **Functional Group Isomerism** Compounds having the same molecular formula but different functional groups are called **functional group isomers** and the phenomenon is known as **functional group isomerism.** e.g. Two functional group isomers are possible for the molecular formula C_3H_6O.

$$\underset{\text{Propanone}}{CH_3-\overset{\overset{\large O}{\|}}{C}-CH_3}\ ; \quad \underset{\text{Propanal}}{CH_3-CH_2-\overset{\overset{\large H}{|}}{C}{=}O}$$

Compounds having the same general formula also exhibit functional isomerism. This is illustrated in the given table:

General Formula for Different Functional Groups

S. No.	General formula	Functional isomers
1.	C_nH_{2n}	Alkene and cycloalkane
2.	C_nH_{2n-2}	Alkyne, cycloalkene and alkadiene
3.	$C_nH_{2n+2}O$	Alcohol and ether
4.	$C_nH_{2n}O$	Aldehydes, ketones and epoxides
5.	$C_nH_{2n}O_2$	Acids, ester, hydroxy aldehyde and hydroxy ketone.

(iv) **Metamerism** If two or more compounds have the same functional group but the alkyl group attached to the same functional group are different then the phenomenon is called **metamerism** and the compounds are called **metamers**. e.g. $C_4H_{10}O$ can be represented by following two formula $CH_3OC_3H_7$ (methoxypropane) and $C_2H_5OC_2H_5$ (ethoxyethane).

(v) **Tautomerism** It is a special type of functional isomerism in which two isomers are readily inter convertible and differs only in the relative position of atleast one atomic nucleus. Isomers which show difference in properties due to wandering nature of hydrogen atom in between two polyvalent atoms, are called **tautomers** and their property is known as **tautomerism.**

To exhibit this phenomenon, a compound must have at least one highly electronegative atom (i.e. O and N) bonded with multiple bonds and at least one acidic hydrogen present on α-carbon atom.

Keto-enol Tautomerism is the best example of this isomerism. It is shown by aldehyde or ketone with α-hydrogen and can be shown in its simplest form as:

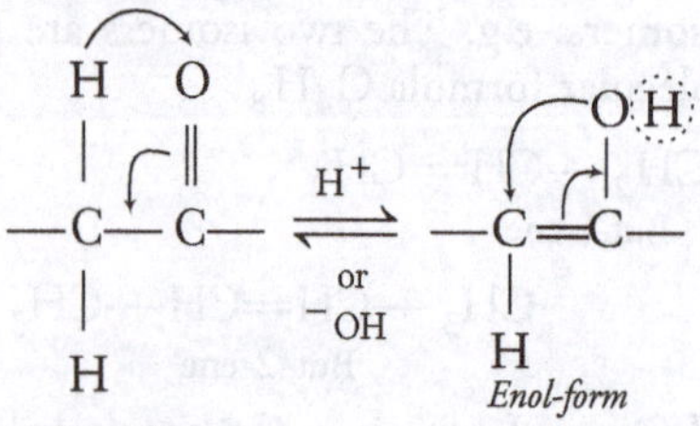

Keto-form *Enol-form*

Keto-enol tautomerism in acetone

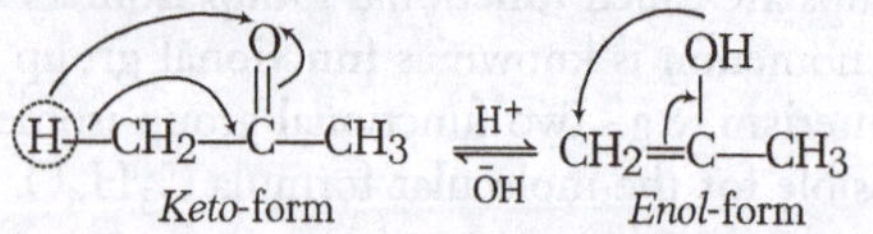

Keto-form *Enol*-form

(vi) **Ring Chain Isomerism** It is also a specialised functional isomerism in which the open chain structure and cyclic structure are isomeric with each other. The phenomenon is called **ring chain isomerism.**

e.g.

(i) C_3H_6 (Alkene and cycloalkane)

$CH_3—CH=CH_2$ and 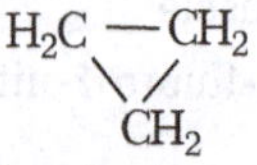

(ii) C_3H_6O (Alkenol and cyclic ether)

$CH_2=CH—CH_2OH$ and 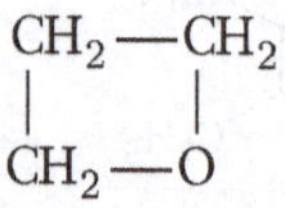

2. Stereoisomerism

Compounds having the same molecular formula (constitution) and the same connectivity of atoms in their molecules, but different 3-dimensional orientation of their atoms in space. are called **stereoisomers** and this phenomenon is called **stereoisomerism.**

Stereoisomerism is of following two types:

(i) Geometrical Isomerism

Isomers which have different properties due to difference in relative spatial arrangement of atoms or groups around the double bonds are called **geometrical isomers** and phenomenon is called **geometrical isomerism.**

Conditions for compounds to exhibit geometrical isomerism:

(a) It results from restricted rotation around.
 (i) Doubly bonded C-atoms in alkenes.
 (ii) Singly bonded C-atoms in cyclic compounds.
 (iii) Doubly bonded C and N-atoms in oximes.
 (iv) Doubly bonded N-atoms in diazo compounds.

(b) Both the atoms of above written bonds should contain different substituents.

e.g. But-2-ene have two geometrical isomers:

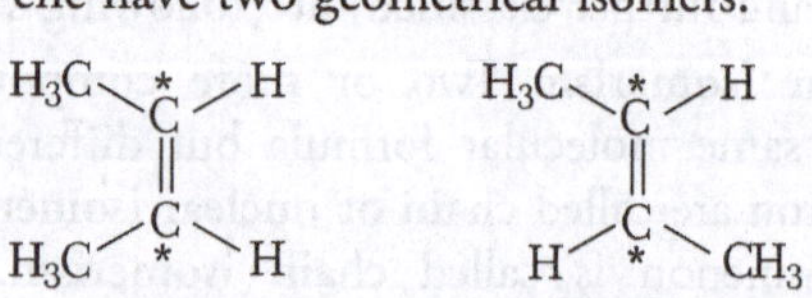

Cis-but-2-ene *Trans*-but-2-ene

1,2-dimethylcyclopropane exists in two isomeric forms:

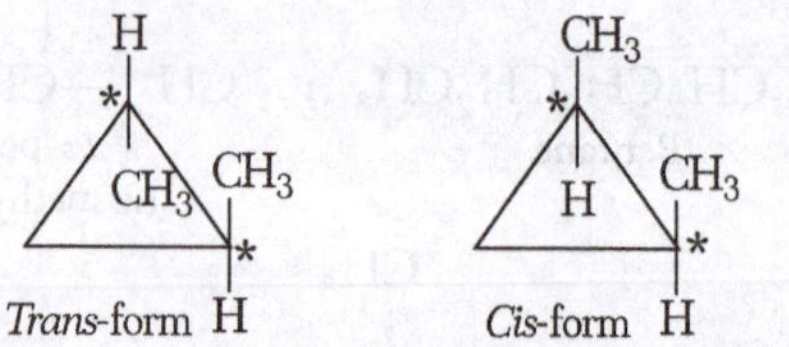

Trans-form *Cis*-form

Note The forms in which similar groups are present on the same side of double bond are called *cis*-forms (*cis* = same side) and the forms in which similar groups are present on the different sides are called *trans*-forms.

Aldoxime have two geometrical isomers:

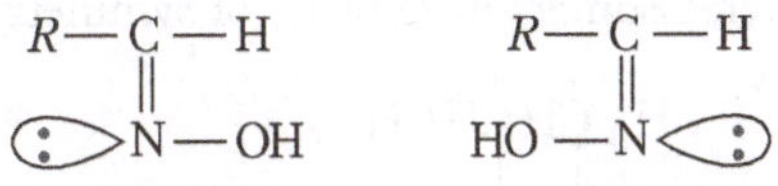

Syn-oxime   *Anti*-oxime

Properties of Geometrical Isomers (*cis-trans* isomers)

Geometrical isomers exhibit following properties:

(i) **Melting points** of *trans* form are greater than the melting point of *cis* form because of symmetrical packing of *trans*-compounds in its crystal lattice.

(ii) **Boiling points** of *cis* form are greater than the boiling point of *trans* form because of steric hinderance and high polarity of *cis*-compound.

(iii) **Solubility** of *cis*-isomer is greater than *trans*-isomer, as molecules of *trans*-isomer are more tightly held in the crystal lattice than the corresponding *cis*-isomer.

(iv) **Stability** *trans*-isomers are more stable than *cis*-isomers because they have greater van der Waals' forces between the groups.

E,Z System of Nomenclature

Cis and *trans*-system of geometrical isomerism cannot work in compounds which do not have identical groups on the sides of double bond. e.g.

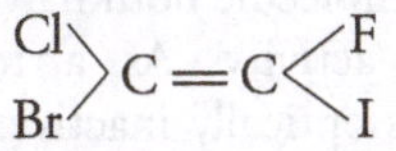

1-bromo-1-chloro-2-fluoro-2-iodoethene

The configuration of these compounds can be specified by using the notations *E* (from German *Entgegen* = opposite) and *Z* (from German *Zusammen* = together).

The rules for assigning the priority are as follows :

(i) The priority can be assigned on the basis of the atomic number of the group attached (in fact the atomic number of that atom of the group is considered which is attached directly to the atom). The group with higher atomic number will get the first priority.

(ii) Now, if two or more atoms are attached to doubly bonded C-atoms with the same atomic number, then the priority is given according to the atomic number of next atom as in the compound written below :

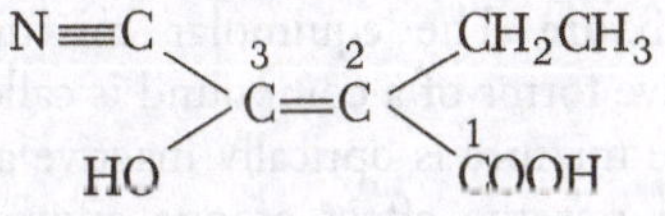

2-ethyl-3-cyano-3-hydroxyprop-2-en-1-oic acid

(ii) Optical Isomerism

Isomers with similar molecular structures and properties but having difference only in their behaviour towards polarised light are called **optical isomers** and phenomenon is known as **optical isomerism.**

Various Terms Used in Optical Isomerism

Before discussing this isomerism in detail, it is better to understand some terms related to optical isomerism.

1. Plane Polarised Light and Optical Activity

A beam of ordinary light consists of electromagnetic waves vibrating in all planes in space. When this light is passed through a **nicol prism,** it becomes plane polarised light, which vibrates only in one plane.

When the solutions of certain organic compounds are placed in the path of plane polarised light, they rotate the path of the light either to left or right, such substances are called as optically active substances. A substance which rotates the plane polarised light to the right is called ***dextro*-rotatory** or ***d*-form** and is indicated by placing a positive (+) sign before the **degree of rotation.** The substance which rotates the plane polarised light towards the left is called ***laevo*-rotatory** or ***l*-form** and a negative (–) sign is placed before the degree of rotation. Such *d* and *l*-forms of compound are called **optical isomers** and the phenomenon is called **optical isomerism.** The angle through which the plane polarised light is rotated can be measured by an instrument called polarimeter.

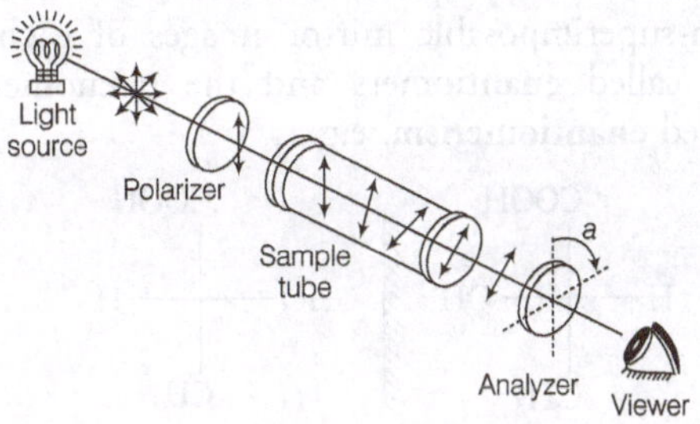

Schematic Diagram of Polarimeter

Conditions for Optical Activity

Following conditions are necessary for optical activity:

(i) Presence of asymmetric carbon.

(ii) Existence of mirror images that are not superimposable.

2. Chiral Molecule

It is the molecule in which carbon is bonded to four different groups. Due to such an arrangement the symmetry of this molecule is completely lost. Word "chiral" in itself is a synonym of asymmetry. Chiral centre is also called stereo centre or stereogenic centre.

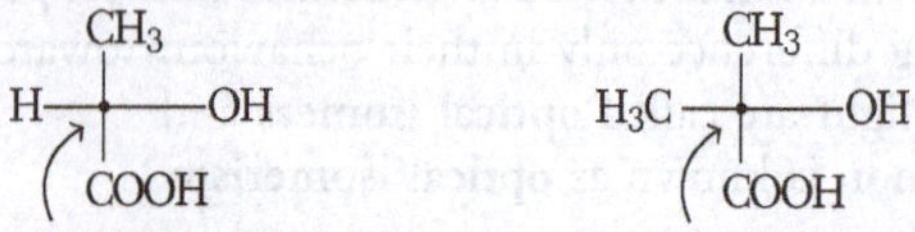

Chiral centre   Achiral centre

3. Specific Rotation [α]

It is the number of degrees of rotation observed in a polarised light of known wavelength at room temperature when it is passed through a 1-decimetre tube containing the compound under study with the extent of 1 g/cc.

$$[\alpha]_\lambda^t = \frac{\alpha}{l \times d} = \frac{\text{Observed rotation (degrees)}}{\text{Length (dm)} \times \text{density (g / cc)}}$$

In $[\alpha]_\lambda^t$, t indicates temperature λ the wavelength of light used.

Types of Optical Isomers

Based on the differential behaviour towards polarised light, optical isomers are broadly categorised into following two types:

Optically Active Isomers

Compounds that have the ability to rotate the plane of polarised light are called **optically active isomers.** *These are as follows :*

(i) **Enantiomers** Optical isomers which are non-superimposable mirror images of each other are called **enantiomers** and the phenomenon is called **enantiomerism.** e.g.

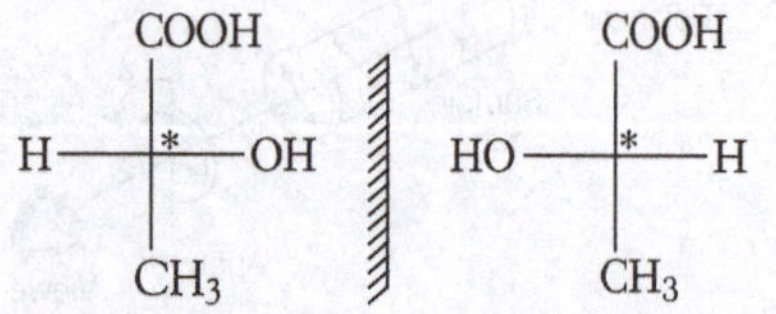

d-(–)-lactic acid   *l*-(+)-lactic acid

Some characteristics of enantiomers are as follows:

- The melting points and boiling points of a pair of enantiomers are identical.
- A pair of enantiomers also have identical densities, refractive index, heats of formation and many other properties.
- A compound and its enantiomer can be distinguished by their effects on polarised light, i.e. they are optically active.

(ii) **Diastereomers** Many molecules have more than one chiral centre. If there are *n* chiral centres, then there are 2^n stereoisomers, number can be less if some of the stereoisomers have plane of symmetry.

e.g. 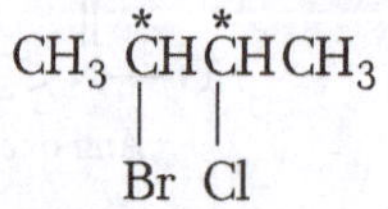

The molecule, has two chiral centres hence, there are four stereoisomers or two pairs of enantiomers.

Some characteristics of diastereomers are as follows:

- The melting and boiling points of a pair of diastereomers are different.
- The chemical properties of diastereomers are different.
- Diastereomers can rotate the path of plane polarised light in the same direction but differ in extent.
- They are optically active and easily separated by fractional crystallisation.

Optically Inactive Isomers

Compounds that do not have the ability to rotate the plane of polarised light are called optically inactive isomers. *These are as follows:*

(i) ***Meso* Compounds** Optical isomers which have the plane of symmetry within the molecule, i.e. the one half of the molecule is dextrorotatory and rest half is laevorotatory are called *meso* compounds.

Thus, within the molecule both halves show equal and opposite optical activity. As a result, the overall molecule becomes optically inactive.

This phenomenon of optical inactivation in which the rotation produced by one half of the molecule is cancelled by its another half is called **internal compensation.** e.g. *meso*-tartaric acid contains two chiral atoms but does not show enantiomerism and is actually optically inactive.

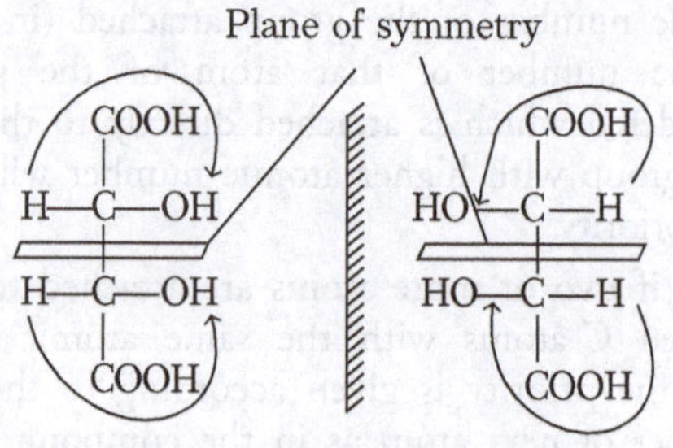

Meso Tartaric acid

(ii) **Racemic Mixture** The equimolar mixture of two optically active forms of a compound is called racemic mixture. The mixture is optically inactive as both the forms cancel out the effect of one another. Such a cancellation effect is called **external compensation.**

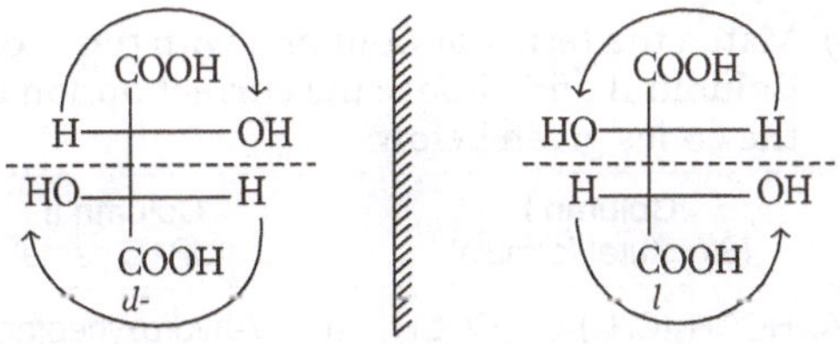

A pair of enantiomers (stereoisomers of tartaric acid).

There are four optical isomers ($2^n = 2^2 = 4$) of tartaric acid, two of which are optically inactive *(meso)* and two are optically active. A mixture of enantiomers in 1 : 1 amount is optically inactive due to external cancellation of optical rotation and is called **racemic mixture.** Separation of enantiomers is called **resolution of a racemic mixture.**

In case of a cyclic compound, the *cis-* isomer will be *meso* compound, thus there will be three optical isomers.

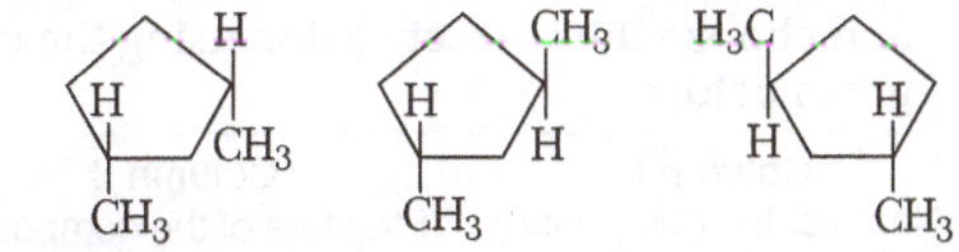

A *meso* compound (*cis*-isomer)

A pair of enantiomers (*trans*-isomer)

Topic Practice 2

Very Short Answer Type Questions

1 Mark

1 Fill in the Blanks

(i) The IUPAC name of $CH_3CH_2CH_2CH_2CH_2CH_3$ is...........

(ii) The IUPAC name of $BrCH_2CH = CH_2$ is...........

(iii) Two or more compounds that have same molecular formula but different carbon skeleton are called...........

(iv) $CH_3\overset{O}{\overset{\|}{C}}CH_3$ and CH_3CH_2CHO exhibit...........isomerism.

2 Objective Type Questions

(i) The structure of *iso*-butyl group in an organic compound is

(a) $(CH_3)_2CH—CH_2—$ (b) $CH_3CH_2—\overset{|}{C}H—CH_3$

(c) $CH_3CH_2CH_2CH_2$ (d) $CH_3—\underset{CH_3}{\overset{CH_3}{\overset{|}{\underset{|}{C}}}}—$

(ii) What is the correct IUPAC name of the given compound?

$CH_3—\underset{CH_3}{\underset{|}{C}H}—CH_2CH_2CH_2\underset{CH_2CH_3}{\underset{|}{C}H}—CH_2CH_2CH_3$

(a) 6-ethyl-2-methylnonane
(b) 2-methyl-6-ethylnonane
(c) 2,6-ethyl methylnonane
(d) None of the above

(iii) Which of the following is not in accordance to IUPAC system?

(a) $Br—CH_2—CH{=}CH_2$
1-bromoprop-2-ene

(b) $CH_3—CH_2—\underset{Br}{\overset{CH_3}{\overset{|}{\underset{|}{C}}}}—CH_2—\underset{CH_3}{\underset{|}{C}H}CH_3$
4-bromo- 2, 4-dimethylhexane

(c) $CH_3—\underset{CH_3}{\underset{|}{C}H}—\underset{C_6H_5}{\underset{|}{C}H}—CH_2—CH_3$
2-methyl-3- phenylpentane

(d) $CH_3—\underset{O}{\underset{\|}{C}}—CH_2—CH_2CH_2COOH$
5-oxohexanoic acid

(iv) What is the correct IUPAC name of the following?

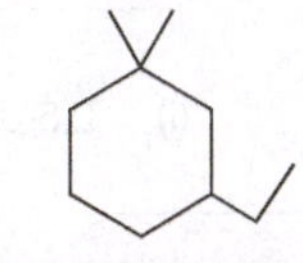

(a) 3-ethyl-1,1-dimethylcyclohexane
(b) 1-ethyl-3,3-dimethylcyclohexane
(c) 1,1-dimethyl-3-ethylcyclohexane
(d) None of the above

(v) The correct IUPAC name of the compound,

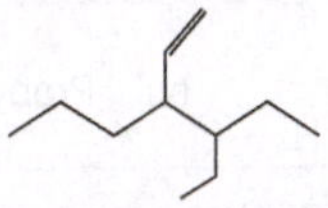

is

(a) 3-(1-ethyl propyl) hex-1-ene
(b) 4-ethyl-3-propylhex-1-ene
(c) 3-ethyl-4-ethenylheptane
(d) 3-ethyl-4-propylhex-5-ene

(vi) Write the correct IUPAC name of the following :

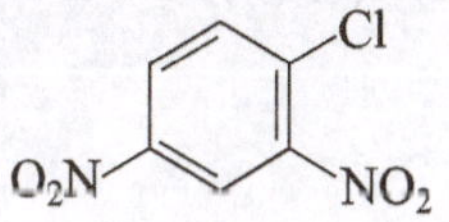

(a) 1-chloro-2, 4-dinitrobenzene
(b) 6-chloro-1, 3-dinitrobenzene
(c) 1-chloro-4, 6-dinitrobenzene
(d) 2-chloro-1, 5-dinitrobenzene

(vii) How many chain isomers are given by the compound, C_5H_{12}?
(a) Three (b) Two (c) Four (d) Only one

(viii) The following compounds show.

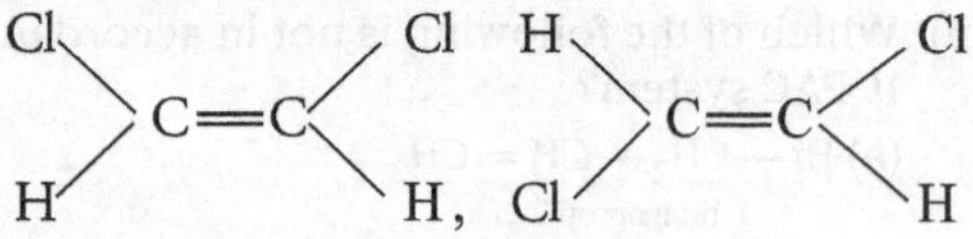

(a) configuration isomerism
(b) conformational isomerism
(c) structural isomerism
(d) geometrical isomerism

(ix) Which of the following compounds will exhibit geometrical isomerism?
(a) 1-phenyl-2-butene
(b) 3-phenyl-1-butene
(c) 2-phenyl-1-butene
(d) 1, 1-diphenyl-1-propane

3. Matching Type Questions

(i) Match terms of Column I with Column II and choose the correct option using the codes given below:

	Column I (Bond-line formula for the molecule)		Column II (Name of the molecule)
A.	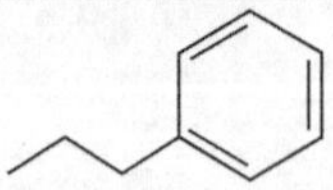	(i)	2,5-dimethylheptane
B.	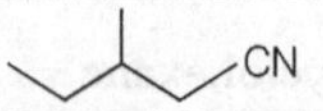	(ii)	3-methylpentanenitrile
C.	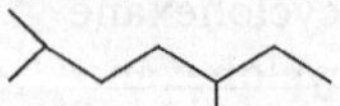	(iii)	3-bromo-3-chloroheptane
D.	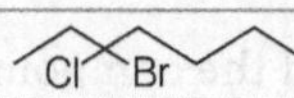	(iv)	4-chlorobutanal
E.	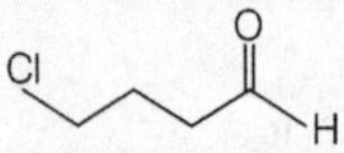	(v)	Propylbenzene

Codes

	A	B	C	D	E
(a)	(v)	(ii)	(i)	(iii)	(iv)
(b)	(i)	(ii)	(iii)	(iv)	(v)
(c)	(ii)	(iii)	(i)	(v)	(iv)
(d)	(iii)	(i)	(v)	(ii)	(iv)

(ii) Match the terms of Column I with those of Column II and choose the correct option using the codes given below:

Column I (Structural formula)		Column II (IUPAC name)
A. $HOCH_2(CH_2)_3CH_2COCH_3$	(i)	7-hydroxyheptan-2-one
B. $BrCH_2CH=CH_2$	(ii)	3-bromoprop-1-ene
C. $CH_2(OH)CH_2(OH)$	(iii)	Ethane-1,2-diol
D. $CH_2=CH-CH=CH_2$	(iv)	But-1,3-diene

Codes

	A	B	C	D		A	B	C	D
(a)	(iv)	(iii)	(ii)	(i)	(b)	(iii)	(i)	(iv)	(ii)
(c)	(i)	(ii)	(iii)	(iv)	(d)	(ii)	(iv)	(i)	(iii)

(iii) Match the terms of Column I with Column II and choose the correct option using the codes given below.

Column I (Name of the compound)		Column II (Structure of the compound)
A. 1,2-dibromobenzene	(i)	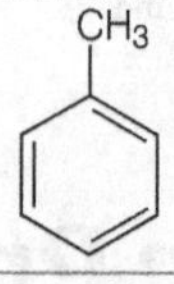
B. Nitrobenzene	(ii)	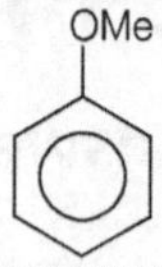
C. Methoxybenzene (Anisole)	(iii)	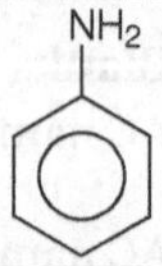
D. Methylbenzene (Toluene)	(iv)	
E. Aminobenzene (Aniline)	(v)	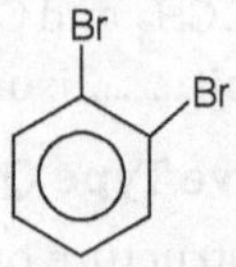

Codes

	A	B	C	D	E		A	B	C	D	E
(a)	(i)	(ii)	(iii)	(iv)	(v)	(b)	(iv)	(iii)	(v)	(ii)	(i)
(c)	(iii)	(iv)	(i)	(ii)	(v)	(d)	(v)	(iv)	(ii)	(i)	(iii)

(iv) Match the items of Column I with the Column II and choose the correct option using the codes given below:

Column I (Structure of Compounds)	Column II (Type of isomerism)
A. $CH_3CH_2CH_2CH_2CH_3$ and $CH_3-CH(CH_3)-CH_2CH_3$	(i) Chain isomerism
B. $CH_3CH_2CH_2OH$ and $CH_3-CH(OH)-CH_3$	(ii) Position isomerism
C. $CH_3-C(=O)-CH_3$ and $CH_3-CH_2-C(H)=O$	(iii) Metamerism
D. $CH_3OC_3H_7$ and $C_2H_5OC_2H_5$	(iv) Functional group isomerism

Codes

	A	B	C	D		A	B	C	D
(a)	(i)	(ii)	(iii)	(iv)	(b)	(ii)	(iii)	(i)	(iv)
(c)	(iv)	(i)	(ii)	(iii)	(d)	(i)	(ii)	(iv)	(iii)

Very Short Answer Type Questions

2 Marks

4 What are primary and secondary suffixes as applied to IUPAC nomenclature?

5 Give the IUPAC name of the following compound

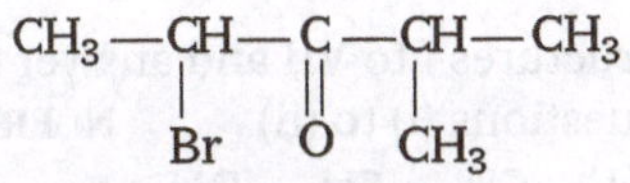

6 Draw all position isomers of an alcohol with molecular formula, C_3H_8O.

Short Answer Type I Questions (2 Marks)

7 Give the common name of :

(i) methanol (ii) ethanol

(iii) ethoxyethane (iv) ethanoic acid

(v) 1,4-dimethyl benzene

8 Which of the following represents the correct IUPAC name for the compounds concerned?

(i) 2,2-dimethylpentane or 2-dimethylpentane

(ii) 2,4,7-trimethyloctane or 2,5,7-trimethyloctane

(iii) 2-choloro-4-methylpentane or 4-chloro-2-methylpentane **NCERT Textbook**

(iv) But -3-yn-1-ol or But-4-ol-1-yne

9 Write structural formulae for compounds named as

(i) 1-bromoheptane

(ii) 5-bromoheptanoic acid

10 Name the compounds whose line formulae are given below.

(i) 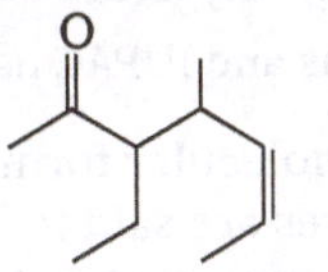

(ii) 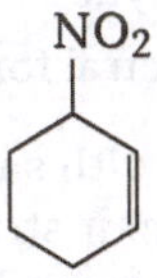

11 Which of the following selected chains is correct to name the given compound according to IUPAC system?

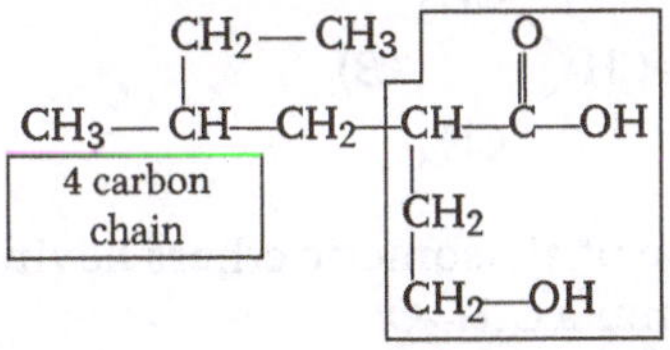

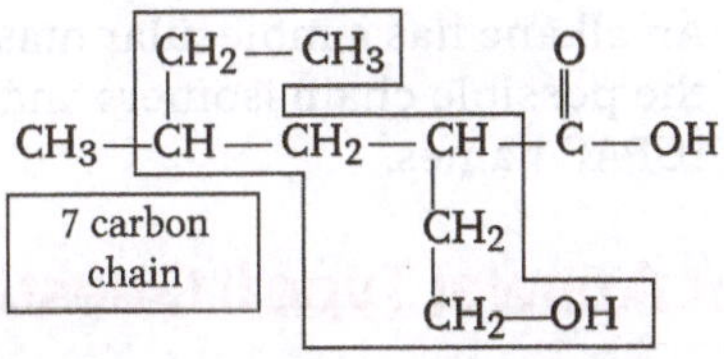

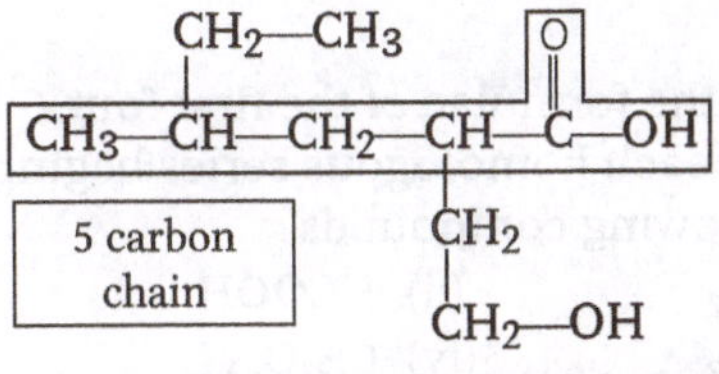

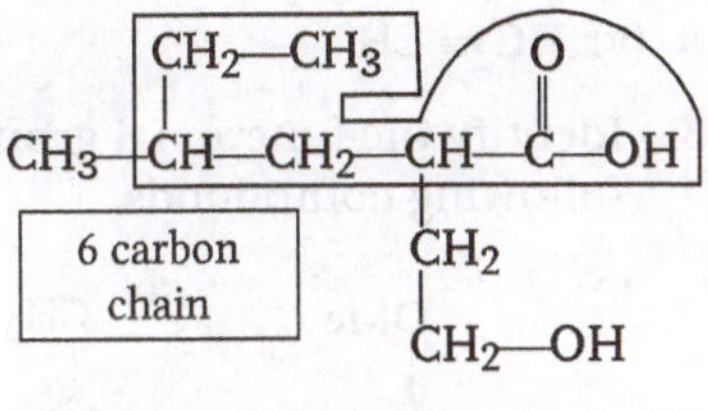

12 Give the IUPAC nomenclature of the following compounds:

(i)

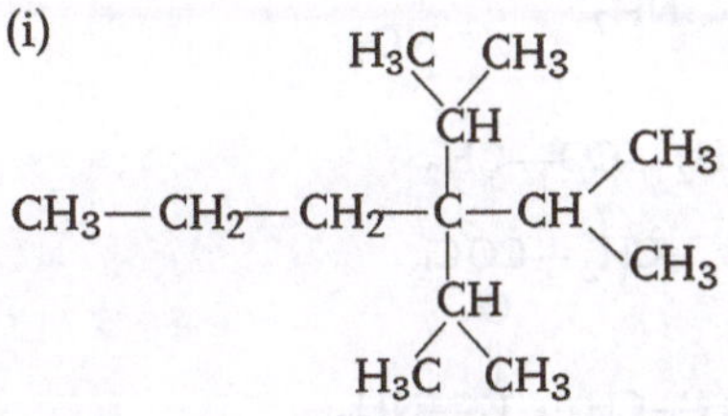

(ii) 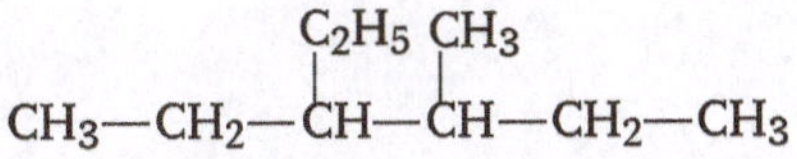

[2]

13 The following organic compounds are popularly known by their common names:

(a) *neo*-Pentane (b) Acetone
(c) Vinyl-Chloride (d) *tert*-Amyl alcohol
(e) *iso-Butyl* bromide (f) Allyl alcohol
(g) Formaldehyde (h) Glycerol

Write the structral formulas and IUPAC names.

14 Compounds with same molecular formula but differing in their structures are said to be structural isomers. What type of structural isomerism is shown by

$CH_3—S—CH_2—CH_2—CH_3$ (*A*)

and $CH_3—S—CH(CH_3)_2$ (*B*)

15 Draw structure of all isomeric ethers having molecular formula $C_5H_{12}O$.

16 An alkane has a molecular mass of 72. Draw all the possible chain isomers and write their IUPAC names.

Short Answer Type II Questions

3 Marks

17 Write down the formulae of the first four members of each homologous series beginning with the following compounds.

(i) $CH_2 = CH_2$ (ii) HCOOH
(iii) CH_3COCH_3 (iv) CH_3OH
(v) $HC \equiv CH$

18 Identify the functional groups present in the following compounds.

(i) 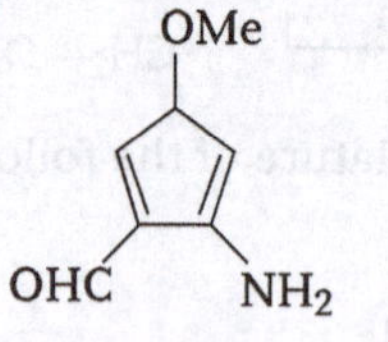

(ii) $CH_2=CH—COOH$

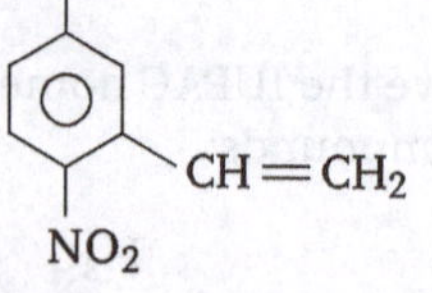

(iii) $CH_3—CH_2—CO—CH_2—CH_2—COCl$

(iv) $CH_2=CH—CH_2—C(=O)—NH_2$

19 Give condensed and bond line structural formulae and identify the functional group(s) present, if any, for

(i) 2,2,4-trimethylpentane
(ii) 2-hydroxy-1,2,3- propanetricarboxylic acid
(iii) Hexanedial. **NCERT Textbook**

20 Give IUPAC names of the following structures.

(i) 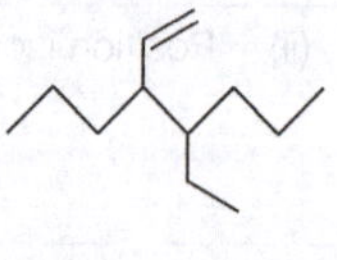

(ii) 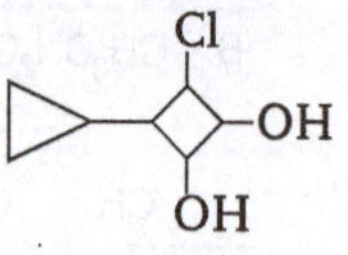

(iii) 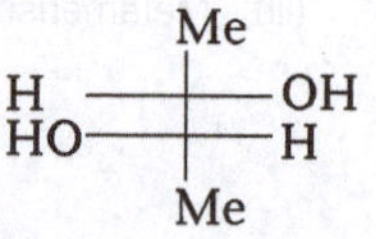

21 Give the IUPAC names of the following compounds :

(i) 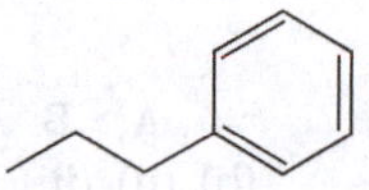

(ii) 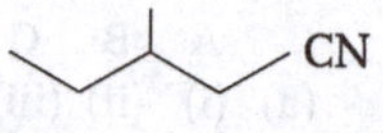

(iii) 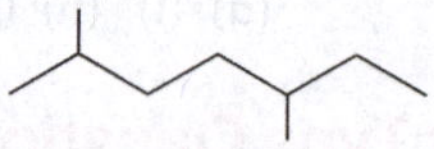

(iv) 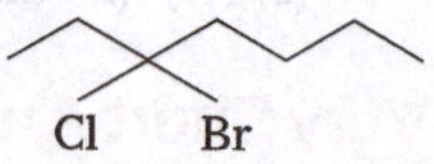

(v) 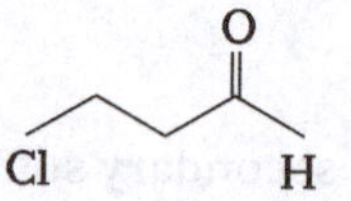

(vi) Cl_2CHCH_2OH

22 Write structural formulae for all the isomeric amines with molecular formula $C_4H_{11}N$.

23 Consider structures I to VII and answer the following questions (i) to (ii). **NCERT Exemplar**

I. $CH_3—CH_2—CH_2—CH_2—OH$

II. $CH_3—CH_2—CH(OH)—CH_3$

III. $CH_3—C(CH_3)(OH)—CH_3$

IV. $CH_3—CH(CH_3)—CH_2—OH$

V. $CH_3—CH_2—O—CH_2—CH_3$

VI. $CH_3—O—CH_2—CH_2—CH_3$

VII. $CH_3—O—CH(CH_3)—CH_3$

(i) Which of the above compounds form pairs of metamers?
(ii) Identify the pairs of compounds which are functional group isomers.
(iii) Identify the pairs of compounds that represent position isomerism.
(iv) Identify the pairs of compounds that represent chain isomerism.

Hints & Solutions

1. (i) hexane (ii) 3-bromoprop-1-ene
(iii) chain isomers (iv) functional group

2. (i) (*a*) '*Iso*' means one Me group is present in side chain. Hence, the structure of *iso*-butyl group is

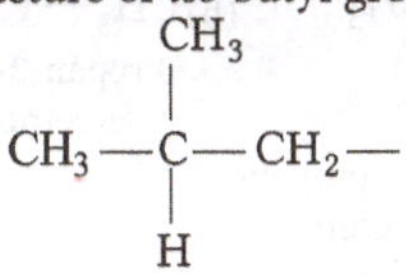

'yl' suffix is used to represent one —H less than the parent hydrocarbon.

(ii) (*a*) The correct IUPAC name of the given compound is

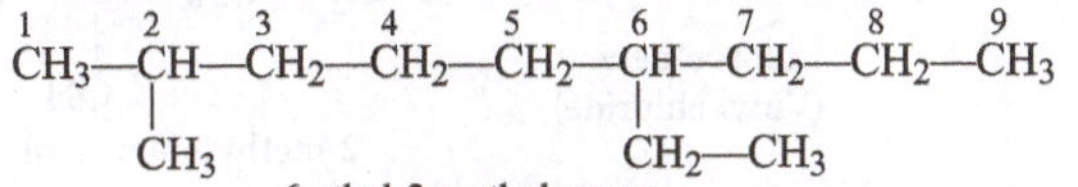

6-ethyl-2-methylnonane
(lowest locant rule and alphabetical order rule is followed.)

(iii) (*a*) In IUPAC system of nomenclature, preference is given to multiple bond than halogen substituent, so the correct name of $Br—\overset{3}{C}H_2—\overset{2}{C}H=\overset{1}{C}H_2$ is 3-bromoprop-1-ene

(iv) (*a*) A saturated monocyclic compound is named by prefixing 'cyclo' to the corresponding straight chain alkane. If side chain are present, then the general rules of naming are applied. Thus, the correct IUPAC name of the following structure is

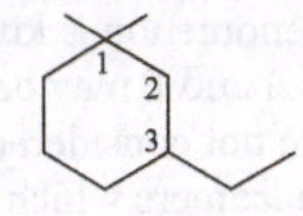

3-ethyl-1,1-dimethylcyclohexane
(Substituent name in alphabetical order)

(v) (*a*)

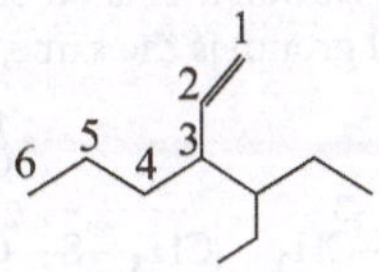

3-(1-ethylpropyl)hex-1-ene

(vi) (*a*) The correct IUPAC name of

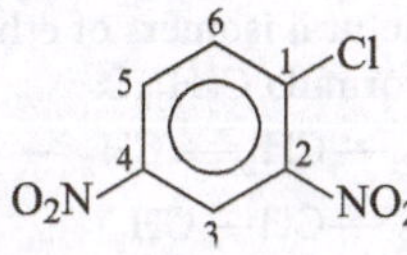

is

1-chloro-2,4-dinitrobenzene (not 4-chloro-1,3-dinitrobenzene).

(vii) Chain isomers for C_5H_{12} represents three compounds:
(a) $CH_3CH_2CH_2CH_2CH_3$: Pentane

(b) 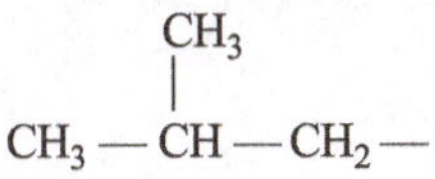 *Iso*-pentane (2-methylbutane)

(c) 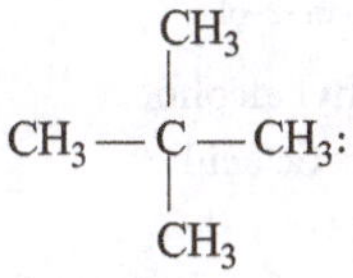 *Neo*-pentane (2,2-dimethylpropane)

(viii) (d)

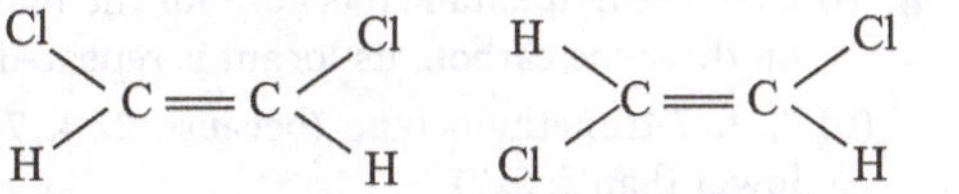

The given compounds show geometrical isomerism and exist as *cis*-and *trans*-isomers.

(ix) (*a*) Alkene in which different groups are attached with the double bonded C-atoms, exhibits geometrical isomerism.

1-phenyl-2-but-2-ene

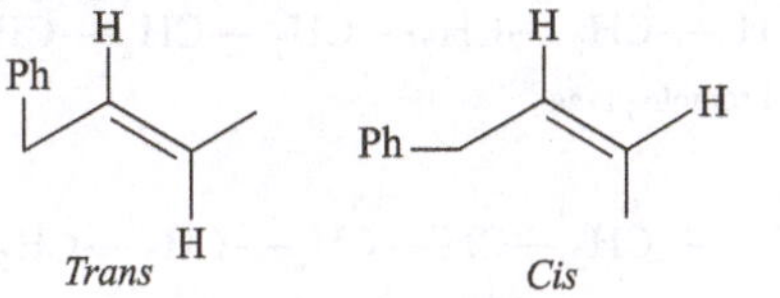

Trans *Cis*

It will show geometrical isomerism.

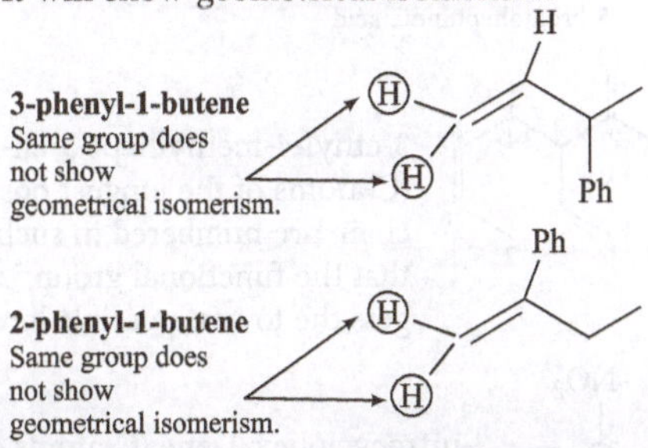

1, 1-diphenyl-1-propene does not show geometrical isomerism.

3. (i) (a) A → (v), B → (ii), C → (i), D → (iii), E → (iv)

(ii) (c) $HOCH_2(CH_2)_3CH_2COCH_3$ will be named as 7-hydroxyheptan-2-one and not as 2-oxoheptan-7-ol. Similarly, $Br\,CH_2\,CH=CH_2$ is named as 3-bromoprop- 1-ene and not 1-bromoprop-1-ene.
If more than one functional group of the same type are present, their number is indicated by adding di, tri etc., before the class suffix. In such cases the full name of the parent alkane is written before the class suffix. e.g. $CH_2(OH)\,CH_2OH$ is named as ethane-1, 2-diol. $CH_2=CH—CH=CH_2$ is named as but-1,3-diene.

(iii) (*d*) A → (v), B → (iv), C → (ii), D → (i), E → (iii)
(iv) (*d*) A → (i), B → (ii), C → (iv), D → (iii)

4. The primary suffix indicates whether the carbon chain is saturated or unsaturated while the secondary suffix indicates the functional group present in the molecule.

5. 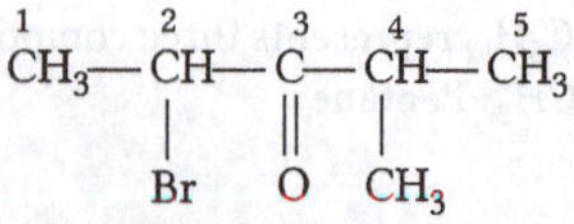

2-bromo-4-methylpentan-3-one

6. $CH_3CH_2CH_2OH$ and $CH_3CH(OH)CH_3$

Propan-1-ol   Propan-2-ol

7. (i) methyl alcohol (ii) ethyl alcohol
(iii) diethyl ether (iv) acetic acid
(v) *p*-xylene **[2]**

8. (i) 2,2-dimethylpentane (because for the two alkyl groups on the same carbon, its locant is repeated twice).

(ii) 2, 4, 7-trimethyloctane (because 2, 4, 7-locant set is lower than 2, 5, 7).

(iii) 2-chloro-4-methylpentane. (Alphabetical order of substituents) (iv) But-3-yn-1-ol (because lower locant for the principal functional group, i.e. alcohol). **[2]**

9. (i)

$\overset{7}{C}H_3-\overset{6}{C}H_2-\overset{5}{C}H_2-\overset{4}{C}H_2-\overset{3}{C}H_2-\overset{2}{C}H_2-\overset{1}{C}H_2-Br$

1-bromoheptane **[1]**

(ii) 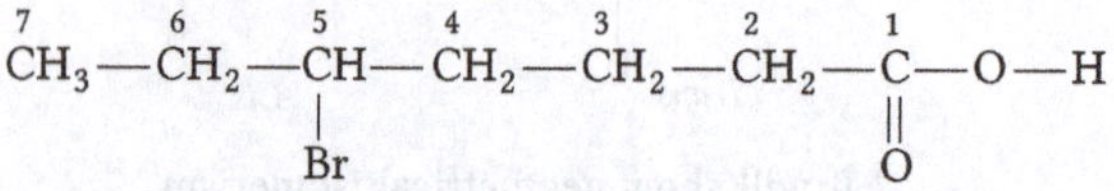

5-bromoheptanoic acid **[1]**

10. (i) 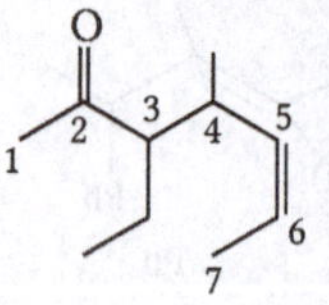

3-ethyl-4-methylhept-5-en-2-one (C-atoms of the longest possible chain are numbered in such a way that the functional group, $>C{=}O$, gets the lowest possible locant).

(ii) 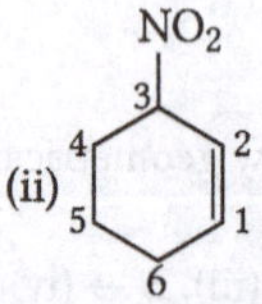

3-nitrocyclohex-1-ene (C-atoms of the ring are numbered in such a manner that double bond gets the lowest possible locant followed by the $-NO_2$ group).

11. According to IUPAC, the longest carbon chain having maximum number of functional group is being selected.

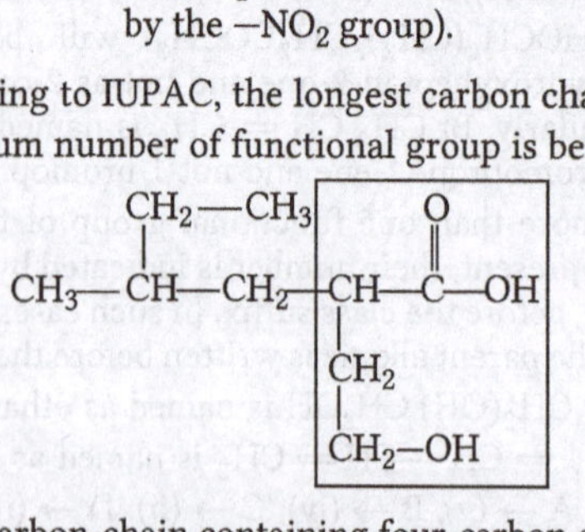

Thus, carbon-chain containing four-carbon atoms which also includes both functional group will be selected. While the other three C-chains are incorrect since none of them contains both the functional groups. **[2]**

12. (i) 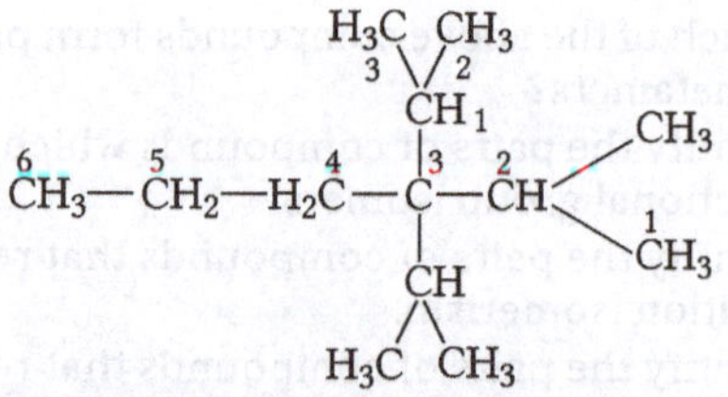

2-methyl - 3,3-*bis*(1-methyl ethyl) hexane

(ii) 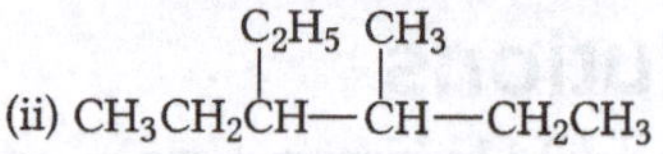

3-ethyl-4-methyl hexane

13. (a) 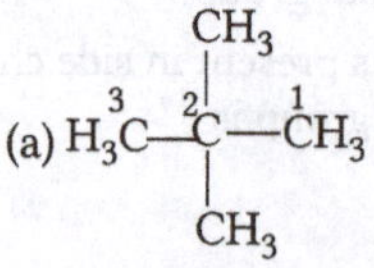

2, 2-dimethylpropane
(*neo*-pentane)

(b) 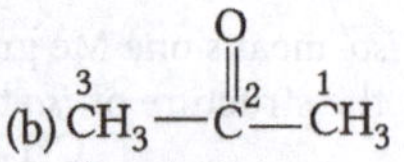

Propan-2-one
(Acetone)

(c) 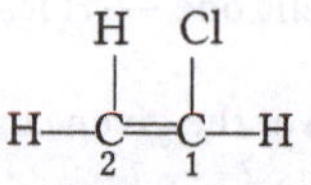

Chloroethene
(Vinyl chloride)

(d) 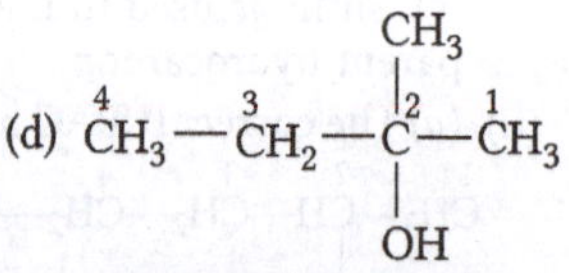

2-methylbutan-2-ol

(e) 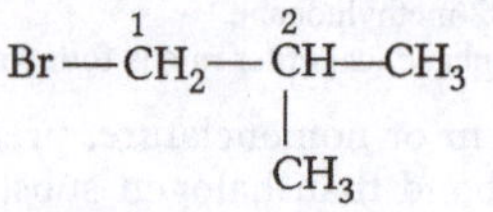

1-bromo-2-methylpropane

(f) $\overset{3}{H_2C}=\overset{2}{C}H\overset{1}{C}H_2OH$

Prop-2-en-1-ol

(g) 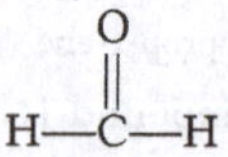

Methanal

(h) 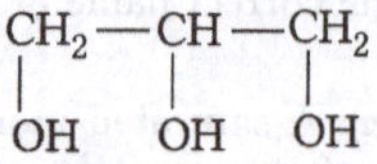

Propan-1,2,3-triol

14. The two isomers which differ in the position of the functional group on the carbon skeleton are called position isomers and the phenomenon is known as **position isomerism**. Thus, *A* and *B* may be regarded as position isomers but they are not considered as metamers since metamers are those isomers which have different number of carbon atoms on either side of the functional group. But here, the number of carbon atoms on either side of sulphur atom (functional group) is the same, i.e. 1 and 3. **[1]**

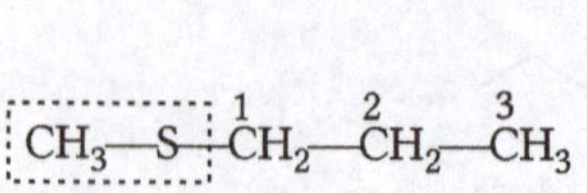

Methyl *n*-propylthioether
(*A*)

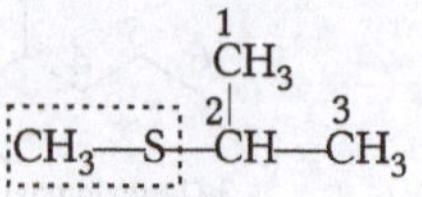

Isopropylthioether
(*B*) **[1]**

15. Six different structural isomers of ethers can be drawn from molecular formula $C_5H_{12}O$:

(i) $CH_3-CH_2-CH_2-CH_2-O-CH_3$

(ii) 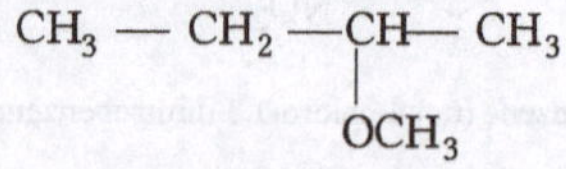

(iii) $CH_3-CH_2-CH_2-OCH_3$
$\quad\quad\quad\quad\quad | $
$\quad\quad\quad\quad CH_3$

$\quad\quad\quad CH_3$
$\quad\quad\quad\ |$
(iv) CH_3-C-CH_3
$\quad\quad\quad\ |$
$\quad\quad\quad OCH_3$

(v) $CH_3-CH_2-CH_2-O-C_2H_5$

(vi) $CH_3-CH-CH_3$
$\quad\quad\quad |$
$\quad\quad\quad OC_2H_5$

16. First of all, we will derive the molecular formula.

Molecular formula of alkane is C_nH_{2n+2}.

$\because$ Molecular mass = 72

$\therefore$ $12n + 2n + 2 = 72$

$n = 5$

The alkane is C_5H_{12}. The possible chain isomers are:

(i) $CH_3-CH_2-CH_2-CH_2-CH_3$
Pentane

(ii) $CH_3-CH-CH_2-CH_3$
$\quad\quad\quad |$
$\quad\quad\quad CH_3$
2-methylbutane

$\quad\quad\quad CH_3$
$\quad\quad\quad |$
(iii) CH_3-C-CH_3
$\quad\quad\quad |$
$\quad\quad\quad CH_3$
2,2-dimethyl propane **[2]**

17. (i) $CH_2=CH_2$, $CH_3CH=CH_2$, $CH_3CH_2CH=CH_2$, $CH_3CH_2CH_2CH=CH_2$

(ii) $HCOOH$, CH_3COOH, CH_3CH_2COOH, $CH_3CH_2CH_2COOH$

(iii) CH_3COCH_3, $CH_3CH_2COCH_3$, $CH_3CH_2CH_2COCH_3$, $CH_3CH_2CH_2CH_2COCH_3$

(iv) CH_3OH, CH_3CH_2OH, $CH_3CH_2CH_2OH$ $CH_3CH_2CH_2CH_2OH$

(v) $HC\equiv CH$, $CH_3C\equiv CH$, $CH_3CH_2C\equiv CH$, $CH_3CH_2CH_2C\equiv CH$ **[3]**

18. (i) Functional groups are $-NH_2$ (amino), $-OMe$ (methoxy) and $-CHO$ (aldehydic).

(ii) Carbon-carbon double bond, $-NO_2$ (nitro) and $-COOH$ (carboxylic).

(iii) $-CO-$ (keto), $-COCl$ (acylchloride).

(iv) $-\overset{|}{C}=\overset{|}{C}-$ (carbon-carbon double bond),

$-\overset{O}{\overset{\|}{C}}-NH_2$ (acetamide). **[3]**

19.

S.No.	Condensed formula	Bond line formula	Functional groups
(i)	$(CH_3)_3CCH_2CH(CH_3)_2$	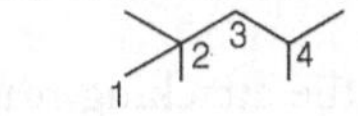	—
(ii)	$HOOCCH_2C(OH)(COOH)CH_2COOH$	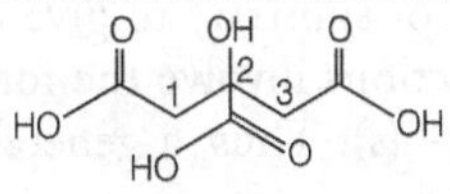	$-\overset{O}{\overset{\|}{C}}-OH$ (carboxyl) and $-OH$ (hydroxyl)
(iii)	$OHC(CH_2)_4CHO$	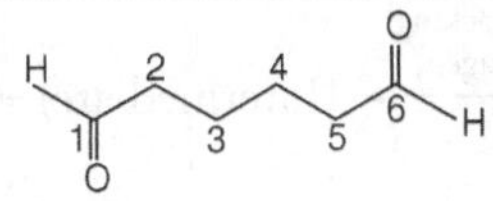	$-\overset{O}{\overset{\|}{C}}-H$ (aldehyde)

20. (i) 4-ethyl-3-propylhept-1-ene.
(ii) 3-chloro-4-cyclopropyl cyclobutane-1,2-diol **[1]**
(iii) Butane-2,3-diol **[1]**

21. (i) Propylbenzene (ii) 3 -methylpentanitrile
(iii) 2,5-dimethylheptane (iv) 3-bromo-3-chloroheptane
(v) 3-chloropropanal (vi) 2,2-dichloroethanol **[6 × 1/2]**

22. All the possible isomeric amines with molecular formula $C_4H_{11}N$ are as follows:

(i) $CH_3-CH_2-CH_2-CH_2-NH_2$

(ii) $CH_3-CH_2-CH-CH_3$
$\quad\quad\quad\quad\quad |$
$\quad\quad\quad\quad\quad NH_2$

(iii) $CH_3-CH-CH_2-NH_2$
$\quad\quad\quad |$
$\quad\quad\quad CH_3$

$\quad\quad\quad CH_3$
$\quad\quad\quad |$
(iv) CH_3-C-NH_2
$\quad\quad\quad |$
$\quad\quad\quad CH_3$

(v) $CH_3-CH_2-CH_2-NH-CH_3$

(vi) $CH_3-CH-NH-CH_3$
$\quad\quad\quad |$
$\quad\quad\quad CH_3$

(vii) $CH_3-CH_2-NH-CH_2-CH_3$

(viii) $CH_3-CH_2-N-CH_3$
$\quad\quad\quad\quad\quad |$
$\quad\quad\quad\quad\quad CH_3$ **[3]**

23. (i) V and VI or VI and VII form a pair of metamers since they differ in the number of carbon atoms on the either side of the functional group, i.e. O-atom.

(ii) I and V, I and VI , I and VII; II and V, II and VI, II and VII ; III and V, II and VI; III and VII; IV and V ; IV and VI and IV and VII are all functional group isomers.

(iii) I and II, III and IV, VI and VII represent position isomerism.

(iv) I and III, I and IV, II and III and II and IV represent chain isomerism. **[3]**

TOPIC 03 Types of Chemical Reactions and their Mechanism

In organic reactions, the attacking reagent reacts with the organic molecule or substrate to give the required product. The reactions involve the formation of one or more intermediate (s). Thus, a general organic reaction can be represented as

$$\text{Organic molecule (Substrate)} \xrightarrow{\text{Attacking reagent}} [\text{Intermediate}] \longrightarrow \text{Product(s)}$$
$$[\text{Intermediate}] \longrightarrow \text{By products}$$

In fact, these reactions involve simultaneous making and breaking of bonds. The energy required for bond breaking is provided by the formation of bonds.

A sequential account of each step, describing details of electron movement, energetics during bond cleavage and bond formation, and the rates of transformation of reactants into products (kinetics) is called the organic reaction mechanism. It helps in predicting the reaction of different organic compounds. It is also helpful in planning the strategy for synthesising different compounds.

In the following sections, we shall learn some of the principles that explain how these reactions take place.

Fission of a Covalent Bond

There are two possible ways through which a covalent bond can get cleaved. These are **homolytic cleavage** and **heterolytic cleavage.**

Heterolytic Cleavage or Heterolysis

If a covalent bond breaks in such a way that both the electrons of shared pair are taken away by one of the bonded atoms, the bond fission is called **heterolytic fission.** e.g.

$$X—Y \xrightarrow{\text{Heterolysis}} X^{+} + Y^{-}$$
(when X is less electronegative than Y)

$$X—Y \xrightarrow{\text{Heterolysis}} X^{-} + Y^{+}$$
(when Y is less electronegative than X)

In the obtained species, one is positively charged and has a sextet (6) of electrons and the other is negatively charged with octet of electrons and atleast one lone pair.

Because of the generation of charged species, reactions involving such cleavage (heterolytic cleavage) are also called **ionic** or **heteropolar** or just **polar reactions.**

e.g. The heterolysis of methylbromide can be represented as

$$H_3C—Br \longrightarrow H_3C^{+} + Br^{-}$$

Carbocation or Carbonium Ion

It is the carbon which has sextet of electrons and a positive charge, then the species is called **carbocation** (earlier called carbonium ion), e.g. CH_3^+ (methyl carbonium ion).

Classification

Depending upon the attachment of one, two or three carbon atoms to the positively charged carbon, the carbocations are categorised as **primary, secondary** or **tertiary carbocations respectively.**

e.g. $CH_3\overset{+}{C}H_2$ Ethyl carbocation 1° ; $(CH_3)_2\overset{+}{C}H$ *Iso*-propyl carbocation 2° ; $(CH_3)_3\overset{+}{C}$ *Tert*-butyl carbocation 3°

Stability

Carbocations are highly reactive and unstable species. As the number of alkyl group attached to positively charged carbon increases, the stability of carbocations increases due to inductive and hyperconjugative effects. (discussed later in this chapter)

Thus, the order of stability of carbocation is

$$\overset{+}{C}H_3 < CH_3\overset{+}{C}H_2 < (CH_3)_2\overset{+}{C}H < (CH_3)_3\overset{+}{C}$$

or methyl carbocation < 1° < 2° < 3°.

Structure

In $\overset{+}{C}H_3$, the carbon atom hybridise to give three sp^2 hybrid orbitals, each of which overlaps with the 1*s* orbital of hydrogen atom to give a (C) sp^3 — H(1*s*) σ bond. Thus, there are in all three σ bonds that are directed towards the corners of a triangle. Thus, its shape is trigonal planar. The remaining orbital (unhybridised orbital) is perpendicular to the molecular plane and is emtpy.

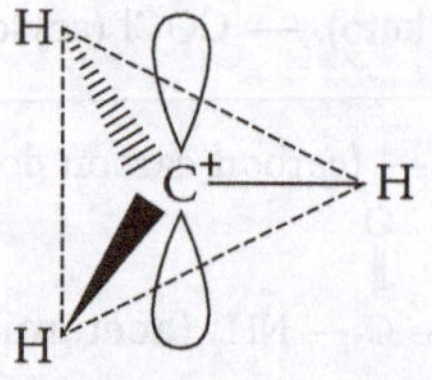

Shape of methyl cation

Example 1 Write structures of various carbocations that can be obtained from 2-methylbutane. Arrange these carbocations in order of increasing stability.

Sol. 2-methyl butane has four different sets of equivalent H atoms.

$$\underset{\displaystyle CH_3}{CH_3—\underset{|}{CH}—CH_2—CH_3}$$

Removal of H-atom from any of C-atom gives four different carbocations.

$$\underset{\displaystyle CH_3}{CH_3 \rightarrow \overset{\beta}{\underset{|}{CH}} \rightarrow \overset{\alpha}{CH_2} \rightarrow \overset{+}{CH_2}} \quad \text{(I) (1°)}$$

$$\underset{\displaystyle CH_3}{CH_3 \rightarrow \underset{\uparrow}{CH} \rightarrow \overset{+}{CH} \leftarrow CH_3} \quad \text{(II) (2°)}$$

$$\underset{\displaystyle CH_3}{CH_3 \rightarrow \underset{\uparrow}{\overset{+}{C}} \leftarrow CH_2 — CH_3} \quad \text{(III) (3°)}$$

$$\underset{\displaystyle CH_3}{\overset{+}{CH_2} \leftarrow \underset{\uparrow}{CH} \leftarrow CH_2 — CH_3} \quad \text{(IV) (1°)}$$

Stability of carbocation decreases in the order 3°> 2°>1°. So, III (3° carbocation) is most stable followed by II (2° carbocation). Out of I and IV (both are 1° carbocation), I has a CH_3 group at β-carbon while II has a CH_3 group at α-carbon. As +*I*-effect decreases with distance, hence IV is more stable than I. Therefore, the overall stability of these four carbocations increases in the order.

I < IV < II < III

Carbanion

The heterolytic cleavage can also give a species in which the carbon atom bears a formal negative charge. It has octet of electrons in its valence shell such a species is called **carbanion**. These are also categorised as 1°, 2° and 3°. The structure of simple carbanions is usually pyramidal with C-atom carrying the negative charge in sp^3 hybrid state and can be seen as

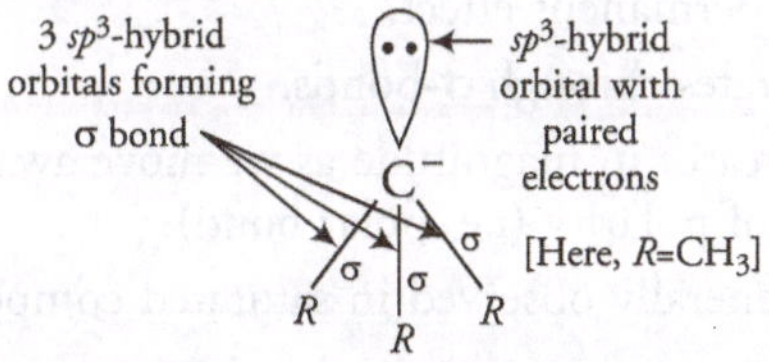

The order of stability of carbanions is as:

$$(C_6H_5)_3\bar{C} > (C_6H_5)_2\bar{C}H > C_6H_5\bar{C}H_2 > \text{allyl} > \bar{C}H_3 > (1° > 2° > 3° \text{ carbanions})$$

Homolytic Cleavage or Homolysis

If a covalent bond breaks in such a way that each atom takes away one electron of shared pair, the fission is called **homolysis** or **homolytic cleavage**. This cleavage involves movement of only one electron, which is represented by **half headed (fish hook)** curved arrow. e.g.

$$R—X \xrightarrow[\text{Light}]{\text{Heat or}} \underset{\text{Alkyl free radical}}{R^\bullet} + X^\bullet$$

Free Radicals

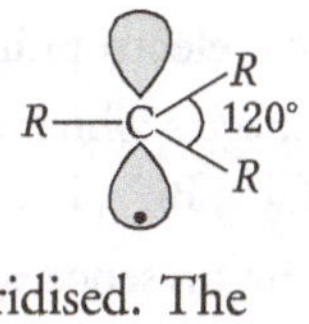

The neutral chemical species, formed by the homolytic cleavage are called **free radicals**. It is a planar species in which the C-atom bearing the odd electron is sp^2-hydridised. The carbon atom lies at the center of the triangle and the three bonds are directed towards the three corners of planar trigonal geometry. The odd electron lies in the unhybridised *p*-orbital perpendicular to the plane.

Classification

Alkyl free radicals are also classified as primary, secondary or tertiary. The relative stability of alkyl free radicals follows the order:

$$(CH_3)_3\dot{C} > (CH_3)_2\dot{C}H > CH_3—\dot{C}H_2 > \dot{C}H_3 > \text{Vinyl}$$

Structure

These species carry a high energy unpaired electron, called the **odd electron**, which makes them highly reactive towards other similar reagents and other non-polar covalent bond. The organic reaction involving homolytic cleavage are called **free radical** or **homopolar** or **non-polar reactions.**

Types of Attacking Reagents

The species which attack on a substrate molecule and bring about the chemical change are called **attacking reagents.** *These are classified into following two categories:*

1. Nucleophiles or Nucleophilic Reagents

An electron rich species having a lone pair of electrons is called a nucleophile (Nu$\mathbf{:}$), i.e. nucleus loving species.

e.g. negatively charged species like, H^-, Cl^-, Br^-, I^-, carbanions, $—\bar{O}H, —\bar{O}R, —\bar{S}R, —CN^-$.

Nucleophiles can also be seen in the form of neutral molecules. Neutral covalent compounds in which central atom has complete octet, has at least one lone pair of electrons and all atoms present on the central atom are not electronegative are called **neutral nucleophile**.

e.g. $H_2\ddot{\underset{\bullet\bullet}{O}}$, $\ddot{N}H_3$, $R\ddot{N}H_2$, $R\ddot{\underset{\bullet\bullet}{O}}H$, $R\ddot{S}H$, etc.

Organic compounds containing carbon-carbon multiple bonds also behave as the nucleophile, e.g. alkene, alkyne, benzene,

$CH_2{=}CH{-}CH{=}CH_2$, $CH_2{=}CH{-}C{\equiv}CH$, etc.

2. Electrophiles or Electrophilic Reagents

An **electrophile** (E^+) is defined as electron deficient species which attacks on electron rich areas such as H^+, Cl^+, Br^+, I^+, NO_2^+, SO_3^+ and carbocations (because of the presence of sextet of electrons).

The electrophiles can also be seen in the form of neutral molecules also, e.g. carbenes ($:CR_2$), nitrenes ($\ddot{N}R$), BF_3 etc. The neutral electrophiles can be:

(i) All neutral covalent compounds in which central atom has incomplete octet. e.g.

$BeCl_2$, BH_3, $ZnCl_2$, AlX_3, FeX_3, $\ddot{C}H_3$, $\ddot{C}X_2$ etc.

(ii) Compounds having functional group like carbonyl group ($>C{=}O$) or alkyl halides (because of the polarity of $C{-}X$ bond).

(iii) All those compounds in which central atom is bonded by two or more than two electronegative atoms, e.g. BX_3, AlX_3, FeX_3, PCl_3, PCl_5, etc.

3. Electron Movement in Organic Reactions

Curved arrows are used to show the movement of electrons in organic reactions. The tail of the arrow shows the point from where the electron pair is shifted and the head of the arrow indicates the point to which the electron pair may move. The shifting of electron pairs in some chemical reactions is shown below:

(i) $=Y{-} \leftrightarrow {-}Y{=}$ from π bond to adjacent bond position.

(ii) $=Y{-} \leftrightarrow {-}\ddot{Y}{-}$ from π bond to adjacent atom

(iii) $-\ddot{Y}{-} \leftrightarrow {-}Y{=}$ from atom to adjacent bond position.

e.g. $H\ddot{\underset{\bullet\bullet}{O}}: + CH_3{-}\ddot{\underset{\bullet\bullet}{Br}}: \longrightarrow CH_3OH + :\ddot{\underset{\bullet\bullet}{Br}}:$

Electron Displacement in Covalent Bonds

The bonding pairs of the covalent bond in organic compounds undergo electronic displacements on their own or under the influence of an attacking agent. These electronic displacements is because of the presence of atom or substituents group in the molecule, it causes permanent polarisation of the bond. Inductive effect and resonance effect involve such type of electron displacements.

If electronic displacement is due to the presence of attacking reagent, it generates temporary polarisation. Such type of displacement is called electromeric or polarisability effects. Now we will discuss about the above mentioned effects one by one.

Inductive Effect

In a polar covalent bond, the electrons are shifted to the more electronegative atom and hence, a polarity is developed in the bond, e.g. in a chain of carbon atoms having C—Cl bond, the C attached directly to the Cl atom because of its less electronegativity acquires some positive charge (δ^+).

The carbon that is bonded directly to the C^{δ^+} also lose some of its electron density due to more polar C^{δ^+} and hence, acquires somewhat less positive charge (δ^{++}). Similarly the next carbon (C_3) also acquires some positive charge but less than (δ^{++}) as shown below.

$$\overset{\delta\delta\delta^+}{\underset{3}{CH_3}}-\overset{\delta\delta^+}{\underset{2}{CH_2}}\rightarrow\overset{\delta^+}{\underset{1}{CH_2}}\rightarrow\overset{\delta^-}{Cl}$$

This induction of polarity, due to the presence of polar bond in an organic molecule, is called **inductive effect**.

Special features of inductive effect are:

(i) It is a permanent effect.

(ii) It operates through σ-bonds.

(iii) It decreases in magnitude as we move away from the cause of polarity (i.e. polar bond).

(iv) It is generally observed in saturated compounds.

For practical purpose, the inductive effect is ignored after the second C-atom. It must be born in mind that the electron pairs although permanently displaced but they do not leave their valence shells.

Two types of inductive effects are given below:

Positive and Negative Inductive Effects

Atoms or groups having greater electron affinity than hydrogen are said to have $-I$-effect (electron withdrawing group). Some of the $-I$-effect producing groups in decreasing order of inductive effect are:

$$R_3\overset{+}{N} > \overset{+}{N}H_3 > NO_2 > CN > SO_3H > CHO > C{=}O > COOH > —COCl > —COOR > CONH_2 > F > Cl > Br > I > —OH > OR > NH_2 > C_6H_5 > H$$

$-I$ power in decreasing order with respect to H

Similarly, atoms or groups having smaller electron affinity than hydrogen are said to have $+I$ effect (electron releasing or donating).

e.g. The order of $+I$-effect of some groups is as follows:

$$3° \text{ or } (CH_3)_3C— > 2° \text{ or } (CH_3)_2CH > 1° \text{ or } CH_3CH_2 > CH_3$$

Applications of Inductive Effect

The various applications of inductive effect are as follows:

(i) It helps in determining the stability of free radicals, carbocations and carbanions. Following relationship are considered :

(a) Stability of carbocation or free radical

$$\propto +I \text{ power of the group}$$

$$\propto \frac{1}{-I \text{ power of the group}}$$

Thus, the stability order for carbocations and free radicals is 1° < 2° < 3°.

(b) Stability of carbanions $\propto -I$ power of the group

$$\propto \frac{1}{+I \text{ power of the group}}$$

and the stability order for carbanions is

1° > 2° > 3°.

(ii) It helps in determining the strength of acids and bases. Following relationship are considered:

(a) Strength of an acid $\propto K_a \propto \frac{1}{pK_a} \propto$ stability of anion.

As stability of acid anion (or conjugate base)

$$\propto -I \text{ power of group present}$$

$$\propto \frac{1}{+I \text{ power of group present}}$$

Thus, strength of acid increases with the attachment of group showing $-I$-effect and decreases with the attachment of group showing $+I$-effect.

Although, Ph group is $-I$-effect showing group, HCOOH (formic acid) is more acidic than benzoic acid (PhCOOH). This is because of $+R$ (resonance effect) of phenyl (Ph or C_6H_5) group.

(b) Similarly, strength of a base $\propto +I$ power of group present in the base $\propto K_b \propto \frac{1}{pK_b}$

$$\propto \frac{1}{-I \text{ power of group present in the base}}$$

However, this relation is not true for amines in their aqueous solutions as here the basicity is decided by combined effect of inductive effect, solvation effect and steric hindrance.

The basicity order of some of the amines are as follows:

R of amine	Relative basic strength
CH_3—	2° > 1° > 3° > NH_3
C_2H_5—	$R_2NH > R_3N > RNH_2 > NH_3$
Me_2CH—	$RNH_2 > NH_3 > R_2NH > R_3N$
Me_3C—	$NH_3 > RNH_2 > R_2NH > R_3N$

The above two relations can be summarised as:

Acid/Base	Group with + *I*-effect	Group with – *I*-effect
Acidic strength of acid	Decreases	Increases
Basic strength of base	Increases	Decreases

Example 2 Arrange the following compounds in increasing order of acidity.

I. $CH_3CH(Br)CH_2COOH$ II. $CH_3CH_2CH(Br)COOH$

III. $CH_3CH_2C(Br)_2COOH$ IV. $CH_2BrCH_2CH_2COOH$

Sol. As we know inductive effect decreases on moving away from the cause of polarity. Here, Br group is the cause of polarity, so as the distance between Br and COOH increases, inductive effect as well as acidity decreases. Thus, the order of acidity is

III > II > I > IV

⟵ More inductive effect

Remember! As the distance between $+I$ showing group and –COOH increases, acidity increases.

Resonance

When a single Lewis dot structure is unable to explain all the properties of a compound, two or more structures, called the **canonical forms** or **resonating structures**, are drawn to explain all the properties of that compound, then the actual structure of the compound is in between these canonical form and is called the resonance hybrid of these canonical forms. This phenomenon is called **resonance**, e.g. benzene is a resonance hybrid of following two canonical forms.

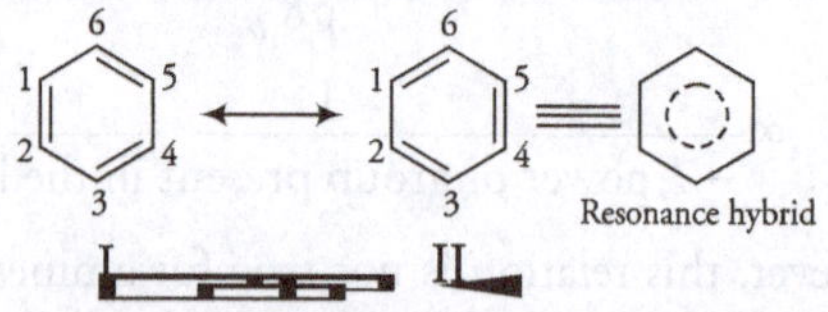

Canonical forms

The resonating structure are hypothetical, i.e. have no real existence. The energy of actual structure (or resonance hybrid is lower than, that of any of the canonical forms. The difference between hybrid and the energy of most stable (lowest energy) canonical form is called the **resonance stabilisation energy** or **resonance energy**. The more the number of important canonical forms, more is the resonance energy. In case of resonating structures of equivalent energy, resonance is of great importance.

Rules for Writing Resonance Structures

While writing resonance structures, the following rules are considered.

(i) The arrangement of atoms must be identical or almost same in every resonance structure.

(ii) The energy content of all the canonical forms must be nearly the same

(iii) Each canonical form must have the same number of unpaired electrons.

Example 3 Draw the resonance structures of the following compounds.

(i) $CH_2 = CH - \ddot{Cl}:$ (ii) $CH_2 = CH - CH = CH_2$

(iii) $CH_2 = CH - \underset{\underset{H}{|}}{C} = O$

Sol.

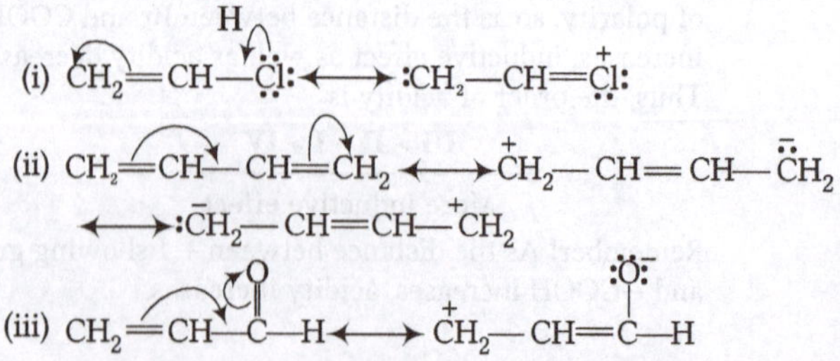

Deciding Stability of Canonical Forms

Among the canonical forms the most stable canonical form can be judged by following rules.

(i) Among all the canonical forms, the form without charges will be the most stable one.

(ii) Among the charged forms:

(a) The structure in which maximum number of covalent bonds are present and octet of all the atoms (except hydrogen which has a duplet) is complete is most stable.

(b) The structure with less charge separation of opposite charge and more dispersal of charge, is more stable than the others.

Example 4 Explain why the following two structures, I and II cannot be the major contributors to the real structure of CH_3COOCH_3. **NCERT Textbook**

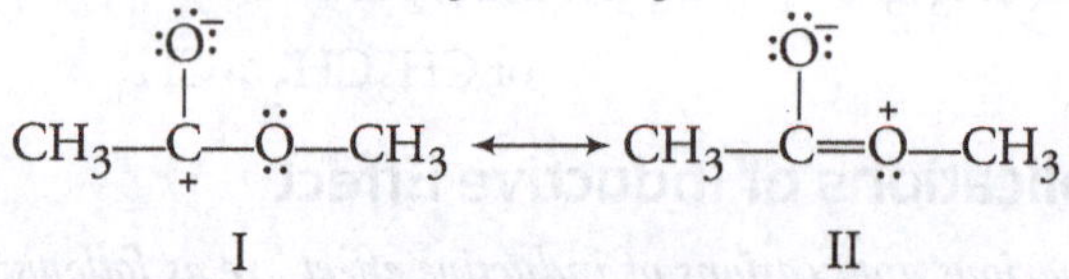

I II

Sol. In both the structures, there is charge separation and in structure I, the octet of one of the carbon is incomplete. That's why these two structures are less important contributors.

Example 5 Which of the following ions is more stable? Use resonance to explain your answer.

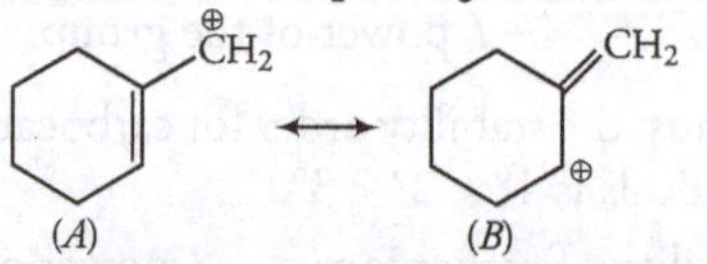

(A) (B)

Sol. Carbocation (*A*) is more stable than carbocation (*B*). Carbocation (*A*) is more planar and, hence stabilised by resonance while carbocation (*B*) is non-planar and hence it does not undergo resonance.

Further, double bond is more stable within the ring in comparison to outside the ring.

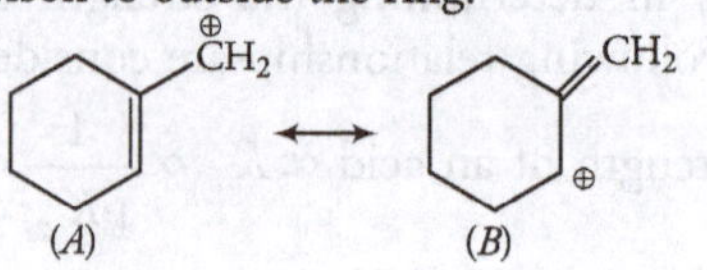

(A) (B)

Resonance Effect

The polarity developed within a molecule due to the interaction of two π-bonds or of a π-bond with the lone pair of electrons present on the adjacent atom is called the resonance effect (*R*). It is a permanent effect.

It is also called the **mesomeric effect** and transmitted through the chain.

Depending upon the direction of transfer of electrons, this effect can be of following two types:

1. Positive Resonance Effect (+ *R*-Effect)

When the electrons move away from the atom or substituent group attached to the conjugated system, the effect is called **positive resonance effect.**

In this effect, electron densities increase at certain places. e.g. groups like halogen, —OH, —O*R*, —OCO*R*, $-NH_2$, — NH*R*, $-NR_2$ show + *R*-effect.

The + *R*-effect of NH_2 group in aniline is shown as:

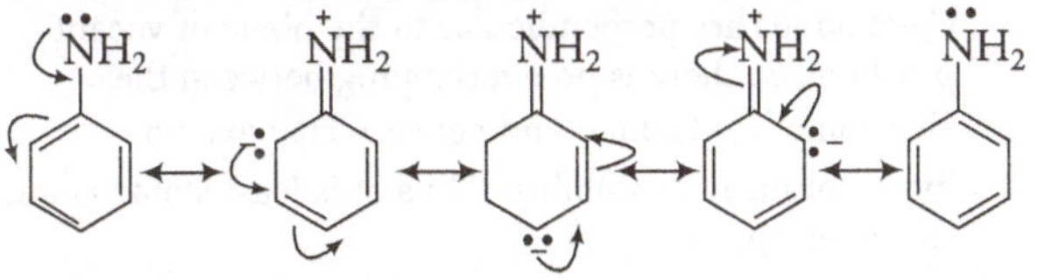

2. Negative Resonance Effect (– *R*-Effect)

When the electrons are transferred towards the atom or substituent group attached to the conjugated system, the effect is called **negative resonance effect.** It results in decrease in density at certain places, i.e. at 2 and 4 or at *o*-and *p*-positions. Thus, now the *meta* (or 3) position becomes electron rich as compared to *o* and *p* -positions and is generally attacked by the electrophile.

—COOH, — CHO, >C=O , —CN and $-NO_2$ show –*R* showing groups effect. The -*R*-effect of $-NO_2$ in nitrobenzene can be represented in the following manner:

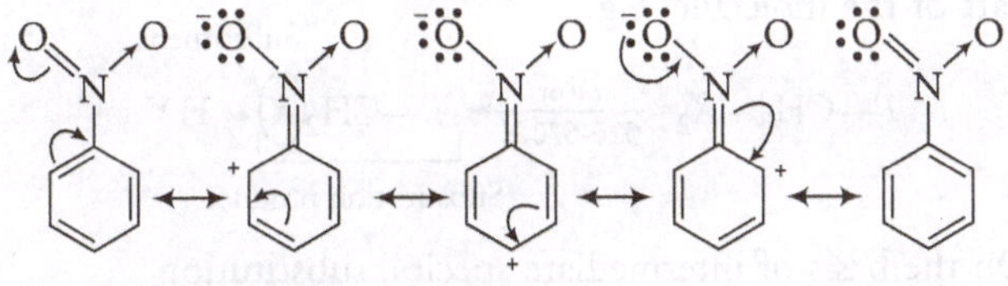

Note When single and double bonds are present alternately either in open chain or in cyclic system, the system is called conjugated system and such system often exhibit abnormal behaviour. In these systems, the π-bonds are delocalised and hence, polarity is developed.

Electromeric Effect (E-effect)

The polarity developed due to complete transfer of a shared pair of π electrons to any of the atoms linked directly to the multiple bond in the presence of an attacking reagent is called the **electromeric effect.** It is a **temporary effect** and operates only in the presence of attacking reagent. It is a strong effect because of the involvement of weak π-bonds.

The electromeric effect is represented by means of a curved arrow beginning at original position of the electron pair and terminating where the pair has migrated. This effect may be classified as + *E* type or – *E* type.

1. Positive Electromeric Effect (+ *E*-Effect)

If the electrons of the π-bond are transferred to that atom of the double bond to which the reagent gets finally attached, it is known as + *E*-effect. e.g.

$$CH_3-CH=CH_2 + H^+ \longrightarrow CH_3-\overset{+}{C}H-CH_3$$

2. Negative Electromeric Effect (– *E*-Effect)

If the electrons of the double bond are transferred to an atom of the double bond other than the one to which the reagent gets finally attached, the effect is known as – *E* effect. e.g.

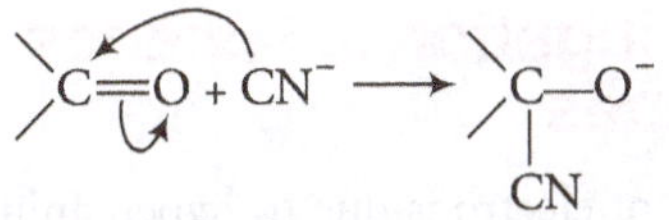

Note
- If π and σ bonds both are present in a compound, the reagent always attacks the π electron cloud first because π electron cloud is always much more exposed than a σ electron cloud.
- If inductive and electromeric effects operate in opposite directions, the electromeric effect predominates over the inductive effect.

Hyperconjugation

The stabilising interaction that involves delocalisation of σ electrons of C—H bond of an alkyl group linked directly to an atom of unsaturated system or to an atom having unshared *p* orbital, is called hyperconjugation.

It is a permanent effect and during it, partial conjugation is developed between the σ electrons of C—H bond and the unsaturated system or the unshared *p*-orbital e.g. The positively charged carbon of ethyl cation ($CH_3CH_2^+$) has empty *p* orbital, with which one of the C—H bonds of the methyl group align in its plane and thus, the electrons of the C—H bonds can be delocalised into the empty *p*-orbital as shown below:

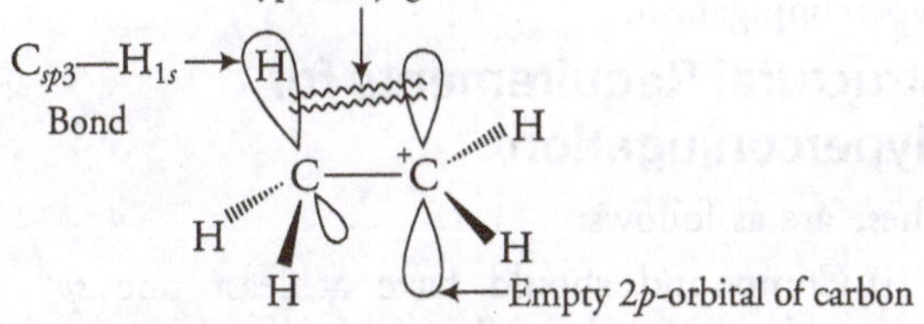

Orbital diagram showing hyperconjugation in ethyl cation

Such type of overlap makes the carbocation more stable because electron density from the adjacent σ bond helps in dispersing the positive charge.

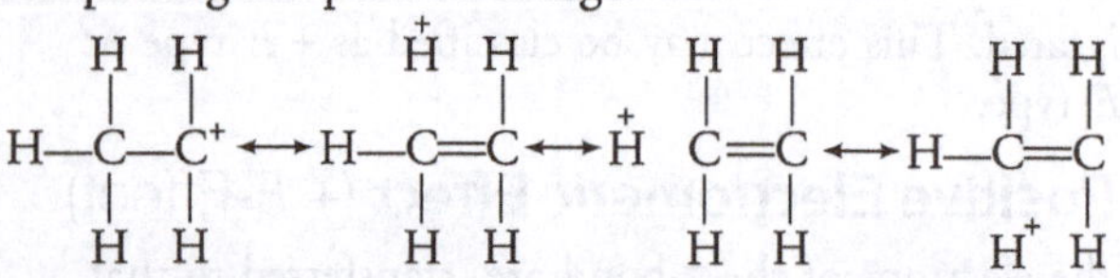

In general, as the number of alkyl groups attached to a positively charged carbon increases, the number of hyperconjugative structures and hence, the stability of cation increases.

Thus, the order of relative stabilities of carbocation is:

$(CH_3)_3C^+$ (9 hyperconjugative structure) > $(CH_3)_2CH^+$ (6 hyperconjugative structure) > $CH_3CH_2^+$ (3 hyperconjugative structure) > CH_3^+

Hyperconjugation in Alkenes and Alkyl Arenes

Delocalisation of electrons due to hyperconjugation in case of alkenes is shown below:

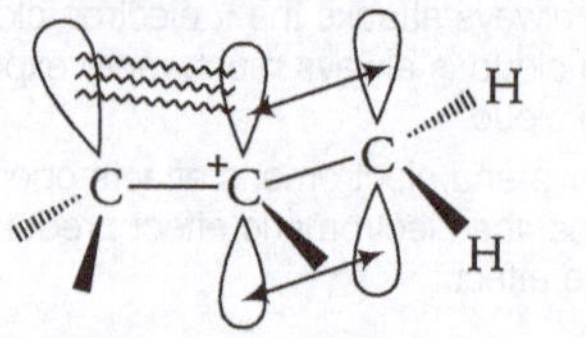

There are several ways to visualise hyperconjugative effect. An important of which is that in which C—H bond is assumed to have partial ionic character because of resonance.

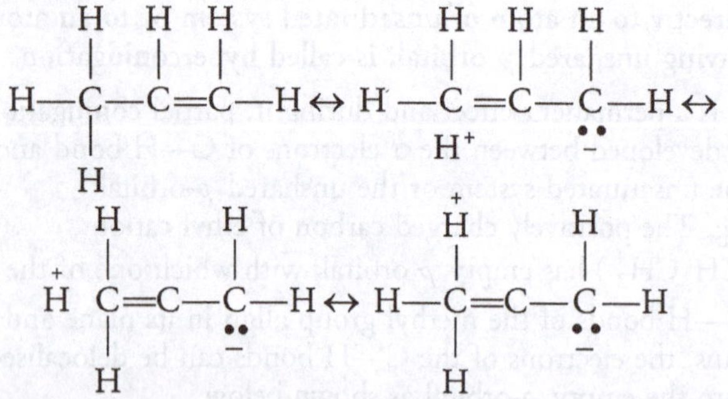

In such a condition, term 'no bond resonance' is used for hyperconjugation.

Structural Requirements for Hyperconjugation

These are as follows:

(i) Compound should have at least one sp^2 hybrid carbon of either alkene, alkyl carbocation or alkyl free radical.

(ii) α-carbon with respect to sp^2 hybrid carbon should have atleast one hydrogen. More the number of H—C bonds attached to the unsaturated system, more stable will be the alkene.

Example 6 Explain why $(CH_3)_3\overset{+}{C}$ is more stable than $CH_3\overset{+}{C}H_2$ and $\overset{+}{C}H_3$ is the least stable cation.

NCERT Textbook

Sol. $(CH_3)_3C^+$ has 9 hyperconjugative structures due to the presence of 9 C—H bonds but $CH_3CH_2^+$ possess only 6 hyperconjugative structures due to the presence of only 6 C—H bonds in conjugation with *p* orbital. Thus, $(CH_3)_3C^+$ is more stable than $CH_3CH_2^+$. In CH_3^+, the C—H bonds are perpendicular to the plane of vacant *p*-orbital, so there is no overlapping between the electron of C—H bond and hence, CH_3^+ have no hyperconjugative stability. Thus, it is least stable among the given species.

Types of Organic Reactions and Mechanisms

The organic reactions can be categorised into following categories:

Substitution Reactions

A substitution reaction is that which involves the direct replacement (displacement or substitution) of an atom or a group of atoms in an organic molecule by another atom or group of atoms without any change in the remaining part of the molecule. e.g.

$$R\text{—}CH_3 + X_2 \xrightarrow[520\text{-}670\ K]{h\nu \text{ or}} R\text{—}CH_2X + HX$$

(Substituent: X; Substitution product: $R\text{—}CH_2X$)

On the basis of intermediate species, substitution reactions can further be classified into three categories. *These are as follows:*

1. Free Radical Substitution Reactions

Substitution reaction brought about by free radicals are called free radical substitution reactions, e.g. halogenation of alkanes. $\underset{\text{Methane}}{CH_4} + Cl_2 \xrightarrow[-HCl]{h\nu} \underset{\text{Chloromethane}}{CH_3Cl}$

2. Electrophilic Substitution Reactions

The substitution reactions which are initiated by electrophiles, are called electrophilic substitution reactions. These reactions are characteristic of aromatic compounds.

e.g.

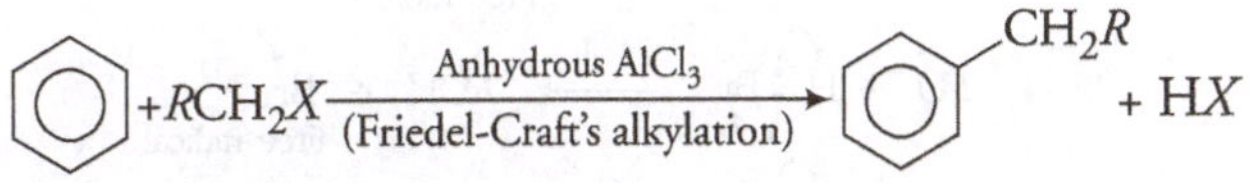

3. Nucleophilic Substitution Reactions

These reactions involve substitution that begins with nucleophilic attack. The atom which departs with its bonding pair of electrons is called leaving group.

$$\underset{\substack{\uparrow \\ \text{Leaving group}}}{R\text{—}X} + Nu^- \longrightarrow R\text{—}Nu + X^-$$

There are two types of nucleophilic substitution reactions:

(i) S_N2 Type (Bimolecular Nucleophilic Substitution)

The term bimolecular means that rate of a reaction depends upon the concentration of substrate and nucleophile. It follows second order kinetics. These reactions are commonly seen in primary alkyl halides and alcohols. This reaction takes place in one step.

$$\text{Rate} \propto \underset{\substack{\downarrow \\ RX}}{[A]}\ \underset{\substack{\downarrow \\ Nu^-}}{[B]}$$

Mechanism

These reactions take place through a transition state in which both the reactants are partially bonded to each other.

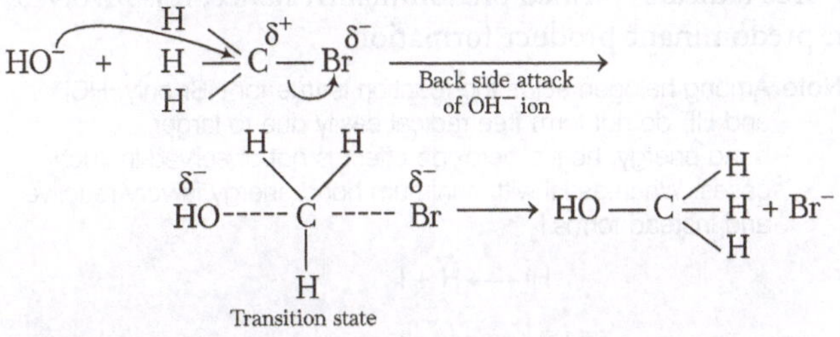

As the hydroxide ion approaches the molecule from the back side, an effective collision take place, the —OH bond is formed and the —Br bond is broken simultaneously with the liberation of bromide ion.

Stereochemistry of S_N2 mechanism The back side attack by a nucleophile in S_N2 reactions produce a product whose configuration is opposite to that of the reactant. Therefore, inversion of configuration occurs, if there is chiral carbon at alkyl halide. It is also known as Walden inversion.

e.g. Optically active, (–)-2-bromooctane was hydrolysed to obtain (+)-octan-2-ol.

Relative reactivity of alkyl halides toward S_N2 reactions

The relative order of alkyl halides toward S_N2 reaction is methyl halides > primary halides > secondary halides > tertiary halides.

(ii) S_N1 Type (Unimolecular Nucleophilic Substitution)

The term unimolecular means that rate of nucleophilic substitution reaction depends upon the concentration of the substrate and not on the nucleophile. It follows first order kinetics. The reaction takes place in two steps:

$$\text{Rate} \propto \underset{\substack{\downarrow \\ RX}}{[\text{substrate}]}$$

Mechanism

These reactions take place in two steps:

Step I $R\text{—}X \underset{\text{Step}}{\overset{\text{Slowest}}{\rightleftharpoons}} R^+ + X^-$

Step II $R^+ + \underset{\text{(Nucleophile)}}{OH^-} \xrightarrow{\text{Fast}} R\text{—}OH$

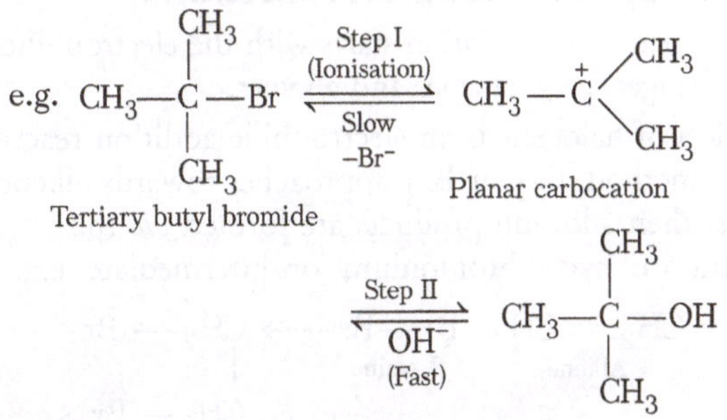

Stereochemistry of S_N1 mechanism The attack of nucleophile can occur from both the faces with almost equal ease, thereby giving a 50:50 mixture of two enantiomers, i.e. a racemic mixture.

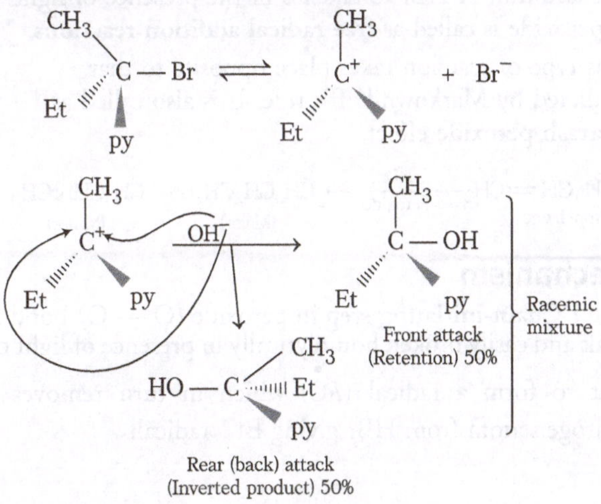

Addition Reactions

Reactions which involve combination between two reacting molecules to give a single molecule as a product are called **addition reactions.** This type of reaction is a characteristic of the compounds containing double or triple bonds. In these reaction, a group add to an unsaturated system. e.g.

$$>C\overset{\sigma}{\underset{\pi}{=}}C< + X_2 \longrightarrow >\underset{X}{C}\overset{\sigma}{-}\underset{X}{C}<$$

$$-C\overset{\sigma}{\underset{\pi}{\equiv}}C- + X_2 \longrightarrow \underset{X}{>}C\overset{\sigma}{\underset{\pi}{=}}C\underset{X}{<} \xrightarrow{X_2} X-\underset{X}{C}\overset{\sigma}{-}\underset{X}{C}-X$$

$$>C\overset{\sigma}{\underset{\pi}{=}}O + HCN \longrightarrow >\underset{OH}{C}\overset{\sigma}{-}CN$$

Types of Addition Reactions

These reactions can be further classified into three categories:

1. Electrophilic Addition Reactions

In these reactions, initiation starts with the electrophilic part of reagent, e.g. alkenes and alkynes.

Addition of halogens is an electrophilic addition reaction. In this method, Cl_2 or Br_2 approaches towards alkene or alkyne, then addition products are formed *via* the formation of cyclic bromonium ion intermediate. e.g.

$$\underset{\text{Alkene}}{CH_2=CH_2} + \underset{\text{Bromine}}{Br-Br} \longrightarrow \underset{\substack{\text{1,2-dibromo}\\ \text{ethane}}}{\begin{matrix} CH_2-Br \\ | \\ CH_2-Br \end{matrix}}$$

2. Free Radical Addition Reactions

The addition of HBr to alkenes in the presence of light or peroxide is called as **free radical addition reactions.** This type of reaction takes place opposite to that predicted by Markownikoff's rule. It is also called as **Kharash peroxide effect.**

$$\underset{\text{Prop-1-ene}}{CH_3CH=CH_2} \xrightarrow[\text{Peroxide}]{HBr} \underset{\text{(Major)}}{CH_3CH_2CH_2Br} + \underset{\text{(Minor)}}{CH_3CHBrCH_3}$$

Mechanism

***Step* I Chain-initiating step** in peroxide (O — O) bond is weak and easily broken homolytically in presence of light or heat to form a radical ($R\dot{O}$) which in turn removes a hydrogen atom from HBr giving $Br^{\bullet}$ radical.

$$RO:OR \xrightarrow[\text{UV}]{\text{Homolytic}} \underset{\text{Free radical}}{2R\dot{O}}$$

$$R\dot{O} + H:Br \longrightarrow ROH + \underset{\text{Free radical}}{\dot{B}r}$$

$$H:Br \longrightarrow \dot{H} + \dot{B}r$$

***Step* II Chain-propagating step** Br radical attacks on the π-bond of the alkene to form a bromine—carbon bond. Bromine radical can join to any of the sp^2-hybridised carbons of the alkene to form primary or secondary free radicals as shown below

$$\dot{B}r + CH_2=CHCH_3 \longrightarrow \underset{\text{(2° free radical)}}{BrCH_2\dot{C}HCH_3}$$

$$\dot{B}r + CH_2=CHCH_3 \longrightarrow \underset{\text{(1° free radical)}}{\dot{C}H_2\underset{Br}{C}HCH_3}$$

Since, stability of 2° free radical is greater than 1° free radical, hence formed predominantly.

***Step* III Chain-terminating step** Alkyl radical that is formed removes a hydrogen atom from another molecule of HBr to produce alkyl halide and bromine radical as:

$$BrCH_2\dot{C}HCH_3 + H:Br \longrightarrow BrCH_2\,CH_2CH_3 + \dot{B}r$$

This step is repeated till one of the substrate is finished. As 2° free radical is formed predominantly hence, it is involved in predominant product formation.

Note Among halogen acids the reaction is true for HBr only. HCl and HF do not form free radical easily due to larger bond-energy, hence peroxide effect is not observed in such cases. Whereas HI with minimum bond energy is very reactive and instead forms I_2.

$$HI \longrightarrow \dot{H} + \dot{I}$$

$$\dot{I} + \dot{I} \longrightarrow I_2$$

3. Nucleophilic Addition Reactions

In these reactions, initiation occur with the nucleophilic part of reagent. These addition readily takes place on carbonyl compounds, nitriles etc., due to the presence of unevenly distributed electron cloud,

e.g.

$$>C=O + \overset{+}{H}\overset{-}{C}N \underset{}{\overset{\text{pH 9-10}}{\rightleftharpoons}} -\underset{OH}{\overset{|}{C}}-CN$$

Mechanism

Step I The cyanide ion formed by ionisation of HCN is the nucleophile.

$$H{-}CN + OH^- \longrightarrow H_2O + :\overset{\ominus}{C}N$$

Cyanide ion

Step II $CN^{\ominus}$ attacks on C-atom of carbonyl group.

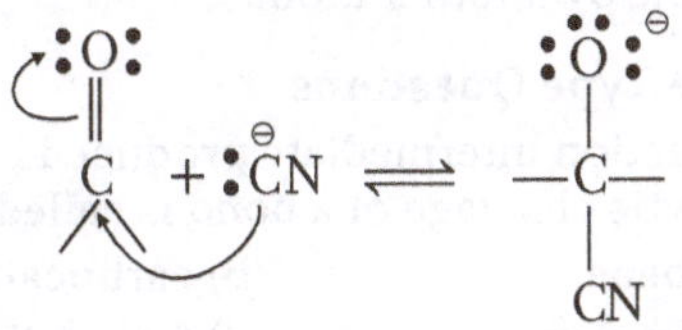

Step III The negatively charged oxygen-(an alkoxide ion) is a relatively strong base and is protonated by either water or HCN to complete the addition.

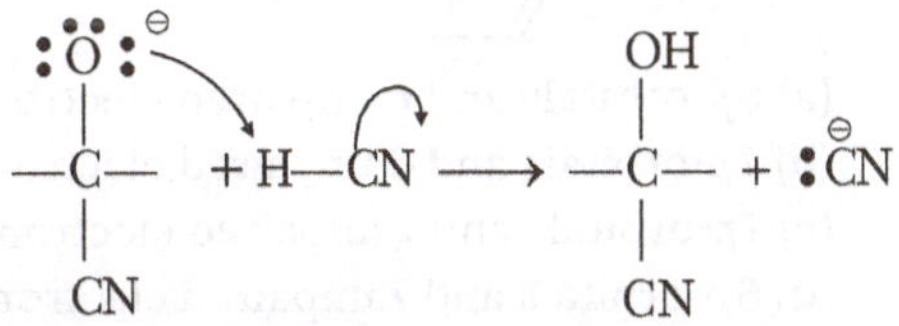

Elimination Reactions

In these reactions, two groups on adjacent atoms or on same atom are lost and a double bond is formed. Therefore, the product is only an alkene or alkyne [multiple bond]. They are just opposite to addition reactions. This type of reaction is given by the compounds which have a nucleophile as leaving group, i.e. X^-, $\bar{O}H$, $C_2H_5O^-$, N_2 etc.

e.g.

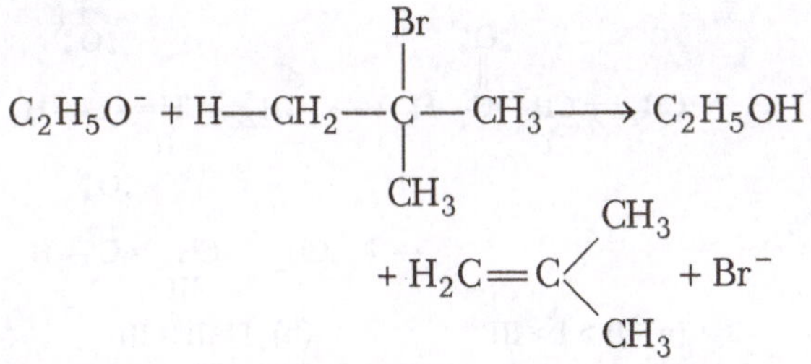

In haloalkanes, halide is lost from α-carbon and hydrogen is lost from β-carbon. The elimination that involves loss of two groups from adjacent carbon is termed as β-elimination.

Types of Elimination Reactions

The two types of elimination reactions are as follows:

1 Bimolecular (E2) Elimination

E2 elimination is a concerted one step process in which abstraction of proton from the β-C atom by base and removal of X^- from the α-C atom take place simultaneously. Due to the formation of transition state, this mechanism is comparable with S_N2 mechanism.

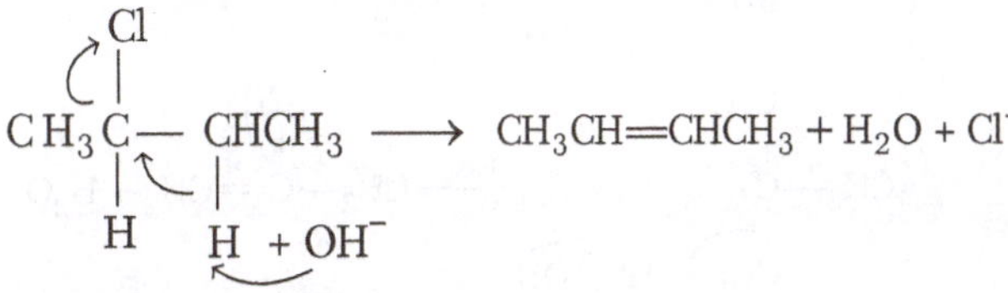

The rate depends on the concentration of alkyl halide as well as on the concentration of base.

$$\text{Rate} \propto [\text{alkyl halide}]\ [\text{base}]$$

Mechanism

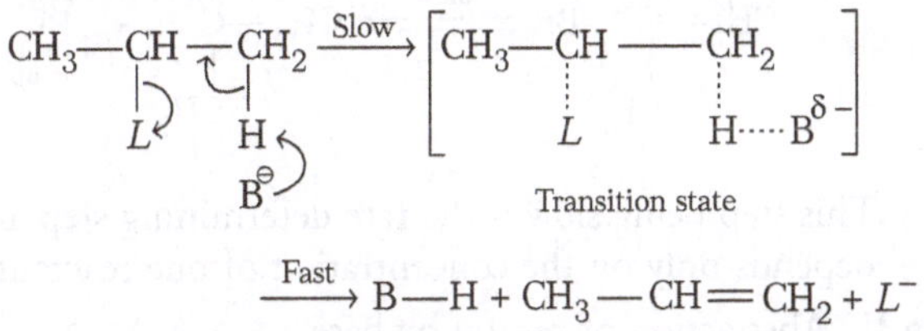

(Here, *L* is the leaving group)

Some important points related to E2 *reactions are:*

(i) Reactivity depends upon both strength and nature of alkyl halide.

(ii) Strong base is required to abstract proton. A more substituted alkyl halide gives more stable alkenes and therefore, more reactive. General order of reactivity is tertiary > secondary > primary

(iii) E2 reaction proceeds at room temperature.

(iv) Polar protic solvent retards E2 reaction as it solvates the base.

(v) Rate of cleavage of C—*X* bond is in order

$$I > Br > Cl > F$$

Fastest → Slowest

Unimolecular (E1) Reaction

Unimolecular (E1) reaction proceed *via* two steps. It is named as unimolecular because the rate of E1 reaction depends only on the concentration of alkyl halide.

$$\text{Rate} = k\ [\text{alkyl halide}]$$

In this reaction, firstly, heterolytic dissociation of alkyl halide occurs, which is a slow and rate determining step. Then, abstraction of proton through a base occurs from a carbon adjacent to the positively charged carbon atom. Due to the formation of carbocation this mechanism is comparable with S_N1 mechanism.

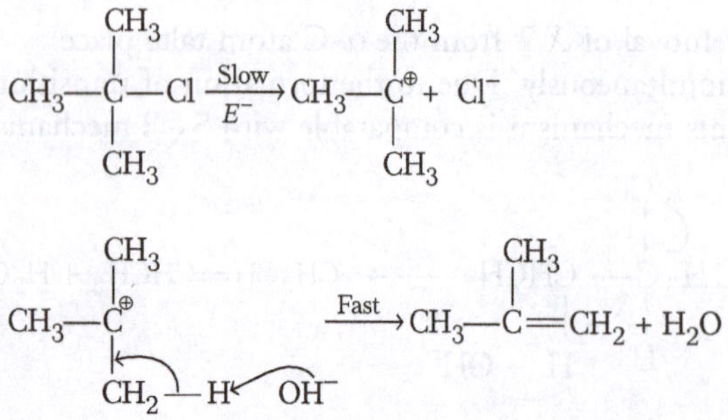

Mechanism

Step I Generation of carbocation

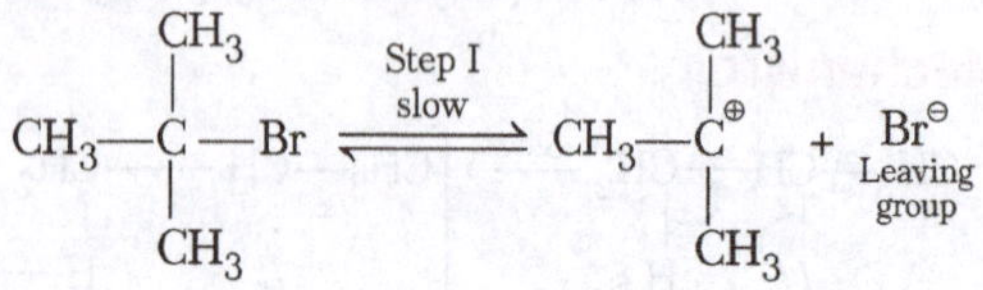

This step being slow is the rate determining step and depends only on the concentration of one reactant.

Step II Abstraction of proton by base

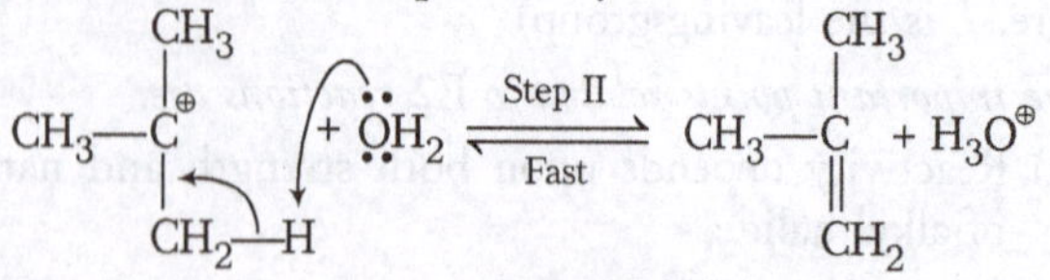

Rearrangement Reactions

Reactions involving the migration of an atom or a group from one atom to another within the same molecule are called rearrangement reactions, e.g. 1-bromobutane rearranges to 2-bromobutane in the presence of anhydrous $AlCl_3$ at 575 K.

$$\underset{\text{1-bromobutane}}{CH_3-CH_2-CH_2-CH_2-Br} \xrightarrow[575\ K]{\text{Anhyd. } AlCl_3} \underset{\text{2-bromobutane}}{CH_3-CH_2-\underset{|}{\overset{Br}{CH}}-CH_3}$$

Topic Practice 3

Very Short Answer Type Questions

(1 Mark)

1 Fill in the Blanks

(i) The species which has sextet of electrons and a positive charge is called ....

(ii) The stability of carbocation increases due to ...... and .... effects.

(iii) An.........is defined as electron deficient species which attacks on electron rich areas.

(iv) .... is a temporary effect.

(v) A ....involves the direct replacement of an atom or a group of atoms in an organic molecule by another atom.

2. Objective Type Questions

(i) The reaction intermediate produced by homolytic cleavage of a bond is called

(a) carbene (b) carbocation

(c) carbanion (d) free radical

(ii) The radical is aromatic because it has

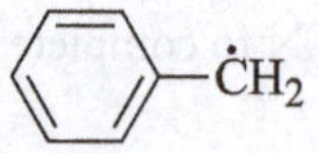

(a) 6*p*-orbitals and 6 unpaired electrons

(b) 7*p*-orbitals and 6 unpaired electrons

(c) 7*p*-orbitals and 7 unpaired electrons

(d) 6*p*-orbitals and 7 unpaired electrons

(iii) Which of the following is the most reactive towards electrophilic reagent?

(a) 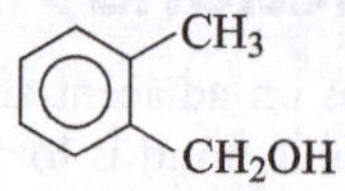

(b) 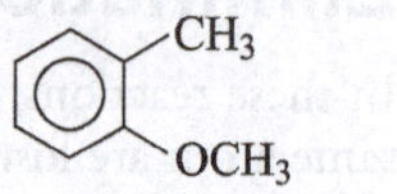

(c) 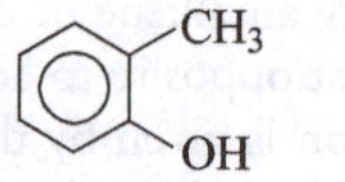

(d) 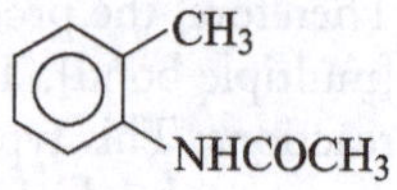

(iv) The order of relative stability of the contributing structures is

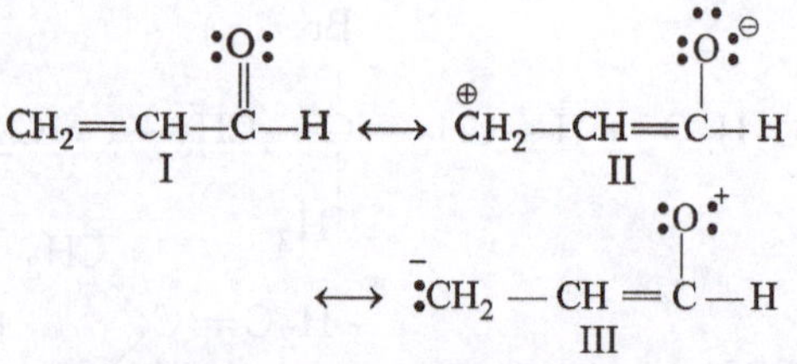

(a) II > I > III (b) I > II > III

(c) III > II > I (d) I = II = III

(v) "The polarity produced in the molecule by the interaction of two π-bonds or between a π-bond and lone pairs of electrons present on an adjacent atom."

This effect is called

(a) inductive effect

(b) electromeric effect

(c) resonance effect

(d) hyperconjugation effect

(vi) Observe the effect carefully and predict the nature of it.

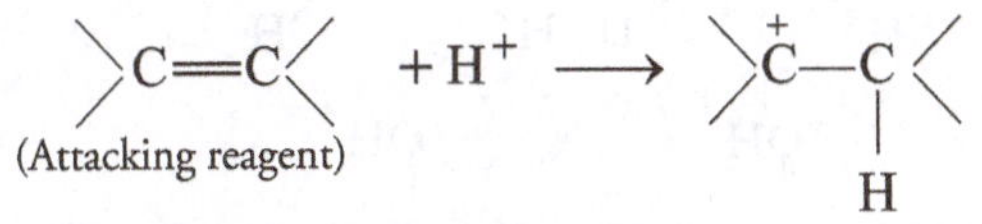

Choose the correct option.

(a) Negative electromeric effect
(b) Resonance effect
(c) Positive electromeric effect
(d) Inductive effect

(vii) Hyperconjugation involves overlapping of which of the following orbitals.

(a) σ-σ (b) σ-p
(c) p-p (d) π-π

(viii) Which one is a nucleophilic substitution reaction among the following?

(a) $CH_3CHO + HCN \longrightarrow CH_3CH(OH)CN$

(b) $CH_3—CH=CH_2 + H_2O \xrightarrow{H^+} CH_3—CH(OH)—CH_3$

(c) $RCHO + R'MgX \longrightarrow R—CH(OH)—R'$

(d) $CH_3—CH_2—CH(CH_3)—CH_2Br + NH_3 \longrightarrow CH_3—CH_2—CH(CH_3)—CH_2NH_2$

3. Match the terms mentioned in Column I with the terms in Column II and choose the correct option using the codes given below: **NCERT Exemplar**

	Column I		Column II
A.	Carbocation	(i)	Cyclohexane and hex-1-ene
B.	Nucleophile	(ii)	Conjugation of electrons of C—H σ bond with empty p-orbital present at adjacent positively charged carbon.
C.	Hyperconjugation	(iii)	sp^2-hybridised carbon with empty p-orbital.
D.	Isomers	(iv)	Ethyne
E.	sp-hybridisation	(v)	Species that can receive a pair of electrons.
F.	Electrophile	(vi)	Species that can supply a pair of electrons.

Codes

	A	B	C	D	E	F
(a)	(i)	(ii)	(iii)	(iv)	(v)	(vi)
(b)	(iii)	(vi)	(ii)	(i)	(iv)	(v)
(c)	(ii)	(iii)	(iv)	(v)	(vi)	(i)
(d)	(vi)	(iii)	(ii)	(i)	(iv)	(v)

4. Write the correct stability order for the following carbocations.

$(CH_3)_2\overset{+}{C}H, (CH_3)_3\overset{+}{C}, CH_3CH_2\overset{+}{C}H_2$

5 Give the structure and hybridisation of
(i) CH_3^+ (ii) CH_3^-

6 $CH_2=\bar{C}H$ is more basic than $HC\equiv C^-$. Explain why?

7 Why does SO_3 act as an electrophile? **NCERT Exemplar**

8 Using curved arrow notation, show the formation of reactive intermediates when the following covalent bonds undergo heterolytic cleavage.
(i) $CH_3—SCH_3$ (ii) $CH_3—CN$ (iii) $CH_3—Cu$

9 Why is benzylic free radical more stable than allylic free radical?

10 Which of the two : $O_2NCH_2CH_2O^-$ or $CH_3CH_2O^-$ is expected to be more stable and why? **NCERT Textbook**

11 Show the polarisation of carbon-magnesium bond in the following structure.
$CH_3—CH_2—CH_2—CH_2—Mg—X$

12 Name the type of organic reaction involved in the following reaction.
$CH_3CH_2I + KOH(aq) \longrightarrow CH_3CH_2OH + KI$

13 Identify electrophilic centre in the following compounds $CH_3CH=O, CH_3CN, CH_3I$.

Short Answer Type I Questions

2 Marks

14 What are reactive intermediates? How are they generated by bond fission?

15 Identify the most stable species in the following set of ions giving reasons. **NCERT Exemplar**
(i) $\overset{+}{C}H_3, \overset{+}{C}H_2Br, \overset{+}{C}HBr_2, \overset{+}{C}Br_3$
(ii) $\bar{C}H_3, \bar{C}H_2Cl, \bar{C}HCl_2, \bar{C}Cl_3$

16 Which of the following compounds will not exist as resonance hybrid. Give reason for your answer.
(i) CH_3OH
(ii) $R—CONH_2$
(iii) $CH_3CH=CHCH_2NH_2$

17 Which bond is more polar in the following pair of molecules?

(i) $H_3C—H$ or $H_3C—Br$
(ii) $H_3C—NH_2$ or $H_3C—OH$
(iii) $H_3C—OH$ or $H_3C—SH$ **NCERT Textbook**

18 Draw the possible resonance structures for $CH_3—\ddot{\underset{\cdot\cdot}{O}}—\overset{+}{C}H_2$ and predict which of the structures is more stable. Give reason for your answer.

19 Resonance structures of propenal are given below. Which of these resonating structures is more stable? Give reason for your answer.

$$\underset{\text{I}}{CH_2 = CH — CH = O} \leftrightarrow \underset{\text{II}}{\overset{\oplus}{C}H_2 — CH = CH — \overset{\ominus}{O}}$$

20 Explain, why alkyl groups act as electron donors when attached to a π-system?

21 Which of the two structures *A and B* given below is more stabilised by resonance. Explain $\underset{A}{CH_3COOH}$ and $\underset{B}{CH_3CO\overset{\ominus}{O}}$

22 What are electrophiles and nucleophiles? Explain with examples.

23 How does (i) an electron withdrawing group (EWG) and (ii) an electron donating group (EDG) influence the acid strength of carboxylic end?

24 What is meant by

(i) delocalisation (ii) resonance energy?

25 Classify the following reactions in one of the reaction type studied in this unit.

(i) $CH_3CH_2Br + HS^- \longrightarrow CH_3CH_2SH + Br^-$
(ii) $(CH_3)_2C = CH_2 + HCl \longrightarrow (CH_3)_2CCl—CH_3$
(iii) $CH_3CH_2Br + HO^- \longrightarrow CH_2 = CH_2 + H_2O + Br^-$
(iv) $(CH_3)_3C—CH_2OH + HBr \longrightarrow (CH_3)_2CBrCH_2CH_3 + H_2O$ **NCERT Textbook**

Short Answer Type II Questions

(3 Marks)

26 What is the relationship between the members of following pairs of structures? Are they structural or geometrical isomers or resonance contributors? **NCERT Textbook**

(i) 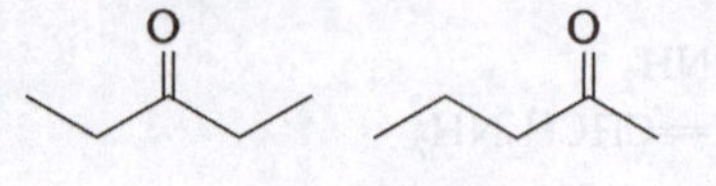

(ii) 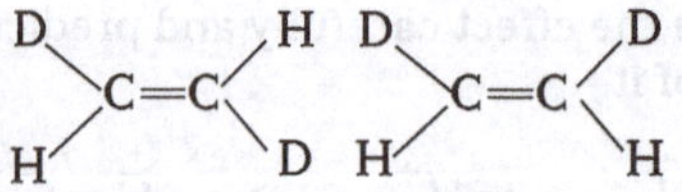

(iii) $H—\overset{\overset{+}{O}H}{\overset{\|}{C}}—OH \quad H—\overset{\overset{OH}{|}}{C^+}—OH$

27 Identify the reagents shown in bold in the following equations as nucleophiles or electrophiles.

(i) $CH_3COOH + \underline{HO^-} \longrightarrow CH_3COO^- + H_2O$
(ii) $CH_3COCH_3 + \underline{^-CN} \longrightarrow (CH_3)_2C(CN)(OH)$
(iii) $C_6H_6 + \underline{CH_3\overset{+}{C}O} \longrightarrow C_6H_5COCH_3$

NCERT Textbook

28 Arrange the following:

(i) $C_6H_5\overset{+}{C}HCH_3$, $C_6H_5\overset{+}{C}HCH = CH_2$, $C_6H_5CH_2\overset{+}{C}H_2$, $C_6H_5\overset{+}{C}(CH_3)_2$ in order of increasing stability.
(ii) $CH_3CH_2^+$, $C_6H_5CH_2^+$, $(CH_3)_3C^+$, $CH_2 = CHCH_2^+$ in order of decreasing stability.
(iii) $HC{\equiv}C^-$, $CH_2 = CH^-$, $CH_3CH_2^-$, CH_3^-, $(CH_3)_2CH^-$, $C_6H_5CH_2^-$ in order of increasing stability.

29 Give three points of differences between inductive effect and resonance effect. **NCERT Exemplar**

30 The structure of triphenylmethyl cation is given below. This is very stable and some of its salts can be stored for months.

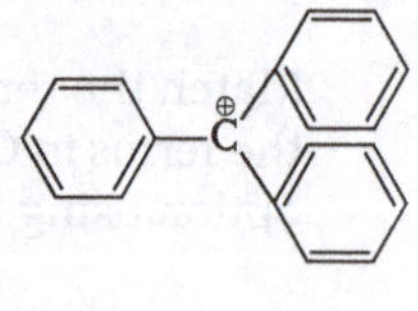

Explain the cause of high stability of this cation.

Long Answer Type Questions

(5 Marks)

31 For the following bond cleavages, use curved-arrows to show the electron flow and classify each as homolysis or heterolysis. Identify reactive intermediate produced as free radical, carbocation and carbanion.

(i) $CH_3O{-}OCH_3 \longrightarrow CH_3\dot{O} + \dot{O}CH_3$

(ii) 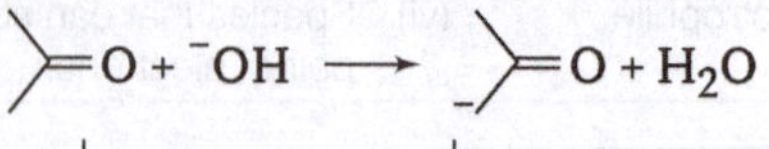

(iii) 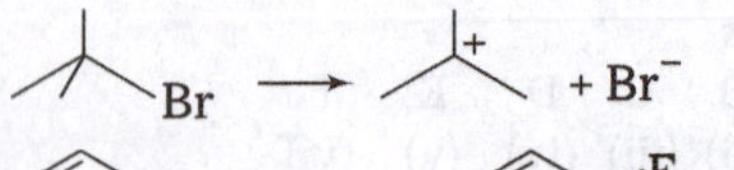

(iv) 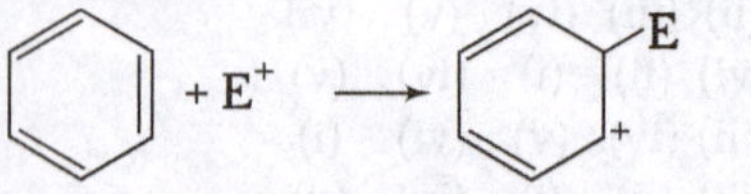

32 Explain the terms inductive and electromeric effects. Which electron displacement effect explains the following correct orders of acidity of the carboxylic acids? **NCERT Textboook**

(i) $Cl_3CCOOH > Cl_2CHCOOH > ClCH_2COOH$

(ii) $CH_3CH_2COOH > (CH_3)_2CHCOOH > (CH_3)_3C \cdot COOH$

33 Draw the resonance structures for the following compounds. Show the electron shift using curved arrow notation. **NCERT Exemplar**

(i) C_6H_5OH (ii) $CH_3CH{=}CHCHO$

(iii) $C_6H_5{-}CHO$ (iv) $C_6H_5{-}\overset{+}{C}H_2$

(v) $CH_3CH{=}CH\overset{+}{C}H_2$

Hints & Solutions

1. (i) carbocation (ii) inductive, hyperconjugative
(iii) electrophile (iv) electromeric effect
(v) substitution reaction

2. (i)(*d*) In homolytic cleavage, covalent bond is cleaved in such a way that each atom take its shared electrons with itself and free radicals are formed.

$$A{-}B \xrightarrow[\text{fission}]{\text{Homolytic}} \underset{\text{Free radicals}}{A^{\bullet} + B^{\bullet}}$$

(ii) (*c*) Because of the presence of 7*p* -orbitals and 7 unpaired electrons, it is aromatic in nature as these unpaired electrons delocalise in *p*-orbitals.

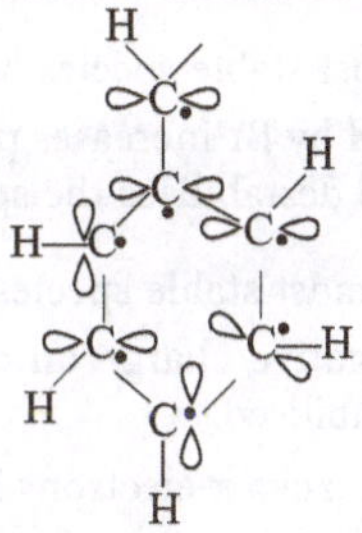

(iii) (*c*) +*R*-effect of OH > $-CH_3$
Hence, 2-methyl phenol is more reactive towards electrophilic reagent.

(iv) (*b*)

$$\underset{\text{I}}{CH_2{=}CH{-}\overset{:\ddot{O}:}{\overset{\|}{C}}{-}H} \longleftrightarrow \underset{\text{II}}{\overset{+}{C}H_2{-}CH{=}\overset{:\ddot{O}:^-}{\overset{|}{C}}{-}H}$$

$$\longleftrightarrow \underset{\text{III}}{:\bar{C}H_2{-}CH{=}\overset{:O:^+}{\overset{|}{C}}{-}H}$$

Stability : I > II > III

Because

I. most stable, more number of covalent bonds, each carbon and oxygen atom has complete octet and no separation of opposite charges.

II. negative charge on more electronegative atom and positive charge on more electropositive atom.

III. does not contribute as oxygen has positive charge and carbon has negative charge, hence least stable.

(v) (*c*) The resonance effect is defined as, the polarity produced in the molecule by the interaction of two π-bonds or between a π-bond and lone pair of electrons present on an adjacent atom. The effect is transmitted through the chain. There are two types of resonance or mesomeric effects designated as +*R* and −*R* or +*M* and −*M* respectively.

(vi) (*c*) In this effect, the π-electrons of the multiple bond are transfered to that atom to which the attacking reagent get attached. So, it is an example of positive electromeric effect (+*E* -effect). e.g.

$$>C{=}C< + \underset{\substack{\text{(Attacking}\\ \text{reagent)}}}{H^+} \longrightarrow >\overset{+}{C}{-}\underset{\underset{H}{|}}{C}<$$

(vii) (*b*) Hyperconjugation involves overlapping of the σ–*p*-orbitals. It is a general stabilising interaction. It involves delocalisation of σ electrons of C—H bond of an alkyl group directly attached to an atom of unsaturated system or to an atom with an unshared system or to an atom with an unshared p -orbital. The σ electrons of C—H bond of the alkyl group enter into partial conjugation with the attached unsaturated system or with the unshared *p* -orbital. It is a permanent effect

(viii) (*d*) $CH_3-CH_2-\underset{}{\overset{CH_3}{\overset{|}{C}H}}-CH_2Br + NH_3 \longrightarrow CH_3-CH_2-\overset{CH_3}{\overset{|}{C}H}-CH_2NH_2$

It is an example of nucleophilic substitution reaction.

3. (b) A→(iii), B→(vi), C→(ii), D→(i), E→(iv), F→(v)

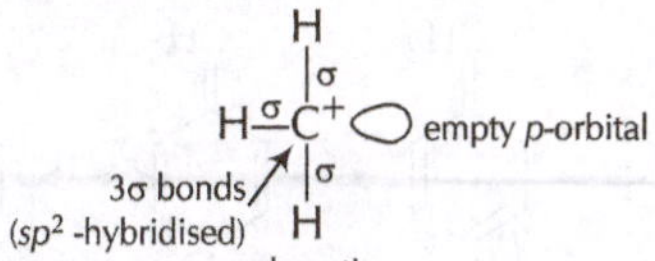

carbocation

- Nucleophile being electron rich can supply a pair of electrons whereas electrophile being electron deficient can receive a pair of electrons.
- Hyperconjugation is found when C—H bonds are in conjugation with carbon having empty *p*-orbital.

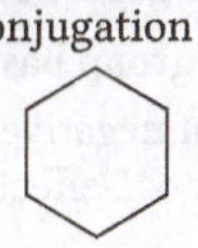 and $CH_3CH_2CH_2CH_2CH{=}CH_2$

Both have C_6H_{12} formula but different structures, so these are isomers.

- $\overset{sp}{CH} \equiv \overset{sp}{CH}$ (Ethyne) exhibits *sp*-hybridisation.

4. (b) The order of stability of carbocation is 3° > 2° > 1°.

$(CH_3)_3\overset{+}{C} > (CH_3)_2\overset{+}{C}H > CH_3CH_2\overset{+}{C}H_2$

3° carbocation, i.e. $(CH_3)_3\overset{+}{C}$ is the most stable carbocation.

5. (i) CH_3^+ (ii) CH_3^-

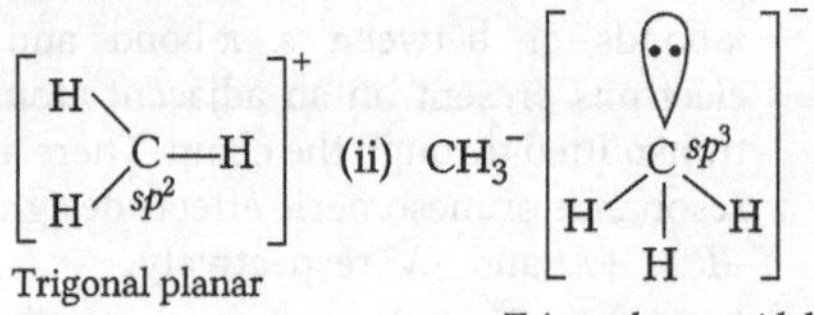

Trigonal planar   Trigonal pyramidal

6. $CH_2{=}\overset{sp^2}{C}H^-$ $HC{\equiv}\overset{sp}{C}^-$

Since, *sp*-carbon is more electronegative than *sp*^{2}-carbon, therefore, $CH \equiv C^-$ is less willing to donate a pair of electrons than $H_2C = CH^-$. In other words, $H_2C = CH^-$ is more basic than $HC \equiv C^-$.

7. In SO_3, three highly electronegative oxygen atoms are attached to sulphur atom. It makes sulphur atom electron deficient. Further, due to resonance, sulphur acquires a positive charge. Both these factors, make SO_3 an electrophile.

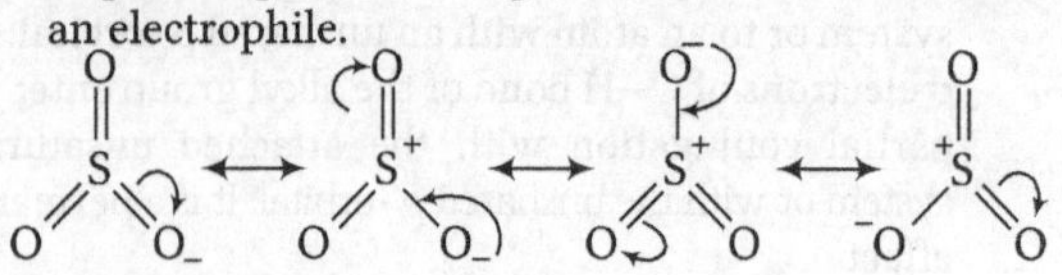

8. (i) $CH_3—SCH_3 \longleftrightarrow \overset{-}{C}H_3 + \overset{+}{S}CH_3$

(ii) $CH_3—CN \longleftrightarrow \overset{+}{C}H_3 + CN^-$
Carbocation

(iii) $CH_3—Cu \longleftrightarrow \overset{-}{C}H_3 + Cu^+$
Carbanion

9. This is due to presence of more resonating structures of benzylic free radical.

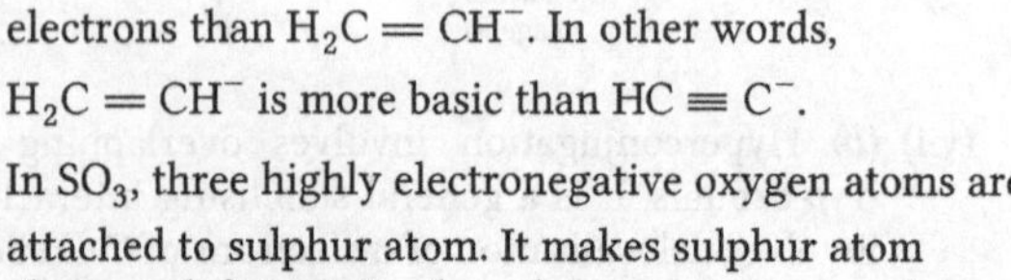

While allylic free radical has only two resonating structures so it has less delocalisation.

$CH_2 = CH—\overset{\bullet}{C}H_2 \longleftrightarrow \overset{\bullet}{C}H_2—CH{=}CH_2$

10. $O_2N—CH_2—CH_2O^-$ is expected to be more stable than $CH_3—CH_2O^-$ because $—NO_2$ group has $-I$-effect, this leads to the dispersal of negative charge. On the other hand — CH_3 group has $+I$-effect, which intensify the negative charge.

Dispersal of the charge leads to the stability of ion while intensification of negative charge leads to the unstability of ion.

$$O_2N \leftarrow CH_2 \leftarrow CH_2 \leftarrow O^-$$
More stable

$$CH_3 \rightarrow CH_2 \rightarrow O^-$$
Less stable

11. Carbon is more electronegative than magnesium therefore, Mg acquires a partial positive charge and carbon acquires a partial negative charge.

$$CH_3—CH_2—CH_2—\overset{-\delta}{C}H_2—\overset{+\delta}{Mg}—X$$

12. This is an example of nucleophilic substitution reaction because the nucleophile I^- is replaced by the nucleophile OH^-.

13. $CH_3\underline{C}H{=}O$, $H_3C\underline{C}{\equiv}N$ and $H_3\underline{C}—I$, the underlined carbon atoms are electrophilic centres as they will have partial positive charge due to polarity of the C—O or C—N or C—I bonds.

14. The reactive intermediates are those chemical species which are produced during the course of the reaction. There are many reactive intermediate, three of which are carbocation, carbanion and the free radical. [1]

Carbocation and carbanion are generated by the heterolytic bond fission while free radicals are generated by homolytic bond fission.

$$CH_3—Cl \longrightarrow CH_3^+ + Cl^-$$

$$(CH_3)_2—Zn \longrightarrow 2CH_3^- + Zn^{2+}$$

(Heterolytic bond fission)

$$CH_3—CH_3 \longrightarrow 2\overset{\bullet}{C}H_3 \text{ (Homolytic bond fission)}$$

[1]

15. (i) $\overset{+}{C}H_3$ is the most stable species because the replacement of H by Br increases positive charge on carbon atom and destabilises the species. [1]

(ii) $\overset{-}{C}Cl_3$ is the most stable species because on replacing H by Cl, negative charge on carbon is reduced and species is stabilised. [1]

16. (i) CH_3OH, as it lacks π-electrons hence it will not exist as resonance hybrid.

(ii) $R—CONH_2$ Due to the presence of non-bonding electrons on N and π-electrons on C=O bond, amide can be represented as a resonance hybrid of the following three resonating structures.

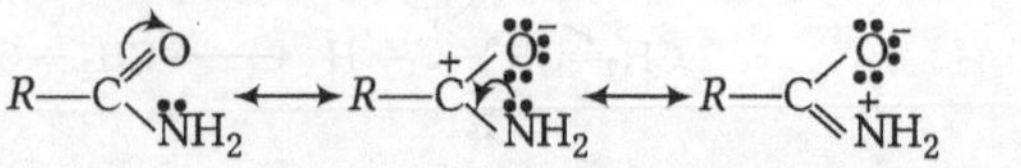

I   II   III

(iii) $CH_3CH = CHCH_2NH_2$ As the lone pair of electrons on the N-atom is not conjugated with the π-electrons of the double bond, thus, resonance is not possible and hence no resonance hybrid will exist.

17. (i) C—Br bond is more polar as Br is more electronegative than H.
(ii) C—O bond is more polar than C—N.
(iii) C—O bond is more polar than C—S as O is more electronegative than S. [2]

18. The given carbocation has two resonance structures:

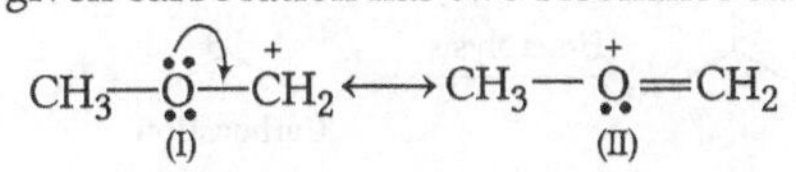

Structure (II) is more stable because both the carbon atoms and the oxygen atom have an octet of electrons. [2]

19. The structure having more covalent bonds in a resonating structure has more stability. Further, there is charge separation in structure (II) and the terminal carbon has only a sextet of electrons in (II). These two factors makes structure (II) less stable.

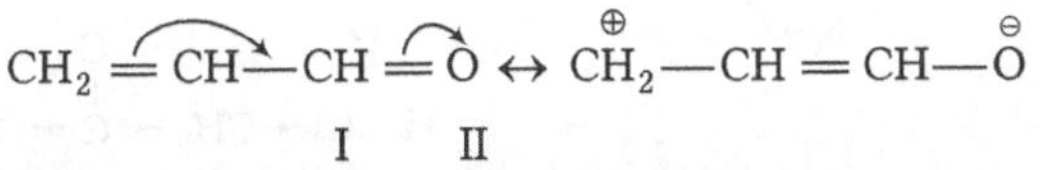

Hence, I > II in terms of stability. [2]

20. Due to hyperconjugation, alkyl groups act as electron donors when attached to a π-system as shown below:

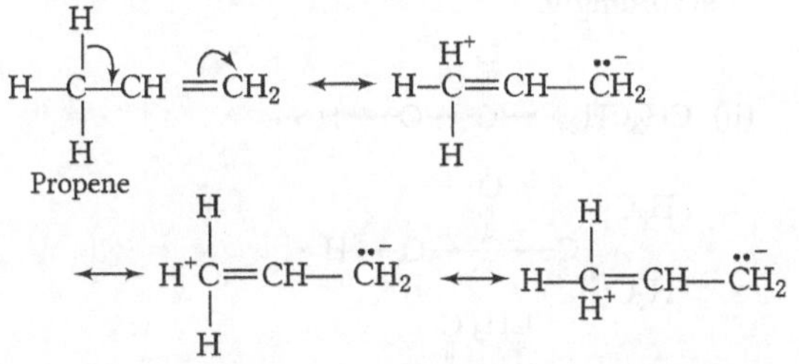

[2]

21. Resonating structures of *A* and *B* are as follows:

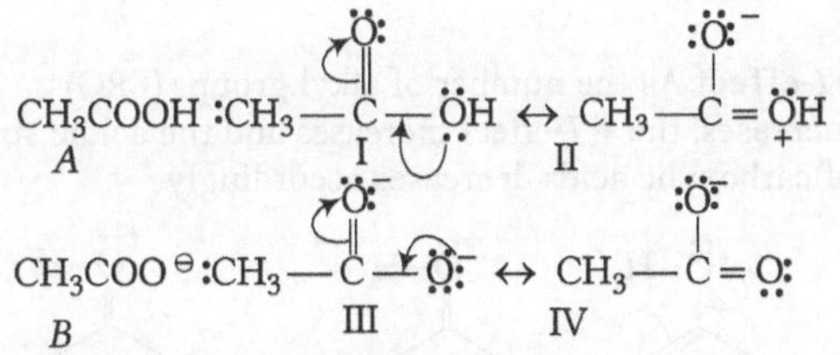

Structure (II) is less stable than structure (I) because later carries separation of positive and negative charges. Therefore, contribution of structure (II) is less than that of (I) towards the resonance hybrid of compound (*A*), i.e. CH_3COOH. On contrary, structure (III) and (IV) are of equal energy and hence contribute equally towards the resonance hybrid of compound (*B*).

Therefore, structure (*B*) is more stable than structure (*A*), i.e. $CH_3COO^{\ominus}$. [2]

22. Refer to text on pages 367 and 368 (Types of attacking reagents).

23. The influence of the inductive effect on acidity is best understood in terms of the conjugate base, $RCOO^-$ and can be summarised as follows.

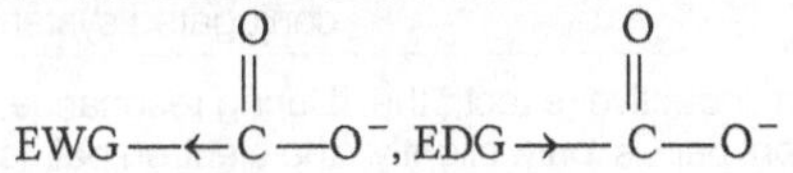

[1]

(i) EWG stabilises $RCOO^-$
(ii) EDG destabilises $RCOO^-$ and hence weakens the acid. [1]

24. (i) **Delocalisation** Delocalisation means that pairs of bonding electrons extend over three or more atoms and belong to the whole molecule. Delocalised π orbital are much larger than the localised π orbital and are therefore more stable. [1]
(ii) **Resonance energy** Refer to text on page 370.

25. (i) Nucleophilic substitution reaction
(ii) Electrophilic addition reaction
(iii) β-elimination reaction
(iv) Nucleophilic substitution reaction with rearrangement. [4 × 1/2]

26. (i) Structural isomers
(differ in position of the functional group) [1]
(ii) Geometrical isomers:

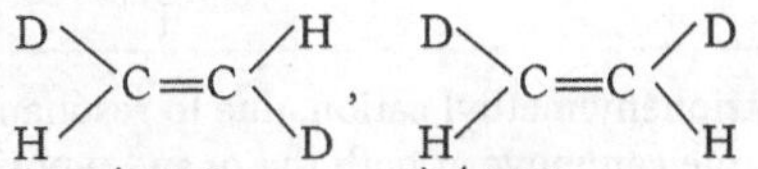

trans–isomer (as similar groups are on opposite side of double bond)   *cis*-isomer (as similar groups are on same side of double bond) [1]

(iii) Resonance contributors
(differ in the position of electrons but not atoms.) [1]

27. (i) HO^- is a nucleophile. [1]
(ii) ^-CN is a nucleophile. [1]
(iii) $CH_3\overset{+}{C}O$ is an electrophile. [1]

28. (i) $C_6H_5CH_2\overset{+}{C}H_2 < C_6H_5\overset{+}{C}HCH_3 < C_6H_5\overset{+}{C}(CH_3)_2 < C_6H_5\overset{+}{C}HCH = CH_2$ [1]

(ii) $(CH_3)_3C^+ > C_6H_5CH_2^+ > CH_2 = CHCH_2^+ > CH_3CH_2^+$ [1]

(iii) $(CH_3)_2CH^- < CH_3CH_2^- < CH_3^- < CH_2 = CH^- < C_6H_5CH_2^- < HC{\equiv}C^-$

29. The main points of difference between inductive and resonance effects are given below.

Inductive Effect	Resonance Effect
It involves displacement of only σ-electrons and hence, occurs only in saturated compounds.	It involves delocalisation of π or n (lone pairs) of electrons and hence occurs in unsaturated and conjugated systems.
During inductive effect, the electron pair is only slightly displaced towards the more electronegative atom and hence only partial positive and negative charges appear.	During resonance effect, the electron pair is completely transferred and hence full positive and negative charge appear.
Inductive effects are transmitted over short distance in saturated carbon chains and the magnitude of the effect decreases rapidly as the distance from the heteroatom increases.	The resonance effect are transmitted all along the length of the conjugated system without suffering much change in magnitude.
The effect almost becomes negligible beyond three carbon atoms from the hetero-atom. $\overset{\delta\delta\delta+}{CH_3}-\overset{\delta\delta+}{CH_2}\rightarrow\overset{\delta+}{CH_2}\rightarrow CH\rightarrow Cl$	In crotonaldehyde C_3, is almost as positive as C_1. $CH_3-CH=CH-CHO$ $\underset{4}{CH_3}-\underset{3}{CH}=\underset{2}{CH}-\overset{+}{\underset{1}{CH}}-\overset{-}{O}$ $\longleftrightarrow \underset{4}{CH_3}-\overset{+}{\underset{3}{CH}}-\underset{2}{CH}=\underset{1}{CH}-O^-$

30. In triphenylmethyl cation, due to resonance, the positive charge can move at both the *o*- and *p*-position of each benzene ring. This is illustrated below.

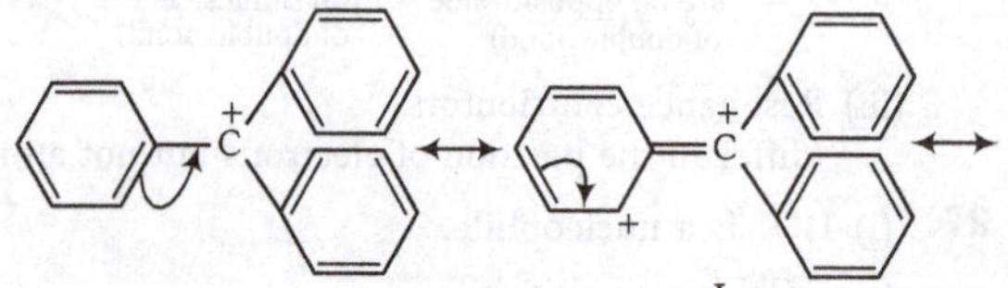

I

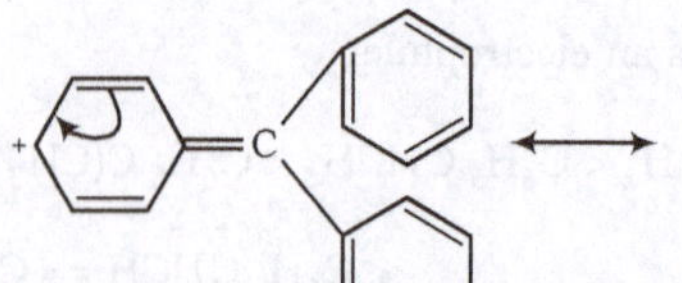

II

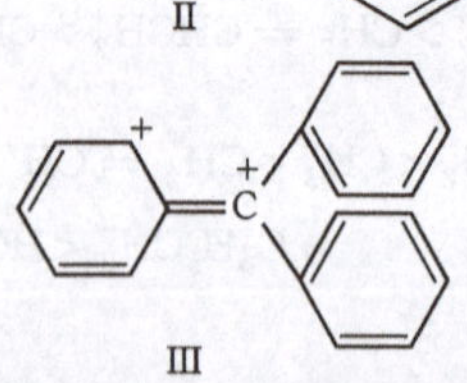

+ Six more such structures are possible due to other two benzene rings.

III

Since, there are three benzene rings, hence, there are, nine resonance structures.
Thus, triphenylmethyl cation is highly stable due to these nine resonance structures. **[3]**

31. (i) $CH_3O-OCH_3 \xrightarrow{\text{Homolysis}} CH_3\dot{O} + \dot{O}CH_3$
Free radicals

(ii)

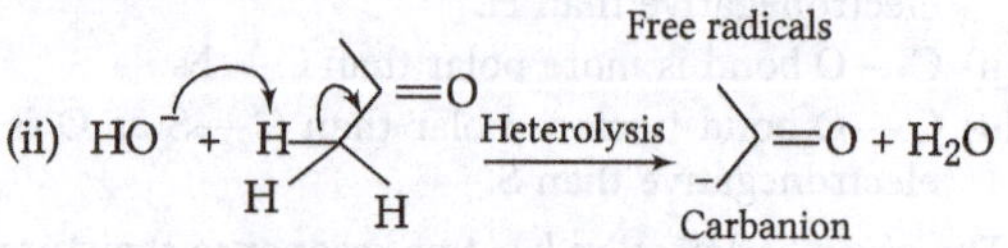

Carbanion

(iii)

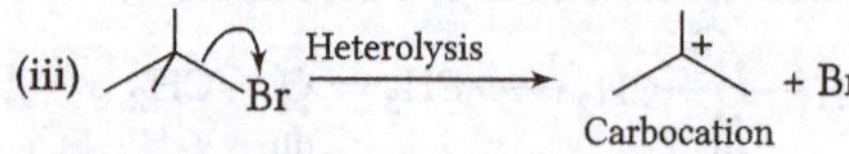

Carbocation

(iv)

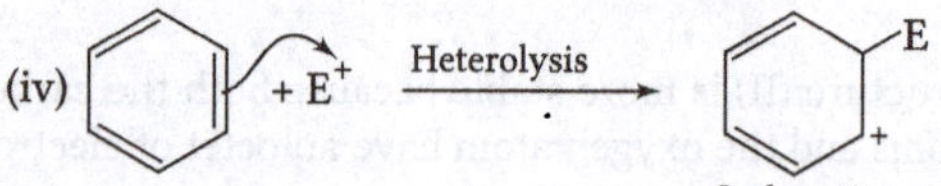

Carbocation

32. Refer to pages 368 and 371 (Inductive and electromeric effect)

(i)

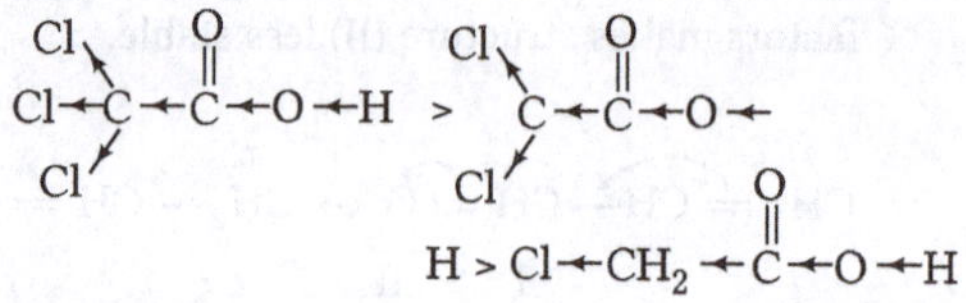

–*I*-effect As the number of halogen atoms (EWG) decreases, the overall–*I*-effect decreases and the acidic strength of carboxylic acids decreases accordingly. **[2]**

(ii)

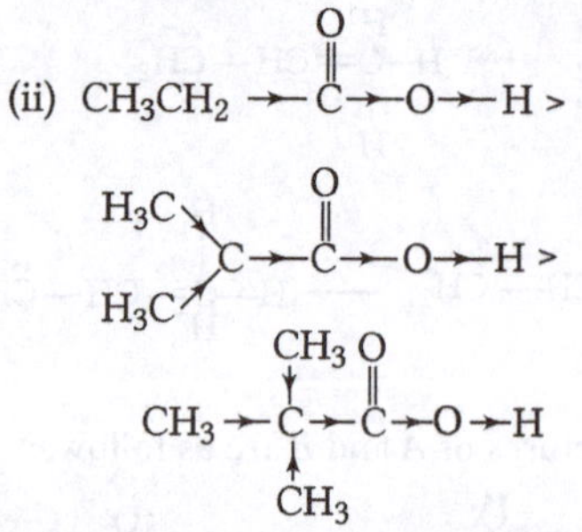

+*I*-effect As the number of alkyl groups (ERG) increases, the + *I*-effect increases and the acidic strength of carboxylic acids decreases accordingly.

33. (i)

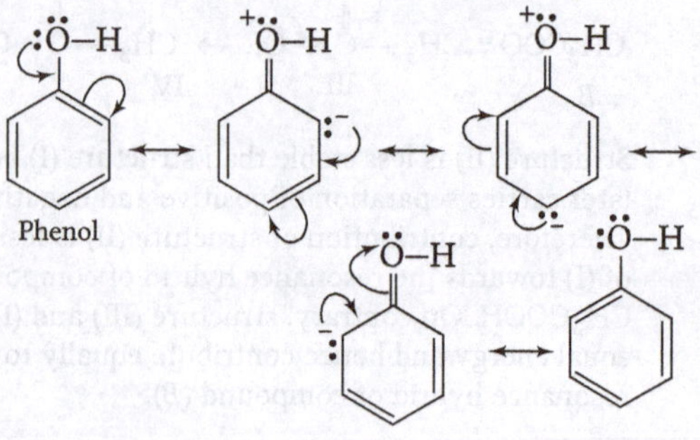

Phenol

(ii)

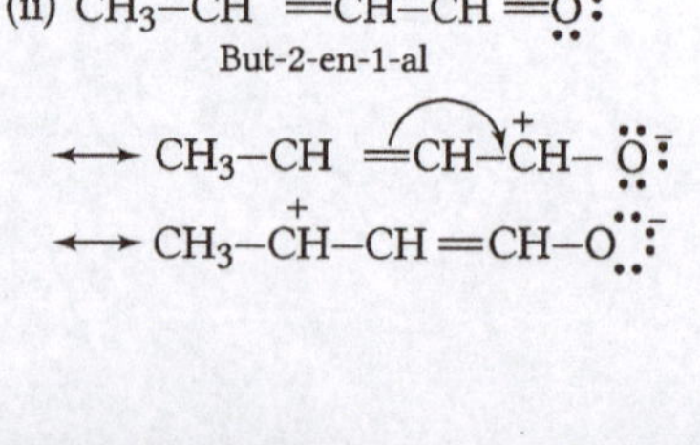

But-2-en-1-al

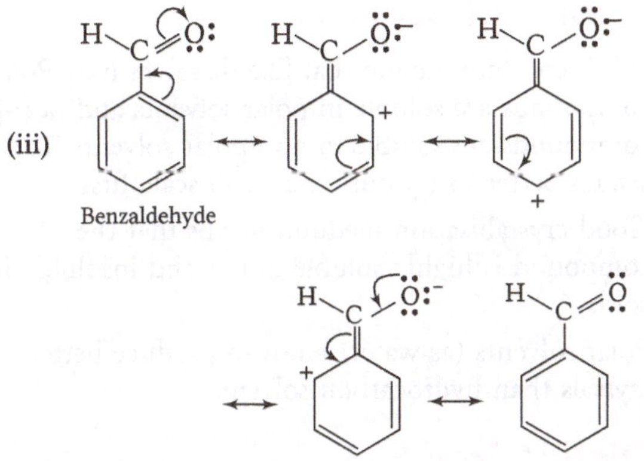

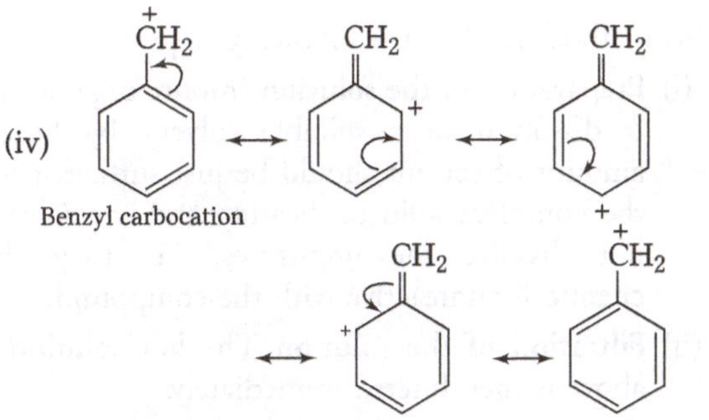

(v) $CH_3-CH=CH-\overset{+}{C}H_2 \longleftrightarrow CH_3-\overset{+}{C}H-CH=CH_2$

But-2-en-1-yl carbocation

TOPIC 04 Characterisation of Organic Compounds (Analysis and Estimation)

When an organic compound is extracted from any natural resource or synthesised in a chemical reaction, then it is always found that some undesired impurities are also present along with the desired product. Hence, it is always necessary to purify the compound before performing any analytical studies over it.

A number of methods are available for the purification. The choice of a particular technique or method depends upon the nature of the compound whether solid or liquid and also on nature of impurities. Analytical studies on the other hand are useful in elucidating structure of organic compounds through quantitative and qualitative means. In this section, we will learn the purification of organic compounds and determination of their structure *via* various means.

Methods of Purification of Organic Compounds

Organic compounds either obtained from natural sources or synthesised in the laboratory. They have some impurities associated with them, i.e. these are not pure. Hence, it is essential to remove these impurities from the organic compound. The process of removal of impurities is called **purification.**

Following techniques are used to purify an organic compound:

Sublimation

This process is employed for those solids which convert directly into vapours on heating without converting into liquid phase and the vapours upon cooling give back the solid.

$$\text{Solid} \underset{\text{Cool}}{\overset{\text{Heat}}{\rightleftharpoons}} \text{Vapour}$$

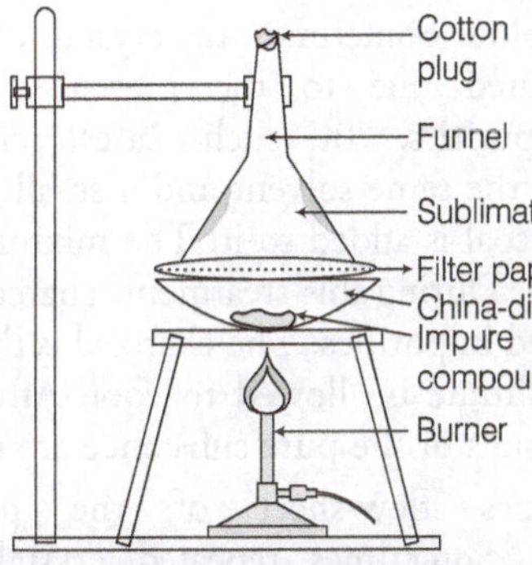

Ordinary sublimation

Thus, non-sublimate impurities from a sublimate compound can be separated by this method.

e.g. Impure samples of naphthalene, anthracene, camphor, benzoic acid, NH_4Cl, $HgCl_2$, dry ice, salicylic acid, iodine etc., can be purified by this method provided that impurities are non-volatile.

Note A mixture of two or more sublimates cannot be separated by sublimation. Such mixtures are separated by chemical methods.

Crystallisation

This is the most common method for purifying organic solids. This method is based on the differences in the solubility of the organic compound and its impurities in a suitable solvent.

This method involves the following steps:

(i) **Preparation of the solution** Impure organic compound is dissolved in a suitable solvent by heating. The amount of solvent should be just sufficient to dissolve the complete solid on heating and the solvent should not dissolve the impurities, i.e. they should be chemically unreactive with the compound.

(ii) **Filtration of the solution** The hot solution obtained above is then filtered immediately.

(iii) **Crystallisation** The hot filtrate is allowed to cool slowly and undisturbed in a beaker. After sometime the crystals of the pure compound are formed. When the crystallisation is complete, the crystals are separated from the mother liquor (supernant liquid) by filtration. The crystals left in the funnel are washed once or twice with a little of the cold solvent to remove adhering impurities, if any.

(iv) **Drying of crystals** The crystals are dried by pressing between the folds of **filter papers** and then placed in a steam or air oven for sometime. The crystals are finally dried over sulphuric acid or calcium chloride in a desiccator.

(v) **Removal of colour** Sometimes, the crystals obtained are slightly coloured due to the presence of certain coloured impurities. In such cases, crystals are redissolved in the same solvent and a small amount of activated charcoal is added to it. The mixture is boiled for 15-20 min. During this treatment, charcoal adsorbs all the coloured impurities. The charcoal is then filtered out and the filtrate is allowed to cool. After that the colourless crystals of the pure substance are **obtained.**

Figure outlines flow-sheet of the process of crystallisation. Sometimes repeated crystallisation is carried out to make it more yield effective.

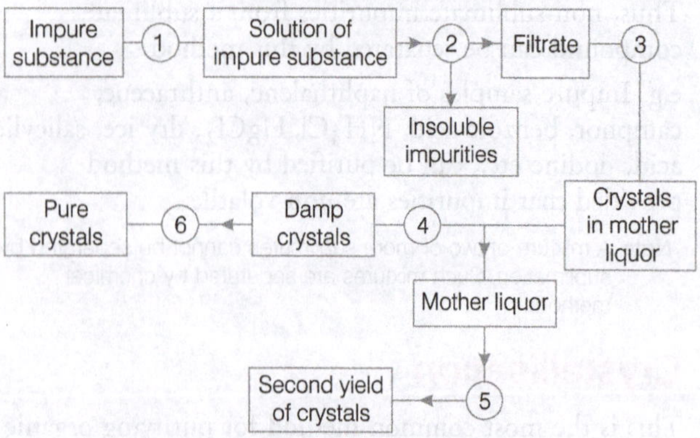

Schematic flow-diagram for crystallisation

Choice of Solvent

It is a common saying that like dissolves like. Polar compounds are soluble in polar solvents and non-polar compounds are soluble in non-polar solvents. It is always better to try out on a small scale first.

Good crystallisation medium means that the compound is highly soluble in hot and insoluble in cold.

Polar solvents (as water) tends to produce better crystals than hydrocarbon solvents.

Distillation

This process is based upon the difference in the boiling points of two liquids or two components. Thus, it is used to separate

(i) a volatile liquid from a non-volatile impurity.

(ii) two liquids having large difference in their boiling points.

In this method, when the mixture of the liquids (having large difference in their boiling point) is heated by taking in a round bottom flask, the vapours of the lower boiling liquid are formed first. These vapours are condensed by the condenser and collected in a receiver. The vapours of higher boiling liquid are formed later and thus, collected separately. The apparatus used for simple distillation is shown in the following figure.

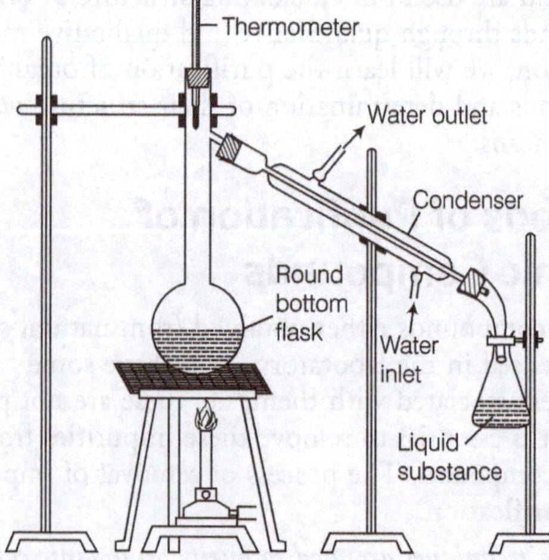

The mixtures of chloroform and aniline, ether and toluene, benzene and aniline etc. are separated by this technique.

Fractional Distillation

It is used to separate the liquids, boiling points of which are nearly equal, i.e. within the limit of 10 to 15 K.

In this method, a fractionating column is fitted over the mouth of the round bottom flask as shown in the following figure.

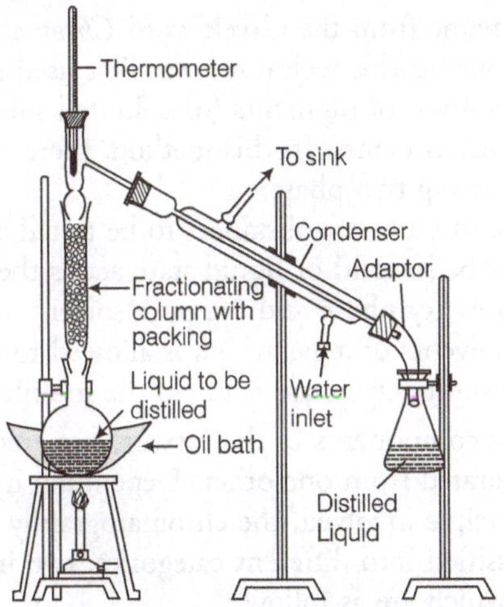

Fractional distillation

The vapour of higher boiling liquid condense before the vapours of lower boiling liquids. As the vapours rise in the fractionating column, it becomes rich in the vapours of more volatile component. Fractionating column provides many surfaces for heat change between the ascending vapours and the descending condensed liquid. Some of the condensing liquid also get heat from the ascending vapours and revaporises.

Thus, the vapours become rich in the low boiling component. The vapours of low boiling component move upward and reach at the top which contains mainly vapours of pure low boiling liquids. The vapours are collected in a receiver by passing through a condenser.

After a series of successive distillations, the remaining liquid in the distillation flask gets enriched in high boiling component. Each successive condensation and vaporisation unit in the fractionating column is called a **theoretical plate**. Commercially columns with hundreds of plates are available.

This method is used to separate different fractions of crude oil in petroleum industry.

Distillation Under Reduced Pressure

It is used for those liquids which have a tendency to decompose at a temperature below their boiling point. As we know at boiling point, vapour pressure of liquid is equal to its atmospheric pressure.

Hence, under reduced pressure the liquid will boil at low temperature. Thus, temperature for decomposition is not reached.

The reduced pressure is achieved by using a water pump or vacuum pump. e.g. boiling point of glycerol is 563 K but it decomposes much before its boiling temperature. However at 12 mm of Hg pressure, glycerol boils at 453 K without decomposition, so glycerol is separated from spent lye in soap industry by using this method. Other examples include H_2O_2, concentration of sugar cane juice in sugar industry.

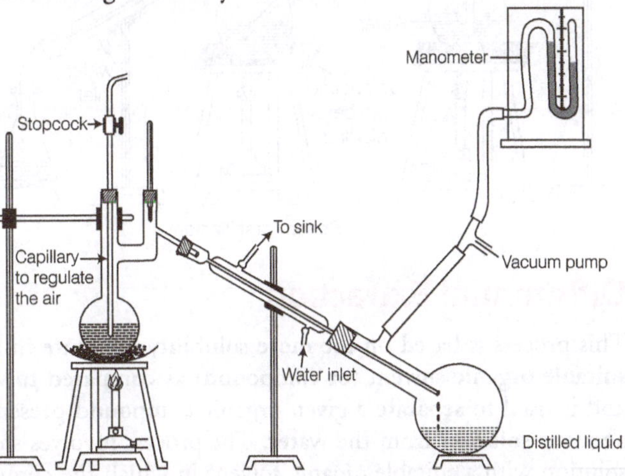

Distillation under reduced pressure

Steam Distillation

This technique is used for purifying steam volatile compounds that are immiscible with water. In this method, the impure liquid is taken in a heated flask and steam is passed over it with the help of a steam generator.

The mixture of steam and the volatile organic compound is condensed and collected in a receiver. From this mixture, water is removed by using separating funnel. During steam distillation, a liquid boils only when the sum of vapour pressure of the liquid (p_1) and of water (p_2) becomes equal to the atmospheric pressure (p) i.e. $p = p_1 + p_2$

Since, $p_1 < p$, so the liquid will vapourise at a temperature much below than its boiling point e.g. a mixture of water and a steam volatile insoluble substance will vapourise close but below 373 K.

The vapour obtained consists of the molecules of both organic liquid as well as water. When the vapour is condensed, a distillate containing both the organic liquid as well as water is obtained. The composition of the distillate is given by the equation, $\frac{w_A}{w_B} = \frac{p_A M_A}{p_B M_B}$.

The above technique is used for separating aniline from aniline-water mixture.

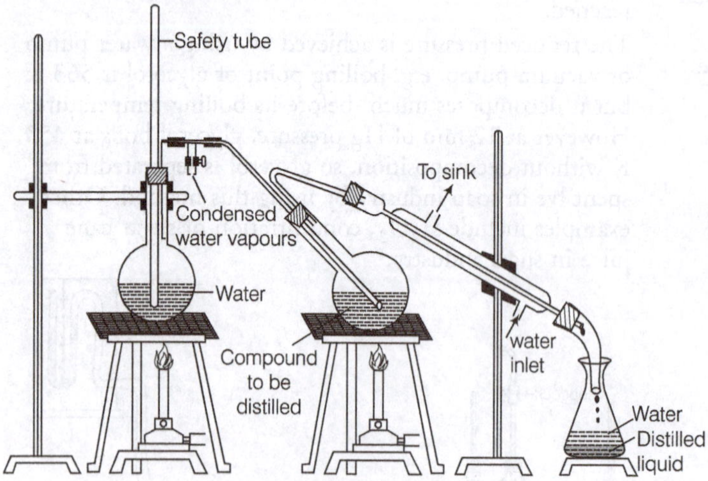

Steam distillation

Differential Extraction

This process is **based on the more solubility of solute in a suitable organic solvent (or compound) as compared to water and is used to separate a given organic compound present in an aqueous solution from the water.** The process involves shaking of solution with a suitable organic solvent in which the compound is more soluble as compared to water such as ether, chloroform or benzene, in a separating funnel (which is shown below in the figure). While performing such an act one point should be kept in mind that solvent and water must form two distinct layers that can be separated by using separating funnel. The organic solvent from the compound can be removed by either distillation or evaporation.

If the solubility of organic compound is very less in the organic solvent then a very large quantity of the solvent is required to extract even a very minute amount of the compound. In such a condition, **continuous extraction** is used, which involves the repeated use of same solvent for the extraction of the compound.

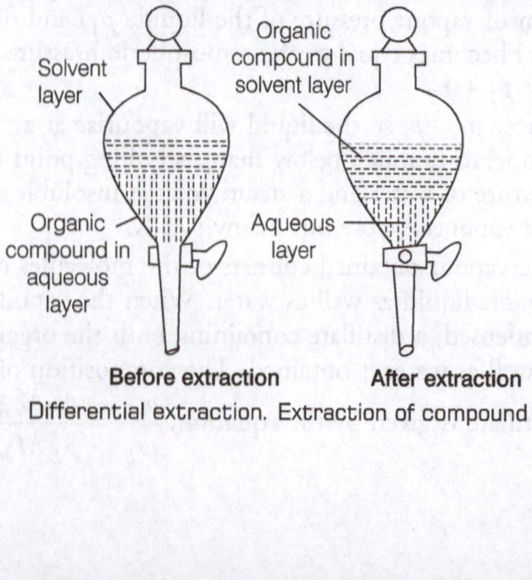

Differential extraction. Extraction of compound

Chromatography

It is an important and modern technique used for the separation, identification and purification of organic compounds. Purity of a compound can also be checked with the help of this technique.

This technique was discovered by Tswett and got its name from the Greek word *Chroma* (means colour) as this technique was first used for the separation of pigments (or coloured substances) found in plants. In this method, there are following two phase.

The mixture of substances to be tested which may be in solid or liquid state act as the **stationary phase** and the pure solvent or mixture of solvents or a gas which is allowed to pass over the stationary phase is called the **mobile phase.**

The components of the mixture get gradually separated from one other. Depending upon the principle involved, the chromatography is classified into different categories, two important of which are as follows:

1. Adsorption Chromatography

This method is based upon the different rates of adsorption of different compounds by an adsorbent. Silica gel and alumina are generally used as adsorbent during this process.

When the mobile phase is passed over the stationary phase (adsorbent), the components of the mixture move by different distance over the stationary phase and thus, they can be separated or identified.

Two main chromatographic methods working on the principle of differential adsorption are as follows :

(i) **Column chromatography** A glass tube containing adsorbent (stationary phase) and is fitted with a stop cock at its lower end is called the column. The mixture of substance to be separated is placed at the top portion of the column over the adsorbent. When the suitable solvent or mixture of solvent, called the **eluant** is allowed to pass through the column, different components due to their different rate of adsorption move different distances and thus, result in the formation of different bands as shown in the following figure.

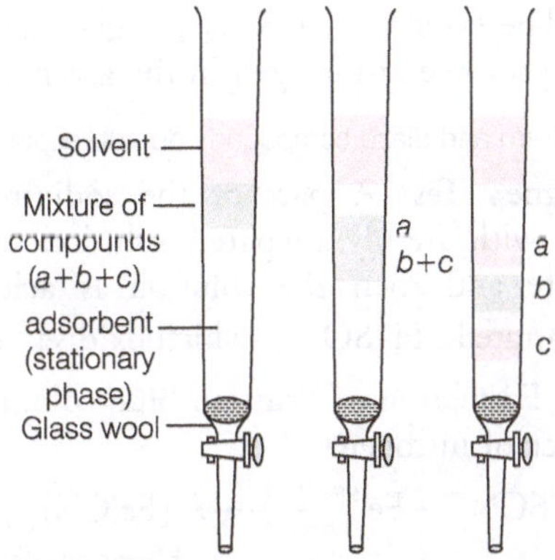

Column chromatography

The most readily adsorbed component is retained at the top and the less readily adsorbed components form separate band below it at various distances.

(ii) **Thin layer chromatography** In this method, a glass plate of suitable size is coated with a thin layer (about 0.2 mm) of adsorbent. This plate is called the **thin layer chromatography plate** or **chromaplate.** On this plate, the solution of mixture to be separated is applied in the form of a small spot, about 2 cm above the one end. The plate is then placed in a closed jar having eluant. As the eluant rises up the plate, the components of the mixture move with it upto different distances depending upon their different rates of adsorption and get separated from one another as shown below:

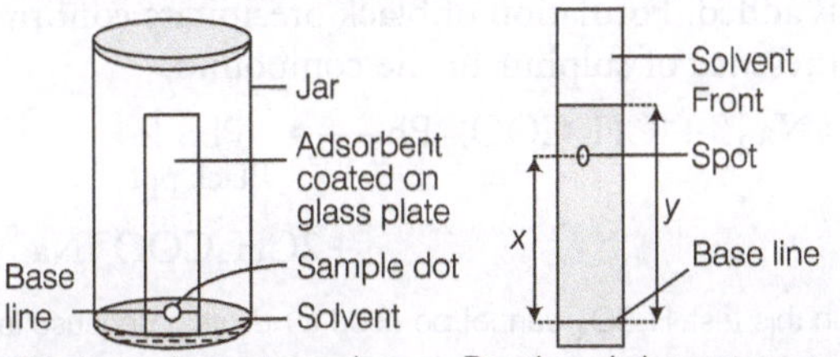

Thin layer chromatography Developed chromatogram

The relative adsorption of different components is expressed in terms of retardation factor (R_f values) which is given as

$$R_f = \frac{\text{Distance moved by the substance from base line } (x)}{\text{Distance moved by the solvent from base line } (y)}$$

The spot of the coloured components are visible on the TLC plate due to their own colour.

However, the spots of colourless substance are made visible by placing the plate

(i) under UV light.

(ii) in a covered jar having few crystals of iodine. (component that adsorb iodine appear in the form of brown spots).

(iii) an appropriate reagent may be spread on the plate e.g. ninhydrin solution is sprayed to detect the presence of amino acids.

2. Partition Chromatography

This method is based on the continuous differential partitioning of components of a mixture between stationary and mobile phases.

Paper chromatography is a type that works on this principle. In this method, a special type of paper, called the **chromatography paper** is used.

This paper contains water trapped in it and act as the **stationary phase.** The mixture of the components to be separated is placed in the form of small spot about 2 cm above from the lower end (at the base line).

When this strip is suspended in a suitable solvent or a mixture of solvents which act as the **mobile phase,** the solvent start rising up the paper due to capillary action and flows over the spot.

The paper selectively retains different components on the basis of their different partition in the two phases.

The paper strip so obtained is called the **chromatogram.** The spots of separated coloured components are visible at different heights from the original spot of the mixture on the chromatogram.

However, the spots of colourless substances are observed by using the same methods as done in thin layer chromatography.

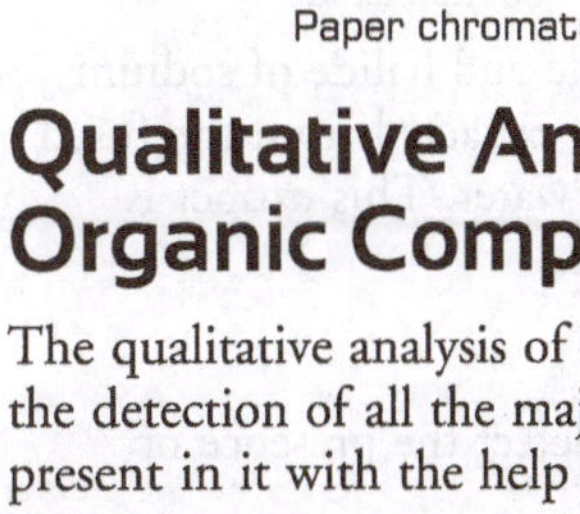

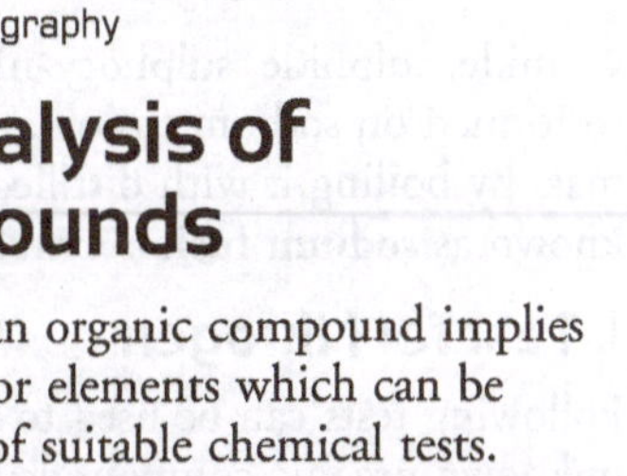

Paper chromatography

Qualitative Analysis of Organic Compounds

The qualitative analysis of an organic compound implies the detection of all the major elements which can be present in it with the help of suitable chemical tests.

Detection of Carbon and Hydrogen

To detect the presence of carbon and hydrogen, the compound is heated with dry copper (II) oxide. By this, carbon is oxidised to CO_2 and hydrogen to water.

$$\text{C of organic compound} + 2CuO \xrightarrow{\Delta} CO_2 + 2Cu$$

$$\text{H of organic compound} + CuO \xrightarrow{\Delta} H_2O + Cu$$

H_2O vapours turn anhydrous $CuSO_4$ blue and CO_2 evolved turns lime water milky.

$$\underset{\text{White}}{CuSO_4} + 5H_2O \longrightarrow \underset{\text{Hydrated copper sulphate (Blue)}}{CuSO_4 \cdot 5H_2O}$$

$$Ca(OH)_2 + CO_2 \longrightarrow \underset{\text{Milky}}{CaCO_3\downarrow} + H_2O$$

Detection of Oxygen

There is no satisfactory qualitative test for oxygen. An indicative test for the presence of oxygen can be performed. It involves the heating of compound in an atmosphere of nitrogen. If water drops are formed, the presence of oxygen is inferred.

Detection of Other Elements : Lassaigne's Test

The elements other than C and H (like N, S, *X*, P) are detected with the help of **Lassaigne's test.** In this test, the compound is fused with small quantity of Na metal in a fusion tube to convert the elements present in it into their ionic forms. Following reactions take place.

$$Na + C + N \xrightarrow{\text{Fusion}} \underset{\text{Sodium cyanide}}{Na^+C{\equiv}N}$$

$$2Na + S \xrightarrow{\text{Fusion}} \underset{\text{Sodium sulphide}}{Na_2S}$$

$$Na + C + N + S \longrightarrow \underset{\text{Sodium sulphocyanide}}{NaSCN}$$

(when N and S both are present)

$$Na + \underset{\text{Halogen}}{X} \longrightarrow \underset{\text{Sodium halide}}{NaX}$$

Cyanide, sulphide, sulphocyanide and halide of sodium so formed on sodium fusion are extracted from the fused mass by boiling it with distilled water. This extract is known as **sodium fusion extract.**

1. Test for Nitrogen

Following tests can be used to detect the presence of unknown organic compounds:

(i) **Soda-lime Test** To the small amount of soda-lime, unknown compound is mixed and heated in a test tube. The evolution of NH_3 gas gives an indication of the presence of nitrogen in the given compound.

Note Nitro and diazo compounds do not respond to this test.

(ii) **Lassaigne's Test** A part of the sodium extract is boiled with freshly prepared solution of iron (II) sulphate and then the solution is acidified with concentrated H_2SO_4 (which oxidise Fe^{2+} into Fe^{3+}). Formation of Prussian blue colour shows the presence of nitrogen.

$$6CN^- + Fe^{2+} \longrightarrow \underset{\text{Hexacyanoferrate}}{[Fe(CN)_6]^{4-}}$$

$$3[Fe(CN)_6]^{4-} + 4Fe^{3+} \xrightarrow{xH_2O} \underset{\substack{\text{Prussian blue} \\ \text{Iron (III) hexacyanoferrate (II)} \\ \text{(ferriferrocyanide)}}}{Fe_4[Fe(CN)_6]_3 \cdot xH_2O}$$

Note Lassaigne's test is positive for nitrogen only when the compound contains carbon alongwith nitrogen. $NH_2NH_2 \cdot HCl$ contains nitrogen but does not contain carbon, thus, NaCN is not formed and hence, test of N is negative.

2. Test for Sulphur

Following two tests are used to detect the presence of sulphur in organic compounds

(i) **Lassaigne's Test** A part of Lassaigne extract is acidified with CH_3COOH and then $(CH_3COO)_2Pb$ solution is added. Formation of black precipitate confirms the presence of sulphur in the compound.

$$Na_2S + (CH_3COO)_2Pb \longrightarrow \underset{\text{Black ppt.}}{PbS\downarrow} + 2CH_3COO^-Na^+$$

Note In this test, H_2SO_4 cannot be used for dilution because lead acetate itself will react with H_2SO_4 to form white ppt of lead sulphate.

$$\underset{\text{Lead acetate}}{Pb(OCOCH_3)_2} + H_2SO_4 \longrightarrow \underset{\text{White ppt.}}{PbSO_4\downarrow} + 2\,CH_3COOH$$

(ii) **Sodium Nitroprusside Test** A few drops of sodium nitroprusside solution are added to a part of soda extract.

The appearance of purple colouration confirms the presence of sulphur.

$$Na_2S + Na_2[Fe(CN)_5NO] \longrightarrow \underset{\text{Purple colour}}{Na_4[Fe(CN)_5NOS]}$$

(iii) **Oxidation Test** Unknown organic compound is fused with sodium carbonate and potassium nitrate mixture in an ignition tube. The sulphur present in compound gets oxidised to sodium sulphate.

$$Na_2CO_3 + S + 3[O] \xrightarrow[\text{Heat}]{KNO_3} Na_2SO_4 + CO_2$$

The mass obtained is filtered. To this, few drops of barium chloride solution are added to the filtrate. A white ppt. indicates the presence of sulphur in the given compound.

$$Na_2SO_4 + BaCl_2 \longrightarrow BaSO_4 \downarrow + 2NaCl$$

3. Test for Nitrogen and Sulphur

If the compound contains sulphur and nitrogen both, sodium sulphocyanide is formed in Lassaigne's extract which gives blood red colouration of $Fe(SCN)_3$ with $FeCl_3$.

$$Na + C + N + S \longrightarrow NaSCN$$

$$Fe^{3+} + SCN^- \longrightarrow \underset{\text{Blood red}}{Fe[(SCN)]^{2+}}$$

If sodium fusion is carried out with excess of sodium, the thiocyanate decomposes to yield cyanide and sulphide. These ions give their usual tests.

$$NaSCN + 2Na \longrightarrow NaCN + Na_2S$$

4. Test for Halogens

Following tests can be used to detect the presence of halogen (Cl, Br, I) in an organic compound.

(i) Lassaigne's Test

The soda extract of organic compound is boiled with conc. HNO_3 to expel the gases. Here, the HNO_3 decomposes NaCN and Na_2S (if present) in the soda extract as:

$$NaCN + HNO_3 \longrightarrow NaNO_3 + HCN\uparrow$$

$$Na_2S + 2HNO_3 \longrightarrow 2NaNO_3 + H_2S\uparrow$$

$$Na + X \longrightarrow \underset{\text{Soda extract}}{NaX} \quad (X = Cl, Br, I)$$

It is then cooled and treated with $AgNO_3$ solution:

Observations

(i) Formation of a white ppt soluble in NH_4OH solution indicates the presence of chlorine in organic compound.

$$NaCl + AgNO_3 \longrightarrow \underset{\text{White ppt.}}{AgCl} + NaNO_3$$

(ii) Formation of dull yellow ppt partially soluble in NH_4OH solution indicates the presence of bromine in the organic compound.

$$NaBr + AgNO_3 \longrightarrow \underset{\text{Dull yellow ppt.}}{AgBr\downarrow} + NaNO_3$$

(iii) Formation of yellow ppt insoluble in NH_4OH indicates the presence of iodine in the organic compound.

$$AgNO_3 + NaI \longrightarrow \underset{\text{Yellow ppt.}}{AgI\downarrow} + NaNO_3$$

Note
- In the detection of halogens if, cyanide and sulphide are not removed before adding silver nitrate solution, these radicals will combine with silver nitrate and produce white and black ppt of AgCN and Ag_2S respectively.
- H_2SO_4 cannot be used instead of HNO_3 as it gives white ppt of Ag_2SO_4 with $AgNO_3$ which interfere with the test of chlorine.

(ii) Beilstein's Test

Here, the copper wire is heated in the oxidising flame of bunsen burner and heating is continued till it does not impart blue or green flame. Upon heating, the halogen present in the compound reacts with Cu to form a volatile Cu halide which imparts blue or green colour in the flame indicates the presence of halogen in the given compound.

5. Test for Phosphorus

For the detection of phosphorus, organic compound is fused with sodium peroxide (oxidising agent) hence, phosphorus is converted into sodium phosphate.

$$5Na_2O_2 + \underset{\text{Compound}}{2P} \xrightarrow{\text{Fuse}} \underset{\text{Sodium phosphate}}{2Na_3PO_4} + 2Na_2O$$

The fused mass is extracted with water and the water extract is boiled with conc. HNO_3. Upon cooling, a few drops of ammonium molybdate solution are added, a yellow ppt confirms the presence of phosphorus in the organic compound.

$$Na_3PO_4 + 3HNO_3 \longrightarrow H_3PO_4 + 3NaNO_3$$

$$H_3PO_4 + 12(NH_4)_2MoO_4 + 21HNO_3 \longrightarrow \underset{\substack{\text{(Yellow ppt.)} \\ \text{Ammonium phosphomolybdate}}}{(NH_4)_3PO_4 \cdot 12MoO_3\downarrow} + 21NH_4NO_3 + 12H_2O$$

Quantitative Analysis

The percentage of different elements present in an organic compound can be determined with the help of following methods.

Estimation of Carbon and Hydrogen

The C and H in an organic compound are estimated by **Liebig method.** In this method, the organic compound is heated with dry cupric oxide in an atmosphere of dry oxygen (or air) free from CO_2. Thus, the C and H present in the organic compound are oxidised to CO_2 and water vapours respectively.

$$C_xH_y + (x + y/4)O_2 \longrightarrow xCO_2 + (y/2)H_2O$$

(i) CO_2 vapours are passed through weighed potash bulb which absorbs CO_2 completely. The increase in the weight of potash bulb corresponds to the weight of CO_2 produced.

$$2KOH + CO_2 \longrightarrow K_2CO_3 + H_2O$$

(ii) Water vapours are passed through weighed calcium chloride tube (U-shaped). Increase in the weight of $CaCl_2$ corresponds to the weight of H_2O formed.

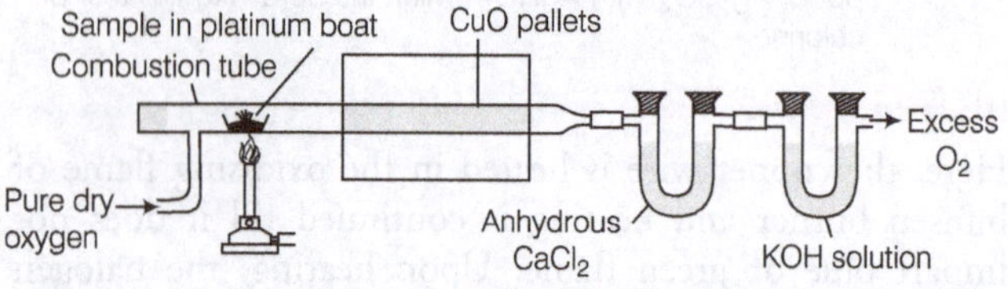

Estimation of carbon and hydrogen

From the respective weights, the percentage of C and H can be determined as:

(i) $\% \text{ of carbon} = \dfrac{12 \times \text{mass of } CO_2 \times 100}{44 \times \text{mass of organic compound}}$

(ii) $\% \text{ of hydrogen} = \dfrac{2 \times \text{mass of } H_2O \times 100}{18 \times \text{mass of organic compound}}$

Example 1 On complete combustion, 0.246 g of an organic compound gave 0.198g of carbon dioxide and 0.1014 g of water. Determine the percentage composition of carbon and hydrogen in the compound.

NCERT Textbook

Sol. Percentage of carbon $= \dfrac{12 \times 0.198 \times 100}{44 \times 0.246} = 21.95\%$

Percentage of hydrogen $= \dfrac{2 \times 0.1014 \times 100}{18 \times 0.246} = 4.58\%$

Estimation of Nitrogen

Following two methods are used to estimate the percentage of nitrogen in an organic compound.

1. Duma's Method

In this method, organic compound is heated with dry cupric oxide in a combustion tube in the atmosphere of CO_2. Upon heating, C and H present are oxidised to CO_2 and water vapours respectively, while N_2 is set free.

$$C_xH_yN_z + (2x + y/2)\,CuO \longrightarrow$$
$$x\,CO_2 + y/2\,H_2O + \frac{z}{2}N_2 + (2x + y/2)\,Cu$$

A small amount of N_2 might be oxidised to its oxides but they are reduced back to N_2 with the help of Cu placed at the end of the combustion tube. The mixture of gases so produced is collected over an aqueous solution of potassium hydroxide which absorbs carbon dioxide. Nitrogen is collected in the upper part of the graduated tube.

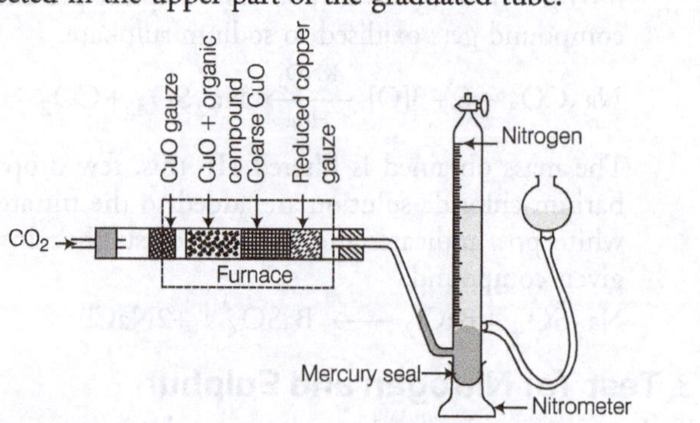

Duma's method for the estimation of nitrogen

Let the mass of organic compound $= m$ g

Volume of nitrogen collected $= V_1$ mL

Room temperature $= T_1$K

Volume of nitrogen at STP $= \dfrac{p_1V_1 \times 273}{760 \times T_1}$

(let it be V mL)

where, p_1 and V_1 are the pressure and volume of nitrogen.

p_1 = Atmospheric pressure − Aqueous tension

$\because$ 22400 mL N_2 at STP weights 28 g

$\therefore$ V mL N_2 at STP weighs $= \dfrac{28 \times V}{22400}$ g

$\therefore$ Percentage of nitrogen $= \dfrac{28 \times V \times 100}{22400 \times m}$

Example 2 In Duma's method for estimation of nitrogen, 0.3 g of an organic compound gave 50 mL of nitrogen collected at 300 K temperature and 715 mm pressure. Calculate the percentage composition of nitrogen in the compound.

(Aqueous tension at 300 K = 15 mm). **NCERT Textbook**

Sol. Volume of nitrogen collected at 300 K and 715 mm pressure = 50 mL

Actual pressure $= 715 - 15 = 700$ mm;

Volume of nitrogen at STP $= \dfrac{273 \times 700 \times 50}{300 \times 760}$

$= 41.9$ mL

$\because$ 22,400 mL of N_2 at STP weighs = 28 g

$\therefore$ 41.9 mL of nitrogen weighs $= \dfrac{28 \times 41.9}{22400}$ g

$\therefore$ Percentage of nitrogen $= \dfrac{28 \times 41.9 \times 100}{22400 \times 0.3}$

$= 17.46\%$

2. Kjeldahl's Method

This method is based on the principle that when the nitrogenous compound is heated with conc. H_2SO_4 in the presence of potassium sulphate, (which raises the boiling point of H_2SO_4) and $CuSO_4$ (catalyst), the nitrogen present in the compound is converted to ammonium sulphate. The ammonium sulphate, so formed is decomposed with excess of alkali (NaOH) and NH_3 get evolved that is estimated volumetrically, using the titration of an acid.

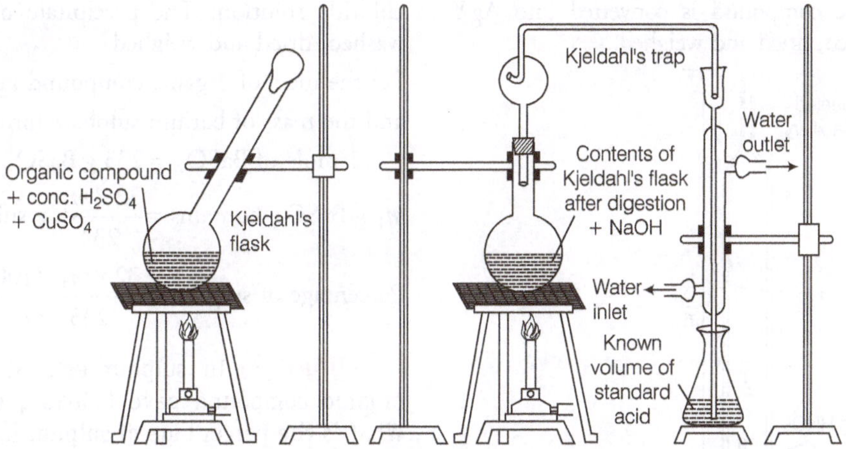

Kjeldahl's method for estimating nitrogen

It is done by estimating unreacted sulphuric acid left after the absorption of ammonia by titrating it with standard alkali solution. The difference between the initial amount of acid taken and that left after the reaction gives the amount of acid reacted with ammonia.

$$\text{Organic compound} + \underset{\text{(Conc.)}}{H_2SO_4} \longrightarrow (NH_4)_2SO_4$$

$$\xrightarrow{2\,NaOH} Na_2SO_4 + 2NH_3 + 2H_2O$$

$$2NH_3 + H_2SO_4 \longrightarrow (NH_2)_4SO_4$$

Let the mass of organic compound taken $= m$ g

Volume of H_2SO_4 of molarity, M taken $= V$ mL

Volume of NaOH of molarity, M, used for titration of excess of $H_2SO_4 = V_1$ mL

V_1 mL of NaOH of molarity M

$$= \frac{V_1}{2} \text{ mL of } H_2SO_4 \text{ of molarity } M$$

Volume of H_2SO_4 of molarity M unused

$$= (V - V_1/2) \text{ mL}$$

$(V - V_1/2)$ mL of H_2SO_4 of molarity M

$= 2(V - V_1/2)$ mL of NH_3 solution of molarity M.

1000 mL of 1 M NH_3 solution contains

$$= 17 \text{ g } NH_3 \text{ or } 14 \text{ g of N}$$

$2(V - V_1/2)$ mL of NH_3 solution of molarity M contains

$$= \frac{14 \times M \times 2(V - V_1/2)}{1000} \text{ g N}$$

$$\text{Percentage of N} = \frac{14 \times M \times 2(V - V_1/2)}{1000} \times \frac{100}{m}$$

$$= \frac{1.4 \times M \times 2(V - V_1/2)}{m}$$

Example 3 During estimation of nitrogen present in an organic compound by Kjeldahl's method, the ammonia evolved from 0.5 g of the compound in Kjeldahl's estimation of nitrogen, neutralized 10 mL of 1 M H_2SO_4. Find out the percentage of nitrogen in the compound.

NCERT Textbook

Sol. 1 M of 10 mL H_2SO_4 = 1 M of 20 mL NH_3

$\because$ 1000 mL of 1 M ammonia contains nitrogen = 14 g

$\therefore$ 20 mL of 1 M ammonia will contain nitrogen $= \frac{14 \times 20}{1000}$ g

$\therefore$ Percentage of nitrogen $= \frac{14 \times 20 \times 100}{1000 \times 0.5}$

$= 56.0\%$

Note Kjeldahl's method is not applicable to compounds containing nitrogen in nitro and azo groups and nitrogen present in the ring, as nitrogen of these compounds is not quantitatively converted into ammonium sulphate.

Estimation of Halogens

In the case of halogens, estimation is done with **Carius method.** Here, the weighed amount of organic compound is heated in a sealed tube called the Carius tube, with fuming HNO_3 in the presence of $AgNO_3$. As a result, halogen present in the organic compound is converted into Ag*X* which is filtered, washed, dried and weighed.

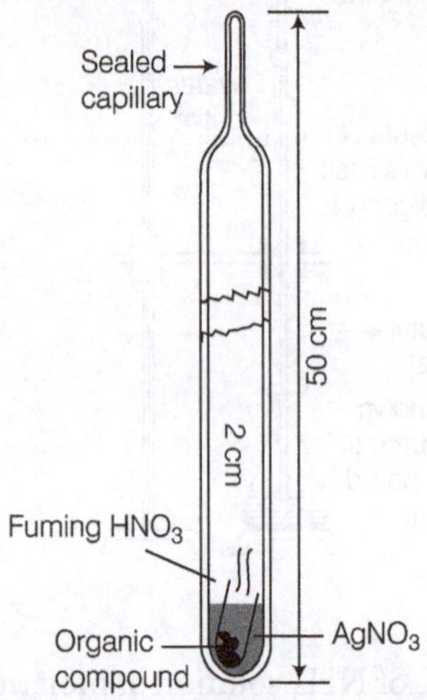

Carius method for estimating halogen

Let the mass of organic compound taken $= m$ g

Mass of Ag*X* formed $= m_1$g

1 mol of Ag*X* contains 1 mol of *X*

Mass of halogen is m_1g of Ag*X*

$$= \frac{\text{atomic mass of } X \times m_1 \text{g}}{\text{molecular mass of Ag}X}$$

$$\text{Percentage of halogen} = \frac{\text{atomic mass of } X \times m_1 \times 100}{\text{molecular mass of Ag}X \times m}$$

$$\text{Thus, \% of chlorine} = \frac{35.5}{143.5} \times \frac{\text{mass of AgCl} \times 100}{\text{mass of compound}}$$

$$\text{\% of bromine} = \frac{80}{188} \times \frac{\text{mass of AgBr} \times 100}{\text{mass of compound}}$$

$$\text{\% of iodine} = \frac{127}{235} = \frac{\text{mass of AgI} \times 100}{\text{mass of compound}}$$

Example 4 In carius method of estimation of halogen, 0.15 g of an organic compound gave 0.12 of AgBr. Find out the percentage of bromine in the compound. **NCERT Textbook**

Sol. $$\text{Percentage of bromine} = \frac{80}{188} \times \frac{\text{mass of AgBr} \times 100}{\text{mass of compound}}$$

$$\text{Percentage of bromine} = \frac{80 \times 0.12 \times 100}{188 \times 0.15} = 34.04\%$$

Estimation of Sulphur

It is also estimated by **Carius method.** In this case, the compound is heated with sodium peroxide or fuming HNO_3, resulting to oxidation of its sulphur to H_2SO_4 which is collected as $BaSO_4$ by using excess of barium chloride solution. The precipitate of $BaSO_4$ is filtered, washed, dried and weighed.

Let the mass of organic compound taken $= m$ g

and the mass of barium sulphate formed $= m_1$ g

$$1 \text{ mole of } BaSO_4 = 233 \text{ g } BaSO_4 = 32 \text{ g sulphur}$$

$$m_1 \text{ g } BaSO_4 \text{ contains} = \frac{32 \times m_1}{233} \text{ g sulphur}$$

$$\text{Percentage of sulphur} = \frac{32 \times m_1 \times 100}{233 \times m}$$

Example 5 In sulphur estimation, 0.157 g of an organic compound gave 0.4813 g of barium sulphate. What is the percentage of sulphur in the compound ? **NCERT Textbook**

Sol. $$\text{Percentage of sulphur} = \frac{32 \times \text{mass of } BaSO_4 \times 100}{233 \times \text{mass of compound}}$$

$$= \frac{32 \times 0.4813 \times 100}{233 \times 0.157} = 42.10\%$$

Estimation of Phosphorus

For the estimation of phosphorus, weighed amount of organic compound is heated with HNO_3 in a Carius tube. Phosphorus present in the compound is converted into phosphoric acid. It is precipitated as ammonium phosphomolybdate,$(NH_4)_3PO_4 \cdot 12MoO_3$, by adding ammonia and ammonium molybdate.

Let the mass of organic compound taken $= m$ g

and mass of ammonium phosphomolybdate $= m_1$ g

Molar mass of $(NH_4)_3PO_4 \cdot 12MoO_3 = 1877$ g

$$\text{Percentage of phosphorus} = \frac{31 \times m_1 \times 100}{1877 \times m} \%$$

Alternatively, the contents of the tube are heated with $MgCl_2$ solution in the presence of NH_4Cl and NH_4OH (magnesia mixture), the $MgNH_4PO_4$ so formed is collected, washed, dried and ignited to get magnesium pyrophosphate $(Mg_2P_2O_7)$ which is weighed and the percentage of P is calculated with the help of following formula.

$$\text{Percentage of P} = \frac{62 \times \text{mass of } Mg_2P_2O_7 \text{ formed}}{222 \times \text{mass of the compound}} \times 100\%$$

Where, 222 u is the molar mass of $Mg_2P_2O_7$ and 62 is the mass of two P atom present in $Mg_2P_2O_7$.

Estimation of Oxygen

If sum of percentage of all other elements present in a compound is less than 100, then % of oxygen = 100 – sum of % of all other elements.

Direct Method for Estimating Oxygen

In this method, a calculated quantity of the organic compound is heated in a stream of nitrogen gas and the obtained oxygen is converted into CO by passing the gaseous mixture over red hot coke. The CO is warmed with I_2O_5 (iodine pentoxide), which oxidises CO to CO_2 and itself gets reduced to I_2.

$$\text{Compound} \longrightarrow O_2 + \text{other gaseous products}$$

$$2C + O_2 \xrightarrow{1373\,K} 2CO\,]\times 5 \quad (A)$$

$$I_2O_5 + 5CO \longrightarrow I_2 + 5CO_2\,]\times 2 \quad (B)$$

From the equation (*A*) and (*B*),

$1 \text{ mol } O_2 \equiv 2 \text{ mol } CO \equiv 2 \text{ mol } CO_2$.

$\therefore$ 88 g CO_2 is obtained from O_2 = 32 g

Let the mass of organic compound taken = m g

Mass of carbon dioxide produced = m_1 g

$\therefore$ m_1 g carbon dioxide is obtained from $= \dfrac{32 \times m_1}{88}$ g O_2

$\therefore$ Percentage of oxygen $= \dfrac{32 \times m_1 \times 100}{88 \times m}$ %

The percentage of oxygen can also be derived from the amount of iodine produced.

Topic Practice 4

Very Short Answer Type Questions

(1 Mark)

1. Fill in the Blanks

(i) A mixture of $CaSO_4$ and camphor can be separated by ....

(ii) .... method can be used to separate two compounds with different solubilities in a solvents.

(iii) Sodium extract is boiled with nitric acid to decompose .... and ...., if present.

(iv) The C and H in an organic compound are estimated by .... method.

(v) .... method is based on the principle that when nitrogenous compound is heated with conc. H_2SO_4 in presence of potassium sulphate and $CuSO_4$, the nitrogen present in the compound convert into NH_4SO_4.

2. Objective Type Questions

(i) Naphthalene can be easily purified by
(a) sublimation (b) crystallisation
(c) distillation (d) vaporisation

(ii) Which of the following method is used to purify liquids having very high boiling points and those which decompose at or below their boiling points?
(a) Simple distillation
(b) Fractional distillation
(c) Distillation under reduced pressure
(d) None of the above

(iii) Glycerol can be separated from spent-lye in soap industry by
(a) chromatography
(b) sublimation
(c) fractional distillation
(d) distillaltion under reduced pressure

(iv) The technique in which extraction of compound takes place on the basis of more solubility of one compound in another solvent, is
(a) differential extraction (b) chromatography
(c) sublimation (d) crystallisation

(v) Which chromatography is based on the fact that different compounds are adsorbed on an adsorbent to different degrees.?
(a) Partition chromatography
(b) Adsorption chromatography
(c) Absorption chromatography
(d) Paper chromatography

(vi) Formation of which of the following complex indicates presence of sulphur in the organic compound when sodium nitroprusside is added to sodium extract of the compound?
(a) $Fe_4[Fe(CN)_6]_3$ (b) $Na_2[Fe(NO)(CN)_5]$
(c) $Fe(CNS)$ (d) $Na_4[Fe(CN)_5NOS]$

(vii) In Kjeldahl's method, the nitrogen present in an organic compound is quantitatively converted into
(a) Nitrogen (b) ammonium sulphate
(c) ammonium phosphate
(d) ammonia

(viii) In Duma's method for estimation of nitrogen, 0.3 g of an organic compound gave 50 mL of nitrogen collected at 300K temperature and 715 mm pressure. The percentage composition of nitrogen in the compound (Aqueous tension at 300K = 15mm) is
(a) 15.46% (b) 17.46%
(c) 18.36% (d) 28%

3. Matching Type Questions

(i) Match the items of Column I with Column II and choose the correct option using the codes given below:

Column I		Column II
A. Adsorbent	(i)	Silica gel or alumina
B. R_f value	(ii)	Brown spots
C. The spots of colourless compounds, which are invisible to eye	(iii)	Ninhydrin solution
D. Crystals of iodine	(iv)	Fluorescent in ultraviolet light.
E. Spraying reagent	(v)	Acts as stationary phase.
F. Chromatography paper contains water trapped in it.	(vi)	$\frac{\text{Distance moved by the substance from base line } (x)}{\text{Distance moved by the solvent from base line } (y)}$

Codes

	A	B	C	D	E	F
(a)	(v)	(vi)	(iv)	(ii)	(iii)	(i)
(b)	(vi)	(iv)	(v)	(i)	(iii)	(ii)
(c)	(ii)	(iii)	(iv)	(v)	(vi)	(i)
(d)	(i)	(vi)	(iv)	(ii)	(iii)	(v)

(ii) Match the Column I and Column II and choose the correct option using the codes given below:

Column I		Column II
A. Glycerol	(i)	Sublimation
B. o-nitrophenol	(ii)	Beilstein's test
C. Anthracene	(iii)	Victor-Meyer's method
D. Halogens	(iv)	Steam distillation
E. Molecular weight	(v)	Vacuum distillation
	(vi)	Eudiometry

Codes

	A	B	C	D	E
(a)	(v)	(iv)	(i)	(ii)	(iii)
(b)	(iv)	(v)	(i)	(vi)	(ii)
(c)	(vi)	(iv)	(i)	(iii)	(ii)
(d)	(v)	(iv)	(vi)	(ii)	(iii)

(iii) Match the items of Column I with Column II and choose the correct option using the codes given below :

Column I (Test for element)		Column II (Products involved in the chemical reaction)
A. Test for nitrogen	(i)	$(NH_4)_3PO_4 \cdot 12MoO_3$ Ammonium phosphomolybdate
B. Test for sulphur	(ii)	$Fe_4[Fe(CN)_6]_3 \cdot xH_2O$ Prussian blue
C. Test for nitrogen and sulphur	(iii)	AgX
D. Test for halogens	(iv)	$[Fe(SCN)]^{2+}$ Blood red
E. Test for phosphorus	(v)	PbS Black

Codes

	A	B	C	D	E
(a)	(i)	(ii)	(iii)	(iv)	(v)
(b)	(ii)	(v)	(iv)	(iii)	(i)
(c)	(v)	(iii)	(iv)	(ii)	(i)
(d)	(iv)	(ii)	(iii)	(i)	(v)

(iv) Match the items of Column I with the items of Column II appropriately and choose the correct option using the codes given below:

Column I		Column II
A. Carius method	(i)	$\frac{1.4 \times M \times 2\,(V - V_1/2)}{m}$
B. Percentage of sulphur	(ii)	$\frac{62 \times m_1 \times 100}{222 \times m}\%$
C. Percentage of phosphorus	(iii)	$\frac{\text{Atomic mass of } X \times m_1 \times 100}{\text{Molecular mass of AgX} \times m}$
D. Percentage of halogen	(iv)	$S = \frac{32 \times m_1 \times 100}{233 \times m}$
E. Percentage of nitrogen	(v)	Organic compound is heated with fuming nitric acid in the presence of silver nitrate.

Codes

	A	B	C	D	E
(a)	(v)	(iv)	(ii)	(iii)	(i)
(b)	(ii)	(iv)	(iii)	(i)	(v)
(c)	(iv)	(v)	(ii)	(i)	(iii)
(d)	(iii)	(i)	(v)	(ii)	(iv)

4. Name a suitable technique of separation of the components from a mixture of calcium sulphate and camphor. **NCERT Textbook**

5 How will you separate a mixture of *o*-nitro phenol and *p*-nitrophenol?

6 If a liquid compound decomposes at its boiling point, which method(s) can you choose for its purification. It is known that the compound is stable at low pressure, steam volatile and insoluble in water. **NCERT Exemplar**

7 Explain, why an organic liquid vapourises at a temperature below its boiling point in steam distillation process?

8 The R_f value of A and B in a mixture determined by TLC in a solvent mixture are 0.65 and 0.42 respectively. If the mixture is separated by column chromatography using the same solvent mixture on a mobile phase, which of the two components A or B will elute first? Explain.

9 Explain the reason for the fusion of an organic compound with metallic sodium for testing nitrogen, sulphur and halogens. **NCERT Textbook**

10 In DNA and RNA, nitrogen atom is present in the ring system. Can Kjeldahl's method be used for the estimation of nitrogen present in these? Give reason. **NCERT Exemplar**

11 Lassaigne's test is not shown by diazonium salts, though they contain nitrogen. Why?

12 Will CCl_4 give white precipitate of AgCl on heating it with silver nitrate? Give reason for your answer.

13 Describe the method, which can be used to separate two compounds with different solubilities in a solvent S. **NCERT Textbook**

14 Two liquids A and B can be separated by the method of fractional distillation. The boiling point of liquid A is less than boiling point of liquid B. Which of the liquids do you expect to come out first in the distillate? Explain. **NCERT Exemplar**

Short Answer Type I Questions

2 Marks

15. Suggest methods for the separation of the following mixtures
   (i) a mixture of liquid A (bp 365K) and liquid B (bp 355 K)
   (ii) a mixture of liquid C (bp 348 K) and liquid D (bp 478 K).

16. Why is it necessary to use acetic acid and not sulphuric acid for acidification of sodium extract for testing sulphur by lead acetate test? **NCERT Textbook**

17. Why is nitric acid added to sodium extract before adding silver nitrate for testing halogens?

18. For testing halogens in an organic compound with $AgNO_3$ solution, sodium extract (Lassaigne's test) is acidified with dilute HNO_3. What will happen if a student acidifies the extract with dilute H_2SO_4 in place of dilute HNO_3? **NCERT Exemplar**

19. Why is a solution of potassium hydroxide used to absorb carbon dioxide evolved during the estimation of carbon present in an organic compound?

20. Differentiate between the principle of estimation of nitrogen in an organic compound by
   (i) Duma's method.
   (ii) Kjeldahl's method.

21. 0.3780 g of an organic chloro compound gave 0.5740 g of silver chloride in Carius estimation. Calculate the percentage of chlorine present in the compound. **NCERT Textbook**

22. In the estimation of sulphur by Carius method, 0.468 g of an organic sulphur compound afforded 0.668 g of barium sulphate. Find the percentage of sulphur in the given compound.

23. Give a brief description of the principles of the following techniques taking an example in each case
   (i) Crystallisation
   (ii) Distillation
   (iii) Chromatography. **NCERT Textbook**

Short Answer Type II Questions

3 Marks

24. Benzoic acid is an organic compound. Its crude sample can be purified by crystallisation from hot water. What characteristic differences in the properties of benzoic acid and the impurity make this process of purification suitable?

25. Explain the principle of paper chromatography. **NCERT Textbook**

26. Suggest a method to purify
   (i) camphor containing traces of common salt.
   (ii) kerosene oil containing water.
   (iii) a liquid which decomposes at its boiling point.

27. Discuss the principle of estimation of halogens, sulphur and phosphorus present in an organic compound. **NCERT Textbook**

28. A sample of 0.50 g of an organic compound was treated according to Kjeldahl's method. The ammonia evolved was absorbed in 50 mL of 0.5 M H_2SO_4. The residual acid required 60 mL of 0.5 M solution of NaOH for neutralisation. Find the percentage composition of nitrogen in the compound. **NCERT Textbook**

29. An organic compound contains 69% carbon and 4.8% hydrogen, the remainder being oxygen. Calculate the masses of carbon dioxide and water produced when 0.20 g of this substance is subjected to complete combustion. **NCERT Textbook**

Long Answer Type Questions

5 Marks

30. Draw a diagram of bubble plate type fractionating column. When do we require such type of a column for separating two liquids. Explain the principle involved in the separation of components of a mixture of liquids by using fractionating column. What industrial applications does this process have? **NCERT Textbook**

31. Discuss the chemistry of Lassaigne's test and also discuss qualitative analysis for phosphorus.

Hints & Solutions

1. (i) sublimation (ii) Crystallisation (iii) NaCN, Na_2S (iv) Liebig (v) Kjeldahl's

2. (i) (*a*) Substances which sublime on heating are usually purified by sublimation. Hence, naphthalene is purified by sublimation

(ii) (*c*) Distillation under reduced pressure is used to purify liquids having very high boiling points and those, which decompose at or below their boiling points.

Such liquids are made to boil at a temperature lower than their normal boiling points by reducing the pressure on their surface. A liquid boils at a temperature at which its vapour pressure is equal to the external pressure. The pressure is reduced with the help of a water pump or vacuum pump.

(iii) (*d*) Glycerol decomposes at its boiling point. So, it is separated from spent-lye by using distillation under reduced pressure.

(iv) (*a*) Differential extraction is the technique where extraction of compound is based on more solubility of the compound in another solvent.

(v) (*b*) Adsorption chromatography is based on the fact that different compounds are adsorbed on an adsorbent to different degrees. Commonly used adsorbents are silica gel and alumina.

(vi) (*d*) Formation of sodium thionitroprusside (purple) shows the presence of sulphur in organic compound.

$$\underset{\text{Sodium extract}}{Na_2S} + \underset{\text{Sodium nitroprusside}}{Na_2[Fe(NO)(CN)_5]} \longrightarrow \underset{\text{Sodium thionitroprusside (Purple)}}{Na_4[Fe(CN)_5NOS]}$$

(vii) (*d*) In Kjeldahl's method, the nitrogen is quantitatively converted into ammonia by heating with NaOH.

$$\underset{\text{From organic compound}}{C+H+N}+H_2SO_4 \xrightarrow{\Delta} (NH_4)_2SO_4 + CO_2 + H_2O$$

$$(NH_4)_2SO_4 + 2NaOH \longrightarrow Na_2SO_4 + 2NH_3 + 2H_2O$$

(viii) (*b*) Volume of N_2 at STP is calculated followed by percentage of N_2. Volume of nitrogen collected at 300 K and 715 mm pressure is 50 mL.

$$\text{Volume of nitrogen at STP} = \frac{p_1V_1 \times 273}{760 \times T_1}$$

where, p_1 = actual pressure
= atmospheric pressure − aqueous tension
= 715 − 15 = 700 mm

V_1 = volume of nitrogen = 50 mL

T_1 = room temperature ≃ 300 K

$$\text{Volume of nitrogen at STP} = \frac{273 \times 700 \times 50}{300 \times 760} = 41.9 \text{ mL}$$

22400 mL of N_2 at STP weighs = 28 g

$$41.9 \text{ mL of nitrogen weighs} = \frac{28 \times 41.9}{22400} \text{ g}$$

per centage of nitrogen

$$= \frac{28 \times 41.9 \times 100}{22400 \times 0.3} = 17.46\%$$

3. (i) (d) A→(i), B→(vi), C→(iv), D→(ii), E→(iii), F→(v)

(ii) (d) A→(v), B→(iv), C→(i), D→(ii), E→(iii)

(iii) (b) A→(ii), B→(v), C→(iv), D→(iii), E→(i)

A. Test for nitrogen, $6CN^- + Fe^{2+} \longrightarrow [Fe(CN)_6]^{4-}$

$$3[Fe(CN)_6]^{4-} + 4Fe^{3+} \xrightarrow{x.H_2O} \underset{\text{Prussian blue}}{Fe_4[Fe(CN)_6]_3 \cdot xH_2O}$$

B. Test for sulphur, $S^{2-} + Pb^{2+} \longrightarrow \underset{\text{Black}}{PbS}$

$$S^{2-} + [Fe(CN)_5NO]^{2-} \longrightarrow \underset{\text{Violet}}{[Fe(CN)_5NOS]^{4-}}$$

C. Test for both nitrogen and sulphur,

$$Na + C + N + S \longrightarrow NaSCN$$

$$Fe^{3+} + SCN^- \longrightarrow \underset{\text{Blood red}}{[Fe(SCN)]^{2+}}$$

$$NaSCN + 2Na \longrightarrow NaCN + Na_2S$$

D. Test for halogen, $X^- + Ag^+ \longrightarrow AgX$

E. Test for phosphorus,

$$Na_3PO_4 + 3HNO_3 \longrightarrow H_3PO_4 + 3NaNO_3$$

$$H_3PO_4 + \underset{\text{Ammonium molybdate}}{12(NH_4)_2MoO_4} + 21HNO_3 \longrightarrow$$

$$\underset{\text{Ammonium phosphomolybdate}}{(NH_4)_3PO_4 \cdot 12MoO_3} + 21NH_4NO_3 + 12H_2O$$

(iv) (a) A→(v), B→(iv), C→(ii), D→(iii), E→(i)

4. A mixture of $CaSO_4$ and camphor can be separated by sublimation. Because camphor is sublimable but $CaSO_4$ is not therefore, sublimation of the mixture gives camphor on the sides of funnel while $CaSO_4$ is left in the China dish.

5. A mixture of *o*-nitrophenol and *p*-nitrophenol can be separated by steam distillation, *o*-nitrophenol being less volatile distiles over along with water while *p*-nitrophenol being non-volatile remains in the flask.

6. If a compound decomposes at its boiling point but is steam volatile, water-insoluble and stable at low pressure, steam distillation can be used for its purification. This technique is applied to separate substances which are steam volatile and immiscible with water.

7. In steam distillation, the mixture consisting of the organic liquid and water boils when the sum of the vapour pressure of the organic liquid (p_1) and that of water (p_2) becomes equal to the atmospheric pressure (p_1), i.e. $p = p_1 + p_2$.
Since, p_1 is lower than p, the orgainc liquid vaporises at lower temperature than its boiling point.

8. R_f value of A is 0.65, therefore, it is less strongly adsorbed as compared to compound B which has R_f value of 0.42. Therefore, A will be eluted first.

9. Nitrogen, sulphur and halogens are present in an organic compound in covalent form so their detection is not easy. By fusing with Na metal, these elements are converted into NaCN or Na_2S or NaX, i.e. in an ionic form. In ionic form, these can be easily detected by ionic reactions.

10. DNA and RNA have nitrogen in the heterocyclic rings. Nitrogen present in rings, azo and nitro groups cannot be converted into $(NH_4)_2SO_4$. That's why Kjeldahl's method cannot be used for the estimation of nitrogen present in these.

11. Diazonium salts ($C_6H_5N_2^+X^-$) readily lose N_2 on heating before reacting with fused sodium metal. Therefore, these do not give positive Lassaigne's test for nitrogen.

12. CCl_4 will not give a white ppt of AgCl with $AgNO_3$ solution because CCl_4 is a covalent compound.
It does not ionise to give Cl^- ions required for the formation of AgCl precipitate.

13. Crystallisation method. To describe this, refer to text on page 383.

14. Refer to text on page 385 (Fractional distillation).

15. (i) Fractional distillation because the boiling points of two liquids differ by only 10°. [1]

(ii) Simple distillation because the boiling points of the two liquids differ much. [1]

16. If H_2SO_4 is used, lead acetate itself will react with H_2SO_4 to form white ppt of lead sulphate.

$$\underset{\text{Lead acetate}}{Pb(OCOCH_3)_2} + H_2SO_4 \longrightarrow \underset{\text{White ppt.}}{PbSO_4\downarrow} + 2\,CH_3COOH$$ [1]

Hence, white precipitate of $PbSO_4$ will interfere with the following test of sulphur.

$$Pb(CH_3COO)_2 + Na_2S \longrightarrow \underset{\text{Black ppt}}{PbS\downarrow} + 2CH_3CO\overset{-}{O}\overset{+}{Na}$$

However, if acetic acid is used, it does not react with lead acetate, so does not interfere in the test. [1]

17. Sodium extract is boiled with nitric acid to decompose NaCN and Na_2S, if present.

$$NaCN + HNO_3 \longrightarrow NaNO_3 + HCN\uparrow$$

$$Na_2S + 2HNO_3 \longrightarrow 2NaNO_3 + H_2S\uparrow$$ [1]

If cyanide and sulphide are not removed, they will react with $AgNO_3$ and hence, will interfere with the silver nitrate test for halogens.

$$NaCN + AgNO_3 \longrightarrow \underset{\text{White ppt.}}{AgCN} + NaNO_3$$

$$Na_2S + 2AgNO_3 \longrightarrow \underset{\text{Black ppt.}}{Ag_2S} + 2NaNO_3$$ [1]

18. On adding dilute H_2SO_4 for testing halogens in an organic compound with $AgNO_3$, white precipitate of Ag_2SO_4 is formed. This will interfere with the test of chlorine and this Ag_2SO_4 may be mistaken for white precipitate of chlorine as AgCl. Hence, dilute HNO_3 is used instead of dilute H_2SO_4. [2]

19. CO_2 is slightly acidic in nature, therefore, it reacts with the strong base KOH to form K_2CO_3 and from the weight of the CO_2 obtained, percentage of carbon in the organic compound is calculated.

$$2\,KOH + CO_2 \longrightarrow K_2CO_3 + H_2O$$ [1]

The increase in the weight of U-tube containing KOH gives the weight of CO_2 produced and from the weight of the CO_2 obtained, percentage of carbon in the organic compound is calculated as:

$$\%\text{ of carbon} = \frac{12}{44} \times \frac{\text{weight of } CO_2 \text{ formed}}{\text{weight of substance taken}} \times 100$$ [1]

20. Refer text on pages 390 and 391 (Estimation of nitrogen).

21. % of chlorine $= \frac{35.5}{143.5} \times \frac{\text{mass of AgCl formed}}{\text{mass of substance taken}} \times 100$

$= \frac{35.5}{143.5} \times \frac{0.5740}{0.3780} \times 100 = 37.566\%$ [2]

22. % of sulphur $= \frac{32}{233} \times \frac{\text{mass of } BaSO_4 \text{ formed}}{\text{mass of substance taken}} \times 100$

$= \frac{32}{233} \times \frac{0.668}{0.468} \times 100 = 19.60\%$ [2]

23. Refer to text on pages 383, 384 and 386 (Crystallisation, distillation and chromatography).

24. Benzoic acid can be purified by hot water because of the following characteristics :

(i) Benzoic acid is more soluble in hot water and less soluble in cold water. [1]

(ii) Impurities present in benzoic acid are either insoluble in water or are more soluble in water to such an extent that they remain in solution as the mother liquor upon crystallisation. [2]

25. Refer to text on page 387 (Partition chromatography).

26. (i) Sublimation camphor sublimes while common salt remains as residue in the China dish. [1]

(ii) Since the two liquids are immiscible, the technique of solvent extraction with a separating funnel is used. The mixture is thoroughly shaken and the separating funnel is allowed to stand. Kerosene being lighter than water forms the upper layer while water forms the lower layer.

The lower water layer is run off using the stop cock of the funnel and kerosene oil is obtained. It is dried over anhydrous $CaCl_2$ or $MgSO_4$ and then distilled to give pure kerosene oil. [1]

(iii) Distillation under reduced pressure. [1]

27. Refer to text on page 392 Estimation of halogens, sulphur and phosphorus)

28. Volume of the acid taken = 50 mL of 0.5 M H_2SO_4

= 25 mL of 1.0 M H_2SO_4

Volume of alkali used for neutralisation of excess acid

= 60 mL of 0.5 M NaOH

= 30 mL of 1.0 M NaOH [1]

$H_2SO_4 + 2NaOH \longrightarrow Na_2SO_4 + 2H_2O$

1 mole of H_2SO_4 = 2 moles of NaOH

Hence, 30 mL of 1.0 M NaOH

= 15 mL of 1.0 M H_2SO_4 [1]

∴ Volume of acid used by ammonia = 25 − 15 = 10 mL

% of nitrogen $= \frac{1.4 \times N_1 \times \text{vol. of acid used}}{w}$

(where, N_1 = normality of acid and w = mass of the organic compound taken)

% of nitrogen $= \frac{1.4 \times 2 \times 10}{0.5} = 56.0$ [1]

29. $\% C = \frac{12}{44} \times \frac{\text{Mass of } CO_2 \text{ formed}}{\text{Mass of substance taken}} \times 100$

$69 = \frac{12}{44} \times \frac{\text{Mass of } CO_2 \text{ formed}}{0.2} \times 100$ [1]

∴ Mass of CO_2 formed

$= \frac{69 \times 44 \times 0.2}{12 \times 100} = 0.506$ g [1]

$\% H = \frac{2}{18} \times \frac{\text{Mass of } H_2O \text{ formed}}{\text{Mass of substance taken}} \times 100$

$4.8 = \frac{2}{18} \times \frac{\text{Mass of } H_2O \text{ formed}}{0.2} \times 100$

∴ Mass of H_2O formed $= \frac{4.8 \times 18 \times 0.2}{2 \times 100} = 0.0864$ g [1]

30. The bubble plate type fractionating column is shown in the figure. The tower is divided into number of compartments by mean of shelves having openings. The openings are covered with caps called **bubble caps.** Each shelf is provided with an overflow pipe which keeps the liquid to a certain level and then allows the rest to trickle down to the lower shelf. Such type of column is used for continuous separation of bulk quantities of liquids. e.g. distillation of fermented liquid for manufacture of rectified spirit.

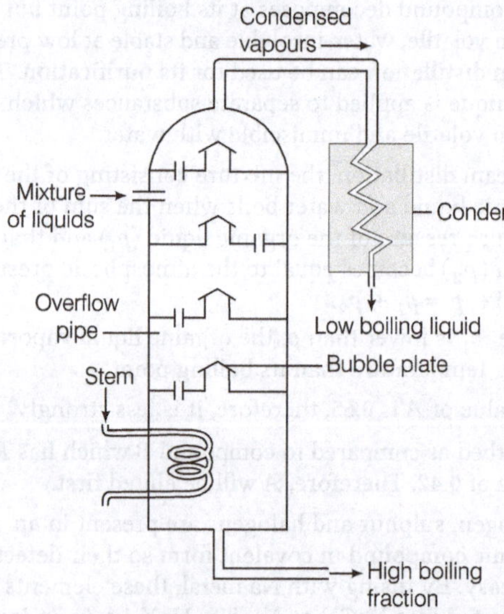

Refer to text on page 385 (Fractional distillation). [3]

Industrial Applications

(i) Separation of crude oil in petroleum industry into various useful fractions such as gasoline, kerosene oil, diesel oil, lubricating oil, etc.

(ii) Separation of acetone and methanol from *pyroligneous acid* obtained by destructive distillation of wood. [2]

31. Refer to text on pages 388 and 389 (Detection of other elements : Lassaigne's test for phosphorus).

SUMMARY

- Hydrides of carbon (hydrocarbon) or their derivatives are known as **organic compounds**.
- **Shapes**

σ-bond	Hybridisation	Shape
4	sp^3	tetrahedral
3	sp^2	trigonal planar
2	sp	linear

- **Structure Representation**
  (i) **Dash structure** All bond pairs are replaced by (–).
  (ii) **Condensed structure** Except ═ and ≡ bonds all bonds are omitted.
  (iii) **Bond line structure** C — C bonds are shown by *zig-zag* lines.
- **Functional group** are atoms or group of atoms responsible for their chemical behaviour, e.g. alcohol group (—OH).
- **Homologous series** is a series of compounds differing from its previous and successive member by $—CH_2$. e.g. alkane (CH_4, C_2H_6).
- **Nomenclature** In trivial system, organic compounds were named after their source or some properties. In IUPAC system compounds are named as prefix + rood word + suffix.
- **Isomerism** This phenomenon arises when compounds have same molecular formula but differ in structures, atoms or spatial arrangement.
- **Structural isomerism** is a phenomenon arises when compounds have same molecular formula but differ in way of bonding.
  When two or more compounds have similar molecular formula but different carbon skeletons, these are referred as **chain isomers.**
  When two or more compounds differ in the position of substituent atom or functional group on the carbon skeleton, they are called **position isomers**.
  Two or more compounds having the same molecular formula but different functional groups are called **functional isomers**.
  Metamerism arises due to different alkyl chains on either side of the functional group in the molecule.
- **Stereo isomerism** is a phenomenon arises when compounds having similar molecular structural formula differ in their spatial arrangements. This can be optical or geometrical.
- **Reaction mechanism** is sequential information of each step in a reaction.
- **Fission/cleavage of bond** Breaking of covalent bond. The two type of cleavage are as follows :
  Homolytic Each atom takes its shared electron and produces free radicals.
  Heterolytic One atom takes shared electrons and produces ions (carbocation and carbanion).
- **Nucleophiles** Electron rich species, having lone pair of electrons e.g. Cl^-, Br^-, H_2O, NH_3 etc.
- **Electrophilics** Electron deficient species e.g. H^+, BF_3, $BeCl_2$, PCl_3 etc.
- **Electron Displacement Effects in Covalent Bond**
  (i) **Inductive effect** (*I*) It is induction of polarity due to presence of polar bond. It is a permanent effect. Atoms or groups having greater/lesser electron affinity than H, shows + *I* or – *I* effect.
  (ii) **Resonance effect** (*R*) It is polarity developed due to interaction of two π-bonds or π-bonds with lone pair of electrons present on the adjacent atoms. It is a permanent effect. When the electrons move away/towards the atom or group attached to the conjugated system (+) *R* or (–) *R* effect is produced.
  (iii) **Electronic effect** (*E*) Polarity developed due to complete transfer of a shared pair of π-electrons to atoms linked with multiple bond. If electron of π-bond are transferred to atoms/neighbouring atom of double bond to which reagent is attacked, it produce +*E* or –*E* effect.
- **Hyperconjugation** is delocalisation of σ-electrons of C — H bond.
- **Types of organic reactions** Substitution, Elimination, Addition Reactions, Addition elimination, Rearrangement.

- **Purification** Process of removal of impuritie:

  (i) **Crytallisation** Used for purifying solid organic compounds and based on the difference in solubilities of compound and impurity in a solvent.

  (ii) **Distillation** Used to separate a volatile liquid from a non-volatile impurity or two liquids having large difference in their boiling point e.g. chloroform and aniline. When difference in boiling point is very low (10-15K), fractional distillation is used. When liquid have tendency to decompose before its boiling point distillation under reduced pressure is used. e.g. glycerol. When compound or impurity is steam volatile, steam distillation is used e.g. aniline.

- **Chromatography** It is based on the difference in the rates at which the components of a mixture are adsorbed on a suitable adsorbent. Various types of chromatography are :

  (i) Adsorption column chromatography (ii) Partition paper chromatography (iii) Thin layer chromatography

- **Qualitative analysis** is used to detect elements present in a sample.
- **Test for C and H** H_2O turns only $CuSO_4$,blue, CO_2 turns lime water milky.
- **Test for N** Sodium extract + $FeSO_4$ + H_2SO_4(conc.)→ Prussian blue colour.
- **Test for S** Sodium extract + acetic acid + lead acetate → black ppt.

  Sodium extract + sodium nitroprusside → purple colour.

- **Test for *X*** (*X* = **Cl, Br, I**):

  Sodium extract + X_2 + $AgNO_2$ → white ppt (Cl).

  Dull yellow ppt (Br)

  Yellow/light violet (I).

- **Test for P** Fused sample with $Na_2O_2 + H_2O +$ Conc. HNO_3 + heat and cooling with ammonium molybdate

  → Yellow ppt.

- **Quantitative Analysis**

  It is used to detect percentage of elements present in a sample.

- **To detect percentage of elements present in the sample.**

$$\%\text{of C} = \frac{12 \times \text{mass of } CO_2 \times 100}{44 \times \text{mass of organic compounds (0.C)}}$$

$$\%\text{of H} = \frac{2 \times \text{mass of } H_2O \times 100}{18 \times \text{mass of (0.C)}}$$

$$\%\text{of N} = \frac{28 \times V \times 100}{22400 \times m} \text{ (Duma's method)}$$

$$= \frac{1.4 \times M \times (V - V_1/2)}{2} \text{ (Kjeldahl's method)}$$

$$\%\text{ of X} = \frac{\text{Atomic mass } X \times \text{mass of Ag (formed)} \times 100}{\text{Molecular mass of AgX} \times \text{mass of (0.C)}}$$

$$\%\text{ of S} = \frac{32 \times \text{mass of } BaSO_4 \times 100}{233 \times \text{mass of (0. C)}}$$

$$\%\text{ of P} = \frac{62 \times \text{mass of } Mg_2P_2O_7 \times 100}{222 \times \text{mass of (0.C)}}$$

Chapter Practice

Very Short Answer Type Questions

(1 Mark)

1. Fill in the Blanks

(i) Organic compounds are formed due to presence of ....

(ii) A .... is an atom or group of atoms bonded together in a unique fashion and also determines the physical and chemical properties.

(iii) Two types of isomerism are .... and ....

(iv) .... and .... carbocations are more stable due to resonance.

(v) .... have both electrophilic and nucleophilic sites hence have dual nature.

(vi) Solid substances soluble in a suitable solvent are purified by ....

(vii) .... is used for separation, isolation, purification and identification of constituents of a mixture.

(viii) Presence of extra elements such as N, S and halogens is detected by ....

2. Objective Type Questions

(i) Which of the following is necessary in the formation of π -bonds?

(a) Parallel orientation of *p*-orbitals

(b) Internuclear orientation of *p*-orbitals

(c) Zero orientation of *p*-orbital

(d) No bonding orientation of *p*-orbitals

(ii) In cyclic compounds, the bond-line formula for chlorocyclohexane is represented by which of the following representations?

(a) 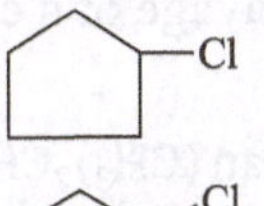

(b) 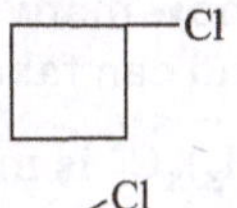

(c) 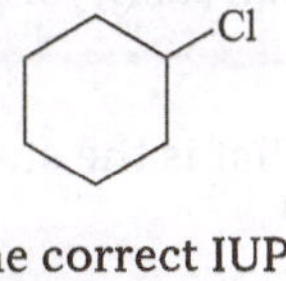

(d) 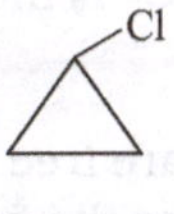

(iii) The correct IUPAC name of the given structures will be

I. $CH_3—\overset{\overset{O}{\|}}{C}—CH_2—CH_2—CH_2—COOH$

II. $CH \equiv C—CH = CH—CH = CH_2$

Choose the correct option.

	I	II
(a)	Hexane-dione,	Hexa-1,3-dien-5-yne
(b)	5-oxohexanoic acid,	Hexa-1,3-dien-5-yne
(c)	5-oxohexanoic acid,	Hexadiene-5-yne
(d)	3-oxohexanoic acid,	Hexa-diene-5-yne

(iv) The correct IUPAC name of the following compounds I and II respectively are

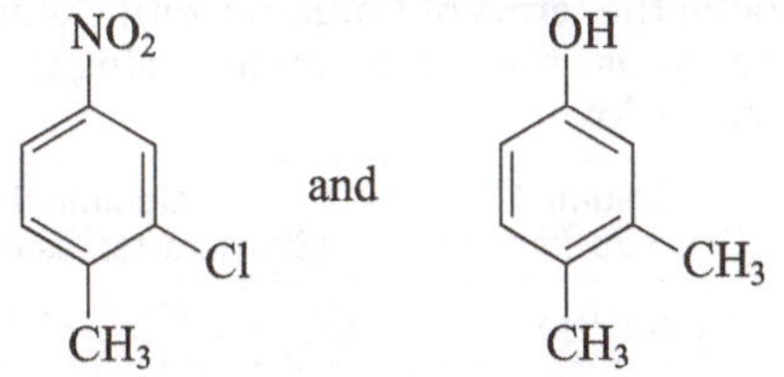

I II

(a) 2-chloro-1-methyl-4-nitrobenzene and 3,4-dimethylphenol

(b) 4-methyl-5-chloronitrobenzene and 3,4-dimethylphenol

(c) 2-methyl-1-chloro-5-nitrobenzene and dimethylphenol

(d) 3-chloro-4-methyl- nitrobenzene and dimethylphenol

(v) Choose the correct order of stability of carbocation using the concept of hyperconjugation.

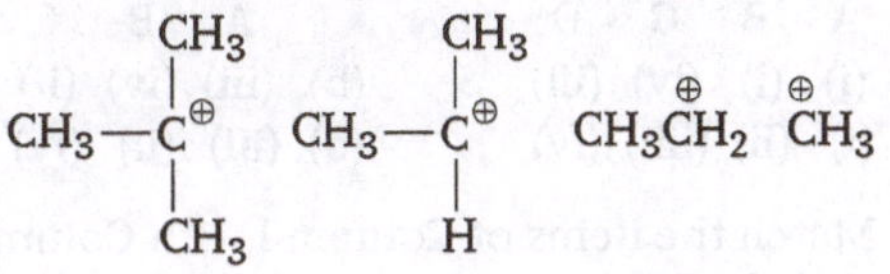

I II III IV

(a) I < II < III < IV (b) IV < III < II < I

(c) III < IV < II < I (d) None of the above

(vi) Hyperconjugation is possible in

(a) carbocation (b) alkene

(c) alkyl arenes (d) All of these

(vii) Which of the following process is used to separate volatile liquid from non-volatile impurities?

(a) Distillation

(b) Sublimation

(c) Differential extraction

(d) Crystallisation

(viii) Which of the following process is not used for the purification of solid impurities?
(a) Distillation (b) Sublimation
(c) Crystallisation (d) Vaporisation

(ix) Acidified sodium fusion extract on addition of ferric chloride solution gives blood red colouration. This confirms the presence of which of the following element(s)?
(a) Both S and Cl (b) Both N and S
(c) Only N (d) Only S

(x) In the estimation of sulphur, which reagent is heated along with organic compound in a Carius tube?
(a) Sodium peroxide (b) Dil. nitric acid
(c) Dil. H_2SO_4 (d) Sodium hydroxide

3. Matching Type Questions

(i) Match the terms of Column I with Column II and choose the correct option using the codes given below:

Column I (Structural formula)		Column II (Structural representations)
A. Complete	(i)	
B. Dot or Lewis	(ii)	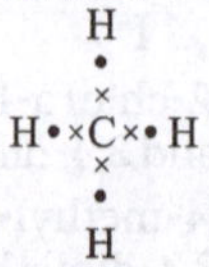
C. Condensed	(iii)	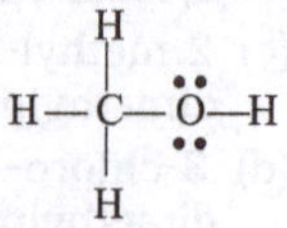
D. Bond-line	(vi)	CH_3CH_3

Codes

	A	B	C	D
(a)	(i)	(i)	(iv)	(iii)
(b)	(iii)	(iv)	(ii)	(i)
(c)	(i)	(ii)	(iiii)	(iv)
(d)	(iii)	(ii)	(iv)	(i)

(ii) Match the items of Column I with Column II and choose the correct option using the codes given below:

Column I (IUPAC name of the molecule)		Column II (Structure of molecule)
A. Hex-1,3-dien-5-yne	(i)	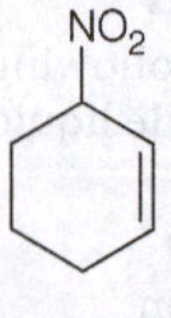
B. 2-chlorohexane	(ii)	$CH_2=CHCH_2CH(OH)CH$
C. Pent-4-en-2-ol	(iii)	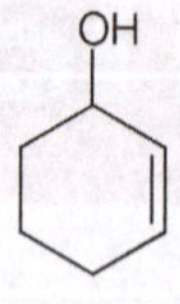
D. 3-nitrocyclohexene	(iv)	$CH_3CH_2CH_2CH_2CH(Cl)CH_3$
E. Cyclohex-2-en-1-ol	(v)	$CH\equiv C—CH=CHCH=CH$
F. 6-hydroxyheptanal	(vi)	$CH_3CH(OH)CH_2CH_2CH_2CH_2CHO$

Codes

	A	B	C	D	E	F
(a)	(v)	(iv)	(ii)	(i)	(iii)	(vi)
(b)	(i)	(ii)	(iii)	(iv)	(v)	(vi)
(c)	(vi)	(iv)	(iii)	(ii)	(i)	(v)
(d)	(iv)	(iii)	(ii)	(i)	(v)	(vi)

4. Calculate the number of sigma bonds in 4-methyl phenol.

5. How many secondary hydrogens are present in (i) *iso*-pentane and (ii) *neo*-pentane?

6. How many σ and π bonds are present in each of the following molecules?
(i) $HC\equiv CCH=CHCH_3$ (ii) $CH_2=C=CHCH_3$

7. Write the structure of the first member of the ketone homologous series. Give its IUPAC name.

8. Draw the structural formula of pentan-3-one.

9. Name the alkyl groups derived from *iso*-butane.

10. Give the IUPAC name of the compound:

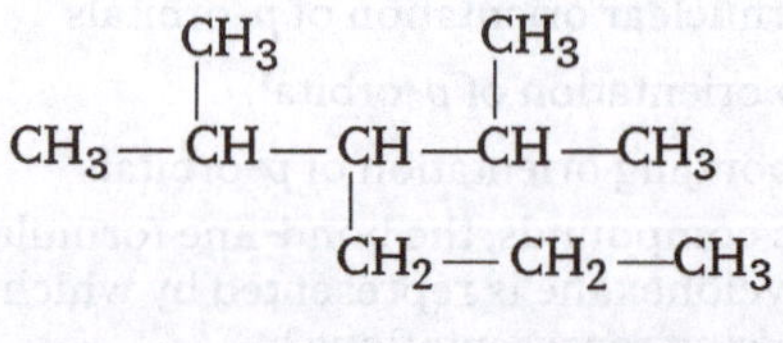

11. In how many ways the cleavage of a covalent bond can take place?

12. $(CH_3)_3C^+$ is more stable than $(CH_3)_2CH^+$. Explain why?

13. What are free radicals? What is the stability order or the free radicals?

14. Select electrophiles from the following: NO_2^+, $C_2H_5O^-$, Cl^+, BF_3, HS^-

15. Classify the following groups as + *I*-effect or – *I*-effect groups.

— NO_2 (nitro), — COOH (carboxyl), CH_3 — O^- (methoxy)

16. How will you separate a mixture of iodine and sodium chloride?

17. How will you separate two miscible liquids which differ in their boiling points by 10°C?

18. What do you understand by the stationary phase and the moving phase in paper chromatography?

19. 0.2570 g of an organic compound in quantitative analysis gave 0.3500 g of barium sulphate. Calculate the percentage of sulphur in the organic compound.

20. How will you qualitatively detect the presence of carbon and hydrogen in an organic compound? Give all relevant equations.

21. What conclusion would you draw if the Lassaigne's extract gives a blood red colour with $FeCl_3$? Write the relevant chemical equations.

22. An organic substance weighing 0.2388 g containing chlorine was heated with strong HNO_3 and $AgNO_3$ in a sealed tube. The weight of dry AgCl obtained was 0.3046 g. Calculate the percentage of chlorine in the substance.

Assertion-Reason

Directions (Q. Nos. 23-27) In the following questions. An Assertion (A) is followed by a corresponding Reason (R). Use the following keys to choose the appropriate answer.

(a) Both (A) and (R) are correct and (R) is the correct explanation of (A).

(b) Both (A) and (R) are correct but (R) is not the correct explanation of (A).

(c) (A) is correct and (R) is incorrect.

(d) (A) is incorrect and (R) is correct.

23. **Assertion** (A) Acyclic compounds consist of straight or branched chain compounds.

Reason (R) Acyclic compounds have aromatic character.

24. **Assertion** (A) All the carbon atoms in $H_2C{=}C{=}C{=}CH_2$ are sp^2-hybridised.

Reason (R) In this molecule, all the carbon atoms are attached to each other by double bonds.

25. **Assertion** (A) The structure of 2, 3-dimethylhept-5-ene is

$$CH_3{-}CH{=}CH{-}\underset{}{\overset{\displaystyle CH_3}{\overset{|}{C}H}}{-}CH_2{-}\overset{\displaystyle CH_3}{\overset{|}{C}H}{-}CH_3$$

Reason (R) The alkyl group do not get preference to the double bond.

26. **Assertion** (A) Free radicals are short lived and highly reactive.

Reason (R) Free radicals are highly unstable.

27. **Assertion** (A) Inductive effect and resonance effect cause permanent polarisation of bond.

Reason (R) These involve electron displacements due to the influence of an atom or a substituted group present in the molecule.

Case-Study

28. An intermediate is a molecular entity, that is formed from the reactants and reacts further to give the directly observed products of a chemical reaction. Most chemical reactions are stepwise, that is they take more than one elementary step to complete.

An intermediate is the reaction product of each of these steps, except for the last one, which forms the final very isolated. Also, owing to the short lifetime, they do not remain in the product mixture.

In certain cases, they are separated and stored. For example matrix isolation and low temperature. Matrix isolation is a technique that is used experimentally in physics and chemistry that included a material that has been trapped with in an unreactive material. Host matrix generally embedded. Guest particles can be molecules, atoms and ions. The guest is isolated within the host matric.

(i) What happen when CH_3CH_2Cl undergoes homolytic fission?

(ii) Define the shape of carbocation.

(iii) Give the correct order of the relative stabilities of the following carbocations.

$$\underset{(A)}{\overset{\oplus}{C}H_3},\ \underset{(B)}{CH_3\overset{\oplus}{C}H_2},\ \underset{(C)}{\overset{\oplus}{C}H_2OCH_3}$$

29. When a single Lewis dot structure is unable to explain all the properties of a compound, two or more structures, called the canonical forms or resonating structures, are drawn to explain all the

structure of the compound is in between these canonical form and is called the resonance hybrid of these canonical forms. This phenomenon is called resonance.

The resonating structure are hypothetical, i.e. have no real existence. The energy of actual structure or resonance hybrid is lower than, that of any of the canonical forms. The difference between hybrid and the energy of most stable (lowest energy) canonical form is called the resonance stabilisation energy or resonance energy.

The more the number of important canonical forms more is the resonance energy. In case of resonating structures of equivalent energy, resonance is of great important.

(i) Write all the resonating structures of phenoxide ion.

(ii) In the given pair of resonating structure which is more stable?

$$\underset{(a)}{R-\overset{\oplus}{C}=\ddot{O}:} \longleftrightarrow \underset{(b)}{R-C\equiv\overset{\oplus}{\underset{\cdot\cdot}{O}}:}$$

(iii) Write the correct relation between resonance and bond order.

Short Answer Type I Questions

2 Marks

30. Draw the formulae for the first three members of each homologous series starting with formic acid and methanol.

31. Write dash, condensed and bond line structural formulae for the isomers of the molecular formulae.

(i) C_8H_{10} (ii) $C_3H_6O_3$ (iii) C_3H_6O

32. What is homologous series? Write its important characteristics.

33. Give the structure of each of the following compounds:

(i) 2, 3-dibromo-3-ethylheptane

(ii) 1-bromo-2-iodocyclobutene

34. Which family of hydrocarbon is represented by the general formula C_nH_{2n-2}? Write the IUPAC and common names of the first three members of this family.

35. Classify the following pairs as position, chain, functional isomers or metamers.

(i) Diethylamine and methylpropyl amine

(ii) Ethanol and dimethyl ether

36. Giving justification, categorise the following molecules/ions as nucleophilies or elecrophiles

$$NO_2^+, HS^-, BF_3, C_2H_5O^-, (CH_3)_3N, Cl^+$$
$$(CH_3)_3C^+ = O, NH_2^-$$

37. Explain the following by giving example:

(i) Inductive effect (ii) Electrophiles

38. Arrange the following.

(i) $(CH_3)_3\overset{+}{C}$, $CH_3CH_2\underset{CH_3}{\overset{+}{C}}$, $CH_3CH_2CH_2\overset{+}{C}H_2$

[Increasing order of stability]

(ii) —I, —Br, —Cl, —F

[Decreasing order of $-I$-effect]

39. By mistake, an alcohol (boiling point 97° C) was mixed with a ketone (boiling point 68° C). Suggest a suitable method to separate the two compounds. Explain the reason for your choice. **NCERT Exemplar**

Short Answer Type II Questions

3 Marks

40. Define the term functional group? Write the functional groups of the following.

(i) Thioalcohol (ii) Isothiocyanate
(iii) Thiocyanate (iv) Sulphonic acid
(v) Sulphones (vi) Sulphoxides

41. Draw all possible isomers of a compound with molecular formula, $C_4H_{10}0$. Classify them as chain and position isomers.

42. Explain the following types of structural isomers with one example each.

(i) Functional isomers

(ii) Metamers

(iii) Position isomers

43. Draw all possible structural isomers with the molecular formula C_6H_{14}. Name all the isomers in IUPAC system. Indicate primary, secondary, tertiary and quaternary carbon atoms in each isomer.

44. What is hyperconjugation effect? How does it differ from resonance effect?

45. What is the difference between distillation, distillation under reduced pressure and steam distillation? Discuss on the basis of boiling points of different substances. **NCERT Textbook**

46. What is the principle of steam distillation for the purification of organic compounds? With the help of diagrams describe the method of steam distillation.

47. A liquid with high boiling point decomposes on simple distillation but it can be steam distilled for its purification. Explain how is it possible?

48. Write the chemical equations involved in the Lassaigne's test for nitrogen in an organic compound.

49. (i) Write the formula of Prussian blue colour formed in Lassaigne's test for nitrogen detection.
(ii) Write the formula for estimation of nitrogen by Kjeldahl's method.
(iii) Name the method used to separate.
(a) glycerol from spent lye in soap industry
(b) aniline from aniline water mixture.

50. Discuss the reactions and the principle underlying the estimation of the following:
(i) Duma's method for eastimation of nitrogen.
(ii) Carius method for the estimation of halogens and sulphur.
(iii) Phosphorus.

Long Answer Type Questions

5 Marks

51. (i) What is the major factor that influences the relative stabilities of carbanions, radicals and carbocations?
(ii) Define the term inductive effect.
(iii) How does the inductive effect of an alkyl group affect the stability of these three intermediates?

52. Draw all possible carboxylic acids and esters for a compound with molecular formula $C_4H_8O_2$. Write the IUPAC name also.

53. (i) What are electrophiles? Give one example of electrophilic substitution reaction.
(ii) Write the chemistry of Lassaigne's test for qualitative analysis of sulphur
(iii) Give one example of position isomerism.

Answers

1. (i) covalent bonding (ii) functional group
(iii) structural and stereoisomerism
(iv) Allylic, benzylic (v) Ambiphiles
(vi) Crystallisation (vii) Chromatography
(viii) Lassaigne's test

2. (i) (*a*) In the formation of π (pi) bond, parallel orientation of the two *p*-orbitals on adjacent atoms is necessary for a proper sideways overlap.
(ii) (*c*) Structure of chlorocyclohexane is

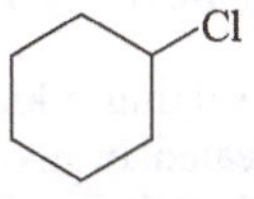

(iii) (*b*) I. $\overset{6}{CH_3}-\overset{5}{\underset{\|}{\overset{O}{C}}}-\overset{4}{CH_2}-\overset{3}{CH_2}-\overset{2}{CH_2}-\overset{1}{COOH}$

5-oxohexanoic acid

II. $\underset{6}{CH}\equiv\underset{5}{C}-\underset{4}{CH}=\underset{3}{CH}-\underset{2}{CH}=\underset{1}{CH_2}$

Hexa-1,3-dien-5-yne

(iv) (*a*)

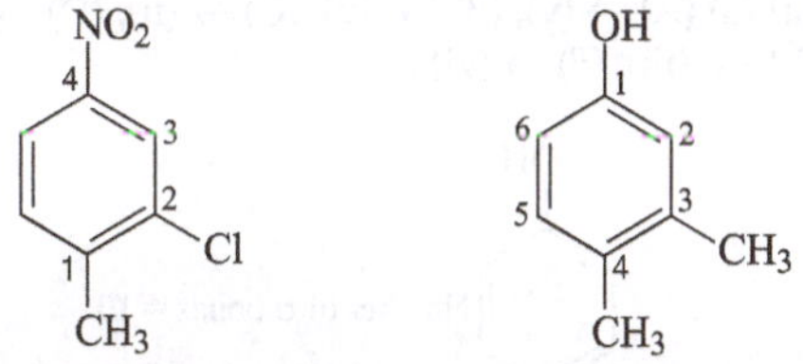

2-chloro-1-methyl-4-nitrobenzene (or 4-methyl-5-chloronitrobenzene) 3,4-dimethylphenol

(v) (*b*) Greater the number of alkyl groups attached to a positively charged carbon atom, the greater is the hyper conjugation interaction and stabilisation of the cation. Thus, we have the following relative stability of carbocation:

$$(CH_3)_3\overset{+}{C} > (CH_3)_2\overset{+}{C}H > CH_3\overset{+}{C}H_2 > \overset{+}{C}H_3$$

(vi) (*d*) Besides carbocation, hyperconjugation is also possible in alkenes and alkyl arenes which can be explained by delocalisation of electrons by hyperconjugation. In the case of alkene, it can be depicted as shown below

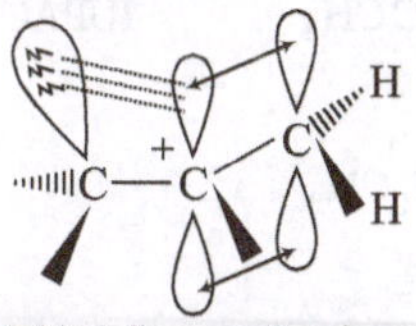

Orbital diagram showing hyperconjugation in propene

(vii) (*a*) Distillation is based on the difference in the boiling points of liquids. Thus, it is used to separate volatile liquid from the non-volatile impurities.

(viii) (*a*) Distillation process is not used for purification of solid impurities. It is used for the purification of liquid which boils without decomposition and contains non-volatile impurities.

(ix) (*b*) Acidified sodium fusion extract on addition of ferric chloride solution gives blood red colouration, which confirms the presence of N and S both.

$$Na + C + N + S \longrightarrow NaSCN$$

$$Fe^{3+} + SCN^- \longrightarrow \underset{\text{Blood red}}{[Fe(SCN)]^{2+}}$$

(x) (*a*) To estimate sulphur a known mass of an organic compound is heated in a Carius tube with sodium peroxide or fuming nitric acid. Sulphur present in the compound is oxidised to sulphuric acid. It is precipitated as barium sulphate by adding excess of barium chloride solution in water. The precipitate is filtered, washed, dried and weighed. The percentage of sulphur can be calculated from the mass of barium sulphate.

3. (i) (d) (A) → (iii), (B) → (ii), (C) → (iv), (D) → (i)
(ii) (a) (A) → (v), (B) → (iv), (C) → (ii), (D) → (i), (E) → (iii), (F) → (vi)

4.

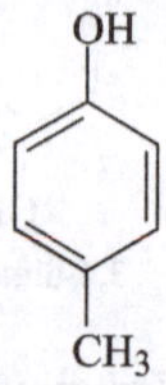

Number of σ bonds = 10

5. (i) $CH_3—CH(CH_3)—CH_2CH_3$

2° H's = 1

(ii) $CH_3—C(CH_3)_2—CH_3$

2° H's = zero

6. (i) 10 σ-bonds, 3 π-bonds
(ii) 9σ-bonds, 2 π-bonds

7. Acetone, CH_3COCH_3 ; IUPAC name = Prop -2-one

8. $\overset{5}{C}H_3\overset{4}{C}H_2\overset{3}{C}(=O)\overset{2}{C}H_2\overset{1}{C}H_3$

Pentan-3-one

9. *iso*-butyl

10. 2-methyl -3-isopropyl hexane

11. **Hint** Homolytic and heterolytic cleavage Refer to text on page 366 (Topic-3, Fission of a covalent bond).

12. Refer to text on page 366 (Topic 3, Carbocation)

13. Refer to page 367 (Topic 3, Free radicals)

14. NO_2^+, Cl^+, BF_3

15. + *I*-effect = $–OCH_3$, – *I*-effect = $–NO_2$, — COOH

16. Sublimation

17. fractional distillation

18. Refer to text on page 387 (Topic 4 : Partition chromatography)

19. Refer to text on page 392 (Topic 4 : Estimation of sulphur) [**Ans.** 18.7%]

20. Refer to text on page 387 and 388 (Topic 4 : Detection of Carbon and Hydrogen)

21. Refer to text on page 389 (Topic 4 : Test for nitrogen and sulphur)

22. Refer to text on page 392 (Topic 4 : Estimation of halogens) [**Ans.** 31-56%]

23. (A) is correct and (R) is incorrect.
Correct Reason Acyclic compounds does not have aromatic character.

24. (*d*) (A) is incorrect and (R) is correct.
Correct Assertion Hybridisation of C can be find out by counting σ-bonds and it bonds present on C-atom.

$$\underset{①}{\overset{3\sigma}{CH_2}} \underset{1\pi}{=} \overset{2\sigma\,②}{C} \underset{2\pi}{=} \overset{3\sigma}{C}\,③ \underset{1\pi}{} \begin{matrix} H \\ H \end{matrix}$$

C_1 and C_3 carbon are sp^2-hybridised while C_2-carbon is *sp*-hybridised.

25. (*d*) (A) is incorrect and (R) is correct.
The correct (A) is 2, 4-dimethyhept-5-ene.

26. (*b*) Both (A) and (R) are correct but (R) is not the correct explanation of (A).
Correct Reason Free radicals contains odd electrons, so they are short lived and they readily try to pair up the odd electrons to become a neutral molecule.

27. (*a*) Both (A) and (R) are correct and (R) is the correct explanation of (A).

28. (i) When CH_3CH_2Cl undergoes homolytic cleavage results in the formation of free radical.

$$CH_3CH_2—Cl \xrightarrow[\text{Fission}]{\text{Homolytic}} CH_3\dot{C}H_2 + \dot{C}l$$

(ii) The shape of carbocation is trigonal planer with positively charged carbon being sp^2-hybridised.

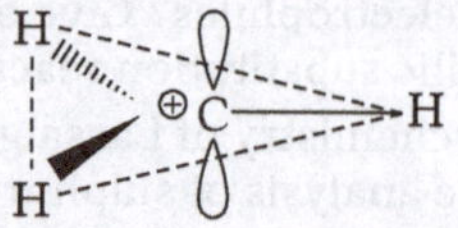

(iii) The dispersal of the charge stabilises the carbocation more the number of alkyl groups, the greater in dispersal of positive charge and therefore, more in the stability of carbocation.
Thus, the correct order relative stability is

$$\underset{(C)}{\overset{\oplus}{C}H_2OCH_3} > \underset{(B)}{CH_3\overset{\oplus}{C}H_2} > \underset{(A)}{\overset{\oplus}{C}H_3}$$

29. (i) The phenoxide ion has 5 resonating structures. These are

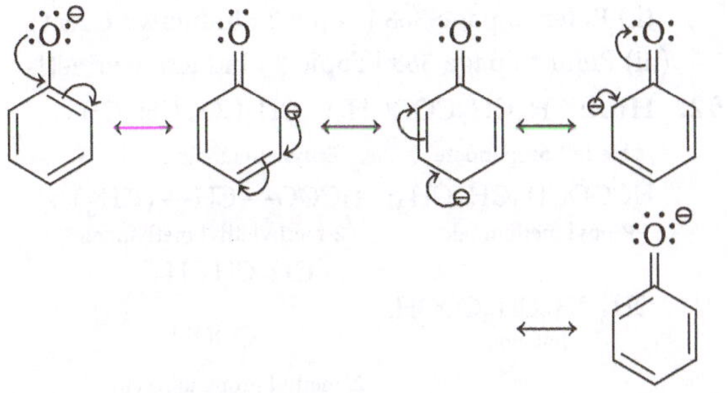

(ii) Structure (a) is more stable than structure (b) because the positive charge is present on the highly electronegative oxygen.

(iii) The correct relation between the resonance and bond order formula is $B.O = \frac{\text{No. of bonds}}{\text{No. of resonating structures}}$

30. **Hint** HCOOH, CH_3COOH, C_2H_5COOH

CH_3OH, C_2H_5OH, C_3H_7OH

31.

(i) C_8H_{10}

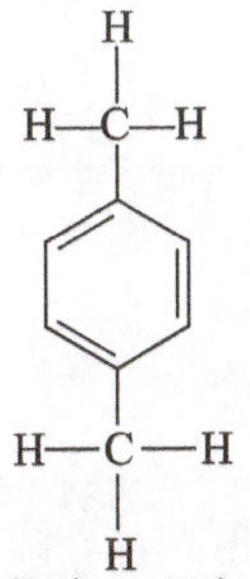

(Dash structure)

$CH_3—C_6H_5—CH_3$

(Condensed structure)

(Bond line structure)

Similarly, with *O* and *m*-isomers.

(ii) $C_3H_6O_3$

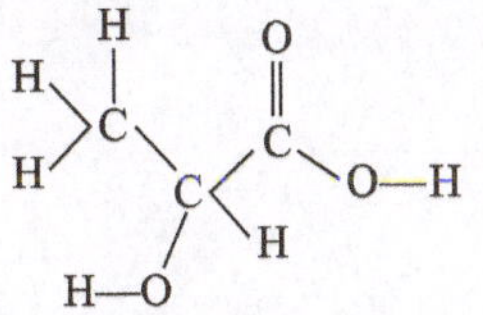

(Dash structure)

$CH_3—CH(OH)—COOH$

(Condensed structure)

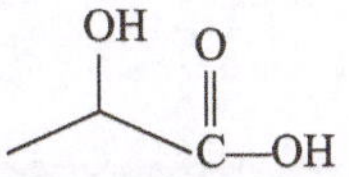

(Bond line structure)

Similarly, with other isomers.

(iii) C_3H_6O

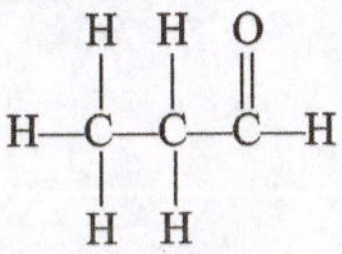

(Dash structure)

H_3CH_2CHO

(Condensed structure)

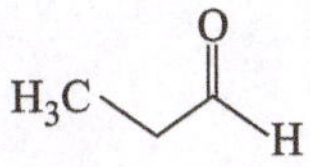

(Bond line structure)

32. Refer to page 341 (Topic-1 : Homologous series)

33. (i)

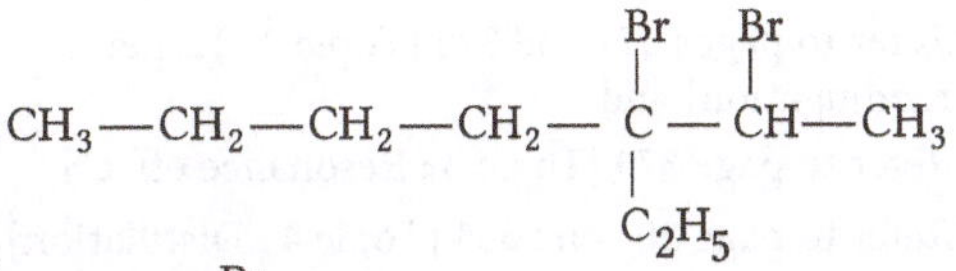

(ii)

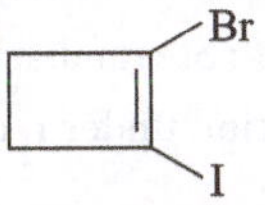

34. Alkyne family, first three members are ethyne, propyne, butyne.

35. **Hint** (i) Metamers (ii) Functional isomers

36. Refer to page 367 and 368 (Topic-3 : Nucleophiles and electrophiles)

37. (i) Refer to page 368 (Topic-3 : Inductive effect)

(ii) Refer to page 368 (Topic-3 : Electrophiles)

38. (i) Refer to page 369 (Topic-3 : Applications of Inductive effect)

(ii) Refer to page 369 (Topic-3 : Positive and negative inductive effect)

39. **Hint:** Simple distillation, Refer to page 384 (Topic-4: Distillation)

40. **Hint:** Refer to page 341 (Topic-1 : Functional group).

(i) —S—H (ii) —N=C=S (iii) —S—C≡N,

(iv) 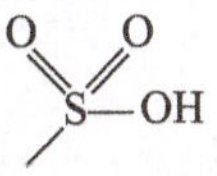 (v) 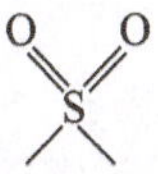 (vi) 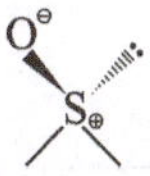

41. **Hint: Possible isomers** $CH_3CH_2CH_2CH_2OH$,

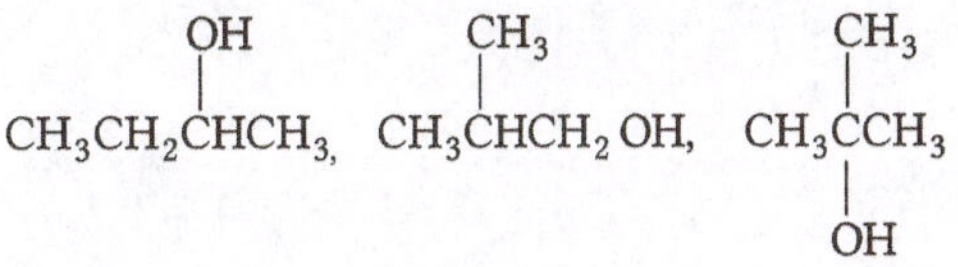

$CH_3CH_2CH_2OCH_3$, $CH_3CH_2OCH_2CH_3$, $(CH_3)_2CHOCH_3$

42. (i) and (iii) Refer page 355 (Topic-2 : Functional group isomerism and position isomerism)

(ii) Refer to page 356 (Topic-2 : metamerism)

43. **Hint:** $\overset{1°}{CH_3}\overset{2°}{CH_2}\overset{2°}{CH_2}\overset{2°}{CH_2}\overset{2°}{CH_2}\overset{1°}{CH_3}$,

(*n*-hexane)

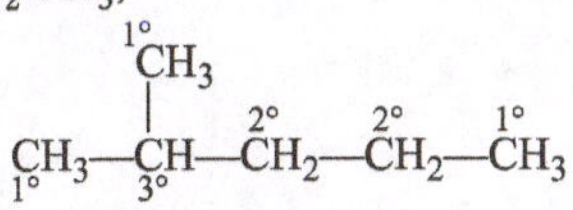

(2-methylpentane)

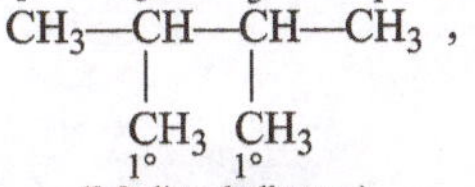

(2,3-dimethylbutane)

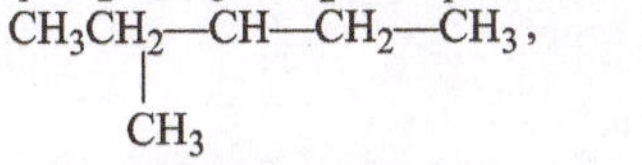

(3-methylpentane)

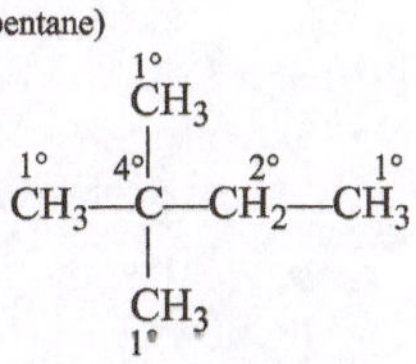

(2,2-dimethyl butane)

44. Refer to pages 371 and 372 [Topic 3 : Hyper rconjugation] and
Refer to page 370 [Topic 3 : Resonance effect]

45. Refer to page 384 and 385 [Topic 4 : Distillation]

46. Refer to pages 385 and 386 [Topic 4 : Steam distillation]

47. Refer to page 385 [Topic 4: Distillation under reduced pressure]

48. Refer to page 388 [Topic 4 : Test for nitrogen]

49. (i) $Fe_4[Fe(CON)_6]_3 \cdot xH_2O$

(ii) **Hint:** % of N = $\frac{1.4 \times M \times 2(V - V_1)_2}{M}$ prussion blue

(iii) (a) Distillation under reduced pressure

(b) Steam distillation

50. (i) Refer to page 390 [Topic 4 : Duma's method]

(ii) Refer to page 392 [Topic 4: Carius method]

(iii) Refer to page 392 [Topic 4 : Estimation of phosphorus]

51. (i) Refer to page 366 and 367 [Topic 3 : carbocation, carbanion, free radicals]

(ii) Refer to page 368 [Topic 3 : Inductive effect]

(iii) Refer to page 368 [Topic 3 : Inductive effect]

52. **Hint:** $CH_3CH_2COOCH_3$; $CH_3COOCH_2CH_3$

Hethyl propanoate; Ethyl ethanoale

$HCOOCH_2CH_2CH_3$; $HCOO—CH—(CH_3)_2$

Propyl methanoale; 2-methylethyl methanoale

$CH_3CH_2CH_2COOH$; CH_3CHCH_3 with COOH on the central C

Butanoic; 2, methyl propanoic acid

53. (i) Refer to page 368 and 372 (Topic-3 : Electrophiles and electrophilic substitution reaction)

(ii) Refer to pages 388 and 389 (Topic-4 : Test for sulphur)

(iii) Refer to page 355 (Topic-2 : Position isomerism)

CHAPTER

09

Hydrocarbons

- Saturated Hydrocarbons (Alkanes)
- Unsaturated Hydrocarbons (Alkenes and Alkynes)
- Aromatic Hydrocarbons

As the name implies, hydrocarbons are the compounds of carbon and hydrogen only. The main sources of these compounds are coal and petroleum.

Classification of Hydrocarbons

Any two carbon atoms of a hydrocarbon may combine through single (—), double (═) or triple (≡) bonds. Depending upon the manner of attachment of carbon atoms, hydrocarbons can be classified in three major classes that are shown below :

Hydrocarbons
(Compounds of C and H only)

- **Saturated hydrocarbons** (Carbon atoms are joined together through single bonds only).
  - Alkanes
    [Open chain, e.g. $CH_3—CH_3$ (ethane)]
  - Cycloalkanes
    (Closed chain) e.g.

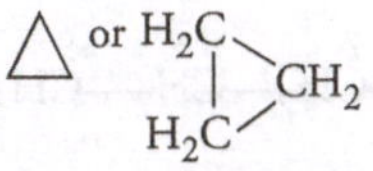

(Cyclopropane)

- **Unsaturated hydrocarbons** (One or more multiple bond(s) are present between the carbon atom).
  - Alkenes
    (have atleast one double bond between carbon atoms). e.g. $CH_2═CH_2$ (ethene), $CH_3—CH═CH_2$(propene) etc.
  - Alkynes
    (have atleast one triple bond between carbon atoms). e.g. $CH≡CH$ (acetylene), $CH_3—C≡CH$ (propyne) etc.
- **Aromatic hydrocarbons** (Alternate single and double bond, $(4n + 2)\pi$ electrons are present). e.g.

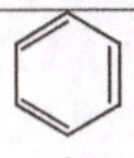

(Benzene)

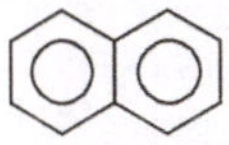

(Naphthalene)

TOPIC 01 Saturated Hydrocarbons (Alkanes)

These are the open chain saturated hydrocarbons, in which carbon atoms are joined together only through single bonds. These are the simplest hydrocarbons and were earlier called '**paraffins**' (*Latin : parum*-little affinis-affinity) because of their inert (non-reactive) nature towards many acids, bases and other reagents.

General molecular formula for these compounds is C_nH_{2n+2} (where, $n = 1, 2, 3, ...$). If $n = 1$, we get CH_4 (methane), the first member of alkane series. By replacing the hydrogen(s) of CH_4 by —CH_3 or other alkyl groups, we get the complete series of members of this group.

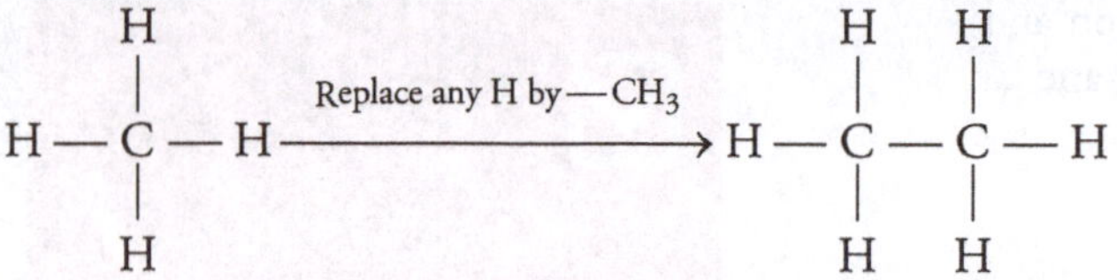

- Groups having one H-atom less than the alkanes are called **alkyl groups.** General molecular formula for these groups is C_nH_{2n+1} e.g. —CH_3 is the alkyl group (methyl group) derived from methane by replacing its one hydrogen atom.

Structure of Alkanes

In alkanes, the central C-atom is sp^3-hybridised and have four half-filled sp^3-hybridised orbitals. These four orbitals form four σ-bonds either with four H-atoms using their 1 *s*-orbitals (sp^3-*s* bonding) or with other carbon atoms (sp^3-sp^3 linkage) or both.

e.g. Consider the structure of methane.

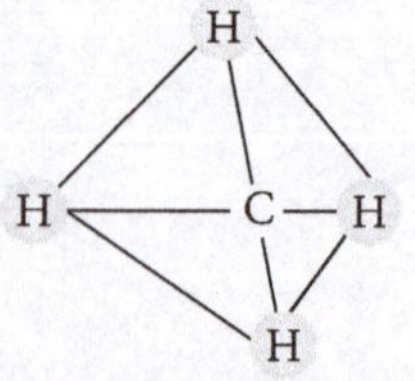

Structure of methane

The four σ-bonds are directed toward the corners of a regular tetrahedron, i.e. they are multiplanar (not in one plane). The H—C—H bond angle are 109.5° and C—C and C—H bond lengths are approximately 154 pm and 112 pm respectively.

Thus, methane have four sp^3-*s* σ bonds formed between sp^3-orbitals of C and 1*s*-orbital of H.

Nomenclature

The nomenclature of hydrocarbons has been discussed below:

1. Writing IUPAC Name From a Given Structure

In the previous chapter, you have read that alkanes are named by adding the suffix 'ane' to the 'root word', i.e. root word + ane = alkane

Further recall that, in complex structures, the numbering is done from the end which gives the lowest sum and in accordance with alphabetical order of the name of substituent. e.g.

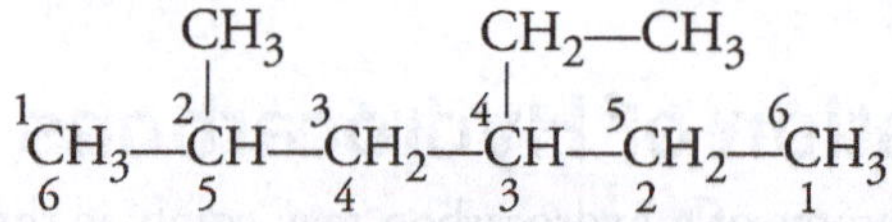

(Sum = 4 + 2 = 6) correct

(Sum = 3 + 5 = 8) incorrect

(4-ethyl-2-methylhexane)

('e' comes first in the alphabetical order)

The prefix *sec*, di, tri etc. are not considered in alphabetical order while writing the IUPAC name. Only the first letter of root word is considered, if arranged in alphabetical order.

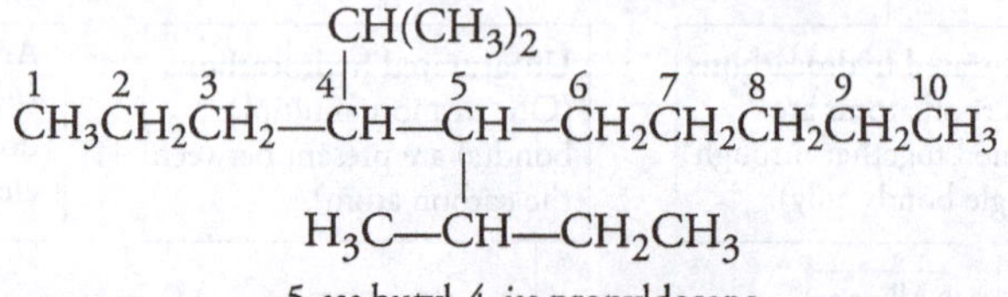

5-*sec*-butyl-4-*iso* propyldecane

('b' comes first in alphabetical order, here 's' of *sec* is not considered).

If the substituent group is also complex then separate numbering is done in it. e.g.

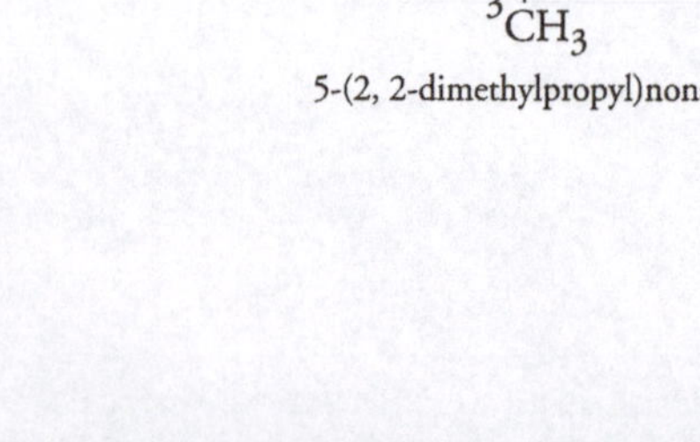

Substituent (number starts from the carbon that is linked with the principal chain).

5-(2, 2-dimethylpropyl)nonane

Example 1 Write the IUPAC names of the following:

(i) $(C_2H_5)_4C$ (ii) $(CH_3)_2\,CHCH(CH_3)_2$

Sol.

(i) 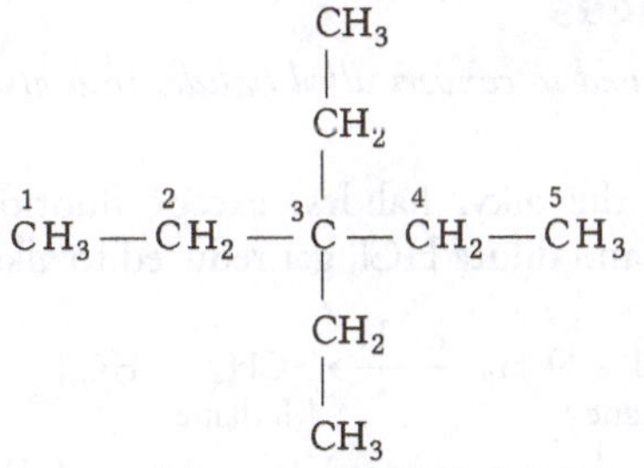

3, 3-diethylpentane

(ii) 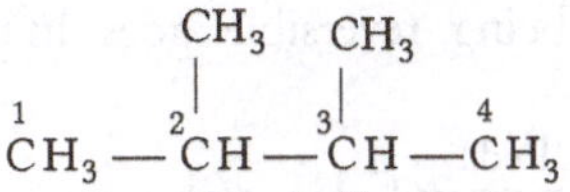

2, 3 -dimethylbutane

2. Writing Correct Structure From the Given IUPAC Name

To write the structure of a compound from its name, first draw the longest chain of carbon atoms (according to root word) and then number it. Now attach the different substituent at the mentioned places and satisfy the valencies of all the C-atoms by putting required number of hydrogen atoms, e.g. the structure of 3-ethyl-2, 2- dimethylpentane can be written as :

Step I. Here 'pent' is the root word, so the principal chain have five C-atoms. Thus, draw five C-atoms in a straight chain.

C—C—C—C—C

Step II. Give number to the carbon atoms (you can give number from either sides)

$C^1—C^2—C^3—C^4—C^5$

Step III. Attach ethyl group at third carbon and two methyl group at second carbon.

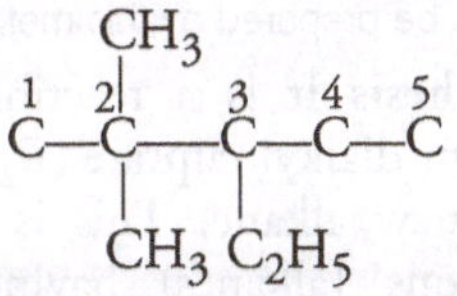

Step IV. Satisfy the valency of each carbon atom by adding the required number of hydrogen atoms.

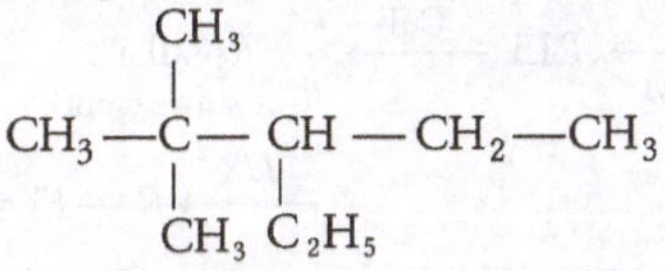

The obtained structure is the correct structure of the given compound.

Example 2 Write structures for each of the following compounds. Why are the given names incorrect? Write correct IUPAC names. **NCERT Textbook**

(i) 2-ethylpentane (ii) 5-ethyl-3-methylheptane

Sol. (i) 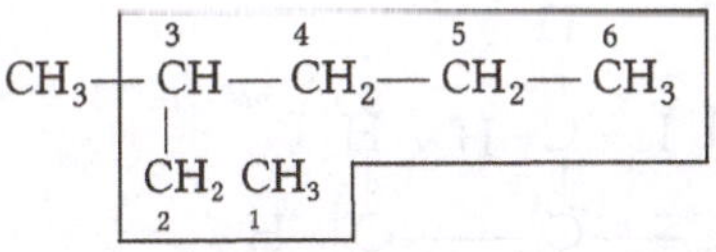

Longest chain is of six carbon atoms and not of five. Hence, the correct name of the compound is 3-methylhexane.

(ii) 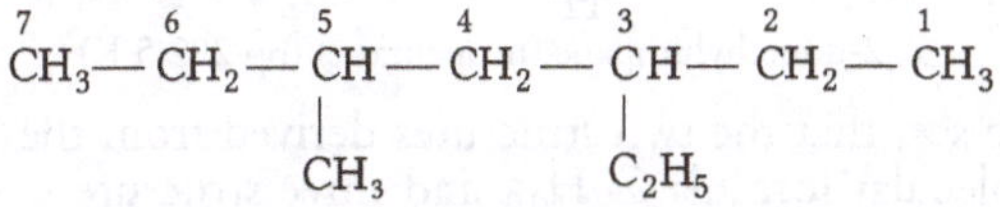

Numbering is always started from the end that gives lower number to the ethyl group as compared to methyl group (because in alphabets 'e' comes first than 'm'). Hence, the correct name is 3-ethyl-5-methylheptane.

Occurrence: Sources of Alkanes

The main sources of alkanes are **natural gas** and **petroleum.** The natural gas is found near petroleum wells and is a mixture of higher solid hydrocarbons. Bee's wax, which is mainly mynicyl palmitate (an ester) also contains small quantities of $C_{27}H_{56}$ and $C_{31}H_{64}$.

Isomerism

First three members of alkane family methane, ethane and propane have only one structure but higher alkanes can have more than one structure. Hence, exhibit isomerism e.g. four carbon atoms can be joined in the following two different ways with molecular formula C_4H_{10}.

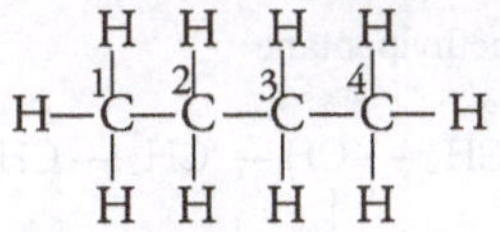

Butane (*n*-butane) (bp 273 K)

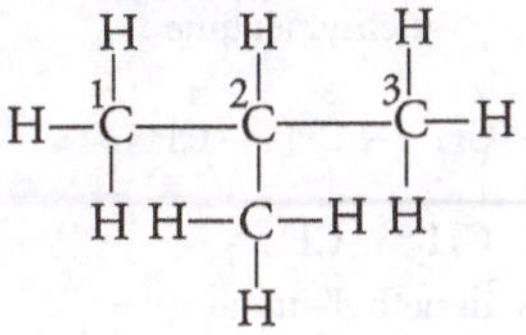

2-methylpropane (isobutane) (bp 261 K)

Similarly, C_5H_{12} can have three different structures which are given below.

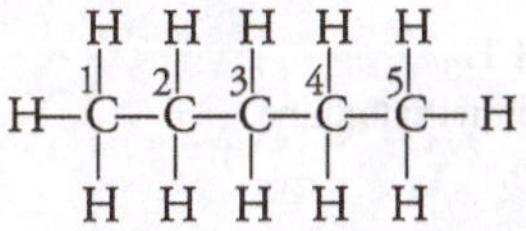

Pentane (*n*-pentane) (bp 309 K)

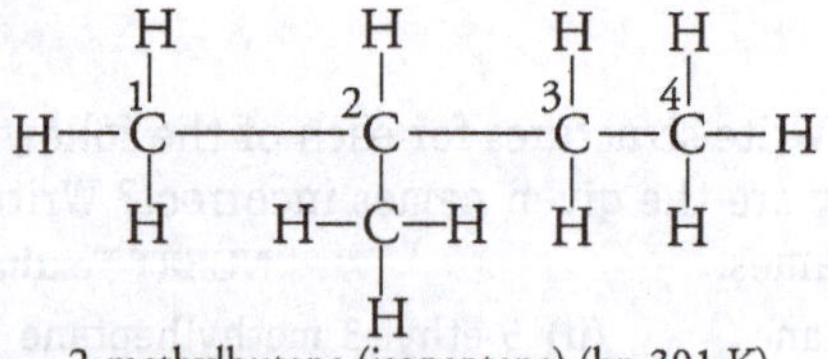

2-methylbutane (isopentane) (bp 301 K)

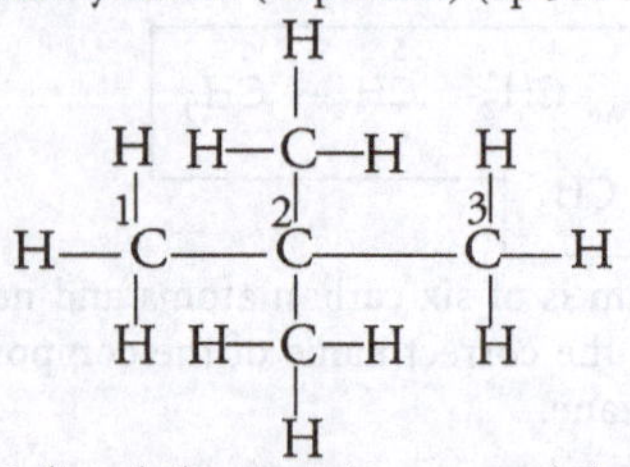

2, 2-dimethylpropane (neopentane) (bp 282.5 K)

We see, that the two structures derived from the molecular formula C_4H_{10} and three structure derived from the molecular formula C_5H_{12} have different properties (boiling point). Such structures which differ in their properties due to difference in thier structures are called structural isomers. And the structural isomers which differ in chain of carbon atoms are known as **chain isomers.**

- The number of possible structural isomers for C_6H_{14} and C_7H_{16} are respectively 9 and 75.

Example 3 Write structures of different chain isomers of alkanes corresponding to the molecular formula C_6H_{14}. Also write their IUPAC names. **NCERT Textbook**

Sol. (i) $\overset{1}{C}H_3—\overset{2}{C}H_2—\overset{3}{C}H_2—\overset{4}{C}H_2—\overset{5}{C}H_2—\overset{6}{C}H_3$

n-hexane

(ii) $\overset{1}{C}H_3—\overset{2}{C}H(CH_3)—\overset{3}{C}H_2—\overset{4}{C}H_2—\overset{5}{C}H_3$

2-methylpentane

(iii) $\overset{1}{C}H_3—\overset{2}{C}H_2—\overset{3}{C}H(CH_3)—\overset{4}{C}H_2—\overset{5}{C}H_3$

3-methylpentane

(iv) $\overset{1}{C}H_3—\overset{2}{C}H(CH_3)—\overset{3}{C}H(CH_3)—\overset{4}{C}H_3$

2,3- dimethylbutane

(v) $\overset{1}{C}H_3—\overset{2}{C}(CH_3)_2—\overset{3}{C}H_2—\overset{4}{C}H_3$

2,2-dimethylbutane

Methods of Preparation

Following methods can be used to prepare alkanes :

1. From Alkyl Halides

Following methods are used to convert alkyl halides into alkanes are as follows :

(i) **Reduction** : All the alkyl halides, except fluorides, when treated with zinc and dilute HCl, get reduced to alkanes. e.g.

$$\underset{\text{Chloromethane}}{CH_3—Cl} + H_2 \xrightarrow{Zn, H^+} \underset{\text{Methane}}{CH_4} + HCl$$

Alkyl iodide can also be reduced by using red P and HI. Here, red P is used to remove iodine as volatile PI_3, otherwise the reaction being reversible goes in backward direction.

$$\underset{\text{Ethyl iodide}}{C_2H_5I} + HI \xrightarrow{\text{Red P}} \underset{\text{Ethane}}{C_2H_6} + I_2$$

(ii) **Wurtz Reaction** When alkyl halides are treated with sodium metal in the presence of dry ether (free from moisture) it results in the formation of an alkane having double the number of carbons as that are present in parent halide. This reaction is called **Wurtz reaction.**

$$\underset{\text{Bromoethane}}{C_2H_5Br} + 2Na + BrC_2H_5 \xrightarrow[-2NaBr]{\text{Dry ether}} \underset{n\text{-butane}}{C_2H_5—C_2H_5}$$

If different alkyl halides are used, the product is non-separable mixture of alkanes, so **this method is more suitable for the synthesis of symmetrical alkanes, i.e. alkanes having even number of carbon atoms.** e.g.

$$CH_3X + 2Na + C_2H_5X \xrightarrow[-NaX]{\text{Ether}} \underset{\text{Ethane}}{CH_3—CH_3} + \underset{\text{Propane}}{CH_3—C_2H_5} + \underset{\text{Butane}}{C_2H_5—C_2H_5}$$

(A small percentage of alkene is also obtained during this reaction).

Note Methane cannot be prepared by this method.

(iii) **Corey-House Synthesis** It is a reaction that involves the reaction of a lithium dialkyl cuprate (R_2CuLi) with an alkyl halide to form a new alkane. This is a good method to prepare hydrocarbons (alkanes) having odd number of carbon atoms. Methane cannot be synthesised using this method.

$$\underset{\text{(Any alkyl halide)}}{R—X} \xrightarrow[\text{Diethyl ether}]{Li} RLi \xrightarrow{CuI} \underset{\text{(Gilman reagent)}}{R_2CuLi} \xrightarrow{R'X} R—R' + RCu + LiX$$

(This R' should be methyl, 1° alkyl or 2° cycloalkyl).

$$(CH_3)_2CHBr \xrightarrow[\text{(ii) Cu}]{\text{(i) Li}} \underset{\text{Lithium di-}iso\text{-propyl cuprate}}{[(CH_3)_2CH]_2LiCu}$$

$$\xrightarrow{CH_3CH_2CH_2Br} (CH_3)_2CHCH_2CH_2CH_3$$

For the second step to give a good yield of the alkane, the alkyl halide (say $R'X$) must be either a methyl halide (a primary alkyl halide) or a secondary cycloalkyl halide.

The alkyl groups of the lithium dialkyl cuprate (also called Gilman reagent) may be methyl, 1°, 2° or 3°. Moreover, the two alkyl groups being coupled need not be different.

2. From Carboxylic Acids

Carboxylic acids can be converted into alkanes by following methods

(i) **Decarboxylation (Removal of $—CO_2$)** When sodium salts of carboxylic acids are heated with sodalime (a mixture of NaOH and CaO), CO_2 is eliminated and alkanes having one carbon atom less than the parent compound is obtained. Thus, sodalime acts as the decarboxylating agent.

$$\underset{\text{Sodium ethanoate}}{CH_3COO^-Na^+} + NaOH \xrightarrow[\Delta]{CaO} \underset{\text{Methane}}{CH_4} + Na_2CO_3$$

Note
- Purpose of using CaO in sodalime
- CaO permits the reaction to be carried out at a relatively higher temperature so that complete decarboxylation is ensured.
- Sodium hydroxide is hygroscopic in nature (i.e. absorbs moisture from air) but CaO present in sodalime keeps it dry.

(ii) **Kolbe's Electrolytic Method** When aqueous solution of sodium or potassium salt of a carboxylic acid is subjected to electrolysis, it gives an alkane having even number of carbon atoms at the anode. In this method, a new C—C linkage is developed.

$$CH_3COO^-Na^+ + H_2O + CH_3COO^-Na^+ \xrightleftharpoons{\text{Electrolysis}} \underbrace{\underset{|}{CH_3}\ CH_3 + CO_2\uparrow}_{\text{At anode}} + \underbrace{H_2\uparrow + 2Na^+OH^-}_{\text{At cathode}}$$

Mechanism

It involves the following steps :

Step I $\quad 2CH_3COO^-Na^+ \xrightleftharpoons[\text{Ionisation}]{} 2CH_3—\overset{\overset{O}{||}}{C}—O^- + 2Na^+$

Step II At anode

$$\underset{\text{Acetate ion}}{2CH_3—\overset{\overset{O}{||}}{C}—O^-} \xrightarrow{-2e^-} \underset{\text{Acetate free radical}}{2CH_3—\overset{\overset{O}{||}}{C}—\ddot{\underset{\cdot\cdot}{O}}\!:} \longrightarrow \underset{\text{Methyl free radical}}{2\dot{C}H_3} + 2CO_2\uparrow$$

Step III $\quad H_3\dot{C} + \dot{C}H_3 \longrightarrow H_3C—CH_3\uparrow$

Step IV **At cathode** $\quad H_2O + e^- \longrightarrow {}^-OH + \dot{H}$

$$2\dot{H} \longrightarrow H_2\uparrow$$

Because of the generation of OH^- ions, the solution becomes alkaline.

Note CH_4 cannot be prepared by this method. This method is not suitable for alkanes having odd number of carbon atoms, as in such case a mixture of hydrocarbons is formed which is difficult to separate.

3. By Reduction of Carbonyl Compounds

(i) Carbonyl compounds are easily reduced with hydrogen iodide in presence of red phosphorus to alkanes.

$$R\overset{\overset{O}{||}}{C}H \xrightarrow{\text{Red P + HI}} RCH_3$$

$$R\overset{\overset{O}{||}}{C}CH_3 \xrightarrow{\text{Red P + HI}} RCH_2CH_3$$

(ii) Carbonyl compounds react with hydrazine (NH_2NH_2) in presence of $C_2H_5\overset{-}{O}\overset{+}{Na}$ to give alkane. This reaction is called as **Wolff-Kishner reduction.**

$$R\overset{\overset{O}{||}}{C}CH_3 \xrightarrow[-H_2O]{NH_2—NH_2} R\overset{\overset{N—NH_2}{||}}{C}CH_3 \xrightarrow[450\text{ K}]{C_2H_5\overset{-}{O}\overset{+}{Na}} RCH_2CH_3$$

(iii) Carbonyl compounds react with zinc amalgam in presence of conc. HCl to give the alkane. This reaction is called as **Clemmensen reduction.**

$$R\overset{\overset{O}{||}}{C}CH_3 \xrightarrow{\text{Zn - Hg + conc. HCl}} RCH_2CH_3$$

4. From Alcohols, Aldehydes and Ketones

The alcohols, aldehydes and ketones on reduction with a mixture of red phosphorus and hydroiodic acid yield corresponding alkanes.

$$\underset{\text{Alcohol}}{R—OH} + 2HI \xrightarrow[423\text{ K}]{\text{Red P}} \underset{\text{Alkane}}{RH} + I_2 + H_2O$$

$$\underset{\text{Alcohol}}{R\text{—CHO}} + 4HI \xrightarrow[473\text{ K}]{\text{Red P}} \underset{\text{Alkane}}{RCH_3} + 2I_2 + H_2O$$

$$\underset{\text{Ketone}}{\begin{matrix}R\\R\end{matrix}\!\!>C{=}O} + 4HI \xrightarrow[523\text{ K}]{\text{Red P}} \underset{\text{Alkane}}{R\text{—}CH_2\text{—}R} + 2I_2 + H_2O$$

For example,

$$\underset{\text{Methanol}}{CH_3OH} + 2HI \xrightarrow[423\text{ K}]{\text{Red P}} \underset{\text{Methane}}{CH_4} + I_2 + H_2O$$

$$\underset{\text{Acetaldehyde}}{CH_3CHO} + 4HI \xrightarrow[473\text{ K}]{\text{Red P}} \underset{\text{Alkane}}{CH_3CH_3} + 2I_2 + H_2O$$

$$\underset{\text{Acetone}}{CH_3\text{—}\overset{\overset{\displaystyle O}{\|}}{C}\text{—}CH_3} + 4HI \xrightarrow[523\text{ K}]{\text{Red P}} \underset{\text{Propane}}{CH_3CH_2CH_3} + 2I_2 + H_2O$$

From Grignard Reagent Grignard reagent is prepared by treating alkyl halides with magnesium in the presence of dry ether. When Grignard reagent is treated with protonic compounds such as water, acids, alcohols, amines etc., the —MgX group is replaced by —H and alkanes are obtained.

$$CH_3MgI + C_2H_5OH \longrightarrow \underset{\text{Methane}}{CH_3H \text{ or } CH_4} + C_2H_5\overset{\delta-}{O}\overset{\delta+}{Mg}I$$

Physical Properties

Alkanes exhibit following physical properties :

1. Physical State

Alkanes possess weak van der Waals' forces. Due to which, their first four members (C_1 to C_4) are gases, C_5 to C_{17} are liquids and all other highest ones (i.e. $>C_{18}$) are waxy solids.

2. Boiling Point

As the number of carbon atoms or molecular mass increases, the boiling point of alkane increases because van der Waals' forces increases due to increased surface area. However, branching results in decrease in boiling point due to decreased surface area which results in weaker van der Waals' forces. e.g. order of boiling point 2, 2-dimethyl propane (282.5) < 2-methylbutane (300.9) < pentane (309.1).

3. Melting Point and Density

Melting point also increases with increase in molecular weights but alkanes with even number of carbon atoms have higher melting point than the preceding and succeeding members, due to their well packed structures.

Alkanes are lighter than water and their density also increases with increase in molecular mass.

Chemical Properties

Although alkanes are almost inert towards most of the reagents, but they show following reactions under suitable conditions of temperature and pressure.

1. Substitution Reactions

The reactions in which hydrogen atom(s) of a hydrocarbon is (are) substituted by other group(s) are called **substitution reactions.** Alkanes undergo several substitution reactions like halogenation, nitration and sulphonation.

(i) **Reaction with Chlorine (Halogenation)** When an alkane is treated with a halogen at higher temperature (573-773 K) or in the presence of diffused sunlight or ultraviolet light, the hydrogen atoms of alkanes are successively replaced by halogen atoms. This reaction is known as **halogenation**. e.g.

$$CH_4 + Cl_2 \xrightarrow{h\nu} \underset{\text{Chloromethane}}{CH_3Cl} + HCl$$

$$CH_3Cl + Cl_2 \xrightarrow{h\nu} \underset{\text{Dichloromethane}}{CH_2Cl_2} + HCl$$

$$CH_2Cl_2 + Cl_2 \xrightarrow{h\nu} \underset{\text{Trichloromethane}}{CHCl_3} + HCl$$

$$CHCl_3 + Cl_2 \xrightarrow{h\nu} \underset{\text{Tetrachloromethane}}{CCl_4} + HCl$$

For this reaction, the order of reactivity of halogens is $F_2 > Cl_2 > Br_2 > I_2$ and the order of rate of replacement of hydrogens from alkane is 3° > 2° > 1°. Thus, **fluorination** is a violent process which is difficult to control so carried out in dark whereas during **iodination** presence of oxidising agent such as HIO_3 or HNO_3 is necessary as the reaction is very slow and reversible.

$$CH_4 + I_2 \rightleftharpoons CH_3I + HI$$

and $$HIO_3 + 5HI \longrightarrow 3I_2\uparrow + 3H_2O$$

Mechanism

Halogenation process proceed through free radical mechanism which involves following three steps :

Step I **Initiation** (Generation of free radical) In the presence of heat or light, the chlorine molecule undergo homolysis to give chlorine free radicals. This is because Cl—Cl bond is weaker than C—C and C—H bonds.

$$Cl\text{—}Cl \xrightarrow[\text{Homolysis}]{h\nu} \underset{\text{Chlorine free radical}}{\dot{C}l + \dot{C}l}$$

Step II **Propagation** The free radicals generated attack on the alkane molecule to give alkyl free radical which in turn reacts with other chlorine molecule to give alkyl chloride and chlorine free radical. These reactions are repeated and thereby setup a chain of reactions.

$$CH_4 + \dot{C}l \xrightarrow{h\nu} \dot{C}H_3 + H{-}Cl$$

$$\dot{C}H_3 + Cl{-}Cl \xrightarrow{h\nu} CH_3{-}Cl + \underset{\text{Chlorine free radical}}{\dot{C}l}$$

The chlorine and methyl free radicals generated above repeat the above steps and thereby setup a chain of reactions.

The above reaction gives the required products but many other side reactions also occur during the process. Two such reactions are as follows:

$$CH_3Cl + \dot{C}l \longrightarrow \dot{C}H_2Cl + HCl$$

$$\dot{C}H_2Cl + Cl{-}Cl \longrightarrow CH_2Cl_2 + \dot{C}l$$

Step III **Termination** The chain reaction is terminated either by complete consumption of reactants or also in the following termination process (due to reaction of two free radicals).

$$\dot{C}l + \dot{C}l \longrightarrow Cl{-}Cl;$$

$$H_3\dot{C} + \dot{C}H_3 \longrightarrow H_3C{-}CH_3$$

$$H_3\dot{C} + \dot{C}l \longrightarrow H_3C{-}Cl$$

Thus, ethane is also produced as by product during the free radical chlorination of methane.

2. Combustion

When alkanes are heated in excess of air or dioxygen, they are oxidised to give carbon dioxide and water. A large amount of heat is evolved during this reaction. Thus, alkanes are used as fuels.

$$CH_4(g) + 2O_2(g) \longrightarrow CO_2(g) + 2H_2O(l); \quad \Delta_C H^{\ominus} = -890 \text{ kJ mol}^{-1}$$

$$C_4H_{10}(g) + \frac{13}{2}O_2(g) \longrightarrow 4CO_2(g) + 5H_2O(l); \quad \Delta_C H^{\ominus} = -2875.84 \text{ kJ mol}^{-1}$$

The general combustion equation for any alkane is

$$C_nH_{2n+2} + \left(\frac{3n+1}{2}\right)O_2 \longrightarrow nCO_2 + (n+1)H_2O$$

If air or dioxygen is insufficient, incomplete combustion of alkanes take place and carbon black is formed as product. Carbon black is used for making ink, printer ink, black pigments and as filters.

$$CH_4(g) + O_2(g) \xrightarrow[\text{combustion}]{\text{Incomplete}} C(s) + 2H_2O(l)$$

3. Catalytic Oxidation (Reaction with Oxygen in Presence of Catalyst)

If alkanes are heated in controlled supply of dioxygen or air and in the presence of suitable catalysts, a variety of oxidation products (alcohol, aldehyde and carboxylic acid) are obtained as follows:

$$\text{(i) } 2CH_4 + O_2 \xrightarrow{\text{Cu/523 K/100 atm}} \underset{\text{Methanol}}{2CH_3OH}$$

$$\text{(ii) } CH_4 + O_2 \xrightarrow[\Delta]{Mo_2O_3} \underset{\text{Methanal}}{HCHO} + H_2O$$

$$\text{(iii) } 2CH_3CH_3 + 3O_2 \xrightarrow[\Delta]{(CH_3COO)_2Mn} \underset{\text{Ethanoic acid}}{2CH_3COOH} + 2H_2O$$

Generally, alkanes do not undergo oxidation but alkanes having tertiary H-atom undergo oxidation to corresponding alcohols by treating them with potassium permanganate.

$$\underset{\text{2-methylpropane}}{(CH_3)_3CH} \xrightarrow[\text{Oxidation}]{KMnO_4} \underset{\text{2-methylpropan-2-ol}}{(CH_3)_3COH}$$

4. Isomerisation

When *n*-alkanes are heated with anhydrous $AlCl_3$ and HCl gas, they isomerise to give branched chain alkanes as the major product which are given below:

$$\underset{n\text{-hexane}}{CH_3(CH_2)_4CH_3} \xrightarrow{\text{Anhyd.}AlCl_3/HCl} \underset{\text{2-methylpentane}}{CH_3CH(CH_3){-}(CH_2)_2{-}CH_3} + \underset{\text{3-methylpentane}}{CH_3CH_2{-}CH(CH_3){-}CH_2{-}CH_3}$$

+ minor products (not reported in organic synthesis)

5. Cyclisation

Alkanes having six or more carbon atoms undergoes cyclisation to give cycloalkane and on subsequent dehydrogenation at a higher temperature in presence of catalyst such as Pt, Pd or Ni.

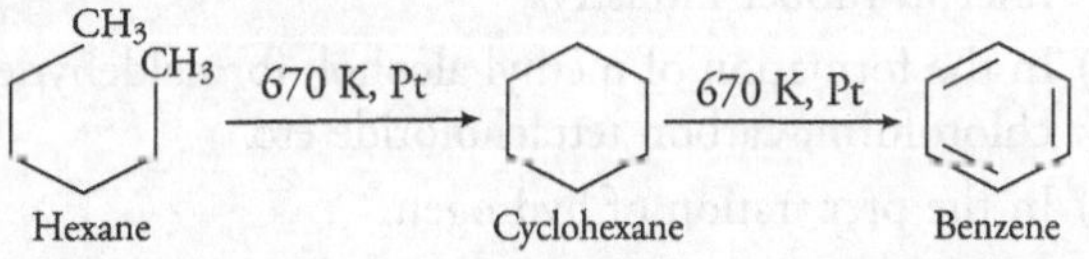

Hexane Cyclohexane Benzene

6. Aromatisation

Straight chain alkanes having 6 or more C-atoms when heated to 773 K at 10-20 atm pressure in the presence of Cr_2O_3, V_2O_5 or Mo_2O_3 supported over alumina gel, get dehydrogenated (i.e. loss hydrogen) and cyclised to give benzene and its homologous.

This reaction is known as **aromatisation** or **reforming**.

e.g.

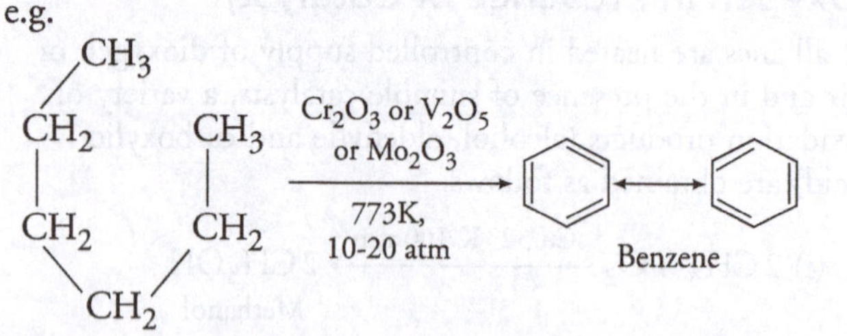

If *n*-heptane is used in place of *n*-hexane, toluene, $(C_6H_5CH_3)$ is obtained as the product.

7. Pyrolysis or Cracking

Higher alkanes when heated at a higher temperature get decompose to give smaller fragments like lower alkanes, alkenes etc. This reaction is called **pyrolysis**.

e.g.

$$\underset{\text{Dodecane}}{C_{12}H_{26}} \xrightarrow[973\text{ K}]{\text{Pt/Pd/Ni}} \underset{\text{Heptane}}{C_7H_{16}} + \underset{\text{Pentane}}{C_5H_{10}} + \text{Other products}$$

This reaction takes place by free radical mechanism and is used to prepare oil gas or petrol gas from kerosene oil.

8. Reaction with Steam

When methane is treated with steam at 1273 K and in the presence of nickel as catalyst, it gives carbon monoxide and dihydrogen gas.

$$CH_4 + H_2O \xrightarrow[\Delta]{\text{Ni}} CO + 3H_2$$

The above reaction is an industrial process for the synthesis of dihydrogen.

Uses

(i) As a fuel and illuminant.

(ii) In the preparation of carbon black which is used for making printing ink, black paints and as a filler in rubber industry.

(iii) In the formation of methyl alcohol, formaldehyde, chloroform, carbon tetracholoride etc.

(iv) In the preparation of hydrogen.

Conformations

The rotation of carbon-carbon single bond (σ-bond), due to cylindrical symmetry of σ-MOs (molecular orbitals) along internuclear axis, in alkanes results into different spatial arrangement of atoms in space, that are interconvertible. These arrangements are called **conformations, conformers** or **rotamers.** In general, alkanes possess infinite number of conformations.

However, weak repulsive interaction are present between the adjacent bonds in alkanes so the rotation of C—C single bond is not completely free and is hindered by a small energy barriers of 1-20 kJ mol^{-1}. The repulsive interaction between the adjacent bond is called **torsional strain.**

Conformations of Ethane

As we write the structure of ethane (C_2H_6) molecule we see that it contains a carbon-carbon single bond with each carbon atom attached to three hydrogen atoms.

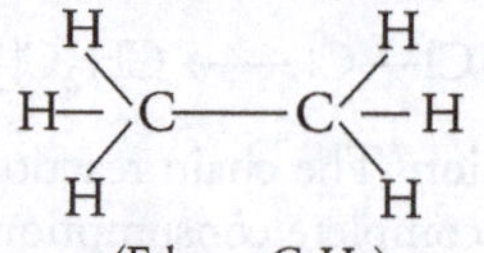

(Ethane, C_2H_6)

Now, considering the ball and stick model of ethane, keep one carbon atom stationary and rotate the other carbon atom around the C—C axis.

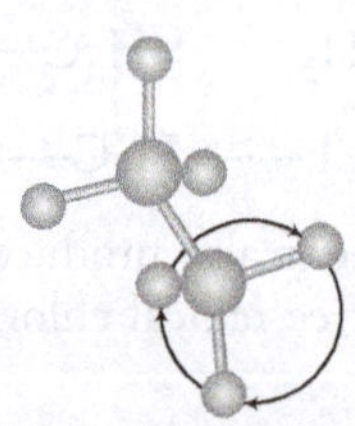

An infinite number of arrangements of the hydrogen atom attached to one carbon atom with respect to the hydrogen atom of the second carbon atom are possible.

These infinite number of different arrangements are called **conformations.** However, there are two extreme cases discussed below.

1. Staggered Conformation

The conformation in which the hydrogen atoms attached to the two carbon atoms are as far apart as possible is called the **staggered conformation.**

2. Eclipsed Conformation

The conformation in which the hydrogen atoms attached to the two carbon atoms are as closed together as possible is called **eclipsed conformation.**

Any intermediate conformation between the above two is called **skew or gauche conformation.**

In all the conformations, the bond angles as well as bond lengths remain the same. The staggered and eclipsed conformations of ethane in three dimensions can be represented by following two projections.

I. **Sawhorse Projections** In this projection, there is a long straight line, upper end of which is slightly tilted towards right or left hand side. This line shows the central C—C bond. The lower end of this line shows the front carbon and upper end represents the rear (the atom away from the eye) carbon atom. Each carbon also has three lines attached to it, that show three carbon atoms inclined at an angle of 120° to each other. Sawhorse projections for eclipsed and staggered conformation of ethane are as follows:

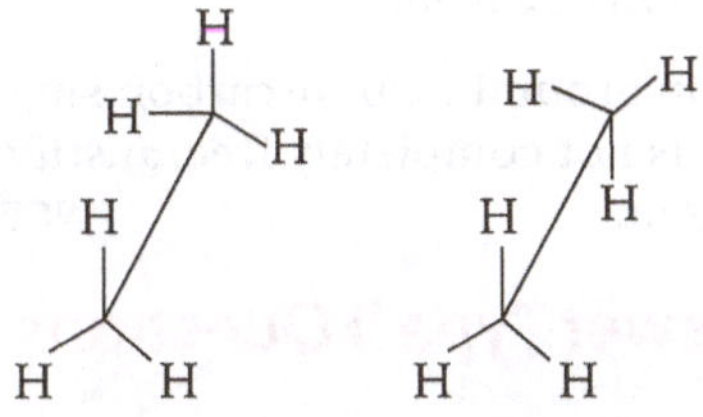

(i) Eclipsed (ii) Staggered

Sawhorse projections of ethane

II. **Newman Projections** In this projection, the front carbon is represented by a point and the three hydrogen attached to it by three lines attached to the point at an angle of 120° from each other.The rear carbon is shown by a circle and three shorter lines arising from the circle at an angle of 120° to each other show the three hydrogen atoms attached to the rear carbon atom. (carbon lying in the back)

The Newman's projections for staggered, eclipsed skew conformations of ethane are shown below :

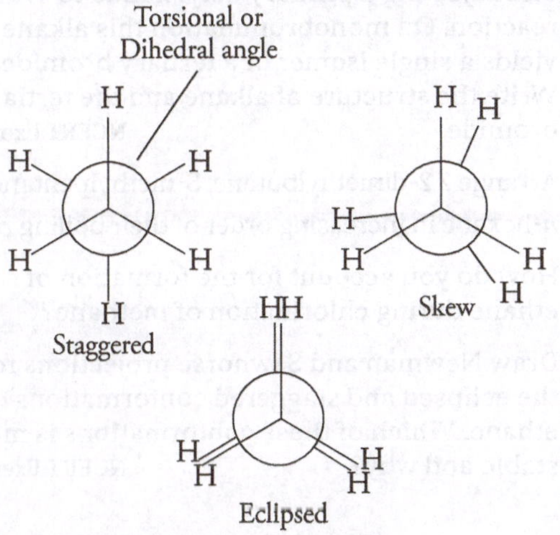

Newman's projections of ethane

Relative Stability of Conformations

In staggered conformation, since the electron clouds of carbon-hydrogen bonds are as far apart as possible, so it has minimum repulsive forces, minimum energy and maximum stability. On the other hand, eclipsed conformation has maximum repulsive forces, maximum energy and minimum stability because in it the electron clouds of carbon hydrogen bonds are too close to each other. The angle of rotation about C—C bond is called the **dihedral angle** or **torsional angle** and is maximum, i.e. 180° in staggered conformation and minimum (0°) in eclipsed conformation.Thus, torsional strain is minimum in staggered conformation and maximum in eclipsed form. The two forms differ in energy by 12.5 kJ mol^{-1}. This energy barrier is so small that small thermal or kinetic energy is sufficient to overcome it by intermolecular collisions, hence the different conformations of ethane cannot be separated and isolated.

Topic Practice 1

Very Short Answer Type Questions

1 Mark

1 Fill in the Blanks

(i) When unsaturated compound i.e alkenes are treated with dihydrogen in the presence of finely divided catalyst ...... are obtained.

(ii) When alkyl halides are treated with ...... in the presence of dry ether (free from moisture) it results in the formation of an alkane having double number of carbons as that present in parent-halide.

(iii) Alkanes are ligher than ....

(iv) Complete the following reaction.

$$C_{12}H_{26} \xrightarrow[973\text{ K}]{\text{Pt/pd/Ni}} \text{.........} + C_5H_{10} + \text{other products.}$$

2 Objective Type Questions.

(i) $C_5H_{11}Cl$ by Wurtz reaction forms 2,2,5,5-tetramethylhexane as the main product. Hence, $C_5H_{11}Cl$ is

(a) 2,2-dimethyl-1-chloropropane
(b) 2-methyl-1-chlorobutane
(c) Both (a) and (b)
(d) None of the above

(ii) R_2CuLi is the intermediate formed in the Corey-House synthesis. It is called

(a) Corey-House reagent (b) Gilman reagent
(c) Frankland reagent (d) Schmidt reagent

(iii) In the iodination of alkane, some HIO_3 is also added so that
(a) reaction is made faster
(b) reaction is made reversible
(c) HI formed is oxidised to I_2
(d) reaction is selective

(iv) Eclipsed form of ethane has higher energy due to
(a) torsional strain (b) steric strain
(c) angle strain (d) Both (a) and (b)

3. Match the hydrocarbons in Column I with the number of 3° carbon in Column II and choose the correct option using the codes given below :

Column I		Column II	
A.	*Neo*-pentane	(i)	3
B.	*Iso*-pentane	(ii)	2
C.	2, 3-dimethylbutane	(iii)	1
D.	1, 2, 3-trimethyl cyclohexane	(iv)	0

Codes

	A	B	C	D		A	B	C	D
(a)	(iv)	(iii)	(ii)	(i)	(b)	(iv)	(iii)	(i)	(ii)
(c)	(iii)	(iv)	(ii)	(i)	(d)	(i)	(ii)	(iii)	(iv)

4 Sodium salt of which acid will be needed for the preparation of propane? Write chemical equation for the reaction. **NCERT Textbook**

5 What effect does branching of an alkane chain has on its boiling point? **NCERT Textbook**

6 Why do hydrocarbon molecules with an odd number of carbon atoms have lower melting points than those with an even number of carbon atoms?

7 Convert 1-bromopropane to 2-bromopropane.

8 *n*-propylmagnesium bromide on hydrolysis gives propane. Is there any other Grignard reagent which also gives propane? If so, give its name, structure and equation for the reaction.

Short Answer Type I Questions

2 Marks

9 Write structural formulaes of the following compounds.
(i) 3, 4, 4, 5-tetramethylheptane
(ii) 2, 5-dimethylhexane **NCERT Textbook**

10 Write the reaction for the preparation of butane by
(i) Wurtz reaction (ii) Kolbe's reaction

11 Why is Wurtz reaction not preferred for the preparation of alkanes containing odd number of carbon atoms? Illustrate your answer by taking one example. **NCERT Textbook**

12 What happens, when
(i) bromoethane is treated with zinc and hydrochloric acid?
(ii) hydrogen is passed into 2-bromopropane in the presence of palladium?

13 Write the structures and names of products obtained in the reactions of sodium with a mixture of 1-iodo-2-methylpropane and 2-iodopropane.

14 Write hydrocarbon radicals that can be formed as intermediates during monochlorination of 2-methylpropane. Which of them is more stable? Give reason.

15 Rotation around carbon-carbon single bond of ethane is not completely free. Justify the statement. **NCERT Exemplar**

Short Answer Type II Questions

3 Marks

16 Write IUPAC names of the following compounds
(i) $(CH_3)_3CCH_2C(CH_3)_3$
(ii) $(CH_3)_2C(C_2H_5)_2$
(iii) Tetra-*tert*-butylmethane. **NCERT Textbook**

17 In the alkane $H_3CCH_2—C(CH_3)_2—CH_2CH(CH_3)_2$, identify 1°, 2°, 3° carbon atoms and give the number of H-atoms bonded to each one of these.

18 An alkane C_8H_{18} is obtained as the only product on subjecting a primary alkyl halide to Wurtz reaction. On monobromination this alkane yields a single isomer of a tertiary bromide. Write the structure of alkane and the tertiary bromide. **NCERT Exemplar**

19 Arrange 2,2-dimethylbutane, 3-methylpentane and *n*-hexane in increasing order of their boiling point.

20 How do you account for the formation of ethane during chlorination of methane?

21 Draw Newman and Sawhorse projections for the eclipsed and staggered conformations of ethane. Which of these conformations is more stable and why? **NCERT Exemplar**

22 Complete the reactions :

(i) $CH_3CH_2CH_3 + HNO_3 \xrightarrow{\text{Vapour phase}}$

(ii) $CH_4 + O_2 \xrightarrow[723-773\text{ K}]{\text{Copper tube}}$

(iii) $C_2H_5CO\overset{-}{O}\overset{+}{Na} + NaOH \xrightarrow{CaO}$

23 An alkane has a molecular mass of 72. Give all the possible structural isomers along with their IUPAC names.

Long Answer Type Questions

(5 Marks)

24 Write structures of different isomeric alkyl groups corresponding to the molecular formula C_5H_{11}. Write IUPAC names of alcohols obtained by attachment of —OH groups at different carbons of the chain. **NCERT Textbook**

25 (i) Arrange the three isomeric pentanes in order of increasing stability at room temperature.

(ii) Give a method of preparation of propane from (a) an alkene (b) an alkyl halide.

(iii) Write the structure of all the alkenes that can be hydrogenated to form 2-methyl butane.

(iv) Why is light or heat necessary to initiate the chlorination reaction?

Hints & Solutions

1. (i) alkanes, (ii) sodium metal (iii) water, (iv) C_7H_{16}
2. (i) → (a), (ii) → (b), (iii) → (c), (iv) → (d)
3. (a) A → (iv), B → (iii), C → (ii), D → (i)
4. Since, decarboxylation of the salt gives such alkane which has one carbon atom less than that present in the acid. Thus, to prepare propane (C_3H_8), a four carbon containing acid salt, (i.e. sodium salt of butanoic acid) is used.

$$CH_3CH_2CH_2COO^-Na^+ + NaOH \xrightarrow{CaO} CH_3CH_2CH_3 + Na_2CO_3$$

5. Refer to text on page 414 (Topic-1, Physical properties of alkanes).
6. Molecules with odd number of carbon atoms have lower melting points because they do not fit into crystal lattice easily whereas, hydrocarbons with even number of carbon atoms can fit into crystal lattice easily.
7. $\underset{\text{1-bromopropane}}{CH_3CH_2CH_2Br} \xrightarrow{\text{KOH (alc.)}} \underset{\text{Propene}}{CH_3—CH=CH_2}$

$$\xrightarrow[\text{Markownikoff addition}]{HBr} \underset{\text{2-bromopropane}}{CH_3\ \underset{}{\overset{Br}{\overset{|}{CH}}}\ CH_3}$$

8. *Iso*-propyl magnesium bromide, $(CH_3)_2CHMgBr$,

$$(CH_3)_2CHMgBr + H_2O \longrightarrow CH_3CH_2CH_3 + Mg(OH)Br$$

9. (i) $\overset{1}{C}H_3—\overset{2}{C}H_2—\underset{\underset{H_3C}{|}}{\overset{3}{C}H}—\underset{\underset{CH_3}{|}}{\overset{\overset{CH_3}{|}}{\overset{4}{C}}}—\underset{\underset{CH_3}{|}}{\overset{5}{C}H}—\overset{6}{C}H_2\overset{7}{C}H_3$ [1]

(ii) $\overset{1}{C}H_3–\overset{\overset{CH_3}{|}}{\overset{2}{C}H}–\overset{3}{C}H_2–\overset{4}{C}H_2–\overset{\overset{CH_3}{|}}{\overset{5}{C}H}–\overset{6}{C}H_3$ [2]

10. (i) Ethyl bromide on reaction with sodium in the presence of dry ether yields butane.

$$2C_2H_5Br + 2Na \xrightarrow{\text{Dry ether}} \underset{\text{Butane}}{CH_3CH_2CH_2CH_3} + 2NaBr$$ [1]

(ii) An aqueous concentrated solution of sodium propanoate on electrolysis yields butane at anode.

$$2CH_3CH_2CO\overset{-}{O}\overset{+}{Na}(aq) + 2H_2O\,(l) \xrightarrow{\text{Electrolysis}}$$
$$CH_3CH_2CH_2CH_3 + 2CO_2 + H_2\uparrow + 2NaOH$$ [1]

11. For the preparation of alkanes containing odd number of carbon atoms, two different alkyl halides are taken and two different alkyl halides can react in three different ways. Therefore, a mixture of alkanes is produced.

e.g. $3CH_3I + 6Na + 3C_2H_5I \xrightarrow{\text{Dry ether}} \underset{\text{Ethane}}{CH_3—CH_3}$
$$+ \underset{\text{Propane}}{CH_3CH_2CH_3} + \underset{\text{Butane}}{CH_3CH_2CH_2CH_3} + 6NaI$$

That's why this method (Wurtz reaction) is not suitable for the preparation of odd number alkanes. [2]

12. (i) Ethane is formed.

$$\underset{\text{Bromoethane}}{CH_3CH_2—Br} + 2[H] \xrightarrow[\text{(Reduction)}]{Zn/HCl} CH_3CH_3 + HBr$$ [1]

(ii) Propane is obtained.

$$CH_3—\underset{\underset{CH_3}{|}}{CH}—Br + H_2 \xrightarrow[\text{(Reduction)}]{Pd} \underset{\text{Propane}}{CH_3—\underset{\underset{CH_3}{|}}{CH_2}} + Br$$ [1]

13. **Key Idea** This question is based upon Wurtz reaction. Wurtz reaction represent that two alkyl groups can be coupled by reacting alkyl halide with sodium

$$2RX + 2Na \xrightarrow[\text{Dry ether}]{\Delta} R—R + 2NaX$$

(i) $\underset{\text{1-iodo-2-methylpropane}}{CH_3\underset{\underset{CH_3}{|}}{CH}CH_2I} + 2Na + ICH_2—\underset{\underset{CH_3}{|}}{CH}—CH_3 \xrightarrow{\Delta}$

$$\underset{\text{2, 5-dimethyl hexane}}{CH_3—\underset{\underset{CH_3}{|}}{CH}—(CH_2)_2—\underset{\underset{CH_3}{|}}{CH}—CH_3} + 2NaI$$ [1/2]

(ii)

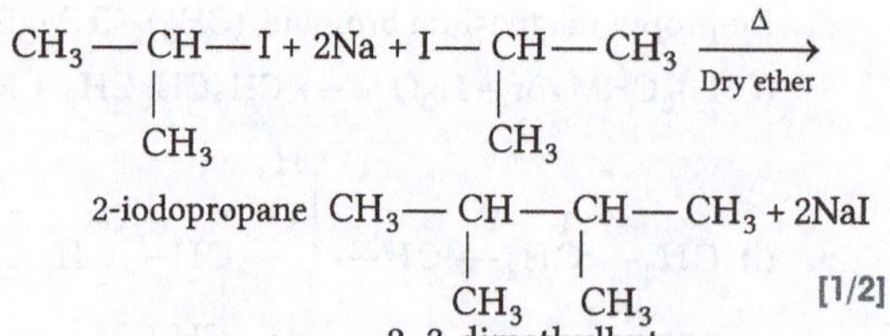

2-iodopropane

2, 3-dimethylbutane [1/2]

(iii)

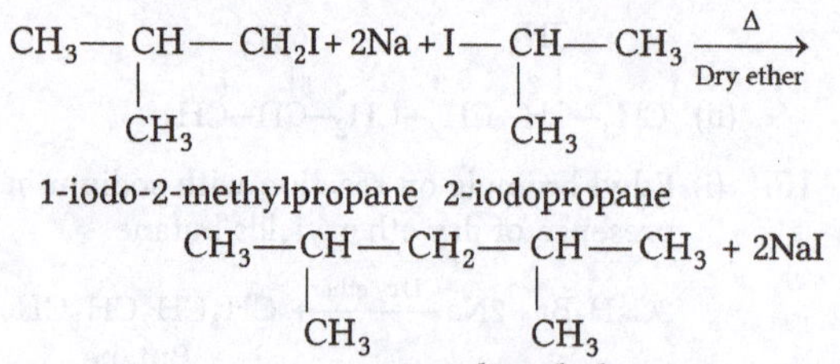

1-iodo-2-methylpropane 2-iodopropane

2, 4-dimethylpentane [1]

14. 2-methylpropane gives two types of radicals.

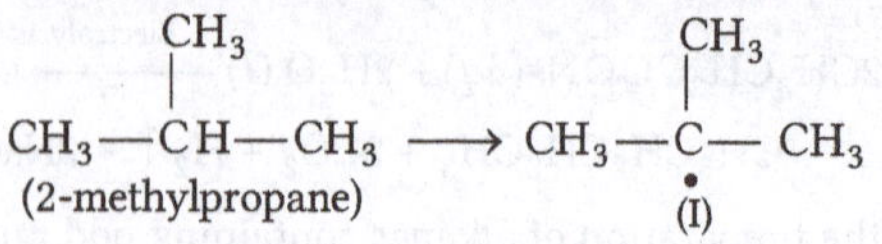

(2-methylpropane) (I) and (II) [1]

Radical (I) is more stable because it is 3° and stabilised by nine hyperconjugative structures (as it has 9 α-hydrogens). Radical (II) is less stable because it is 1° and stabilised by only one hyperconjugative structure (as it has only 1 α-hydrogen). [1]

15. Alkanes can have infinite number of conformations by rotation around C — C single bonds. This rotation around a C — C single bond is hindered by a small energy barrier of 1-20 kJ mol^{-1} due to weak repulsive interaction between the adjacent bonds. Such a type of repulsive interaction is called torsional strain. In staggered form of ethane, the electron cloud of carbon hydrogen bonds are far apart.

Hence, minimum repulsive force. In eclipsed electron cloud of carbon-hydrogen become close resulting in increase in electron cloud repulsion. This repulsion affects stability of a conformer.

In all the conformations of ethane the staggered form has least torsional strain and the eclipsed form has the maximum torsional strain. Hence, rotation around C— C bond in ethtane is not completely free.

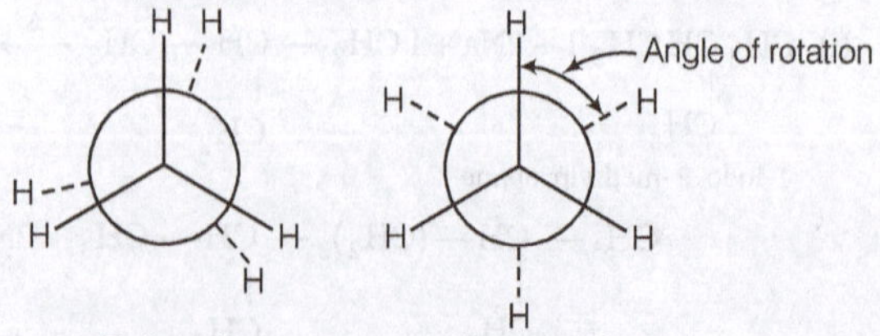

Newman's projection of ethane

16. The expanded structures of these alkanes are:

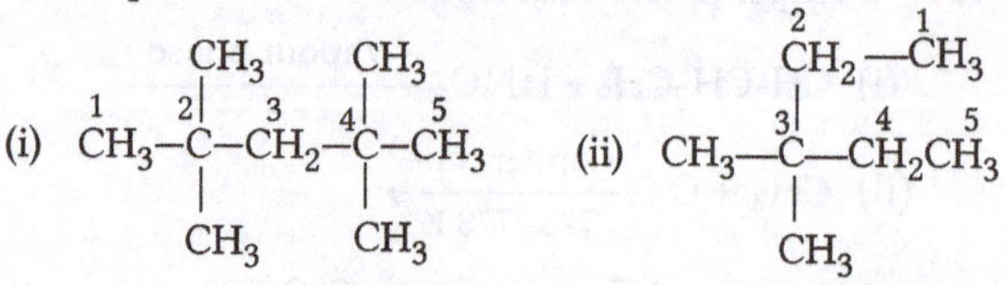

(i) 2,2,4, 4-tetramethylpentane (ii) 3, 3-dimethylpentane

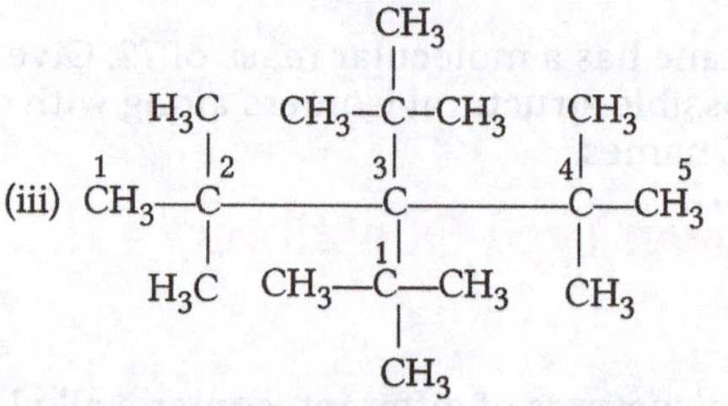

(iii) 3, 3-di-*tert*-butyl-2,2,4,4-tetramethylpentane or 3,3-*bis* (1, 1-dimethylethyl)-2,2,4,4-tetramethylpentane

17. **Key Idea** The carbon which is attached with only 1 or no other carbon atom, is called 1° carbon. Similarly, carbon attached with 2, 3 or 4 other carbon atoms is called 2°, 3°, or 4° carbon atoms respectively. Similarly, hydrogens attached with 1°, 2° or 3° carbon atoms are called 1°, 2° or 3° hydrogens respectively.

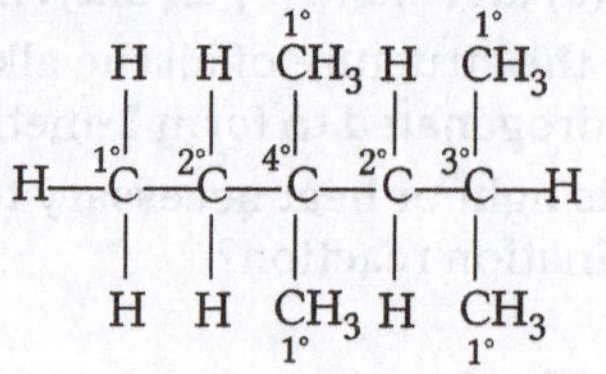

15 H-bonded to five 1°C-atoms [1]

4 H-bonded to two 2°C-atoms [1]

1 H-bonded to one 3°C-atom [1]

18. Since, alkane C_8H_{18} on monobromination yields a single isomer of a tertiary bromide, therefore alkane must contain tertiary hydrogen. [1]

This is possible if primary alkyl halide (which undergoes Wurtz reaction) has a tertiary hydrogen.

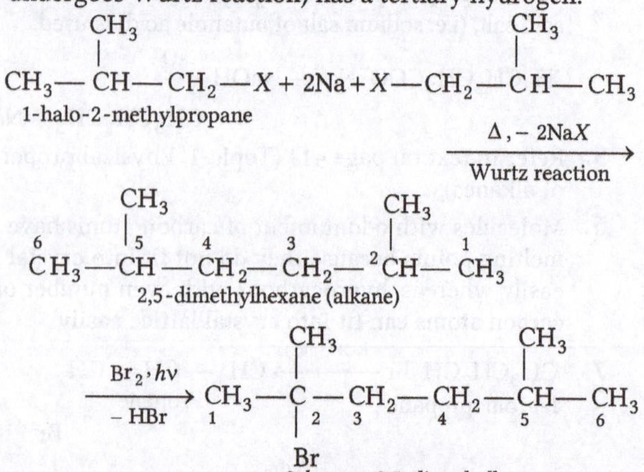

1-halo-2-methylpropane; Wurtz reaction; 2,5-dimethylhexane (alkane); 2-bromo-2,5-dimethylhexane (3° bromide) [2]

19. $H_3C-CH_2-C(CH_3)_2-CH_3$ (two CH_3 groups on the central C), $CH_3-CH_2-CH(CH_3)-CH_2-CH_3$,

2, 2-dimethylbutane
Molecular formula = (C_6H_{14})

3-methylpentane
Molecular formula = (C_6H_{14})

$CH_3CH_2CH_2CH_2-CH_2-CH_3$

n-hexane
Molecular formula = (C_6H_{14})

The three given compounds are isomers of molecular formula C_6H_{14}, *n*-hexane has the longest chain and therefore has the highest boiling point. 2, 2-dimethylbutane is the most spherical and has the smallest surface area. In this case, the van der waals' force will be weakest and so it has the lowest boiling point.Thus, the increasing order of boiling point of the three isomers is as follows:

2, 2-dimethylbutane < 3-methylpentane < *n*-hexane **[2]**

20. Refer to pages 414 and 415. (Topic-1, Free radical chain mechanism for the chlorination of methane). From the mechanism, it is evident that methyl free radicals are produced during propagation step. If two methyl free radicals combine with each other a molecule of ethane is formed. **[3]**

21. Refer to pages 416 and 417 (Topic-2, Conformations of ethane).

Staggered form of ethane is more stable than the eclipsed conformation by about 12.5 kJ mol^{-1}.

This is because any two hydrogen atoms on adjacent carbon atoms of staggered conformation are maximum apart while in eclipsed conformation, they cover or eclipse each other in space. Thus, in staggered form, there is minimum repulsive forces, minimum energy and maximum stability of the molecule. **[3]**

22. (i) $CH_3CH_2CH_3 + HNO_3 \xrightarrow{\text{Vapour phase}} \underset{\text{Nitroethane}}{CH_3CH_2NO_2} + \underset{\text{Nitropropane}}{CH_3CH_2CH_2NO_2} + \underset{\text{Nitromethane}}{CH_3NO_2} + H_2O$ **[1]**

(ii) $CH_4 + O_2 \xrightarrow[723-773\text{ K}]{\text{Copper tube}} \underset{\text{Methanol}}{2CH_3OH}$

(iii) $C_2H_5CO\overset{-}{O}\overset{+}{Na} + NaOH \xrightarrow{CaO} \underset{\text{Ethane}}{C_2H_6} + Na_2CO_3$ **[1]**

23. The general formula of alkanes is $C_nH_{2n+2} \Rightarrow$

$12 \times n + 1 \times (2n+2) = 72$ or $12n + 2n + 2 = 72$ or $n = 5$

Thus, the molecular formula of the alkane is C_5H_{12}. For structural isomers and their IUPAC names.

(i) $CH_3-CH_2-CH_2-CH_2-CH_3$
Pentane

(ii) $CH_3-CH_2-CH(CH_3)-CH_3$
(2-methyl butane)

(iii) $CH_3-C(CH_3)_2-CH_3$
2, 2-dimethyl propane

24.

	Structures of $—C_5H_{11}$ group	Corresponding alcohols	Name of alcohols
(i)	$CH_3-CH_2-CH_2-CH_2-CH_2-$	$CH_3-CH_2-CH_2-CH_2-CH_2-OH$	Pentan-1-ol
(ii)	$CH_3-CH(-)-CH_2-CH_2-CH_3$	$CH_3-CH(OH)-CH_2-CH_2-CH_3$	Pentan-2-ol
(iii)	$CH_3-CH_2-CH(-)-CH_2-CH_3$	$CH_3-CH_2-CH(OH)-CH_2-CH_3$	Pentan-3-ol
(iv)	$CH_3-CH(CH_3)-CH_2-CH_2-$	$CH_3-CH(CH_3)-CH_2-CH_2-OH$	3-methylbutan-1-ol
(v)	$CH_3-CH_2-CH(CH_3)-CH_2-$	$CH_3-CH_2-CH(CH_3)-CH_2-OH$	2-methylbutan-1-ol
(vi)	$CH_3-C(CH_3)(-)-CH_2-CH_3$	$CH_3-C(CH_3)(OH)-CH_2-CH_3$	2-methylbutan-2-ol

	Structures of $-C_5H_{11}$ group	Corresponding alcohols	Name of alcohols
(vii)	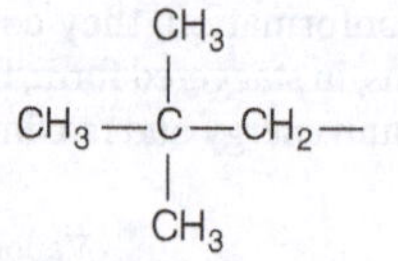	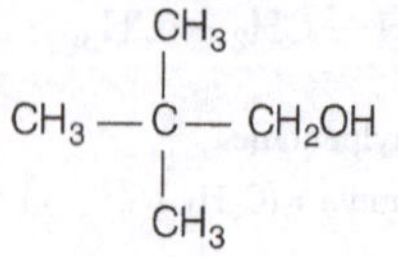	2,2-dimethyl propan-1-ol
(viii)	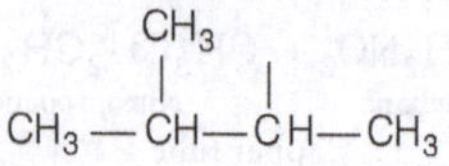	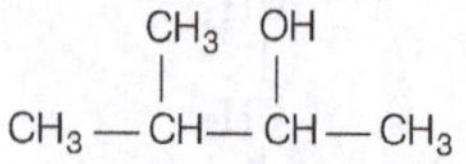	3-methylbutan-2-ol

25. (i) The stability of structural isomers generally increases with increase in branching. Thus, Pentane $[CH_3(CH_2)_3CH_3]$ < *iso*-pentane, $[(CH_3)_2CHCH_2CH_3]$ < *neo*-pentane, $[(CH_3)_4C]$ [1]

(ii) (a) $\underset{\text{Propene}}{CH_3CH=CH_2} + H_2 \xrightarrow[\text{Catalyst}]{\text{Pt, Pd or Ni}} \underset{\text{Propane}}{CH_3CH_2CH_3}$ [1]

(b) $CH_3-CH_2-CH_2Cl \xrightarrow[\text{or LiAlH}_4]{\text{Zn/HCl}} CH_3-CH_2-CH_3$ [1]

(iii) The alkenes must have the same carbon skeleton as 2-methylbutane.

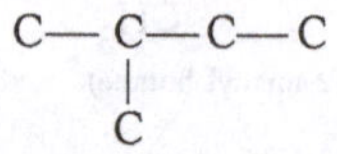

There are three different positions for the double bond; hence the three different alkenes are:

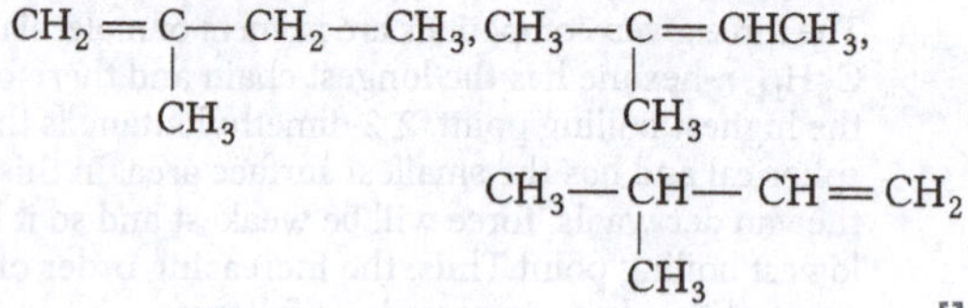

[1]

(iv) The Cl—Cl bond must be broken to form Cl radical before the reaction with methane. This homolysis requires energy, which is supplied either by heat or light. [1]

TOPIC 02 Unsaturated Hydrocarbons (Alkenes)

The unsaturated hydrocarbons having atleast one double bond are called **alkenes.** Their general formula is C_nH_{2n} (where, $n=2, 3, 4...$) as they have two carbon atoms less than the alkanes. These are also named as **olefins** (oil forming) as the first member of this class, i.e. ethene forms oily liquid when treated with chlorine.

Structure of Double Bond

In alkenes, double bond between two carbon atoms consists of one strong σ - bond formed by the head on overlapping of the sp^2-hybrid orbitals and one weak π-bond formed by the sideways overlapping of two 2 *p*-orbitals of two C-atoms. The orbital diagram of ethene molecule is shown as:

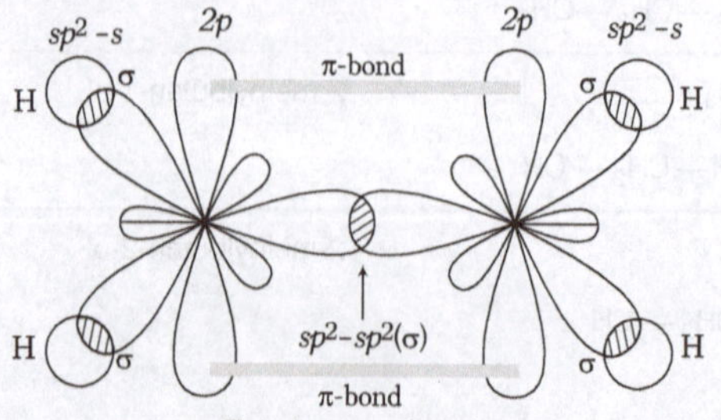

Ethylene molecule

Both the C-atoms shown above are sp^2-hybridised with triangular shape. The C=C double bond (134 pm) is shorter than C—C single bond (154 pm).

As π-bond is a weak bond therefore, can be easily attacked by the electron deficient species called **electrophiles.** Hence, the presence of exposed π-bond makes alkene an easier target for the electrophiles.

Nomenclature

While naming alkenes, follow the following rules (according to IUPAC system).

(i) Choose the longest chain bearing double bond.

(ii) Number the chain from the end that is closer to the double bond.

(iii) Write the root word and add suffix 'ene'.

(iv) If any substituent is present, write its name before the root word. The general formula of alkene is C_nH_{2n}. For $n=1$, we get : CH_2 (methene). It has very short half-life. If $n=2$, we get C_2H_4, the first stable member of alkene series. Its common name is ethylene and IUPAC name is ethene.

IUPAC names of other alkenes are as follows :

Structure	IUPAC name
$CH_3-CH=CH_2$	Propene
$CH_3-CH_2-CH=CH_2$	But-1-ene
$CH_3-CH=CH-CH_3$	But-2-ene
$CH_2=CH-CH=CH_2$	Buta-1, 3-diene
$CH_2=\underset{\underset{CH_3}{\mid}}{C}-CH_3$	2-methylprop-1-ene
$CH_2=CH-\underset{\underset{CH_3}{\mid}}{CH}-CH_3$	3-methylbut-1-ene

Isomerism

Alkenes can exhibit structural as well as stereoisomerism.

1. Structural Isomerism

Because of the possibility of several structures for a single molecular formula, alkenes having atleast 4C-atoms are able to exhibit structural isomerism. e.g. Alkene with molecular formula C_4H_8 can have following three structures.

$$\text{I. } \overset{1}{C}H_2=\overset{2}{C}H-\overset{3}{C}H_2-\overset{4}{C}H_3$$
But-1-ene (C_4H_8)

$$\text{II. } \overset{1}{C}H_3-\overset{2}{C}H=\overset{3}{C}H-\overset{4}{C}H_3$$
But-2-ene (C_4H_8)

$$\text{III. } \overset{1}{C}H_2=\underset{\underset{CH_3}{\mid}}{\overset{2}{C}}-\overset{3}{C}H_3$$
2-methylprop-1-ene (C_4H_8)

Structure I and II differ in the position of double bond, so these are called **position isomers.** But structure I and III differ in the chain of carbon atoms, so these are called **chain isomers.** Thus, it is obvious that alkenes generally exhibit chain and position isomerism.

Example 11 Write structures and IUPAC names of different structural isomers of alkenes coresponding to C_6H_{12}.

Sol. (a) $CH_2=CH-CH_2CH_2CH_2CH_3$
Hex-1-ene

(b) $CH_3-CH=CH-CH_2CH_2CH_3$
Hex-2-ene

(c) $CH_3-CH_2-CH=CH-CH_2CH_3$
Hex-3-ene

(d) $CH_3-\overset{CH_3}{\overset{\mid}{C}}=CH-CH_2-CH_3$
2-methylpent-2-ene

(e) $CH_3-\overset{CH_3}{\overset{\mid}{CH}}-CH=CH-CH_3$
4-methylpent-2-ene

(f) $CH_3-CH_2-\overset{CH_3}{\overset{\mid}{C}}=CH-CH_3$
3-methylpent-2-ene

(g) $CH_2=\overset{CH_3}{\overset{\mid}{C}}-CH_2CH_2CH_3$
2-methylpent-1-ene

(h) $CH_2=CH-\overset{CH_3}{\overset{\mid}{CH}}-CH_2CH_3$
3-methylpent-1-ene

(i) $CH_2=CH-CH_2\overset{CH_3}{\overset{\mid}{CH}}CH_3$
4-methylpent-1-ene

(j) $H_3C-\underset{\underset{CH_3}{\mid}}{\overset{CH_3}{\overset{\mid}{C}}}-CH=CH_2$
3, 3-dimethylbut-1-ene

(k) $H_3C-\overset{CH_3}{\overset{\mid}{CH}}-\overset{CH_3}{\overset{\mid}{C}}=CH_2$
2,3-dimethylbut-1-ene

(l) $H_3C-\overset{CH_3}{\overset{\mid}{C}}=\overset{CH_3}{\overset{\mid}{C}}-CH_3$
2, 3-dimethylbut-2-ene

2. Stereoisomerism (Geometrical Isomerism)

Alkenes also exhibit geometrical isomerism (a type of stereoisomerism) due to the possibility of different geometrical arrangements in space, as rotation around the double bond is restricted, not free.

Thus, alkenes having the general formula $YXC=CXY$ or $XYC=CXZ$ or $XYC=CZW$ generally exist in following geometrical arrangements.

(i) *Cis-form* If the identical atoms or groups lie on the same side of the double bond, the isomer is called *cis*-form. e.g.

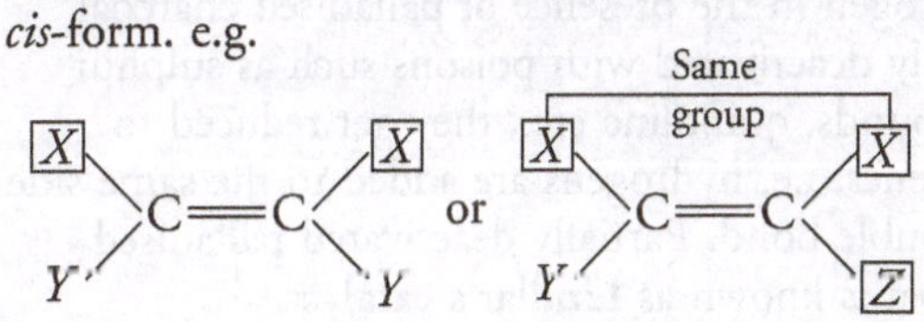

(ii) ***Trans*-form** If the identical atoms or groups lie on the opposite side of the double bond, the isomer is called *trans*-form. e.g.

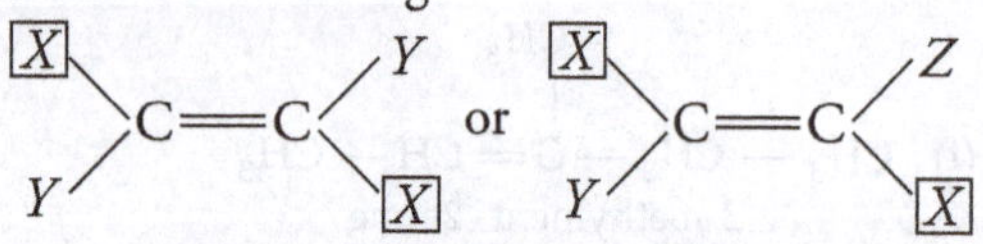

Due to different geometrical arrangement in space, the *cis* and *trans*-isomers differ in their properties like boiling and melting points, solubility, dipole moment etc; e.g. the *cis, trans*-isomers of but-2-ene have the following structures.

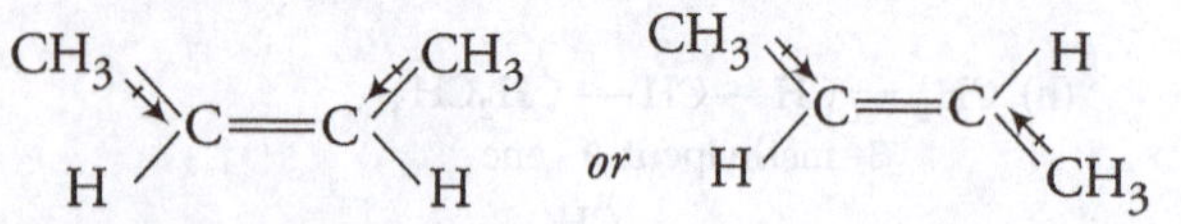

Cis-but-2-ene (bp 277 K) (Dipole moment $\mu = 0.33$ D, polar) *or* *Trans*-but-2-ene (bp 274 K) $\mu = 0$ (Non-polar)

The bond dipoles of C—CH_3 in *trans*-form cancel each other and thus, makes the molecule non-polar.
However, melting point of *trans*-form is higher than that of *cis*-form. (For more details about the nomenclature and isomerism of alkenes, also see the previous chapter.)

Example 12 Which of the following compounds will show *cis-trans* isomerism?

(i) $(CH_3)_2C=CH—C_2H_5$ (ii) $CH_2=CBr_2$
(iii) $C_6H_5CH=CH—CH_3$ **NCERT Textbook**
(iv) $CH_3CH=CClCH_3$

Sol. For exhibiting *cis-trans* (or geometrical isomerism, a molecule must fulfill the following conditions.

(i) It must have atleast one double bond.
(ii) The groups attached to each double bonded carbon atom must be different.
(iii) Atleast one same group is present on the two double bonded carbon. Structure (iii) and (iv) fulfill all the above conditions, so both will exhibit *cis-trans* isomerism.

Methods of Preparation

Following methods can be used to prepare alkenes from different substances:

1. From Alkynes

When alkynes are treated with calculated quantity of dihydrogen in the presence of palladised charcoal partially deactivated with poisons such as sulphur compounds, quinoline etc., they get reduced to *cis*-alkenes, i.e. hydrogens are added to the same side of the double bond. Partially deactivated palladised charcoal is known as **Lindlar's catalyst**.

However, if Na in liquid ammonia is used in place of Pd/C, *trans*-alkenes are the major product.

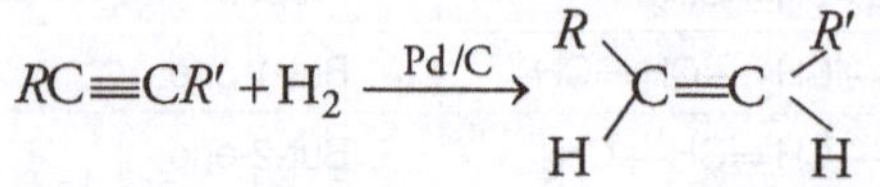

Cis-alkene

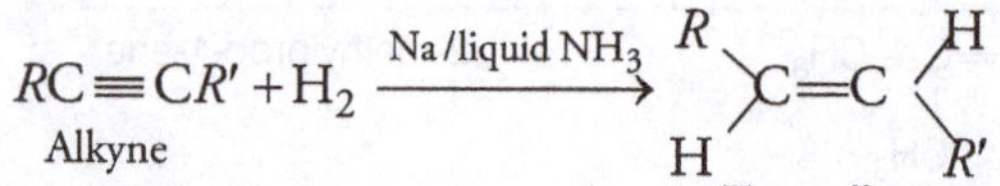

Trans-alkene

2. From Dehydrohalogenation of Alkyl Halides

When alkyl halides are heated with alcoholic potash (KOH in alcohol or ethanol), a HX (halogen acid) molecule is eliminated to give alkene.

Due to the elimination of H as well as halogen, the reaction is called **dehydrohalogenation**.

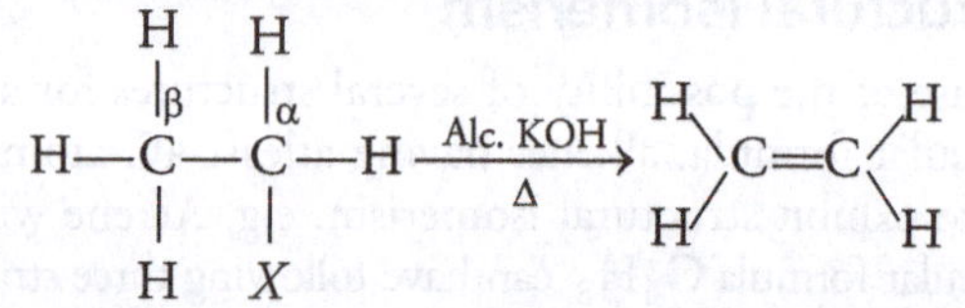

$(X = Cl, Br, I)$

This reaction is also known as **β-elimination reaction**, since hydrogen atom is eliminated from the β-carbon atom (carbon atom next to the carbon to which halogen is attached). The order of reactivity of halogens towards this reaction is $I_2 > Br_2 > Cl_2$.

This is because as the size of halogen increases, C—X bond strength decreases, i.e. it becomes weaker. Further, the order of reactivity of alkyl group is 3°>2°>1°.

Saytzeff Rule The above elimination is governed by Saytzeff rule, according to which, more substituted (or more stable, i.e. symmetrical) alkenes are the major product of an elimination reaction

i.e. 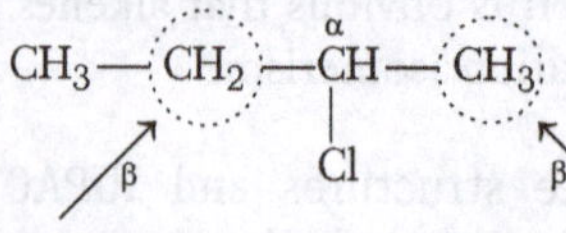

With lesser H-atoms. Thus forms more preferred or major product, i.e. $CH_3—CH=CH—CH_3$

With more H-atoms. Thus forms less preferred or minor product, i.e. $CH_3—CH_2—CH=CH_2$

The above rule is not followed in the case given below

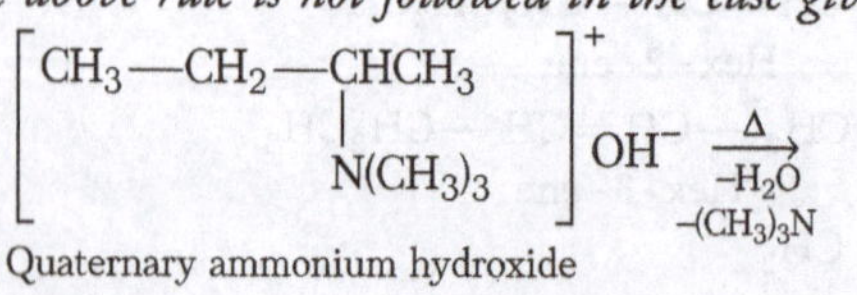

Quaternary ammonium hydroxide

$CH_3CH_2CH=CH_2 + CH_3CH=CHCH_3$
Major Minor

Such findings were given by Hofmann while working on β-elimination in quaternary ammonium compounds. He explained the difference in result on the basis of the presence of bulky $N(CH_3)_3$ group in the compound which destabilises transition state in this case. The findings of Hofmann are known as **Hofmann rule** (Hofmann elimation). Et_3N (triethyl amine) can also be used in place of alcoholic KOH. Et_3N is a bulky base and poor nucleophile thus minimises, S_N2 reaction.

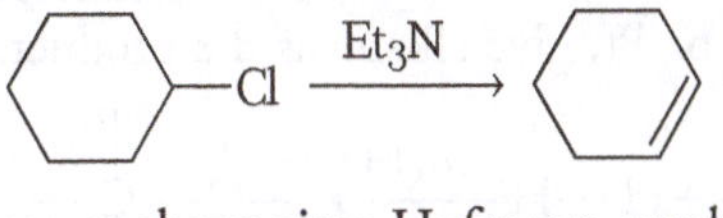

Also bulky base as above gives Hofmann product (less-substituted) as major product.

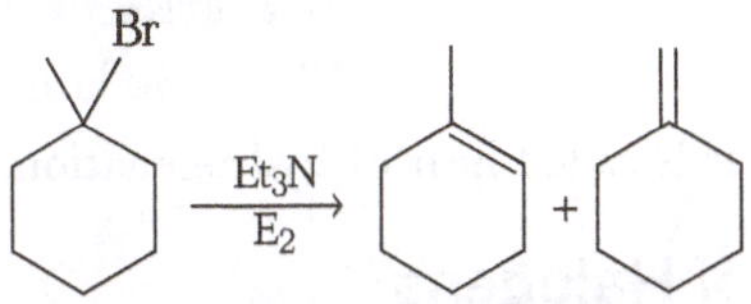

Minor Major

Tertiary butoxide is also a bulky base. Hence, gives less substituted (Hofmann product) as major product.

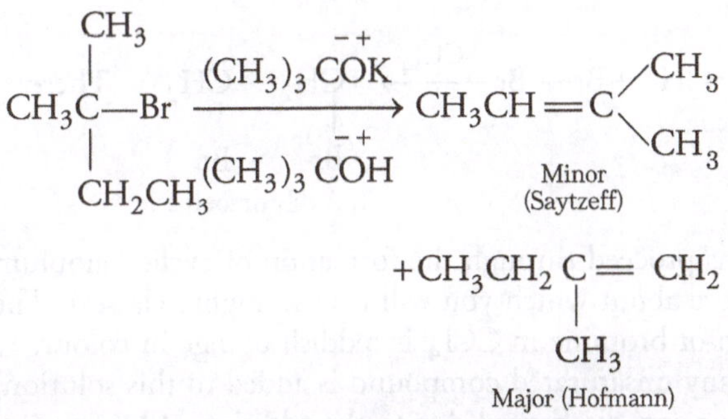

Dehydrohalogenation occur faster when alkyl halide on reaction with KOH gives a conjugated product as shown below

$$CH_3\underset{\displaystyle Br}{\underset{|}{C}}HCH{=}CH_2 \xrightarrow[\Delta]{KOH\ (alc.)} \underbrace{CH_2{=}CHCH{=}CH_2}_{\pi\text{-bonds in conjugation}}$$

However, it occurs with difficulty in cases where conjugation is already present in substrate. e.g.

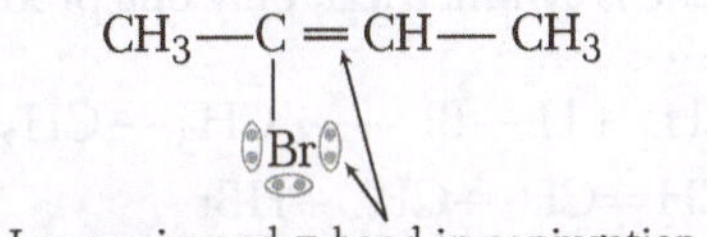

Lone pairs and π-bond in conjugation

- Ease of the formation of alkenes is in order

$$R_2C{=}CR_2 > R_2C{=}CHR > R_2C{=}CH_2$$

$$\text{or } RCH{=}CHR > RCH{=}CH_2 > CH_2{=}CH_2$$

and same is the stability order of alkenes.

Ease of formation for geometrical isomers follow the order:

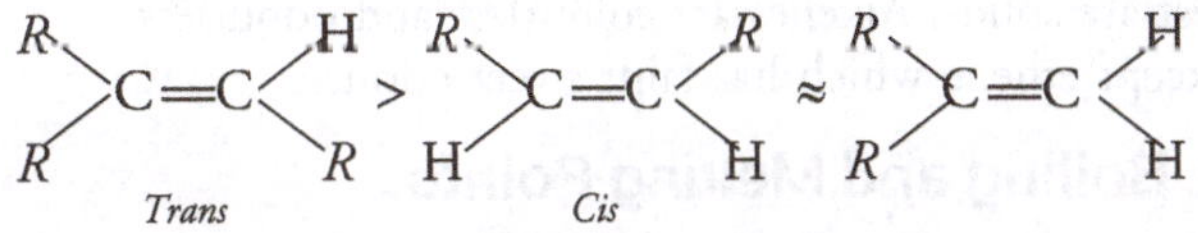

By general rule The more stable the alkene, the more easily it is formed.

3. From *Vicinal* Dihalides

Dihalides having two halogen atoms at adjacent carbon atoms are called **vicinal dihalides.** When such halides are treated with zinc metal, both the halogen atoms are taken up by Zn to give an alkene. Due to the removal of halogen atoms, the reaction is called **dehalogenation,** e.g.

$$CH_2Br{-}CH_2Br + Zn \longrightarrow CH_2{=}CH_2 + ZnBr_2$$

$$CH_3CHBr{-}CH_2Br + Zn \longrightarrow CH_3CH{=}CH_2 + ZnBr_2$$

4. From Dehydration of Alcohols

Alcohols (R—OH) when treated with concentrated sulphuric acid at 170°C, alkene is obtained. i.e.

$$\underset{\text{Ethanol}}{CH_3CH_2OH} \xrightarrow[170°C]{Conc.H_2SO_4} \underset{\text{Ethene}}{CH_2{=}CH_2} + H_2O$$

Because of the elimination of a molecule of water, the reaction is called **dehydration.** Since, presence of an acid is essential for the dehydration process, so the reaction is also known as **acidic dehydration of alcohols.** It is also an example of β -elimination reaction, because of the removal of H from β -carbon atom.

5. From Salts of Carboxylic Acid : Kolbe's Electrolysis

The electrolysis of sodium or potassium salts of dicarboxylic acid solutions releases alkene and carbon dioxide at anode. This process is known as **Kolbe's electrolysis.**

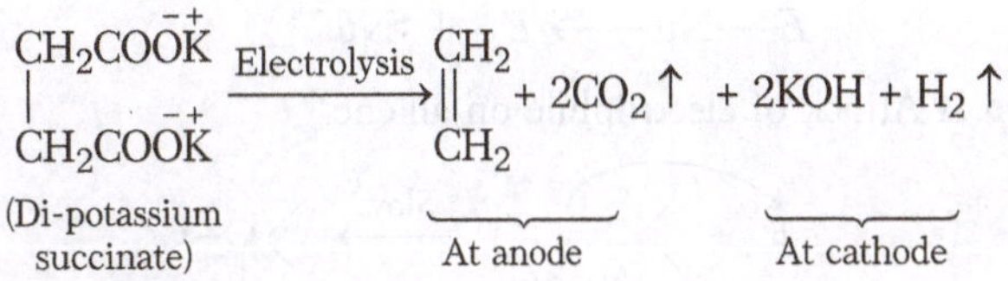

The resulting solution contains KOH and hence alkaline.

Physical Properties

1. Physical State, Colour and Odour

First three alkenes are gases, next 14 are liquids and rest are solids. Alkenes are colourless and odourless except ethene which has faint sweet odour.

2. Boiling and Melting Points

Alkenes show similar trend of boiling and melting points as alkanes (i.e. increases with increase in molecular mass but decreases with branching) but geometrical isomers behave differently. *Cis*-alkenes have higher boiling point as compared to their *trans*-isomers. However, melting point is higher in case of *trans*-isomers.

3. Dipole Moment and Density

In general, *trans*-form has almost zero dipole moment and thus, exhibits weaker intermolecular attractions. These are lighter than water and the density gradually increases with rise in molecular mass.

Chemical Properties

Alkenes generally undergo **electrophilic addition reactions** because of the presence of a double bond (a strong σ and a weaker π-bond), π electrons of which being loosely held are easily polarisable.

These reactions involve cleavage of a π-bond and formation of two new σ-bonds.

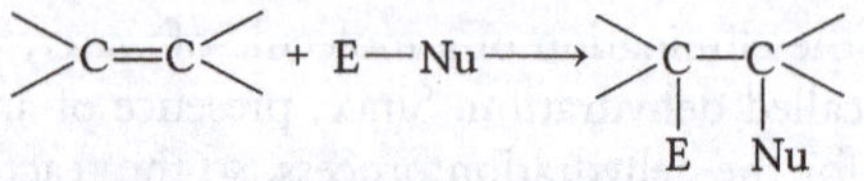

In polar solvents, addition proceed by ionic mechanism (at low temperature), whereas in the presence of light or non-polar solvents, the addition occurs by free radical mechanism (at high temperature). Apart from addition reactions, alkenes also participate in the oxidation, ozonolysis and polymerisation reaction.

The mechanism involved in ionic electrophilic addition reaction are as follows :

***Step* I** Ionisation of reagent to generate electrophile and nucleophile.

$$E\text{—Nu} \longrightarrow E^+ + :\text{Nu}^-$$

***Step* II** Attack of electrophile on alkene.

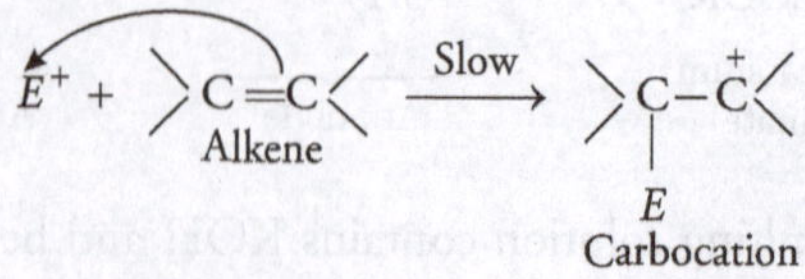

***Step* III** Attack of nucleophile to give addition product.

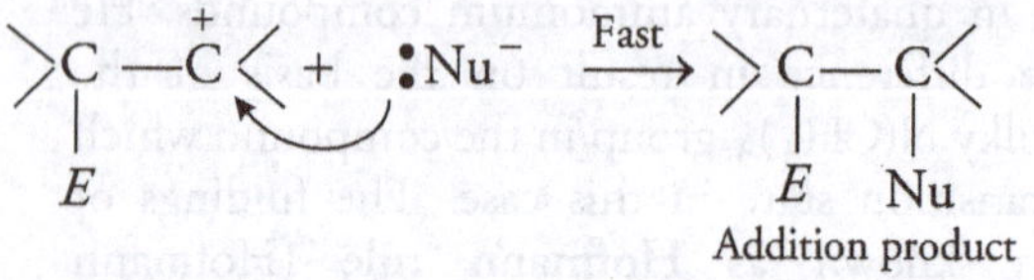

A brief description of the reactions given by alkenes is as follows :

1. Addition of Hydrogen

Alkenes when treated with H_2 in the presence of finely divided Ni, Pd or Pt, give alkane as the product.

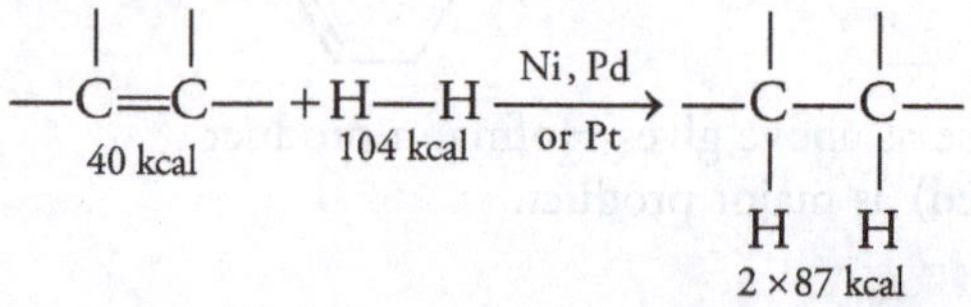

$$\Delta H = -30 \text{ kcal mol}^{-1}$$

The evolved heat is called **heat of hydrogenation.**

2. Addition of Halogens

Alkenes give addition product, i.e. *vicinal* dihalides, when treated with halogens like Cl_2 or Br_2. I_2 does not give this reaction under normal conditions of temperature and pressure.

$$\underset{\text{Ethene}}{CH_2{=}CH_2} + Br\text{—}Br \xrightarrow{CCl_4} \underset{\text{1, 2-dibromoethane}}{CH_2(Br)\text{—}CH_2(Br)}$$

These reactions proceed through the formation of cyclic halonium ion (more about which you will read in higher classes). The solution of bromine in CCl_4 is reddish orange in colour. When any unsaturated compound is added to this solution, its colour gets discharged due to the addition of bromine at the unsaturation site (=bond). This reaction is used as a test for unsaturation.

3. Addition of Hydrogen Halides

When alkenes react with hydrogen halides (HCl, HBr, HI), alkyl halides are obtained. The order of reactivity of hydrogen halides toward this reaction is

$$HI > HBr > HCl$$

(i) If the alkene is symmetrical, only one product is formed. e.g.

$$CH_2{=}CH_2 + H\text{—}Br \longrightarrow CH_3\text{—}CH_2\text{—}Br$$

$$CH_3\text{—}CH{=}CH\text{—}CH_3 + HBr \longrightarrow CH_3\text{—}CH_2\text{—}\underset{\substack{|\\Br}}{CH}CH_3$$

(ii) If the alkene is unsymmetrical, several products are obtained and the nature of major product depends upon the reaction conditions. e.g. If HBr is added to an unsymmetrical alkene, say propene, the following products are possible.

$$CH_3{-}CH{=}CH_2 + H{-}Br \longrightarrow \begin{cases} CH_3{-}\underset{\substack{|\\Br}}{CH}{-}CH_3 \ \text{2-bromopropane (I)} \\ CH_3{-}CH_2{-}CH_2{-}Br \ \text{1-bromopropane (II)} \end{cases}$$

However, I is the major product in accordance with **Markownikoff's rule** It states that negative part of the addendum (adding molecule) gets attached to that carbon atom which possesses lesser number of hydrogen atom. This can also be understood by considering the mechanism of the reaction.

Mechanism

***Step* I** Generation of electrophile $HBr \longrightarrow H^+ + Br^-$

***Step* II** Attack of electrophile on double bond (generation of carbocation)

$$H_3C{-}\overset{2}{C}H{=}\overset{1}{C}H_2 + H{-}Br \xrightarrow{H^+}$$

$$H_3C{-}CH_2{-}\overset{+}{C}H_2 + Br^- \qquad H_3C{-}\overset{+}{C}H{-}CH_3 + Br^-$$

(a) Less stable primary carbocation (b) More stable secondary carbocation (so readily attacked by Nu^-)

***Step* III** Attack of nucleophile (here Br^-) on the more stable carbocation.

$$Br^- + H_3C{-}\overset{+}{C}H{-}CH_3 \longrightarrow H_3C{-}\underset{\substack{|\\Br}}{CH}{-}CH_3$$

2-bromopropane (major product)

Note Less stable carbocation is also attacked by Br^- but with a slower rate so, gives a lesser amount of product.
Anti-Markownikoff addition or peroxide effect or Kharash effect.
If HBr is added to an unsymmetrical alkene say propene, in the presence of peroxide, 1-bromopropane is the major product in accordance with anti Markownikoff or Kharash rule (It states that the negative part of the addendum goes to that carbon atom which has more number of hydrogen atoms).
This is also called **peroxide effect** or **Kharash effect** (first observed by M S Kharash and F R Mao in 1933).

$$CH_3{-}CH{=}CH_2 + HBr \xrightarrow{(C_6H_5CO)_2O_2} CH_3{-}\underset{\substack{|\\CH_2Br}}{CH_2}$$

1-bromopropane

Formation of 1-bromopropane as major product can also be understood by the following mechanism of the reaction.

Mechanism

This reaction takes place by free radical mechanism and involves the following steps:

***Step* I Initiation** Generation of free radical ($\dot{B}r$)

$$C_6H_5{-}\overset{\overset{O}{||}}{C}{-}O{-}O{-}\overset{\overset{O}{||}}{C}{-}C_6H_5 \xrightarrow{\text{Homolysis}}$$

Benzoyl peroxide

$$2C_6H_5{-}\overset{\overset{O}{||}}{C}{-}\dot{\ddot{O}}: \longrightarrow 2\dot{C}_6H_5 + 2CO_2$$

$$\dot{C}_6H_5 + H{-}Br \xrightarrow{\text{Homolysis}} C_6H_6 + \dot{B}r$$

***Step* II Propagation** Attack of $Br^\bullet$ at double bond

(i)

$$CH_3{-}CH{=}CH_2 + \dot{B}r \xrightarrow{\text{Homolysis}}$$

$$CH_3{-}\underset{\substack{|\\Br}}{CH}{-}\dot{C}H_2 \qquad CH_3{-}\dot{C}H{-}CH_2{-}Br$$

(a) (Less stable primary free radical) (b) (More stable secondary free radical)

$$\text{(ii)}\ CH_3{-}\dot{C}H{-}CH_2Br + H{-}Br \xrightarrow{\text{Homolysis}} CH_3{-}CH_2{-}CH_2Br + \dot{B}r$$

(Major product)

$$\text{(iii)}\ CH_3{-}\underset{\substack{|\\Br}}{CH}{-}\dot{C}H_2 + H{-}Br \xrightarrow{\text{Homolysis}} CH_3{-}\underset{\substack{|\\Br}}{CH}{-}CH_3 + \dot{B}r$$

(Minor product)

***Step* III Termination** $\dot{B}r + \dot{B}r \longrightarrow Br_2$

In case of HF, HCl and HI, the major product remain the same whether the alkene is symmetrical or unsymmetrical in case of anti-markownikoff's addition.

This is because

(a) The bonds between halogen and hydrogen is very strong in HF and HCl that's why $RO^{\bullet}$, free radical is unable to break them homolytically. Thus, reaction procedure is not modified.

(b) In the case of HI, although $RO^{\bullet}$ free radical produces homolytic cleavage but $I^{\bullet}$, free radical formed has more tendency to form I_2 as compared to form free radical of carbon.

Example 14 Write IUPAC names of the products obtained by addition reactions of HBr to hex-1-ene. **NCERT Textbook**

(i) In the absence of peroxide (ii) In the presence of peroxide.

Sol. (i)

$$\underset{\text{Hex-1-ene}}{CH_2{=}CH{-}CH_2{-}CH_2{-}CH_2{-}CH_3} + H{-}Br \xrightarrow[\text{No peroxide}]{} \underset{\text{2-bromohexane (according to Markownikoff's rule)}}{CH_3{-}\underset{\substack{|\\ Br}}{CH}{-}CH_2{-}CH_2{-}CH_2{-}CH_3}$$

(ii)

$$CH_2{=}CH{-}CH_2{-}CH_2{-}CH_2{-}CH_3 + H{-}Br \xrightarrow[\text{Peroxide}]{} Br{-}CH_2{-}CH_2{-}CH_2{-}CH_2{-}CH_2{-}CH_3$$

1-bromohexane (according to anti-Markownikoff's rule)

4. Addition of Sulphuric Acid

Alkenes react with cold concentrated sulphuric acid to give an addition product in accordance with Markownikoff's rule.

$$H_3C{-}CH{=}CH_2 + H{-}O{-}\overset{\substack{O\\ \|}}{\underset{\substack{\|\\ O}}{S}}{-}O{-}H \longrightarrow CH_3{-}\overset{\substack{OSO_2OH\\ |}}{CH}{-}CH_3 \text{ or } C_3H_7HSO_4$$

Ethyl hydrogensulphate

5. Addition of Water (Hydration)

When alkenes are treated with a few drops of concentrated sulphuric acid, addition of water takes place in accordance with Markownikoff's rule and alcohols are obtained as the product.

$$\underset{\text{2-methylpropene}}{CH_3{-}\underset{\substack{|\\ CH_3}}{C}{=}CH_2} + \overset{+\ \ -}{HOH} \xrightarrow{H^+} \underset{\text{2-methylpropan-2-ol}}{(H_3C)_2\underset{\substack{|\\ OH}}{C}{-}CH_3}$$

Note

If an alkene is treated with $Hg(OCOCH_3)_2$, $NaBH_4$ / NaOH, the reaction is called oxymercuration-demercuration reaction and the product is obtained by adding a water molecule in accordance with Markownikoff's rule.

$$(CH_3)_3CCH{=}CH_2 \xrightarrow[\text{THF}]{Hg(OCOCH_3)_2} \xrightarrow{NaBH_4/NaOH} (CH_3)_3C{\cdot}\underset{\substack{|\\ OH}}{CH}CH_3$$

If an alkene is treated with B_2H_6/H_2O_2, OH^- the reaction is called hydroboration-oxidation and the product is obtained by adding a water molecule in accordance with Kharash effect.

$$\underset{\text{Propene}}{CH_3CH{=}CH_2} \xrightarrow[H_2O_2,\ OH^-]{B_2H_6} \underset{\text{Propanol}}{CH_3CH_2CH_2OH}$$

6. Oxidation

(i) **Complete Combustion** In the presence of oxygen, alkenes burn to give carbon dioxide and water (steam) along with large amount of heat

e.g. $$C_xH_y + \left(x + \frac{y}{4}\right)O_2 \longrightarrow xCO_2 + \frac{y}{2}H_2O + \text{heat}$$

$$C_2H_4 + 3O_2 \longrightarrow 2CO_2 + 2H_2O + \text{heat}$$

Heat of combustion of alkanes containing more hydrogen atoms is greater than the corresponding alkenes. The *cis*-isomer, which is destabilised by the interaction of two large groups (steric repulsion) on the same side of the double bond, has a higher heat of combustion than does the *trans*-isomer. Since the reaction is exothermic, smaller the ΔH is (numerically), the more stable is the alkene relative to its parent alkane. For isomeric alkenes, ΔH increases with increase in stability.

(ii) **Cold Alkaline $KMnO_4$ or Baeyer's Reagent** Cold Alkaline $KMnO_4$ oxidises alkene to glycol and its pink colour fades (decolourises). It is also considered as a test for unsaturated hydrocarbons called Baeyer test and alk.$KMnO_4$ is called Baeyer reagent.

$$3CH_2{=}CH_2 + 2KMnO_4 + 4H_2O \xrightarrow{298\text{-}303K} 3\begin{array}{l} CH_2{-}OH \\ | \\ CH_2{-}OH \end{array} + 2MnO_2 + 2KOH$$

The reagent is used at room temperature, otherwise at higher temperature carboxylic acid and ketone are formed. The addition of 2 — OH groups by alk. $KMnO_4$ is *syn*-addition.

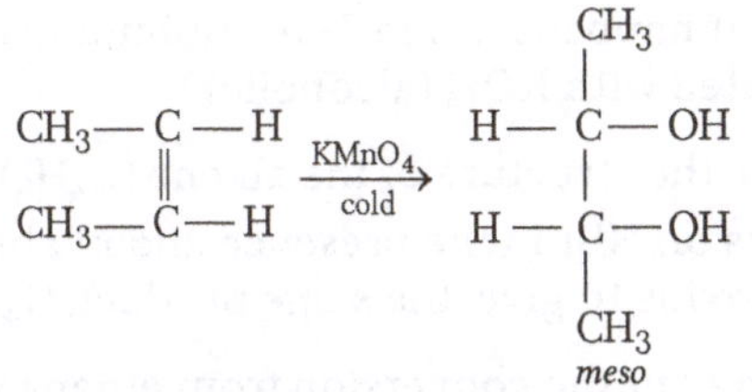

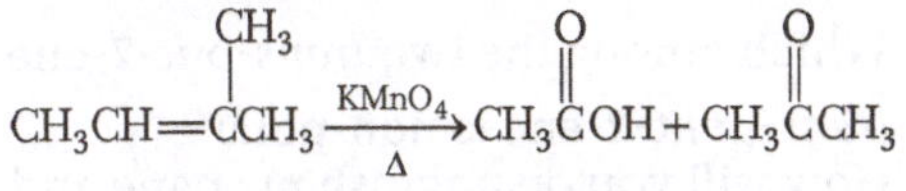

$$C_3H_7CH{=}CH_2 \xrightarrow[\Delta]{KMnO_4} C_3C_7\overset{O}{\overset{\|}{C}}\,OH + CO_2$$

Above reaction also concludes that **heat or acidic** $KMnO_4$ is the stronger oxidising agent than alkaline or cold $KMnO_4$ or Bayer's reagent.

(iii) **Ozonolysis** Alkenes react with O_3 to give ozonide which on reduction with $Zn{-}H_2O$ cleaved to give smaller molecule. e.g.

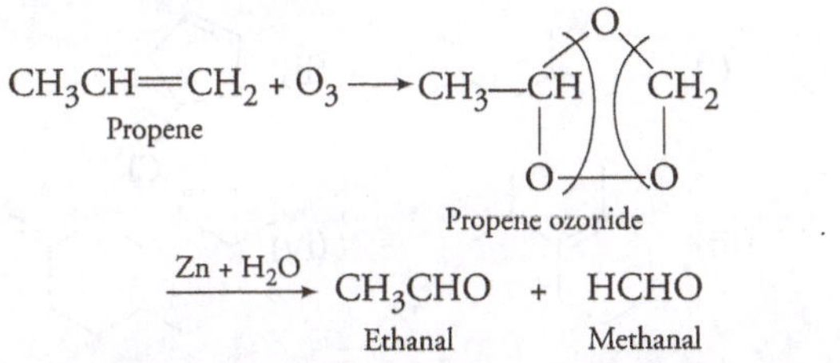

Note (i) To determine product by ozonolysis of alkenes, break C=C bond and place oxygen at breaking point.

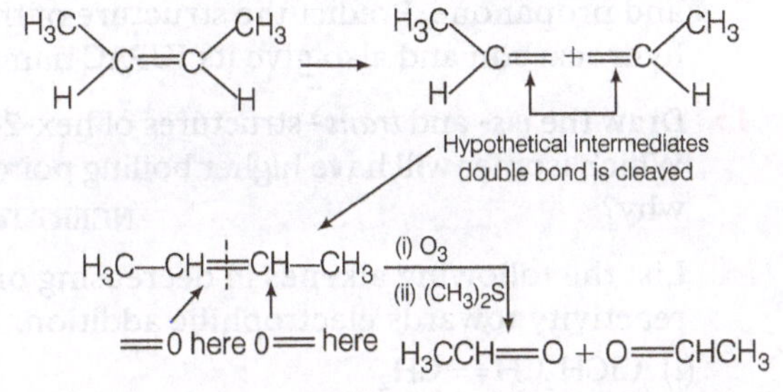

(ii) This reaction is also **helpful for deciding the structure of alkene and location of double bond**. To decide the structure of alkene from ozonolysis products, bring the products together in such a way that their O-atoms are face to face, replace O by C=C bond. Thus,

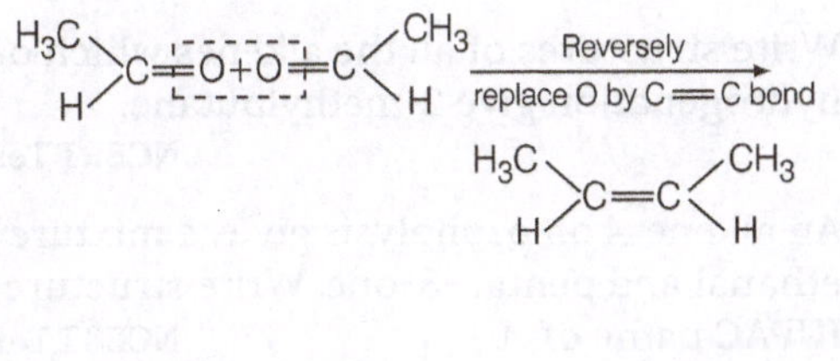

7. Polymerisation

When a large number of **monomers** (small molecules) combine to give a molecule bearing high molecular mass, called the **polymer**, the process is called **polymerisation**. The polymerisation reactions can be seen as :

$$\underset{\text{Ethene}}{n(CH_2{=}CH_2)} \xrightarrow[\text{Catalyst}]{\text{High temperature/pressure}} \underset{\text{Polythene}}{-\!(CH_2{-}CH_2)\!-_n}$$

$$\underset{\text{Propene}}{n(CH_3{-}CH{=}CH_2)} \xrightarrow[\text{Catalyst}]{\text{High temperature/pressure}} \underset{\text{Polypropene}}{-\!(\underset{CH_3}{\underset{|}{CH}}{-}CH_2)\!-_n}$$

Polymers are used for making plastic bags, squeeze bottles, refrigerator, dishes, toys, pipes, radio and TV cabinets etc. Polypropene is used for making milk crates, plastic buckets and other moulded articles. Polythene is a polymer of ethene. Excessive use of polythene and polypropylene is a matter of great concern.

Uses

The important uses of ethylene are as follows:

(i) It is used for the artificial ripening of fruits.

(ii) Ethylene is used to prepare the polythene which is an important plastic and finds a variety of applications.

(iii) It is used as a general anaesthetic.

(iv) It is used as a starting material for the synthesis of a large number of organic compounds such as ethylene glycol, ethyl halides, ethyl alcohol etc.

Topic Practice 2

Very Short Answer Type Questions

1 Mark

1. Fill in the Blanks

(i) The general formula of alkene is ....

(ii) Alcohols when treated with concentrated sulphuric acid at 170°C ...... is obtained.

(iii) Complete the following reaction :

$$CH_3{-}CH{=}CH_2 + HBr \xrightarrow{......} CH_3{-}\underset{CH_2Br}{\underset{|}{CH_2}}$$

(iv) Alkynes on hydrogenation with .... or with Na or Li in liquid ammonia gives alkenes.

2. Objective Type Questions

(i) Major product of the dehydration of the following compound is $(CH_3)_3C\underset{\displaystyle OH}{\underset{|}{C}H}CH_3$

(a) $(CH_3)_3CCH=CH_2$

(b) $(CH_3)_2CH\underset{\displaystyle CH_3}{\underset{|}{C}}=CH_2$

(c) $(CH_3)_2C=C(CH_3)_2$

(d) $CH_3CH_2CH=CHCH_2CH_3$

(ii) Select the major product of the reaction.

$$CH_3CH_2\overset{\displaystyle CH_3}{\overset{|}{\underset{\displaystyle Br}{\underset{|}{C}}}}CH(CH_3)_2 \xrightarrow[C_2H_5OH]{C_2H_5\overset{-}{O}\overset{+}{Na}} ?$$

(a) $CH_3CH_2\overset{\displaystyle CH_3}{\overset{|}{C}}=C(CH_3)_2$

(b) $CH_3CH_2\overset{\displaystyle CH_2}{\overset{\|}{C}}CH(CH_3)_2$

(c) $CH_3CH=\overset{\displaystyle CH_3}{\overset{|}{C}}CH(CH_3)_2$

(d) $CH_2=CH\overset{\displaystyle CH_3}{\overset{|}{C}H}CH(CH_3)_2$

3. Match the compounds given in Column I with suitable properties/reagent given in Column II and choose the correct option using codes given below:

	Column I	Column II
A.	*Cis*-but-2-ene, *trans*-but-2-ene	(i) Alkaline $KMnO_4$
B.	*n*-butane, propane	(ii) Dipole moment
C.	Ethene, ethane	(iii) Melting point
D.	But-1-ene, but-2-ene	(iv) Ozonolysis

Codes

	A	B	C	D
(a)	(ii)	(iii)	(i)	(iv)
(b)	(iii)	(ii)	(i)	(iv)
(c)	(i)	(iv)	(ii)	(iii)
(d)	(i)	(ii)	(iii)	(iv)

4. Arrange the following alkenes in the decreasing order of stability.

(i) $CH_3\overset{\displaystyle CH_3}{\overset{|}{C}}=CHCH_3$ (ii) $CH_3\overset{\displaystyle CH_3}{\overset{|}{C}H}CH=CH_2$

(iii) $CH_2=\overset{\displaystyle CH_3}{\overset{|}{C}}CH_2CH_3$

5. What happens, when 2-bromobutane is being treated with KOH (alcoholic)?

6. Give the structure of the alkene (C_4H_8) which adds on HBr in the presence and in absence of peroxide to give the same product, C_4H_9Br.

7. Bring out the conversion from ethane to ethene.

8. Which among the two *trans*-but-2-ene or *trans*-pent-2-ene is non-polar?

9. How will you distinguish propane and propene by giving chemical tests?

Short Answer Type I Questions

2 Marks

10 A common method for the preparation of alkenes from alcohols involve heating the alcohol with a mineral acid.

11 Give the IUPAC names of each of the following:

(i) 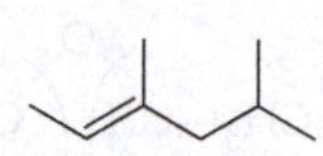 (ii) 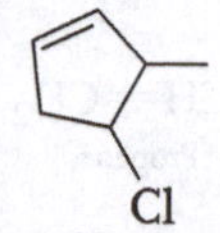

(iii) 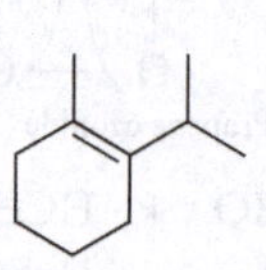 (iv) 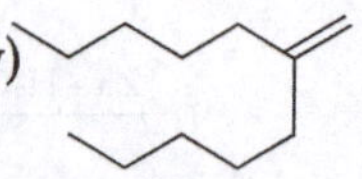

12 A hydrocarbon containing two double bonds on reductive ozonolysis produces glyoxal, ethanal and propanone. Predict the structure of the hydrocarbon and also give its IUPAC name.

13 Draw the *cis*- and *trans*- structures of hex-2-ene. Which isomer will have higher boiling point and why? **NCERT Textbook**

14 List the following alkenes in decreasing order of reactivity towards electrophilic addition.

(i) $ClCH_2CH=CH_2$

(ii) $(CH_3)_2C=CH_2$

(iii) $CH_3CH=CH_2$

(iv) $CH_2=CHCl$

Explain your order.

15 Write structures of all the alkenes which on hydrogenation give 2-methylbutane. **NCERT Textbook**

16 An alkene *A* on ozonolysis gives a mixture of ethanal and pentan-3-one. Write structure and IUPAC name of *A*. **NCERT Textbook**

17 Propanal and pentan-3-one are the ozonolysis products of an alkene. What is the structural formula of the alkene? **NCERT Textbook**

18 The intermediate carbocation formed in the reactions of HI, HBr and HCl with propene is the same and the bond energy of HCl, HBr and HI is 430.5 kJ mol^{-1}, 363.7 kJ mol^{-1} and 296.8 kJ mol^{-1} respectively. What will be the order of reactivity of these halogen acids? **NCERT Exemplar**

19 Name the organic products of the reaction of but-2-ene with each of the following reagents and write a balanced equation for each reaction.

(i) Hydrogen bromide

(ii) Bromine dissolved in tetrachloromethane

20 Complete the following reactions :

(i) *Iso*-propyl bromide $\xrightarrow[\text{Heat}]{\text{Alc. KOH}} A \xrightarrow[\text{Peroxide}]{\text{HBr}} B$

(ii) *n*-propyl alcohol $\xrightarrow[\text{443 K}]{\text{Conc. } H_2SO_4} A \xrightarrow[\text{Heat}]{O_2,\ Ag} B$

21 An alkene (molecular weight = 56) on reaction with trioxygen followed by zinc/CH_3COOH gave only ethanal. Identify the structure of the alkene.

Short Answer Type II Questions

3 Marks

22 Write IUPAC names of the following compounds. **NCERT Textbook**

(i) $CH_3CH=C(CH_3)_2$

(ii) $CH_2=CH-C\equiv C-CH_3$

(iii) 

(iv) $CH_3CH=CH-CH_2-CH=CH-\underset{\displaystyle C_2H_5}{\underset{|}{C}H}-CH_2-CH=CH_2$

23 For the following compounds, write structural formulae and IUPAC names for all possible isomers having the number of double or triple bond as indicated

(i) C_4H_8 (one double bond)

(ii) C_5H_8 (one triple bond)

24 An alkene *A* contains three C—C σ-bonds, eight C—H σ-bonds and one C—C π-bond. *A* on ozonolysis gives two moles of an aldehyde of molar mass 44 u. Write IUPAC name of *A*.

25 Write IUPAC name of the products obtained by the ozonolysis of the following compounds : **NCERT Textbook**

(i) Pent-2-ene

(ii) 3,4-dimethylhept-3-ene

(iii) 2-ethylbut-1-ene

(iv) 1-phenylbut-1-ene

26 Predict the major product(s) of the following reactions and explain their formation.

$H_3C-CH=CH_2 \xrightarrow[\text{HBr}]{(Ph-CO-O)_2}$ **NCERT Exemplar**

$H_3C-CH=CH_2 \xrightarrow{\text{HBr}}$

27 An alkyl halide (*X*) of formula $C_6H_{13}Cl$ on treatment with alcoholic KOH or potassium *tert*-butoxide gives two isomeric alkenes *Y* and *Z* (C_6H_{12}). Both alkenes on hydrogenation give 2, 3-dimethylbu- tane. Predict the structure of *X*, *Y* and *Z*.

28 Give the structures of *A* and *B*.

$$\underset{\text{(Isomers of formula } C_3H_6O)}{C} + D \xleftarrow{\text{Hot } KMnO_4} \underset{(C_6H_{12})}{A} \xrightarrow[\text{(ii) Zn, } H_2O]{\text{(i) } O_3} \underset{\text{(Isomers of formula } C_3H_6O)}{B + C}$$

29 Addition of HBr to propene yields 2-bromopropane, while in the presence of benzoyl peroxide, the same reaction yields 1-bromopropane. Explain and give mechanism. **NCERT Textbook**

30 In the presence of peroxide, addition of HBr to propene takes place according to anti-Markownikoff's rule but peroxide effect is not seen in the case of HCl and HI. Explain.

Long Answer Type Questions

5 Marks

31 Write the IUPAC names of the following compounds. **NCERT Textbook**

(i) $(CH_3)_2CH-CH=CHCH_2CH=CH-\underset{\displaystyle C_2H_5}{\underset{|}{C}H}CH_3$

(ii) 

(iii) $CH_2=C(CH_2CH_2CH_3)_2$

(iv) $CH_3-\overset{\displaystyle CH_3-CH_2CH_2CH_2}{\overset{|}{C}H}-CH=\overset{\displaystyle CH_2CH_3}{\overset{|}{C}}CH_2-\overset{\displaystyle CH_3}{\overset{|}{C}H}-CH_3$

Also, calculate the number of σ and π-bonds.

Hints & Solutions

1. (i) C_nH_{2n} (ii) alkene
(iii) $(C_6H_5CO)_2O_2$ (iv) Lindlar's catalyst
2. (i) → (c), (ii) → (a)
3. (a) A → (2), B → (3), C → (1), D → (4)
4. Stability of an alkene increases with increase in the number of electron donating substituent at the double bonded carbon atom. Thus, (*i*) > (*iii*) > (*ii*).
5. 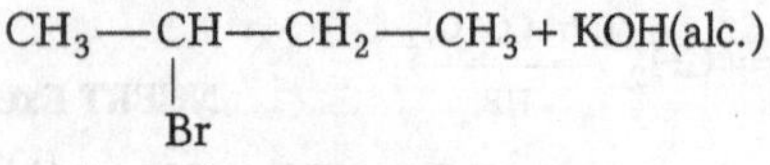

2-bromobutane

$\longrightarrow CH_3—CH=CH—CH_3 + KBr + H_2O$
(But-2-ene)

6. $CH_3—CH=CH—CH_3$
(Symmetrical alkene)

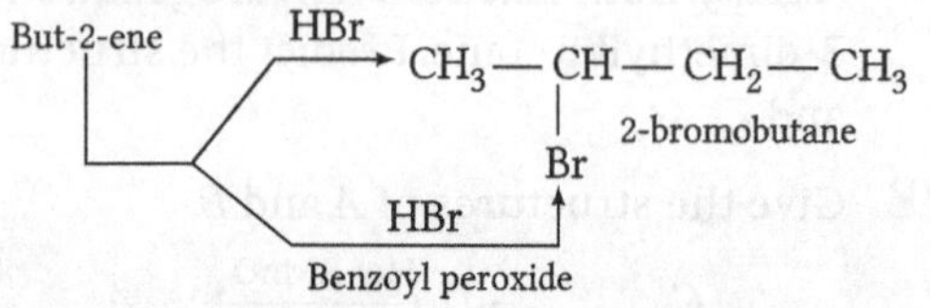

7. $CH_3CH_3 \xrightarrow[-HI]{I_2/HNO_3} CH_3CH_2I \xrightarrow{KOH\ (alc.)} CH_2=CH_2$
Ethane, Ethyl iodide, Ethene

8. In *trans*-but-2-ene, the dipole moments of the two $C—CH_3$ bonds are equal and opposite. Therefore, they cancel out each other. Hence, *trans* but-2-ene is non-polar.

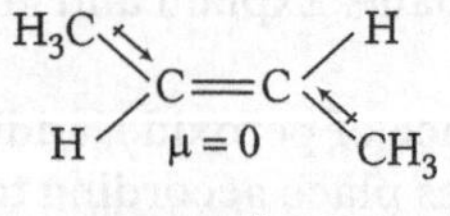

9. Propane and propene can be distinguished by bromine water test and alkaline $KMnO_4$ test.
$CH_3CH_2CH_3 + Br_2/H_2O \longrightarrow$ No change

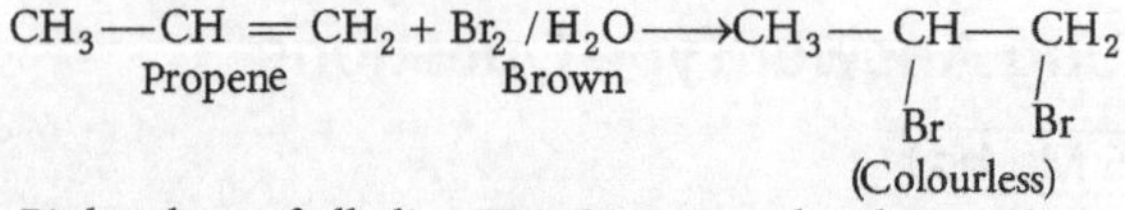

Pink colour of alkaline $KMnO_4$ turns colourless in the presence of unsaturated compound.

10. Refer to pages 424 to 425. (Methods of preparation).
11. (i) 3, 5-dimethyl-2-hexene or 3,5-dimethylhex-2-ene
(ii) 4-chloro-3-methylcyclopentene
(iii) 1-*sec*-butyl-2-methylcyclohexene or 1-methyl-2-(1-methylpropyl) cyclohexene
(iv) 2-pentyl-1-heptene or 2-pentylhept-1-ene [4 × 1/2]
12. *Step* I. Write the structures of the products with their carbonyl group facing one another.

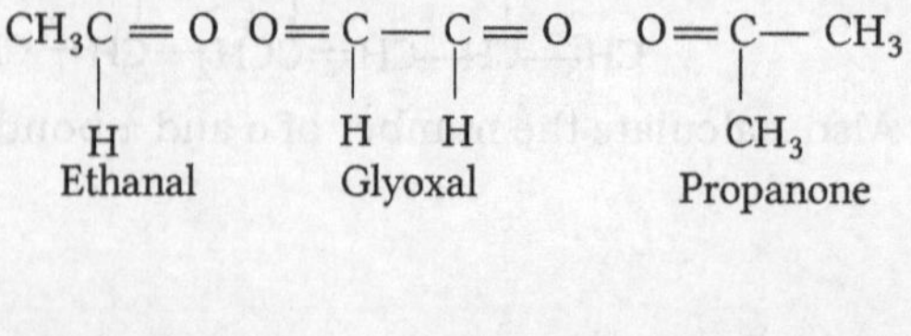

[1]

Step II. Remove oxygen and put double bonds between the carbonyl carbons.

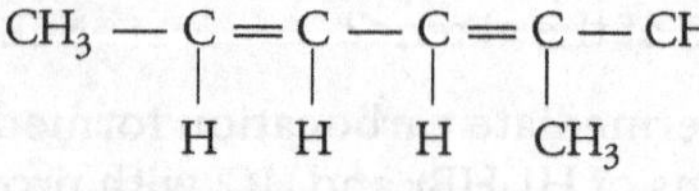

Thus, the compound is 2-methyl-2, 4-hexadiene. [1]

13. Hex-2-ene is $CH_3—CH_2—CH_2—CH=CH—CH_3$.
The structures of *cis*- and *trans*- isomers of hex-2-ene are

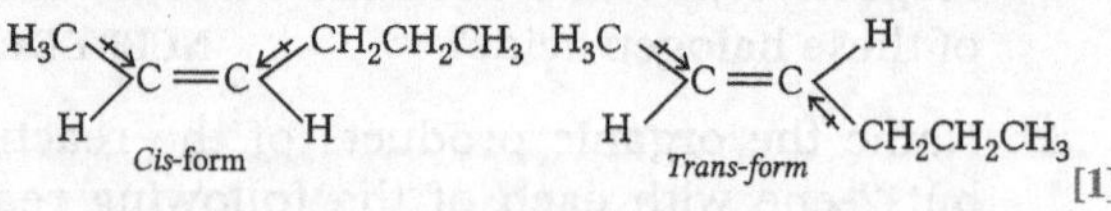

[1]

Cis- form is more polar than *trans*-form, i.e. *cis*-form has higher dipole moment than *trans*-form. Thus, the boiling point of *cis*-isomer is greater than that of *trans*-isomer because of the greater dipole-dipole interactions between the molecules in it. Furthermore, *trans*-isomer of hex-2-ene is almost non-polar. [1]

14. Electron donating alkyl groups make the π-bond more electron rich and more reactive. Conversely, electron withdrawing groups such as Cl make the π-bond more electron deficient and less reactive. The order is

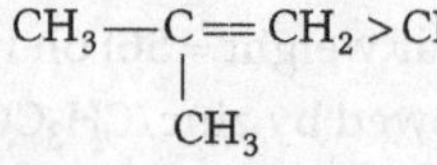
(two CH_3 groups) $> CH_3—CH=CH_2$ (one CH_3 group)

$> Cl—CH_2CH=CH_2$ (one alkyl group with Cl atom) $> CH_2=CH—Cl$ (Cl is directly bonded to double bonded carbon) [2]

15 Structure of 2-methylbutane is

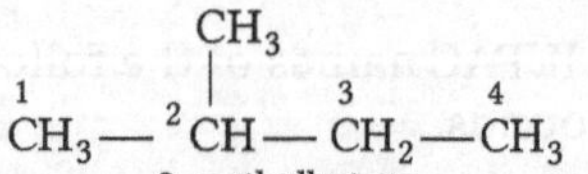

2-methylbutane

Put the double bonds at different positions and also satisfy the tetravalency of each carbon atom in the molecule. [1]

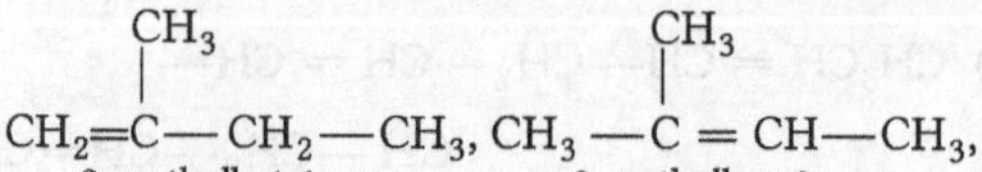

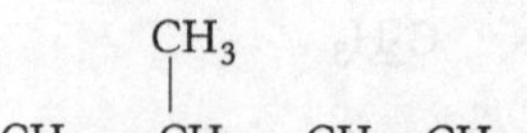

[1]

16 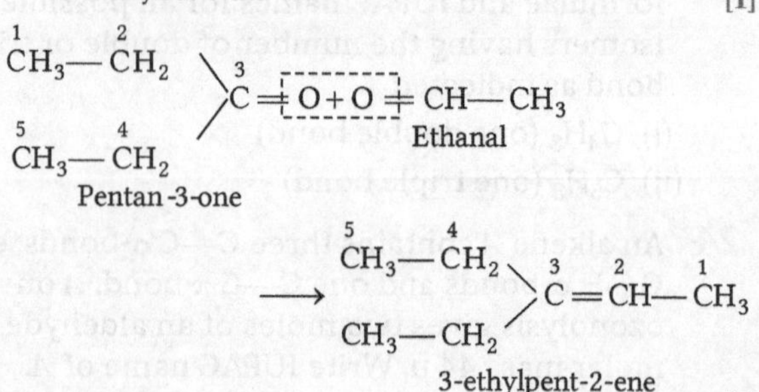

[2]

17.

> **Key Idea** Write the structures of the products of ozonolysis in such a way that their oxygen atoms pointing towards each other. Join the two ends through a double bond after removal of oxygen atoms to obtain structure of alkene *A*.

$$\overset{3}{CH_3}\,\overset{2}{CH_2}\,\overset{1}{CH}{=}O + O{=}\overset{3}{C}(\overset{2}{CH_2}\overset{1}{CH_3})(\overset{4}{CH_2}\overset{5}{CH_3})$$

Propanal   Pentan-3-one

$$\longleftarrow \overset{6}{C}H_3\overset{5}{C}H_2\overset{4}{C}H{=}\overset{3}{C}(\overset{2}{C}H_2\overset{1}{C}H_3)(CH_2CH_3)$$

3-ethylhex-3-ene **[2]**

18 Addition of halogen acids to an alkene is an electrophilic addition reaction.

$$CH_3{-}CH{=}CH_2 + H^+ \xrightarrow[\text{Ist step}]{\text{Slow}}$$

$$CH_3{-}\overset{+}{C}H{-}CH_3 \xrightarrow[\text{IInd step}]{X^-,\text{fast}} CH_3{-}\underset{\substack{|\\X}}{CH}{-}CH_3$$ **[1]**

First step is slow so, it is rate determining step. The rate of this step depends on the availability of proton. This in turn depends upon the bond dissociation enthalpy of the H—*X* molecule.

Lower the bond dissociation enthalpy of H—*X* molecule, greater the reactivity of halogen halide. Since, the bond dissociation energy decreases in the order; HI (296.8 kJ mol^{-1}) < HBr (363.7 kJ mol^{-1}) < HCl (430.5 kJ mol^{-1})

Therefore, the reactivity of the halogen acids decreases from HI to HCl, i.e. HI > HBr > HCl. **[1]**

19. (i) $CH_3{-}CH{=}CH{-}CH_3 + HBr \longrightarrow$

$$CH_3{-}\underset{\substack{|\\Br}}{CH}{-}CH_2{-}CH_3$$

2-bromobutane **[1]**

(ii) $CH_3{-}CH{=}CH{-}CH_3 + Br_2 \xrightarrow{CCl_4}$

$$CH_3{-}\underset{\substack{|\\Br}}{CH}{-}\underset{\substack{|\\Br}}{CH}{-}CH_3$$

2,3-dibromobutane **[1]**

20. (i) $$CH_3\underset{\substack{|\\Br}}{CH}CH_3 \xrightarrow[\text{Heat}]{\text{Alc. KOH}} \underset{(A)}{CH_3CH{=}CH_2}$$

Iso-propyl bromide   Propene

$$\xrightarrow[\text{Peroxide}]{\text{HBr}} \underset{(B)}{CH_3CH_2CH_2Br}$$

1-bromopropane **[1]**

(ii) $$\underset{n\text{-propyl alcohol}}{CH_3CH_2CH_2OH} \xrightarrow[443\text{ K}]{\text{Conc. }H_2SO_4} \underset{\text{Propene}}{\underset{(A)}{CH_3CH{=}CH_2}}$$

$$\xrightarrow[\text{Heat}]{O_2,\ Ag} CH_3CH{-}CH_2 \text{ (with O bridging the two carbons)}$$

(*B*)
Propylene oxide **[1]**

21. First of all we will derive the molecular formula of alkene, $C_nH_{2n}; 12n + 2n = 56$ or $14n = 56$ **[1]**

$\therefore \quad n = 4$

Thus, the molecular formula of alkene is C_4H_8.

As it is giving only ethanal on reaction with O_3 followed by reduction, the alkene is symmetrical and its structure is

$$H{-}\underset{\substack{|\\H}}{\overset{\substack{H\\|}}{C}}{-}\underset{\substack{|\\H}}{C}{=}\underset{\substack{|\\H}}{C}{-}\underset{\substack{|\\H}}{\overset{\substack{H\\|}}{C}}{-}H$$

But-2-ene **[1]**

22. Find the longest chain including functional group and write the root word.

Write suffix of the functional group with its position.

Write the name of the substituents with their positions before the root word, in alphabetical order.

(i) $$\overset{4}{C}H_3{-}\overset{3}{C}H{=}\overset{2}{\overset{\substack{CH_3\\|}}{C}}{-}\overset{1}{C}H_3$$

2-methylbut-2-ene

(ii) $$\overset{1}{C}H_2{=}\overset{2}{C}H{-}\overset{3}{C}{\equiv}\overset{4}{C}{-}\overset{5}{C}H_3$$

Pent-1-en-3-yne

(iii)

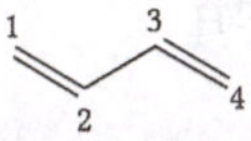

Buta-1,3-diene

(iv) $$\overset{10}{C}H_3{-}\overset{9}{C}H{=}\overset{8}{C}H{-}\overset{7}{C}H_2{-}\overset{6}{C}H{=}\overset{5}{C}H{-}$$

$$\underset{\substack{|\\C_2H_5}}{\overset{4}{C}H}{-}\overset{3}{C}H_2{-}\overset{2}{C}H{=}\overset{1}{C}H_2$$

4-ethyldeca-1,5,8-triene

Note Numbering is done from the side which gives lowest locant to the principle functional group.

23. (i) Isomers of C_4H_8 having one double bond are :

(a) $$\overset{4}{C}H_3\overset{3}{C}H_2{-}\overset{2}{C}H{=}\overset{1}{C}H_2$$

But-1-ene

(b) 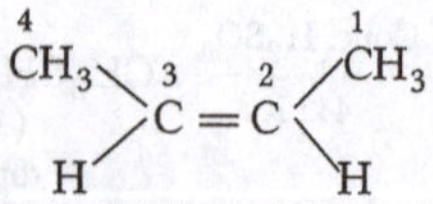

Cis-but-2-ene

(c) 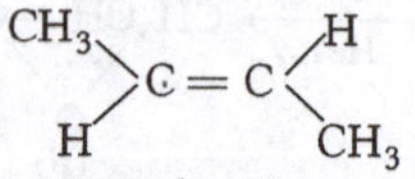

Trans-but-2-ene

(d) $\overset{\displaystyle CH_3}{\overset{|}{CH_3-C=CH_2}}$

2-methylprop-1-ene [2]

(ii) (a) $\overset{5}{C}H_3\overset{4}{C}H_2\overset{3}{C}H_2\overset{2}{C}\equiv\overset{1}{C}H$

Pent-1-yne

(b) $\overset{5}{C}H_3\overset{4}{C}H_2-\overset{3}{C}\equiv\overset{2}{C}-\overset{1}{C}H_3$

Pent-2-yne

(c) $\overset{4}{C}H_3-\overset{3}{C}H(CH_3)-\overset{2}{C}\equiv\overset{1}{C}H$

3-methylbut-1-yne [1]

24. **An aldehyde having molar mass 44 u is ethanal, CH_3CHO. Write the structures of two molecules of ethanal in such a way that their oxygen atoms point towards each other. Join the two ends through the double bond with the removal of both of the oxygen atoms to obtain alkene *A*.**

$$\underset{\text{Ethanal}}{CH_3CH=O}+\underset{\text{Ethanal}}{O=CHCH_3}\longleftarrow \underset{(A)\ \text{But-2-ene}}{CH_3-CH=CH-CH_3}$$

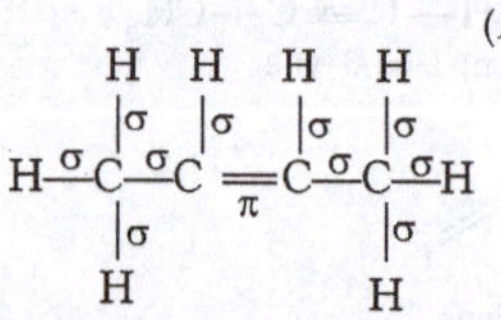 [2]

Hence, alkene (*A*) is but-2-ene which contains three C—C, eight C—H σ-bonds and one C—C π bond (as given in the question). [1]

25. **Key Idea** To find the product of ozonolysis, break the double bond and add two O-atoms, one with each double bonded C-atom.

Give the IUPAC name of product obtained.

(i) $\underset{\text{Pent-2-ene}}{\overset{5}{C}H_3-\overset{4}{C}H_2-\overset{3}{C}H=\overset{2}{C}H-\overset{1}{C}H_3}\xrightarrow[\text{(ii) } Zn/H_2O]{\text{(i) } O_3/CH_2Cl_2,\ 196\ K}$

$$\underset{\text{Propanal}}{\overset{3}{C}H_3-\overset{2}{C}H_2-\overset{1}{C}H=O}+\underset{\text{Ethanal}}{O=\overset{1}{C}H-\overset{2}{C}H_3}$$ [1]

(ii) $\underset{\text{3,4-dimethylhept-3-ene}}{\overset{7}{C}H_3-\overset{6}{C}H_2-\overset{5}{C}H_2-\overset{4}{C}(CH_3)=\overset{3}{C}(CH_3)-\overset{2}{C}H_2-\overset{1}{C}H_3}\xrightarrow[\text{(ii) } Zn/H_2O]{\text{(i) } O_3/CH_2Cl_2,\ 195\ K}$

$$\underset{\text{Pentan-2-one}}{\overset{5}{C}H_3-\overset{4}{C}H_2-\overset{3}{C}H_2-\overset{2}{C}(=O)-\overset{1}{C}H_3}+\underset{\text{Butan-2-one}}{\overset{4}{C}H_3-\overset{3}{C}H_2-\overset{2}{C}(=O)-\overset{1}{C}H_3}$$ [1]

(iii) $\underset{\text{2-ethylbut-1-ene}}{\overset{4}{C}H_3-\overset{3}{C}H_2-\overset{2}{C}(CH_2-CH_3)=\overset{1}{C}H_2}\xrightarrow[\text{(ii) } Zn/H_2O]{\text{(i) } O_3/CH_2Cl_2,\ 195\ K}$

$$\underset{\text{Pentan-3-one}}{\overset{1}{C}H_3\overset{2}{C}H_2-\overset{3}{C}(=O)-\overset{4}{C}H_2\overset{5}{C}H_3}+\underset{\text{Methanal}}{HCHO}$$

(iv) $\underset{\text{1 - phenylbut - 1 - ene}}{\overset{4}{C}H_3-\overset{3}{C}H_2-\overset{2}{C}H=\overset{1}{C}H-C_6H_5}\xrightarrow[\text{(ii) } Zn/H_2O]{\text{(i) } O_3/CH_2Cl_2,\ 195\ K}$

$$\underset{\text{Propanal}}{CH_3-CH_2CHO}+\underset{\text{Benzaldehyde}}{C_6H_5CHO}$$ [1]

26. **In presence of organic peroxide, the addition of HBr to propene follows anti-Markownikoff's rule (or peroxide effect) to form 1-bromopropane (*n*-propyl bromide)**

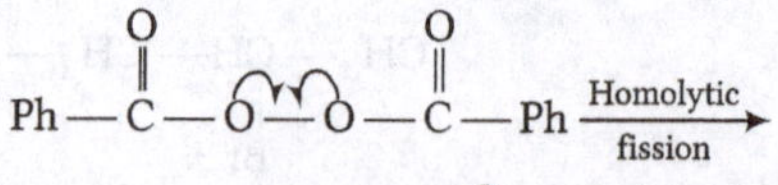

$$2Ph-C(=O)-O^{\bullet}\longrightarrow 2Ph^{\bullet}+2CO_2$$

$$Ph^{\bullet}+HBr\longrightarrow C_6H_6+Br^{\bullet}$$

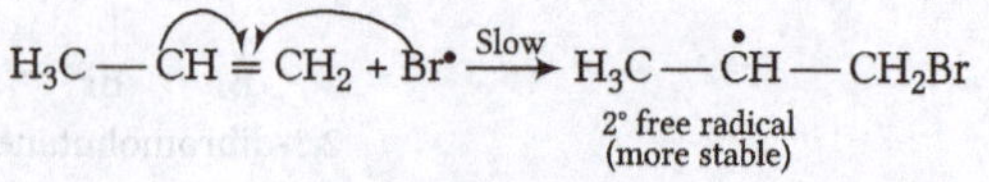

$$\xrightarrow{HBr}\underset{\text{1-bromopropane}}{H_3C-CH_2-CH_2Br}+\dot{B}r$$ [2]

However, in absence of peroxide, addition of HBr to propene follows Markownikoff's rule and gives 2-bromopropane as major product.

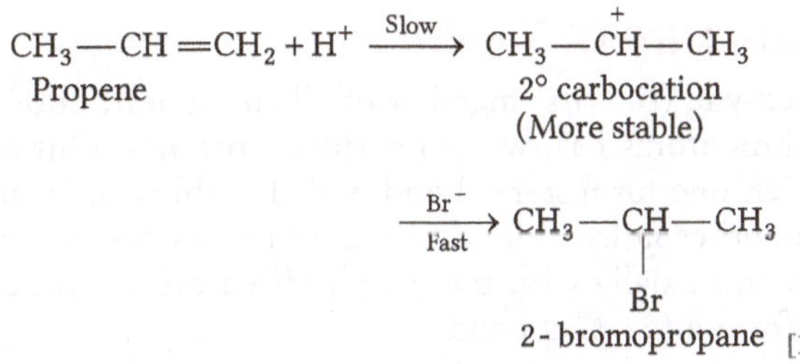

[1]

27. 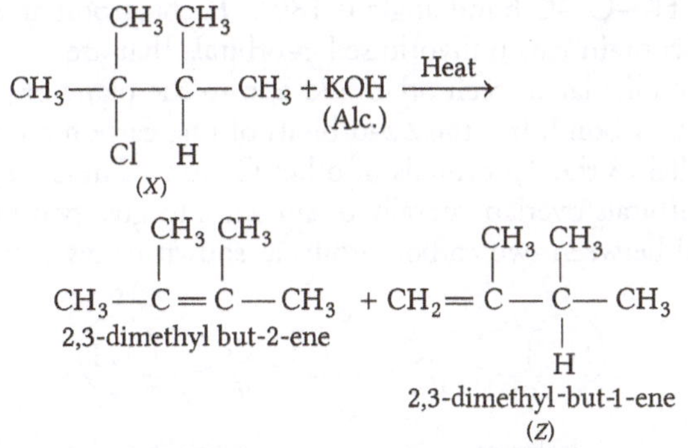

[3]

28. (*B*) and (*C*) are CH_3CH_2CHO (propanal) and CH_3COCH_3 (propanone). Hence, *A* is

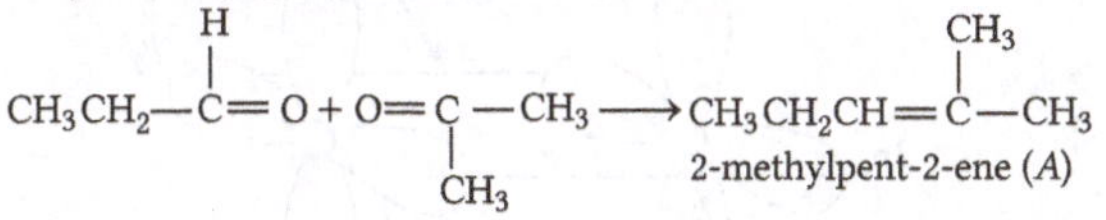

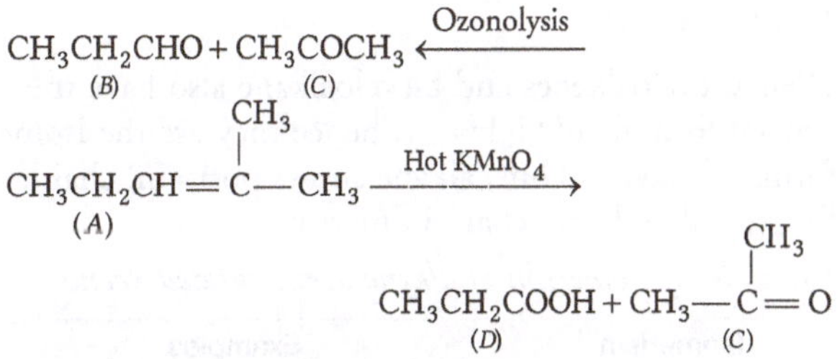

29 Refer to the text on pages 426 and 427. (Chemical properties of alkenes)

30. Peroxide effect is not observed in addition of HCl and HI. This is due to the fact that the H—Cl bond being stronger (430.5 kJ mol^{-1}) than H—Br bond (363.7 kJ mol^{-1}) is not cleaved by the free radical whereas the H—I bond is weaker (296.8 kJ mol^{-1}) and iodine free radicals combine to form iodine molecules instead of adding to the double bond.

31. (i) 2, 8-dimethyldeca-3, 6-diene
σ-bonds = 33, π-bonds = 2
(ii) Octa-1, 3, 5, 7-tetraene
σ-bonds = 17, π-bonds = 4
(iii) 2-propylpent-1-ene
σ-bonds = 23, π-bonds = 1
(iv) 4-ethyl-2, 6-dimethyldec-4-ene
σ-bonds = 41, π-bonds = 1

TOPIC 03 Unsaturated Hydrocarbons (Alkynes)

The compounds containing atleast one triple bond are called **alkynes**. It is another class of unsaturated compounds, having 4C-atoms less than the alkanes, so, general formula of these compounds is C_nH_{2n-2} (where $n = 2, 3, 4$). The first stable member of this series is **ethyne** (or **acetylene**) which is commonly used for arc welding in the form of oxyacetylene flame obtained by mixing acetylene and oxygen gas.

Nomenclature

Nomenclature of alkynes can be done by the following systems :

1. Common System

According to this system, higher members of alkyne are named as the derivatives of acetylene, i.e. $CH \equiv CH$, e.g. $CH_3 — C \equiv CH$, methylacetylene.

2. IUPAC System

The IUPAC name of alkyne is written by replacing -'ane' of alkane by a suffix -'yne'.

The position of triple bond is indicated by arabic numbers, the numbering being started from that end which lies closer to the triple bond.

Common and IUPAC name of alkynes (C_nH_{2n-2})

Formula	Structure	Common name	IUPAC name
C_2H_2	$H—C \equiv C—H$	Acetylene	Ethyne
C_3H_4	$H_3C—C \equiv CH$	Methylacetylene	Prop-1-yne
C_4H_6	$H_3C—C \equiv C—CH_3$	Dimethylacetylene	But-2-yne
C_5H_8	$H_3C—C \equiv C—CH_2CH_3$	Ethylmethylacetylene	Pent-2-yne

Isomerism

Dienes, cycloalkenes and bicycloalkane also have the general formula of C_nH_{2n-2}, hence they are the isomeric forms of alkyne. Thus, alkyne shows position, chain, functional and ring chain isomerism.

Examples of isomerism of alkyne are tabulated below :

Isomerism	Examples
Positional isomerism	$CH\equiv CCH_2CH_3$ and $CH_3C\equiv CCH_3$
Chain isomerism	$CH_3CH_2CH_2C\equiv CH$ and $(CH_3)_2CH-C\equiv CH$
Functional isomerism	$CH_3-CH_2-C\equiv CH$, $CH_2=CH-CH=CH_2$ and $CH_2=C=CH-CH_3$
Ring-chain isomerism	$CH_3C\equiv CH$ and 

Note Alkynes are linear molecules that have an angle of 180°. Therefore, alkynes does not show geometrical and stereoisomerism.

Example 5 Write structure of different isomers corresponding to the 5th member of alkyne series. Also write IUPAC names of all the isomers. What type of isomerism is exhibited by different pairs of isomers?

NCERT Textbook

Sol. Molecular formula of 5th member of alkyne is C_6H_{10}.

The possible isomers are :

(a) $HC\equiv C-CH_2-CH_2-CH_2-CH_3$
Hex-1-yne

(b) $CH_3-C\equiv C-CH_2-CH_2-CH_3$
Hex-2-yne

(c) $CH_3-CH_2-C\equiv C-CH_2-CH_3$
Hex - 3 - yne

(d) $HC\equiv C-\underset{\underset{CH_3}{|}}{CH}-CH_2-CH_3$
3-methylpent-1-yne

(e) $HC\equiv C-CH_2-\underset{\underset{CH_3}{|}}{CH}-CH_3$
4-methylpent-1-yne

(f) $CH_3-C\equiv C-\underset{\underset{CH_3}{|}}{CH}-CH_3$
4-methylpent-2-yne

(g) $HC\equiv C-\overset{\overset{CH_3}{|}}{\underset{\underset{CH_3}{|}}{C}}-CH_3$
3,3-dimethylbut-1-yne

Structure of Triple Bond

In ethyne (the first member of alkyne series), both the carbon atoms has two *sp* hybridised orbitals. Out of which one form *sp-s* σ bond with 1*s* orbital of H atom. The other *sp*-hybridised orbital of one carbon atom overlaps axially with the *sp*-hybridised orbital of other to form a C—C σ bond.

The H—C—C bond angle is 180°. Each carbon atom also contain two unhybridised *p*-orbitals that are perpendicular to each other and also to the plane of C—C σ bond, but the 2*p*-orbitals of one carbon atom are parallel to the 2*p*-orbitals of other C-atom. These two 2*p*-orbitals overlap laterally or sideways to give two pi (π) bond between two carbon atoms as shown below :

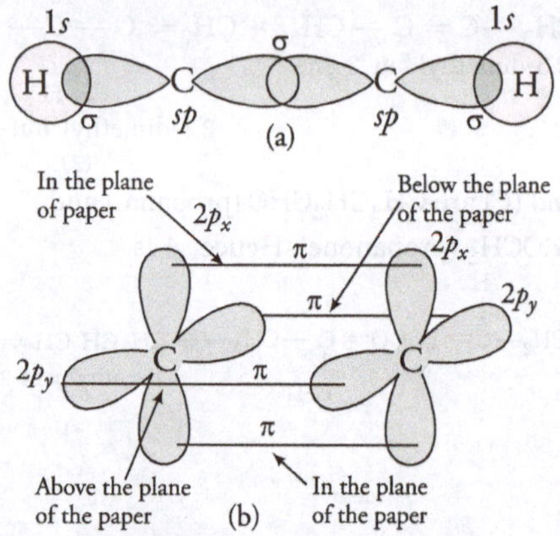

Orbital picture of ethyne showing
(a) sigma overlap (b) pi overlap

Thus, in ethyne molecule, there are one C—C σ bond, two C—H σ bonds and two C—C π bonds. The C≡C bond is stronger (bond enthalpy 823 kJ mol^{-1}) and shorter (120 pm) than the C=C and C—C. Electron cloud between two C-atoms of ethyne is cylindrically symmetrical about the internuclear axis, so ethyne is a linear molecule.

Methods of Preparation

Following methods are used to prepare alkynes.

1. From Calcium Carbide

When calcium carbide is treated with water, ethyne is obtained.

$$CaC_2 + 2H_2O \longrightarrow Ca(OH)_2 + C_2H_2$$

Calcium carbide is prepared by heating the lime stone and then treating the obtained quicklime with coke at high temperature.

$$CaCO_3 \xrightarrow{\Delta} CaO + CO_2\uparrow$$

$$CaO + 3C \longrightarrow \underset{\text{Calcium carbide}}{CaC_2} + CO$$

Note Other metallic carbide of group II (alkaline earth metals) also give the similar reaction with water.

2. From Natural Gas

Natural gas (mostly CH_4) can be converted into acetylene when it is heated for a shorter period.

$$6CH_4 + 2O_2 \xrightarrow[\text{Cracking}]{1770\text{ K}} 2CH{\equiv}CH + 2CO_2 + 10H_2$$

$$2CH_4 \xrightarrow[0.01\text{ s}]{1800\text{ K}} HC{\equiv}CH + 3H_2$$

This method is also considered as industrial method for the preparation of ethyne.

3. Kolbe's Electrolysis

Electrolysis of concentrated solution of sodium or potassium salt of fumaric acid gives acetylene. Other alkynes can also be obtained by this method.

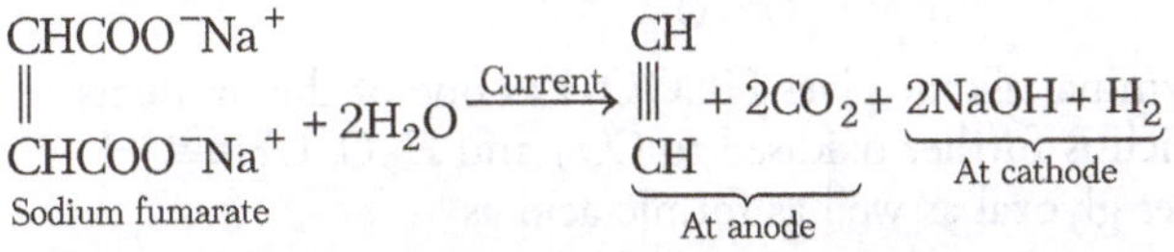

4. From *Vicinal* Dihalides (Dehydrohalogenation)

Vicinal dihalides when treated with alcoholic KOH and $NaNH_2$ undergo dehydrohalogenation to give respective alkynes. e.g.

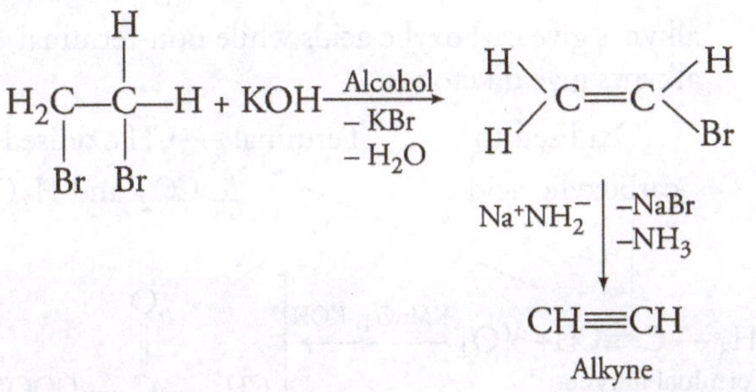

Physical Properties

(i) First three members of alkynes are gases, next eight are liquids and higher alkynes are solids.

(ii) All alkynes are colourless and odourless except acetylene which has garlic odour.

(iii) Melting and boiling points and densities of alkynes are slightly higher than that of corresponding alkenes and alkanes. These properties generally increases with increase in molecular mass.

(iv) These are lighter than water and also insoluble in it. However, they are soluble in non-polar solvents like benzene, ether etc. Alkynes are weakly polar in nature.

Chemical Properties

Alkynes exhibit the following characteristic reactions.

1. Acidic Character of Alkyne

In ethyne (or alkynes) the *sp*-hybridised carbon atom possesses maximum *s*-character and hence, maximum electronegativity. Due to which, it attracts the shared electron pair of C—H bond to a greater extent and makes removal of proton easier. That's why the hydrogen(s) attached with the triply bonded carbon atoms are acidic in nature and gives the following reactions.

(i) **Reaction of alkyne with Na in liq. NH_3 or $NaNH_2$** : Alkynes form monosodium ethynide and disodium ethynide.

$$CH_3{-}C{\equiv}C{-}H + Na^+NH_2^- \longrightarrow \underset{\text{Sodium propynide}}{CH_3{-}C{\equiv}C^-Na^+} + NH_3$$

(ii) **Reaction with Tollen's reagent** With Tollen's reagent (ammoniacal $AgNO_3$), a white precipitate of silver salt is obtained.

$$H{-}C{\equiv}C{-}H + 2AgNO_3 + 2NH_4OH \longrightarrow \underset{\substack{\text{Silver acetylide}\\ \text{(white ppt.)}}}{Ag{-}C{\equiv}C{-}Ag} + 2NH_4NO_3 + 2H_2O$$

These reactions are not shown by alkenes and alkanes, hence used for distinction between alkynes, alkenes and alkanes. The order of acidity of different compounds is

(i) $HC{\equiv}CH > H_2C{=}CH_2 > CH_3{-}CH_3$

(ii) $HC{\equiv}CH > CH_3{-}C{\equiv}CH >> CH_3{-}C{\equiv}C{-}CH_3$

2. Addition Reaction

Alkynes also undergo electrophilic addition reactions. Because of the presence of a triple bond, two moles of the reagent are added to it.

Mechanism

It involves the formation of vinylic cation and then addition product.

$$-C{\equiv}C- + H{-}Z \xrightarrow{H^+} \underset{\text{Vinylic cation}}{-\overset{H}{\overset{|}{C}}{=}\overset{\oplus}{C}-} + :\!Z \longrightarrow -\overset{H}{\overset{|}{C}}{=}\overset{Z}{\overset{|}{C}}-$$

The addition product obtained depends upon the stability of vinylic cation.

The addition of reagent takes place in accordance to Markownikoff's rule.

(i) **Addition of Dihydrogen**

$$HC\equiv CH + H_2 \xrightarrow{Pt/Pd/Ni} \underset{\text{Alkene}}{[H_2C{=}CH_2]} \xrightarrow{H_2} \underset{\text{Alkane}}{CH_3{-}CH_3}$$

(ii) **Addition of Halogens**

$$CH_3{-}C\equiv CH \xrightarrow{Br_2} \underset{\text{1, 2-dibromopropene}}{[CH_3CBr{=}CHBr]} \xrightarrow{Br_2} \underset{\text{1,1,2,2-tetrabromopropane}}{CH_3CBr_2CHBr_2}$$

Note Alkynes also decolourise the red brown colour of bromine water (in CCl_4). This is used as a test for unsaturation.

(iii) **Addition of Hydrogen Halide**

$$CH_3{-}C\equiv CH + H{-}Br \longrightarrow \underset{\text{2-bromopropene}}{[CH_3{-}C(Br){=}CH_2]} \longrightarrow \underset{\text{2,2-dibromopropane}}{CH_3{-}C(Br)_2{-}CH_3}$$

(iv) **Addition of Water** It occurs in the presence of mercuric sulphate and dilute sulphuric acid at 333 K. Carbonyl compounds are the product of this reaction.

$$\underset{\text{Ethyne}}{CH\equiv CH} + H{-}OH \xrightarrow[333\,K]{Hg^{2+}/H^+} CH_2{=}C(OH){-}H \xrightarrow{\text{Isomerisation}} \underset{\text{Ethanal}}{CH_3{-}C({=}O){-}H}$$

3. Oxidation Reactions

Alkynes give following types of oxidation reactions by combining with different oxidising agents.

(i) **Complete Combustion** In the presence of air (or O_2), alkynes undergo combustion to give carbon dioxide and water along with large amount of heat and light energy. The generalised combustion reaction is

$$C_nH_{2n-2} + \left(\frac{3n-1}{2}\right)O_2 \longrightarrow nCO_2 + \left(\frac{2n-2}{2}\right)H_2O + \text{Energy}$$

(ii) **Ozonolysis** It is more or less similar to alkenes except the fact that an additional bond is present in ozonide. Its presence modify the products as follows

***Step* I** Ozonide formation

***Step* II** Ozonide hydrolysis

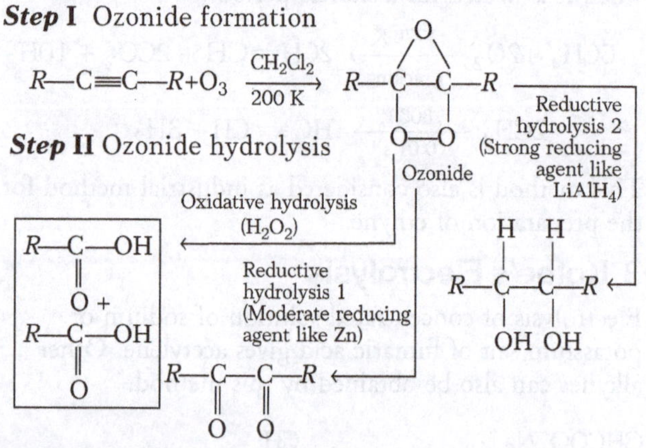

Terminal alkyne gives HCOOH as one of the products which is further oxidised to CO_2 and H_2O. $CH\equiv CH$ gives glyoxal as well as formic acid as

$$CH\equiv CH \xrightarrow[\text{(ii) } H_2O]{\text{(i) } O_3} \underset{\text{Glyoxal}}{\begin{matrix} CHO \\ | \\ CHO \end{matrix}} + \underset{\text{Formic acid}}{HCOOH}$$

(iii) **Oxidation with $KMnO_4$**

(a) **With cold alk. $KMnO_4$** (Baeyer's reagent) terminal alkynes give carboxylic acids while non-terminal alkynes give diketones.

Oxidised to carboxylic acid; Terminal —CH oxidised to CO_2 and H_2O

$$\underset{\text{Terminal alkyne}}{CH_3{-}C\equiv CH} + 3[O] \xrightarrow{KMnO_4,\ KOH} \left[CH_3{-}\overset{O}{\overset{\|}{C}}{-}COOH\right] \xrightarrow{[O]} CH_3COOH + CO_2\uparrow + H_2O$$

$$\underset{\text{Non-terminal alkyne}}{CH_3{-}C\equiv C{-}CH_3} + 2[O] \xrightarrow{KMnO_4,\ KOH} \underset{\text{Butan-2, 3-dione}}{CH_3{-}\overset{O}{\overset{\|}{C}}{-}\overset{O}{\overset{\|}{C}}{-}CH_3}$$

However, acetylene under these conditions give oxalic acid.

$$\begin{matrix} CH \\ \| \! | \\ CH \end{matrix} + 2[O] \xrightarrow[373-383\,K]{KMnO_4/KOH} \underset{\text{Glyoxal}}{\left[\begin{matrix} CH{=}O \\ | \\ CH{=}O \end{matrix}\right]} \xrightarrow{2[O]} \underset{\text{Oxalic acid}}{\begin{matrix} COOH \\ | \\ COOH \end{matrix}}$$

(b) **With hot $KMnO_4$** Cleavage occurs at the $C \equiv C$ resulting in the formation of carboxylic acids. With non-terminal alkynes a mixture of two carboxylic acids are obtained while with terminal alkynes, one carboxylic acid and CO_2 is produced. In general, $\equiv CH$ is oxidised to CO_2 and $\equiv CR$ is oxidised to RCOOH.

$$CH_3-C\equiv C-CH_2CH_3 \xrightarrow[373-383\,K]{KMnO_4/KOH} CH_3COOH + CH_3CH_2COOH$$

$$CH_3-C\equiv CH + 4[O] \xrightarrow[373-383\,K]{KMnO_4/KOH} CH_3COOH + CO_2$$

However, acetylene under these conditions gives CO_2 and H_2O.

$$\begin{matrix} CH \\ \|\| \\ CH \end{matrix} + 4[O] \xrightarrow[373-383\,K]{KMnO_4/KOH} \left[\begin{matrix} COOH \\ | \\ COOH \end{matrix}\right] \xrightarrow{[O]} 2CO_2 + H_2O$$

4. Polymerisation

(i) **Linear Polymerisation** Under suitable conditions, ethyne molecules undergo linear polymerisation to give a high molecular weight polyene, called polyacetylene $-\!\!\left[CH=CH-CH=CH\right]\!\!-_n$, which is a conductor of electricity under special conditions. Thin film of polyacetylene is good conductor, lighter and cheaper than the metal conductors, so it is used as electrode in batteries.

(ii) **Cyclic Polymerisation** When ethyne is passed through red hot iron tube at 873 K, it undergoes cyclic polymerisation to give benzene, an aromatic compound. Thus, this reaction is the best route for entering from aliphatic to aromatic compounds.

$$3CH\equiv CH \xrightarrow[873\,K]{\text{Red hot iron tube}}$$

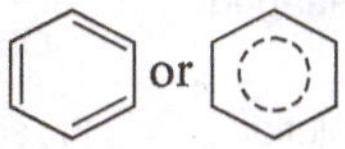

Uses

(i) It is used for the artificial ripening of fruits and vegetables.

(ii) It is used as a starting meterial for the formation of acetaldehyde, acetic acid, ethyl alcohol etc.

(iii) It is used as a starting material for the preparation of plastics, synthetic rubbers and synthetic fibre orlon.

(iv) It is used for cutting and welding of iron and steel.

Distinguishing Test between Alkane, Alkene and Alkyne

Different distinguishing tests are as follows:

Ethane and Ethyne

S. No.	Reagent	Ethane		Ethyne	
		Observation	Reaction	Observation	Reaction
1.	Br_2 solution (in CCl_4)	No effect	—	Br_2 solution is decolourised due to electrophilic addition.	$CH\equiv CH + \underset{\text{Red}}{2Br_2} \xrightarrow{CCl_4} \underset{\text{Colourless}}{CHBr_2-CHBr_2}$
2.	Aqueous $KMnO_4$ (neutral)	No effect	—	Aqueous $KMnO_4$ (pink) is decolourised and black/ brown precipitate of MnO_2 are formed.	$3CH\equiv CH + 4MnO_4^- + 2H_2O \longrightarrow 3\,\begin{matrix} CHO \\ | \\ CHO \end{matrix} + 4MnO_2 + 4OH^-$
3.	Warm alkaline $KMnO_4$	No effect	—	Warm alkaline $KMnO_4$, gives oxidative cleavage of ($C\equiv C$) bond to form salts of carboxylic acids.	$RC\equiv CR \xrightarrow[\Delta]{MnO_4^-/OH^-} 2RCO^-$ (C=O); $CH_3C\equiv CCH_2CH_3 \xrightarrow[\Delta]{MnO_4^-/OH^-} CH_3\overset{O}{\overset{\|}{C}}O^- + CH_3CH_2\overset{O}{\overset{\|}{C}}O^-$

S. No.	Reagent	Ethane Observation	Ethane Reaction	Ethyne Observation	Ethyne Reaction
4.	Ammoniacal $AgNO_3$ (Tollen's reagent)	No effect	—	White precipitate of silver acetylide is formed.	$CH\equiv CH + 2AgNO_3 + 2NH_4OH \longrightarrow \underset{\text{White precipitate}}{Ag^+C^-\equiv C^-Ag^+}\downarrow + 2NH_4NO_3 + 2H_2O$
5.	Ammoniacal Cu_2Cl_2 (Fehling's solution)	No effect	—	Red precipitate of cuprous acetylide is formed.	$CH\equiv CH + Cu_2Cl_2 + 2NH_4OH \longrightarrow \underset{\text{Red precipitate}}{Cu^+C^-\equiv C^-Cu^+}\downarrow + 2NH_4Cl + 2H_2O$

Ethene and Ethyne

S. No.	Reagent	Ethene Observation	Ethene Reaction	Ethyne Observation	Ethyne Reaction
1.	Br_2 solution (in CCl_4)	Br_2 solution (in CCl_4) is decolourised	$CH_2{=}CH_2 + \underset{\text{Red}}{Br_2} \xrightarrow{CCl_4} \underset{\text{Colourless}}{CH_2Br{-}CH_2Br}$	Br_2 solution (in CCl_4) is decolourised	As in set 1
2.	Baeyer's reagent (MnO_4^-/OH^-)	It is decolourised	$3\,CH_2{=}CH_2 + \underset{\text{Purple}}{2MnO_4^-} + 4H_2O \longrightarrow 3\,\underset{\text{Diol}}{CH_2OH{-}CH_2OH} + 2OH^- + \underset{\text{(Brown/black) ppt}}{2MnO_2}$	It is decolourised	As in set 1
3.	Ammoniacal $AgNO_3$ (Tollen's reagent)	No reaction	—	White precipitate of silver acetylide	$CH\equiv CH + 2AgNO_3 + 2NH_4OH \longrightarrow \underset{\text{White ppt}}{AgC\equiv C-Ag}\downarrow + 2NH_4NO_3 + 2H_2O$
4.	Ammoniacal cuprous chloride (Fehling's solution)	No reaction	—	Red precipitate of cuprous acetylide	$CH\equiv CH + Cu_2Cl_2 + 2NH_4OH \longrightarrow \underset{\text{Red ppt.}}{CuC\equiv CCu}\downarrow + 2NH_4Cl + 2H_2O$

Topic Practice 3

Very Short Answer Type Questions

(1 Mark)

1 Fill in the Blanks.

(i) Stability of alkynes is relatively ...... than corresponding to alkenes and alkanes.

(ii) Alkynes are ...... in water but are .... in non-polar solvent.

(iii) Acetylenic bond is............and stronger than single or double bond.

(iv) Due to the linear structure acetylenic bond does not participate in a........... isomerism.

2 Objective Type Questions

(i) The correct IUPAC name of the given structure

$H_3C-\underset{\underset{CH_3}{|}}{CH}-C\equiv CH$ is

(a) 2-methylbut-1-yne (b) 1-methylbut-3-yne

(c) 2-methylbut-3-yne (d) 3-methylbut-1-yne

(ii) The common name and IUPAC name of $CH_3CH_2-C\equiv CH$, respectively are

(a) dimethylacetylene and but-2-yne

(b) ethylacetylene and but-1-yne

(c) acetylene and but-2-yne

(d) methylacetylene and but-2-yne

(iii) $CH_3-C\equiv CH + Br-Br \longrightarrow A$.

Here, A refers to

(a) $BrCH_2-CH=CHBr$
(b) $CH_3-CH=CBr_2$
(c) $Br-CH_2-CBr=CH_2$
(d) $CH_3-CBr=CHBr$

(iv) When $CH_3-C\equiv CH$ reacts with one mole of HBr then product obtained is

(a) bromoethene (b) dibromopropane
(c) 2-bromopropene (d) 1-bromopropane

(v) Which of the following reaction will yield 2,2-dibromopropane?

(a) $CH_3-CH=CH_2 + HBr \longrightarrow$
(b) $CH_3-C\equiv CH + HBr \longrightarrow$
(c) $CH_3-CH=CHBr + HBr \longrightarrow$
(d) $CH\equiv CH + HBr \longrightarrow$

3 Match the Column I with Column II and choose the correct option from the codes given below.

	Column I		Column II
A.	$RC\equiv CR \xrightarrow[CH_3COOH]{BH_3,\ THF}$	(i)	$CH_3-C\equiv C-Na$
B.	$RC\equiv CR \xrightarrow[H_2]{Pd/Ni}$	(ii)	$R-CH_2-\overset{O}{\overset{\parallel}{C}}-R$
C.	$CH_2(Br)CH_2Br \xrightarrow[NaNH_2]{Alc.\ KOH}$	(iii)	$CH_3-C\equiv C-OH$
D.	$CH_3C\equiv CH \xrightarrow{NaNH_2}$	(iv)	$R-CH_2-CH_2-R$
		(v)	$CH\equiv CH$

Codes

	A	B	C	D		A	B	C	D
(a)	(ii)	(iv)	(v)	(i)	(b)	(ii)	(iv)	(v)	(iii)
(c)	(ii)	(v)	(iv)	(i)	(d)	(ii)	(iv)	(iii)	(v)

4 What is the IUPAC name of $H_3C-C\equiv CH$

5 How can you prepare ethyne from calcum carbride?

6 What is the correct order of acidity of alkyne.
$HC\equiv CH$, $H_2C=CH_2$, CH_3-CH_3

7 Complete the following reaction.

$$CH\equiv CH \xrightarrow[373\text{-}383\ K]{KMnO_4/KOH}$$

8 Explain, why alkynes are less reactive than alkenes toward addition of Br_2.

9 Write an equation of the reaction of propyne with water in the presence of H_2SO_4 and $HgSO_4$. Show the intermediate.

10 Alkynes on reduction with sodium in liquid ammonia form *trans*-alkenes. Will the butene thus formed on reduction of 2-butyne show geometrical isomerism? **NCERT Exemplar**

11 Write chemical equation for the combustion of hexyne. **NCERT Textbook**

12 How would you distinguish between
(i) But-1-yne and but-2-yne
(ii) Propene and propyne

13 How will you separate propene from propyne?

Short Answer Type II Questions

3 Marks

14 Write equations for the preparation of
(i) $HC\equiv CD$
(ii) $DC\equiv CD$

15 Hydrocarbon A (molecular formula is C_5H_8) gave a white precipitate with ammoniacal silver nitrate. Oxidation of A with hot alkaline $KMnO_4$ gave 2-methyl propanoic acid. What is the structural formula of A?

16 How would you convert the following compound into benzene? **NCERT Textbook**
(i) Ethyne
(ii) Ethene

Long Answer Type Questions

5 Marks

17 An alkyl halide $C_5H_{11}Br(A)$ reacts with ethanolic KOH to give an alkene 'B', which reacts with Br_2 to give a compound 'C', which on dehydrobromination gives an alkyne 'D'. On treatment with sodium metal in liquid ammonia, one mole of 'D' gives one mole of the sodium salt of 'D' and half a mole of hydrogen gas. Complete hydrogenation of 'D' yields a straight chain alkane. Identify A, B, C and D. Give the reactions involved. **NCERT Exemplar**

Hints & Solutions

1. (i) higher, (ii) insoluble, soluble, (iii) shorter, (iv) *cis-trans*
2. (i) d, (ii) b, (iii) d, (iv) c, (v) b
3. (a) A-2, B-4, C-5, D-1
4. Prop-1-yne
5. Refer on text page 424 to 425 (Topic-3, Methods of preparation).
6. $HC \equiv CH > H_2C = CH_2 > CH_3—CH_3$
7. $$CH \equiv CH \xrightarrow[373\text{-}383\ K]{KMnO_4/KOH} \begin{matrix} COOH \\ | \\ COOH \end{matrix} \quad \text{(Oxalic acid)}$$
8. The three-membered ring bromonium ion formed from the alkyne (*A*) has a full double bond causing it to be more strained and less stable than the one from the alkene (*B*),

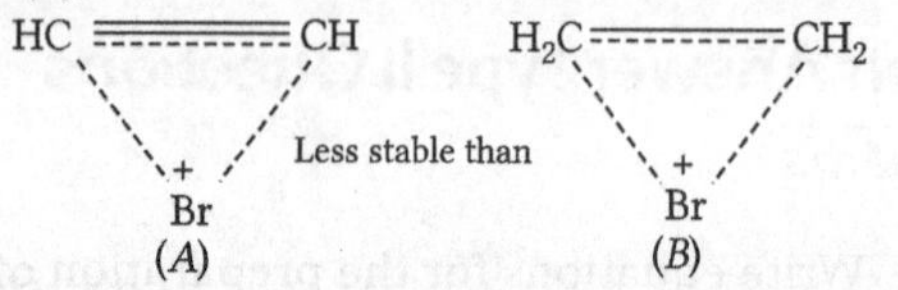

Also, the carbon's of (*A*) that are part of the bromonium ion have more *s*-character than (*B*), further making (*A*).

9. $$CH_3—C \equiv CH + H_2O \xrightarrow{HgSO_4/H_2SO_4}$$
$$\left[\begin{matrix} CH_3—C = CH_2 \\ \quad | \\ \quad OH \end{matrix}\right] \xrightarrow{\text{Tautomerism}} \begin{matrix} CH_3—C—CH_3 \\ \| \\ O \end{matrix}$$
(Enol) unstable — Acetone (a ketone stable)

The Markownikoff's addition of H_2O gives an unstable enol form that rearranges to the more stable ketone.

10. $$\overset{4}{C}H_3—\overset{3}{C} \equiv \overset{2}{C}—\overset{1}{C}H_3 \xrightarrow[196-200\ K]{Na,\ liquid\ NH_3}$$
2-butyne
$$\begin{matrix} H_3C & & H \\ & C = C & \\ H & & CH_3 \end{matrix}$$

Trans-2-butene formed by the reduction of 2-butyne is capable of showing geometrical isomerism.

11. $$C_6H_{10}\ (g) + \frac{17}{2} O_2(g) \xrightarrow{Heat} 6\ CO_2(g) + 5H_2O\ (g)$$
12. (i) Upon treatment with ammoniacal solution of $AgNO_3$. But-1-yne would give white ppt whereas but-2-yne does not react.
(ii) Upon treatment with ammoniacal solution of $AgNO_3$, propyne would give white ppt. whereas propene does not react.
13. On passing the mixture through ammoniacal $AgNO_3$ solution or ammoniacal $CuCl_2$ solution when propyne reacts while propene passes over.
14. (i) $HC \equiv CH \xrightarrow{NaNH_2} HC \equiv C^-Na^+ \xrightarrow{D_2O} HC \equiv CD$ [1/2]
(ii) $HC \equiv CH \xrightarrow{2\ Na} Na^+C^- \equiv C^-Na^+ \xrightarrow{D_2O} DC \equiv CD$ [1/2]
15. The structural formula of *A* is
$$CH_3—CH(CH_3)—C \equiv CH$$
3-methyl-1-butyne [1]
$$\begin{matrix} CH_3—CH—C \equiv CH \\ | \\ CH_3 \\ (A) \end{matrix} \xrightarrow{\text{Alk. } KMnO_4} \begin{matrix} CH_3—CH—COOH \\ | \\ CH_3 \end{matrix}$$
$$(A) \xrightarrow{AgNO_3} \begin{matrix} CH_3—CH—C \equiv CAg \\ | \\ CH_3 \end{matrix}$$
16. (i) Refer to text on page 576 (Topic-3, Polymerisation).
(ii) $$\underset{\text{Ethene}}{CH_2 = CH_2} \xrightarrow{Br_2/CCl_4} \begin{matrix} CH_2—CH_2 \\ | \quad\ \ | \\ Br \quad Br \end{matrix}$$
$$\xrightarrow[\text{Dehydrobromination}]{\text{Alc. KOH, }\Delta} \underset{\text{Vinyl bromide}}{CH_2 = CHBr}$$
$$\xrightarrow[196\ K,\ \text{dehydrobromination}]{NaNH_2/liq.NH_3} \underset{\text{Ethyne}}{HC \equiv CH}$$
$$\xrightarrow[373\ K]{\text{Red hot Fe tube}}$$

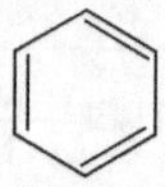

Benzene

17. 1 mole of alkyne *D* gives 1 mole of sodium alkynide and 1/2 mole of H_2. Furthermore, *D* gives straight chain alkane on hydrogenation, and is obtained from five membered compound therefore, *D* must be five membered straight chain terminal alkyne, i.e. 1-pentyne. Since, alkene B on reaction with Br_2 forms a compound ' *C*' which on dehydrohalogenation, gives 1-pentyne, therefore, '*C*' must be 1,2-dibromopentane and alkene '*B*' must be 1-pentene. Since, alkene '*B*' is obtained by dehydrogenation of alkyl halide, therefore, alkyl halide A must be 1-bromopentane. Reactions are as follows
$$\underset{\text{1-bromopentane }(A)}{CH_3CH_2CH_2CH_2CH_2Br} \xrightarrow[- HBr]{\text{Alc. KOH, }\Delta}$$
$$\underset{\text{1-pentene (B)}}{CH_3CH_2CH_2CH = CH_2} \xrightarrow{Br_2 \text{ in } CS_2}$$
$$\underset{\text{1, 2-dibromopentane }(C)}{CH_3CH_2CH_2—\overset{2}{C}HBr—\overset{1}{C}H_2Br}$$
$$\xrightarrow[- 2HBr]{\text{Alc. KOH,}} \underset{\text{1-pentyne }(D)}{CH_3CH_2CH_2C \equiv CH}$$
$$\xrightarrow{Na \textit{ in liq. } NH_3} \underset{\text{Sodium 1-pentynide}}{CH_3CH_2CH_2C \equiv C^-Na^+} + \frac{1}{2} H_2$$

TOPIC 04 Aromatic Hydrocarbons (Benzene)

Aromatic hydrocarbons are specialised cyclic compounds which are known for their characteristic unique smell. (Greek Aroma = fragrance). The group is also called arenes.

Most of the aromatic compounds were found to contain benzene ring. Benzene ring is highly unsaturated and is involved in most of the reactions of aromatic hydrocarbon. The unsaturation of benzene ring is retained.

Benzene and its derivatives are called the **benzenoid compounds**. However, there are many aromatic hydrocarbons also that do not have benzene ring. Such compounds are called **non-benzenoid compounds.** e.g.

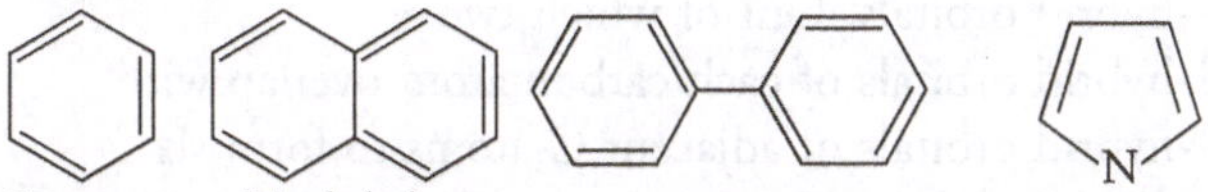

Benzene (benzenoid) | Naphthalene (benzenoid) | Biphenyl (benzenoid) | Pyrrole (non-benzenoid)

Nomenclature and Isomerism of Benzenoid Compounds

(For nomenclature and isomerism of aromatic compounds see chapter 12). Since, all the six hydrogen atoms of benzene are equivalent, so it gives only one type of product on monosubstitution.

However, disubstitution gives three products *viz* 1,2 or 1,6 (or *ortho*), 1,3 or 1,5 (or *meta*) and 1,4 (or *para*).

e.g.

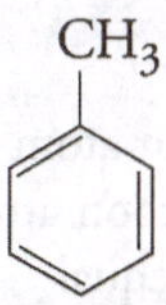

Methylbenzene (toluene)

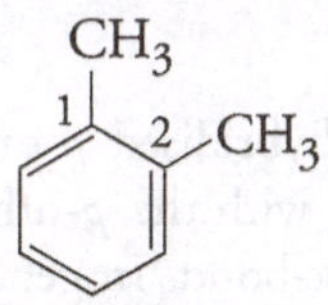

1, 2-dimethylbenzene (*o*-xylene)

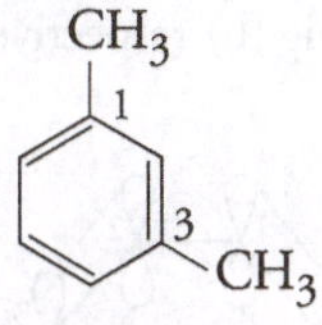

1, 3-dimethylbenzene (*m*-xylene)

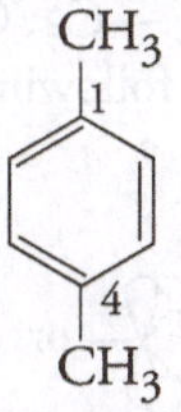

1, 4-dimethylbenzene (*p*-xylene)

Structure of Benzene

Based on the following facts, structure of benzene was obtained :

(i) Molecular formula of benzene is C_6H_6 which indicated that it is highly unsaturated compound (it has eight hydrogen atoms less than normal saturated alkane C_6H_{14}).

(ii) On ozonolysis it forms triozonide by adding three atoms of oxygen, that indicates the presence of three double bonds.

(iii) Benzene produces only one monosubstituted derivative, it means that all the six carbon and six hydrogen atoms present in benzene are identical.

Cyclic Structure of Benzene : Kekule's Hypothesis

On the basis of above observations in 1865, Kekule proposed the ring structure for benzene. Kekule suggested that the six carbon atoms of benzene are in a ring and are bonded to each other by alternating single and double bonds. One hydrogen atom is attached to each carbon atom of a ring.

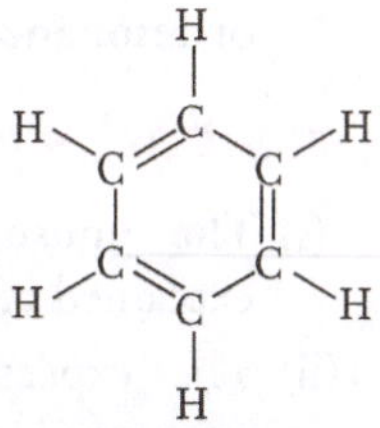

The given Kekule structure predicts the formation of two types of 1, 2-dibromobenzene I and II.

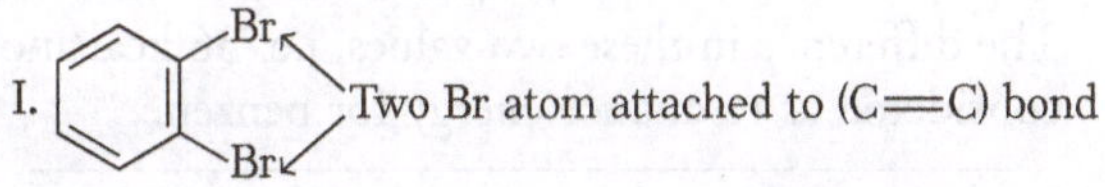

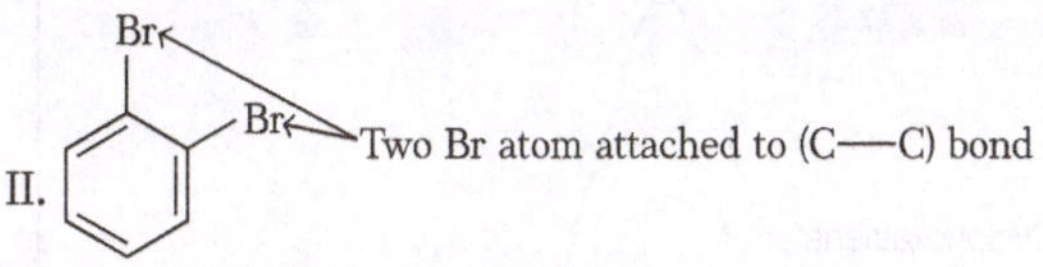

But only one type of 1, 2-disubstributed product is formed. Thus, all the hydrogen atoms of benzene are equivalent. Kekule assumed that the double bonds in the structure of benzene are not fixed but are wandering in continuous state of oscillation back and forth between two carbon atoms. Thus, each bond has single bond character for some fraction of time and double bond character for the other fraction.

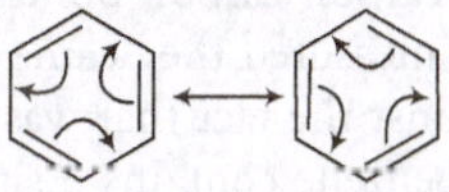

Evidences in Favour of Kekule's structure

(i) Benzene on hydrogenation in the presence of nickel catalyst gives cyclohexane (C_6H_{12}). It also combines with three molecules of chlorine to give benzene hexachloride.

These reactions confirm the presence of three double bonds.

$$\underset{\text{Benzene}}{C_6H_6} + 3H_2 \xrightarrow[220-250^\circ C]{Ni} \underset{\text{Cyclohexane}}{C_6H_{12}}$$

(ii) The synthesis of benzene from three molecules of acetylene also favours Kekule's structure.

$$3CH \equiv CH \xrightarrow{\Delta}$$ 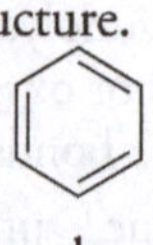

(iii) Benzene combines with three molecules of ozone to form triozonide.

(iv) A compound with delocalised electrons is more stable than localised electron compound. The extra stability that a compound gets as a result of having delocalised electrons is called **delocalisation energy** or **resonance energy**.

Drawbacks of Kekule's structure

(i) The unusual stability of benzene could not be explained *via* Kekule structure.

(ii) The expected heat of hydrogenation of Kekule structure was 85.8 kcal/mol. But the calculated heat of hydrogenation of benzene is 49.8 kcal/mol.

This statistics suggests that in real sense benzene is more stable than the proposed Kekule structures. The difference in these two values, i.e. 36 kcal/mol is considered as resonance energy for benzene.

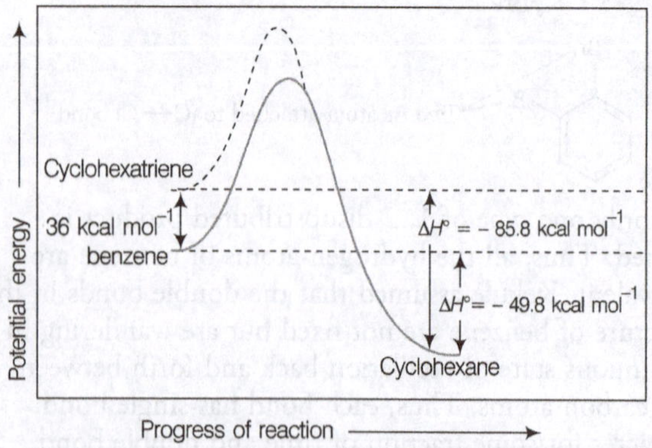

(iii) When all the carbon-carbon bond length of benzene molecule was measured they came equal (1.39Å). This was against the fact that was proposed by Kekule, i.e. benzene contains 3 single and 3 double bonds of bond length 1.44 and 1.36 Å.

Resonance and Stability of Benzene

The stability of benzene can be explained on the basis of concept of resonance.

According to Kekule, benzene is a resonance hybrid of the two structures (*A*) and (*B*) and the hybrid structure may be represented by inserting a circle or a dotted circle in the hexagon as shown in (*C*). The circle represent the six electrons which are delocalised between the six carbon atoms of the benzene ring.

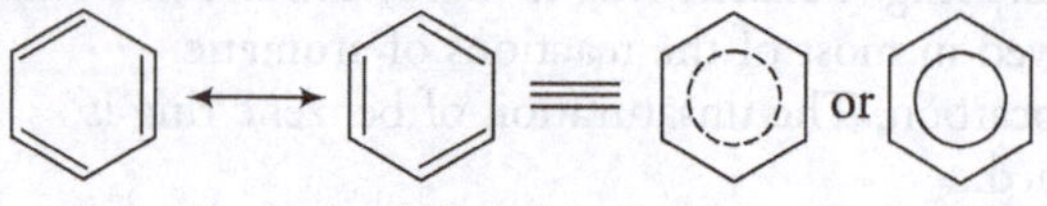

(*A*) (*B*) (*C*)

Orbital Structure of Benzene

In benzene, all the six carbon atoms contain three sp^2-hybrid orbitals. Out of which two sp^2-hybrid orbitals of each carbon atom overlap with sp^2-hybrid orbitals of adjacent C-atoms to form six C—C σ bonds which lie in the hexagonal plane. The remaining sp^2-hybrid orbital of each carbon atom overlaps with the 1*s*-orbital of a hydrogen atom to give six C—H σ bonds. Each C also has one unhybridised *p*-orbital which is perpendicular to the plane of the ring as shown in the figure.

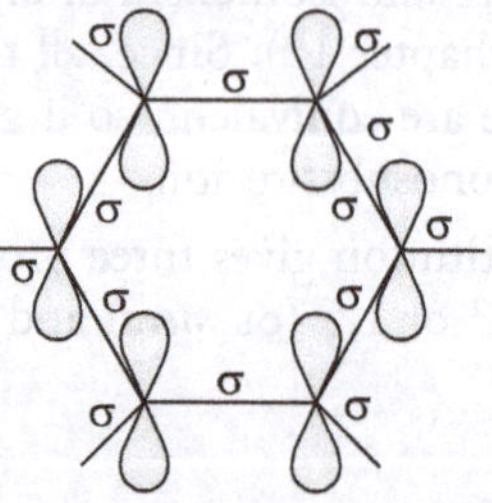

The unhybridised *p*-orbital of each carbon atom overlaps laterally with the *p*-orbital of adjacent carbon atom to form a π-bond. In general, there are two equal possibilities of three π-bonds by the overlap of *p*-orbitals of C_1—C_2, C_3—C_4, C_5—C_6 Fig. (a) C_2—C_3, C_4—C_5, C_6—C_1 Fig.(b) respectively as shown in the following figures :

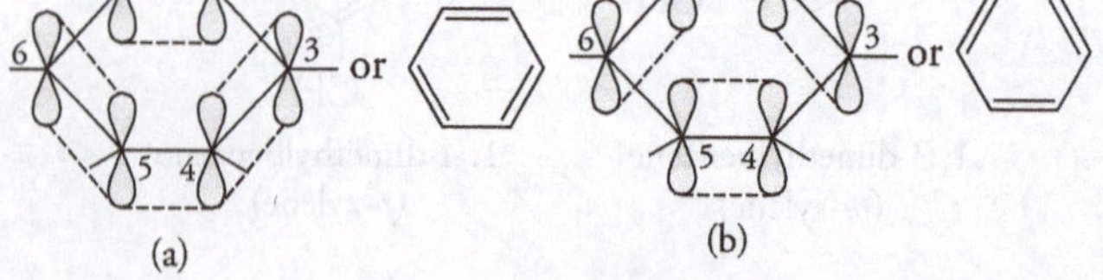

(a) (b)

The above fact is also supported by X-ray diffraction which showed that all the C—C bond lengths are equal (139 pm) and intermediate of single and double bond lengths. The overlapping of *p*-orbitals of adjacent carbon atoms can also be represented in the form of two doughnuts (rings) of electron clouds, one above and one below the plane of the hexagonal ring as shown below:

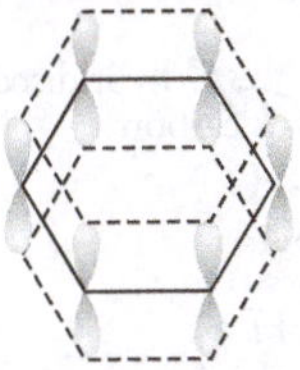

or

Electron cloud

The six π-electrons are, thus, delocalised and can move freely about the six carbon nuclei. This delocalised π-electron cloud is attracted more strongly by the nuclei of the carbon atoms than the electron cloud localised between two carbon atoms. These delocalised π-electrons makes the benzene ring more stable.

Further, absence of pure double bond shows the non-reactivity of benzene towards usual reactions of alkenes and also explains its unusual behaviour.

Aromaticity

A compound can be considered as aromatic if it follows the given three rules :

(i) An aromatic compound must be cyclic and planar.

(ii) An aromatic compound must have the conjugated system in it.

(iii) An aromatic compound must follow **Huckel's rule** which states that the number of π-electrons $=(4n+2)$; where $n=$ integer 0, 1, 2, 3 etc.

e.g.

(a) Cyclopropenyl cation

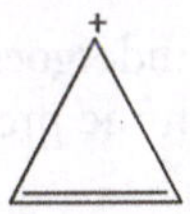

Number of π-electrons $=2$

$(4n+2)=2$ and $n=0$ thus, Huckel's rule is followed.

(b) 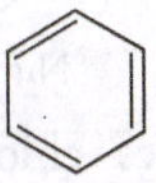

Benzene

Cyclopentadienyl anion

Cycloheptatrienyl cation

Number of π-electrons $=6$

$(4n+2)=6$ and $n=1$ thus, Huckel rule is followed.

(c) Napthalene

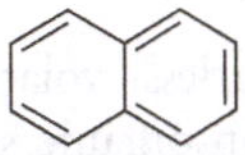

Number of π-electrons $=10$

$4n+2=10$ and $n=2$ thus, Huckel rule is followed.

(d)

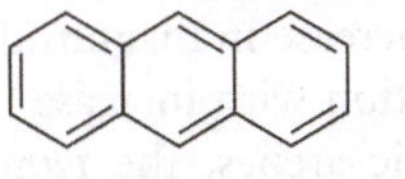

Anthracene

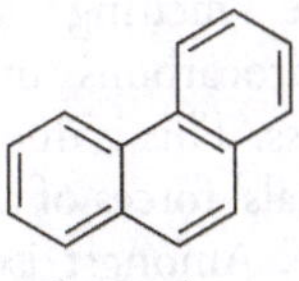

Phenanthrene

Number of π-electrons $=14$.

$4n+2=14$ and $n=3$ thus, Huckel rule is followed.

Those compounds which does not follow the above 3 rules are called **non-aromatic.** These non-aromatic compounds may be cyclic with conjugated system.

e.g. 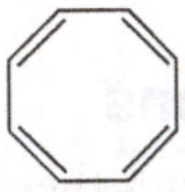 (cyclooctatetraene) is cyclic with conjugated system but it does not follow Huckel rule and its plane is also distorted that's why it is non-aromatic.

Methods of Preparation

Benzene is commercially obtained from coal tar but in laboratory, *it is prepared by following processes :*

1. Decarboxylation of Aromatic Acids (From Sodium Benzoate)

When sodium salt of benzoic acid is heated with sodalime (NaOH + CaO), it gives benzene.

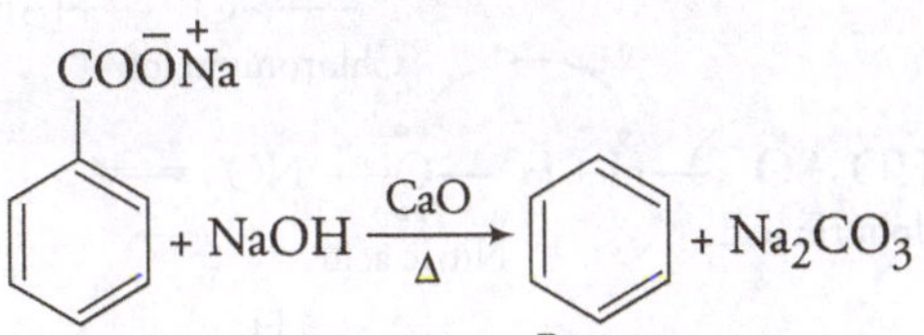

Benzene

2. Reduction of Phenol

When vapours of phenol are passed over heated zinc dust, benzene is obtained.

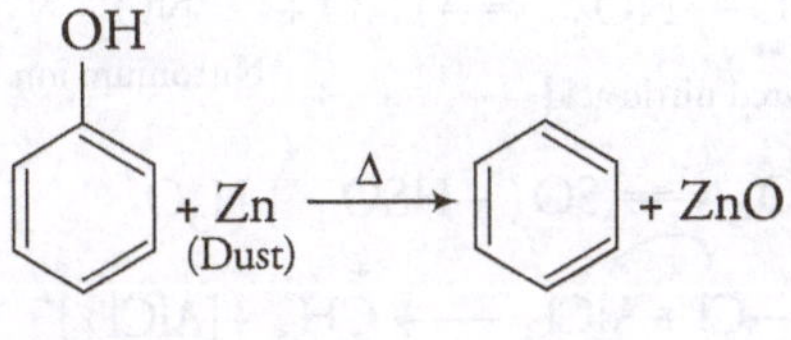

Physical Properties

(i) Benzene is a colourless, volatile liquid insoluble in water but soluble in organic solvents (ether, ethanol etc.).

(ii) It is inflammable and burns with sooty flame.

(iii) The melting and boiling point of aromatic hydrocarbons increases with increasing molecular mass. This is due to increase in magnitude of van der Waals' forces of attraction with increase in molecular size. Amongst isomeric arenes, the *para*-isomer has highest melting point because it is most symmetrical.

(iv) They are toxic and carcinogenic in nature.

Chemical Properties

Benzene readily undergoes electrophilic substitution reactions and addition reactions. Important chemical reactions exhibited by benzene are as follows :

1. Electrophilic Substitution Reactions

The reactions in which an electrophile substitutes the hydrogen atom of the benzene ring, are called **electrophilic substitution reactions.**

Mechanism

It involves following steps :

***Step* I Generation of electrophile, E^+** The electrophile generated during chlorination, nitration, sulphonation, alkylation and acylation are respectively Cl^+, NO_2^+, SO_3^+, R^+, RCO^+ (acylium ion).

(i) $Cl—Cl + AlCl_3 \longrightarrow Cl^+ + Cl^{\delta+}—Al^{\delta-}Cl_3$

$\longrightarrow Cl^+ + [AlCl_4]^-$

Chloronium ion

(ii) $HO_3SO—H + H—\ddot{O}—NO_2 \rightleftharpoons$ (Sulphuric acid, Nitric acid)

$H—\overset{+}{\underset{H}{O}}—NO_2 + HSO_4^-$

$H—\overset{+}{\underset{H}{O}}—NO_2 \rightleftharpoons H_2O + \overset{\oplus}{N}O_2$

Protonated nitric acid — Nitronium ion

(iii) $2H_2SO_4 \rightleftharpoons SO_3 + HSO_4^- + H_3O^+$

(iv) $CH_3—Cl + AlCl_3 \longrightarrow \overset{+}{C}H_3 + [AlCl_4]^-$

(v) $CH_3—\underset{\underset{O}{||}}{C}—Cl + AlCl_3 \longrightarrow CH_3—\underset{\underset{O}{||}}{\overset{+}{C}} + [AlCl_4]^-$

***Step* II Formation of carbocation** (arenium ion)

E^+ attacks on the benzene ring to give σ-complex or arenium ion, in which one of the carbon is sp^3-hybridised.

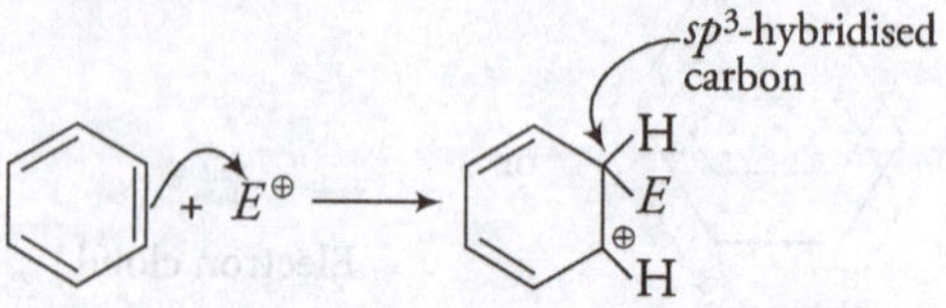

Sigma complex (arenium ion)

The arenium ion gets stabilised by resonance.

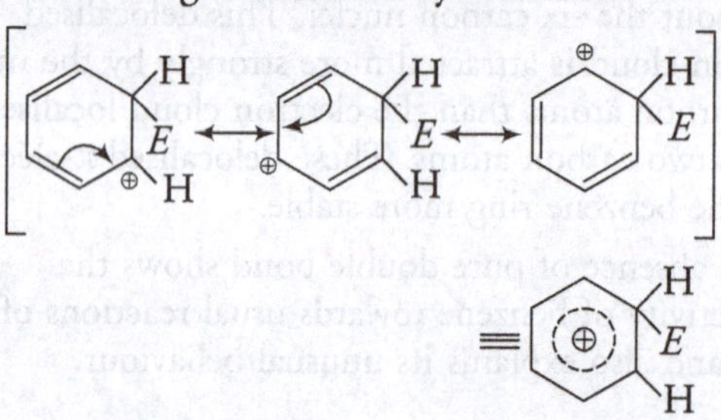

***Step* III Removal of proton** To regain aromatic character, the σ-complex lose one proton to $AlCl_4^-$ or HSO_4^- as shown below :

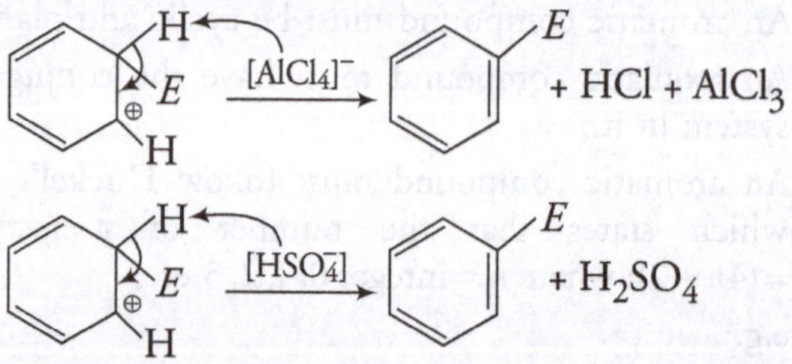

Various electrophilic substitution reactions are as follows :

(i) **Nitration** Benzene undergoes nitration when treated with conc. HNO_3 in the presence of conc. sulphuric acid.

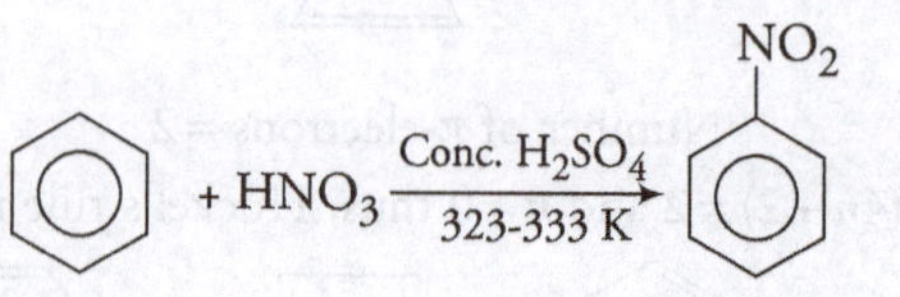

Nitrobenzene

(ii) **Halogenation** Benzene undergoes chlorination or bromination when it is treated with chlorine or bromine in the presence of Lewis acid catalyst, aluminium chloride or ferric chloride or ferric bromide in the absence of light.

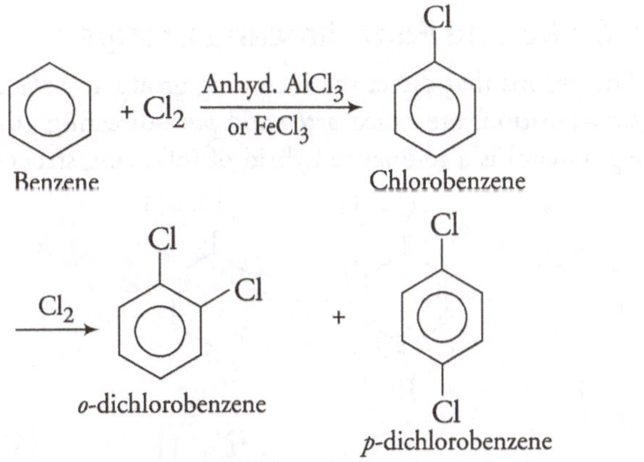

If E^+ is in excess, further substitution takes place, e.g. benzene on treatment with excess of chlorine in the presence of anhydrous $AlCl_3$ can be chlorinated to hexachlorobenzene (C_6Cl_6).

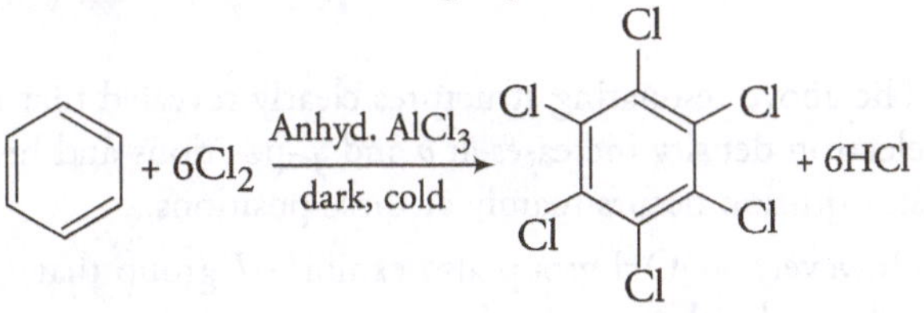

Hexachlorobenzene
(C_6Cl_6)

(iii) **Sulphonation** It is done by heating benzene with fuming sulphuric acid (oleum).

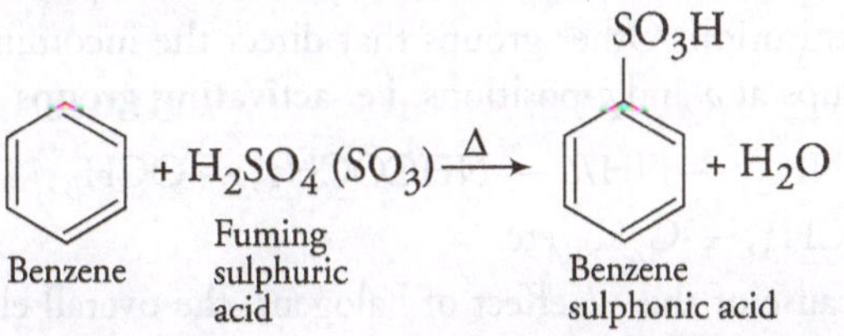

(iv) **Friedel-Crafts Alkylation** When benzene is treated with alkyl halide in the presence of anhyd. $AlCl_3$, it gives alkyl benzene. This reaction is called Friedel-Crafts alkylation.

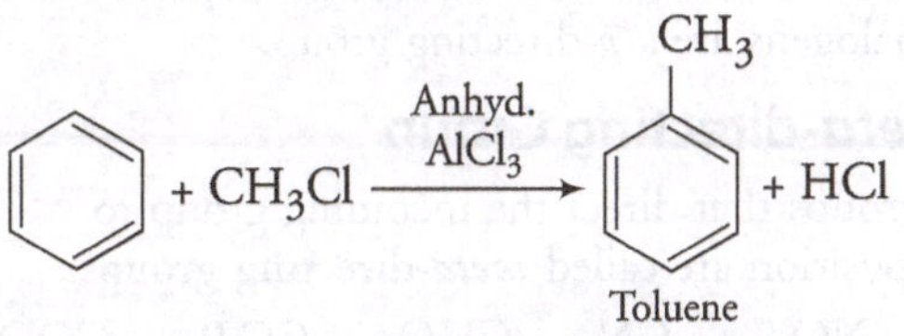

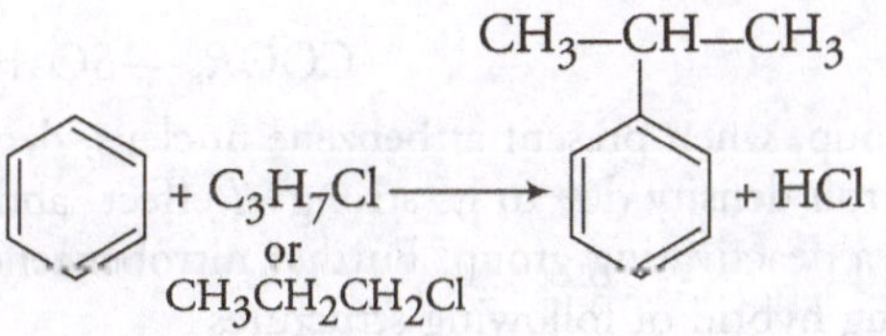

$$[\because CH_3CH_2CH_2Cl + AlCl_3 \xrightarrow[AlCl_4^-]{} \underset{1°\text{(less stable)}}{CH_3CH_2\overset{+}{C}H_2}$$

$$\xrightarrow{\text{Rearrangement}} \underset{2°\text{(more stable)}}{CH_3\overset{+}{C}HCH_3}\,]$$

(v) **Friedel-Crafts acylation** When benzene is treated with alkyl halide or acid anhydride in the presence of a Lewis acid (like $AlCl_3$), acyl benzene is obtained as a product.

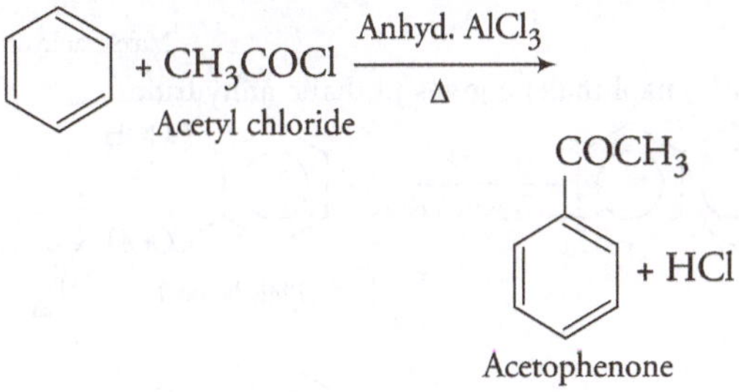

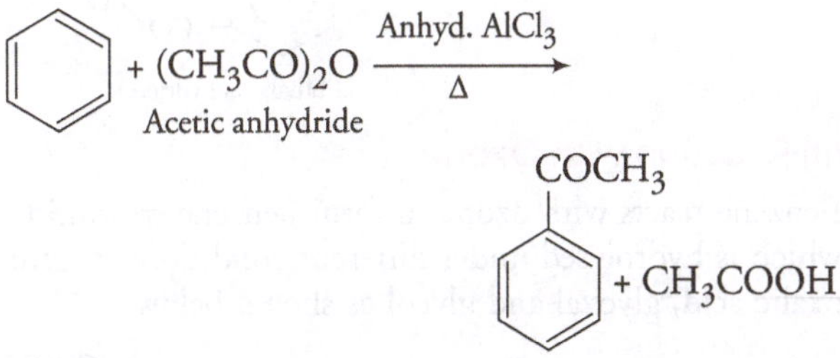

2. Addition Reactions

(i) **Addition of Hydrogen** When benzene is treated with hydrogen in the presence of nickel catalyst, under vigorous conditions, i.e. at high temperature and/or pressure, it gets reduced to cyclohexane.

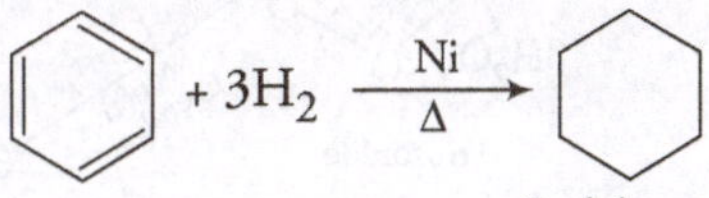

Cyclohexane

(ii) **Addition of Chlorine** When benzene is treated with chlorine molecules in the presence of UV light, addition of Cl takes place and benzene hexachloride, $C_6H_6Cl_6$ or **gammaxane** is obtained.

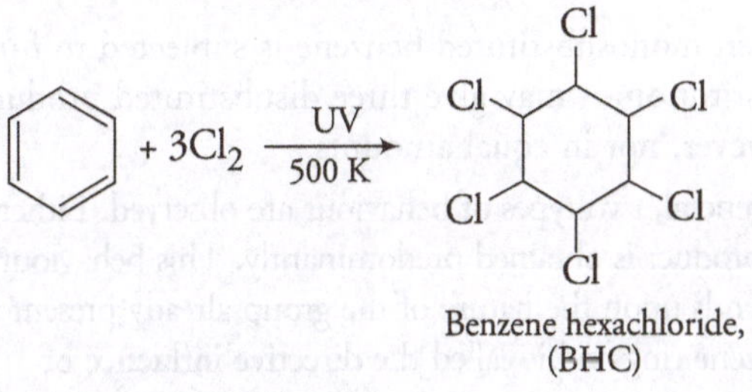

Benzene hexachloride,
(BHC)

3. Oxidation

(i) **Catalytic Oxidation** (Reaction with Oxygent) Benzene reacts with controlled amount of air at 773K in presence of a vanadium pentaoxide as catalyst to give maleic anhydride. e.g.

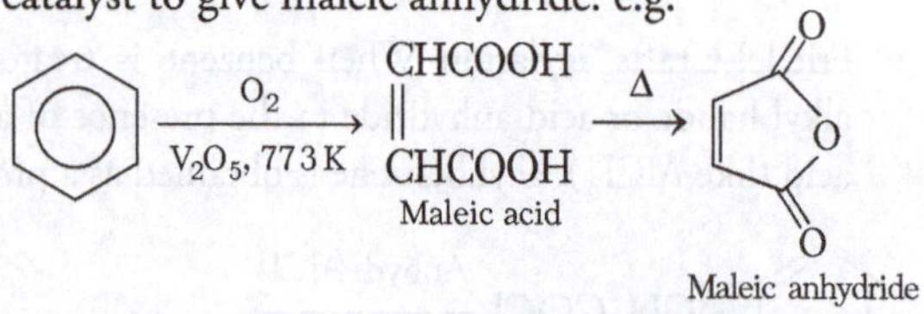

Similarly, naphthalene gives phthalic anhydride.

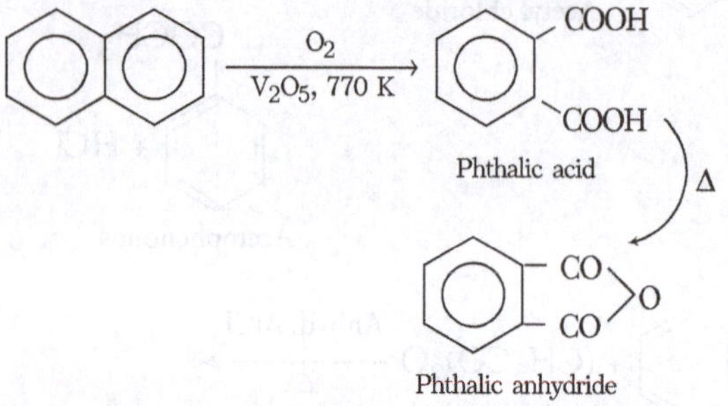

(ii) Reaction with Ozone

Benzene reacts with ozone to form benzene triozonide which is hydrolysed under different conditions to give oxalic acid, glyoxal and glycol as shown below

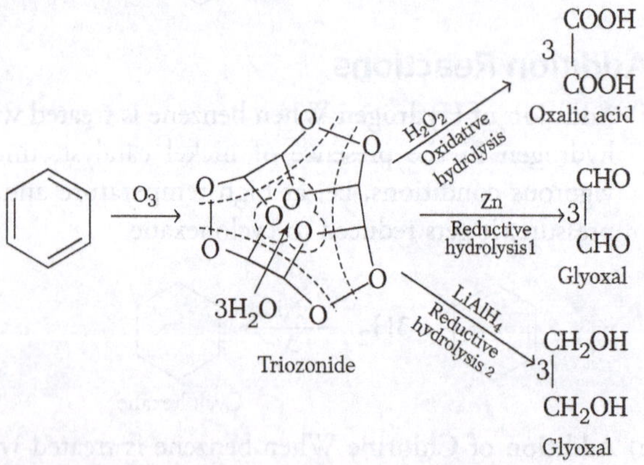

Directive Influence of a Functional Group in Monosubstituted Benzene

When monosubstituted benzene is subjected to further substitution, it may give three disubstituted products, however, not in equal amounts.

In general, two types of behaviour are observed. Either *o*/*p* or *m* product is obtained predominantly. This behaviour depends upon the nature of the group already present in the benzene ring and is called the **directive influence of substituents.**

1. *Ortho* and *Para*-directing Groups

The groups that direct the incoming group at *ortho* and *para*-positions are called *ortho* and *para*-directing groups. e.g. phenol is a resonance hybrid of following structures :

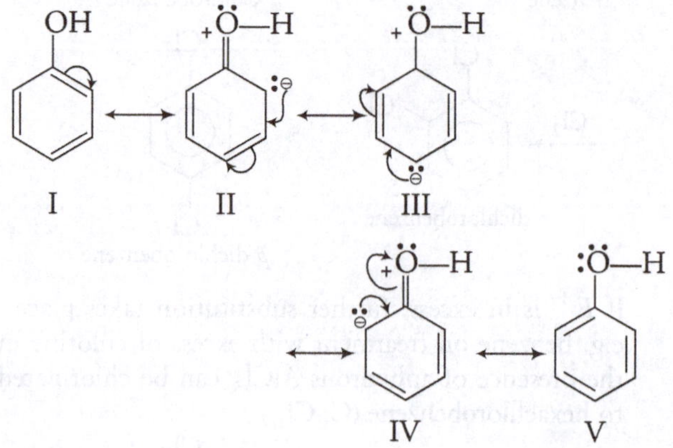

The above resonating structures clearly revealed that the electron density increases at *o* and *p*-positions and hence, substitution occurs mainly at these positions.

However, —OH group also exhibit $-I$ group that reduces the electron density to some extent at *ortho* and *para* -positions. But overall electron density increases at these positions of the ring due to resonance. Thus, —OH is an activating group and activates the *ortho* and *para*-positions of benzene nucleus for electrophilic substitution. Other groups that direct the incoming groups at *o* and *p*-positions, i.e. **activating groups** are

$—NH_2$, —NH*R*, $—NHCOCH_3$, $—OCH_3$, $—CH_3$, $—C_2H_5$ etc.

Because of the $-I$-effect of halogens, the overall electron density on the benzene ring decreases. It makes substitution difficult therefore halogens are **moderately deactivating.**

But due to resonance the electron density or *o*-and *p*-position is greater than that at the *m*-position. That's why halogens are *o*/*p*-directing group.

2. *Meta*-directing Group

The groups that direct the incoming group to *meta*-position are called ***meta*-directing groups.**

e.g. $—NO_2$, —CN, —CHO, —COR, —COOH, —COOR, $—SO_3H$ etc.

NO_2 group, when present at benzene nucleus, decreases the electron density due to its strong $-I$-effect and hence is called a deactivating group. Further nitrobenzene is a resonating hybrid of following structures

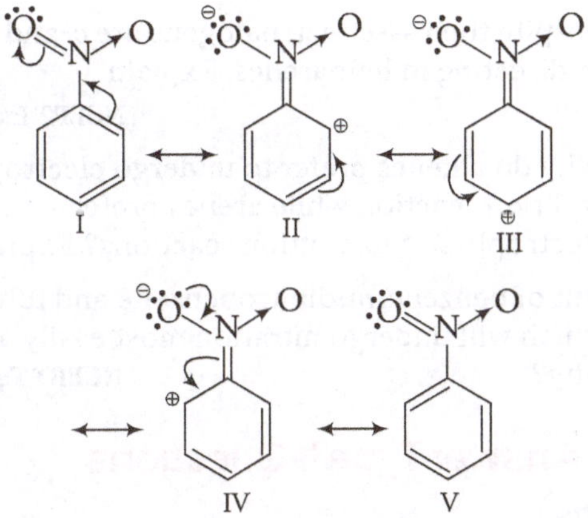

I II III IV V

The given structures show that the overall electron density on the benzene ring decreases and thus, the electrophilic substitution becomes difficult. The electron density on *o*-and *p*-position is comparatively lesser than that at *m*-position. So, electrophile attacks at *meta*-position, i.e. substitution occurs at *meta*-position.

Carcinogenicity and Toxicity

The polynuclear hydrocarbons having two or more fused benzene rings are toxic and have carcinogenic (cancer producing) property. These are obtained by incomplete combustion of organic materials like tobacco, coal and petroleum. They reach into the human body and undergo several biochemical reactions. They damage DNA and cause cancer. Some examples of carcinogenic hydrocarbons are as follows :

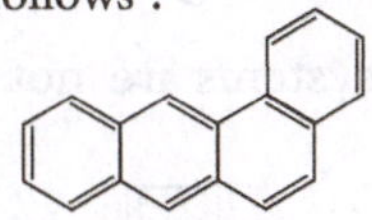

1, 2-benzanthracene

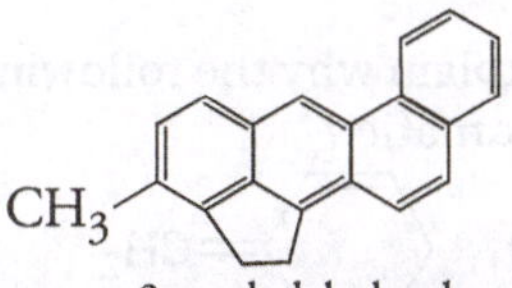

3-methylcholanthrene

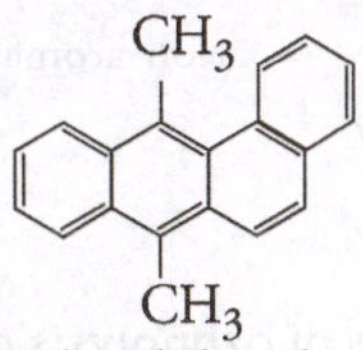

9, 10-dimethyl-1,2-benzanthracene

Uses

(i) It is used in the manufacture of styrene, gammaxene, nitrobenzene, chlorobenzene, phenol, nylon, detergent, insecticides etc.

(ii) It is used in dry cleaning of woollen clothes.

(iii) Benzene is blended with petrol to improve its octane number.

(iv) Benzene is used as a solvent for resins, rubbers, paints etc.

Topic Practice 4

Very Short Answer Type Questions

(1 Mark)

1 Fill in the Blanks

(i) Aromatic hydrocarbon burn with .... flame.

(ii) When benzene is treated with alkyl halide in the presence of anhydrous $AlCl_3$, it gives ....

(iii) Complete the following reaction.

$$C_6H_6 + \text{........} \xrightarrow[500\text{ K}]{\text{UV}} \text{BHC}$$

(iv) The polynuclear hydrocarbons having two or more fused benzene rings are toxic and have .... property.

2 Objective Type Questions.

(i) Benzene is obtained from which of the following oils after fractional distillation of coal-tar?

(a) Light oil (b) Heavy oil
(c) Middle oil (d) Anthracene oil

(ii) Which of the following compound possesses the C—H bond with the lowest bond dissociation energy?

(a) Toluene
(b) Benzene
(c) *n*-pentane
(d) 2, 2-dimethylpropane

(iii) Birch reduction (dissolving metal reduction) of *o*-xylene gives

(a) 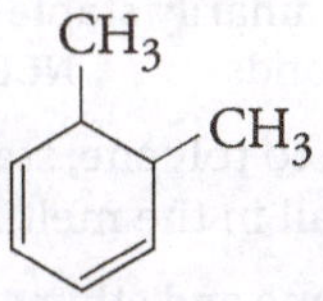 (b) 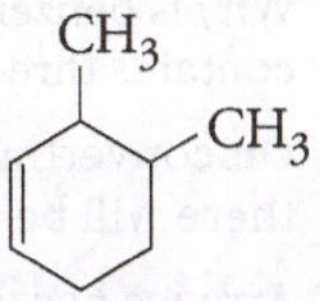

(c) 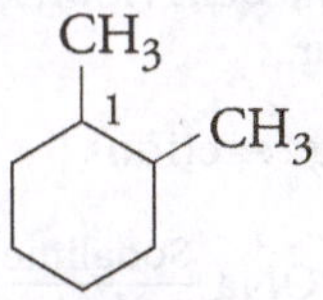 (d) 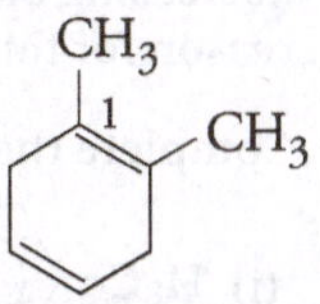

(iv) Aromatisation of *n*-heptane by passing over heated Al_2O_3 and Cr_2O_3 at 773 K gives

(a) benzene (b) toluene
(c) xylene (d) hepthylene

3 Match the groups in Column I with their *o*, *p* and *m*-directing influence along with electronic factor in Column II and choose the correct option using the codes given below:

	Column I		Column II
A.	—alkyl	(i)	*ortho*, *para*, resonance > inductive and activating
B.	—OH	(ii)	*ortho*, *para*, inductive > resonance and deactivating
C.	—Cl	(iii)	*meta*, resonance = inductive and deactivating
D.	—CN	(iv)	*ortho*, *para*, inductive > resonance and activating

Codes

	A	B	C	D		A	B	C	D
(a)	(iv)	(i)	(ii)	(iii)	(b)	(i)	(iii)	(ii)	(iv)
(c)	(i)	(iv)	(iii)	(ii)	(d)	(i)	(ii)	(iii)	(iv)

4 Explain, why *p*-xylene has higher melting point than the corresponding *ortho* or *meta*-isomers?

5 Suggest the name of a Lewis acid other than anhydrous aluminium chloride which can be used during ethylation of benzene. **NCERT Textbook**

6 Why does benzene undergo electrophilic substitution reactions easily and nucleophilic substitutions with difficulty?

7 Suggest a route for the preparation of nitrobenzene starting from acetylene? **NCERT Exemplar**

8 Why iodination of benzene is carried out in the presence of nitric acid or iodic acid?

Short Answer Type I Questions (2 Marks)

9 Why is benzene extra ordinarily stable though it contains three double bonds? **NCERT Textbook**

10 On converting benzene to toluene, state whether there will be a rise or fall in the melting point.

11 Arrange benzene, *n*-hexane and ethyne in decreasing order of acidic behaviour. Also give reason for this behaviour.

12 Complete the following reactions :

(i) 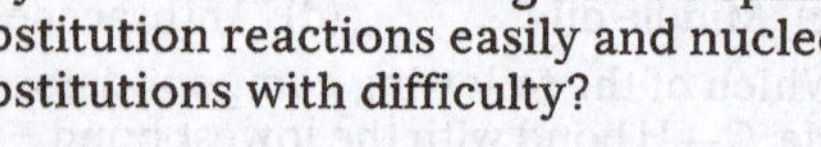

(ii) 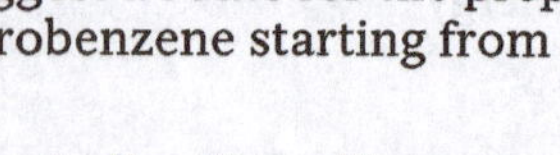

13 What will be the product obtained as a result of the following reaction and why? **NCERT Exemplar**

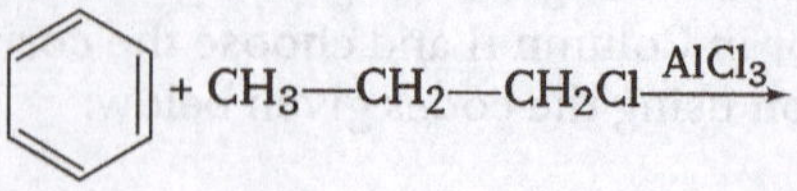

14 Despite their –*I*-effect, halogens are *o*-and *p*-directing in haloarenes. Explain **NCERT Exemplar**

15 Why do alkenes prefer to undergo electrophilic addition reaction while arenes prefer electrophilic substitution reactions? Explain

16 Out of benzene, *m*-dinitrobenzene and toluene which will undergo nitration most easily and why? **NCERT Textbook**

Short Answer Type II Questions (3 Marks)

17 Which of the following compounds are aromatic according to Huckel's rule?

(A) 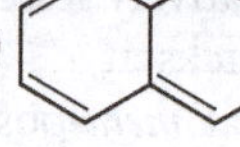 (B) 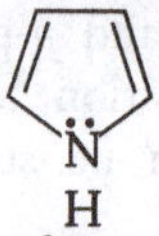

(C) 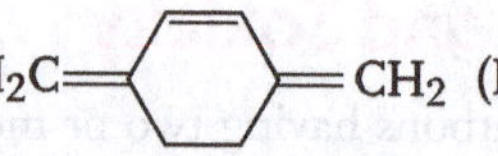 (D) 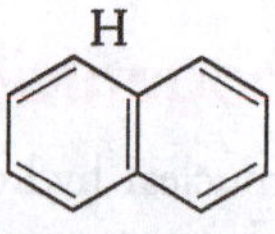

(E) 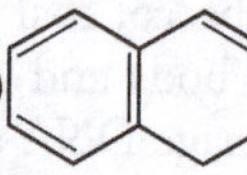 (F) 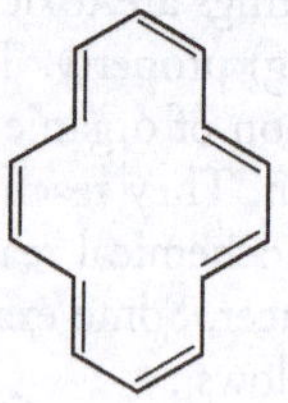

18 Explain why the following systems are not aromatic ?

(i) 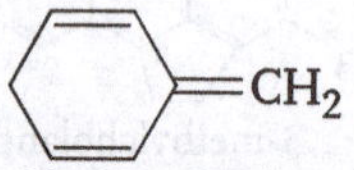
Non-aromatic

(ii) 
Non-aromatic

(iii) 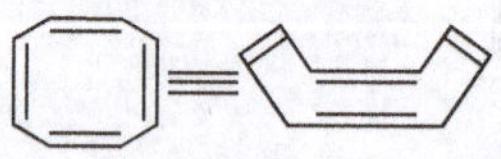
Non-aromatic

19 Write down the products of ozonolysis of 1, 2-dimethyl benzene (*o*-xylene). How does the result support Kekule structure of benzene?

20 Arrange the following set of compounds in order of their decreasing relative reactivity with an electrophile, E^+. **NCERT Textbook**

(i) Chlorobenzene, 2, 4-dinitrochlorobenzene, *p*-nitrochlorobenzene

(ii) Toluene, *p*-H_3C—C_6H_4—NO_2, *p*-O_2N—C_6H_4—NO_2

Also, explain your answer.

21 7-bromo-1, 3, 5-cycloheptatriene exists as an ion whereas 5-bromo-1, 3-cyclopentadiene does not form an ion even in presence of Ag^+. Explain.

Long Answer Type I Questions

(5 Marks)

22 How will you convert benzene into
(i) *p*-nitrobromobenzene
(ii) *m*-nitrochlorobenzene
(iii) *p*-nitrotoluene
(iv) acetophenone? **NCERT Textbook**

23 Assign structures to the following.
(i) An alkyne (*X*) has molecular formula C_5H_8. It reacts neither with sodamide nor with ammoniacal cuprous chloride.
(ii) A hydrocarbon '*Y*' decolourises bromine water. On ozonolysis it gives 3-methyl butanal and formaldehyde. Give the name of the compound.
(iii) A hydrocarbon (*Z*) has molecular formula C_8H_{10}. It does not decolourise bromine water and is oxidised to benzoic acid on heating with $K_2Cr_2O_7$. It can also have three other isomers *A*, *B* and *C*. Write the structures of *Z*, *A*, *B* and *C*.

24 The ring systems having following characteristics are aromatic.
(i) Planar ring containing conjugated π-bonds.
(ii) Complete delocalisation of the π-electrons in ring system. i.e. each atom in the ring has unhybridised *p*-orbital, and
(iii) Presence of $(4n+2)$ π- electrons in the ring where *n* is an integer ($n = 0, 1, 2, \ldots\ldots$) [Huckel rule].
Using this information classify the following compounds as aromatic/non-aromatic. **NCERT Exemplar**

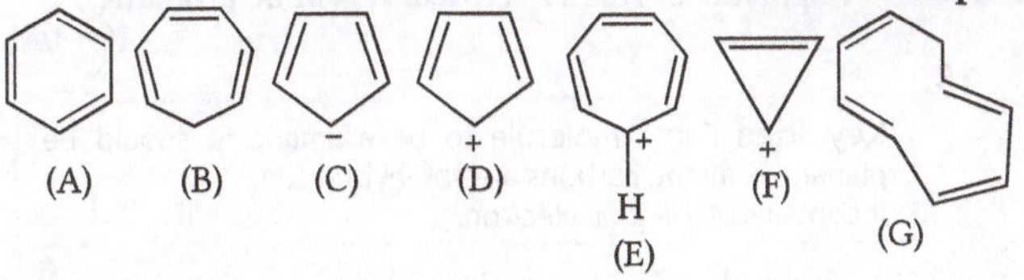

Hints & Solutions

1. (i) sooty, (ii) alkyl benzene, (iii) $3Cl_2$, (iv) carcinogenic
2. (i) → (a), (ii) → (a), (iii) → (d), (iv) → (b)
3. (a) A → (iv), B → (i), C → (ii), D → (iii)
4. The *para*-isomer has a more symmetrical structure, allowing it to fit better into the crystal lattice than the other or *meta*-isomer.
5. In this reaction, anhydrous $FeCl_3$ or $SnCl_4$ can be used in place of anhydrous $AlCl_3$ as a catalyst.
6. Due to the presence of delocalised 6π-electrons, benzene acts as a rich source of electrons. So, it attracts the electrophilic reagent (electron deficient species) towards itself but repels the nucleophilic reagents. That's why benzene gives electrophilic substitution reactions easily and nucleophilic substitution reaction with difficulty.
7.

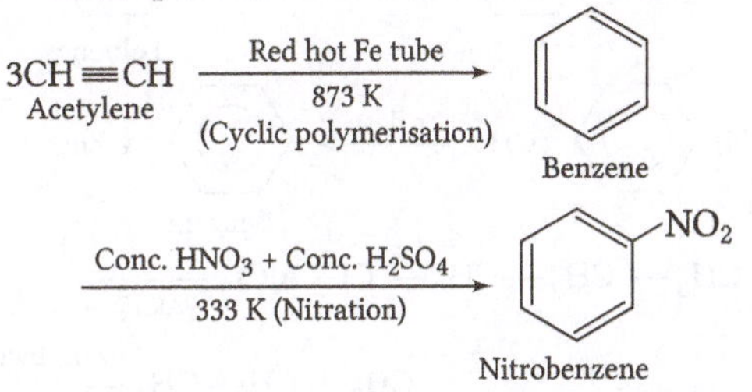

8. The iodination of benzene is usually brought about by refluxing benzene with iodine and conc. HNO_3 or HIO_3.

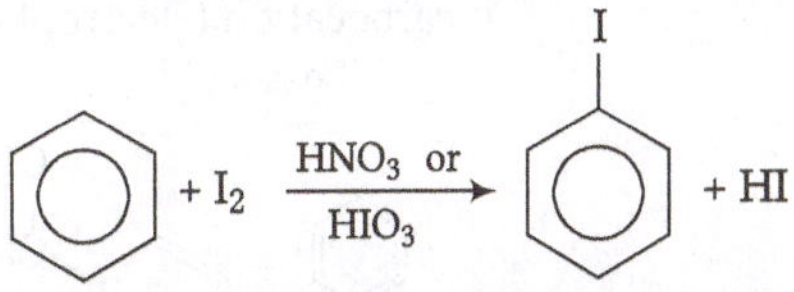

HNO_3 or HIO_3 oxidises HI to I_2 and prevents the backward reaction to occur.

9. Resonance and delocalisation of electrons generally lead to the stability of benzene molecule.

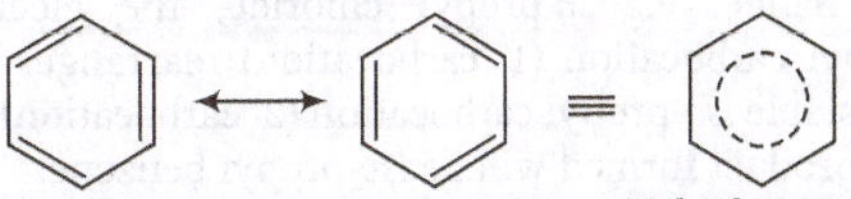

Hybrid structure [1]

The dotted circle in the hybrid structure represents the six electrons which are delocalised between the six carbon atoms of the benzene ring.
Therefore, presence of delocalised π-electrons in benzene makes it more stable than the hypothetical cyclohexatriene. [1]

10. On converting benzene to toluene, there is a fall in the melting point although toluene has the higher molecular mass. This is because the planar molecules of benzene can pack more closely in the crystal lattice and the cohesive forces are strong, whereas the methyl group in toluene prevents such close packing. [2]

11.

> **Key Idea** Higher the s-character, higher is the acidity, so first find hybridisation of all the given compounds and then compare their acidity.

The hybridisation state of carbon in the given compounds is

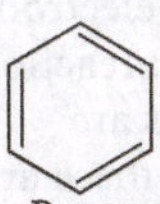

; $CH_3-(CH_2)_4-CH_3$; $H-C\equiv C-H$

Benzene, *n*-hexane, Ethyne [1]

Type of hybridisation	sp^2	sp^3	sp
s-character	33.33%	25%	50%

Acidic character increases with increase in *s*-character of the orbital. Hence, decreasing order of acidic behaviour of ethyne > benzene > hexane [1]

12. (i) 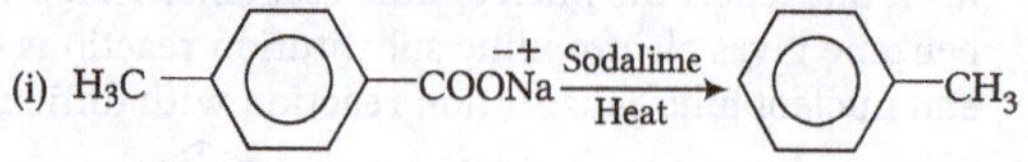

Toluene [1]

(ii) 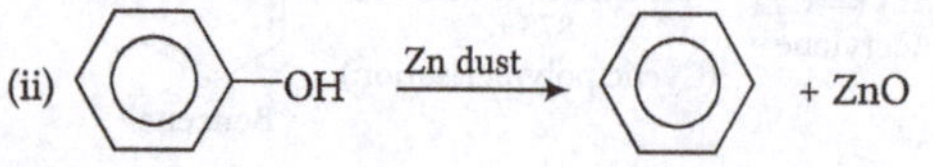

Benzene [1]

13. 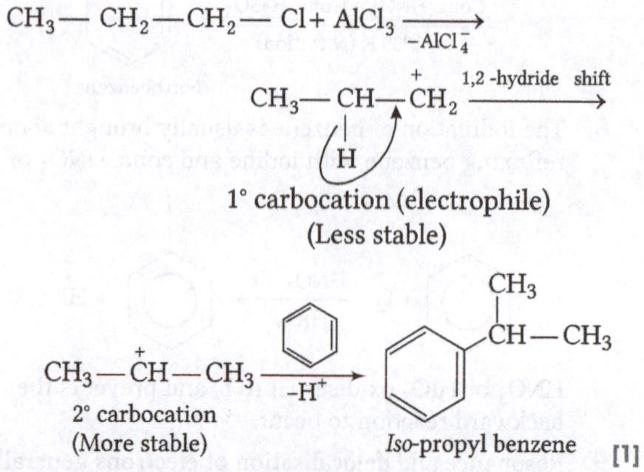

[1]

When Friedel Crafts alkylation is carried out with higher alkyl halide, e.g. *n*-propyl chloride, the electrophile, *n*-propyl carbocation (1° carbocation) rearranges to form more stable *iso*-propyl carbocation (2° carbocation) and the main product formed will be *iso*-propyl benzene. [1]

14. Halogens are moderately deactivating group. Because of their strong –*I* effect, overall electron density on benzene ring decreases. However, due to resonance the electron density on *o* and *p*-positions is greater than that at *m*-position.
Hence, they are also *o* and *p*-directing groups.

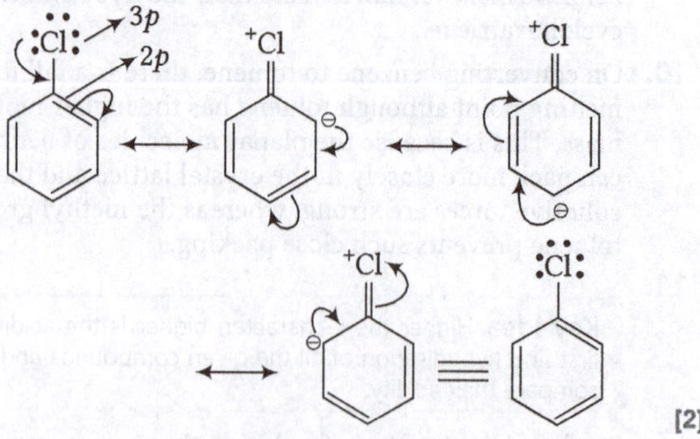

[2]

15. Alkenes are rich source of loosely held π-electrons, due to which they show electrophilic addition reaction. Electrophilic addition reactions of alkenes are accompanied by large energy changes so these are energetically favourable than that of electrophilic substitution reactions.
In special conditions alkenes also undergo free radical substitution reactions. [1]

In arenes during electrophilic addition reactions aromatic character of benzene ring is destroyed while during electrophilic substitution reactions it remains intact. Electrophilic substitution reactions of arenes are energetically more favourable than that of electrophilic addition reaction. That's why alkenes prefer to undergo electrophilic addition reaction while arenes prefer electrophilic substitution reactions. [1]

16.

> **Key Idea** Nitration is an electrophilic substitution reaction and reactivity of benzene nucleus towards E^+ decreases in the presence of electron withdrawing group while increases in the presence of electron releasing group.

Nitration of benzene is an electrophilic substitution reaction. Presence of electron releasing group such as — CH_3 activates the benzene nucleus towards electrophilic substitution while presence of electron withdrawing group such as —NO_2 deactivates the benzene nucleus towards electrophilic substitution. Therefore, the ease of nitration decreases in the order :

Toluene > benzene > *m*-dinitrobenzene

Thus, toluene will undergo nitration most easily. [2]

17. A. The compound has 8π-electrons. It will be non-aromatic. Both rings are non-benzenoid (delocalisation of e^-s is not possible).

B. The compound is aromatic. It has $6\pi e^-$ delocalised electron ($4\pi e^-$ + 2 lone pair electrons), all the four carbon atoms and the N-atom are sp^2-hybridised.

C. The compound contains 6π-electrons but not in the ring hence it is non-aromatic.

D. 10π electron obeying Huckel rule and the ring is planar. It is aromatic.

E. In this compound, one six membered planar ring has 6π electron although it has 8π-electrons in two rings. It is therefore aromatic.

F. It has 14π-electrons in conjugation and in the planar ring, Huckel rule is verified. It will be aromatic.

[6 × 1/2]

18.

> **Key Idea** For a molecule to be aromatic. It should be planar, i.e. all the carbons are sp^2-hybridised. It contains $(4n + 2)$ π-electron.

(i) The molecule is non-planar because of the presence of sp^3 hybridised carbon atom. It contains six π-electrons but its π-electron cloud does not surround all the carbon atoms of the ring. Therefore, it is non-aromatic compound. [1]

(ii) The molecule is not planar because of the presence of sp^3-hybridised carbon atom Moreover, it contains only 4π-electrons. Thus, the molecule is not aromatic as it does not contain planar cyclic electron cloud, having $(4n+2)$ π-electrons. [1]

(iii) Cyclo octatetraene is non-planar with 8π-electrons and hence, it is not aromatic. [1]

19.

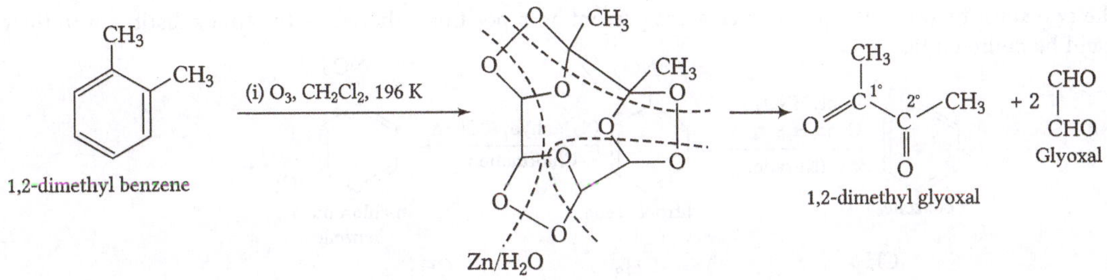

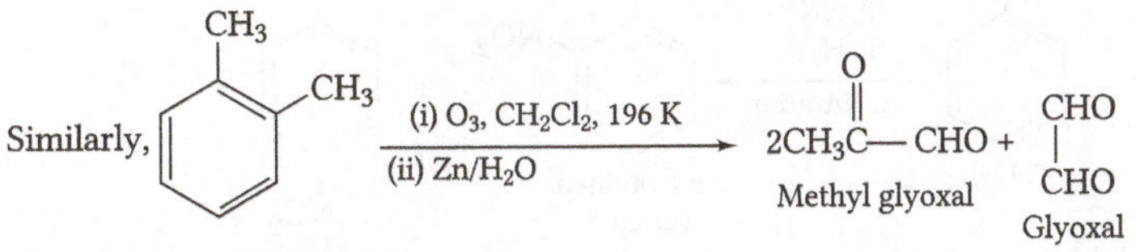

[2]

All the three products cannot be obtained from any one of the two Kekule structures. This indicates that *o*-xylene is a resonance hybrid of two Kekule structures I and II.

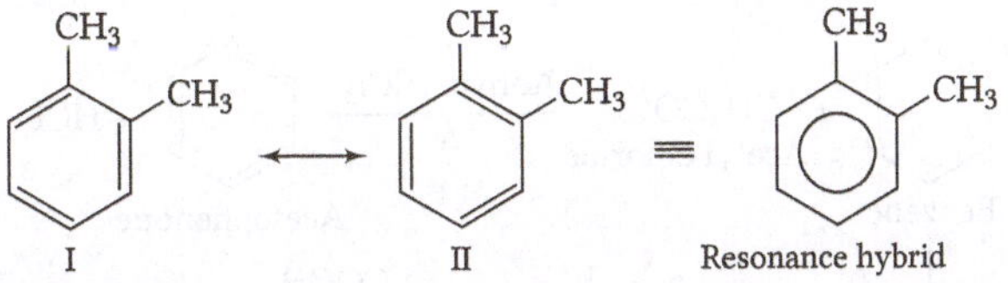

[1]

20. Presence of electron releasing group (or activating group) increases the electron density in benzene nucleus. Therefore, electrophile will attack benzene nucleus easily. But, the presence of electron withdrawing group like $—NO_2$ decreases the electron density in benzene ring. Therefore, electrophile will attack benzene nucleus with difficulty. The order of reactivity towards electrophile, E^+ in order of their decreasing relative reactivity is

(i) Chlorobenzene > *p*-nitrochlorobenzene > 2, 4-dinitrochlorobenzene [2]

(ii) Toluene> *p*-$CH_3—C_6H_4—NO_2$ >*p*-$O_2N—C_6H_4—NO_2$

[1]

21. 7-bromo-1, 3, 5-cycloheptatriene, on ionisation, gives tropylium ion. Since, tropylium ion contains 6π-electrons which are completely delocalised, therefore, according to Huckel rule, it is aromatic and hence stable. Being highly stable, it is easily formed. [1]

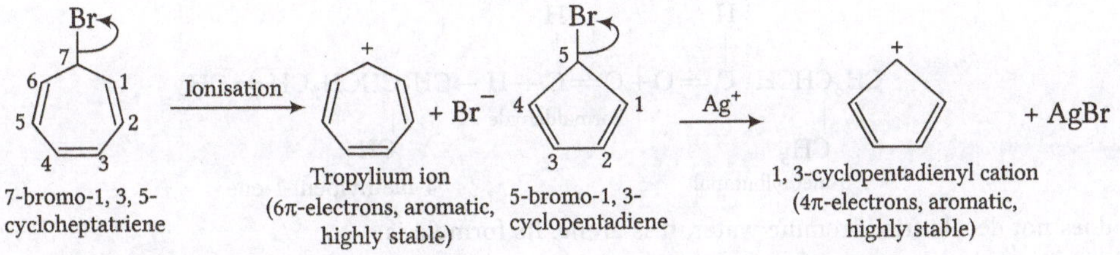

[1]

In contrast, 5-bromo-1,3-cyclopentadiene, on ionisation, will give 1, 3-cyclopentadienyl cation which contains 4 π-electrons and hence, is anti-aromatic. Being anti-aromatic, it is highly unstable and hence is not formed even in the presence of Ag^+ ion which otherwise facilitates ionisation. [1]

22. (i) Since, the two substituents in the benzene ring are present at *p*-position, therefore, the first substituent in the benzene ring should be an *o*, *p*-directing group

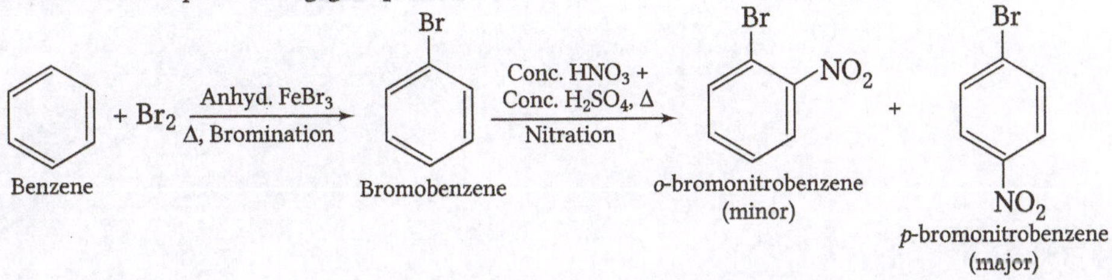

[1]

(ii) Since, the two substituents in the benzene ring are present at *m*-positions, therefore, the first substituent in the benzene ring should be *m*-directing.

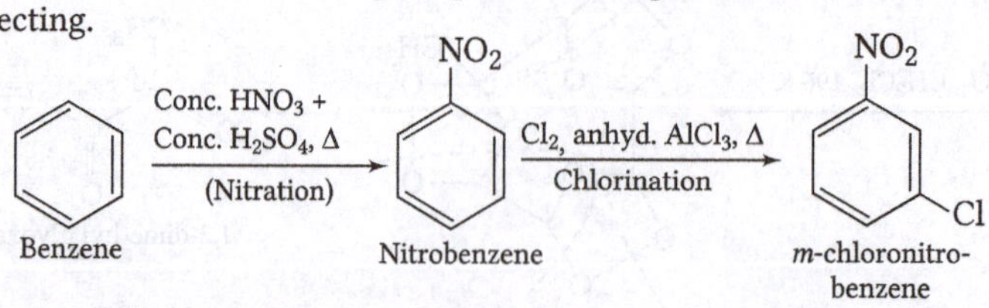

[1]

(iii)

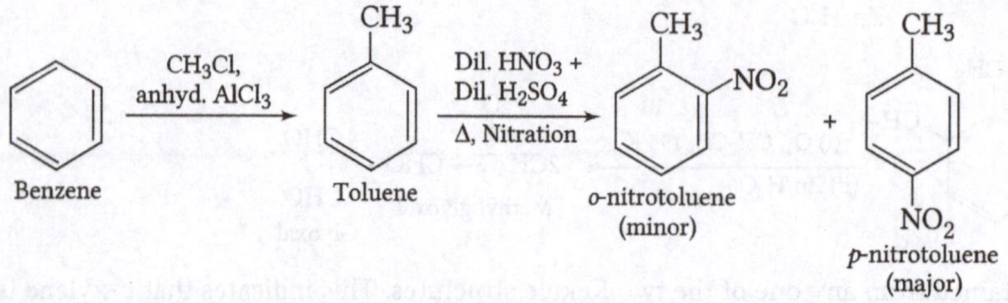

[1]

(iv) Acetophenone can be prepared by Friedel Crafts acylation.

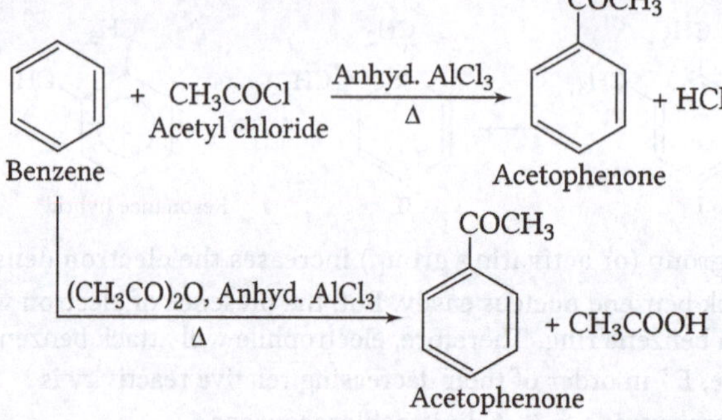

[2]

23. (i) Alkyne *X* is C_5H_8. Since, it does not react with sodamide or ammoniacal cuprous chloride, the triple bond cannot be terminal.

∴ *X* is $CH_3CH_2C\equiv CCH_3$ Pent-2-yne [1]

(ii) Hydrocarbon '*Y*' is alkene because it decolourises bromine water. From the products of ozonolysis, the structure of alkene can be predicted.

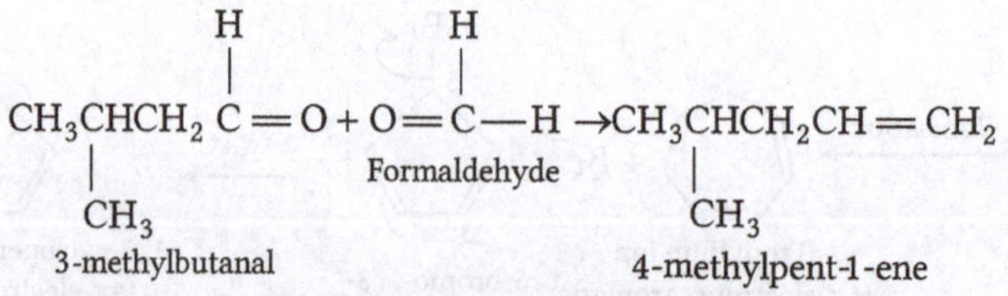

[2]

(iii) Since, it does not decolourise bromine water, it is arene. Its formula is

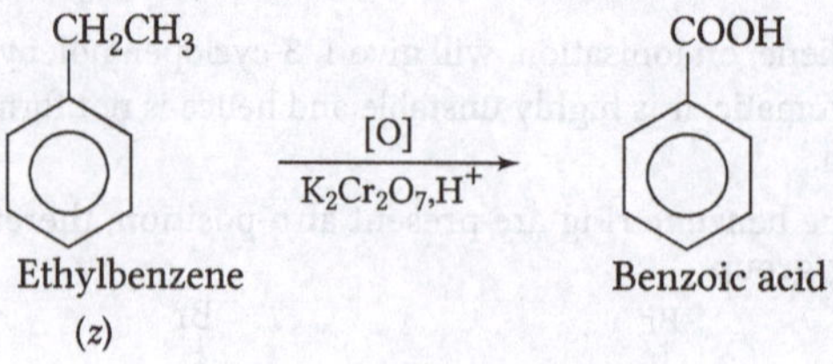

[2]

The other three isomers are

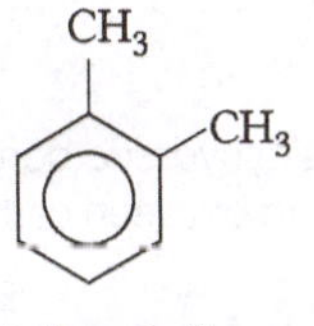

1, 2-dimethylbenzene
(*o*-xylene)

(*A*)

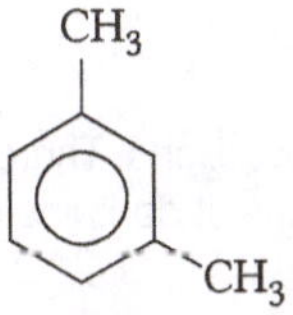

1, 3-dimethylbenzene
(*m*-xylene)

(*B*)

1, 4-dimethylbenzene
(*p*-xylene)

(*C*)

[2]

24.

	Compound	Planar ring	Complete delocalisation of π-electron	Huckel rule (4*n* + 2) π electron	Aromatic or non-aromatic
A.		✓	✓	6π e⁻ Huckel rule obeyed	Aromatic
B.		×	× Incomplete (sp^3-hybrid carbon)	6πe⁻	Non-aromatic
C.		✓	✓	6πe⁻ (4*n* + 2+lone pair e⁻) Huckel rule obeyed	Aromatic
D.	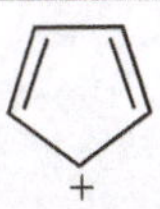	✓	×	4πe⁻	Anti-aromatic
E.	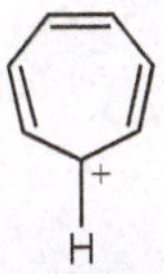	✓	✓	6πe⁻ Huckel rule obeyed	Aromatic
F.		✓	✓	(2πe⁻) *n* = 0 Huckel rule obeyed	Aromatic
G.	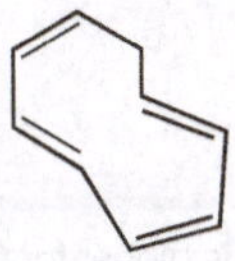	✓	×	8πe⁻ Huckel rule not obeyed	Non-aromatic

SUMMARY

- Compounds of carbon and hydrogen are known as hydrocarbons. There are two types of hydrocarbons; saturated and unsaturated.
- **Saturated hydrocarbons** (Alkanes) also called as paraffins. It contains only single bond between carbon atoms. It's general formula C_nH_{2n+2}. e.g. methane (CH_4), ethane (C_2H_6) etc.

Structure They have tetrahedral geometry with sp^3-hybridisation and 109°28′ bond angle.

Nomenclature Root word + ane = alkane (name).

Isomerism Exhibit only chain isomerism if when 4 or more C-atoms are present.

Preparation

(i) $CH_2{=}CH_2 + H_2 \xrightarrow{Ni/Pt/Pd} CH_3{-}CH_3$ (ethane)

(ii) $R{-}Cl \xrightarrow{Zn,\ H_2} R{-}H + HCl$

(iii) $2R{-}Cl \xrightarrow[\text{dry ether}]{2Na} R{-}R$

(iv) $RMg{-}X + H_2O \longrightarrow R{-}H + Mg(OH)X$

(v) $R\cdot CO\bar{O}\overset{+}{Na} \xrightarrow{NaOH + CaO} R{-}H$

(vi) $RCO\bar{O}\overset{+}{Na} \xrightarrow{\text{Electrolysis}} R{-}R$ (at anode)

Properties

(i) Boiling and melting points increases with molar mass and boiling point decreases with branching.

(ii) $CH_4 \xrightarrow[h\nu]{Cl_2} CH_3{-}Cl + HCl$ (Halogenation)

(iii) $C_nH_{2n+2} + \frac{(3n+1)}{2}O_2 \longrightarrow n\cdot CO_2 + (n+1)H_2O$

(iv) $CH_4 + O_2 \xrightarrow[Mo/O_2]{Cu} CH_3OH$

(v) n-alkane $\xrightarrow{AlCl_3(\text{anhy.})}$ Branched alkane

(vi) n-alkane $\xrightarrow[\text{Or } v_2O_5]{Cr_2O_3}$ Aromatic hydrocarbon

(vii) Higher alkane $\xrightarrow[973\ K]{\text{Pd or Pt}}$ Aromatic hydrocarbon

Conformations are different arrangements due to rotation of C—C bond.

(i) **Staggered** The most stable form in which groups are as far apart as possible.

(ii) **Eclipsed** The least stable form in which groups are as close as possible.

(iii) **Skew or Gauche** Intermediate conformation.

- **Unsaturated Hydrocarbons** have atleast one (=) or (≡) bond.
- **Alkenes** also called olefins and have atleast one (=) bond. Its general formula is C_nH_{2n}.

Structure Double bonded C are sp^2-hybridised with trigonal planer shape and 120° angle.

Nomenclature Root word + ene.

Isomerism They exhibit position and chain isomerism.

They also exhibit geometrical isomerism which is shown by the compounds of the type $y\cdot x\cdot c = cx\cdot y$ or $x\cdot yc = c\cdot x\cdot z$.
In *cis* form same groups lie on same side and in trans form they lie on opposite sides.

Preparation

(i) $R{-}C{\equiv}C{-}R \xrightarrow[H_2]{Pd/C}$ *cis*-alkene.

(ii) Alkyne $\xrightarrow[\text{Liq. } NH_3]{Na}$ *trans*-alkene.

(iii) $CH_3{-}CH_2X \xrightarrow[-HX]{KOH(alc.)} CH_2{=}CH_2$

(iv) $CH_3{-}CH_2OH \xrightarrow[170°C]{H_2SO_4} CH_2{=}CH_2 + H_2O$

Properties

(i) Their boiling and melting point increases with increase in molar mass. Boiling point of *cis*-form is higher but melting point is higher for *trans* form.

(ii) $CH_2 = CH_2 + HBr \longrightarrow CH_3{-}CH_2{-}Br$, (–)ve part goes to that C-atom which has less H-atom but in the presence of peroxide opposite is true.

(iii) Alkene + $H_2O \longrightarrow$ alcohol.

(iv) $CH_2 = CH_2 + H_2O + O \xrightarrow[273\ K]{KMnO_4\ (dil)} CH_2(OH){-}CH_2(OH)$

(v) $R{-}CH{=}CH{-}R + O_3 \xrightarrow{Zn/H_2O} 2R{-}CHO$

(vi) n-alkene $\xrightarrow{\text{High } T \text{ and } P}$ Polythene.

- **Alkynes** Have at least one (≡) bond. General formula is C_nH_{2n-2}.

Structure Triple bonded C-are sp-hybridised with linear shape and 180° bond angle.

Nomenclature Root word + yne.

Isomerism Exhibit chain and position isomerism.

Preparation

(i) $CaC_2 + 2H_2O \longrightarrow Ca(OH)_2 + C_2H_2$ (ii) $CH_2—Br—CH_2Br \xrightarrow{NaNH_2} CH \equiv CH$

Properties

(i) Their melting and boiling points increases with increase in molecular mass.

(ii) These are lighter than water.

(iii) These are acidic due to the presence of H-atom at ($\equiv$) bonded C-atoms. Some chemical reactions are as follows :

$$CH_3\ C \equiv CH \xrightarrow{Na/NaNH_2} CH_3C \equiv C^-\ Na^+$$

(iv) $—C \equiv C— \xrightarrow{Br_2} —C(Br_2)—C(Br_2)—$ (v) $—C \equiv C— \xrightarrow{Hg^{2+}/H^+} —CH = C(OH)— \xrightarrow{\text{Isomerisation}} CH_2—C(=O)—$

(vi) Polymerisation n-acetylene $\longrightarrow$ Polyacetylene (vii) Acetylene $\xrightarrow[\text{Red hot iron tube}]{873\text{ K}}$ Benzene.

- **Aromatic hydrocarbons** Cyclic compounds having benzene nucleus.

Aromaticity For a compound to be aromatic. It must be cyclic, planar, have conjugate system and $(4n + 2)\pi \cdot e^-$ (Huckel's rule).

Benzene is C_6H_6. Due to resonance in it, all the C—C bond length are equal. All carbons are sp^2-hybridised.

Preparation

(i) $CH \equiv CH \xrightarrow[1500°C]{\text{Red hot tube}}$ Benzene (ii)

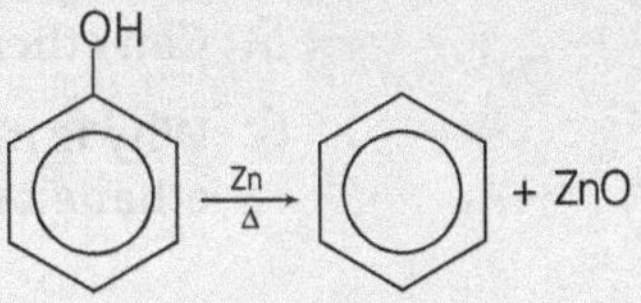

Properties

(i) They burn with sooty flame.

(ii) Various chemical reaction are as follows

(a) $C_6H_6 \xrightarrow{HNO_3\ (conc.) H_2SO_4} C_6H_5—NO_2$ (b) $C_6H_6 + Cl_2 \xrightarrow{AlCl_3(anhy.)} C_6H_5—Cl$ (Electrophile $= Cl^+$)

(c) $C_6H_6 + CH_3Cl \xrightarrow{AlCl_3(anhy.)} C_6H_5—CH_3$ (toluene) (d) $C_6H_6 + CH_3COCl \xrightarrow{AlCl_3(anhy.)} C_6H_5—COCH_3$

(e) $C_6H_6 + 3H_2 \xrightarrow[\Delta]{Ni} C_6H_{12}$ (f) $C_6H_6 + 3Cl_2 \xrightarrow[500\text{ K}]{UV} C_6H_5—Cl_6$(BHC)

- **Directive Influence of functional groups towards electrophilic substitution.**

(i) $—NH_2$, $—NHR$, $—NHCOCH_3$, —OH, $—CH_3$, $—C_2H_5$ etc; are o/p-directing activating groups.

(ii) Halogens are o/p directing but deactivating.

(iii) $—NO_2$, —CN, —CHO, —COOH, $—SO_3H$, —CO etc., are *meta*-directing and deactivating groups.

Chapter Practice

Very Short answer Type Questions

1 Mark

1. Fill in the Blanks

(i) The fluorination of alkane is a............process.

(ii) Alkenes exhibit geometrical isomerism due to the possibility of different............arrangements in space, as rotation around the double bond is restrictd, not free.

(iii) Baeyer's reagent is............

(iv) NO_2 group is............directing group.

2. Objective Type Questions

(i) Major product A of the reaction is

$$(CH_3)_2C{=}CH_2 \xrightarrow{ICl} A$$

(a) 2-chloro-1-iodo-2-methyl propane
(b) 1-chloro-2-iodo-2-methyl propane
(c) 1, 2-dichloro-2-methyl propane
(d) 1, 2-diiodo-2-methyl propane

(ii) Which one of the following has the minimum boiling point?

(a) *n*-butane (b) 1-butyne
(c) 1-butene (d) *Iso*-butene

(iii) Which of the following compounds has a double bond that is conjugated with the π-system of the benzene ring?

(a) *p*-benzyltoluene
(b) 2-phenyl-1-butene
(c) 3-phenylcyclohexene
(d) 3-phenyl-1,4-pentadiene

(iv) Out of resonance stabilised compounds are

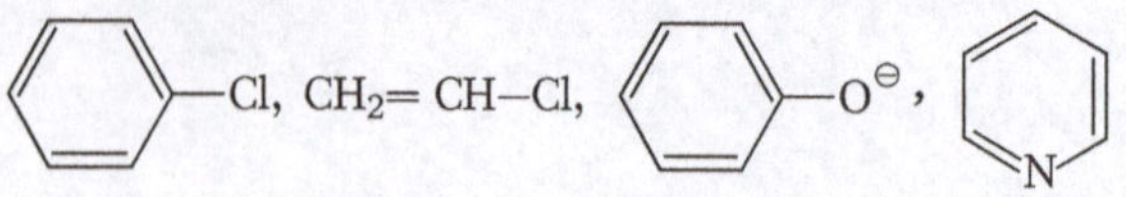

I II III IV

(a) Both I and II (b) I, III and IV
(c) I, II, III and IV (d) II, III and IV

3. Match the hydrocarbons in Column I with the properties shown by them in Column II and choose the correct option using the codes given below.

Column I	Column II
A. Ethyne	(i) Reacts with 1 mole H_2 to form alkane
B. Propyne	(ii) Reacts with 2 moles H_2 to form alkane
C. Cyclopropane	(iii) Reacts with Cu_2Cl_2/NH_4OH
D. Cyclobutene	(iv) Has sp^3 and sp-hybridised carbon

Codes

	A	B	C	D		A	B	C	D
(a)	(iv)	(i)	(ii)	(iii)	(b)	(ii)	(iii)	(i)	(iv)
(c)	(i)	(iv)	(ii)	(iii)	(d)	(ii)	(i)	(iii)	(iv)

4. What is electrophile in sulphonation reactions?

5. Can ethene show conformations? Why?

6. Why is it not possible to have pure staggered ethane or pure eclipsed ethane?

Assertion-Reason

Directions (Q. Nos. 7-11) In the following questions, a statement of assertion is followed by a corresponding statements of reason of the following statements, choose the correct one.

(a) Both (A) and (R) are correct and (R) is the correct explanation of (A).
(b) Both (A) and (R) are correct but (R) is not the correct explanation of (A).
(c) (A) is correct but (R) is incorrect.
(d) (A) is incorrect but (R) is correct.

7. **Assertion** (A) The boiling point of alkanes increases steadily with increase in size of chain.

Reason (R) Greater the length of the chain, greater is the surface area and hence, larger the van der Waals' attractive forces.

8. **Assertion** (A) Cyclopropane is easily reduced to propane.

Reason (R) There is cleavage of C—C bond due to strain in cyclopropane.

9. **Assertion** (A) Among isomeric pentanes, 2, 2-dimethylpentane has the lower boiling point.

Reason (R) Branching in hydrocarbon does not affect the boiling point.

10. **Assertion** (A) CH_4 does not react with Cl_2 in dark.

Reason (R) Chlorination of CH_4 takes place in sunlight.

11. **Assertion** (A) Addition of HBr on 2-butene does not give isomeric products.

Reason (R) Addition of HBr on 2-butene follows Markownikoff's rule.

Case-Study

12. Alkenes generally undergo electrophilic addition reactions because of the presence of a double bond (a strong σ and a weaker π-bond), π-electrons which being loosely held are easily polarised. These reactions involve cleavage of a π-bond and formation of two new σ-bonds.

In polar solvents, addition proceed by ionic mechanism (at low temperature), whereas in the presence of light or non-polar solvents, the addition occurs by free radical mechanism (at high temperature).

Apart from addition reactions alkenes also participate in the oxidation, ozonolysis and polymerisation reaction.

(i) Give the reaction of 1-butene with HBr in the presence of a peroxide.

(ii) Name the organic products of the reaction of but -2-ene with bromine dissolved in tetrachloromethane

(iii) Write the reaction of polymerisation of ethylene.

13. Aromaticity is defined as a property of the conjugated cycloalkenes which enhances the stability of a molecule due to the delocalisation of electrons present in the π-π orbitals.

Aromatic molecules are said to be very stable and they do not break so easily and also reacts with other types of substances. The organic compounds which are not said to be aromatic are known as aliphatic compounds. These might be in cyclic form, but only the aromatic rings have a special kind of stability.

We encounter aromaticity in our day-to-day lives. Even our bodies function with the help of certain aromatic compounds.

Aromatic compounds are essential in the industry and around 35 million tonnes of these compounds are known to be produced worldwide every year in the form of polymers and chemicals, such as the nylon and polyester. These compounds are important even in the field of the biochemistry of all the living things.

Aromatic compounds are less stable compounds and they have many kinds of chemicals as well as synthetic uses.

In fact, the nucleic acids and the amino acids that make up our cell structure make use of these aromatic compounds. But, the main thing is what makes aromatic compounds? The aromatic compounds are said to exhibit some special characteristics or called as rules which are given below.

- The aromatic compounds are always cyclic structures.
- Each element of the ring within the structure must and should have a *p*-orbital ring which is in perpendicular form to the ring and this makes it a planar molecule.
- All the compounds obey the Huckel's rule, i.e. all the aromatic compounds should have the $(4n+2)\pi$ number of electrons.
- The last one is that the organic compound has to be flat.

(i) Why C_6H_6 doesn't undergo addition like all alkenes?

(ii) Which of the following follows Huckel's rule?

A. 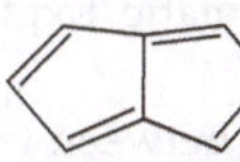 B. 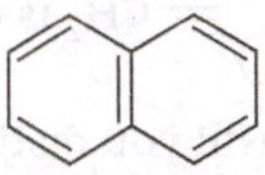

(iii) Explain why 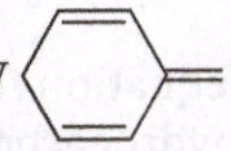 CH_2 is not aromatic.

Short Answer Type I Questions

2 Marks

14. Write the structures for the compound having the following IUPAC names

(i) 3-ethyl-2-methyl pentane

(ii) 3, 4, 8-trimethyl decane

15. Starting from ethanoic acid, how will you prepare

(i) methane (ii) ethane

16. Complete the following and give IUPAC name of the major product

(i) $CH_3—\underset{\displaystyle CH_3}{\underset{|}{C}}=CH_2 + HCl \longrightarrow$

(ii) 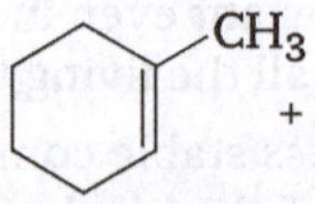 $+ HBr \longrightarrow$

17. What are addition reactions ? Which of the following will not give the addition reactions and why?
Propane, propyne, propene, benzene.

18. Explain, the mechanism of electrophilic addition reactions of alkenes.

19. A hydrocarbon '*X*' takes up two molecules of hydrogen and is converted into a saturated hydrocarbon. On ozonolysis, *X* gives a mixture of three carbonyl compounds namely, acetaldehyde, acetone and propan-1, 3-dial. Assign structure to compound *X*.

20. Explain the term polymerisation with two examples.

21. Show the formation of the electrophile in the following reactions

(i) $Cl_2 + FeCl_3$ (ii) $HNO_3 + H_2SO_4$
(iii) $Br_2 + Fe$ (iv) H_2SO_4

Short Answer Type II Questions
3 Marks

22. (i) 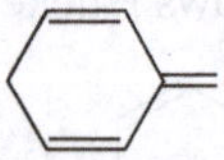 $=CH_2$ is not aromatic. Explain.

(ii) How will you distinguish between 1-butene and butane?

(iii) Write chemical equation for combustion reaction of the hydrocarbon pentene.

23. (i) Arrange HCl, HBr, HI and HF in order of decreasing reactivity towards alkene.

(ii) Give a chemical test to distinguish between ethane and ethyne.

24. (i) Write chemical equation for combustion reaction of the following hydrocarbons.

(a) Butane (b) Pentene

(ii) Identify *A* and *B*

$$CaC_2 \xrightarrow{H_2O} A \xrightarrow[\text{(ii) } B]{\text{(i) } 2NaNH_2} CH_3—C\equiv C—CH_3$$

25. (i) Explain how —OH is *o* and *p*-directing group whereas $—NO_2$ is *m*-directing.

(ii) What conclusion is drawn from the fact that benzene forms a single C_6H_5Br product when it is monobrominated?

(iii) How does benzene react with fuming sulphuric acid ? Give reaction.

26. How will you convert benzene into

(i) acetophenone and
(ii) methyl benzene

27. Explain the terms substitution and addition reactions? Methane gives substitution reaction while ethylene gives addition reaction. Justify the statement giving two examples in each case.

28. Explain the following :

(i) Friedel-Crafts acylation
(ii) Kolbe's electrolytic method.

Long Answer Type Questions
5 Marks

29. (i) Which one is more polar, *cis*-2-butene or *trans*-2-butene.

(ii) If one mole of HBr is added to the following compounds, write down the structures of the product/products expected to the formed.

(a) Buta-1, 3-diene (b) Penta-1, 3-diene
(c) Penta-1, 2-diene (d) Buyhept-1-ene.

Answers

1. (i) violent (ii) geometrical
(iii) cold, dilute (1%) alkaline solution of $KMnO_4$.
(iv) *Meta*

2. (i) → (a), (ii) → (d), (iii) → (b), (iv) → (c),

3. (a) A → (iv), B → (i), C → (ii), D → (iii)

4. SO_3^+

5. Ethene cannot show conformations due to the presence of double bond. The bond rotation is restricted around the double bond.

6. Refer to text on page 416 (Topic-1, Conformations).

7. (*a*) Both (A) and (R) are correct and (R) is the correct explanation of (A).

8. (*a*) Both (A) and (R) are correct and (R) is the correct explanation of (A).

9. (*c*) (A) is correct and (R) is incorrect.
On branching in hydrocarbon, boiling point decreases.

10. (*b*) Both (A) and (R) are correct but (R) is not the correct explanation of (A).

Chlorination of CH_4 does not take place in dark, free radicals can be generated only in the presence of sunlight as this reaction follows free radical mechanism and which is necessary for the reaction to proceed further.

11. (*a*) (A) is correct and (R) is incorrect. As 2-butene is a symmetrical molecular, thus it does not give any isomer and also Markownikoff's rule is not applicable in this case (applicable for unsymmetrical alkene).

12. (i) The complete reaction is given below.

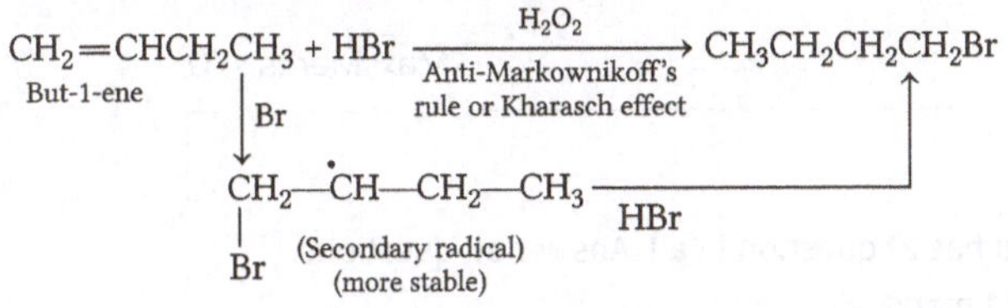

(ii) $CH_3—CH=CH—CH_3 + HBr \longrightarrow CH_3—\underset{\underset{Br}{|}}{CH}—CH_2—CH_3$

But-2-ene 2-bromobutane

(iii) Alkenes in the presence of trace of oxygen and at high temperature and pressure undergo self addition.

$$nCH_2=CH_2 \xrightarrow[\text{traces of } O_2]{473\text{ K, 1500 atm}} -\!\!\left(CH_2—CH_2\right)\!\!-_n$$

13. (i) C_6H_6 being on aromatic compound does not react with any electrophile like alkene as then it would lose its aromaticity which makes the compound very stable.

(ii) Only*B* follows Huckel's rule. According to Huckel's rule, all aromatic compounds should have $(4n+2)\pi$ electrons *B* has 10 electron or 5π bonds.

$\therefore \quad 4n+2=10 \Rightarrow 4n=8$

$\Rightarrow \quad n=2$

As *n* is a natural number *B* follows Huckel's rule.

(iii) The molecule is non-planar because of the presence of sp^3-hybridised carbon atom. It contains six π-electron cloud does not surround all the carbon atoms of the ring. Therefore, it is not an aromatic compound.

14.

(i) $CH_3—\overset{\overset{CH_3}{|}}{CH}—\overset{\overset{C_2H_5}{|}}{CH}—CH_2—CH_3$

(ii) $CH_3CH_2—\underset{\underset{CH_3}{|}}{CH}—CH_2CH_2CH_2—\underset{\underset{CH_3}{|}}{CH}$

$—\underset{\underset{CH_3}{|}}{CH}—CH_2CH_3$

15. (i) Refer to text on page 413 (Topic-1, Preparation from carboxylic acid decarboxylation).

(ii) Refer to text on page 413 (Topic-1, Kolbe's electrolysis).

16. (i) Refer to text on pages 426 and 427 (Topic-2, Addition of hydrogen halides).

(ii) Refer to text on pages 426 and 427 (Topic-2, Addition of hydrogen halides).

17. Refer to text on page 426 (Topic-2, Chemical properties of alkenes).

18. Refer to text on page 427 (Topic-2, Chemical properties of alkenes).

19. The three compounds obtained are :

CH_3CHO, $CH_3\overset{\overset{O}{\|}}{CH}CH_3$ $OHC—CH_2—CHO$

The alkene is

$CH_3CH=CH—CH_2—CH=\overset{\overset{CH_3}{|}}{CH}—CH_3$

20. Refer to text on page 429 (Topic-2, Polymerisation).

21. Refer to text on page 446 and 447 (Topic-4, Chemical properties).

22. (i) Refer to text on page 452 Q. Nos. 18(i) Part.

(ii) Butene decolourises Br_2/CCl_4 water, while butane does not decolurises it.

(iii) Refer to text on page 428 (Topic-2, Oxidation).

23. (i) Refer to text on pages 426 and 427 (Topic-2, Addition of hydrogen halide).

(ii) Refer to text on page 439 and 440 (Topic-3, Distinguishing Test between Alkane, Alkene, Alkynes).

24. (i) Refer to text on page 415 (Topic-1, Combustion).

(ii) Refer to text on page 436. (Topic-3 Methods of preparations (1) from calcium carbide)

25. (i) Refer to text on page 448 and 449 (Topic-4) *Ortho* and *Para*-directing groups.

(ii) Refer to text on pages 446 and 447 (Topic-4, Halogenation).

(iii) Refer to text on page 447 (Topic-4, Sulphonation).

26. (i) Refer to text on page 447 (Topic-4, Friedal-Crafts acylation).

(ii) Refer to text on page 447 (Topic-4, Friedel-Crafts alkylation).

27. (i) Refer to text on page 414 (Topic-1, Substitution reactions).

(ii) Refer to text on page 426 (Topic-2, Chemical properties of alkenes).

28. (i) Refer to text on page 447 (Topic-4, Friedel-Crafts acylation).

(ii) Refer to text on page 425 (Topic-2, From salt of carboxylic acid).

29. (i) Refer to text on page 426 (Topic-2, Physical properties).

(ii) Refer to text on pages 426 and 427 (Topic-2, Addition of hydrogen halides).

SAMPLE QUESTION PAPER 1

A Highly Simulated Sample Question Paper for ISC Class XI

CHEMISTRY (Fully Solved)

FULLY SOLVED

Time : 3 hours | **Max. Marks : 70**

GENERAL INSTRUCTIONS

- This paper is divided into four Section A, B, C and D and has 21 question in all. Answer all questions.
- **Section A** has fourteen subparts. Each question carries 1 mark.
- While attempting **Multiple Choice Questions** in Section A, you are required to write only ONE option as the answer.
- **Section B** has **ten question**. Each question carries 2 marks.
- **Section C** has **seven questions**. Each question carries 3 marks.
- **Section D** has **three questions**. Each question carries 5 marks.
- Internal choices have been provided in **one question each in Section B, C and D.**
- The intended marks for questions are given in brackets [].
- All working, including rough work, should be done on the same sheet as, and adjacent to the rest of the answer.
- Balanced equations must be given wherever possible and diagrams where they are helpful.
- When solving numerical problems, all essential working must be shown.
- In working out problems, use the following data:
  Gas constant $R = 1.987$ cal deg^{-1} mol^{-1} = 8.314 J K^{-1} mol^{-1} = 0.0821 dm^3 atm K^{-1} mol^{-1},
  1 L atm = 1 dm^3 atm = 101.3 J, 1 Faraday = 96500 coulombs. **Avogadro's number** = 6.023×10^{23}.

Section-A

[14 Marks]

1. (A) Fill in the blanks by choosing the appropriate word(s) from those given in the brackets. **[4 × 1]**

[subshell, main shell, increases, decreases, isobaric, orbitals, isothermal, adiabatic, matter, mass, heat, energy, Dalton, SO_2, CO_2, O_3]

(i) ...... and ...... are mainly produced by burning of fossil fuels. *• Recall*

(ii) Principal quantum number and azimuthal quantum number represents .... and .... respectively. *• Recall*

(iii) Electronegativity generally .... across a period and .... on moving down a group. *• Understanding*

(iv) An open system can exchange .... as well as .... with its surroundings. *• Recall*

(B) Select and write the correct alternative from the choices given below. **[7 × 1]**

(i) The ratio of K_p/K_C for the reaction,

$CO(g) + \frac{1}{2}O_2(g) \rightleftharpoons CO_2(g)$, is *• Application*

(a) 1 (b) RT

(c) $(RT)^{1/2}$ (d) $(RT)^{-1/2}$

(ii) If 500 mL of a 5M solution is diluted to 1500 mL, what will be the molarity of the solution obtained?

(a) 1.5 M (b) 1.66 M

(c) 0.017 M (d) 1.59 M

• *Evaluate*

(iii) Which of the following ions forms a hydroxide highly soluble in water? • *Understanding*

(a) Ni^{2+} (b) K^{+}

(c) Zn^{2+} (d) Al^{3+}

(iv) Number of angular nodes for $4d$ orbital is • *Evaluate*

(a) 4 (b) 3

(c) 2 (d) 1

(v) The valence bond theory explains the shape, the formation and directional properties of bonds of polyatomic molecules like CH_4, NH_3 and H_2O, etc., in terms of • *Recall*

(a) overlapping of atomic orbitals

(b) hybridisation of atomic orbitals

(c) Both (a) and (b)

(d) dipole moment

(vi) **Assertion** F—F bond has low bond dissociation energy.

Reason The fluorine has least reactivity. • *Analysis*

(a) Both Assertion and Reason are true and Reason is the correct explanation of Assertion.

(b) Both Assertion and Reason are true but Reason is not correct explanation of Assertion.

(c) Assertion is true but Reason is false.

(d) Assertion is false but Reason is true.

(vii) **Assertion** The dissolution of NH_4Cl in water is endothermic but it dissolves in water.

Reason On dissolution of NH_4Cl, entropy increases. • *Analysis*

(a) Both Assertion and Reason are true and Reason is the correct explanation of Assertion.

(b) Both Assertion and Reason are true but Reason is not correct explanation of Assertion.

(c) Assertion is true but Reason is false.

(d) Assertion is false but Reason is true.

(C) Read the passage given below carefully and answer the questions that follow. [3 × 1]

Dipole moment is the measure of degree of polarity and is defined as the product of the magnitude of the charge and the distance between the centres of positive and negative charge. It is usually represented by a Greek letter μ (mu).

It is a result of polarisation.

Mathematically, it is expressed as:

Dipole moment (μ) = Charge (Q) × Distance of separation (r)

It is usually expressed in Debye units (D).

$1\ D = 3.33564 \times 10^{-30}$ C m

where, C is coulomb and m is metre.

or $1\ D = 1 \times 10^{-18}$ esu (or, stat C m)

Here, esu = electrostatic unit stat C cm = static coulomb centimeter

It is a vector quantity and is represented by the crossed arrow ($\leftarrow\!\!\!+\!\!\!\rightarrow$) pointing towards the more electronegative atom.

$\overset{+\!\!\rightarrow}{H - \ddot{F}:} \rightarrow$ More electronegative atom

This arrow symbolises the direction of the shift of electron density in the molecule.

(i) What is the relation between resultant dipole moment of NH_3 and NF_3? • *Analysis*

(ii) Why the dipole moments of CO_2, BF_3 and CCl_4 are zero? • *Understanding*

(iii) In BF_3, BeF_2 and H_2O, which have highest dipole moment? • *Analysis*

Section-B [20 Marks]

2. Explain the trend in the first ionisation energy of the transition elements. [2]
• *Understanding*

3. If bond energy for H — H and Cl—Cl bonds respectively are 430kJ/mol and 242 kJ/mol and heat of formation of HCl is –91 kJ/mol. • *Evaluate*
Calculate the bond energy of H—Cl bond. [2]

4. Complete the following reactions • *Understanding*

(i) *Iso*-propyl bromide $\xrightarrow[\text{Heat}]{\text{Alc. KOH}} A \xrightarrow[\text{Peroxide}]{\text{HBr}} B$

(ii) *n*-propyl alcohol $\xrightarrow[443\text{ K}]{\text{Conc. } H_2SO_4} A \xrightarrow[\text{Heat}]{O_2,\text{ Ag}} B$ [2]

Or Complete the following • *Understanding*

(i) 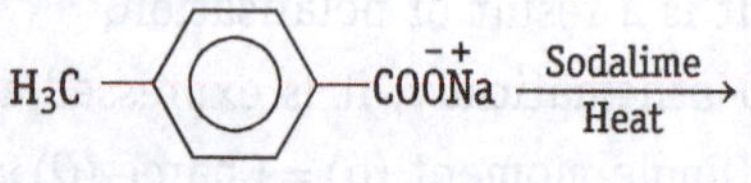

(ii) 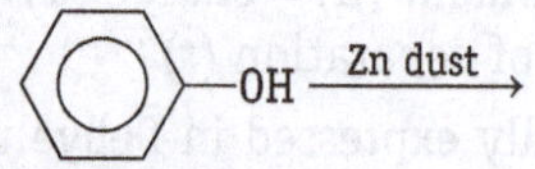

5. Compare the size of • *Understanding*

(i) Cl atom with Cl^- ion.

(ii) Na atom with Na^+ ion. [2]

6. Why does SO_3 act as an electrophile? [2]
• *Understanding*

7. Give a reason for the following. • *Understanding*

(i) $CH{=}\overset{\ominus}{C}H$ is more basic than $HC \equiv \overset{\ominus}{C}$.

(ii) Benzylic free radical is more stable than allylic free radical. [2]

8. Identify (*A*) and (*B*) in the following reaction:

$CH_3—CH_2—COOH \xrightarrow{\text{KOH}} (A) \xrightarrow{\text{Kolbe's electrolysis}} (B)$ [2]
• *Understanding*

9. Why Wurtz reaction is not preferred for the preparation of alkanes containing odd number of carbon atoms? Give one example. [2]
• *Analysis*

10. An alkane has molecular mass of 72, how many carbon atoms does the alkane molecule contain? [2]
• *Analysis*

11. An alkene gives propanal and pentan-3-one on ozonolysis, what is the name and structure formula of the alkane? [2]
• *Evaluate*

Section-C [21 Marks]

12. How will you convert benzene into

(i) *p*-bromonitrobenzene • *Understanding*

(ii) *m*-chloronitrobenzene

(iii) *p*-nitrotoluene [3]

13. Arrange the following according to bond length giving reasons. • *Analysis*

(i) H—F, H—Cl, H—Br, H—I

(ii) C— C, C=C, C≡C

(iii) C—H bond length in CH_4, C_2H_4 and C_2H_2 [3]

14. (i) Calculate total number of angular nodes and radial nodes present in 3*p*-orbital.
• *Evaluate*

(ii) How d_{xy} and $d_{x^2-y^2}$ orbitals are related?
• *Recall*

(iii) Nickel (Ni) atom can lose two electrons to give Ni^{2+} ion. From which orbital will nickel lose the electrons? (Z for Ni = 28) [3]
• *Analysis*

15. What are the features of long form of periodic table? [3]
• *Recall*

16. What are disproportional reactions? Explain with example. [3]
• *Recall*

Or Permaganate ions react with bromide ions in basic medium to give manganese dioxide and bromate ions. Write the balanced ionic equation for the said reaction. • *Recall*

17. For the reaction, $2A(g)+B(g) \longrightarrow 2D(g)$; $\Delta U° = -10.5$ kJ mol^{-1} and $\Delta S° = -44.1$ J K^{-1}. Calculate $\Delta G°$ for the reaction and predict whether the reaction may occur spontaneously. • *Application*
($R = 8.314 \times 10^{-3}$ kJ K^{-1}mol^{-1}, $T = 298$ K) [3]

18. (i) At 450 K, $K_p = 2 \times 10^{10}$/bar for the following reaction at equilibrium:
$$2SO_2(g) + O_2(g) \rightleftharpoons 2SO_3(g)$$
What is the K_c at this temperature? • *Application*

(ii) For the reaction,
$$2NO(g) + O_2(g) \rightleftharpoons 2NO_2(g), \Delta H = -117 \text{ kJ}.$$
(a) Predict the effect of increase in concentration of NO on the equilibrium concentration of NO_2. • *Analysis*

(b) Predict the effect of pressure decrease as a result of increased volume on equilibrium concentration of NO_2. [3] • *Analysis*

Section-D [15 Marks]

19. The ionisation constant of acetic acid is 1.74×10^{-5}. Calculate the degree of dissociation of acetic acid in its 0.05 M solution. Calculate the concentration of acetate ion in the solution and its pH. [5] • *Application*

Or Write short note on • *Recall*
(i) Bronsted-Lowry acids and bases.
(ii) Solubility product constant.

20. Discuss the shape of the following molecules using VSEPR model [5] • *Application*
$BeCl_2$, $SiCl_4$, AsF_5, H_2S, PH_3

21. (i) Write short note on aromaticity. • *Recall*
(ii) Show addition reaction in benzene. • *Understanding*
(iii) Write combustion reaction for benzene. • *Recall*
(iv) Give Friedel-Crafts alkylation of benzene. • *Recall*
(v) Show nitration of benzene. • *Recall* [5]

FULLY SOLVED

SOLUTIONS

1. (A) (i) SO_2, CO_2 (ii) main shell, subshell
(iii) increases, decreases (iv) matter, energy

(B) (i) (d)
$$\Delta n_g = 1 - \left(1 + \frac{1}{2}\right) = -\frac{1}{2}$$
$$\therefore \quad K_p = K_C(RT)^{-\frac{1}{2}}$$
$$\frac{K_p}{K_C} = (RT)^{-\frac{1}{2}}$$

(ii) (*b*) For dilution, a general formula is
$$\underset{\text{(Before dilution)}}{M_1V_1} = \underset{\text{(After dilution)}}{M_2V_2}$$
$$500 \times 5 \text{ M} = 1500 \times M$$
$$M = \frac{5}{3} = 1.66\text{M}$$

(iii) (b) Alkali metal hydroxides, i.e. KOH is highly soluble in water.

(iv) (c) Angular nodes = *l*. For 4*d*, *l* = 2, so angular nodes = 2

(v) (c) This theory was proposed by Heitler and London. The shape of molecules, overlapping of atomic orbitals and the hybridisation of atomic orbitals are explained by the valence bond theory.

(vi) (c) Fluorine is highly reactive because F—F bond has low bond dissociation energy.
Thus, Assertion is true but Reason is false.

(vii) (b) The dissolution of NH_4Cl in water is endothermic but it dissolves in water because on dissolution, entropy increases i.e., $\Delta S = +$ve. This increase in entropy outweights the energy absorbed as ΔH is + ve and $T\Delta S$ becomes greater than ΔH ($T\Delta S > \Delta H$). Then, according to the equation, $\Delta G = \Delta H - T\Delta S$, ΔG becomes – ve and the process is spontaneous.
Thus, both Assertion and Reason are true but Reason is not the correct explantion for Assertion.

(C) (i) The dipole moment of NH_3 is larger than NF_3 because in NH_3, the dipole moment vector of the bond and the lone pairs are in same direction, but in NF_3 these are opposite in direction. So, the net dipole moment will be the substractive of the two in NF_3.

(ii) The dipole moment of CO_2, BF_3 and CCl_4 are zero because these molecules have symmetrical shapes and thus, the dipoles get cancelled and the net dipole moment becomes zero.

(iii) Among the given molecules, H_2O has highest dipole moment.

2. In case of transition elements, opposite trends are observed for ionisation energy. Thus, $(IE)_1$ of the corresponding elements of 3*d* and 4*d*-series are almost similar but these are smaller than the $(IE)_1$ of the 5*d*-series elements. Certainly the higher values of ionisation energies of the 5*d*-transition elements are consistent with the relatively small size of the atoms.

3. Given, $H_2 + Cl_2 \longrightarrow 2HCl, \Delta_f H = -91 \text{ kJ mol}^{-1}$

$\because$ In this reaction, two moles of HCl are produced,

$\Delta_r H = 2 \times \Delta_f H = 2 \times -91 = -182 \text{ kJ mol}^{-1}$

Let the bond energy of H—Cl bond is *x*.

$\therefore$ The bond energy for 2 moles of HCl = 2*x*.

For the reaction,

$$H—H + Cl—Cl \longrightarrow 2H—Cl,$$

$$\Delta_r H = \Sigma BE_{(reactants)} - \Sigma BE_{(products)}$$

$$-182 = 430 + 242 - 2x$$

$$-182 = 672 - 2x$$

$$\therefore \quad x = \frac{854}{2} = 427 \text{ kJ mol}^{-1}$$

4. (i) $CH_3CH(Br)CH_3$ (*Iso*-propyl bromide) $\xrightarrow[\text{Heat}]{\text{Alc. KOH}}$ $CH_3CH{=}CH_2$ (*A*) Propene $\xrightarrow[\text{Peroxide}]{\text{HBr}}$ $CH_3CH_2CH_2Br$ (*B*) 1-bromopropane

(ii) $CH_3CH_2CH_2OH$ (*n*-propyl alcohol) $\xrightarrow[\text{443 K}]{\text{Conc. } H_2SO_4}$ $CH_3CH{=}CH_2$ (*A*) Propene

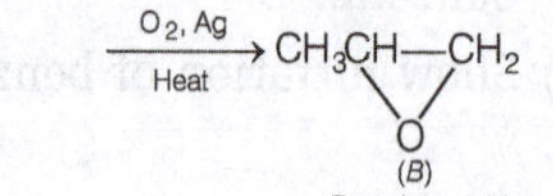

(*B*) Propylene oxide

Or

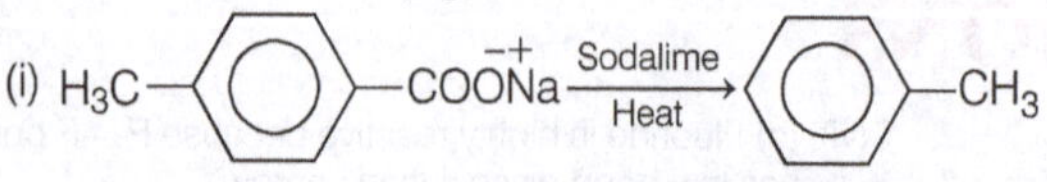

Toluene

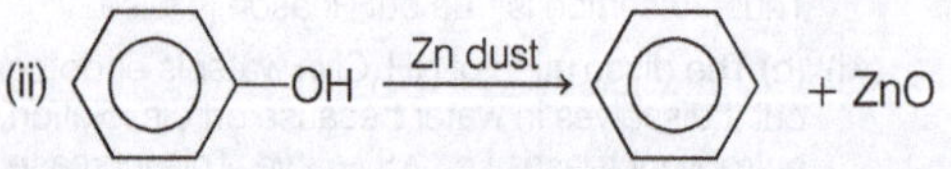

Benzene

5. Refer to text on page 113 (Ionic radius: Comparison of the ionic radii with corresponding atomic radii).

6. In SO_3, three highly electronegative oxygen atoms are attached to sulphur atom. It makes sulphur atom electron deficient. Further, due to resonance, sulphur acquires positive charge. Both these factors, make SO_3 an electrophile.

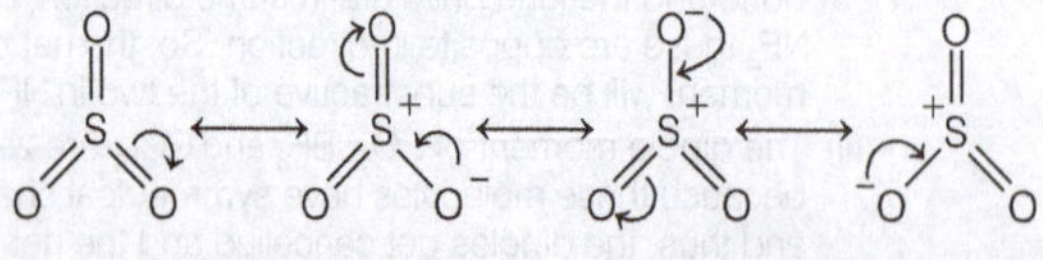

7. (i) $\overset{sp^2}{CH_2 = CH^-}$, $\quad HC \equiv \overset{sp}{C^-}$

Since, *sp*-hybridised carbon is more electronegative than sp^2-hybridised carbon, therefore, $CH \equiv C^-$ is less willing to donate a pair of electrons than $H_2C{=}CH^-$. In other words, $H_2C{=}CH^-$ is more basic than $HC \equiv C^-$.

(ii) This is due to more resonance of benzylic free radical.

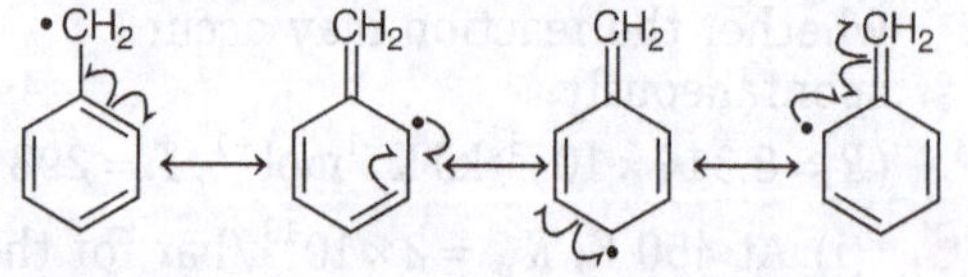

While allylic free radical has only two resonating structures so, it has less delocalisation.

$$CH_2{=}CH—\dot{C}H_2 \longleftrightarrow \dot{C}H_2—CH{=}CH_2$$

8. $A \longrightarrow CH_3—CH_2COO^-K^+$;

$B \longrightarrow CH_3—CH_2—CH_2—CH_3$ (Butane)

9. For the preparation of alkanes containing odd number of carbon atoms, two different alkyl halides are taken and two different alkyl halides can react in three different ways. Therefore, a mixture of alkanes is produced. e.g.

$$3CH_3I + 6Na + 3C_2H_5I \xrightarrow{\text{Dry ether}} \underset{\text{Ethane}}{CH_3—CH_3} + \underset{\text{Propane}}{CH_3CH_2CH_3} + \underset{\text{Butane}}{CH_3CH_2CH_2CH_3} + 6NaI$$

That's why this method (Wurtz reaction) is not suitable for the preparation of odd number alkanes.

10. The general formula of alkanes is C_nH_{2n+2}.

$$\therefore \quad 12 \times n + 1 \times (2n + 2) = 72$$

$$\text{or} \quad 12n + 2n + 2 = 72 \quad \text{or} \quad n = 5$$

Hence, number of carbon atoms = 5.

11. $\overset{3}{C}H_3\overset{2}{C}H_2\overset{1}{C}H{=}O$ (Propanal) $+$ $O{=}\overset{3}{C}(\overset{2}{C}H_2\overset{1}{C}H_3)(\overset{4}{C}H_2\overset{5}{C}H_3)$ (Pentan-3-one)

$\longrightarrow \overset{6}{C}H_3\overset{5}{C}H_2\overset{4}{C}H{=}\overset{3}{C}(\overset{2}{C}H_2\overset{1}{C}H_3)(CH_2CH_3)$

3-ethylhex-3-ene

12. (i) Since, the two substituents in the benzene ring are present at *p*-position, therefore, the first substituent in the benzene ring should be an *o*, *p*-directing group.

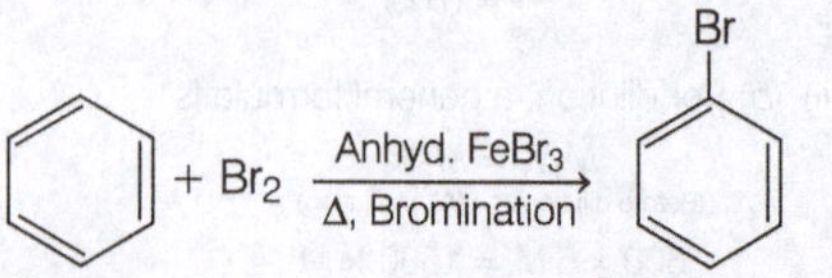

Benzene   Bromobenzene

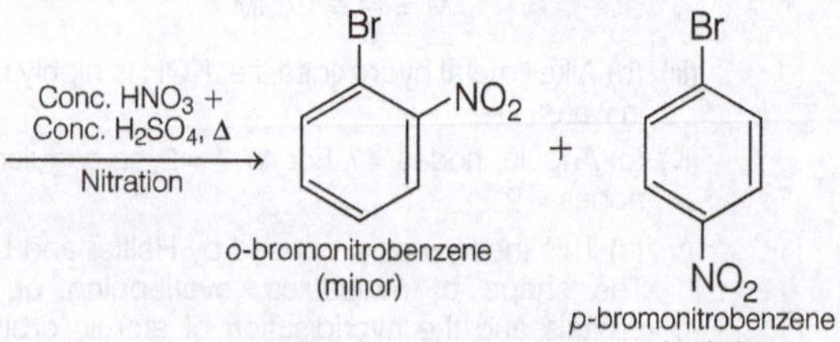

o-bromonitrobenzene (minor)   *p*-bromonitrobenzene (major)

(ii) Since, the two substituents in the benzene ring are present at *m*-positions, therefore, the first substituent in the benzene ring should be *m*-directing.

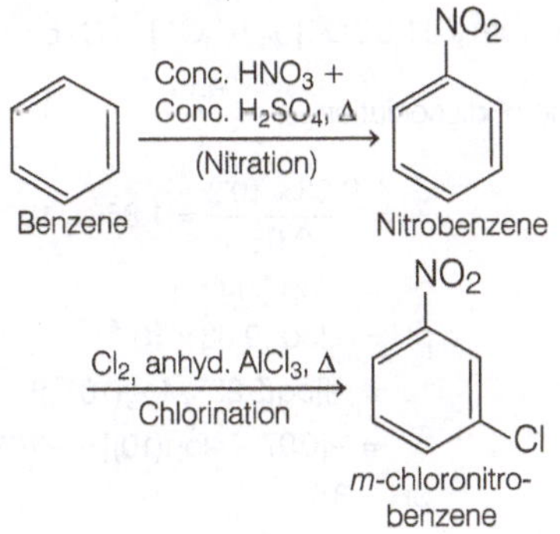

(iii)

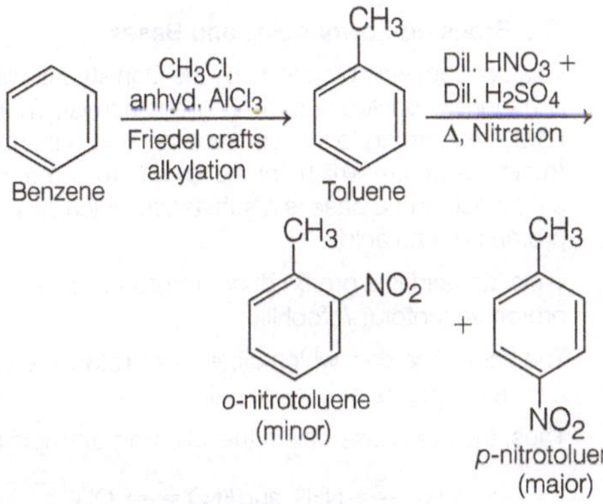

13. (i) Refer to text on page 146 (Topic-1, Bond length, various factors that affect bond length, (i)]

(ii) Refer to text on page 146 and 147 (Topic-1, Bond length, various factors that affect bond length, (ii)]

(iii) $C_2H_2 < C_2H_4 < CH_4$

14. (i) For 3*p*-orbital, principal quantum number, $n = 3$ and azimuthal quantum number, $l = 1$.

Number of angular nodes $= l = 1$.

Number of radial nodes $= n - l - 1 = 3 - 1 - 1 = 1$

(ii) The d_{xy} orbital is exactly like $d_{x^2-y^2}$ orbital except that its lobes are at an angle of 45° to the lobes of $d_{x^2-y^2}$ orbital.

(iii) ${}_{28}Ni = 1s^2 2s^2 2p^6 3s^2 3p^6 3d^8 4s^2$, nickel will lose 2 electrons from 4s (outermost shell) to form Ni^{2+} ion.

15. Features of Long Form of Periodic Table

This table is based on the electronic configuration of the elements and is also called the **Bohr's table** as it follows the Bohr's scheme to arrange various electrons around the nucleus.

Salient features of this table are as follows :

(i) In this table, there are 18 vertical columns, called the groups or families. These groups are numbered from 1 to 18 (according to IUPAC, International Union of Pure and Applied Chemistry, recommendations) replacing the older notations of groups IA...VIIA, VIII, IB, ...VIIB and 0. Each group or family contains a number of elements with same electronic configuration of valence shell (i.e., the outermost shell).

(ii) Elements of 1, 2 and 13 to 17 are called the main group or typical or representative elements. Elements of group 1 and 2 are also called alkali metals and alkaline earth metals respectively.

(iii) Elements of group 3 to 12 are called transition elements.

(iv) Element with atomic numbers 58 to 71 are called lanthanoids and elements with atomic number 90 to 103 are called actinoids. Lanthanoids and actinoids are placed in two separate rows below the periodic table in order to avoid the unnecessary sidwise expansion of the periodic table. These are also known as inner transition elements.

(v) This periodic table has seven horizontal rows, called the periods, which are numbered as 1, 2, 3, 4, 5, 6, 7 from top to bottom. The period number represents the highest principal quantum number (*n*) of the element.

(vi) There are two elements in the first period and 8, 8, 18, 18 and 32 elements in the subsequent periods.

The numbers 2, 8, 8, 18, 18, 32 are sometimes referred as magic numbers as the repetition in properties is observed after these number of elements in successive periods.

Although the seventh period is incomplete, but its maximum tendency is to have 32 elements (on the basis of quantum numbers).

Thus, first period is known as the shortest period, second and third are called the short periods. Fourth and fifth are known as long period and sixth is called the longest period.

(vii) Each period begins with an element having one electron in a new energy level (or new shell). Thus, the first element of each period is an alkali metal (with an exception of hydrogen) and the last element of each period is a noble gas.

16. These are a special kind of redox reactions in which the same element undergoes oxidation as well as reduction.

Only the compound in which element having intermediate oxidation state is present, undergo disproportionation reactions. In other words, the element must exhibit atleast three oxidation states to undergo disproportionation reaction.

e.g. In hydrogen peroxides, oxidation state of O is −1 which is an intermediate oxidation state, so it will oxidise to O_2 (in which oxidation state of O is 0) as well as reduce to give H_2O (in which oxidation state of O is −2). In other words, it undergoes disproportionation reaction.

Reduction

$$\overset{+1\ -1}{2H_2O_2(aq)} \longrightarrow \overset{+1\ -2}{2H_2O(l)} + \overset{0}{O_2(g)}$$

Oxidation

Or

***Step* I** The skeletal ionic equation is

$$MnO_4^-(aq) + Br^-(aq) \longrightarrow MnO_2(s) + BrO_3^-(aq)$$

***Step* II** Assign oxidation numbers for Mn and Br

$$\overset{+7}{Mn}O_4^-(aq) + \overset{-1}{Br^-}(aq) \longrightarrow \overset{+4}{Mn}O_2(s) + \overset{+5}{Br}O_3^-(aq)$$

This indicates that permanganate ion is the oxidant and bromide ion is the reductant.

***Step* III** Calculate the increase and decrease of oxidation number, and make the increase equal to the decrease.

$$2\overset{+7}{Mn}O_4^-(aq) + \overset{-1}{Br^-}(aq) \longrightarrow 2\overset{+4}{Mn}\,O_2(s) + \overset{+5}{Br}O_3^-(aq)$$

Step IV As the reaction occurs in the basic medium and the ionic charges are not equal on both sides, add 2 OH^- ions on the right to make ionic charges equal.

$$2\,MnO_4^-(aq) + Br^-(aq) \longrightarrow 2MnO_2(s) + BrO_3^-(aq) + 2OH^-(aq)$$

Step V Finally, count the hydrogen atoms and add appropriate number of water molecules (i.e. one H_2O molecule) on the left side to achieve balanced redox reaction).

$$2MnO_4^-(aq) + Br^-(aq) + H_2O(l) \longrightarrow 2MnO_2(s) + BrO_3^-(aq) + 2OH^-(aq)$$

17. We know that $\Delta G° = \Delta H° - T\Delta S°$, so first find $\Delta H°$ by using the formula, $\Delta H° = \Delta U° + \Delta n_g RT$ and then $\Delta G°$ by putting the values of $\Delta H°$, T and $\Delta S°$.

For a spontaneous reaction, $\Delta G \leq 0$.

$$2A(g) + B(g) \longrightarrow 2D(g);$$

$$\Delta n_g = \Sigma n_p - \Sigma n_r = 2 - 3 = -1$$

$$\Delta H° = \Delta U° + \Delta n_g RT$$

$$\Delta H° = -10.5\text{ kJ mol}^{-1} + (-1 \times 8.314 \times 10^{-3}\text{ kJ K}^{-1}\text{ mol}^{-1} \times 298\text{ K})$$

$$= -12.977\text{ kJ mol}^{-1}$$

$$\Delta G° = \Delta H° - T\Delta S°$$

$$\Delta G° = -12.977\text{ kJ mol}^{-1} - (298\text{ K} \times -44.1 \times 10^{-3}\text{ kJ K}^{-1}\text{mol}^{-1})$$

$$= +0.1648\text{ kJ mol}^{-1}$$

The reaction will not occur spontaneously because $\Delta G°$ is positive.

18. (i) $2SO_2(g) + O_2(g) \rightleftharpoons 2SO_3(g)$

$\therefore$ $\Delta n_g = 2 - 3 = -1$

$$K_c = \frac{K_p}{(RT)^{\Delta n_g}} = \frac{K_p}{(RT)^{-1}}$$

$$K_c = K_p \times RT = 2.0 \times 10^{10}\text{ bar}^{-1} \times 0.0831\text{L bar K}^{-1}\text{mol}^{-1} \times 450\text{ K}$$

$$= 7.479 \times 10^{11}\text{ L mol}^{-1}$$

(ii) $2NO(g) + O_2(g) \rightleftharpoons 2NO_2(g); \Delta H = -117$ kJ

(a) If we increase the concentration of NO, the rate of forward reaction will increase, i.e., more NO_2 will be formed.

(b) Decrease in pressure will favour backward reaction (side with more number of moles) i.e., less NO_2 will be formed.

19.

	CH_3COOH + H_2O	$\rightleftharpoons$ CH_3COO^-	+ H_3O^+
Initially	C	0	0
At time, t	$C - C\alpha$	$C\alpha$	$C\alpha$

$$\because \quad K_a = \frac{[CH_3COO^-]\,[H_3O^+]}{[CH_3COOH]}$$

$$\because \quad [CH_3COO^-] = [H_3O^+]$$

$$\therefore \quad [CH_3COO^-] = [H_3O^+] = \sqrt{K_a \cdot [CH_3COOH]}$$

Given, $K_a = 1.74 \times 10^{-5}$, $[CH_3COOH] = 0.05$ M

$$\therefore \quad [CH_3COO^-] = [H_3O^+] = \sqrt{1.74 \times 10^{-5} \times 0.05}$$

$$= 9.33 \times 10^{-4}\text{ M}$$

Again, from $[CH_3COO^-] = [H_3O^+] = C \cdot \alpha$

$$\text{Degree of dissociation, } \alpha = \frac{[H_3O^+]}{C}$$

$$= \frac{9.33 \times 10^{-4}}{0.05} = 1.866 \times 10^{-2} \approx 1.87 \times 10^{-2}$$

$$pH = -\log[H_3O^+]$$

$$pH = -\log[9.33 \times 10^{-4}]$$

$$= -[\log(9.33) + \log(10^{-4})]$$

$$= -[0.97 - 4\log(10)] = -0.97 + 4$$

$$pH = 3.03$$

Or

(i) **The Bronsted-Lowry Acids and Bases**

This concept was proposed by the Danish chemist, Johannes Bronsted and the English chemist, Thomas M. Lowry. According to this concept, an acid is a substance (molecule or ion) which can donate H^+ to some other substance and a base is a substance which can accept a proton from an acid.

Thus, an acid is a proton donor (protogenic) and a base is proton acceptor (protophilic).

The acid-base pair, which differ by a proton, are said to form a conjugate acid-base pair.

Thus, the acid-base pair in the following example are

$$NH_3 \underset{-H^+}{\overset{+H^+}{\rightleftharpoons}} NH_4^+ \text{ and } H_2O \underset{+H^+}{\overset{-H^+}{\rightleftharpoons}} OH^-$$

The general form of such reactions is,

Add proton

Acid + Base $\rightleftharpoons$ Conjugate base + Conjugate acid

Lose proton

Or

$$Acid_1 + Base_2 \rightleftharpoons Base_1 + Acid_2$$

It is also interesting to note that some substance exhibit dual behaviour, i.e., they have the tendency of accepting as well as donating the protons or in other words, they behave as acid and base both. Such substances are called amphoteric or amphiprotic substances.

e.g. NH_3, H_2O, CH_3COOH, etc.

$$H_2O + H_2O \rightleftharpoons H_3O^+ + OH^-$$

$$NH_3 + NH_3 \rightleftharpoons NH_4^+ + NH_2^-$$

$$CH_3COOH + CH_3COOH \rightleftharpoons CH_3\overset{+}{C}OOH_2 + CH_3COO^-$$

(ii) **Solubility Product Constant**

The concentration of substance in a saturated solution is defined as its solubility (s). Its value depends upon the nature of solvent and the temperature.

Consider saturated solution of sparingly soluble electrolyte, AB.

$$\underset{\text{Solid}}{AB} \rightleftharpoons \underset{\substack{\text{Unionised}\\\text{(dissolved)}}}{AB} \rightleftharpoons \underbrace{A^+ + B^-}_{\text{Ions}}$$

Applying the law of mass action, $K = \frac{[A^+][B^-]}{[AB]}$

Since, the solution is saturated, the concentration of unionised molecules of the electrolyte will be constant at a particular temperature. i.e.

$$[AB] = \text{constant} = K'$$

Hence, $[A^+][B^-] = KK' = K_{sp}$

This new constant K_{sp} is called **solubility product** and is defined as the product of the concentration of ions in a saturated solution of an electrolyte at a given temperature.

For general electrolyte of A_xB_y type $K_{sp} = x^x y^y S^{(x+y)}$

(where, S = solubility per mol)

20. The shape of the given molecules using VSEPR model are shown below.

(i) **$BeCl_2$** The central atom Be has only 2 valence electrons which are bonded to Cl, so there are only 2 bond pairs and no lone pairs. It is of the type AB_2 and hence, the shape is linear. **[1]**

Cl—Be—Cl or Cl**:** Be **:** Cl

(ii) **$SiCl_4$**

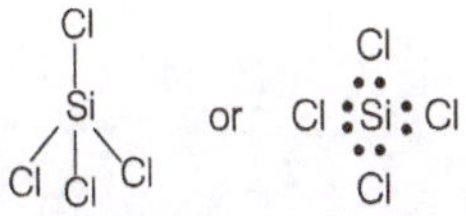

Similarly, the central atom Si has only 4 bond pairs and no lone pair. It is of the type AB_4 and hence, the shape is tetrahedral. **[1]**

(iii) **AsF_5**

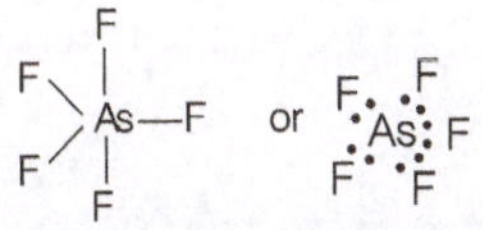

The central atom As has only 5 bond pairs and no lone pair. It is of the type AB_5 and hence, the shape is trigonal bipyramidal. **[1]**

(iv) **H_2S**

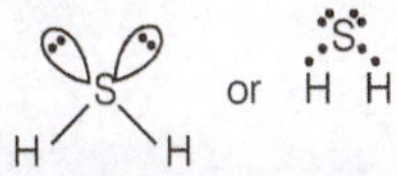

The central atom S has 6 valence electrons. Out of these only two are used in bond formation with two H-atoms, while four (two pairs) remains as non-bonding electrons (i.e., lone pairs). So, it contains 2 bond pairs and 2 lone pairs. It is of the type AB_2E_2 and hence, the shape is bent or V- shaped. **[1]**

(vi) **PH_3**

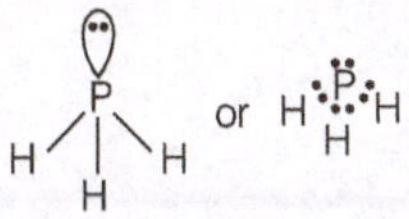

The central atom P has 5 valence electrons. Out of which three are utilised in bonding with H atoms and one pair remains as lone pair. So, it contains 3 bond pairs and one lone pair. It is of the type AB_3E and hence the shape is pyramidal. **[1]**

21. (i) **Aromaticity**

A compound can be considered as aromatic if it follows following three rules.

(a) An aromatic compound must be cyclic and planar.

(b) An aromatic compound must have the conjugated system in it.

(c) An aromatic compound must follow **Huckel rule** which states that the number of π-electrons involved in conjugation is $(4n + 2)$; where n = integer 0, 1, 2, 3 etc. For example, in

Number of π-electrons = 2

$(4n + 2) = 2$ and $n = 0$, thus Huckel rule is followed.

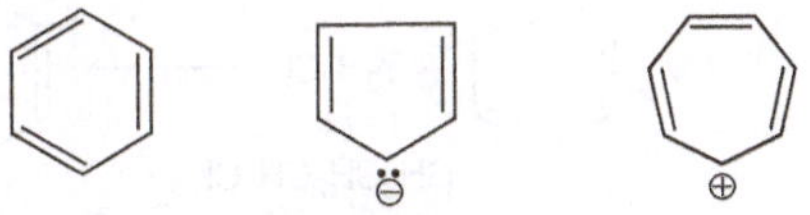

Benzene | Cyclopentadienyl anion | Cycloheptatrienyl cation

Number of π-electron = 6

$(4n + 2) = 6$ and $n = 1$, thus Huckel rule is followed.

Those compounds which does not follow the above 3 rules are called **non-aromatic.** These non-aromatic compounds may be cyclic with conjugated system.

e.g.  (cyclooctatetraene) is cyclic with conjugated system but it does not follow Huckel rule and its plane is also distorted that's why it is non-aromatic.

(ii) **Addition Reactions in Benzene**

(a) When benzene is treated with hydrogen in the presence of nickel catalyst, under vigorous conditions, i.e., at high temperature and/or pressure, it gets reduced to cyclohexane.

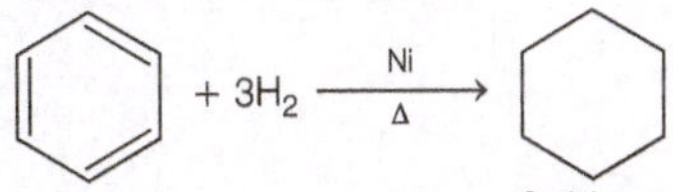

Cyclohexane

(b) When benzene is treated with chlorine molecules in the presence of UV light, addition of Cl takes place and benzene hexachloride, $C_6H_6Cl_6$ or **gammaxane** is obtained.

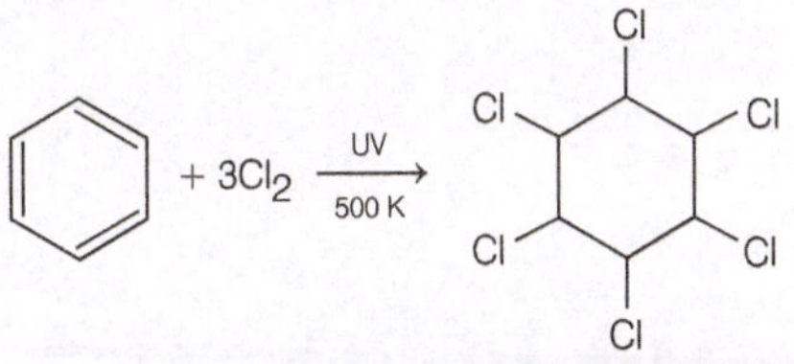

Benzene hexachloride (BHC)

(iii) **Combustion**

When benzene is burnt in excess of air, it burns with sooty flame to give CO_2 and H_2O.

$$C_6H_6 + \frac{15}{2}O_2 \longrightarrow 6CO_2 + 3H_2O$$

The general reaction for the combustion of aromatic hydrocarbons is

$$C_xH_y + \left(x + \frac{y}{4}\right)O_2 \longrightarrow xCO_2 + \frac{y}{2}H_2O$$

(iv) **Friedel-Crafts alkylation**

When benzene is treated with alkyl halide in the presence of anhyd. $AlCl_3$, it gives alkyl benzene. This reaction is called Friedel-Crafts alkylation.

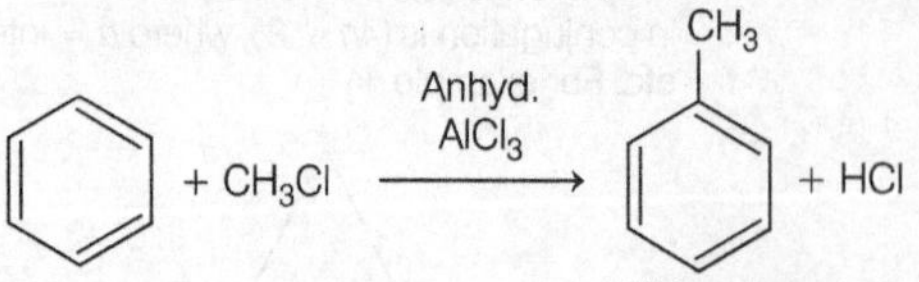

Toluene

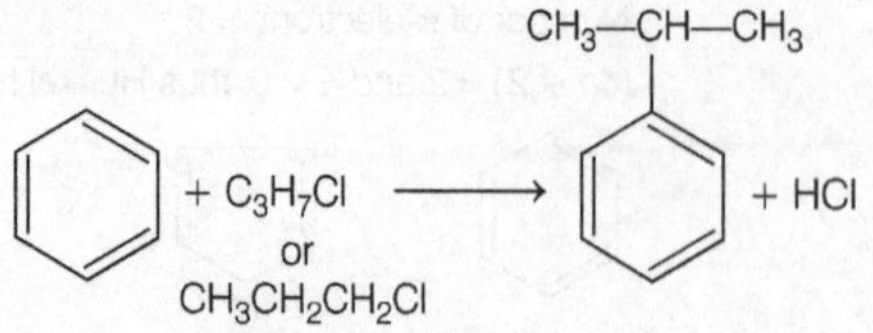

[$\because$ $CH_3CH_2CH_2Cl + AlCl_3 \xrightarrow[AlCl_4^-]{} CH_3CH_2\overset{+}{C}H_2$ 1° (less stable)

$\xrightarrow{\text{Rearrangement}} CH_3\overset{+}{C}HCH_3$] 2° (more stable)

(v) **Nitration of Benzene**

Benzene undergoes nitration when treated with conc. HNO $_3$ in the presence of conc. sulphuric acid.

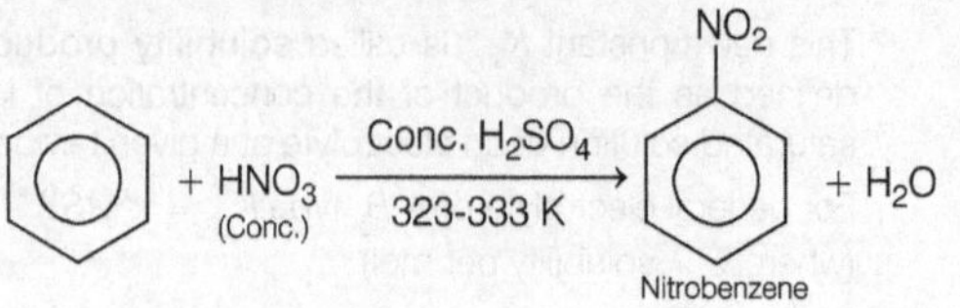

Nitrobenzene

SAMPLE QUESTION PAPER 2

A Highly Simulated Sample Question Paper for ISC Class XI

CHEMISTRY (Unsolved)

See Instruction Sample Paper 1

Section-A

[14 Marks]

1. (A) Fill in the blanks by choosing the appropriate word(s) from those given in the brackets. [4 × 1]

[molality, molarity, negative, positive, exothermic, alkanes, water, alcohol, solvent, solution, chlorine, fluorine, free energy, enthalpy, spontaneous].

(i) ...... is defined as the number of moles of the solute in 1 liter of ...... • *Recall*

(ii) Decrease in .... of a reacting system indicates an .... reaction. • *Recall*

(iii) .... are lighter than .... • *Analysis*

(iv) .... has highest .... electron gain enthalpy. • *Recall*

(B) Select and write the correct alternative from the choices given below. [7 × 1]

(i) The compound which contains both ionic and covalent bonds is • *Analysis*

(a) CH_4 (b) H_2

(c) KCN (d) KCl

(ii) If K_1 and K_2 are the equilibrium constants of the equilibria (I) and (II) respectively, what is the relationship between the two constants?

(I) $SO_2(g) + \frac{1}{2}O_2(g) \xrightleftharpoons{K_1} SO_3(g)$

(II) $2SO_3(g) \xrightleftharpoons{K_2} 2SO_2(g) + O_2(g)$ • *Application*

(a) $(K_1)^2 = \frac{1}{K_2}$ (b) $K_2 = (K_1)^2$

(c) $K_1 = \frac{1}{K_2}$ (d) $K_1 = K_2$

(iii) What is the pH of a 10^{-4} M OH^- solution at 330K, if K_w at 330K is $10^{-13.6}$? • *Evaluate*

(a) 4 (b) 9.0 (c) 10 (d) 9.6

(iv) Enthalpy of sublimation of a substance is equal to • *Recall*

(a) enthalpy of fusion + enthalpy of vapourisation

(b) enthalpy of fusion

(c) enthalpy of vapourisation

(d) twice the enthalpy of vaporisation

(v) The types of hybrid orbitals of nitrogen in NO_2^+, NO_3^- and NH_4^+ respectively are expected to be • *Application*

(a) *sp*, sp^3 and sp^2

(b) *sp*, sp^2 and sp^3

(c) sp^2, *sp* and sp^3

(d) sp^2, sp^3 and *sp*

(vi) **Assertion** A negative value of $E°$ means that the redox couple is a weaker reducing agent than the H^+/H_2 couple.

Reason A negative $E°$ means that the redox couple is stronger reducing agent than the H^+/H_2. • *Analysis*

(a) Both Assertion and Reason are true and Reason is the correct explanation of Assertion.

UNSOLVED

(b) Both Assertion and Reason are true but Reason is not correct explanation of Assertion.

(c) Assertion is true but Reason is false.

(d) Assertion is false but Reason is true.

(vii) **Assertion** Graphite conducts electricity.

Reason Delocalisation of electrons occurs in graphite. • *Analysis*

(a) Both Assertion and Reason are true and Reason is the correct explanation of Assertion.

(b) Both Assertion and Reason are true but Reason is not correct explanation of Assertion.

(c) Assertion is true but Reason is false.

(d) Assertion is false but Reason is true.

(C) Read the passage given below carefully and answer the questions that follow.

When a single Lewis dot structure is unable to explain all the properties of a compound, two or more structures, called the canonical forms or resonating structures, are drawn to explain all the properties of that compound, then the actual structure of the compound is in between these canonical forms and is called the resonance hybrid of these canonical forms. This phenomenon is called resonance.

The resonating structure are hypothetical, i.e., have no real existence. The energy of actual structure or resonance hybrid is lower than that of any of the canonical forms. The difference between hybrid and the energy of most stable (lowest energy) canonical form is called the resonance stabilisation energy or resonance energy. The more the number of important canonical forms, more is the resonance energy. [1×3]

(i) Write all the resonating structures of phenoxide ion. • *Understanding*

(ii) In the given pair of resonating structures which is more stable? • *Understanding*

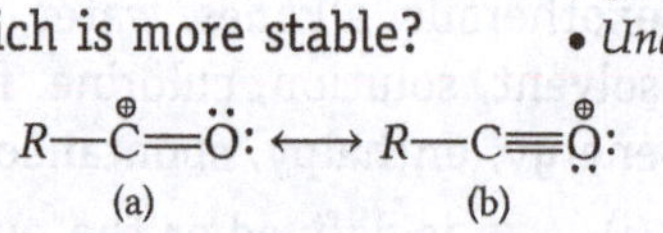

(iii) Write the correct relation between resonance and bond order. • *Recall*

Section-B

[20 Marks]

2. Give a reason for the following. • *Understanding*

(i) $AlCl_3$ and C_2H_4 have same bond angles.

(ii) Ice melts slowly at high altitudes. [2]

3. (i) Why solution of sugar in water does not conduct electricity whereas that of common salt in water does? • *Understanding*

(ii) K_b for NH_4OH is 1.8×10^{-5} and for CH_3NH_2 is 4.4×10^{-4}. Which of them is strongest base and why? [2]
• *Analysis*

Or

(i) At 0°C, ice and water are present in equilibrium. What will happen on increasing the pressure? • *Application*

(ii) What is the effect of reducing volume on the following system, $2C(s) + O_2(g) \rightleftharpoons 2CO(g)$? • *Application*

4. Despite their $-I$-effect, halogens are *o*-and *p*-directing in haloarenes. Explain. [2]
• *Understanding*

5. (i) How does an electron withdrawing group (EWG) and an electron donating group (EDG) influence the acid strength of carboxylic acid? • *Understanding*

(ii) Identify the most stable species in the following set of ions giving reasons,

(a) $\overset{+}{C}H_3, \overset{+}{C}H_2Br, \overset{+}{C}HBr_2, \overset{+}{C}Br_3$ • *Analysis*

(b) $\overset{-}{C}H_3, \overset{-}{C}H_2Cl, \overset{-}{C}HCl_2, \overset{-}{C}Cl_3$ [1+1]

6. (i) Which of the following represents the correct IUPAC name for the compounds concerned? • *Analysis*

(a) 2,2-dimethylpentane or 2-dimethylpentane

(b) 2,4,7-trimethyloctane or 2,5,7-trimethyloctane

(ii) Give the common name of • *Recall*

(a) methanol

(b) ethanol [1+1]

7. (i) Write the conjugate acid for NH_2^- and NH_3. • *Understanding*

(ii) What is the relationship between pK_a and pK_b values? [2] • *Recall*

8. The equilibirum constant for a reaction is 10. What will be the value of $\Delta G°$? • *Application*
$R = 8.314\ J\ K^{-1}mol^{-1}$, $T = 300\,K$.
[**Ans.** 5.744 kJ mol^{-1}] [2]

9. Give correct reason for the following. • *Understanding*

(i) BF_3 has a zero dipole moment although the B—F bonds are polar.

(ii) All carbon to oxygen bonds in CO_3^{2-} are equivalent. [2]

10. Carbon monoxide is allowed to expand isothermally and reversibly from $10\,m^3$ to $20\,m^3$ at 300 K and work obtained is 4.754 kJ. Calculate then number of moles of carbon monoxide. • *Evaluate*
[**Ans.** 2.75 moles] [2]

11. How will the following be converted? • *Understanding*

(i) Bromoethane to *n*-butane

(ii) Acetone to *n*-propane [2]

Section-C [21 Marks]

12. The ionisation constant of 0.05 M solution of phenol is 1.0×10^{-10}. What will be the degree of ionisation if the solution is also 0.01 M in solution phenolate? • *Evaluate*
[**Ans.** 1×10^{-8}] [3]

13. (i) Which among the following is a state function and why? q, W and $q + W$. • *Analysis*

(ii) Calculate the entropy change in surroundings when 1.00 mole of $H_2O(l)$ is formed under standard conditions. $\Delta_f H° = -286$ kJ mol^{-1}. • *Evaluate*
[**Ans.** 959.73 J mol^{-1}] [3]

14. Arrange the following as stated: • *Analysis*

(i) Increasing order of basic character; MgO, SrO, K_2O, NiO, Cs_2O

(ii) Increasing first ionisation energy; Mg, Al, Si, Na

(iii) Increasing acidic proeprty; ZnO, Na_2O_2, P_2O_5, MgO [3]

15. How will you convert? • *Understanding*

(i) Benzoic acid to benzene

(ii) Toluene to benzene

(iii) Acetic acid to methane [3]

16. Write the anode reaction, the cathode reaction and the net cell reaction in the following cells. Which electrode would be positive terminal in each cell ? [3] • *Understanding*

(i) $Zn(s)|Zn^{2+}||\ Br_2|\ Br^-|\ Pt(s)$

(ii) $Cr(s)|Cr^{3+}||I_2|\ I^-|\ Pt(s)$

(iii) $Pt(s)|H_2(g)|\ H^+(aq)\ ||\ Cu^{2+}|\ Cu(s)$

Or Identify the type of redox reaction taking place in the following. [3] • *Analysis*

(i) $3\overset{0}{Mg}(s) + \overset{0}{N_2}(g) \longrightarrow \overset{+2\,-3}{Mg_3N_2}(s)$

(ii) $\overset{+5\,-2}{V_2O_5}(s) + 5\overset{0}{Ca}(s) \longrightarrow 2\overset{0}{V}(s) + 5\overset{+2\,-2}{CaO}(s)$

(iii) $2\overset{+1\,+5\,-2}{KClO_3}(s) \longrightarrow 2\overset{+1\,-1}{KCl}(s) + 3\overset{0}{O_2}(g)$

(iv) $\overset{0}{Ca}(s) + 2\overset{+1\,-2}{H_2O}(l) \longrightarrow \overset{+2\,-2\,+1}{Ca(OH)_2}(aq) + \overset{0}{H_2}(g)$

(v) $\overset{0}{Br_2}(l) + 2\overset{-1}{I^-}(aq) \longrightarrow 2\overset{-1}{Br^-}(aq) + \overset{0}{I_2}(s)$

(vi) $\overset{0}{Cl_2}(g) + 2OH^-(aq) \longrightarrow \overset{+1}{ClO^-}(aq) + \overset{-1}{Cl^-}(aq) + H_2O\ (l)$

17. (i) How many σ-bonds and π-bonds are present in the second member of the alkene series? • *Analysis*

(ii) What is the shape of the following compounds? • *Understanding*

(a) $H_2C{=}O$ (b) CH_3F

(c) $HC{\equiv}N$

(iii) What is the hybridisation of each carbon in, $H_2C{-}C{=}CH_2$? [3] • *Evaluate*

UNSOLVED

18. Write down the quantum numbers n, and l for the following orbitals. • *Evaluate*

(i) $3d_{x^2-y^2}$ (ii) $4d_{z^2}$ (iii) $3d_{xy}$ (iv) $4d_{xz}$ (v) $2p_z$ (vi) $3p_x$ [3]

Section-D [15 Marks]

19. (i) The molar solubility of lead iodate, $Pb(IO_3)_2$ is 4.0×10^{-5} mol/L at 25°C. Calculate its K_{sp}. • *Evaluate*

$Pb(IO_3)_2 \rightleftharpoons Pb^{2+} + 2IO_3$

[**Ans.** $K_{sp} = 2.56 \times 10^{-13}$]

(ii) What will be the pH of 1 M Na_2SO_4 solution? [pH = 7] • *Application*

(iii) What is K_C for the following equilibrium when the equilibrium concentration of each substance is, • *Evaluate*

$[SO_2] = 0.60M$, $[O_2] = 0.82$ M and $[SO_3] = 1.90$ M?

$$2SO_2(g) + O_2(g) \rightleftharpoons 2SO_3(g)$$

[$K_c = 12.299$ L mol^{-1}] [5]

20. How will you convert benzene into • *Understanding*

(i) benzoic aicd (ii) hexachlorobenzene

(iii) *p*-dichlorobenzene (iv) acetophenone

(v) iodobenzene [5]

Or

(i) An alkyne (X) has molecular formula C_5H_8. It reacts neither with sodamide nor with ammoniacal cuprous chloride. Write the name and structure of X. • *Understanding*

(ii) A hydrocarbon 'Y' decolourises bromine water. On ozonolysis it gives 3-methyl-butanal and formaldehyde. Give the name and structure of the compound. • *Understanding*

(iii) A hydrocarbon (Z) has molecular formula C_8H_{10}. It does not decolourise bromine water and is oxidised to benzoic acid on heating with $K_2Cr_2O_7$. It can also have three other isomers A, B and C. Write the structures of Z, A, B and C. • *Understanding* [5]

21. (i) Complete the following reactions. • *Recall*

(a) $(CH_3)_2CHBr \xrightarrow[\text{(ii) Cu}]{\text{(i) Li}} A \xrightarrow{CH_3CH_2CH_2Br} B$

(b) Ethanol $\xrightarrow[\Delta]{\text{Alc. KOH}} A \xrightarrow[CCl_4]{Br_2} B$ [2]

(ii) Hydrocarbon A (molecular formula is C_5H_8) gave a white precipitate with ammoniacal silver nitrate.

Oxidation of A with hot alkaline $KMnO_4$ gave 2-methyl propanoic acid. What is the structural formula of A? Explain. • *Understanding* [3]

UNSOLVED

Answer key

1. (B) (i)-(c), (ii)-(a), (iii)-(d), (iv)-(a), (v)-(b), (vi)-(d), (vii)-(a)

SAMPLE QUESTION PAPER 3

A Highly Simulated Sample Question Paper for ISC Class XI

CHEMISTRY (Unsolved)

Time : 3 hours

Max. Marks : 70

GENERAL INSTRUCTIONS

- This paper is divided into four Section A, B, C and D and has 21 question in all. Answer all questions.
- **Section A** has fourteen subparts. Each question carries 1 mark.
- While attempting **Multiple Choice Questions** in Section A, you are required to write only ONE option as the answer.
- **Section B** has **ten question.** Each question carries 2 marks.
- **Section C** has **seven questions.** Each question carries 3 marks.
- **Section D** has **three questions.** Each question carries 5 marks.
- Internal choices have been provided in **one question each in Section B, C and D.**
- The intended marks for questions are given in brackets [].
- All working, including rough work, should be done on the same sheet as, and adjacent to the rest of the answer.
- Balanced equations must be given wherever possible and diagrams where they are helpful.
- When solving numerical problems, all essential working must be shown.
- In working out problems, use the following data:

  Gas constant $R = 1.987$ cal deg^{-1} mol^{-1} = 8.314 J K^{-1} mol^{-1} = 0.0821 dm^3 atm K^{-1} mol^{-1},

  1 L atm = 1 dm^3 atm = 101.3 J, 1 Faraday = 96500 coulombs. **Avogadro's number** = 6.023×10^{23}.

UNSOLVED

Section-A

[14 Marks]

1. (A) Fill in the blanks by choosing the appropriate word(s) from those given in the brackets.

[number of moles, number of neutrons, directly, inversely, isoenergy, pressure, temperature, degenerated, exclusive, directional, spherical, non-directional, cubicle, +2, +5, +7]. [4 × 1]

(i) The volume of a gas at constant pressure and temperature is .... proportional to the .... of gas present. • *Recall*

(ii) According to Boyle's law, "At a given temperature the volume of a given mass of a gas is ...... proportional to its ....". • *Recall*

(iii) Oxidation state of manganese in $KMnO_4$ in acidic medium changes from .... to .... • *Recall*

(iv) *s*-subshell is .... in nature, while *p*-subshell is .... • *Recall*

(B) Select and write the correct alternative from the choices given below. [7 × 1]

(i) 5 mL of *N*/HCl, 20 mL of *N*/2 H_2SO_4 and 30 mL of *N*/3 HNO_3 are mixed together and volume made to 1 L. The normality of resulting solution is • *Evaluate*

(a) *N*/40

(b) *N*/10

(c) *N*/20

(d) *N*/5

(ii) A measured temperature on Fahrenheit scale is 200°F. What will this reading be on Celsius scale? • *Evaluate*

(a) 40°C (b) 94°C
(c) 93.3°C (d) 30°C

(iii) When heat is absorbed by the system at constant pressure then • *Recall*

(a) $\Delta H = q_V$
(b) $\Delta U = q_p$
(c) $\Delta H = q_p$
(d) $\Delta U = q_V$

(iv) The molecule of hydrogen atom is formed due to the overlapping of orbitals of two hydrogen atoms. Which of the following types of overlapping takes place in the formation of H_2 molecule? • *Analysis*

(a) 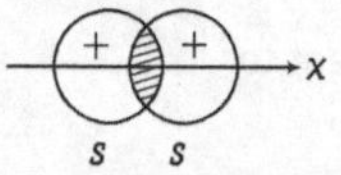

(b) 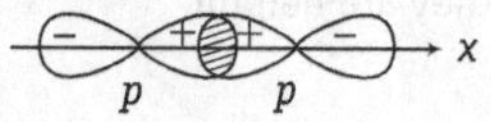

(c) 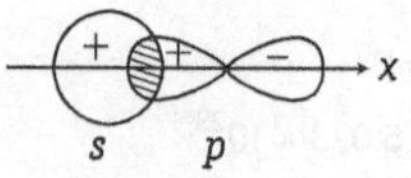

(d) All of these

(v) Which of the following has minimum bond length? • *Analysis*

(a) O_2 (b) O_2^+
(c) O_2^- (d) O_2^{2-}

(vi) **Assertion:** The atomic and ionic radii generally decreases toward right in a period.
Reason: The ionisation enthalpy increases on moving towards left in a period. • *Analysis*

(a) Both Assertion and Reason are true and Reason is the correct explanation of Assertion.
(b) Both Assertion and Reason are true but Reason is not correct explanation of Assertion.
(c) Assertion is true but Reason is false.
(d) Assertion is false but Reason is true.

(vii) **Assertion:** 1 mole of acetone requires more heat to vaporise than the 1 mole of water to vaporise.
Reason: There is strong hydrogen bonds between water molecules but weaker intermolecular dipole-dipole interactions in acetone. • *Analysis*

(a) Both Assertion and Reason are true and Reason is the correct explanation of Assertion.
(b) Both Assertion and Reason are true but Reason is not correct explanation of Assertion.
(c) Assertion is true but Reason is false.
(d) Assertion is false but Reason is true.

(C) Read the passage given below carefully and answer the questions that follow.

Chemical bonding, involves interactions that account for the association of atoms into molecules, ions, crystals, and other stable species that make up the familiar substances of the everyday world. When atoms approach one another, their nuclei and electrons interact and tend to distribute themselves in space in such a way that the total energy is lower than it would be in any alternative arrangement. If the total energy of a group of atoms is lower than the sum of the energies of the component atoms, then the energy lowering is the bonding energy.

The ideas that helped to establish the nature of chemical bonding came during early 20th century, after the electron had been discovered and quantum mechanics had provided a language for the description of the behaviour of electrons in atoms. However, even though chemists need quantum mechanics to attain a detailed quantitative understanding of bond formation, much of their pragmatic understanding of bonds is expressed in simple intuitive models. These models treat bonds as primarily of two kinds-namely, ionic and covalent.

The type of bond that is most likely to occur between two atoms can be predicted on the basis of the location of the elements in the periodic table, and to some extent the properties of the substances so formed can be related to the type of bonding.

A key concept in a discussion of chemical bonding is that of the molecule. Molecules are the smallest unit of compounds that can exist. One feature of molecules that can be predicted with reasonable success is their shape. Molecular shapes are of considerable importance for understanding the reactions that compounds can undergo. [1 × 3]

(i) According to molecular orbital theory, H_2^{2-} molecule does not exist, why? • *Understanding*

(ii) In PO_4^{3-}, calculate formal charge on each oxygen atom and P—O bond order. • *Analysis*

(iii) Acetophenone has higher dipole moment than ethanol. Explain? • *Understanding*

Section-B [20 Marks]

2. For an isolated system, $\Delta U = 0$, what will be ΔS? • *Analysis* [2]

3. Presence of lone pairs distorts the geometry of a molecule. Explain with example. • *Understanding* [2]

4. Write the resonance structures of CO_3^{2-} and HCO_3^-. • *Understanding*

5. Enthalpy of combustion of carbon to CO_2 is -393.5 kJ mol^{-1}. Calculate the heat realeased upon formation of 35.2 g of CO_2 from carbon and dioxygen gas. (Molar mass of CO_2 = 44 g mol^{-1}). • *Evaluate*

[Ans : 314.8 kJ mol^{-1}**]** [2]

6. Calculate the number of kJ of heat necessary to raise the temperatureof 60.0 g of aluminium from 35°C to 55°C. (Molar heat capacity of Al is 24 J mol^{-1}K^{-1}. Molar mass of Al = 27 g mol^{-1}) • *Application*

[Ans : 1.067 kJ**]** [2]

7. On complete combustion, 0.246 g of an organic compound gave 0.198 g of carbon dioxide and 0.1014 g of water. Determine the percentage composition of carbon and hydrogen in the compound. • *Evaluate*

[Ans : %C = 21.95%, %H = 4.58%**]** [2]

Or

Explain the reason for the fusion of an organic compound with metallic sodium for testing nitrogen, sulphur and halogens. Also give the reactions. • *Understanding*

8. What are transition elements? Which of the following are not transition elements? • *Analysis*

Cu ($Z = 29$), S ($Z = 16$), Ga ($Z = 31$), Pd ($Z = 46$) and U ($Z = 92$). [2]

9. (i) Why do the C—C bonds rather than C—H bonds break during cracking of alkanes? • *Understanding*

(ii) Convert 1-brompropane to 2-bromopropane. • *Understanding* [2]

10. Balance the following equation. • *Recall*

(i) $Cr_2O_7^{2-} + H^+ + I^- \longrightarrow Cr^{3+} + I_2 + H_2O$

(ii) $MnO_4^- + SO_3^{2-} + H^+ \longrightarrow Mn^{2+} + SO_4^{2-} + H_2O$ [2]

11. The relative reactivity of 1°, 2°, 3° hydrogen's towards chlorination is 1 : 3.8 : 5. Calculate the percentages of all monochlorinated products obtained from 2-methylbutane.

[Ans : 1° = 41.7%, 2° = 35.2%, 3° = 23.1%**]** • *Evaluate* [2]

UNSOLVED

Section-C

[21 Marks]

12. Arrange the following: • *Analysis*

(i) $C_6H_5\overset{+}{C}HCH_3$, $C_6H_5\overset{+}{C}HCH{=}CH_2$, $C_6H_5CH_2\overset{+}{C}H_2$, $C_6H_5\overset{+}{C}(CH_3)_2$ in order of increasing stability.

(ii) $CH_3CH_2^+$, $C_6H_5CH_2^+$, $(CH_3)_3C^+$, $CH_2{=}CHCH_2^+$ in order of decreasing stability.

(iii) $HC{\equiv}C^-$, $CH_2{=}CH^-$, $CH_3CH_2^-$, CH_3^-, $(CH_3)_2CH^-$, $C_6H_5CH_2^-$ in order of increasing stability. [3]

13. (i) One millilitre solution of 0.01 M HCl is added to 1L of sodium chloride solution. What will be the pH of the resulting solutions? [Ans : pH = 5] • *Evaluate*

(ii) Neutral solutions have pH = 7 at 298 K. A sample of pure water is found to have pH < 7. Does it mean that it is acidic? • *Anslysis*

(iii) Find the conjugate acid/base for the following species.
HNO_2, CN^-, $HClO_4$, F^-, OH^-, CO_3^{2-} and S^{2-} • *Application* [3]

14. Calculate the oxidation number of sulphur, chromium and nitrogen in H_2SO_5, $Cr_2O_7^{2-}$ and NO_3^-. Suggest the structure of these compounds. Count for the fallacy. • *Analysis* [3]

15. (i) Arrange the following in order of decreasing bond angles. • *Analysis*

CH_4, NH_3, H_2O, BF_3, C_2H_2

(ii) What is the total number of σ and π bonds in the following molecules? [3]

(a) C_2H_2 (b) C_2H_4 • *Analysis*

Or Explain the following on the basis of valence bond theory. • *Understanding*

(i) BF_3 is planar but NH_3 is not.

(ii) CCl_4 and $SiCl_4$ are tetrahedral.

(iii) The HSH bond angle is H_2S is closer to 90° than HOH bond angle in H_2O.

16. Write IUPAC names of the following compounds. • *Understanding*

(i) $CH_3CH{=}C(CH_3)_2$

(ii) $CH_2{=}CH{-}C{\equiv}C{-}CH_3$

(iii) 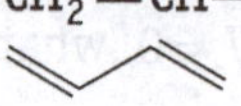

(iv) $CH_3CH{=}CH{-}CH_2{-}CH{=}CH{-}\underset{\underset{C_2H_5}{|}}{CH}{-}CH_2{-}CH{=}CH_2$ [3]

17. Which bond is more polar in the following pair of molecules? Explain with reason.

(i) $H_3C{-}H$ or $H_3C{-}Br$ • *Analysis*

(ii) $H_3C{-}NH_2$ or $H_3C{-}OH$

(iii) $H_3C{-}OH$ or $H_3C{-}SH$ [3]

18. Two moles of an ideal gas initially at 27°C and one atmospheric pressure are compressed isothermally and reversibly till the final pressure of gas is 10 atm. Calculate q, W and ΔU for the process.

[**Ans** : $W = 11488.3$ J $q = -11488.3$ J $\Delta U = 0$ J] • *Evaluate* [3]

Section-D

[15 Marks]

19. (i) For the reaction, $N_2(g) + 3H_2(g) \rightleftharpoons 2NH_3(g)$, the partial pressures of N_2 and H_2 are 0.80 and 0.40 atmosphere respectively at equilibrium. The total pressure of the system is 2.80 atmosphere. What is K_p for the above reaction? • *Evaluate*

[**Ans** : $K_p = 50\ atm^{-2}$]

(ii) Explain, why pure liquids and solids can be ignored while writing the equilibrium constant expression? • *Understanding* [5]

Or (i) Give the p versus V graph for isobaric process. • *Recall*

(ii) For an exothermic reaction, what happens to the equilibrium constant if temperature is increased? • *Application*

(iii) Which of the following reactions involve homogeneous equilibrium and which involve heterogeneous equilibrium? • *Analysis*

(a) $2NH_3(g) \rightleftharpoons N_2(g) + 3H_2(g)$

(b) $2Cu(NO_3)_2(s) \rightleftharpoons 2CuO(s) + 4NO_2(g) + O_2(g)$

(c) $CH_3COOC_2H_5(aq) + H_2O(l) \rightleftharpoons CH_3COOH(aq) + C_2H_5OH(aq)$ [5]

20. What are the main points of similarity and difference between valence bond theory and molecular orbital theory. [5]

21. Give the main products of the reactions. • *Understanding*

(i) $C_6H_6 \xrightarrow[\text{Conc. } H_2So_4]{\text{Conc. } HNO_3}$

(ii) $C_6H_5CH_3 \xrightarrow{CrO_2Cl_2}$

(iii) $C_6H_5CH_2CH_2CH_3 \xrightarrow{\text{Alk. } KMnO_4}$

(iv) $C_6H_6 + Cl_2 \xrightarrow{\text{Sunlight}}$

(v) $C_6H_6 + CH_3COCl \xrightarrow{\text{Anhyd. } AlCl_3}$ [5]

Answer key

1. (B) (i)-(a), (ii)-(c), (iii)-(c), (iv)-(a), (v)-(b), (vi)-(c), (vii)-(d)

SAMPLE QUESTION PAPER 4

A Highly Simulated Sample Question Paper for ISC Class XI

CHEMISTRY (Unsolved)

See Instruction Sample Paper 1

UNSOLVED

Section-A [14 Marks]

1. (A) Fill in the blanks by choosing the appropriate word(s) from those given in the brackets. [4 ×1]

[heat capacity, specific heat, alcohol, alkene, Markovnikov's, anti-Markovnikov's, optical, geometrical, single, double, 1°, 100°, state, path, O_3, CO].

(i) .... isomerism arises due to restricted rotation of .... bond. • *Recall*

(ii) Work is not a .... function but it is a .... function. • *Recall*

(iii) Addition of water to alkenes takes place in accordance with .... rule and .... are obtained as products. • *Understanding*

(iv) .... is the quantity of heat required to raise the temperature of one unit of mass by .... • *Recall*

(B) Select and write the correct alternative from the choices given below. [7 × 1]

(i) Which one of the following has the minimum boiling point? • *Analysis*

(a) *n*-butane (b) 1-butyne
(c) 1-butene (d) *Iso*-butane

(ii) When an electron is excited from ground level to 5th orbit, the number of spectral lines obtained in Bohr spectrum of H-atoms is • *Evaluate*

(a) 5 (b) 8
(c) 10 (d) 15

(iii) In which case, a spontaneous reaction is possible at any temperature? • *Application*

(a) $\Delta H(-\text{ve}), \Delta S(+\text{ve})$
(b) $\Delta H(-\text{ve}), \Delta S(-\text{ve})$
(c) $\Delta H(+\text{ve}), \Delta S(+\text{ve})$
(d) None of the above

(iv) $N_2(g) + 3H_2(g) \rightleftharpoons 2NH_3(g), K_1$ ...(i)

$N_2(g) + O_2(g) \rightleftharpoons 2NO(g), K_2$ ...(ii)

$H_2(g) + \frac{1}{2}O_2(g) \rightleftharpoons H_2O(g), K_3$ ...(iii)

The equation for the equilibrium constant of the reaction,

$2NH_3(g) + \frac{5}{2}O_2(g) \rightleftharpoons 2NO(g) + 3H_2O(g)$,

(K_4) in terms of K_1, K_2 and K_3 is • *Application*

(a) $\frac{K_1K_2}{K_3}$ (b) $\frac{K_1K_3^2}{K_2}$

(c) $K_1K_2K_3$ (d) $\frac{K_2K_3^3}{K_1}$

(v) The pair of electron in the given carbanion, $CH_3C \equiv C^-$, is present in which orbitals? • *Understanding*

(a) sp^3 (b) sp^2 (c) sp (d) $2p$

(vi) **Assertion** There is an equilibrium between the gaseous molecules and dissolved molecules of the gas under pressure.

Reason Such equilibrium is governed by Henry's law. • *Analysis*

(a) Both Assertion and Reason are true and Reason is the correct explanation of Assertion.
(b) Both Assertion and Reason are true but Reason is not correct explanation of Assertion.
(c) Assertion is true but Reason is false.
(d) Assertion is false but Reason is true.

(vii) **Assertion** In the electrophilic substitution of ary halides, the incoming electrophile gets attached to the *meta*-position.

Reason Aryl halides are moderately deactivating. • *Analysis*

(a) Both Assertion and Reason are true and Reason is the correct explanation of Assertion.
(b) Both Assertion and Reason are true but Reason is not correct explanation of Assertion.
(c) Assertion is true but Reason is false.
(d) Assertion is false but Reason is true.

(C) Read the passage given below carefully and answer the questions that follow. [3 ×1]

In the modern periodic table, elements are arranged in order of increasing atomic numbers which is related to the electronic configuration.

Depending upon the type of orbitals receiving the last electron, the elements in the periodic table have been divided into four blocks, *viz, s, p, d* and *f*.

The modern periodic table consists of 7 periods and 18 groups. Each period begins with the filling of a new energy shell. In accordance with the Aufbau principle, the seven periods (1 to 7) have 2, 8, 8, 18, 18, 32 and 32 elements respectively.

The seventh period is still incomplete. To avoid the periodic table being too long, the two series of *f*-block elements, called lanthanoids and actinoids are placed to the bottom of the main body of the periodic table.

(i) Write the outermost electronic configuration of last element of *p*-block in 6th period. • *Understanding*

(ii) In terms of period and group, where would you locate the element with $Z = 114$. • *Analysis*

(iii) Assign the position of the element having outer electronic configuration of $(n-2)f^7(n-1)d^1ns^2$ for $n = 6$, in the periodic table. • *Analysis*

UNSOLVED

Section-B [20 Marks]

2. What is the basic difference between the terms electron gain enthalpy and electronegativity? • *Recall* [2]

3. Classify the following species into Lewis acids and Lewis bases and show how these act as Lewis acid/base? • *Application* [2]

(i) OH^- (ii) F^- (iii) H^+ (iv) BCl_3

4. The solubility of $Sr(OH)_2$ at 298 K is 19.23 g / L of solution. Calculate the concentrations of strontium and hydroxyl ions and the pH of the solution. • *Application*

[Ans : Sr^{2+} – 0.1581 M, OH^- = 0.3163 M, pH = 13.5] [2]

Or One mole of H_2O and one mole of CO are taken in a 10 L vessel and heated to 725 K. At equilibrium, 40% of water (by mass) reacts with CO according to the equation, $H_2O(g) + CO(g) \rightleftharpoons H_2(g) + CO_2(g)$. Calculate the equilibrium constant for the reation.

[Ans : 0.444] • *Evaluate*

5. (i) Identify the substance that get reduced in the following reaction, • *Analysis*

$$Fe_2O_3(s) + 3CO(g) \longrightarrow 2Fe(s) + 3CO_2(g)$$

(ii) Zn rod is immersed in $CuSO_4$ solution. What will you observe after an hour? Explain your observation in terms of redox reaction. • *Analysis*

[2]

6. A gold coloured metal object has a mass of 365 g and a volume of 22.12 cm^3. Is the object composed of pure gold? [Density of pure gold = 19.32 g cm^{-3}]. • *Analysis* [2]

7. What are the possible structures for a carboxylic acid with a molecular formula $C_4H_8O_2$ and label each C atom as *sp*, sp^2 and sp^3? • *Understanding* [2]

8. Is it possible for any process to have $\Delta H = \Delta E$? If yes, state under what conditions? If no, state why not? • *Understanding* [2]

9. Write the cell reaction and calculate the standard $E°$ of the cell.

$$Zn \mid Zn^{2+}(1\ M) \parallel Cd^{2+}(1\ M) \mid Cd$$

Given, $E^{\circ}_{Zn/Zn^{2+}} = 0.763$; $E^{\circ}_{Cd/Cd^{2+}} = 0.403$ V • *Analysis*

[**Ans** : $E_{cell} = 0.36$ V] [2]

10. Calculate the molar solubility of $Ni(OH)_2$ in 0.10 M NaOH. The ionic product of $Ni(OH)_2$ is 2.0×10^{-15}. • *Evaluate*

[**Ans** : $S = 2.0 \times 10^{-3}$ M] [2]

11. Explain the term polymerisation with two examples. • *Recall* [2]

Section-C

[21 Marks]

12. Write the electronic configuration of ${}_9F^{19}$, ${}_{16}S^{32}$ and ${}_{18}Ar^{38}$ and then point out the element with • *Analysis*

(i) maximum nuclear charge

(ii) minimum number of neutrons

(iii) maximum number of unpaired electrons. [3]

13. Write shortnotes on • *Recall*

(i) resonance (ii) σ and π – bonds

(iii) covalent bond. [3]

14. A sample of 0.50 g of an organic compound was treated according to Kjeldahl's method. The ammonia evolved was absorbed in 50 mL of 0.5 M H_2SO_4. The residual acid required 60 mL of 0.5 M solution of NaOH for neutralisation. Find the percentage composition of nitrogen in the compound. • *Evaluate*

[**Ans** : 56%] [3]

15. Explain the following types of structural isomers with one example each. • *Recall*

(i) Functional isomers

(ii) Metamers

(iii) Position isomers [3]

16. (i) What are primary and secondary suffixes as applied to IUPAC nomenclature? • *Recall*

(ii) Draw all position isomers of an alcohol with molecular formula, C_3H_8O. • *Understanding*

(iii) Arrange the following in increasing order of C—C bond length:

C_2H_6, C_2H_4, C_2H_2. • *Analysis* [3]

Or

What is the shape and hybridisation of the following compounds? • *Application*

(i) $H_2C=O$

(ii) CH_3F

(iii) $HC\equiv N$

17. Calculate degree of hydrolysis and pH of 0.25 M NaCN solution at 25°C. $K_a = 4.8 \times 10^{-10}$. [$h = 8.33 \times 10^{-5}$, pH = 9.32] • *Application* [3]

18. Explain, why the following systems are not aromatic ? • *Understanding*

(i) 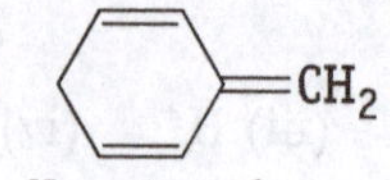

Non-atomatic

(ii) 

Non-aromatic

(iii) 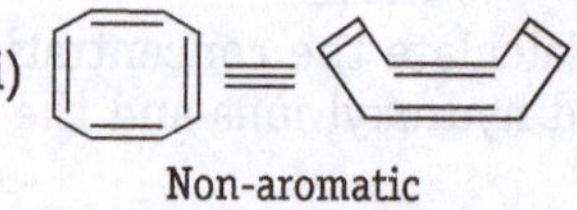

Non-aromatic [3]

Section-D [15 Marks]

19. (i) The enthalpy of a vaporisation of CCl_4 is 30.5 kJ mol^{-1}. Calculate the heat required for the vaporisation of 284 g of CCl_4 at constant pressure (molar mass of $CCl_4 = 154$ g mol^{-1}). • *Evaluate*

[Ans : 56.25 kJ]

(ii) Acetic acid (ethanoic acid) and hydrochloric acid reacts with KOH solution. The enthalpy of neutralisation of ethanoic acid is –55.8 kJ mol^{-1} while that of hydrochloric acid is –57.3 kJ mol^{-1}. Can you think of why are these different? • *Analysis*

[5]

20. (i) Give the structures of *A* and *B* in the following reactions • *Understanding*

(a) 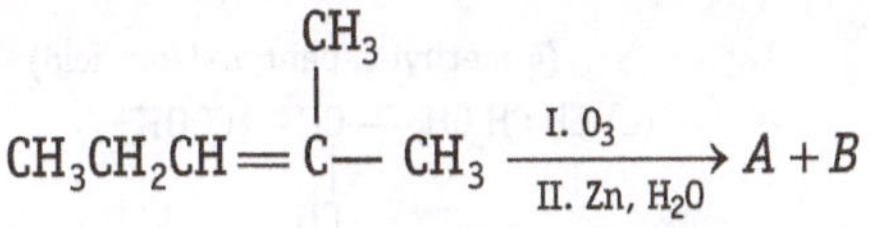

(b) 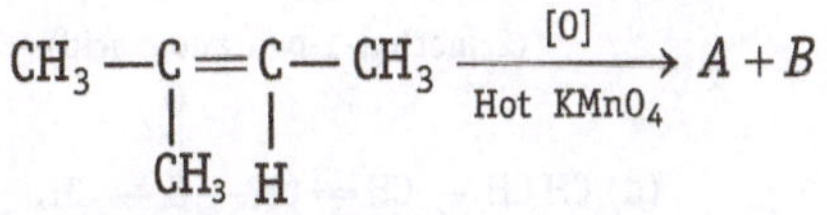

(ii) How will you convert • *Understanding*

(a) ethyne to 1, 2-dibromoethane?

(b) ethene to methanoic acid?

(c) ethene to ethanol?

[5]

Or An alkyl halide $C_5H_{11}Br(A)$ reacts with ethanolic KOH to give an alkene '*B*', which reacts with Br_2 to give a compound '*C*', which on dehydrobromination gives an alkyne '*D*'. On treatment with sodium metal in liquid ammonia, one mole of '*D*' gives one mole of the sodium salt of '*D*' and half a mole of hydrogen gas. Complete hydrogenation of '*D*' yields a straight chain alkane. Identify *A*, *B*, *C* and *D*. Give the reactions involved. • *Understanding*

21. (i) Why is benzene extra ordinarily stable though it contains three double bonds? • *Understanding*

(ii) On converting benzene to toluene, state whether there will be a rise or fall in the melting point. • *Analysis*

(iii) Complete the following reactions.

(a) $CH_3CH_3 \xrightarrow[h\nu]{Br_2} A \xrightarrow{\text{Aq. KOH}} B$

(b) $CH_3CH_2Br \xrightarrow[\Delta]{\text{alc. KOH}} A \xrightarrow{H_2/Ni} B$

(iv) What do you mean by isomerism? • *Recall*

[5]

Answer key

1. (B) (i)-(d), (ii)-(c), (iii)-(a), (iv)-(d), (v)-(c), (vi)-(a), (vii)-(d)

SAMPLE QUESTION PAPER 5

A Highly Simulated Sample Question Paper for ISC Class XI

CHEMISTRY (Unsolved)

See Instruction Sample Paper I

UNSOLVED

Section-A

[14 Marks]

1. (A) Fill in the blanks by choosing the appropriate word(s) from those given in the brackets. [4 ×1]
[limiting reagent, same, different, solute, solvent, particles, water, CO_2, radius, distance, partly, completely, resonance, dipole moment, hybridisation, stereoisomers, gram, moles, graphite.]

(i) The substance which is .... consumed in a reactions is called a .... • *Recall*

(ii) .... is defined as the product of magnitude of charge (q) and the .... separating the centers of positive and negative charges. • *Recall*

(iii) The compounds having .... molecular formula but .... spatial arrangement of atoms or group of atoms are called structural isomer. • *Recall*

(iv) Molarity is defined as the number of .... of the .... dissolved in 1 L of the solution. • *Recall*

(B) Select and write the correct alternative from the choices given below. [7 ×1]

(i) The orbital diagram in which Aufbau principle is violated is • *Analysis*

(a) [⇅] [⇅|↑|] (b) [↑] [⇅|↑|↑]

(c) [⇅] [↑|↑|↑] (d) [⇅] [⇅|⇅|↑]

(ii) Nitric oxide acts as a reducing agent in the reaction, • *Analysis*

(a) $4NH_3 + 5O_2 \longrightarrow 2NO + 6H_2O$

(b) $2NO + 3I_2 + 4H_2O \longrightarrow 2NO_3^- + 6I^- + 8H^+$

(c) $2NO + H_2SO_3 \longrightarrow N_2O + H_2SO_4$

(d) $2NO + H_2S \longrightarrow N_2O + S + H_2O$

(iii) In a set of degenerate orbitals, the electrons distribute themselves to retain like spins as far as possible. This statement belongs to • *Understanding*

(a) Pauli's exclusion principle

(b) Aufbau principle

(c) Hund's rule of maximum multiplicity

(d) Slater's rule

(iv) Indicate the incorrectly named compound. • *Analysis*

(a) $CH_3-\underset{\displaystyle CH_3}{\underset{|}{CH}}-CH_2-CH_2-CHO$
(4-methyl-1-pentanal)

(b) $CH_3-\underset{\displaystyle CH_3}{\underset{|}{CH}}-C\equiv C-COOH$
(4-methyl-2-pentyn-1-oic acid)

(c) $CH_3CH_2CH_2-\underset{\displaystyle CH_3}{\underset{|}{CH}}-COOH$
(2-methyl-1-pentanoic acid)

(d) $CH_3CH_2-CH=CH-\overset{\displaystyle O}{\overset{||}{C}}-CH_3$
(3-hexen-5-one)

(v) Which of the following pair of ions are isoelectronic and isostructural? • *Analysis*

(a) CO_3^{2-}, SO_3^{2-} (b) ClO_3^-, CO_3^{2-}

(c) SO_3^{2-}, NO_3^- (d) ClO_3^-, SO_3^{2-}

(vi) **Assertion** BrF_5 and SF_6 both have same hybridisation.
Reason BrF_5 is square pyramidal, while SF_6 molecule is octahedral. • *Analysis*

(a) Both Assertion and Reason are true and Reason is the correct explanation of Assertion.

(b) Both Assertion and Reason are true but Reason is not correct explanation of Assertion.

(c) Assertion is true but Reason is false.

(d) Assertion is false but Reason is true.

(vii) **Assertion** A liquid crystallises into a solid and is accompanied by decrease in entropy.
Reason In crystals, molecules arrange in an ordered manner. • *Analysis*

(a) Both Assertion and Reason are true and Reason is the correct explanation of Assertion.

(b) Both Assertion and Reason are true but Reason is not correct explanation of Assertion.

(c) Assertion is true but Reason is false.

(d) Assertion is false but Reason is true.

(C) Read the passage given below carefully and answer the questions that follow.

Chemical bonding, involve interactions that account for the association of atoms into molecules, ions, crystals and other stable species that make up the familiar substances of the everyday world. When atoms approach one another, their nuclei and electrons interact and tend to distribute themselves in space in such a way that the total energy is lower than it would be in any alternative arrangement. If the total energy of a group of atoms is lower than the sum of the energies of the component atoms, then the energy lowering is the bonding energy.

The ideas that helped to establish the nature of chemical bonding came to fruition during the early 20th century, after the electron had been discovered and quantum mechanics had provided a language for the description of the behaviour of electrons in atoms.

However, even though chemists need quantum mechanics to attain a detailed quantitative understanding of bond formation, much of their pragmatic understanding of bonds is expressed in simple intuitive models. These models treat bonds as primarily of two kinds—namely, ionic and covalent.

[3 ×1]

(i) In O_3, what is the fomal charge on each O-atom? • *Evaluate*

(ii) Which compound of chlorine contains both ionic as well as covalent bonds? • *Analysis*

(iii) According to molecular orbital theory, does He_2^+ molecule exist? • *Understanding*

Section-B [20 Marks]

2. Differentiate between the principle of estimation of nitrogen in an organic compound by • *Recall*

(i) Duma's method.

(ii) Kjeldahl's method. [2]

3. At 298K, K_p for the reaction, • *Application*

$N_2O_4(g) \rightleftharpoons 2NO_2(g)$ is 0.98. Predict whether the reaction is spontaneous or not. [2]

4. (i) In the equation, $N_2(g)+3H_2(g) \rightleftharpoons 2NH_3(g)$, what would be the sign of work done? • *Analysis*

(ii) Predict the change in internal energy for an isolated system at constant volume. • *Analysis* [2]

5. (i) Heat capacity (C_p) is an extensive property but specific heat (C) is an intensive property. What will be the relation between C_p and C for 1 mole of water? • *Understanding*

(ii) For the same increase in volume, why work done is more if the gas is allowed to expand reversibly at higher temperature? • *Understanding* [2]

6. An ion with mass number 56 contains 3 units of positive charge and 30.4% more neutrons than the electrons. Assign the symbol to this ion. • *Analysis* [2]

7. Among the molecules, NO^+, N_2 and NO_2^-, identify the species which are isoelectronic with CO. • *Analysis*

Or Write the lewis dot structure of • *Understanding*

(a) nitrite ion (b)carbon dioxide

8. (i) Why do elements in the same group have similar physical and chemical properties? • *Understanding*

(ii) What is the IUPAC name, official name and symbol of the element with atomic number 110? • *Evaluate* [2]

9. In the estimation of sulphur by Carius method, 0.468 g of an organic sulphur compound afforded 0.668 g of barium sulphate. Find the percentage of sulphur in the given compound. • *Evaluate*

[Ans : 19.6%] [2]

10. Ionisation constant of a weak base MOH ,is given by the expression $K_b = \frac{[M^+][OH^-]}{[MOH]}$

Values of ionisation constant of some weak bases at a particular temperature are given below.

Base	Dimethyl amine	Urea	Pyridine	Ammonia
K_b	5.4×10^{-4}	1.3×10^{-14}	1.77×10^{-9}	1.77×10^{-5}

Arrange the bases in decreasing order of the extent of their ionisation at equilibrium. Which of the above base is the strongest? • *Analysis* [2]

11. A common method of preparation of alkenes from alcohols involve heating the alcohol with a mineral acid. What is the mechanism of this dehydration? • *Evaluate* [2]

Section-C [21 Marks]

12. (i) Define octet rule. Write its significance and limitations. • *Recall*

(ii) Draw the Lewis structures for the following molecule and ions. H_2S, $SiCl_4$. • *Understanding* [3]

Or

(i) What is valence bond theory? • *Recall*

(ii) Write two differences between σ and π bonds. • *Recall*

UNSOLVED

UNSOLVED

13. The enthalpy change for the reaction,
$Zn\ (s) + 2H^+(aq) \longrightarrow Zn^{2+}(aq) + H_2(g)$, is -154.40 kJ mol^{-1}. The formation of 2 g of hydrogen expands the system by 22.4 L at 1 atm pressure. What is the internal energy change of the reaction? • *Applicaiton*

[**Ans** : $\Delta U = -156.67$ kJ] [3]

14. (i) A 0.02 M solution of pyridinium hydrochloride has pH = 3.44. Calculate the ionisation constant of pyridine. • *Application*

[**Ans** : 1.52×10^{-9}]

(ii) What will be the pH of 0.1 M ammonium acetate solution ? [$pK_a = pK_b = 4.74$]. • *Application*

[**Ans** : pH = 7.0]

(iii) The ionisation constant of formic acid is 1.8 $\times 10^{-4}$. Calculate the ratio of sodium formate and formic acid in a buffer of pH 4.25. • *Application*

[**Ans** : 3.24] [3]

15. (i) Write chemical equation for combustion reaction of the following hydrocarbons.
(a) Butane (b) Pentene • *Recall*

(ii) Identify *A* and *B* • *Understanding*

$$CaC_2 \xrightarrow{H_2O} A \xrightarrow[373\text{-}383K]{KMnO_4/KOH} B$$

[3]

16. (i) State the principle that suggests the presence of only two electrons in an orbital. • *Recall* [3]

(ii) Account for the following: • *Understanding*
(a) Chromium has configuration $3d^5\ 4s^1$ and not $3d^4\ 4s^2$.
(b) Bohr's orbits are called stationary orbits or states. [3]

17. Account for the following
(i) Benzene undergo electrophilic substitution reactions easily as compared to nucleophilic substitution. • *Understanding*
(ii) Suggest a route for the preparation of nitrobenzene starting from acetylene? • *Understanding*
(iii) Write chemical equation for combustion reaction of toluene. • *Recall* [3]

18. Write the structures of *A* and *B* in the following reactions. • *Understanding*

(i) $CH_2 = CH_2 \xrightarrow{Br_2} A \xrightarrow{Alc.\ KOH} B$

(ii) $CH \equiv CH \xrightarrow{NaNH_2} A \xrightarrow{CH_2Br} B$

(iii) $CH_3CH = CH_2 \xrightarrow{HBr} A \xrightarrow[Dry\ ether]{Na} B$ [3]

Section-D [15 Marks]

19. (i) Illustrate the following:
(a) Friedel-Crafts alkylation in benzene. • *Recall*
(b) Nitration in benzene. • *Recall*
(c) Ozonolysis of 1, 3-dimethyl benzene (*o*-xylene). • *Understanding*

(ii) Arrange the following set of compounds in order to their decreasing relative reactivity with an electrophile, E^+. • *Analysis*
(a) Chlorobenzene, 2,4-dinitrochlorobenzene, *p*-nitrochlorobenzene
(b) Toluene, $p\text{-}H_3C—C_6H_4—NO_2$, $p\text{-}O_2N—C_6H_4—NO_2$.
Also, explain your answer. [5]

20. In each of the following pairs, predict which has higher value of the property mentioned and why? • *Analysis*
(i) HF, HCl [Polar character]
(ii) NH_3, H_2O [Bond angle]
(iii) KCl, KF [Lattice enrhalpy]
(iv) NF_3, NH_3 [Dipole moment]
(v) C_2H_2, C_2H_4 [*s*-character in the hydridisation of carbon] [5]

21. What are the oxidation numbers of the underlined elements in each of the following and how do you rationalise your results? • *Evaluate*
(i) $K\underline{I}_3$ (ii) $H_2\underline{S}_4O_6$
(iii) $\underline{Fe}_3O_4$ (iv) $CH_3\underline{C}H_2OH$
(v) $\underline{C}H_3COOH$

Or

Justify that the following reactions are redox reactions. • *Analysis*
(i) $CuO(s) + H_2(g) \longrightarrow Cu(s) + H_2O\ (g)$
(ii) $Fe_2O_3(s) + 3CO\ (g) \longrightarrow 2Fe\ (s) + 3CO_2(g)$
(iii) $4BCl_3(g) + 3LiAlH_4(s) \longrightarrow 2B_2H_6(g) + 3LiCl(s) + 3AlCl_3(s)$
(iv) $2K(s) + F_2(g) \longrightarrow 2K^+F^-\ (s)$
(v) $4NH_3(g) + 5O_2(g) \longrightarrow 4NO(g) + 6H_2O(g)$ [5]

Answer key

1. (B) (i)-(b), (ii)-(b), (iii)-(c), (iv)-(d), (v)-(d), (vi)-(b), (vii)-(a)